Greece

THE ROUGH GUIDE

written and researched by

Mark Ellingham, Marc Dubin, Natania Jansz and John Fisher

additional contributions by

Lance Chilton, Nick Edwards, Geoff Garvey and Chris Nicholas

THE ROUGH GUIDES

THE ROUGH GUIDES

TRAVEL GUIDES • PHRASEBOOKS • MUSIC AND REFERENCE GUIDES

 We set out to do something different when the first Rough Guide was published in 1982. Mark Ellingham, just out of university, was travelling in Greece. He brought along the popular guides of the day, but found they were all lacking in some way. They were either strong on ruins and museums but went on for pages without mentioning a beach or taverna. Or they were so conscious of the need to save money that they lost sight of Greece's cultural and historical significance. Also, none of the books told him anything about Greece's contemporary life – its politics, its culture, its people, and how they lived.

So with no job in prospect, Mark decided to write his own guidebook, one which aimed to provide practical information that was second to none, detailing the best beaches and the hottest clubs and restaurants, while also giving hard-hitting accounts of every sight, both famous and obscure, and providing up-to-the-minute information on contemporary culture. It was a guide that encouraged independent travellers to find the best of Greece, and was a great success, getting shortlisted for the Thomas Cook travel guide award,

and encouraging Mark, along with three friends, to expand the series.

The Rough Guide list grew rapidly and the letters flooded in, indicating a much broader readership than had been anticipated, but one which uniformly appreciated the Rough Guide mix of practical detail and humour, irreverence and enthusiasm. Things haven't changed. The same four friends who began the series are still the caretakers of the Rough Guide mission today: to provide the most reliable, up-to-date and entertaining information to independent-minded travellers of all ages, on all budgets.

We now publish more than 150 titles and have offices in London and New York. The travel guides are written and researched by a dedicated team of more than 100 authors, based in Britain, Europe, the USA and Australia. We have also created a unique series of phrasebooks to accompany the travel series, along with an acclaimed series of music guides, and a best-selling pocket guide to the Internet and World Wide Web. We also publish comprehensive travel information on our web site:

www.roughguides.com

HELP US UPDATE

We've gone to a lot of effort to ensure that the eighth edition of *The Rough Guide to Greece* is accurate and up-to-date. However, things change – places get "discovered", opening hours are notoriously fickle, restaurants and rooms raise prices or lower standards. If you feel we've got it wrong or left something out, we'd like to know, and if you can remember the address, the price, the time, the phone number, so much the better.

We'll credit all contributions, and send a copy of the next edition (or any other Rough Guide if you prefer) for the best letters. Please mark letters: "Rough Guide Greece Update" and send to:
Rough Guides, 62–70 Shorts Gardens, London WC2H 9AB, or Rough Guides, 375 Hudson St, 4th floor, New York NY 10014.
Or send email to: mail@roughguides.co.uk
Online updates about this book can be found on Rough Guides' Web site at www.roughguides.com

THE AUTHORS OF THE ROUGH GUIDE TO GREECE

Mark Ellingham and Natania Jansz wrote the original edition of this book – the first ever Rough Guide – in 1981. They couldn't believe their good fortune in being paid by a publisher to spend time roaming around Classical ruins and medieval castles, and island-hopping in the Aegean. Mark continued writing Rough Guides and still works for the company as Series Editor. He is currently spending most of his time developing publication of the guides on the Internet but would be happier roaming the ruins, etc. Natania divides her time between Clinical Psychology and writing; she has edited the Rough Guide special, More Women Travel. Natania and Mark have a toddler, Miles, who rates Greek food (and sand) high on his list of life's good things.

John Fisher has also been involved with Rough Guides from the start. One of the original authors of the Greek guide, he has since written numerous other Rough Guide titles including the Rough Guide to Crete. Between travels, John can usually be found chained to a desk at Rough Guide HQ in London. He lives in south London with his wife and two young sons.

Marc Dubin first arrived in Greece in 1978, able to ask only for yoghurts, and the loo, in the local tongue. Since 1981 he has returned yearly, thereby acquiring fluency in Greek, and from 1989 onwards has lived part-time on the island of Sámos, where he recently restored an old cottage. Marc writes regularly for various publications on topics as diverse as Greek cuisine, music and backcountry trekking. When not in Greece, he lives in London or ranges across the Mediterranean in the course of updating his other Rough Guides: Turkey, Cyprus, and the Pyrenees.

READERS' LETTERS

We'd like to thank the readers of previous editions, who took time to write in with comments and suggestions. For this edition, we were helped by letters from:

Cyrille Altheritiere, Dave and Elaine Andrews, George Androvik, Chris Arthur, D.J. Authers, Judith Azrael, Orazio Belsito, Kate Bennett, David Bensley, Beth Bernstein, Debra Black, D. Blackburn, Nancy-Kim Blake, Jan Blakeley, Reverend and Mrs R.J. Blakeway-Phillips, Gregory Bouras, S. Braun, John Broadbent, Jane Brodie and Jan Cookson, Michael Brown, Christopher Burns, Peter Ceulemans, Roland Chapman, Andreas Charalambous, Vickie Chatzigeorgiou, Yannis Christopoulos, Clare Clarke, Peter Crane, Hugh Cunniam, Dennis Cunningham, A. David, Joanne Davies, Michael Davies, Siôn Huw Davies, Barbara Dorf, Dirk Drijbooms, Sarah Durrant and Joanne Burrell, Josephine Dyer, Marc and Mary Eady, Gary Eastwood, Imogen Edwards, Jenny Eldred, Jane Elliott, Samantha Evans, Alan Everett, Hanneke Faber, Sally Fairish, Henry Fan, Frances Faux, N. Foot, Jo Foster and Susannah Mayne, Gillian Foxon, Richard Francis, Fiona Fry and Simon Discombe, Michael Garcia and Zoe Scott, Steve Gardiner, Mina Gavala, Hans Geluk, C. Gipson, Professor Benita Goldman, Ceri Greenwood, Philip and Judy Greenwood, Emanuele Habib, Jane Hacker, Olga Hadjilambri, Elizabeth Halliday, Janet and Harry Hannaby, Chris Hardy, Paul Hargrave, R.J. Hartley, Mrs S.C. Hawsher, Annabel Hayward, Arthur Hohler, John Holden, Peter Hooch, Jessica Horsley and Jürgen Banholzer, Dennis Howard-Jones, Ian Hughes, Howy Jacobs, Eric Jensen and Julie Nishimura-Jensen, Mr and Mrs R.A. Jones, Niki Kapari, Lynne Kelly, Andreas Kitidis, Professor A.S. Knowland,

Michael Krokos, Kate Lackie and Caroline Ray, D.H. Laity, Christine Lea, Rebecca Lisle-Taylor, Melanie Loake, Jane Low, Katy Lumb, Franka Van Der Loo Bno, Alan Lovejoy, Linda and Peter Ludlow, Anne Marie Luijendijk, Deborah Lyons and Fred Bohrer, Patrick McCarmack, Daniel McDonnell, Monica MacKaness and John Garratt, Ellie Mckinlay, Amanda Mackinnon, Dermott McMeel, Allegra Madgwick, Peter Marsh, Charles Manton, K.M. Marriott, Mary and Alan Miller, Elda Molla and Barbara Halatas, Emma and Matthew Morrall, Gareth Morris Jones, Alexandra Morriss, Leigh Murphy, Emilie Nangle, Richard Nelsson, Carla and John Nesbitt, Nick and Sova, Raphaella Nicol, Elly Nijenhuis, Apostolos Nikolakopoulos, Jonathan Oades, Michael O'Hare and Sally Manders, Anna Paliastead, Tessa Parsons and Mark Brandon, James Pettifer, David Phillips, Giorgios Pittas and Lorentzos Halkoussis, Martin Potter, R.W. Price, Manuelle Prunier, E. Randall, David Reilly, Ashleigh Rinchey, Lezlee Roberts and Andy Wilcox, P. Robinson, John H. Rose, James Ryan, Carola Saipham, Ian and Janet Sampson, Ken Shaw and Carolyn Spice, Shona, Joyce B. Siegel, Carola Singham, Neil Smart, Clare Smedley, Janette Smith, Simon Squires, Matthew Stanley, Derek G. Stevens, Paul Stevens, Phillip Stiveno, Colin Stubley, Murray Sugden, Ian Sutherland, Ed and Brenda Swidler, Wanda and Barry Syner, Robert K. Thompson, P. Travers, Yiannis Triandafillou, Urszula Truszkowska, Andrew Tyrer, Siouzos Vasilis, Peter A. Verity, A. Vernardos, D. Walker, Mike Webber, Kate Welch, Simon Whittaker, Rosemary Wilkinson, Stuart Wilson, Tom Winnifrith, John Winstanley, Peggy A. Wright, Matthew Wright and M.C. O'Halloran, Laura Wyatt, Lisa Wycherley, Yvonne and Dave, Rhea Zambellas.

CONTENTS

- ## CHAPTER 3: THESSALY AND CENTRAL GREECE 267–322

- ## CHAPTER 4: EPIRUS AND THE WEST 323–371

- ## CHAPTER 5: THE NORTH: MACEDONIA AND THRACE 372–459

PART THREE THE ISLANDS 461

- ## CHAPTER 6: THE ARGO-SARONIC 465–481

- ## CHAPTER 7: THE CYCLADES 482–563

PART FOUR   CONTEXTS   838

LIST OF MAPS

MAP SYMBOLS

━━━	Railway	◓	Cave
═══	Major paved road	⋆	Viewpoint
═══	Minor paved road	⬤	Refuge
━━━	Unpaved road	⚠	Campsite
- - - - -	Footpath	◉	Accommodation
⊞⊞⊞⊞	Steps	■	Restaurant
— —	Ferry route	✕	Airport
▬▬▬	Waterway	P	Parking
- - - -	Chapter division boundary	Ⓜ	Metro station
-·-·-	International boundary	★	Bus stop
◆	Point of interest	☼	Lighthouse
⍜	Mosque	(*i*)	Information office
✡	Synagogue	✉	Post office
‡	Church	(*c*)	Telephone
⋔	Monastery or convent	■	Building
♯	Castle	+■	Church
⫽	Hill	+⁺+	Christian cemetery
∴	Archeological site	▨	Park
▲	Peak	▨	National park
⋀	Mountains	▬	Pedestrianized area
⋆	Marshland	▨	Beach
◊	Waterfall		

INTRODUCTION

With well over a hundred inhabited islands and a territory that stretches from the Mediterranean to the Balkans, Greece has interest enough to fill months of travel. The **historic sites** span four millennia, encompassing the legendary and renowned – such as Mycenae, Olympia, Delphi and the Parthenon – and the obscure, where a visit can still seem like a personal discovery. The **beaches** are parcelled out along a convoluted coastline equal to France's in length, and they range from those of islands where the boat calls twice a week to resorts as cosmopolitan as any in the Mediterranean. Perhaps more surprisingly, the country's mountainous interior offers some of the best and least exploited **hiking** in Europe.

Modern Greece is the result of an extraordinary diversity of **influences**. Romans, Arabs, Latin Crusaders, Venetians, Slavs, Albanians, Turks, Italians, to say nothing of the Orthodox Byzantine empire, have been and gone since the time of Alexander the Great. All have left their mark: the Byzantines in countless churches and monasteries and in ghost towns like Mystra; the Venetians in impregnable fortifications at Náfplio, Monemvasía and Methóni in the Peloponnese; and other Latin powers, such as the Knights of Saint John and the Genoese, in magnificent castles throughout the eastern Aegean. Most obvious of all is the heritage of four hundred years of Ottoman Turkish rule which, while universally derided, exercised an inestimable influence on music, cuisine, language and way of life. The contributions, and continued existence, of substantial minorities – Vlachs, Muslims, Catholics, Jews, Gypsies – have also helped to forge the Hellenic identity.

All these players have been instrumental in forming a hard-to-define but powerful sense of **Greekness**, which has kept alive the people's sense of themselves throughout their turbulent history. With no local ruling class or formal Renaissance period to impose a superior model of taste or to patronize the arts, medieval Greek peasants, fishermen and shepherds created a vigorous and truly popular culture. It is still manifest in a thousand instinctively tasteful ways, ranging from traditional music, intricate embroidery, woven goods and carved furniture, to the stereotypically white cubist houses of popular images.

Of course there are formal cultural activities as well: **museums** that shouldn't be missed in Athens, Thessaloníki and Iráklion; the compelling **monasteries** of the Metéora and Mount Áthos; the magnificent **mansions** of Zagóri and Pílion; **castles** such as those in the Dodecanese, northeast Aegean, central Greece and the Peloponnese; as well, of course, as the great **ancient sites** dating from the Mycenaean, Minoan, Classical, Hellenistic, Roman and Byzantine eras. The country hosts some excellent summer **festivals** too, bringing international theatre, dance and musical groups to perform in ancient theatres at Epidaurus, Dodona and Athens, as well as castle courtyards and more contemporary venues in coastal and island resorts.

But the call to cultural duty should never be too overwhelming on a Greek holiday. The **hedonistic pleasures** of languor and warmth – always going lightly dressed, swimming in balmy seas at dusk, talking and drinking under the stars – are just as appealing. But despite recent improvements to the tourism "product", Greece is still essentially a land for adaptable sybarites, not for those who crave five-star treatment with super-soft beds, faultless plumbing, Cordon-Bleu cuisine and attentive service. Except at the growing number of luxury facilities in new or restored buildings, hotel and pension rooms can be box-like, campsites offer the minimum of facilities, and the food at its best is fresh and uncomplicated.

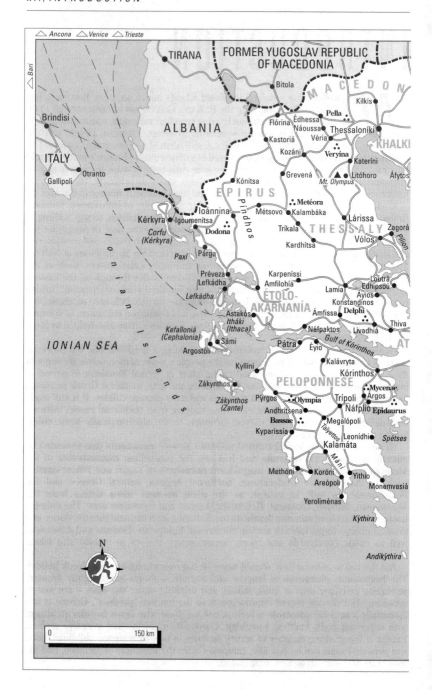

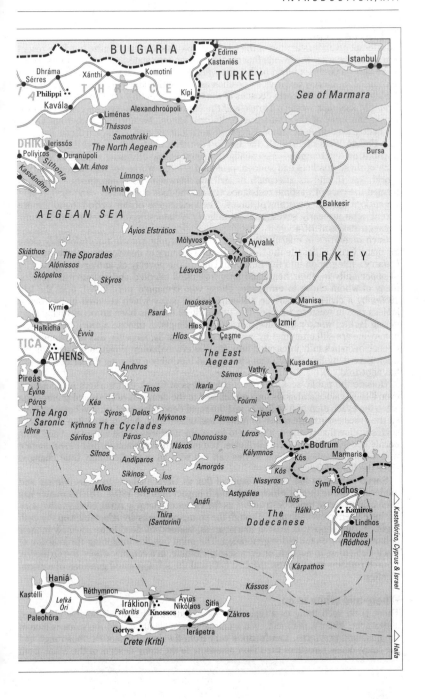

The Greek people

To attempt an understanding of the Greek people, it's useful to realize just how recent and traumatic were the events that created the modern state and **national character** – the latter a complex blend of the extroverted and the pessimistic, which cannot be accounted for merely by Greece's position as a natural bridge between Europe and the Middle East. Until the early decades of the twentieth century many parts of Greece – Crete, Macedonia, western Thrace and the entire eastern Aegean – were in Ottoman (or in the case of the Dodecanese, Italian) hands. Meanwhile, numerous Greek Orthodox lived in Asia Minor, Egypt, western Europe and in the northern Balkans. The Balkan Wars of 1912–13, the Greco-Turkish war of 1919–22 and the organized **population exchanges** – essentially regulated ethnic cleansing — which followed each of these conflicts had sudden, profound effects. Worse yet was to come during World War II, and its aftermath of civil war between the Communists – who had formed the core of wartime resistance against the Axis occupation – and the UK- and US-backed rightist government forces. The viciousness of this period found a more recent echo in nearly seven years of military dictatorship under the colonels' junta between 1967 and 1974.

Such memories of misrule, diaspora and catastrophe remain uncomfortably close for many Greeks, despite the last quarter of a century of democratic stability and the country's integration into the European Union. The poverty of, and enduring paucity of opportunity in, their homeland long frustrated talented and resourceful Greeks, many of whom chose to **emigrate**. Those who remained were lulled, until the late 1980s, by a civil-service-driven full-employment policy which resulted in the lowest jobless rate in western Europe. The downside of this has been an occasionally staggering lack of worker initiative, but official attempts to impose a more austere economic line are still often met by waves of strikes. Lately, however, this has changed as Greece becomes fully integrated into the Western economy, privatization and competition have demolished state monopolies, and inevitably a growing disparity in wealth has appeared.

Outside the public sector, the meticulousness of Greek craftworkers is legendary, even if their values and skills took a back seat to the demands of crisis and profiteering when the evacuation of Asia Minor and the rapid depopulation of rural villages prompted the graceless **urbanization** of Athens and other cities. Amidst the often superficial sophistication that resulted, it's easy to forget the nearness of the village past and stubbornly lingering Third World attributes. You may find, for example, that buses operate with Germanic efficiency, but ferries can sail with an unpredictability little changed since the time of Odysseus.

Social attitudes too, are in a state of flux as Greece adapts to mass tourism and modern times, neither of which made much impact until the 1960s. The encounter has been painful and at times destructive, as the values of a largely rural, conservative society have been irrevocably lost. Though the younger Greeks are adaptable and the cash registers ring happily, at least in tourist areas, visitors still need to be sensitive in their behaviour towards the older generation. The mind boggles imagining the reaction of black-clad elders to nudism, or even scanty clothing, in a country where the Orthodox Church remains an all-but-established faith and the self-appointed guardian of national identity.

Where and when to go

There is no such thing as a typical Greek island; each has its distinctive character, appearance, history, flora and even a unique tourist clientele. And the same is true of the mainland provinces. **Landscapes** vary from the mountainous Píndhos range and the rainy, dense forests of the Pílion peninsula to the stony deserts of the Máni, from the soft theatricality of the Peloponnesian coastal hills to the poplar-studded plains of Macedonia, from the pine-scented ridges of Skiáthos and Sámos to the wind-blown rocks of the central Aegean. The inky plume of cypress, the silver green of olive groves, the purplish outline of distant hills, an expanse of shimmering cobalt sea: these are the enduring and unfailingly pleasing motifs of the Greek landscape.

Most places and people are far more agreeable, and resolutely Greek, outside the **peak period** of early July to the end of August, when soaring temperatures and crowds of foreigners and locals alike can be overpowering. You won't miss out on **warm weather** if you come in **June** or **September**, excellent times almost everywhere but particularly in the islands. An exception to this pattern, however, is the north-mainland coast – notably the Halkidhikí peninsula – and the islands of Samothráki and Thássos, which only really operate during July and August. In **October** you might hit a stormy spell, especially in western Greece or in the mountains, but for most of that month the "summer of Áyios Dhimítrios" (the Greek equivalent of Indian summer) prevails, and the southerly Dodecanese and Crete are extremely pleasant. Autumn in general is beautiful; the light is softer, the sea often balmier than the air, and the colours subtler.

December to **March** are the coldest and least reliable months, though even then there are many fine days of perfect crystal visibility, and the glorious lowland flowers begin to bloom very early in spring. The more northerly latitudes and high altitudes of course endure far colder and wetter conditions, with the mountains themselves under snow from November to May. The mildest **winter climate** is to be found on Rhodes, or in the southeastern parts of Crete. As spring slowly warms up, **April** is still uncertain, though superb for wildflowers, green landscapes and photography; by **May** the weather is more generally predictable, and Crete, the Peloponnese, the Ionian islands and the Cyclades are perhaps at their best, even if the sea is still a little cool for swimming.

AVERAGE TEMPERATURES AND RAINFALL

	Jan		March		May		July		Sept		Nov	
	°F	Rain	°F	Rain	°F	Rain	°F	Rain	°F	Rain	°F	Rain
	Max Min	days	Max Min	days	Max Min	days	Max Min	days	Max Min	days	Max Min	days
Athens	54 44	13	60 46	10	76 60	9	90 72	2	84 66	4	65 52	12
Crete (Haniá)	60 46	17	64 48	11	76 56	5	86 68	0	82 64	3	70 54	10
Cyclades (Mýkonos)	58 50	14	62 52	8	72 62	5	82 72	0.5	78 68	1	66 58	9
North Greece (Halkidhikí)	50 36	7	59 44	9	77 58	10	90 70	4	83 64	5	60 47	9
Ionian (Corfu)	56 44	13	62 46	10	74 58	6	88 70	2	82 64	5	66 52	12
Dodecanese (Rhodes)	58 50	15	62 48	7	74 58	2	86 70	0	82 72	1	68 60	7
Sporades (Skiáthos)	55 45	12	58 47	10	71 58	3	82 71	0	75 64	8	62 53	12
East Aegean (Lésvos)	54 42	11	60 46	7	76 60	6	88 70	2	82 66	2	64 50	9

Other factors that affect the timing of your Greek travels have to do with the level of tourism and the amenities provided. Service standards, particularly in tavernas, slip under the peak-season pressures, and room rates are at their highest from July to September. If you can only visit during mid-summer, reserve a package well in advance, or plan your itinerary off the beaten track. Explore the less obvious parts of the Peloponnese or the northern mainland, or island-hop with an eye for the more obscure places – where ferries call less than daily and there's no airport.

Out of season, especially between November and April, you have to contend with reduced ferry services to the islands (and non-existent hydrofoils), plus fairly skeletal facilities when you arrive. You will, however, find reasonable service on all the main routes and at least one hotel and taverna open in the port or main town of all but the tiniest isles. On the mainland, winter travel poses no special difficulties except, of course, in mountain villages either cut off by snow or (at weekends especially) monopolized by avid Greek skiers.

BASICS

GETTING THERE FROM BRITAIN

It's close on 2000 miles from London to Athens, so for most visitors flying is the only viable option. There are direct flights to a variety of Greek destinations from all the major British airports. Flying time is around three and a half hours and the cost of charter flights is reasonable – sample return fares to Athens from London in midsummer start from around £160 (Manchester £180, Glasgow £200), but there are always bargains to be had. Easter and Christmas are also classed as high season, but outside these periods flights can be snapped up for as little as £120 return. Costs can often be highly competitive, too, if you buy a flight as part of an all-in package: see pp. 6–7 for details of holiday operators.

Road or **rail** alternatives take a minimum of three days, and are only worth considering if you plan to visit Greece as part of an extended trip through Europe. The most popular route is down through Italy, then across to Greece by ferry. The old overland route through the former Yugoslavia will remain impractical for the foreseeable future, but a much longer route via Hungary, Romania and Bulgaria is still possible.

BY PLANE

Most of the cheaper flights from Britain to Greece are **charters**, which are sold either with a package holiday or as a flight-only option. The flights have fixed and unchangeable outward and return dates, and often a maximum stay of one month.

For longer stays or more flexibility, or if you're travelling out of season (when few charters are available), you'll need a **scheduled** flight. As with charters, these are offered under a wide variety of fares, and are again often sold off at discount by agents. Useful sources for discounted flights are the classified ads in the travel sections of newspapers like the *Independent*, *Guardian*, *Observer* and *Sunday Times*, as well as weekly listings magazines such as *Time Out*. Teletext is also worth checking, as are **Internet sites** such as:

www.lastminute.com
www.travelselect.com
www.bargainholidays.com
www.cheapflights.co.uk.

Although **Athens** remains the prime destination for cheap fares, there are also **direct flights** from Britain to **Thessaloníki**, **Kalamáta**, **Kavála** and **Préveza** on the Greek mainland, and to the islands of **Crete**, **Rhodes**, **Kós**, **Kárpathos**, **Corfu**, **Páros**, **Mýkonos**, **Zákynthos**, **Kefalloniá**, **Skiáthos**, **Sámos**, **Lésvos** and **Límnos**. And with any flight to Athens, you can buy a **domestic connecting flight** (on the national carrier, Olympic) to one of three dozen or so additional Greek mainland and island airports.

CHARTER FLIGHTS

Travel agents throughout Britain sell **charter flights** to Greece, which usually operate from late April or May to late October or mid-November (depending on destination); late-night departures and early-morning arrivals are common, though you usually have a choice of more civilized hours. Even the high-street chains frequently promote "flight-only" deals, or discount all-inclusive holidays, when their parent companies need to off-load their seat allocations. In any case, phone around for a range of offers. Charter airlines include Air 2000, Flying Colours, Britannia, Caledonian, Sabre and Monarch, but you can often only book tickets on these through travel agents.

The greatest variety of **flight destinations** tends to be from London and Manchester. In summer, if you book in advance, you should have a choice of most of the Greek regional airports listed above. Flying from elsewhere in Britain (Birmingham, Cardiff, Glasgow or Newcastle), or looking for last-minute discounts, you'll find options more limited, most commonly to Athens, Corfu, Rhodes, Kós and Crete.

It's worth noting that **non-EU nationals** who buy charter tickets to Greece must buy a return ticket, to return after no fewer than three days and no more than four weeks, and must accompany it with an **accommodation voucher** for at least the first few nights of their stay – check that the ticket satisfies these conditions or you could be refused entry. In practice, the "accommodation voucher" has become a formality; it has to name an existing hotel but you're not expected to use it (and probably won't be able to if you try).

The other important condition regards travel to **Turkey** (or any other neighbouring country). If you travel to Greece on a charter flight, you may visit another country only as a day-trip; if you stay overnight, you will invalidate your ticket. This rule is justified by the Greek authorities because they subsidize charter airline landing fees, and are therefore reluctant to see tourists spending their money outside Greece. Whether you go along with that rationale or not, there is no way around it, since the Turkish authorities clearly stamp all passports, and the Greeks usually check them. The package industry on the east Aegean and Dodecanese islands bordering Turkey, however, does sometimes prevail upon customs officials to back-date re-entry stamps when bad weather strands their tour groups overnight in Anatolia.

Student/youth charters are allowed to be sold as one-way flights only. By combining two one-way charters you can, therefore, stay for over a month. Student/youth charter tickets are available to anyone under 26, and to all card-carrying full-time students under 32.

Finally, remember that **reconfirmation** of return charter flights is vital and should be done at least 72 hours before departure. If you've travelled out with a package company, this service will usually be included as part of the rep's duties, but you should not assume that it has been done. Personal visits to the airline's representative office are best, as phone numbers given on ticket wallets are usually engaged.

SCHEDULED FLIGHTS

The advantages of **scheduled flights** are that they can be booked well in advance, have longer ticket validities (30, 60, 90 or even 180 days), involve fewer or none of the typical restrictions

---

SCHEDULED AIRLINES

British Airways ☎0345/222111
Cronus Airlines ☎020/7580 3500
EasyJet ☎0870/600 0000 or www.easyjet.com
Olympic Airways ☎020/7409 3400
Virgin Atlantic Airways ☎01293/747747

---

applicable to charters, and often leave at more sociable hours. However, many of the cheaper, shorter-duration SuperPEX or APEX fares do have advance-purchase and/or minimum-stay requirements, and also severe restrictions on date changes or refunds. As with charters, discount fares on scheduled flights are available from most high-street travel **agents**, as well as from a number of specialist flight and student/youth agencies – though it's always well worth contacting the airlines direct, using the telephone numbers in the box above. Like charters, they must be reconfirmed within 72 hours of the return leg.

The widest choice of scheduled flights is with the Greek national carrier **Olympic Airways** and with **British Airways**, who both fly from London Heathrow to Athens (twice daily on BA, three times daily on Olympic), mostly direct, but on Olympic stopping four times weekly in Thessaloníki. BA also offers one daily Athens service from Gatwick, but nothing to Thessaloníki. Both airlines have a range of special fares, and even in July and August, discount flight agents can come up with deals, valid for sixty days away, for as low as £190 return, including tax; more realistically, you'll pay around £250 return during high season. It may be worth avoiding absolutely rock-bottom fares, as Olympic no longer allows changes to your return date on tickets of under ninety days' validity. In the spring or autumn, return fares to Athens run to about £160 including taxes, and in winter dip to about £140. As this route is common-rated between these airlines, you'll also be able to book onward connections simultaneously to domestic Greek airports, though discounts will apply only if using Olympic on all legs of the journey.

Virgin Atlantic Airways also has a near-daily service from Gatwick to Athens, arriving in the late afternoon, plus daily (in summer) departures from Heathrow to Athens, though that flight arrives in the small hours. Fares, in a bewildering array of structures and limited-time special offers, tend to

FLIGHT AGENTS

Argo Holidays, 100 Wigmore St, London W1H 9DR (☎020/7331 7000). *Designated consolidator for Olympic, BA, and Virgin Atlantic; consistently some of the lowest fares, and good service.*

Avro, 1 Weir Rd, London SW19 8UX (☎020/8715 1999). *Seat-only sales of all Monarch charter flights to Athens, Corfu, Iráklion (Crete) and Rhodes from a selection amongst Gatwick, Luton, Manchester and Glasgow.*

Campus Travel, 52 Grosvenor Gardens, London SW1 0AG (☎020/7730 3402); 541 Bristol Rd, Selly Oak, Birmingham B29 6AU (☎0121/414 1848); 39 Queens Rd, Clifton, Bristol BS8 1QE (☎0117/929 2494); 5 Emmanuel St, Cambridge CB1 1NE (☎01223/324283); 53 Forest Rd, Edinburgh EH1 2QP (☎0131/668 3303); 166 Deansgate, Manchester M3 3FE (☎0161/273 1721); 105–106 St Aldates, Oxford OX1 1DD (☎01865/242067). *Student/youth travel specialists, with branches also in YHA shops and on university campuses all over Britain, and its own student/youth charter flights to Athens during the summer.*

Eclipse Direct ☎0161/742 2277 or 0990/010203. *Seat-only deals on Air 2000, and fly-drives to Rhodes and Kós from various UK airports.*

Greece & Cyprus Travel Centre, 44 Birmingham Rd, Sutton Coldfield, West Midlands B72 1QQ (☎0121/355 6955). *Flight consolidator and general Greek packages specialists.*

Mondial Travel, 8 Moscow Rd, London W2 4BT (☎020/7792 3333). *Good ticketing agency for scheduled flights to Greece.*

North South Travel, Moulsham Mill Centre, Parkway, Chelmsford, Essex CM2 7PX (☎01245/492882). *Discount flight agency, with added bonus in a portion of profits going to aid Third World development projects.*

STA Travel, 86 Old Brompton Rd, London SW7 3LH (☎020/7361 6161); 25 Queens Rd, Bristol BS8 1QE (☎0117/929 4399); 38 Sidney St, Cambridge CB2 3HX (☎01223/366966); 75 Deansgate, Manchester M3 2BW (☎0161/834 0668); and personal callers at 117 Euston Rd, London NW1 2SX; 88 Vicar Lane, Leeds LS1 7JH; 36 George St, Oxford OX1 2OJ; and branches at the universities of Birmingham, Kent, London and Loughborough. *Discount fares, particularly good for students and under-26s.*

Sunset Air Fares, Sunset Business Centre, Manchester Rd, Bolton BL4 8RT (☎0870/607 5085). *Flight-only and fly-drive deals from regional airports to Kalamáta, Préveza and Kavála (for Thássos) in addition to the usual destinations; typically on Flying Colours.*

Thomson/Britannia Flights ☎0990/502555. *Limited flight-only deals to Corfu, Rhodes, Iráklion (Crete), Thessaloníki, Zákynthos, Kós, Sámos, Kefalloniá, Skiáthos and Kavála (for Thássos) on Britannia Airways.*

Trailfinders, 42–50 Earls Court Rd, London W8 6FT (☎020/7937 5400); 194 Kensington High St, London W8 7RG (☎020/7938 3939); 22–24 The Priory, Queensway, Birmingham B4 6BS (☎0121/236 1234); 48 Corn St, Bristol BS1 1HQ (☎0117/929 9000); 254–284 Sauchiehall St, Glasgow G2 3EH (☎0141/353 2224); 58 Deansgate, Manchester M3 2FF (☎0161/839 6969). *One of the best-informed and most efficient agents, for scheduled flights only; all branches open daily until 6pm, Thurs until 7pm.*

work out slightly pricier than BA or Olympic. A sixty-day midweek ticket, tax inclusive, might set you back £220 during low season, £235 in summer; changing your return date will incur a small charge, but at least (unlike at Olympic) it's allowed.

Cronus Airlines, so far the only Greek airline to challenge Olympic on international routes, offers daily late-evening services to Athens, arriving at dawn the next day. Advertised flights to Thessaloníki all currently go via Athens, with a whopping three-hour layover, but Cronus plans to introduce three weekly direct services to Thessaloníki in 2000. Fares to either city weigh in at about £160 low season, tax included, or £235 high season.

Note that flights from **British regional airports** route through Heathrow in the first instance, with a supplement applicable. Olympic has a code-sharing partnership with British Midland, which should ease the pain (and possibly the cost) of connections from Leeds and Manchester in particular.

Potentially the cheapest, no-frills service is provided by **EasyJet**, out of London Luton to Athens only; fares vary from £49 to £159 **one way**, tax included, with the exact amount depending on the season, how far in advance you book and availability for the particular flight. Departures also vary with time of year, but typically there are two flights daily, at around noon and late in the evening. The cheaper tickets are obviously very restrictive, and there's no on-board meal service. On the plus side, EasyJet usually offers special train fares from central London to Luton in co-operation with Thameslink.

PACKAGES AND TOURS

Virtually every British **tour operator** includes Greece in its programme, though with many of the larger groups you'll find choices limited to the established resorts – notably the islands of Rhodes, Kós, Crete, Skiáthos, Zákynthos and

---

SPECIALIST PACKAGE OPERATORS

VILLA OR VILLAGE ACCOMMODATION

Argo Holidays, 100 Wigmore St, London W1H 9DR (☎020/7331 7070). *Packages to luxury hotels and top villas on more than thirty islands; special strengths the Argo-Saronic, northeast Aegean and Dodecanese (including "Winter Sun" on Rhodes).*

CV Travel, 43 Cadogan St, London SW3 2PR (☎020/7591 2800). *Quality villas on Corfu and Paxí.*

Direct Greece, Granite House, 31–33 Stockwell Street, Glasgow G1 4RY (℀0141/559 7111 or in Manchester at 0161/236 2838) *Moderately priced villas, apartments and restored houses on Rhodes, Hálki, Lésvos, Corfu, Crete, Lefkádha, Zákynthos and (on the mainland) Párga and the outer Máni.*

Elysian Holidays, 16 High St, Tenterden, Kent TN30 6AP (☎01580/766599). *Began as Híos restored-house specialists, now have a wide programme of quality premises on Páros, Sýros, Spétses, Mýkonos, Pátmos and the Candíli Estate on Évvia.*

Filoxenia/Grecofile, Sourdock Hill, Barkisland, Halifax, West Yorkshire HX4 0AG (☎01422/375999). *Tailor-made itineraries and bespoke packages to unspoiled areas of the mainland such as the Peloponnese and Epirus; flight arrangements on scheduled or charter airlines.*

Greek Islands Club, 10–12 Upper Square, Old Isleworth, Middlesex TW7 7BJ (☎020/8232 9780). *Extremely high-quality villas throughout the Ionian and Sporades islands; also Kýthira, Crete and Sývota on the Epirot mainland.*

Greek Sun Holidays, 1 Bank St, Sevenoaks, Kent TN13 1UW (☎01732/740317). *Good-value package holidays, including some fly-drive options, in the Dodecanese, northeast Aegean, Cyclades and on Mount Pílion; also tailor-made island-hopping itineraries.*

Hidden Greece ☎020/8766 7868. *A bespoke agency running for forty years now, arranging accommodation on and transport to thirty less-visited islands, mostly in the Cyclades and Dodecanese.*

Houses of Pilion ☎01963/210667 (calls are forwarded automatically to the proprietors, who live full-time on the peninsula). *Longest-running operator for the area, offering an excellent collection of inland cottages and coastal apartments.*

Laskarina Holidays, St Marys Gate, Wirksworth, Derbyshire DE4 4DQ (☎01629/822203). *Top-end villas, quality hotels and restored houses on Spétses, Skópelos, Alónissos, Hálki, Sými, Tílos, Kálymnos, Télendhos, Léros, Lipsí, Pátmos, Ikaría and Sámos; consistently high marks for customer service.*

Pure Crete, 79 George St, Croydon CR10 1LD (☎020/8760 0879 or info@pure-crete.com). *Characterful, converted cottages and farmhouses in western Crete.*

Simply Simon Holidays, 45 Nevern Square, London SW5 9PF (☎020/7373 1933). *Cyclades specialist, focusing on small hotels and studios; direct charters to Mýkonos and Santoríni.*

Simply Travel, Chiswick Gate, 598–608 Chiswick High Rd, London W4 5RT. Administers three separate programmes: Greece (☎020/8275 0955) for the mainland; Simply Ionian (☎020/8995 1121); and Simply Crete (☎020/8994 4462). *Offers high-quality apartments, villas and small hotels for each area.*

Skiathos Travel, 4 Holmesdale Rd, Kew Gardens, Richmond, Surrey TW9 3J2 (☎020/8940 5157). *Long-running Sporades specialist; also a small Cyclades programme, and some flight-only deals.*

Sunvil Holidays, Sunvil House, 7–8 Upper Square, Old Isleworth, Middlesex TW7 7BJ (☎020/8568 4499). *Durable and consistently high-quality outfit specializing in upmarket hotels and villas in the Ionian islands, the Sporades, select Cyclades, western Crete, Límnos, Thássos, the Peloponnese, Párga and Sývota. Also main-*

Corfu, plus Tólo and the Halkidhikí peninsula on the mainland. If you buy one of these at a last-minute discount, especially in spring or autumn, you may find it costs little more than a flight – and you can use the accommodation offered as much or as little as you want.

For a more low-key and genuinely "Greek" resort, however, it's better to book your holiday through one of the **specialist agencies** listed below. Most of these are fairly small-scale operations, providing competitively priced packages with flights (unless otherwise stated) and often

land fly-drives, and sailing holidays in the Ionian islands.

Tapestry Holidays, 24 Chiswick High Rd, London W4 1TE (☎020/8235 7788). *Top-rated Turkey specialists now branched out into quality apartments on Kefalloniá and Pílion.*

Travel à la Carte, The Whitehouse, Bucklebury Alley, Cold Ash, Newbury, Berks RH16 9NN (☎01635/201140 or *www.travelalacarte.co.uk*). *Established Corfu specialist, now branched out to beach and rural villas on Alónissos, Hálki, Paxí, Skiáthos, Skópelos and Sými as well.*

Travelux, 40 High St, Tenterden, Kent TN30 6AR (☎01580/765000; *www.travelux.co.uk*). *Long-established Lefkádha villa specialists; also the only operator to Zagóri, with the best hotels there and a range of activity holidays (such as hiking, painting, photography, Alexander technique).*

WALKING HOLIDAYS

Alternative Travel Group ☎01865/315678. *Somewhat pricey guided walks on Ándhros, Náxos and select mainland destinations.*

Headwater, 146 London Rd, Northwich, Cheshire CW9 5HH (☎01606/813399). *Treks on Mount Taïyettos, the Máni and Amorgós island.*

Ramblers Holidays, Longcroft House, Fretherne Rd, Welwyn Garden City, Herts AL8 6PQ (☎01707/331133). *An outfit which has shed its former fusty image and now offers fairly challenging treks in Crete and the Máni; also easier outings on Sámos, Pátmos, Náxos and Amorgós.*

Sherpa Expeditions, 131a Heston Rd, Hounslow, Middlesex TW5 0RD (☎020/8577 2717). *Good range of more difficult mainland treks on Mount Ólympos and in the Píndhos, though some of these may be self-guiding.*

Waymark Holidays, 44 Windsor Rd, Slough SL1 2EJ (☎01753/516477). *Spring and autumn walking holidays on Sámos, Mílos, Pílion and Crete.*

NATURE AND WILDLIFE

Limosa ☎01263/578143. *Birding on Lésvos, and in the wetlands and forests of Thrace.*

Marengo Guided Walks, 17 Bernard Crescent, Hunstanton P36 6ER (☎01485/532710 or *marengo@supanet.com*). *Annually changing programme of easy walks guided by ace botanist Lance Chilton; past one-week offerings have included Sámos, Sými, northern Lésvos, Crete and Thássos.*

Naturetrek, The Cadcam Centre, Bighton, near Alresford, Hampshire SO24 9RE (☎01962/733051 or *www.naturetrek.co.uk*). *Fairly pricey but expertly led one-week birdwatching expeditions on Sámos and Lésvos, plus a two-week natural history tour of the Píndhos.*

SAILING HOLIDAYS

Explore Worldwide, 1 Frederick St, Aldershot, Hampshire GU11 1LQ (☎01252/760 1000). *Kaïki-based island-wanderer trips, mostly in the Cyclades, with light walking ashore.*

Nautilus Yachting ☎01732/867445. *Bareboat yacht charter out of Corfu, Lefkádha, Kós, Rhodes and Skiáthos; also flotilla holidays from Lefkádha and Póros.*

Sunsail, The Port House, Port Solent, Portsmouth, Hampshire, PO6 4TH (☎02392/222222). *Resort-based tuition in dinghy sailing, yachting and windsurfing at five locations in Greece, including the south Pílion; one- or two-week flotilla sailings northward out of Kós Town, Lefkádha, Kefalloniá and the Sporades.*

The Moorings, Bradstowe House, Middle Wall, Whitstable, Kent CT5 1BF (☎01227/776677). *Operates bareboat charters out of Athens, Corfu and Kós Town.*

Top Yacht Charter, Andrew Hill Lane, Hedgerley, Bucks SL2 3UW (☎01753/646636). *Bareboat charters from six bases around Greece, including Kós and Rhodes.*

MIND AND BODY

Skyros Centre, 92 Prince of Wales Rd, London NW5 3NE (☎020/7267 4424). *Holistic health, fitness and "personal growth" holidays at two centres on the island of Skýros, as well as prestigious writers' workshops tutored by big names.*

more traditional village-based accommodation. They also make an effort to offer islands and corners of the mainland without overdeveloped tourist resorts. Such agencies tend to divide into two types: those which, like the major chains, contract a block of accommodation and flight seats (or even their own plane) for a full season, and an increasing number of bespoke agencies which tailor holidays at your request, making all transport and accommodation arrangements on the spot. These can work out somewhat more expensive, but the quality of flights and lodging is often correspondingly higher.

The **walking** holiday operators listed in the box on p.7 run trekking groups of ten to fifteen people plus an experienced guide. Walks tend to be day-long hikes from one or more bases, or point-to-point treks staying in village accommodation en route. Camping out is not usually involved.

Sailing holidays usually involve small flotillas of four- to eight-berth yachts, and can be based on shore or at sea. All levels of experience are catered for. Prices start at around £520 per person, flights included, in a group of four on a two-week flotilla. Alternatively, confident sailors can simply arrange to charter a yacht from a broker; the Greek National Tourist Organization has lists of companies.

BY TRAIN

Travelling by **train** from Britain to Greece takes around three and a half days and fares work out much more expensive than flights. However, with a regular ticket stopovers are possible – in France, Switzerland and Italy – while with an InterRail or Eurail train pass you can take in Greece as part of a wider rail trip around Europe.

ROUTES

The most practical route from Britain takes in France, Switzerland and Italy before crossing on the ferry from Bari or Brindisi to Pátra (Patras). Book seats well in advance, especially in summer (for ferry information, see the box on p.10).

Until 1990, the route through **former Yugoslavia** was the most popular; for obvious reasons this is a non-starter for the foreseeable future. A more rambling alternative from Budapest runs via **Bucharest** and **Sofia** to **Thessaloníki**, which is advised as your first stop, since Athens is nearly nine hours further on the train.

RAIL TICKET OFFICES

Eurotrain, 52 Grosvenor Gardens, London SW1 (☎020/7730 3402).

Rail Europe, 179 Piccadilly, London W1 (☎0990/848848).

Wasteels, Victoria Station, London SW1 (☎020/7834 7066).

BUS TICKET OFFICES

National Express Eurolines, 52 Grosvenor Gardens, London SW1 (☎0990/808080).

TICKETS AND PASSES

Regular train tickets from Britain to Greece are not good value; London to Athens costs at least £380 return. If you are **under 26**, you can get a **BIJ ticket**, discounting these fares by around 25 percent; these are available through Eurotrain and Wasteels (see box above for addresses). Both regular and BIJ tickets have two months' return validity, or can be purchased as one ways, and the Italy routes include the ferry crossing. The tickets also allow for stopovers, so long as you stick to the route prescribed.

Better value by far is to buy an **InterRail youth pass** which is available to European residents and offers unlimited travel on a zonal basis on up to 25 European rail networks. The only extras you pay are supplements on certain express trains, plus half-price fares in Britain (or the country of issue) and on the cross-Channel ferries. The pass includes the ferry from Brindisi in southern Italy to Pátra in Greece. There are several types: to reach Greece from the UK you'll need a pass valid for at least two zones (£209 for 22 days), though if you're intending to travel further in Europe you might invest in an all-zone card for £259; Greece is zoned with Italy, Turkey and Slovenia. The **Adult InterRail pass**, dubbed the 26+, operates on a similar basis, costing £279 for one zone and £359 for an all-zone card.

Finally, anyone over sixty and holding a British Rail Senior Citizen Railcard, can buy a **Rail Europe Senior Card** (£5 for a year). This gives up to thirty percent reductions on rail fares throughout Europe and thirty percent off sea crossings.

BY BUS

With charter flights and no-frills airlines like EasyJet offering such competitive rates, it's hard to find good reasons for wanting to spend three or four days on a bus to Greece. However, it's still a considerably cheaper option than taking the train.

National Express Eurolines (bookable through any National Express office; see box opposite) is the only coach company still offering this line, and only during summer. The **route** is either Belgium, Germany and Austria, or via France, to Italy, and then a ferry across to Greece. Stops of about twenty minutes are made every five or six hours, with the odd longer break for roadside café meals.

BY CAR

If you have the time and inclination, **driving to Greece** can be a pleasant proposition. Realistically, though, it's really only worth considering if you have at least a month to spare, are going to stay in Greece for an extended period, or want to take advantage of various stopovers en route.

It's important to plan ahead. The **Automobile Association** (AA) provides a comprehensive service offering general advice on all facets of driving to Greece and the names and addresses of useful contact organizations. Their European Routes Service (contact the AA on ☎01256/20123) can arrange a detailed print-out of a route to follow.

The most popular **route** is down through France and Italy to catch one of the Adriatic ferries. A longer alternative through Eastern Europe (Hungary, Romania and Bulgaria) is just about feasible.

SHUTTLE AND THE FERRIES

The **Shuttle** train operates trains 24 hours a day, carrying cars, motorcycles, buses and their passengers, and taking 35 minutes between Folkestone and Calais. At peak times, services operate every fifteen minutes, making advance bookings unnecessary; during the night, services still run hourly. Through trains connect London with Paris in just over three hours. Return fares from May to August cost around £280–310 per vehicle (passengers included), with discounts in the low season; passenger fares from London to Paris cost £95–135 return, depending on when you book.

The alternative **cross-Channel** options for most travellers are the **ferry** or **hovercraft** links between Dover and Calais or Boulogne (the quickest and cheapest routes), Ramsgate and Dunkerque, or Newhaven and Dieppe.

CROSS-CHANNEL INFORMATION

Hoverspeed ☎01304/240101. To Boulogne and Calais.
P&O European Ferries
Dover (☎01304/203388);
Portsmouth (☎02392/772244);
London (☎0990/980980). To Calais.
Sally Line ☎01843/595522. To Dunkerque.
Shuttle ☎0990/353535 (Customer Services Centre Information and ticket sales).
Stena Sealink Line, Ashford
(☎01233/647047). To Calais and Dieppe.

Ferry **prices** vary according to the time of year and, for motorists, the size of your car. The Dover–Calais/Boulogne runs, for example, start at about £180 return low season, £220 return high season for a car with up to five passengers. **Foot passengers** should be able to cross for about £50 return year round; taking a **motorbike** costs from £80–90 return.

VIA ITALY

Heading for western Greece or the Ionian islands, it has always made most sense to drive **via Italy** – and whatever your final destination, taking a ferry on the final leg makes for a more relaxed journey. Initial routes down to Italy through **France** and **Switzerland** are very much a question of personal taste. One of the most direct is Calais–Reims–Geneva–Milan and then down the Adriatic coast to the Italian port of your choice. Even on the quickest autoroutes (with their accompanying tolls), the journey will involve two overnight stops.

Once in Italy, there's a choice of five **ports**. Regular car and passenger ferries link **Ancona**, **Bari** and **Brindisi** with **Igoumenítsa** (the port of Epirus in western Greece) and/or **Pátra** (at the northwest tip of the Peloponnese and the closest port to Athens). Most sail via the island of **Corfu**, and a very few companies link other Ionian islands such as **Paxí**, **Itháki** or **Kefalloniá** en route to Pátra during the summer; you can stop over at no extra charge if you get these halts specified on your ticket. Generally, these ferries run year round, but services are greatly reduced out of season. Ferries also sail regularly from **Venice** and less frequently from **Trieste**. For more details see the box on p.10.

FERRIES FROM ITALY

Note: all timings are approximate.

From Ancona Strintzis, ANEK, and Minoan to Igoumenítsa (16–23hr) or Pátra (20–31hr); daily or nearly so year round. Strintzis via Corfu and Igoumenítsa or direct to Pátra; Minoan and ANEK via Igoumenítsa only. Most sailings 8–10pm, but there are a number of afternoon departures. Also Superfast direct to Pátra in 19hr almost daily year round.

From Bari Ventouris to Igoumenítsa direct (11hr 30min), roughly every other day March–Sept; late June–early Sept calls at Corfu (10hr) en route; Marlines to Igoumenítsa (13hr) daily late June–mid-Sept; Superfast heads almost daily year-round for Igoumenítsa (9hr) and then Pátra (15hr 30min). All sailings 6–9pm.

From Brindisi Adriatica to Corfu (7hr 30min), Igoumenítsa (9hr 30min) and Pátra (19hr) every other day year round; direct to Pátra (14hr) summer only. Fraglines to Corfu/Igoumenítsa (10hr) almost daily March–Oct; Agoudimos to Igoumenítsa most days June–Dec (12hr); Diler to Igoumenítsa (7–8hr 30min) almost daily May–Sept, via Corfu Aug. Hellenic Mediterranean Lines to Corfu/Igoumenítsa (8hr/9hr 30min), 3–7 weekly April–Oct; to Kefalloniá (15hr), most days late June–early Sept; Paxí and Zákynthos, several weekly early

July–early Sept. European Seaways, 4 to 6 weekly April–Sept to Corfu and usually Igoumenítsa (10hr). Med Link Lines, daily to Pátra (13hr) April–Sept; via Kefalloniá (11hr) 4–7 weekly July–Aug. Strintzis almost daily late March–Oct to Corfu (7hr) and Igoumenítsa (8hr 30min); Ventouris, every other day May–June & Sept, daily July–Aug to Igoumenítsa (8hr), via Corfu (6hr) July–Aug. Most ferries leave Brindisi 8–11pm, but Ventouris, Fragline, Agoudimos, and European Seaways offer 9–10am departures at peak season, Strintzis and Diler consistently so across the year. There's usually at least one daily boat in winter, except between Christmas and New Year's Eve.

From Trieste ANEK to Igoumenítsa (24–28hr), 2–5 weekly almost year-round; continues to Corfu 1–2 times weekly April–Oct, to Pátra (32–35hr) 3–4 weekly April–Oct. Departs mid- to late afternoon.

From Venice Strintzis, 2–3 weekly Nov–March, 4 weekly otherwise to Igoumenítsa (28hr), Corfu and Pátra (38hr); Minoan 4–5 weekly late Oct–late March, daily otherwise to the same ports (25hr & 36hr respectively). Note that, along with Ancona, this is one of the more reliable departure ports out of season. Departures about 5pm.

SAMPLE FARES

Prices below are one-way high/low season fares; port taxes (£3–5 per person in each direction) are not included. Substantial reductions apply on many lines for both InterRail or Eurail pass-holders, and for those under 26. Slight discounts are usually available on return fares. Many companies allow you to sleep in your van on board, sparing you the cost of a cabin berth; ask about reduced "camping" fares.

Igoumenítsa from Bari or Brindisi: deck class £18–£24/£12–£20; car from £24–£32/£13–£20. Superfast fares are £32/£22 (deck) & £32/£19 (car), also valid all the way to **Pátra**.

Pátra from Ancona: deck class £42/£28; car from £65/£35. Superfast fares £52/£36 (deck) & £74/£40 (car).

Pátra from Brindisi: deck class £25–£35/£15–£24; car from £28–£46/£18–£25.

Pátra from Trieste: deck class £39/£29; car from £79/£39.

Pátra from Venice: deck class £43/£32; car from £86/£43.

The crossing to Igoumenítsa is usually, but not always, substantially cheaper than to Pátra; the cheapest of all the crossings is from Brindisi to Igoumenítsa. However, drivers will discover that the extra cost in Italian motorway tolls and fuel offsets the Brindisi route's savings over those from Bari, Ancona or Venice; the shipping compa-

nies are well aware of this and set their prices accordingly.

In summer, it is essential to **book tickets** a few days ahead, especially in the peak July–August season. During the winter you can usually just turn up at the main ports (Ancona and Venice have the most reliable departures at that

ITALIAN AGENTS

The dialling code for Italy is ☎39.

Adriatica, c/o Adria Shipping, Corso Garibaldi 85/87, Brindisi (☎0831/523825, fax 590758).

Agoudimos, c/o Hellas Ferry Lines, Corso Garibaldi 81, Brindisi (☎0831/529091, fax 529217)

ANEK, Ancona: Stazione Marittima (☎071/205959); Trieste, Stazione Marittima (☎040/302888, fax 311881).

Diler, c/o Italian Ferries, Corso Garibaldi 96/98, Brindisi (☎0831/590305, fax 590191).

European Seaways, c/o Adriatico, Corso Garibaldi 54, Brindisi (☎0831/523355, fax 561014)

Fraglines, Corso Garibaldi 88, Brindisi (☎0831/590196, fax 590181).

Hellenic Mediterranean Lines, Corso Garibaldi 8, Brindisi (☎0831/528531, fax 526872)

Marlines, c/o Pier Paolo Santelia, Stazione Marittima, Bari (☎080/52 31 824, fax 52 30 287).

Med Link Lines, c/o Discovery Shipping, Corso Garibaldi 49, Brindisi (☎0831/527667, fax 564070).

Minoan Lines, Ancona: Via Astagno 1 (☎071/201708, fax 201933); Venice, Santa Marta (San Basilio) Magazzino 17 (☎041/27 12 345, fax 52 12 929).

Strintzis Lines, Brindisi: Corso Garibaldi 65 (☎0831/562200, fax 568300); Ancona: Stazione Marittima (☎071/20 71 068, fax 20 70 874); Venice: Stazione Marittima 103 (☎041/27 70 559, fax 27 70 367).

Superfast Ferries, Ancona: Morandi & Co, Via XXIX Settembre 2/0 (☎071/202033, fax 202219); Bari, c/o Portrans, Corso A. de Tullio 6 (☎080/52 11 416, fax 57 20 427).

Ventouris, Bari: c/o P. Lorusso & Co, Stazione Marittima Booths 3–4 (☎080/52 17 118, fax 52 17 734); Brindisi, c/o Venmare, Corso Garibaldi 56 (☎0831/5212614, fax 521654).

UK AGENTS

The following are UK agents for advance bookings:

Serena Holidays, 40 Kenway Rd, London SW5 (☎020/7373 6548).
For Adriatica Lines.

Viamare Travel Ltd, Graphic House, 2 Sumatra Rd, London NW6 (☎020/7431 4560).
Agents for Agoudimos, ANEK, Fragline, Marlines, Med Link, Strintzis, Superfast, Ventouris.

DIRECT CONTACTS

Most of the more durable shipping companies have Web sites or email addresses for making bookings. They include:

Adriatica *www.adriatica.it*
adrnav@interbusiness.it
ANEK *www.anek.gr*
Hellenic Mediterranean Lines
hml@mail.otenet.gr
Marlines *www.marlines.gr*
info@marlines.gr

Minoan Lines *www.minoan.gr*
booking-eta@minoan.gr
Strintzis Lines *www.strintzis.gr*
sales@strintzis.gr
Superfast *www.superfast.com*
superfast@superfast.com

time of year), but it's still wise to book in advance, certainly if you are taking a car or want a cabin. A few phone calls or Internet searches before leaving are, in any case, advisable, as the range of fares and operators (from Brindisi especially) is considerable; if you do just turn up at the port, spend some time shopping around the agencies.

VIA HUNGARY, ROMANIA AND BULGARIA

Avoiding former Yugoslavia involves a pretty substantial diversion through Hungary, Romania and Bulgaria. This is not a drive to contemplate unless you actively want to see some of the countries en route – too exhausting and too problematic. However, it's all simpler than it was, with visas easier to obtain at the borders, if you haven't fixed them in advance.

From **Budapest**, the quickest route **through Romania** is via Timisoara, then to head towards Sofia in Bulgaria and on across the Rila mountains to the border at Kulata. Once at the Greek border, it's a three- to four-hour drive to Thessaloníki or Kavála. Bear in mind that road conditions are often poor and border crossings difficult. Contact the respective embassies and the AA for more advice.

GETTING THERE FROM IRELAND

Summer charters operate from Dublin and Belfast to Athens and there are additional services to Mýkonos, Rhodes, Crete and Corfu. A high-season charter from Dublin to Athens costs upwards of IR£200 return, while a week's package on one of the above islands costs from IR£440 per person for two weeks.

Year-round **scheduled services** with Aer Lingus and British Airways operate from both Dublin and Belfast via Heathrow to Athens, or from Dublin via Heathrow on British Midland and Olympic, but you'll find them pricey compared to charters. Youth and student fares are offered by USIT (see box below for address).

Travelling **via London** is an alternative if flights are in short supply, and may sometimes

AIRLINES IN IRELAND

Aer Lingus 46–48 Castle St, Belfast (☎02890/245151); 2 Academy St, Cork (☎021/274331); 41 Upper O'Connell St, Dublin (☎01/844 4777).

British Airways 9 Fountain Centre, College St, Belfast (☎02890/899131). British Airways does not have a Dublin office; for reservations from Eire, call ☎0141/222 2345, or contact Aer Lingus.

British Midland Suite 2, Fountain Centre, College St, Belfast (☎02890/241188); Nutley, Merrion Rd, Dublin (☎01/283 8833).

Olympic Airways, c/o Travel Cuts, Frankin House, 142 Pembroke Rd, Dublin (☎01/608 0090).

Ryanair, Phoenix House, Conyngham Rd, Dublin (☎01/609 7800).

TRAVEL AGENTS IN IRELAND

Balkan Tours, 37 Ann St, Belfast (☎02890/246795). *Direct charter flights.*

Joe Walsh Tours, 8–11 Baggot St, Dublin (☎01/676 3053). *General budget fares agent.*

Thomas Cook, 118 Grafton St, Dublin (☎01/677 1721). *Package holiday and flight agent, with occasional discount offers.*

Trailfinders, 4–5 Dawson Street, Dublin 2 (☎01/677 7888). *Branch of the reliable scheduled-flight discount agents.*

USIT, Fountain Centre, Belfast (☎02890/324073); 10–11 Market Parade, Patrick St, Cork (☎021/270900); 33 Ferryquay St, Derry (☎01504/371888); Aston Quay, O'Connell Bridge, Dublin (☎01/679 8833); Victoria Place, Eyre Square, Galway (☎091/565177); Central Buildings, O'Connell St, Limerick (☎061/415064); 36–37 Georges St, Waterford (☎051/72601). *Student and youth specialist.*

save you a little money, but on the whole it's rarely worth the time and effort. For the record,

budget flights to London are offered by British Midland, Aer Lingus and Ryanair.

GETTING THERE FROM NORTH AMERICA

Only a few carriers fly directly to Greece from North America, so most North Americans travel to a gateway European city, and pick up a connecting flight on from there with an associated airline. If you have time, you may well discover that it's cheaper to arrange the final Greece-bound leg of the journey yourself, in which case your only criterion will be finding a

suitable and good-value North America–Europe flight; for details of onward flights from the UK, see "Getting There from Britain" above.

The **Greek national airline**, Olympic Airways, flies out of New York (JFK), Boston, Montréal and Toronto, though the airline can offer reasonably priced add-on flights within Greece, especially to the Greek islands, leaving from the same Athens terminal that you will fly into.

Another option to consider is picking up a flight to Europe and making your way to Greece by train, in which case a **Eurail Pass** makes a reasonable investment – all the details are covered below. For details of train routes, see "Getting There from Britain".

SHOPPING FOR TICKETS

Discount ticket outlets – advertised in the Sunday travel sections of major newspapers – come in several forms. **Consolidators** buy up blocks of tickets that airlines don't think they'll be able to sell at their published fares, and unload them at a discount. Many advertise fares on a one-way basis, enabling you to fly into one city and out

AIRLINES IN NORTH AMERICA

Air Canada Canada, call directory enquiries, ☎1-800/555-1212, for local toll-free number; US, ☎1-800/776-3000.

Air France US, ☎1-800/237-2747; Canada, ☎1-800/667-2747.

Alitalia ☎1-800/223-5730.

British Airways US, ☎1-800/247-9297; Canada, ☎1-800/AIRWAYS or 1-800/668-1055.

Canadian Airlines Canada, ☎1-800/665-1177; US, ☎1-800/426-7000.

Czech Airlines ☎1-800/223-2365 or 212/765-6022; Montreal ☎1-800/561-5171; Toronto ☎1-800/641-0641.

Delta Airlines ☎1-800/241-4141.

Iberia ☎1-800/772-4642.

KLM US, ☎1-800/374-7747; Canada, ☎1-800/361-5073.

LOT Polish Airlines ☎1-800/223-0593.

Lufthansa ☎1-800/645-3880.

Olympic Airways ☎1-800/223-1226 or 212/838-3600.

Sabena ☎1-800/955-2000.

Swissair ☎1-800/221-4750.

United Airlines ☎1-800/538-2929.

from another without penalty. Consolidators normally don't impose advance purchase requirements (although in busy times you should book ahead just to be sure of getting a ticket), but they do often charge very stiff fees for date changes. **Discount agents** also deal in blocks of tickets offloaded by the airlines, but they typically offer a range of other travel-related services like insurance, rail passes, youth and student ID cards, car rentals and tours. These agencies tend to be most worthwhile for students and under-26s, who can benefit from special fares and deals. **Travel clubs** are another option – most charge an annual membership fee, which may be worth it for their discounts on air tickets and car rental. Some agencies specialize in **charter flights**, which may be even cheaper than anything available on a scheduled flight, but again there's a trade-off: departure dates are fixed, and withdrawal penalties are high (check the refund policy). Student/youth fares can sometimes save you money, though again the best deals are usually those offered by seat consolidators advertising in Sunday newspaper travel sections.

Don't automatically assume that any tickets purchased through a travel specialist will be the

---

DISCOUNT TRAVEL COMPANIES

Air Brokers International, 323 Geary St, Suite 411, San Francisco, CA 94102 (☎1-800/883-3273, www.airbrokers.com). *Consolidator.*

Air Courier Association, 191 University Boulevard, Suite 300, Denver, CO 80206 (☎303/278-8810). *Courier flight broker.*

Airhitch, 2472 Broadway, Suite 200, New York, NY 10025 (☎212/864-2000). *Standby-seat broker. For a set price, they guarantee to get you on a flight as close to your preferred destination as possible, within a week.*

Council Travel, Head Office: 205 East 42nd St, New York, NY 10017 (☎1-800/226-8624, 1-888 COUNCIL, 212/822-2700, www.counciltravel.com). *Student travel organization with sixty branches in the US.*

Educational Travel Center, 438 North Frances St, Madison, WI 53703 (☎1-800/747-5551 or 608/256-5551). *Student/youth discount agent.*

Encore Travel Club, 4501 Forbes Blvd, Lanham, MD 20706 (☎1-800/444-9800). *Discount travel club.*

Interworld Travel, 800 Douglass Rd, Miami, FL 33134 (☎305/443-4929). *Consolidator.*

Last Minute Travel Club, 100 Sylvan Rd, Suite 600, Woburn, MA 01801 (☎1-800/LAST-MIN). *Travel club specializing in standby deals.*

Moment's Notice, 7301 New Utrecht Ave, Brooklyn, NY 11204 (☎212/486-0500). *Discount travel club.*

New Frontiers/Nouvelles Frontières, 12E 33rd St, New York, NY 10016 (☎1-800/366-6387); 1001 Sherbrook East, Suite 720, Montréal, H2L 1L3 (☎514/526-8444) and other branches in LA, San Francisco and Québec City. *French discount travel firm.*

Now Voyager, 74 Varick St, Suite 307, New York, NY 10013 (☎212/431-1616). *Courier flight broker and consolidator.*

STA Travel, 10 Downing St, New York, NY 10014 (☎1-800/781-4040 or 212/627-3111) and other branches in the Los Angeles, San Francisco and Boston areas. *Worldwide specialist in independent travel.*

TFI Tours International, Head Office: 34 West 32nd St, New York, NY 10001 (☎1-800/745-8000). *Consolidator; other offices in Las Vegas, San Francisco, Los Angeles and Miami.*

Travac, 989 6th Ave, New York, NY 10018 (☎1-800/872-8800 or 212/563-3303). *Consolidator and charter broker. If you have a fax machine you can have a list of fares faxed to you by calling toll-free ☎1-888/872-8327.*

Travel Avenue, 10 South Riverside, Suite 1404, Chicago, IL 60606 (☎1-800/333-3335 or 312/876-6866). *Discount travel agent.*

Travel CUTS, 243 College St, Toronto, ON M5T 1P7 (☎1-800/667-2887), and other branches all over Canada. *Student/youth travel organization with branches all over the country.*

Travelers Advantage, 801 Royal Parkway, Suite 200, Nashville, TN 37214 (☎1-800/548-1116). *Discount travel club; annual membership required.*

UniTravel, 1177 North Warson Rd, St Louis, MO 63132 (☎1-800/325-2222). *Consolidator.*

Worldtek Travel, 111 Water St, New Haven, CT 06511 (☎1-800/243-1723). *Discount travel agency.*

Worldwide Discount Travel Club, 1674 Meridian Ave, Miami Beach, FL 33139 (☎305/534-2082). *Discount travel club.*

cheapest – once you get a quote, check with the airlines and you may turn up an even better deal. In addition, exercise caution and never deal with a company that demands cash up front or refuses to accept payment by credit card.

For destinations not handled by discounters – which applies to most regional airports – you'll have to deal with airlines' published fares. The cheapest of these is an **APEX** (Advance Purchase Excursion) ticket. This carries certain restrictions. For instance, you may be expected to book – and pay – at least 21 days before departure, keep to a minimum/maximum limit on your stay, and be liable to penalties if you change your schedule. On transatlantic routes there are also winter **Super APEX** tickets, sometimes known as "Eurosavers" – slightly cheaper than ordinary Apex, they limit your stay to between seven and 21 days. Some airlines also issue **Special APEX** tickets to those under 24, often extending the maximum stay to a year.

Note that fares are heavily dependent on **season**, and are highest from June to September; they drop either side of this, and you'll get the best deals during the low season (November– February, excluding Christmas). Note that flying on weekends ordinarily adds $50 or so to the round-trip fare; price ranges quoted in the sections below assume midweek travel.

FLIGHTS FROM THE US

The twice-weekly non-stop flights to Athens out of **New York** and **Boston** on Olympic start at around US$500 round trip in winter, rising to around $950 in summer for a maximum thirty-day stay with seven-day advance purchase. Delta has a daily direct service from New York to Athens for the same APEX fare. Prices are usually similar on British Airways, Lufthansa, Swissair, Sabena and United, although their flights are via European gateway cities. However, it is worth checking for discounts with these carriers. Swissair for example was offering a summer fare of $730 from New York at time of writing and Lufthansa and Sabena were even lower at $649. LOT Polish Airlines had special deals on their round-trip high season APEX fares from several US cities to Athens, via Warsaw ($749 from New York, $739 from Chicago, $879 from LA). United also flies to Athens from **Washington DC** for a high/low season rate of around $1140/$560. Flying in the "mid season" of September or October can make for

EUROPEAN CONNECTIONS

There are direct flights to:
Thessaloníki from Amsterdam, Brussels, Copenhagen, Dusseldorf, Frankfurt, London, Munich, Stuttgart, Vienna, Zurich.
Corfu from Amsterdam, Dusseldorf, Frankfurt, Geneva, London, Milan, Stuttgart.

significant savings. United's fare from Washington DC for instance falls from the summer high to about $790 on September 5 and Olympic will bring you from New York to Athens for $730 in the same period.

As with the service from the Eastern cities, the stiff competition between the different airlines dictates that fares to Athens from the **Mid-west** or **West Coast** are virtually identical: high/low season fares on Olympic, Delta, United, Iberia and so on start at $1040/$600 from Chicago or $1310/$1010 from LA, San Francisco or Seattle. With little else to choose between the major carriers, you might look into the stopover time at the different European gateway cities, as these can sometimes be overnight; check with your ticket agent.

FLIGHTS FROM CANADA

As with the US, air fares from **Canada** to **Athens** vary tremendously depending upon where you start your journey. Olympic fly non-stop out of Montréal and Toronto twice a week for a scheduled fare of CDN$1380 round trip in winter or CDN$1540 in summer.

Northwest/KLM operates several flights a week to Athens via Amsterdam, from Toronto, Montréal, Vancouver and Edmonton. From Toronto, expect to pay around CDN$1850 in low season, CDN$2050 in high season; and from Vancouver CDN$2100 (low) or CDN$2400 (high). Travellers from Montréal can also try the European carriers Air France, Alitalia, British Airways, Iberia, Lufthansa and Swissair, all of which operate several flights a week to Athens via major European cities. One unlikely source for good deals is Czech Airlines, which flies out of Montreal to Athens via Prague for CDN$880 (low) or CDN$1285 (high).

Air Canada, flying in conjunction with Lufthansa, quote the following low/high season fares to Athens: from Toronto/Montréal around CDN$1360/CDN$1540, and from Vancouver around CDN$1740/CDN$1970. Canadian Airlines offers a much cheaper option from Toronto at about CDN$950/CDN$1320.

RAIL PASSES

A **Eurail Pass** is not likely to pay for itself if you're planning to stick to Greece, though it's worth considering if you plan to travel to Greece across Europe from elsewhere. The pass, which must be purchased before arrival in Europe, allows unlimited free train travel in Greece and sixteen other countries. The **Eurail Youthpass** (for under-26s) costs $388 for fifteen days, $499 for 21 days or $623 for one month; if you're 26 or over you'll have to buy a first-class pass, available in fifteen-day ($554), 21-day ($718) and one-month ($890) versions. You stand a better chance of getting your

---

SPECIALIST TOUR OPERATORS

US

Astro Tours, 2359 East Main St, Columbus, OH 43209 (☎1-800/543-7717 or 614/237-7798). *Cruise packages to the Greek islands.*

Brendan Tours, 15137 Califa St, Van Nuys, CA 91411 (☎1-800/421-8446). *City highlights, cruise packages and car rental.*

Caravan Tours Inc, 401 North Michigan Ave, Suite 2800, Chicago, IL 60611 (☎1-800/621-8338). *All kinds of packages covering the entire country.*

Classic Adventures, PO Box 153, Hamlin, NY 14464-0153 (☎1-800/777-8090, www.classicadventures.com). *Trekking, biking and walking tours in May–June and Sept–Oct, covering archeological sites and coastal trips.*

Classic Holidays, 350 Park St, Suite 204, North Reading, MA 01864 (☎1-800/752-5055). *Packages from eight to 21 days, group tours and cruises.*

Classic Journeys, 5580 La Jolla Blvd. No. 104, La Jolla, CA 92037 (☎1-800/200-3887). *Walking tours of the Greek isles.*

Cloud Tours Inc, 645 Fifth Ave, New York, NY 10022 (☎1-800/223-7880 or 212/753-6104). *Affordable escorted tours and Mediterranean cruises.*

Educational Tours and Cruises, 9 Irving St, Medford, MA 02155 (☎1-800/275-4109). *Custom-designed tours to Greece and the islands, specializing in art, history, food and wine, ancient drama, painting and birdwatching.*

Elderhostel, 75 Federal St, Boston, MA 02110 (☎877/426-8056). *Educational and activity programmes for senior travellers (companions may be younger).*

Globus and Cosmos, Littleton,CO (☎1-800/221-0090, www.cosmostours.com). *Group tours and packages.*

Guaranteed Travel, 83 South St, Morristown, NJ 07963 (☎973/540-1770). *Specializes in "Greece-Your-Way" independent travel.*

Hellenic Adventures, 4150 Harriet Ave South, Minneapolis, MN 55409 (☎1-800/851-6349 or 612/827-0937). *A vast range of small group and independent tours: cultural, historical, horseback riding, hiking, wilderness, culinary and family-oriented.*

Homeric Tours, 55 East 59th St, New York, NY 10017 (☎1-800/223-5570). *All-inclusive tours from nine to 23 days, as well as cruises and charter flights.*

Insight International Tours, 745 Atlantic Ave, Suite 720, Boston, MA 02111 (☎1-800/582-8380). *General Greek vacations.*

ST Cultural Tours, 225 West 34th St, New York, NY 10122 (☎1-800/833-2111 or 212/563-1202). *A wide range of package and independent educational tours.*

Valef Yachts, Box 391, Ambler, PA 19002 (☎1-800/223-3845 or 215/641-1624). *Yachting trips and charters.*

CANADA

Adventures Abroad, 20800 Westminter Highway, Suite 2148, Richmond, BC V6V 2W3 (☎1-800/665-3998 or 604/303-1099). *General operator, offering group and individual tours and cruises.*

Auratours, 1470 Peel St, Suite 252, Montreal, Quebec H3A 1TL (☎1-800/363-0323 or 514/282-

9056). *General operator, offering group and individual tours and cruises.*

Chat Tours, 241 Bedford Rd, Toronto, Ontario M5R 2K9 (☎1-800/268-1180). *Motorcoach and sea tours, and cruises.*

money's worth out of a **Eurail Flexipass**, which is valid for a certain number of travel days in a two-month period. This, too, comes in under-26/first-class versions: ten days, costing $458/$654, and $599/$862 for fifteen days.

A further alternative is to attempt to buy an InterRail Pass in Europe (see "Getting There from Britain") – most agents don't check residential qualifications, but once you're in Europe it'll be too late to buy a Eurail Pass if you have problems. You can purchase Eurail passes from the agents listed in the box on this page.

North Americans are also eligible to purchase more specific passes valid for travel in Greece only, for details of which see "Getting Around", p.35.

RAIL CONTACTS IN NORTH AMERICA

CIT Tours, 342 Madison Ave, Suite 207, New York, NY 10173 (☎1-800/223-7987).

DER Tours/GermanRail, 9501 W Divon Ave, Suite 400, Rosemont, IL 60018 (☎1-800/421-2929 or 1-800/782-2424).

Online Travel, 9501 W Devon Ave, Suite 502, Rosemont, IL 60018 (☎1-800/660-5300)

Rail Europe, 226–230 Westchester Ave, White Plains, NY 10604 (☎1-800/438-7245).

ScanTours, 1535 6th St, Suite 205, Santa Monica, CA 90401 (☎1-800/223-7226).

GETTING THERE FROM AUSTRALIA & NEW ZEALAND

It's fairly easy to track down flights from Australia to Athens, less so from New Zealand, but given the prices and most people's travel plans, you'll probably do better looking for some kind of Round-the-World ticket that includes Greece. **If London is your first destination in Europe, and you've picked up a reasonably good deal on a flight there, it's probably best to wait until you reach the UK before arranging your onward travel to Greece; see "Getting There from Britain" for all the details.**

Fares are seasonally adjusted with low season from mid-January to the end of February and October–November; high season mid-May to August, December to mid-January; and shoulder seasons the rest of the year. Tickets purchased direct from the airlines tend to be expensive; travel agents offer much better deals on fares and have the latest information on limited specials, round-the-world fares and stopovers. Some of the best discounts are through **Flight Centres** and **STA**, who can also advise on visa regulations.

FLIGHTS FROM AUSTRALIA

Cheapest fares to Athens **from Australia** are with Gulf Air or Olympic Airways from A$1450 low season, while Alitalia via Milan, Aeroflot via Moscow and Thai Airways via Bangkok all start around A$1540. In addition Singapore Airlines has a good connecting service to Athens from $1750. Qantas and British Airways offer a free return flight within Europe for A$1850–2300 which differs only slightly from their "Global Explorer" Pass (A$2000–3000), a **Round-the-World** fare that allows six stopovers worldwide wherever these two airlines fly to. An alternative covering more destinations is the BA/Qantas "One World" deal in conjunction with American Airlines and Cathay Pacific, costing A$2400–3500. Also worth considering is Garuda's A$1600 fare from Sydney, Brisbane or Cairns via Jakarta or Denpasar to various European cities, from where you could pick up a cheap onward flight or continue **overland** to Athens.

AGENTS AND AIRLINES IN AUSTRALIA AND NEW ZEALAND

DISCOUNT TRAVEL AGENTS

Anywhere Travel, 345 Anzac Parade, Kingsford, Sydney (☎02/9663 0411, *anywhere@ozemail.com.au*).

Budget Travel, 16 Fort St, Auckland, plus branches around the city (☎09/366 0061 or 0800/808 040).

Destinations Unlimited, 3 Milford Rd, Auckland (☎09/373 4033).

Flight Centres Australia: 82 Elizabeth St, Sydney, plus branches nationwide (☎13 1600), 205 Queen St, Auckland (☎09/309 6171), plus branches nationwide. *Good discounts on fares.*

STA Travel, Australia: 702 Harris St, Ultimo, Sydney; 256 Flinders St, Melbourne; other offices in state capitals and major universities (nearest branch ☎13 1776, fastfare telesales ☎1300/360 960); New Zealand: 10 High St, Auckland (☎09/309 0458, fastfare telesales ☎09/366 6673), plus branches in Wellington, Christchurch, Dunedin, Palmerston North, Hamilton and at major universities (*www.statravelaus.com.au*). *Fare discounts for students and under-26s.*

Status Travel, 22 Cavenagh St, Darwin (☎08/8941 1843).

Student Uni Travel, 92 Pitt St, Sydney (☎02/9232 8444) plus branches in Melbourne, Darwin, Brisbane, Cairns and Perth. *Special backpacker and student rates.*

Thomas Cook, Australia: 175 Pitt St, Sydney; 257 Collins St, Melbourne plus branches in other state capitals (nearest branch ☎13 1771; telesales 1800/063 913). New Zealand: Level 5, Telstra Business Centre, Auckland (☎09/359 5200, *www.thomascook.com.au*). *Travellers' cheques and airfares.*

Trailfinders, 8 Spring St, Sydney (☎02/9247 7666). *Australian branch of UK-based fare discounter.*

Travel.com.au, 80 Clarence St, Sydney (☎02/9290 1500, *www.travel.com.au*). *Web-based travel agency, with special discounts for booking online.*

USIT Beyond, corner of Shortland and Jean Batten Place, Auckland (☎09/379 4224) plus branches in Christchurch, Hamilton, Palmerston North and Wellington (*www.usitbeyond.co.nz*). *Specialists in student and independent travel.*

SPECIALIST AGENTS

Adventure Travel Company, 164 Parnell Rd, Parnell, Auckland (☎09/379 9755). *New Zealand agent for Peregrine Adventures.*

Adventure World, 73 Walker St, North Sydney; plus branches in Adelaide, Brisbane, Melbourne and Perth (☎02/956 7766 or 1800/221 931). *Agents for a vast array of international adventure travel companies that operate trips to mainland Greece and islands.*

Australians Studying Abroad, 1/970 High St, Armadale, Melbourne (☎03/9509 1955 or 1800/645 755, *www.asatravinfo.com.au*). *Study tours exploring Greek culture and art; Anatolian tour includes Turkey too.*

Grecian Tours Travel, 237a Lonsdale St, Melbourne (☎03/663 3711). *Offers a variety of accommodation, and sightseeing tours.*

House of Holidays, 539 Main St, Mordialloc, Victoria (☎03/9580 4488). *Wholesalers with a wide selection of Greek holidays.*

Kompas Holidays, 232 Boundary St, Spring Hill, Brisbane (☎07/3222 3333 or 1800/269 968). *City stopovers, sightseeing tours, cruises, traditional accommodation and yacht charter. Booking through travel agents only.*

Kyrenia Travel Services, 92 Goulburn St, Sydney (☎02/9283 2144). *Mainland and island accommodation, land tours and island hopping.*

Peregrine Adventures, 258 Lonsdale St, Melbourne (☎03/9663 8611), plus offices in Brisbane, Sydney, Adelaide and Perth (*www.peregrine.net.au*). *Walking and cycling trips, visiting historical towns and monuments.*

Travel Market, 11th floor, 141 Queen St, Brisbane (☎07/3210 0323). *Individually tailored holidays in the Greek islands, for a range of budgets.*

AIRLINES

Aeroflot, Australia (☎02/9262 2233). *Once-a-week flight from Sydney to Athens via transfers in Moscow and Singapore.*

Air New Zealand, Australia (☎02/9223 4666); New Zealand (☎09/357 3000). *Several flights weekly to Athens via LA or Bangkok from major Australian and New Zealand cities (in partnership with the "Star Alliance" and other code-share arrangements).*

Alitalia, Australia (☎1300/653 747); New Zealand (☎09/379 4455). *Three flights per week from Sydney (plus Brisbane, Canberra and Melbourne under code-share agreements with other airlines) to Athens via Milan.*

British Airways, Australia (☎02/8904 8800); New Zealand (☎09/356 8690). *Daily flights to London from major Australasian cities: code share with Qantas in their "Global Explorer" and "One World" RTW fares.*

Garuda, Australia (☎1300/365 330); New Zealand (☎09/366 1855). *Several flights weekly from Australian and New Zealand cities to London, Frankfurt and Amsterdam via either a transfer or stopover in Denpasar/Jakarta.*

Gulf Air, Australia (☎02/9244 2199). *Once-weekly flight to Athens via Singapore and Bahrain.*

Olympic Airways, Australia (☎02/9251 2044); no New Zealand office. *Thrice-weekly flights to Athens from Sydney and Melbourne, with onward connections to other Greek destinations.*

Qantas Australia (☎13 1313); New Zealand (☎09/357 8900 and 0800/808 767). *Daily flights to London from major Australasian cities; code share with British Airways in their "Global Explorer" and "One World" RTW fares.*

Singapore Airlines, Australia (☎13 1011); New Zealand (☎09/379 3209). *Daily flights to Athens from Brisbane, Sydney, Melbourne, Perth and Auckland via Singapore.*

Thai Airways Australia (☎1300/651 960); New Zealand (☎09/377 3886). *Three flights a week to Athens via either a transfer or stopover in Bangkok from Brisbane, Sydney, Melbourne, Perth and Auckland.*

FLIGHTS FROM NEW ZEALAND

From New Zealand, the best deals to Athens are with Thai Airlines via Bangkok from $1999, and Singapore Airlines via Singapore and Alitalia via Milan, both for around NZ$2275. There's also a very versatile offer with Lufthansa from $2299, who can route you through anywhere that Air New Zealand or Qantas flies – including Los Angeles, Singapore, Sydney, Hong Kong or Tokyo – for a stopover. Lufthansa are also partners in the "Star Alliance" **RTW fare**, starting at NZ$3299. British Airways/Qantas can get you to a variety of European destinations, including Athens for $2475, but you may be better off with their "Global Explorer" or "One World" RTW fares from NZ$2999.

TRAVELLERS WITH DISABILITIES

It is all too easy to wax lyrical over the attractions of Greece: the stepped, narrow alleys, the ease of travel by bus and ferry, the thrill of clambering around the great archeological sites. It is almost impossible, on the other hand, for the able-bodied travel writer to see these attractions as potential

hazards for anyone who has difficulty in walking, is wheelchair-bound or suffers from some other disability.

However, don't be discouraged. It is possible to enjoy an inexpensive and trauma-free holiday in Greece if some time is devoted to gathering **information** before arrival. Much existing or readily available information is out of date – you should always try to double-check. A number of addresses of contact organizations are published below. The Greek National Tourist Office is a good first step as long as you have specific questions to put to them; they publish a useful questionnaire which you could send to hotels or owners of apartment/villa accommodation.

PLANNING A HOLIDAY

There are **organized tours** and **holidays** specifically for people with disabilities; many companies in Britain will advise on the suitability of holidays or villas advertised in their brochures. If you want to be more independent, it's perfectly possible, provided that you do not leave home with the vague hope that things will turn out all right, and that "people will help out" when you need assistance. This cannot be relied on. You must either be completely confident that you can manage alone, or travel with an able-bodied friend (or two).

It's important to become an authority on where you must be self-reliant and where you may expect help, especially regarding transport and accommodation. For example, to get between the terminals at Athens airport, you will have to fight for a taxi; it is not the duty of the airline staff to find you one.

It is also vital to **be honest** – with travel agencies, insurance companies, companions and, above all, with yourself. Know your limits and

make sure others know them. If you do not use a wheelchair all the time but your walking capabilities are limited, remember that you are likely to need to cover greater distances while travelling (often over tougher terrain and in hotter weather) than you are used to. If you use a wheelchair, have it serviced before you go, and carry a repair kit.

Read your travel **insurance** small print carefully to make sure that people with a pre-existing medical condition are not excluded. And use your travel agent to make your journey simpler: **airlines** or bus companies can cope better if they are expecting you, with a wheelchair provided at airports and staff primed to help. A **medical certificate** of your fitness to travel, provided by your doctor, is also extremely useful; some airlines or insurance companies may insist on it.

Make a **list** of all the facilities that will make your life easier while you are away. You may want a ground-floor room, or access to a large elevator; you may have special dietary requirements, or need level ground to enable you to reach shops, beaches, bars and places of interest. You should also keep track of all your other special needs, making sure, for example, that you have extra supplies of drugs – carried with you if you fly – and a prescription including the generic name in case of emergency. Carry spares of any kind of drug, clothing or equipment that might be hard to find in Greece; if there's an association representing people with your disability, contact them early in the planning process.

VISAS AND RED TAPE

UK and all other EU nationals need only a valid passport for entry to Greece; you are no longer stamped in on arrival or out upon departure, and in theory at least enjoy uniform civil rights with Greek citizens. US, Australian, New Zealand, Canadian and most non-EU Europeans receive mandatory entry and exit stamps in their passports and can stay, as tourists, for ninety days. If you arrive on a flight or boat from another EU state, such nationals may not be stamped in routinely – make sure this is done to avoid unpleasantness on exit.

If you are planning to **travel overland**, you should check current visa requirements for Hungary, Romania and Bulgaria at their closest consulates; transit visas for most of these territories are at present issued at the borders, though at a higher price than if obtained in advance at a local consulate.

VISA EXTENSIONS

If you wish to remain in Greece for longer than three months, you should officially apply for an **extension**. This can be done in the larger cities like Athens, Thessaloníki, Pátra, Rhodes and Iráklio through the *Ypiresía Allodhapón* (Aliens' Bureau); prepare yourself for concerted bureaucracy. In other locations you visit the local police station, where the staff are apt to be more co-operative.

Unless they are of Greek descent, visitors from **non-EU** countries are currently allowed only one six-month extension to a tourist visa, which costs 11,000dr. In theory, **EU nationals** are allowed to stay indefinitely but, at the time of writing, must still present themselves every six months or every year, according to whether they have a non-employment resident visa or a work permit; the first extension is free, but you will probably be charged for subsequent extensions. In all cases, the procedure should be set in motion a couple of weeks before your time runs out. If you don't have a work permit, you will be required to present pink, personalized bank **exchange receipts** (see "Currency Regulations", p.29) totalling at least 500,000dr for the preceding three months, as proof that you have sufficient funds to support yourself without working. Possession of unexpired credit cards, a Greek savings account passbook or travellers' cheques can to some extent substitute for the pink receipts.

Certain individuals get around the law by leaving Greece every three months and re-entering a few days later, ideally via a different frontier post, for a new, ninety-day tourist stamp. However, with the recent flood of Albanian and Eastern European refugees into the country, all looking for work, security and immigration personnel don't always look very kindly on this practice.

If you **overstay** your time and then leave under your own power – ie are not deported – you'll be given a 22,000dr spot fine upon departure, effectively a double-priced retroactive visa extension; no excuses will be entertained except perhaps a doctor's certificate stating you were immobilized in hospital. It cannot be overemphasized just how exigent Greek immigration officials often are on this issue.

GREEK EMBASSIES ABROAD

Australia 9 Turrana St, Yarralumla, Canberra, ACT 2600 (☎02/6273 3011).
Britain 1a Holland Park, London W11 3TP (☎020/7221 6467).
Canada 80 Maclaren St, Ottawa, ON K2P 0K6 (☎613/238-6271).
Ireland 1 Upper Pembroke St, Dublin 2 (☎01/676 7254).
New Zealand 5–7 Willeston St, Wellington (☎04/473 7775).
US 2221 Massachusetts Ave NW, Washington DC 20008 (☎202/939-5800).

INSURANCE

British and other EU nationals are officially entitled to free medical care in Greece (see "Health Matters", p.25) upon presentation of an E111 form, available from most post offices. "Free", however, means admittance only to the lowest grade of state hospital (known as a *yenikó nosokomío*), and does not include nursing care or the cost of medication. Occasionally, hospital staff greet E111s with uncomprehending looks, in which case you may have to request reimbursal by the NHS upon your return home. If you need prolonged medical care, you should make use of private treatment, which is expensive – 8000dr minimum for a brief clinic consultation.

Some form of **travel insurance**, therefore, is advisable – and essential for **North Americans** and **Australasians**, whose countries have no formal health-care agreements with Greece (other than allowing for free emergency trauma treatment). For **medical claims**, keep receipts, including those from pharmacies. You will have to pay for all private medical care on the spot (insurance claims can be processed if you have hospital treatment) but it can all be (eventually) claimed back.

A typical travel insurance policy provides cover for the **loss** of baggage, tickets and – up to a certain limit – cash or cheques, as well as **cancellation or curtailment** of your journey. Most of them exclude "**dangerous sports**" unless an extra premium is paid: in the Greek islands this means motorbiking, windsurfing and possibly sailing, with most visitors engaging in one or the other at some point. Read prospective policies carefully; coverage can vary wildly for roughly similar premiums and many policies can be adapted to exclude cover you don't need. If you take medical coverage, ascertain whether benefits will be paid as treatment proceeds or only after return home, and whether there is a **24-hour**

TRAVEL INSURANCE COMPANIES

AUSTRALIA
Cover More ☎02/9202 8000 or ☎1800/251881
Ready Plan ☎03/9791 5077 or ☎1300/557 017

BRITAIN
Columbus Direct Insurance ☎020/7375 0011
Endsleigh Insurance ☎020/7436 4451
Marcus Hearne & Co Ltd ☎020/7739 3444
STA Travel ☎020/7361 6161
USIT Campus ☎0870/240 1010 (national call centre)
Worldwide Travel Insurance Services Ltd ☎01892/833 338

IRELAND
USIT Now ☎01/602 1600 or 679 8833

NEW ZEALAND
Ready Plan ☎09/300 5333

NORTH AMERICA
Access America ☎1-800/284 8300; Canada, ☎1-800/654-1908
Carefree Travel Insurance ☎1-800/323 3149
STA Travel ☎1-800/777 0112
Travel Guard ☎1-800/826 1300; Canada, ☎715/345-0505
Travel Insurance Services ☎1-800/937 1387
Worldwide Assistance ☎1-800/821 2828

medical emergency number. When securing baggage cover, make sure that the **per-article limit** (typically under £500 equivalent) will cover your most valuable possession.

EUROPEAN COVER

In **Britain and Ireland**, travel insurance schemes (from around £25 for three weeks) are sold by a number of specialist insurance companies and travel agents, listed in the box on p.23, as well as by banks or credit-card companies (such as American Express). Policies issued through the specialist companies listed are all good value; annual, multi-trip policies are available from about £75.

Most **banks** and **credit-card** issuers also offer some sort of vacation insurance, which is often automatic if you pay for the holiday with their card. However, it's vital to check just what these policies cover – usually only death or dismemberment.

Travel agents and tour operators are likely to **require** some sort of insurance when you book a package holiday, though after a change in the UK law in late 1998 they can no longer require you to buy their own. If you have a good "all risks" **home insurance policy** it *may* cover your possessions against loss or theft even when overseas. Many **private medical schemes** (such as BUPA or PPP) also offer coverage plans for abroad, which include baggage loss, cancellation or curtailment and cash replacement as well as sickness or accident.

NORTH AMERICAN COVER

Before buying an insurance policy, check that you're not already covered. **Canadians'** provincial health plans usually provide partial cover for medical mishaps overseas. Holders of official **student/teacher/youth cards** are entitled to (admittedly very meagre) accident coverage and hospital in-patient benefits. Students will often find that their student health coverage extends during the vacations and for one term beyond the date of last enrolment. **Bank and credit cards** often have certain levels of medical or other insurance included – as in the UK, check their limitations – and you may automatically get travel insurance if you use a major credit card to pay for

your trip. **Homeowners' or renters' insurance** often covers theft or loss of documents, money and valuables while overseas, though conditions and maximum amounts vary from company to company.

After exhausting the possibilities above, you might want to contact a specialist **travel insurance company**; your travel agent can usually recommend one, or see the box on p.23. The best deals are usually to be had through student/youth travel agencies – ISIS now offers STA Travel Insurance for travellers under the age of sixty. Coverage is worldwide and comes in packages covering seven days ($35), fifteen days ($55), one month ($115), 45 days ($155), two months ($180) and one year ($730) – add an extra $35–50 for each additional month on longer stays.

Most North American travel policies apply only to items lost, stolen or damaged while in the custody of an identifiable, responsible third party such as a hotel porter, an airline or a luggage consignment. Note also that very few insurers will arrange on-the-spot payments in the event of a major expense or loss; you will usually be **reimbursed** only after you've returned home.

AUSTRALIAN AND NEW ZEALAND COVER

In Australasia, travel insurance is put together by the airlines and travel agent groups (see box on p.23) in conjunction with insurance companies. Policies are all comparable in cost and coverage; a typical one costs A$110/NZ$130 for two weeks, A$180/NZ$215 for one month, A$260/NZ$315 for two months.

INSURANCE REPORTS

In all cases of theft or loss of goods, you must contact the local police within a certain time limit to have a **report** made out so that your insurer can process the claim. This can occasionally prove tricky in Greece, since many officials simply won't accept that anything could be stolen on their turf, or at least don't want to take responsibility for it. Moreover, there have been enough fraudulent claims in recent years to make the police justifiably wary. Be persistent, and if necessary enlist the support of the local **tourist police** or tourist office.

HEALTH MATTERS

There are no required inoculations for Greece, though it's wise to ensure that you are up to date on tetanus and polio. Don't forget to take out travel insurance (see "Insurance", p.23), so that you're covered in case of serious illness or accidents.

The **water** is safe pretty much everywhere, though you will come across shortages or brackish supplies on some of the drier and more remote islands. Bottled water is widely available if you're feeling cautious.

SPECIFIC HAZARDS

The main health problems experienced by visitors have to do with **overexposure to the sun**, and the odd nasty from the sea. To combat the former, don't spend too long in the sun, cover up limbs, wear a hat, and drink plenty of fluids in the hot months to avoid any danger of **sunstroke**; remember that even hazy sun can burn. For seagear, goggles or a dive mask for swimming and footwear for walking over wet or rough rocks are useful.

HAZARDS OF THE DEEP

In the sea, you may have the bad luck to meet an armada of **jellyfish** (*tsoúkhtres*), especially in late summer; they come in various colours and sizes ranging from purple "pizzas" to invisible, minute creatures. Various over-the-counter remedies are sold in resort pharmacies; baking soda or diluted ammonia also help to lessen the sting. The welts and burning usually subside of their own accord within a few hours; there are no deadly man-of-war species in Greek waters.

Less vicious but more common are black, spiky **sea urchins** (*ahiní*), which infest rocky shorelines year-round; if you step on or graze one, a sewing needle (you can crudely sterilize it by heat from a cigarette lighter) and olive oil are effective for removing spines; if you don't extract them they'll fester. You can take your revenge by eating the roe of the reddish-purple ones, which is served as a delicacy in a few seafood restaurants.

The worst maritime danger – fortunately very rare – is the **weever fish** (*dhrákena*) which buries itself in tidal-zone sand with just its poisonous dorsal and gill spines protruding. If you tread on one, the sudden pain is excruciating, and the exceptionally potent venom can cause permanent paralysis of the affected area. Imperative first aid is to immerse your foot in water as hot as you can stand, which degrades the toxin and relieves the swelling of joints and attendant pain, but you should still seek medical attention as soon as possible.

Somewhat more common are **stingrays and skates** (Greek names include *platý, seláhi, vátos* or *trígona*), which mainly frequent bays with sandy bottoms where they can camouflage themselves. Though shy, they can give you a nasty lash with their tail if trodden on, so shuffle your feet a bit when entering the water.

When snorkelling in deeper water, especially around Crete or the Dodecanese, you may happen upon a brightly coloured **moray eel** (*smérna*) sliding back and forth out of its rocky lair. Keep a respectful distance – their slightly comical air and clown-colours belie an irritable temper and the ability to inflict nasty bites or even sever fingers.

SANDFLIES, DOGS AND MOSQUITOES

If you are sleeping on or near a **beach**, it's wise to use insect repellent, either lotion or wrist/ankle bands, and/or a tent with a screen to guard against **sandflies**. Their bites are potentially dangerous, as these flies spread leishmaniasis, a parasitic infection characterized by chronic fever, listlessness and weight loss. It's difficult to treat, requiring long courses of medication.

In Greece, the main reservoirs for leishmaniasis are **dogs**. Transmission of the disease to humans by fleas has not been proven, but it's wisest not to befriend strays as they also carry echinococcosis, a debilitating liver fluke. In humans these form nodules and cysts which can only be removed surgically.

Mosquitoes (*kounóupia*) in Greece carry nothing worse than a vicious bite, but they can be infuriating. One solution is to burn pyrethrum incense coils (*spíres* or *fidhákia*), which are widely and cheaply available, if pungently malodorous. Better, if you can get them, are the small electrical devices (trade names Vape-Net or Bay-Vap) that vaporize an odourless insecticide tablet; many accommodation proprietors supply them routinely. Insect repellents such as Autan are available from most general stores and kiosks.

CREEPY-CRAWLIES

Adders (*ohiés*) and **scorpions** (*skorpií*) are found throughout Greece; both creatures are shy, but take care when climbing over dry-stone walls where snakes like to sun themselves, and don't put hands or feet in places, like shoes, where you haven't looked first.

Snakebites cause very few deaths in Europe. Many snakes will bite if threatened, whether they are venomous or not. If a bite injects venom, then swelling will normally occur within thirty minutes. If this happens, get medical attention; keep the bitten part still; and make sure all body movements are as gentle as possible. If medical attention is not nearby then bind the limb firmly to slow the blood circulation, but not so tightly as to stop the blood flow.

Many reptiles, including snakes, can harbour *Salmonella* bacteria, so should be handled cautiously and preferably not at all. This applies particularly to **tortoises**.

In addition to munching its way through a fair fraction of Greece's surviving pine forests, the **pine processionary caterpillar** – taking this name from the long, nose-to-tail convoys which individuals form at certain points in their life cycle – sports highly irritating hairs, with a poison worse than a scorpion's. If you touch one, or even a tree-trunk they've been on recently, you'll know all about it for a week, and the welts may require antihistamine to heal.

PHARMACIES AND DRUGS

For **minor complaints** it's enough to go to the local **farmakío**. Greek pharmacists are highly trained and dispense a number of medicines which elsewhere could only be prescribed by a doctor. In the larger towns and resorts there'll usually be one who speaks good English. Pharmacies are usually closed evenings and Saturday mornings, but all should have a monthly schedule (in both English and Greek) on their door showing the complete roster of night and weekend duty pharmacists in town. **Homeopathic and herbal remedies** are quite widely available, too, and the largest towns have dedicated homeopathic pharmacies, identified by the characteristic green cross. There is a large homeopathic centre in Athens at Nikosthénous 8, Platía Plastíra, Pangráti (☎70 98 199); the Centre of Homeopathic Medicine is at Perikléous 1, Maroússi (☎80 52 671).

If you regularly use any form of **prescription drug**, you should bring along a copy of the prescription, together with the generic name of the drug; this will help should you need to replace it, and also avoids possible problems with customs officials. In this regard, it's worth being aware that **codeine is banned** in Greece. If you import any you might find yourself in serious trouble, so check labels carefully; it's the core ingredient of Panadeine, Veganin, Solpadeine, Codis and Empirin-Codeine, to name just a few common compounds.

Contraceptive pills are more readily available every year, but don't count on getting these – or spermicidal jelly/foam – outside of a few large island towns, over-the-counter at the larger *farmakía*; Greek women tend not to use any sort of birth control systematically, and have an average of four abortions during their adult life. **Condoms**, however, are inexpensive and ubiquitous – just ask for *profylaktiká* (the slangy terms *plastiká* or slightly vulgar *kapótes* are even better understood) at any pharmacy or corner *períptero* (kiosk).

Women's hygienic supplies are sold in pharmacies (*farmakía*), or in supermarkets near the toilet paper and diapers. Napkins ("Always" brand) are ubiquitous; tampons, known by the trademark catch-all of "Tampax", can be trickier to find in remoter spots, especially on the smaller islands. Where there are no Tampax as such you may have to make do with "OB".

Lastly, **hayfever** sufferers should be prepared for the early Greek pollen season, at its height from April to June. If you are taken by surprise, pharmacists stock tablets and creams, but it's cheaper to come prepared. Commercial antihistamines like Triludan are difficult to find in smaller towns, and local brands can cost upwards of £10/$16 equivalent for a pack of ten.

DOCTORS AND HOSPITALS

You'll find English-speaking **doctors** in any of the bigger towns or resorts; the tourist police, hotel staff or even your consulate should be able to come up with some names if you have any difficulty.

For **an ambulance**, phone ☎166. In **emergencies** – cuts, broken bones, etc – treatment is given free in **state hospitals**, though you will only get the most basic level of nursing care. Greek families routinely take in food and bedding for relatives, so as a tourist you'll be at a severe disadvantage. Somewhat better are the ordinary state-run **out-patient clinics** (*yiatría*) attached to most public hospitals and also found in rural locales. These operate on a first-come, first-served basis, so go early; usual hours are 8am to noon.

Don't forget to obtain **receipts** for the cost of all drugs and medical treatment; without them you won't be able to claim back the money on your travel insurance.

COSTS, MONEY AND BANKS

The cost of living in Greece has spiralled during the years of EU membership: the days of renting an island house for a few thousand drachmas a week are long gone, and food prices at corner shops now differ little from those of other member countries. However, outside the established resorts, travel between and around the islands remains reasonably priced, with the cost of restaurant meals, short-term accommodation and public transport still cheaper than anywhere in northern or western Europe except parts of Portugal.

Prices depend on where and when you go. Mainland cities, larger tourist resorts and the trendier small islands (such as Sými, Sífnos and Pátmos) are more expensive, and costs everywhere increase sharply in July, August and at Christmas, New Year or Easter. **Students** with an International Student Identity Card (ISIC) can get fifty percent discount off admission fees at many archeological sites and museums; those over 65 can rely on site-admission discounts of 25 to 30 percent. These, and other occasional discounts, tend to be more readily available to EU nationals.

SOME BASIC COSTS

On most islands a **daily per-person budget** of £21–24/US$34–39 will get you basic accommodation, breakfast, picnic lunch, a ferry or bus ride and a simple evening meal, as one of a couple. Camping would cut costs marginally. On £33–36/$54–59 a day you could be living quite well, plus sharing the cost of renting a large motorbike or small car.

Inter-island **ferries**, a main unavoidable expense, are reasonably priced, subsidized by the government in an effort to preserve remote island communities. A deck-class ticket for the four-hour trip from Rhodes to Kós costs about £7/US$10.50, while Sámos to Híos, another four- or five-hour journey, runs to just £6/US$10. For even less you can catch a ferry to the numerous small islands that lie closer to Rhodes, Kós and Sámos, the most likely touchdown points if you're flying in on a direct charter.

The simplest double **room** generally costs around £11–15/$18–25 a night, depending on the location and the plumbing arrangements. Bona fide single rooms are rare, and cost about seventy percent double rates. Organized **campsites** are little more than £2.50/US$3.75 per person, with similar charges per tent and perhaps 25 percent more for a camper van. With discretion you can camp for free in the more remote, rural areas.

A basic taverna **meal** with local wine can be had for around £6/US$10 a head. Add a better bottle of wine, seafood or more careful cooking, and it could be up to £10/US$16 a head; you'll rarely pay more than that except in Ródhos Town. Sharing seafood, Greek salads and dips is a good way to keep costs down in the better restaurants, and even in the most developed of resorts, with inflated "international" menus, you'll often be able to find a more earthy but decent taverna where the locals eat.

CURRENCY

The Greek currency is the **drachma** (*dhrakhmí*), and the exchange rate is currently around 500dr to the pound sterling, or 310dr to the US dollar.

The most common **notes** in circulation are those of 100, 500, 1000, 5000 and 10,000 drachmas (*dhrakhmés*), while **coins** come in denominations of 5, 10, 20, 50 and 100dr; you might come across 1dr and 2dr coins, and 50dr bills, too, though they're rarely used these days. In 1998 a new, compact 5000dr note was introduced which is very easily confused with the 500dr bill, so beware. In practice, shopkeepers rarely bother with differences of under 20dr – whether in your favour, or theirs.

BANKS AND EXCHANGE

Greek **banks** are normally open Monday to Thursday 8.30am–2pm, Friday 8.30am–1.30pm. Certain branches in the major towns or tourist centres are open extra hours in the evenings and on Saturday mornings for exchanging money. Always take your passport with you as proof of identity and be prepared for at least one long line; sometimes you have to line up once to have the transaction approved, and again to pick up the cash.

Outside these times, the largest hotels and **travel agencies** can often provide this service, albeit sometimes with hefty commissions. On small islands with no full-service bank, "authorized" bank agents will charge yet another extra fee (1–2 percent) to cover the cost of posting a travellers' cheque or Eurocheque to the main branch.

The safest way to carry money is in **travellers' cheques**. These can be obtained from banks (even if you don't have an account) or from offices of Thomas Cook and American Express; you'll usually pay a commission of between one and two percent, though it pays to be aware of any special commission-free deals. You can cash the cheques at most banks, though rarely elsewhere. Each travellers' cheque transaction in Greece will incur a **commission** charge of 400–800dr, so you won't want to change too many small amounts.

Small-denomination **foreign bank notes** are also extremely useful, and relatively unlikely to be stolen in Greece (see "Police and Trouble", p.69). Since the freeing up of all remaining currency controls in 1994, a number of authorized brokers for exchanging foreign cash have emerged in Athens and other major tourist centres. When changing small amounts, choose those bureaux that charge a flat percentage commission (usually one percent) rather than a high minimum. There also a small number of 24-hour automatic **foreign-note-changing machines** in a few resorts, but again a high minimum commission tends to be deducted.

Alternatively, most British banks can issue current account holders with a **Eurocheque** card and chequebook, with which you can pay for expensive items in certain shops, and withdraw money from cash machines (if the card has a PIN number) or at bank counters. An annual or biennial fee is charged for issuing the card, while each cheque attracts a two percent processing charge on the debit facility subject to a minimum of £1.75, but there's no on-the-spot commission levied on transactions. Indeed, if you use this scheme to obtain over £85 equivalent, it is one of the cheaper ways of getting money abroad, and unlike with travellers' cheques the money stays in your account until the Eurocheque is presented from Greece, usually three weeks later. The current limit is 50,000dr per cheque, and the bank or merchant does not need to know the prevailing exchange rate – useful if bank computers have gone down.

In 1998, the Greek **post office** abandoned the business of changing money – a nuisance, as many tiny islands have a post office but no bank. If you have a UK-based Girobank account, you may still be able to use your chequebook to get money at remote post offices.

Finally, there is no need to purchase drachmas **before arrival** unless you're coming in at some ungodly hour to one of the remoter land or sea frontier posts, or on a Sunday. Airport arrival lounges will always have an exchange booth or autoteller for passengers on incoming international flights.

CREDIT CARDS AND CASH DISPENSERS

Major **credit cards** are not usually accepted by cheaper tavernas or hotels, but they're almost essential for renting cars, for buying Olympic Airways tickets and for expensive souvenirs. If you run short of money, you can get a **cash advance** on a credit card, but be warned that the minimum amount is 15,000dr. The Emboriki Trapeza (Commercial Bank) handles Visa, while the Ethniki Trapeza (National Bank) services Access/Mastercard customers. However, there is usually a two percent charge on the total, high additional transaction fees and always interminable delays while approval is sought by telex.

It is far simpler to use the growing network of Greek **cash dispensers**, by learning the PIN numbers for your debit/credit cards. Larger airports (such as Athens, Crete, Rhodes and Thessaloníki) have at least one of these in the arrivals hall, and almost any town or island with a population larger than a few thousand (or a substantial tourist traffic) also has them. The most well distributed are those of the National Bank/Ethniki Trapeza and the Commercial Bank/Emboriki Trapeza, which happily and interchangeably accept Visa, Mastercard, Plus, Cirrus and Eurocheque cards; those of the Alfa Trapeza Pisteos/Alpha Credit Bank and its subsidiary the Ionian Bank/Ioniki Trapeza are less widespread and somewhat more restrictive – for example, Alpha Credit cash dispensers accept only American Express and Visa cards.

Cash dispenser transactions with **debit cards** linked to a cheque account via the Plus/Cirrus systems attract charges of two percent on the sterling transaction value, subject to a minimum of £1.50, making them slightly cheaper than Eurocheques, and indeed the **least expensive** way of getting money in Greece as long as you withdraw more than £75 equivalent. By contrast, using **credit cards** at a cash dispenser is one of the **dearest** ways of obtaining cash: a cash advance per-transaction fee of £1.50 minimum, plus a "foreign transaction" fee of up to 2.75 percent on the total, depending on the card issuer.

EMERGENCY CASH

All told, learning and using the PIN numbers for any debit or credit cards you have is the quickest and least expensive way of securing moderate amounts of emergency funds from abroad. In an emergency, however, you can arrange to have **money sent** from home to a bank in Greece.

Receiving funds via telex takes a minimum of three days and often up to seven days, so be prepared for delays. From the UK, a bank charge of three percent, or minimum £17, maximum £35, is levied. Bank drafts can also be sent, with higher commission rates. You can retrieve the amount in foreign currency, or even as travellers' cheques, but still more onerous commissions will apply.

Funds can also be sent via Western Union Money Transfer (☎0800/833833 in the UK, 1-800/325-6000 in North America). Exact fees depend on the amount being transferred and the destination, but as examples, wiring £400–500 should cost around £37, while $1000 will cost around $75. The American Express MoneyGram (☎0800/894887 in the UK, 1-800/543-4080 in North America) is now only available to American Express cardholders. Funds should be available for collection at Amex's or Western Union's local office within minutes of being sent.

CURRENCY REGULATIONS

Since 1994, Greek **currency restrictions** no longer apply to Greek nationals and other EU member citizens, and since Greece's entry into the European ERM in 1998, the drachma is totally convertible. Arcane rules may still apply to arrivals from North America, Australia or non-EU nations, but you would have to be extremely unlucky to run foul of them.

If you have reason to believe that you'll be acquiring large quantities of drachmas – from work or sale of valuables (though the latter is officially illegal) – declare all monetary devices on arrival, then request (and save) pink, personalized receipts for all **bank exchange transactions**. Otherwise you may find that you can only re-exchange a limited sum of drachmas on departure; even at the best of times many banks stock a limited range of foreign notes – your best bet is often the exchange booth in airport arivals (not departures). These pink receipts are also essential for obtaining a non-employment resident visa (see p.22).

INFORMATION AND MAPS

The National Tourist Organization of Greece (*Ellinikós Organismós Tourismoú*, or EOT; GNTO abroad) maintains offices in most European capitals, plus major cities in North America and Australia (see box opposite for addresses). It publishes an impressive array of free, glossy, regional pamphlets, which are good for getting an idea of where you want to go, even if the actual text should sometimes be taken with an occasional pinch of salt. Also available from the EOT are a reasonable fold-out map of the country and a large number of brochures on special interests and festivals.

TOURIST OFFICES

In Greece, you will find official **EOT offices** in most of the larger towns and resorts. The principal Athens office is at Amerikís 2, just up from Stadhíou. Here, in addition to the usual leaflets, you can pick up weekly **schedules** for the inter-island **ferries** – not one hundred percent reliable, but useful as a guideline. The EOT staff are themselves very helpful for advice on **ferry**, **bus** and **train** departures as well as new opening hours for sites and museums, and occasionally can give assistance with accommodation.

Where there is no EOT office, you can get information (and often a range of leaflets) from municipally run tourist offices, for example in Ioánnina, Kós and Mólyvos – these are often very good and highly motivated. In the absence of any of these, you can visit the **Tourist Police**, essen-

tially a branch (often just a single delegate) of the local police. They can sometimes provide you with lists of rooms to let, which they regulate.

MAPS

No authoritative, authentic maps . . . . Well, isn't that as it should be? Why does anybody need maps? If an individual wants them he's a spy. If a country needs maps it's moribund. A well-mapped country is a dead country. A complete survey is a burial shroud. A life with maps is a tyranny!

That extract from Alan Sillitoe's 1971 satire, *Travels in Nihilon*, pretty much sums up the prevailing attitude towards **maps** in Greece, which are an endless source of confusion and often outright misinformation. Each cartographic company seems to have its own peculiar system of transcribing Greek letters into English – and these, as often as not, do not match the semi-official transliterations on the road signs.

The most reliable **general touring maps** of Greece are those published by Athens-based Road Editions (*www.road.gr*). They're available in Greece at selected bookstores, including their own retail outlet in Athens, or in Britain at Stanfords and other quality travel shops. In case of difficulty, contact (in Britain) Portfolio, Unit 1C, West Ealing Business Centre, Alexandria Road, London W13 0NJ (☎020/8579 7748). In the US, they're sold exclusively through Map Link (see address in box on p.33) or Omni Resources, PO Box 2096, Burlington NC 27216 (☎910/227-8300). These are not perfect – no Greek map is – but, based on large-scale military maps not available to the public, they're the best you will find. Road covers the mainland in five folding sheets at 1:250,000 scale, entitled "Thrace", "Macedonia", "Epiros/Thessaly", "Central Greece", and "Peloponnese". Their 1:60,000 hiking map of Mount Pílion doubles nicely as a road map.

If Road products are unavailable, good second choices are the GeoCenter maps "Greece and the Islands" and "Greek Islands/Aegean Sea", which together cover the country at a scale of 1:300,000. The single-sided fold-up Freytag-Berndt 1:650,000, with an index, is very nearly as good, and easier to use when driving. Despite recent revisions and updating, Michelin #980

GREEK NATIONAL TOURIST OFFICES ABROAD

Australia
51 Pitt St, Sydney NSW 2000 (☎02/9241 1663)

Britain
4 Conduit St, London W1R 0DJ (☎0171/734 5997)

Canada
1300 Bay St, Upper Level, Toronto, ON M5R 3K8 (☎416/968-2220); 1233 rue de la Montagne, H3G 1Z2, Montréal, Quebec ☎514/871-1535

Denmark
Copenhagen Vester Farimagsgade 1, 2 DK 1606-Kobenhavn V (☎325-332)

Netherlands
Leidsestraat 13, NS 1017 Amsterdam (☎20/254-212)

Norway
Ovre Stottsgate 15B, 0157 Oslo 1 ☎2/426-501

Sweden
Grev Turigatan 2, PO Box 5298, 10246 Stockholm (☎8/679 6480)

USA
645 Fifth Ave, New York, NY 10022 (☎212/421-5777); 168 North Michigan Ave, Chicago, IL (☎312/782-1084); 611 West 6th St, Suite #2198 Los Angeles, CA (☎213/626-6696)

If your home country isn't listed here, apply to the embassy. Note that there are no Greek tourist offices in Ireland or New Zealand.

remains a fourth choice. All these are widely available in Britain and North America, though less easily in Greece; see the list of map outlets in the boxes on pp.32–3. Freytag-Berndt also publishes a series of more detailed maps on various regions of Greece, such as the Peloponnese, the Cyclades and the northeast Aegean islands (in two sheets); these are best bought overseas from specialist outlets, though in Greece they are re-jacketed and distributed by Efstathiadis.

Maps of **individual islands** are more easily available on the spot, and while most are wildly inaccurate or obsolete, with strange hieroglyphic symbology, a rare few are reliable and up-to-date. These include the Road Editions product for Crete, plus a steadily growing number of Road titles for smaller islands, including Rhodes, Kós and Corfu.

The most useful foreign-produced map of **Athens**, with a decent index, is the Falkplan, available from most specialist outlets. If you can read Greek, and plan to stay for some time in the city, the Athina-Pireás Proastia Alpha-Omega street atlas, published by Kapranidhis and Fotis, is invaluable, though pricey. It has a complete index, down to the tiniest alley – of which there are many – and also shows cinemas, most hotels and the outlines of important buildings.

HIKING/TOPOGRAPHICAL MAPS

Hiking/topographical maps, subject to uneven quality and availability, are gradually improving.

Road Editions, in addition to their road maps, have produced 1:50,000, GSM-compatible topographical maps for Mount Párnitha, Mount Pílion, Mount Ólymbos and Mount Íti, usually with rudimentary route directions in English. The Greek mountaineering magazine **Korfes** also publishes 1:50,000 maps of select alpine areas, with Roman-alphabet lettering appearing on a few sheets. More than eighty maps have been published, and new ones are issued periodically as a centrefold in the magazine – though many are revisions of previous areas. To get back issues you may need to visit the magazine's office at Platía Kentrikí 16, Aharnés, Athens (ring first on ☎24 61 528), although the more central bookstore Iy Folia tou Vivliou (see p.134) also has an extensive back stock.

Compared to the Road titles, the Korfes maps are, unfortunately, unreliable in the matter of trails and new roads, but extremely accurate for natural features and village position, based as they are on the older maps of the **Yeografikí Ipiresía Stratoú** (Army Geographical Service, or YIS). If you want to obtain these for islands, and mainland areas not covered by Road or Korfes, visit the YIS at Evelpídhon 4, north of Aréos Park in Athens, on Monday, Wednesday or Friday from 8am to noon only. All foreigners must leave their passport with the gate guard; EU citizens may proceed directly to the sales hall, where efficient, computerized transactions take just a few minutes. Other nationals will probably have to go

MAP OUTLETS

AUSTRALIA

Adelaide
The Map Shop, 16a Peel St, Adelaide (☎08/8231 2033).

Brisbane
Worldwide Maps & Guides, 187 George St, Brisbane (☎07/3221 4330).

Melbourne
Mapland, 372 Little Bourke St, Melbourne (☎03/9670 4383).

Perth
Perth Map Centre, 891 Hay St, Perth (☎08/9322 5733).

Sydney
Travel Bookshop, 3/175 Liverpool St, Sydney (☎02/9261 8200).

CANADA

Montréal
Ulysses Travel Bookshop, 4176 St-Denis, Montréal, PQ H2W 2M5 (☎514/289-0993).

Toronto
Open Air Books and Maps, 25 Toronto St, Toronto ON M5R 2C1 (☎416/363-0719).

Vancouver
International Travel Maps and Books, 552 Seymour St, Vancouver V6Z 1G3 (☎604/687-3320).
World Wide Books and Maps, 1247 Granville St, Vancouver, BC V6Z 1E4 (☎604/687-3320).

IRELAND

Easons Bookshop, 40 O'Connell St, Dublin 1 (☎01/873 3811).
Fred Hanna's Bookshop, 27–29 Nassau St, Dublin 2 (☎01/677 1255).
Hodges Figgis Bookshop, 56–58 Dawson St, Dublin 2 (☎01/677 4754).
Waterstone's, Queens Building, 8 Royal Ave, Belfast BT1 1DA (☎02890/247355); 69 Patrick St, Cork (☎021/276522); 7 Dawson St, Dublin 2 (☎01/679 1415).

NEW ZEALAND

Specialty Maps, 58 Albert St, Auckland (☎09/307 2217).

BRITAIN

London

Daunt Books, 83 Marylebone High St, London W1M 3DE (☎020/7224 2295).

National Map Centre, 22–24 Caxton St, London SW1H 0QU (☎020/7222 2466).

Stanfords, 12–14 Long Acre, London WC2E 9LP (☎020/7836 1321); inside Campus Travel at 52 Grosvenor Gardens, London SW1W 0AG (☎020/7730 1314); inside British Airways at 156 Regent St, London W1R 5TA (☎020/7434 4744). Maps available by mail or phone order.

The Travel Bookshop, 13–15 Blenheim Crescent, London W11 2EE (☎020/7229 5260).

The rest of England and Wales

Austick's City Bookshop, 91 The Headrow, Leeds LS1 6OJ (☎0113/243 3099).

Blackwell's, 156–160 West St, Sheffield S1 3ST (☎0114/273 8906); 13–17 Royal Arcade, Cardiff CF1 2PR (☎029/2039 5036); 32 Stonegate, York YO1 2AP (☎01904/624531); also trading as Blackwell's University Bookshop, Alsop Building, Brownlow Hill, Liverpool L3 5TX (☎0151/709 8146) and Blackwell's Map and Travel Shop, 53 Broad St, Oxford OX1 3BQ (☎01865/568467).

Heffers Map Shop, 20 Trinity St, Cambridge, and 19 Sidney St, 3rd Flr, Cambridge CB2 3HL (☎01223/568467).

The Map Shop, 30a Belvoir St, Leicester LE1 6QH (☎0116/247 1400).

Newcastle Map Centre, 55 Grey St, Newcastle upon Tyne NE1 6EF (☎0191/261 5622).

Stanfords, 29 Corn St, Bristol BS1 1HT (☎0117/929 9966).

Waterstone's, 91 Deansgate, Manchester M3 2BW (☎0161/832 1992).

Scotland

Aberdeen Map Shop, 74 Skene St, Aberdeen AB10 1QE (☎01224/637999).

James Thin Melven's Bookshop, 29 Union St, Inverness IV1 1QA (☎01463/233500).

John Smith and Sons, 57–61 St Vincent St, Glasgow G2 5TB (☎0141/221 7472).

MAP OUTLETS CONTINUED

US

Book Passage, 51 Tamal Vista Blvd, Corte Madera, CA 94925 (☎415/927-0960).

The Complete Traveler Bookstore, 199 Madison Ave, New York, NY 10016 (☎212/685-9007); 3207 Fillmore St, San Francisco, CA 92123 (☎415/923-1511).

Eliot Bay Book Company, 101 S Main St, Seattle, WA 98104 (☎206/624-6600).

Forsyth Travel Library, 226 Westchester Ave, White Plains, NY 10604 (☎1-800/367-7984).

Map Link Inc, 30 S La Patera Lane, Unit 5, Santa Barbara, CA 93117 (☎805/692-6777).

Phileas Fogg's Books & Maps, #87 Stanford Shopping Center, Palo Alto, CA 94304 (☎1-800/533-FOGG).

Rand McNally, 444 N Michigan Ave, Chicago, IL 60611 (☎312/321-1751); 150 E 52nd St, New York, NY 10022 ☎(212/758-7488); 595 Market St, San Francisco, CA 94105 (☎415/777-3131); 1201 Connecticut Ave NW, Washington, DC 20003 (☎202/223-6751). Or call ☎1-800/333-0136 (ext 2111) for the address of your nearest store/direct mail order.

Sierra Club Bookstore, 6014 College Ave, Oakland, CA 94618 (☎510/658-7470).

Traveler's Choice Bookstore, 22 W 52nd St, New York, NY 10019 (☎212/664-0995).

---

upstairs for an interview; if you don't speak reasonably good Greek, it's best to have a Greek friend get them for you.

As of writing, maps covering Crete, the Dodecanese, the east Aegean, Skýros, most of Corfu and much of Epirus, Macedonia and Thrace are still off-limits to all foreigners, as well as to Greeks. With matters unsettled across the Balkans, previous plans to lift such restrictions have been shelved indefinitely. A German company, **Harms**, has released a series of five maps at 1:80,000 scale which cover Crete from west to east and show, with about fifty percent accuracy, many hiking routes; despite these defects, they're invaluable until and unless the YIS declassifies this area, and they are available overseas at specialist map outlets.

Finally, for hiking in particular areas of Crete, Corfu, Sámos, Rhodes, Sými, Thássos and Lésvos, **maps-with-guide-booklets** published by Marengo Publications in Britain also prove very useful. Stanfords keeps a good stock of these, or order from Marengo direct at 17 Bernard Crescent, Hunstanton PE36 6ER (☎01485/532710).

GETTING AROUND

The standard means of land transport in Greece is the bus. Train networks are usually slow and limited, though service on the Pátra line and the northern mainland lines is improving. Buses, however, cover just about every route on the mainland – albeit infrequently on minor roads – and provide basic connections on the islands. The best way to supplement buses is to rent a moped, motorbike or car, especially on the islands, where in any substantial town or resort you can find a rental outlet.

Inter-island travel of course means taking **ferries**. These again are extensive, and will eventually get you to any of the 166 inhabited isles. Planes are expensive, at three to four times the cost of a deck-class ferry ticket and almost twice as much as the cheapest cabin berth.

BUSES

Bus services on the **major routes**, both on the mainland and islands, are highly efficient and frequent. On **secondary roads** they're less regular, with long gaps, but even the most remote villages will be connected – at least on weekdays – by a school or market bus to the provincial capital. As these often leave shortly after dawn, an alarm clock can be a useful travel aid. Coming in the opposite direction, these local buses usually leave the provincial capital at about 2pm. On the **islands** there are usually buses to connect the port and main town for ferry arrivals or departures.

The network is nationally run by a single syndicate known as the **KTEL** (Kratikó Tamío Ellinikón Leoforíon). However, even in medium-sized towns there can be several scattered terminals for services in different directions, so make sure you have the right station for your departure.

Some sample one-way fares from Athens are: Thessaloníki (9000dr), Pátra (3500dr) and Delphi (2500dr).

Buses are amazingly **prompt** as a rule, so be there in plenty of time for scheduled departures. For the major, inter-city lines such as Athens–Pátra, ticketing is computerized, with assigned seating, and such buses often get fully booked. On smaller rural/island routes, it's generally first come, first served, with some standing allowed, and tickets dispensed on the spot by an *ispráktoros* or conductor.

TRAINS

The Greek railway network, run by **OSE**, is limited to the mainland, and with a few exceptions trains are slower than the equivalent buses. However, they're also much cheaper – nearly fifty percent less on non-express services, even more if you buy a return ticket – and some of the lines are enjoyable in themselves. The best, a real treat, is the rack-and-pinion line between Diakoftó and Kalávryta in the **Peloponnese** (see p.261).

Timetables are sporadically available during May or June as small, Greek-only booklets; the best place to obtain them are the OSE offices in Athens at Sína 6, or in Thessaloníki at Aristotélous 18, or the main train stations in these cities. Always check the station schedule boards, since with the once-yearly printing changes often crop up in the interim. Trains tend to leave promptly at the outset, though on the more circuitous lines they're invariably late by the end of the journey.

If you're starting a journey at the initial station of a run you can (at no extra cost) **reserve a seat**; a carriage and seat number will be written on the back of your ticket. At most intermediate points, it's first come, first served.

There are two basic classes: first and second. **First class** may be worth the extra money, insomuch as the wagons may be emptier and the seats more comfortable. An express category, the **Intercity**, exists on certain routes between Alexandhroúpoli, Thessaloníki, Vólos, Athens, Pátra, Korinthos and Kalamata. German-made rolling stock is relatively sleek, and much faster than the bus if the timetable is adhered to;

Belgrade △   △ Belgrade   △ Sofia   △ Sofia

Plovdiv

Skopje
**FORMER YUGOSLAV
REPUBLIC OF
MACEDONIA**

Svilengrad   Edirne
Kastaniés
Pýthio
Uzunköprü

△ *Istanbul*

Dhráma   Komotiní

B U L G A R I A

Kilkís   Xánthi
Sérres

Polýkastro
A L B A N I A   Flórina
Amýndeo   Édhessa
Véria

Thessaloníki
Alexandhroúpoli

Kozáni

Kateríni

TURKEY

Kalambáka   Lárissa
Igoumenítsa   Tríkala
Kardhítsa

Vólos

Lamía

Livadhiá   Halkhídha

Pátra   Dhiakoftó
Kalávrita
Olympía   Kórinthos
Pýrgos   Trípoli   Árgos
Megalópoli   Náfplio
Kyparissía

ATHENS
Pireás

Kalamáta

N

GREECE: TRAINS

0   100 km

accordingly, stiff supplements are charged depending on the distance travelled. There is also one nightly **sleeper** in each direction between Athens and Thessaloníki, again with fairly hefty surcharges. Note that any kind of ticket issued on board a train carries a fifty percent surcharge.

InterRail and **Eurail** Pass holders (see appropriate "Getting There" sections) can use their pass in Greece but must secure reservations like everyone else, and may need to pay express **supplements** on a few lines. InterRail passes and Eurotrain tickets are available in Greece through the International Student and Youth Travel Service (ISYTS), Níkis 11, 2nd floor, Athens, or at Wasteels, Mnisikléous 10a, Platía Mitropóleos, Athens.

North Americans can also buy the Greek Rail pass, valid any three days in a month for first class travel ($86) or five days in a month ($120). There's also a Greek Flexi Rail and Flight Pass which entitles the holder to three days' first class rail and two days' air travel (on Olympic) within a month. The price is $163 for adults, $97 for children aged 2–11. Both these passes must be purchased prior to departure and are available from DER (see box on p17).

FERRIES

Ferries are of use primarily for travel to and between islands, though you may also want to make use of the routes between Athens and certain ports in the southeastern Peloponnese. There are three different varieties of vessel: medium-sized to large **ordinary ferries** (which operate the main services), **hydrofoils** (run by Minoan "Flying Dolphins", Samos Hydrofoils and Dodecanese Hydrofoils, among several companies), and local **kaïkia** (small boats which do short hops and excursions in season). Costs are very reasonable on the longer journeys, though proportionately more expensive for shorter, inter-island connections. Short-haul lines with monopolies – for example Alexandhroúpoli–Samothráki and Kými–Skýros – are invariably overpriced.

We've indicated most of the **ferry connections**, both on the maps (see pp.462–3 for a general pattern) and in the "Travel Details" at the end of each chapter. Don't take our listings as exhaustive or wholly reliable, however, as schedules are notoriously erratic, and must be verified each year; details given are essentially for departures between June and September. **Out-of-season** departure frequencies are severely reduced, with many islands connected only once or twice a week. However, in spring or autumn those ferries that do operate are often compelled by the transport ministry to call at extra or unusual islands, making possible some interesting connections.

The most reliable, up-to-date information is available from the local **port police** (*limenarhío*), which maintains offices at Pireás (☎01/42 26 000) and on or near the harbours of all fair-sized islands. Smaller places may only have a *limenikós stathmós* (marine post), often just a single room with a VHF radio. Their officers rarely speak much English, but keep complete schedules posted – and, meteorological report in hand, are the final arbiters of whether a ship will sail or not in stormy weather conditions. *Apagorevtikó*, or obligatory halt of all seaborne traffic, is applied for weather in excess of force 7 on the Beaufort scale; hydrofoils are confined to port at force 6 or above.

Few ferry companies, with the exceptions of Miniotis Lines and NEL Lines, produce regular **schedule** sheets. The only attempt at an all-inclusive Greek ferry guide is the yearly "Greek Travel Routes, Domestic Sea Schedules", co-produced by the GNTO and the Greek travel agents' manual the GTP; be prepared to master an array of bewildering abbreviations for ports and shipping companies The printed guide is available at GNTO/EOT offices, but you'll find a regularly updated version at *www.gtpnet.com*.

REGULAR FERRIES

On most **ferry** routes, your only consideration will be getting a boat that leaves on the day, and for the island, that you want. However, when sailing from **Pireás**, the port of Athens, to the Cyclades or Dodecanese islands, you should have a choice of at least two, often three, sailings and may want to bear in mind a few of the factors below.

Most importantly, bear in mind that **routes** taken and the speed of the boats vary enormously. A journey from Pireás to Thíra (Santoríni), for instance, can take anything from nine to fourteen hours. Prior to buying a ticket it's wise to establish how many stops there will be before your island, and the estimated time of arrival. Many agents act just for one specific boat (they'll blithely tell you that theirs is the only available service), so you may have to ask around to uncover alternatives. Especially in high season, early arrival is critical in getting what may be a very limited stock of accommodation.

The **boats** themselves have improved somewhat since the early 1990s, with a fair number of elderly rustbuckets consigned to the scrap heap or dumped overseas. Just about the only ferries you might want to avoid if you have the choice, especially for overnight journeys, is Agapitos Lines' *Golden Vergina* (on the line to Páros, Ikaría and Sámos) and the *Ayios Rafael*, run by NEL in the northeast Aegean. You will more often than not be surprised to encounter a former English Channel or Scandinavian fjord ferry, rechristened and enjoying a new lease of life in the Aegean.

Regular ferry **tickets** are, in general, best bought on the day of departure, unless you need to reserve a cabin berth or space for a car. Buying tickets in advance will tie you down to a particular ferry at a particular time – and innumerable factors can make you regret that. Most obviously there's bad weather, which, particularly off-season, can play havoc with the schedules, causing some small boats to remain at anchor and others to alter their routes drastically. (The ticket price is refunded if a boat fails to sail.) There are only three periods of the year – March 23–25, the week before and after Easter, and mid-August – when ferries need to be booked at least a couple of days in advance.

Following cases in 1996 of captains loading ferries to double their rated capacity, **obligatory advance ticketing** was universally introduced in 1998. Larger, reputable companies such as ANEK and DANE have been computerized for some years anyway. Staff at the gangway may bar you from embarking if you don't have a ticket, and should you succeed in sneaking aboard, you will find that tickets sold at the *loyistírio* (purser's office) will have a stiff surcharge attached (usually 20–30 percent). **Fares** for each route are currently set by the transport ministry and should not differ among ships or agencies, though curiously, tickets for journeys towards Athens are marginally more expensive than those in the opposite direction.

The cheapest class of ticket, which you'll probably automatically be sold, is **deck class**, variously called *tríti* or *gámma*. This gives you the run of most boats except for the upper-class restaurant and bar. On the shorter, summer journeys the best place to be, in any case, is on deck – space best staked out as soon as you get on board. However, boats acquired recently seem, with their glaring overhead lights and moulded-plastic bucket seats, expressly designed to frustrate those attempting to sleep on deck. In such cases it's well worth the few thousand extra drachmas for a cabin bunk, especially if you can share with friends (cabins are usually quadruple). Class consciousness has increased of late, so deck-class passengers may find themselves firmly locked out of second-class facilities at night to prevent them from crashing on the plush sofas, and may have to make do with pullman-type seats. First-class cabins usually cost scarcely less than a plane flight and are not terrific value – the main difference between first and second being the presence of a bathroom in the cabin, and sometimes two bunks rather than four. Most cabins, incidentally, are overheated or overchilled, and pretty airless; ask for an *exoterikí* (outer) cabin if you want a porthole (though these are always bolted shut).

Occasionally, with non-computerized companies, you will be sold a cabin berth at an intermediate port only to find that they are "full" when the boat arrives. Pursers will usually not refund you the difference between a cabin and third class. Your first- or second-class fare entitles you to a bunk, and this is clearly stated (in Greek) on the verso of your ticket. Make a scene if necessary until you are accommodated – there are often cabins in the bilge, set aside for the crew but generally unused, where you can sleep.

Motorbikes and **cars** get issued extra tickets, in the latter case up to four times the passenger fare. This obviously limits the number of islands you'll want to drag a car to – it's really only worth it for the larger ones like Crete, Rhodes, Híos, Lésvos, Sámos, Corfu or Kefalloniá. Even with these, unless you're planning a stay of more than four days, you may find it cheaper to leave your car on the mainland and rent another on arrival. Technically, written permission is required to take rental motorbikes and cars on ferries, though in practice few crew will bother to quiz you on this.

Some ferries sell a limited range of **food on board**, though it tends to be overpriced and mediocre. Honourable exceptions are the meals served by DANE, NEL and all ferries to Crete on their overnight sailings. On the short, daytime hops between the various islands of the Argo-Saronic, Cyclades and Sporades, it's a good idea to stock up beforehand with your own provisions; most ferries on these lines offer nothing other than biscuits, coffee and soft drinks.

HYDROFOILS

Hydrofoils – commonly known as *dhelfínia* (after the Minoan "Flying Dolphins") – are roughly twice as fast (and at least twice as expensive) as ordinary ferries. However, they're a useful alternative to regular ferries if you are pushed for time, and their network can also neatly fill gaps in ferry scheduling. Their drawback is that they were originally designed for cruising on placid Russian or Polish rivers, and are quite literally out of their depth on the open sea; thus they are extremely sensitive to bad weather, and even in moderate seas are not for the seasick-prone. Most of these services don't operate – or are heavily reduced – from October to June and are prone to arbitrary cancellation if not enough passengers turn up.

At present, hydrofoils operate among the **Argo-Saronic islands** close to Athens, down the east coast of the **Peloponnese** to Monemvassiá and Kýthira, among the **northern Sporades** (Évvia, Skýros, Skiáthos, Skópelos and Alónissos), between Thessaloníki and certain resorts on **Halkidhikí**, between Kavála and **Thássos**, between Alexandhroúpoli and Samothráki, among certain of the **Cyclades** (Ándros, Tínos, Mýkonos, Páros, Náxos, Amorgós, the minor islets, Íos, Thíra), and in the **Dodecanese** and east Aegean among Rhodes, Kós, Kálymnos, Léros and Pátmos, with regular forays up to Sámos, Ikaría and Foúrni, or over to Tílos and Níssyros. The principal **mainland ports** are Zea and Flísvos marinas in Pireás, Rafína,

Vólos, Áyios Konstandínos and Thessaloníki, as well as Kavála and Alexandhroúpoli.

Schedules and **tickets** for the Minoan Flying Dolphins company, which also operates high-speed catamarans to the Cyclades, are available from their head office in Athens at Filellínon 3, off Platía Sýndagma (☎01/32 44 600); in Pireás at Aktí Themistokléous 8 (☎01/42 80 001); in Vólos from Andonopoúlou 9–11 (☎0421/39 786); and in Thessaloníki from Kriti Travel, Íonos Dhragoúmi 1 (☎031/547 454). The Cyclades catamarans have separate booking numbers (☎01/75 12 356, fax ☎01/68 98 344). Samos Hydrofoils, based on Sámos in Vathý, tends to be more reliable than Dodecanese Hydrofoils, which has hubs on Kós and Rhodes. You may see craft with other livery, but we have excluded them, as they are chartered by tour agencies and do not offer scheduled services controlled by the Ministry of Transport.

KAΪKIA AND OTHER SMALL FERRIES

In season **kaïkia** (caiques) and small ferries of a few hundred tonnes' displacement sail between adjacent islands and to a few of the more obscure ones. These can be extremely useful and often very pleasant, but are no cheaper than mainline services. In fact, if they're classified as **tourist agency charters**, and not passenger lines controlled by the transport ministry, they tend to be quite expensive, with pressure to buy return fares (one-ways almost always available). The more consistent kaïki links are summarized in the "Travel Details" section of each island chapter, though inevitably departures depend on the whims of local boat-owners, so the only firm information is to be had on the quayside. Kaïkia and small ferries, despite appearances, have a good safety record; indeed it's the larger, overloaded car-ferries that have in the past run into trouble.

MOTORBIKES, MOPEDS AND BIKES

The cult of the **motorcycle** is highly developed in Greece, presided over by a jealous deity apparently requiring regular human sacrifice. Accidents among both foreign and local bikers are routine occurrences, with annual fatalities edging into two figures on the busier islands. Some package companies have even taken to warning clients in print against renting motorbikes (thereby making a bit extra on organized overland excursions), but with caution and common sense – and an eye to increasingly enforced regulations – riding a two-wheeler through a resort should be a lot safer than piloting one through London or New York.

Many tourists come to grief on rutted dirt tracks or astride mechanically dodgy machines. In other cases **accidents** are due to attempts to cut corners, in all senses, by riding two to an under-powered scooter simply not designed to propel such a load. Don't be tempted by this apparent economy – you won't regret getting two separate mopeds, or one powerful 100cc bike to share – and remember that you're likely to be charged an exorbitant sum for any repairs if you do have a wipeout. Also, verify that your travel insurance policy covers motorcycle accidents.

One worthwhile precaution is to wear a **crash helmet** (*kránio*); most rental outfits will offer you one, and some will make you sign a waiver of liability if you refuse it. Helmet-wearing is in fact required by law, but few riders (except army conscripts) wear them – though compliance is increasing as police set up random roadblocks to catch offenders. Reputable establishments demand a full motorcycle driving licence for any engine over 90cc (the law actually stipulates "over 50cc"), and you will usually have to leave your passport as security. For smaller models, any driving licence will do.

Mopeds and small **motor scooters**, known in Greek as **papákia** (little ducks) after their characteristic noise, are good transport for all but the hilliest islands. They're available for rent on many islands and in a few of the popular mainland resorts for 3000dr a day (mopeds) or 4000–5500dr (scooters and small motorbikes). These specimen rates can be bargained down out of peak season, or if you negotiate for a longer period of rental.

Before riding off, make sure you check the bike's mechanical state, since many are only cosmetically maintained. Bad brakes and worn or oil-fouled spark plugs are the most common defects; dealers often keep the front brakes far too loose, with the commendable intention of preventing you going over the handlebars. If you break down it's your responsibility to return the machine, so take down the phone number of the rental agency in case it gives out in the middle of nowhere. Better outlets often offer a free retrieval service.

Among **moped models**, the usual offerings are the surprisingly powerful Piaggio Si or Piaggio

Monte Carlo, which can take one person only along almost any road, carry two baskets or bags and are automatic with a pedal or push-start. Bungee cords (*khtapódi* in slang) for tying down bundles are supplied on request.

As far as **scooters** go, the Piaggio Vespa or Peugeot are more comfortable than mopeds for long trips, with capacious baskets, but have considerably less stability on unpaved surfaces. The latest generation of these models are ultra-trendy and practical enough, but thirsty on fuel and a few don't have kick-starts as backups to the battery.

In the family of true **motorbikes**, the favourites, in descending order of reliability, are the Honda 50, Yamaha Townmate and Suzuki FB Birdie; gears are shifted with an easy-to-learn left-foot pedal action, and (very important) these can all be push-started if the battery fails. They can carry two, though if you have a choice, the Honda Cub 70–90cc series give more power at nominal extra cost, as does the Yamaha 80 Townmate. Best of all is the 1997-vintage Honda Astrea 100, very powerful but scarcely bigger than older models.

CYCLING

Cycling in Greece is not such hard going as you might imagine (except in mid-summer), especially on one of the mountain bikes that are rapidly supplanting the old bone-shakers at rental outfits; they rarely cost more than 1500dr a day. You do, however, need steady nerves, as roads are generally narrow with no verges or bike lanes (except on Kós), and many Greek drivers consider bicyclists a lower form of life.

If you have your own mountain or touring bike, you might consider taking it along by **train** or **plane** (it's free if within your 23kg international allowance). Once in Greece you should be able to take a bike for free on most of the **ferries**, in the guard's van on most trains (for a small fee – it goes on a later goods train otherwise), and with a little persuasion on the roof of **buses**. Any small spare parts you might need, however, are best brought along, since **specialist bike shops** are only found in the provincial capitals and main cities.

DRIVING AND CAR RENTAL

Cars have obvious advantages for getting to the more inaccessible parts of mainland Greece, but this is one of the more expensive countries in Europe to **rent a car**. If you drive **your own** **vehicle** to and through Greece, via EU member states, you no longer require a Green Card. In accordance with recent directives, **insurance** contracted in any EU member state is valid in any other, but in many cases this is only third party cover – the statutory legal minimum. Competition in the industry is so intense, however, that many UK insurers will throw in full, pan-European cover for free or for a nominal sum, up to sixty days; shop around if necessary.

Upon arrival with EU number plates, your EU passport should no longer get a carnet stamp, and the car is in theory free to circulate in the country until its road tax or insurance expires. Beware, however, that the rules governing car import are in a constant state of flux, and there are reports of people being only allowed to use their cars for six-month periods each year (you choose the time period). Other nationalities will get a non-EU car entered in their passport; the **carnet** normally allows you to keep a vehicle in Greece for up to six months, exempt from road tax. It is difficult, though not impossible, to leave the country without the vehicle; the nearest customs post will seal it for you (while you fly back home for a family emergency, for example) but you must find a Greek national to act as your guarantor, and possibly pay storage. This person will assume ownership of the car should you ultimately abandon it.

CAR RENTAL

Car rental within Greece starts at £190/$305 a week in high season for the smallest, A-group vehicle, including unlimited mileage, tax and insurance. Tour operators' and local agents' brochures threaten alarming rates of £230/$370 for the same period but, except in August, no rental company expects to fetch that price for a car. Outside peak season, at the smaller local outfits, you can sometimes get terms of about £22/$36 per day, all inclusive, with slightly better rates for three days or more. **Comparison shopping** among agencies in the larger resorts can yield a variation in quotes of up to fifteen percent for the same conditions over a four-to-seven-day period; the most negotiable variable is whether or not kilometres in excess of one hundred per day (a common hidden catch) are free. Open **jeeps**, an increasingly popular extravagance, begin at about £45/$72 per day, rising to as much as £60/$96 at busy times and places.

Note that brochure prices in Greece almost never include tax, **collision damage waiver**

CAR RENTAL AGENCIES

UK
Alamo ☎0990/993000
Autos Abroad ☎020/7287 6000
Avis ☎0990/900500
Budget ☎0800/181 181
Eurodollar ☎0990/365365
Europcar/InterRent ☎0345/222 525
Hertz ☎0990/996699
Holiday Autos ☎0990/300400
Suncars ☎0870/500 5566
Transhire ☎020/7978 1922

NORTH AMERICA
Alamo ☎1-800/522-9696; Canada, ☎1-800/GO-ALAMO
Auto Europe ☎1-800/223-5555
Avis ☎1-800/331-1084; Canada, ☎1-800/879-2847

Budget ☎1-800/527-0700; Canada, ☎1-800/268-8900
Camwell Holiday Autos ☎1-800/422-7737; Canada, ☎1-800/678-0678
Dollar ☎1-800/800-6000
Europe by Car ☎1-800/223-1516 or 212/245-1713
Hertz ☎1-800/654-3001
National ☎1-800/CAR RENT

AUSTRALIA
Avis ☎1800/225 533
Budget ☎1300/362 848
Hertz ☎1800/550 067

NEW ZEALAND
Avis ☎09/526 2847
Budget ☎09/375 2222
Hertz ☎09/367 6350

(CDW) and personal insurance. CDW in particular is absolutely vital, as the coverage included by law in the basic rental fee is generally inadequate, so check the fine print on your contract. Be careful of the hammering that cars get on dirt tracks; tyres, windshield and the underside of the vehicle are almost always excluded from even supplementary insurance policies. All agencies will want either a credit card or a large **cash deposit** up front; minimum age requirements vary from 21 to 25. Driving licences issued by any European Union state are honoured, but in theory (and increasingly, in practice) an **International Driving Licence** is required by all other drivers, including Australasians and North Americans. This must be arranged before departure, as ELPA (the Greek motoring association) no longer issues IDLs to foreign nationals.

In peak season, you may get a better price through one of the **overseas booking companies** that deal with local firms than if you negotiate for rental in Greece itself; this may also be the only way to get hold of a car, at any price, at such times. Competitive companies in Britain include Holiday Autos, Suncars and Transhire (see box above). Payless, European, Kosmos, Alamo, Reliable, Thrifty, Eurodollar and Just are dependable Greek, or smaller international, chains with

branches in many towns; all are considerably cheaper than the biggest international operators Budget, Europcar, Hertz and Avis. Specific local recommendations are given in the guide.

In terms of **models**, the more competitive companies tend to offer the Subaru M80 or Vivio, the Fiat Cinquecento or Seisento and the Suzuki Alto 800 as A-group cars, and Opel (Vauxhall) Corsa 1.2, Fiat Uno/Punto or Nissan Micra in the B group. Any more than two adults, with luggage, will generally require B category. The Suzuki Alto 600, Fiat Panda 750/900 and Seat Marbella should be avoided if at all possible, and are being phased out by the more reputable agencies. The standard four-wheel-drive option is a Suzuki jeep, mostly open – great for bashing down rutted tracks to remote beaches.

DRIVING IN GREECE

Greece has the highest **accident rate** in Europe after Portugal, and on mainland motorways or the larger tourist islands it's easy to see why. **Driving habits** amongst locals can be atrocious: overtaking is erratic, lane lines and turn signals may as well not exist, and motorbikes hog the road or weave from side to side. **Drunk driving** is also a major problem; Sunday afternoons in rural areas are particularly bad, and for the same reason you should avoid driving late at night on weekends or holidays.

Matters are made worse by poor **road conditions**: signposting is absent or badly placed, pavement markings are faded, asphalt can turn into a one-lane surface or a dirt track without warning on secondary routes, railway crossings are rarely guarded, and you're heavily dependent on magnifying mirrors at blind intersections in congested villages. Uphill drivers insist on their **right of way**, as do those first to approach a one-lane bridge; **flashed headlights** mean the opposite of what they do in the UK or North America, here signifying that the other driver insists on coming through or overtaking.

There are a limited number of **express highways** between Pátra, Athens, Vólos and Thessaloníki, on which tolls are levied – currently between 500dr and 700dr at each sporadically placed gate. They're nearly twice as quick as the old roads, and well worth using. But even on these so-called motorways, there may be no proper far-right lane for slower traffic, which is expected to straddle the solid white line at the verge and allow rapid traffic to pass.

Wearing a **seatbelt** is compulsory, as is keeping a first-aid kit in the boot, and children under the age of 10 are not allowed to sit in the front seats. It's illegal to drive away from any kind of accident, and you can be held at a police station for up to 24 hours. If this happens, you have the right to ring your consulate immediately to summon a lawyer; don't make a statement to anyone who doesn't speak, and write, very good English. In practice, once police are informed that there was no personal injury, they rarely come out to investigate.

Tourists with proof of AA/RAC/AAA membership are given free road assistance from ELPA, the Greek equivalent, which runs **breakdown services** on several of the larger islands; in an emergency ring their road assistance service on ☎104. Many car rental companies have an agreement with ELPA's equally widespread competitors Hellas Service and Express Service, but they're prohibitively expensive to summon on your own – over 40,000 drachmas to enrol as an "instant member".

RUNNING A VEHICLE

Petrol/gasoline currently costs 215–245dr a litre for either regular unleaded (*amólyvdhi*) or super unleaded; as throughout the EU, leaded four-star

is to be unavailable after January 1, 2000. It is easy to run out of fuel after dark or on weekends in both rural and urban Greece; most stations close at 7 or 8pm sharp, and nearly as many are shut all weekend. There will always be at least one pump per district open on a rota basis, but it's not always apparent which one it is. This is not so much of a problem on the major highways, but it is a factor everywhere else. So always fill up, or insist on full rental vehicles at the outset, and if you've brought your own car, keep a full jerrycan at all times. Filling stations run by international companies (BP, Mobil and Texaco) often take credit cards; Shell, and Greek chains like EKO, Mamidhakis, Jetoil, Revoil and Elinoil usually don't (except in tourist areas).

Incidentally, the smallest grade of **mopeds** and **scooters** consume **mix** – a red- or green-tinted fuel dispensed from a transparent cylindrical device. This contains a minimum of three percent two-stroke oil by volume; when unavailable, you brew it up yourself by adding to supergrade fuel the necessary amount of separately bottled two-stroke oil (*ládhi dhýo trohón* in Greek). It's wise to err on the generous side – say five percent – or you risk the engine seizing up.

In terms of **maintenance**, the easiest models to have serviced and buy parts for in Greece are VWs (including combi and Transporter vans), Mercedes, Opels, Ladas, Skodas and virtually all French, Italian, Korean and Japanese makes. British models are a bit more difficult, but you should be fine as long as you haven't brought anything too esoteric.

In general, both mechanics' **workshops** and **parts retailers** are clustered at the approach and exit roads of all major towns, usually prominently signposted. For the commonest makes, emergency spares like fan belts and cables are often found at surprisingly remote service stations, so don't hesitate to ask at an unlikely-looking spot. Rural mechanics are okay for quick patch-up jobs like snapped clutch cables, but for major problems it's best to limp into the nearest sizable town to find a mechanic who is factory-trained for your make.

HITCHING

Hitching carries the usual risks and dangers, and is inadvisable for women travelling alone, but overall Greece is one of the safer countries in which to do it. It's fairly reliable, too, as a means of getting around, so long as you're not overly concerned about time; lifts are fairly frequent but tend to be short.

Hitching is easier on islands and in rural areas than as a means of getting out of big cities, whose suburbs tend to sprawl for miles. At its best, hitching is a wonderful method of getting to know the country – there's no finer way to take in the Peloponnese than from the back of a truck that looks like it has been converted from a lawn-mower – and a useful way of picking up some Greek. While you'll often get lifts from Greeks eager to display or practise their English, there will be as many where to communicate you're forced to try the language.

TAXIS

Greek **taxis** are among the cheapest in western Europe – so long as you get an honest driver who switches the meter on (see the caveats about Athens on p.81). Use of the meter is mandatory within city or town limits, where Tariff "1" applies, while in rural areas or between midnight and 5am, Tariff "2" is in effect. On certain islands, such as Kálymnos and Léros, set rates apply on specific fixed routes for "collective" taxis – these only depart when full. Otherwise, throughout Greece the flag falls at 200dr (though you can expect this figure to inch up); any baggage not actually on your lap is charged at 50dr apiece. Additionally, there are **surcharges** of 200dr for leaving (but not entering) an airport, and 100dr for leaving a harbour area. If you summon a taxi by phone on spec, there's a 400dr charge, while a pre-arranged rendevous is 500dr; in either case the meter starts running from the moment the driver begins heading towards you. For a week or so before and after Orthodox Easter, and Christmas, a *filodhórima* or gratuity of about ten percent is levied. Any or all of these extras will legitimately bump up the basic meter reading of about 1300dr for ten rural kilometres.

Incidentally, **Athens taxi-drivers** are not obliged to take a fare if free and, if you're going somewhere obscure, expect to navigate and/or to provide them with a street map.

A special warning needs to be sounded about **unlicensed taxi-drivers** who congregate outside major train stations, particularly Athens and Lárissa. These shady characters may offer to shuttle you several hundred kilometres for the same price as the train/KTEL bus, or less; upon arrival you will discover that the fare quoted is per

person, not per vehicle, and that along the way stops are made to cram several more passengers in – who again do not share your fare. Moreover, the condition of the vehicles usually leaves a lot to be desired.

DOMESTIC FLIGHTS

Olympic Airways and its subsidiary Olympic Aviation operate most of the **domestic flights** within Greece. They cover a fairly wide network of islands and larger mainland towns, though most routes are to and from Athens or Thessaloníki. Airline operation has been officially deregulated in Greece since 1993, but few private airlines have successfully challenged the state-run carrier: Air Greece and Cronus both offer high-volume routes between Crete, Rhodes, Athens and Thessaloníki; while Air Manos has about a dozen routes, but only reliably runs from June to October – with booking via local travel agents. All three airlines offer prices that undercut Olympic by a fair margin, though frequencies tend to be sparse. This, of course, could change drastically if financially troubled Olympic goes under, as is frequently threatened, and a successor state carrier offers inevitably reduced service.

For the moment, Olympic **schedules** can be picked up at their offices abroad (see "Getting There" sections) or through their branch offices and representatives in Greece, which are maintained in almost every town or island of any size; Greek-only small booklets, which include prices for domestic routes, appear twice yearly (early April and late June), while English-language books geared more for an international readership are published twice yearly (March and October).

Fares for flights to and between the islands, including the domestic airport tax of about £7/$11/3400dr, work out around three to four times the cost of a ferry journey, but on certain inter-island hauls that are poorly served by boat (Rhodes–Kastellórizo or Kárpathos–Kássos, for example), you should consider this time well bought. For obscure reasons, flights between Athens and Mílos, Kýthira, Préveza or Kalamáta are slightly better value per air mile, so take advantage.

Island flights are often full in peak season; if they're an essential part of your plans, it is worth trying to make a **reservation** at least a week to ten days in advance. Domestic air tickets are nonrefundable, but you can change your flight, space permitting, without penalty as late as a day before your original departure.

Incidentally, the only surviving Olympic-run **shuttle buses** between the main town and the airport are on Kós and Kastellórizo; others have long since been axed as a cost-cutting exercise. In several instances (Athens, Thessaloníki, Ioánnina, Híos, Rhodes), municipally run services have picked up the slack, but otherwise you're at the mercy of the taxi-drivers who congregate outside the arrivals gate.

Like ferries, flights are subject to **cancellation** in bad weather, since many services are on small, 50- or 68-seat ATR prop planes, or even tinier Dornier 18-seaters, none of which will fly in strong winds or (depending on the destination airport) after dark. Despite these uncertainties, a flight on a Dornier puddle-jumper is a highly recommended experience. You can watch the crew, who are often on first-name basis with passengers, flicking switches in the cockpit; virtually every seat has a view, and you fly low enough to pick out every island feature – you might even select beaches in advance.

Size restrictions also mean that the 15-kilo **baggage weight limit** is fairly strictly enforced; if, however, you've just arrived from overseas or purchased your ticket outside Greece, you are allowed the 23-kilo standard international limit. All services operated on the domestic network are **non-smoking**.

ACCOMMODATION

There are huge numbers of beds for tourists in Greece, so most of the year you can rely on turning up pretty much anywhere and finding a room – if not in a hotel, then in a private house or block of rooms (the standard island accommodation). Only from mid-July to early September, the country's high season, are you likely to experience problems. At these times, if you don't have accommodation reserved well in advanced, you'd be wise to keep well off the main tourist trails, turning up at each new place early in the day, and taking whatever is available – you may be able to exchange it for something better later on.

Out of season, you face a slightly different problem: most private rooms – and campsites – operate only from late April or early May to October, leaving hotels your only option. During winter you may have no choice but to stay in the main towns or ports. There will often be very little life outside these places anyway, with all the seasonal beach bars and restaurants closed. On many smaller islands, you will often find just one hotel – and perhaps one taverna – staying open year-round.

HOTELS

Hotels in the larger resorts are often contracted out on a seasonal basis by foreign package holiday companies, though there are often vacancies available (especially in spring or autumn) for walk-in trade. The tourist police set official **categories** for hotels, which range from "De Luxe" down to the rarely encountered "E-class"; all except the top category have to keep within set price limits. There is talk, but so far only just that, of replacing the letter system with a star grading system as in other countries. While they last, letter ratings are supposed to correspond to **facilities** available, though in practice categorization often depends on location within a resort and "influence" with the tourism authorities. It is mandatory for D-class rooms to have attached baths; C-class must additionally have a bar or designated breakfast area. The presence of a pool and/or tennis court will attract a B-class rating, while A-category hotels should have a restaurant, bar and extensive common areas. Often these, and the De Luxe outfits (essentially self-contained complexes), back onto a quasi-private beach.

Mainland town hotels are almost invariably poor value for money, used as they are to a business clientele on expense accounts, and thus charging the same inflated rates all year. In ski resorts and other areas with significant October-to-April leisure tourism, such as Galaxídhi, Náfplio and Mount Pílion, rates are markedly higher at weekends and holidays, and generally so during winter when heating bills must be accounted for. The only exceptions to this are the Peloponnese – which has enough foreign tourism to generate some healthy competition – and to a certain extent Athens.

In terms of **food**, C-class hotels are required only to provide the most rudimentary of continental breakfasts – you may choose not to take, or pay, for it – while B-class and above will usually offer some sort of buffet breakfast including cheese, cold cuts, sausages, eggs and so on. With some outstanding exceptions, noted in the guide, lunch or supper at hotel-affiliated restaurants is bland and poor value.

HOT WATER

A key variable in both rooms and hotels is the type of water heating. Rooftop **solar units** (*iliaká*), with their nonexistent running costs, are more popular than electric **immersion heaters** (*thermosífona*). Under typical high-season demand, however, solar-powered tanks tend to run out of hot water with the post-beach shower crunch at 6pm, with no more available until the next day. A heater, either as a backup or primary source, is more reliable; proprietors may either jealously guard the **boiler controls** or entrust you with its workings, which involves either a circuit breaker or a rotary switch turned to "I" for fifteen minutes. You should never shower with a *thermosífono* powered up (look for the glow-lamp indicator on the tank) – besides the risk of shock from badly earthed plumbing, it would be fairly easy to empty smaller tanks and burn out the heating element.

PRIVATE ROOMS

The most common island and mainland-resort accommodation is **privately let rooms** (*dhomátia*). Like hotels, these are regulated and officially divided into three classes (A down to C), according to facilities. These days the bulk of them are in new, purpose-built, low-rise buildings, but a few are still actually in people's homes, where you'll occasionally be treated to disarming hospitality.

Rooms are almost always scrupulously clean, whatever their other amenities. At their simplest, you'll get a bare, concrete room, with a hook on the back of the door and toilet facilities outside in the courtyard. At the fancier end of the scale, they are modern, fully furnished places with an en-suite, marble-clad bathroom and a fully equipped kitchen shared by guests. Between these extremes there will be a choice of rooms at various prices – owners will usually show you the most expensive first. Some of the cheap places will also have more expensive rooms with en-suite facilities – and vice versa, with singles often tucked under stairways or in other less desirable corners of the building. Price and quality are not necessarily directly linked, so always ask to see the room before agreeing to take it.

Areas to **look for rooms**, along with recommendations of the best places, are included in the guide. As often as not, however, the rooms find you: owners descend on ferry or bus arrivals to fill any space they have, sometimes waving photos of the premises. In smaller places you'll often see rooms advertised, sometimes in German (*Zimmer*); the Greek signs to look out for are "ENIKIAZÓMENA DHOMÁTIA" or "ENIKIÁZON-TEH DHOMÁTIA". In the more developed island resorts, where package holidaymakers predominate, *dhomátia* owners will often require you to stay for at least three days, or even a week.

It has become standard practice for rooms proprietors to ask to keep your **passport** – ostensibly "for the tourist police", who do require customer particulars – but in reality to prevent you skipping out with an unpaid bill. Some owners may be satisfied with just taking down your details, as is done in hotels, and they'll almost always return the documents once you get to know them, or if you need them for another purpose.

If you are **stranded**, or arrive very late in a remote mountain or island village, you may very

---

ROOM PRICES

Establishments listed in this book have been **price-coded** according to the scale outlined below. The rates quoted represent the **cheapest available double room** in high season. Out of season, rates can drop by up to fifty percent, especially if you negotiate for a stay of three or more nights. Bona fide single rooms, where available, cost around seventy percent of the price of a double.

① up to 6000dr   ③ 9000–12,000dr   ⑤ 16000–20,000dr
② 6000–9000dr   ④ 12000–16,000dr   ⑥ above 20,000dr

£1=500dr; $1=300dr

Note: Youth hostels typically charge 2000–2500dr for a dormitory bed.

Old-fashioned, 1970s-vintage rooms on the remoter islets, occasionally still without private bath, tend to fall into the ① price category. Standard, en-suite rooms without cooking facilities weigh in at ②; newer, state-of-the-art rooms and self-catering studios occupy the top end of the ③ niche, along with the more modest government-rated C-class hotels, the better among these edging into ④. The top half of ④ corresponds fairly well to the better-value B-class hotels, while ⑤ tallies with most of B-class, and ⑥ with A- and De Luxe class.

Prices in any establishment should by law be displayed on the back of the door of your room, or over the reception desk. If you feel you're being overcharged at a place which is officially registered, threaten to report it to the tourist office or police, who will generally adopt your side in such cases. Small amounts over the posted price may be legitimately explained by municipal tax or out-of-date forms. More commonly you will find that you have bargained so well, or arrived so far out of high season, that you are actually paying less than you're supposed to.

---

well find that there is someone prepared to earn extra money by putting you up. This should not be counted on, but things work out more often than not. Otherwise, the most polite course is to have a meal or drink at the taverna or kafenío and then, especially in summer, enquire as to the possibility of sleeping either in the vacant schoolhouse or in a spare room at the *kinotikó grafío* (community records office).

In **winter**, officially from November until early April, private rooms – except in Ródhos Old Town – are closed pretty much across the board to keep the hotels in business. There's no point in traipsing about hoping to find exceptions; most owners obey the system very strictly. If they don't, the room-owners will find you themselves and, watching out for hotel rivals, guide you back to their place.

VILLAS AND LONG TERM RENTALS

The easiest – and usually most economical – way to arrange a **villa rental** is through one of the package holiday companies detailed on p.6. They represent some superb places, from fairly simple to luxurious, and costs can be very reasonable, especially if shared between a few people. Several of the companies we list will arrange **"multi-centre"** stays on two or more islands.

On the islands, a few local travel agents arrange villa rentals, though they are often places the overseas companies gave a miss on or could not fill. **Out of season**, you can sometimes get a good deal on villa or apartment rental for a month or more by asking around locally, though in these days of EU convergence and the increasing desirability of the islands as year-round residences, "good deal" means anything under 50,000dr for a large studio (*garsoniéra*) or 60,000dr for a small one-bedroom flat.

YOUTH HOSTELS

Greece is not exactly packed with **youth hostels** (*xenón neótitos* in the singular), and those that do exist tend, with few exceptions, to be very run-down and/or filthy, and thus a far cry from similar north European institutions. Competition from unofficial "student hostels" (see below) and inexpensive rooms means that they are not as cost-effective as elsewhere in Europe. It's best to have a valid IYHF card, but you can often buy one on the spot, or maybe just pay a little extra for your bed. Charges for a dormitory bed are around £4–5/$6.50–8 a night; most hostels have a curfew at 11pm or midnight and many places only open in spring and summer.

Hostels on the **mainland** include: Athens, Mycenae, Olympia, Pátra and Thessaloníki. On the islands you'll find them only on Thíra (3), Rhodes (1) and Crete (4). Not all of these are officially recognized by the IYHF.

A number of alternatives to official youth hostels exist, particularly in Athens. These inexpensive dormitory-style **student hostels** are open to anyone but can be rather insalubrious. Some offer **roofspace**, providing a mattress and a pleasantly cool night under the stars.

MONASTERIES

Greek **monasteries** and **convents** have a tradition of putting up travellers (of the appropriate sex). On the mainland, this is still a customary – if steadily decreasing – practice, used mostly by villagers on pilgrimage; on the islands, far less so, where you should always ask locally before heading out to a monastery or convent for the night. Also, dress modestly – shorts for men and women, and short skirts are total anathema – and try to arrive early in the evening, not later than 8pm or sunset (whichever is earlier).

For **men**, the most exciting monastic experience is a visit to the "Monks' Republic" of **Mount Áthos** (see p.427), on the Halkidhikí peninsula, near Thessaloníki. This is a far from casual travel option, involving a fair amount of advance planning and the securing of a permit.

CAMPING

Officially recognized campsites range from ramshackle compounds on the islands to highly organized and rather soulless complexes, formerly run by the EOT (Greek Tourist Organization) prior to privatization. Most places cost 900dr a night per person, slightly less per tent and 1500dr per camper van, but at the fanciest sites, rates for two people plus a tent can almost add up to the price of a basic room. Generally, you don't have to worry about leaving tents or other equipment unattended at wardened campsites; Greeks are very honest. The main risk, alas, comes from other campers. The Greek Camping Association, Solonós 102, 106 80 Athens (☎01/36 21 560), publishes an annual booklet covering most officially recognized Greek campsites and the facilities they offer; it's available from EOT offices.

Camping rough – outside authorized campsites – is such an established element of Greek travel that few people realize that it's officially illegal. Since 1977 "free" camping, as EOT calls it, has actually been forbidden by a law originally enacted to harass gypsies, and regulations are increasingly enforced. Another drawback is the increased prevalence of theft in rural areas, often from marauding bands of refugees from Albania and other north Balkan states. All told, you will feel less vulnerable inside a tent, camper van or even a rock-cave – not that rain is likely during the long Greek summer, but some protection is essential from wind, sun, insects (see "Health", p.25) and stray animals raiding your food. You will always need at least a light sleeping bag, since even summer nights can get cool and damp; a foam pad is also recommended for pitching on harder ground.

If you do camp rough, it's vital to exercise sensitivity and discretion. Police will crack down on people camping (and especially littering) around popular tourist beaches, particularly when a large community of campers develops. Off the beaten track, however, nobody is very bothered, though it is always best to ask permission locally in the village taverna or café. During high season, when everything – even the authorized campsites – may be full, attitudes towards freelance camping are more relaxed, even in the most touristed places. At such times the best strategy is to find a sympathetic taverna, which in exchange for regular patronage will probably be willing to guard small valuables and let you use their facilities.

EATING AND DRINKING

Greeks spend a lot of time socializing outside their homes, and sharing a meal is one of the chief ways of doing it. The atmosphere is always relaxed and informal, and pretensions (and expense-account prices) are rare outside of the more chi-chi parts of Athens and major resorts. Greeks are not prodigious drinkers – tippling is traditionally meant to accompany food – although since the mid-1990s a whole range of bars and pubs have sprung up, both in tourist resorts and as pricey music halls at the outskirts of the major towns.

BREAKFASTS, PICNIC FARE AND SNACKS

Greeks don't generally eat **breakfast**, so the only egg-and-bacon kind of places are in resorts where foreigners congregate, or where there are returned North American or Australian Greeks. Such spots can sometimes be fairly good value (1200–1900dr for the works, with coffee), especially if there's competition. More indigenous alternatives are yogurts at a *galaktopolío* (milk bar), or cheese pies and pretzel rings from a street stall (see "Snacks", p.48).

PICNIC FARE

Picnic fare is good, cheap and easily available at bakeries and *manávika* (fruit-and-veg stalls). **Bread**, alas, is often of minimal nutritional value and inedible within a day of purchase. It's worth paying extra at the bakery (*foúrnos* or *psomádhiko*) for *olikís* (wholemeal), *sikalísio* (rye bread),

oktásporo (eight-grain) or even *enneásporo* (nine-grain), the latter types most commonly baked where large numbers of Germans or Scandinavians are about. When buying **olives**, go for the fat Kalamáta or Ámfissa ones; they're more expensive, but tastier. The best **honey** is reckoned to be the pure-thyme variety from the more barren islands (such as Límnos, Náxos and Astypálea) or areas of the mainland, although it's about double the price of ordinary honeys.

Honey is an ideal topping for the famous local **yoghurt**, which is not confined to the bland Fage-brand stuff of the UK supermarket. All of the larger island towns have at least one dairy shop where locally produced yoghurts are sold in plastic or (better) clay containers of various sizes. Sheep-milk yoghurt is richer and sweeter, scarcely requiring honey; cow-milk yoghurt is tarter but more widely available. Side by side with these will be *krémes* (custards) and *ryzógala* (rice puddings) in one-serving plastic containers.

Féta cheese is ubiquitous – often, ironically, imported from Holland or Denmark, though local brands are usually better and not much more expensive. The goat's-milk variety can be very dry and salty, so ask for a taste before buying. If you have access to a fridge, leaving the cheese overnight in a plastic container filled with water will solve both problems. This sampling advice goes for other indigenous cheeses as well, the most palatable of which are the expensive gruyère-type *graviéra*.

Despite membership of the EU, plus growing personal incomes and exotic tastes, Greece imports very little garden produce from abroad, aside from bananas and a few mangoes. **Fruit** in particular is relatively expensive and available only by season, though in the more cosmopolitan spots it is possible to find such things as **avocados** (light-green ones from Crete are excellent). Reliable picnic fruits include *yiarmádhes*, a variety of **peach** available during August and September; *krystália*, tiny, hard green **pears** that ripen a month or two later and are heavenly; and the *himoniátiko* **melon** (called casava in North America) which appears at the same time, in its yellow, puckered skin with green flecks. Greece also has a burgeoning **kiwi** industry, and while the first crop in October coincides with the end of the tourist season, the harvest carries over into the following April. Less portable, but succulent, are **figs** (*sýka*); there's a crop of large fruits in May, followed by smaller ones in August. Salad **vegetables** are more reasonably priced; besides the famous, enormous tomatoes (June to September), there is a bewildering variety of springtime greens, including rocket, dill, enormous spring onions and lettuces. Useful **expressions** for shopping are *éna tétarto* (250g) and *misó kiló* (500g).

SNACKS

Traditional **snacks** can be one of the distinctive pleasures of Greek eating, though they are being increasingly edged out by an obsession with *tóst* (toasted sandwiches) and other Western junk/fast food at nationwide chains such as Goody's (burgers), Roma Pizza and Theios Vanias (baked pastries) – somewhat less insipid for being homegrown. However, independently produced kebabs (*souvlákia*) are widely available, and in most larger resorts and towns you'll find *yíros* – doner kebab with garnish in thick, doughy *píta* bread that's closer to Indian naan bread.

Other common snacks include *tyrópites* (cheese pies) and *spanokópites* (spinach pies), which can usually be found at the baker's, as can *kouloúria* (crispy pretzel rings sprinkled with sesame seeds) and *voutímata* (dark biscuits heavy on the molasses, cinnamon and butter).

RESTAURANTS

Greek cuisine and **restaurants** are simple and straightforward. There's usually no snobbery about eating out; everyone does it regularly, and it's still reasonable – around 2900–3800dr per person for a substantial meal with a measure of house wine. That said, there's a lot of lazy cooking about – especially in resorts, menus are dominated by pizza, spaghetti and chops – and you'll now find growing numbers of what the Greeks call **"kultúra" restaurants**, often pretentious attempts at Greek nouvelle cuisine which tend to be long on airs and graces, and (at 5000–7000dr a head) short on value. The exceptions which succeed have been singled out in the text.

In choosing a restaurant, the best strategy is to go where the Greeks go. And they go late: 2pm to 3pm for **lunch**, 9pm to 11pm for **supper**. You can eat earlier, but you're likely to get indifferent service and cuisine if you frequent establishments catering to the tourist schedule. Chic appearance

is not a reliable guide to quality; often the more ramshackle, traditional outfits represent the best value. One good omen is the waiter bringing a carafe of refrigerated water, unbidden, rather than pushing you to order bottled stuff.

In busy resort areas, it's wise to keep a wary eye on the **waiters**, who are inclined to urge you into ordering more than you want, then bring things you haven't ordered. They often don't actually write anything down and may work out the **bill** by examining your empty plates. Although cash-register receipts are now required in all establishments, these are often only for the grand total, and itemized tabs will be in totally illegible Greek script. Where prices are printed on menus, you'll be paying the right-hand (higher) of the two columns, inclusive of all taxes and usually **service charge**, although a small extra tip of about ten percent directly to the waiter is hugely appreciated – and usually not expected.

Bread costs extra, but consumption is not obligatory; unless it is assessed as part of the cover charge, you have the right to send it back without paying for it. You'll be considered deviant for refusing it, but so much Greek bread is inedible sawdust that there's little point in paying extra unless you actually want to use it as a scoop for dips.

Children are always welcome, day or night, at family tavernas, and Greeks don't mind in the slightest if they play tag between the tables or chase the **cats** running in mendicant packs – which you should not feed, as signs often warn you.

ESTIATÓRIA

There are two basic types of restaurant: the **estiatório** and the **taverna**. Distinctions between the two are slight, though the former is more commonly found in towns and tends to have the slightly more complicated dishes termed **mayireftá** (literally, "cooked").

An estiatório will generally feature a variety of such oven-baked **casserole** dishes: *moussakás*, *pastítsio*, meat or game stews like *kokinistó* and *stifádho*, *yemistá* (stuffed tomatoes or peppers), the oily vegetable casseroles called *ladherá* and oven-baked meat and fish. Usually you go into the kitchen and point at the desired steam trays to choose these dishes.

Batches are cooked in the morning and then left to stand, which is why this *mayireftá* food is often **lukewarm** or even cold. Greeks don't mind this (most actually believe that hot food is bad for you), and dishes like *yemistá* are actually enhanced by being allowed to cool off and stand in their own juice. Similarly, you have to specify if you want your food with little or no oil (*horís ládhi*), but once again you will be considered a little strange since Greeks regard olive oil as essential to digestion (and indeed it is the healthiest of the vegetable oils, even in large quantities).

Desserts (*epidhórpia* in formal Greek) of the pudding-and-pie variety don't exist at estiatória, and yoghurt or cheese only occasionally. Fruit, however, is always available in season; watermelon (often on the house), melon and grapes are the summer standards. Autumn treats worth asking after include *kydhóni* or *akhládhi stó foúrno*, baked quince or pear with some sort of syrup or nut topping.

TAVERNAS & PSISTARIÉS

Tavernas range from the glitzy and fashionable to rough-and-ready huts set up under a reed canopy, behind a beach. Really primitive ones have a very limited (often unwritten) menu, but the more established will offer some of the main *mayireftá* dishes mentioned above, as well as the standard taverna fare. This essentially means **mezédhes** (hors-d'oeuvres) or **orektiká** (appetizers) and *tís óras* (meat and fish, fried or grilled to order). A handful of tavernas, especially on the mainland offer **game** (*kynígi*) – rabbit, quail or turtle dove, especially during autumn shooting season. In the mountains of the north where there are rivers, trout, pike and freshwater crayfish are to be found in some eating places.

Psistariés or grill-houses serve spit-roasted lamb, pork or goat (generically termed *kondosoúvli*), grilled chicken (*kotópoulo skáras*) or *kokorétsi* (grilled offal roulade) – in remote mountain villages, often plonked straight onto your table upon a sheet of waxed paper. They will usually have a limited selection of mezédhes, but no *mayireftá* at all.

Since the idea of courses is foreign to Greek cuisine, starters, main dishes and salads often arrive together unless you request otherwise. The best thing is to order a selection of mezédhes and salads to share, in true Greek fashion. Waiters encourage you to take the *horiátiki* **salad** – the so-called Greek salad, including *féta* cheese – because it is the most expensive. If you only want tomato, or tomato and cucumber, ask for *domatosaláta* or *angourodomáta*. *Láhano* (cab-bage) and *maroúli* (lettuce) are the typical winter and spring salads respectively.

The most interesting **mezédhes** are *tzatzíki* (yoghurt, garlic and cucumber dip), *melitzanosaláta* (aubergine/eggplant dip), *kolokythákia tiganitá* (courgette/zucchini slices fried in batter) or *melitzánes tiganités* (aubergine/eggplant slices fried in batter), *yígandes* (white haricot beans in vinaigrette or hot tomato sauce), *tyropitákia* or *spanakópittes* (small cheese and spinach pies), *revythókeftedhes* or *pittaroúdhia* (chickpea patties similar to falafel), *okhtapódhi* (octopus) and *mavromátika* (black-eyed peas).

Among **meats**, *souvláki* (shish kebab) and *brizóles* (chops) are reliable choices. In both cases, pork (*hirinó*) is usually better and cheaper than veal (*moskharísio*). The best *souvláki*, though not often available, is lamb (*arnísio*). At psistariés, meaty lamb shoulder chops (*kopsídha*) are more substantial than the scrawny rib chops called *païdhákia*; roast lamb (*arní psitó*) and roast kid (*katsíki stó fournó*) are considered estiatório fare. *Keftédhes* (breadcrumbed meatballs), *biftékia* (similar, but meatier) and the spicy, home-made sausages called *loukánika* are cheap and good. *Kotópoulo* (chicken), especially grilled, is also usually a safe bet.

Seaside *psarotavérnes* offer **fish**, though for the inexperienced, ordering can be fraught with peril. Summer visitors get a relatively poor choice of fish, most of it frozen, farmed or imported from Egypt and North Africa. Drag-net-trawling is prohibited from the end of May until the beginning of October, when only lamp-lure, trident and multi-hook line methods are allowed. During these warmer months, such few fish as are caught tend to be smaller and dry-tasting, and are served with butter sauce. Taverna owners often comply only minimally with the requirement to indicate when seafood is **frozen** (look for the abbreviation "kat." on the Greek-language side of the menu). Given these considerations, it's often best to set your sights on the **humbler**, seasonally migrating or perennially local species. The cheapest consistently available fish are *gópes* (bogue), *atherína* (sand smelts) and *marídhes* (picarel), eaten head and all, but rolled in salt and sprinkled with lemon juice. In autumn especially you may encounter *psarósoupa* or *kakaviá* (fish stew).

The **choicer** varieties, such as *barboúni* (red mullet), *tsipoúra* (gilt-head bream), *lavráki* (sea bass) or *fangrí* (common bream), will be expensive; if the price seems too good to be true, it's

A FOOD AND DRINK GLOSSARY

BASICS

Alát	Salt	*Lahaniká*	Vegetables	*Olikís*	Wholemeal bread
Avgá	Eggs	*O logariasmós*	The bill	*Sikalísio*	Rye bread
(Horís) ládhi	(Without) oil	*Méli*	Honey	*Thalassiná*	Seafood
Hortofágos	Vegetarian	*Neró*	Water	*Tyrí*	Cheese
Katálogo/lísta	Menu	*Psári(a)*	Fish	*Yiaoúrti*	Yoghurt
Kréas	Meat	*Psomí*	Bread	*Zákhari*	Sugar

COOKING TERMS

Akhnistó	Steamed	*Sto foúrno*	Baked
Pastó	Marinated in salt	*Tiganitó*	Pan-fried
Psitó	Roasted	*Tis óras*	Grilled/fried to order
Saganáki	Rich red sauce	*Yakhní*	Stewed in oil and tomato sauce
Skáras	Grilled	*Yemistá*	Stuffed (squid, vegetables, etc)
Sti soúvla	Spit roasted		

SOUPS AND STARTERS

Avgolémono	Egg and lemon soup	*Krítamo*	Rock samphire
Dolmádhes	Stuffed vine leaves	*Mavromátika*	Black-eyed peas
Fasoládha	Bean soup	*Melitzanosaláta*	Aubergine/eggplant dip
Florínes	Canned red Macedonian peppers	*Revýth keftédhes*	Chickpea (garbanzo) patties
		Skordhaliá	Garlic dip
Kápari	Pickled caper leaves	*Soúpa*	Soup
Kopanistí, khtypití	Spicy cheese purée	*Taramosaláta*	Cod roe paté
Tzirosaláta	cured mackerel dip	*Tzatzíki*	Yoghurt and cucumber dip

VEGETABLES

Angináres	Artichokes	*Koukiá*	Broad fava beans
Angoúri	Cucumber	*Maroúli*	Lettuce
Ánitho	Dill	*Melitzána*	Aubergine/eggplant
Bámies	Okra, ladies' fingers	*Papoutsákia*	Stuffed aubergine/eggplant
Bouréki, bourekákia	Courgette/zucchini, potato and cheese pie	*Patátes*	Potatoes
		Piperiés	Peppers
Briám	Ratatouille	*Pligoúri, pinigoúri*	Bulgur wheat
Domátes	Tomatoes	*Radhíkia*	Wild chicory
Fakés	Lentils	*Rízi/Piláfi*	Rice (usually with *sáltsa* – sauce)
Fasolákia	French beans		
Horiátiki (saláta)	Greek salad (with olives, fétta etc)	*Rókka*	Rocket greens
		Saláta	Salad
Hórta	Greens (usually wild)	*Spanáki*	Spinach
Kolokyhákia	Courgette/zucchini	*Yígandes*	White haricot beans

FISH AND SEAFOOD

Astakós	Aegean lobster	*Gávros*	Mild anchovy	*Koutsomoúra*	Goatfish (small barboúni)
Atherína	Sand smelt	*Glóssa*	Sole		
Bakaliáros	Cod	*Gópa*	Bogue	*Kydhónia*	Cherrystone clams
Barboúni	Red mullet	*Kalamarákia*	Baby squid		
Fangrí	Common bream	*Karavídhes*	Crayfish	*Lakérdha*	Light-fleshed premium tuna
Galéos	Dogfish, hound shark	*Kalamária*	Squid		
		Kefalás	Axillary bream	*Marídhes*	Whitebait
Garídhes	Shrimp, prawns	*Koliós*	Chub mackerel	*Melanoúri*	Saddled bream

Mýdhia	Mussels	*Selákhi*	Skate, ray	*Tsipoúra*	Gilt-head bream
Okhtapódhi	Octopus	*Synagrídha*	Dentex	*Vátos*	Skate, ray
Platý	Skate, ray	*Skathári*	Black bream	*Xifías*	Swordfish
Sardhélles	Sardines	*Skoumbrí*	Atlantic mackerel		
Sargós	White bream	*Soupiá*	Cuttlefish		

MEAT AND MEAT-BASED DISHES

Arní	Lamb	*Moussakás*	Aubergine, potato and
Biftéki	Hamburger		meat pie with bechamel topping
Brizóla	Pork or beef chop	*Païdhákia*	Lamb rib chops
Hirinó	Pork	*Pastítsio*	Macaroni baked with meat
Keftédhes	Meatballs	*Patsás*	Tripe and trotter soup
Kokorétsi	Liver/offal roulade, spit-roasted	*Salingária*	Garden snails
Kopsídhia	Lamb shoulder chops	*Sykóti*	Liver
Kotópoulo	Chicken	*Soutzoukákia*	Mincemeat rissoles/beef patties
Kounélli	Rabbit	*Stifádho*	Meat stew with tomato
Loukánika	Spicy homemade sausages	*Youvétsi*	Baked clay casserole
Moskhári	Veal		of meat and short pasta

SWEETS AND DESSERT

Baklavás	Honey and nut pastry	*Karydhópita*	Walnut cake
Bougátsa	Salt or sweet cream pie served	*Kréma*	Custard
	warm with sugar and	*Loukoumádhes*	Dough fritters in honey
	cinnammon		syrup and sesame seeds
Galaktobóureko	Custard pie	*Pagotó*	Ice cream
Halvás	Sweetmeat with	*Pastélli*	Sesame and honey bar
	sesame or semolina	*Ryzógalo*	Rice pudding

FRUIT AND NUTS

Akhládhia	Big pears	*Kerásia*	Cherries	*Pepóni*	Melon
Aktinídha	Kiwis	*Krystália*	Miniature pears	*Portokália*	Oranges
Fistíkia	Pistachio nuts	*Kydhóni*	Quince	*Rodhákino*	Peach
Fráoules	Strawberries	*Lemóni*	Lemon	*Sýka*	(Dried) figs
Karpoúzi	Watermelon	*Míla*	Apples	*Stafýlia*	Grapes

CHEESE

Féta	Salty, white cheese	*Kasséri*	Medium-sharp cheese
Graviéra	Gruyère-type hard cheese	*Myzíthra*	Sweet cream cheese
Katsikísio	Goat cheese	*Próvio*	Sheep cheese

DRINKS

Bíra	Beer	*Krasí*	Wine	*Portokaládha*	Orangeade
Boukáli	Bottle	*áspro*	white	*Potíri*	Glass
Gála	Milk	*kokkinélli/rozé*	rosé	*Stinyássas!*	Cheers!
Galakakáo	Chocolate milk	*kókkino/mávro*	red	*Tsáï*	Tea
Gazóza	Generic fizzy drink	*Limonádha*	Lemonade	*Tsáï vounoú*	"Mountain"
Kafés	Coffee	*Metalikó neró*	Mineral water		(sage) tea

probably farmed. Prices are usually quoted by the kilo, and should not be more than double the street market rate, so if squid is 2500dr a kilo at the fishmongers, that sum should fetch you two 250-gramme portions. Standard procedure is to go to the glass-fronted cooler and pick your own specimen.

Cheaper **seafood** (*thalassiná*) such as *kalamarákia* (fried baby squid) and *okhtapódhi* (octopus) are a summer staple of most seaside tavernas, and occasionally *mýdhia* (mussels), *kydhónia* (cockles) and *garídhes* (small prawns) will be on offer at reasonable prices. Keep an eye out, however, to freshness and season – mussels in particular are a common cause of stomach upsets or even mild poisoning.

As the more favoured species have become overfished, **unusual seafoods**, formerly the exclusive province of the poor, are putting in a greater appearance on menus. Ray or skate (variously known as *platý, seláhi, trígona* or *vátos*) can be fried or used in soup, and is even dried for decoration. Sea urchins (*ahiní*) are also a humble favourite, being split and emptied for the sake of their (reputedly aphrodisiac) roe that's eaten raw. Only the reddish ones are gravid; special shears are sold for opening them if you don't fancy a hand full of spines.

As in estiatória, traditional tavernas offer fruit rather than sticky **desserts**, though nowadays these are often available, along with coffee, in tavernas frequented by foreigners.

WINES

Both estiatória and tavernas will usually offer you a choice of bottled **wines**, and many still have their own house variety: kept in barrels, sold in bulk by the quarter-, half- or full litre, and served either in glass flagons or the brightly coloured tin "monkey-cups" called *kantária*. Not as many tavernas stock their own wine as once did, but it's worth asking whether they have wine *varelísio* (barrelled) or *hýma* (in bulk). You should expect to pay no more than about 1200dr per litre, with smaller measures priced proportionately. Non-resinated wine is almost always more than decent. **Retsína** – pine-resinated wine, a slightly acquired taste – is also usually better straight from the barrel, though the bottled Yeoryiadhi brand from Thessaloníki is excellent.

Among the **bottled wines** available **nationwide**, Cambas, Boutari Lac de Roches, Calliga and the Rhodian CAIR products (especially the Moulin range) are good, **inexpensive** whites, while Boutari Nemea or Naoussa are decent, **mid-range** reds. If you want something better but still moderately priced, Tsantali Agioritiko is an excellent white or red. But especially if you're travelling around wine-producing islands, you may as well go for **local bottlings**. Almost anything produced on **Límnos** is decent; the Alexandrine muscat is now used for whites, the local *límnio* grape for reds and rosés. **Santoríni**, another volcanic island, has a number of premium products such as Nykhteri and Vysanto, and the Robola white of **Kefalloniá** is justly esteemed. **Páros** and **Náxos** also both have acceptable local vintages, while **Crete** is now beginning to have labels superior to the bog-standard Logado. On **Rhodes**, Alexandris products from Émbonas are well thought of, as is the Emery label with its Villaré white.

Curiously, island red wines (except for Rhodes's CAIR Moulin and Emery Mythiko) are almost uniformly mediocre; in this respect you're better off pushing the boat out for **reds from the mainland**. The Halkidhikí peninsula vintner Carras does the excellent Porto Carras, and Ktima Papaïoannou Nemea (Peloponnese), Averof Katoï (Métsovo, Epirus) and Tsantali Rapsani (Thessaly) are all superb, velvety reds – and likely to be found only in the better *kultúra* tavernas or *káves* (**bottle shops**). The other **premium microwineries** on the mainland whose products have long been fashionable, in both red and white, include Hatzimihali (Atalánti, central Greece), Spyropoulos Mantinia (central Peloponnese), Athanasiadhi (central Greece), Skouras and Lazaridhi (east Macedonia). For any of these you can expect to pay 2000–3000dr per bottle in a shop, double that at a taverna.

Last but not least, CAIR on Rhodes makes its very own "**champagne**" ("naturally sparkling wine fermented *en boteille*", says the label), in both brut and demi-sec versions. It's not Moet & Chandon quality by any means, but at about £4 equivalent per bottle, who's complaining....

CAFÉS, CAKE SHOPS AND BARS

The Greek eating and drinking experience encompasses a variety of other places beyond restaurants. Most importantly, there is the institution of the **kafenío**, found in every town, village and hamlet in the country. In addition, you'll come across **ouzerís**, **zaharoplastía** (Greek patisseries) and **barákia**.

THE KAFENÍO

The **kafenío** (plural, kafenía) is the traditional Greek coffee shop or café. Although its main business is "Greek" (Middle Eastern) coffee – prepared *skéto* or *pikró* (unsweetened), *métrio* (medium) or *glykó* (sweet) – it also serves spirits such as oúzo (see below), brandy (usually Metaxa or Botrys brand, in three grades), beer, tea (either sage-based tea known variously as *alisfakiá* or *tsáï vounoú*, or British-style) and soft drinks. Another refreshing drink sold in cafés is *kafés frappé*, a sort of iced instant coffee with or without milk and sugar – uniquely Greek despite its French-sounding name. Like Greek coffee, it is always accompanied by a welcome glass of cold water. Standard fizzy soft drinks are also sold in all kafenía.

Usually the only **edibles** available are *glyká koutalioú* (sticky, syrupy preserves of quince, grape, fig, citrus fruit or cherry) and the traditional *ipovrýhio*, a piece of mastic submerged in a glass of water like a submarine – which is what the word means in Greek.

Like tavernas, kafenía range from the plastic and sophisticated to the old-fashioned, spit-on-the-floor variety, with marble or brightly painted metal tables and straw-bottomed chairs. An important institution anywhere in Greece, they form the pivot of life in the country villages. You get the impression that many men spend most of their waking hours there. Greek women are rarely to be seen in the more traditional places – and foreign women may sometimes feel uneasy or unwelcome in these establishments. Even in holiday resorts, you will find that there is at least one coffeehouse that the local men have reserved for themselves.

Some kafenía close at siesta time, but many remain open from early in the morning until late at night. The chief summer socializing time is 6–8pm, immediately after the siesta. This is the time to take your pre-dinner oúzo, as the sun begins to sink and the air cools down.

OÚZO, MEZÉDHES AND OUZERIS

Oúzo and the similar *tsípouro* (mainland) and *tsikoudhiá* (Crete), are simple **spirits** of up to 48 percent alcohol, distilled from wine-mash residue left over from wine-making, and then flavoured with herbs such as anise or fennel. There are nearly a score of brands, with the best reckoned to be from Lésvos, Sámos and Týrnavos on the mainland; inferior ones are either weak (such as the Rhodian Fokiali, at forty percent) or spiked with molasses or grain alcohol to "boost" them.

When you order, you will be served two glasses: one with the oúzo, and one full of water to be tipped into your oúzo until it turns a milky white. You can drink it straight, but the strong, burning taste is hardly refreshing if you do. It is increasingly common to add **ice cubes** (*pagáki*), a bowl of which will be provided upon request.

A much smoother variant of oúzo is **soúma**, found chiefly on Rhodes and Sámos, but in theory anywhere grapes are grown. The smoothness is deceptive – two or three glasses of it and you had better not have any other firm plans for the afternoon.

Until the 1980s, every oúzo you ordered was automatically accompanied by a small plate of **mezédhes**, on the house: bits of cheese, cucumber, tomato, a few olives, sometimes octopus or even a couple of small fish. Unfortunately these days you usually have to ask, and pay, for this.

Though they are confined to the better resorts and select neighbourhoods of the larger islands and towns, one kind of drinking establishment specializes in oúzo and mezédhes. These are called **ouzerí** (same in the Greek plural, we've added 's' to the hybrid), and are well worth trying for the marvellous variety of mezédhes they serve (though lately numbers of mediocre tavernas have counterfeited the name). At the genuine article, several plates of mezédhes plus drinks will effectively substitute for a more involved meal at a taverna (though it usually works out more expensive if you have a healthy appetite). Faced with an often bewilderingly varied menu, you might opt for the *pikilía* (medley, assortment) available in several sizes, the largest and most expensive one usually heavy on the seafood. At other ouzeris the language barrier may be overcome by the waiter wielding an enormous **dhískos** or tray laden with all the current cold offerings – you pick the ones you like the looks of.

SWEETS AND BREAKFAST

Similar to the kafenío is the **zaharoplastío**, a cross between café and patisserie, serving coffee, alcohol, yoghurt with honey and sticky cakes.

The better establishments offer an amazing variety of pastries, cream-and-chocolate confections, honey-soaked Greco-Turkish sweets like *baklavás, kataïfi* (honey-drenched "shredded wheat"), *loukoumádhes* (deep-fried batter puffs dusted with cinnamon and dipped in syrup), *galaktoboúreko* (custard pie) and so on.

If you want a stronger slant towards the dairy products and away from the pure sugar, seek out a **galaktopolío**, where you'll often find *ryzógalo* (rice pudding – rather better than the English canned variety), *kréma* (custard) and locally made *yiaoúrti* (yoghurt), best if it's *próvio* (from sheep's milk).

Ice cream, sold principally at the gelaterie which have swept over Greece of late (Dhodhoni is the posh chain), can be very good and almost indistinguishable from Italian prototypes. A scoop (*baláki*) costs 250–400dr; you'll be asked if you want it in a cup (*kypelláki*) or a cone (*konáki*), and whether you want toppings like *santí* (whipped cream). By contrast, the mass-produced brands like Delta or Evga are pretty average, with the exception of Floca Poème and Nirvana labels; Häagen-Dazs is also widely available. A sign reading "PAGOTÓ POLÍTIKO" or "KAÏMÁKI" means that the shop concerned makes its own Turkish-style ice cream – as good as or better than the usual Italian version – and the proprietors are probably of Asia Minor or Constantinopolitan descent.

Both zaharoplastía and galaktopolía are more family-oriented places than the kafenío, and many also serve a basic **continental breakfast** of *méli me voútyro* (honey poured over a pat of butter) or jam (all kinds are called *marmeládha* in Greek; ask for *portokáli* – orange – if you want proper marmalade) with fresh bread or *friganiés* (melba-toast-type slivers). You are also more like-

ly to find proper (*evropaïkó*) tea and non-Greek coffee. *Nescafé* has become the generic term for all instant coffee, regardless of brand; it's generally pretty vile, and in resort areas smart proprietors have taken to offering filter coffee, dubbed *gallikós* (French).

BARS – AND BEER

Bars (*barákia* in the plural), once confined to towns, cities and holiday resorts, are now found all over Greece, especially in pedestrian areas. They range from clones of Parisian cafés or Spanish *bodegas* to seaside cocktail bars, or imitation English "pabs" (sic), with videos running all day. At their most sophisticated, however, they are well-executed theme venues in ex-industrial premises or Neoclassical houses that can hold their own against close equivalents in Spain or London, with Western (currently techno) soundtracks.

For this and other reasons, drinks are invariably more expensive than in a café. Bars are, however, most likely to stock a range of **beers**, mostly foreign labels made locally under licence. However, since 1996 three new **homegrown brews** have appeared, rapidly capturing a slice of market: Mythos, a smooth lager in a green bottle, put out by the Boutari vintners; Veryina, brewed in Komotiní and common in eastern Macedonia and Halkidhikí; and Fisher, a sharp pilsner. Kronenberg 1664 and Kaiser are two of the more common quality **foreign-licence** varieties, with the latter available in both light and dark. Bland, inoffensive Amstel and the increasingly rare, yeasty Henninger are the two ubiquitous cheapies; the Dutch themselves claim that Amstel is better than the one available in Holland, and Amstel also makes a very palatable, strong (seven percent) **bock**. Heineken, still referred to as a "*prássini*" by bar and taverna staff after its green bottle, despite the advent of Mythos, is too harshly sharp for many. Since 1993 a tidal wave of even pricier, genuinely imported German beers, such as Bitburger and Warstein (plus a few British ones), has washed over the fancier resorts.

Incidentally, try not to get stuck with the one-third litre cans, vastly more expensive (and more of a rubbish problem) than the returnable half-litre bottles.

COMMUNICATIONS

POSTAL SERVICES

Post offices are open Monday to Friday from 7.30am to 2pm, though certain main branches have hours through the evening and on Saturday morning.

Airmail letters from the mainland take three to seven days to reach the rest of Europe, five to twelve days to get to North America, and a bit longer for Australia and New Zealand. Generally, the larger the island (and the planes serving its airport), the quicker the service. Postal rates fall within the normal EU range: 170dr (35p equivalent) for postcards or letters to Europe, 200dr (42p equivalent) to North America or Australasia. For a modest fee (about 500dr), you can shave a day or two off delivery time to any destination by using the **express service** (*katepígonda*). **Registered** (*systiméno*) delivery is also available for a similar amount, but proves quite slow unless coupled with express service. If you are sending large purchases home, note that **parcels** should and often can only be handled in the main provincial or county capitals. This way, your bundle will be in Athens, and on an international flight, within a day.

For a simple letter or card, a **stamp** (*grammatósima*) can also be purchased at a *períptero* (kiosk). However, the proprietors charge ten percent commission on the cost of the stamp, and never seem to know the current international rates.

Ordinary **post boxes** are bright yellow, express boxes dark red, but it's best to use only those by the door of an actual post office, since days may pass between collections at other street-corner or wall-mounted boxes. If you are confronted by two slots, "ESOTERIKÓ" is for domestic mail, "EXOTERIKÓ" for overseas.

The **poste-restante** system is reasonably efficient, especially at the post offices of larger towns. Mail should be clearly addressed and marked "poste restante", with your surname underlined, to the main post office of whichever town you choose. It will be held for a month and you'll need your passport to collect it.

PHONES

Making **telephone calls** is relatively straightforward, though the **OTE** (*Organizmós Tiliepikinoníon tís Elládhos*, the state-run telecom) has historically provided some of the worst service in the EU. However, since the mid-1990s this has improved drastically, and rates have dropped dramatically, under the twin threats of privatization and thriving competition from local mobile networks.

In theory, all exchanges are to become **digital** (*psifiakó*) by the year 2002, but in the meantime you may still encounter a few **pulse-analogue** (*palmikó*) exchanges. When ringing long-distance on such circuits, you must wait for a critical series of six electrical crunches on the line after dialling the country or Greek area code, before proceeding.

Call boxes, invariably sited at the noisiest street corners, work only with phone cards; these come in two denominations – 100, 500 and 1000 units – and are available from kiosks, OTE offices and newsagents. Not surprisingly, the more expensive cards are the best value. Despite numbers hopefully scribbled on the appropriate tabs, call boxes **cannot be rung back**, certainly not from abroad.

If you won't be around long enough to use up a phone card – the cheapest one costs £2 equivalent – it's probably easier to make **local calls** from a *períptero* or **street kiosk**. Here the phone may be connected to a meter (if not, there'll be a sign saying *móno topikó*, "local only"), and you pay after you have made the call. Local, one-unit calls are reasonable enough (30dr for the first three minutes), but long-distance ones add up quickly.

Other options for calling include **counter coin-op phones** in bars, kafenía and hotel lobbies; these take 10-, 20-, 50- and 100dr coins and, unlike kerbside phone boxes, can be rung back. Most of them are made in northern Europe and bear instructions in English. Avoid making long-distance calls from hotel rooms, as a hundred percent surcharge will be slapped on.

For **international** (*exoterikó*) **calls**, it's better to use either kerbside card phones or the very few remaining inside the premises of the nearest OTE office. As of writing, many OTE branches have withdrawn from the business of providing call facilities, with opening hours drastically shortened, and now generally resemble a UK high-street BT Phone Store with their array of phones

and fax machines for sale. **Faxes** are best sent from post offices and some travel agencies – at a price; receiving a fax may also incur a small charge.

Overseas phone calls with a 100-unit card will **cost**, approximately, £2 for six minutes to all EU countries and much of the rest of Europe, and $5 for the same time to North America or Australia – more than double what you'd pay at night rates on a private line, whose economy is only approached if you buy the 1000-unit card. **Cheap rates**, a reduction of ten to fifty percent depending on call distance, apply from 10pm to 8am daily, plus all day Sunday, for calls **within Greece**; calling **internationally**, cheap rates take effect from 10pm to 6pm for Europe, 11pm to 8am for North

---

PHONING GREECE FROM ABROAD

Dial the international access code (given below) + 30 (country code) + area code (minus initial 0) + number

Australia ☎0011   Canada ☎011   Ireland ☎010   New Zealand ☎00   UK ☎0   USA ☎011

PHONING ABROAD FROM GREECE

Dial the country code (given below) + area code (minus any initial 0) + number

Australia ☎0061   Canada ☎001   Ireland ☎00353   New Zealand ☎0064   UK ☎0044   USA ☎001

GREEK PHONE CODES

Athens ☎01	Mobiles ☎093, ☎094,	Pátra ☎061	Thessaloníki ☎031
Corfu ☎0661	☎095, ☎097	Rhodes ☎0241	Zákynthos ☎0695
Iráklion ☎081	Mýkonos ☎0289	Santoríni ☎0286	
Kós ☎0242	Páros ☎0284	Skiáthos ☎0427	

USEFUL GREEK TELEPHONE NUMBERS

Ambulance ☎166	Forest fire reporting ☎191	Police/Emergency ☎100
ELPA Road Service ☎104	Operator ☎132 (Domestic)	Speaking clock ☎141
Fire brigade, urban ☎199	Operator ☎161 (International)	Tourist police ☎171

PHONE CREDIT-CARD OPERATOR ACCESS NUMBERS FROM GREECE

AT&T USA Direct ☎00 800 1311	British Telecom ☎00 800 4411
Australia ☎00 800 61 11	Cable & Wireless ☎00 800 4422
Australia (Ortus) ☎00 800 6121	Canada ☎00 800 1611
Bell Atlantic ☎00 800 1821	MCI ☎00 800 1211
Bell South ☎00 800 1721	Sprint ☎00 800 1411

America, and 8pm to 6am for Australia. Discounts for other destinations are minimal. With access to a subscriber line, night rates to any EU country are about 19p per minute equivalent.

British Telecom, as well as North American long-distance companies like AT&T, MCI and Sprint, provide **credit-card call** services from Greece, but only back to the home country. There are now a few local-dial numbers with some providers (given in the box opposite) which enable you to connect to the international network for the price of a one-unit call, and then charge the call to your home number – usually cheaper than the alternatives.

Mobile phones are an essential fashion accessory in Greece, which has the highest per-capita usage in Europe outside of Italy. There are three networks at present: Panafon, Telestet and Cosmote. Ringing any of them from Britain, you will find that costs are exactly the same as calling a fixed phone, though of course such

numbers are pricey when rung locally. UK users should note that only GSM phones will work in Greece. Coverage country-wide is fairly good, though there are a number of "dead" zones in the shadows of mountains, or on really remote islets. Pay-as-you-go, contract-free plans are being heavily promoted in Greece (such as Telestet B-Free and Panafon À La Carte), and if you're going to be around for a while – for example, working a season in the tourist industry – an outlay of £80 or less will see you to a decent apparatus and your first calling card, which lasts six months rather than the sixty-day norm in Britain.

Email and **Internet** use is catching on slowly but surely in Greece; electronic addresses or Web sites are given for the few travel companies and hotels that have them. For your own email needs, you're best off using the various Internet cafés which have sprung up in the larger towns – street addresses are given where appropriate.

THE MEDIA

Although the Greek press and airwaves have been relatively free since the fall of the colonels' dictatorship in 1974, nobody would ever put forth the Greek media as a paradigm of responsible or objective journalism. Papers are almost uniformly sensational, state-run radio and TV often biased in favour of the ruling party, and private channels imitative of the worst American programming. Most visitors will tune all this out, however, seeking solace in the music of private radio stations, or the limited number of English-language publications.

British **newspapers** are fairly widely available in Greece at a cost of 500–700dr for dailies, or 900–1000dr for Sunday editions. You'll find day-old copies of *The Independent* and *The Guardian*'s European edition, plus a few of the tabloids, in all the resorts as well as in major towns. American and international alternatives include the turgid *USA Today* and the more readable *International Herald Tribune*, the later including as a major bonus a free, abridged English translation of the respected Greek daily *Kathemerini* (see below). *Time* and *Newsweek* are also widely available.

Among locally produced monthly **English-language magazines**, the late lamented *The Athenian* folded in 1997 after 23 years, with a rather sloppy successor, *Atlantis*, rising less than phoenix-like from the ashes. Slightly better is the expensive, glossy *Odyssey*, produced every other month by and for wealthy diaspora Greeks, and little different from the average in-flight magazine. **English-language newspapers** are the *Athens News* (daily except Monday, 300dr) in colour with good features and Balkan news, plus entertainment listings on Friday, available in most resorts, and the less commonly encountered *Hellenic Times* (Fridays, 300dr).

GREEK PUBLICATIONS

Many papers are funded by **political groups**, which tends to decrease the already low quality of Greek dailies. Among these, only the **centrist** *Kathemerini* – whose former proprietress Helen Vlahos attained heroic status for her defiance of the junta – approaches the standards of a major European newspaper. *Eleftherotypia*, once a PASOK mouthpiece, now aspires to more independence, and has links with the UK's *Guardian*; *Avriani* has taken its place as the PASOK cheerleading section. *Ta Nea* is mostly noted for its extensive small ads. On the far **Left**, *Avyi* is the Eurocommunist/Synaspismós forum with literary leanings, while *Rizospastis* acts as the organ of the KKE (unreconstructed Communists). *Ethnos* became notorious some years back by receiving covert funding from the KGB to act as a disinformation bulletin. At the other end of the political spectrum, *Apoyevmatini* generally supports the **centre-right** Néa Dhimokratía party, while *Estia*'s no-photo format and reactionary politics are both stuck somewhere at the turn of the century. The **ultra-nationalist**, lunatic fringe is staked out by paranoid *Stohos* ("Our Goal: Greater Greece; Our Capital: Constantinople").

Among **magazines** not merely translations of overseas titles, *Takhydhromos* is the respectable news-and-features weekly; *Ena* is more sensationalist, *Klik* a crass rip-off of *The Face*, while *To Pondiki* (The Mouse) is a satirical weekly revue in the same vein as Britain's *Private Eye*; its famous covers are spot-on and accessible to anyone with minimal Greek. More specialized niches are occupied by low-circulation titles such as *Adhesmatos Typos* (a slightly rightist, muckraking journal) and *Andi*, an intelligent bi-weekly somewhat in the mould of Britain's *New Statesman and Society*.

RADIO

If you have a **radio** on your personal stereo, playing dial roulette can be rewarding. Greek music programmes are always accessible (if variable in quality), and since abolition of the government's former monopoly of wavelengths, regional stations have mushroomed; indeed the airwaves are now positively cluttered as every island town sets up its own studio and transmitter.

On Rhodes, 102 FM International (also on 104.3FM) features foreign DJs and mostly rock, as well as regular news bulletins in English. The Turkish state radio's third channel is also widely (if somewhat unpatriotically) listened to on border islands for its classical, jazz and blues programmes. The **BBC World Service** broadcasts on short wave throughout Greece; 9.41, 15.07 and 12.09 MHz are the most common frequencies.

The **Voice of America**, with its transmitters on Rhodes, can be picked up in most of the Dodecanese on medium wave.

TV

Television first appeared in Greece in 1965, but it only became dominant during the 1967–74 junta, with the ruling colonels using it as a means of social control and to purvey anodyne variety revues, sports events and so on. As in many countries, it transformed the Greeks from a nation of live performers and coffee-house habitués to introverted stay-at-homes, which dovetailed nicely with the junta's "family values".

Greece's centralized, government-controlled **TV stations**, ET1, NET and (out of Thessaloníki) ET3,

nowadays lag behind private, decidedly right-wing channels – Mega, Antenna, Star, Skaï and Seven-X – in the ratings. On NET, news summaries in English are broadcast daily at 6pm. Programming on all stations has evolved little since junta days, tending to be a mix of soaps (especially Italian, Spanish and Latin American), game shows, westerns, B-movies and sports. All foreign films and serials are broadcast in their original language, with Greek subtitles. Except for the round-the-clock channels Mega, Skaï and Antenna, channels broadcast from breakfast time, or just after, until the small hours. Numerous **cable and satellite** channels are received, including CNN, MTV, Filmnet, Euronews (in English), French TV5 and Italian Rai Due. The range available depends on the area (and hotel) you're in.

OPENING HOURS AND PUBLIC HOLIDAYS

It is virtually impossible to generalize about Greek opening hours, except to say that they change constantly. The traditional timetable starts at a relatively civilized hour, with shops opening between 8.30 and 9.30am, then runs through until lunchtime, when there is a long break for the hottest part of the day. Things (except banks and government offices) may then reopen in the mid- to late afternoon.

Tourist areas tend to adopt a slightly more northern timetable, with shops and offices, as well as the most important archeological sites and museums, usually open throughout the day.

BUSINESS AND SHOPPING HOURS

Most **government agencies** are open to the public on weekdays from 8am to 2pm. In general, however, you'd be optimistic to show up after 1pm expecting to be served the same day. Private businesses, or anyone providing a service, frequently operate a 9am to 6pm schedule. If someone is actually selling something, then they are more likely to follow a split shift as detailed below.

Shopping hours during the hottest months are theoretically Monday, Wednesday and Saturday from approximately 9am to 2.30pm, and

Tuesday, Thursday and Friday from 8.30am to 2pm and 6 to 9pm. During the cooler months the morning schedule shifts slightly forward, the evening trade a half or even a full hour back. In Athens recently many enterprises have taken to keeping continuous hours (*synéhies óres*) during the winter, but this is by no means universally observed. Thus, there are so many exceptions to these rules by virtue of holidays and professional idiosyncrasy that you can't count on getting anything done except from Monday to Friday, between 9.30am and 1pm. It's worth noting that **delis** and **butchers** are not allowed to sell fresh meat during summer afternoons (though some flout this rule); similarly **fishmongers** are only open in the morning until they sell out (usually by noon), as are **pharmacies**, which additionally are shut on Saturday (except for the duty pharmacist).

All of the above opening hours will be regularly thrown out of sync by the numerous **public holidays and festivals**. The most important, when almost everything will be closed, are listed in the box on p.60.

ANCIENT SITES AND MONASTERIES

All the major **ancient sites** are now fenced off and, like most **museums**, charge admission fees ranging from a token 500dr to a whopping 2000dr,

PUBLIC HOLIDAYS

January 1
January 6
March 25
First Monday of Lent (variable Feb/March; see below)
Easter weekend (variable April/May; see below)

May 1
Pentecost or Whit Monday (50 days after Easter; see below)
August 15
October 28
December 25 & 26

VARIABLE RELIGIOUS FEASTS

Lenten Monday		**Easter Sunday**		**Whit Monday**	
2000	March 13	2000	April 30	2000	June 19
2001	February 26	2001	April 15	2001	June 4
2002	March 18	2002	May 5	2002	June 24

with an average fee of around 800dr. At most of them reductions of twenty-five to thirty percent apply to senior citizens, and fifty percent to students with proper identification. In addition, entrance to all state-run sites and museums is **free** to all EU nationals on Sundays and public holidays outside of peak season – non-EU nationals are unlikely to be detected as such unless they go out of the way to advertise the fact.

Opening hours vary from site to site. As far as possible, individual times are quoted in the text, but bear in mind that these change with exasperating frequency, and at smaller sites may be subject to the whim of a local keeper. Unless specified, the times quoted are generally summer hours, in effect from around late April to the end of September. Reckon on similar days but later opening and earlier closing in winter.

Smaller sites generally close for a long lunch and **siesta** (even where they're not supposed to),

as do **monasteries**. The latter are generally open from 9am to 1pm and 5 to 8pm (3.30 to 6.30pm in winter) for limited visits. Most monasteries impose a fairly strict **dress code** for visitors: no shorts on either sex, with women expected to cover their arms and wear skirts; the necessary wraps are sometimes provided on the spot.

It's free to take **photos** of open-air sites, though museum photography and the use of videos or tripods anywhere requires an extra fee and written permit. This usually has to be arranged in writing from the nearest Department of Antiquities (*Eforía Arheotíton*). It's also worth knowing that Classical studies students can get a free annual pass to all Greek museums and sites by presenting themselves at the office on the rear corner (Tossítsa/Bouboulínas) of the National Archeological Museum in Athens – take documentation, two passport-sized photographs and be prepared to say you're a teacher.

FESTIVALS AND CULTURAL EVENTS

Many of the big Greek popular festivals have a religious basis so they're observed in accordance with the Orthodox calendar. Give or take a few saints, this is similar to the regular Catholic liturgical year, except for Easter, which can fall as many as five (but usually one or two) weeks to either side of the Western festival. Other festivals are cultural in nature, with the highlight for most people being to catch a performance of Classical drama in one of the country's ancient theatres. There's also a full programme of cinema and modern theatre, best in Athens, but with something on offer in even the smallest town at some point during the year.

EASTER

Easter is by far the most important festival of the Greek year – infinitely more so than Christmas – and taken much more seriously than it is anywhere in western Europe. From Wednesday of Holy Week until the following Monday, the state radio and TV networks are given over solely to religious programmes.

The **festival** is an excellent time to be in Greece, both for its beautiful religious ceremonies and for the days of feasting and celebration that follow. The mountainous island of **Ídhra** with its alleged 360 churches and monasteries is the prime Easter resort, but unless you plan well in advance you have no hope of finding accommodation at that time. Other famous Easter celebrations are held at Corfu, Pyrgí on Híos, Ólymbos on Kárpathos and St John's monastery on Pátmos.

The first great public ceremony takes place on **Good Friday** evening as the Descent from the Cross is lamented in church. At dusk the Epitáfios, Christ's funeral bier, lavishly decorated by the women of the parish (in large villages there will be more than one, from each church), leaves the sanctuary and is paraded solemnly through the streets. In many places, Crete especially, this is accompanied by the burning of effigies of Judas Iscariot.

Late **Saturday** evening sees the climax in a majestic Anástasis Mass to celebrate Christ's triumphant return. At the stroke of midnight all the lights in every crowded church are extinguished, and the congregation plunged into the darkness which envelops Christ as He passes through the underworld. Then there's a faint glimmer of light behind the altar screen before the priest appears, holding aloft a lighted taper and chanting *"Avtó to Fós . . . "* (This is the Light of the World). Stepping down to the level of the parishioners, he touches his flame to the unlit candle of the nearest worshippers, intoning *"Dévteh, léveteh Fós"* (Come, take the Light). Those at the front of the congregation and on the aisles do the same for their neighbours until the entire church – and the outer courtyard, standing room only for latecomers – is ablaze with burning candles and the miracle re-affirmed.

Even the most committed agnostic is likely to find this moving. The traditional greeting, as fireworks explode all around you in the street, is *"Khristós Anésti"* (Christ is risen), to which the response is *"Alithós Anésti"* (Truly He is risen). In the week up to Easter Sunday you should wish people a Happy Easter: *"Kaló Páskha"*; on or after the day, you say *"Khrónia Pollá"* (Many happy returns).

Worshippers then take the burning **candles** home through the streets; they are said to bring good fortune to the house if they arrive still burning. On reaching the front door it is common practice to make the sign of the cross on the lintel with the flame, leaving a black smudge visible for the rest of the year. The **Lenten fast** is traditionally broken early on Sunday morning with a meal of **mayerítsa**, a soup made from lamb tripe, rice, dill and lemon. The rest of the lamb will be roasted on a spit for Sunday lunch, and festivities often take place through the rest of the day.

The Greek equivalent of **Easter eggs** are hard-boiled eggs (painted red on Holy Thursday), which are baked into twisted, sweet bread-loaves (*tsouréki*) or distributed on Easter Sunday. People rap their eggs against their friends' eggs, and the owner of the last uncracked egg is considered lucky.

THE FESTIVAL CALENDAR

Most of the other Greek festivals are celebrations of one or other of a multitude of **saints**; the most important are detailed below. A village or church bearing the saint's name is a fair guarantee of some sort of observance – sometimes right across the town or island, otherwise quiet, local and consisting of little more than a special liturgy and banners adorning the chapel in question. Saints' days are also celebrated as **name days**; if you learn that it's an acquaintance's name day, you wish them "*Khrónia Pollá*" ("Many years", as in "Many happy returns"). Also listed are a few more **secular** holidays, most enjoyable of which are the pre-Lenten carnivals.

In addition to the specific dates mentioned, there are literally scores of **local festivals**, or **paniyíria**, celebrating the patron saint of the main village church. With hundreds of possible name-saints' days (calendars list two or three, often arcane, for each day) you're unlikely to travel around Greece for long without stumbling on something.

It is important to remember the concept of the **paramoní**, or **eve of the festival**. Most of the events listed below are celebrated on the night before, so if you show up on the morning of the date given you will very probably have missed any music, dancing or drinking.

January 1

New Year's Day (*Protokhroniá*) in Greece is the feast day of Áyios Vassílios, and is celebrated with church services and the baking of a special loaf, the *vasilópitta*, in which a coin is baked which brings its finder good luck throughout the year. The traditional New Year greeting is "*Kalí Khroniá*".

January 6

Epiphany (*Ayía Theofánia*, or *Fóta* for short), when the *kalikántzari* (hobgoblins) who run riot on

earth during the twelve days of Christmas are rebanished to the nether world by various rites of the Church. The most important of these is the blessing of baptismal fonts and all outdoor bodies of water. At lakeside, seaside or riverside locations, the priest traditionally casts a crucifix into the deep, with local youths competing for the privilege of recovering it.

January 8

The **Yinekokratía** of certain villages in Thrace is a festival where St Domenica (Dhomníka in Greek), patroness of midwives, is celebrated by men and women reversing roles for the day: the women hold forth in the kafenía while the men do the domestic chores.

Pre-Lenten carnivals

These – known in Greek as *Apokriátika* – span three weeks, climaxing during the seventh weekend before Easter. *Katharí Dheftéra* (Lenten Monday) of the first carnival week is always seven weeks before Easter Sunday. **Pátra Carnival**, with a chariot parade and costume parties, is one of the largest and most outrageous in the Mediterranean, with events from January 17 until "Clean Monday", the last day of Lent; on the last Sunday before Lent there's a grand parade, with the city's large **gay population** in conspicuous participation. Interesting, too, are the *boúles* or masked revels which take place around Macedonia (particularly at Náoussa), Thrace (Xánthi) and the outrageous **Goat Dance** on Skýros in the Sporades. The Ionian islands, especially Kefalloniá, are also good for carnival, while Athenians "celebrate" by going around hitting each other on the head with plastic hammers. In Thebes, a mock shepherd wedding occurs, while most places celebrate with colourful pageants reflecting local traditions.

March 25

Independence Day and the feast of the **Annunciation** (*Evangelismós* in Greek) is both a religious and a national holiday, with, on the one hand, military parades and dancing to celebrate the beginning of the revolt against Turkish rule in 1821, and on the other church services to honour the news being given to Mary that she was to become the Mother of Christ. There are major festivities on Tínos, Ídhra (Hydra) and any locality with a monastery or church named Evangelístria or Evangelismós.

April 23

The feast of **Áyios Yeóryios** (St George), the patron of shepherds, is a big rural celebration, with much feasting and dancing at associated shrines and towns. Good venues include Aráhova, near Delphi, and the island of Skýros, of which George is patron saint. If April 23 falls before Easter, ie during Lent, the festivities are postponed until the Monday after Easter.

May 1

May Day is the great urban holiday when townspeople traditionally make for the countryside to picnic, returning with bunches of wild flowers. Wreaths are hung on their doorways or balconies until they are burnt in bonfires on St John's Eve (June 23). There are also large demonstrations by the Left, claiming the *Ergatikí Protomayiá* (Working-Class First of May) as their own.

May 21

The feast of **Áyios Konstandínos** (St Constantine) and his mother, Ayía Eléni (St Helen), the first pro-Orthodox Byzantine rulers. There are firewalking ceremonies in certain Macedonian villages; elsewhere celebrated rather more conventionally as the name day for two of the more popular Christian names in Greece.

May/June

The Monday of **Áyio Pnévma** (the Holy Spirit) marks the descent of same to the assembled disciples, fifty days after Easter. Usually a modest liturgy at rural chapels of the Holy Spirit, gaily decked out with pennants.

June 29

The joint feast of **Áyios Pétros and Áyios Pávlos** (Peter and Paul), two of the more widely celebrated name days.

July 17

The feast of **Ayía Marína**: a big event in rural areas, as she's an important protector of crops. The eponymous port town on Léros will be en fête, as will Ayía Marína village on Kássos. Between mid-July and mid-September there are religious festivals every few days, especially in the rural areas, and between these and the summer heat, ordinary business comes to a virtual standstill.

July 20

The feast of **Profítis Ilías** (the Prophet Elijah) is widely celebrated at the countless hill- or mountaintop shrines of Profítis Ilías. The most famous is on Mount Taïyettos, near Spárti, with an overnight vigil.

July 26

Ayía Paraskeví is celebrated in parishes or villages bearing that name, especially in Epirus.

August 6

Metamórfosis toú Sotíros (Transfiguration of the Saviour) provides another excuse for celebrations, particularly at Khristós Ráhon village on Ikaría, and at Plátanos on Léros. On Hálki the date is marked by messy food fights with flour, eggs and squid ink (!), so beware.

August 15

Apokímisis tis Panayías (Assumption or Dormition of the Blessed Virgin Mary). This is the day when people traditionally return to their home village, and in most places there will be no accommodation available on any terms. Even some Greeks will resort to sleeping in the streets. There is a great pilgrimage to Tínos, and major festivities at Páros, at Ayiássos on Lésvos, on Lipsí and at Ólymbos on Kárpathos.

August 29

Apokefálisis toú Prodhromou (Beheading of John the Baptist). Popular pilgrimages and celebrations at Vrykoúnda on Kárpathos.

September 8

Yénisis tis Panayías (Birth of the Virgin Mary) sees special services in churches dedicated to the event, and a double cause for rejoicing on Spétses where they also celebrate the anniversary of the battle of the straits of Spétses, which took place on September 8, 1822. A re-enactment of the battle takes place in the harbour, followed by fireworks and feasting well into the night. Elsewhere, a lively festival at Vourliótes, Sámos, and a pilgrimage of childless women to the monastery at Tsambíka, Rhodes.

September 14

A last major summer festival, the **Ípsosis toú Stavroú** (Exaltation of the Cross), keenly observed on Hálki.

September 24

The feast of **Áyios Ioánnis Theológos** (St John the Divine), observed on Níssyros and Pátmos.

October 26

The feast of **Áyios Dhimítrios** (St Demetrius), another popular name day, particularly celebrated in Thessaloníki, of which he is the patron saint. In rural areas the new wine is traditionally broached on this day, a good excuse for general inebriation.

October 28

Ókhi Day, the year's major patriotic shindig – a national holiday with parades, folk-dancing and speeches to commemorate Metaxas's apocryphal one-word reply to Mussolini's 1940 ultimatum: "*Okhi!*" (No!).

November 8

Another popular name day, the feast of the **Archangels Michael and Gabriel** (Mihaïl and Gavriïl, or *tón Taxiárhon*), marked by rites at the numerous churches named after them, particularly at the rural monastery of Taxiárhis on Sými, and the big monastery of Mandamádhos, Lésvos.

December 6

The feast of **Áyios Nikólaos** (St Nicholas), the patron of seafarers, who has many chapels dedicated to him.

December 25

A much less festive occasion than Greek Easter, **Christmas** (*Khristoúyenna*) is still an important religious feast celebrating the birth of Christ, and in recent years it has started to take on more of the trappings of the Western Christmas, with decorations, Christmas trees and gifts. December 26 is not Boxing Day as in England but the **Sýnaxis tis Panayías**, or Meeting of the Virgin's Entourage.

December 31

New Year's Eve (Paramoní Protokhroniá), when, as on the other twelve days of Christmas, children go door-to-door singing the traditional *kálanda* (carols), receiving money in return. Adults tend to sit around playing cards, often for money. The *vassilópitta* is cut at midnight (see January 1).

CULTURAL FESTIVALS

As well as religious festivals, Greece has a full range of **cultural festivals** – highlights of which include classical **drama** in ancient theatres at Athens, Epidaurus, Dodona and Dion. A leaflet entitled "Greek Festivals", available from GNTO offices abroad, includes details of smaller, **local festivals** of music, drama and dance, which take place on a more sporadic basis.

MAJOR FESTIVALS

Athens: the **Athens Festival** (June–Sept) encompasses a wide range of performances including modern and ancient theatre, ballet, opera, jazz and classical music, held mostly at the open-air Herodes Atticus Odeion. The Athens International Jazz and Blues Festival (June) puts on big-name acts at the modern open-air theatre on Lykavitós Hill. Details and tickets for events can be obtained from the Athens Festival box office (Stadhíou 4, ☎32 21 459), or at Herodes Atticus itself on the day from 6 until 9pm, when most performances start. It's worth calling in very soon after you arrive in Greece, since the more prestigious events often sell out.

Epidaurus: the **Epidaurus Festival** (July–Aug) hosts strictly open-air performances of Classical drama in the ancient theatre.

Pátra: the **International Festival** (mid-June to Sept) sees ancient drama, theatre and classical music up in the castle, as well as in the ancient odeion.

Thessaloníki: hosts the **Dhimitría Cultural Festival** (Oct) and a film festival (Nov) as well as Philoxenia, a large international trade and tourism exhibition (Nov).

MINOR FESTIVALS

Itháki Music Festival (July)

Ippokrateia Festival, Kós (July–Aug)

Kassándhra Festival, Síviri and Áfytos (July–Aug)

Manolis Kalomiris Festival, Sámos (July–Aug)

Réthymnon Renaissance Fair (July–Aug)

Sými Festival (July–Sept)

Philippi/Thássos Festival, mostly at Kavála castle (early July–early Sept)

Sáni Festival, Kassándhra, Halkidhikí (early July–early Sept)

Ólymbos Festival, Platamónas castle/ancient Dion (mid-July–early Sept)

Lefkádha Arts Jamboree (Aug)

Makrinítsa/Vólos Festival (Aug)

Ioánnina Cultural Summer (Aug–Sept)

Iráklion Festival (early Aug)

Santoríni Music Festival (Aug–Sept)

Rhodes Festival (Aug–Oct)

CINEMA AND THEATRE

Greek **cinemas** show a large number of American and British movies, always in the original soundtrack with Greek subtitles, though fly-posters tend to be Greek-only. **Indoor screenings** are highly affordable, currently 1700–2000dr depending on location and plushness of facilities; they shut from mid-May to late September unless they have air conditioning or a roll-back roof. Accordingly in summer vast numbers of outdoor cinemas operate; an **outdoor movie** (marginally cheaper) is worth catching at least once for the experience alone, though it's best to opt for the early screening (about 9pm) since the sound on the 11pm show gets turned down or even off to avoid complaints of noise from adjacent residences.

Theatre gets suspended during the summer months but from late September to May there's a lot of activity; Athens alone has scores of theatres, with playbills ranging from the classics to satirical revues (all in Greek).

SPORTS AND OUTDOOR PURSUITS

The Greek seashore offers endless scope for water sports, with windsurfing-boards for rent in most resorts and, less reliably, waterskiing and parasailing facilities. On land, the greatest attraction lies in hiking, through what is one of Europe's more impressive mountain terrains. Winter also sees possibilities for skiing at one of a dozen or so underrated centres.

As far as spectating goes, the twin Greek obsessions are **football** (soccer) and **basketball**, with **volleyball** a close third in popularity.

WATER SPORTS

The years since the mid-1980s have seen a massive growth in the popularity of **windsurfing** in Greece. The country's bays and coves are ideal for beginners, and boards can be rented in literally hundreds of resorts. Particularly good areas, with established schools, include Vassilikí on Lefkádha island, Kéfalos on Kós, Zákynthos, western Náxos, Kokkári on Sámos, Lésvos, Corfu and Crete, and Methóni in the Peloponnese. You can almost always pay for an initial period of instruction, if you've not tried the sport previously. Board rental rates are very reasonable – about £6/$10 an hour.

Waterskiing is available at a number of the larger resorts, and a fair few of the smaller ones too. By the crippling rental standards of the ritzier parts of the Mediterranean it is a bargain, with twenty minutes' instruction often available for around £8–10/$13–16. At many resorts, **parasailing** (*parapént* in Greek) is also possible; rates start at £10/$16 a go.

A combination of steady winds, appealing seascapes and numerous natural harbours have long made Greece a tremendous place for **sailing**. Holiday companies offer all sorts of packaged and tailor-made cruises (see pp.7 & 16 in "Getting There"). In Greece, small boats and motorized dinghies are rented out by the day at many resorts. Spring and autumn are the most pleasant and least expensive seasons; meltémi winds make for pretty nauseous sailing between late June and early September, and summer rates for the same craft can be three times as high as shoulder-season prices. For more details, pick up the informative brochure "Sailing the Greek Sea" from GNTO offices, or contact the Hellenic Yachting Federation, Aktí Navárhou Koundourióti 7, 185 34 Pireás (☎01/41 37 351, fax 01/41 31 119).

Because of the potential for pilfering submerged antiquities, **scuba diving** is severely restricted, its legal practice confined to certain coasts around Attica, Kálymnos, Kalamáta, Préveza, Rhodes, Skiáthos, Corfu, Zákynthos and

Mýkonos. For more information and an update on new, approved sites, contact the Union of Greek Diving Centres (☎01/92 29 532 or 41 18 909), or request the information sheet "Regulations Concerning Underwater Activities" from the nearest branch of the GNTO/EOT.

Greece also has lots of white water, especially in the Peloponnese and Epirus, so if you're into **river rafting** there is much potential. There are periodically articles and advice (in Greek) in the outdoors magazine *Korfes*.

SKIING

Skiing is a comparative newcomer to Greece, in part because snow conditions are unpredictable, and runs generally short. However, there are now more than a dozen ski centres scattered about the mountains, and what they may lack in professionalism is often made up for by a very easy-going and unpretentious après-ski scene. Costs are an attraction, too – much lower than in northern Europe, at around £11/$18 a day for rental of skis and boots, plus £7/$11 a day for a lift pass. The season generally lasts from the beginning of January to the end of April, with a few extra weeks possible at either end, depending on snow conditions.

The most developed of the resorts, originally established as R&R for the local bauxite miners, is on **Parnassós**, the legendary mountain near Delphi. It's easily accessible from Athens; throughout the season Athenian operators run buses up to the resort, returning the same day. Avoid weekends (which can be chaos) and you may have the resort more or less to yourself. The leading operator is Klaoudatos, a big department store on Dhimarhíou street, near Platía Omónia. In winter they devote a floor to skiing, including ski rental (though this is simpler at Parnassós itself). The resort has runs for all grades up to black. Its main problem is that the lifts are often closed due to high winds.

Other major **ski centres** include **Veloúhi** (Mount Tymfristós), near Karpeníssi in central Greece; **Helmós**, near Kalávryta on the Peloponnese; and **Vérmion**, near Náoussa in Macedonia. Minor areas, at lower altitudes and thus with shorter seasons, and where the skiing may be secondary to other local attractions, are **Pisodhéri** near Flórina, also in Macedonia; **Métsovo** in Epirus; and **Agriólefkes** (Hánia) on Mount Pílion.

Further details are available from the EOT, which publishes a leaflet entitled "Ski Centres and Mountaineering Shelters".

WALKING

Greeks are just becoming used to the notion that anyone should want to **walk** for pleasure, yet if you have the time and stamina it is probably the single best way to see the remoter back country. This guide includes descriptions of a number of the more accessible mountain hikes, as well as suggestions for more casual walking.

In addition, you may want to acquire one or both of the specific Greek **hiking guidebooks**; see p.910 in *Contexts*. See also p.31 for details of hiking maps available, and pp.7, 16 and 18 for details of companies offering walking holidays in the mountains.

FOOTBALL AND BASKETBALL

Football (soccer) is far and away the most popular sport in Greece – both in terms of participating and watching. The most important (and most heavily sponsored) teams are Panathanaïkós and AEK of Athens, Olympiakós of Pireás and PAOK of Thessaloníki. Other major teams in the provinces include Lárissa and the Cretan Ofí. If you're interested, matches (usually played on Wednesday nights and Sunday afternoons) are easy enough to catch from September to May. In mid-autumn you might even see one of the Greek teams playing European competition. The Greek national team qualified for the 1994 World Cup in some style, and then proceeded to lose all their three games heavily and returned from the US without scoring a goal.

The nation's **basketball** team is one of the continent's strongest and won the European Championship in 1987 – cheered all the way with enormous enthusiasm. At club level, many of the football teams maintain basketball squads.

FINDING WORK

Since Greece's full accession to the European Union in early 1993, a citizen of any EU state has (in theory) the right to work in Greece. In practice, however, there are a number of bureaucratic hurdles to overcome. Formerly, the most common job for foreigners was teaching English in the numerous private cramming academies (*frondistíria*), but lately severe restrictions have been put on the availability of such positions for non-Greeks, and you will more likely be involved in a commercial or leisure-oriented trade. Similarly, that other long-standing fallback of long-haul backpackers, picking fruit or greenhouse vegetables, is now the exclusive province of Albanian males.

SHORT-TERM WORK

EU membership notwithstanding, short-term work in Greece is always on an unofficial basis and for this reason it will generally be where you can't be seen by the police or you're badly paid – or, more often, both. The recent influx of between 500,000 and a million Albanians, Serbs, Bulgarians and Russians has resulted in a surplus of unskilled labour and severely depressed wages. Note that **youth hostels** are a good source of information on temporary work – indeed a few may even offer you a job themselves, if you turn up at the right time.

TOURISM-RELATED WORK

Most women working casually in Greece find jobs in **bars** or **restaurants** around the main resorts. Men, unless they are "trained" chefs, will be edged out by Albanians even when it comes to washing up.

If you're waiting or serving, most of your wages will probably have to come from tips but you may well be able to get a deal that includes free food and lodging; evening-only hours can be a good shift, leaving you a lot of free time. The main drawback may be the machismo and/or chauvinist attitudes of your employer. (Ads in the local press for "girl bar staff" are certainly best ignored; see "Sexual Harassment" on p.70)

Corfu, with its big British slant, is an obvious choice for bar work; Rhodes, Crete, Skiáthos,

Páros, Íos and Santoríni are also promising. Start looking, if you can, around April or May; you'll get better rates at this time if you're taken on for a season.

On a similar, unofficial level you might be able to get a sales job in **tourist shops** on Corfu, Ídhra, Rhodes or Crete, or (if you've the expertise) helping out at one of the **windsurfing** schools that have sprung up all around the coast. **Yacht marinas** can also prove good hunting-grounds though less for the romantic business of crewing, than scrubbing down and repainting. Again, the best possibilities are likely to be on Rhodes, Corfu or Kálymnos; the Zéa port at Pireás is actually the biggest marina, but non-Greek owners don't tend to rest up there for long.

Perhaps the best type of tourism-related work, however, is that of courier/greeter/group co-ordinator for a **package holiday company**. All you need is EU nationality and language proficiency compatible with the clientele, though knowledge of Greek is a big plus. English-only speakers are pretty well restricted to places with a big British package trade, namely Crete, Rhodes, Skiáthos and the Ionian islands.

Many such staff are recruited through ads in newspapers issued outside Greece, but it's by no means unheard of to be hired on the spot in April or May. A big plus, however you're taken on, is that you're usually guaranteed about six months of steady work, and that if things work out you may be re-employed the following season with contract and foreign-currency wages from the home company, not from the local affiliate.

SELLING AND BUSKING

You may do better by working for yourself. Travellers report rich pickings during the tourist season from **selling jewellery** on island beaches, or on boats – trinkets from Asia are especially popular with Greeks. Once you've managed to get the stuff past the customs officials (who will be sceptical, for instance, that all those trinkets are presents for friends), there rarely seem to be problems with the local police, though it probably pays to be discreet.

Busking can also be quite lucrative. Playing on the Athens metro or the city's streets, it's possible to make around 3000dr in a two-hour session.

DOCUMENTATION FOR LONG-TERM EMPLOYMENT

If you plan to work professionally for someone else, you first visit the nearest Department of Employment and collect two forms: one an **employment application** which you fill in, the other for the formal offer of work by your prospective employer. Once these are vetted, and revenue stamps (*hartósima*, purchased at kiosks) applied, you take them to the Alien's Bureau (*Ypiresía Allodhapón*) or, in its absence, the central police station, to support your application for a **residence permit** (*ádhia paramonís*). For this, you will also need to bring your passport, six photographs, more *hartósima* and a stable address (not a hotel). Permits are given for terms of one year (green triptych booklets), or five years (blue booklets) if they've become well acquainted with you. A **health examination** at the nearest public hospital is required, to screen for TB, hepatitus and HIV.

As a **self-employed professional**, you must satisfy the requirements of the Greek state with equivalent qualifications to native Greeks plying the same trade. You should also befriend a good accountant, who will advise you on which of the several varieties of incorporation are to your advantage; trading under a fictitious name is vastly more expensive tax-wise than doing business as a private person. You will need to sign on with **TEBE**, the Greek National Insurance scheme for self-employed people (analogous to Class 4 National Insurance contributions in the UK). If you are continuing to contribute to a social insurance scheme in a country which has reciprocal agreements with Greece (all EU states do), this must be proved in writing – a tedious and protracted process.

Once you're square with TEBE, visit the tax office or *eforía* to be issued a **tax number** (abbre-viated "ah-fi-mi" in Greek, similar to a UK Schedule D number) which must be cited in all transactions. You will be required to prepare receipt and invoice books with your tax number professionally printed on them, or have a rubber stamp made up for applying that number to every sheet. The tax office will also determine which rate of VAT (the "fi-pi-ah") you should pay for each kind of transaction; VAT returns must be filed every two months, which is where the friendly accountant who chose your incorporation type comes in handy again.

The self-employed tend to be issued one- or five-year residence permits, and these are supposed to be free of charge. **EU nationals** who do not wish to work in Greece but still need a residence permit (such as property-owners needing to set up a bank account) will still get a "white" pass gratis, but must present evidence of financial solvency; personalized pink exchange receipts, travellers' cheques or credit cards are all considered valid proofs.

At the present time, **non-EU nationals** who wish to work in Greece do so surreptitiously, with the ever-present risk of denunciation to the police and instant deportation. Having been forced to accept large numbers of EU citizens looking for jobs in a climate of rising unemployment, Greek immigration authorities are cracking down hard on any suitable targets, be they Albanian, African, Swiss or North American. That old foreigners' standby, teaching English, is now available only to TEFL certificate-holders, preferably Greek, non-EU nationals of Greek descent, and EU nationals in that order. If you are a non-EU foreign national of Greek descent, you are termed *omólogos* (returned Greek diaspora member) and in fact have tremendous employment and residence rights – you can, for example, open your very own *frondistírio* without any qualifications.

POLICE AND TROUBLE

As in the past, Greece remains one of Europe's safest countries, with a low crime rate and a deserved reputation for honesty. If you leave a bag or wallet at a café, you'll most likely find it scrupulously looked after, pending your return. Similarly, Greeks are relatively relaxed about leaving possessions unlocked or unattended on the beach, in rooms or on campsites.

However, in recent years there has been a large increase in **theft** and **crimes against persons** (blamed largely on Albanian and Romanian refugees) in towns, remote villages and resorts, so it's wise to lock things up and treat Greece like any other European destination. Following are also a few pointers on offences that might get you into trouble locally, and some advice on **sexual harassment** – all too much a fact of life given the classically Mediterranean machismo of Greek culture.

SPECIFIC OFFENCES

The most common causes of a brush with authority are nude bathing or sunbathing, and camping outside an authorized site.

Nude bathing is legal on only a very few beaches (most famously on Mýkonos), and is deeply offensive to the more traditional Greeks – exercise considerable sensitivity to local feeling and the kind of place you're in. It is, for example, very bad etiquette to swim or sunbathe nude within sight of a church. Generally, if a beach has become fairly well established as naturist, or is

well secluded, it's highly unlikely that the police are going to come charging in. Where they do get bothered is if they feel a place is turning into a "hippie beach" or nudity is getting too overt on mainstream tourist stretches. Most of the time, the only action will be a warning, but you can officially be arrested straight off – facing up to three days in jail and a stiff fine.

Topless (sun)bathing for women is technically legal nationwide, but specific locales often opt out of the "liberation" by posting signs, which should be heeded.

Very similar guidelines apply to **camping rough**, which has been theoretically illegal nationwide since 1977 (see "Accommodation", p.46). Even for this you're still unlikely to incur anything more than a warning to move on. The only real risk of arrest is if you are told to clear off and fail to do so. In either of the above cases, even if the police do take any action against you, it's more likely to be a brief spell in their cells than any official prosecution.

Incidentally, any sort of **disrespect** towards the Greek state or Orthodox Church in general, or Greek civil servants in particular, may be construed as offences in the most literal sense, so it's best to keep your comments on how things are working (or not) to yourself. Every year a few foreign louts find themselves in deep trouble over a drunken indiscretion. This is a society where verbal injuries count, with a consistent backlog of court cases dealing with the alleged public utterance of *malákas* (wanker). In the nonverbal field, ripped or soiled clothes and untucked-in shirts are considered nearly as insulting. Don't expect a uniformly civil reception if dressed in grunge attire, since many Greeks – for whom poverty is an uncomfortably close memory – may consider that you're making light of hard times.

Drug offences are treated as major crimes, particularly since there's a mushrooming local use and addiction problem. The maximum penalty for "causing the use of drugs by someone under 18", for example, is life imprisonment and an astronomical fine. Theory is by no means practice, but foreigners caught in possession of even small amounts of grass do get long jail sentences if there's evidence that they've been supplying the drug to others.

In an emergency, dial ☎100 for the police; ☎171 for the tourist police in Athens, ☎01-171 outside of it; ☎166 for an ambulance; and ☎199 for the fire brigade.

If you get arrested for any offence, you have a right to contact your **consulate**, who will arrange a lawyer for your defence. Beyond this, there is little they can, or in most cases will, do. Details of full-ranking consulates in Athens and Thessaloníki appear in their respective "Listings" sections. There are honorary British consulates on Rhodes, Crete and Corfu as well.

SEXUAL HARASSMENT

Thousands of women travel independently in Greece without being **harassed** or feeling intimidated. Greek machismo, however, is strong, if less upfront than in, for example, southern Italy. Most of the hassle you are likely to get is from a small minority of Greek men, known as *kamákia* (fish harpoons), who migrate in summer to the beach bars and discos of the main resorts and towns, specifically in pursuit of "liberated, fun-loving" tourists.

Indigenous Greeks, who become increasingly protective of you as you become more of a fixture in any one place, treat these outsiders with contempt; their obvious stakeouts are waterfront cafés, beach bars and dance clubs. Words worth remembering as unambiguous responses include "*pápsteh*" (stop it), "*afístemeh*" (leave me alone) and "*fíyeteh*" (go away), the latter intensified if followed by "*dhrómo*"! (road, as in "Hit the road!").

Hitching is not advisable for lone women travellers, but **camping** is generally not a problem, though away from recognized sites it is often wise to attach yourself to a local family by making arrangements to use nearby private land. In the more remote mountains and islands you may feel more uncomfortable travelling alone. The intensely traditional Greeks may have trouble understanding why you are unaccompanied, and might not welcome your presence in their exclusively male kafenía – often the only place where you can get a drink. Travelling with a man, you're more likely to be treated as a *xéni*, a word meaning both (female) stranger and guest.

Lone men need to be aware of one long-established racket in the largest mainland towns and island ports. Near Sýndagma in Athens, in particular, you may be approached by dubious gents asking the time or your origins, and then offering to take you for a drink in a nearby bar. This is invariably staffed with hostesses (who may also be on the game) whose main job is to convince you to treat them to drinks. At the end of the night you'll be landed with an outrageous bill, some of which goes for the hostess's "commission"; physical threats are brought to bear on reluctant payers.

CONSUMER PROTECTION ON HOLIDAY

In a tourist industry as developed as in Greece there are inevitably a number of cowboys and shady characters amongst the taxi-drivers, hoteliers and car rental agencies in particular. **EKPI-ZO**, the **Greek Consumers' Association**, has established a "Legal Information and Assistance for Tourists" programme, to be run yearly from June to September. Their main branch is in Athens (☎01/33 04 444), with offices also in Vólos, Pátra, Crete and Kavála. EKPIZO issues a pamphlet about holidaymakers' rights, available in airports and tourist offices. They are always prepared to pursue serious cases, by friendly persuasion or court action if necessary.

DIRECTORY

BARGAINING This isn't a regular feature of life, though you'll find it possible with private rooms and some hotels out of season. Similarly, you may be able to negotiate discounted rates for vehicle rental, especially for longer periods. Services such as shoe, watch and camera repair don't have iron-clad rates, so use common sense when assessing charges (advance written estimates are not routine practice).

CHILDREN Kids are worshipped and indulged in Greece, arguably to excess, and present few problems when travelling. Baby foods and nappies/diapers are ubiquitous and reasonably priced, plus concessions are offered on most forms of transport. Private rooms establishments and luxury hotels are more likely to offer some kind of babysitting service than the mid-range, C-class hotels.

DEPARTURE TAX This is levied on all international ferries – currently 1500dr per person and per car or motorbike. To non-EU states (Turkey, Egypt and Israel), it's 4000–5000dr per person, sometimes arbitrarily levied twice (on entry and exit). There's also an airport departure tax of £7 equivalent (currently 3400dr) for destinations less than 750 miles away, £13.50/6600dr if it's further, but this is always included in the price of the ticket – there's no collection at the airport itself. This tax, nicknamed the *spatósima* locally, is supposed to fund ongoing construction of the new Athens airport at Spáta, so it may be abolished upon completion in March 2001.

ELECTRICITY Voltage is 220 volt AC throughout the country. Wall outlets take double round-pin plugs as in the rest of continental Europe. Three-to-two-pin adapters should be purchased beforehand in the UK, as they can be difficult to find locally; standard 5-, 6- or 7-amp models permit operation of a hair dryer or travel iron. North American appliances will require both a step-down transformer and a plug adapter (the latter easy to find in Greece).

FILMS Fuji and Kodak print films are reasonably priced and easy to have processed – you practically trip over "One Hour Foto" places in resorts. Kodak and Fuji slide films can be purchased, again at UK prices or better, in larger towns, but cannot be processed there – whatever you may be told, exposed rolls will be sent to Athens for handling, so wait until you get home.

GAY LIFE For men, overtly gay behaviour in public remains taboo in rural areas, and only visible at certain resorts like Ídhra, Rhodes or Mýkonos, still the most popular European gay resort after Ibiza in Spain. Eressós on Lésvos, the birthplace of Sappho, is (appropriately) an international mecca for lesbians. Homosexuality is legal over the age of 17, and (male) bisexual behaviour common but rarely admitted. Greek men are terrible flirts, but cruising them is a semiotic minefield and definitely at your own risk – references in gay guides to male cruising grounds should be treated sceptically. "Out" gay Greeks are rare, and "out" local lesbians rarer still; foreign same-sex couples will be regarded in the provinces with some bemusement but accorded the standard courtesy as foreigners. The gay movement in Greece is represented by Akoe Amphi, PO Box 26022, 10022 Athens (☎01/77 19 221). See also p.130 and Athens "Listings", p.137.

GREEK LANGUAGE COURSES These abound in Athens – see the city's "Listings" section for addresses.

LAUNDRIES *Plindíria*, as they're known in Greek, are beginning to crop up in most of the main resort towns; sometimes an attended service wash is available for little or no extra charge over the basic cost of 1500–1700dr per wash and dry. Otherwise, ask rooms owners for a *skáfi* (laundry trough), a bucket (*kouvás*) or the special laundry area often available; they freak out if you use bathroom washbasins, Greek plumbing and wall-mounting being what they are.

PERÍPTERA These are street-corner kiosks, or sometimes a hole-in-the-wall shopfront. They sell everything from pens to disposable razors, stationery to soap, sweets to condoms, cigarettes to plastic crucifixes, yoghurts to milk-in-cartons – and are often open when nothing else is.

TIME As throughout the EU, Greek summer time begins at 2am on the last Sunday in March, when the clocks go forward one hour, and ends at 2am the last Sunday in October when they go back. Be alert to this, as the change is not well publicized, leading scores of visitors to miss planes and ferries every year. Greek time is thus always two hours ahead of Britain. For North America, the difference is seven hours for Eastern Standard Time, ten hours for Pacific Standard Time, with an extra hour plus or minus for those weeks in April and October when one place is on daylight saving and the other isn't. A recorded time message (in distinctly slow Greek, 24-hour convention) is available by dialling ☎141.

TOILETS Public toilets are usually in parks or squares, often subterranean; otherwise try a bus station. Except in areas frequented by tourists, public toilets tend to be pretty filthy – it's best to use those in restaurants and bars. Remember that throughout Greece, you drop paper in the adjacent wastebins, *not* in the bowl.

USEFUL THINGS TO BRING A high-quality, porcelain-lined canteen or drinking-water bottle; a small alarm clock for early buses and ferries; a flashlight if you're camping out; sunscreen of high SPF (25 or above, generally unavailable in Greece); pocket knife (Swiss Army type or similar), with tweezers, mini-screwdriver and other similar accessories; ear plugs for noisy ferries or hotels; and good-quality tea bags.

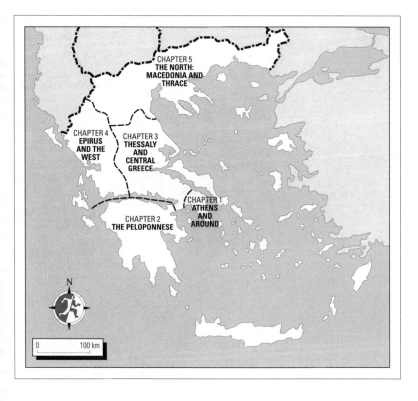

CHAPTER ONE

ATHENS AND AROUND

Athens is not a graceful city. It looks terrible from just about every approach, its air pollution is dire, and its traffic and postwar architecture are a disaster. For many of the four million-plus visitors who pass through each year, it can seem a dutiful stop. Their priorities usually include visits to the Acropolis and the National Archeological Museum and an evening or two amid the tavernas of Pláka, the

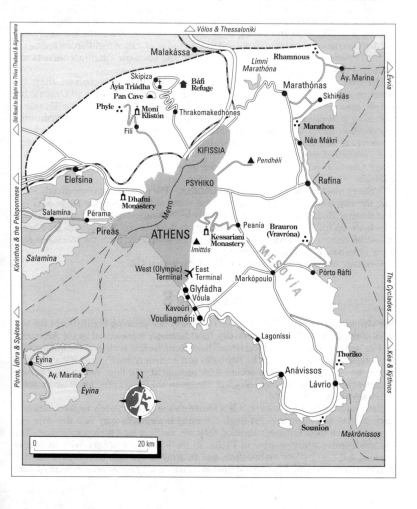

Map labels:
Vólos & Thessaloníki
Old Road to Delphi via Thíva (Thebes) & Aigosthena
Malakássa
Límni Marathóna
Rhamnous
Ay. Marina
Évvia
Skipiza
Báfi Refuge
Ávia Triádha
Pan Cave
Marathónas
Phyle
Moní Klistón
Thrakomakedhónes
Skhiniás
Filí
Marathon
Néa Mákri
KIFISSIA
Pendhéli
Kórinthos & the Peloponnese
Elefsina
PSYHIKO
Rafina
Metro
Salamína
Pé1ama
Dhafní Monastery
Pireás
ATHENS
Peanía
Brauron (Vravróna)
Kessariani Monastery
Imittós
MESOYÍA
Salamína
West (Olympic) Terminal
East Terminal
Markópoulo
Pórto Ráfti
The Cyclades
Póros, Ídhra & Spétses
Glyfádha
Vóula
Kavoúri
Vouliagméni
Lagoníssi
Thoriko
Éyina
Kéa & Kýthnos
Ay. Marina
Éyina
N
Anávissos
Lávrio
Sounion
Makrónissos
0   20 km

one surviving old quarter. Most tourists then get out fast, disillusioned with such sparse evidence of the past and so little apparent charm.

Such are the basic facts – yet somehow the city has the character to transcend them. An exhausting but always stimulating mix of metropolis and backwater, First and Third World, West and East, Athens has seen its population soar from 700,000 to well over four million – over a third of the nation's people – since World War II. The pace of this transformation is reflected in the city's chaotic mix of urban and rural: chickens roost in yards with state-of-the-art cars parked nearby, while eastern-style bazaars vie for space with outlets for Armani and Benetton. And the city's hectic modernity is tempered with an air of intimacy and hominess; as any Greek will tell you, Athens is merely the largest village in the country.

Once you accept this, you'll find that the **ancient sites** and the **Acropolis** – supreme monument though it is – are only the most obvious of **Athens' attractions**. There are startling views to be had from the hills of **Lykavitós** and **Filopáppou**; and, around the foot of the Acropolis, the **Pláka** has scattered monuments of the Byzantine and medieval town that seemed so exotic to Byron and the Romantics. As you might expect, the city also offers the best **eating** to be found in Greece, with some beautiful cafés, garden tavernas and street markets – as well as the most varied nightlife, including traditional **music and films** in the winter months, and **open-air cinema, concerts** and **classical drama** in summer.

Outside Athens, the emphasis shifts more exclusively to ancient sites; the beaches along the Attic coast are functional enough escapes for Athenians, but hardly priorities if you are moving on to the islands. Of the sites, the Temple of Poseidon at **Sounion** is the most popular trip, and rightly so, with its dramatic cliff-top position above the cape. Lesser-known and less-visited are the sanctuaries at **Rhamnous** and **Brauron** (Vravróna), both rewarding ruins with beaches nearby. The committed might also take in the burial mound at **Marathon** – though this is more Classical pilgrimage than sightseeing – and the Sanctuary of Demeter at **Eleusis** (Elefsína).

Walkers may want to head for the **mountains – Párnitha**, most compellingly – that ring the city, where springtime hikes reveal some of the astonishing range of Greek wild flowers. Hedonists, however, will already be making escape plans for **the islands**, which are served by ferries and hydrofoils from the Athenian port-suburb (and heavy industrial centre) of **Pireás** (Piraeus) and, more selectively, from the two other Attic ferry terminals at **Rafína** and **Lávrio**.

Coverage of the ports and sights of Attica starts on p.138.

ATHENS

For visitors, **ATHENS** (Athína in modern Greek) has stunning highlights in the vestiges of the ancient, Classical Greek city, most famously represented by the **Acropolis** and its surrounding archeological sites. These form the first section of the guide to the city's sights in this chapter – "The Acropolis and Ancient Athens" – and, if it's your first trip to the city, they're likely to occupy a fair amount of your time. An essential accompaniment is the **National Archeological Museum**: the finest collection of Greek antiquities anywhere in the world.

Even on a brief visit, however, it is a shame to see Athens purely as the location of ancient sites and museums. Although the **neighbourhoods** may lack the style and monuments of most European capitals, they are worth at least some exploration. The old nineteenth-century quarter of **Pláka**, in particular, is a delight, with its mix of Turkish and Greek-island architecture, and an array of odd little museums devoted to traditional arts, ceramics and music. Just to its north, the **bazaar** area, around Athinás and Eólou, retains an almost Middle Eastern atmosphere in its life and trade, while the **National Gardens**, elegant **Kolonáki** and the hill of **Lykavitós** offer respite from the maelstrom. Further afield, but still well within the limits of Greater Athens, are the monasteries of **Kessarianí** and **Dhafní**, the latter with Byzantine mosaics the equal of any in Greece.

Some history

Athens has been inhabited continuously for over 7000 years. Its acropolis, supplied with spring water, commanding views of all seaward approaches and encircled by protective mountains on its landward side, was a natural choice for prehistoric settlement and for the Mycenaeans, who established a palace-fortress on the rock. Its development into a city-state and artistic centre continued apace under the Dorians, Phoenicians and various dynastic rulers, reaching its apotheosis in the fifth century BC. This was the **Classical period**, when the Athenians, having launched themselves into an experiment in radical democracy, celebrated their success with a flourish of art, architecture, literature and philosophy that has influenced Western culture ever since. (An account of the Classical period is given with the main sites of ancient Athens on pp.89–91; Athens' Roman history is outlined in the box on p.105.)

The discontinuity from ancient to medieval Athens was due, essentially, to the emergence of **Christianity**. Having survived with little change through years of Roman rule, the city lost its pivotal role in the Roman–Greek world after the division of the Roman empire into Eastern and Western halves, and the establishment of Byzantium (Constantinople) as capital of the Eastern – **Byzantine** – empire. There, a new Christian sensibility soon outshone the prevailing ethic of Athens, where schools of philosophy continued to teach a pagan Neoplatonism. In 529 these schools were finally closed by Justinian I, and the city's temples, including the Parthenon, were reconsecrated as churches.

Athens featured rarely in the chronicles of the time, enjoying a brief revival under the foreign powers of the Middle Ages: in the aftermath of the piratical Fourth Crusade, Athens – together with the Peloponnese and much of central Greece – passed into the hands of the **Franks**. At the Acropolis they established a ducal court (of some magnificence, according to contemporary accounts) and for a century Athens was back in the mainstream of Europe. Frankish control, however, was based on little more than a provincial aristocracy. In 1311 their forces battled **Catalan** mercenaries, who had a stronghold in Thebes, and were driven to oblivion in a swamp. The Catalans, having set up their own duchy, in turn gave way to **Florentines** and, briefly, Venetians, before the arrival in 1456 of **Sultan Mehmet II**, the Turkish conqueror of Constantinople.

Turkish Athens was never much more than a garrison town. The links with the West, which had preserved a sense of continuity with the Classical and Roman city, were severed, and the flood of visitors was reduced to a trickle of French and Italian ambassadors to the Sublime Porte, and the occasional traveller or painter. The town does not seem to have been oppressed by Ottoman rule, however: the Greeks enjoyed some autonomy, and both Jesuit and Capuchin monasteries continued to thrive. Although the Acropolis became the home of the Turkish governor and the Parthenon was used as a mosque, life in the village-like quarters around the Acropolis drifted back to a semi-rural existence. Similarly, the great port of **Pireás**, still partially enclosed within its ancient walls, was left to serve just a few dozen fishing boats.

Four centuries of Ottoman occupation followed until, in 1821, in common with the inhabitants of a score of other towns across the country, the Greeks of Athens rose in **rebellion**. They occupied the Turkish quarters of the lower town – the current Pláka – and laid siege to the Acropolis. The Turks withdrew, but five years later were back to reoccupy the Acropolis fortifications, while the Greeks evacuated to the countryside.

ATHENS AND ITS ENVIRONMENT

The enormous and rapid population increase and attendant industrial development that characterized the postwar period had a disastrous effect on the **environment** of Athens. With a third of the Greek population, half the country's industry and over a half of its cars crammed into Greater Athens, the capital has found itself with one of the world's worst **pollution** problems. A noxious cloud, the *néfos*, trapped by the circle of mountains and aerial inversion layers, can frequently be seen hovering over the city. Despite what your burning eyes and throat may tell you, some improvement in the situation has been registered in recent decades, though not in the critical pollutant, nitrogen dioxide. Moreover, the level of pollution still aggravates acute respiratory diseases and arguably contributed to the high death toll in the freak heatwaves or *káfsones* during the summers of 1987 and 1988. Alarmingly, the *néfos* is also gnawing away at the very fabric of the ancient city, including the Parthenon marbles. As sulphur dioxide settles on the columns and statuary, it becomes a friable coating of calcium sulphate, which is washed off by the winter rains, taking a thin layer of stone with it.

Despite the severity of the situation, the main anti-pollution measure of recent years has been restrictions on the use of **private cars**. Successive governments have toyed with limitations on weekday use of vehicles in a central restricted zone, stipulating alternate days for odd- and even-numbered numberplates, but their efforts are undermined by the fact that most shops, offices and businesses persist in closing for a three-hour summer siesta – making for four rush hours a day and double the amount of pollution and traffic problems. At least fuller integration into the EU and concomitant lowering of the once crippling import duties on private cars mean that Athenians can now upgrade their vehicles more regularly and those that use lead-free petrol are now cheaper to buy and thus far more common.

More far-reaching measures are at last being taken to help the city's **public transport** system rise to the challenge: the extra airport at Spata creeps slowly towards realization and, back in the heart of the city, virtually every landmark square is being excavated for the expansion of the metro system in time for the 2004 Olympic Games. The three-line metro will be complemented by a circular tram system downtown and the operation of passenger ferries between the coastal suburbs and metro stations at Pireás and Fáliro.

Furthermore, all electricity, most heating and some cooking is now fuelled by copious supplies of Russian natural gas, installed (by pipeline) in Athens in 1997. With air inversion layers prompting pollution alerts in both summer and winter, there is still a long way to go, but these policies do at least offer a ray of hope.

When the Ottoman garrison finally left in 1834, and the Bavarian architects of the new German-born monarchy moved in, Athens was arguably at its nadir.

For all the claims of its ancient past, and despite the city's natural advantages, Athens was not the first-choice capital of modern Greece. That honour went instead to Náfplio in the Peloponnese, where the **War of Independence** was masterminded by Kapodistrias and where the first Greek National Assembly met in 1828. Had Kapodistrias not been assassinated, in 1831, the capital would most likely have remained in the Peloponnese, if not at Náfplio, then at Trípoli, Corinth or Pátra, all much more established and sizable towns. But following Kapodistrias's death, the "Great Powers" of Western Europe intervened, inflicting on the Greeks a king of their own choosing – **Otho**, son of Ludwig I of Bavaria – and, in 1834, transferring the capital and court to Athens. The reasoning was almost purely symbolic and sentimental: Athens was not only insignificant in terms of population and physical extent but was then at the edge of the territories of the new Greek state, which had yet to include northern Thessaly, Epirus or Macedonia, or any of the islands beyond the Cyclades or Sporades.

The **nineteenth-century development** of Athens was a gradual and fairly controlled process. While the archeologists stripped away all the Turkish and Frankish embellishments from the Acropolis, a modest city took shape along the lines of the Bavarians' Neoclassical grid. **Pireás**, meanwhile, grew into a port again, though until this century its activities continued to be dwarfed by the main Greek shipping centres on the islands of Sýros and Ídhra (Hydra).

The first mass expansion of both municipalities came suddenly, in 1923, as the result of the tragic Greek–Turkish war in **Asia Minor**. The peace treaty that resolved the war entailed the exchange of Greek and Turkish ethnic populations, their identity being determined solely on the basis of religion. A million and a half Greeks, mostly from the age-old settlements along the Asia Minor coast, but also many Turkish-speaking peoples from the communities of inland Anatolia, arrived in Greece as refugees. Over half of them settled in Athens, Pireás and the neighbouring villages, changing at a stroke the whole make-up of the capital. Their integration and survival is one of the great events of the city's history, and has left its mark on the Athens of today. The web of suburbs that straddles the metro line from Athens to Pireás, and sprawls out into the hills, bears nostalgic names of the refugees' origins – Néa Smýrni (New Smyrna), Néa Iónia, Néa Filadhélfia – as do many streets. Originally, these neighbourhoods were exactly that: refugee villages with populations primarily from one or another Anatolian town, built in ramshackle fashion, often with a single water source for two dozen families.

The merging of these shanty-suburbs and their populations with the established communities of Athens and Pireás dominated the years leading up to **World War II**. With the war, however, new concerns emerged. Athens was hit hard by German occupation: during the winter of 1941–2 there were an estimated 2000 deaths from starvation each day. In late 1944, when the Germans finally left (Allied policy was to tie them down in the Balkans), the capital saw the first skirmishes of **civil war**, with the British forces being ordered to fight against their former Greek allies in the Communist-dominated resistance army, ELAS. Physical evidence of the ensuing month-long battle, the *Dhekemvriuná*, can still be seen in a handful of bullet-pocked walls. From 1946 to 1949 Athens was a virtual island in the civil war, with road approaches to the Peloponnese and the north only tenuously kept open.

But during the 1950s, after the civil war, the city started to expand rapidly. A massive **industrial investment** programme – financed largely by the Americans, who had won Greece for their sphere of influence – took place, and the capital saw huge **immigration** from the war-torn, impoverished countryside. The open spaces between the old refugee suburbs began to fill and, by the late 1960s, Greater Athens covered a continuous area from the slopes of mounts Pendéli and Párnitha down to Pireás and Elefsína.

On a visual level, much of the modern city is unremittingly ugly, since old buildings were demolished wholesale in the name of quick-buck development, particularly during the colonels' junta of 1967–74 (see p.850). Only now are planning and preservation measures being enforced – in a last-ditch attempt to rescue the city from its engulfing **pollution** (see box opposite). The PASOK administration of the late 1980s endowed the city with thousands of trees, shrubs, patches of garden and an ever-growing number of pedestrian-only streets – though Athens still lags far behind Paris or London in terms of open space. There is also increasing awareness of the nineteenth-century architectural heritage – what's left of it – with many old houses being restored and repainted.

Long-term solutions are proving more elusive: priorities include decanting industry and services into the provinces to ease the stresses on the city's environment (see box opposite) and its ailing infrastructure, and creating a mass transport network capable of meeting the needs of a modern capital city.

Orientation, arrival and information

As a visitor, you're likely to spend most time in the central grid of Athens, a compact, walkable area. Only on arrival at, or departure from, the various far-flung stations and terminals (see below), do you have to confront the confused urban sprawl. Once in the centre, it's a simple matter to orient yourself. There are four strategic reference points: the squares of **Sýndagma** ("Syntagma" on many English-language maps) and **Omónia** and the hills of the **Acropolis** (unmistakable with its temple crown) and (to the northeast) **Lykavitós**. Once you've established these as a mental compass you should not be lost for long – anyone will point you back in the direction of Sýndagma or Omónia.

Sýndagma (Platía Sindágmatos, "Constitution Square", to give it its full title) lies midway between the Acropolis and Lykavitós. With the Greek Parliament building – plus mammoth metro tunnelling and traffic diversions – on its uphill side, and banks and airline offices clustered around, it is to all intents and purposes the centre of the capital. Almost everything of daytime interest is within twenty to thirty minutes' walk of the square.

To the northeast, the ritzy **Kolonáki** quarter curls around the slopes of **Lykavitós**, with a funicular up the hillside to save you the final climb. To the east, behind the Parliament, the jungly **National Gardens** function as the city's chief lung and meeting place; beyond them are the 1896 Olympic stadium and the attractive neighbourhoods of **Pangráti** and **Méts**, both crammed with restaurants and bars.

To the southwest, up to the base of the **Acropolis**, spread the ramshackle but much-commercialized lanes of **Pláka**, the lone surviving area of the nineteenth-century, pre-independence village. Beyond the Acropolis itself is **Filopáppou hill**, an area of parkland bordered by the neighbourhoods of **Koukáki** and **Áno Petrálona**, also good choices for accommodation and meals. (Filopáppou Hill itself should be avoided at night, when it has a reputation for rapes and muggings.)

Northwest of Sýndagma, two broad thoroughfares, **Stadhíou** and **Panepistimíou** (officially but ineffectually named Venizélou), run in just under a kilometre to **Omónia** (fully, Platía Omonías, "Concord Square"). This is an approximate Athenian equivalent of Piccadilly Circus or Times Square: more than a bit seedy, with fast-food cafés, gypsies, pickpockets and a scattering of porno shows in the backstreets around. To the northeast, beyond Panepistimíou, is the student neighbourhood of **Exárhia**, a slightly "alternative" district, with a concentration of lively tavernas and bars there and in its extension **Neápoli**. South of Omónia, stretching down to **Ermoú** street and the **Monastiráki** bazaar district on the borders of Pláka, lies the main commercial centre, crammed with offices and shops offering everything from insurance to machine tools.

Points of arrival

Athens airport – **Ellinikón** – is 9km out of the city, southeast along the coast towards Glyfádha. It has two distinct sections – **west** (*dhitikó*) and **east** (*anatolikó*) – whose separate entrances are ten to fifteen minutes' drive apart on either side of the perimeter fence. **Olympic Airways** flights, domestic and foreign, operate from the western terminal; all **other international flights** use the eastern, which adjoins the charter-flight terminal. Both the east and west terminals have **money exchange** facilities, open 24 hours at the eastern terminal, but only from 8am to 7.30pm at the western one (though there are two cash dispensers that accept Visa, Mastercard, Cirrus and Plus); insist on some small-denomination notes for paying for your bus ticket or taxi ride.

FINDING AN ADDRESS

The Greek for street is **odhós** but – both when addressing letters and in speech – people usually refer only to the name of the street: Ermoú, Márkou Moussoúrou, etc. The practice is different with **platía** (square) and **leofóros** (avenue), which always appear before the name. In written addresses, the house number is written after the street name, thus: Ermoú 13. We have adopted the same practice.

To get into the city, the quickest and simplest way is to get a **taxi**, which, at 1600–2400dr to central Athens or Pireás, is a modest cost split two or more ways. Make sure before setting out that the metre is switched on, and visible; overcharging of tourists can be brutal. If the driver resists or claims the metre is broken, any mention of the police should quickly change his tack. You may have fellow passengers in the cab; each drop-off will pay the full fare.

If you're willing to wait a bit, and carry your bags around, an **express bus** calls at both terminals on a variable schedule around the clock, dropping you at selected points in the city centre. You should note that the wait can be up to an hour at night, and 30 minutes during the day. Service from the west terminal tends to be less consistent but from there it is just as easy to walk out onto the main road and take buses #A2 or #B2 from the stop just to the right of the entrance road (tickets are available from the kiosks outside the terminal). The express bus fare is currently 250dr (500dr midnight–5am); tickets should be bought from a booth beside the stops when open but can be purchased on the bus late at night if you have small change.

The express bus link to the centre is numbered #092 on its way into town and #091 on the trip to the airport. At the international terminal the stops are clearly marked to avoid confusion. The main stops in the centre are at the **Stíles** for Koukáki and parts of Pláka, **Sýndagma** for the square itself and the top of Pláka, and the turning-round point at **Omónia** – best for Exárhia or Viktória. The bus calls first at the charter terminal, then the nearby international (east) terminal before heading round to the Olympic (west) terminal. In high season you may find that the services to the terminals have been separated into #091 for the east terminal, #092 for the west terminal and #093 for a short shuttle between the charter and other two terminals. When this happens the routes retain the same number in each direction. There is also an express bus #019 from the airport (all terminals) direct to the port of **Pireás** for anyone planning to head straight for the ferries.

Train stations

There are two train stations, almost adjacent, a couple of hundred metres northwest of Omónia, off Dheliyáni street. The **Stathmós Laríssis** handles the main lines coming from the north (Lárissa, Thessaloníki, the Balkans, western Europe and Turkey). The **Stathmós Peloponníssou** three blocks south, is the terminal for the narrow-gauge line circling the Peloponnese, including the stretch to Pátra (the main port for ferries from Italy and Corfu).

From either station, you are five to fifteen minutes' walk away from the concentration of hotels around Platía Viktorías and Exárhia, both handy for the National Archeological Museum and excellent restaurants. For hotels elsewhere, the yellow trolley **bus #1** southbound passes along Sámou, one block east of the Laríssis station (to get to it from the Peloponníssou terminal, use the giant metal overpass, then detour around the metro works) and makes a strategic loop down through Omónia, along Stadhíou to Sýndagma, then down Filellínon to Hadrian's Arch (for Méts), and finally along Veïkoú to Koukáki (on the southeast side of Filopáppou hill). **Bus #057** from the Peloponníssou terminal also passes through both central squares and down to Leofóros Syngroú.

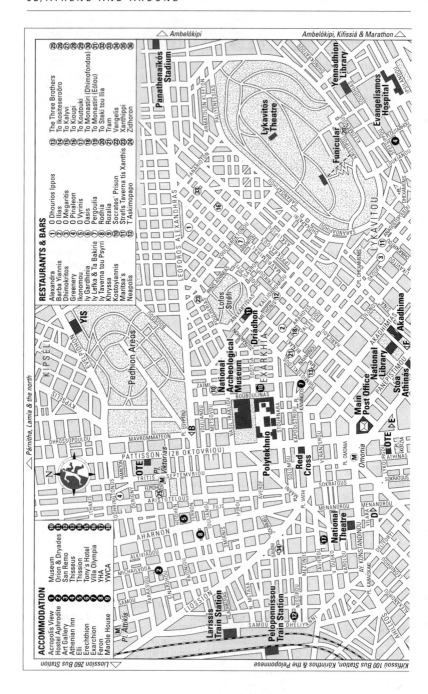

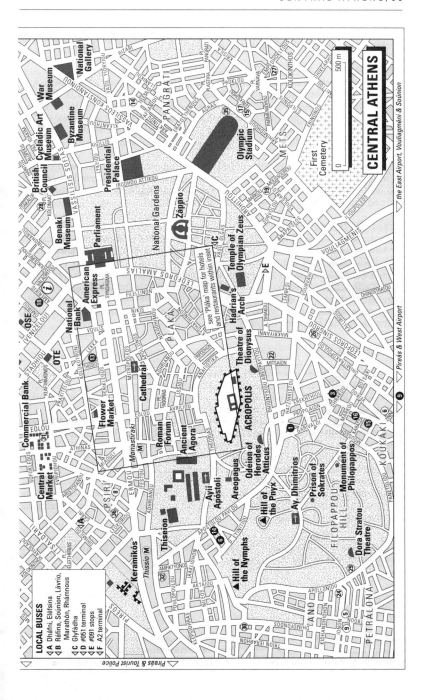

CENTRAL ATHENS

0 _____ 500 m

▷ the East Airport, Vouliagméni & Soúnion

▷ Pireás & West Airport

▷ Pireás & Tourist Police

LOCAL BUSES

◁A Dháfni, Eléfsina
◁B Ráfina, Soúnion, Lávrio, Marathón, Rhámnous
◁C Glyfádha
◁D #051 terminal
◁E #091 stops
◁F A2 terminal

National Gallery

War Museum

Byzantine Museum

Cycladic Art Museum

British Council

Presidential Palace

Benaki Museum

Parliament

American Express

National Bank

Commercial Bank

Central Market

Flower Market

Cathedral

Roman Forum

Ancient Agora

Monastiráki

Keramikós

Thisíon

Ayii Apóstoli

Areopagus

Odeíon of Herodes Atticus

ACROPOLIS

Theatre of Dionysus

Hadrian's Arch

Temple of Olympian Zeus

Záppio

National Gardens

Olympic Stadium

First Cemetery

Hill of the Pnyx

Ay. Dhimítrios

Prison of Sokrates

Monument of Philopáppos

Dora Stratou Theatre

Hill of the Nymphs

see 'Pláka' map for hotels and restaurants within inset

PANGRÁTI

METS

PLÁKA

PSIRÍ

KOUKÁKI

PETRÁLONA

ÁNO PETRÁLONA

FILOPÁPPOU HILL

OSE

OTE

Be wary of **taxis** (both official and unlicensed) at the train stations – some thrive on newly arrived tourists, shuttling them a couple of blocks for highly inflated fares.

Bus stations

Again, there are two principal terminals. Coming into Athens from northern Greece or the Peloponnese, you'll find yourself at **Kifissoú 100**, a ten-minute bus ride from the centre. The least expensive way into town is to take city bus #051 to the corner of Zínonos/Menándhrou, just off Omónia and only a block or two from a yellow trolley-bus stop. Routes from central Greece (see p.151 for specific destinations) arrive at **Liossíon 260**, north of the train stations; to get into the centre, take the blue city bus #024 to Omónia or Sýndagma.

In addition, there are international **OSE buses**, run by the railway company, which arrive at the Stathmós Peloponnísou. Private **international bus companies** arrive at, and leave from, a variety of locations. Most will take you to the train station or to Kifissoú 100; a few drop passengers right in the city centre.

Pireás: the ferries

If you arrive by boat at **Pireás**, the simplest access to Athens is by **metro** to the stations at Monastiráki, Omónia or Viktorías. Trains run from 6am to midnight, with fares varying from 120 to 180dr according to a zone system (you will only need to pay more than 120dr if you are going up to the northern suburbs). For the airport, take express bus #019 (see p.81). **Taxis** between Pireás and central Athens should cost around 1800dr, including baggage, although rates per kilometre double at night – again, see the comments opposite.

There's a full account of Pireás, together with a map of the central area, showing the metro station and harbours, on p.139.

Information

The main EOT tourist office (Mon–Fri 9am–7pm, Sat 9am–2pm; ☎33 10 692 or 32 71 300) is at Amerikís 2, just up from Stadhíou; it dispenses ferry timetable sheets (use these as guidelines only), along with maps and pamphlets, and is also a source of information about the **Athens Festival** (see p.131).

To complement our plans and the free EOT map, the street-indexed **Falk-Plan** is a good, **large-scale map** of the city (available from the shops listed on p.134). The Historical Map of Athens produced by the Greek Ministry of Culture is well worth its 1200dr price. It has a good map of central Athens and, on the other side, a clear, large-scale map of Pláka. Both maps number all the sites by period, and the museums.

If you are planning a long stay, the **Athína-Pireás Proástia** A–Ω atlas, co-published by Kapranidhis and Fotis, is available from kiosks and bookshops, but is in Greek only and is quite pricey at 6000dr. It does, however, show absolutely everything, including cinemas and concert venues.

> The **telephone code** for Greater Athens and Pireás is ☎01; when calling from overseas, omit the zero.

City transport

Athens is served by slow but wide-ranging **buses**, and a fast but very limited **metro** system; taxis fill in the gaps. Public transport networks operate from around 5am to midnight, with a skeleton service on some of the buses in the small hours.

Buses

The **bus network** is extensive and cheap, with a flat fare of 120dr. Tickets must be bought in advance from kiosks, certain shops and newsagents, or from the limited number of booths run by bus personnel near major stops – look for the brown, red and white logo proclaiming *Isitíria edhó* (tickets here). They're sold individually or in bundles of ten, and must be cancelled in a special machine when boarding. Fare-dodgers risk an on-the-spot fine equivalent to forty times the current fare. Cancelled tickets apply only to a particular journey and vehicle; there are no transfers. If you're staying long enough, it would be worth buying a monthly pass for 6000dr.

Buses are very crowded at peak times, unbearably hot in summer traffic jams, and chronically plagued by strikes and slow-downs; walking is often a better option. Express services run to and from the airport – see p.81. Other **routes**, where relevant, are detailed in the text. The most straightforward are the **yellow trolley buses**: #1 connects the Laríssis train station with Omónia, Sýndagma and Koukáki; #2, #3, #4, #5 and #12 all link Sýndagma with Omónia and the National Archeological Museum on Patissíon. In addition, there are scores of **blue city buses**, all with three-digit numbers and serving an infinity of routes out into the straggling suburbs and beyond.

The metro

The single-line **metro** (120dr two-zone fare, 180dr for all three zones) runs from Pireás in the south to Kifissiá in the north; in the centre, there are stops at Thissío, Monastiráki, Omónia and Platía Viktorías. Long-awaited work on the lateral extensions to the system is well under way and should be ready early in the new millennium. Metro and bus tickets are not interchangeable.

Taxis

Athenian **taxis** are the cheapest of any EU capital – fares around the city centre will rarely run above 700dr, with the airport and Pireás only 1600–2400dr – the exact amount determined by traffic and amount of luggage. All officially licensed cars are painted yellow and have a special red-on-white numberplate. You can wave them down on the street, pick them up at ranks at the train station, airport or the National Gardens corner of Sýndagma, or get your hotel to phone one for you. They are most elusive during the rush hours of 1.30–2.30pm and 7.30–8.30pm.

Make sure the **metre** is switched on when you get in, with its display visible and properly zeroed; theoretically, it's illegal to quote a flat fare for a ride within city limits – the meter must be used. If it's "not working", find another taxi. Attempts at **overcharging** tourists are particularly common with small-hours arrivals at the airport; a threat to have hotel staff or the police adjudicate usually elicits co-operation, as they will very likely take your side and the police have the power to revoke a driver's operating permit.

Legitimate surcharges can considerably bump up the final bill from the total shown on the meter. Currently the flag falls at 200dr, there's an automatic 300dr supplement for entering the confines of the airport, and a 150dr surcharge for journeys involving train or ferry terminals; luggage is 50dr extra for each bag over 10 kg; the rate per kilometre doubles between midnight and 5am; and there are Easter and Christmas bonuses which seem to extend for a week or two either side of the actual date. Every taxi must have a plastic dash-mounted placard listing regular rates and extra charges in English and Greek.

To try and make ends meet on government-regulated fare limits, taxi-drivers will often pick up a whole string of passengers along the way. There is no fare-sharing: each passenger (or group of passengers) pays the full fare for their journey. So if you're picked up by an already-occupied taxi, memorize the meter reading at once; you'll pay from that point on, plus the 200dr minimum. When hailing an occupied taxi, call out your destination, so the kerb-crawling driver can decide whether you suit him or not.

Accommodation

Hotels and **hostels** can be packed to the gills in midsummer – August especially – but for most of the year there are enough beds in the city to go around, and to suit most wallets and tastes. It makes sense to **phone** before turning up: if you just set out and do the rounds, you'll find somewhere, but in summer, unless you're early in the day, it's likely to be at the fourth or fifth attempt.

For cheaper places, you're on your own. Find a street kiosk (there are hundreds in Athens) and ask to use their phone; you pay 30dr per unit after you've finished making all the calls – there's no need to find coins. Virtually every hotel and hostel in the city will have an English-speaking receptionist. Once you locate a vacancy, ask to see the room before booking in – standards vary greatly even within the same building, and you can avoid occasional overcharging by checking the government-regulated room prices displayed by law on the back of the door in each room.

Our listings are grouped into four main areas. The quarters of **Pláka and Sýndagma**, despite their commercialization, are highly atmospheric – and within easy walking distance of all the main sites and the Monastiráki metro station (a useful gateway for the port of Pireás). Occasionally gritty and sleazy, the **bazaar area** is the city at its most authentic, while nearby **Thissío** is rather smarter and airier. The downside of some of the hotels in these areas is that they are subject to round-the-clock noise; if you want uninterrupted sleep, you're better off heading for one of the quieter neighbourhoods a little further out. **Koukáki** and **Pangráti** are attractive parts of the city, and though slightly out of the way – twenty minutes' walk from Sýndagma or the heart of Pláka – compensate with excellent neighbourhood tavernas and cafés. Koukáki is easiest reached from Pireás via the #9 trolley bus, whose terminus is just outside the Petrálona metro station, while Pangráti is on the #4 or #12 trolleys from Záppio. Around **Exárhia** and **Platía Viktorías** (officially Platía Kyriákou), to the north of Omónia, you are again out of the tourist mainstream, but benefit from good-value local restaurants and the proximity of cinemas, clubs and bars. These areas now have clusters of very good-value, mid-range hotels, just a short walk away from the train stations (and metros Omónia or Viktorías).

The city's **campsites** are out in the suburbs, not especially cheap, and only worth using if you have a camper van to park; phone ahead to book space in season. Camping rough in Athens is not a good idea. Police patrol many of the parks, especially those by the train stations, and muggings are commonplace. Even the train stations are no real refuge; they close when services stop and are cleared of stragglers.

ACCOMMODATION PRICE CODES

Throughout the book we've used the following **price codes** to denote the cheapest available double room in each establishment in high season. Out of season, rates can drop by more than fifty percent, especially if you are staying for three or more nights. Single rooms, where available, cost around seventy percent of the price of a double.

① Up to 6000dr	④ 12,000–16,000dr
② 6000–9000dr	⑤ 16,000–20,000dr
③ 9000–12,000dr	⑥ 20,000dr and upwards

Note: Youth hostels typically charge 2000–2500dr for a dormitory bed.
For more accommodation details, see pp.43–6.

Pláka and Sýndagma

Achilleas, Lékka 21 (☎32 33 197, fax 32 22 412). Great central location. All rooms with a/c and TV. Breakfast served on roof terrace. ⑤.

Acropolis House, Kódhrou 6 (☎32 22 344, fax 32 44 143). A very clean, well-sited pension; some rooms have shared baths. TV lounge. Rates include breakfast. ④.

Adams, Herefóndos cnr Thálou (☎32 25 381, fax 32 38 553). Rather average small hotel, with some Acropolis views, in the heart of Pláka. ④.

Adonis, Kódhrou 3 (☎32 49 737, fax 32 31 602). A modern but unobjectionable low-rise pension across the street from *Acropolis House*, with some suites. ⑤.

Adrian, Adhrianoú 74 (☎32 21 553, fax 32 50 461). Small very plush hotel with TV, a/c and mini-bar in all rooms. Pricier third-floor rooms have Acropolis view. ⑥.

Dioskouri, Pittákou 6 (☎32 48 165, fax 32 10 907). This renovated pension benefits from a breakfast garden and a good locale (one block in from Leofóros Amalías); shared bathrooms. ③.

George's Guest House, Níkis 46 (☎32 26 474). One of the most enduring of the hostel-type places, located just a block west of Sýndagma. Maximum 4-bed dorms and some doubles, but cramped bathrooms are consistently grubby and the place is not noted for its courtesy. ②.

Kouros, Kódhrou 11 (☎32 27 431). Slightly faded pension, but with adequate facilities: shared baths and sinks in rooms. Located on a pedestrianized street (the continuation of Voulís – two blocks southwest of Sýndagma). ③.

Nefeli, Iperídhou 16 (☎32 28 044, fax 32 25 800). Actually situated at Hatzimiháli 2 this mid-range hotel has TV and a/c in all rooms. ④.

Phaedra, Herefóndos 16 at the Adhrianoú junction (☎32 27 795). Very plain and ripe for an overhaul, but clean and quiet at night – thanks to its location at the junction of two pedestrian malls. Polite welcoming management but only shared facilities. ②.

Student Inn, Kydhathinéon 16 (☎32 44 808, fax 32 100 65). A former hostel, now a bona fide hotel: singles, doubles and triples with shared baths. Prone to nocturnal noise from outside, but otherwise acceptable. Small courtyard and Internet facilities open to non-residents. ③.

Thisseus Hostel, Thisséos 10 (☎32 45 960). You don't get much more central than this – three blocks west of Sýndagma – nor much cheaper. No frills, but clean enough, and with a kitchen for guests' use. Some 3- and 4-bed dorms.

XEN (YWCA), Amerikís 11, (☎36 24 291, fax 36 22 400). Women-only hostel just north of Sýndagma that provides clean, relatively quiet rooms, a self-service restaurant and Greek classes. Recommended.

The Bazaar area and Thissío

Attalos, Athinás 29 (☎32 12 801, fax 32 43 124). A bit pricey but comfortable. ④.

Erechthion, Flammaríou 8, Thissío (☎34 59 606, fax 34 62 756). Reasonable mid-range option in this lively area behind the Acropolis. All rooms with a/c and TV. ④.

Pella Inn, Ermoú 104 (☎32 50 598, fax 32 50 598). A family-run hotel under new enthusiastic management. From the third floor up the views of the Acropolis and Hephaisteon are startling. ③.

Tembi, Eólou 29 (☎32 13 175, fax 32 54 179). Used to foreigners: book exchange, drinks, fridge, plus handy affiliated travel agency. ②.

Thission, Apostólou Pávlou 25, Thissío (☎34 67 634, fax 34 62 756). Somewhat better value than the nearby *Erechthion*, this friendly place has a/c and TV in all rooms and fine views from the roof terrace. ③.

Koukáki and Pangráti

Acropolis View, Webster 10, Koukáki (☎92 17 303, fax 92 30 705). Stone-clad, smallish hotel whose front rooms and roof café live up to its name. ⑥.

Art Gallery, Erekhthíou 5, Koukáki (☎92 38 376, fax 92 33 025). Original paintings on the walls lend this average pension its name. ④.

Marble House, cul-de-sac off A. Zínni 35, Koukáki (☎92 34 058, fax 92 26 461). Probably the best value in Koukáki, with a very helpful management. Often full, so call ahead. Most rooms with bath; also two self-catering studios. ③.

Tony's Hostel, Zaharítsa 26, Koukáki (☎92 36 370). Decent hostel with some en-suite bathrooms and a friendly atmosphere.

Villa Olympia, Karatzá 16, Koukáki (☎92 37 650). Ideally designed for longer stays, this cosy pension run by an English lady provides a hearty breakfast. Good value. ②.

Youth Hostel #5, Damaréos 75, Pangráti, off map near the huge Profítis Ilías church (☎75 19 530). A bit out of the way but friendly, no curfew and in a decent, quiet neighbourhood; trolleys #2 and #11 from downtown stop just around the corner.

Exárhia and Platía Viktorías

Athenian Inn, Háritos 22, Kolonáki (☎72 38 097, fax 72 42 268). Actually in Kolonáki, adjacent to Exárhia, this mid-range hotel is small, elegant and convenient for most of the museums around the National Gardens. ⑤.

Hostel Aphrodite, Inárdhou 12, cnr Mikhaïl Vódha 65 (☎88 39 249, fax 88 16 574). Friendly and clean, providing hot water in shared bathrooms, a safe, a roof for sunning and free storage. A few blocks northwest of the Viktória metro station.

Elli, Heïdhen 29, Platía Viktorías (☎88 15 876, fax 88 15 876). Characterful pension in refurbished Neoclassical building on a quiet tree-lined street. TV and shower in all rooms. Best deal in the area. ②.

Exarchion, Themistokléous 55, Platía Exárhia (☎36 01 256, fax 38 03 296). Big 1960s high-rise hotel that's surprisingly inexpensive and well placed, if a bit noisy. ③.

Feron, Férron 43, Platía Viktorías (☎82 32 083). Small hotel with en-suite baths in all rooms. Good value. ②.

Museum, Bouboulínas 16 (☎36 05 611, fax 38 00 507). Nicely placed, reasonable-value hotel, right behind the National Archeological Museum and parkland. ③.

Orion and **Dryades**, Anexartisías 5, Exárhia (☎36 27 362, fax 38 05 193). Very quiet, well-run twin hotels across from the Lófos Stréfi park – a steep uphill walk. Reception in the cheaper *Orion*, which also has a self-service kitchen and communal area on the roof with an amazing view of central Athens. ②–③.

San Remo, Nisýrou 8, near Stathmós Laríssis (☎52 33 245). Small, inexpensive hostel offering clean but basic accommodation in a grubby neighbourhood.

YHA, Victor Hugo 16 (☎52 34 170, fax 52 34 015). Between the train station and Omónia, the only official youth hostel in Athens is friendly, informative and includes a café and left luggage store. Membership 700dr per day on top of bed price still makes it cheaper than other dorm deals. Annual membership 4200dr.

Campsites

Camping Nea Kifissia (☎80 75 579: open all year round), with a swimming pool, is in the cool, leafy suburb of Kifissiá. Take bus #A7 from Platía Kánningos or metro to Kifissiá and transfer onto bus #528 to the terminal close to the campsite.

Voula Camping (☎89 52 712: open all year round), on the beach but with swimming pool, bar and restaurant. Bus A2 from Panepistimíou or Sýndagma Square.

The Acropolis and Ancient Athens

This section covers the **Acropolis** and the assorted Classical and Roman sites on its slopes; the hills of the **Pnyx** and **Philoppapus (Filopáppou)** over to the southwest; and the neighbouring **Ancient Agora** (marketplace) and **Keramikos** (cemetery) to the northwest. This is essentially the core of the ancient, Classical Greek city, though a few further pockets and Roman extensions are covered in the Pláka section, beginning on p.101.

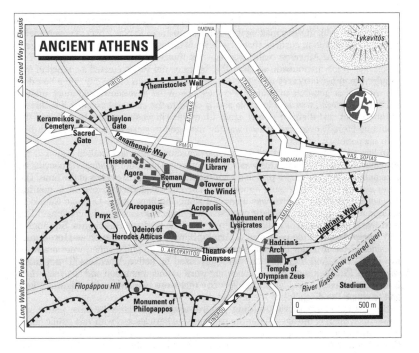

Classical Athens: some history

Perhaps the most startling aspect of ancient, Classical Athens is how suddenly it emerged to the power and glory for which we remember it – and how short its heyday proved to be. In the middle of the **fifth century BC**, Athens was little more than a country town in its street layout and buildings. The latter comprised a scattered jumble of single-storey houses or wattled huts, intersected by narrow lanes. Sanitary conditions were notoriously lax: human waste and rubbish were dumped outside the town with an almost suicidal disregard for plague and disease. And on the rock of the Acropolis, a site reserved for the city's most sacred monuments, stood blackened ruins – temples and sanctuaries burned to the ground during the Persian invasion of 480 BC.

There was little to suggest that the city was entering a unique phase of its history in terms of power, prestige and creativity. But following the victories over the Persians at Marathon (490 BC) and Salamis (480 BC), Athens stood unchallenged for a generation. It grew rich on the export of olive oil and of silver from the mines of Attica, but above all it benefited from its control of the **Delian League**, an alliance of Greek city-states formed as insurance against Persian resurgence. The Athenians relocated the League's treasury from the island of Delos to their own acropolis, ostensibly on the grounds of safety, and with its revenues their leader **Pericles** was able to create the so-called **Golden Age** of the city. Great endowments were made for monumental construction, arts in all spheres were promoted, and – most significantly – a form of **democracy** emerged.

This democracy had its beginnings in the sixth-century BC reforms of Solon, in which the political rights of the old land-owning class had been claimed by farmer- and craftsmen-soldiers. With the emergence of Pericles the political process was radically overhauled, aided in large part by the Delian League's wealth – which enabled office-holders to be paid, thereby making it possible for the poor to play a part in government. Pericles's constitution ensured that all policies of the state were to be decided by a general assembly of Athenian male citizens – six thousand constituted a quorum. The assembly, which met outside at either the **Agora** or the **Pnyx**, elected a council of five hundred members to carry out the everyday administration of the city and a board of ten *strategoi* or generals to guide it. Pericles, one of the best-known and most influential of the *strategoi*, was as vulnerable as any other to the electoral process: if sufficient numbers had cast their lot (*ostra*) against him, his citizenship would be forfeited (he would be literally ostracized); as it was, he managed to stave off such a fate and died with his popularity intact.

In line with this system of democratic participation, a new and exalted notion of the Athenian citizen emerged. This was a man who could shoulder political responsibility, take public office and play a part in the **cultural** and **religious events** of the time. The latter assumed ever-increasing importance. The city's Panathenaic festival, honouring its protectress deity Athena, was upgraded along the lines of the Olympic Games to include drama, music and athletic contests. Athenians rose easily to the challenge. The next five decades were to witness the great dramatic works of **Aeschylus**, **Sophocles** and **Euripides**, and the comedies of **Aristophanes**. Foreigners such as **Herodotus**, considered the inventor of history, and **Anaxagoras**, the philosopher, were drawn to live in the city. And they, in turn, were surpassed by native Athenians. **Thucydides** wrote *The Peloponnesian War*, a pioneering work of documentation and analysis, while **Socrates** posed the problems of philosophy that were to exercise his follower **Plato** and to shape the discipline to the present day.

But it was the great civic **building programme** that became the most visible and powerful symbol of the age. Under the patronage of Pericles and with vast public funds made available from the Delian treasury, the architects **Iktinos**, **Mnesikles** and **Callicrates**, and the sculptor **Pheidias**, transformed the city. Their buildings, justified in part as a comprehensive job-creation scheme, included the Parthenon and Erechtheion on the Acropolis; the Thiseon (or Hephaisteion) and several *stoas* (arcades) in the Agora; a new odeion (theatre) on the south slope of the Acropolis hill; and, outside the city, the temples at Sounion and Rhamnous.

Athenian culture flourished under democracy, but the system was not without its contradictions and failures. Only one in seven inhabitants of the city were actual citizens; the political status and civil rights that they enjoyed were denied to the many thousands of women, *metics* (foreigners) and slaves. While the lives of men became increasingly public and sociable, with meetings at the Agora or Pnyx and visits to the gymnasiums and theatres, **women** remained secluded in small and insanitary homes.

THE SITES: OPENING HOURS AND FEES

Summer opening hours for the **sites** and **museums** in Athens are included with some trepidation. They are notorious for changing without notice, from one season to another, or from one week to the next, due to staff shortages.

To be sure of admission, it's best to visit between 9am and noon, and to be wary of Monday – when many museums and sites close for the whole day. Last tickets are sold at the time given for closure, although the site may be open fifteen minutes more. For (generally) reliable and up-to-the-minute details, ask at the EOT office at 2 Ameríkas Street for their printed list of opening hours.

For many years, during the off-season (from Oct–March), entrance has been free on Sundays. During the summer months some sites and museums may let students in for half price (EU students free) and there may be a reduced price if you are over 65. The response will vary from site to site, but ask.

Their subordination was in fact reinforced by a decree in 451 BC, which restricted their property rights, placing them under the control of fathers, husbands or guardians. At any one time, only forty women could be appointed priestesses – one of the few positions of female power. Aeschylus summed up the prevailing attitude when he declared that the mother does no more than foster the father's seed.

The city's democracy was also sullied by its **imperialist** designs and actions, which could be brutal and exploitative, although acts of mercy against rebellious allies were also documented. Atrocities included the wholesale massacre of the male population of Melos – and the building programme of Pericles itself relied on easy pickings from weaker neighbours and allies. In the *polis* of Athens the achievements of democracy could be overshadowed, too, with attacks on the very talents it had nurtured and celebrated: Aristophanes was impeached, Pheidias and Thucydides were exiled, Socrates was tried and executed.

But, historically, the fatal mistake of the Athenian democracy was allowing itself to be drawn into the **Peloponnesian War** against Sparta, its persistent rival, in 431 BC. Pericles, having roused the assembly to a pitch of patriotic fervour, died of the plague two years after war began, leaving Athens at the mercy of a series of far less capable leaders. In 415 BC a disastrous campaign in Sicily saw a third of the navy lost; in 405 BC defeat was finally accepted after the rest of the fleet was destroyed by Sparta in the Dardanelles. Demoralized, Athens succumbed to a brief period of oligarchy.

Through succeeding decades Athens was overshadowed by Thebes, though it recovered sufficiently to enter a new phase of democracy, the **age of Plato**. However, in 338 BC, nearly one and a half centuries after the original defeat of the Persians, Athens was again called to defend the Greek city-states, this time against the incursions of **Philip of Macedon**. Demosthenes, said to be as powerful an orator as Pericles, spurred the Athenians to fight, in alliance with the Thebans, at Chaironeia. There they were routed, in large part by the cavalry commanded by Philip's son, Alexander, and Athens fell under the control of the Macedonian empire.

The city continued to be favoured, particularly by **Alexander the Great**, a former pupil of Aristotle, who respected both Athenian culture and its democratic institutions. Following his death, however, came a more uncertain era, which saw periods of independence and Macedonian rule, until 146 BC when the **Romans** swept through southern Greece and it was incorporated into the Roman province of Macedonia (see box on p.105).

The Acropolis

April–Sept daily 8am–7pm; Oct–March Mon–Fri 8am–4.30pm, Sat & Sun 8am–2.30pm; site and museum 2000dr, Oct–March free on Sun.

The **rock of the Acropolis**, with the ruins of the Parthenon rising above it, is one of the archetypal images of Western culture. A first glimpse of it above the traffic is a revelation, and yet feels utterly familiar. Pericles had intended the temple to be a spectacular landmark, a "School for Hellas" and a symbol of the city's imperial confidence – as such, it was famous throughout the ancient world. Even Pericles, however, could not have anticipated that his ruined temple would come to symbolize the emergence of Western civilization – nor that, two millennia on, it would attract some three million tourists a year.

As Donald Horne points out in *The Great Museum*, it would be hard to imagine the ruins having such a wide appeal if they had retained more of their former glory: if, for example, the Parthenon "still had a roof, and no longer appealed to the modern stereotype for outline emerging from rough stone", or if "we repainted it in its original red, blue and gold and if we reinstalled the huge, gaudy cult-figure of Athena festooned in bracelets, rings and necklaces". Yet it's hard not to feel a sense of wonder as you catch

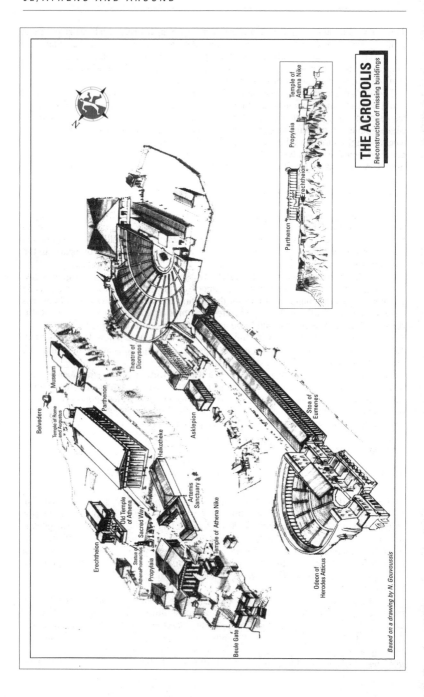

THE ACROPOLIS
Reconstruction of missing buildings

Parthenon · Propylaia · Temple of Athena Nike
Erechtheion

Belvedere

Museum

Temple of Rome and Augustus

Parthenon

Theatre of Dionysos

Hälkotheke

Asklepion

Stoa of Eumenes

Erechtheion

Old Temple of Athena

Statue of Athena Promachos

Sacred Way

Artemis Sanctuary

Temple of Athena Nike

Propylaia

Odeon of Herodes Atticus

Beulé Gate

Based on a drawing by N. Gouvoussis

glimpses of the ancient ruins from the city below. The best of these street-level **views** are along Eólou, where the Parthenon forms the focal point of the horizon. Calmer and quieter vantage points higher up include the nearby hills of **Lykavitós**, **Ardhittós** and **Filopáppou**, where you can look on, undisturbed, from among the pine groves; a walk to one of these is highly recommended.

The main **approach** to the ruins is the path that extends above Odhós Dhioskoúron, where it joins Theorías at the northwest corner of Pláka. Two alternative options – though both perhaps better as ways down from the rock – are to make your way through the ancient Agora (entrance on Adhrianoú; see p.99) or, from the south side of the slope, around the footpath beside the Odeion of Herodes Atticus.

The Propylaia and Athena Nike temple

Today, as throughout its history, the Acropolis offers but one entrance – from a terrace above the Agora. Here in Classical times the Panathenaic Way extended along a steep ramp to a massive monumental double-gatehouse, the **Propylaia**; the modern path makes a more gradual, zigzagging ascent through an arched Roman entrance, the **Beule Gate**, added in the third century AD.

The **Propylaia** were constructed by Mnesikles upon completion of the Parthenon, in 437 BC, and their axis and proportions aligned to balance the temple. They were built from the same Pentelic marble (from Mount Pendéli, northeast of the city), and in grandeur and architectural achievement are no mean rival to the Parthenon temple. In order to offset the difficulties of a sloping site, Mnesikles combined for the first time standard Doric columns with the taller and more delicate Ionic order. The ancient Athenians, awed by the fact that such wealth and craftsmanship should be used for a purely secular building, ranked this as their most prestigious monument.

The halls had a variety of uses, even in Classical times. To the left of the central hall (which before Venetian bombardment supported a great coffered roof, painted blue and gilded with stars), the Pinakotheke – currently in scaffolding – exhibited paintings of Homeric subjects by Polygnotus. Executed in the mid-fifth century BC, these were described 600 years later by Pausanias in his Roman-era *Guide to Greece*. There was to have been a similar wing-room to the right, but Mnesikles's design trespassed on ground sacred to the Goddess of Victory and the premises had to be adapted as a waiting room for her shrine – the Temple of Athena Nike.

Simple and elegant, the **Temple of Athena Nike** was begun late in the rebuilding scheme (probably due to conflict over the extent of the Propylaia's south wing) and stands on a precipitous platform overlooking the port of Pireás and the Saronic Gulf. Pausanias recounts that it was from this bastion that King Aegeus maintained a vigil for the tell-tale white sails that would indicate the safe return of his son Theseus from his mission to slay the Minotaur on Crete. Theseus, flushed with success, forgot his promise to swap the boat's black sails for white. On seeing the black sails, Aegeus assumed his son had perished and, racked with grief, threw himself to his death. The temple's frieze, with more attention to realism than triumph, depicts the Athenians' victory over the Persians at Plateia.

Amazingly, the whole temple was reconstructed, from its original blocks, in the nineteenth century; the Turks had demolished the building two hundred years previously, using it as material for a gun emplacement. Recovered in this same feat of jigsaw-puzzle archeology were the reliefs from its parapet – among them *Victory Adjusting her Sandal*, the most beautiful exhibit in the Acropolis Museum.

In front of this small temple are the scant remains of a **Sanctuary of Brauronian Artemis**. Although its function remains obscure, it is known that the precinct once housed a colossal bronze representation of the Wooden Horse of Troy. More noticeable is a nearby stretch of **Mycenaean wall** (running parallel to the Propylaia) that was incorporated into the Classical design.

The Parthenon

Seen from the Propylaia, the Acropolis is today dominated by the Parthenon, set on the rock's highest ground. In Classical times, however, only the temple's pediment could be viewed through the intervening mass of statues and buildings. The ancient focus was a ten-metre-high bronze statue of *Athena Promachos* (Athena the Champion), moved to Constantinople in Byzantine times and there destroyed by a mob who believed that its beckoning hand had directed the Crusaders to the city in 1204. The statue was created by Pheidias as a symbol of the Athenians' defiance of Persia; its spear and helmet were visible to sailors approaching from Sounion.

THE ACROPOLIS: PERICLES TO ELGIN – AND BEYOND

The Acropolis's natural setting, a craggy mass of limestone plateau, watered by springs and rising an abrupt hundred metres out of the plain of Attica, has made it a focus and nucleus during every phase of the city's development.

The site was one of the earliest settlements in Greece, its slopes inhabited by a **Neolithic** community around 5000 BC. In **Mycenaean** times it was fortified with Cyclopean walls (parts of which can still be seen), enclosing a royal palace and temples which fostered the cult of Athena. City and goddess were integrated by the **Dorians** and, with the union of Attic towns and villages in the ninth century BC, the Acropolis became the heart of the first Greek city-state, sheltering its principal public buildings. So it was to remain, save for an interval under the **Peisistratid tyrants** of the seventh and sixth centuries BC, who re-established a fortified residence on the rock. But when the last tyrant was overthrown in 510 BC, the Delphic Oracle ordered that the Acropolis should remain forever the **province of the gods**, unoccupied by humans.

It was in this context that the monuments visible today were built. Most of the substantial remains date from the **fifth century BC** or later; there are outlines of earlier temples and sanctuaries but these are hardly impressive, for they were burned to the ground when the Persians sacked Athens in 480 BC. For some decades, until Pericles promoted his grand plan, the temples were left in their ruined state as a reminder of the Persian action. But with that threat removed, in the wake of Athenian military supremacy and a peace treaty with the Persians in 449 BC, the walls were rebuilt and architects drew up plans for a reconstruction worthy of the city's cultural and political position.

Pericles's **rebuilding** plan was both magnificent and enormously expensive but it won the backing of the democracy, for many of whose citizens it must have created both wealth and work – paid for from the unfortunate Delian League's coffers. The work was under the general direction of the architect and sculptor **Pheidias** and it was completed in an incredibly short time. The Parthenon itself took only ten years to finish: "every architect", wrote Plutarch, "striving to surpass the magnificence of the design with the elegance of the execution".

Their monuments survived unaltered – save for some modest Roman tinkering – for close to a thousand years, until in the reign of Emperor Justinian the temples were converted to **Christian** worship. In subsequent years the uses became secular as well as religious, and embellishments increased, gradually obscuring the Classical designs. Fifteenth-century Italian princes held court in the Propylaia, the entrance hall to the complex, and the same quarters were later used by the **Turks** as their commander's headquarters and as a powder magazine. The Parthenon underwent similar changes from Greek to Roman temple, from Byzantine church to Frankish cathedral, before several centuries of use as a Turkish mosque. The Erechtheion, with its graceful female figures, saw service as a harem. A Venetian diplomat, Hugo Favoli, described the Acropolis in 1563 as "looming beneath a swarm of glittering golden crescents", with a minaret rising from the Parthenon. For all their changes in use, however, the buildings would have resembled – very much more than today's bare ruins – the bustling and ornate ancient Acropolis, covered in sculpture and painted in bright colours.

To the right of the statue passed the Panathenaic Way, the route of the quadrennial festival in honour of the city's patroness, the goddess Athena. Following this route up today, you can make out grooves cut for footholds in the rock and, to either side, niches for innumerable statues and offerings.

The **Parthenon** was the first great building in Pericles's scheme. Designed by Iktinos, it utilizes all the refinements available to the Doric order of architecture to achieve an extraordinary and unequalled harmony. Its proportions maintain a universal 9:4 ratio, not only in the calculations of length to width, or width to height, but in such relationships as the distances between the columns and their diameter. Additionally,

Sadly, such images remain only in the prints and sketches of that period: the Acropolis buildings finally fell victim to the demands of war, blown up during the successive attempts by the Venetians to oust the Turks. In 1684 the Turks demolished the temple of Athena Nike to gain a brief tactical advantage. Three years later the Venetians, laying siege to the garrison, ignited a Turkish gunpowder magazine in the Parthenon, and in the process blasted off its roof and set a **fire** that raged within its precincts for two days and nights. The apricot-tinged glow of the Parthenon marbles so admired by the Neoclassicists of the eighteenth century was one of the more aesthetic results.

Arguably surpassing this destruction, at least in the minds of modern Greeks, were the activities of Western looters at the start of the nineteenth century: the French ambassador Fauvel gathering antiquities for the Louvre, and **Lord Elgin** levering away sculptures from the Parthenon in 1801. As British Ambassador to the Porte, Elgin obtained permission from the Turks to erect scaffolding, excavate and remove stones with inscriptions. He interpreted this concession as a licence to make off with almost all of the bas-reliefs from the Parthenon's frieze, most of its pedimental structures and a caryatid from the Erechtheion – which he later sold to the British Museum. There were perhaps justifications for Elgin's action at the time – not least the Turks' tendency to use Parthenon stones in their lime kilns, and possible further ravages of war – though it was controversial even then. Byron, a more sympathetic character who roundly disparaged all this activity, visited in 1810–11, just in time to see the last of Elgin's ships loaded with the marbles. Today, however, the British Museum's continued retention of the "Elgin Marbles" (a phrase that Greek guides on the Acropolis, who portray Elgin unequivocally as a vandal, do not use) rests on legal rather than moral claims. Hopefully the British Museum will soon find a graceful pretext to back down; the long-awaited completion of the new Acropolis Museum, slated to occupy land around the Makriyánni barracks just south of the bluffs, would be a perfect opportunity, but the project – originally scheduled for completion in 1996 – seems to have stalled indefinitely.

As for the Acropolis **buildings**, their fate since the Greeks regained the Acropolis after the War of Independence has not been entirely happy. Almost immediately, Greek archeologists began clearing the Turkish village that had developed around the Parthenon-mosque; a Greek regent lamented in vain that they "would destroy all the picturesque additions of the Middle Ages in their zeal to lay bare the ancient monuments". Much of this early work was indeed destructive: the iron clamps and supports used to reinforce the marble structures were, contrary to ancient example, not sheathed in lead, so they have since rusted and warped, causing the stones to crack. Meanwhile, earthquakes have dislodged the foundations; generations of feet have slowly worn down surfaces; and, more recently, sulphur dioxide deposits, caused by vehicle and industrial pollution, have been turning the marble to dust.

Since a 1975 report predicted the collapse of the Parthenon, visitors have been barred from its actual precinct, and a major, long-term restoration scheme of the entire Acropolis embarked upon. Inevitably this has its frustrations, with many of the buildings scaffolded and the Acropolis at times taking on the appearance of a building site. Of late, progress has been delayed by disputes between the architect in charge of the restoration, Manolis Korres, and the committee of non-specialists which has been put over him.

any possible appearance of disproportion is corrected by meticulous mathematics and craftsmanship. All seemingly straight lines are in fact slightly curved, an optical illusion known as *entasis* (intensification). The columns (their profile bowed slightly to avoid seeming concave) are slanted inwards by 6cm, while each of the steps along the sides of the temple was made to incline just 12cm over a length of 70 metres.

Built on the site of earlier archaic temples, the Parthenon was intended as a new sanctuary for Athena and a home for her cult image – a colossal wooden statue of *Athena Polias* (Athena of the City) overlaid with ivory and gold plating, with precious gems as eyes and sporting an ivory gorgon death's-head on her breast. Designed by Pheidias, the statue was installed in the semi-darkness of the *cella* (cult chamber), where it remained an object of prestige and wealth, if not veneration, until at least the fifth century AD. The sculpture has been lost since ancient times but its characteristics are known through numerous later copies (including a fine Roman one in the National Archeological Museum).

The name "Parthenon" means "virgins' chamber", and initially referred only to a room at the west end of the temple occupied by the priestesses of Athena. However, the temple never rivalled the Erechtheion in sanctity and its role tended to remain that of treasury and artistic showcase, devoted rather more to the new god of the *polis* than to Athena herself. Originally its columns were painted and it was decorated with the finest frieze and pedimental sculpture of the Classsical age, depicting the Panathenaic procession, the birth of Athena and the struggles of Greeks to overcome giants, Amazons and centaurs. Of these, the best surviving examples are in the British Museum, but the greater part of the pediments, along with the central columns and the *cella*, were destroyed by the Venetian bombardment in 1687.

The Erechtheion

To the north of the Parthenon, beyond the foundations of the Old Temple of Athena, stands the **Erechtheion**, the last of the great works of Pericles to be completed. It was built over ancient sanctuaries, which in turn were predated by a Mycenaean palace. Here, in a symbolic reconciliation, both Athena and the city's old patron of Poseidon-Erechtheus were worshipped; the site, according to myth, was that on which they had contested possession of the Acropolis. The myth (which probably recalls the integration of the Mycenaeans with earlier pre-Hellenic settlers) tells how an olive tree sprang from the ground at the touch of Athena's spear, while Poseidon summoned forth a sea-water spring. The Olympian gods voted Athena the victor.

Pausanias wrote of seeing both olive tree and seawater in the temple, adding that "the extraordinary thing about this well is that when the wind blows south a sound of waves comes from it."

Today, in common with all buildings on the Acropolis, entrance is no longer permitted, but its series of elegant Ionic porticoes are worth close attention, particularly the north one with its fine decorated doorway and frieze of blue Eleusinian marble. On the south side is the famous **Porch of the Caryatids**, whose columns are transformed into the tunics of six tall maidens holding the entablature on their heads. The statues were long supposed to have been modelled on the widows of Karyai, a small city in the Peloponnese that was punished for its alliance with the Persians by the slaughter of its menfolk and the enslavement of the women. There is, though, little suggestion of grieving or humbled captives in the serene poses of the Caryatid women. Some authorities believe that they instead represent the Arrephoroi, young, high-born girls in the service of Athena. The ones in situ are now, sadly, replacements. Five of the originals are in the Acropolis Museum, a sixth was looted by Elgin, who also removed a column and other purely architectural features – pieces that become completely meaningless out of context in the British Museum and which are replaced here by casts in a different colour marble. The stunted olive tree growing in the precinct was planted by an American archeologist in 1917.

The Acropolis Museum

Placed discreetly on a level below that of the main monuments, the **Acropolis Museum** contains all of the portable objects removed from the site since 1834 (with the exception of a few bronzes displayed in the National Archeological Museum). Over recent years, as increasing amounts of stone and sculptures have been removed from the ravages of environmental pollution, the collection has grown considerably. Labelling is rudimentary at best; a supplementary guide is useful.

In the first rooms to the left of the vestibule are fragments of pedimental sculptures from the **Old Temple of Athena** (seventh to sixth century BC), whose traces of paint give a good impression of the vivid colours that were used in temple decoration. Further on is the **Moschophoros**, a painted marble statue of a young man carrying a sacrificial calf, dated 570 BC and one of the earliest examples of Greek art in marble. Room 4 displays one of the chief treasures of the building, a unique collection of **Korai**, or maidens, dedicated as votive offerings to Athena at some point in the sixth century BC. Between them they represent a shift in art and fashion, from the simply contoured Doric clothing to the more elegant and voluminous Ionic designs; the figures' smiles also change subtly, becoming increasingly loose and natural.

The pieces of the **Parthenon frieze** in Room 8 were sundered from the temple by the Venetian explosion and subsequently buried, thereby escaping the clutches of Lord Elgin. They portray scenes of Athenian citizens in the Panathenaic procession; the fact that mortals featured so prominently in the decoration of the temple indicates the immense collective self-pride of the Athenians at the height of their Golden Age. This room also contains a graceful and fluid sculpture, known as **Iy Sandalízoussa**, which depicts **Athena Nike** adjusting her sandal. Finally, in the last room are four authentic and semi-eroded **caryatids** from the Erechtheion, displayed behind a glass screen in a carefully rarefied atmosphere.

West and south of the Acropolis

Most visitors to the Acropolis leave by the same route they arrived – north through Pláka. For a calmer and increasingly panoramic view of the rock, it's worth taking the time to explore something of the area to the **west of the Acropolis**, punctuated by the hills of the Areopagus, Pnyx and Filopáppou, each of which had a distinct function in the life of the ancient city.

The **south slope** is rewarding, too, with its Greek and Roman theatres and the remains of *stoas* and sanctuaries. It can be approached from the Acropolis, with an entrance just above the Herodes Atticus theatre, though its main entrance is some way to the south along Leofóros Dhionissíou Areopayítou.

No less important, these sites all give access to the neighbourhoods of **Koukáki** and **Áno Petrálona**, two of the least spoilt quarters in Athens, and with some of the city's best tavernas (see p.125).

The Areopagus, Pnyx and Filopáppou Hill

Rock-hewn stairs ascend the low hill of the **Areopagus** immediately below the entrance to the Acropolis. The "Hill of Mars" was the site of the Council of Nobles and the Judicial Court under the aristocratic rule of ancient Athens. During the Classical period the court lost its powers of government to the Assembly (held on the Pnyx) but it remained the court of criminal justice, dealing primarily with cases of homicide. Aeschylus used this setting in *The Eumenides* for the trial of Orestes, who, pursued by the Furies' demand of "a life for a life", stood accused of murdering his mother Clytemnestra.

The hill was used as a campsite by the Persians during their siege of the Acropolis in 480 BC, and in the Roman era by St Paul, who preached the "Sermon on an Unknown God" here, winning amongst his converts Dionysius "the Areopagite", who became the city's patron saint. Today, there are various foundation cuttings on the site, and the ruins of a church of Áyios Dhioníssios (possibly built over the court), though nothing is actually left standing. The Areopagus's historic associations apart, it is notable mainly for the views, not only of the Acropolis, but down over the Agora and towards Kerameikos – the ancient cemetery (see p.100).

Following the road or path over the flank of the Acropolis, you come out onto Leofóros Dhionissíou Areopayítou, by the Herodes Atticus theatre. Turning right, 100m or so down (and across) the avenue, a network of paths leads up **Filopáppou Hill**, also known as the "Hill of the Muses" (*Lófos Moussón*). This strategic height has played an important, if generally sorry, role in the city's history. It was from here that the shell which destroyed the roof of the Parthenon was lobbed; more recently, the colonels placed tanks on the slopes during their coup of 1967. (Avoid the area at night, as it has a reputation for rapes and muggings.)

The hill's summit is capped by a somewhat grandiose monument to a Roman senator and consul, Filopappus, who is depicted driving his chariot on its frieze. Again, it is a place above all for views. To the west is the Dora Stratou Theatre (or Filopáppou Theatre) where Greek music and dance performances (see p.131) are held. Northwest, along the main path, and following a line of truncated ancient walls, is the church of **Áyios Dhimítrios**, an unsung gingerbread gem, which has kept its original Byzantine frescoes. In the cliff-face across from this to the south you can make out a kind of cave dwelling, known (more from imagination than evidence) as the **prison of Socrates**.

Further to the north, above the church, rises the **Hill of the Pnyx**, an area used in Classical Athens as the meeting place for the democratic assembly, which gathered more than forty times a year. All except the most serious political issues, such as ostracism, were aired here, the hill on the north side providing a convenient semicircular terrace from which to address the crowd. All male citizens could vote and, at least in theory, all could voice their opinions, though the assembly was harsh on inarticulate or foolish speakers. There are remains of the original walls, used to form the theatre-like court, and of *stoas* for the assembly's refreshment. The arena is today used for the *son et lumière* (not greatly recommended) of the Acropolis, which takes place on most summer evenings.

Beyond the Pnyx, still another hill, **Lófos Nymfón** (Hill of the Nymphs), is dominated by a nineteenth-century observatory and gardens, occasionally open to visitors.

The south slope of the Acropolis

Entrance on Leofóros Dhionysíou Areopayítou; daily: summer 8am–7pm; winter 8am–2.45pm; 500dr.

The second-century Roman **Odeion of Herodes Atticus**, restored for performances of music and Classical drama during the summer festival (see p.131), dominates the south slope of the Acropolis hill. It is open only for shows, though; the main reason to come here otherwise is the earlier Greek sites to the east.

Pre-eminent among these is the **Theatre of Dionysos**, beside the main site entrance. One of the most evocative locations in the city, it was here that the masterpieces of Aeschylus, Sophocles, Euripides and Aristophanes were first performed. It was also the venue for the annual festival of tragic drama, where each Greek citizen would take his turn as member of the chorus. The ruins are impressive. Rebuilt in the fourth century BC, the theatre could hold some 17,000 spectators – considerably more than the Herodes Atticus's 5000–6000 seats; twenty of the theatre's sixty-four tiers of seats survive. Most notable are the great marble thrones in the front row, each inscribed with the name of an official of the festival or of an important priest; in the middle sat the priest of Dionysos and on his right the representative of the Delphic Oracle. At the rear of the stage along the Roman *bema* (rostrum) are reliefs of episodes in the life of Dionysos flanked by two squatting Sileni, devotees of the satyrs. Sadly, all this is roped off to protect the stage-floor **mosaic** – itself a magnificent diamond of multicoloured marble best seen from above.

Above the theatre – reached by steps, then a path to the right – looms a vast grotto, converted perhaps a millennium ago into the chapel of **Panayía Khryssospiliótissa**; it's worth a look for the setting rather than its kitsch iconography. To the west of the theatre extend the ruins of the **Asklepion**, a sanctuary devoted to the healing god Asklepios (see p.178) and built around a sacred spring. The curative centre was probably incorporated into the Byzantine church of the doctor-saints Kosmas and Damian, of which there are prominent remains. Nearer to the road lie the foundations of the Roman **Stoa of Eumenes**, a colonnade of stalls that stretched to the Herodes Atticus Odeion.

The Ancient Agora

Southeastern entrance down the path from the Areopagus; northern entrance on Adhrianoú; Tues–Sun 8.30am–2.30pm; 1200dr.

The **Agora** (market) was the nexus of ancient Athenian city life. Competing for space were the various claims of administration, commerce, market and public assembly. The result was ordered chaos. Eubolus, a fourth-century poet, observed that "you will find everything sold together in the same place at Athens: figs, witnesses to summonses, bunches of grapes, turnips, pears, apples, givers of evidence, roses, medlars . . . water clocks, laws, indictments". Women, however, were not in evidence; secluded by custom, they would delegate any business in the Agora to slaves. Before shifting location to the Pnyx, the assembly also met here, and continued to do so when discussing cases of ostracism for most of the fifth and fourth centuries BC.

Originally the Agora was a rectangle, divided diagonally by the Panathenaic Way and enclosed by temples, administrative buildings, and long porticoed *stoas* (arcades of shops) where idlers and philosophers gathered to exchange views and listen to the orators. In the centre was an open space, defined by boundary stones at the beginning of the fifth century BC; considered sacred and essential to the life of the community, those accused of homicide or other serious crimes were excluded from it by law.

The site today is a confused, if extensive, jumble of ruins, dating from various stages of building between the sixth century BC and the fifth century AD. The best overview is from the Areopagus, by the southeast entrance. For some idea of what you are surveying, however, the place to head for is the **Museum**, housed in the reconstructed **Stoa of Attalos**. The stoa itself was a US$1.5 million project of the American School of Archeology in Athens. It is, in every respect bar one, an entirely faithful reconstruction of the original. What is missing is colour: in Classical times the exterior would have been painted in bright red and blue (like the Minoan palaces of Crete). Of the displays – mostly pottery from the sixth to fourth century BC, plus some early Geometric grave offerings – highlights are the red-figure dishes depicting athletes, musicians and minor deities, together with the adjacent oil flask in the form of a kneeling boy (both exhibits are in the centre of the hall).

Around the site, the most prominent ruins are of various other stoas, including the recently excavated "Painted Stoa" where **Zeno** expounded his Stoic philosophy, and those of the city's gymnasiums and council hall (*bouleuterion*). Somewhat above the general elevation, to the west, is the **Thiseon**, or Temple of Hephaistos. Because exploits of Theseus were displayed on the metopes and frieze this temple was long thought to be dedicated to Theseus. The name Thiseon lingers for the train station and the area to the southwest. The best preserved, though perhaps least admired, of all Doric temples, it lacks the curvature and "lightness" of the Parthenon's design. Dedicated to the patron of blacksmiths and metalworkers – hence its popular name – it was the first building of Pericles's programme, though not the first completed. Its remaining *metopes* depict the labours of Hercules and the exploits of Theseus, while the barrel-vaulted roof dates from the Byzantine conversion of the temple into a church of St George. The other bona fide church on the site – that of **Áyii Apóstoli** (the Holy Apostles), by the south entrance – is worth a glance inside for its fresco fragments, exposed during a 1950s restoration of the eleventh-century shrine.

Kerameikos (Keramikós)

Entrance at Ermoú 148; Tues–Sun 8.30am–2.30pm; 500dr.

The Kerameikos site, encompassing the principal cemetery of ancient Athens, provides a fascinating and quiet retreat from the Acropolis. It is little visited and in addition has something of an oasis feel about it, with the lush Iridhanós channel, speckled with water lilies, flowing across it from east to west.

From the entrance can be seen the double line of the **Long Walls**, which ran to the port at Pireás; the inner wall was hastily cobbled together by the men, women and children of Athens while Themistocles was pretending to negotiate a mutual disarmament treaty with Sparta in 429 BC. The barriers are interrupted by the great **Dipylon Gate**, where travellers from Pireás, Eleusis and Boeotia entered the ancient city, and the **Sacred Gate**, used for the Eleusinian and Panathenaic processions. These followed the Sacred Way, once lined by colonnades and bronze statues, into the Agora. Between the two gates are the foundations of the **Pompeion**, where preparations for the processions were made and where the main vehicles were stored.

Branching off from the Sacred Way is the **Street of the Tombs**, begun in 394 BC and now excavated along a hundred or so metres. Both sides were reserved for the plots of wealthy Athenians. Some twenty, each containing numerous commemorative monuments, have been excavated, and their original stones, or replicas, reinstated. The flat vertical *stelai* were the main funerary monuments of the Classical world; the sarcophagus belonged to Hellenistic and Roman times. The sculpted crescent with the massive conglomerate base to the left of the path is the *Memorial of Dexileos*, the twenty-year-old son of Lysanias of Thorikos, who was killed in action at Corinth in 394 BC. The adjacent plot contains the *Monument of Dionysios of Kollytos*, in the shape of a pillar *stele* supporting a bull carved from Pentelic marble. As with any cemetery, however, it is the more humble monuments, such as the statue of a girl with a dog on the north side of the street, that connect past and present in the shared experience of loss. From the terrace overlooking the tombs, Pericles delivered his famous funeral oration dedicated to those who died in the first years of the Peloponnesian War. His propaganda coup inspired thousands more to enlist in a campaign during which one-third of the Athenian force was wiped out.

The **Oberlaender Museum**, named after the German-American manufacturer who financed it, contains an extensive collection of *stelai*, terracotta figures, vases and sculptures from the site. Among them, Room 1's *Ampharete Holding Her Infant Grandchild*, and *The Boxer*, with a cauliflower ear and the thongs of a glove tied around his wrist, are remarkable in their detailed execution. The terracotta figures and vases of Room 2 include some of the earliest art objects yet found in Greece.

Pláka and Monastiráki

Pláka, with its alleys and stairs built on the Turkish plan, is the most rewarding Athenian area for daytime wanderings – not least because of its pedestrianization, with cars banished from all but a few main streets. In addition to a scattering of Roman sites and various offbeat and enjoyable museums, it offers glimpses of an exotic past, refreshingly at odds with the concrete blocks of the metropolis. If you can, time your visit to coincide with the Sunday morning **flea market** around Monastiráki square and along that side of the Agora.

Roughly delineated by Sýndagma, Odhós Ermoú and the Acropolis, the district was basically the extent of nineteenth-century, pre-independence Athens, and provided the core of the city for the next few decades. Once away from Sýndagma, the narrow winding streets are lined with nineteenth-century Neoclassical houses, some grand, some humble, with gateways opening onto verdant courtyards overlooked by wooden verandas. Tiled roofs are edged with terracotta medusa-heads, goddesses and foliage designs, ornaments known collectively as *akrokerámata*; the grander facades are decorated with pilasters and capitals and wrought-iron balconies. Poor and working class for most of this century, the district has lately been extensively gentrified and renovated.

From Sýndagma to Adhrianoú

An attractive approach to Pláka is to follow **Odhós Kydhathinéon**, a pedestrian walkway that starts near the **English and Russian churches** on Odhós Filellínon, south of Sýndagma. It leads gently downhill, past the Greek Folk Art Museum, on a leafy square with one of the few remaining old-time cafés on the corner, on through café-crowded Platía Filomoússou Eterías to Hadrian's street, **Odhós Adhrianoú**, which runs nearly the whole length of Pláka from Hadrian's Arch past the ancient Agora.

The **Museum of Greek Folk Art** (Tues–Sun 10am–2pm; 500dr), at Kydhathinéon 17, is one of the most enjoyable in the city. Its five floors are mostly devoted to collections of weaving, pottery, regional costumes and embroidery, which reveal both the sophistication and the strong Middle Eastern influence of Greek popular arts. On the second floor, the carnival tradition of northern Greece, and the all-but-vanished shadow-puppet theatre, are featured. The fourth floor dazzles with its exhibits of gold and silver jewellery and weaponry. Most compelling of all, on the third floor, is the reconstructed village room with a series of murals by the primitive artist **Theophilos** (1873–1934). Theophilos was one of the characters of turn-of-the-century Greece, dressing in War of Independence outfits and painting tavernas and cafés for a meal or a small fee. A museum of his work is at Variá on Lésvos, and other paintings – usually scenes from peasant life or battles during the War of Independence – survive in situ in the Peloponnese, on Lésvos and on Mount Pílion, though they have only in the last few decades been recognized as being worth preserving.

Down and across the street from the Museum of Greek Folk Art, the **Hellenic Children's Museum**, Kydhathinéon 14 (Mon–Wed 9.30am–1.30pm, Fri 9.30am–1.30pm & 5–8pm, Sat & Sun 10am–1pm; free) is more a playschool than a museum: chaotic but fun. It includes workrooms, playrooms and displays on stuff like the building of the new Athens metro lines, which children can enter complete with hard hats. On a similar theme, the **Museum of Greek Children's Art**, Kódhrou 9 (Mon–Sat 10am–2pm, Sun 11am–2pm; closed Aug; 200dr) has changing displays of children's art, including sculpture, but also tables and drawing materials for children to use. Some paintings are for sale, as well as a large range of eye-catching cards painted by Greek children.

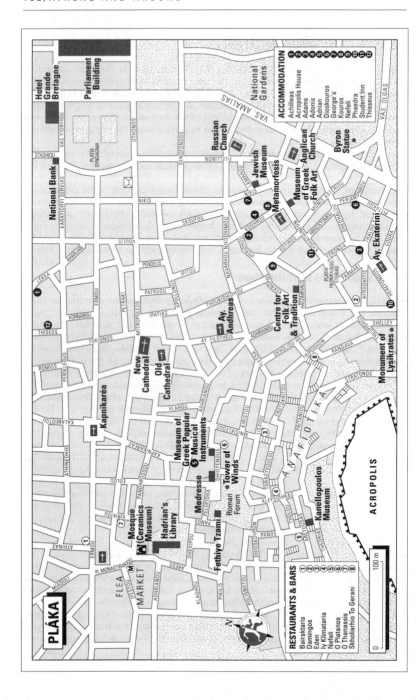

PLÁKA

ACCOMMODATION
1 Achilleas
2 Acropolis House
3 Adams
4 Adonis
5 Adrian
6 Dioskouros
7 George's
8 Kouros
9 Nefeli
10 Phaedra
11 Student Inn
12 Thisseus

RESTAURANTS & BARS
1 Bairaktaris
2 Damingos
3 Eden
4 Iy Klimataria
5 Nefeli
6 O Platanos
7 O Thanassis
8 Skholiarhio To Gerani

Hotel Grande Bretagne
Parliament Building
National Bank
PLATIA SYNDAGMA
Russian Church
Jewish Museum
Metamorfosis
Museum of Greek Folk Art
Anglican Church
Byron Statue
Ay. Ekaterini
Centre for Folk Art & Tradition
Ay. Andhreas
New Cathedral
Old Cathedral
Kapnikaréa
Museum of Greek Popular Musical Instruments
Tower of the Winds
Roman Forum
Medresse
Fethiye Tzami
Hadrian's Library
Mosque (Ceramics Museum)
Kanellopoulos Museum
Monument of Lysikrates
ACROPOLIS
FLEA MARKET
ANAFIOTIKA

STADHIOU
VAS YIORYIOU
OTHONOS
VAS AMALIAS
National Gardens
KARAYIORYI SERVIAS
AHARNON
LEKKA
ERMOU
KORNAROU
THISEOS
ROMVIS
PERIKLEOUS
FOKIONOS
KALAMIOTOU
ATHINEDHOS
MIAOULI
ATHINAS
IFESTOU
ERMOU
PL MONASTIRAKIOU
ADHRIANOU
KLADHOU
PIKILIS
POLIGNOTOU
AREOS
DHEXIPOU
PANOS
PELOPIDHA
PANDHROSSOU
VRISAKIOU
VLAHOU
KAPNIKAREAS
MITROPOLEOS
FOTHINOS
PANDROSSOU
EOLOU
XIRIOU
NIKIS
VOULIS
PENDELIS
IPITOU
PATROOU
APOLLONOS
IPATIAS
PETRAKI
AY FILOTHEIS
THOUKIDHIDHOU
ADHRIANOU
NAVARHOU NIKODHIMOU
FILELLINON
XENOFONDOS
SKOUFOU
KODHROU
PERIVOLIOU
NIKIS
SOTIROS
KIKILIAS
HATZIMIHALI
AFRODHITIS
SHELLEY
SHOLEIOU
RANGAVA
STRATONOS
TRIPODHON
PRITANIOU
EPIHARMOU
ERECHTHEOS
THESPIDHOS
KIRISTOU
MNISIKLEOUS
THOLOU
KLEPSIDHRAS
MARKOU AVRILIOU
DHIOYENOUS
THRASYVOULOU
SHOLIOU HILL
VYRONOS
YERONDA
FARMAKI
MONIS ASTERIOU
MNISSIKLEOUS
NIKODHIMOU
DHEDHALOU
VAKHOU
FLAMIN
PERIANDHROU
MISSISTOMON
PITTAKOU
GOURA
ETERIAS
PLATIA FILOMOUSOU
HERODHOTOU
SHELLEY
AFRODHITIS
ANTINOROS

100 m

PLÁKA

Two other museums are close by. A couple of blocks to the northwest, at Angelikís Hatzimiháli 6, the **Centre of Folk Art and Tradition** (Tues–Fri 9am–1pm & 5–9pm, Sat & Sun 9am–1pm; closes for a movable month during summer; free) features costumes, cloth, musical instruments, and so forth, in another grand Pláka mansion. A short distance to the east, at Níkis 39, is the **Jewish Museum of Greece** (Mon–Fri 9am–2.30pm, Sun 10am–2pm; 300dr). Displaying art and religious artefacts from the very ancient Jewish communities scattered throughout Greece, the centrepiece is the reconstructed synagogue of Pátra, dating from the 1920s, whose furnishings have been moved here en bloc and remounted.

The Monument of Lysikratos and around

At the eastern end of Pláka, Odhós Lissikrátous gives onto a small, fenced-off archeological area at one end of Odhós Tripódhon, the **Street of the Tripods**, where winners of the ancient dramatic contests dedicated their tripod-trophies to Dionysos. Here you can see the **Monument of Lysikratos**, a tall and graceful stone and marble structure from 335 BC, which stands as a surprisingly complete example of these ancient exhibits. A four-metre-high stone base supports six Corinthian columns rising up to a marble dome on which, in a flourish of acanthus leaf carvings, a winning tripod was placed. The inscription on its architrave tells us that "Lysikratos of Kikyna, son of Lysitheides was *choregos* (sponsor); the tribe of Akamantis won the victory with a chorus of boys; Theon played the flute; Lysiades of Athens trained the chorus; Evainetos was archon." The monument was incorporated into a French Capuchin convent in 1667, and tradition asserts that Byron used the convent as a study, writing part of *Childe Harold* here; at the time Athens had no inn, and the convent was a regular lodging for European travellers.

The street beyond, **Výronos**, is named after the poet (*O Lórdhos Výronas* to Greeks). At its far end, facing you across the road, is the old Makriyánni police barracks, revered by Greek rightists for its stout resistance to Communist attack during December 1944. Part of it has been transformed into the so-called **Acropolis Study Centre** (daily 8.30am–3pm; free), flanked by the metro construction and containing little beyond plaster casts of the Elgin Marbles and models of the winning designs for the hypothetical **Acropolis Museum**.

Hadrian's Arch and the Temple of Olympian Zeus

Taking the other street at the Lysikratos monument crossroads, Odhós Lyssikrátous, you emerge at the edge of Pláka near one of the most hazardous road junctions in Athens, the meeting of Dhionyssíou Areopayítou, Amalías and Singroú. Across the way, facing Leofóros Amalías, stands **Hadrian's Arch**, erected by that emperor to mark the edge of the Classical city and the beginning of his own. On the near side its frieze is inscribed "This is Athens, the ancient city of Theseus", and on the other "This is the City of Hadrian and not of Theseus". Since there are few obvious signs of a Roman city, this makes little sense to today's visitor, but there are Roman remains south of the Temple of Olympian Zeus and recent excavations suggest that the Roman city occupied at least the Záppio area.

Directly behind the arch, the colossal pillars of the **Temple of Olympian Zeus** (Tues–Sun 8am–2.30pm; 500dr; entrance on Vasilíssis Ólgas) dominate their surroundings. The largest temple in Greece, and according to Livy, "the only temple on earth to do justice to the god", it was dedicated by Hadrian in 131 AD, some 700 years after the tyrant Peisistratos had laid its foundations. Hadrian marked the occasion by contributing a statue of Zeus and a suitably monumental one of himself, although both have since been lost. Just fifteen of the temple's original 104 Pentelic marble pillars remain erect, though the column drums of another, which fell in 1852, litter the ground, giving a startling idea of the project's size. Almost equally impressive is the fact that in the Byzantine era, a stylite made his hermitage on the temple architrave.

From the Olympian Zeus temple, a shady route up to Sýndagma or Kolonáki leads through the Záppio and the **National Gardens** (see p.113).

Anafiótika and the Kanellópoulos Museum

Continuing straight ahead from the Kydhathinéon–Adhrianoú intersection, up **Odhós Thespídhos**, you reach the edge of the Acropolis precinct. Up to the right, the white-washed cubist houses of **Anafiótika** cheerfully proclaim an architect-free zone amid the higher slopes of the Acropolis rock. The pleasingly haphazard buildings here were erected by workers from the island of Anáfi in the southern Aegean, who were employed in the mid-nineteenth-century construction of Athens. Unable to afford land, they took advantage of a customary law to the effect that if a roof and four walls could be thrown up overnight, the premises were yours at sunrise. The houses, and the two churches that serve them, are the image of those the Cycladic islanders had left behind.

Follow Rangavá or Stratoús anticlockwise around the Acropolis rock and you will eventually emerge on Theorías, outside the eclectic **Kanellópoulos Museum** (Tues–Sun 8am–2.30pm; 500dr). Though there is nothing here that you won't see examples of in the bigger museums, this collection of treasures, exhibited in the top-most house under the Acropolis, has a calm appeal. The bulk of the ground-floor exhibits are icons but there is also Byzantine jewellery, bronze oil-lamps and crosses, and Roman funerary ornaments from Fayum. The top floor is given over entirely to Geometric, Classical and Hellenistic art, primarily pottery and votive figurines, generally of a high standard and distinguished by whimsical execution. The middle floor and the stairwells are devoted to Near Eastern and Cypriot art of various periods from the Bronze Age on, including some exquisite Persian goldwork and flamboyantly painted "Phoenician" vials.

The Roman Forum and Tower of the Winds

The western reaches of Adhrianoú, past the newly restored Neoclassical Demotic School, is largely commercial – souvenir shops and sandals – as far as the **Roman Forum** (entrance cnr Pelopídha/Eólou; Tues–Sun 8am–2.30pm; 500dr), a large irregularly shaped excavation site bounded by railings.

The forum was built by Julius Caesar and Augustus (Octavian) as an extension of the older ancient Greek *agora* to its west. It has undergone substantial excavation in recent years, but the majority of it is now open to visitors. Its main entrance, on the west side, was through the relatively intact **Gate of Athena Archegetis**, which consisted of a Doric portico and four columns supporting an entablature and pediment. On the pilaster facing the Acropolis is engraved an edict of Hadrian announcing the rules and taxes on the sale of oil.

The Tower of the Winds

The best-preserved and easily the most intriguing of the forum ruins is the graceful octagonal structure known as the **Tower of the Winds** (Aéridhes in Greek). Designed in the first century BC by Andronikos of Kyrrhos, a Syrian astronomer, it served as a compass, sundial, weather vane and water clock – the latter powered by a stream from one of the Acropolis springs.

Each face of the tower is adorned with a relief of a figure floating through the air, personifying the eight winds. On the **north** side (facing Eólou) is Boreas blowing into

---

When the **Romans** ousted Athens' Macedonian rulers and incorporated the city into the vast new province of Achaia in 146 BC, Athens continued to enjoy rare political privileges. Its status as a respected seat of learning and great artistic centre had already been firmly established throughout the ancient world: Cicero and Horace were educated here and Athenian sculptors and architects were supported by Roman commissions. Unlike Corinth, though, which became the administrative capital of the province, the city was endowed with relatively few imperial Roman **monuments**, Hadrian's Arch being perhaps the most obvious. Athenian magistrates, exercising a fair amount of local autonomy, tended to employ architects who would reflect the public taste for the simpler *propylaion*, gymnasium and old-fashioned theatre, albeit with a few Roman amendments.

The city's Roman **history** was shaped pre-eminently by its alliances, which often proved unfortunate. The first major onslaught occurred in 86 BC, when Sulla punished Athens for its allegiance to his rival Mithridates by burning its fortifications and looting its treasures. His successors were more lenient. Julius Caesar proffered a free pardon after Athens had sided with Pompey; and Octavian, who extended the old *agora* by building a forum, showed similar clemency when Athens harboured Brutus following the Ides of March. The most frequent visitor was the **Emperor Hadrian**, who used the occasions to bestow grandiose monuments, including his eponymous arch, a magnificent and immense library and (though it had been begun centuries before) the Temple of Olympian Zeus. A generation later **Herodes Atticus**, a Roman senator who owned extensive lands in Marathon, became the city's last major benefactor of ancient times.

---

a conch shell; **northwest**, Skiron holding a vessel of charcoal; **west**, Zephyros tossing flowers from his lap; **southwest**, Lips speeding the voyage of a ship; **south**, Notos upturning an urn to make a shower; **southeast**, Euros with his arm hidden in his mantle summoning a hurricane; **east**, Apiliotis carrying fruits and wheat; and **northeast**, Kaikias emptying a shield full of hailstones. Beneath each of these, it is still possible to make out the markings of eight sundials.

The semicircular tower attached to the south face was the reservoir from which water was channelled in a steady flow into a cylinder in the main tower; the time was read by the water level viewed through the open northwest door. On the top of the building a bronze Triton revolved with the winds. In Ottoman times dervishes used the tower as a *tekke* or ceremonial hall, terrifying their superstitious Orthodox neighbours with their chanting, music and exercises.

Other forum ruins and Hadrian's library

The other forum ruins open to view are somewhat obscure. Among the more prominent Roman bits and pieces are a large public latrine, a number of shops and a stepped *propylaion* or entrance gate just below the Tower of the Winds. To the northwest is the oldest Ottoman mosque in Athens, the **Fethiye Tzami**, built in 1458. It was dedicated by Sultan Mehmet II, who conquered Constantinople in 1453 (*Fethiye* means "Conqueror" in Turkish). It now is used as an archeological warehouse.

Bordering the north end of the forum site, stretching between Áreos and Eólou, stand the surviving walls of **Hadrian's Library**, an enormous building which once enclosed a cloistered court of a hundred columns. **Odhós Áreos**, alongside, signals the beginning of the Monastiráki flea market area (see p.106). At its end, round behind the forum, are some of the quietest, prettiest and least spoiled streets in the whole of Pláka – many of them ending in steps up to the Anafiótika quarter (see opposite).

Across the street from the Tower of the Winds stands another Turkish relic – a gateway and single dome from a **medresse**, an Islamic school. During the last years of Ottoman rule and the early years of Greek independence it was used as a prison and was notorious for its bad conditions; a plane tree in the courtyard was used for hangings. The prison was closed early in this century and torn down.

The Museum of Greek Popular Musical Instruments

Just beside the *medresse*, at Dhioyénous 1–3, is the **Museum of Greek Popular Musical Instruments** (Tues & Thurs–Sun 10am–2pm, Wed noon–6pm; free). Superbly accommodated in the rooms of a Neoclassical building, this wonderful display traces the history and distribution of virtually everything that has ever been played in Greece, including (in the basement) some not-so-obvious festival and liturgical instruments such as triangles, strikers, livestock bells and coin garlands worn by carnival masquers. Reproductions of frescoes show the Byzantine antecedents of many instruments, and headphone sets are provided for sampling the music made by the various exhibits.

After all this plenty, it's difficult to resist the stock of the museum shop, which includes many of the recommendations in our section on music (see Contexts, p.885), albeit at a slight mark-up.

Monastiráki: the Flea Market area

The northwest districts of Pláka, along Ermoú and Mitropóleos, are noisier, busier and more geared to the Greek life of the city. Neither street lays any claim to beauty, though the bottom (west) half of **Ermoú**, with its metalworkers and other craftsmen, has an attractive workaday character. The top third, from Eólou just west of the pretty Byzantine church of the Kapnikaréa east to Sýndagma Square has been made into an attractive pedestrian mall.

Churches are also the chief feature of **Odhós Mitropóleos** (Cathedral Street). The dusty, tiny chapel of **Ayía Dhynámis** crouches surreally below the concrete piers of the Ministry of Education and Religion; the **Mitrópolis** itself, an undistinguished nineteenth-century cannibal of dozens of older buildings, carves out a square midway along; and the **old cathedral** stands alongside it, a beautiful little twelfth-century church cobbled together from plain and carved blocks, some of which are as ancient as Christendom itself.

Pandhróssou, Platía Monastirakioú and the Mosque of Tzisdarákis

From the bottom corner of the pedestrianized cathedral square, **Odhós Pandhróssou** leads the way into the **Monastiráki Flea Market** – not that its name is really justified by the rich and conventional jewellery and fur shops that pack the first section. In fact, not many genuine market shops remain at all this side of Platía Monastirakíou. With the exception of a couple of specialist icon dealers, everything is geared to the tourist. Most quirky among them is the shop of Stavros Melissinos, the "poet-sandalmaker of Athens", at Pandhróssou 89. Melissinos enjoyed a sort of fame in the 1960s, hammering out sandals for the Beatles, Jackie Onassis and the like; it is said that John Lennon sought him out specifically for his poetic musings on wine and the sea, which Melissinos continues to sell alongside the footwear.

Platía Monastirakioú, full of nut sellers, lottery sellers, fruit stalls, kiosks – and currently metro-digging paraphernalia – gets its name from the little monastery church (*monastiráki*) at its centre, possibly seventeenth century in origin and badly restored in the early twentieth century. The area around has been a marketplace since Turkish times, and maintains a number of Ottoman features. On the south side of the square, rising from the walls of Hadrian's Library and the shacks of Pandhróssou, is the eighteenth-century **Mosque of Tzisdarákis**, now minus minaret and home to the **Museum of Greek Folk Art Kyriazopoulos Ceramic Collection** (daily except

Tues; 9.30am–2pm; 500dr). Donated by a Thessaloníki professor, the collection is devoted to folk sculpture and pottery, together with some decorated household items from various points in the Hellenic world.

The mosque itself, especially its striped *mihrab* (the niche indicating the direction of Mecca) is equally interesting. Above the entrance is a calligraphic inscription recording the mosque's founder and date, and a series of niches used as extra *mihrabs* for occasions when worshippers could not fit into the main hall.

West of Platía Monastirakioú: the flea market proper

West of Monastiráki square, the **flea market** caters more and more for local needs, with clothes, iron- and copperware, tools and records in **Odhós Iféstou**; old furniture, bric-à-brac and camping gear in **Platía Avyssinías**; chairs, office equipment, wood-burning stoves, mirrors, canaries and sundry other goods in **Astíngos**, **Ermoú** and nearby. Beside the church of **Ayíou Filípou**, there's a market in hopeless jumble-sale rejects, touted by a cast of eccentrics (especially on Sundays); of late this extends around the corner, along Adhrianoú, as far as Platía Thisíou.

The north entrance to the **Agora** (see p.99) is just south of Platía Avyssinías on Adhrianoú, across the cutting where the metro line for Pireás re-emerges into the open air after tunnelling under the city centre. Odhós Adhrianoú is here at its most appealing, with a couple of interesting antique shops, a shady kafenío above the metro tunnel, and good views of the Acropolis. (It is also along this stretch that the Sunday second-hand market unfolds itself.) Following the Agora fence around to the southwest, you'll come to another good café vantage-point on busy **Apostólou Pávlou**. On the hill above is the old **Observatory**, surrounded by a last enclave of streets untroubled by tourism or redevelopment. There's nothing of particular interest here, just a pleasant wander through the very north end of Áno Petrálona, although the area is lively at night with a selection of trendy bars and cafés.

North from Pláka: the Bazaar, Omónia square and the National Archeological Museum

When the German Neoclassicists descended on Athens in the 1830s, the land between Pláka and present-day **Omónia square** was envisaged as a spacious European expansion of the Classical and medieval town. Time and the realities of Athens' status as a commercial capital have made a mockery of that grandiose vision: the main **bazaar area** is no less crowded and oriental than Monastiráki, while Omónia itself stubbornly retains a mix of gritty bad taste. For visitors, the focus of interest is the **National Archeological Museum**, which, with its neighbour, the **Polytekhnío**, fronts the student/alternative quarter of **Exárhia**, currently the city's liveliest option for nights out.

The Bazaar: Ermoú to Omónia

A broad triangle of streets, delineated by Pireós (officially Tsaldhári) in the west and Stadhíou in the east, reaches north to its apex at Omónia square. Through the middle run **Athinás** and **Eólou streets** – the modern **bazaar**, whose stores, though stocked mainly with imported manufactured goods, still reflect their origins in their unaffected decor, unsophisticated packaging and, most strikingly, their specialization. Each street has a concentration of particular stores and wares, flouting modern marketing theory. Hence the Monastiráki end of Athinás is dedicated to tools; food stores are gathered around the central market in the middle, especially along Evripídhou; there's glass to the west; paint and brasswork to the east; and clothes in Eólou and Ayíou Márkou. Praxitélous is full of lettering merchants; Platía Klafthmónos and Aristídhou of electrical goods; and department stores cluster around Omónia. Always raucous and teeming with shoppers, *kouloúri* (bread-ring) sellers, gypsies and other vendors, the whole area is great free entertainment. Eólou is now for pedestrians only and is much more pleasant though perhaps not so dramatic to walk along as Athinás.

The best bit is the central **meat** and **seafood** market, on the corner of Athinás and Evripídhou. The building itself is a grand nineteenth-century relic, with fretted iron awnings sheltering forests of carcasses and mounds of hearts, livers and ears – no place for the squeamish. In the middle section of the hall is the fish market, with all manner of bounty from the sea squirming and glistening on the marble slabs. Across Athinás is the fruit and vegetable bazaar arrayed around a suspended archeological dig. On the surrounding streets are rows of grocers, their stalls piled high with sacks of pulses, salt cod, barrels of olives and wheels of cheese.

To the north is the **flower market**, gathered around the church of Ayía Iríni on Eólou. This has stalls through the week but really comes alive with the crowds on a Sunday morning. An additional feature of **Eólou** is its views: walk it north to south, coming from Omónia, and your approach takes you towards the rock of the Acropolis, with the Erechtheion's slender columns and pediment peeking over the edge of the crag.

Around Omónia square

Omónia itself has little to offer. A continuous turmoil of people and cars, it is Athens at its sleaziest and most urban. There are sporadically functioning escalators (the only public ones in Greece) down to the **metro**, and, at the top, *períptera* selling everything from watch straps to porn. The centre is another metro building site. The palms around the perimeter are replacements for their predecessors, which were cut down in the 1950s lest foreigners think Greece "too Asiatic". Destitute Albanian refugees congregate near the square, which has recently developed a reputation for hustle and petty crime, while after dark the area is also frequented by prostitutes and their customers (the main red-light district is on nearby Sofokléous).

To the north, just beside the National Archeological Museum on Patissíon, is the **Polytekhnío**, a Neoclassical building housing the university's school of engineering and science. It was here in late 1973 that students launched their protests against the repressive regime of the colonels' junta, occupying the building and courtyards, and broadcasting calls for mass resistance from a pirate radio transmitter. Large numbers came down to demonstrate support and hand in food and medicines. The colonels' answer came on the night of November 16. Snipers were positioned in neighbouring houses and ordered to fire indiscriminately into the courtyards while a tank broke down the entrance gate. Even today nobody knows how many of the unarmed students were killed – figures range from twenty to three hundred. Although the junta's leader, Papadhópoulos, was able publicly to congratulate the officers involved before being overthrown by secret police chief Ioannídhes, a new, more urgent sense of outrage was spreading; within a year the dictatorship was toppled.

The anniversary of the massacre is invariably commemorated by a march on the US Embassy, outpost of the colonels' greatest ally; it's a bit apathetic nowadays, but still a day out for the Left. The date is also a significant one for the shadowy terrorist group *Dhekaeftá Noémvri* (17 November), which has operated since the early 1980s. With just two or three low-ranking members caught to date, rumour has it that the group enjoys semi-official protection from rogue elements of the powers-that-be.

The National Archeological Museum

Mon 12.30–7pm, Tues–Sun 8am–7pm; 2000dr.

The National Archeological Museum, Patissíon 28, is an unrivalled treasure house of Cycladic, Minoan, Mycenaean and Classical Greek art – and an essential Athens experience. Despite inadequate labelling and generally unimaginative displays, it elbows its way into the list of the world's top ten museums. To avoid disappointment, give yourself a clear morning or afternoon for a visit; better still, take in the collection – which can be overwhelming if you delve beyond the obvious highlights – in two or more separate trips.

The museum's main divisions are: **prehistoric**, with Mycenae predominating; **sculpture** from the Archaic (eighth century BC) to Hellenistic (third to second centuries BC) periods; and **pottery** from the Geometric period (ninth century BC) to the

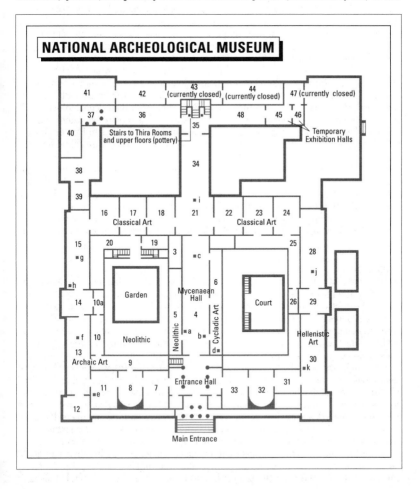

end of the fourth century AD. Smaller self-contained collections include **bronzes** in Rooms 36 to 40; immensely covetable **jewellery** in Room 32; and the brilliant Minoan-style **frescoes** from Thíra (Santoríni) upstairs in Room 48.

Mycenaean and Cycladic art

The biggest crowd-puller is the **Mycenaean hall**, in Room 4. Schliemann's gold finds from Grave Circle A at Mycenae (see p.167) are the big attraction; as hard to get a look at on a summer's day as the Louvre's *Mona Lisa* is the so-called funerary *Mask of Agamemnon* **[a]** in Case 3. Despite the proof offered by modern dating techniques, which indicate that it belonged to some more ancient Achaian king, crowds are still drawn by its correspondence with the Homeric myth.

The Mycenaeans' consummate art was small-scale decoration of rings, cups, seals and inlaid daggers – requiring eye-tiring scrutiny of the packed showcases to appreciate. As well as the death masks, there's a superb golden-horned *Bull's Head* **[b]** in Case 18, and in Case 1 a lovely duck-shaped vase of rock crystal; in Case 3, with the "Agamemnon" mask, is a magnificent inlaid dagger. Case 8 has jewellery, daggers and a miniature golden owl and frog from Nestor's palace at Pylos; alongside, in Case 9, are baked tablets of Linear B, the earliest Greek writing.

On the left wall there are Cretan-style frescoes from Tiryns which depict chariot-borne women watching spotted hounds in pursuit of boar, and bull-vaulting reminiscent of Knossos. More finds from Tiryns, in Case 15, include a large krater with a chariot and warriors. In Case 32 **[c]** are the superb *Vafio* cups, with their scenes of wild bulls and long-tressed, narrow-waisted men, while in Case 33 an equally eye-catching cup is decorated with twining octopuses and dolphins. Further references to Homer abound: in the small Room 3 to the left there's a magnificent *Boar's Tusk Helmet* and an ivory lyre with sphinxes adorning the soundboard.

To the right of the Mycenaean hall, Room 6 houses a large collection of **Cycladic art** – pre-Mycenaean pieces from the Aegean islands. Many of these suggest the abstract forms of modern Cubist art – most strikingly in the much-reproduced *Man Playing a Lyre* **[d]**. Another unusual piece, at the far end of the room, is a sixteenth-century BC cylindrical vase depicting a ring of fishermen carrying fish by their tails. Room 5, to the left of the Mycenaean hall, contains **Neolithic** finds, primarily from excavations in Thessaly.

Sculpture

Most of the rest of the ground floor is occupied by **sculpture**. Beginning in Room 7, on the left of the museum's main entrance, the exhibition proceeds chronologically (and this is the best way to see it) from the Archaic through the Classical and Hellenistic periods (Rooms 7–31) to the Roman- and Egyptian-influenced periods (Rooms 41–43). The gradual development from the stiff, stylized representations of the seventh century BC towards ever freer and looser naturalism is excitingly evident as you go through these cold and rather shabby rooms.

Early highlights include the Aristion *Stele of a Young Warrior* **[e]**, with delicately carved beard, hair and tunic-folds in Room 11, and the Croesus *kouros* (statue of an idealized youth) in Room 13 **[f]**; both are from the late sixth century BC. You need sharp eyes not to miss some of the less obvious delights. Behind the Croesus *kouros*, for instance, and quite untrumpeted, a statueless plinth is carved with reliefs showing, on one side, young men exercising in the gymnasium, on the other a group of amused friends setting a dog and cat to fight each other – a common enough sight in contemporary Greece.

Room 15, which heralds the **Classical art** collection, leaves you in rather less doubt as to its central focus. Right in the middle stands a mid-fifth-century BC *Statue of Poseidon* **[g]**, dredged from the sea off Évvia in the 1920s. The god stands poised to throw his trident – weight on the front foot, athlete's body perfectly balanced, the model of idealized male beauty. A less dramatic, though no less important, piece in the same room is the *Eleusinian Relief* **[h]**. Highly deliberate in its composition, the relief shows the goddess of fertility, accompanied by her daughter Persephone, giving to mankind an ear of corn – symbol of the knowledge of agriculture.

Other major Classical sculptures include the *Little Jockey* (Room 21; **[i]**) seeming too small for his galloping horse, found in the same shipwreck as the *Poseidon*; the fourth-century BC bronze *Ephebe of Antikíthira* **[j]**; the bronze head of a **boxer**, burly and battered, in Room 28; and the third-century BC bronze head of a *Philosopher*, with furrowed brow and unkempt hair, in Room 30. The most reproduced of all the sculptures is also in Room 30: a first-century AD statue of a naked and indulgent *Aphrodite* **[k]** about to rap Pan's knuckles for getting too fresh – a far cry (a long fall, some would say) from the reverent, idealizing portrayals of the gods in Classical times. Room 31 has an extraordinary bronze equestrian portrait statue of the Roman *Emperor Augustus*.

Too numerous to list, but offering fascinating glimpses of everyday life and changing styles of craftsmanship and perception of the human form, are the many **stelai** or carved gravestones found in several of the Classical rooms. Also worth a mention is Room 20, where various Roman copies of the lost Pheidias *Athena*, the original centre-piece of the Parthenon, are displayed.

Upstairs: the Thíra rooms, pottery and coins

Keep a reserve of energy for the **Thíra rooms** upstairs. A visual knockout, these have been reconstructed as they were originally arranged, with their frescoes of monkeys, antelopes and flowers, and furnishings of painted wooden chairs and beds. Discovered at Akrotíri on the island of Thíra (Santórini), they date from around 1450 BC, contemporary with the flourishing Minoan civilization on Crete.

The other upper rooms are occupied by a dizzying array of **pottery**. Rooms 49 and 50 are devoted to the Geometric Period (1000–700 BC), 52 and 53 to sixth-century black-figured pottery, 54 to black- and red-figured pots, and 55 and 56 to funerary white urns and fourth-century pottery. Beautiful though many of the items are, there is absolutely nothing in the way of explanation, and this is probably the section to omit if you are running short of time or stamina.

Exárhia and back towards Sýndagma

Exárhia, fifty-odd blocks squeezed between the National Archeological Museum and Stréfi hill, is perhaps the city's liveliest and most enjoyable night-time destination. Since the early 1980s it has become home to a concentration of ouzeris, nightclubs and genuine music tavernas, many relocated from the Pláka; student budgets confronting bistro prices results in the nursing of a single drink all evening.

In the 1980s, the area was linked – in the press at least – with Athens' disaffected youth, and became synonymous with the so-called anarchists who frightened the sedate and respectable by staving in car windscreens, splattering walls with black graffiti and drug-dealing. Since then, Exárhia has been cleaned up and gentrified, and the reality is not so extreme as Athenians – who like their city pretty savoury – would lead you to believe, though you still see the odd leftover punk or wasted individual.

Back towards Sýndagma

Between the counter-culturality of Exárhia and the occasional frowsiness of the bazaar, the broad busy avenues of Stadhíou, Panepistimíou and Akadhimías are lined with mainstream retailers, usually tucked into cavernous, often opulent arcades that would have gained the approval of the original Bavarian planners.

Except for the blue city buses peeling off behind on Akadhimías and the metro works along Panepistimíou, the grounds of the Neoclassical **National Library** and **University** buildings, bang in the middle of all this, are an oasis of calm. The scattered buildings, designed by the Dane, Christian Hansen, deserve a look, since their garish decoration gives an alarming impression of what the Classical monuments might have looked like when their paintwork was intact. Also worth a stop if you've time are three minor but quite enjoyable museums.

The first of these, on Platía Kolokotróni, housed the parliament from 1874 until 1935, but since 1961 has been home to the **National Historical Museum** (Tues–Sun 8am–2.30pm; 500dr). Its exhibits are predominantly Byzantine and medieval, though there is also a strong section on the War of Independence that includes Byron's sword and helmet.

The second, the **City of Athens Museum** (Mon, Wed & Fri–Sun 8am–2.30pm; 500dr) is at Paparigopoúlou 7, on Platía Klafthmónos. This was the residence of the German-born King Otho in the 1830s before the new palace (now the Parliament, on Sýndagma) was completed in 1842. Exhibits – mainly prints, and still somewhat sparse – feature an interesting model of the city as it was in 1842, with just three hundred houses.

The trio is completed by the **Numismatic Museum** (Tues–Sun 8am–2.30pm; 800dr), newly housed in a grand building at Panepistimíou 12, just up the road from the main university complex. The vast collection of over 400,000 coins, ranging from Mycenean times through Classical, Macedonian and Roman to Byzantine and the modern era, was transferred in 1998 from the National Archeological Museum.

Sýndagma, the National Gardens and south

All roads lead to Platía Syndágmatos – **Sýndagma** (Syntagma) square – so you'll find yourself there sooner or later. Catering to tourism, with a post office (extended hours), American Express, airline and travel offices grouped around – not to mention *McDonalds, Arby's Roast Beef* and *Wendy's* – it has convenience but not much else to recommend it.

The square

Most of the square's buildings are modern and characterless, except on the uphill (east) side where the **Voulí**, the Greek National Parliament, presides. This was built as the royal palace for Greece's first monarch, the Bavarian King Otho, who moved in in 1842. In front of it, goose-stepping **Evzónes** in tasselled caps, kilt and woolly leggings – a prettified version of traditional mountain costume – change their guard at intervals in front of the **Tomb of the Unknown Soldier**, to the rhythm of camera shutters. Hemingway, among others, impugned their masculinity but they are in fact a highly trained elite corps with rigorous height and weight requirements; formerly they were recruited almost exclusively from mountain villages.

Other flanking buildings to have survived postwar development include the vast **Hotel Grande Bretagne** – Athens' grandest. In the course of one of the more nefarious episodes of British meddling in Greek affairs, it nearly became the tomb of Winston Churchill. He had arrived on Christmas Day 1944 to sort out the *Dhekemvrianá*, the "events of December", a month of serious street-fighting between British forces and the Communist-led ELAS resistance movement, whom the British were trying to disarm. ELAS saboteurs had placed an enormous explosive charge in the drains, intending to blow up various Greek and Allied VIPs; according to whom you believe, it was either discovered in time by a kitchen employee, or removed by ELAS themselves when they realized they might get Churchill as well.

"Sýndagma" means "constitution" and the name derives from the fact that Greece's first one was proclaimed by a reluctant King Otho from a palace balcony in 1843. The square is still the principal venue for mass **demonstrations**, whether trade-union protests against the government's austerity programmes or "drive-in" sabotage by taxi-drivers outraged at proposals to curtail their movements in the interest of cleaner air. In the run-up to elections, the major political parties stage their final campaign rallies here – a pretty intimidating sight, with around 100,000 singing, flag-waving Greeks packed into the square. At such times, overground city transport in the area comes to a halt.

The National Gardens

At the back of the Voulí, the **National Gardens** (sunrise to sunset; free) are the most refreshing acres in the whole city – not so much a flower garden as a luxuriant tangle of trees, whose shade and duck ponds provide palpable relief from the heat and smog of summer. They were originally the private palace gardens – a pet project of Queen Amalia in the 1840s; purportedly the main duty of the minuscule Greek navy in its early days was the fetching of rare plants, often the gifts of other royal houses, from remote corners of the globe.

Of late, however, the gardens have fallen on hard times: pond-cleaning and pruning are done only when funding permits, a botanical museum is closed more often than not, and a sorry excuse for a mini-zoo has become the target of criticism by environmental and animal-welfare groups. To add insult to injury, the metro project has requisitioned a large area of the gardens for air vents and site bungalows. The general air of derelic-tion is reinforced by the numerous cats abandoned here and fed only intermittently. Nonetheless, there are few better places in the city to read or wait for an evening ferry or plane.

The southern extension of the gardens, open 24 hours, consists of the graceful crescent-shaped grounds of the **Záppio**. This grand Neoclassical exhibition hall, another creation of the Danish architect Hansen (he of the university), was for a peri-od the Greek State Radio headquarters but is now used mainly for press conferences and commercial exhibitions. A well-shaded **café**, the *Kipos*, is up at the east (uphill) exit of the park on to Iródhou Attikoú (see "Eating and drinking", p.119, for more on these).

Iródhou Attikoú also fronts the **Presidential Palace**, the royal residence until Constantine's exile in 1967, where more *evzónes* stand sentry duty. The surrounding streets, with a full complement of foreign embassies and hardly a store or taverna, are very posh and heavily policed. The centre-right party, *Néa Dhimokratía*, has its head-quarters in Odhós Rigílis nearby, as does the army's Officers' Club, scene of much anti-democratic intriguing in the past.

The Olympic Stadium

A walk to the base of Iródhou Attikoú and across busy Leofóros Ardhittoú will bring you to the **Olympic Stadium**, a nineteenth-century reconstruction on Roman founda-tions, slotting tightly between the pine-covered spurs of Ardhittós hill; access is via the gate on Arhimídhous.

This site was originally marked out in the fourth century BC for the Panathenaic ath-letic contests, but in Roman times, as a grand gesture to mark the reign of the emper-or Hadrian, it was adapted for an orgy of blood sports, with thousands of wild beasts baited and slaughtered in the arena. Herodes Atticus (see p.105) later undertook to refurbish the 60,000 seats of the entire stadium; his white marble gift was to provide the city with a convenient quarry through the ensuing seventeen centuries.

The stadium's reconstruction dates from the modern revival of the Olympic Games in 1896 and to the efforts of another wealthy benefactor, the Alexandrian Greek Yiorgos Averoff. Its appearance – pristine whiteness and meticulous symmetry – must be very much as it was when first restored and reopened under the Roman senator, and indeed it's still used by local athletes and as the finishing point for marathons in major athletic meets. Above the stadium to the south, on the secluded **Hill of Ardhittós**, are a few scant remnants of a Temple of Fortune, again constructed by Herodes Atticus.

Mets and Pangráti

South and east of Ardhittós are the only two central neighbourhoods outside Pláka to have retained something of their traditional flavour – **Mets** and **Pangráti**. Particularly in Mets, a steep hillside quarter on the southwest side of the stadium, there are still nearly intact streets of pre-World War II houses, with tiled roofs, shuttered windows, and courtyards with spiral metal staircases and potted plants. They're a sad reminder of how beautiful this out-of-control city once was, even quite recently.

Mets and the Próto Nekrotafío

More specific attractions in **Mets** are the concentration of tavernas and bars around Márkou Moussoúrou and Arhimídhous (see p.124), and the Próto Nekrotafío (First Cemetery), at the top end of Anapáfseos (Eternal Rest) street, itself lined with shops catering to the funerary trade.

The **Próto Nekrotafío** shelters just about everybody who was anybody in nineteenth- and twentieth-century Greek public life: the humbler tombs of singers, artists and writers are interspersed with ornate mausolea of soldiers, statesmen and "good" families, whose descendants come to picnic, stroll and tend the graves. One of the "unregarded wonders of Athenian life", Peter Levi called it: "the neoclassical marbles run riot, they reflower as rococo, they burst into sunblasts of baroque." The graveside statuary occasionally attains the status of high art, most notably in the works of Ianoulis Halepas, a Belle Epoque sculptor from Tínos generally acknowledged to be the greatest of a school of fellow-islanders. Halepas battled with mental illness for most of his life and died in extreme poverty in 1943; his masterpiece is the idealized **Kimiméni** (Sleeping Girl), on the right about 300 metres in.

Pangráti

Pangráti is the unremarkable but pleasant quarter to the north and east of the Stadium. Platía Plastíra, Platía Varnáva and Platía Pangratíou are the focal points, the first with a vast old-fashioned kafenío where you can sit for hours on a leafy terrace for the price of a coffee. Pangratíou, fringed by the local *álsos* or grove-park, is the rallying place for the neighbourhood's youthful posers. Several good tavernas are tucked away between (and on) Platía Varnáva and nearby Odhós Arhimídhous, and the latter has an impressive *laïkí agorá* – **street market** – every Friday.

More Pangráti eating places are down towards Leofóros Vas. Konstandínou, among the rather claustrophobic alleys opposite the **statue of Harry Truman** – repeatedly restored to his pedestal after being blown off it by leftists in reprisal for his bringing the US into the Greek civil war. The Nobel-laureate poet **George Seferis** lived not far away in Odhós Ágras, an attractive stair-street flanking the northeast wall of the Olympic Stadium.

North of Sýndagma: Kolonáki, Lykavitós and the Benáki and Cycladic Art museums

Athens is at its trendiest north of Sýndagma, and if you have money to spend, **Kolonáki** is the place to do it, catering to every Western taste from fast food to high fashion. The quarter is not especially interesting for visitors to the city – though it's a fond haunt of expatriates – but it does give access to **Lykavitós hill**, where a funicular hauls you up for some of the best views of the city. Also close by are two fine museums: one devoted to **Cycladic Art**, the other, the **Benáki**, an assembly of just about all things Greek, from Mycenaean artefacts to twentieth-century memorabilia. Here too, what is believed to be the fourth-century BC foundations of **Aristotle's Lyceum** were recently unearthed, during routine excavation work for a new Museum of Modern Art. The discovery of the Lyceum, where Aristotle taught for thirteen years and Socrates was a frequent visitor, is of immense importance to scholars.

Kolonáki

Kolonáki is the city's most chic central address and shopping area. Although no great shakes architecturally, it enjoys a superb site on the southwest-facing slopes of Lykavitós (Lycabettus), looking out over the Acropolis and National Gardens. From its summit, on one of those increasingly rare clear days, you can see the mountains of the Peloponnese. The lower limits of Kolonáki are defined by Akadhimías and Vasilíssis Sofías streets, where in grand Neoclassical palaces Egypt, France and Italy have their embassies. The middle stretches of the quarter are for shopping, while the highest are purely residential.

The heart of the district is officially called Platía Filikís Eterías, but is known to all as **Kolonáki square**, after the ancient "little column" that hides in the trees on the southwest side. Other diversions include the kiosks with their stocks of foreign papers and magazines, the **British Council** on the downhill side, and numerous cafés on Patriárhou Ioakím to the east – the principal display ground for Kolonáki's well-heeled natives. Assorted cafés and pubs nearby on pedestrianized Tsakálof, Milióni and Valaorítou are better and slightly cheaper options for snacks and drinks.

Kolonáki's streets also contain an amazing density of small, classy **shops**, with the accent firmly on **fashion** and **design**. In a half-hour walk around the neighbourhood you can view the whole gamut of consumer style. Patriárhou Ioakím and Skoufá, with its cross-streets to the northwest, comprise the most promising area, along with the pedestrianized Voukourestíou-Valaorítou-Kriezótou block, just below Akadhimías.

For more random strolling, the highest tiers of Kolonáki are pleasant, with steep streets ending in long flights of steps, planted with oleander, jasmine and other flowering shrubs. The one **café** spot up here is at **Platía Dhexamenís**, a small and attractive square close to the Lykavitós loop road, where for most of the year tables are set under the trees around the **Dhexamení**, a covered reservoir begun by the emperor Hadrian.

Lykavitós Hill

Not far away from Kolonáki square, at the top of Ploutárhou, a **funicular** (Mon–Wed & Fri–Sun 8.45am–12.40am, Thurs 10.30am–12.40am, every 10min in summer, less frequent the rest of the year; 500dr) begins its ascent to the summit of **Lykavitós hill**. For the more energetic, the principal path up the hill begins by the bus stop across from the St George Lycabettus Hotel above Platía Dhexamenís and rambles through woods to the top. There's a small café half way up eyeball-to-eyeball with the Acropolis. On the summit, the chapel of **Áyios Yeóryios** dominates – a spectacular place to celebrate the saint's name-day if you're around on April 23. An expensive restaurant commands the adjacent terrace facing the Acropolis and the sea. The restaurant also operates a café on the terrace facing inland.

The road up the hill goes to the open-air **Lykavitós Theatre**, which is used primarily as a music venue during the Athens Summer Festival (see p.131) and hosts other diverse acts between May and October. If you come down by the southeast slopes, you emerge near the lovely little enclave that the British and American archeological schools have created for themselves on Odhós Souidhías. Here, too, is the **Yennádhion Library**, with large collections of books on Greece and an unpublicized drawer full of Edward Lear's watercolour sketches; good-quality and reasonably priced reproductions are on sale.

The Benáki Museum

Once it reopens from a lengthy refit (scheduled for 2000), this overlooked **museum** at Koumbári 1/cnr Vasilíssis Sofías, should not be missed. Housing a private collection given to the state by **Emmanuel Benakis**, a collector who had grown wealthy on the Nile cotton trade, it is constantly surprising and fascinating, with exhibits ranging from Mycenaean jewellery, Greek costumes and folk artefacts to Byronia, and memorabilia of the Greek War of Independence – even a reconstructed Egyptian palace reception hall. These, together with displays of jewellery and other items from the Hélène Stathatos collection (of National Archeological Museum fame) are worth an hour or two of anyone's time.

Among the more unusual exhibits are collections of early Greek Gospels, liturgical vestments and church ornaments rescued by Greek refugees from Asia Minor in 1922; dazzling embroideries and body ornaments; and some unique historical material – on the Cretan statesman Eleftherios Venizelos, Asia Minor and the Cretan Revolution.

An additional attraction, especially if you've been dodging traffic all day, is the **rooftop café**, with good snacks and views over the nearby National Gardens. A **shop** (Mon–Sat 9am–3pm), by the entrance, has remained open during the museum's extended closure and stocks a fine selection of books on Greek folk art, records of regional music and some of the best posters and postcards in the city. The nineteenth-century **Stathatos House** now functions as a wing of the museum, containing Greek art collection of the Academy of Athens.

Goulandhrís Museum of Cycladic and Ancient Greek Art

For display, labelling, explanation and comfort, the small private **Goulandhrís Museum of Cycladic and Ancient Greek Art** (Mon, Wed–Fri 10am–4pm, Sat 10am–3pm; 1000dr, Sat 500dr) on Neofýtou Dhouká, is way ahead of anything else in Athens. The collection includes objects from the Cycladic civilization (third millennium BC), pre-Minoan Bronze Age (second millennium BC) and the period from the fall of Mycenae to the beginning of historic times around 700 BC, plus a selection of Archaic, Classical and Hellenistic pottery; you learn far more about these periods than from the corresponding sections of the National Archeological Museum.

If Cycladic art seems an esoteric field, don't be put off. The distinctive marble bowls and folded-arm figurines with their sloping wedge heads are displayed in a way that highlights their supreme purity and simplicity, and elucidates their appeal to twentieth-century artists like Moore, Picasso and Brancusi. You can also see in the figurines the remote ancestry of the Archaic style that evolved into the great sculptures of the

Classical period. The exact purpose of the mostly female effigies is unknown but, given their frequent discovery in grave-barrows, it has been variously surmised that they were spirit-world guides for the deceased, substitutes for the sacrifice of servants and attendants, or representations of the Earth Goddess in her role of reclaiming yet another of her children.

Much of the top floor is devoted to a collection of painted Classical bowls, often showing two unrelated scenes on opposite sides. The curators consider the one with a depiction of revellers on one face and three men in cloaks conversing on the other to be the star exhibit, but there is not one dud. Most of the more exquisite items date from the fifth century BC – not for nothing was it referred to as a "Golden Age".

To round off the experience, there's a good **shop**, **snack bar** and shaded courtyard.

Other nearby museums

A number of other museums of somewhat more specialist interest are grouped conveniently close together near the angled intersection of Vasilíssis Sofías and Vasiléos Konstandínou, close by the Benáki and Cycladic Art museums.

Byzantine Museum

The setting of the **Byzantine Museum** (Tues–Sun 8am–2.30pm; 500dr) at Vasilíssis Sofías 22 is perhaps its best feature: a peaceful, courtyarded villa that once belonged to the Duchesse de Plaisance, an extravagantly eccentric French philhellene and widow of a Napoleonic general who helped fund the War of Independence. To enjoy the exhibits – almost exclusively icons, housed in two restored side galleries – requires some prior interest, best developed by a trip to the churches at Mystrás, Dhafní or Ósios Loukás. Labelling is generally Greek-only and you are told little of the development of styles, which towards the sixteenth century show an increasing post-Renaissance Italian influence, due to the presence of the Venetians in Greece. The rear hall contains marble artefacts, plus a reconstructed basilica. An annexe is currently under construction, which will hopefully mean better exposure for artefacts previously held in storage.

War Museum

The only "cultural" endowment of the 1967–74 junta, the **war museum** (Tues–Fri 9am–2pm, Sat & Sun, 9.30am–2pm; free) at Vasilíssis Sofías 24 becomes predictably militaristic and right-wing as it approaches modern events: the Asia Minor campaign, the civil war, Greek forces in Korea, etc. Earlier times, however, are covered with a more scholarly concern and this gives an interesting insight into changes in warfare from Mycenae through to the Byzantines and Turks. Among an array of models is a fascinating series on the acropolises and castles of Greece, both Classical and medieval.

National Gallery of Art

The **National Gallery Alexandros Soutsos** (Mon & Wed–Sat 9am–3pm, Sun 10am–2pm; 1000dr) at Vasiléos Konstandínou 50, has a rather disappointing core collection of Greek art from the sixteenth century to the present although a planned refurbishment in 1999 promises to introduce some new blood. Until then one of the few modern painters to stand out is Nikos Hatzikyriakos-Ghikas (Ghika), who is well represented on the ground floor. On the mezzanine is a small group of canvases by the primitive painter Theophilos (more of whose work can be seen at the Museum of Greek Folk Art in Pláka – see p.101). Temporary exhibitions can be worth catching; keep an eye out for posters or check in *The Hellenic Times* or *Athens News*.

The outskirts: Dhafní, Kessarianí and Kifissiá

Athens pushes its suburbs higher and wider with each year and the **monasteries of Dhafní** and **Kessarianí**, once well outside the city limits, are now approached through more or less continuous cityscape. However, each retains a definite countryside setting and makes for a good respite from the central sights.

The monasteries are easily reached by taxi or by local **city transport**. For Dhafní (9km west of the centre), take bus A16, B16 or A16 from Platía Elesthérias, 300m down Pireós from Omónia; the monastery is to the left of the road, about twenty minutes' ride (Platía Eleftthérias is popularly known as Platía Koumoundoúrou and the return buses are so marked). For Kessarianí, take blue bus #224 from Akadhimías to the last stop, from where the church is a thirty- to forty-minute climb further up the lower slopes of Mount Imittós.

The northern suburb of **Kifissiá** is included in this section as an insight into wealthy Athenian life – it has long been where the rich have their villas – and for natural history students, who may want to check out the Goulandhrís Museum. Kifissiá is the most northerly stop on the metro.

Classical enthusiasts may want to continue from Dhafní to the site of **Eleusis** (see p.149), a further twenty-minute ride on the A16 bus route.

Dhafní

Dhafní Monastery (daily 8am–2.30pm; 500dr) is one of the great buildings of Byzantine architecture. Its classic Greek-cross-octagon design is a refinement of a plan first used at Ósios Loukás, on the road to Delphi (see p.274), and its mosaics are considered among the great masterpieces of the Middle Ages.

The monastic church replaced a fortified fifth-century basilica, which in turn had been adapted from the ruins of a sanctuary of Apollo – the name is derived from the *daphnai* (laurels) sacred to the god. Both the church and the fortifications which enclose it incorporate blocks from the ancient sanctuary; a porch featuring Classical columns was present up until two centuries ago, when it was hauled off among Lord Elgin's swag.

The Byzantines only occupied the building for little over a century. When the monastery was established, in 1070, the Greek Church was undergoing an intellectual revival, but the state was in terminal collapse. The following year the Normans took Bari, the last Byzantine possession in southern Italy, and the Seljuk Turks defeated the Byzantine army in Armenia – a prelude to the loss of Asia Minor and, before long, Greece itself. The fortifications and remains of a Gothic cloister show evidence of later building under the Cistercians, who replaced Dhafní's Orthodox monks after the Frankish conquest of Athens in 1204. The monastery today is unoccupied; the Cistercians were banished by the Turks, and Orthodox monks, allowed to return in the sixteenth century, were duly expelled for harbouring rebels during the War of Independence.

Inside the church, the **mosaic cycle** is remarkable for its completeness: there are scenes from the life of Christ and the Virgin, saints (a predominance of Eastern figures from Syria and elsewhere in the Levant), archangels and prophets. The greatest triumph is the *Pandókrator* (Christ in Majesty) on the dome: lit by the sixteen windows of the drum, and set against a background of gold, this stern image directs a tremendous and piercing gaze, his finger poised on the Book of Judgement. A perfect encapsulation of the strict orthodoxy of Byzantine belief, the scene is rendered poignant by the troubled circumstances in which it was created.

Kessarianí

What it loses in a strict architectural comparison with Dhafní, **Kessarianí monastery** makes up for in its location. Although just five kilometres from the centre of the city, it is high enough up the slopes of Mount Imittós to escape the *néfos* and the noise. The sources of the river Ilissos provide for extensive gardens hereabouts, as they have since ancient times (Ovid mentions them); Athenians still come to collect water from the local fountains, though it may have become contaminated and should not be drunk.

The monastery buildings date from the eleventh century, though the frescoes in the chapel are much later – executed during the sixteenth and seventeenth centuries. In contrast to Dhafní's clerics, Kessarianí's abbot agreed to submit to Roman authority when the Franks took Athens, so the monastery remained in continuous Greek (if not quite Orthodox) occupation through the Middle Ages. Today the monastery is maintained by a small group of monks, who allow **visits** (Tues–Sun 8am–2.30pm; 800dr). Outside these hours you can while away the time in the well-maintained grounds, full of picnickers in summertime.

On the way up to the monastery, which is fairly obvious from the bus terminal, don't overlook the refugee neighbourhood of Kessarianí. With an attractively casual, ramshackle aspect, its streets were used as a 1920s location for the Greek movie *Rembetiko*. You can also catch a glimpse, not far to the north, of the uniform modern blocks of Panepistimioúpoli, the university campus.

Kifissiá

Kifissiá, one of Athens's most desirable suburbs, edges up the leafy slopes of Mount Pendéli, about ten kilometres north of the city centre. A surprising 300m above sea level and a good 5°F cooler than central Athens, it appealed to the nineteenth-century bourgeoisie as a suitable site for summer residence. Their villas – Neoclassical, Swiss, Alsatian and fantasy-melange – still hold their own amid the newer concrete models. Indeed, despite the encroachments of speculators' apartment buildings and trendy boutiques, the suburb's village-like character prevails.

The centre of the old "village" is the crossroads called Plátanos – though the mighty plane tree that gave it its name has long since fallen under the axe of the traffic planners – just at the uphill end of the gardens opposite the Kifissiá metro station. The hub is the two or three streets around Plátanos: *Varsos*, in the middle of the block up Kassavéti from Platía Platánou, an old-fashioned patisserie specializing in home-made yoghurts, jams and sticky cakes, acts as a meeting place for the whole neighbourhood. Most other watering holes are trendy and pricey cafés and bars, full of young locals preening themselves, checking out the designer competition and yakking on their mobiles.

If you want some direction to your wanderings around trees and gardens, head for the **Goulandhrís Natural History Museum** (Sat & Sun 9am–2pm; 800dr) at Levídhou 13, fifteen minutes' walk from the metro. The collection has especially good coverage of Greek birds and butterflies and endangered species like the monk seal (*Monachus monachus*; see p.776) and sea turtle (*Caretta caretta*; see p.834) and a 250,000-specimen herbarium. The museum has a café and a shop selling superb illustrated books, postcards, posters and prints.

Eating and drinking

As you'd expect in a city that houses almost half the Greek population, Athens has the best and the most varied **restaurants** and **tavernas** in the country – and most places are sources not just of good food but of a good night out.

Starting with **breakfast**, most Athenians survive on a thimbleful of coffee, but if you need a bit more to set you up for the day, you'll easily find a bakery, yoghurt shop or fruit stall. Koukáki is particularly good for this, with the *Nestoras Tzatsos* bakery at Veïkoú 45, another at no. 75, and still another on pedestrianized Olymbíou, just off Platía Koukáki, offering excellent wholegrain bread and milk products. Alternatively, you could try one of the places listed under "Tea houses and patisseries" on p.126. For a regular **English breakfast**, there are several options in and around Pláka. The cheapest and friendliest place is at Níkis 26; a second choice is at Kydathinéon 10, near the corner of Moní Asteríou; or try the omelettes and croissants at Neon, Mitropóleos 3.

Later in the day, a host of **snack** stalls and outlets gets going. If your budget is low you can fill up at them exclusively, avoiding sit-down restaurants altogether. The standard **snacks** are *souvláki me píta* (kebab in pitta bread), *tyrópites* (cheese pies) and *spanakópites* (spinach pies), along with *bougátses* (cream pies) and a host of other speciality pastries. One of the best **souvláki** stands in Pláka is widely acknowledged to be *Kostas'*, at Adhrianoú 116, which usually has a queue, and there is a cluster of good ones around Exárhia square, while those in the immediate vicinity of Omónia are best avoided. At Omónia, however, and at several other points in the city look out for the Everest chain, which does a nice line in pastries, sandwiches and ice cream. There is a *Bagel Café* at 9b Karayeóryi Servías, just below Sýndagma, while the *Arístoπ* around the corner at Voulís 10 has been famous for years for its good, inexpensive *tirópites*.

For **main meals**, Pláka's hills and lanes are full of character, and provide a pleasant evening setting, despite the aggressive touts and general tourist hype. But for good value and good quality, only a few of the quarter's restaurants and tavernas are these days worth a second glance. For quality Greek cooking, if you're staying any length of time in the city, it's better to strike out into the ring of **neighbourhoods** around: to Méts, Pangráti, Exárhia/Neápoli, Koukáki, Áno Petrálona or the more upmarket Kolonáki. None of these is more than a half-hour's walk, or a quicker trolley bus or taxi ride, from the centre – effort well repaid by more authentic menus, and often a livelier atmosphere.

Restaurants

The listings below are devoted mainly to **restaurant meals**, grouped according to district and divided into cheap (under 4000dr per person) and less so (over 4000dr). Note that some of our recommendations are closed in summer (usually in August), and for five days or so around Easter; this is usually due to hot, un-air-conditioned locales, or the exodus of their regular business trade.

Pláka

Selections here represent just about all of note that **Pláka** has to offer; most are on the periphery of the quarter, rather than on the more travelled squares and stairways. At the latter, don't be bamboozled by the touts, positioned at crucial locations to lure you over to their tavernas' tables – invariably a bad sign.

UNDER 4000DR

Damingos, Kydhathinéon 41. Tucked away in the basement, this place has dour service, but is good value, with barrelled wine and excellent *bakaliáro skordhaliá* (cod with garlic sauce). Evenings only; closed mid-July to end August.

Iy Klimataria, Klepsýdhras 5. Recently celebrated its centenary and still going strong, this unpretentious and pleasant taverna has decent food, with live, unamplified music in the winter. In the summer the roof opens and the quiet shaded street becomes an oasis. Mainly grilled meat and fish. There's a good combination bar and sweetshop just down the steps.

Skholiarhio To Gerani, Tripódhon 14. Attractive split-level taverna which serves a good selection of mezédhes like flaming sausages and *bouréki* (thin pastry filled with ham and cheese) and good house red wines; it has a perennially popular summer terrace.

OVER 4000DR

Eden, Lissíou 12, off Mnesikléous. The city's oldest vegetarian restaurant offers dishes you'll pine for on travels around Greece such as mushroom stew, chili and lasagna; the setting is pleasant as well, on the ground floor of an old house. Portions not huge but very tasty.

Nefeli, cnr Aretoúsas & Pános. Rather touristy with live music but a great setting high up towards the Acropolis and an interesting selection of beef and lamb dishes in unusual sauces. The adjacent synonymous ouzerí is a more genuine local hangout.

O Platanos, Dhioyénous 4. One of the oldest tavernas in Pláka, with outdoor summer seating under the namesake tree. Serves lunch and supper. Specialities include cuttlefish and roast beef with various vegetables. Closed Sun.

Monastiráki, Psyrrí and the Bazaar
The shift from Pláka to the more genuinely commercial quarter of **Monastiráki** is refreshing, since the area attracts serious eaters. There is a definite character about the streets, too, at its best around the flea market. A few blocks west of Athinás the up and coming area of **Psyrrí** is now home to a throng of trendy *mezedhopolía* and bars that line the crossroads of Ayíon Anaryíron and Táki. The trio of places within the **meat market** are open through the night and offer a fascinating glimpse of the capital's high and low life at nocturnal play.

UNDER 4000DR

Bairaktaris, Platía Monastirakioú 2. Large modernized old restaurant whose walls are lined with wine barrels and paintings. Straightforward menu of grilled and oven dishes. Daily 7am–3am.

To Monastiri, central meat market (entrance from Eólou 81). The best of the three restaurants here; the raw ingredients are certainly fresh, and there's *patsás* (tripe and trotter soup) if you're in desperate need of a hangover cure. Daily 24hrs.

Iy Taverna Tou Psyrrí, Eskhýlou 12, Psyrrí. One of the most original and cheapest establishments in the area, there is a tasty selection of fare like *thrápsalo* (huge squid), rare fish and chunky *tyrópites*.

O Thanasis, Mitrópoleos 69. Reckoned to be the best *souvláki* and kebab place in this part of Athens. Always packed with locals at lunchtime.

OVER 4000DR

Zidhoron, Táki 10, Psyrrí. *Mezedhopolío,* fairly typical of the area, painted bright yellow and featuring foods with a Middle Eastern flavour like *pastourmás, haloúmi* and hummus.

Exárhia/Platía Viktorías
Exárhia is still surprisingly untrodden by tourists, considering its proximity to the centre. Its eating and drinking establishments are conveniently close to the National Archeological Museum and several recommended hotels, and exploring them gives some insight into how the student/youth/alternative crowd carries on.

UNDER 4000DR

Barba Yannis, Emm. Benáki 94, Exárhia. Varied menu of home-style oven food (changes daily) in a relaxed atmosphere, aided and abetted by barrel wine. Tables outside on pedestrianized street in summer. Very popular and open all day until the small hours.

O Dhourios Ippos, Koletti 21b, Exárhia. Grill with winter basement and leafy summer roof terrace. Fine liver, fried courgettes and tiny *tyropittákia.*

Oasis, Valtetsíou 44, Exárhia. A wonderful taverna with seating in the garden, and a varied menu of largely meat dishes..

Rozalia, Valtetsíou 58, Exárhia. The best mezédhes-plus-grill taverna immediately around the platía, with highly palatable white and red barrelled wine. You order from the proffered tray as the waiters thread their way through the throng. Garden opposite in summer.

The Three Brothers, Elpídhos 7, Platía Viktorías. Wide range of grilled meat and fish plus mezédhes.

Vangelis, Sahíni, off Liossíon (200m up from Platía Váthis). Simply one of the friendliest and most traditional tavernas in the city. Oven casseroles and 1950s decor. Grilled food available in the evening, including great *kokorétsi* and *kondosoúvli*. Open garden at the back.

OVER 4000DR

Kostoyiannis, Zaími 37, behind the National Archeological Museum. One of the city's best restaurants – much frequented by crowds from the theatres and cinemas around. Quality mezédhes and delicacies like rabbit stew. Evenings only. Closed Sun.

FOREIGN CUISINE RESTAURANTS

Healthy as it may be, you may tire of Greek food, especially during an extended visit. Unlike the rest of the country, Athens offers a fair selection, from highly chi-chi **French** places, through **Eastern European**, **Armenian** and **Arabic**, to **Japanese** and **Korean**. Listed below are some of the more central places, which don't require a large outlay in taxi fares to reach – others are to be found at the beach suburbs to the south. Eating non-Greek in Athens is comparatively expensive: budget for 5000–8000dr per person.

Unless otherwise indicated, the places listed below are closed in high summer and on Sunday, but otherwise stay open until 1.30am. Reservations are advisable.

ARMENIAN-TURKISH

Tria Asteria, Mélitos 7, Néa Smyrni, at end of #10 trolley line (☎93 58 134). Specialities include *tandir kebab* and *kionefe*, a special stuffed-filo dessert. Open in summer.

BRAZILIAN

Planeta Samba, Sarandapígou 15–17, Neápoli, on the Lykavitós ringroad (☎36 15 488). *Vatapa*, *muceca* and a filling buffet to the tune of lively samba sounds.

CHINESE

Dragon Palace, Andínoros 3, Pangráti, off map not far from the National Gallery (☎72 42 795). Cantonese dishes such as Peking duck. Open in summer.

Golden Dragon, Olymbíou 27–29/Syngroú 122, Koukáki, off map down Syngroú (☎92 32 316). A cut above average: ginger chicken, stuffed chicken wings, beef sate etc. Open in summer.

The Great Wall, Asklipíou 74, Neápoli (☎36 18 973). Wide range of soups, meat and seafood dishes, including spicier Sechuan style. Small courtyard in summer. Free delivery.

CZECH

Bohemia, Dhímou Tséliou, Ambelókipi, a few blocks north of the old Panathinaikos stadium on Leofóros Alexándras(☎64 26 341). *Knedliki*, *svitsova* and Czech beers; open in summer.

Svejk, Roúmbesi 8a, Néos Kósmos, off map east of Syngroú (☎90 18 389). Rich stew-like main courses, also duck and carp according to season. Closed Mon.

ETHIOPIAN

Axum, Dhrossopoúlou 183, Platía Koliátsou, close to Patissíon trolley routes #5 & 12 (☎20 11 774). Genuine African cuisine, eaten with the fingers and accompanied by traditional music at weekends. Very good value. Closed Tues but open all year.

Neápoli

Neápoli is a long walk or short bus ride up Hariláou Trikoúpi from Exárhia, with a concentration of calmer clubs, bars and cinemas that make it a favourite dining-out area for savvy locals. The food here is good, teetering to either side of the 4000dr divider. Mavromiháli is parallel to and one street higher up the slopes of **Lykavitós** from Hariláou Trikoúpi.

Alexandra, Zonára 21. Aubergine croquettes, beetroot salad with walnuts and meat in various sauces are among the imaginative dishes in this converted old house.

Ta Bakiria, Mavromiháli 119. Among the less usual dishes are salads with mayonnaise and beef in a mushroom sauce. Atmospheric but smoky interior for wintertime and a small summer courtyard. Closed Sun.

Iy Lefka, Mavromiháli 121. Standard taverna fare, including great *fava*, black-eyed beans, baked and grilled meat with barrelled retsina. Summer seating in a huge garden enclosed by barrels.

FRENCH

L'Abreuvoir, Xenokrátous 51, Kolonáki (☎72 29 106). Modern ambience with rare specialities like duck steak in cherry vinegar and a wide selection of French wines. Open daily and summer.

Prunier, Ipsilándou 63, Kolonáki (☎72 27 379). Central and unpretentious bistro. Imported French wines.

GERMAN

Ritterburg, Formíonos 11, Pangráti, off map past Platía Plastíra (☎72 38 421). Schnitzels, sausages and the like.

ITALIAN

Al Convento, Anapíron Polémou 4–6, Kolonáki (☎72 39 163). Claims to be the oldest Italian restaurant in Athens; the speciality is pasta and scallopine. Open in summer. Closed Sun.

Liberty, Loukianoú 36, Kolonáki (☎72 47 283). Some more interesting main courses like stuffed chicken, fafales and pennes – not just the usual pasta variations.

JAPANESE

Michiko, Kydhathinéon 27, Pláka (☎32 20 980). Touristy and expensive – but very central and surprisingly authentic. Open in summer.

The Sushi Bar, Platía Varnáva, Mets (☎75 24 354). Decent range of sushi, tempura and soups in an authentic bright atmosphere. Takeaway and delivery too. Open daily and summer.

KOREAN

Seoul, Evritanías 8, off Panórmou in Ambelókipi (☎69 24 669). Speciality Korean barbecue. Garden seating in summer.

Orient, Lékka 26, Sýndagma (☎32 21 192). Also Chinese and Japanese dishes. Open in summer.

MEXICAN

Senor Frog, Anapíron Polémou 10, Kolonáki (☎72 24 524). Wider international menu as well as the standard chili dishes.

RUSSIAN

Valentina, Lykoúrgou 235, Kallithéa, not far from metro station (☎94 31 871). An array of dishes like borscht and stroganoff at taverna prices. Open in summer.

O Pinaleon, Mavromiháli 152. Rich mezédhes (choose from tray brought to table) and meaty entrées, washed down with homemade wine, lovingly brewed by the chef/owner from Híos. Open mid-Oct to late May.

Strefis Taverna tis Xanthis, Irínis Athinéas 5. House specialities include rabbit stew and schnitzel. A pleasant old mansion with a roof garden that offers fine view across northern Athens. Mon–Sat 9pm–2am.

Tram, Mavromiháli 168. Fine Neoclassical building with spacious roof terrace and unusual dishes like stuffed onions, beef with bacon and mushrooms and *pastourmadhopittákia*.

Kolonáki

Kolonáki has a ritzy, upmarket reputation that puts off a lot of tourists. Nonetheless, among the boutiques are some surprising finds.

UNDER 4000DR

To Kioupi, Platía Kolonáki. Subterranean taverna. Good standard Greek food. Closed Sun & Aug.

OVER 4000DR

Dhimokritos, Dhimokrítou 23. A bit snooty, but a beautiful building and well-prepared food from a vast menu. Open lunchtime and evenings. Closed late summer and Sundays.

Maritsa's, Voukourestíou 47. Posh interior and pavement seating. Specializes in seafood like crawfish fritters, lobster spaghetti and grilled mussels.

Rodhia, Aristípou 44, near the base of the *funicular*. Main courses include beef in lemon sauce and lamb fricassee. Closed Sun.

Pangráti and Méts

These two neighbourhoods feature some of the city's best eating places. All the places below are a short (if generally uphill) walk across busy Ardhitóu and past the Olympic stadium, or accessible via a #2, #4 or #12 trolley ride to Platía Plastíra. **Goúva** is an extension of Méts, just south of the First Cemetery.

UNDER 4000DR

O Ilias, cnr Stasínou/Telesílis, Pangráti. A very good and very popular taverna with standard menu. Evenings only. Tables outside in summer.

To Kalyvi, Empedhokléous 26 (off Platía Varnáva), Pangráti. Excellent, traditional mezédhes-type fare. Rustic decor and live music. Closed late May–late Sept.

Karavitis, Arktínou 35, off Leofóros Vas. Konstandínou, Pangráti. Old-style taverna with bulk wine, mezédhes and clay-cooked main courses. Indoor and outdoor seating.

O Megaritis, Ferekídhou 2, Pangráti. Casserole food, barrel wine, indoor and terrace seating. Open all year.

Prasino, John Kennedy 23 (cnr Vrioúlon), Pangráti, off map beyond Filoláou. Caters to refugee clientele with Anatolian-style food, including brains. Tables out on pavement in summer. Closed Mon.

O Vyrinis, Arhimídhous 11 (off Platía Plastíra), Pangráti. Good-quality taverna, with its own house wine and a wide variety of mezédhes. Tables in garden in summer.

OVER 4000DR

Pergoulia, Márkou Moussoúrou 16, Pangráti. Delicious, unusual mezédhes – being English-run there are some set meals options. Air-conditioned in summer.

To Strateri, Platía Plíta 3, Goúva, off map below the cemetery. A good, slightly upmarket psistariá. Outdoor seating in the park in summer.

Xanthippi, Arhimídhous 14, Pangráti. Just behind the stadium this converted old house offers interesting mezédhes, crepes and meat combos.

Koukáki

This is one of the most pleasant parts of the city in which to while away the middle of a day or round off an evening, having wandered down from the south slope of the Acropolis or Filopáppou hill. It's very much middle-class, residential Athens – uneventful and a bit early-to-bed, except for the lively pedestrianized streets of Dhrákou, Zínni and Olymbíou, teeming with trendy bars, cafeterias and eateries. The districts straddle the #1, #5 and #9 trolley lines.

UNDER 4000DR

Iy Gardhinia, Zínni 29. Extremely basic, inexpensive casserole food and barrel wine in a cool, cavernous setting. Lunchtime only in summer.

To Ikositseroöro, Syngroú 42/44. The name means "open round-the-clock", and that's its main virtue. Fair, if rather overpriced, portions of anti-hangover food such as lamb tongues and *patsás*. At its liveliest after midnight in summer.

To Meltemi, Zínni 26. A modest-priced ouzerí that shields its customers from street traffic with banks of greenery. Offers a wide range of mezédhes dishes, but the emphasis is on seafood. Closed Sun.

Ouzeri Evvia, Olymbíou 8, off map further down Veíkou. Hearty food as well as drink served on the pedestrian way, very reasonable and informal.

Iy Rouga, Olymbíou 2, off map further down Veíkou. Lunchtime oven food and evening grill with friendly service.

OVER 4000DR

Socrates' Prison, Mitséon 20 (below Herodes Atticus theatre), Makriyánni. Long a justifiably popular but touristy taverna, with sidewalk tables. Unusual dishes include chickpeas with bacon and spicy meatballs in a clay pot. Closed Sun and 20 days in Aug.

Áno Petrálona

Áno Petrálona, an old refugee neighbourhood on the west flank of Filopáppou Hill, is the least touristy district of central Athens. Just why is a mystery: the range of tavernas is excellent, the #9 trolley bus appears regularly, there's a nearby metro station, and it's a natural choice for eating after an evening at the Dora Stratou folk-dance theatre. There's a trolley stop on the Platía Amalías Merkoúri, from where the main artery of Dhimifóndos is a short stroll northwest. The places listed below are in or just beyond the bottom left corner of our "Central Athens" map.

UNDER 4000DR

Ikonomou (sign in Greek), cnr Tróön/Kydhandídhon. Basic home cooking served to packed pavement tables in summer.

To Koutouki, Lakíou 9. Inexpensive traditional taverna with good *fáva* and grilled meat. Like a country house with roof seating overlooking Filopáppou Hill. Closed Sun.

To Monastiri, Dhimifóndos 46. Very popular, moderately priced neighbourhood place with standard fare. Occasional guitar music on an informal basis after 11.30pm.

To Steki tou Ilia, Eptahálkou 5. This establishment on the pedestrianized road up towards Thissío station is so popular the owners have opened a namesake 200m further down. Fine lamb chops.

OVER 4000DR

T'Askimopapo, Iónon 61. A wonderful winter taverna with unusual dishes like meat in creamy sauces. Closed Sun and all summer.

Khryssa, Dhimofóndos 81. This classy restaurant with some pavement seating boasts international cuisine like smoked salmon and duck in various sauces, including curry.

Tea houses and patisseries

With a couple of honourable exceptions, **tea houses** and continental-style **patisseries** are a recent phenomenon in Athens. Quiet, rather consciously sophisticated places, they're essentially a reaction against the traditional and basic kafenía. Most are concentrated around Pláka and in Kolonáki and the more upmarket suburbs. The pedestrianized streets of Milióni and Valaorítou in Kolonáki, in particular, seem to be one uninterrupted pavement café.

De Profundis, Angelikís Hatzimihális 1, Pláka. A trendy-looking tea house but reasonably priced: herb teas, quiches, small main courses, pastries. Mon–Fri 5pm–2am; Sat & Sun noon–2am; closed Aug.

Gelateria Leonardo da Vinci, Dhimitrakopoúlou 42, cnr Dhrákou, Koukáki. Athens' most extensive range of rich and wonderful Italian *gelati* – not exorbitant for the quality. Seating indoors and out.

Galaktopolio Iy Amalthea, Tripódhon 16, Pláka. Tasteful if pricey, serving mostly crepes as well as non-alcoholic drinks.

La Chocolatiere, Skoufá, Kolonáki. Exquisite chocolates and cakes; also light snacks, shakes and drinks, served under trees on the platía opposite. A good place to come for a present if you're invited to a Greek's name day.

La Tasse, Milióni 8, Kolonáki. One of the most popular of the establishments on this pedestrianized lane, just north of Kolonáki square.

Oasis, west side of National Gardens, opposite cnr of Amalías and Filellínon. An unexpected haven just off the main avenue, offering ice cream and snacks in the shade.

Strofes, Akarnanías 10, Ambelókipi, off our map near Alexándras/Kifissías junction. Claims to serve sixty varieties of tea.

To Tristrato, cnr Dedhálou/Angélou Yéronda, Pláka. Coffee, fruit juices, and salads, eggs, desserts, cakes. Comfortable but expensive. Daily 2pm–midnight.

Zonar's, Panepistimíou 9. Traditional upmarket patisserie – still much as it was described, as a haunt of Harriet and Guy Pringle and Yakimov, in Olivia Manning's *Fortunes of War*.

Ouzeris

Ouzeris – also called *ouzádhika* or *mezedhopolía* – are essentially bars selling oúzo, beer and wine (occasionally just oúzo), along with mezédhes (hors d'oeuvres) to reduce the impact. A special treat is a *pikilía* (usually 1500–3000dr), a selection of all the mezédhes available; this will probably include fried shrimp, pieces of squid, cheese, olives, tongue, cheese pies, sausage and other delicacies. Ordinarily, you should allow about 7000dr for two, with drinks, and you never need reservations. As in a Spanish *tapas* bar, the drink is of equal importance to the food so you don't tend to get as full as in a taverna for the same price. Ouzeris that are more food-oriented are to be found in the restaurant listings.

By far the **best hunting ground** for ouzeris is along the two parallel roads of Themistokléous and Emm. Benáki and their cross streets between Panepistimíou and Exárhia Square. Those included below are typical of at least twenty decent establishments in that area.

Athinaikon, Themistokléous 2, cnr Panepistimíou. An old ouzeri in a new location, but retaining its style – marble tables, old posters, etc. Variety of good-sized mezédhes, such as shrimp croquettes and mussels in cheese sauce. Closed Sun.

Dhexameni, Platía Dhexamenís, Kolonáki. Café-ouzerí that serves drinks and snacks in summer under the trees. Shaded and moderately expensive.

Epistrofi Stin Ithaki, cnr Kolléti and Benáki, Exárhia. Featuring Santorini wine, this one has a good line in fish and seafood mezédhes. Closed Sun.

Iy Gonia, Arahóvis 59, Exárhia. Mushroom *saganáki,* meatballs, spicy sausages and octopus are among the delights at this place near the square.

Iy Lesvos, Emm. Benáki 38. Split-level establishment with lots of fish and seafood mezédhes and barrelled wine as well as a selection of ouzos.

O Mitsos, Platía Halandríou, Haláudhri (take bus #A6 or #B6 from Har. Trikoúpi or Leofóros Alexándras to the terminal and it's across the square near the big church). Wonderful cheap spot with divine mussels in mustard sauce, fried fish, sausages and various dips. Well worth the trip out into the suburbs. Closed Sun.

Iy Oréa Ellás, Mitropóleos 59, Monastiráki. Tucked inside a first-floor cultural centre with fine Acropolis view, this atmospheric spot has a decent selection of mezédhes at good prices.

Music and nightlife

Traditional **Greek music** – rembétika and *dhimotiká* – can, at its best, provide the city's most compelling night-time entertainment. To partake, however, you really need to visit during the winter months; from around May to October most clubs and *boîtes* close their doors, while the musicians head off to tour the countryside and islands. Most of the places that remain open are a tourist travesty of over-amplified and over-priced *bouzouki* noise – at their nadir, not surprisingly, in Pláka.

As for other forms of live music, there are small, indigenous **jazz** and **rock** scenes, perennially strapped for funds and venues but worth checking out. **Classical** music performances tend to form the core of the summer Athens Festival, but with the completion in 1991 of the city's concert hall out on Vasilíssis Sofías there is now a long-running winter season as well. **Discos** and **music bars** are very much in the European mould. The clubs in the city tend to close during the summer, unless they have roof terraces; Athenian youth, meanwhile, move out to a series of huge hangar-like disco-palaces in the coastal suburbs.

For **information** and knowledgeable advice on all kinds of Athenian music – traditional, rock and jazz – look in at the **record shops** 7+7, Iféstou 7, Monastiráki, or Happening, Hariláou Trikoúpi 13; see "Records and CDs", p.135. Both of these generally display posters for the more interesting events and have tickets on sale for rock, jazz or festival concerts.

Traditional music

For an introduction to Greek **traditional** and **folk music** see Contexts, p.885. In Athens, the various styles can coexist or be heard on alternate evenings at a number of music clubs or *boîtes*. There are purely traditional music venues (such as *To Armenaki*, especially for island music from the Cyclades and Crete), where people go to dance, or to celebrate weddings and other occasions. Most gigs start pretty late – there's little point in arriving much before 10.30pm – and continue until 3 or 4am. After midnight (and a few drinks) people tend to loosen up and start dancing; at around 1am there's generally an interval, when patrons may move to other clubs down the street or across

---

LISTINGS INFORMATION

The **listings** and recommendations in this section are up to date at the time of going to press, but obviously venues change fast and often. Useful additional sources of information include the English-language daily *Athens News*, whose Friday edition has a complete events programme for the weekend, and the Greek-language *Athinórama* (every Friday), the single most reliable source, with screening times for all films and an exhaustive catalogue of night spots and events. The weekly *Hellenic Times* has good coverage of forthcoming art exhibitions and events, including the summer Athens Festival.

town. Prices tend to be pretty stiff, with expensive drinks (and sometimes food), plus an admission fee or a minimum consumption per set.

Rembétika

For anyone with an interest in folk sounds, **rembétika**, the old drugs-and-outcast music brought over by Asia Minor Greeks, is worth catching live. The form was revived in the late 1970s and, though the fad has waned, there are still good sounds to be heard. If possible, phone to make a reservation and check who's playing. Some of these venues tend more towards **laïkó** (popular) sounds, the descendant of rembétika (see p.890).

CENTRAL ATHENS

Boemissa, Solomoú 19, Exárhia (☎36 43 836). Rembétika, old folk songs and music from the Cyclades – the most popular with Greeks, irrespective of their place of origin. Drinks 1500dr. Closed Mon.

Iy Palia Markiza, Próklou 41, Pangráti (☎75 25 074). Claims to offer rembétika "as you would have heard it in Smyrna and Pireás". Housed in a fine old turn-of-the-century building above Platía Varnáva. Open Wed–Sun 11pm–5am, and occasionally 3.30–8pm; afternoon sessions are cheaper, otherwise count on 3000dr per person.

Rembetikí Istoría, Ippokrátous 181, Neápoli (☎64 24 967). Fairly genuine sounds from Pávlos and company in a large old house. Drinks 1500dr. Closed Wed.

Reportaz, cnr Athanasíou Dhiákou and Syngroú, Koukáki (☎92 32 114). Owned by the chief editor of a Sunday newspaper, this joint is popular with journalists. Good singing and fine folk atmosphere. Drinks 1500dr.

Stoa Athanaton, Sofokléous 19 (in the old meat market) (☎32 14 362). Fronted by bouzouki veterans Hondronakos and Koulis Skarpelis. Good taverna food; 2000dr minimum. Open 3–6pm and midnight–6am. Closed Sun.

Taximi, Isávron 29, off Hariláou Trikoúpi, Exárhia (☎36 39 919). Crowded salon on third floor of a Neoclassical building; no food, no cover, but drinks 2000dr. Closed Sun, also July & Aug.

FURTHER AFIELD

Kendro Dhaskalakis, Leofóros Marathónos (☎66 77 255). Out-of-town taverna run by veteran *bouzouki* star Mihalis Daskalakis. Open Wed–Sat.

Marabou, Panórmou 113, near Leofóros Alexándhras in Ambelókipi (look for a sign with a toucan). One of the first rembétika revival clubs, and still one of the most popular – mobbed at weekends. For four nights of the week the music is taped, but on Friday and Saturday they feature *laterna* (hurdy-gurdy). Expensive food and drink, at around 3000–4000dr a head. No reservations. Open year-round.

Nikhtes Mayikes, Vouliagménis 85, Glifádha (☎94 47 600). Plays host to some of the big names. Drinks at the bar 2000dr; menu 7500dr; whisky 24,000dr per bottle.

Dhimotiká (folk) music

There's a real mix of styles at these clubs – everything from Zorba-like Cretan *santoúri* music to wailing clarinet from the mountains of Epirus, from ballroom dancing to lyrical ballads from Asia Minor. Venues are scattered throughout the city and are often pricier than their rembétika equivalents; reservations are advisable.

Elatos, Trítis Septemvríou 16, nr Omónia Square (☎52 34 262). An eclectic assortment of *dhimotiká*. Closed Wed.

Elliniko Horio, Menándroú 60, nr Omónia Square (☎52 26 531). Features the wild, clarinet-dominated music of Epirus. Closed Tues.

Enallax, Mavromiháli 139, Neápoli (☎64 37 416). Lively and friendly venue which hosts acts of various folk styles. No cover charge or reservation needed. Drinks 1500dr.

Kriti, Ayíou Thomá 8, Ambelókipi, off map past Leofóros Alexándras (☎77 58 258). Specializes in Cretan music. Closed Mon.

Pinakothíki, Ayías Théklas 5, Psyrrí (☎32 47 741). Small but cosy venue with appearances from revered but less well known artists like the Cretan Psarandonis and some foreign acts. Closed Sun.

To Armenaki, Patriárkhou Ioakím 1, short taxi ride from Venizélou/Távros metro station (☎34 74 716). Island music, with the classic singer Irini Konitopoulou-Legaki often putting in an appearance. Closed Mon & Tues.

Jazz and Latin

Jazz has a rather small following in Greece, but the main club, *Half-Note*, has a pleasant environment and usually good musicians. The major events take place as part of the **Jazz and Blues Festival** at the end of June; information and tickets are available from the Athens Festival box office (see p.131) and select record stores. Latin and other ethnic music styles are slowly increasing in popularity and the venues where it can be heard are generally very pleasant.

Café Asante, Damáreos 78, Pangráti, off our "Central Athens" map behind the huge Profítis Ilías church (☎75 60 102). Excellent atmosphere and interesting range of live acts from Latin through Armenian to African and even some rock. 2000dr entrance.

Half-Note, Trivonianoú 17, Ambelókipi, off our map beyond Leofóros Alexándras(☎64 49 236). Live jazz most nights, often provided by good musicians brought in from abroad, but closed Tues and for much of the summer.

Hi-Hat Café, Krousóvou 1, Ilísia, nr *Hilton Hotel* (☎72 18 171). Small venue with sporadic live gigs (jam night on Mon) and mixture of jazz, funk and soul. 1500dr minimum.

La Joya, Tsókha 43, nr American Embassy, Ambelókipi, off map along Vas. Konstandínou (☎64 40 030). Great atmosphere. The live or taped rock, jazz and Latin accounts for some of its considerable success – as does beautiful decor, adventurous food and its popularity as a venue for celebrity parties. Open until 2.30am.

Take Five, Patriárkhou Ioakím 37, Kolonáki (☎72 40 736). Supper club with live jazz bands. Reservations suggested. Closed Mon & Thurs.

Rock: live venues and music bars

The indigenous Greek **rock scene** is small but very solid and its public knowledgeable. Obscure Aussie bands, for example, who would hardly draw a handful of people in London, can be greeted like mini messiahs here. There are occasional appearances by better-known international bands and the annual **Rock Wave Festival**, established in 1997 and held down in Pireás in mid-July, has been attracting the likes of Blur, Garbage, Prodigy and Patti Smith. Local bands still face some difficulties like costly instruments and disfavour from the authorities, but they survive, and groups such as Echo Tattoo, Purple Overdose, Make Believe and Bokomolech are well worth catching if you can. Clubs pop up and disappear like mushrooms, though there are a number of fairly permanent music bars, especially in Exárhia. Many of these host the occasional gig and generally have a dance floor of sorts.

An Club, Solomoú 13–15, Exárhia (☎33 05 056). Basement club featuring local and lesser-known foreign rock bands. Entrance from 2000dr.

Berlin, Iraklidhón 8, Thissío. Up-to-date indie rock sounds in the air-con interior. Pavement seating but you can't hear the music.

Decadence, Poulherías 2/Voulgaroktónou, Exárhia. Features the savviest indie/alternative sounds. Best in winter, when Dhaskalopoulos, the Greek John Peel, spins the discs on Thurs.

Kittaro Retro Club, Ipírou 48, nr Aharnón. Open Thurs–Sun; it features live bands, usually playing solid seventies-style rock.

Memphis, Vendíri 5, Ilísia, behind *Hilton Hotel*. Roomy and comfy bar with good sound system pumping out rock and dance. Goth night on Tues.

Mo Better, Kolétti 32, Exárhia. Cramped but fun bar on the first floor of an old building. Garage, punk and indie rock. 1500dr entrance includes drink.

Rodhon, Márni 24, Platía Váthis (☎52 47 427). The city's most important venue for foreign and Greek rock, soul and reggae groups. Good atmosphere in a converted cinema. Closed in summer.

Discos and clubs

As you would expect of a European capital, Athens has a fair selection of nineties dance, trance, hip-hop and rave showcases. **Rave parties** do happen, with local and foreign DJs, but, as elsewhere, the business operates underground, so look out for posters or ask compulsive clubbers. Expect the unexpected at these clubs: most play recent hits, but don't be surprised if the sound shifts to Greek or belly-dancing music towards the end of the night. Some central Athens air-conditioned clubs remain open through the summer but with the rising temperature the scene really moves out to the coast beyond the airport, where Athens youth congregate at weekends in the beach suburbs of Kalamáki, Glyfádha and Voúla. If you join them, bear in mind that the taxi fare will be the first of several hefty bills, although admission prices usually include a free drink.

Central Athens

Müller, Emm. Benáki 62, Exárhia (☎38 30 550). Small club featuring eclectic trip-hop and drum'n'bass.

Q Base, Evripídhou 49, nr Omónia Square (☎32 18 256). Disco, house and techno grooves.

R-Load, Ermoú 161, Thisío (☎34 56 187). This is the best central venue for spacing out to trance and such ambient vibes.

Beach suburbs

Black Hole, Astéria, Glyfádha (☎89 46 898). One of the places to be seen and strut your stuff. Drinks 2000dr.

Bouzios, Vasiléos Yeoryíou 2, Kalamáki (☎98 12 004). Heavyweight clubbing spot. Spacious, glamorous and very popular with celebrities. Open year-round.

Kingsize-Arena (Show Centre), Leofóros Posidhónos 5, Ellinikó, opposite the airport (☎89 44 138). Vast place that does expensive food to go along with the latest disco faves.

Plus Soda, Evryális 2, Glyfádha (☎89 40 205). Currently one of the most hip spots for shaking your booty to drum'n' bass or techno sounds.

Gay venues

The gay scene is fairly discreet but Athens has its share of clubs, especially in the Makriyánni district to either side of Syngroú, with an established reputation. For further ideas, check the (brief and not entirely reliable) gay sections in the listings magazines *Athinórama* and *Exodus*.

Alekos Island, Tsakálof 42, Kolonáki. Easy-going atmosphere, with rock/pop music. Owned by Alekos, who claims to be known around Europe.

Alexander's, Anagnostopoúlou 44. Relaxed, slightly middle-of-the-road gay bar in the Kolonáki district.

Granazi, Lembéssi 20, near Syngroú. Gay bar close by the transvestite cruising area.

Koukles, Zan Moreás & Syngroú, Koukáki. The name means "Dolls" and there are humorous live drag acts.

Lambda, Lembéssi 15 & Syngroú 9. Popular, with Greek and international music, live shows and gay films.

Arts and culture

Unless your Greek is fluent, the contemporary **Greek theatre** scene is likely to be inaccessible. As with Greek music, it is essentially a winter pursuit; in summer, the only theatre tends to be satirical and (to outsiders) totally incomprehensible revues. **Dance**, however, is more accessible and includes a fine traditional Greek show, while **cinema** is undubbed – and out of doors in summer.

In addition, in winter months, you might catch **ballet** (and **world music** concerts) at the convenient but acoustically awful Pallas Theatre, at Voukourestíou 1; **opera** from the Greek National Opera Lyrikí Skiní, in the Olympia Theatre at Akadhimías 59; and **classical events** either in the Hall of the Friends of Music (Mégaro Mousikís), out on Leofóros Vasilíssis Sofías next to the US embassy, or at the Filippos Nakas Concert Hall, at Ippokrátous 41. Also worth looking out for are events at the various **foreign cultural institutes**. Among these are: the Hellenic American Union, Massalías 22; the British Council, Platía Kolonáki 17; the French Institute, Sína 29/Massalías 1; and the Goethe Institute, Omírou 14–16.

Athens Festival

The summer **Athens Festival** has, over the years, come to encompass a broad spectrum of cultural events: most famously **ancient Greek theatre** (performed, in modern Greek, at the Herodes Atticus theatre on the south slope of the Acropolis), but also traditional and contemporary dance, classical music, jazz, traditional Greek music and even a smattering of rock shows. The **Herodes Atticus theatre**, known popularly as the *Iródhio*, is memorable in itself on a warm summer's evening – although you should avoid the cheapest seats, or you won't see a thing. Other festival venues include the open-air Lycabettus Theatre on **Lykavitós Hill**, the **mansion of the Duchess of Plaisance** in Pendéli and the great ancient **theatre at Epidaurus** (see p.177), which is best taken in as part of a Peloponnesian tour as excursions from Athens are expensive and exhausting.

Events are scheduled from early June until September, although the exact dates may vary each year. Programmes of performances are best picked up as soon as you arrive in the city, and for theatre, especially, you'll need to move fast to get tickets. The **festival box office** is in the arcade at Stadhíou 4 (☎32 21 459 or 32 23 111, ext 240; Mon–Sat 8.30am–2pm & 5–7pm, Sun 10.30am–1pm); most events are held in the Herodes Atticus theatre, where the box office is open 5–9pm on the day of performance. Schedules of the main drama and music events are available in advance from EOT offices abroad (though they don't handle tickets). For student discounts, you must buy tickets in advance.

Dance

On the **dance** front, one worthwhile "permanent" performance is that of the **Dora Stratou Ethnic Dance Company** in their own theatre on Filopáppou hill. Gathered on a single stage are traditional music, choreography and costumes you'd be hard put to encounter in many years' travelling around Greece. Performances are held nightly at 10.15pm (extra show Wed & Sun 8.15pm) from June to September. To reach the theatre, walk up the busy Areopayítou street, along the south flank of the Acropolis, until you see the signs. Tickets (3000–4000dr) can almost always be picked up at the door; take your own refreshments, or rely on the somewhat pricey snacks on offer.

Cinema

Athens is a great place to catch up on movies. There are literally dozens of indoor cinemas in the city, some of them very new and plush, some relics of the 1920s and 1930s,

HAT-TRICKS AND HOOLIGANS

Greeks are fanatical about football, both their own brand and the big European leagues. They have a particular affinity to the English game and Greek commentaries are sprinkled with English terms like "offside", "foul" and "hat-trick". Sadly, less savoury aspects of the game have also been adopted, and the nineties have seen an upswing in hooliganism, just as it has been on the wane in Britain, although it is usually of the destructive rather than murderous variety.

Contrary to the British spirit of the underdog, Greeks like a successful side and so most people all over the country claim to support one of the big three teams of greater Athens; Panathinaïkós, AEK or Olympiakós. The league title has only occasionally been snatched from the hands of this trio by one of the Thessaloníki outfits and gloriously in 1988 by Lárissa. Of late the Pireás team Olympiakós has been in the ascendancy again, winning three consecutive championships in 1997–9 under the expert coaching of Serb Dusan Bajevic, who was at the helm of AEK's similar hat-trick between 1992 and 1994. On either side of that, Panathinaïkós bagged two pairs of titles, completing the nineties' carve-up.

Most fans stick to their armchairs or kafenío seats throughout the game, and matches are often surprisingly poorly attended apart from local derbies and European games. This makes it easy for the casual visitor to gain admission on the day and even the big matches are not too difficult to obtain tickets for. With Greece currently having places in the Champions League, the chances of catching a famous English, Italian, Spanish or German side in the future are quite good. Look out for kiosks in the centre of town selling advance tickets or details in the press.

The thrilling fields

Panathinaïkós (colours green & white) play at the Olympic Stadium (OAKA) up in the northern suburb of Kalogréza; take the metro to Iríni station and it's a five-minute walk through the sports complex. Buses to Kifissiá also pass nearby but take much longer.

AEK (colours yellow & black) play at the Níkos Goumás stadium in Néa Filadhélfia; take the metro to Perissós station, from where it's less than ten minutes' walk under the lines and through residential streets.

Olympiakós (colours red & white) play at Karaïskaki stadium in Néo Fáliro, which is right opposite the metro station of the same name, the last before Pireás itself.

Note that AEK and Olympiakós often switch their European games to OAKA in order to attract larger gates.

If you've got a liking for the underdog you can always try to see one of the less famous first division teams like Paniónios in Néa Smýrni, Apóllon in Perissós (near AEK), Ethnikós, who share Karaïskaki with Olympiakós, or the redoubtable Atrómitos (Intrepid) Athinón out in Peristéri, who are now languishing in the lower divisions and are likened to Millwall for their small but diehard support.

---

whilst in summer **outdoor** screens seem to spring up all over the place. Unless they have air conditioning or a roll-back roof, the indoor venues tend to be closed between mid-May and October.

Admission, whether at indoor or outdoor venues, is reasonable: count on 1700–1800dr for outdoor screenings, 1900–2000dr for first-run fare at a midtown theatre. Films are always shown in the original language with Greek **subtitles** (a good way to increase your vocabulary). For **listings**, the weekly magazine *Athinórama* (every Fri; 500dr), is the most reliable source of programme information if you can decipher Greek script, although foreign film titles are also given in the original language. Films are divided according to category and geographical location of the cinema. English-language cinema listings – less complete – can be found in the *Athens News* (daily, except Monday) or *The Hellenic Times* and *Hellenic Star* weekly paper.

Among **indoor cinemas**, a cluster showing regular English-language films can be found in three main central areas: Patissíon/Kypséli; downtown, on the three main thoroughfares connecting Omónia and Sýndagma; and Ambelókipi, around the junctions of Leofóros Alexándhras and Kifissías. The new, posh Village Center in Maroúsi (just off Kifissías, near the Aïdhonákia amusement park) has ten theatres showing current films year round, with the added advantage that you can reserve tickets by phone (☎68 05 950). **Oldies** and **art films** tend to be shown at the Asty on Koraï downtown; the Orfeus, Artémonos 57 (a fifteen-minute walk from Pangráti or Koukáki); the Alfaville, Mavromiháli 168; the Aavora, Ippokrátous 180; and the Studio, Stavropoúlou 33, Platía Amerikís (off map up Patissíon). Catch **horror/cult films** at the Petit-Palais (cnr Vasilíou Yeoryíou Víta/Rizári); the Plaza, Kifissías 118, Ambelókipi; the Philip, Platía Amerikís/Thássou 11 (off map up Patissíon); the Amalia, Dhrossopoúlou 197 (off map parallel to Patissíon); the Nirvana, Leofóros Alexándhras 192; the Rialto, Kypsélis 54, Kypséli (off map north of Leofóros Alexándhras); and the Zina, Leofóros Alexándhras 74.

The summer **outdoor screens** are less imaginative in their selections – second-run offerings abound – though to attend simply for the film is to miss much of the point. You may in any case never hear the soundtrack above the din of Greeks cracking *passatémpo* (pumpkin seeds), drinking and conversing; at late screenings (11pm), the sound is turned right down anyway, so as not to disturb local residents. The most central and reliable outdoor venues are Sine Pari, Kydathinéon 22, Pláka; Thissio, Apostólou Pávlou 7, under the Acropolis; Nea Panathinea, Mavromiháli 165, Neápoli; Zefyros, Tróön 36, Áno Petrálona, and the two in Exárhia, Vox on the platía and Riviera at Valtetsíou 46.

Markets and shops

You can buy just about anything in Athens and even on a purely visual level the city's **markets** and **bazaar** areas are worth an hour or two's wandering. Among the markets, don't miss the Athinás food halls, nor, if you're into bargain-hunting through junk, the Sunday morning **flea markets** in Monastiráki, Thissíon and Pireás. The **Athens flea market** spreads over a half-dozen or so blocks around Monastiráki square each Sunday from around 6am until 2.30pm. In parts it is an extension of the tourist trade – the shops in this area are promoted as a "flea market" every day of the week – but there is authentic Greek (and nowadays Soviet refugee-Greek) junk, too, notably along (and off) Iféstou and Pandhróssou streets. The real McCoy, most noticeable at the Thissío metro station end of Adhrianoú and the platía off Kynéttou near the church of Áyios Fílippos, is just a bag of odds and ends strewn on the ground or on a low table; dive in.

The **Pireás flea market** – at similar times on Sunday mornings – has fewer tourists and more goods. The market is concentrated on Alipédou and Skilítsi streets parallel to the railroad tracks about 500 yards from the sea (see the map on p.139). It is a venue for serious antique trading, as well as the sale of more everyday items.

In addition, many Athenian neighbourhoods have a *laikí agorá* – **street market** – on a set day of the week. Usually running from 7am to 2pm, these are inexpensive and enjoyable, selling household items and dry goods, as well as fresh fruit and vegetables. The most centrally located ones are: Hánsen in Patissíon on Monday; Lésvou in Kypséli (off map) and Láskou in Pangráti (off map), both on Tuesday; Xenokrátous in Kolonáki, Tsámi Karatássou in Koukáki and Arhimídhous in Méts, all on Friday; and Plakendías in Ambelókipi (one of the largest; off map) and Kallidhromíou in Exárhia, both on Saturday. Finally, if you're after live Greek **plants** or **herbs**, there's a Sunday morning gathering of stalls on Vikéla street in Patissíon (off map) and plants and flowers on sale daily at the Platía Ayías Irínis near Ermoú.

If you are after electrical gear, now about as cheap in Greece as elsewhere in Europe, the best place to look is in the streets off Patissíon, just north of Omónia square. The selections below include some of the most enjoyable shops for souvenir-hunting, plus a few more functional places for those in search of books, music and outdoor gear.

Books

Archeological Service Bookstore, Panepistimíou 57, in stoa on left. Outlet for the high-quality if dry archeological service publications.

Compendium, Níkis 28 (upstairs), off Sýndagma. The friendliest and best value of the English-language bookstores, featuring Penguins, Picadors, Rough Guides and other paperbacks, plus a small secondhand section.

Eleftheroudhakis, Panepistimíou 17. Five floors of English books provide space for an extensive stock.

Estia-Kollarou, Sólonos 60. Big Greek-language bookshop, strong on modern history, politics, folk traditions and fiction.

Iy Folia tou Vivliou (The Book Nest), Panepistimíou 25, in the arcade and upstairs. The city's biggest selection of English-language fiction, with a good collection of recent academic work on Greece, and back issues of the *Korfes* hiking magazine.

Pyrinos Kosmos, Ippokrátous 16. The best shop in town for Greek and English books on philosophy, religion and mysticism.

Reymondos, Voukourestíou 18. Good for foreign periodicals in particular.

Crafts and antiques

Greek handicrafts are not particularly cheap but the workmanship is usually very high. In addition to the stores listed below, consider those at the **National Archeological Museum**, **Benáki Museum** and **Cycladic Art Museum**, which sell excellent, original designs as well as reproductions, and the cluster of antique shops at the base of **Adhrianoú**, near the corner of Kynéttou, which are good for Ottoman and rural Greek items like backgammon boards, hubble-bubbles, kilims, etc; the best is at Adhrianoú 25.

Athens Design Centre, Valaorítou 4. A highly original modern potter has her base here. Prices aren't exorbitant considering the quality.

Gravoures, Kolokotróni 15, Sýndagma. Engravings and prints.

Karamichos, Voulís 31–33. A central outlet for *flokátes*, those hairy-pile wool rugs that are still the best thing to warm up a cold stone floor.

To Kati yia Sas, Iperídhou 23, Pláka. Eclectic stock of craft items.

Kendro Ellinikis Paradosis, Mitropóleos 59, Monastiráki. As the name suggests, this pleasant upstairs emporium has a wide selection of traditional arts and crafts and is mercifully free of the hard sell often encountered in the nearby flea market.

Lalaounis, Panepistimíou 6. Home-base outlet of the world-renowned family of goldsmiths, whose designs are superbly imaginative and very expensive.

Les Amis de Livres, Valaorítou 9, in a cul-de-sac. Prints and engravings.

Manos Faldaïs, Hariláou Trikoúpi 75, Exárhia. Unusual crafts like hand-made puppets, wind chimes and scented candles.

National Welfare Organization, Ipatías 6, cnr Apóllonos, Pláka. Rugs, embroideries, copperware – traditional craft products made in remote country districts.

Stavros Melissinos, Pandhróssou 89, off Monastiráki. The "poet-sandalmaker" of Athens – see p.106. The sandals translate better than the poems but nevertheless an inspiring (and not especially inflated) place to be cobbled.

Skyros, cnr Makriyánni/Hadzikhrístou, Koukáki. Traditional, if not very portable, Greek village furniture (particularly from Skýros), and more practical cushions, lamps, etc.

Health and speciality food

Herbs and herb teas are sold dry and fresh at most street markets and at the Athinás bazaar. Otherwise, the following central outlets are useful.

AB Vassilopoulos The three huge main stores are at Leofóros Kifissías, Psihikó, by the east airport and above Kifissiá on the National Road (all off map), but there are several other outlets throughout the city. Gigantic supermarket stocking esoteric ingredients (their well-known sales pitch is that they stock birds' milk) for just about every cuisine or diet.

Aralus, Sofokléous 17, Central Bazaar. Fruits, nuts, wholegrain bread, pasta and so on. Also supplements and vitamins.

Kendro Fyzikis Zois keh Iyias, Panepistimíou 57. Headquarters of the Greek Green Party, but also a tremendously well-stocked store and vegetarian snack bar with a pleasant loft where afternoon snacks are served.

To Stakhi, Mikrás Asías 61–63, Ambelókipi (off map, nr Leofóros Alexándhras/Kifissías junction). Well-stocked store.

Outdoor supplies

Aegean Dive Shop, Pandhóras 31, Glyfádha, off map, on the coast to the southeast (☎89 45 409). Good-value one-day dive trips to a reef near Vouliagméni, sporadically during the week but regularly on weekends.

Alberto's, Patissíon 37, in the arcade; plus many others on same street heading towards Omónia. This is in effect the "bike bazaar", for repairs, parts and sales. For mountain bikes, try Gatsoúlis at Thessaloníkis 8 in Néa Filadhélfia (off map; #18 trolley bus).

Alpamayo, Panepistimíou 44. Small hiking store which also stocks some *Korfes* back issues (see also "Books", opposite).

Kazos, in the arcade between Panepistimíou and Koraï. A bit pricey due to its central location, but handy for small items like socks, knives, water bottles, etc.

Marabout, Sólonos 74, behind the university. Soft goods only – parkas, packs, sleeping bags, etc.

Mediterranean Dive Shop, Vas. Pávlou 95, Kastélla, nr Pireás (☎41 25 376). Efficient and reasonably priced shop for the hire of reliable diving equipment.

No-Name Bike Shop, Trítis Septemvríou 40/cnr Stournári. Bicycles and accessories.

Pindhos, Patissíon 52. Extensive state-of-the-art hiking/climbing gear: Lowe packs, ice axes, stoves, water containers, parkas, foam pads, etc.

Survival, Kynéttou 4, on Ayíou Filíppou square. Good for ponchos, stoves, mess kits, boots, knives and survival gear in general.

Records and CDs

If you hear music you like, or want to explore Greek sounds of bygone days (or today), refer to the discographies in Contexts (p.885) and then try the outlets below. When shopping, beware of records warped by poor stacking in the racks. The big advantage of shopping here is that the **vinyl industry** is still alive and well, having survived the CD onslaught; you may find pressings discontinued elsewhere.

Happening, Harilaou Trikoupi 13. Good range of heavy metal and indie rock plus tickets, info and magazines.

Jazz Rock, Akadhimías 45. Specializes in just that with forays into rock and ethnic music, also a good source of information and tickets for upcoming concerts.

Metropolis, Panepistimíou 64. Strictly CDs; the branch at #54 sells just vinyl. Often has discounted items.

7+7, Iféstou 7, Monastiráki. This shop in the flea market has a choice selection of old and new rock and Greek music on vinyl and CD.

Tzina, Panepistimíou 57. Stop in here if Metropolis or Xylouris doesn't have what you're after; it has its own label of Greek folk.

Xylouris, Panepistimíou 39, in the arcade. Run by the widow of the late, great Cretan singer Nikos Xylouris, this is currently one of the best places for Greek popular, folk and (of course) Cretan music. On the expensive side, but stocks items unavailable elsewhere.

Listings

Airlines Most of the following are within 100m or so of Sýndagma: Olympic, ticket office at Fillelínon 15 (☎92 67 555 for reservations or ☎96 66 666), main office at Syngroú 96 (☎92 69 111); Air Canada, Óthonos 10d (☎32 23 206); Air France, Vouliagménis 18, Glyfádha (☎96 01 100); Air Greece, Níkis 20 (☎32 55 011); Air Manos, Panepistimíou 39 (☎32 34 900); Alitalia, Vouliagménis 577, near airport (☎99 88 888); American Airlines, Panepistimíou 15 (☎33 11 045); British Airways, Vouliagménis 130, cnr Themistokléous, Glyfádha (☎89 06 666); Canadian Airlines (Amfitreon Air Services), 3rd floor, Syngroú 7 (☎92 12 470); Cronus, Óthonos 10 (☎33 15 510); CSA, Panepistimíou 15 (☎32 32 303); Cyprus Airways, Filellínon 10 (☎32 47 801); Delta, Óthonos 4 (☎33 11 660); Easyjet, airport only (☎96 00 000); Egyptair, Vouliagménis 26 (☎92 12 818); El Al, Voukourestíou 16 (☎92 12 818); Kenya Airways, c/o KLM; KLM, Vouliagménis 41, Glyfádha (☎96 05 000); Lufthansa, Vas. Sofías 11 (☎36 92 11); Malev, Panepistimíou 15 (☎32 41 116); Qantas (represented by British Airways); Sabena, Vouliagménis 41, Glyfádha (☎96 00 071); Singapore Airlines, Xenofóndos 9 (☎32 39 111); South African Airways, Merlin 8, Kolonáki (☎36 16 305); Swissair, Óthonos 4 (☎32 35 811); Thai, Sekéri 1, Kolonáki (☎36 47 610); Turkish Airlines, Fillelínon 19 (☎32 46 024); TWA, Syngroú 8 (☎92 13 400); Virgin Atlantic, Tziréon 8–10 (behind Athens Gate Hotel) (☎92 49 100).

Airport enquiries ☎93 69 111 for Olympic flight enquiries; ☎96 94 111 for all other carriers.

American Express Poste restante and money changing at the main branch at Ermoú 2 (1st floor), cnr Sýndagma. Mail pick-up desk open in summer Mon–Fri 7.30am–8pm, Sat 7.30am–2pm; shorter weekday hours in winter.

Banks The normal banking hours are Mon–Thurs 8am–2pm and Fri 8am–1.30pm and just about all banks can do exchange during those hours. The National Bank of Greece at Sýndagma stays open for **exchange** Mon–Thurs 8am–2pm & 3.30–6.30pm, Fri 8am–1.30pm & 3–6.30pm, Sat 9am–3pm & Sun 9am–1pm. The nearby, less crowded Yenikí Trápeza/General Bank cnr Ermoú and Sýndagma, has longer hours: Mon–Thurs 8am–6.30pm, Fri 8am–6pm, Sat 8am–2pm, closed Sun.

Buses For information on buses out of Athens (and the respective terminals), see "Travel Details" at the end of this chapter.

Camera repair Most central at Pikópoulos, Lékka 26, off Ermoú, 3rd floor and Kriton Kremnitsios, Karayeóryi Servías 7, 5th floor.

Car rental A number of companies are to be found along Leofóros Syngroú, including InterRent/EuropCar, at no. 4, Holiday Autos (no. 8), Thrifty (no. 24), Eurodollar (no. 29), Just (no. 43), Avanti (no. 50), Antena (no. 52) and Autorent (no. 118); the latter three give student discounts, while Payless is just off Syngroú at Hatzikhrístou 20.

Car repairs, tyres, and assistance VW vans are well looked after at Grigoris Steryiadhis, Melandhías 56, Goúva (between Pangráti and Néos Kósmos; off map down Vouliagménis). Mechanics for virtually any make are scattered around Néos Kósmos district, while spares stores congregate along and between Kalliróis and Vouliagménis. If they don't have the part, or the know-how, they'll refer you to someone who does. Tyre stores are grouped between Trítis Septemvríou 60–80 (north of Omónia). **ELPA** – the Greek automobile association – gives free **help and information** to foreign motorists at Leofóros Mesoyíon 2 (northeast of Lykavitós, off map) and at the Athens Tower in Ambelókipi. For **emergency assistance** call ☎104 (free, though you'll pay for any parts).

Dentists Free treatment at the Evangelismos Hospital, Ipsilándou 45, Kolonáki and at the Pireás Dentistry School (*Odhondoiatrikó Skholío*), cnr Thívon/Livadhías, well north of the metro and public buses. For private treatment, check the ads in the *Athens News* or ask your embassy for addresses.

Embassies/Consulates include: Albania, Karakhrístou 1 (☎72 34 412); Australia, Dhimitríou Soútsou 37 (☎64 50 405); Britain, Ploutárhou 1, Kolonáki (☎72 36 211); Bulgaria, Stratigoú

Kallári 33a, Paleó Psihikó (☎67 48 105, Mon–Fri 10am–noon); Canada, Ioánnou Yennadhíou 4 (☎72 73 400); Denmark, Vas. Sofías 11 (☎36 08 315); Egypt, Vas. Sofías 3 (☎36 18 612); France, Vas. Sofías 7 (☎33 91 000); Germany, Karaóli Dhimitríou 3 (☎72 85 111); Hungary, Kálvou 16, Paleó Psihikó (☎67 25 337, Mon–Fri 9am–noon); India, Kleánthous 3 (☎72 16 227); Ireland, Vas. Konstandínou 7 (☎72 32 771); Israel, Marathonodhrómou 1, Paleó Psihikó (☎67 19 530); Italy, Sekéri 2, Kolonáki (☎36 17 227); Japan, Vas. Sofías 64 (☎72 33 732); Netherlands, Vassiléos Konstandínou 5–7 (☎72 39 701); New Zealand (consulate), Xenías 24, Ambelókipi (☎77 10 112); Norway, Vassiléos Konstandínou 7 (☎72 47 605); Romania, Emm. Benáki 7, Paleó Psihikó (☎67 28 875, Mon–Fri 10am–noon); South Africa, Kifissías 60, Maroússi (☎68 06 645); Sweden, Vas. Konstandínou 7 (☎72 90 421); Turkey, Vas. Yeorgíou Vita 8, (☎72 45 915); US, Vas. Sofías 91 (☎72 12 951).

Emergencies Dial the tourist police (☎171; 24hr) for medical or other assistance. In a **medical emergency**, don't wait for an ambulance if you can travel safely – get a taxi straight to the hospital address that the tourist police gives you. If your Greek is up to it, ☎166 summons an ambulance, ☎105 gets you a rota of night-duty doctors, and ☎106 ascertains the best hospital for you to head for. Otherwise, KAT, way out in Kifissiá at Níkis 2, is excellent for trauma and acute complaints if you can hold out that long – it's the designated casualty ward for Greater Athens.

Environment Greenpeace, Zoödhóhou Piyís 52, Exárhia (☎38 40 774). Mon–Sat 9am–4pm. Stop by if you want information, or are staying long-term in Greece and would like to participate in volunteer work and campaigns. WWF Greece, Filellínon 26, 4th floor (☎32 47 586) has many excellent field programmes.

Ferries Most central offices for major lines like ANEK, Strintzis, Hellenic Mediterranean, G&A and Ventouris flank Leofóros Amalías between Sýndagma and Hadrian's Arch; a prominent exception is Minoan Lines, on Vasiléos Konstandínou, next to the Olympic Stadium. Phone ☎143 for recorded timetable in Greek or pick up schedule for coming days from the EOT office. Minoan Flying Dolphin tickets are sold an hour before departure at the quay in Marína Zéas (☎42 80 001), although it's wise to book tickets in advance during high season at an agent in Athens or Pireás. For Minoan High Speed catamarans to the Cyclades phone ☎75 12 356.

Gay groups Akoe Amphi, the (predominantly male) Greek Gay Liberation Movement, has an office at Zalóngou 6 (Mon–Fri 6–11pm).

Greek language courses Athens Centre, Arhimídhous 48, Pangráti (☎70 12 268, fax 70 18 603), is considered the best for foreigners. The Hellenic American Union, Massalías 22, is more geared to the needs of Greeks learning English.

Hiking Trekking Hellas, Filellínon 7, 3rd floor, arrange hiking tours throughout Greece.

Hospital clinics For minor injuries the Hellenic Red Cross, Trítis Septemvríou/Kapodhistríou, is fairly good. For **inoculations**, try the Vaccination Centre, Leofóros Alexándras 196/cnr Vasilíssis Sofías, Ambelókipi (Mon–Fri 8.30am–12.30pm), where most jabs are free; phone ☎64 60 493.

Internet cafés Internet cafés with full email capabilities and access to the Net have been sprouting up all over the city. Some of the more central and reliable places are: Info Café, branches at Ippokrátous 31 (☎36 15 094) and cnr Botási & Solomoú, Exárhia (☎33 04 002); Museum Internet Café, Patission 46 (☎88 33 418); Sofokleous.com Internet Café, Stadhíou 5 (☎32 48 105); and Tafnet, Pendélis 3 cnr Mitropóleos, Pláka (☎32 49 282). The standard rate is about 1500dr per hour.

Laundry Numerous dry/wet cleaners will do your laundry for you, or there are coin-ops at Dhidhótou 46, Exárhia; cnr Ploutárhou & Karneádhou, Kolonáki; and Ioulianoú 72–78, near the Archaeological Museum.

Lost property The transport police have a lost property office (*Grafío Haménon Andikiménon*) at Alexándras 173, 7th floor (☎64 21 616).

Luggage storage Best arranged with your hotel; many places will keep the bulk of your luggage for free or a nominal amount while you head off to the islands.

Motorbike rental Available from Motorent, whose head office is at Falírau 5, cnr Makriyánni, Koukáki (☎92 34 939, fax 92 34 885).

Mt Áthos permits See p.431 for details if you're planning a trip to Áthos. In Athens, the Ministry of Foreign Affairs, Akadhimías 3, in the arcade, 5th floor, is the first stop in securing a permit; office hours are Mon, Wed & Fri 11am–1pm.

Opticians Quick repairs at Paraskevopoulos in the arcade between Voukourestíou and Kriezótou, by the parcel post office.

Pharmacies (*farmakía*) The Marinopoulos branches in Patissíon and Panepistimíou streets are particularly good and also sell homeopathic remedies, as does (supposedly) any establishment with a green cross outside. Bakakos, on Omónia square is the largest general pharmacy in Athens and stocks just about anything. Call ☎107 for after-hours pharmacies, or consult daily listings in *Athens News*. If you can read Greek, all pharmacies display a daily list of those open after-hours – sometimes the list is in English.

Phones You can phone locally from a *períptero* (kiosk), where you pay afterwards. Phone boxes all require phone cards, which cost 1000dr for 100 units. These are quite handy to have and can be used for a quick call home. Metered international calls are best made at the central OTE offices at Stadhíou 15 and Patissíon 85; the latter is open 24hr.

Police Dialling ☎100 gets the flying squad; for thefts, problems with hotel overcharging, etc, contact the **tourist police** at Dimitrakoupoúlou 77, Koukáki (☎171).

Post offices (*Tahydhromía*) For ordinary letters and parcels up to 2kg, the branch on Sýndagma (cnr Mitropóleos) is open Mon–Fri 7.30am–8pm, Sat 7.30am–2pm, Sun 9am–1.30pm. To send home parcels of personal effects, use the post office in the arcade between Voukourestíou and Kriezótou (Mon–Fri 7.30am–2pm) or, closer to Omónia, at Koumoundoúrou 29. Paper and string are supplied – you bring box and twine. "Surface/air lift" will get parcels home to North America or Europe in two weeks. For souvenirs, a branch at Níkis 37 expedites shipments and minimizes duty/declaration problems.

Poste restante The main post office for Athens is at Eólou 100, just off Omónia (Mon–Fri 7.30am–8pm, Sat 7.30am–2pm, Sun 9am–1.30pm).

Scuba diving Greece has gradually been opening up to diving although there are still restrictions because of underwater antiquities. If you want to do an introductory dive or a full PADI course, instruction in English and certification can be given by bilingual Greek South African Peter Kastrinoyiannakis (☎98 43 851).

Train information, reservations and tickets The most central OSE offices are at Filellínon 17 and Sína 6.

Travel agencies Most budget and youth/student agencies are to be found just off Sýndagma, on and around Filellínon and Níkis streets. The cheapest ferry tickets to Italy are usually sold through USIT, Filellínon 1 (☎32 41 884), or Transalpino, Níkis 28, still trading despite the demise of its namesake. Among other agencies, Highway Express, Níkis 42; Periscope, Filellínon 22; Himalaya, Filellínon 7, and Arcturus, Apóllonos 20, are worth scanning for air travel deals. For the hardy, the widest range of north-bound buses is available at Magic Bus, Filellínon 20.

Work/residence permits/visa extensions at the Aliens' Bureau (*Ipiresía Allodhapón*), Leofóros Alexándhras 173; open Mon–Fri 8am–1pm, but go early or you won't get seen. Also, come armed with small notes for revenue stamps, large notes for the extension fee(s), wads of passport photos, pink personalized bank receipts and plenty of patience.

AROUND ATHENS: ATTICA

Attica (Attikí), the region encompassing the capital, is not much explored by tourists. Only the great romantic ruin of the **Temple of Apollo** at Sounion is on the excursion circuit. The rest, if seen at all, tends to be en route to the islands – from the ports of **Pireás**, **Rafina** (a fast and cheap route to many of the Cyclades) or **Lávrio** (which serves Kéa).

The neglect is not surprising. The mountains of **Imittós**, **Pendéli** and **Párnitha**, which surround Athens on three sides, are progressively less successful in confining the urban sprawl, and the routes out of the city to the south and west are unenticing to say the least. But if you're planning on an extended stay in the capital, a day trip or two or a brief circuit by car can make a rewarding break, with much of Greece in microcosm to be seen within an hour or two's ride: mountainside at **Párnitha**, minor archeological sites in **Brauron** and **Rhamnous** and the odd unspoilt beach, too.

Pireás (Piraeus)

PIREÁS has been the port of Athens since Classical times. Today it is a substantial metropolis in its own right, containing much of Greater Athens' industry, as well as the various commercial activities associated with a port: banking, import–export, freight and so on. For most visitors, though, it is Pireás's inter-island ferries that provide the reason for coming (see "The Ferries" below for details).

The port at Pireás was founded at the beginning of the fifth century BC by **Themistocles**, who realized the potential of its three natural harbours. His work was consolidated by Pericles with the building of the **"Long Walls"** to protect the corridor to Athens, and it remained active under Roman and Macedonian rulers. Subsequently, under Turkish rule, the place declined to the extent that there was just one building there, a monastery, by the end of the War of Independence. From the 1830s on, though,

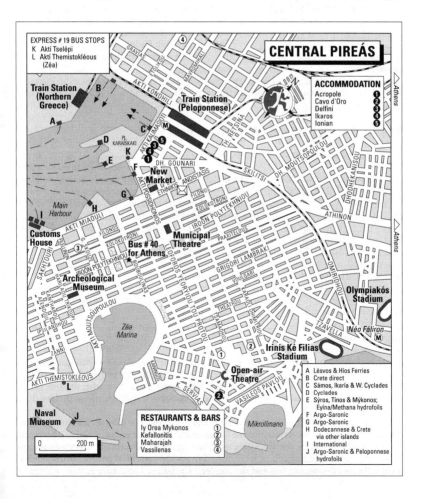

EXPRESS # 19 BUS STOPS
K Aktí Tselépi
L Aktí Themistokléous
   (Zéa)

CENTRAL PIREÁS

Train Station (Northern Greece)

Train Station (Peloponnese)

ACCOMMODATION

Acropole	❶
Cavo d'Oro	❷
Delfini	❸
Ikaros	❹
Ionian	❺

Athens

PL. KARAÏSKAKI

DH. GOUNARI

New Market

Main Harbour

Customs House

Municipal Theatre

Bus # 40 for Athens

Archeological Museum

Zéa Marina

Olympiakós Stadium

Néo Fáliron

Irinís Ké Filías Stadium

Open-air Theatre

Mikrolímano

Naval Museum

0   200 m

RESTAURANTS & BARS

ly Orea Mykonos	①
Kefallonitis	②
Maharajah	③
Vassilenas	④

A Lésvos & Híos Ferries
B Crete direct
C Sámos, Ikaría & W. Cyclades
D Cyclades
E Sýros, Tínos & Mýkonos;
   Eyína/Methana hydrofoils
F Argo-Saronic
G Argo-Saronic
H Dodecannese & Crete
   via other islands
I International
J Argo-Saronic & Peloponnese
   hydrofoils

Pireás grew by leaps and bounds. The original influx into the port was a group of immigrants from Híos, whose island had been devastated by the Turks; later came populations from Ídhra, Crete and the Peloponnese. By World War I, Pireás had outstripped the island of Sýros as the nation's first port, its strategic position enhanced by the opening of the Suez and Corinth canals in 1862 and 1893 respectively. Like Athens, the city's great period of expansion began in 1923, with the exchange of populations with Turkey. Over 100,000 Asia Minor Greeks decided to settle in Pireás, doubling the population almost overnight – and giving a boost to a pre-existing semi-underworld culture, whose enduring legacy was rembétika, outcasts' music played in hashish dens along the waterside.

The city these days is almost indistinguishable from Athens, with its scruffy web of suburbs merging into those of the capital. Economically, it is at present on a mild upswing, boosted by two successive go-ahead mayors and the prominence of its late MP, former actress and Minister of Culture, Melina Mercouri. An unashamedly functional place, with its port despatching up to sixty ships a day in season – both to the islands and to a range of international destinations – there are few sights beyond the numbers and diversity of the sailors in the harbour. The ancient walls are long gone, and the junta years saw misguided demolition of many buildings of character. On the plus side, there's a nice enough **park** (three blocks back from the main harbour, intersected by Vas. Konstandínou); a scattering of genuine antique/junk shops, full of peasant copper and wood, plus a big Sunday morning **flea market**, near Platía Ipodhamías, at the top end of Goúnari (behind the train station); and a couple of more than respectable museums.

The Archeological and Maritime museums

The **Archeological Museum** at Hariláou Trikoúpi 31 (Tues–Sun 8.30am–2.30pm; 500dr) is the best time-filler in Pireás, and enthusiasts will certainly want to make a special trip out here. Upper-floor exhibits include a *kouros* (idealized male statue) dedicated to Apollo, which was dragged out of the sea in 1959. Dating from 520 BC, this is the earliest known life-size bronze, and is displayed with two other fifth-century bronzes of Artemis and Athena found in the same manner at about the same time.

On the ground floor are more submarine finds, this time second-century AD stone reliefs of battles between Greeks and Amazons, apparently made for export to Rome. The sea's effect on them was far more corrosive than in the case of the bronzes, but you can still tell that some scenes are duplicated – showing that the ancients weren't above a bit of mass artistic production.

A few blocks away, on Aktí Themistokléous, adjacent to Zéa, the **Maritime Museum** (Tues–Sat 9am–2pm; 400dr) is more specialized, tracing developments with models and the odd ancient piece.

The ferries

If you're staying in Athens prior to heading out to the islands, it's worth going to the tourist office at Amerikís 2 to pick up a **schedule of departures** from Pireás. These can't be relied upon implicitly, but they do give a reasonable indication of what boats are leaving when and for where; note that the Argo-Saronic sailings and ships based on Sýros or Páros are omitted.

The majority of the boats – for the Argo-Saronic, Ikaría or Sámos, and the popular Cyclades – leave between 8 and 9am. There is then another burst of activity between noon and 3pm towards the Cyclades and Dodecanese, and a final battery of sailings from 4 to 10pm (sometimes later), bound for a wide variety of ports, but especially Crete, the northeast Aegean and the western Cyclades. The frequency of sailings is such that, in high season at least, you need never spend the night in Athens or Pireás.

There's no need to **buy tickets** for conventional ferries before you get here, unless you want a cabin berth or are taking a car on board (in which case, consult agents in Athens or Pireás); Flying Dolphin reservations are a good idea during July and August. In general, the best plan is to get to Pireás early, say at 7am, and check with the various **shipping agents** around the metro station and along the quayside Platía Karaïskáki. Keep in mind that many of these act only for particular lines, so for a full picture of the various boats sailing you will need to ask at three or four outlets. Prices for all domestic boat journeys are standard, but the quality of the craft and circuitousness of routes vary greatly. If you are heading for Thíra (Santoríni) or Rhodes, for example, try to get a boat that stops at only three or four islands en route; for Crete settle for direct ferries only.

Boats for different destinations leave from a variety of points along the main harbour, usually following the pattern in the box below, though it's wise to leave time for wayward ships and look for the signs (indicating name of boat and a clockface with departure time) hung in front of the relevant boats on the waterside railings or on the stern

---

FERRY DEPARTURE POINTS

Aegean islands (Cyclades/Dodecanese)
These leave from either Aktí Kalimasióti, the quay right in front of the metro station (#3 on the map), from just the other side of Platía Karaïskáki (#4) or from the points listed for specific islands below. The big boats going to the major Dodecanese usually share point #8 with some of the Cretan ferries.

Crete
Those going via the Cyclades or on to the Dodecanese use the dock on Aktí Miaoúli (#8), while direct services leave from #2 on Aktí Kondhíli.

Sýros, Tínos, Mýkonos
The morning departures tend to go from #5, next to the Éyina hydrofoils.

Western Cyclades
The ferries for these islands usually depart from Aktí Kalimasióti (#3), right in front of the metro station.

Sámos/Ikaría
Boats ending up at these islands, whether morning or evening services, use the Aktí Kalimasióti (#3) dock as well.

Híos/Lésvos
Most Híos and Mytilíni (Lésvos) boats leave from the newly opened quay (#1) round the harbour past the train station for northern Greece.

Argo-Saronic
Ordinary ferries leave from Aktí Possidhónios (#6) and also just round the corner with Aktí Miaoúli (#7), a ten-minute walk from the metro.

International destinations (Limassol, Haifa, Izmir, etc)
These leave from further around the main harbour (#9), towards the customs house (where you should check passports before boarding).

Hydrofoils
Except for departures direct to Éyina, which leave from Aktí Tselépi (#5), hydrofoils for Argo-Saronic and Peloponnesian destinations leave from the Zéa marina (#10), a twenty-minute overhill walk from the metro.

Tickets are on sale from the Flying Dolphins office at the quay from about an hour before departure. To be sure of a particular sailing in high season, it is wise to book ahead in Athens. Equally, if your schedule is tight, book your seat back to Pireás when you arrive.

of the boats themselves. The ticket agent should know the whereabouts of the boat on the particular day.

Practicalities

The easiest way to get to Pireás from Athens is on the **metro**. There are central stops in Athens at Platía Viktorías, Omónia and Monastiráki squares, plus Thissío for those in Veïkou, and Petrálona for those in Koukáki; the journey takes about 25 minutes from Omónia to the Pireás train station stop (the end of the line). Metro trains run from 6am, early enough to catch the first ferries, until midnight, long after the arrival of all but the most delayed boats. Tickets cost 120dr a journey, 180dr if you start your journey north of Attikí station.

Alternatively, you could take a **bus** or a taxi. Bus #40 (about every 20min during the day; hourly 1am–5am) will deposit you on Vasiléos Konstandínou, half a dozen blocks from the docks, but it's very slow – allow nearly an hour from Sýndagma, the most obvious boarding point. The **express buses** (see p.81) are quicker and provide a particularly useful link with the airport. **Taxis** cost about 1700dr at day tariff from the centre of Athens or the airport – worth considering, especially if you're taking one of the hydrofoils from the Zéa marina, which is a fair walk from the metro.

Accommodation

Few visitors stay in Pireás, and most of the port's **hotels** are geared to a steady clientele of seamen, resting between ships. For this reason, picking somewhere at random is not always a good idea. There are, however, a few reasonably priced and wholesome places close to the port. One of the nicest, tucked in a sidestreet a block from the metro station is the family-style *Ionion Hotel*, Kapodhistríou 10 (☎41 77 537, fax 41 10 613; ③), a clean place with TV in all the renovated rooms. Opposite each other in the next street along are the functional and very cheap *Hotel Delfini*, Leohárous 7 (☎41 23 512, fax 42 27 517; ②) and *Ikaros*, Leohárous 18 (☎41 29 305, 41 77 024; ④), which has TV and a/c in all rooms. Also close by is the *Acropole*, Goúnari 7 (☎41 73 313; ③), a safe but slightly run-down standby with a rooftop bar. A much posher place in a fine setting over the hill in Kastélla is the *Cavo d'Oro*, Vas. Pávlou 19–21 (☎41 13 744; ⑥), complete with piano music in the lounge bar.

Sleeping rough in Platía Karaïskáki, as some exhausted travellers attempt to do, is unwise. If thieves or the police don't rouse you, street-cleaners armed with hoses certainly will – at 5am.

Eating and drinking

If you're simply looking for food to take on board, or breakfast, you'll find numerous places around the market area, back from the waterside Aktí Miaoúli/Ethnikís Andistáseos, open from 6.30am. Along the waterfront and down its sidestreets there are also an array of standard *souvlaki* and oven food joints.

For a real blowout, the *Vassilenas* at Etolikoú 72 (the street running inland from Aktí Kondhíli) is a fine choice. Housed in an old grocery store, its set menu provides mezédhes enough to defy all appetites; at 5000dr a head, drinks extra, it's not especially cheap, but enough Athenians consider it worth the drive that most evenings you need to book a table (☎46 12 457). There's a string of ouzeris and seafood tavernas along Aktí Themistokléous, west of the Zéa marina, most of them pretty good and reasonably priced, or try the Indian restaurant *Maharajah (Shere-e-Punjab)* at Notará 122 or snack-bar-style *Punjab* at Kolokotróni 136, both genuine and cheap by Greek standards.

Otherwise, a good bet for seafood is *Kefalonitis*, on the corner of Rethýmnis and Tsakálof, up by the open-air theatre. As the name implies, this place is run by a

Kefallonian family, and is far superior to the tourist-traps on Mikrolímano. A nearby and equally authentic alternative is *Iy Orea Mykonos*, a simple island-style fish taverna on the corner of Kilkís and Sfakión.

Entertainment and nightlife

Culturally, there's not a great deal going on at Pireás, though a **summer festival**, run alongside that of Athens, features events in the open-air theatre set back from the yacht harbour of Mikrolímano (or Tourkolímano, as it has been called for centuries). In winter there's always **football** (see box, p.132): Olympiakós is the port's big team, rival to the capital's AEK and Panathenaïkós, and it plays at Stádhio Karaïskáki beside Néo Fáliro metro station, while **basketball** and other gymnastic events take place in the indoor arena, Stádhio Irínis & Filías, on the opposite side of the tracks.

Finally, a word for the port's best **rembétika venue** (see p.890), the *Ondas tis Konstandinas* at Koundouriótou 109 on the corner of Karóli Dhimitríou (☎42 20 459; closed Sun & Mon, and in summer). This is a very friendly taverna, with rembétika music each night and a special *Smyrneïka* show every Tuesday. On Friday and Saturday nights there's a minimum charge of 4000dr per person.

The "Apollo Coast", Cape Sounion and Lávrio

The seventy kilometres of coast south of Athens – the tourist-board-dubbed "**Apollo Coast**" – has some good but highly developed beaches. At weekends, when Athenians flee the city, the sands fill fast, as do the innumerable bars, restaurants and discos at night. If this is what you're after, then resorts like **Glyfádha** and **Vouliagméni** are functional enough. But for most foreign visitors, the coast's lure is at the end of the road, in the form of the Temple of Poseidon at **Cape Sounion**.

Access to Sounion (Soúnio in the modern spelling) is straightforward. There are buses on the hour and half-hour from the KTEL terminal on Mavromatéon at the southwest corner of the Pedíou e Áreos Park; there's also a more central (but in summer, very full) stop ten minutes later at point "D" on Filellínon, south of Sýndagma (corner of Xenofóndos, in front of the Middle East Airways office). There are both coastal (*paraliakó*) and inland (*mesoyiakó*) services, the latter slightly longer and more expensive. The coast route normally takes around two hours; last departures back to Athens are posted at the Sounion stop.

For Glyfádha/Voúla and Vouliagméni/Várkiza – the main resorts – take the A3 trunk line from Sýndagma or E2 express bus from opposite the National Gardens and transfer onto local services #114 and #115. The A2 trunk-line bus for Glyfádha/Voúla also leaves from Panepistimíou.

The resorts: Glyfádha to Anávissos

Although some Greeks swim at Pireás itself, few would recommend the sea much before **GLYFÁDHA**, half an hour's drive southeast from the city centre. The major resort along the "Apollo Coast", merged almost indistinguishably with its neighbour **VOÚLA**, this is lined with seafood restaurants, ice-cream bars and discos, as well as a couple of marinas and a golf course. Its popularity, though, is hard to fathom, built as it is in the shadow of the airport. The only possible appeal is in the beaches, the best of which is the **Astir**, privately owned and with a stiff admission charge; others are gritty. Hotels are all on the expensive side, and in any case are permanently full of package tours; there is a campsite at Voúla (☎01/89 52 712).

VOULIAGMÉNI, which in turn has swallowed up **Kavoúri**, is a little quieter than Glyfádha, and a little ritzier. Set back from a small natural saltwater lake, it boasts a water-ski school, some extremely chi-chi restaurants, and an EOT pay-beach. Again, budget accommodation is hard to come by, though there is a **camp-site** – and another EOT pay-beach – just to the south at **Várkiza**. There is also pleasant free swimming to be enjoyed from the popular rocks between Vouliagméni and Várkiza.

South from Várkiza, there are further beaches en route to Sounion, though unless you've a car to pick your spot they're not really worth the effort. The resorts of **Lagoníssi** and **Anávissos** are in the Glyfádha mould, and only slightly less crowded, despite the extra distance from Athens.

Cape Sounion

Cape Sounion – Aktí Souníou – is one of the most imposing spots in Greece, for centuries a landmark for boats sailing between Pireás and the islands, and an equally dramatic vantage-point in itself to look out over the Aegean. On its tip stands the fifth-century BC **Temple of Poseidon**, built in the time of Pericles as part of a major sanctuary to the sea god.

The Temple of Poseidon

The temple (Tues–Sun 10am–sunset; 800dr) owes its fame above all to **Byron**, who visited in 1810, carved his name on the nearest pillar (an unfortunate precedent) and commemorated the event in the finale of his hymn to Greek independence, the "Isles of Greece" segment of *Don Juan*:

> *Place me on Sunium's marbled steep,*
> *Where nothing, save the waves and I,*
> *May hear our mutual murmurs sweep;*
> *There, swan-like, let me sing and die:*
> *A land of slaves shall ne'er be mine –*
> *Dash down yon cup of Samian wine!*

In summer, at least, there is faint hope of solitude, unless you slip into the site before the tour groups arrive. But the temple is as evocative a ruin as any in Greece. Doric in style, it was probably built by the architect of the Thiseon in the Athens *agora*. That it is so admired and visited is in part due to its site, but also perhaps to its picturesque state of ruin – preserving, as if by design, sixteen of its thirty-four columns. On a clear day, the view from the temple takes in the islands of Kéa, Kýthnos and Sérifos to the southeast, Éyina and the Peloponnese to the west.

The rest of the site is of more academic interest. There are remains of a fortification wall around the sanctuary; a **Propylaion** (entrance hall) and **Stoa**, and cuttings for two shipsheds. To the north are the foundations of a small **Temple of Athena**.

Beaches – and staying at Sounion

Below the promontory are several **coves** – the most sheltered a five-minute walk east from the car park and site entrance. The main Sounion beach is more crowded, but has a couple of tavernas at the far end – pretty reasonably priced, considering the location. *O Ilias* has the slightly better view and a fair selection of grilled meat and fish.

If you want to stay, there are a couple of **campsites** just around the coast: *Camping Bacchus* (the nearest; ☎0292/39 262) and *Sounion Beach Camping* (5km; ☎0292/39 358). The 1960s-style *Hotel Aegeon* (☎0292/39 262; ⑥) is right on the Sounion beach and predictably pricey, so *Hotel Saron* (☎0292/39 144; ④), just round the coast by the second campsite, is a better deal and has a pool into the bargain.

Lávrio

Ten kilometres north of Sounion, around the cape, is the port of **LÁVRIO**. This has daily ferry connections with Kéa and a single weekly boat to Kýthnos, though extra high-speed services are supposed to be starting up. It can be reached by **bus** from the Mavromatéon terminal in Athens, or from Sounion.

The port's ancient predecessor, Laurion, was famous for its silver mines – a mainstay of the classical Athenian economy – which were worked almost exclusively by slaves. The port today remains an industrial and mining town, though nowadays for less precious minerals (cadmium and manganese) and also hosts the country's principal transit camp for political refugees: mostly Kurds from Iraq and Turkey at present, with a scattering of eastern Europeans, awaiting resettlement in North America, Australia or Europe. The island offshore, **Makrónissos**, now uninhabited, has an even more sinister past, for it was here that hundreds of ELAS members and other leftists were imprisoned in "re-education" labour camps during and after the civil war.

As you might imagine, this is not really a place to linger between buses and ferries, though the *To Koralli* fish taverna by the boat jetty provides adequate but rather pricey sustenance. If you have more time to kill, the site of **ancient Thoriko** is of some interest. It lies down a zigzag track from the village of Pláka, 5km north of Lávrio. A defensive outpost of the mining area in classical times, its most prominent ruins are of a theatre, crudely engineered into an irregular slope in the hill.

East of Athens: the Mesóyia and Brauron

The area east of Athens is one of the least visited parts of Attica. The mountain of **Imittós** (Hymettus) forms an initial barrier, with Kessarianí monastery (see p.119) on its cityside flank. Beyond extends the plateau of the **Mesóyia** (Midland), a gentle landscape whose villages have a quiet renown for their *retsina* and for their churches, many of which date to Byzantine times. On towards the coast, there is the remote and beautiful site of **ancient Brauron**, and the developing resort of **Pórto Ráfti**.

The Mesóyia

The best-known attraction of the Mesóyia is at the village of **PEANÍA**, on the east slope of Imittós: the **Koutoúki cave** (daily 9.30am–4.30pm; 500dr), endowed with spectacularly illuminated stalactites and stalagmites and multicoloured curtains of rock. It is fairly easily reached by taking the Athens–Markópoulo bus, stopping at Peanía and then walking up. Close by the village – just to the east on the Spáta road – is the chapel of **Áyios Athanásios**, built with old Roman blocks and fragments.

MARKÓPOULO, the main Mesóyia village, shelters a further clutch of chapels. Within the village, set in a walled garden, stand the twin chapels of **Ayía Paraskeví** and **Ayía Thékla**; ring for admission, and a nun will open them up to show you the seventeenth-century frescoes. Over to the west, on the road to Koropí, is one of the oldest churches in Attica, the tenth-century **Metamórfosi**, the keys to which can be obtained from the Análipsi church in Koropí.

Heading east from Markópoulo, the road runs past the unusual double-naved **Ayía Triádha** (2500m out) and on to the coast at **PÓRTO RÁFTI**, whose bay, protected by islets, forms an almost perfect natural harbour. Buses to here from the Mavromatéon terminal sometimes give the final destination as Avláki. The area has been comprehensively developed, with an EOT pay-beach at Avláki and a fair number of tavernas, but remains a good place to **stay** if you can find a room. The *Kiani Akti,* Ayías Marínas

40 (☎0299/86 400, fax 86 050; ⑤) is a smart modern hotel on the road to Avláki. As for **food**, the most genuine and reasonably priced places are on the old harbour 2km before the bus terminal – try *To Limani*. On the small island in the harbour is a large Roman statue of a woman whose now missing arm held the "first fruits" of crops that were sent each year to the sacred island of Delos. During the sixteenth century the statue was thought to hold scissors, and the port came to be known as the tailor's port, Pórto Ráfti.

From here, if you've your own vehicle, you can make your way over the mountain to the village of Vravróna and the site of **ancient Brauron**.

Brauron

Brauron (site and museum Tues–Sun 8.30am–2.30pm; 500dr) is one of the most enjoyable minor Greek sites. It lies just outside the modern village of Vravróna (40km from Athens), in a marshy area at the base of a low, chapel-topped hill. The marsh and surrounding fields are alive with birdsong, only rarely drowned out by traffic noise from the nearby busy road.

The remains are of a **Sanctuary of Artemis**, centred on a vast *stoa*. This was the chief site of the Artemis cult, legendarily founded by Iphigeneia, whose "tomb" has also been identified here. It was she who, with Orestes, stole the image of Artemis from Tauris (as commemorated in Euripides's *Iphigeneia at Tauris*) and introduced worship of the goddess to Greece. The main event of the cult was a quadrennial festival, now shrouded in mystery, in which young girls dressed as bears to enact a ritual connected with the goddess and childbirth.

The **Stoa of the Bears**, where these initiates stayed, has been substantially reconstructed, along with a stone **bridge**; both are fifth century BC and provide a graceful focus to the semi-waterlogged site. Somewhat scantier are the ruins of the temple itself, whose stepped foundations can be made out; immediately adjacent, the sacred spring still wells up, today squirming with tadpoles. Nearby, steps lead up to the chapel, which contains some damaged frescoes. At the site **museum**, left off the main road over a kilometre from the ruins, various finds from the sanctuary are displayed.

Getting to Brauron from Athens will involve a walk if you're dependent on public transport. Bus #304 from the Záppio passes through **Loútsa** and terminates within two kilometres of the site. Loútsa itself is also served by buses #316 and #321 and is a lively little spot with a decent sandy beach and row of tavernas and cafés.

Rafína, Marathon and Rhamnous

The port of **RAFÍNA** has **ferries,** the **catamaran** (in fact a sort of jet-boat) and **hydrofoils** to a wide assortment of the Cyclades, the Dodecanese and the northeast Aegean, as well as to nearby Évvia. It is connected regularly by bus with Athens: a forty-minute trip (from Mavromatéon) through the "gap" in Mount Pendéli.

Boats aside, the appeal of the place is mainly gastronomic. Though much of the town has been spoilt by tacky seaside development, the little fishing harbour with its line of **roof-terrace seafood restaurants** remains one of the most attractive spots on the Attic coast. Of these, *Ta Kavouria tou Asimaki*, the first as you descend to the harbour from the square, is the cheapest and best. A lunchtime outing is an easy operation, given the frequency of the bus service. Evenings, when it's more fun, you need to arrange your own transport back, or make for the beachside **campsite** at nearby Kókkino Limanáki. The town's few **hotels** are often full in summer, so you need to phone ahead to be sure of a room; the best value is the *Corali* (☎0294/22 477; ②) located in the central Platía Nikifórou Plastíra, while the *Avra* (☎0294/22 780, fax 23 320; ⑥), just down from the square and overlooking the sea, is large and rather overpriced.

If you want a **swim**, the pleasant little bay of **Blé Limanáki** is just ten minutes' walk north over the headland above the harbour and avoids the pollution of the longer town beach. There is nothing to eat or drink here though. Alternatively, you can walk the extra fifteen minutes to **Kókkino Limanáki**, which has a good shady beach and some restaurants and shops.

Marathon

The site of the most famous military victory in Athenian history is not far from the village of **MARATHÓNAS**, 42km from Athens. Buses also leave from the Mavromatéon terminal in Athens, some of them calling first at Rafína. Just over three kilometres after Néa Mákri (4km before the village of Marathónas there is a turn to the right; the **Týmfos Marathóna** stands to the left of the road 700 yards after this turn. The ancient burial mound was raised over 192 Athenians who died in the city's famous victory over the Persians in 490 BC. Consisting only of overgrown earth piled ten metres high, it is a quietly impressive monument. Another mound, this for the eleven Plataian allies of the Athenians (including a ten-year-old boy) who died in the battle, is about 5km away, near the edge of the mountain. To reach the **Mound of the Plataians** and the **archeological museum**, return to the Rafína–Marathónas road and turn right towards the village of Marathónas. Turn left and follow the small yellow signs for 2.5km to the museum (open, as is the mound precinct, Tues–Sun 8.30am–2.30pm; 500dr) with a sparse collection of artefacts mainly from the local Cave of Pan, a deity felt to have aided the victory.

Marathónas village itself is a dull place, with just a couple of cafés and restaurants for the passing trade. Nearby, though, to the west, and quite an impressive site, is **Límni Marathóna** – Marathon Lake – with its huge marble dam. This provided Athens' entire water supply until the 1950s and it is still used as a storage facility for water from the giant Mórnos project in central Greece. You can drive or walk across the top of the dam and there is a scenically situated café/restaurant on the east side.

The coast around ancient Marathon takes in some good stretches of sand, walkable from the tomb if you want to cool off. The best and most popular **beach** is to the north at **SKHINIÁS**, a long, pine-backed strand with shallow water, crowded with Athenians at weekends. There is a **campsite**, *Camping Marathon*, midway along the road from Marathónas. Of the tavernas, *Iy Avra* is the best bet and stays open most of the year, at least at weekends.

Rhamnous

Further to the north, the ruins of **RHAMNOUS** (Tues–Sun 8.30am–2.30pm; 500dr) occupy an isolated site above the sea. Among the scattered and overgrown remains is a Doric **Temple of Nemesis**, goddess of retribution. Pausanias records that the Persians who landed nearby before their defeat incurred her wrath by carrying off a marble block – upon which they intended to commemorate their conquest of Athens. There are also the remains of a smaller temple dedicated to Themis, goddess of justice. Rhamnous can be reached just five times daily by bus from the Mavromatéon terminal; the village name to look for is Káto Soúli.

Mount Párnitha and Phyle

Scarcely an hour's bus ride north from the city centre, **Mount Párnitha** is an unexpectedly vast and – where it has escaped fire damage – virgin tract of forest, rock and ravine. If you've no time for expeditions further afield, it will give you a taste of what Greek mountains are all about, including a good selection of mountain flowers. If you're here in March or April, it merits a visit in its own right. Snow lies surprisingly late on the north side and, in its wake, carpets of crocus, alpine squills and mountain windflower spring from the mossy ground, while lower down you'll find aubretia, tulips, dwarf iris and a whole range of orchids.

There are numerous **waymarked paths** on the mountain (look for red discs and multicoloured paint splodges on the trees). The principal and most representative ones are the approach to the Báfi refuge up the **Houni** ravine, and the walk to the Skípiza spring. These, along with a couple of lesser excursions, to the ancient fort at Phyle and one of the many legendary **caves of Pan**, are detailed below.

The hike to the Báfi refuge

On Saturdays and Sundays bus A12 runs from the corner of Aharnón and Stournári (north side of Platía Váthis) twice a day (6.30am and 2.30pm) up to Párnitha. During the week take the trunk-line bus A10 or B10 to the end of the line (Mesiníti) and then the local buses #724 or #737 to the suburb of Thrakomakedhónes, whose topmost houses are beginning to steal up the flanks of the mountain beside the mouth of the **Houni** ravine. Get off at the highest stop and keep on, bearing left, up Odhós Thrákis to where the road ends at the foot of a cliff beside two new blocks of flats. Keep straight ahead along the foot of the cliff and in a few metres you come to the start of the path, turning down left into a dry streambed, before crossing and continuing on the opposite bank.

The refuge is about two hours' walk away. The track curves slowly leftwards up the craggy, well-defined ravine, at first through thick scrub, then through more open forest of Greek fir, crossing the stream two or three times. At a junction reached after about 45 minutes, signposted "Katára–Mesanó Neró–Móla", keep straight ahead. At the next fork, some ten minutes later, keep right. After a further five minutes, at the top of a sparsely vegetated slope, you get your first glimpse of the pink-roofed refuge high on a rocky spur in front of you. Another twenty minutes brings you to the confluence of two small streams, where a sign on a tree points left to Ayía Triádha (see below), and a second path branches right to Móla and Koromiliá. Take the third, middle, path, up a scrubby spur. At the top a broad path goes off left to meet the ring road leading to Ayía Triádha.

From here, turn right, down into the head of a gully, where the path doubles back and climbs up to the refuge. Normally the refuge warden provides **board and lodging**, particularly on weekends, but it would be wise to check opening times and accommodation policy with the Atharnés EOS (☎24 69 777) in advance, as the schedule changes periodically. Water is usually available at the back of the building, except in winter.

To the Skípiza spring

For the walk to the Skípiza spring, you need to get off at the chapel of Ayía Triádha in the heart of the mountains. On the weekends there are two A12 connections a day: at 6.30am, returning at 8am; and at 2.30pm, returning at 4pm. If you get stuck, you can continue to the *Hotel Mount Parnes* and take the téléférique down if it's operating – otherwise there's a rough trail down a gully near the *Xenia Hotel*, spilling out near the Metóhi picnic grounds.

The **Skípiza spring** is an hour and a half to two hours' walk away. From the bus stop by the chapel, walk west past the *Hotel-Chalet Kyklamina*, continuing straight on to the ring road. After the first ascent and descent, you come after fifteen minutes to the Paliohóri spring on the right of the road in the middle of a left-hand bend, opposite a piece of flat ground marked with pointed-hat pipes. A beautiful and well-defined path is clearly marked by discs on trees, beginning by the spring and following the course of a small stream up through the fir woods.

From Skípiza you can continue right around the summit to **Móla** (about 90min) and from there, in another hour, back to the Báfi refuge. Alternatively, by setting your back to the Skípiza spring and taking the path that charges up the ridge almost directly behind, you can get to **Báfi** in around forty minutes. Turn left when you hit the paved road after about half an hour; follow it ten minutes more down to the ring road and turn left again. In a few paces you are in the refuge car park. To get back to Ayía Triádha by the road it's about 6km (an hour's walk).

The Cave of Pan

Another highly evocative spot for lovers of classical ghosts is the **Cave of Pan**, which Menander used as the setting for one of his plays. The best approach is by track and trail from the chapel of Ayía Triádha: a map showing local landmarks (labelled in Greek), superimposed on a topographical map, is posted just behind the church.

Phyle

Over to the west of the main Párnitha trails, another route up the mountain will take you to the ruined but still impressive fourth-century BC Athenian fort of **Phyle**, about an hour and three-quarters on foot beyond the village of Filí (known locally as Khasiá). Buses to Filí leave near the Aharnón/Stournára stop on Sourméli.

On the way up to the fort you pass the unattractively restored fourteenth-century **monastery of Klistón** in the mouth of the Goúra ravine that splits through the middle of the Párnitha range. The walking, unfortunately, is all on asphalt.

Eleusis and west to the Peloponnese

The main **highway to Kórinthos** (Corinth) is about as unattractive a road as any in Greece. For the first thirty or so kilometres you have little sense of leaving Athens, whose western suburbs merge into the industrial wastelands of first Elefsína and then Mégara. Offshore, almost closing off the bay, is **Salamína** (ancient Salamis), not a dream island in anyone's book but a nicer escape than it looks, and accessible by ferries from the mainland here at Lákki Kaloírou (and at Pérama, near Pireás).

A train or bus direct to Kórinthos or beyond, though, is perhaps the wisest option. Only the site of **ancient Eleusis** is in any way a temptation to stop, and even this is strictly for classical enthusiasts. **Drivers** should note that the Athens–Kórinthos non-toll road is one of the most dangerous in the country, switching from four-lane highway to a rutted two-laner without warning; it is best driven in daytime, or preserve your sanity and pay the toll.

Eleusis

The **Sanctuary of Demeter** at **ELEUSIS**, at the beginning of the Sacred Way to Athens, was one of the most important in the Greek world. For two millennia, the ritual ceremonies known as the Mysteries were performed, which had an effect on their ancient initiates the equal of any modern cult. According to Pindar, who experienced the rites in classical times and, like all others, was bound by pain of death not to reveal their content, anyone who had "seen the holy things [at Eleusis] and goes in death beneath the earth is happy, for he knows life's end and he knows the new divine beginning."

Established in Mycenaean times, perhaps as early as 1500 BC, the cult centred around the figure of Demeter (Ceres to the Romans), the goddess of corn, and the myth of her daughter Persephone's annual descent into and resurrection from the underworld, which came to symbolize the rebirth of the crops (and the gods responsible for them) in the miracle of fertility. By the fifth century BC the cult had developed into a sophisticated annual festival, attracting up to 30,000 people from all over the Greek world. Participants gathered in Athens, outside the Propylaia on the Acropolis, and, after various rituals, including mass bathing and purification in Phaleron Bay, followed the Sacred Way to the sanctuary here at Eleusis. It has been speculated by some, such as the late ethnomycologist R. Gordon Wasson, that one of the rituals entailed the ingestion of a potion containing grain-ergot fungus, the effects of which would be almost identical to those of modern psychedelic drugs. The Mysteries eventually fell foul of Christianity and died out. It is interesting that there was supposedly a curse that Demeter would render the land permanently barren if her worship there ever ceased. Looking at the ecological havoc wreaked by the area's industry, it would seem that the curse has been fulfilled.

The site

The **ruins** (Tues–Sun 8.30am–2.30pm; 500dr) are obscure in the extreme, dating from several different ages of rebuilding and largely reduced to foundations; any imaginings of mystic goings-on are further hampered by the spectacularly unromantic setting. The best plan is to head straight for the **museum**, which features models of the site at various stages in its history. This will at least point you in the direction of the **Telesterion**, the windowless Hall of Initiation, where the priests of Demeter would exhibit the "Holy Things" – presumably sheaves of fungus-infected grain, or vessels containing the magic potion – and speak "the Unutterable Words".

To reach the site from Athens, take **bus** A16 from Platía Eleftherías, down Pireós from Omónia. Ask to be dropped at the *Heröön* (Sanctuary), to the left of the main road, a short way into Elefsína. The trip can easily be combined with a visit to the monastery at Dhafní (see p.118), on the same road and bus route.

On from Elefsína

Northwest from Elefsína, the **old road to Thebes and Delphi** heads into the hills. This route is described in Chapter Three, and is highly worthwhile, with its detours to **ancient Aegosthena** and the tiny resort of **Pórto Yermenó**. At Mégara another, more minor road heads north to reach the sea at the village of Alepohóri, where it deteriorates to a track to loop around to Pórto Yermenó.

Heading directly west, on towards the Peloponnese, there are shingle beaches – more or less clear of pollution – along the old, parallel coastal road at Kinéta and Áyii Theódhori. This highway, with the Yeránia mountains to the north and those of the Peloponnese across the water, has a small place in pre-Homeric myth, as the route where Theseus slew the bandit Sciron and threw him off the cliffs to be eaten by a giant sea turtle. Thus, Sciron met the same fate as the generations of travellers he had preyed upon.

You leave Attica at Isthmía, a village beside the **Corinth Canal** (see p.163), where most of the buses break the journey for a drink at the café by the bridge. To the north of the canal, Loutráki and Perahóra are technically part of Attica but, as they are more easily reached from Kórinthos, are covered in the Peloponnese chapter.

travel details

Trains

Trains for **Kórinthos and the Peloponnese** leave from the **Stathmós Peloponníssou**, those for **northern Greece** from **Stathmós Laríssis**. The stations adjoin each other, just west of Deliyánni, on the #1 trolley bus route. To reach the Peloponnese station, use the metal overpass next to the Laríssis station. The new Inter-City trains are considerably faster and more reliable but there is a hefty extra charge (also levied on rail passes).

Destinations from Stathmós Peloponníssou include: Árgos (6 daily; 3hr 10min); Kalamáta (4 daily; 6hr 30min–8hr); Kórinthos (12 daily; 1hr 30min–2hr); Pátra (8 daily; 3hr 30min–4hr 30min); Pýrgos (7 daily; 5hr 30min–6hr 30min).

Destinations from Stathmós Laríssis include: Alexandhroúpoli (2 daily; 16hr); Halkídha (17 daily; 1hr 30min); Thessaloníki (10 daily; 6hr 10min–8hr); Vólos (3 daily; 5–7hr).

Buses

Attica Buses for most destinations in Attica (ie within this chapter) leave from the Mavromatéon terminal (250m north of the National Archeological Museum, at the junction with Leofóros Alexándhras, "B" on the Athens map). Exceptions are specified in the text.

Destinations include: Lávrio (every 30min until 6pm, then hourly until 9pm; 1hr 30min); Marathon Tomb (every 30min until 2pm, hourly thereafter; 1hr 15min); Rafína (every 30min; 1hr); Sounion by the coast (hourly on the half hour; 1hr 30min); Sounion by the inland route (hourly on the hour; 1hr 45min).

Peloponnese and western/northern Greece Most buses leave from the terminal at Kifissoú 100, a good 4km northeast of the city centre, in the industrial district of Peristéri; the easiest way to get there is on the #051 bus from the corner of Vilára and Menándhrou (near Omónia; "E" on the map).

Destinations include: Árgos (hourly; 2hr 15min; Árta (8 daily; 6hr); Corfu (3 daily; 11hr); Igoumenítsa (3 daily; 8hr 30min); Ioánnina (8 daily; 7hr 30min); Kalamáta (10–11 daily; 4hr 30min); Kefallonía (4–5 daily; 8hr); Kórinthos (every 30min; 1hr 30min); Lefkádha (4 daily; 6hr); Mycenae/Náfplio (hourly; 2hr 30min); Olympia (4 daily; 6hr); Pátra (every 30min; 3hr); Pýlos (2 daily; 6hr); Spárti (11 daily; 4hr); Thessaloníki (10 daily; 7hr 30min); Trípoli (12 daily; 3hr); Zákynthos (4 daily; 7hr).

Central Greece Buses for most other destinations in central Greece leave from the Liossíon 260 terminal, easiest reached by taxi. Alternatively, take either bus #024 at the Amalías entrance of the National Gardens (by Sýndagma), or on Panepistimíou almost to the end of its route (about 25min; the stop is 200m south of the terminal); or the metro from Omónia/ Monastiráki to the Áyios Nikólaos station (800m southeast of the terminal; coming out, go under the rail line, turn left and look out for the buses).

Destinations include: Áyios Konstandínos (hourly at quarter past the hour; 2hr 30min); Delphi (6 daily; 3hr); Halkídha (every 30min; 1hr 15min); Karpeníssi (3 daily; 6hr); Kými, for Skýros ferries (6 daily; 3hr 30min); Ósios Loukás (2 daily; 4hr); Thíva/Thebes (hourly; 1hr 30min); Tríkala (9 daily; 5hr 30min); Vólos (9–12 daily; 5hr).

Island ferries and hydrofoils

Information For details of ferries from **Rafína** or **Lávrio** call their respective port police offices (Rafína: ☎0294/22 300; Lávrio: ☎0292/25 249). For **hydrofoils** call (☎0294/23 500 or 23 561).

Pireás Ferries and hydrofoils to the Argo-Saronic, Monemvassía, Crete, the Cyclades, Dodecanese and northeast Aegean islands. See p.142 for details of how to get to Pireás.

Lávrio Ferries daily to Kéa; one weekly to Kýthnos. Bus from Mavromatéon.

Rafína Ferries daily to Mármari, Kárystos and Stýra on Évvia; most days to Ándhros, Tínos, Sýros, Mýkonos, Páros and Náxos, plus less frequently to Amorgós; and two or three weekly to Híos, Lésvos and Límnos. Hydrofoils to Évvia (Stýra, Mármari and Kárystos), Ándhros, Tínos, Mýkonos, Páros, Náxos and beyond. Most ferries from Rafína to the Cyclades leave in the **late afternoon** – a boon if you've missed the morning Pireás boats. Bus from Mavromatéon.

International ferries

From Pireás Destinations include: Izmir or Çeşme, Turkey (once weekly); Kuşadası, Turkey (once weekly May–Oct); Limassol, Cyprus and Haifa, Israel (at least weekly, via Rhodes or Crete.

Domestic flights

Olympic Airways operates regular flights from the **west airport** to the following destinations: Alexandhroúpoli, Astypálea, Haniá (Crete), Híos, Ikaría Iráklion (Crete), Ioánnina, Kalamáta, Kárpathos, Kastoriá, Kavála, Kefalloniá, Kérkyra (Corfu), Kýthira, Kós, Kozáni, Léros, Límnos, Mílos, Mýkonos, Mytilíni (Lésvos), Náxos, Páros, Préveza, Ródhos (Rhodes), Sámos, Skiáthos, Sýros, Sitía (Crete), Skýros, Thessaloníki, Thíra (Santórini) and Zákynthos.

Island services are heavily reduced out of season.

CHAPTER TWO

THE PELOPONNESE

T he appeal of the Peloponnese (Pelopónnisos in Greek) is hard to overstate. This southern peninsula, technically an island since the cutting of the Corinth Canal, seems to have the best of almost everything Greek. Its ancient sites include the Homeric palaces of Agamemnon at **Mycenae** and of Nestor at **Pýlos**, the best preserved of all Greek theatres at Epidaurus, and the lush sanctuary of **Olympia**, host for a millennium to the Olympic Games. The medieval remains are scarcely less rich, with the fabulous Venetian, Frankish and Turkish castles of **Náfplio**, **Methóni** and **Kórinthos**; the strange battle towers and frescoed churches of the **Máni**; and the extraordinarily well-preserved Byzantine shells of **Mystra** and **Monemvasiá**.

Beyond this incredible profusion of cultural monuments, the Peloponnese is also a superb place to relax and wander. Its **beaches**, especially along the west coast, are among the finest and least developed in the country, and the **landscape** inland is superb – dominated by range after range of forested mountains, and cut by some of the lushest valleys and gorges to be imagined. Not for nothing did its heartland province of **Arcadia** give its name to the concept of a classical rural idyll.

The Peloponnese is at its most enjoyable and intriguing when you venture off the beaten track: to the old hill towns of Arcadia like **Karýtena**, **Stemnítsa** and **Dhimitsána**; the Maniot tower villages such as **Kítta** or **Váthia**; at **Voïdhokiliá** and **Elafónissos** beaches in the south; or the trip along the astonishing **rack-and-pinion railway** leading inland from the north coast at **Dhiakoftó** to **Kalávryta**.

Anciently known as the **Moreas**, from the resemblance of the outline to that of a mulberry leaf (*morá*), rounded at the top, with three long fingers below (from west to east, Messinía, the Máni and Monemvasiá), plus the thumb of the Argolid, it will amply repay any amount of time that you devote to it. The **Argolid**, the area richest in ancient history, is just a couple of hours from Athens, and if pushed you could complete a circuit of the main sights here – **Corinth**, **Mycenae** and **Epidaurus** – in a couple of days, making your base by the sea in Náfplio. Given a week, you could take in the two large sites of Mystra and Olympia at a more leisurely pace. To get to grips with all this, however, plus the wonderful southern peninsulas of the Máni and Messinía, and the hill towns of Arcadia, you'll need at least a couple of weeks.

If you were planning on a combination of Peloponnese-plus-islands, the Argo-Saronic or Ionian islands are the most convenient, although you would be better off limiting yourself to the mainland on a short trip. The **Argo-Saronic** islands (see p.465) are linked by hydrofoil with the Argolid and Pireás. Of the **Ionian** islands, isolated **Kýthira** is covered in this chapter since closest access is from the southern Peloponnese ports, but **Zákynthos** (see p.830) or **Kefalloniá** (see p.818) can also be reached from the western port of Kyllíni, and Greece's second port city of **Pátra** serves as a gateway to Corfu – and to southern Italy.

Travelling about the peninsula by **public transport**, you'll be dependent mostly on the **buses**. These are fast and regular on the main routes between the seven provincial capitals, and from these towns go to most other places at least once a day; travelling between smaller towns in different provinces is considerably more complicated. The Peloponnese **train line**, now over a century old, is in a poor state, especially on its highly scenic southern loop, with trains risking mishaps on defective sleepers if they exceed

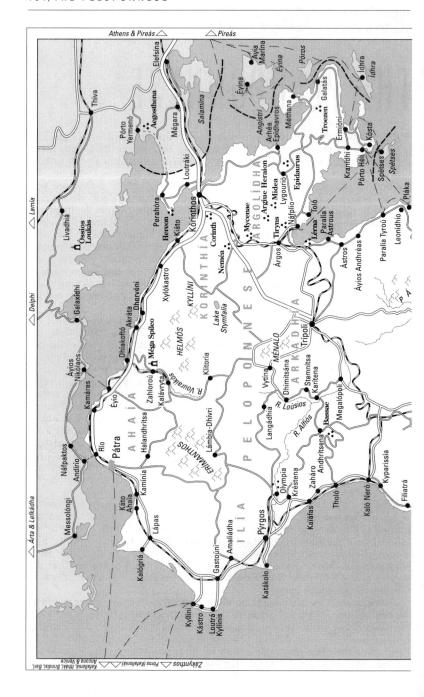

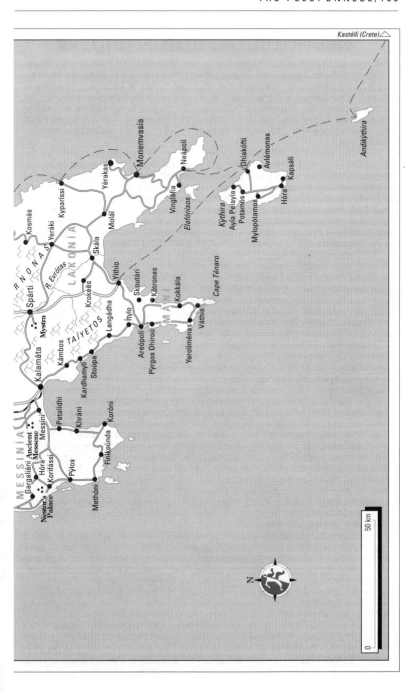

PELOPÓNNISSOS – MOREAS: SOME HISTORY

The **ancient history** of the Peloponnese is very much that of the Greek mainstream. During the **Mycenaean period** (around 2000–1100 BC), the peninsula hosted the semi-legendary kingdoms of Agamemnon at Mycenae, Nestor at Pýlos and Menelaus at Sparta. In the **Dorian** and **Classical** eras, the region's principal city-state was Sparta, which, with its allies, brought down Athens in the ruinous Peloponnesian War. Under **Roman** rule, Corinth was the capital of the southern Greek province. For more on all these periods, see "The Historical Framework" on p.841, and the individual accounts in this chapter.

From the decline of the Roman empire, through to the Ottoman conquest, the Peloponnese pursued a more complex and individual course. A succession of occupations and conquests, with attendant outposts and castles, left an extraordinary legacy of medieval remains throughout the region.

The Peloponnese retained a nominally Roman civilization, well after the colonial rule had dissipated, with Corinth at the fore until the city was destroyed by two major earthquakes in the fourth and sixth centuries. Around this time, too, came attacks from barbarian tribes of Avars and Slavs, who were to pose sporadic problems for the new rulers – the **Byzantines**, the eastern emperors of the now divided Roman empire.

The Byzantines established their courts, castles and towns from the ninth century onward; their control, however, was only partial, as large swathes of the Moreás fell under the control of the Franks and Venetians. The **Venetians** settled along the coast, founding trading ports at Monemvasiá, Pýlos and Koróni, which endured, for the most part, into the fifteenth century. The **Franks**, led by the Champlitte and Villehardouin clans, arrived in 1204, bloodied and eager from the sacking of Constantinople in the piratical Fourth Crusade. They swiftly conquered large tracts of the peninsula, and divided it into feudal baronies under a prince of the Morea.

Towards the middle of the thirteenth century, there was a remarkable **Byzantine revival**, which spread from the court at Mystra to reassert control over the peninsula. A last flicker of "Greek" rule, it was eventually extinguished by the **Turkish conquest** between 1458 and 1460, and was to lie dormant, save for sporadic rebellions in the perennially intransigent Máni, until the nineteenth-century **War of Greek Independence**.

In this, the Peloponnese played the major part. The banner of rebellion was raised near **Kalávryta** on March 25, 1821, by Yermanos, Archbishop of Pátra, and the Greek forces' two most successful leaders – the great, flawed heroes **Petros Mavromihalis** and **Theodhoros Kolokotronis** – were natives of, and carried out most of their actions in, the Peloponnese. As you journey around with all the benefits of a present-day transport infrastructure, you will be in the footsteps of Kolokotronis almost everywhere you go. The international naval battle that accidentally decided the war, **Navarino Bay**, was fought off the west coast at Pýlos; and the first Greek parliament was convened at **Náfplio**. After independence however, power swiftly drained away from the Peloponnese to Athens, where it was to stay. The peninsula's contribution to the early Greek state became a disaffected one, highlighted by the assassination in Náfplio of Capodistrias, the first Greek president, by Maniots.

Throughout the **nineteenth** and **early twentieth centuries**, the region developed important ports at Pátra, Kórinthos and Kalamáta, but its interior reverted to back-water status, starting a population decline that continues today. It was little disturbed until **World War II**, during which the area saw some of the worst German atrocities; there was much brave resistance in the mountains, but also some of the most shameful collaboration. The **civil war** which followed left many of the towns polarized and physically in ruins. In its wake there was substantial **emigration** from both towns and countryside, to North America in particular, as well as to Athens and other Greek cities. Earthquakes still cause considerable disruption, as at Kórinthos in 1981 and Kalamáta in 1986.

Today, the southern Peloponnese has a reputation for being one of the most traditional and politically **conservative** regions of Greece. The people are held in rather poor regard by other Greeks, though to outsiders they seem unfailingly hospitable.

the leisurely timetable; however they do provide some direct connections and landscape views unavailable on buses. Renting a **car** is worthwhile if you can afford it, even for just a few days – to explore the south from Kalamáta or Spárti, or heartland and coastal Arcadia from Náfplio or Trípoli.

CORINTH AND THE ARGOLID

The usual approach from Athens to the Peloponnese is along the highway through Elefsína and across the Corinth Canal to modern-day **Kórinthos** (Corinth); buses and trains come this way at least every hour, the former halting at the canal (see p.150). Another, more attractive approach to the peninsula is by ferry or hydrofoil, via the **Argo-Saronic** islands (see p.465); routes run from Pireás through those islands, with brief hops over to the Argolid ports of Ermióni, Pórto Héli – plus Náfplio and Paleá Epídhavros in season.

The region that you enter, to the south and southeast of Kórinthos, is known as the **Argolid** (Argolídha in modern Greek), after the city of Árgos, which held sway in Classical times. The greatest concentration of ancient sites in Greece is found in this compact little peninsula, its western boundary delineated by the main road south from Kórinthos. Within an hour or so's journey of each other are Agamemnon's fortress at **Mycenae**, the great theatre of **Epidaurus**, and lesser sites at **Tiryns**, **Árgos** and **Lérna**. Inevitably, these, along with the great Roman site at **Ancient Corinth**, draw the crowds, and in peak season you may want to see the sites early or late in the day to realize their magic.

When ruin-hopping palls, there are the small-town pleasures of elegant **Náfplio**, and a handful of pleasant **coastal resorts**. The best beaches in these parts, however, are to be found along the coast road south from Árgos – at the beaches of Ástros and Tyrós, where there are some good campsites. Technically outside the Argolid, both of these are easiest reached by bus from Árgos or by hydrofoil from Náfplio (summer only), Pórto Héli or the island of Spétses. The southern continuation of these hydrofoil routes takes you on down the coast to the Byzantine remains of Monemvasiá.

Kórinthos

Like its ancient predecessor, the city of **KÓRINTHOS** (modern Corinth) has been levelled on several occasions by earthquakes – most recently in 1981, when a serious quake left thousands in tented homes for most of the following year. Repaired and reconstructed, with buildings of prudent but characterless concrete, the modern city has little of interest to the outsider; it is largely an industrial-agriculture centre, its economy bolstered by the drying and shipping of currants, for centuries one of Greece's few successful exports (the word "currant" itself derives from Corinth). Perhaps unexpectedly, the hottest and driest part of the peninsula in summer is Kórinthos.

You could do worse than base yourself here for a night or two, for the setting, with the sea on two sides and the mountains across the gulf, is good; however you are unlikely to escape from the continuous traffic noise anywhere in the centre of town, so you might consider **Arhéa Kórinthos** – 7km to the southwest – as a quieter, slightly cooler alternative, with magnificent views at night, and close to the remains of ancient and medieval Corinth. Kórinthos itself provides access to Perahóra and a couple of other minor sites (see p.164).

The only specific sight in the modern city itself is the **Folklore Museum** (daily 8am–1pm; free), located in a tasteful modern building near the harbour. This contains the usual array of peasant costumes, old engravings and dioramas of traditional crafts.

Arrival and information

Orientation is straightforward. The centre of Kórinthos is its **park**, bordered on the longer side by Ermoú street and bisected by the parallel Ethnikís Andistásis (formerly Konstandínou). The **bus station for Athens** and some local destinations (including Loutráki and the northeast) is on the Ermoú side of the park, at the corner with Koliátsou. **Buses** to Arhéa Kórinthos, Léheo, Kiáto, Xylókastro and Dhervéni go from outside a well-stocked zaharoplastío on Koliátsou, west of the park, while buses to other parts of Korinthía province go from Ethnikís Andistásis on the southwest corner of the park. **Long-distance buses** (to Spárti, Kalamáta, Trípoli, Mycenae, Árgos and Náfplio) use a café near the *Ephira* hotel on the other side of the park, at the corner of Ethnikís Andistásis and Arátou. Unlike the others, this station – the most used by tourists – has no signboard for destinations and times. Information and tickets are grudgingly provided by the café staff. The **train station** is a few blocks to the east.

You'll find the National and Commercial **banks** along Ethnikís Andistásis, and the main **post office** on Adhimandoú, on the south side of the park. There's a **tourist police** post at Ermoú 5 (☎0741/23 282), near the Athens bus station, and **taxis** wait along Ethnikís Andistásis side of the park. If you want to rent your own transport, for **mopeds** and **bikes** check out Liberopoulos, at Ethnikís Andistásis 27 (☎0741/72 937), and for **cars**, try Vasilopoulos at Adhimandoú 30 (☎0741/28 437); both are near the southern end of the park.

Accommodation

At most times of year, **hotel rooms** are reasonably easy to find, with two or three on the road into town from the train station, and others nearer the centre – though most suffer from road noise. There are a couple of **campsites** along the gulf to the west: *Korinth Beach* (☎0741/27 967; April–Oct) is 3km out at Dhiavakíta – to reach the beach, such as it is, you must cross the coastal road and the railway line. *Blue Dolphin* (☎0741/25 766; April–Oct) is a bit further away at Léheo, but it is on the seaward side of the tracks, and for that alone is preferable. For both sites, take the bus to Léheo (a part of Ancient Corinth) from alongside the park in modern Kórinthos.

Acropolis, Ethnikís Anexartisías 25 (☎0741/22 430). On the way into town from the train station. ⑤.

Ephira, Ethnikís Andistásis 52 (☎0741/24 021, fax 24 514). One block from the park and nearest the long-distance bus station. A modern hotel and a good mid-priced choice. ④.

Korinthos, Dhamaskínou 26 (☎0741/22 631, fax 23 693). Near the *Acropolis*; there's little to choose between them. ⑤.

Eating and drinking

Kórinthos has a few **tavernas**, and rather more fast-food places along the waterfront, all modestly priced. Most other eating places are directly onto very busy streets.

Anaxagoras, Ayíou Nikoláou 31. Good range of mezédhes and grilled meats.

Arhontiko (☎0741/27 968). A favourite with the locals. As this place is out near the campsites, you might want to phone first.

24 Ores, Áyiou Nikoláou, on the eastern side of the marina. A good and tasty selection of snacks and more traditional food.

Ancient Corinth

Buses to Ancient Corinth, **ARHÉA KÓRINTHOS**, leave modern Kórinthos ten past every hour from 8am to 9pm and return on the half-hour. The ruins of the **ancient city**, which displaced Athens as capital of the Greek province in Roman times, occupy a rambling sequence of sites, the main enclosure of which is given a sense of scale by the majestic ruin of the Temple of Apollo. Most compelling, though, are the ruins of the medieval city, which occupy the stunning acropolis site of **Acrocorinth**, towering 565m above.

The ruins of Ancient Corinth spread over a vast area, and include sections of ancient walls (the Roman city had a fifteen-kilometre circuit), outlying stadiums, gymnasiums and necropolises. Only the central area, around the Roman forum and the Classical Temple of Apollo, is preserved in an excavated state; the rest, odd patches of semi-enclosed and often overgrown ruin, you come across unexpectedly while walking about the village and up to Acrocorinth.

The overall effect is impressive, but it only begins to suggest the majesty of this once supremely wealthy city. Ancient Corinth was a key centre of the Greek and Roman

---

SITE OPENING HOURS

Summer opening hours for the **sites** and **museums** in the Peloponnese are included with some trepidation. They are notorious for changing without notice, from one season to another, or from one week to the next due to staff shortages.

To increase the chances of admission, it's best to visit between 9am and 2pm, and to be wary of Monday, when most museums and sites close for the whole day. Finally, always be prepared with alternative plans for the day you arrive at a site which, despite the opening hours clearly stated on the gate in front of you, is firmly closed.

---

worlds, whose possession meant the control of trade between northern Greece and the Peloponnese. In addition, the twin ports of **Lechaion**, on the Gulf of Corinth, and **Kenchreai**, on the Saronic Gulf, provided a trade link between the Ionian and Aegean seas – the western and eastern Mediterranean. Not surprisingly, this meant that the city's ancient (and medieval) history was one of invasions and power struggles which, in Classical times, was dominated by Corinth's rivalry with Athens – against whom it sided with Sparta in the Peloponnesian War.

Despite this, Corinth suffered only one major setback, in 146 BC, when the Romans, having defeated the Greek city-states of the Achaean League, razed the site to the ground. For a century the city lay in ruins before being rebuilt, on a majestic scale, by Julius Caesar in 44 BC: initially intended as a colony for veterans, it was later made the provincial capital. Once again Corinth grew rich on trade – with Rome to the west, Syria and Egypt to the east.

Roman Corinth's reputation for wealth, fuelled by its trading access to luxury goods, was soon equalled by its appetite for earthly pleasures – including sex. Corinthian women were renowned for their beauty and much sought after as *hetairai* (courtesans); a temple to Aphrodite/Venus, on the acropolis of Acrocorinth, was served by over a thousand sacred prostitutes. **St Paul** stayed in Corinth for eighteen months in 51–52 AD, though his attempts to reform the citizens' ways were met only by rioting – tribulations recorded in his two Letters to the Corinthians. The city endured until rocked by two major earthquakes, in 375 and 521, which brought down the Roman buildings, and again depopulated the site until a brief Byzantine revival in the eleventh century.

The excavations

Daily: spring/autumn 8am–7pm; summer 8am–9pm; winter 8am–5pm; museum hours same; 1200dr for both.

Inevitably, given successive waves of earthquakes and destruction, the **main excavated site** is dominated by the remains of the Roman city. Entering from the north side, just behind the road where the buses pull in, you find yourself in the **Roman agora**, an enormous marketplace flanked by the substantial foundations of a huge *stoa*, once a structure of several storeys, with 33 shops on the ground floor. Opposite the *stoa* is a *bema*, a marble platform used for public announcements. At the far end are remains of a **basilica**, while the area behind the *bema* is strewn with the remnants of numerous Roman administrative buildings. Back across the *agora*, almost hidden in a swirl of broken marble and shattered architecture, there's a fascinating trace of the Greek city – a **sacred spring**, covered over by a grille at the base of a narrow flight of steps.

More substantial is the elaborate Roman **Fountain of Peirene**, which stands below the level of the *agora*, to the side of a wide excavated stretch of what was the main approach to the city, the marble-paved **Lechaion Way**. Taking the form of a colonnaded and frescoed recess, the fountain occupies the site of one of two natural springs in Corinth – the other is up on the acropolis – and its cool water was channelled into a magnificent fountain and pool in the courtyard. The fountain house was, like many of Athens' Roman public buildings, the gift of the wealthy Athenian and friend of Emperor Hadrian, Herodes Atticus. The waters still flow through the underground cisterns and supply the modern village.

The real focus of the ancient site, though, is a rare survival from the Classical Greek era, the fifth-century BC **Temple of Apollo**, whose seven austere Doric columns stand slightly above the level of the forum and are flanked by foundations of another marketplace and baths. Over to the west is the site **museum**, housing a large collection of domestic pieces, some good Roman mosaics from nearby villas and a frieze depicting some of the labours of Heracles (Hercules), several of which were performed nearby – at Neméa, Stymfalía and Lérna. The city's other claim to mythic fame, incidentally, is as the home of the infant Oedipus and his step-parents, prior to his travels of discovery to Thebes.

A number of miscellaneous smaller excavations surround the main site. To the west, just across the road from the enclosing wire, there are outlines of two **theatres**: a Roman **odeion** (once again endowed by Herodes Atticus) and a larger Greek theatre, adapted by the Romans for gladiatorial sea battles. To the north are the inaccessible but visible remains of an **Asclepion** (dedicated to the healing god).

Acrocorinth

Summer daily 8am–7pm; winter Tues–Sun 8am–2.30pm; free.

Rising almost sheer above the lower town, **Acrocorinth** is sited on an amazing mass of rock, still largely encircled by two kilometres of wall. The ancient acropolis of Corinth, it became one of Greece's most powerful fortresses during the Middle Ages, besieged by successive waves of invaders, who considered it the key to the Moreás.

Despite the long, four-kilometre climb to the entrance gate (an hour's walk) – or a taxi ride from Ancient Corinth, reasonable if shared – a visit to the summit is unreservedly recommended. Looking down over the Saronic and Corinthian gulfs, you really get a sense of the strategic importance of the fortress's position. Amid the sixty-acre site, you wander through a jumble of chapels, mosques, houses and battlements, erected in turn by Greeks, Romans, Byzantines, Frankish crusaders, Venetians and Turks.

The Turkish remains are unusually substantial. Elsewhere in Greece evidence of the Ottoman occupation has been physically removed or defaced, but here, halfway up the hill, you can see a midway point in the process: the still functioning **fountain of Hatzi Mustafa**, which has been Christianized by the addition of great carved crosses. The outer of the citadel's **triple gates**, too, is largely Turkish; the middle is a combination of Venetian and Frankish, the inner, Byzantine, incorporating fourth-century BC towers. Within the citadel, the first summit (to the right) is enclosed by a **Frankish keep** – as striking as they come – which last saw action in 1828 during the War of Independence. Keeping along the track to the left, you pass some interesting (if perilous) cisterns, remains of a Turkish bath house and crumbling Byzantine chapels.

In the southeast corner of the citadel, hidden away in the lower ground, is the **upper Peirene spring**. This is not easy to find: look out for a narrow, overgrown entrance, from which a flight of iron stairs leads down some five metres to a metal screen. Here, broad stone steps descend into the dark depths, where a fourth-century BC arch stands guard over a pool of water that has never been known to dry up. To the north of the fountain, on the second and higher summit, is the site of the **Temple of Aphrodite** mentioned opposite; after its days as a brothel, it saw use as a church, mosque and belvedere.

Practicalities

To explore both ancient and medieval Corinth you need a full day, or better still, to stay here overnight. A modern **village** spreads around the edge of the main ancient site, and there is a scattering of **rooms** to rent in its backstreets – follow the signs or ask at the cafés. A good cheap option, by the Avin garage on the road from Kórinthos, is the hospitable *Hotel Shadow* (☎0741/31 481; ③), with great views from the rear rooms; a free museum in the lobby includes an extensive and labelled collection of minerals, fossils, petrified wood and local relics. In the centre of the village is *Marinos* rooms (☎0741/31 209; ④) with an enthusiastically illustrated restaurant. The *Tasos* serves good, traditional Greek taverna food at low prices. The solitary modern building up in Acrocorinth is the *Acrocorinthos* café; there is a fully operational restaurant here until early evening during summer months.

Around Corinth

As well as the **Corinth Canal**, which you can't help but cross en route between Kórinthos and Athens, a number of minor sites are accessible by bus (at least most of the way) from Kórinthos, both on the Peloponnese and the western Attic peninsula of Yeránia. Just south of the canal is ancient **Ísthmia**, site of the Panhellenic Isthmian Games. To the northwest are the spa of Loutráki and the classical **sanctuary of Hera** at **Perahóra** on Cape Melangávi. If you have a car, there's a grand and rather wild route east from the cape, around the **Alkyonidhón Gulf** to Pórto Yermenó (see p.270). There are beaches along the way, though little settlement or development, and the final stretch of road beyond Káto Alepohóri is scarcely better than a jeep track.

Back in the Peloponnese proper, **Neméa** – as in the Lion of Hercules' labour – is a brief detour southwest of Kórinthos, off the road to Mycenae and Árgos. **Sikyon** is a bit more remote, 25km up the coast towards Pátra, but again accessible by bus.

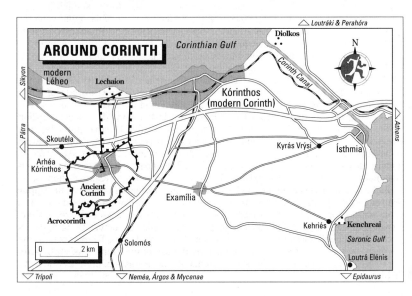

The Corinth Canal

The idea for a **Corinth Canal**, providing a short cut and safe passage between the Aegean and Ionian seas, dates back at least to Roman times, when the emperor Nero performed initial excavations with a silver shovel and Jewish slave labour. It was only in the 1890s, however, that the technology became available to cut right across the six-kilometre isthmus. Opened in July 1893, the canal, along with its near-contemporary Suez, helped establish Pireás as a major Mediterranean port and shipping centre, although the projected toll revenues were never realized. Today supertankers have made it something of an anachronism and the canal has fallen into disrepair, but it remains a memorable sight nonetheless.

Approaching on the Athens road, you cross the canal near its southeastern end. From Kórinthos you can use the Loutráki buses to get here and back. At the **bridge** there's a line of **cafés**, where buses from Athens usually stop if they're going beyond Kórinthos. Peering over from the bridge, the canal appears a tiny strip of water until some huge freighter assumes toy-like dimensions as it passes nearly eighty metres below. If you were to take one of the cruise ships from Pireás to the Ionian, you would actually sail through the canal – a trip almost worthwhile for its own sake. At the western end of the canal, by the old Kórinthos–Loutráki ferry dock, there are remains of the **diolkos**, a paved way along which a wheeled platform used to carry boats across the isthmus. In use from Roman times until the twelfth century, the boats were strapped onto the platform after being relieved temporarily of their cargo.

Ancient Ísthmia

Modern Ísthmia (Isthmía) lies either side of the Saronic Gulf entrance to the canal, and is served by regular buses from Kórinthos. To the south of the modern settlement, on a hillock alongside the present-day village of Kyranós Vrýsi, is the site of ancient **ÍSTHMIA** (summer Tues–Sun 8.45am–3pm; winter daily 8am–2.30pm; free).

There is nothing very notable to see at the site, though the ancient settlement was an important one, due to its **sanctuary of Poseidon** – of which just the foundations remain, much having been incorporated into the seven-kilometre Byzantine Hexamillian Wall – and the Panhellenic Isthmian games. The latter ranked with those of Delphi, Neméa and Olympia, though they have left scant evidence in the form of a **stadium** and **theatre**, together with a few curiosities – including starting blocks used for foot races – in the small adjacent **museum** (same times as site), which also houses some of the finds from Kenchreai. There are decent swimming spots and some accommodation at Kekhriés and Loutrá Elénis on the coast heading south towards Arhéa (Paleá) Epídhavros.

Loutráki

Six kilometres north of the canal is the spa resort of **LOUTRÁKI**. The epicentre of the 1981 Corinth earthquake, it has today straight lines of unmemorable concrete buildings. The resort is nonetheless immensely popular, with a larger concentration of hotels than anywhere else in the Peloponnese. The visitors are mostly Greek, or Italian, coming here since 1847 for the "cure" at the hot springs, and to sample Loutráki mineral water – the country's leading bottled brand. A sign of the times is the new Pepsi-Cola bottling plant on the outskirts of Loutráki. Others come for the renovated and reopened casino, Greece's oldest, on Posidhónos on the southwest seafront. Near the train station, there is a helpful **tourist kiosk** on E.Venizélou, the main road through town, four blocks south of the bus station, and a second near the thermal baths. The local council has a choice range of well-produced brochures and a town map.

With your own transport, you'd be better off using the town simply as a staging post en route to the site of ancient Perahóra and making Lake Vouliagméni your base (see p.164). Otherwise, Loutráki is connected by bus and special summer trains with

Athens, and by half-hourly bus with Kórinthos. Travel agency facilities are available from 24 Hours Travel (☎0744/67 666, fax 67 667) on Y. Lékka, near the thermal baths. If you end up staying, *Hotel Brettagne*, at Y. Lékka 28 (☎0744/22 349; ③), makes a refreshing change from the many expensive spa-resort **hotels**; *Hotel Pappas* (☎0744/23 026; ⑤), to the left of the Perahóra road, has better facilities and fine views across the gulf. The friendly, family-run *Acropole*, P. Tsaldhári 11 (☎0744/22 265, fax 61 171; ④) is recently refurbished and comfortable. The *Harama* psistariá at the corner of Kanári and Ethnikís Andistásis has good grills at decent rates.

Perahóra

The road to **Cape Melangávi** is enjoyable in itself, running above the sea in the shadow of the Yeránia mountains, whose pine forests are slowly recovering from fire devastation in 1986. En route the road offers a loop through the modern village of **PERAHÓRA** (11km) before heading out to the cape along the shore of **Lake Vouliagméni**, a beautiful two-kilometre-wide lagoon with sheltered swimming, a new hotel, the *Philoxenia* (☎0741/91 294; all year; ②), and a small campsite, *Limni Heraiou* (☎0741/91 230; all year). Perahóra is connected by hourly bus with Loutráki; one daily bus makes the journey between Loutráki and Lake Vouliagméni, but runs in summer only.

Ancient Perahóra (daily 8am–2.30pm) – also known as Peréa or the Heraion Melangávi – stands just 1km from the western tip of the peninsula, commanding a marvellous, sweeping view of the coastline and mountains along both sides of the gulf. The site's position is its chief attraction, though there are the identifiable ruins of a sanctuary in two parts, the **Hera Akraia** (*akron* is the extremity of the peninsula) and **Hera Limenia** (of the port), as well as the **stoa** of the ancient harbour, which provides great snorkelling opportunities.

The initial excavation of Perahóra, between 1930 and 1933, is described by Dilys Powell in *An Affair of the Heart*. Humfry Payne, her husband, directed the work until his death in 1936; he was then buried at Mycenae. The site also features in myth, for it was here that Medea, having been spurned by her husband Jason at Corinth, killed their two children.

Neméa

Ancient **NEMÉA**, the location for Hercules' (Herakles) slaying of its namesake lion (his first labour), lies 6km off the road from Kórinthos to Árgos. By public transport, take the bus to modern Neméa and ask to be dropped en route at Arhéa Neméa, also the name of a village just 300m west of the ruins. Moving on from the site, you can walk back up to the Árgos road and possibly wave down a bus on to Fíkhti for Mycenae.

Like Olympia and Ísthmia, Neméa held athletic games for the Greek world from the sixth century BC, until these were transferred to Árgos in 270 BC. A sanctuary rather than a town, the principal remains at the **site** (summer Tues–Sun 8.30am–3pm, winter daily 8am–2.30pm; 500dr) are of the **Temple of Nemean Zeus**, currently three slender Doric columns surrounded by other fallen and broken drums, but slowly being reassembled by a team of University of California archeologists. Nearby are a **palaestra** with **baths** and a Christian basilica, built with blocks from the temple. Outside the site, half a kilometre east, is a **stadium** whose starting line has been unearthed. There is also a **museum** (same hours), with excellent contextual models, displays relating to the biennial games and items from the area.

The Stymphalian Lake

If you have transport, it's possible to cut across the hills from Neméa towards Arcadia, detouring into another Herculean locale, the **Stymphalian Lake** (around 35km from ancient Neméa). In myth, this was the nesting-ground of man-eating birds who preyed upon travellers, suffocating them with their wings, and poisoned local crops with their excrement. Hercules roused them from the water with a rattle, then shot them down – one of the more straightforward of his labours.

The lake is known in modern Greek as **Límni Stymfalías**, though it is really more of a swamp: an enormous depression with seasonal waters, ringed by woods and the dark peaks of Mount Olíyirtos on the south. There are no buildings for miles around, save for the ruins of the thirteenth-century Frankish Cistercian **Abbey of Zaráka** (beside the road), one of the few Gothic buildings in Greece.

If you don't have your own transport, the most promising approach to the lake is from Kiáto on the Gulf of Corinth, where there are several hotels and rooms to rent; the road, much better than that from Neméa, has the occasional bus. The nearest places to stay are the *Hotel Stymfalia* (☎0747/22 072; ②) at **Stymfalía** village, just before the abbey (though it is reportedly shut), or the *Xenia* (☎0747/31 283; ⑤) 3km outside **Kastaniá**, a mountain village 20km to the west that's famed for its butterflies.

Ancient Sikyon

Six kilometres inland from Kiáto (see above), ancient **SIKYON** (Sikyóna) (Tues–Sun, 8am–2.30pm; free) is a fairly accessible if little-known site, which deserves more than the few dozen visitors it attracts each year. Six buses a day run from Kiáto (on the bus and train routes from Kórinthos) to the village of Vasilikó, on the edge of a broad escarpment running parallel to the sea, from where it's a kilometre's walk to the site.

In ancient history, Sikyon's principal claim to fame came early in the sixth century BC, when the tyrant Kleisthenes purportedly kept a court of sufficient wealth and influence to entertain suitors for his daughter's hand for a full year. After his death the place was rarely heard from politically, except as a consistent ally of the Spartans, but a mild renaissance ensued at the end of the fourth century when Demetrios Polyorketes moved Sikyon to its present location from the plain below. The town became renowned for sculptors, painters and metallurgic artisans, and flourished well into Roman times; it was the birthplace of Alexander the Great's chief sculptor, Lysippus, and, allegedly, of the art of sculptural relief.

The road from Vasilikó cuts through the site, which is fenced off into a number of enclosures. To the right is the **Roman baths museum** which shelters mosaics of griffins from the second to third centuries AD. To the left are the majority of the public buildings, with a theatre and stadium on the hillside above. As you enter the **main site** (unrestricted access), opposite the Roman baths, the foundations of the **Temple of Artemis** are visible to your left. Beyond it are traces of a **bouleuterion** (senate house) dating from the first half of the third centuries BC. The most important remains in this section are of the **Gymnasium of Kleinias** in the far right-hand corner, at the base of the hill; this is on two levels, the lower dating from around 300 BC, the other from Roman times.

Although only the first ten rows of seats have been excavated, the outline of the **theatre** – larger than that of Epidaurus – is impressive and obvious. Pine trees have grown in the upper half, from where there's a marvellous view encompassing the rest of the site, the village of Vasilikó, the lemon and olive groves around Kiáto, plus gulf and mountains in the distance.

Xylókastro and the coast westward

A string of resorts, popular with Greeks, runs westwards along the Korinthian coast, accessible by bus or train from Kórinthos. There are hotels in Vraháti, Kokkóni, Kiáto,

Melíssi and Sykiá, but **XYLÓKASTRO** is of more interest, with both good beaches and accommodation, and a pleasant setting backed by Mount Kyllíni. The main beach, Pefkiás, is backed by a strip of pine woodland. Cheapest of its dozen **hotels** is the hospitable *Hermes* (☎0743/22 250; ②), I. Ioánnou 95, near Pefkiás. More expensive are the *Kyani Akti*, near the sea at Tsaldhári 68 (☎0743/28 930; ③), and the air-conditioned *Apollon*, housed in a fine old building at I. Ioánnou 119 (☎0743/22 571, fax 25 240; ⑤). The long seafront boasts a number of **restaurants**, of which *Zesti Gonia* is friendly, with good fish, while *Palea Exedhra* has more variety. In the hills behind, the Panayía Korfiótissa monastery has wonderful views over the sea and the Fónissa valley. **DHERVÉNI**, another 18km west, is less attractive, and there is no hotel or campsite; there are **rooms** for rent, and those offered by Konstandinos Stathakopoulos (☎0743/31 223; ②), near the centre and the beach, have kitchen facilities and are comfortable. The area around the village of Evrostíni, 12km inland and the site of the seventeen-domed church of Áyios Yeóryios of Zahóli, is attractively rural. It is only possible to connect westwards with Pátra and Ahaïa by train, not by local bus, since the latter only run to and from Kórinthos.

Mycenae (Mykínes)

Tucked into a fold of the hills just east of the road from Kórinthos to Árgos, Agamemnon's citadel at **MYCENAE** fits the legend better than any other place in Greece. It was uncovered in 1874 by the German archeologist Heinrich Schliemann (who also excavated the site of Troy), impelled by his single-minded belief that there was a factual basis to Homer's epics. Schliemann's finds of brilliantly crafted gold and sophisticated tomb architecture bore out the accuracy of Homer's epithets of "well-built Mycenae, rich in gold".

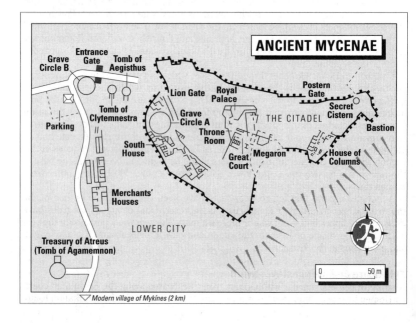

ANCIENT MYCENAE

Grave Circle B · Entrance Gate · Tomb of Aegisthus · Lion Gate · Royal Palace · Postern Gate · Tomb of Clytemnestra · Grave Circle A · THE CITADEL · Secret Cistern · Parking · Throne Room · Bastion · South House · Megaron · House of Columns · Great Court · Merchants' Houses · LOWER CITY · Treasury of Atreus (Tomb of Agamemnon) · N · 0 50 m

▽ Modern village of Mykínes (2 km)

Mycenaean history and legend

The Mycenae–Árgos region is one of the longest occupied in Greece, with evidence of Neolithic settlements from around 3000 BC. But it is to a period of three centuries at the end of the second millennium BC – from around 1550 to 1200 BC – that the citadel of Mycenae and its associated drama belong. This period is known as **Mycenaean**, a term which covers not just the Mycenae region but a whole Bronze Age civilization that flourished in southern Greece at the time.

According to the **legend** related in Homer's *Iliad* and *Odyssey* and Aeschylus' *Oresteia*, the city of Mycenae was founded by Perseus, the slayer of Medusa the gorgon, before it fell into the bloodied hands of the **House of Atreus**. In an act of vengeance for his brother Thyestes' seduction of his wife, Atreus murdered Thyestes' children, and fed them to their own father. Not surprisingly, this incurred the wrath of the gods. Thyestes' own daughter, Pelopia, subsequently bore him a son, Aegisthus, who promptly murdered Atreus and restored his father to the throne.

The next generation saw the gods' curse fall upon Atreus' son Agamemnon. On his return to Mycenae after commanding the Greek forces in the Trojan War – a role in which he had earlier consented to the sacrifice of his own daughter, Iphigeneia – he was killed in his bath by his wife Clytemnestra and her lover, the very same Aegisthus who had killed his father. The tragic cycle was completed by Agamemnon's son, Orestes, who took revenge by murdering his mother, Clytemnestra, and was pursued by the Furies until Athena finally lifted the curse on the dynasty.

The **archeological remains** of Mycenae fit remarkably easily with the tale, at least if it is taken as a poetic rendering of dynastic struggles, or, as most scholars now believe it to be, a merging of stories from various periods. The buildings unearthed by Schliemann show signs of occupation from around 1950 BC, as well as two periods of intense disruption, around 1200 BC and again in 1100 BC – at which stage the town, though still prosperous, was abandoned.

No coherent explanation has been put forward for these events, since the traditional "Dorian invasions" theory (see p.842) has fallen from favour, but it seems that war among the rival kingdoms was a major factor in the Mycenaean decline. These struggles appear to have escalated as the civilization developed in the thirteenth century BC, and excavations at Troy have revealed the sacking of that city, quite possibly by forces led by a king from Mycenae, in 1240 BC. The citadel of Mycenae seems to have been replanned, and heavily fortified, during this period.

The Citadel

Daily: summer 8am–7pm (Aug 8am–9pm); winter 8am–5pm; 1500dr.

The **Citadel of Mycenae** is entered through the famous **Lion Gate**, whose huge sloping gateposts bolster walls were termed "Cyclopean" by later Greeks in bewildered attribution to the only beings deemed capable of their construction. Above them a graceful carved relief stands out in confident assertion: Mycenae at its height led a confederation of Argolid towns (Tiryns, Árgos, Assine, Hermione – present-day Ermióni), dominated the Peloponnese and exerted influence throughout the Aegean. The motif of a pillar supported by two muscular lions was probably the symbol of the Mycenaean royal house, for a seal found on the site bears a similar device. Inside the walls to the right is **Grave Circle A**, the royal cemetery excavated by Schliemann and believed by him to contain the bodies of Agamemnon and his followers, murdered on their triumphant return from Troy. Opening one of the graves, he found a tightly fitting and magnificent gold mask that had somehow preserved the flesh of a Mycenaean noble; "I have gazed upon the face of Agamemnon," he exclaimed in an excited cable to the king of Greece. For a time it seemed that this provided irrefutable evidence of the truth of Homer's tale. In fact, the burials date from about three centuries before the Trojan

War, though given Homer's possible accumulation of different and earlier sagas, there's no reason why they should not have been connected with a Mycenaean king Agamemnon. They were certainly royal graves, for the finds (now in the National Archeological Museum in Athens) are among the richest that archeology has yet unearthed.

Schliemann took the extensive **South House**, beyond the grave circle, to be the Palace of Agamemnon. However, a building much grander and more likely to be the **Royal Palace**, was later discovered near the summit of the acropolis. Rebuilt in the thirteenth century BC, this is an impressively elaborate and evocative building complex; although the ruins are only at ground level, the different rooms are easily discernible. Like all Mycenaean palaces, it is centred around a **great court**: on the south side, a staircase would have led via an anteroom to the big rectangular **throne room**; on the east, a double porch gave access to the **megaron**, the grand reception hall with its traditional circular hearth. The small rooms to the north are believed to have been **royal apartments**, and in one of them the remains of a red stuccoed bath have led to its fanciful identification as the scene of Agamemnon's murder.

With the accompaniment of the sound of bells drifting down from goats grazing on the hillsides, a stroll round the ramparts is evocative. A more salutary reminder of the nature of life in Mycenaean times is the **secret cistern** at the eastern end of the ramparts, created in the twelfth century BC. Whether it was designed to enable the citadel's occupants to withstand siege from outsiders, rival Mycenaeans or even an increasingly alienated peasantry is not known. Steps lead down to a deep underground spring; it's still possible to descend the whole way, though you'll need to have a torch and be sure-footed, since there's a seventy-metre drop to the water (depth unknown) at the final turn of the twisting passageways. Nearby is the **House of Columns**, a large and stately building with the base of a stairway that once led to an upper storey.

Only the ruling Mycenaean elite could live within the citadel itself. Hence the main part of town lay outside the walls and, in fact, extensive remains of **merchants' houses** have been uncovered near to the road. Their contents included Linear B tablets recording the spices used to scent oils, along with large amounts of pottery, the quantity suggesting that the early Mycenaeans may have dabbled in the perfume trade. The discovery of the tablets has also prompted a reassessment of the sophistication of Mycenaean civilization, for they show that, here at least, writing was not limited to government scribes working in the royal palaces as had previously been thought, and that around the citadel there may have been a commercial city of some size and wealth.

Alongside the merchants' houses are the remains of another **Grave Circle** (B), dating from around 1650 BC and possibly representing an earlier, rival dynasty to the kings buried in Grave Circle A, and two **tholos** (circular chamber-type) tombs, speculatively identified by Schliemann as the **tombs of Aegisthus** and **Clytemnestra**. The former, closer to the Lion Gate, dates from around 1500 BC and has now collapsed, so is roped off; the latter dates from some two centuries later – thus corresponding with the Trojan timescale – and can still be entered.

The Treasury of Atreus

Same hours as the Citadel; admission included in Citadel entrance fee.

Four hundred metres down the road from the Citadel site is another, infinitely more startling *tholos*, known as the **Treasury of Atreus** or – the currently preferred official name – "Tomb of Agamemnon". This was certainly a royal burial vault at a late stage in Mycenae's history, contemporary with the "Clytemnestra Tomb", so the attribution to Agamemnon or his father is as good as any – if the king was indeed the historic leader of the Trojan expedition. In any case, it is an impressive monument to Mycenaean building skills, a beehive-like structure built without the use of mortar. Entering the tomb through a majestic fifteen-metre corridor, you come face to face with the chamber doorway, above which is a great lintel formed by two immense slabs of stone – one of which, a staggering nine metres long, is estimated to weigh 118 tonnes.

Practicalities: Mykínes

The modern village of **MYKÍNES** is 2km from the Kórinthos–Árgos road and the train station, but not all trains on the Kórinthos–Árgos–Trípoli line stop here. Buses from Athens to Árgos or Náfplio usually drop passengers at the turning, Fíkhti (the café here sells bus tickets) rather than in the village; local buses from Náfplio serve the village itself. The walk in from the main highway is along a beautiful straight road partly lined with eucalyptus trees, through which glimpses of the citadel appear, flanked by the twin mountains of Zára and Ilías. The site is a further two-kilometre uphill walk from the village.

Accommodation and eating

Unless you have your own transport, you might want to stay at Mykínes, which can be heavily touristy by day but quiet once the site has closed and the tour buses depart. Along the village's single street, there is quite an array of hotels – most of their names taken from characters in the House of Atreus saga – as well as a number of signs for rooms. Mycenae's two **campsites** are both centrally located, on the way into the village. Both open all year; there's not a great deal to choose between them, though *Camping Mykines* (☎0751/76 121, fax 76 247) is smaller and a little closer to the site than *Camping Atreus* (☎0751/76 221).

All the hotels listed below have **restaurants** catering for the lunchtime tour-group trade; therefore don't raise your expectations too high. Other eating places worth trying are the *Electra* (☎ 0751/76 447), the *King Menelaos* (☎0751/76 300) and the *Menelaos* (☎0751/76 311), all along the main street.

Belle Hélène (☎0751/76 225, fax 76 179). The village's most characterful hotel, with a good restaurant; converted from the house used by Schliemann during his excavations. Signatures in its visitors' book include Virginia Woolf, Henry Moore, Sartre and Debussy. ③.

Klytemnestra (☎0751/76 451, fax 76 731). Pleasant, modern hotel run by a friendly young Australian. Open all year. ②.

Petite Planète (☎0751/76 240, fax 76 610). A comfortable hotel at the top end of the village, with great views and a swimming pool. Owned by another of the Dassis clan, this is the nearest hotel to the site. ⑤.

Rooms Dassis (☎0751/76 123, fax 76 124). A pleasant, well-organized setup, run, along with a useful travel agency below, by Canadian Marion Dassis, who married into the local Dassis dynasty. Good for groups or families. ②–③.

The Argive Heraion and ancient Midea

The little-visited **Argive Heraion** (daily 8.30am–3pm; free) is an important sanctuary from Mycenaean and Classical times and the site where Agamemnon is said to have been chosen as leader of the Greek expedition to Troy. It lies 7km south of Mycenae, off the minor road which runs east of Árgos through Hónikas, and on to Náfplio. The lonely site is above the village of Hónikas (Néo Iréo); before you reach the village, look out for signs to "Ancient Ireo". There are various Mycenaean tombs near the site, but the principal remains of a temple complex, baths and a *palaestra* (wrestling/athletics gym), built over three interconnnecting terraces, all date from the fifth century BC.

The Heraion makes a pleasant diversion for anyone driving between Mycenae and Náfplio, or an enjoyable afternoon's walk from Mykínes – it takes a little over an hour on foot if you can find the old track southeast from the village, running parallel to the minor road to Ayía Triádha and Náfplio. Hónikas has the occasional bus to Árgos; Ayía Triádha, 5km on, has more frequent connections to Náfplio.

Ancient Midea, in gorgeous countryside between the villages of Midhéa and Dhéndhra, was the third fortified Mycenaean palace of the area, after Mycenae and Tiryns. Excavations have uncovered a fortified area of some six acres, the remains of a young girl – apparently an earthquake victim in the thirteenth century BC – and numerous workshop items, but its most famous find is the remarkable Dendra cuirass, bronze body armour now in the archeological museum in Náfplio.

Árgos

ÁRGOS, 12km south of the Mykínes junction, is said to be the oldest inhabited town in Greece, although you wouldn't know it from first impressions. However, this turn-of-the-century trading centre has some pleasant squares and Neoclassical buildings, and a brief stop is worthwhile for the excellent museum and mainly Roman ruins. Try to time your visit to coincide with the regular **Wednesday market**, which draws locals from all the surrounding hill villages.

A confusing plethora of signs, none of them useful, won't help direct you to the modern **Archeological Museum** (Tues–Sun 8am–2.30pm; 500dr) which is just off the semi-pedestrianized street between the market square and the main church square, Platía Ayíou Pétrou. It makes an interesting detour after Mycenae, with a good collection of Mycenaean tomb objects and armour as well as extensive pottery finds. The region's Roman occupation is well represented here, in sculpture and mosaics, and there are also finds from Lerna on display.

Before you leave Árgos, ask to be pointed in the direction of the town's ancient remains – a few minutes' walk down the Trípoli road. The **site** (daily 8am–3pm; free) is surprisingly extensive; the **theatre**, built by Classical Greeks and adapted by the Romans, looks oddly narrow from the road, but climb up there and it feels immense. Estimated to have held 20,000 spectators – six thousand more than Epidaurus – it is matched on the Greek mainland only by the theatres at Megalópolis and Dodóna. Alongside are the remains of an **odeion** and **Roman baths**.

Above the site looms the ancient **acropolis**, capped by the largely Frankish **medieval castle** of Lárissa (daily 8am–2.30pm; free), built on sixth-century BC foundations and later augmented by the Venetians and Turks. Massively walled, cisterned and guttered, the sprawling ruins offer wonderful views – the reward for a long, steep haul up, either on indistinct trails beyond the theatre, or a very roundabout road.

Practicalities

You may well need to change **buses** in Árgos: its connections are considerably better than those of Náfplio. There are two KTEL offices, both near the southeast corner of the market square; the one to the south is for buses back towards Athens and various points in the Argolid; the other is for Trípoli, Spárti and down the coast towards Leonídhi.

For a good meal between buses, try the *Retro Restaurant* on the central square, although there are cheaper in the backstreets. Staying overnight shouldn't prove necessary, unless you find Náfplio full – a possibility in high season. **Hotels** on the Ayíou Pétrou main square include *Palladion* (☎0751/66 248; ③), the comfortable *Telesilla* (☎0751/ 68 317; ④) and *Mycenae* (☎0751/68 754, fax 68 332; ⑤) – the last prefers longer-stay guests, groups, families and archeologists.

Tiryns (Tírynthos)

In Mycenaean times **TIRYNS** stood by the sea, commanding the coastal approaches to Árgos and Mycenae. The Aegean shore gradually receded, leaving the fortress stranded on a low hillock in today's plains, surrounded by citrus groves, and alongside the Argolid's principal modern prison. It's not the most enchanting of settings, which in part explains why this accessible, substantial site is relatively empty of visitors. After the crowds at Mycenae, however, the opportunity to wander about Homer's "wall-girt Tiryns" in near-solitude is worth taking. The site lies just to the east of the main Árgos–Náfplio road, and frequent local buses drop off and pick up passengers opposite.

The Citadel

Daily: summer 8am–8pm; winter 8am–2.30pm; 500dr.

As at Mycenae, Homer's epigrams correspond remarkably well to what you can see on the ground at Tiryns. The fortress, now over three thousand years old, is undeniably impressive, and the site itself had been occupied for four thousand years before that. The walls, 750m long and up to 7m thick, formed of huge Cyclopean stones, dominate the site; the Roman guidebook writer Pausanias, happening on the site in the second century AD, found them "more amazing than the Pyramids" – a claim that seems a little exaggerated, even considering that the walls then stood twice their present height.

The entrance is on the far side of the fortress from the road, and visitors are restricted to exploring certain passages, staircases and the palace. Despite this, the sophistication and defensive function of the citadel's layout are evident as soon as you climb up the **entrance ramp**. Wide enough to allow access to chariots, the ramp is angled so as to leave the right-hand, unshielded side of any invading force exposed for the entire ascent, before forcing a sharp turn at the top – surveyed by defenders from within. The **gateways**, too, constitute a formidable barrier; the outer one would have been similar in design to Mycenae's Lion Gate, though unfortunately its lintel is missing, so there is no heraldic motif that might confirm a dynastic link between the sites.

Of the **palace** itself only the limestone foundations survive, but the fact that they occupy a level site makes them generally more legible than the ruins of hilly and boulder-strewn Mycenae, and you can gain a clearer idea of its structure. The walls themselves would have been of sun-dried brick, covered in stucco and decorated with frescoes. Fragments of the latter were found on the site: one depicting a boar hunt, the other a life-sized frieze of courtly women, both now in the Náfplio museum. From the forecourt, you enter a spacious **colonnaded court** with a round sacrificial altar in the middle. A typically Mycenaean double porch leads directly ahead to the **megaron** (great hall), where the base of a throne was found – it's now in the Archeological Museum in Athens, with miscellaneous finds and frescoes from the site. The massive round clay hearth that's characteristic of these Mycenaean halls – there's a perfect example at Nestor's Palace (see p.241) – is no longer to be seen at Tiryns, because some time in the sixth century BC this part of the palace became the site of a temple to Hera, a structure whose column bases now pepper the ground. **Royal apartments** lead off on either side; the women's quarters are thought to have been to the right, while to the left is the bathroom, its floor – a huge, single flat stone – intact. The **lower acropolis**, north of the megaron, is currently out of bounds due to the excavation of two underground cisterns discovered at its far end in the late 1980s.

A tower further off to the left of the megaron gives access to a **secret staircase**, as at Mycenae, which winds down to an inconspicuous **postern gate**, although currently both are closed off. The site beyond the megaron is separated by an enormous inner wall and can only be viewed from a distance.

Náfplio

NÁFPLIO (which you may also see as Nauplia or Navplion) is a rarity amongst Greek towns. A lively, beautifully sited place, it exudes a rather grand, fading elegance, inherited from the days when it was the fledgling capital of modern Greece. The seat of government was here from 1829 to 1834 and it was in Náfplio that the first prime minister, Kapodistrias, was assassinated by vengeful Maniot clansmen. It was here that the Bavarian Prince Otho, put forward by the European powers to be the first King of Greece, had his initial royal residence from 1833 to 1834. Since the 1980s the town has served as a popular weekend retreat year-round, with the result that hotel rooms and meals have crept up to Athens rates and above, but it remains by far the most attractive base for exploring the Argolid and resting up for a while by the sea.

Arrival and accommodation

Wedged between the sea and a doubly fortressed headland, the old part of Náfplio is an easy town to find your way around. Arriving by **bus**, you are set down at one of two adjacent terminals just south of the interlocking squares, **Platía Trion Navárhon** and **Platía Kapodhístria**, on Syngroú. The **train** will deposit you at the junction of Polyzoïdhou and Irakléous, where a new station has been built, with two old red carriages serving as ticket office and waiting room.

Accommodation

Accommodation in Náfplio is generally overpriced for what you get, though out of season most **hotels** drop their prices significantly. There are a number of private **rooms** advertised – and sometimes touted to new arrivals; most cluster on the slope above the main squares. A few other hotels and rooms, generally the last to fill, are located out on the road to Árgos. There is nowhere to **camp** in Náfplio itself, but southeast on the stretch of coast from Toló (11km from Náfplio) to Íria (26km away), there are a dozen or so campsites (see p.177).

Acronafplia, Ayíou Spyrídhonos 6 (☎0752/24 481). Good-value pension in five refurbished buildings around town. ①–⑤.

Agamemnon, Aktí Miaoúli 3 (☎0752/28 021, fax 28 022). On the waterfront, with an upmarket restaurant and roof garden giving great views. ⑤.

Byron, Plátonos 2 (☎0752/22 351, fax 26 338; *byronhotel@otenet.gr*). A beautifully restored old mansion just above Áyios Spyrídhon church. ④–⑥.

Dioscouri, Zygomála and Výronos 6 (☎0752/28 550, fax 21 202). A friendly hotel, reached via a steep flight of steps. Rooms at the front overlook the old town and the port. Open all year. ⑤.

Economou, Arganáftón 22 (☎0752/23 955). Opposite the now-closed Youth Hostel, and worth the walk from the centre. Recently refurbished and excellent value; some dorm beds available. ②.

Epidauros, Kokkínou 2 (☎ & fax 0752/27 541). Small but well-furnished rooms, set in narrow streets of the old town, behind the waterfront. Nearby is the *Tiryns* owned by the same people, with similar priced rooms. ④.

King Othon, Farmakopoúlou 2 (☎0752/27 585, fax 27 595). Popular, well-placed hotel, beautifully refurbished with an impressive staircase. Close to the waterfront and Platía Syndágmatos. ④.

Leto, Zygomála 28 (☎0752/28 093). Located at the base of the Akronafplía fortress; some cheaper rooms available next door. ③.

Park, Dhervenakíou 1, off Platía Kapodhístria (☎0752/27 428, fax 27 045). Large, well-run 1960s hotel which may well have space when the smaller old-town places are full. ③.

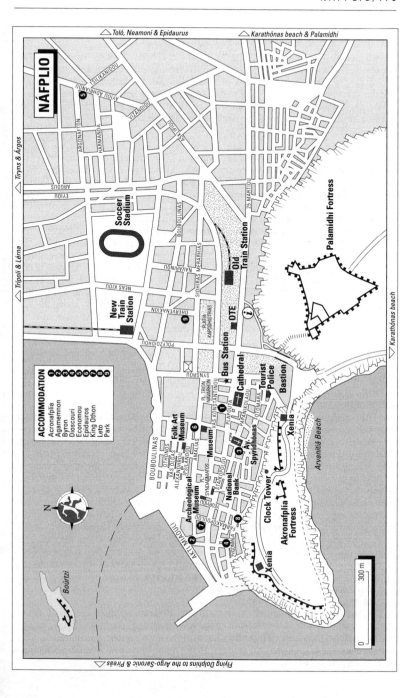

NÁFPLIO

△ Tripoli & Lérna △ Tiryns & Árgos △ Toló, Neamoní & Epidaurus △ Karathónas beach & Palamídhi

△ Flying Dolphins to the Argo-Saronic & Piréas ▷ Karathónas beach

ACCOMMODATION
Acronafplia ❶
Agamemnon ❷
Byron ❸
Dioscouri ❹
Economou ❺
Epidauros ❻
King Othon ❼
Leto ❽
Park ❾

Bourtzi

Soccer Stadium

New Train Station

Old Train Station

Palamídhi Fortress

Folk Art Museum ❻
Archeological Museum ❼
National Bank
Museum
Ay. Spyridhónas
Clock Tower
Akronafplia Fortress
Xenia
Xenia
Cathedral
Bus Station
Tourist Police
Bastion
OTE

Arvanitiá Beach

0   300 m

The Town

There's ample pleasure in just wandering about Náfplio: looking around the harbourfront, walking over to the rocky town beach and, when you're feeling energetic, exploring the great twin fortresses of Palamídhi and Akronafplía on the headland. Náfplio also offers some of the best restaurants and shops in the eastern Peloponnese, plus a range of useful facilities including car rental and, in summer, hydrofoils down the coast to Monemvasiá or east to the Argo-Saronic islands.

Palamídhi

The **Palamídhi**, Náfplio's principal fort, was one of the key military flashpoints of the War of Independence. The Greek commander Kolokotrónis – of whom there's a majestically bewhiskered statue down in the Platía Kapodhístria – laid siege to the castle for over a year before finally gaining control. After independence, ironically, he was imprisoned in the fortress by the new Greek government; wary of their attempts to curtail his powers, he had kidnapped four members of the parliament.

The most direct approach to the **fortress** (daily: summer 8am–6.45pm; winter 8.30–3pm; 800dr) is by a stairway from the end of Polyzoïdhou street, beside a Venetian bastion, though there is also a circuitous road up from the town. On foot, it's a pretty killing climb up 899-plus stone-hewn steps and, when you reach the summit, you're confronted with a bewilderingly vast complex. Within the outer walls there are three self-contained castles, all of them built by the Venetians between 1711 and 1714, which accounts for the appearance of that city's symbol, the Lion of St Mark, above the various gateways. The middle fort, San Niccolo, was the one where Kolokotrónis was imprisoned; it later became a notorious prison during the civil war.

The fortress takes its name, incidentally, from Náfplio's most famous and most brilliant legendary son, **Palamedes** – the inventor of dice, lighthouses and measuring scales. He was killed by the Greeks at Troy, on charges of treachery trumped up by Odysseus, who regarded himself as the cleverest of the Greeks.

Akronafplía and Boúrtzi

The **Akronafplía** (Its Kalé – "Three Castles" – in Turkish), to the west of the Palamídhi, occupies the ancient acropolis, whose walls were adapted by three successive medieval restorers – hence the name. The fortifications are today far less complete than those of the Palamídhi, and the most intact section, the lower Torrione castle, has been adapted to house the *Xenia Hotel*. There's little of interest, but the hotel has meant a road has been carved out over the headland, and this brings you down to a small pay **beach**, **Arvanitía** (said to be so named from running red with the blood of Albanian mercenaries slaughtered by Hasan Pasha in 1779), overcrowded in season but nevertheless an enjoyable spot to cool off in the shelter of the forts. In the early evening, it is the province of just a few swimmers, though the refreshment kiosks operate only at peak hours and in season. If you walk along the path that continues from the end of the road just past the beach entrance for about ten minutes, you can pick your way down to a couple of small stone beaches below the cliffs; take provisions if you want to stay for a few hours to relax, or you can take the attractive paved route around the western end of Akronafplía, to the main town harbour. A dirt road to the left of Arvanitía leads to Karathónas beach (see opposite).

The town's third fort, the much-photographed **Boúrtzi**, occupies the islet offshore from the harbour. Built in the fifteenth century, the castle has seen various uses in modern times: from the nineteenth-century home of the town's public executioner to a luxury hotel earlier in the twentieth century. In her autobiography *I Was Born Greek*, the late actress and politician, Melina Mercouri, claimed to have consummated her first marriage there.

Mosques and museums

In the town itself there are a few minor sights, mainly from the town's Turkish past, and two excellent museums. **Platía Syndágmatos**, the main square of the old town, is the focus of most interest. In the vicinity, three converted **Ottoman mosques** survive: one, in the southeast corner of the square, is an occasional theatre and cinema; another, just off the southwest corner, was the modern Greek state's original **Voulí** (parliament building). A third, fronting nearby Staïkopoúlou, has been reconsecrated as the cathedral of **Áyios Yeóryios**, having actually started life as a Venetian Catholic church. In the same area are a pair of handsome **Turkish fountains** – one abutting the south wall of the theatre-mosque, the other on Kapodhistría, opposite the church of Áyios Spyrídhon. On the steps of the latter, Ioannis Kapodistrias was assassinated by two members of the Mavromihalis clan from the Máni in September 1831; you can still see a scar left in the stone by one of the bullets. The Catholic church, which has also been a mosque, on Fotómara, has a monument to foreigners who died in the War of Independence, including Byron.

The **Archeological Museum** (Tues–Sun 8am–2.30pm; 500dr) occupies a dignified Venetian mansion on the west side of Syndágmatos. It has some good collections, as you'd expect in a town at the heart of the Argolid sites, including a unique and more or less complete suit of Mycenaean armour, the Dendra cuirass from around 1400 BC, and reconstructed frescoes from Tiryns.

The fine **Folk Art Museum** on Ipsilándou, just off Solróni, which won a European "Museum of the Year" award when it opened in 1981 and features some gorgeous embroideries, costumes and traditional household items, is closed for renovation and is not expected to open until 2000; recommended if open. At Staïkopoúlou 25 is the **Komboloï (Worry-Beads) Museum**, while a little further down at number 4 you can see shadow puppets being made at To Enotion. The **War Museum** (Tues–Sat 9am–2pm; Sun 9.30am–2pm; free) has weaponry, uniforms, illustrations and other military memorabilia.

Ayía Moní

More handicrafts are on sale at the convent of **Ayía Moní**, 4km east of Náfplio on the Epidaurus road, just south of the suburb of Ária. The monastic church, one of the most accomplished Byzantine buildings in the Peloponnese, dates back to the twelfth century. From the outer wall bubbles a nineteenth-century fountain, identified with the ancient spring of Kanthanos, in whose waters the goddess Hera bathed each year to restore her virginity. Modern Greeks similarly esteem the water, though presumably with less specific miracles in mind.

Karathónas beach

The closest proper beach to Náfplio is at **Karathónas**, a fishing hamlet just over the headland beyond the Palamídhi fortress, which can be reached by a short spur off the drive going up to the ramparts. A more direct dirt road – theoretically closed to traffic – around the base of the intervening cliffs makes a pleasant 45-minute walk, and there are four morning bus services in season.

The **sandy beach** stretches for a couple of kilometres, with a summer taverna at its far end. There were plans to develop it during the junta years, when the old road here was built, along with the concrete foundations of a hotel, but the project was suspended in the 1970s and has yet to be revived. At present Karathónas attracts quite a few Greek day-trippers in season, along with a handful of foreigners in camper vans; there are cafés in summer, plus windsurf boards for rent.

Eating, drinking and nightlife

A good place to start restaurant menu-gazing in Náfplio is the waterside **Bouboulínas**, where the locals take their early evening vólta, or **Staïkopoúlou**, off which may many enjoyable tavernas. For **breakfast or coffee**, it's hard to beat the *Propylaion* right beside the bus station; assorted bakeries and juice bars around Platía Syndágmatos are also worth investigating. **Nightlife** is low key, with a few late-night bars and the occasional seasonal disco on and around Bouboulínas and Syngroú. A quieter drink can be had at the **cafés** on Platía Syndágmatos, which stay open late. The real night-out haunts around town are the numerous huge discos and nightclubs such as *Perama* on the beach road out towards Néo Kíos, or *Zorba's* outside Toló.

Byzantio, Vas. Aléxandrou 15. Excellent and friendly Serbian taverna, on a quiet corner, with unusual specialities.

Kakanarakis, Vas. Ólgas 18 (☎0752/25 371). A lively place serving a variety of dependably good mezédhes. Open evenings only; popular with Greeks so arrive early or book ahead.

Omorfi Tavernaki, Vas. Ólgas 16. Local specialities include *kolokotroneïko* (pork in a rich wine and basil sauce), and courgette balls.

Posidonas/Haras, Sidhirás Merarhías. Eating out in the park, with tasty, well-prepared mezédhes, at low prices.

Listings

Banks are concentrated around Platía Syndágmatos and along Amalías. The National Bank branch on Sidhirás Merarhías has an automatic exchange machine.

Bookshops Odyssey, on Platía Syndágmatos (April–Oct 8am–10pm, Nov–March 8am–2pm), has a good stock of English-language books, newspapers, cassettes, CDs and videos.

Car rental Pick from: Safeway (☎0752/22 155), Eyíou 2; AutoEurope (☎0752/24 160, fax 24 164), Bouboulínas 51; or Sundy Tours (☎ & fax 0752/24 411), next door to the bus station.

Hydrofoils Náfplio is a stop for Flying Dolphin hydrofoils from June to September only. Services connect the town with Spétses and the other Argo-Saronic islands, plus Pireás and Monemvasiá; some involve a change at Pórto Héli. The ticket office, Yannopoulos (☎0752/28 054, fax 22 393), is at Platía Syndágmatos.

Laundries Two near the bus station end of Papanikoláou.

Moped, motorbike and bicycle rental From Nikopoulos, Bouboulínas 49; or MotorTraffic, Sidhirás Merarhías 15 (☎0752/22 702).

Post office The main branch (Mon–Fri 7.30am–2pm) is on the northwest corner of Platía Kapodhístria.

Taxis There's a rank on Syngroú, opposite the bus station.

Tourist office (☎0752/24 444). 25-Martíou 2; open daily, officially 9am–1pm, 4pm–8pm, but hours unpredictable and usually shorter.

Tourist police (☎0752/28 131). On the right at top of Syngroú. Helpful and open daily 7.30am–9pm.

Beaches around Náfplio: Toló, Kastráki and beyond

Southeast from Náfplio are the ever-expanding resorts of **Toló** and **Kastráki** – popular and established enough to feature in some British package-holiday brochures. Inevitably, this means that they get packed at the height of the season, although they're still more tranquil than the big island resorts; you can always seek refuge at the low-key places further along the coast.

Toló (Tolon)

TOLÓ, 11km from Náfplio (hourly buses in season; last back at 10pm), is frankly overdeveloped, with a line of thirty or more hotels and campsites swamping its limited sands. Out of season it can still be quite a pleasant resort, but in summer it is about as un-Greek an experience as you'll find in the Peloponnese. Redeeming features include views of the nearby islets of Platía and Romví, and in summer a good range of watersports (windsurfing, waterskiing, paragliding), but the local mosquitoes can be a problem.

Hotels in Toló tend to be block-booked through the summer but you could try some of the smaller places, like the *Hotel Artemis* (☎0752/59 458; ④) and *Hotel Tolo* (☎0752/59 248; ⑤). If they're full or beyond your budget, it's usually possible to find **rooms** by asking around or following the signs, but be prepared for inflated summer prices. The **campsites** charge similar rates: first try *Sunset* (☎0752/59 556; March–Oct); failing that, there's the quieter *Lido II* (☎0752/59 369). The taverna closest to the *Sunset* is highly rated.

In July and August, there are **hydrofoils** to the Argo-Saronic islands of Ídhra (Hydra) and Spétses.

Kastráki and ancient Assine

A pleasant alternative to Toló, especially if you're looking for an inexpensive campsite, is the longer beach at **KASTRÁKI**, 2km to the east; coming from Náfplio by bus, ask to be let off where the road reaches the sea – it forks right to Toló and left (500m) to Kastráki, marked on some maps as Paralía Asínis. Here, too, development is under way, but it's a fair bit behind that of Toló, limited to a scattering of small-scale hotels and campsites. *Camping Kastraki* (☎0752/59 386; April–Oct) is on the beach, and has windsurfing equipment, pedalos and canoes for hire.

If you get tired of the water, wander along the beach to the scrub-covered rock by the Náfplio road junction. This is, or was, **ancient Assine** (Tues–Sun 8am–2.30pm; free), an important Mycenaean and Classical city destroyed by the jealous and more powerful Árgos in retribution for the Asinians having sided with the Spartans against them. There's little to see other than a 200-metre length of ancient wall, but it's an oddly atmospheric spot.

East to Íria

Further around the coast, to the east of Kastráki, the road runs on to **DHRÉPANO**, a sizable village with four **campsites** and a very expensive **hotel**. The best campsite is *Triton* (☎0752/92 228; March–Nov); it's 1200m from the main square of Dhrépano – follow signs to the beach. Beyond Dhrépano, the **Vivári lagoon** has a couple of good fish tavernas on its shore. If you continue this way for another 13km, you reach a turning and poor track down to the beach and the *Poseidon* campsite (☎0752/913 41; May–mid-Oct) at Paralía Iríon, below **ÍRIA** village.

For the coast southeast of here towards Pórto Héli, Ermióni, Galatás and Méthana (each a local port for the Argo-Saronic islands) see pp.181–3.

Epidaurus (Epídhavros)

EPIDAURUS is a major Greek site, visited for its stunning **ancient theatre**, built by Polykleitos in the fourth century BC. With its extraordinary acoustics, this has become a very popular venue for the annual Athens Festival productions of **Classical drama** which are staged on Friday and Saturday nights from June through until the last weekend in August. The works are principally those of Sophocles, Euripides and Aeschylus;

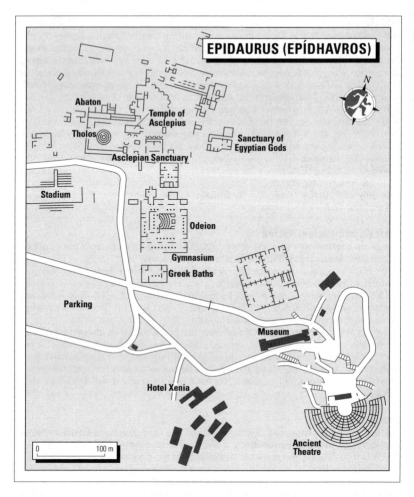

given the spectacular setting, they are worth arranging your plans around, whether or not you understand the modern Greek in which they're performed.

The theatre, however, is just one component of what was one of the most important sanctuaries in the ancient world, dedicated to the healing god, Asclepius, and a site of pilgrimage for half a millennium, from the sixth century BC into Roman times, and now a World Heritage site.

The Ancient Theatre and Asklepion

Daily: summer 8am–9pm; winter 8am–5pm; 1500dr. For festival performances you are admitted to the theatre after 7pm, but not to the rest of the site.

The dedication of the sanctuary at Epidaurus to **Asklepios**, the legendary son of Apollo, probably owes its origin to an early healer from northern Greece who settled in the area. There were Asklepian sanctuaries throughout Greece (Athens has ruins of one on the south slope of its Acropolis) and they were sited, rationally enough, alongside natural springs. Epidaurus, along with the island of Kós, was the most famous and inspirational of them all, and probably the richest. The sanctuary was much endowed by wealthy visitors and hosted a quadrennial festival, including drama in the ancient theatre, which followed the Isthmian games. Its heyday was in the fourth and third centuries BC; Rome, when ravaged by an epidemic in 293 BC, sent for the serpent that was kept in the sanctuary.

This aspect of the site, however, along with most of the associated Asclepian ruins, is incidental for most visitors; Epidaurus's **ancient theatre** is simply a wonderful sight. With its backdrop of rolling hills, this 14,000-seat arena merges perfectly into the landscape, so well in fact that it was rediscovered and unearthed only in the nineteenth century. Constructed with mathematical precision, it has an extraordinary equilibrium and, as guides on the stage are forever demonstrating, near-perfect natural acoustics – such that you can hear coins, or even matches, dropped in the circular orchestra from the highest of the 54 tiers of seats. Constructed in white limestone (red for the dignitaries in the front rows), the tiered seats have been repaired, but otherwise restoration has been minimal, with the beaten earth stage being retained, as in ancient times.

The museum

Close by the theatre is a small **museum** (summer daily 8am–7pm; winter Tues–Sun 8am–5pm, Mon noon–5pm; entrance fee included in site ticket price), which is best visited before you explore the sanctuary. The finds displayed here show the progression of medical skills and cures used at the Asclepion; there are tablets recording miraculous and outrageous cures – like the man cured from paralysis after being ordered to heave the biggest boulder he could find into the sea – alongside quite advanced surgical instruments.

In 86 BC, by which time Epidaurus's reputation was in decline, the Roman consul Sulla, leader of the forces invading the Peloponnese, looted the sanctuary and destroyed its buildings. Hence, most of the ruins visible today are just foundations and a visit to the museum helps identify some of the former buildings.

The sanctuary

The **Asklepian sanctuary**, as large a site as Olympia or Delphi, holds considerable fascination, for the ruins here are all of buildings with identifiable functions: hospitals for the sick, dwellings for the priest-physicians, and hotels and amusements for the fashionable visitors to the spa. Their setting, a wooded valley thick with the scent of thyme and pine, is evidently that of a health farm.

The reasonably well-labelled **site** begins just past the museum, where there are remains of **Greek baths** and a huge **gymnasium** with scores of rooms leading off a great colonnaded court; in its centre the Romans built an **odeion**. To the southwest is the outline of the **stadium** used for the ancient games, while to the southeast, a small **sanctuary of Egyptian Gods** reveals a strong presumed influence on the medicine used at the site.

North of the stadium are the foundations of the **Temple of Asclepius** and beside it a rectangular building known as the **Abaton** or **Kimitirion**. Patients would sleep here to await a visitation from the healing god, commonly believed to assume the form of a serpent. He probably appeared in a more physical manifestation than expected; harmless snakes are believed to have been kept in the building and released at night to bestow a curative lick.

The deep significance of the serpent at Epidaurus is elaborated in the circular **Tholos**, one of the best-preserved buildings on the site and designed, like the theatre, by Polykleitos. Its inner foundation walls form a labyrinth which is thought to have been used as a snakepit and, according to one theory, to administer a primitive form of shock therapy to the mentally ill. The afflicted would crawl in darkness through the outer circuit of the maze, guided by a crack of light towards the middle, where they would find themselves surrounded by writhing snakes. Presumably, on occasions, it worked. Another theory is that the labyrinth was used as an initiation chamber for the priests of Asclepius, who underwent a symbolic death and rebirth in it.

Practicalities

Most people take in Epidaurus as a day-trip, though there's a **hotel** at the site, the unattractive and expensive *Xenia* (☎0753/22 003; ②–⑤ by season). There are better and more modestly priced hotels on the way to and in nearby **LYGOURIÓ** village, 25km from Náfplio and 5km northwest of the site. Possibilities here include the *Hotel Alkion* (☎ & fax 0753/22 552; ③) at the turning off the main road to the village, or *Hotel Koronis* (☎0753/22 267; ④) in the village itself; both are open all year but fully booked long in advance for the festival period. Alternatively, it's possible to **camp** in the grass car park on days of performances, though you must wait until an hour after the play's end before setting up a tent. Pleasant beachside accommodation is available at Arhéa (Paleá) Epídhavros, 15km to the northeast (see following). Lygourió itself has a few tavernas and cafés, but little of interest other than the Byzantine church of Áyios Ioánnis Elémonos and a Mycenaean pyramid on the northeast road.

For meals, the nearest **restaurant** is the *Oasis* on the Lygourió road, although there is a café at the site *Xenia*. Much better is *Taverna Leonides* (☎0752/22 115), in the village proper, a friendly spot with a garden out the back; you'd be wise to book ahead if your visit coincides with a performance at the ancient theatre. Actors eat here after shows, and photos on the wall testify to the patronage of Melina Mercouri, the Papandreous, François Mitterrand and Peter Hall.

TICKETS AND TRANSPORT

Theatre tickets cost 4000–8000dr. In recent years there have been chaotic scenes with overselling and ticket-holders being turned away at the gates. Tickets for the plays are available at the site on the day of performance, or in advance in Athens (at the festival box office) or possibly in Náfplio. Advance information is usually unavailable until just before the festival. In Athens you can buy all-inclusive tickets for performances and return bus travel. There are also special evening buses from the site to Náfplio after the show. English translations of the plays are available at the site and at the Odyssey bookshop in Náfplio. Normally there are six buses daily from Náfplio to the site; they are marked "Theatre", "Asklipion" or "Epidhavros" and shouldn't be confused with those to the modern villages of Néa or Arhéa (Paleá) Epídhavros (see below).

Paleá Epídhavros

The closest beach resort to Epidaurus is **Paleá Epídhavros**, which has expanded since the recent improvement of the direct coast road from Kórinthos, but remains pleasantly small-scale. The recent discovery of ancient remains at the village means that some road signs for the beach now indicate "Ancient Epidavros", while the main inland site is referred to as "Ancient Theatre of Epidavros". As far as the remains are concerned, excavations are still in progress but they are worth a quick visit. A smaller classical theatre on the headland, past the small town beach, is a festival venue for weekend musical shows in July and August, for which advance information is available at the hotel *Christina* or from Athens (☎01/728 2333). You can find some small, open, Mycenaean *thólos* tombs behind the main street through town; turn inland up Odhós Ippokrátous by the BP petrol station, then left just above.

Facing the harbour and town beach, there are a number of **hotels** and purpose-built **rooms**, with more, plus campsites, on the road south to Yialási beach. All are full with festival patrons in season. If you want to book ahead, two friendly hotels to try are the *Christina* (☎0753/41 451, fax 41 655; ④) with excellent homemade breakfasts, on the waterfront square, and the *Paola Beach* (☎0753/41 397 fax 41 697; closed in winter; ④), the last hotel beyond the church at Vayioniá beach. The *Elena* rooms (☎0753/41 207; ②–③) are comfortable apartments, with air-conditioning for an extra charge. Three of the four **campsites** are on the beach to the south of the village in the district known as Yialási: they are *Verdelis* (☎0753/41 425; March–Oct), *Bekas* (☎0753/41 714; March–Oct) and *Nicholas II* (☎0753/41 445; April–Oct). **Buses** from Náfplio are scheduled to run late morning and return mid-afternoon, some via Epidaurus, though they can be unreliable – the central bus stop is at the *Platanos* café. Taxis are summonable on ☎0753/41 723 if you are stuck. A hydrofoil route from Pireás via Éyina during summer months provides alternative easy access from Athens – the local agents are Syroyiannouli (☎0753/42 010).

The Saronic ports: Méthana to Pórto Héli

The roads across and around the southern tip of the Argolid are sensational scenic rides, but the handful of resorts here are lacking in character, have disappointing beaches and are generally overdeveloped. With a car, you can pick your route and take a leisurely drive back to Náfplio, perhaps exploring the site of **ancient Troezen** and the **Lemonodhássos** lemon groves. Otherwise, you'll probably travel this way only if heading for one of the **Argo-Saronic islands**: **Méthana** has local connections to Éyina (Aegina) and Póros; **Galatás** to Póros; **Ermióni** to Ídhra (Hydra) and Spétses; **Kósta** and **Pórto Héli** to Spétses. Geographically part of the Peloponnese, Galatás, Trizína and Méthana are, like the Argo-Saronic islands, administratively in the province of Pireás, and sometimes prices are inflated to match those on the islands.

Méthana and ancient Troezen

It's a sixty-kilometre drive from Epidaurus to **MÉTHANA**, the last section along a cliff-hugging corniche road. Set on its own volcanic peninsula, Méthana is a disappointing spa-town, whose devotees are attracted by foul-smelling sulfur springs. Of the half-dozen hotels, the most pleasant is the seafront *Avra* (☎0298/92 382; ③). The agent for the **hydrofoil** is Palli (☎0298/92 460). The **volcano** at Kaϊméni Hóra ("Burnt Village"), on the northwest side of the peninsula is semi-dormant, though Strabo recorded an eruption two thousand years ago. Access paths have been blocked to discourage casual visitors.

Two kilometres west of the village of Trizína, itself just south and inland of the turning to the Méthana peninsula, are the ruins of ancient **TROEZEN**, the legendary birthplace of Theseus and location of his domestic dramas. The root of his problems was Aphrodite, who, having been rejected by Theseus's virgin son Hippolytus, contrived to make Phaedra – Theseus's then wife – fall in love with the boy (her stepson). Phaedra, too, was rejected and responded by accusing Hippolytus of attempted rape. Hippolytus fled, but, when his horses took fright at a sea monster and he was killed, Phaedra confessed her guilt and committed suicide. Originally told by Euripides (later reworked by Racine), a full account of the tragedy, together with a map of the remains, is on sale for 300dr in the modern village. For romantics, Theseus's autobiography in Mary Renault's *The King Must Die*, starts, "The Citadel of Troizen, where the palace stands, was built by giants before anyone remembers. But the Palace was built by my great-grandfather. At sunrise . . . the columns glow fire-red and the walls are golden. It shines bright against the dark woods on the mountainside."

Such **remains** as exist of the ancient town are spread over a wide site. Most conspicuous are three ruined Byzantine chapels, constructed of ancient blocks, and a structure known as the Pýrgos Dhiatihísmatos or **Tower of Theseus**, whose lower half is third century BC and top half is medieval. This stands near the lower end of a gorge, the course of an ancient **aqueduct**, which you can follow in fifteen minute's walk up a dirt road; a short, signed path leads to the **Dhiavoloyéfyro** ("Devil's Bridge"), natural rock formations spanning the chasm. On the far side, a short path to the right leads down to the lower bridge; a path to the left continues upstream past attractive rockpools – a rare black butterfly is said to be endemic in the valley here.

Galatás and Lemonodhássos

Workaday **GALATÁS** lies only 350m across the water from the upmarket island of Póros, with which it is connected by skiffs, sailing more or less continuously in the summer months (5min; 80–100dr). The town has a cluster of **hotels**, of which the best value are the *Saronis* (☎0298/22 356; ③) and the friendly *Papasotiriou* (☎0298/22 841; ④), with taverna; plus **rooms** for rent, a **bike rental** place and **taxis**. The town is connected by daily buses with Epidaurus and Náfplio.

On the coast road to the south is the small, unattractive **Pláka** beach (2km); two left turns shortly after bring you to the slightly better **Alykí** beach (4km), backed by a small salt lake; from a church on the main paved road behind Alykí, a route, signposted "Taverna Kardassi", leads into the **Lemonodhássos** – a vast, irrigated lemon grove. Paths meander through 30,000 lemon trees, heading upwards to an inspiringly positioned **taverna**, where a charming old man serves fresh lemonade as you sit on the shady terrace. Henry Miller recounts a visit here in *The Colossus of Maroussi*, hyperbolizing that "in the spring young and old go mad from the fragrance of sap and blossom." There is also a café and a good seafront taverna at Alykí beach, both seasonal. Further along the main road is the longer, cleaner Lemonodhássos beach (5km).

Ermióni, Kósta and Pórto Héli

Continuing clockwise around the coast from Galatás, you follow a narrow, modern road, cut from the mountainside to open up additional resorts close to Athens. Plépi (part of Aktí Ídhras – "Hydra Beach") is a villa-urbanization, visited by boats from beachless Ídhra opposite. **ERMIÓNI** (ancient Hermione) is better: a real village, enclosed by a rocky bay, overlooking Dhokós and Ídhra, and perhaps saved from development by lack of a sandy beach. It has two modest **hotels**: the *Akti* (☎0754/31 241; ②), and the *Ganossis Filoxenia* (☎0754/31 218; ④); plus the *Ganossis Filoxenia* apartments (☎0754/31 218; ④) along the beach. Aris Skouris, on the seafront south of the harbour, has bikes and mopeds for rent. The agent for the **hydrofoil** is Koustas (☎0754/31 170, fax 31 600).

Further round, **KÓSTA** facing Spétses, and much larger **PÓRTO HÉLI**, squeezed between two enclosed bays, are purpose-built resorts that have swallowed up their original hamlets. Beyond the pretty waterfront views, both feature a rather soulless mix of package-tour hotels and facilities for yachters exploring the Argo-Saronic islands. If you want or have to stay in Kósta, there is a campsite – *Camping Costa* (☎0754/51 571) to the west of Kósta – as well as some fairly upmarket hotels like the *Hotel Lido* (☎0754/57 393; ⑤). There are more reasonable options near the harbourfront in Pórto Héli:

Flisvos (☎0754/51 316, fax 51 011; ②) on Platía Karaïskáki, as is the bus stop; *Limani* (aka *Porto* ☎0754/51 410; ②) is on the war-memorial square, as is Hellenic Vision Travel (☎0754/51 453, fax 52 375) which books hydrofoils and can find accommodation. There are numerous restaurants and cafés as well as car and bike rental. Pórto Héli is the only Argolid port which has direct **hydrofoil** connections to Monemvasiá and Kýthira. Kósta connects four times a day by **ferry** to Spétses; tickets 140dr on the boat. About 2km east of Kósta is the excellent *Limanaki* taverna, at the attractive small beach at **Áyios Emilianós**. With your own transport, you can go further to the very long, part-sand, part-pebble beach of Kranídhi bay, east across the peninsula from Pórto Héli; there are no facilities.

The circuitous route back to Náfplio from Pórto Héli runs inland, via attractive Kranídhi (7km), then scrambling its way up through the mountains past the 1121m viewpoint peak of Mount Dhídhymo. It is covered 3–4 times daily by a bus, which usually dovetails in Pórto Héli and Kósta with ferries and hydrofoils to and from Spétses and elsewhere; in low season however, you may have to change buses in Kranídhi.

The east coast: Náfplio to Leonídhi

The **coastline** between Náfplio and Leonídhi is mountainous terrain, increasingly so as you move south towards Monemvasiá where the few villages seem carved out of their dramatic backdrop. Considering its proximity to Náfplio – and Athens – the whole stretch is enjoyably low key and remarkably unexploited, remaining more popular with Greek holidaymakers than with foreign tourists; the accommodation at resorts before Leonídhi may be fully booked well in advance for the mid-June to mid-August Greek school holidays.

Getting to the **beaches** – Parália Ástrous, Áyios Andhréas, Parália Tyroú and Pláka – is perhaps best done by car, though there are also **buses** twice daily from Árgos to Leonídhi, while **Parália Tyroú** and **Pláka** (the port/beach of Leonídhi) are served by the Flying Dolphin **hydrofoils** en route from Spétses/Pórto Héli to Monemvasiá. However you travel, change money in advance, as there are few **banks** between Náfplio and Leonídhi.

Right at the beginning of the route, around the coast from Náfplio, the minor site of **ancient Lérna** makes an interesting halt. If you are travelling by train from Árgos to Trípoli, you could stop off at the station of Mýli, only 500m from the site; alternatively, a trip there makes a nice ride around the coast via Néo Kíos beach if you rent a bike in Náfplio.

Ancient Lérna

The site of ancient **LÉRNA** (Tues–Sun 8.30am–3pm; 500dr) lies 10km south of Árgos and 12km from Náfplio by the minor road around the coast via Néa Kíos. On the way in from Árgos there is an interesting detour possible to the cave-lake **monastery** at Kefalári, and 4km further on to the Bronze Age **pyramid** at Ellinikó village, actually a stockade on the ancient road to Arcadia, standing nearly to full height. The nearest village is Mýli, at the foot of Mount Pontínus, on the bus and train routes from Árgos to Trípoli. Just beyond the straggle of the village a narrow, poorly signposted lane leads to the prehistoric site, which now lies between the main road and the railway; surrounded by an orange grove and close to the sea, it makes a fine picnic spot. The warden, unused to visitors, may volunteer to show you around this, one of Greece's most important Bronze Age sites. American excavations carried out in the 1950s unearthed ruins of an early **Neolithic house** and a well-preserved **fortification wall**, revealing it as one of the most ancient of Greek settlements, inhabited from as early as 5500 BC.

Another large house at the north end of the site is thought to have been an early palace, but was superseded, by a much larger and more important structure known as the **House of Tiles**. Measuring approximately 24m by 9m, this dwelling, labelled as another palace, takes its name from the numerous terracotta roof tiles found inside, where they are thought to have fallen when either lightning or enemy raiders set the building ablaze in approximately 2200 BC. The house represents the earliest known instance of the use of terracotta as a building material, and is the most impressive pre-Helladic structure to have been unearthed on the Greek mainland. A symmetrical ground plan of small rooms surrounding larger interior ones is today sheltered by a huge canopy, with stairs mounting to a now-vanished second storey. The substantial walls, made of sun-dried brick on stone foundations, were originally covered with plaster. Even after its destruction, this palace may have retained some ritual significance, since two Mycenaean **shaft graves** were sunk into the ruins in around 1600 BC, and the site was not completely abandoned until around 1250 BC at the end of the Mycenaean period. Further excavations are taking place in Mýli itself, and an archeological park has been proposed, to connect the two sites.

As implied by the chronology, the founders and early inhabitants of Lérna were not Greeks. Certain similarities in sculpture and architecture with contemporary Anatolia suggest an Asiatic origin but this has yet to be proved conclusively. Excavated finds, however, demonstrate that the Lerneans traded across the Aegean and well up into the Balkan peninsula, cultivated all the staple crops still found in the Argolid and raised livestock, as much for wool and hides as for food. Elegant terracotta sauce tureens and "teaspoons", which may be seen in the Árgos archeological museum (see p.170), hint at a sophisticated cuisine.

According to myth, Hercules performed the second of his labours, the slaying of the nine-headed Hydra, at Lérna. As if in corroboration of the legend, the nearby swamps are still swarming with eels.

Coastal Arcadia: Ástros and Paralía Tyroú

The initial section of coast from Lérna to Ástros and Áyios Andhréas is low-lying: less spectacular than the sections further south, but pleasant enough, with a scattering of accommodation at Xiropigádho. The first resort of any size is **PARÁLIA ÁSTROUS**, whose older houses are tiered against a headland shared by a medieval **fort** (Tues–Sun 8am–2.30pm; free) and the ruins of a thirteenth-century BC acropolis. Back from the northern end of the sand and gravel beach, which extends 6km south of the fishing harbour, there are a few tavernas, more cafés, numerous rooms to let and some **hotels**: the *Golden Beach* (☎0755/51 294; ③) has a seafront main square setting, while inland nearby the larger *Hotel Crystal* (☎0755/51 313; ④–⑤) rooms have fridges; both of them have air-conditioning. The new *Castro* rooms (☎0755/51 313, fax 51 764; ④) are well appointed and good value, sleeping up to four per apartment. The *Thirea* campsite (☎0755/51 002; May–Oct) is a lively spot.

To the west and south, a trio of surprisingly neat and compact villages – Ástros (site of the second National Assembly in 1823), Korakavoúni and Áyios Andhréas – perch at the foothills of **Mount Párnon** as it drops to meet the lush, olive-green plain. The **Kynouria Archeological Museum** (Tues–Fri 8.30am–2.30pm) in a traditional building in Ástros contains local items – including a collection from the Roman villa of Herodes Atticus at Éva Dholianón, 5km inland on the road to Trípoli. A little beyond Áyios Andhréas (10km from Ástros), the road curls down to the coast and the first in a series of fine-pebbled swimming coves, crammed between the spurs of Párnon. There are seasonal **rooms** at several of the coves, plus the *Arcadia* campsite (☎0755/31 190; May–Oct) on the main road, 6km beyond Áyios Andhréas; popular with middle-aged

Greeks, the site has a friendly atmosphere but is noisy, particularly at weekends. Few concessions are made to tourists along this stretch of coast, apart from the occasional makeshift taverna; out of season, you'll definitely need your own supplies.

PARALÍA TYROÚ is a fair-sized town, with banks and a post office, and is a popular resort, mostly with older Greeks; younger Greeks tend to go further south along the coast, to Pláka. The place feels sedate, with comfortable, mid-range hotels and cafés spread back from its long pebble beach. **Hydrofoils** call in high season; the agent is Politis (☎0757/41 692). **Hotel** accommodation options at the southern end of the beach include: *Apollon* (☎0757/41 393; ③) with fridges in the rooms, and which also has apartments; *Kamvyssis* (☎0757/41 424; ④) with TV and air-conditioning; and *Galazia Thalassa* (aka *Blue Sea*; ☎0757/41 369; ④). The well-equipped **campsite**, *Zaritsi* (☎0757/41 429; April–Oct), is a few kilometres north at Zarítsi beach. Southwards 12km, en route to Leonídhi, there is a good fish taverna, the *Klimataria*, above pretty Sambatiká beach.

Leonídhi, Pláka and south towards Monemvasiá

Gigantic red cliffs that wouldn't look out of place in deserts of the American Southwest or the Canary Islands, confine **LEONÍDHI** (Leonídhion in formal Greek), the terminus of the Árgos bus route. Set inland, with rich agricultural land spreading down to the sea, this prosperous and traditional market town sees little need to pander to tourists, most of whom head for the coast at Leonídhi's diminutive port, Pláka. The **Tsakonic dialect** – a form of ancient Doric – is still used locally, notably for the Easter Sunday Mass. Also unique is the streaky, pale purple, sweet-tasting Tsakonikí aubergine, celebrated in a Pláka festival each August. If you prefer to stay inland, you might find space in the town's one modest **hotel**, the *Alexaki* (aka *Neon*; ☎0757/22 383; ③–⑤), or the few advertised **rooms** for rent such as the *Ithaki* (☎0757/23 394; ②) or the *Kostarini* (☎0757/22273; ②), both with air-conditioning and open all year. There are some enjoyable, small-town tavernas, such as the *Mouria* near the small square.

Pláka to Yérakas
PLÁKA, 4km away, is a delightful place consisting of a harbour, a couple of **hotels** and some **eating places**. It also has a fine pebble beach, which in recent years has become popular with Greek and European tourists, plus a sporadic influx of yachties. In summer, it would be wise to phone ahead to reserve a balconied room with sea view in the first-choice *Hotel Dionysos* (☎0757/23 455; ②), owned by the Bekarou family who have run the *Michael & Margaret* taverna opposite since 1830. Eat here and you may be rewarded with tales of wartime derring-do by the taverna owner's father. There are excellent meals also to be had at picturesquely situated little places like *Tou Psara* taverna near the harbour. The agent for the **hydrofoils** is Kounia (☎0757/22 206).

The small resort of **POÚLITHRA**, 3km south of Pláka around the bay, marks the end of the coast road – which heads inland to small, isolated, mountain villages. There are tavernas close by the narrow strip of beach; a **hotel**, the *Akroyiali* (☎0757/51 262; ④); and rooms such as *Kekes* (☎0757/51205; ④) and *Spanoudakis* (☎0757/51 325; ③).

South of Leonídhi, in Lakonía province, the coastline is wilder and sparsely inhabited, with just a couple of coastal settlements cut into the cliffs. To reach the two little settlements – **KYPARÍSSI** and **YÉRAKAS** – you're better off taking the Flying Dolphin **hydrofoil**, which stops at both on the way to Monemvasiá. By road, it's a very roundabout route (though in better shape than it looks on the map) from Molaï, on the Spárti–Monemvasiá road.

Inland from Leonídhi

The route inland from **Leonídhi** is worth taking for its own sake, climbing through the huge **Dhafnón gorge**, past the **monastery of Élonas** – although the views are even better if this route is covered in the reverse direction, descending through the gorge to Leonídhi. The road peaks at the high mountain village of **Kosmás**, providing a temperature shock in the height of summer but a great place to stop and enjoy the fresh mountain air over a drink in the atmospheric square, shaded by a huge plane tree. The whole route is a decent road for cars, and brings you out near the Byzantine site of **Yeráki**; from there, you have a choice of roads – to Spárti or Yíthio (Gythion) via Skála, or to Monemvasiá and Neápoli via Molái. Without a car, you'll have to plan very carefully: a daily bus runs from Leonídhi to Yeráki, and goes on to Spárti twice a week – but check first.

Moní Élonas

Visible from Leonídhi, the **Panayía tis Élonas** (Elónis) monastery stands out as a white slash in the mountainside – though as you twist around and up the ravine, it drops away from view. The turn-off to the monastery (visitors permitted from sunrise to sunset) comes 13km from Leonídhi, via a short approach road which ends at a gateway. A cliff path takes you on to the main building, where you can wander down to a small chapel (closed during siesta) crammed with icons and lanterns, and to a spring, whose icy-cold water has supposedly curative powers. Most of the monastery, originally founded in medieval times following the appearance of a miraculous and inaccessible icon by St Luke, was rebuilt following the War of Independence, becoming a nunnery in 1972. Today, it is maintained by four nuns, who sell a classic little history (in Greek only) of the monastery's legends and vicissitudes.

Kosmás

Continuing south, 15km past the Élonas turning, you reach **KOSMÁS**, a handsome alpine village set about a grand platía and giant plane tree, with several tavernas. Straddling the most important pass of Párnon, at 1150m, it can be a chilly place during the spring or winter, but very beautiful, too, with its streams, cherries and walnut trees, and would make a pleasant base for mountain walking. The *Maleatis Apollo* guesthouse (☎0757/31 494; ②) has rooms with kitchens, sleeping two to four, and a small taverna, in an attractively refurbished eighteenth-century building. Just at the edge of the village, on the Leonídhi side, are the *Kosmas* studios (☎0757/31 483; ②), also with kitchens. Beyond the village the road runs through a pass, then sweeps downvalley through fir forests to the village and Byzantine ruins of Yeráki (see opposite).

THE SOUTHEAST: LAKONÍA

Draw a line on the map, from south of Leonídhi to north of Spárti and then to the high ridge of Taïyetos. Broadly, everything below this line is **Lakonía**, the ancient territories of the Spartans. Exclude the lush Evrótas valley, with Spárti itself and Mystra, and you are left with a dramatic and underpopulated landscape of harsh mountains and poor, dry, rocky soil. Landforms apart, the highlights here are the extraordinarily preserved Byzantine town of **Monemvasiá** – an essential visit for any tour of the southern Peloponnese – and the aridly remote **Máni** peninsula, with its bizarre history of violence and piety, of feuds and unique tower houses and frescoed churches with barrel roofs. Monemvasiá is a regular stop for Flying Dolphin hydrofoils from Pireás and the Argo-Saronic islands, and would make a superb entry point to the peninsula. In summer, the Maniot port of **Yíthio** (Gythion), and **Neápoli**, south of Monemvasiá, are additional stops on the hydrofoil and provide the easiest links to **Kýthira**, technically an Ionian island under the administration of Pireás, but covered – due to its Peloponnesian access – in this chapter.

South from Leonídhi: Yeráki

If you choose the southeastern route over Mount Párnon from Leonídhi then it is well worth making the effort to visit the **Byzantine antiquities** at **Yeráki**. With its **Frankish castle** and fifteen **chapels** spread over a spur of the mountain, Yeráki stands a creditable third to the sites of Mystra and Monemvasiá.

Medieval Yeráki

Yeráki (Tues–Sun 8am–2.30pm; free) was one of the original twelve **Frankish baronies** set up in the wake of the Fourth Crusade, and remained through the fourteenth century an important Byzantine town, straddling the road between Mystra and its port at Monemvasiá. The site is spectacular, with sweeping vistas over the olive-covered Evrótas plain and across to Taïyetos. It stands four kilometres outside and overlooking the current village of Yeráki (see below).

All the main churches are kept locked, and to visit them you should, theoretically, enquire at the café on the village square for one of the caretakers, one of whom may give a tour, clambering around the rocks to the best-preserved **chapels**. However it appears they will usually only open nowadays for organized excursions, and there are reports of hostility at the cafés to lone women.

The most substantial remains of the medieval town are of its fortress, the **Kástro**, built in 1256 by the local Frankish baron, Jean de Nivelet, who had inherited Yeráki, with six other lordships, from his father. Its heavily fortified design is based on that of the Villehardouin fortress at Mystra, for this was one of the most vulnerable Frankish castles of the Morea, intended to control the wild and only partially conquered territories of Taïyetos and the Máni. In the event, Jean retained his castle for less than a decade, surrendering to the Byzantines in 1262 and buying an estate near Kórinthos on the proceeds. In the late seventeenth century it became Venetian, then Turkish in 1715 until being abandoned in the late eighteenth century. Within the fortress are huge **cisterns** for withstanding sieges, and the largest of Yeráki's churches: the thirteenth-century **mitrópolis**, also known as **Áyios Yeóryios**, which features blackened Byzantine frescoes, a Frankish iconostasis and the Villehardouin arms.

The churches on the slope below also mix Frankish and Byzantine features, and many incorporate material from Yeráki's ancient predecessor, Geronthrai. The caretaker may be prepared to unlock two or three, including **Áyios Dhimítrios**, **Zoödhóhos Piyí** and **Ayía Paraskeví** (at the base of the hill), each of which has restored frescoes.

Practicalities

The "modern" village of **Yeráki** has no regular accommodation, though rooms may be negotiable through the café or taverna in the square. If you're dependent on public transport, you'll need to take in Yeráki as day-trip from Spárti: **buses** run several times daily, but only twice a week along the splendid route over Mount Párnon to Leonídhi.

Monemvasiá

MONEMVASIÁ standing impregnable on a great island-like irruption of rock, was the medieval seaport and commercial centre of the Byzantine Peloponnese, the secular

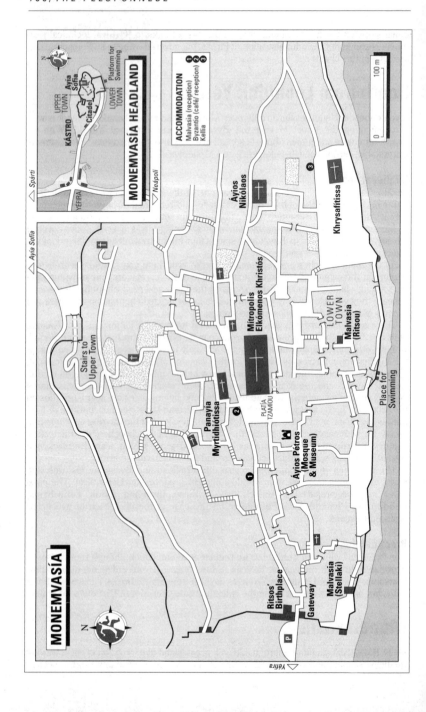

MONEMVASÍA

MONEMVASÍA HEADLAND

KASTRO

UPPER TOWN

Avia Sofia

Citadel

Platform for Swimming

LOWER TOWN

△ Spárti

▽ Neápoli

△ Avia Sofia

ACCOMMODATION
Malvasia (reception)
Byzantio (café/ reception)
Kellia

Áyios Nikólaos

Khrysafítissa

Stairs to Upper Town

Mitrópolis
Elkómenos Khristós

LOWER TOWN

Malvasía
(Ritsou)

Panayía
Myrtidhiótissa

PLATÍA
TZAMÍOU

Áyios Pétros
(Mosque
& Museum)

Place for Swimming

Ritsos'
Birthplace

Gateway

Malvasía
(Stellaki)

N

0   100 m

▽ Yéfira

counterpart of Mystra. Nowadays the lower town is a curious mixture of atmospheric heritage combined with tacky souvenir shops and gawping tourists.

The town's name, an elision of *Moni Emvasis*, "single entrance", is a reference to its approach from the mainland, across a kilometre of causeway and a small bridge built this century to replace a sequence of wooden bridges. Such a defensible and strategic position gave it control of the sea lanes from Italy and the West to Constantinople and the Levant. Fortified on all approaches, it was invariably the last outpost of the Peloponnese to fall to invaders, and was only ever taken through siege.

Some history

Founded by the **Byzantines** in the sixth century, Monemvasiá soon became an important port. It remained in Byzantine possession for almost seven hundred years, passing only very briefly to the Franks – who took it in 1249 after a three-year siege but had to ransom it back for the captured Guillaume de Villehardouin. Subsequently, it served as the chief commercial port of the Despotate of Mystra and was for all practical purposes the Greek Byzantine capital. Mystra, despite the presence of the court, was never much more than a large village; Monemvasiá at its peak had a population of almost 60,000.

Like Mystra, Monemvasiá had something of a golden age in the thirteenth century; during this period, it was populated by a number of noble Byzantine families, and reaped considerable wealth from estates inland, from the export of wine (the famed Malmsey – *Malvasia* – mentioned by Shakespeare; now being replanted locally – to be available initially at the Lazareto hotel restaurant) and from roving corsairs who preyed on Latin shipping heading for the East. When the rest of the Moréas fell to the Turks in 1460, Monemvasiá was able to seal itself off, placing itself first under the control of the papacy, later under the **Venetians**. Only in 1540 did the **Turks** gain control, the Venetians having abandoned their garrison after the defeat of their navy at Préveza.

Turkish occupation precipitated a steady decline, both in prestige and population, though the town experienced something of a revival during the period of Venetian control (1690–1715) of the Peloponnese. Monemvasiá was again thrust to the fore in the **War of Independence**, being the first of the major Turkish fortresses to fall, after a terrible siege and wholesale massacre of the Turkish inhabitants, in July 1821.

After the war, there was no longer the need for such strongholds, and, at the end of the nineteenth century, shipping routes changed too, with the opening of the Corinth Canal. The population plummeted and the town drifted into a village existence, its buildings for the most part allowed to fall into ruin. By the time of World War II – during which 4000 New Zealand troops were dramatically evacuated from the rock – only eighty families remained. Today there are just ten in permanent residence, but much restoration work has been done to the walls and many of the churches.

The rock: medieval Monemvasiá

From the mainland village of **Yéfira** – where the causeway to **Monemvasiá** (or **Kástro**, as locals call it) begins – nothing can be seen of the medieval town, which is built purely on the seaward face of the rock. Little more is revealed as you walk across the causeway, past a Mobil garage, but the long entrance road, used for parking, brings you to huge castellated walls. Once through the fortified entrance gate, narrow and tactically Z-shaped, everything looms into view: piled upon one another, amid narrow stone streets and alleyways, are houses with tiled roofs and walled gardens, distinctively Byzantine churches. High above, the improbably extended castle walls protect the upper town on the summit.

The Lower Town

The **Lower Town** once numbered forty churches and over eight hundred homes, an incredible mass of building, which explains the intricate network of alleys. A single main street – up and slightly to the left from the gateway – shelters most of the restored houses, and is lined with cafés, tavernas and souvenir shops. One of the tavernas is owned by the Ritsos family, relatives of the late Yannis Ritsos, one of Greece's leading poets and a lifelong communist, who was born on the rock; a plaque on a house above the main gate commemorates his birthplace.

At the end of this street is the lower town's main square, a beautiful public space, with a cannon and a well in its centre, with the great, vaulted **cathedral** built by the Byzantine emperor Andronikos II Komnenos when he made Monemvasiá a see in 1293. The largest medieval church in southern Greece, it is dedicated to Christ in Chains, and is thus known as *Elkómenos Khristós*. Across the square is the domed church of **Áyios Pétros**, originally a sixteenth-century mosque, which was reconverted by the Turks back into a mosque and now houses a small museum of local finds (open, but keeps unpredictable hours). Unusually for Ottoman Greece, the Christian cathedral was allowed to function during the occupation, and did beside this mosque – hence the name of this square, Platía Tzamíou, the square of the mosque.

Down towards the sea is a third notable church, the **seventeenth-century Khrysafítissa**, whose bell hangs from a bent-over old acacia tree in the courtyard. It was restored and adapted by the Venetians in their second, eighteenth-century, occupation. The **Portello** is a small gate in the sea wall, due south of Platía Tzamíou; you can **swim** safely off the rocks here.

In peaceful times, the town was supplied from the tiny harbour, **Kourkoúla**, outside the town and below the road as you approach the entrance gateway. There are two minor churches just off the main street. **Panayía Myrtidhiótissa**, to the north of the cathedral, is a small, single-aisled basilica with a single dome; inside there is a beautifully carved iconostasis – ask around for the priest if the basilica is locked. The big grey church built alongside the main street, above the Khrysafítissa, is **Áyios Nikólaos**; it dates from the early eighteenth century, and was used for many years as a school.

The Upper Town

The climb to the **Upper Town** is highly worthwhile – not least for the solitude, since most day-trippers stay down below. To get the most from the vast site, it's a good idea to bring some food and drink (from Yéfira – Monemvasiá has no supermarket), to enable you to explore at leisure. There are sheer drops from the rockface, and unguarded cisterns, so descend before dusk and if you have young children, keep them close by.

The fortifications, like those of the lower town, are substantially intact; indeed the **entrance gate** retains its iron slats. Within, the site is a ruin, unrestored and deserted – the last resident moved out in 1911 – though many structures are still recognizable. The only building that is relatively complete, even though its outbuildings have long since crumbled to foundations, is the beautiful thirteenth-century **Ayía Sofía**, by the gateway. Founded as a monastery by Andronikos II, along a plan similar to that of Dhafní, its chapel candles still flicker perilously in the wind.

Beyond the church extend acres of ruins; in medieval times the population here was much greater than that of the lower town. Among the remains are the stumpy bases of Byzantine houses and public buildings, and, perhaps most striking, a vast **cistern** to ensure a water supply in time of siege. Monemvasiá must have been more or less self-sufficient in this respect, but its weak point was its food supply, which had to be entirely imported from the mainland. In the last siege, by Mavromihalis's Maniot army in the War of Independence, the Turks were reduced to eating rats and, so the propagandists claimed, Greek children.

Practicalities

Monemvasiá can be approached by road or sea. **Ferries** from Pireás are currently suspended, but there are regular **hydrofoils** in season, linking the town to the north with Leonídhi, Pórto Héli, Spétses and Pireás, and to the south with Neápoli and the island of Kýthira; currently there is no hydrofoil link with Yíthio. Direct **buses** connect with Spárti three times daily and twice (in season only) with Yíthio; occasionally a change at Moláï is necessary. Out of season it's better to alight at Skála, 17km from Yíthio, and take a local bus or taxi.

The hydrofoil will drop you at a mooring midway down the causeway; buses arrive in the modern mainland village of Yéfira. This is little more than a straggle of hotels, rooms and restaurants for the rock's tourist trade, with a pebble beach; for a **beach** day-trip, it's best to head 3–4km north along the coast.

Accommodation on the rock is expensive – in season and out – and from June to September, you'll need to book ahead. Within the walls, the choice is between three very upmarket **hotels**, each of which has attractively restored and traditionally furnished rooms. The most renowned is the *Malvasia* (☎0732/61 323, fax 61 722; ③–⑥), which occupies three separate locations between the main street and the sea; call first at the hotel reception, well signposted from just inside the main gateway. The similarly characterful *Byzantino* (☎0732/61 254, fax 61 331; ④–⑥) further along the main street is marginally more expensive: ask at the café of the same name. Down near the Khrysafítissa, looking out over the sea, is the EOT's *Kellia* (☎0732/61 520, fax 617 67; ⑤), a small and rather isolated place, very exposed to the sun; advance booking is recommended. Several other **furnished apartments** on the rock are available for long-term rental. If you ask around at the shops and taverna on the main street, it's just possible that you might get one of these on a more temporary basis, out of season. Or you could seek the help of Malvasia Travel in Yéfira (see below). The *Byzantino* has recently opened the *Lazareto* hotel (☎0732/61 991, fax 61 992; ⑥), in the old hospital at the island end of the causeway, with luxurious rooms sympathetically converted. Their *Castellano* restaurant has local specialities and a Peloponnesian wine list (soon to include local Malvasia). **Eating out** in the old village is enjoyable, as much for location as food. Of the several restaurants, the best all-round place is *Matoula*, going since the 1960s, which has a leafy garden overlooking the sea.

Yéfira

There's more accommodation in **YÉFIRA**, along with various other useful tourist services: **bank**, **post office**, and a **travel agent**, Malvasia Travel (☎0732/61 432), which can help with rooms, ferry (if any) tickets and **moped** rental; the Mobil garage just across the bridge towards the rock (☎0732 /61 219) handles the **hydrofoils**. There are several **hotels** near or just north of the causeway. The cheapest is the refurbished *Akroyiali* (☎0732/61 360; ②). The *Aktaion* (☎0732/61 234; ③) and posher *Filoxenia* (☎0732/61 716; ④) are under the same management. The friendly *Monemvasia* (☎0732/61 381; ③) is good value, with a restaurant and large balconies overlooking the sea, while just over the road the *Flower of Monemvasia* (☎0732/61 395, fax 61 391; ③) has rooms with a fridge and TV. If these are full, there are others to choose from, plus **rooms** for rent, advertised along the waterfront. The nearest **campsite** is 3km to the south, along the coast road; *Kapsis Paradise* (☎0732/61 123) is open year-round, and has water skis and mopeds for rent. Back in the village, the best **taverna** is undoubtedly the *Nikolaos*; if you have transport, you could also try the *Pipinelis* (☎0732/61 044; May–Oct), about 2km out on the road south to the campsite, but ring first to be sure it's open and to make a reservation if the weather's cool, as indoor seating is limited. Even closer to the campsite is the pleasant *Kamares* taverna with good grilled and oven food. For nightlife in Yéfira, try the popular *Rock Café* or the *Santé* bar which plays hardcore Greek music.

South to Neápoli and Elafónissos

The isolated southeasternmost "finger" of the Peloponnese below Monemvasiá, locally known as **Vátika**, is little visited by tourists, except for the area around **Neápoli**, the southernmost town in mainland Greece, which offers access to the islet of Elafónissos, just offshore, and to the larger islands of Kýthira and Andikýthira, midway to Crete. From Monemvasiá the southerly route high over the central ridge via Ellinikó village is the more attractive of the two roads to Neápoli.

Neápoli

NEÁPOLI is a mix of old buildings and modern Greek concrete behind a grey sand beach – and mainly of interest for its ferry and hydrofoil connections. For such an out-of-the-way place, it is surprisingly developed, catering mostly to Greek holidaymakers. Besides **rooms**, there are three modest hotels: *Aïvali* (☎0734/22 287; ③) and *Arsenakos* (☎0734/22 991; ④) on the seafront and, just behind, the newer, friendly *Vergina* (☎0734/23443; ③) with fridges in the rooms; all may need to be booked ahead in summer. If you are waiting for the ferry or hydrofoil, you can eat extremely well at *To Konaki tou Zaharia*, by the bridge on the seafront. The agency for the Kýthira ferry is Vatica Bay Travel (☎0734/22 660, fax 23 981), and for the hydrofoil, Dimitris Alexandrakis (☎0734/22 214, fax 23 590). Neápoli has three **banks**; **taxis** are on ☎0734/22 590.

Neápoli **beach** extends north to the village of Vingláfia and the recently upgraded harbour of Poúnda, which has between five and eighteen daily ferry crossings (☎0734/61 117) over the short strait to the islet of Elafónissos. Currently there is only one early morning sailing from Neápoli to the islet. Nearby Lake Strongýli, south of Áyios Yeóryios, has been proposed as an EU NATURA 2000 habitat conservation site.

Elafónissos island

Like Neápoli, **Elafónissos** is relatively busy in summer, and again is frequented mainly by Greek visitors. The island's lone village is largely modern and functional, but has plenty of rooms and some good fish tavernas. Three **pensions**, the *Asteri* (☎0734/61 271; ③) with a fridge in the rooms, *Elafonisos* (☎0734/61 210; ③) and *Lafotel* (☎0734/61 138; ④), are worth booking.

Although otherwise scenically unexciting, the island has one of the best **beaches** in this part of Greece at **Símos**, a large double bay of fine white sand heaped into dunes; it's 5km southeast of the village, from where a caique leaves every morning in summer. There's one basic sandwich-and-drinks stand at the beach, and usually a small community of people camping here. Another beach, **Káto Nisí**, to the southwest of the village is quieter but almost as beautiful, with views to Kýthira.

Arhángelos

Further up the coast from Neápoli, just off the more northerly route from Monemvasiá, **ARHÁNGELOS** is a pleasant little resort at the southern end of a quiet sandy and deserted bay. By a quaint twist the village's name means "archangel", yet it is the harbour of Dhemonía ("devilry"), several kilometres inland. Rooms are to be had at a good restaurant, *Limanaki* (☎0732/44 123; ③; March–Oct), or at the smart, apricot-coloured *Hotel Palazzo* (☎0732/44 111, fax 44 113: *palazzo@travelling.gr*; ⑥), open all year. The *Anokato* bar is a popular hangout for the whole peninsula, especially in winter.

Kýthira island

Isolated at the foot of the Peloponnese, the island of **Kýthira** traditionally belongs to the Ionian islands, and shares their history of Venetian, and later, British rule; under the former it was known as Cerigo. Administratively part of Pireás – like the Argo-Saronic islands – it is listed, confusingly, in the main Peloponnese phone directory under the village of Skála in Lakonía. For the most part, similarities end there. The island architecture, whitewashed and flat-roofed, looks more like that of the Cyclades, albeit with a strong **Venetian** influence. The landscape is different, too: wild scrub- and gorse-covered hills, or moorland sliced by deep valleys and ravines.

Depopulation has left the land underfarmed and the abandoned fields overgrown, for, since the war, most of the islanders have left for Athens or Australia, giving Kýthira a reputation of being the classic emigrant island; it is known locally as "Australian Colony" or "Kangaroo Island", and Australia is referred to as "Big Kýthira". Many of the villages are deserted, their platías empty and the schools and kafenía closed. Kýthira was never a rich island, but, along with Monemvasiá, it did once have a military and economic significance – which it likewise lost with Greek independence and the opening of the Corinth Canal. These days, tourism has brought a little prosperity (and a few luxury hotels), but most summer visitors are Greeks and especially Greek Australians. For the few foreigners who reach Kýthira, it remains something of a refuge, with its fine and remarkably undeveloped **beaches** the principal attraction. However, in 1998 a popular Greek television serial filmed on the island attracted a huge amount of domestic attention and, consequently, holidaymakers from the mainland. Much of the accommodation is now fully booked well in advance for the entire Greek school-summer-holiday period.

Arrival and getting around

Arrival on the island has changed in recent years. In 1997 a huge new all-weather **harbour** was opened at Dhiakófti, and now all hydrofoils and all ferries are docking here instead of Ayía Pelayía or Kapsáli. The airport is deep in the interior, 8km south of Potamós; taxis meet arrivals, as they do the boats. Sadly, there is no other **public transport** at the moment; although a bus has been purchased, the owner is still awaiting a permit to carry passengers. Until it is running the only alternative to pricey taxis is to hitch or, more advisedly, hire a **car** or **moped**. The roads are now well surfaced all over the island and there are reliable petrol stations at Potamós, Kondoliánika and Livádhi.

Dhiakófti

Dhiakófti, until recently an unsung and relatively inaccessible backwater towards the bottom of the northeast coast, has been catapulted into the forefront of activity by the opening of the harbour, constructed by joining the islet of Makrónisi to the shore by a causeway. There is also a nice white sandy beach, and although no major expansion has taken place yet, it seems inevitable that the developers will not be long in seizing their opportunity. For the time being there are just a couple of tavernas, including the friendly *Notaras* by the causeway, a good kafenío and a few rooms and apartments such as the *Porto Diakofti* (☎0735/33 041; ⑤–⑥; April–Oct). Transport is the main problem but there may be a branch of Panayiotis car rental soon. If there isn't, you can arrange to be brought by car by phoning their Kapsáli office, or that of Porfyra in Livádhi.

Ayía Pelayía and northern Kýthira

There's a reasonable choice of **tavernas** and **rooms** in Ayía Pelayía; the *Faros Taverna* (☎0735/33 282; ③) offers both, from its waterfront location. Best value of the upmarket

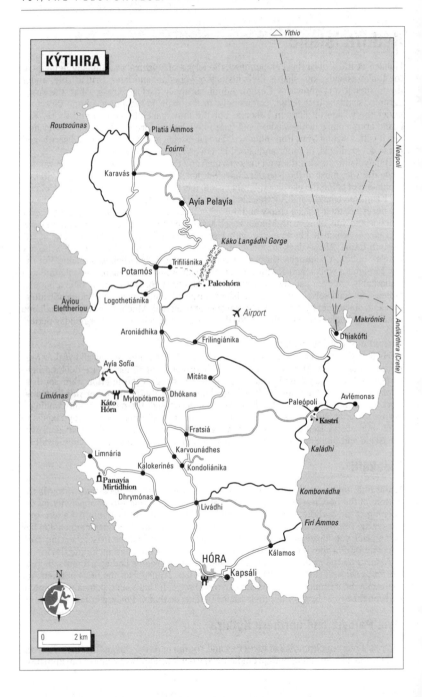

KÝTHIRA

hotels is *Venardos* (☎0735/34 205, fax 33 850; ⑤), which is open all year and can offer very good deals off season. The clean and comfortable *Hotel Kytherea* (☎0735/33 321; ③–④) is more luxurious, as are the more recent *Filoxenia Apartments* (☎0735/33 100, fax 33 610; ⑥; April–Oct), with striking blue shutters and an imaginative layout around small courtyards. Ferry and hydrofoil **tickets** are available from Conomos Travel (☎0735/33 490, fax 33 890), inside the tourist shop on the ground floor of the *Kytherea*. The *Paleo* ouzerí is recommended.

Potamós and around

From Ayía Pelayía, the main road winds up the mountainside towards **POTAMÓS**, Kýthira's largest village – a pleasant and unspoiled place which, if you have a rented vehicle, makes a good base for exploring the island. It has a few **rooms**, such as those at the *Pension Porfyra* (☎0735/33 329; ④) which have a fridge and TV, and *Alevizopoulos* (☎0735/33 245; ③), together with **tavernas**, a **bank**, a **post office**, Olympic Airways office (☎0735/33 688) and two petrol stations. Most of the shops on the island are here, too, as is the **Sunday market**, Kýthira's liveliest regular event.

From **Logothetiánika**, just south of Potamós, an unpaved road leads down to Ayíos Eleftheríos, where you can **swim** from the rocks on the west coast, backed by high cliffs. At Logothetiánika itself, there is a popular taverna, *Karydhies* (☎0735/33 664) with live music Thursday–Saturday, when booking is advisable.

Paleohóra

The main reason for visiting Potamós is to get to **PALEOHÓRA**, the ruined **medieval capital** of Kýthira, 3km to the east of the town. Few people seem to know about or visit these remains, though they constitute one of the best Byzantine sites around. The most obvious comparison is with Mystra: although Paleohóra is much smaller, a fortified village rather than a town, its natural setting is equally spectacular. Set on a hilltop at the head of the **Káko Langádhi gorge**, it is surrounded by a sheer 100m drop on three sides.

The site is lower than the surrounding hills and invisible from the sea and most of the island, something which served to protect it from the pirates that have plagued Paleohóra through much of its history. The town was built in the thirteenth century by Byzantine nobles from Monemvasiá, and when Mystra fell to the Turks, many of its noble families also sought refuge here. Despite its seemingly impregnable and perfectly concealed position, the site was discovered and sacked by **Barbarossa**, commander of the Turkish fleet, in 1537, and the island's seven thousand inhabitants were sold into slavery.

The town was never rebuilt, and tradition maintains that it is a place of ill fortune, which perhaps explains the emptiness of the surrounding countryside, none of which is farmed today. The hills are dotted with Byzantine **chapels**, which suggests that, in its heyday, the area must have been the centre of medieval Kýthira; it is rumoured to have once had eight hundred inhabitants and 72 churches. Now the principal remains are of the surviving churches, some still with traces of frescoes (and kept firmly locked), and the castle. The site is unenclosed and has never been seriously investigated, although excavations are now planned.

If you have your own transport, there's a rough dirt road to Paleohóra, signposted off the main road from Potamós to Aroniádhika. By foot, it's quicker and more interesting to take the path from the tiny village of Trifyliánika, just outside Potamós – look out for a rusting sign to the right as you enter the village. The path is overgrown in parts and not easy to follow; the ruins only become visible when you join the road above the gorge.

Karavás

KARAVÁS, 6km north of Potamós, is untypical of the island's villages – its architecture and the setting, in a deep wooded valley with a stream, are more reminiscent of the other Ionian islands. One of Kýthira's most pleasant villages, it would be a superb base, though there is (as yet) nowhere to stay. There is, however, a restaurant *Amir Ali*, with frequent live music.

Platiá Ámmos, at the end of the valley, is a sandy beach with a seasonal fish **taverna**. There is also an ouzerí and café and a few rooms at *Moudheas* restaurant (☎0735/33 960; ④). The little pebble beach at **Foúrni**, 2km south, is quieter and more attractive.

Kapsáli

KAPSÁLI, in addition to its harbour function, is the one place on Kýthira largely devoted to tourism. Most foreign visitors to Kýthira stay here, and it's a popular port of call for yachts heading from the Aegean to the Ionian islands and Italy. Set behind double pebble-sand bays, it is certainly picturesque. The larger of its two bays has a line of **tavernas**; *To Venetsianiko*, half way along the front, has good food at reasonable prices, but the best is *Hydragogio* at the Hóra end of the beach which serves up good veggie options. For nightlife the liveliest place is *Shaker*, playing the standard mix of Greek and foreign hits.

The best **accommodation** is in high demand and expensive. Top of the tree is the *Porto Delfino* (☎0735/31 940; ⑤–⑥; April–Oct); a few hundred metres above the bay are *Kalokerines Katikies* (☎ & fax 0735/31 265; ⑥; May–Oct) and *Hotel Raikos* (☎0735/31 629, fax 31 801; ⑤; May–Sept). The *Aphrodite Apartments* (☎0735/31 328; ⑤–⑥) have slightly more reasonable rates, as do *Megaloudis* rooms (☎0735/31 340; ④). A fairly basic **campsite** (June–Sept) nestles in the pine trees behind the village.

There's a mobile **post office** in summer, and a couple of travel agents near the harbour: Kytheros International (☎0735/31 925) arranges travel, accommodation and vehicle rental, while Roma Travel (☎0735/31 561) deals with accommodation only. Panayiotis (☎0735/31 600) and Nikos (☎0735/31 5700) both rent **cars**, **motorbikes** and **mopeds**. As well as watersports facilities the former has a friendly reliable service; you can call off season (☎0735/31 551) and get wheels when most places are closed.

Hóra

HÓRA (or Kýthira town), a steep 2km haul above Kapsáli, has an equally dramatic site, its Cycladic-style houses tiered about the walls of a Venetian castle. Within the **castle**, most of the buildings are ruined, but there are spectacular views of Kapsáli and, out to sea, to the islet of Avgó (Egg), legendary birthplace of Aphrodite. Below the castle are the remains of older Byzantine walls, and 21 Byzantine churches in various states of dereliction. A small **museum** (Tues–Sun 8.30am–2.30pm) houses modest remnants of the island's numerous occupiers, in particular Minoan finds from excavations at Paleópoli and an archaic stone lion.

Compared with Kapsáli, Hóra stays quiet and many places are closed out of season. A few **tavernas** open in summer, of which *Zorba* is by far the best, but the climb from Kapsáli discourages the crowds. Out of season, only one café/fast-food place stays open, near the square. **Accommodation** is slightly easier to find than in Kapsáli. The homeliest and best deal is the pension run by Yiorgos Pissis (☎0735/31 070; ②) with shared facilities including kitchen and some balcony views. Other options are the *Castello Studios* (☎0735/31 068; ④) and the old-style *Hotel Margarita* (☎0735/31 711; ⑤–⑥) with air-conditioning and TV in the rooms. At **MANITOHÓRI**, 2km further inland, are the *Hotel Keiti* (☎0735/31 318; ③; April–Oct) and the *Pension Kythera* (☎0735/31 563; ②–③; May–Sept). Other facilities include a couple of **banks**, **post office**, and branches of Panayiotis (☎0735/31 004) and Nikos (☎0735/31 767) vehicle rental. The only real bar is *Mercato*, which stays open in the winter and also has exhibitions of local art.

The southeast coast

The beach at Kapsáli is decent but gets very crowded in July and August. For quieter, undeveloped beaches, it's better to head out to the east coast, towards Avlémonas.

Firí Ámmos and Kombonádha

Firí Ámmos, the nearest good sand beach to Kapsáli, is popular but not overcrowded, even in summer. To get there, you can follow a paved road as far as the sleepy village of Kálamos (take the northerly side road between Kapsáli and Hóra); the beach is signposted down a dirt track on the far side of the village. Firí Ámmos can also be reached from the inland village of Livádhi, on the Hóra–Aroniádhika road – as can **Kombonádha**, the next beach north. There are summer canteens at both beaches, and the *Filio* taverna in Kálamos has good traditional food.

Paleópoli and Avlémonas

PALEÓPOLI, a hamlet of a few scattered houses, is accessible by a paved road from Aroniádhika. The area is the site of the ancient city of **Skandia**, and excavations on the headland of **Kastrí** have revealed remains of an important Minoan colony. There's little visible evidence, apart from shards of pottery in the low crumbling cliffs, but happily, tourist development in the area has been barred because of its archeological significance. Consequently, there's just one solitary **taverna**, the *Skandia* (June–Oct), on the excellent two-kilometre sand-and-pebble **beach** that stretches to either side of the headland. This place has recently been taken over by seven hippyish Anglo-Greek siblings and has great atmosphere with home cooking and frequent musical evenings.

The surrounding countryside, a broad, cultivated valley surrounded by wild hills, is equally attractive. **Paleokástro**, the mountain to the west, is the site of ancient Kýthira and a sanctuary of Aphrodite, but again, there's little to be seen today. Heading across the valley and turning right, an unpaved road leads up to a tiny, whitewashed church above the cliffs. From there, a track leads down to **Kaládhi**, a beautiful pebble beach with caves and rocks jutting out to sea.

AVLÉMONAS, 2km east of Paleópoli, is a tiny fishing port with two tavernas, of which *Sotiris* is recommended for fish, plus a few rooms including the large *Sklavos* apartments (☎0735/33 066; ⑤) and those run by Petrohilos (☎0735/33 034; ④) and his sister Mandy (☎0735/33 039; ④). There is a rather small, unimpressive Venetian fortress, the coast is rocky, the scenery bleak and exposed, and the village has something of an end-of-the-world feel.

North and west of Hóra

LIVÁDHI, 4km north of Hóra, has **rooms** and, on the main road, the newish *Hotel Aposperides* (☎0735/31656, fax 31 688; ⑤) which, together with the adequate *Toxotis* restaurant opposite, would make a good base if you had transport. Livádhi is also home to the most efficient travel agency on the island, Porfyra Travel, which is the main ANEK and Olympic agent (☎0735/31 888, fax 31888; *porfyra@kythira.com*), with exchange and car rental; they can arrange accommodation or transfers, plus group or individual hiking tours of the island. At **Katoúni** (2km out), there is an incongruous arched bridge, a legacy of the nineteenth century when all the Ionian islands were a British protectorate; it was built by a Scottish engineer. From the village, a fork heads west to Kalokerinés, and continues 3km further to the island's principal monastery, **Panayía Myrtidhíon**, set among cypress trees above the wild and windswept west coast. Beyond the monastery, a track leads down to a small anchorage at Limnária; there are few beaches along this rocky, forbidding shore. At **Káto Livádhi**, a kilometre to the east of Livádhi, there is an excellent museum of Byzantine and post-Byzantine art (Tues–Sun 8.30am–2.30pm; free) next to the large central church. It contains frescoes, painstakingly removed from island churches, dating from the sixth to the eighteenth centuries, a seventh-century mosaic floor and some portable icons. Not far away there is also a co-operative pottery workshop (open all day except 2–4pm) and, near an old bridge built by the English, a popular taverna called *Eleni*.

Mylopótamos, Káto Hóra and the Ayía Sofía cave

North of Livádhi, the main road crosses a bleak plateau whose few settlements are nearly deserted. At Dhókana it's worth making a detour off the main road for **MYLOPÓTAMOS**, a lovely traditional village and an oasis in summer, set in a wooded valley occupied by a small stream. The shady *Platanos* kafenío makes a pleasant stop for a drink. *To Kamari*, in an old restored building serves snacks and drinks on a water-side terrace. Follow the sign for "Neraidha" to find a waterfall, hidden from view by lush vegetation. The valley below the falls is overgrown but contains the remains of the watermill that gave the village its name.

Káto Hóra, 500m down the road, was Mylopótamos's predecessor. Now derelict, it remains half-enclosed within the walls of a Venetian fortress. The fortress is small and has a rather domestic appearance: unlike the castle at Hóra, it was built as a place of refuge for the villagers in case of attack, rather than as a base for a Venetian garrison. All the houses within the walls, and many outside, are abandoned. Beyond here, a paved but precipitous road continues 5km through spectacular cliff-scapes to **Limiónas**, a rocky bay with a small beach of fine white sand.

The reason most visitors come to Mylopótamos is to see the **cave of Ayía Sofía**, the largest and most impressive of a number of caverns on the island. A half-hour sign-posted walk from the village, the cave is open regularly from mid-June to mid-September (Mon–Fri 3–8pm, Sat & Sun 11am–5pm; 800dr). When the cave is closed, you can probably find a guide in Mylopótamos; ask at the village, giving a day's notice, if possible. The cave is worth the effort to see: the entrance has been used as a church and has an iconostasis carved from the rock, with important Byzantine frescoes on it. Beyond, the cave system comprises a series of chambers which reach 250m into the mountain, although the thirty- minute guided tour (in Greek and English) only takes in the more interesting outer chambers. These include some startling formations like the "shark's teeth", but you have to ask to be shown "Aphrodite's chambers". A minute new species of disc-shaped insect has been discovered here.

Andikýthira island

The tiny island of **Andikýthira** has a once-weekly ferry from and to Ayía Pelayía, plus a once-weekly connection with Crete on the Kýthira–Kastélli–Kýthira run; theoreti-cally it should be possible to use the latter service for a day-trip with about four and a half hours on the island. Rocky and poor, it only received electricity in 1984. Attractions include good birdlife and flora, but it's not the place if you want company. With only fifty or so inhabitants divided between two settlements – **Potamós**, the harbour, and **Sohória**, the village – people are rather thin on the ground. A resident doctor and a teacher serve the dwindling community (there are three children at the village school, as compared with nearly forty in the 1960s). The only official accom-modation is the set of **rooms** run by the local community at Potamós, which also has the sole **taverna**. In Sohória the only provisions available are basic foodstuffs at the village shop.

Yíthio (Gythion)

YÍTHIO, Sparta's ancient port, is the gateway to the dramatic Máni peninsula, and one of the south's most attractive seaside towns in its own right. Its somewhat low-key harbour, with occasional ferries to Pireás and Kýthira, gives onto a graceful nineteenth-century waterside of tiled-roof houses – some of them now showing their age. There's a beach within walking distance and rooms are relatively easy to find. In the bay, tethered by a long narrow mole, is the **islet of Marathonísi**, ancient Kranae, where Paris of Troy, having abducted Helen from Menelaus's palace at Sparta, dropped anchor, and where the lovers spent their first night.

The Town

Marathónisi is the town's main sight, a pleasant place to while away an hour or so in the early evening, with swimming off the rocks towards the lighthouse (beware sea urchins). Amid the island's trees and scrub stands the restored Tzannetákis tower-fortress built around 1810 by the Turkish-appointed Bey of the Máni, to guard the harbour against his lawless countrymen. It now houses a **Museum of the Máni** (9.30am–5pm; 500dr), which deals with the exploration of the Máni from Ciriaco de Pizzicoli (1447) to Henri Belle (1861), with captions in Greek and English.

For an aerial view of the islet and town, climb up through Yíthio's stepped streets on to the hill behind – the town's ancient acropolis. The settlement around it, known as **Laryssion**, was quite substantial in Roman times, enjoying wealth from the export of murex, the purple-pigmented mollusc used to dye imperial togas.

Much of the ancient site now lies submerged but there are some impressive remains of a **Roman theatre** to be seen at the northeast end of the town. Follow the road past the post office for about 300m, until you reach an army barracks, where a sign in the road says "stop" – the site stands just to the left. With most of its stone seats intact, and 50m in diameter, the theatre illustrates perfectly how buildings in Greece take on different guises through the ages: built to one side is a Byzantine church (now ruined) which, in turn, has been pressed into service as the outer wall of the barracks. The archeological museum is currently under restoration, but possesses items from Yíthio and the Lakonian Máni.

Beaches near Yíthio

For swimming, there are a number of coves within reach of Yíthio, on both sides of which rise an intermittent sequence of cliffs. The long **beach** at Mavrovoúni, by the campsites detailed below, is one of the best but can be very busy; a smaller one, north of the town, has a nominal admission charge. Many of the buses serving Yíthio from Spárti routinely continue to Mavrovoúni – ask on board. Alternatively, if you've transport, there are the superb beaches in Váthy Bay, further along, off the Areópoli road (see p.204). To the north (7km) the little beach of Trínisa ("three islands") is kept clean by the *Afroditi* café. The coastline eastwards from Trínisi to Kokkiniá has nesting turtles, and the Evrótas delta and Dhivári lagoon are significant migratory bird sites, while the extensive dune areas around the Evrótas are botanically important.

Practicalities

Buses drop you close to the centre of town, with the main waterfront street, **Vassíleos Pávlou**, right ahead of you. There are three **banks** near the bus station. Moto Máni by the causeway, on the Areópoli road (☎0733/22 853), has scooters for rent, and Supercycle, on the main square (☎0733/24 407), rents out **motorcycles** by the day or, by negotiation, for longer periods. You can check **ferry** sailings at the Rozaki Shipping and Travel Agency (☎0733/22 207) on the waterfront; the latter will also change travellers' cheques and money. A trip of at least three days is worth considering for the Máni; the Ladopoulou and Andreikos **bookstores** are worth scouring for books on the area.

Accommodation

Finding **accommodation** shouldn't be hard, with a fair selection of hotels and rooms in town – most along the waterfront, signposted up the steps behind, or facing Marathonísi islet. Despite double-glazing in many waterfront rooms on Vassiléos Pávlou, there will be late-night noise from the many music-bars. Out along Mavrovoúni beach there are numerous rooms and three **campsites**; it begins 3km south of the town off the Areópoli road. The nearest and best of these is the *Meltemi* (☎0733/23 260; April–Oct); a couple of kilometres further on are the *Gythion Beach* (☎0733/22 522; year-round) and *Mani Beach* (☎0733/23 450; mid-April to mid-Oct).

Cava Grosso, (☎0733/22 897, fax 23 823). Luxury apartments in Mavrovoúni village. ⑥.

Githion, Vas. Pávlou 33 (☎0733/23 452, fax 23 523). A fine old (1864) hotel on the waterfront, the site of the first poker game played in Greece; good value for money. ④.

Kalypso, (☎0733/24 449, fax 22 265). Just off the main road, in Mavrovoúni. Very good-value rooms with kitchens, air-con and magnificent sea views over Yíthio Bay. ④.

Kondogiannis, Vas. Pávlou 19 (☎0733/22 518). A small, friendly pension, recently refurbished, up steep steps alongside – and above – the management's jewellery shop, and next to the police station. ③.

Kranai, Vas. Pávlou 17 (☎ & fax 0733/24 394). On the waterfront, near *Kondogiannis*; try for a room at the front with a balcony. The restaurant below is very popular. ④.

Saga, Tzanetáki (☎733/23 220, fax 24 370). Pension run by a French family, with a restaurant on the ground floor, overlooking the Marathonísi islet. Recommended. ③.

Spanakas rooms (☎0733/22 490). Homely pension on the route into town from Spárti. ③.

Eating and drinking

For **meals**, the waterside is the obvious location – though choose carefully from among the tavernas since most have inflated prices for fish and seafood. By the small square and taxi rank, the *Korali Ouzeri* has well-prepared food at reasonable prices. *Kostas*, by the bus station and facing the shore, is also a no-nonsense place. Besides these, the restaurant by the *Kranai* pension is popular with locals.

The Máni

The southernmost peninsula of Greece, **the Máni**, stretches from Yíthio in the east to Kardhamýli in the west and terminates at Cape Ténaro, the mythical entrance to the underworld. Its spine, negotiated by road at just a few points, is the vast grey mass of Mount Taïyetos and its southern extension, Sangiás. It is a wild landscape, an arid Mediterranean counterpart to Cornwall, or the Scottish highlands, with an idiosyncratic culture and history to match. Nowhere in Greece does a region seem so close to its violent medieval past – which continued largely unaltered until the end of the nineteenth century. Despite, or perhaps because of this, the sense of hospitality is, like nearby Crete, as strong as anywhere in Greece.

The peninsula has two distinct regions: the Éxo (Outer) Máni and the Mésa (Inner or Deep) Máni. The **Mésa Máni** – that part of the peninsula south of a line drawn betweeen Ítylo and Váthy bays – is the classic Máni territory, its jagged coast relieved

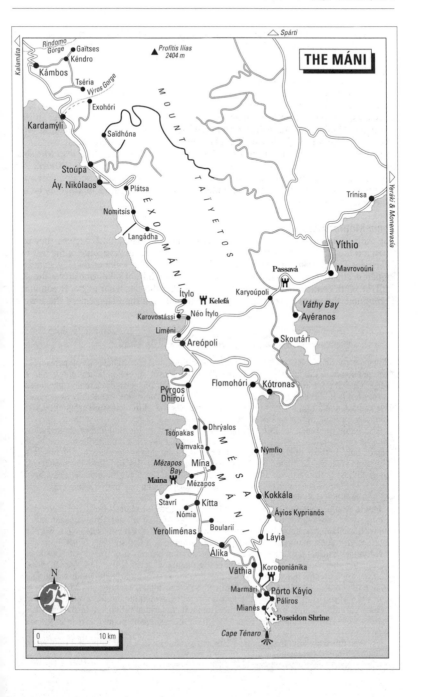

only by the occasional cove, and its land a mass of rocks. It has one major sight, the remarkable caves at **Pýrgos Dhiroú**, which are now very much on the tourist circuit. Beyond this point tourist numbers thin out fast. The attractions include the coastal villages, like **Yeroliménas** on the west coast, or **Kótronas** on the east, but the pleasure is mainly in exploring the **tower houses** and **churches**, and in the solitude. A fair number of the towers survive, their groupings most dramatic at **Kítta**, **Váthia** and **Flomohóri**. The churches are subtler and harder to find, often hidden away from actual villages, but worth the effort. Many were built during the tenth and twelfth centuries, when the Maniots enthusiastically embraced Christianity; almost all retain at least traces of frescoes though almost all are kept locked, with elusive wardens.

The **Éxo Máni** – the coast up from Areópoli to Kalamáta, much of it in Messinía province – sees the emphasis shift much more to walking and beaches. **Stoúpa** and **Kardhamýli** are both beautiful resorts, developing now but far from spoiled. The road itself is an experience, threading precipitously up into the foothills of Taïyetos before looping down to the sea.

Some Maniot history

The **mountains** offer the key to Maniot history. Formidable natural barriers, they provided a refuge from, and bastion of resistance to, every occupying force of the last two millennia. The Dorians never reached this far south in the wake of the Mycenaeans. Roman occupation was perfunctory and Christianity did not take root in the interior until the ninth century (some five hundred years after the establishment of Byzantium). Throughout the years of Venetian and Turkish control of the Peloponnese there were

---

MANIOT BLOOD FEUDS

These were the result of an intricate **feudal society** that seems to have developed across the peninsula in the fourteenth century. After the arrival of refugee Byzantine families, an aristocracy known as **Nyklians** arose, and the various clans gradually developed strongholds in the tightly clustered villages. The poor, rocky soil was totally inadequate for the population and over the next five centuries the **clans clashed** frequently and bloodily for land, power and prestige.

The feuds became ever more complex and gave rise to the building of strongholds: marble-roofed **battle towers** which, in the elaborate customs of the peninsula, could be raised only by those of Nyklian descent. From these local forts the clans – often based in the same village – conducted vendettas according to strict rules and aims. The object was to annihilate both the tower and the male members of the opposing clan. The favoured method of attack was to smash the prestigious tower roofs; the forts consequently rose to four and five storeys.

Feuds would customarily be signalled by the ringing of church bells and from this moment the adversaries would confine themselves to their towers, firing at each other with all available weaponry. The battles could last for years, even decades, with women (who were safe from attack) shuttling in food, ammunition and supplies. With the really **prolonged feuds**, temporary truces were declared at harvest times; then with business completed the battle would recommence. Ordinary villagers – the non-Nyklian peasantry – would, meanwhile, evacuate for the duration of the conflict. The feuds would end in one of two ways: destruction of a family in battle, or total surrender of a whole clan in a gesture of **psyhikó** (a thing of the soul), when they would file out to kiss the hands of enemy parents who had lost "guns" (the Maniot term for male children) in the feud; the victors would then dictate strict terms by which the vanquished could remain in the village.

The last full-scale feud took place as late as 1870, in the village of Kítta, and required a full detachment of the regular army to put down.

PRACTICALITIES IN THE MÁNI

Getting around can be time-consuming unless you have your own transport, and you may want to consider renting a **moped** or **motorbike** from Yíthio or Kalamáta, or a **car** from Stoúpa or Kalamáta. Without a vehicle, you will need to walk or hitch to supplement the buses. In Mésa Máni, there are just two services: Areópoli–Yeroliménas–Váthia (daily in summer; 3 weekly out of season) and Areópoli–Kótronas–Láyia (daily), with the Váthia section being unreliable.

An alternative is to make use of the handful of **taxis**, generally negotiable at Areópoli, Yeroliménas and Kótronas, as well as at Yíthio. Currently, for example, a taxi from Areópoli to Váthia would cost 6000–7000dr, and then you could return by bus.

The Mésa Máni has a **bank** at Areópoli (Mon, Wed, Fri 9am–noon). You can sometimes change Giro cheques or cash at the **post offices** (Mon–Fri 7.30am–2pm) in Yeroliménas or Areópoli, but it's wiser to bring as much as you think you'll need from either Yíthio or Kalamáta.

---

constant rebellions, climaxing in the Maniot uprising on March 17, 1821, a week before Archbishop Yermanos raised the Greek flag at Kalávryta to officially launch the War of Independence.

Alongside this national assertiveness was an equally intense and violent internal tribalism, seen at its most extreme in the elaborate tradition of **blood feuds** (see box opposite), probably prolonged, and certainly exploited, by the **Turks**. The first Maniot uprising against them had taken place in 1571, a year after the Ottoman occupation. There were to be renewed attempts through the succeeding centuries, with plots involving the Venetians, French and Russians. But the Turks, wisely, opted to control the Máni by granting a level of local autonomy, investing power in one or other clan whose leader they designated "Bey" of the region. The position provided a focus for the obsession with arms and war and worked well until the nineteenth-century appointment of **Petrobey Mavromihalis**. With a power base at Liméni he united the clans in revolution, and his Maniot army was to prove vital to the success of the War of Independence.

Unsurprisingly, the end of the war and the formation of an **independent Greece** did not mark the end of Maniot rebellion. Mavromihalis swiftly fell out with the first president of the nation, Kapodistrias and, with other members of the clan, was imprisoned by him at Náfplio – an act which led to the president's assassination at the hands of Petrobey's brothers. The monarchy fared little better until one of the king's German officers was sent to the Máni to enlist soldiers in a special Maniot militia. The idea was adopted with enthusiasm, and was the start of an enduring tradition of Maniot service in the modern Greek military.

In this century, sadly, all has been decline, with persistent **depopulation** of the villages. In places like Váthia and Kítta, which once held populations in the hundreds, the numbers are now down to single figures, predominantly the old. Socially and politically the region is notorious as the most conservative in Greece. The Maniots reputedly enjoyed an influence during the colonels' junta, when the region first acquired roads, mains electricity and running water. They voted almost unanimously for the monarchy in the 1974 plebiscite, and this is one of the very few parts of Greece where you may still see visible support for the ex-king or the far-right National Party.

Into the Máni: Yíthio to Areópoli

The road from Yíthio into the Máni begins amid a fertile and gentle landscape, running slightly inland of the coast and Mavrovoúni beach, through tracts of citrus and olive groves. About 12km beyond Yíthio, the Máni suddenly asserts itself as the road enters a gorge below the Turkish **castle of Passavá**. The castle is one of a pair (with Kelefá to the west) guarding the Máni or perhaps, more accurately, guarding against the Máni. From the Avin petrol station just to the west it's quite a scramble up, with no regular path, but the site is ample reward, with views out across two bays and for some miles along the defile from Areópoli. There has been a fortress on Passavá since Mycenaean times; the present version is an eighteenth-century Turkish rebuilding of a Frankish fort that the Venetians destroyed on their flight from the Peloponnese in 1684. It was abandoned by the Turks in 1780 following the massacre of its garrison and their civilian dependants by the Maniot Grigorakis clan – their vengeance for the arrest and execution by the Turks of the clan chief.

Shortly after Passavá a turning to the left, signposted "Belle Hélène", leads down to a long sandy beach at **Váthy Bay**, which is dominated by German tourists. Before you reach the beach, there is the *Pension Tassia* (☎0733/93 433; ②), with four comfortable rooms, each with a kitchen. At the southern end of the beach is the grand *Hotel Belle Hélène* (☎0733/93 001, fax 98 006; ④; April–Oct), often block-booked by German groups; towards the north end, behind the reasonable *Gorgona* restaurant, the *Kronos* campsite (☎0733/93 320; mid-April to Oct) is well suited to families.

The road beyond the beach deteriorates rapidly, though it is possible to continue through woods to the village of **Ayéranos**, with a couple of tower houses, and from there – if you can find your way among the numerous rough tracks – to Skoutári, below which is another reasonable beach with some Roman remains. A better road to Skoutári leaves the main Yíthio–Areópoli road near Karyoúpoli, itself dominated by an imposing tower house.

Continuing towards Areópoli from Passavá, the landscape remains fertile until the wild, scrubby mass of Mount Kouskoúni signals the final approach to the Mésa Máni. You enter another pass, with **Kelefá castle** (see p.209) above to the north, and beyond it several southerly peaks of the Taïyetos ridge. Areópoli, as you curl down from the hills, radiates a real sense of arrival.

Areópoli and around

An austere-looking town, **AREÓPOLI** sets an immediate mood for the region. It was, until the last century, secondary to Ítylo, 6km north, as the gateway to the Mésa Máni, but the modern road has made it, to all intents, the region's centre. Formerly Tsímova, its present name ("Town of Ares" – the god of war) was bestowed for its efforts during the War of Independence. It was here that Mavromihalis (commemorated by a statue in the main platía) declared the uprising.

The town's sights are archetypically Maniot in their anachronisms. The **Áyii Taxiárhes** cathedral, for example, has primitive reliefs above its doors which look twelfth century until you notice their date of 1798. Similarly, the tower houses could readily be described as medieval, though most of them were built in the early 1800s. On its own, in a little platía, is the church of **Áyios Ioánnis**, the Mavromihalis family church; the interior has strip-cartoon frescoes. Nearby a Byzantine museum is under construction in the Nikolakis tower.

Buses leave Areópoli from the main square; if you are heading north into Messinía, towards Kalamáta, you may need to change in Ítylo. On or just off the main platía are a **bank** (Mon, Wed, Fri 9am–noon), a **post office**, a bookshop, several zaharoplastía and a useful **supermarket**.

There are several **rooms** around the cathedral and two **hotels**: the *Kouris* (☎0733/51 340; ④) on the main square, and the good-value *Mani* (☎0733/51 190, fax 51 269; ③) a few minutes from the square and near the bank. One of the towers, the *Pyrgos Kapetanakou* (☎0733/51 479; ④), was restored by the EOT as a traditional guesthouse;

the rooms are austerely beautiful and well priced. Nearby is the upmarket *Londas* (☎0733/51 360, fax 51 012; ⑤), another converted tower house. The cheaper *Pyrgos Tsimova* (☎0733/51 301; ④) has more of a lived-in feel. There is a private war museum in the living room, with a Lewis gun perched on top of the dresser; the owner is a staunch royalist – the heroic "George of England", referred to in conversation about World War II, is King George VI.

There are a number of **café-restaurants** around the main square; the most popular (and the bus agent) is *Nikola's Corner*, which does good mezédhes. *Barba Petros* has a little courtyard off a pedestrian street towards *Pyrgos Kapetanakou*.

South to the Pýrgos Dhiroú caves

Eight kilometres south from Areópoli, at the village of **PÝRGOS DHIROÚ**, the road forks off to the underground caves – the Máni's major tourist attraction. The village itself has an isolated 21-metre tower house, but is otherwise geared to the cave trade, with numerous tavernas and cafés, and a number of **rooms** for rent. The closest to the caves, and the sea, are at the *Panorama* restaurant (☎0733/52 280; ③). The rooms have TV, air-conditioning and impressive sea views; the establishment has its own fishing boat. If you want to stay in the village itself, the run-down and overpriced *Hotel Diros* (☎0733/52 306; ④) is an option.

The **Pýrgos Dhiroú caves** (June–Sept 8am–5.30pm; Oct–May 8am–2.30pm; 3500dr) are 4km beyond the main village, set beside the sea and a small beach. They are very much a packaged attraction but, unless caves leave you cold, they are worth a visit, especially on weekday afternoons when the wait is shorter. A visit consists of a thirty-minute punt around the underground waterways of the **Glyfádha (Vlyhádha) caves**, well lit and crammed with stalactites, whose reflections are a remarkable sight in the two- to twenty-metre depth of water. You are then permitted a brief tour on foot of the **Alepótrypa caves** – huge chambers (one of them 100m by 60m) in which excavation has unearthed evidence of prehistoric occupation. Unfortunately there is no foreign-language commentary.

You should buy a ticket as soon as you arrive at the caves: this gives you a priority number for the tours. On a mid-season weekend you can wait for an hour or more, so it's best to arrive as early as possible in the day with gear to make the most of the adjacent beach. If time is short, taxis from Areópoli will take you to the caves, then wait and take you back; prices, especially split four ways, are reasonable.

The nearby – on a bend of the road – **museum** (Tues–Sun 8.30am–3pm; 500dr) of Neolithic finds from the caves is interesting, but the few captions are in Greek; a multilingual guide leaflet is promised. There is a café down at the end of the road.

South to Yeroliménas

The narrow, raised coastal plain between Pýrgos Dhiroú and Yeroliménas is one of the more fertile parts of the Mésa Máni with a uniform sprinkling of dwarf olive trees. This seventeen-kilometre stretch of the so-called "shadow coast" supported, until this century, an extraordinary number of small villages. The main road carefully avoids most of them, but many are sited just a kilometre or so to east or west of it. Very few villages have shops, or facilities such as public phones, so you should carry sufficient water if walking. The area retains a major concentration of **churches**, many of them Byzantine, dating from the ninth to the fourteenth centuries. These are especially hard to find, though well detailed in Peter Greenhalgh's *Deep Into Mani*. The main feature to look for is a barrel roof. Almost all are kept locked, though a key can sometimes be found by asking around.

Among Greenhalgh's favourites on the seaward side are the eleventh-century **church of the Taxiárhis** at Haroúdha (3km south of Pýrgos Dhiroú), **Trissákia**

church by a reservoir near Tsópakas (5km south of Pýrgos Dhiroú) and **Ayía Varvára** at Érimos (8km south of Pýrgos Dhiroú).

Mézapos and the Castle of the Maina

An easier excursion from the main road is to the small village of **MÉZAPOS**, whose deep-water harbour made it one of the chief settlements of Máni, until the road was built this century. From the main road, take the side road to Áyios Yeóryios and then to Mézapos, where there are a few rooms. The best of some fine coastal walks leads to the twelfth-century **church of Vlahérna**, which has a few fresco fragments, including a memorable John the Baptist. If you ask at one of the cafés in Mézapos it's sometimes possible to negotiate a boat trip out to Tigáni, or even around the cape to Yeroliménas.

The nearby village of **STAVRÍ** offers traditional **tower-house accommodation** in the converted *Tsitsiris Castle* complex (☎0733/56 297; ⑤), much the same price as the tower hotels in Areópoli and Váthia, though much bigger and in a remoter, more exciting setting. The broader plateau here has a network of small roads, and even the best maps are hopelessly inadequate. To the north of Stavrí, but within walking distance, is the twelfth-century **church of Episkopí**; the roof has been restored, while inside there are some fine but faded frescoes, and columns crowned by Ionic capitals, with a surprising marble arch at the entry to the iconostasis. Head from Stavrí to the deserted hamlet of **Ayía Kyriakí** for good views, and access to the castle on the bare **Tigáni** ("Frying Pan") **peninsula**. The fortress, by general consensus, seems to have been the **Castle of the Maina**, constructed like those of Mystra and Monemvasiá by the Frankish baron, Guillaume de Villehardouin, and ceded with them to the Byzantines in 1261. Tigáni is as arid a site as any in Greece – a dry Monemvasiá in effect – whose fortress seems scarcely man-made, blending as it does into the terrain. It's a jagged walk out to the castle across rocks fashioned into pans for salt-gathering; within the walls are ruins of a huge Byzantine church and numerous cisterns.

Kítta and Boulariï

Continuing along the main road, **KÍTTA**, once the largest and most powerful village in the region, boasts the crumbling remains of more than twenty tower houses. It was here in 1870 that the last feudal war took place, only being suppressed by a full battalion of four hundred regular soldiers. Over to the west, visible from the village, is another eruption of tower houses at Kítta's traditional rival, Nómia.

Two kilometres south of Kítta and east of the main road, **BOULARIÏ** is one of the most interesting and accessible villages in the Mésa Máni. It is clearly divided into "upper" and "lower" quarters, both of which retain well-preserved tower houses and, in varying states of decay, some twenty churches. The two most impressive are tenth-century **Áyios Pandelímon** (enclosed and locked, with two frescoes that are the earliest in the Máni) and eleventh-century **Áyios Stratigós**, which is just over the brow of the hill at the top of the village. This second church is also locked and there are keys with the priest at Eliá village and possibly at the Yeroliménas post office. Entry is well rewarded for the church possesses a spectacular series of frescoes from the twelfth to the eighteenth centuries.

Cape Ténaro (Yeroliménas and south to Mátapan)

After the journey from Areópoli, **YEROLIMÉNAS** (Yerolimín) has an end-of-the-world air, and it makes a good base for exploring the southern extremities of the Máni. Despite appearances, the village was only developed in the 1870s – around a jetty and warehouses built by a local (a non-Nyklian migrant) who had made good on the island of Sýros. There are a few shops, a **post office**, a couple of **cafés** and two **hotels**. Of these, the *Akroyiali* (☎0733/54 204, fax 54 272; ④) is the more comfortable, with some air-conditioned rooms and apartments; a new wing is being added, in traditional style stonework. The *Akrotenaritis* (☎ & fax 0733/54 205; ③–④)), in two buildings, has cheaper rooms with shared facilities in the old part. A couple of other places have rooms with kitchenettes. There are several **places to eat** between the two hotels, but the baked fish in lemon juice and olive oil served at the *Akroyiali* takes some beating.

At the dock, occasional boat trips are offered – when the local owners feel like it – around Cape Ténaro, formerly known as Cape Mátapan (see below).

Álika to Pórto Káyio and Marmári

South from Yeroliménas, a good road (and the bus) continues to **Álika**, where it divides. One fork leads east through the mountains to Láyia (see opposite), and the other continues to Váthia and across the Marmári isthmus to Páliros. Between Álika and Váthia there are good coves for swimming. One of the best is a place known as **Kypárissos**, reached by following a riverbed (dry in summer) about midway to Váthia. On the headland above are scattered Roman remains of ancient Kaenipolis, including (amid the walled fields) the excavated ruins of a sixth-century basilica.

VÁTHIA, a group of tower houses set uncompromisingly on a scorching mass of high hillside rocks, is one of the most dramatic villages in the Mésa Máni. It features in Colonel Leake's account of his travels, one of the best sources on Greece in the early nineteenth century. He was warned to avoid going through the village in 1805 as a feud had been running between two families for the previous forty years. Today it has the feel of a ghost town. The EOT finally completed its lengthy restoration of a dozen tower houses to accommodate guests, but the project fell into disuse in 1998.

From Váthia the road south to the cape starts out uphill, edging around the mountain, before slowly descending to a junction. Left brings you down to the beach and laidback hamlet of **PÓRTO KÁYIO** (7km from Váthia). There are comfortable rooms at the *Akroteri* (☎0733/52 013; ③), and two or three tavernas, the best of which is the *Hippocampos*. Across the bay, on the north side are the spectacular ruins of a Turkish fortress contemporary with Kelefá and the monastery of Korogoniánika. Above the village, the right branch of the road goes south along the headland, capped by a Maniot tower, to pleasant sandy **beaches** at the double bay of Marmári. Rooms and good food with a sea view are available above the first beach at *To Marmari* (☎0733/52 101; ③), under the same management as the *Kastro* in Kokkála.

On to Cape Ténaro

Starting from the bullet-ridden sign to Páliros and the left fork before Marmári, follow the signs on the dirt road – after the second Páliros junction – for the fish taverna, *To Akrotenaro*. After you've wound your way over the Maní's last barren peninsula and down to the taverna, where rooms should be available, the road ends in a knoll crowned with the squat **chapel of Asómati**, constructed largely of materials from an ancient temple of Poseidon.

To the left (east) as you face the chapel is the little pebbly **bay of Asómati**; on the shore is a small **cave**, another addition to the list of sites said to be the mythical entrance to the underworld. Patrick Leigh Fermor, in *Mani*, writes of yet another "Gates of Hades" cave, which he swam into on the western side of the point, just below Marmári. To the right (west) of the Asómati hill, the main path, marked by red dots, continues along the edge of another cove and through the metre-high foundations of a **Roman town** that grew up around the Poseidon shrine; there is even a mosaic in one structure. From here the old trail, which existed before the road was bulldozed, reappears as a walled path, allowing 180-degree views of the sea on its 25-minute course to the lighthouse on **Cape Ténaro**.

The east coast

The east coast of the Mésa Máni is most easily approached from **Areópoli**, where there's a daily **bus** through Kótronas to Láyia. However, if you have transport, or you're prepared to walk and hitch, there's satisfaction in doing a full loop of the peninsula, crossing over to Láyia from Yeroliménas or Pórto Káyio. The east coast landscape is more barren than the west, little more than scrub and prickly pears. This is the Mésa Máni's "sunward coast", harsher than the "shadow coast" of the west side. There are few beaches, and less coastal plain, with most of the scattered villages hanging on the hillsides.

Láyia to Kokkála

From the fork at Álika (see above), it is about a ninety-minute walk by road to **LÁYIA**. Coming from Pórto Káyio it takes around three hours, though the route, at times on narrow tracks, is more dramatic, passing the virtually deserted hilltop village of **Korogoniánika**. A turning off left to Moundanístika, not far above Álika and the Máni's highest village, is recommended for spectacular views. Láyia itself is a multi-towered village that perfectly exemplifies the feudal setup of the old Máni. Four Nyklian families lived here, and their four independently sited settlements, each with its own church, survive. One of the taller towers, so the locals claim, was built overnight by the four hundred men of one clan, hoping to gain an advantage at sunrise. During the eighteenth century the village was home to a Maniot doctor – a strategic base from which to attend profitably to the war-wounded all across the peninsula. Today there is a single kafenío, with a few snacks, but the village is showing healthy signs of revival, with ongoing repair and refurbishment of a number of houses.

The first village beyond Láyia, down near the sea, is **ÁYIOS KYPRIANÓS**. It has a few rooms, though the proprietor may prove elusive. Five kilometres on is **KOKKÁLA**, a larger, though visually unexciting, village, enclosed by a rare patch of greenery. It has a small harbour and scruffy beach, a longer beach to the north and walking possibilities. Three kilometres to the northwest, on the mountainside above Nýmfio, is one of the area's few ancient sites, a spot known as Kiónia (columns), with the foundations of two Doric temples. The village boasts several café-restaurants, and pleasant but expensive rooms for rent above the *Taverna Marathos* (summer only; ☎0733/21 118; ③) on the beach. Overlooking the village is the *Kastro* (☎0733/21 620; ④), another refurbished tower. Newer is the smart but friendly *Hotel Soloteri* (☎0733/21 126; ③), which may be the only place open out of high season.

Flomohóri and Kótronas

A further 22km northwards along this comparatively empty coastline, brings you to **FLOMOHÓRI**; the land below is relatively fertile, and the village has maintained a reasonable population as well as a last imposing group of tower houses. **KÓTRONAS**, a few kilometres downhill, feels like another, softer country. It is still a fishing village, and its pebble beach (there are sandy strips further around the bay) and causeway-islet make it a good last stop in the region. The village is frequented by a fair number of tourists (mainly Germans) each summer, and has a trio of pensions. The most pleasant is the well-priced *Kali Kardia* (aka *4-Asteria*, ☎0733/21 246; ③) above a seafront café. The coastal dirt road from here to Skoutári, and hence Yíthio, is being widened and paved – when completed this will obviate the current necessity to go westwards across the peninsula back to Areópoli.

The Éxo Máni: Areópoli north to Kalamáta

The forty kilometres of road into Messinía, between Areópoli and Kalamáta is as dramatic and beautiful as any in Greece, almost a corniche route between the **Taïyetos** ridge and the **Gulf of Messinía**. The first few settlements en route are classic Maniot villages, their towers packed against the hillside. As you move north, with the road dropping to near sea level, there are three or four small resorts, which are becoming increasingly popular but are as yet relatively unspoiled. For walkers, there is a reasonably well-preserved *kalderími* parallelling (or short-cutting) much of the paved route, with a superb **gorge hike** just north of Kardhamýli, and Stoúpa as a good base for local exploration and touring.

North to Liméni

Areópoli stands back a kilometre or so from the sea. **LIMÉNI**, the town's tiny traditional port, lies 3km to the north: a scattering of houses dominated by the restored tower house of Petrobey Mavromihalis, which resembles nothing so much as an English country parish church. On one of the bends on the road down to Liméni is the newish *Limeni Village* (☎0733/51 111; ⑥), a re-creation of Maniot houses, high above the rocky shore and with its own swimming pool. Further round the bay, on the waterside, there are a few tavernas including *To Limeni* (☎0733/51 458; ③), which has basic rooms.

Ítylo and around

ÍTYLO (OÍTYLO), 11km from Areópoli, is the transport hub for the region. If you are heading into Messinía province towards Kalamáta, either from Yíthio or Areópoli, you may need to change here. It looks tremendous from a distance, though close up it is a little depressing; its population is in decline, and many of the tower houses are collapsing into decay. In better days, Ítylo was the capital of the Máni, and from the sixteenth to the eighteenth century it was the region's most notorious base for piracy and slave trading. The Maniots traded amorally and efficiently in slaves, selling Turks to Venetians, Venetians to Turks, and, at times of feud, the women of each others' clans. Irritated by the piracy and hoping to control the important pass to the north, the Turks built the **castle of Kelefá** in 1670. This is just a kilometre's walk from Ítylo across a gorge, and its walls and bastions, built for a garrison of five hundred, are substantially intact. Also worth exploring is the **monastery of Dhekoúlou**, down towards the coast; its setting is beautiful and there are some fine eighteenth-century frescoes in the chapel.

There are a few **rooms** to rent in Ítylo, and a smart guesthouse with pool just south of town: the *Pyrgos Alevras* (☎0733/59 388; ④), with self-catering studios and views – very good value if you have your own transport. Another option is to look for accommodation by the beach in **NÉO ÍTYLO**, which is just round the bay from Ítylo's ancient seaport, Karavostássi. Néo Ítylo is a tiny hamlet, but as well as rooms for rent it boasts the luxury *Hotel Itylo* (☎ & fax 0733/59 222; ⑤), which also runs the slightly cheaper *Alevras* (④) guesthouse.

Langádha, Nomitsís and Thalamés

If you want to walk for a stretch of the onward route, you can pick up the *kalderími* just below the main road out of Ítylo. As it continues north, the track occasionally crosses the modern road, but it is distinct at least as far as Kotróni or Rínglia. The most interesting of the villages along the way are **LANGÁDHA**, for its setting that bristles with towers, and **NOMITSÍS**, for its trio of frescoed Byzantine churches strung out along the main street. A couple more churches are to be found off the road just to the north; in one of these, that of **Metamórfosis**, there are delightful sculpted animal capitals. Just before Nomitsís, you pass the hamlet of **THALÁMES**, where a local enthusiast has set up a widely advertised **Museum of Maniot Folklore and History** (April–Sept daily 9am–4pm; 800dr). The tag "museum" is perhaps a bit inflated for what is really an unlabelled collection of junkshop items, but it's a nice stop nonetheless and sells jewellery, local honey and olive oil.

Áyios Nikólaos and Stoúpa

The beaches of the Éxo Máni begin south of **ÁYIOS NIKÓLAOS** (Selenítsa), at the pleasant, tree-shaded Pantázi beach. The village's delightful little harbour is flanked by old stone houses, cafés and tavernas overlooking the fishing boats. The taverna at the southern end of the harbour, with a small shaded extension over the water, does excellent fresh fish. There is a scattering of **rooms** and apartments; a good choice is the *Lofos* (π0721/77 371; ②), just above the village, with a nice garden for breakfast.

Just to the north, **STOÚPA** is much more developed, and justifiably so. It has possibly the best sands along this coast, with two glorious **beaches** (Stoúpa and the smaller, deeper Kalogriá) separated by a headland, each sloping into the sea and superb for children. Submarine freshwater springs gush into the bay, keeping it unusually clean – if also a bit cold. Ten minutes to the north of Kalogriá beach is the delightful and often deserted cove of Dhelfíni. A further 600m brings you to the pebble beach of Fonéa, wrapped around a rock outcrop and tucked into a corner of the hillside. Stoúpa was home in 1917–18 to the wandering Cretan writer, Nikos Kazantzakis, who is said to have based his character *Zorba the Greek* on a worker at the coal mine in nearby Pástrova, though the book itself was written later on Éyina island in the Saronics Gulf (see p.468).

Out of peak season, Stoúpa is certainly recommended, though in July and August, and any summer weekend, you may find the crowds a bit overwhelming and space at a premium. The area is an excellent base for walkers, with interesting villages and a network of paths that include some magificently engineered *kalderímia*. A popular walking guide booklet and large-scale map are available: ask at the helpfully efficient Doufexis Travel (π0721/77 677) who can also find accommodation, provide exchange and organize car hire. Accommodation in the resort includes numerous **rooms** and apartments, and several **hotels**. The *Lefktron* (π0721/77 322; ④) and the *Stoupa* (π0721/77 485; ⑤) are upmarket but very friendly. A good rooms option is the *Petros Nikolareas* studios (π0721/77 063; ②), seaward of the main church. Over the road from Kalogriá beach is *Kalogria Camping* (π0721/77 319; June–Oct). Towards Kardhamýli, above Dhelfíni beach, there is another livelier campsite, *Ta Delfinia* (π0721/77 318; April–Sept). There are plenty of **tavernas**, but *Akroyali* at the southern end of the main beach not only has well-prepared food, including fresh fish, but has views after dark of the lights of the mountain village Saïdhóna which look remarkably like an extra constellation of stars. The *Gelateria* homemade ice-cream place at the other end of the beach is justifiably famous. **Bus** services can be unreliable on the Kalamáta–Ítylo route, and **taxis** are in short supply locally; the Stoúpa taxi is on π0721/77 477 and the nearest to Áyios Nikólaos is at Plátsa on π0721/74 226.

Kardhamýli

KARDHAMÝLI, 10km north of Stoúpa, is also a major resort, by Peloponnese standards at least, with ranks of self-catering apartments and pensions, block-booked by the package trade in season. But once again the **beach** is good, though not sandy – a long pebble strip north of the village and backed by acres of olive trees.

Inland from the platía, it's a nice walk up to "Old Kardhamýli"; here a partly restored citadel of abandoned tower houses is gathered about the eighteenth-century church of **Áyios Spyrídhon** with its unusual multistorey bell tower, and the courtyard where the Maniot chieftains Kolokotronis and Mavromihalis played human chess with their troops during the War of Independence. Further back, on the *kalderími* up to Ayía Sofía, is a pair of ancient tombs, said to be of the **Dioskoúri** (the Gemini twins).

On the main road near the platía, you'll find a branch of the Agricultural Bank (Mon–Thur; summer only) and a **post office** (Mon–Fri). Bookable **hotels** include the *Kardamyli Beach* (☎0721/73 180, fax 73 184; ④). Also on the way along the beach, near the campsite, is *Lela's* (☎0721/73 541; ③), a good taverna with fine sea-view **rooms** which should be booked well ahead in summer. The **campsite**, *Melitsina* (May–Sept; ☎0721/73 461), is 2km from the village and has an aggressive proprietor. Among Kardhamýli's **tavernas**, try *Kiki's*, as well as *Lela's* whose eponymous owner was once housekeeper to Patrick Leigh Fermor. Otherwise, all along the through road there are a few low-key bars.

Inland to the Výros gorge

North of Kardhamýli the road leaves the coast, which rises to cliffs around a cape, before finally dropping back to the sea in the bay near Kalamáta. But before moving on, a day or two spent exploring Kardhamýli's immediate environs on foot is time well spent.

The giant **Výros gorge** plunges down from the very summit ridge of Taïyetos to meet the sea just north of the resort, and tracks penetrate the gorge from various directions. From Kardhamýli, the *kalderími* from the citadel continues to the church and village of Ayía Sofía, and then proceeds on a mixture of tracks and lanes either across the plateau up to the hamlet of Exohóri, or down into the gorge, where two **monasteries** nestle deep at the base of dramatic cliffs. An hour or so inland along the canyon, more cobbled ways lead up to either Tséria on the north bank (taverna, but no accommodation) or back towards Exohóri on the south flank. Linking any or all of these points is a reasonable day's hiking at most; forays further upstream require full hiking gear and detailed topographical maps.

Kardhamýli to Kalamáta

Divert west of the road to Kalamáta and you reach the small resorts of Avía and Akroyiáli, and Sántova beach. The *Santova Bungalows* (☎0721/58 496; ③) are good value, with the apartments sleeping four; there are kitchen facilities, good views and plenty of tavernas nearby.

THE HEARTLAND: SPÁRTI, MYSTRA AND TAÏYETOS

In the central core of the Peloponnese is luxuriantly spreading Mount Ménalo, surrounded by some of the most beautiful and verdant landscapes in Greece. Due south in the Lakonian Evrótas valley is Spárti and its Byzantine companion, Mystra, both overlooked and sheltered from the west by the massive and astonishing wall of the Taïyetos mountain ridge.

Spárti (Sparta)

Thucydides predicted that if the ancient city of **Sparta** were deserted, "distant ages would be very unwilling to believe its power at all equal to its fame." The city had no great temples or public buildings and throughout its period of greatness remained unfortified: Lycurgus, architect of the Spartan constitution, declared that "it is men not walls that make a city." Consequently, modern **SPÁRTI**, laid out grid-style in 1834, has few ancient ruins, and is today the pleasant organizational centre of a huge agricultural plain. Spárti's appeal is its ordinariness – its pedestrianized side-streets, café-lined

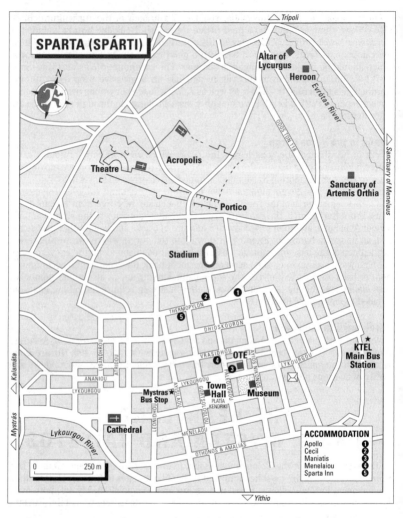

squares, orange trees and evening vólta. The reason for coming here is basically to see **Mystra**, the Byzantine town, 5km to the west, which once controlled great swathes of the medieval world (see p.214).

Ancient Sparta

Descending from the mountains that ring Spárti on three sides, you get a sense of how strategic was the location of the ancient city-state of **SPARTA**. The ancient "capital" occupied more or less the site of today's town, though it was in fact less a city than a grouping of villages, commanding the Lakonian plain and fertile Evrótas valley from a series of low hills to the west of the river.

The Greek city was at the height of its power from the eighth to the fourth century BC, a period when Sparta structured its society according to the laws of **Lycurgus**, defeated Athens in the Peloponnesian War, established colonies around the Greek world, and eventually lost hegemony through defeat to Thebes. A second period of prosperity came under the Romans – for whom this was an outpost in the south of Greece, with the Máni never properly subdued. However, from the third century AD Sparta declined as nearby Mystra became the focus of Byzantine interest.

The sites

All daily: 8.30am–3pm; free.

Traces of ancient Spartan glory are in short supply, but there are some ruins to be seen to the north of the city: follow the track behind the football stadium towards the old **Acropolis**, tallest of the Spartan hills. An immense **theatre** here, built into the side of the hill, can be quite clearly traced, even though today most of its masonry has gone – hurriedly adapted for fortification when the Spartans' power declined and, later still, used in the building of Byzantine Mystra. At the top of the acropolis sit the knee-high ruins of a **tenth-century Byzantine church** and **monastery** of Osíos Níkon.

About 500m along the Trípoli road, a path descends to the remains of the **sanctuary of Artemis Orthia**, where Spartan boys underwent endurance tests by flogging. The Roman geographer and travel writer Pausanias records that young men often expired under the lash, adding that the altar had to be splashed with blood before the goddess was satisfied. Perhaps it was the audience potential of such a gory spectacle that led the Romans to revive the custom: the main ruins here are of the spectators' grandstand they built. They also added shops to supply the audiences at performances. Neither of these sites is enclosed, and you can explore them along pleasant walkways.

Further out is the **Menelaion**, a late Mycenaean settlement and a sanctuary of Menelaus and Helen, about 5km to the southeast of town, on the far side of the river. At the modern village of Amýkles, 7km south of Spárti on the road to Yíthio, is the Amyklaion acropolis and **sanctuary of Apollo Amyklaios**, which until the Roman period was the most important Spartan site after the city itself and location for the Hyacinthia festival which celebrated the reconciliation of the Dorians and the Achaians.

The Archeological Museum

All movable artefacts and mosaics have been transferred to the town's small **Archeological Museum** (Tues–Sun 8.00am–2.30pm; 500dr). Among its more interesting exhibits are a number of votive offerings found on the sanctuary site – knives set in stone that were presented as prizes to the Spartan youths and solemnly rededicated to the goddess – and a marble bust of a running Spartan hoplite, found on the acropolis and said to be Leonidas, the hero of Thermopylae (see p.289).

Practicalities

If it is Mystra that brings you here, and you arrive early in the day, you may well decide to move straight on. Getting out of Spárti is straightforward. The **main bus terminal** (for Trípoli, Athens, Monemvasiá, Kalamáta and the Máni) has been moved recently to the eastern edge of town at Thivrónos at the eastern end of Lykoúrgou. Buses for **Mystra** leave (hourly on weekdays; less frequently at lunchtime and at weekends) from the main terminal and the corner of Lykoúrgou and Leonídhou; schedules are posted on the window of the café there. To reach Áyios Ioánnis, trailhead for hikes up **Mount Taïyetos**, you'll need to take a bus from the bottom of Paleológou on the south side of town. Most of the **banks** are on Paleológou.

Accommodation

There are usually enough **hotels** to go around, many of them on the main avenue of Paleológou. **Camping** is available at two sites out along the Mystra road; both can be reached via the Mystra bus, which will stop by the sites on request. The nearest, 2.5km from Spárti, is *Camping Mystra* (☎0731/22 724) and is open year-round. Two kilometres closer to Mystra is the *Castle View* (☎0731/93 303), a very clean, well-managed site, with a pool, and a bus stop outside.

Apollon, Thermopýlon 84, cnr Tripoléos (☎0731/22 491, fax 23 936). Open all year; parking area. ③.

Cecil, Paleológou 125, cnr Thermopýlon (☎0731/24 980, fax 81 318). Small and very friendly, recently renovated, all rooms with bathrooms and TV. ③.

Maniatis, Paleológou 72, cnr Lykoúrgou (☎0731/22 665, fax 29 994). Modern, with good facilities at a reasonable price. The in-house *Dias* restaurant is recommended. ④.

Menelaïon, Paleológou 91 (☎0731/22 161, fax 26 332). A modernized turn-of-the-century hotel, with a swimming pool. Rooms at the front are best avoided as there's an all-night taxi rank outside. ⑤.

Sparta Inn, Thermopýlon 105, cnr Gortsológlou (☎0731/25 021, fax 24 855). Huge and modern, with a roof garden and two swimming pools. ④.

Eating and drinking

There is a wide choice for meals, with most **restaurants** and **tavernas** concentrated on the main street of Paleológou – including several good psistariés towards the south end of Paleológou. One of the most popular music **bars** at present is *Ministry* opposite the *Menelaïon* hotel.

Averof, Paleológou 77. A long-established and reasonably priced taverna with tasty Greek home cooking; outdoor tables in summer.

Diethnes, Paleológou 105. Highly rated by the locals with a wide range of traditional dishes. The interior lacks atmosphere, but a delightful garden behind with orange and lemon trees compensates.

Dionysos. Recently moved 2km out on the road towards Mystra, this restaurant offers expensive dishes, but they're served with style – outdoors on a summer's evening.

Finikas, Thermopýlon 51. Fine taverna cum psistariá.

Semiramis, Paleológou 58. Taverna, tucked away in the basement, with a traditional Greek menu; the house speciality is roast pork with aubergine.

Mystra (Mystrás)

A glorious, airy place, hugging a steep flank of Taïyetos, **Mystra** is the most exciting and dramatic site that the Peloponnese can offer. Winding up the lushly vegetated hillside is an astonishingly complete Byzantine town that once sheltered a population of some 20,000, and through which you can now wander. Winding alleys lead through monumental gates, past medieval houses and palaces and above all into the churches, several of which yield superb and radiant frescoes. The overall effect is of straying into a massive museum of architecture, painting and sculpture – and into a different age.

There are no facilities at the site itself, so you'll need to base yourself at either Spárti (see above) or the modern settlement of Néos Mystrás (see p.219).

Some history

Mystra was basically a Frankish creation. In 1249, Guillaume II de Villehardouin, fourth Frankish prince of the Morea, built a castle here – one of a trio of fortresses (the others were at Monemvasiá and in the Máni) designed to garrison his domain. The Franks, however, were driven out of Mystra by the Byzantines in 1262, and this isolated triangle of land in the southeastern Peloponnese, encompassing the old Spartan territories, became the **Despotate of Mystra** by the mid-fourteenth century. This was the last province of the Greek Byzantine empire and for years, with Constantinople in terminal decay, was its virtual capital.

During the next two centuries, Mystra was the focus of a defiant rebirth of Byzantine power. The despotate's rulers – usually the son or brother of the eastern emperor, often the heir-apparent – recaptured and controlled much of the Peloponnese, which became the largest of the ever-shrinking Byzantine provinces. They and their province were to endure for two centuries before eventual subjugation by the Turks. The end came in 1460, seven years after the fall of Constantinople, when the despot Demetrius, feuding with his brothers, handed the city over to the Sultan Mehmet II.

Mystra's political significance, though, was in any case overshadowed by its **artistic achievements**. Throughout the fourteenth and the first decades of the fifteenth centuries it was the principal cultural and intellectual centre of the Byzantine world, sponsoring, in highly uncertain times, a renaissance in the arts and attracting the finest of Byzantine scholars and theologians – among them a number of members of the imperial families, the Cantacuzenes and Paleologues. Most notable of the court scholars was the humanist philosopher **Gemisthus Plethon**, who revived and reinterpreted Plato's ideas, using them to support his own brand of revolutionary teachings, which included the assertions that land should be redistributed among labourers and that reason should be placed on a par with religion. Although his beliefs had limited impact in Mystra itself – whose monks excommunicated him – his followers, who taught in Italy after the fall of Mystra, exercised wide influence in Renaissance Florence and Rome.

More tangibly, Mystra also saw a last flourish of **Byzantine architecture**, with the building of a magnificent palace for the despots and a perfect sequence of churches, multi-domed and brilliantly frescoed. It is these, remarkably preserved and sensitively restored, that provide the focus of this extraordinary site. In the painting, it is not hard to see something of the creativity and spirit of Plethon's court circle, as the stock Byzantine figures turn to more naturalistic forms and settings.

The town's **post-Byzantine history** follows a familiar Peloponnesian pattern. It remained in Turkish hands from the mid-fifteenth to late seventeenth centuries, then was captured briefly by the Venetians in 1687, under whom the town prospered once more attaining a population of 40,000. Decline set in with a second stage of Turkish control, from 1715 onwards, culminating in the destruction that accompanied the War of Independence, the site being evacuated after fires in 1770 and 1825. Restoration began in the first decades of this century, was interrupted by the civil war – during which it was, for a while, a battle site, with the ruins of the Pantánassa convent sheltering children from the lower town – and renewed in earnest in the 1950s when the last inhabitants were relocated.

The Byzantine city

Daily: summer 8am–8pm; winter 8am–2pm; 1200dr.

The site of the Byzantine city comprises three main parts: the **Káto Hóra** (lower town), with the city's most important churches; the **Áno Hóra** (upper town), grouped around the vast shell of a royal palace; and the **Kástro** (castle). There are two entrances to the site, at the base of the lower town and up below the kástro; once inside, the site is well signposted. A road loops up from the modern village of Néos Mystrás (see following) to Trýpi, passing near both upper and lower entrances. Buses from Spárti always stop at the lower entrance, and usually go up to the top too. It's a good idea to stock up on refreshments before setting out; there's a hygenic mobile snack bar at the lower gate, serving freshly pressed orange or lemon juices, but nothing at the upper one or in the site itself. This lack of commercialism within the site contrasts distinctly with Monemvasiá and contributes to the powerfully historic atmosphere at Mystra.

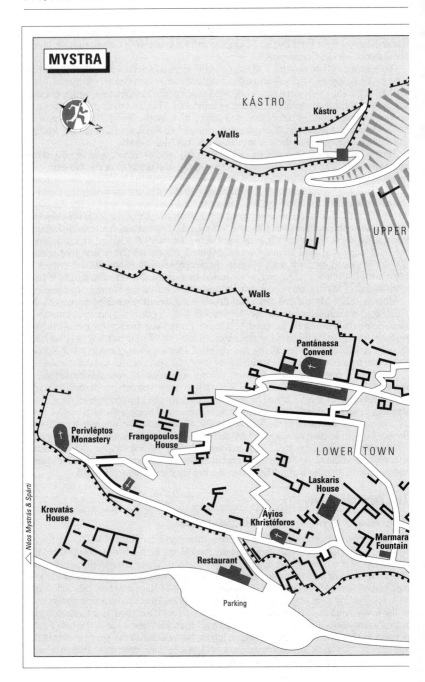

MYSTRA

KÁSTRO

Kástro

Walls

UPPER

Walls

Pantánassa
Convent

Perivléptos
Monastery

Frangopoulos
House

LOWER TOWN

Laskaris
House

Néos Mystrás & Spárti

Krevatás
House

Áyios
Khristóforos

Marmara
Fountain

Restaurant

Parking

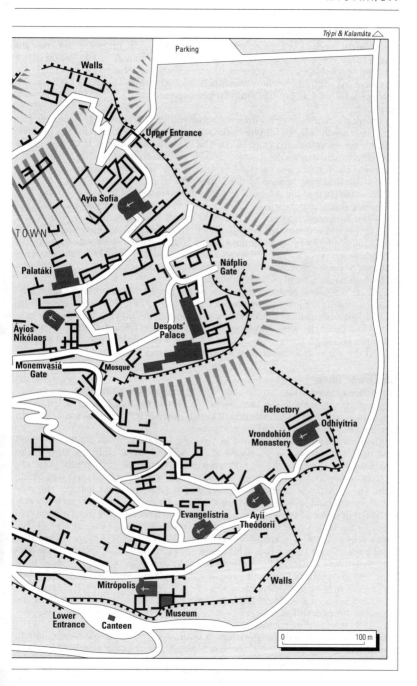

Trýpi & Kalamáta ◁

Parking

Walls

Upper Entrance

Ayía Sofía

TOWN

Palatáki

Náfplio Gate

Áyios Nikólaos

Despots' Palace

Monemvasiá Gate

Mosque

Refectory

Odhiyítria

Vrondohión Monastery

Evangelístria

Ayíi Theódorii

Walls

Mitrópolis

Lower Entrance

Canteen

Museum

0   100 m

The Upper Town and Kástro

The **Kástro**, reached by a path direct from the upper gate, maintains the Frankish design of its original thirteenth-century construction, though it was repaired and modified by all successive occupants. There is a walkway around most of the keep, with views allowing an intricate panorama of the town below. The castle itself was the court of Guillaume II de Villehardouin but in later years was used primarily as a citadel.

Following a course downhill from the upper entrance, the first identifiable building you come to is the church of **Ayía Sofía**, which served as the chapel for the Despots' Palace – the enormous structure below. The chapel's finest feature is its floor, made from polychrome marble. Its frescoes, notably a *Pandokrátor* (Christ in Majesty) and *Nativity of the Virgin*, have survived reasonably well, protected until recent years by coatings of whitewash applied by the Turks, who adapted the building as a mosque. Recognizable parts of the refectory and cells of its attached monastery also remain.

Heading down from Ayía Sofía, there is a choice of routes. The right fork winds past ruins of a Byzantine mansion, the **Palatáki** (Small Palace), and **Áyios Nikólaos**, a large seventeenth-century building decorated with unsophisticated paintings. The left fork is more interesting, passing the fortified **Náfplio Gate**, which was the principal entrance to the upper town, and the vast, multi-storeyed, Gothic-looking complex of the **Despots' Palace** (currently closed for extensive rebuilding and restoration that looks set to continue for a number of years ahead).

Parts of the palace probably date back to the Franks. Most prominent among its numerous rooms is a great vaulted audience hall, built at right angles to the line of the building, with ostentatious windows regally dominating the skyline; this was once heated by eight great chimneys and sported a painted facade. Behind it were various official public buildings, while to the right of the lower wing, flanking one side of a square used by the Turks as a marketplace, are the remains of a **mosque**.

The Lower Town

At the **Monemvasiá Gate**, which links the upper and lower towns, there is a further choice of routes: right to the Pantánassa and Perivléptos monasteries or left to the Vrondohión monastery and cathedral. If time is running out, it is easier to head right first, then double back down to the Vrondohión.

When excavations were resumed in 1952, the last thirty or so families who still lived in the lower town were moved out to Néos Mystrás. Only the nuns of the **Pantánassa** ("Queen of the World") **convent** have remained; currently, there are seven in residence and they have a reception room where they sell their own handicrafts and sometimes offer a cooling *vyssinádha* (cherryade) to visitors. The convent's church, built in 1428, is perhaps the finest surviving in Mystra, perfectly proportioned in its blend of Byzantine and Gothic. The **frescoes** date from various centuries, with some superb fifteenth-century work, including one in the gallery (entered by an external staircase but currently closed) which depicts scenes from the life of Christ. David Talbot Rice, in his classic study *Byzantine Art*, wrote of these frescoes that "Only El Greco in the west, and later Gauguin, would have used their colours in just this way." Other frescoes were painted between 1687 and 1715, when Mystra was held by the Venetians.

Further down on this side of the lower town is a balconied Byzantine mansion, the **House of Frangopoulos**, once the home of the despotate's chief minister – who was also the founder of the Pantánassa.

Beyond it is the diminutive **Perivléptos monastery**, whose single-domed church, partially carved out of the rock, contains Mystra's most complete cycle of frescoes, almost all of which date from the fourteenth century. They are in some ways finer than those of the Pantánassa, blending an easy humanism with the spirituality of the Byzantine icon traditions, and demonstrating the structured iconography of a Byzantine church. The position of each figure depended upon its sanctity and so here upon the dome, the image of heaven, is the *Pandokrátor* (the all-powerful Christ in glory after the Ascension); on the apse is the Virgin, and the higher expanses of wall portray scenes from the life of Christ. Prophets and saints could only appear on the lower walls, decreasing in importance according to their distance from the sanctuary.

Along the path leading from Perivléptos to the lower gate are a couple of minor, much-restored churches, and, just above them, the **Laskaris House**, a mansion thought to have belonged to relatives of the emperors. Like the Frangopoulos House, it is balconied; its ground floor probably served as stables. Close by, beside the path, is an old Turkish fountain.

The **mitrópolis** or cathedral, immediately beyond the gateway, is the oldest of Mystra's churches, built between 1270 and 1292 under the first Paleologue ruler. A marble slab set in its floor is carved with the double-headed eagle of Byzantium, commemorating the spot where Constantine XI Paleologos, the last Eastern emperor, was crowned in 1448; he was soon to perish, with his empire, in the Turkish sacking of Constantinople in 1453. Of the church's frescoes, the earliest, in the northeast aisle, depict the torture and burial of Áyios Dhimítrios, the saint to whom the church is dedicated. The comparative stiffness of their figures contrasts with the later works opposite. These, illustrating the miracles of Christ and the life of the Virgin, are more intimate and lighter of touch; they date from the last great years before Mystra's fall. Adjacent to the cathedral, a small **museum** (included in main admission charge) contains various fragments of sculpture and pottery, though staff may be irritable at having to climb the stairs to keep an eye on you.

Finally, a short way uphill, is the **Vrondohión monastery**. This was the centre of cultural and intellectual life in the fifteenth-century town – the cells of the monastery can still be discerned – and was also the burial place of the despots. Of the two attached churches, the further one, **Odhiyítria (Afendikó)** has been beautifully restored, revealing early fourteenth-century frescoes similar to those of Perivléptos, with startlingly bold juxtapositions of colour.

Practicalities: Néos Mystrás

Buses run regularly through the day from Spárti to the lower Mystra site entrance, stopping en route at the modern village of **NÉOS MYSTRÁS**. This small roadside community has a half-dozen tavernas, crowded with tour buses by day but reverting to a low-key life at night, except at the end of August when the place buzzes with live music and a gypsy market during the week-long annual *paniyíri* (fête).

In general, staying in Néos Mystrás is worth the bit extra over Spárti, for the setting and early access to the site, though you will need to book ahead, or arrive early in the day, to find a place. **Accommodation** is limited to a single hotel, the recently refurbished *Byzantion* (☎0731/83 309, fax 20 019, *medotels@otenet.gr*; ⑤; closed in winter), which is pleasant but oversubscribed for most of the year, and a small number of private rooms – those run by Hristina Vahaviolou (☎0731/20 047; ③) are especially recommended. There are **campsites** along the Mystrás–Spárti road: see under accommodation details for Spárti on p.214.

The Vahaviolos family also has an excellent **taverna**, while the restaurant opposite the hotel, *To Kastro*, is also good, if a bit on the expensive side. Between the village and the site, *Taverna Marmara* is fine – and quieter in the evenings after the tour buses have gone.

Mount Taïyetos and the Langádha pass

Moving on from Spárti there is a tough choice of routes: west over the Taïyetos ridge, either on foot or by road through the dramatic **Langádha pass** to Kalamáta; east to the Byzantine towns of **Yeráki** and **Monemvasiá**; or south, skirting the mountain's foothills, to **Yíthio** and the **Máni**. For anyone wanting to get to grips with the Greek mountains, there is **Mount Taïyetos** itself. Although the range is one of the most beautiful, dramatic and hazardous in Greece, with vast grey boulders and scree along much of its length, it has one reasonably straightforward path to the highest peak, Profítis Ilías. Three areas, covering different and specialized ecological habitats, in the higher mountains and the gorges of Langádha and Nédhondas, have been proposed for conservation in the millennium under the EU's NATURA 2000 programme.

Mount Taïyetos

Gazing up at the crags above the castle at Mystra, Mount Taïyetos (Taygettus) looks daunting and inviting in pretty equal measure. If all you want is a different perspective on the mountain, then the simplest course is to take a bus from Spárti to **ÁYIOS IOÁNNIS**, a little way to the south of Mystra and closer to the peaks. From there a spectacular *kalderími* (cobbled way) leads up from the gravel-crushing mill behind the village to **ANAVRYTÍ**, which boasts superb vistas, a single friendly hotel the *Anemodharména Ípsi* ("Wuthering Heights"; ☎0731/21 788; ③) and one basic taverna aside from the one in the hotel. An alternative, more popular approach involves following the marked E4 overland route, partly on track, partly on trail, up from Néos Mystrás via the **monastery of Faneroméni**. Neither the E4 nor the *kalderími* takes more than two hours uphill, and they can be combined as follows for a wonderful day's outing: bus to Áyios Ioánnis, taxi to rock-crushing mill (2.5km), hike up to Anavrytí for a look around and a meal, then descend via Faneroméni to Néos Mystrás. Note that this route is best tackled from Áyios Ioánnis; the downhill start of the *kalderími* just east of Anavrytí isn't marked, and can be difficult to locate.

Spárti to Kalamáta: the Langádha pass

The **Langádha pass**, the sixty-kilometre route over the Taïyetos from **Spárti to Kalamáta**, was the second ancient crossing after the Kakí Skála (see box opposite) and is still the only paved road across the mountain. Remote and barren, with long uninhabited sections, it unveils a constant drama of peaks, magnificent at all times but startling at sunrise – sadly the pine forests have suffered extensive damage in the fires of 1998. This route was taken by Telemachus in the *Odyssey* on his way from Nestor's palace at Pýlos to that of Menelaus at Sparta. It took him a day by chariot – good going by any standards, since today's buses take three hours.

Heading from Spárti, the last settlement is **TRÝPI**, 9km out, where there is one of the best tavernas in the Spárti area, *Vozola*, and a small **hotel**, the *Keadas* (☎0731/98 222; ②), open Easter to late autumn. Just beyond the village, the road climbs steeply into the mountains and enters the **gorge of Langádha**, a wild sequence of hairpins through the pines. To the north of the gorge, at the rock of Keádhas, the Spartans used to leave their sick or puny babies to die from exposure. Beyond the gorge, just before the summit of the **pass**, 22km from Spárti and 37km from Kalamáta, the *Canadas* **guesthouse** (☎0721/76 821; ①) is built in the style of an alpine chalet, and is excellent value, with a restaurant that serves good *bakaliáros* (cod), *loukániko* (sausage), smoked pork and bean soup. It's also a good place to sample mountain tea, made from the local herb *sidherítis*. At the pass, 3km further on and 125m higher at 1375m, is the

HIKING IN THE TAÏYETOS RANGE

Most **hikes** beyond Anavrytí need experience and proper equipment, including the relevant *Korfes* or *YIS* maps, and should definitely not be undertaken alone – a sprained ankle could be fatal up here. The area is prone to flash floods, so seek advice locally. If you are confident, however, there are various routes to the Profítis Ilías summit and beyond.

The only straightforward route is to follow the **E4 long-distance footpath**, here marked variously by yellow diamonds or red-and-white stripes, for five hours south to the **alpine refuge** at Ayía Varvára (see below).

The classic approach to the 240-metre **Profítis Ilías summit** used to entail a dusty, eleven-kilometre road-walk up from the village of Paleopanayía, a short bus ride south of Spárti off the Yíthio road, to the spring and ex-trailhead at Bóliana (Kryonéri), where there's a single ramshackle hut that serves drinks and sometimes meals in summer. You now have to proceed past Bóliana towards Anavrytí on the E4 track for about thirty minutes, then bear left near a picnic ground and spring (the last reliable water on the mountain). Another half-hour above this, following E4 blazes, what's left of the old trail appears on the right, signposted "EOS Spárti Katafíyio". This short-cuts the new road except for the very last 50m to the Ayía Varvára refuge.

A more challenging option, requiring mountaineering skills and camping equipment, is to adopt the red-dotted trail veering off the E4 early on out, and follow it to a point just below the 1700-metre saddle described by Patrick Leigh Fermor in *Mani*, where you must choose between dropping over the pass to the far side of the range or precarious ridge-walking to the Profítis Ilías summit. Crossing the pass would land you at the head of the **Ríndomo gorge**, where you can camp at the chapel-monastery of Panayía Kavsodhematoúsa before descending the next day to either Gaïtses or Pigádhia, towards the Messinian coast. Keeping to the watershed it is seven tough hours to the peak even in optimum conditions and with a light load, involving exposed rock pinnacles, sheer drops and difficult surfaces. This is not a hike to be lightly undertaken.

AYÍA VARVÁRA TO THE SUMMIT

The **Ayía Varvára refuge** (unstaffed, but open sporadically – more likely at weekends), above Bóliana, sits on a beautiful grassy knoll shaded by tremendous storm-blasted black pines. The conical peak of Profítis Ilías rises directly above; if you can get your climb to coincide with a full moon you won't regret it. There is plenty of room for camping, and the hut has a porch to provide shelter in bad weather.

The path to the **summit** starts at the rear left corner of the refuge and swings right on a long reach. Level and stony at first, it leaves the treeline and loops up a steep bank to a sloping meadow, where it is ineffectually marked by twisted, rusting signs with their lettering long obliterated. Keep heading right across the slope towards a distinct secondary peak until, once around a steep bend, the path begins to veer left in the direction of the summit. It slants steadily upward following a natural ledge until, at a very clear nick in the ridge above you, it turns right and crosses to the far side, from where you look down on the Gulf of Messinía. Turn left and you climb steeply to the summit in around 25 minutes.

There is a squat stone chapel and outbuildings on the **summit**, used during the celebrations of the feast of the Prophet Elijah (Profítis Ilías) on July 18–20. The views, as you would expect, are breathtaking, encompassing the sea to east and west.

SUMMIT TO THE COAST

The ridge terrain **beyond the peak** is beyond the ambitions of casual hikers. The easiest and safest way off the mountain towards the Messinian coast is to follow the E4 from Ayía Varvára to the gushing springs at Pendávli, and then over a low saddle to the summer hamlet of **Áyios Dhimítrios**. This takes just a couple of hours and you can camp in the beautiful surroundings. In the morning you're well poised, at the head of the **Výros gorge**, to handle the all-day descent to Kardhamýli through the other great Taïyetan canyon. At one point you must negotiate stretches of the **Kakí Skála**, one of the oldest paths in Greece, built to link ancient Sparta and Messene. Dirt roads now also link Áyios Dhimítrios with Saïdhóna (24km), above Stoúpa and Kardhamýli in the west, and with Yíthio in the southeast.

Touristiko Taïyetou (☎0721/76236; ②) hotel and restaurant, also open all year. From here paths and tracks head off north and south along the mountain ridge.

The first actual village on the Kalamáta side is **Artemisía**, where you often have to change buses, before entering the **Nédhondas** gorge for the final zigzagging descent to Kalamáta. There is basic accommodation here, in rooms above one of the cafés, but the *Canadas* and *Touristiko Taïyetou* are far better value for little more cost.

ARCADIA

Arcadia (Arkadhía in modern Greek), the heartland province of the Peloponnese, lives up to its name. It contains some of the most beautiful landscapes in Greece: verdant and dramatic hills crowned by a string of medieval towns, and the occasional Classical antiquity. The best area of all is around **Andhrítsena**, **Stemnítsa** and **Karýtena**, where walkers are rewarded with the luxuriant (and rarely visited) **Loúsios gorge**, and archeology buffs by the remote, though permanently covered, **Temple of Bassae** (Apollo Epikourios). En route, if approaching from Trípoli, you may also be tempted by the ancient theatre at **Megalópoli**.

Trípoli

Trípoli is a major crossroads of the Peloponnese, from where most travellers either head **northwest** through Arcadia towards Olympia or Pátra, or **south** to Spárti and Mystra or Kalamáta (see below). To the **east**, a recently improved road, looping around Mount Kteniás, connects Trípoli with Árgos and Náfplio, via Lérna. A second road, under improvement, runs southeast across the Tegean plain, then east down to Ástros. To the **west**, you can reach the coast on a reasonably fast road to Kyparissía, via the evocative, scattered ruins of ancient Megalopolis. To the **northeast**, a new fast highway links Trípoli with Kórinthos and Athens.

The Peloponnese **railway** also passes through Trípoli, continuing its meandering course from Kórinthos and Árgos to Kyparissía and Kalamáta. Those with passes might be tempted to use the train to Trípoli and then take a bus to Spárti, but it's not a good idea, as Árgos–Spárti buses are not scheduled to meet trains in Trípoli and furthermore they often pass through full; it's better to take a direct bus (seven to nine daily from Athens to Spárti, via Árgos and Trípoli), or approach Spárti more enjoyably via the hydrofoil to Monemvasiá.

The Town

The Arcadian capital doesn't live up to expectations: **TRÍPOLI** is a large, modern town, and home to one of the country's biggest army barracks. It doesn't overwhelm you with its charm and has few obvious attractions, although the **Panarcadic Archeological Museum** (Tues–Sun; summer 8.30am–5pm, winter 8am–2.30pm; 500dr), signposted off Vasiléos Yeoryíou and housed in a Neoclassical building with a beautiful rose garden, makes a pleasant diversion; the collection includes finds from much of Arcadia, from Neolithic to Roman. The town's altitude of 650m means an often markedly cooler summer climate (but harsh winters). Traffic is chaotic and you may wish to escape to the quiet greenery of Platía Áreos. Medieval Tripolitsa was destroyed by retreating Turkish forces during the War of Independence; the Greek forces, led by Kolokotronis in one of their worst atrocities, having earlier massacred the town's Turkish population. Tripolitsa's ancient predecessors, the rival towns of Mantinea to the north and Tegea to the south, are the main points of interest to the tourist.

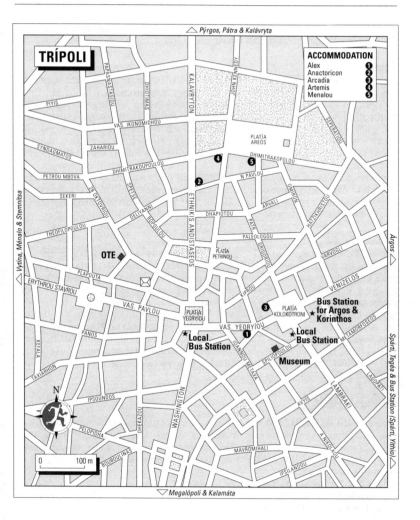

Getting in and out of the town can be fairly complicated. The major **bus terminal**, serving all destinations in Arcadia and the northern Peloponnese, is on Platía Kolokotróni, one of the three main squares. Services to Pátra, Messinía, Kalamáta, the outer Máni, Pýlos and Spárti leave from the "milk" shop directly opposite the train station, at the southeastern edge of town. If you need to spend a night here, there are a number of reliable **hotels** including the *Arcadia* on Platía Kolokotróni (☎071/225 551, fax 222 464; ⑤); the *Alex*, Vas. Yioryíou 26 (☎071/223 465; ③); the very friendly *Anactoricon* on Ethnikís Andistásis 48 (☎071/ 22 2545; ③); the *Menalou* on Platía Áreos (☎071/222 450; ③); and the *Artemis*, Dhimitrakopoúlou 1 (☎071/225 221, fax 233 629; ④). Cheaper **rooms** are advertised on Lambráki on the way into town from the train station. Eating establishments are mostly of the functional variety, but for decent food in more pleasant surroundings there are a couple of tavernas, *Neos Dionysos* and the more homely *Klimataria*, almost adjacent to one another on Kalavrýton, beyond the Aello cinema and about 100m past the far end of Platía Áreos.

Ancient Mantinea

Ancient **MANTINEA** (Tues–Sun 8am–3pm), known to Homer as "pleasant Mantinea", was throughout its history a bitter rival of nearby Tegea, invariably forming an alliance with Athens when Tegea stood with Sparta, then switching allegiance to Sparta when Tegea allied with Thebes. Its site stands 15km north of Trípoli, between the road to Pátra and the new Trípoli–Kórinthos highway, and is served by hourly buses from Platía Kolokotróni in Trípoli. The principal remains are a circuit of fourth-century BC **walls**, still more or less intact, though much reduced in height, and a few tiers of its ancient theatre.

Alongside the site, however, is one of the most bizarre sights in Greece: a modern **church** of Ayía Fotiní constructed in an eccentric pastiche of Byzantine and Egyptian styles. Put together in the 1970s by a Greek-American architect, it is dedicated to "The Virgin, the Muses and Beethoven".

Ancient Tegea

Ancient **TEGEA**, 8km south of Trípoli, was the main city of the central Peloponnese in Classical and Roman times, and, refounded in the tenth century, was an important town again under the Byzantines. The diffuse and partially excavated site lies just outside the village of Aléa (modern Tegea), on the Spárti road. Local buses from Trípoli stop in the village beside a small **museum** (daily 8.30am–3pm; 500dr), which is well stocked with sculptures from the site. Take the road to the left as you leave, which leads in 100m to the main remains, the **Temple of Athena Alea**, in whose sanctuary two kings of Sparta once took refuge. Keeping on the road past the site, it's a twenty-minute walk to the village of Paleá Episkopí, whose church – a huge modern pilgrim shrine – incorporates part of ancient Tegea's theatre and a number of Byzantine mosaics.

Megalópoli

Modern **MEGALÓPOLI** (Megalopolis) is an important road and bus junction, and your first thoughts on arrival may be directed towards getting out. Like Trípoli, it's a rather characterless place, with a military presence and two vast power stations; there's little in the way of hotels or food. The adoption of its ancient name, "Great City", was an altogether empty joke.

However, the impulse to leave should be resisted, at least for an hour or two, because just outside the city to the northwest is one of the most extensive and least touristy sites in the Peloponnese: **ancient Megalopolis**.

Practicalities

Megalópoli has **bus connections** with Trípoli (and on to Árgos and Athens) and Kalamáta. Arrive at a reasonable hour and you should be able to make either of these connections. Moving north or west into Arcadia is slightly more problematic, with just two buses daily to Karýtena/Andhrítsena (currently at noon and 7pm). However, hitching is a viable proposition along this route, as local drivers are aware of the paucity of transport, and it's also possible to negotiate a **taxi** to Karítena. Facilities such as **banks** and a **post office** are also to be found around the central Platía Gortynías.

There are four or five **hotels** in Megalópoli, catering mostly to local business travellers rather than tourists. The cheapest are all in the vicinity of the central platía and include the *Pan*, Papanastasíou 7 (☎0791/22 270; ②), which is rather old but acceptable, with private facilities in the more expensive rooms; the better-presented *Paris*, Ayíou Nikoláou 5 (☎0791/22 410; ③); and the *Achillion*, Papaioánnou 67 (☎0791/22 311; ④), which has clean, comfortable rooms with en-suite showers. The *Leontara* restaurant on the main square is recommended for baked dishes.

Some 28km southwest of Megalópoli by indirect roads, on the flank of 1389-metre Mount Tetrázio, is the mountain village of **Vástas** with its small but remarkable Ayía Theódora church which is dwarfed by the seventeen large trees sprouting from the roof.

Ancient Megalopolis

Ancient Megalopolis (Tues–Sun 8.30am–3pm; free) was one of the most ambitious building projects of the Classical age, a city intended by the Theban leader Epaminondas, who oversaw construction from 371 to 368 BC, to be the finest of a chain of Arcadian settlements designed to hold back the Spartans. However, although no expense was spared on its construction, nor on its extent – nine kilometres of walls alone – the city never took root. It suffered from sporadic Spartan aggression, and the citizens, transplanted from forty local villages, preferred, and returned to, their old homes. Within two centuries it had been broken up, abandoned and ruined.

As you approach the site, along a tree-lined track off the Andhrítsena road (signposted "Ancient Theatre"), the countryside is beautiful enough; a fertile valley whose steaming cooling towers seem to give it added grandeur; beyond the riverbed is just a low hill, and no sign of any ruins. Suddenly, you round the corner of the rise and its function is revealed: carved into its side is the largest **theatre** built in ancient Greece. Only the first few rows are excavated, but the earthen mounds and ridges of the rest are clearly visible as stepped tiers to the summit where, from the back rows, trees look on like immense spectators. Restoration work is planned.

The theatre was built to a scale similar to those at Argos and Dodona, and could seat 20,000; the **Thersileion** (Assembly Hall) at its base could hold 16,000. Today you're likely to be alone at the site, save perhaps for the custodian (who has plans of the ruins). Out beyond the enclosed part of the site you can wander over a vast area, and with a little imagination make out the foundations of walls and towers, temples, gymnasiums and markets. "The Great City", wrote Kazantzakis in *Journey to the Morea*, "has become a great wasteland." But it's the richest of wastelands, gently and resolutely reclaimed by nature.

Megalópoli to Dhimitsána

North of Megalópoli the best of Arcadia lies before you: minor roads that curl through a series of lush valleys and below the province's most exquisite medieval hill towns. The obvious first stop is **Karýtena**.

Moving on from Karýtena, there is a choice of roads. The "main" route loops west through **Andhrítsena** to Kréstena, from where irregular buses run to Olympia. An alternative route to the northwest winds around the edge of the Ménalo mountains to the delightful towns of **Stemnítsa** and **Dhimitsána**, meeting the main Trípoli–Langádhia–Olympia–Pýrgos road at Karkaloú. From either of these you can visit the dramatic and remote site of **ancient Gortys** and explore the **Loúsios gorge**, above which, outrageously sited on 300-metre-high cliffs, is the eleventh-century **Ayíou Ioánnou Prodhrómou monastery** (commonly abbreviated just to Prodhrómou). If you have time on your hands, perhaps the most attractive option is to explore the region north as far as Dhimitsána, then backtrack to Karýtena to proceed on to Olympia via Andhrítsena.

Karýtena

Set high above the Megalópoli–Andhrítsena road, **KARÝTENA** may look familiar; with its medieval bridge over the River Alfiós (Alpheus), it graces the 5000-drachma note. Like many of the Arcadian hill towns hereabouts, its history has Frankish, Byzantine and Turkish contributions, the Venetians having passed over much of the northern interior. It was founded by the Byzantines in the seventh century and had attained a population of some 20,000 when the Franks took it in 1209. Under their century-long rule, Karýtena was the capital of a large barony under Geoffroy de Bruyères, the paragon of chivalry in the medieval ballad *The Chronicle of the Morea*, and probably the only well-liked Frankish overlord.

The village these days has a population of just a couple of hundred; there were at least ten times that figure until the beginning of this century. Approaching, you can stop on the modern bridge over the Alfíos and peer down at the **medieval bridge**, which is immediately adjacent. It is missing the central section, but is an intriguing structure nonetheless, with a small Byzantine chapel built into one of the central pillars.

From the main road, there's a winding three-kilometre road up to the village, in the upper part of which is a small central platía with a kafenío. Off the platía are signposted two Byzantine churches: the fourteenth-century **Zoödhóhos Piyí** (with a Romanesque bell-tower) and the late seventeenth-century **Áyios Nikólaos** (with crumbling frescoes) to the west, down towards the river; ask at the kafenío for the keys. Also off the platía is the **Frourio**, the castle built in 1245 by the Franks, with added Turkish towers. It was repaired by Theodoros Kolokotronis and it was here that he held out against Ibrahim Pasha in 1826 and turned the tide of the War of Independence; hence the view of Karýtena on the 5000-drachma note and a portrait of Kolokotronis on the reverse.

There are only two places to rent **rooms**: one signposted opposite the post office, the *Kondopoulos* (☎0791/31 262; ①); the other, under an isolated house 1km beyond the platía, the *Papadopoulos* (☎0791/31 203; ②); both are basic, with shared facilities, and the hotel in Stemnítsa, 15km away, is far better value. *To Konaki*, a good taverna with typical fare, is on the square.

North through the Loúsios River valley

The site of **ancient Gortys** can be approached either from Karýtena or from Stemnítsa (8km northwest of the site). From Karýtena the most direct route to the valley runs up and through the town to Astílohos (11km), a village 2km southwest of the site; a taxi should cost in the region of 3000dr return. This route is no more than a jeep track, and twenty minutes from the site it becomes a trail. If you don't have a car, it is easier to follow the road north towards Stemnítsa and Dhimitsána for 6km to the hamlet of Ellinikó. From the edge of Ellinikó, a dirt track signposted "Gortys" descends west; after a rough six kilometres (ignore the right-hand fork at the five-kilometre point – this heads north to Prodhrómou before winding east towards Stemnítsa) it ends at the bank of the Loúsios River. Here is an old bridge, which you cross to reach the site of ancient Gortys. It is possible to camp overnight at Gortys, or to stay at the nearby monastery of Prodhrómou. The town of Stemnítsa, with its excellent hotel, probably makes the best base for exploring the area, and walkers may want to do so by following the Stemnítsa–Prodhrómou–Gortys–Ellinikó–Stemnítsa circuit (see below). There are new dirt roads being made above the Loúsios, which may affect the following routes.

Ancient Gortys

Ancient Gortys is one of the most stirring of all Greek sites, set beside the rushing river known in ancient times as the Gortynios. The remains are widely strewn amongst the vegetation on the west (true right) bank of the stream, but the main attraction, below contemporary ground level and not at all obvious until well to the west of the little chapel of Áyios Andhréas (by the old bridge), is the huge excavation containing the remains of a **temple to Asclepius** (the god of healing) and an adjoining **bath**, both dating from the fourth century BC.

The most curious feature of the site is a circular **portico** enclosing round-backed seats which most certainly would have been part of the therapeutic centre. It's an extraordinary place, especially if you camp with the roar of the Loúsios to lull you to sleep. The only drawback is the climate: temperatures up here plummet at night, no matter what the season, and heavy mists, wet as a soaking rain, can envelop the mountains from midnight to mid-morning.

The Loúsios gorge and monastery of Prodhrómou

The farmland surrounding ancient Gortys belongs to the monks of the nearby **Prodhrómou monastery**, who have carved a donkey path along the **gorge of the Loúsios** between Áyios Andhréas and the monastery. It's about forty minutes' walk upstream, with an initially gradual and later steady ascent up a well-graded, switch-backed trail. A set of park benches by a formal gate heralds arrival, and the whole area is well stamped about by the monks' mules. If you look up through the trees above the path, the monastery, stuck on to the cliff like a swallow's nest, is plainly visible a couple of hundred metres above.

The interior of the monastery does not disappoint this promise; the local villagers accurately describe it as *politisméno* (cultured) as opposed to *ágrio* (wild). Once inside it is surprisingly small; there were never more than about fifteen tenants, and currently there are twelve monks, many of them very young and committed. Visitors are received in the *arhondaríki* (guest lounge and adjoining quarters), and then shown the tiny frescoed *katholikón*, and possibly invited to evening services there. The strictest rules of dress apply, but the monks welcome visitors who wish to stay the night. The only problem, especially on weekends, is that there are only a dozen or so beds, and people from Trípoli and even Athens make pilgrimages and retreats here, arriving by the carload along a circuitous dirt track from Stemnítsa. Be prepared for this possibility, and arrive in time to get back to level ground to camp.

Prodhrómou to Stemnítsa

Beyond Prodhrómou the path continues clearly to the outlying monasteries of **Paleá** and **Néa Filosófou**. The older dates from the tenth century but, virtually ruined, is easy to miss since it blends into the cliff on which it's built. The newer (seventeenth-century) monastery has been restored, but retains frescoes inside; there is now a permanent caretaker monk to show you around.

At Prodhrómou you can pick up the dirt track (described above as the fork off the Ellinikó–Gortys track) and head for Stemnítsa. If you are walking it is more pleasant, and quicker, to follow instead the old *kalderími* from Prodhrómou to Stemnítsa – a climb, but not a killing one, of about ninety minutes through scrub oak with fine views over the valley. Usually one of the monks or lay workers will be free to point out the start of the path; once clear of the roadhead confusion by the modern little chapel at the edge of the canyon, there's little possibility of getting lost.

If Stemnítsa is your base rather than your destination, you can take this route in reverse by heading out of town on the paved road to Dhimitsána and (500m after the town-limits sign) bear down and left onto the obvious beginning of the upper end of the *kalderími*. The loop can be completed by following the track all the way back to Ellinikó, where a proper trail leads north back to Stemnítsa.

Stemnítsa

Fifteen kilometres north of Karýtena and at an altitude of 1050m, **STEMNÍTSA** (or Ipsoúnda in its official Hellenicized form – Ipsoús on many maps) was for centuries one of the premier metal-smithing and goldworking centres of the Balkans. Although much depopulated, it remains a fascinating town, with a small folklore museum, an artisan school and a handful of quietly magnificent medieval churches.

The town is divided by ravines into three distinct quarters: the Kástro (the ancient acropolis hill), Ayía Paraskeví (east of the stream) and Áyios Ioánnis (west of it). The **Folklore Museum** (Mon & Wed–Fri 6–8pm, Sat 11am–1pm & 6–8pm, Sun 11am–1pm; closed in Feb; free) is just off the main road in the Ayía Paraskeví quarter, and repays the trip out in itself. The ground floor is devoted to mockups of the workshops of indigenous crafts such as candle-making, bell-casting, shoe-making and jewellery. The next floor up features re-creations of the salon of a well-to-do family and a humbler cottage. The top storey is taken up by the rather random collections of the Savopoulos family: plates by Avramides (a refugee from Asia Minor and ceramics master), textiles and costumes from all over Greece, weapons, copperware and eighteenth- and nineteenth-century icons. Across the way the **Artisan School** is temporarily closed for refurbishment. Next door to the school is the seventeenth-century **basilica of Trión Ierarhón**, the most accessible of the town's Byzantine churches; its caretaker lives in the low white house west of the main door.

To visit the other churches, all of which are frescoed and locked, requires more determined enquiries to find a key. The *katholikón* of the seventeenth-century **monastery of Zoödhóhos Piyí** has perhaps the finest setting, on the hillside above Ayía Paraskeví, but the tiny windows do not permit much of an interior view. The little adjoining monastery hosted the first *yerousía* (convention) of guerrilla captains in the War of Independence, giving rise to the local claim that Stemnítsa was Greece's first capital.

Near the summit of the Kástro hill are two adjacent chapels: the tenth-century **Profítis Ilías** (with a convenient window for fresco-viewing) and the twelfth-century **Panayía Vaferón** (with an unusual colonnade). The last of the town's five churches, **Áyios Pandelímon**, is located at the western edge of the town, to the left of the paved road to Dhimitsána.

Accommodation is limited to the very pleasant and hospitable *Hotel Trikolonion* (☎0795/81 297, fax 81 483; ②), which has rooms and suites in a fine traditional building in the centre of town; the inclusive breakfasts are substantial and the restaurant is cheap and very good. The hotel represents the best value in accommodation between Trípoli and Olympía, and is popular, so advance booking is recommended. You can eat well here, or in town at the simple *Klinitsa* on the square or pleasant *Kastro* near the hill. There is one **bus** a day linking Stemnítsa with Trípoli via Dhimitsána.

Dhimitsána

Like Stemnítsa, **DHIMITSÁNA** has an immediately seductive appearance, its cobbled streets and tottering houses straddling a twin hillside overlooking the Loúsios River. Views from the village are stunning: it stands at the head of the gorge, and looking downriver you can just see the cooling towers of the Megalópoli power plant and the bluff that supports Karýtena. To the east are the lower folds of the Ménalo mountains, most visible if you climb up to the local **Kástro**, whose stretch of Cyclopean walls attests to its ancient use.

In the town, a half-dozen churches with tall, squarish belfries recall the extended Frankish, and especially Norman, tenure in this part of the Morea during the thirteenth century. Yet none should dispute the deep-dyed Greekness of Dhimitsána. It was the birthplace of Archbishop Yermanos, who first raised the flag of rebellion at Kalávryta in 1821, and of the hapless patriarch, Grigoris V, hanged in Constantinople upon the sultan's receiving news of the insurrection mounted by the patriarch's coreligionist and of the massacre at Tripolitsa. Grigoris's house is now an **Ecclesiastical Museum** (daily except Wed & Fri, 10am–1.30pm, 5–7pm). During the hostilities the ubiquitous Kolokotronis maintained a lair and a powder mill in the then almost inaccessible town. Before the War of Independence, the nunnery of **Emyalón** (daylight hours except 2–5pm), 3km south towards Stemnítsa, was used by the Kolokotronis clan as a hideout. About 2km south of Dhimitsána, the new **Open-Air Water Power Museum** (daily summer 10am–2pm, 5pm–7pm, Wed–Mon winter 10am–4pm; 400dr) has a reconstructed watermill, tannery and powder mill, with restored equipment, and exhibitions on the processes involved. It is possible to follow a marked route down to a bridge over the Loúsios, starting on the low road signed to the Emyalón monastery, then joining a *kalderími* via Paleohóri.

Accommodation is available in rooms such as *Velissaropoulos* (✆0795/31 617: ①) or *Tsialas* (✆0795/31 583; ②) and others; the modern and well-appointed, but somewhat pricey hotel *Dimitsana* (✆0795/31 518; ④), 1km out on the road to Stemnítsa, is popular with rambling groups. The **taverna** *Kali Thea*, just across the road from the hotel, is Dhimitsána's best and not too expensive.

Moving on to Olympia

Keep in mind that through buses from Dhimitsána are scarce, and you may well need to hitch (or take a taxi) to Karkaloú or Vytína, on the main Trípoli–Pýrgos road, where you can pick up buses more easily. Once on the road to Olympia, the most enjoyable halt is **LANGÁDHIA** (18km from Dhimitsána), whose tiers of houses and bubbling sluices tumble downhill to the river far below the road. Often you can stop on a late-morning bus, eat lunch and pick up the next through service with little lost time. If you decide to stay the night, there are a couple of well-priced **hotels** on the main road: the central *Kentrikon* (✆ and fax 0795/43 221; ②) and the *Langadia Motel* (✆0795/43 202; ①) at the western end.

You may well find that you have fewer changes and stops if you backtrack south to join the **Karýtena–Andhrítsena route** and travel on to Olympia from there. Alternatively, if you're approaching Olympia from the north, through Arcadia from Pátra, then a pleasant staging post is the twin village of **LÁMBIA-DHÍVRI**, roughly halfway between Trípoli and Pátra. There is a good psistariá, *Iy Divri*, as well as the *Lambia Pension* (✆0624/81 205; ②), both of which enjoy fine views.

Andhrítsena and the Temple of Bassae

Moving west from Karýtena towards Andhrítsena, the Alfiós River falls away to the north and the hills become mountains – Lýkeo to the south and Mínthi to the west. The route, only slightly less remote than the twists of road around Dhimitsána, is a superb one for its own sake, with the added attractions of **Andhrítsena**, a traditional mountain town, and the **Temple of Apollo Epikourios** at **Bassae** up in the flanks of Mount Lýkeo.

Andhrítsena
ANDHRÍTSENA, 28km west of Karýtena, is a beautiful stop, and the traditional base from which to visit the Temple of Apollo at Bassae up in the mountains to the south.

Though very much a roadside settlement today, it too was a major hill town through the years of Turkish occupation and the first century of independent Greece. It remains remarkably untouched, with wooden houses spilling down to a stream, whose clear ice-cold headwaters are channelled into a fountain set within a plane tree in the central platía. There is a small **folk museum**, which opens on demand (200dr). Contact Vassiliki Tsigouri (☎0626/22 197) at the *Tsigouris* restaurant on a side-street near the plane tree.

Hotel accommodation is available only at the *Theoxenia* (☎0626/22 219; ⑤) on the Karýtena side of town. For **meals**, try any of the restaurants on the main platía, and especially the one up the steps beside the old (and closed) *Vassae* hotel.

The Temple of Apollo Epikourios at Bassae

Summer daily 8am–8pm (closes earlier in wimter); 500dr.

Fourteen kilometres into the mountains south from Andhrítsena, the **Temple of Apollo** at **BASSAE** (Vásses) is the most remote and arguably the most spectacular site in Greece. In addition, it is, after the Thiseion in Athens, the best-preserved Classical monument in the country, and for many years was considered to have been designed by Iktinos, architect of the Parthenon – though this theory has recently fallen from favour.

There the superlatives must cease. Romantic though the temple was in the past, for the forseeable future it is swathed in a gigantic grey marquee supported on metal girders and set in concrete with wire stays; its entablature and frieze lie dissected in neat rows on the ground to one side. No doubt the **restoration** is badly needed for its preservation – and the marquee is quite a sight in itself – but it has to be said that visitors are likely to be a bit disappointed. If you are not put off, take the Kréstena road out of town and then, almost immediately, turn off to the left and you begin the climb to the temple. The simplest approach is to share a taxi, which should charge 3500–4000dr for the round trip, waiting an hour at the site. On foot it's a tiring ascent, with little likelihood of a lift. The site is not enclosed, but has a full-time guardian who lives alongside. It's a lonely place, and must have felt even more isolated in ancient times.

The temple was erected in dedication to **Apollo Epikourios** ("the Succourer") by the Phigalians. It's known that they built it in gratitude for being spared from plague, but beyond this it is something of a puzzle. It is oddly aligned on a north–south axis and, being way up in the mountains, is only visible when you are comparatively near. There are oddities, too, in the architecture: the columns on its north side are strangely thicker than in the rest of the building, and incorporated into its *cella* was a single Corinthian column, the first known in Greece (though now vanished save for its base). Unusually again, the cult statue, probably a four-metre-high bronze, would have stood in front of this pillar.

Moving on from Bassae or Andhrítsena

Leaving the Bassae/Andhrítsena area, you've a number of choices. From Andhrítsena there are two daily **buses** back up towards Karýtena/Megalópoli and two down to Pýrgos. If you are headed for **Olympia**, take the Pýrgos bus and get off in Kréstena, from where you can hitch or take a taxi along the 12km side road up to the site. You'll certainly save time and maybe some money.

For the adventurous, a partly surfaced road winds through the mountains from Bassae down to the coast at **Tholó** (see p.244). It takes quite a while to cover the 46km and the road is pretty bumpy in places, but for the unhurried there's an opportunity to stop at Perivólia (10km) which is a surprisingly lively little place with a couple of restaurants, cafés and even a bar full of well-dressed youth. This mountain hamlet has a two-kilometre dirt road connecting it with the similarly diminutive Figália, close by the ruins of the enormous Classical walls of **ancient Phigalia**.

MESSINÍA:
KALAMÁTA TO KYPARISSÍA

The province of **MESSINÍA** stretches from the western flank of the Taïyetos ridge across the plain of **Kalamáta** to the hilly southwesternmost finger of the Peloponnese. Green, fertile and luxuriant for the most part, it's ringed with a series of well-preserved castles overlooking some of the area's most expansive beaches. The pale curve of sand at **Voïdhokiliá**, sandwiched between sea, rock and lagoon, is one of the most beautiful in Greece. Smaller beaches at **Koróni**, **Methóni** and **Finikoúnda** draw the crowds, but its important archeological sites, such as **Nestor's Palace** near Hóra, rarely see visitors in the quantity of the Argolid sites.

Kalamáta

KALAMÁTA is by far the largest city of the southern Peloponnese, spreading for some four kilometres back from the sea, and into the hills. It's quite a metropolitan shock after the small-town life of the rest of the region. The city has a long-established export trade in olives and figs from the Messinian plain, and, until recently, it had a prospering industrial base. In 1986, however, Kalamáta was near the epicentre of a severe **earthquake** that killed twenty people and left 12,000 families homeless. But for the fact that the quake struck in the early evening, when many people were outside, the death toll would have been much higher. As it was, large numbers of buildings were levelled throughout the town. The intensity of the damage was in part due to the city's position over several subterranean streams, but mostly, it seems, the legacy of poor 1960s construction. The result was an economic depression across the whole area, from which the town is only now recovering properly.

The City

Few visitors plan to linger here; however, if you are travelling for a while, it's a good place to get things done, and there are other simple pleasures such as eating at untouristy tavernas on the waterfront or around the centre, which comprises the wide avenue formed by Platía Yeoryíou and the larger Platía Konstandínou Dhiadhókhnou.

With a little time to fill, a twenty-minute walk north of the centre will bring you to the most pleasing area of the city, around the **Kástro**. Built by the Franks and destroyed and adapted in turn by the Turks and Venetians, the Kástro survived the quake with little damage; an **amphitheatre** at its base hosts summer concerts. A short way south of the Kástro on Benákiou is the excellent **Benaki Archeological Museum** (Tues–Sun 8am–2pm; 300dr), which houses a modest but well-labelled collection of tomb reliefs, sculptures and smaller artefacts from the surrounding areas, as well as a colourful Roman mosaic from Desylla.

Kalamáta's **beach,** along Navarínou, a ten-minute bus ride (#1) south of the centre, is always crowded along the central section. The gritty sands are functional but the harbour itself has a welcome touch of life and activity. If you prefer to walk to the harbour from the centre, it's a thirty-minute walk down Aristoménous, and you can wander in the park alongside the narrow bottom end of the street and admire the old steam engines, rolling stock and mechanical paraphernalia at the open-air Railway Museum.

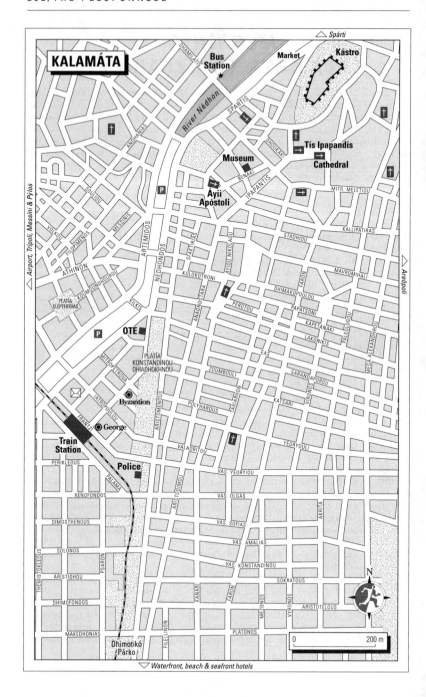

KALAMÁTA

Spárti △

Bus Station

Market

Kástro

Areópoli ▷

Airport, Tripoli, Messíni & Pýlos ◁

River Nédhon

DIAMILATIS

SPÁRTIS

DHOUKAKI

Tís Ipapandis

Museum

Cathedral

BENAKI

IPAPANTIS

MITR. MELETIOU

Áyii Apóstoli

ANDHANIAS

SOULIOU

VOLKOU

FLOMENOS

MESSINIS

ARTEMIDOS

NEDHONDOS

S. AKYIRAS

AYIOU NIKOLAOU

KOLOKOTRONI

STADHIOU

KALLIPATIRAS

MAVROMIHALI

FARON

DHIMAKOPOULOU

PAPATSONI

KAPETANAKI

LAKONIKIS

MEGA ALEXANDHROU

PALEOLOGOU

ATHINON

KOUMOUNDHOUROU

PLATÍA ELEFTHERÍAS

KILKIS

ANAGNOSTARA

PEROTOU

EAS

ZOUMBOULI

SARANDAPOROU

VIRONOS

KATSARI

TAXIARHON

POLYHAROUS

YEORYOULI

OTÉ

P

MITROPETROVA

IATROPOULOU

FRANTZI

PERIKLEOUS

PALAMA

PLATÍA KONSTANDÍNOU DHIADHÓKHNOU

Byzantion

George

Train Station

Police

VALAORITOU

VAS. YEORYIOU

ARISTOMENOUS

ARISTODIMOU

XENOFONDOS

DIMOSTHENOUS

SOLONOS

PSARON

THEMISTOKLEOUS

ARISTIDHOU

DHIMOFONDOS

MAKEDHONIAS

FILELLINON

KANARI

FARON

MEZONOS

VYRONOS

VAS. OLGAS

VAS. SOFIAS

VAS. AMALIAS

VAS. KONSTANDINOU

SOKRATOUS

AKRITA

ARISTOTELOUS

PLATONOS

N

0   200 m

Dhimotikó Párko

▽ Waterfront, beach & seafront hotels

Practicalities

If you're looking to get transport straight through, arrive early to make connections. The **bus station** is about 600m north of the centre; follow the river, partly covered with car-parks, along Nédhondos. The Wednesday/Saturday produce market is nearby, alongside the road to Spárti, and one of the region's most colourful. The most regular buses run north to Megalópoli and Trípoli and west to Messíni, Koróni or Pýlos; the magnificent route over the Taïyetos ridge to Spárti is covered twice daily, and the one to Kardhamýli, Stoúpa and Ítylo (connection to Areópoli) four times daily.

The **train station** is 300m to the west of Platía Konstandínou Dhiadhókhnou, on Frantzí. Kalamáta is the railhead for trains chugging along the pretty, but slow and at times uncomfortable, route to Kyparissía (and ultimately to Pátra, with a possible detour to Olympia) or inland even more scenically to Trípoli and Árgos. Anyone arriving by slow train from Athens or Trípoli, and heading towards Pýlos or Koróni by bus, could get off at **Aspróhoma** station and catch the buses nearby, to avoid the long transfer between rail and bus terminals in Kalamáta itself. There are three **flights** a week to and from Athens; tickets are sold at the Olympic Airways office across from the train station. The **airport** is 6km west on the road to Messíni, Pýlos and Koróni, and buses to these destinations pass the entrance. In season there are four charters a week from the UK, all on Sundays. The small terminal is remarkably clean and civilized, for a Greek airport, and has an automatic **exchange** machine.

Taxis usually meet trains; otherwise there is a taxi rank on Platía Konstandínou Dhiadhókhnou and another on Navarínou. Three rival agencies offer **car rental**: Maniatis, Iatropoúlou 1 (☎0721/27 694), Theodorakopoulos, Kessári 2 (☎0721/20 352), and Stavrianos, Nédhondos 89 (☎0721/23 041). There are two **moped rental** outlets: Bastakos, Fáron 190 (☎0721/26 638), and Alpha, Výronos 156 (☎0721/93 423).

Most facilities, including the **banks** and **post office**, are in the streets around Platía Konstandínou Dhiadhókhnou, though there is a second **post office** near the customs house at the seaward end of Aristoménous. In the summer, Hobby at Fáron 237 sells English-language newspapers and books.

Accommodation

In the city centre, there are very few mid-range **hotels** left. Two of the best in terms of value for money are the *George*, Frantzí 5 (☎0721/27 225; ④) and the larger *Byzantion*, Stathmoú 13 (☎0721/86 824; ③). Both belong to the same management, are very close to the train station, not too far from the buses, and have TV in all rooms. Otherwise you'll do better down by the waterfront, where there are many more hotels. Some of these are expensive, though they seem to have spent more on the reception areas than the bedrooms. Even so, they are often full by mid-afternoon and if you have not booked ahead, particularly at weekends, you may have to shop around.

Choices include the *Flisvos*, Navarínou 135 (☎0721/82 177; ③), which has quiet, comfortable rooms on the waterfront next to the church of Ayía Anástasi. Nearby and next to the platía, the *Haikos*, Navarínou 115 (☎0721/88 902; ④), is a modern hotel with pleasant rooms, TV, air-conditioning and helpful staff. The cosy *Nevada*, Santaróza 9 (☎0721/82 429; ②), is carefully tended by a Greek matriarch; there are a number of house rules (in Greek and interpreted by her son). There is no breakfast, but you can eat very cheaply on the waterfront close by.

The nearest **campsites** are to be found along the stretch of beach to the east of the city. The first, about 5km from the waterfront, is the *Elite* (☎0721/80 365; April–Oct). It is behind the *Hotel Elite* (☎0721/25 015; ③), where campers can eat, and swim in the pool. If you want to swim off the pebble beach you will have to cross the Areópoli–Kalamáta highway, or stay at the *Maria*, also known as the *Sea and Sun*, (☎0721/41 060), a popular and friendly campsite 500m down the road, which fronts onto the sea. However, unless you are stuck, you'd do better heading west towards Petalídhi (see following).

Eating and drinking

The best **restaurants** in the summer months are down by the **harbour**, which has been set up as a yacht marina. Moving from west to east, you have quite a selection: *Krini* at Evangelistrías 40, is a neighbourhood fish-and-wine taverna open most of the year; *Pyrofani* on Salamínos, west of the marina, has a large selection of meat and vegetarian dishes and good local wine; *Katofli* on Salamínos near the marina, has outdoor summer seating and a huge menu; *Meltemi*, near the corner of Navarínou and Fáron, is a basic psistariá with tasty food; *Tabaki*, Navarínou 91, features a wide menu and cheerful service; next door, the *Petrino* has a good selection of mezédhes. There is a well-priced café-ouzeri directly opposite the bus station.

Only in winter does the older **centre** of town get into its culinary stride. At this time, pick from *Kannas*, Lakonikís 18, an atmospheric place with occasional live music which featured in Sheelagh Kanelli's novel, *Earth and Water*, or *Kioupi*, Alexíki 52 (off the Areópoli road), idiosyncratically decorated and with clay-pot cooking (as the name implies). For afternoon or evening drinks, the cafés along the broad Platía Konstandínou Dhiadhókhnou are very pleasant, and less noisy with traffic than Navarínou. Round the corner, the pace heats up in the bars along Frantzí, towards the train station. There are several cinemas nearby, some with family entertainment.

If you're not after a full meal, Kalamáta has plenty of *mezedhopolía*, the better among them serving the traditional local snack – roast pork and potatoes. Down at the harbour, the ouzerí west of the post office does nice fish mezédhes; and there's another good one at the bottom of Fáron, *Diethnes*.

Ancient Messene

The ruins of ancient **MESSENE** (Ithómi) lie 25km northwest of Kalamáta and 20km northwest of modern Messíni. The ancient city was the fortified capital of the Messenians, and achieved some fame in the ancient world as a showcase of military architecture. The highlights of the widely dispersed site are the outcrops of its giant walls, towers and gates.

The ruins share the lower slopes of Mount Ithómi (800m) with the pretty village of **MAVROMÁTI**. A climb to the summit is rewarded with spectacular views of the region of Messinía and the southern Peloponnese. If you wish to stay and see the sunset from the site of the temple of Zeus which crowns this peak, there are **rooms** at the *Zeus* (☎0724/51 025; ①), a pension in the village.

The site is a tricky place to get to, unless you're driving. Buses run only twice a day from Kalamáta (earliest departure 6am). With a car it's a fairly easy detour en route to either Kyparissía, Pýlos or Petalídhi/Koróni.

The site

Messene's fortifications were designed as the southernmost link in a defensive chain of **walled cities** (others included Megalópolis and Árgos) masterminded by the Theban leader Epaminondas to keep the Spartans at bay. Having managed to halt them at the battle of Leuctra (near Stoúpa) in 371 BC, he set about building a nine-kilometre circuit of walls and restoring the Messenians to their native acropolis. The Messenians, who had resisted Spartan oppression from the eighth century BC onwards, wasted no time in re-establishing their capital; the city, so chronicles say, was built in 85 days.

The most interesting of the remains is the **Arcadia gate** at the north end of the site, through which the side road to Meligalás still runs. It consisted of an outer and inner portal separated by a circular courtyard made up of massive chunks of stone precisely cut to fit together without mortar. The outer gate, the foundations of which are fairly evident, was flanked by two square towers from where volleys of javelins and arrows would rain down on attackers. The inner gate, a similarly impregnable barrier, comprised a huge monolithic doorpost, half of which still stands. You can still trace the ruts of chariot wheels in paved stretches of ancient road within the gateway.

Further south, and signposted "Ithomi: Archeological site" on the road running northwest from Mavromáti, is a newly excavated **sanctuary of Asclepius**. This site, which was first mistakenly marked out as the *agora*, consisted of a temple surrounded by a porticoed courtyard. The bases of some of the colonnades have been unearthed along with traces of benches. Next to it you can make out the site of a theatre or meeting place. Excavations continue in the summer with archeologists digging in the shade of semi-permanent canopies.

Other remains are to be seen up Mount Ithómi, an hour's hike along a steep path forking north from the track at the Laconia gate, which is to the southeast of the site. Along the way you pass remains of an Ionic **temple of Artemis**. At the top, on the site of a temple of Zeus, are the ruins of the small **monastery of Vourkanó**, founded in the eighth century but dating in its present form from the sixteenth. Spread below are the lush and fertile valleys of Messinía.

Around the coast to Koróni

Beaches stretch for virtually the entire distance southwest from Kalamáta to Koróni, along what is steadily developing as a major resort coast. At present, however, it is more popular with Greeks than foreigners, and the resorts, tucked away in the pines, consist primarily of campsites, interspersed with the odd room for rent.

The beach at Boúka, 5km south of modern Messíni, is a fine stretch of sand with views of the Máni. It is popular with the locals, especially as a place to go for Sunday lunch. The best of the beaches are around **PETALÍDHI**, 25km west around the coast from Kalamáta. The small town itself is not unattractive and there are a couple of good **campsites**: *Petalidi Beach* (☎0722/31 154; April–Sept), 3km north of the village, is well established and reasonably priced; *Sun Beach* (☎0722/31 200; May–Oct), 500m south of the village, is not on the beach, which is reached by a subway under the road. There are ample tavernas and cafés around the spacious sea-facing square and some cheap rooms. Moving on south, if you have your own transport, there are numerous restaurants, rooms and hotels along the stretch of coast – and busy road – to Koróni. The *Kalami* and *Sokrates* tavernas in Khráni are recommended, the latter having very good mezédhes, and the *Sunrise Village* has an unusually good restaurant for a hotel.

Koróni and Methóni

The twin **fortresses** at Koróni and Methóni were the Venetians' oldest and longest-held possessions in the Peloponnese: strategic outposts on the route to Crete and known through the Middle Ages as "the eyes of the Serene Republic". Today they shelter two of the more attractive small resorts in the south.

Public transport around the Messinian peninsula has improved of late and there are good connections between Kalamáta and Koróni, or Pýlos, with several buses a day from Pýlos to Methóni and Finikoúnda. Direct connections between Methóni and Koróni are still elusive, although a new fast road has been built from Koróni via Vasilítsi to Finikoúnda, and is being continued along the coast to Methóni.

Koróni

KORÓNI has one of the most picturesque sites in Greece, stacked against a fortified bluff and commanding grand views across the Messenian gulf to the Taïyetos peaks. The town is beautiful in itself, with tiled and pastel-washed houses arrayed in a maze of stair-and-ramp streets that can have changed little since the medieval Venetian occupation. Buses terminate in the square below the main church, outside an excellent zaharoplastía and one row back from the waterfront. Koróni's **citadel** is one of the least militaristic-looking in Greece, crowning rather than dwarfing the town. Much of the interior is given over to private houses and garden plots, but the greater part is occupied by the flower-strewn nunnery of **Timíou Prodhrómou**, whose chapels, outbuildings and gardens occupy nearly every bastion.

From the southwest gate of the fortress, stairs descend to the park-like grounds of **Panayía Elestrías**, a church erected at the end of the last century to house a miraculous icon – unearthed with the assistance of the vision of one Maria Stathaki (buried close by). The whole arrangement, with fountains, shrubbery and benches for watching the sunset seems more like the Adriatic than the Aegean.

Continuing downhill, you reach **Zánga beach**, a two-kilometre stretch of sand and preternaturally clear water that sets the seal on Koróni's superiority as a place to relax, drink wine and amble about a countryside lush with vineyards, olives and banana trees. Turtles nest in the area.

Practicalities

To be sure of a room in summer, it's worth trying to phone ahead. The only large hotel, the *Hotel de la Plage* (☎0725/22 401; ⑤) is way out on the road towards Mémi beach. Looking for **private rooms** on arrival, try the places to the right of the fishing port as you face the water, and don't leave it too late in the day; there are also cheaper, quieter rooms in Panórama district, up behind Zánga beach. Several of the town tavernas rent rooms on a regular basis, including the *Parthenon* (☎0725/22 146; ②) near the port and the *Pension Koroni* (☎0725/22 385; ②) above the *Symposium* restaurant on the main street. An attractive and slightly more expensive option, with a leafy setting and views of the bay and castle, is *Marinos Bungalows* (☎0725/22 522; ③) on the road north out of town. There are two **campsites**: *Memi Beach* (☎0725/22 130; May–Oct) is 2km before Koróni as you approach from Petalídhi or Methóni, and *Koroni* (☎0725/22 119; May–Sept) on the road into town; both have sandy beaches, though from *Memi Beach* you have to cross the road.

There is a reasonable selection of **restaurants** on the waterfront, and some authentic **tavernas** (barrel-wine and oven-food places) along the main shopping street. The *Parthenon* has good food and efficient service, and the *Symposium* serves moussaka, grills and seafood. The *Flisvos* remains a good restaurant despite its closure as a hotel.

Many people make wine or rakí in their basement and the heady local tipple figures prominently in the nightlife. There are two or three tavernas on the beach and by night a solitary disco, though all of these close down by mid-September. Otherwise, there are two **banks** for money matters and a **post office**. The main venue for nightlife is the sprawling *Astra Club* out towards Mémi beach.

Finikoúnda

FINIKOÚNDA, 20km west of Koróni, is a small fishing village with a superb cove-beach plus another to the east, and a gigantic strand to the west. Over recent years it gained a reputation as a backpackers' – and especially windsurfers' – resort, with half the summer intake at a pair of campsites on either side of the village, the others housed in a variety of rooms including some taken by British package companies. It can be a fun, laid-back place.

To book **rooms** in advance, try the **hotels** *Finikounda* (☎ & fax 0723/71 208; ④) and *Porto Finissia* (☎0723/71 358, fax 71 458; ④; summer only), or the hospitable *Korakakis Beach* (☎0723/71 221, fax 71 232; ④) which also has self-catering apartments with air-conditioning at similar prices. The local **campsites** are the well-equipped *Anemomilos* (☎0723/71 360, fax 71 121; all year), 500m west of town, *Ammos* (☎0723/71 262; May–Oct), 3km west of the village, and the *Loutsa* (☎0723/71 445; June–Sept), 2km to the east. Among the **tavernas**, *Elena* is recommended for good traditional fare and for a drink with a harbour view, while *Psychos* has tasty food, including pasta and pizzas, at good prices; *Theasis* features a mixture of old and new rock **music**.

Methóni

In contrast to the almost domestic citadel at Koróni, the fortress at **METHÓNI** is as imposing as they come – massively bastioned, washed on three sides by the sea, and cut off altogether from the land by a great moat. It was maintained by the Venetians in part for its military function, in part as a staging post for pilgrims en route, via Crete and Cyprus, to the Holy Land, and from the thirteenth to the nineteenth centuries it sheltered a substantial town.

Within the **fortress** (Mon–Sat 8am–8pm, Sun 9am–8pm; closes 3pm in winter; free), entered across the moat along a stone bridge, are the remains of a Venetian cathedral (the Venetians' Lion of St Mark emblem is ubiquitous), along with a Turkish bath, the foundations of dozens of houses and some awesome underground passages, the last mostly cordoned off. Walking around the walls, a sea gate at the southern end leads out across a causeway to the **Boúrtzi**, a small fortified island. The octagonal tower was built by the Turks in the sixteenth century to replace an earlier Venetian fortification. Unusually, and for no obvious reason, photography is forbidden inside the site – probably because of archeological excavations; it seems unlikely that the Greek military regard it as still of strategic significance.

Practicalities

The modern village, on the landward side of the moat, has a **bank** and **post office**, all easily located in the three-street-wide grid. The bus stops at the first forked junction in town; there is a timetable in a nearby shop window. The rather scruffy beach runs eastwards from the castle. In high season, there may be boat trips out to the southern islands.

Methóni is geared more conspicuously to tourism than Koróni and gets very crowded in season, when accommodation can be expensive and often oversubscribed. Out of season, the **hotels** are cheaper and a number stay open all year. The well-priced *Castello* (☎0723/31 300; ③) is near the entrance to the fortress, with beautiful gardens, balconies and a stunning view; the friendly *Aris* (☎0723/31 336; ④) is on a small platía behind *Castello*. The recently renovated *Anna* (☎0723/31 332; ④) is also friendly – all rooms have TV and there's a good restaurant. In addition, there is the usual collection of cheaper **rooms** such as the *Mintziras* (☎0723/31123; ②) on the hill. At the east end of the beach is a municipal **campsite**, the *Methoni* (☎0723/31 228; May–Oct); it's popular and gets crowded, but the facilities are good and the beach tolerable.

Methóni has several **restaurants**, including the slightly pricey *Klimataria* (☎0723/31 544; May–Oct, evenings only), which serves a well-prepared selection of dishes (including good veggie choices) in a courtyard garden. At the adequate *Rex*, which is open all day, you can eat in the shade of tamarisk trees. Among the dozen or so other eateries, *Inousses* 150m along the beach is also recommended for waterfront dining.

Pýlos and around

PÝLOS (Pýlos) is a little like a small-scale, less sophisticated Náfplio – quite a stylish town for rural Messinía. It is guarded by a pair of medieval castles and occupies a superb position on one of the finest natural harbours in Greece, the landlocked **Navarino Bay** (see box on p.240). Given the town's romantic associations with the Battle of Navarino,

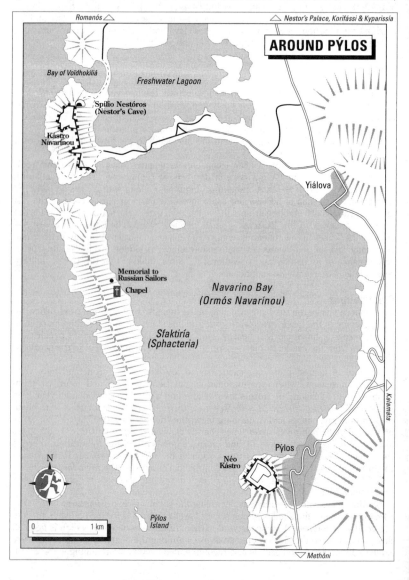

AROUND PÝLOS

Romanós △

△ Nestor's Palace, Korifássi & Kyparissía

Bay of Voïdhokiliá

Freshwater Lagoon

Spílio Nestóros
(Nestor's Cave)

Kástro
Navarínou

Yiálova

Memorial to
Russian Sailors

Chapel

Navarino Bay
(Ormós Navarínou)

Sfaktiría
(Sphacteria)

Kalamáta ▷

Pýlos

Néo
Kástro

N

0   1 km

Pýlos
Island

▽ Methóni

and, more anciently, with Homer's "sandy Pylos", the domain of "wise King Nestor" whose palace (see p.241) has been identified 16km to the north, a better base for exploring this part of the Peloponnese is hard to imagine – particularly if equipped with a car or moped (both for rent here). Relying on public transport, however, you'll find the long afternoon gaps in services make complex day-trips impractical.

The Town

The main pleasures of Pýlos are exploring the hillside alleys, waterside streets and fortress. Getting your bearings is easy as it's not a large town, and buses drop you at the inland end of the central Platía Tríon Navárhon which faces the port.

Shaded by a vast plane tree and scented by limes, **Platía Tríon Navárhon** is a beautiful public platía, completely encircled by cafés and very much the heart of the town. At its centre is a **war memorial** commemorating admirals Codrington, de Rigny and von Heyden, who commanded the British, French and Russian forces in the Battle of Navarino (see box on p.240). Nearby, just uphill on the Methóni road, the little **Antonopouleion Museum** (Tues–Sun 8am–2.30pm; 500dr) boasts remains from the battle, along with archeological finds from the region.

Further memories of the Navarino battles can be evoked by a visit to the **island of Sfaktiría**, across the bay, where there are various tombs of Philhellenes, a chapel and a memorial to the Russian sailors.

The principal sight in town, however, is the **Néo Kástro** (Tues–Sun 8.30am–3pm; 800dr), close by the port on the south side of the bay (further up the Methóni road). The hugely spreading "new castle" was built by the Turks in 1572, and allows a walk around much of the 1500m of arcaded battlements, although unsafe segments are now closed. For much of the eighteenth and nineteenth centuries, it served as a prison and its inner courtyard was divided into a warren of narrow yards separated by high walls, a design completely at odds with most Greek prisons, which were fairly open on the inside. This peculiar feature is explained by the garrison's proximity to the Máni. So frequently was it filled with Maniots imprisoned for vendettas, and so great was the crop of internal murders, that these pens had to be built to keep the imprisoned clansmen apart. The pens and walls have been pulled down as part of an ongoing programme to restore and convert the castle into a planned **museum** for underwater archeology. So far, the only attraction is a collection of René Puaux pictures of the 1821 revolution.

Practicalities

The National Bank is to be found on the central platía, and the **post office** just west from the bus station, on Niléos. **Mopeds** and **cars**, ideal for taking in both Methóni and Nestor's Palace, are available through AutoEurope (☎0723/22 393, fax 23 400) on the Kalamáta road. Mopeds and motorbikes can also be rented from Sapienza Travel (☎0723/23 207) near the *Miramare* (see below), and cars from the *Miramare* itself. You can hire a **boat** from the port to visit Sfaktiría island, where you can snorkel and see the remains of the Turkish fleet lying on the sea bed; ask at the harbourmaster's office or cafés by the port.

Pýlos has somewhat limited accommodation and in the summer months you should definitely try to phone ahead. Among the **hotels**, the friendly, air-conditioned *Arvaniti* (☎0723/23 050, fax 22 934; ②; March–Oct) – up beyond the post office on Niléos – is the best value. The rather faded *Galaxy*, on the platía (☎0723/22 780; ④), is a fall-back choice if the *Arvaniti* is closed or full, as is the posher *Karalis*, Kalamátas 26 (☎0723/22 960, fax 22 970; ④), an attractive seaview hotel with a good restaurant. The *Miramare*, Myrtidhiotíssis 35 (☎0723/22 751; ⑥), has a restaurant and bar and fine views by the

---

THE BATTLES OF NAVARINO BAY

Arriving at Pýlos your gaze is inevitably drawn to the bay, almost landlocked by the long offshore island of Sfaktiría (Sphacteria). Its name, Ormós Navarínou – Navarino Bay – marks the battle that effectively sealed Greek independence from the Turks on the night of October 20, 1827, though the battle itself seems to have been accidental. The Great Powers of Britain, France and Russia, having established diplomatic relations with the Greek insurgent leaders, were attempting to force an armistice on the Turks. To this end they sent a fleet of 27 warships to Navarino, where Ibrahim Pasha had gathered his forces – 16,000 men in 89 ships. The declared intention was to coerce Ibrahim into leaving Messinía, which he had been raiding.

In the confusion of the night an Egyptian frigate, part of the Turks' supporting force, fired its cannons, and full-scale battle broke out. Without intending to take up arms for the Greeks, the "allies" responded to attack and, extraordinarily, sank and destroyed 53 of the Turkish fleet without a single loss. There was considerable international embarrassment when news filtered through to the "victors" but the action had nevertheless ended effective Turkish control of Greek waters and within a year Greek independence was secured and recognized.

Navarino Bay also features in one of the most famous battles of Classical times, described in great detail by Thucydides. In 425 BC, during the Peloponnesian War, an Athenian force encamped in Kástro Navarínou (the old castle of Pýlos) laid siege to a group of Spartans on the island of **Sfaktiría**, just across the straits. In a complete break with tradition, which decreed fighting to the death, the Spartans surrendered. "Nothing that happened in the war surprised the Hellenes as much as this," commented Thucydides.

---

port, but is also closed between October and March. There are many rooms around the winding main road on the hill out towards Kalamáta and Kyparissía.

For **drinks**, the Platía Tríon Navárhon cafés are the obvious choice. Among **tavernas**, try *Grigori's*, on the road up left of the police station on the platía; the *Lykourgos* opposite is also good. Nightlife revolves around bars on the square, and the larger, summer-only discos *Gigi's* and *Zoglo Summer Matter*, both a little out of town. There is also a summer outdoor cinema.

The northern rim of Navarino Bay

Pýlos's northern castle, and ancient acropolis, **Kástro Navarínou** (Paleó Kástro), stands on a hill ridge almost touching the island of Sfaktiría, at the end of the bay. It has substantial walls, and identifiable courtyards and cisterns within fortifications which are a mix of Frankish and Venetian, set upon ancient foundations. It's a ten- to twelve-kilometre trip from the town, for which you'll need some transport. To get there, follow the main road north towards Hóra, but when the road swings right to Korifássi, go left on a side road signed to Romanós and Navarino castle. If you find your way, you will end up at one of the best beaches in the Peloponnese – a lovely sweep of sand curling around the spectacular **bay of Voïdhokiliá**. A simpler alternative is to go north through Yiálova, turn left at the sign to Voïdhokiliá and Golden Beach (the Pýlos–Hóra bus will bring you this far); at the end of the paved road, near Golden Beach's seasonal café, go left until the dirt road ends below the castle hill. From here go right with the footpath between the lagoon and the hill until you reach the dunes and beach. The lagoons have been proposed as an important bird conservation area for NATURA 2000, and it is strongly recommended that vehicles are not driven on the road around the eastern rim of the lagoon.

A path from the beach ascends to the **Spílio toú Nestóros** (Nestor's Cave), and then more steeply up to the castle. This impressive bat-cave with a hole in the roof is fancifully identified as the grotto in which, according to the *Odyssey*, Nestor and Neleus kept their cows, and in which Hermes hid Apollo's cattle. It is not impossible that the cave sparked Homer's imagination, for this area is reckoned by archeologists to have been the Mycenaean-era harbour of King Nestor (see below).

The Bay of Navarino encompasses a couple of additional **beaches** and hamlets. **YIÁLOVA**, 6km out of Pýlos and the first resort around the bay, has tamarisk trees shading the sands, the *Navarino Beach* **campsite** (☎0723/22 761; April–Oct), with good facilities including a recommended restaurant. Nearer the centre there are two **hotels** – the delightful *Zoe* (☎0723/22 025; ④) which has the *Voula Apartments* (④) back towards Pýlos, and *Helonaki House* (☎0723/23 080; ②) with a variety of rooms and apartments for rent. Just north of here, the beach of **Maïstrós** is a popular windsurfing strip. For eating, you can't beat the excellent home cooking at *Oasis* by the corner of the pier, with a good view across the bay.

North to Nestor's Palace

Nestor's Palace (also known as the Palace of Englianós, after the hill on which it stands) was discovered in 1939, but left virtually undisturbed until after World War II; thus its excavation – unlike Mycenae, or most of the other major Greek sites – was conducted in accordance with modern archeological techniques. In consequence, its remains are the best preserved of all the Mycenaean royal palaces, though they shelter rather prosaically beneath a giant metal roof. The site guide by Carl Blegen and Marion Rawson is an excellent buy.

The palace is located some 16km from modern Pýlos, a half-hour drive. Using public transport, take any of the **buses** from Pýlos towards Kyparissía; these follow the main road inland past Korifássi to the site and its museum at Hóra (4km to the east).

The palace site

Flanked by deep, fertile valleys, the **palace site** (Tues–Sun 8.30am–3pm; 500dr) looks out towards Navarino Bay – a location perfectly suiting the wise, measured and peaceful king described in Homer's *Odyssey*. The scene from the epic that is set here is the visit of Telemachus, son of Odysseus, who had journeyed from Ithaca to seek news of his father from King Nestor. As Telemachus arrives at the beach, accompanied by the disguised goddess Pallas Athena, he comes upon Nestor with his sons and court making a sacrifice to Poseidon. The visitors are welcomed and feasted, "sitting on downy fleeces on the sand", and although the king has no news of Odysseus he promises Telemachus a chariot so he can enquire from Menelaus at Sparta. First, however, the guests are taken back to the palace, where Telemachus is given a bath by Nestor's "youngest grown daughter, beautiful Polycaste", and emerges, anointed with oil, "with the body of an immortal".

By some harmonious twist of fate, a bathtub was unearthed on the site, and the palace ruins as a whole are potent ground for Homeric imaginings. The walls stand a metre high, enabling you to make out a very full plan. Originally, they were half-timbered (like Tudor houses), with upper sections of sun-baked brick held together by vertical and horizontal beams, and brilliant frescoes within. Even in their diminished state they suggest a building of considerable prestige. No less should be expected, for Nestor sent the second largest contingent to Troy – a fleet of "ninety black ships". The remains of the massive complex are in three principal groups: the **main palace** in the middle, on the left an earlier and **smaller palace**, and on the right either **guardhouses** or **workshops**.

The basic design will be familiar if you've been to Mycenae or Tiryns: an internal court, guarded by a sentry box, gives access to the main sections of the principal palace. This contained some 45 rooms and halls. The **megaron** (throne room), with its characteristic open hearth, lies directly ahead of the entrance, through a double porch. The finest of the frescoes was discovered here, depicting a griffin (perhaps the royal emblem) standing guard over the throne; this is now in the museum at Hóra. Arranged around are domestic quarters and **storerooms**, which yielded literally thousands of pots and cups during excavations; the rooms may have served as a distribution centre for the produce of the palace workshops. Further back, the famous **bathroom**, with its terracotta tub in situ, adjoins a smaller complex of rooms, centred on another, smaller megaron, identified as the **queen's quarters**. Finally, on the other side of the car park there is a *tholos* (beehive) tomb, a smaller version of the famous ones at Mycenae.

Archeologically, the most important find at the site was a group of several hundred tablets inscribed in **Linear B**. These were discovered on the first day of digging, in the two small rooms to the left of the entrance courtyard. They were the first such inscriptions to be discovered on the Greek mainland and proved conclusively a link between the Mycenaean and Minoan civilizations; like those found by Sir Arthur Evans at Knossos on Crete, the language was unmistakably Greek. The tablets were baked hard in the fire which destroyed the palace around 1200 BC, perhaps as little as one generation after the fall of Troy.

The museum at Hóra

At Hóra, the **museum** (Tues–Sun 8am–2.30pm, but can be erratic; 500dr) on S. Marinátou, signed above the main square, adds significantly to a visit to the site. If you've no transport, it might be better to take a bus here first, to the central bus station stop, and then walk the 45 minutes to the site after viewing the exhibits. In spring or autumn this is a pleasure; shy golden orioles have been seen in trees alongside the road. In hot weather, or if pressed for time, you can hitch fairly easily or get a taxi.

Pride of place in the display goes to the **palace frescoes**, one of which, bearing out Homer's descriptions, shows a warrior in a boar-tusk helmet. Lesser finds include much pottery, some beautiful gold cups and other objects gathered both from the site and from various Mycenaean tombs in the region.

The coast north of Pýlos

The stretch of **coast** between Pýlos and Pýrgos is defined by its **beaches**, which are on a different scale to those elsewhere in the Peloponnese, or indeed anywhere else in Greece – fine sands, long enough (and undeveloped enough) to satisfy the most jaded Australian or Californian. Their relative anonymity is something of a mystery, though one accounted for in part by the poor communications. For those without transport this entails slow and patient progress along the main "coast" road, which for much of the way runs two to five kilometres inland, and a walk from road junction to beach.

Heading north from the Bay of Voïdhokiliá, near the turning inland to Korifássi and Nestor's Palace, you can take a beautiful recently paved road, flanked by orange and olive orchards. This keeps close to the sea for most of the way to Kyparissía, allowing access to isolated beaches and villages.

If you're travelling to Olympia by **train** from this coast, you can save the detour to Pýrgos (not an exhilarating town – see p.252) by getting a connection at Alfiós, a tiny station at the junction of the Olympia line and as bucolic a halt as any on the network.

Marathópoli and Filiatrá

If you are looking for the rudiments of accommodation and a little more than a village café then Marathópoli holds most promise. **MARATHÓPOLI** has a long beach, rockier than most along this coast and facing the little islet of Próti. It has two **hotels**: on the beach, the *Artina* (☎0723/61 400; ④) has en-suite facilities and should be booked in advance; in the village, the *Rania* (☎0723/61 404; ④) is a new hotel which opens all year. The rooms all have small kitchenettes. There are some **rooms** for rent; a **campsite**, *Proti* (☎0723/61 211; May–Oct), with a swimming pool on account of the rocky beach; and two or three summer tavernas by the sea. A small taxi boat makes the short crossing to the islet of Próti, with its sandy beach and monastery, for a reasonable fixed rate.

Further on the road passes through Ayía Kyriakí, a fishing village with a sweet little harbour and a few rooms, before reaching **FILIATRÁ**, which is on the bus route between Pýlos and Kyparissía. By a curious pattern of emigration, just as Kýthira is home to Greek-Australians, the villages along the Kyparissía coast have a concentration of returned Greek-Americans, virtually all of them having done a stint of work in New York or New Jersey. Disgraced American ex-Vice President (1968–73) Spiro Agnew was perhaps the most infamous local boy. However, the Greek-American who has left most mark on his home domain is one Haris Fournakis, also known as **Harry Fournier**, a doctor from Chicago who came back in the 1960s and started building his fantasies. At the northern entrance to Filiatrá, Fournier constructed a garden-furniture version of the **Eiffel Tower** (illuminated at night by fairy lights) and a mini-replica of the globe from the 1964 New York Expo. His most ambitious project, however, was his **Kástro tón Paramythíon** ("Castle of the Fairytales"; 9am–2pm & 5pm–8pm; 500dr), a truly loopy folly with white concrete battlements and outcrops of towers, plus thirty- to forty-foot-high statues of Poseidon's horse (flanked by vases of flowers) and the goddess Athena. The castle is located right on the sea, and can be reached from Filiatrá by following the road for 6km north, through the hamlet of Agríli. Apart from Fournier's castle, the only feature of the town is the pleasant central square with a large, functioning fountain, the bus station and numerous cafés. There is little to detain you, but there is one **hotel**, in the town itself, the recently renovated *Trifylia* (☎0761/34 290; ②) which is more like a pension, though the rooms have en-suite facilities including a small kitchenette and TV. There is no good beach.

Kyparissía

KYPARISSÍA is a small, congenial market town, positioned in the shadow of the eponymous peak, part of the spectacular Egáleo mountain ridge. On a lower outcrop of the range is a Byzantine-Frankish **castle** (free), around which spreads the **old town**. The ochre-hued mansions stand abandoned, having suffered heavy damage in the civil war, though a couple of tavernas still function here, lovely old places and very welcoming.

Below the hill, the modern town goes about its business, with a small harbour and real shops. A few tourist boutiques and a night club or two have sprung up recently, but it's still a pleasant place to rest up, and possibly preferable to a night in Kalamáta if you're on your way to Olympia by bus or train (Kyparissía is the junction of the Kalamáta and Pýrgos lines). Within walking distance of town are long, near-deserted sands and rocky cliff paths.

Practicalities

The centre of the modern town, just south of the adjacent bus and train stations, is Platía Kalantzákou, where you'll find three **banks**, the **post office** and numerous cafés. Accommodation consists of a half-dozen **hotels**, divided between the modern town and the beach. The cheapest place to stay in town is the *Trifolia*, 25-Martíou 40 (☎0761/22 066; ①), just east of the square, towards the market, a down-to-earth and welcoming pension. Other hotels are the *Vasilikon*, Alexopoúlou 7 (☎0761/22 655; ②), further east above the large church, which is well kept, though without any particular charm, and the comfortable *Ionion* (☎0761/22 511, fax 22 512; ④), facing the train station. By the beach there is the **campsite**, *Kyparissia* (☎0761/23 491); beyond this beach, over a small rocky headland is a better beach used by naturists, though with strong currents at times. There are a handful of no-nonsense **restaurants** and pizzerias in Platía Kalantzákou and in the adjacent streets; one of the best is *Nynio*, at 25-Martíou 52. For atmosphere it's better to eat down at the beach, where the taverna *Ta Porákia*, towards the campsite, is a fine choice, or up at the old town, where the liveliest place to eat is the *Psistariá Arcadia*.

Beaches north from Kyparissía

Between Kyparissía and Lake Kaïáfas, the road and rail lines continue, a kilometre or so back from the coast, with the occasional **campsite** advertising its particular stretch of beach. These include the *Apollo Village* (☎0625/61 200; May–Oct) at **Yianitsohóri** (18km along), and a better site at **Tholó** (8km further on) – the *Tholo Beach* (☎0625/61 345; March–Oct). Neohóri, just past Tholó, has a few rooms to rent, as does Yianitsohóri. Just south of there, unofficial camping in the pine forest behind the beach at Eliá is possible. On the beach itself there's an ecological kiosk with information about the turtles that nest there; behind the forest there's a good shady taverna, *O Mythos*.

All of the hamlets on this coast have superb stretches of sandy beach, edged with olive groves, reed-beds or pinewoods – their lack of development seems almost miraculous. One of the nicest of all the beaches is at **KAKÓVATOS** (5km beyond Tholó), which combines breakers with incredibly shallow, slowly shelving waters. The area is slightly more commercialized now with the *Grigoris* taverna and the *Baywatch* café (complete with watchtower) on the beach, while the village has a number of pensions, including *Kallifidhas* (☎0625/31 167; ②) and *Timoleon* (☎0625/32 253; ③).

Just north, at **ZAHÁRO**, the largest town between Kyparissía and Pýrgos, and a train stop, there are a numerous shops and four **hotels**. Near the main crossroads, on the railway station side, are the *Rex* (☎0625/31 221; ③) with kitchenettes in some of its rooms. The *Nestor* (☎0625/31 206; ③) has clean rooms and old-fashioned hospitality; while the *Sugar Town* (☎0625/31 985; ④) opposite is newer and above a café. The *Diethnes* (☎0625/31 208; ②) is near the church at the top, inland end of the village. The railway station is just under a kilometre from the crossroads, on the road to the sea; midway from the station to the excellent beach is the *Banana Place* (☎0625/34 400; ③; April to Oct), which offers chalet-type accommodation with cooking facilities – booking is advisable. Afternoon buses through the Zaháro bus station – east of the crossroads and right – are few and far between; the Zaháro **taxis** are on ☎0625/31357.

Another enormous strand, backed by sand dunes and pine groves, is to be found just before the roads loop inland at **Kaïáfas**. At the beach there's just a single, rather uninspired taverna and the train station. A couple of kilometres inland, however, the village of **LOUTRÁ KAÏÁFAS** assumes the atmosphere of a spa. Strung out alongside the lagoon are a dozen or so hotels and pensions, frequented mainly by Greeks seeking hydrotherapy cures. Each morning a small shuttle-boat takes the patients from their hotels to the hot springs across the lagoon. The best deal for accommodation is probably at the friendly *Hotel Jenny* (☎0625/32 234; ②), which also has a decent restaurant. Two kilometres north of the lake, as the national road loops around a spur in the hills, you can just make out the walls of ancient Samikón on the hillside.

Olympia (Olymbía)

The historic associations and resonance of **OLYMPIA**, which for over a millennium hosted the most important **Panhellenic games**, are rivalled only by Delphi or Mycenae. It is
one of the largest and most beautiful sites in Greece, and the setting is as perfect as could
be imagined: a luxuriant valley of wild olive and plane trees, spread beside twin rivers of
Alfiós (Alpheus) and Kládhios, and overlooked by the pine-covered hill of Krónos. Sadly,
the actual ruins of the sanctuary are jumbled and confusing, and seem to cry out for reconstruction, even on a modest scale. The great temple columns lie half-buried amid the trees
and undergrowth: picturesque and shaded, perfect ground for picnics, but offering little
real impression of their ancient grandeur or function. Their fame, however, prevails over
circumstance, and walking through the arch from the sanctuary to the stadium it is hard
not to feel in awe of the Olympian history. Despite the crowds, the tour buses, the souvenir
shops and other trappings of mass tourism, it demands and deserves a lengthy visit.

The modern village of Olymbía acts as a service centre for the site, and has little in
the way of distractions, save a somewhat dutiful **Museum of the Olympic Games**
(Mon–Sat 8am–3.30pm, Sun 9am–4pm; 500dr), on the street above the *Hotel Phedias*,
with commemorative postage stamps and the odd memento from the modern games,
including the box that conveyed the heart of Pierre de Coubertin (reviver of the modern games) from Paris to its burial at Olympia.

The site

*Daily: May to mid-Oct 8am–7pm (Aug till 9pm; Sept till 8pm); mid-Oct to April
8am–5pm, Sat & Sun 8.30am–3pm; 1200dr.*

From its beginnings the site was a sanctuary, with a permanent population limited to
the temple priests. At first the games took place within the sacred precinct, the walled,
rectangular **Altis**, but as events became more sophisticated a new **stadium** was built
to adjoin it. The whole sanctuary was, throughout its history, a treasure trove of public
and religious statuary. Victors were allowed to erect a statue in the Altis (in their like-
ness if they won three events) and numerous city-states installed treasuries. Pausanias,
writing in the second century AD, after the Romans had already looted the sanctuary
several times, fills almost a whole book of his *Guide to Greece* with descriptions.

The entrance to the site leads along the west side of the **Altis wall**, past a group of
public and official buildings. On the left, beyond some Roman baths, is the **Prytaneion**,
the administrators' residence where athletes were lodged and feasted at official
expense. On the right are the ruins of a **gymnasium** and a **palaestra** (wrestling
school), used by the competitors during their obligatory month of pre-games training.

Beyond these stood the Priests' House, the **Theokoleion**, a substantial colonnaded
building in the southeast corner of which is a structure adapted as a Byzantine church.
This was originally the **studio of Pheidias**, the fifth-century BC sculptor responsible
for the great cult statue in Olympia's Temple of Zeus. It was identified by following a
description by Pausanias, and through the discovery of tools, moulds for the statue and
a cup engraved with the sculptor's name. The studio's dimensions and orientation are
exactly those of the *cella* in which the statue was to be placed, in order that the final
effect and lighting matched the sculptor's intentions.

To the south of the studio lie further administrative buildings, including the
Leonidaion, a large and doubtless luxurious hostel endowed for the most important of
the festival guests. It was the first building visitors would reach along the original
approach road to the site.

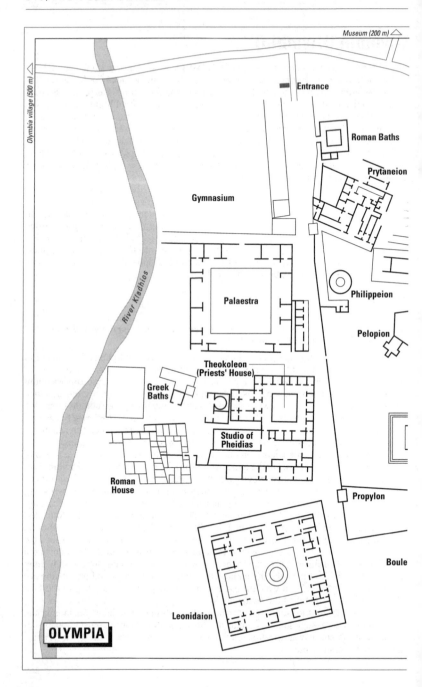

Museum (200 m) △

Olympia village (500 m) ◁

Entrance

Roman Baths

Prytaneion

Gymnasium

River Kladhios

Palaestra

Philippeion

Pelopion

Theokoleon
(Priests' House)

Greek
Baths

Studio of
Pheidias

Roman
House

Propylon

Boule

Leonidaion

OLYMPIA

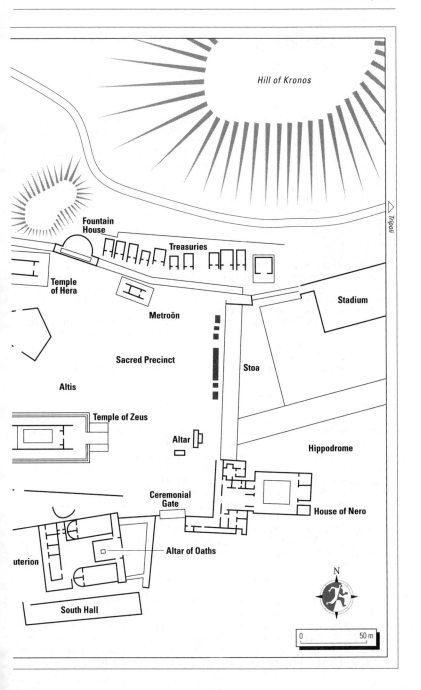

Hill of Kronos

Tripoli

Fountain House

Treasuries

Temple of Hera

Metroön

Stadium

Sacred Precinct

Stoa

Altis

Temple of Zeus

Altar

Hippodrome

Ceremonial Gate

House of Nero

Altar of Oaths

uterion

South Hall

N

0   50 m

THE OLYMPIC GAMES: SOME HISTORY

The origins of the games at Olympia are rooted in **legends** – the most predominant relating to the god **Pelops**, revered in the region before his eclipse by Zeus, and to Hercules (**Herakles**), one of the earliest victors. Historically, the contests probably began around the eleventh century BC, growing over the next two centuries from a local festival to the quadrennial celebration attended by states from throughout the Greek world.

The impetus for this change seems to have come from the **Oracle of Delphi**, which, with the local ruler of Elis, **Iphitos**, and the Spartan ruler **Lykourgos**, helped to codify the Olympic rules in the ninth century BC. Among their most important introductions was a **sacred truce**, the *Ekeheiria*, announced by heralds prior to the celebrations and enforced for their duration. It was virtually unbroken throughout the games' history (Sparta, ironically, was fined at one point) and as host of the games, Elis, a comparatively weak state, was able to keep itself away from political disputes, meanwhile growing rich on the associated trade and kudos.

From the beginning, the main Olympic **events** were athletic. The earliest was a race over the course of the stadium – roughly 200m. Later came the introduction of two-lap (400m) and 24-lap (5000m) races, along with the most revered of the Olympiad events, the **pentathlon**. This encompassed running, jumping, discus and javelin events, the competitors gradually reduced to a final pair for a wrestling-and-boxing combat. It was, like much of these early Olympiads, a fairly brutal contest. More brutal still was the **pancratium**, introduced in 680 BC and one of the most prestigious events. *Pancratium* contestants fought each other, naked and unarmed, using any means except biting or gouging each others' eyes; the olive wreath had on one occasion to be awarded posthumously, the victor having died at the moment of his opponent's submission. Similarly, the **chariot races**, introduced in the same year, were extreme tests of strength and control, only one team in twenty completing the seven-kilometre course without mishap.

The great gathering of people and nations at the festival extended the games' importance and purpose well beyond the winning of olive wreaths; assembled under the temporary truce, **nobles** and **ambassadors** negotiated treaties, while **merchants** chased

The Altis

Admission to the **Altis** was in the earlier centuries of the games limited to free-born Greeks – whether spectators or competitors. Throughout its history it was a male-only preserve, save for the sanctuary's priestess. An Olympian anecdote records how a woman from Rhodes disguised herself as her son's trainer to gain admission, but revealed her identity in joy at his victory. She was spared the legislated death penalty, though subsequently all trainers had to appear naked.

The main focus of the precinct, today as in ancient times, is provided by the great Doric **Temple of Zeus**. Built between 470 and 456 BC, it was as large as the almost contemporary Parthenon, a fact quietly substantiated by the vast column drums littering the ground. The temple's decoration, too, rivalled the finest in Athens; partially recovered, its sculptures of Pelops in a chariot race, of Lapiths and Centaurs, and the Labours of Hercules, are now in the museum. In the *cella* was exhibited the (lost) gold-and-ivory cult statue by Pheidias, one of the seven wonders of the ancient world. Here, too, the Olympian flame was kept alight, from the time of the games until the following spring – a tradition continued at an altar for the modern games.

The smaller **Temple of Hera**, behind, was the first built in the *Altis*; prior to its completion in the seventh century BC, the sanctuary had only open-air altars, dedicated to Zeus and a variety of other cult gods. The temple, rebuilt in the Doric style in the sixth century BC, is the most complete building on the site, with some thirty of its columns surviving in part, along with a section of the inner wall. The levels above this wall were composed only of sun-baked brick, and the lightness of this building material must contacts and foreign markets. **Sculptors** and **poets**, too, would seek commissions for their work. Herodotus read aloud the first books of his history at an Olympian festival to an audience that included Thucydides – who was to date events in his own work by reference to the winners of the *pancratium*.

In the early Olympiads, the **rules of competition** were strict. Only free-born – and male – Greeks could take part, and the rewards of victory were entirely honorary: a palm, given to the victor immediately after the contest, and an olive branch, presented in a ceremony closing the games. As the games developed, however, the rules were loosened to allow participation by athletes from all parts of the Greek and Roman world, and nationalism and professionalism gradually crept in. By the fourth century BC, when the games were at their peak, the athletes were virtually all professionals, heavily sponsored by their home states and, if they won at Olympia, commanding huge appearance money at games elsewhere. Bribery became an all-too-common feature, despite the solemn religious oaths sworn in front of the sanctuary priests prior to the contests.

Under the **Romans**, predictably, the commercializing process was accelerated. The palms and olive branches were replaced by rich monetary prizes, and a sequence of new events was introduced. The nadir was reached in 67 AD when Emperor Nero advanced the games by two years so that he could compete in (and win) special singing and lyre-playing events – in addition to the chariot race in which he was tactfully declared victor despite falling twice and failing to finish.

Notwithstanding all this abuse, the Olympian tradition was popular enough to be maintained for another three centuries, and the games' eventual **closure** happened as a result of religious dogma rather than lack of support. In 393 AD Emperor Theodosius, recently converted to Christianity, suspended the games as part of a general crackdown on public pagan festivities. This suspension proved final, for Theodosius's successor ordered the destruction of the temples, a process completed by barbarian invasion, earthquakes and, lastly, by the Alfiós River changing its course to cover the sanctuary site. There it remained, covered by seven metres of silt and sand, until the first excavation by German archeologists in the 1870s.

have helped to preserve the sculptures – most notably the *Hermes of Praxiteles* – found amid the earthquake ruins.

Between the temples of Hera and Zeus is a grove described by Pausanias, and identified as the **Pelopeion**. In addition to a cult altar to the Olympian hero, this enclosed a small mound formed by sacrificial ashes, among which excavations unearthed many of the terracotta finds in the museum. The sanctuary's principal altar, dedicated to Zeus, probably stood just to the east.

West of the Temple of Hera, and bordering the wall of the *Altis*, are remains of the circular **Philippeion**, the first monument in the sanctuary to be built to secular glory. It was begun by Philip II after the Battle of Chaironea gave him control over the Greek mainland, and may have been completed by Alexander the Great. To the east of the Hera temple is a small, second-century AD **fountain house**, the gift of the ubiquitous Herodes Atticus. Beyond, lining a terrace at the base of the Hill of Kronos, are the **state treasuries**. All except two of these were constructed by cities outside of Greece proper, as they functioned principally as storage chambers for sacrificial items and sporting equipment used in the games. They are built in the form of temples, as at Delphi; the oldest and grandest, at the east end, belonged to Gela in Sicily. In front of the treasuries are the foundations of the **Metroön**, a fourth-century BC Doric temple dedicated to the mother of the gods.

The ancient ceremonial entrance to the **Altis** was on the south side, below a long **stoa** taking up almost the entire east side of the precinct. At the corner was a house built by the Roman emperor Nero for his stay during the games. He also had the entrance remodelled as a triumphal arch, fit for his anticipated victories. Through the arch, just outside the precinct, stood the **Bouleuterion** or council chamber, where before a great statue of Zeus the competitors took their oaths to observe the Olympian rules. As they approached the stadium, the gravity of this would be impressed upon them: lining the way were bronze statues paid for with the fines exacted for foul play, bearing the name of the disgraced athlete, his father and city.

The stadium

In the final analysis, it is neither foundations nor columns that make sense of Olympia, but the 200-metre track of the **stadium** itself, entered by way of a long arched tunnel. The starting and finishing lines are still there, with the judges' thrones in the middle and seating ridges banked to either side.

Originally unstructured, the stadium developed with the games' popularity, forming a model for others throughout the Greek and Roman world. The tiers here eventually accommodated up to 20,000 spectators, with a smaller number on the southern slope overlooking the **hippodrome** where the chariot races were held. Even so, the seats were reserved for the wealthier strata of society. The ordinary populace – along with slaves and all women spectators – watched the events from the hill of Krónos to the north, then a natural, treeless grandstand.

The stadium was unearthed only in World War II, during a second phase of German excavations between 1941 and 1944, allegedly on the direct orders of Hitler. It's a sobering thought to see this ancient site in the context of the 1936 Berlin Olympics.

The Archeological Museum

May to mid-Oct Mon 12.30–7pm, Tues–Sun 8am–9pm; mid-Oct to April Mon 10.30am–5pm, Tues–Fri 8am–5pm, Sat & Sun 8am–2.30pm; 1200dr.

Olympia's site museum lies a couple of hundred metres north of the sanctuary; some of the signposts still refer to it as the "New Museum". It contains some of the finest Classical and Roman sculptures in the country, all superbly displayed.

The most famous of the individual sculptures are the **head of Hera** and the **Hermes of Praxiteles**, both dating from the fourth century BC and discovered in the Temple of Hera. The Hermes is one of the best preserved of all Classical sculptures, and remarkable in the easy informality of its pose; it retains traces of its original paint. On a grander scale is the **Nike of Paionios**, which was originally ten metres high. Though no longer complete (it's well displayed in a special area), it hints at how the sanctuary must once have appeared, crowded with statuary.

The best of the smaller objects include several fine bronze items, among them a **Persian helmet**, captured by the Athenians at the Battle of Marathon, and (displayed alongside) the **helmet of Miltiades**, the victorious Athenian general; both were found with votive objects dedicated in the stadium. There is also a superb terracotta group of **Zeus abducting Ganymede** and a group of finds from the workshop of **Pheidias**, including the cup with his name inscribed.

In the main hall of the museum is the centrepiece of the Olympia finds – statuary and sculpture reassembled from the **Temple of Zeus**. This includes three groups, all of which were once painted. From the *cella* is a frieze of the **Twelve Labours of Hercules**, delicately moulded and for the most part identifiably preserved. The other groups are from the east and west pediments. The east, reflecting Olympian pursuits, depicts Zeus presiding over a **chariot race** between Pelops and Oinamaos. The story has several versions. King Oinamaos, warned that he would be killed by his son-in-law, challenged each of his daughter Hippomadeia's suitors to a chariot race. After allowing them a start he would catch up and kill them from behind. The king (depicted on the left of the frieze) was eventually defeated by Pelops (on the right with Hippomadeia), after – depending on the version – assistance from Zeus (depicted at the centre), magic steeds from Poseidon or, most un-Olympian, bribing Oinamaos's charioteer to tamper with the wheels.

The west pediment, less controversially mythological, illustrates the **Battle of the Lapiths and Centaurs** at the wedding of the Lapith king, Peirithous. This time, Apollo presides over the scene while Theseus helps the Lapiths defeat the drunken centaurs, depicted, with fairly brutal realism, attacking the women and boy guests. Many of the metope fragments are today in the Louvre in Paris, and some of what you see here are plaster-cast copies.

In the last rooms of the museum are a collection of objects relating to the games – including *halteres* (jumping weights), discuses, weightlifters' stones and so on. Also displayed are a number of **funerary inscriptions**, including that of a boxer, Camelos of Alexandria, who died in the stadium after praying to Zeus for victory or death.

Practicalities: Olymbía

Modern **OLYMBÍA** is a village that has grown up simply to serve the excavations and tourist trade. It's essentially one long main avenue, **Praxitéles Kondhýli**, with a few side-streets. Nevertheless, Olymbía is quite a pleasant place to stay, and is certainly preferable to Pýrgos (see p.252), with the prospect of good countryside walks along the Alfiós River and around the hill of Krónos.

Most people arrive at Olympia **via Pýrgos**, which is on the main Peloponnese rail line and has frequent bus connections with Pátra and four daily with Kyparissía. The last of five daily **trains** from Pýrgos to Olympia leaves at 7.20pm; if you have time to kill between buses or trains, the city square Platía Karayiórga, two blocks north of the bus station, is tolerable in an otherwise uninspiring town. **Buses** leave hourly between Pýrgos and Olympia, some signed to "Vasiláki" beyond Olymbía; the last service is at 9pm. The only other direct buses to Olympia are **from Trípoli**, via Langádhia. These run twice daily in either direction. If you are approaching **from Andhrítsena**, either take the bus to Pýrgos and change, or stop at Kréstena and hitch or take a taxi the final 12km on from there.

There is a most helpful **tourist office** (May–Oct daily 9am–10pm; Nov–April Mon–Sat 11am–5pm; ☎0624/23 100), on the right of Praxitéles Kondhýli as you head towards the site. Olymbía has three **banks** on the main avenue, and a **post office** just uphill. **English-language books** are to be found in a couple of shops next to the tourist office.

Accommodation

Accommodation is fairly easy to come by, with a swift turnaround of clientele and a range of hotels and private rooms whose prices are kept modest by competition. A few **rooms** are signposted on Stefanopoúlou or on the road parallel to and above Praxitéles Kondhýli, though you may well be offered one on arrival. As elsewhere, rates can drop substantially out of season, though many of the smaller and cheaper places close during the off season (never precisely defined), and it's best to check in advance. There are three **campsites**, closest of which is *Diana* (☎0624/22 314), 1km from the site, with a pool and good facilities. The others are *Alphios* (☎0624/22 950; April–Sept), 1km out on the Kréstena road, and *Olympía* (☎0624/22 745; April–Oct), 2km out on the Pýrgos road.

Achilles, Stefanopoúlou 4 (☎0624/22 562). A pension on a side-street behind the National Bank; large and comfortable if somewhat noisy rooms above a snack bar. ②.

Antonios (☎0624/22 348). A hotel in the woods on the Kréstena road; expensive and not particularly well furnished, but peaceful, with a swimming pool and a stunning view; open April–Oct. ⑥.

Hercules (☎0624/22 696). A welcoming hotel by the church and school on a side-street off Praxitéles Kondhýli; big breakfasts and small balconies. ②.

Hermes (☎0624/22 577). A comfortable hotel near the Shell garage 400m out on the Pýrgos road; rooms have private facilities and there is a good restaurant. ②.

Pelops, Barélas 2 (☎0624/22 543, fax 22 213). On a square by the church and school; a hotel run by a Greek/Australian couple and strongly recommended by those who stay there. Open March–Oct. ③.

Praxiteles, Spiliopoúlou (☎0624/22 592). Quiet hotel next to the police station; there's an acceptable restaurant, and both meals and rooms are competitively priced. ③.

Eating and drinking

Many of the hotels have reasonable **restaurants** where non-residents can eat. The main avenue is lined with **tavernas**, which offer standard tourist meals at mildly inflated prices in high season, and there is a growing number of fast-food kerbside cafés which are often far better value. The *Kladhios* taverna, out of the village on the banks of the Kládhios River, serves good food in a pleasant setting. In **Miráka** village (1km out on the Trípoli road), the family-run *Taverna Drosia* offers a friendly service and fresh, homemade food; the excellent house wine is made by the owner's father. For picnics, bread from the bakery on the road to Créstena is very good.

The northwest coast to Pátra

Beaches are not a highlight in this northwest corner of the Peloponnese, nor along the north coast from Pátra to Dhiakoftó – in the province of Ahaïa. Despite the proximity of Olympia and Pátra, the northwest corner of the Peloponnese is not much explored by foreign visitors. Admittedly, it's not the most glamorous of coasts, except for the glorious beach at **Kalogriá**, but a visit to the old port of **Katákolo** or around **Loutrá Kyllínis/Arkoúdhi** can provide a pleasant enough diversion. If you are travelling this way, or are arriving in or leaving Greece at the port of Pátra, a detour along the rack-and-pinion **Kalávryta railway** should not be missed; this takes off through a gorge into the mountains at Dhiakoftó.

If heading for Delphi, or central or western Greece, car-drivers and pedestrians alike can save backtracking to Athens by using the **ferry links** across the Gulf of Kórinthos at either Río–Andírio (the shortest and most frequent) or Éyio–Áyios Nikólaos. From Kyllíni there are regular crossings to Zákynthos, and in summer to Kefalloniá, while Katákolo has (summer-only) kaïkia to Zákynthos.

Pýrgos

PÝRGOS has a grim recent history. When the Germans withdrew at the end of World War II, it remained under the control of Greek Nazi collaborators. These negotiated surrender with the Resistance, who were met by gunfire as they entered the town. Full-scale battle erupted and for five days the town burned. Today, it's a drab, 1950s-looking place, which earns few plaudits from casual visitors. If you can avoid an enforced overnight stay, do so. The hotels are overpriced, the food uninspiring and diversions nonexistent. If you have to stay the night, the cheapest hotels are the *Marily*, Deliyiánni 48 (☎0621/28 133, fax 27 066; ④), and the *Pantheon*, Themistokléous 7 (☎0621/29 748; ④).

The main escape routes are by **train** or **bus** to Pátra, Olympia or Kyparissía – though services to the last are not well timed for onward connections; the bus station is at the top of the hill, on Manolopoúlou, and the train station 400m away at the bottom on Ipsilándou, so allow a little time for interchange. There is a daily, but often crowded bus to Itéa, usually in the morning and this should put you within striking distance of Delphi on the same day. Closer to hand, there are frequent buses to Katákolo by local bus #4; these go from opposite the Dhikastikón Mégaron building on 28-Oktovríou, which is parallel to and next above Manolopoúlou (but buy tickets first from the Manolopoúlou bus station).

Katákolo

Thirteen kilometres west of Pýrgos, **KATÁKOLO** is somewhat more enticing: a decayed, ramshackle old port with good beaches close by. Until the last few decades, when new roads improved connections with Pátra, it controlled the trade for Ilía province. Today only a few tramp steamers rust at anchor, though the navy calls occasionally and, oddly, the port remains a stop for Italian summer-cruise ships. Consequently, the town has become aware of a potentially lucrative tourist trade, and most of the old warehouses have been converted into boutiques and trinket shops. But arriving from Pýrgos it feels an easy place to settle into, and to the south there's a pleasant twenty-minute walk out to the **lighthouse**, set on a plateau among arbutus and pine.

There are several **room** establishments with cabins fronted by peach and apricot trees. Try to avoid staying on the main drag, which can be noisy at night, belying the town's torpid daytime appearance. For **meals**, there is a handful of excellent tavernas on the quay.

Beaches

Katákolo's beach, the **Spiándza**, stretches away for miles to the southeast, a popular spot with Greeks, many of whom own shuttered little cottages set just back from the sea. It is sandy, though hard-packed, and is more of a spot for football or jogging, with the sea too shallow for real swimming. However, a thirty-minute walk north, past the overgrown Byzantine-Frankish **castle of Pondikón (Beauvoir)**, will take you to much better swimming at **Áyios Andhréas** beach: two hundred metres of sloping, outcrop-studded sand, with views over a few attendant islets and out to Zákynthos. There are summer tavernas here and a few rooms to let. An even better beach is to be found at **Skafidhiá**, 3km north of Katákolo and accessible by road via Korakohóri.

The cape north of Pýrgos

North from Pýrgos, road and rail meander through a series of uneventful market towns, but there are two forks west to a sandy cape and the coast. The first is at Gastoúni and heads for the spa of **Loutrá Kyllínis** (occasional buses from Pýrgos and Pátra); the second is at Kavásilas, where a side road (buses from Pátra) heads down to **Kyllíni** (port) proper. Take care not to confuse the two.

LOUTRÁ KYLLÍNIS has a long beach, and at its north end you'll find a crop of upmarket **hotels** catering for the resort's spa trade, including the overpriced and under-resourced *Kyllini Spa Xenia Tourist Complex*. It's better to walk south where the development soon gives way to sand dunes. There are two **campsites** – the *Anginara Beach* (☎0623/96 411) and the *Ionian Beach* (☎0623/96 395), both bordered by trees and beaches of fine shingle and sand – further to the southeast and best approached via Lygiá on the road from Gastoúni.

Only a few kilometres south of the EOT complex, at the point where this most westerly coast of the Peloponnese bends back east into the long bay that curves towards Katákolo, is **ARKOÚDHI**, a far better place to stay. This compact village resort has something of an island feel to it and a fine sandy bay enclosed by a rocky promontary. As well as a campsite, there is a surprising number of hotels and rooms. On the edge of the village is the posh but good-value hotel *Arkoudi* (☎0623/96 480; ④), which has a pool. In the village centre more spacious apartments with kitchen and fridge are available at *Soulis* (☎0623/96 379; ③) or the very friendly *Elena* (☎0623/96 493; ③). For meals try the central *Spyros* psistariá, or the *Akrogiali*, which offers a sea view and a wide selection of dishes.

Cheerless little **KYLLÍNI** (accessible by taxi from Loutrá Kyllínis) has little more to offer than its **ferry connections**. It is the principal port for **Zákynthos** (7–9 daily in summer, 5 in winter; ☎0623/92 385; car 2100dr, passengers 1200dr) and **Kefalloniá** (to Argostoli 2–3 daily in summer, 1–2 in winter; to Póros 3 daily in summer, 1–2 in winter; ☎0623/92 351). If you're stuck overnight in Kyllíni, **places to stay** are limited: the choice is between the *Hotel Ionian* (☎0623/92 318; ④) on the main street where some rooms have private facilities, rooms (also on the main street) – or sleeping on the beach. The *Taverna Anna*, beyond the harbour, serves a wide range of traditional dishes and is particularly popular with locals at Sunday lunchtimes.

Using Loutrá Kyllínis, Arkoúdhi or Kyllíni as a base, it's worth taking time to hitch or walk to the village of **KÁSTRO**, at the centre of the cape. Looming above the village is the Frankish **castle of Khlemoútsi** (summer 8.30am–8pm, winter 8am–2.30pm; free), a vast hexagonal structure built in 1220 by Guillaume de Villehardouin, the founder of Mystra. Its function was principally to control the province of Ahaïa, though it served also as a strategic fortress on the Adriatic. Haze permitting, there are sweeping views across the straits to Zákynthos, and even to Kefalloniá and Itháki, from the well-preserved and restored ramparts. Kástro has a hotel, the welcoming *Chryssi Avgi* at Loutrópoleos 9 (☎0623/95 224; ④), which is open from May to mid-October as well as numerous rooms. You can eat here by arrangement, or dine equally well at the nearby *Apollon* taverna.

Kalogriá and Niforéïka Patrón

Midway between Kyllíni and Pátra, **KALOGRIÁ** is an eight-kilometre strand of beach, partly naturist, bordered by a swathe of **pine forests**. A fair proportion of Pátra descends here at the weekend as it's the nearest good **beach** to the city, but it's also a respected place (the beach for its sands and the forest for its birdlife) and permanent development remains low key. It is not actually a village – the nearest bona fide town is Metóhi – but rather a cluster of tavernas and stores. At the far north end of the beach there's the *Kalogria Beach* (☎0693/31 276; ⑤), a large hotel complex with many facilities. There's not much official accommodation apart from that, but free camping is tolerated among the pines behind the beach. A novelty for wildlife aficionados are the estuaries nearby in which you may find yourself swimming alongside harmless metre-long watersnakes.

Around the northwest coast towards Pátra, 3km west of Káto Ahaïa, another busy little resort is that of **NIFORÉÏKA PATRÓN**, where accommodation options include the pricey *Hotel Acheos* complex (☎0693/25 370; ⑤), with cheaper bungalows attached, and *Aliki* camping. There is a choice of several restaurants.

Pátra

PÁTRA (Patras) is the largest town in the Peloponnese and, after Pireás, the major port of Greece; from here you can go to Italy as well as to certain Ionian islands. The city is also a hub of the Greek-mainland transport network, with connections throughout the Peloponnese and, via the ferry at Río, across the straits to Delphi or western Greece.

Unless you arrive late in the day from Italy, you shouldn't need to spend more than a few hours in the city. A conurbation of close to a quarter of a million souls, it's not the

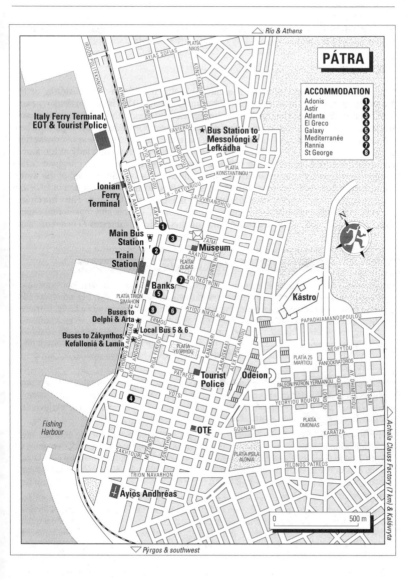

PÁTRA

ACCOMMODATION
Adonis ❶
Astir ❷
Atlanta ❸
El Greco ❹
Galaxy ❺
Mediterranée ❻
Rannia ❼
St George ❽

△ Río & Athens

PLATÍA
NIKIS

AYÍAS SOFÍAS

IRON POLITECHNIOU

KONSTANDINOUPOLEOS

Italy Ferry Terminal,
EOT & Tourist Police

FAVIEROU

★ Bus Station to
Messolóngi &
Lefkádha

PLATÍA
KONSTANTINOU

Ionian
Ferry
Terminal

28 OKTOVRÍOU

SATOVRIANDHOU

Main Bus
Station ❶

Train
Station

Museum

PLATÍA
OLGAS

KOLOKOTRONI

KORINTHOU

Banks ❺

PLATÍA TRION
SIMAHON

❽ ❻

AYÍOU NIKOLAOU

Kástro

PAPADHIAMANDOPOULOU

Buses to
Delphi & Arta ★

ERMOU

Local Bus 5 & 6

Buses to Zákynthos,
Kefalloniá & Lamia

PLATÍA
YEORYÍOU

RIGA FERÉOU

KANAKARÍ

KARAISKAKÍ

ALEX. YPSILANDOU

PLATÍA 25
MARTIOU

NEOFYTOU

PANDOKRATOROS

AV. DHIMITRIOU

BOÚ SARI

Tourist
Police

Odeion

PATREOS

VÓTSÍ

PALEON PATRON YERMANOU

YEORYIOU ROUFOU

LONDOU

KOUKOULI

Achaïa Clauss Factory (7 km) & Kalávryta △

Fishing
Harbour

OTHONOS & AMALIAS

AYÍOU ANDHREOU

SAKHTOURÍ

KORÍNTHOU

GOÚNARI

OTE

PLATÍA
OMONIAS

KARATZA

PLATÍA PSILÁ
ALÓNIA

HILONOS PATREOS

TRION NAVARHON

Áyios Andhréas

0   500 m

▽ Pýrgos & southwest

ideal holiday retreat: there are no beaches and no particular sights. Traffic noise goes
on well into the night and starts earlier than you'd want to get up. Nor has there been
much effort to make the place attractive to visitors, save for a **summer festival** which
sponsors events from late June to mid-September. These include classical plays and the
occasional rock concert in the Roman **odeion**, and art and photographic exhibitions
that bring a bit of life to the warehouses by the harbour (details from the EOT, tourist
police or the theatre on Platía Yeoryíou). The three-week **carnival** (ending on the

Sunday before Lent Monday – *Kathará Dheftéra*) is one of the biggest in the country, with a grand parade through the city centre on the final day.

The Town

The best places to make for are the café-table-studded **Platía Psilá Alónia** or the **Kástro** (daily 8am–7pm; free), a mainly Byzantine citadel. This is not particularly exciting, but it is away from the city bustle, surrounded by a park and a fifteen-minute walk up from the water. Like many a Greek metropolis in summer, Pátra is perhaps at its best after dark, when the heat is less oppressive, the concrete structures less overpowering, and the city life and lights rather brighter; a stroll down to the huge jetty at the foot of Ayíou Nikoláou can bring you to cool sea breezes – and some of the cheapest coffee around, at the port kiosk just over the railway lines. At the southwest end of the waterfront itself is the neo-Byzantine **church of Áyios Andhréas**, which opened in 1979 and houses relics of St Andrew, said to have been martyred on this spot. The church is a massive confection of yellow and cream walls, blue-tiled domes and marmoreal excess that takes in the pillars and arches. A small **archeological museum** (Tues–Sun, sum-

---

FERRY ROUTES AND COMPANIES

Innumerable ticket agents along or near the waterfront each sell different permutations of **ferry crossings** to Italy on one or more of the lines detailed below. It is worth spending an hour or so researching these, especially if you're taking a car, since costs, journey times and routes all differ from one company to another. Glossy ferry company **brochures** quoting times and prices are freely available from the agents. En route to Italy, it is possible to make stopovers on Kefalloniá and Itháki or, more commonly, Igoumenítsa and Corfu (Kérkyra). Domestic tickets to Kefalloniá and Itháki are also available from Pátra.

ROUTES Pátra–Ancona has become the standard route. Until recently this entailed two nights on board, but high-speed ferries operated by ANEK, Minoan Lines, Strintzis and Superfast Ferries can now complete the crossing in 18–24hr. Other routes include Pátra–Brindisi, Pátra–Bari, Pátra–Trieste and Pátra–Venice.

HIGH SEASON All frequencies of ferry crossings detailed below are for the high season, the definition of which varies slightly from company to company. Broadly, for crossings from Italy to Greece, high season is between early July and mid-August; from Greece to Italy, it is between early August and early September. Check with company agents for exact dates. Out of season, all services are reduced.

FARES All companies offer a variety of fares for cabin, airline-type seats, and deck passage, with reductions according to age and student or rail-card status. High-speed ferries cost only fractionally more than the normal ones. All ferry companies offer a substantial discount (normally thirty percent) on return trips if booked together with the outward journey. Travellers with camper vans are often allowed to sleep in them, thus often saving the cost of a cabin.

EMBARKATION TAX All international departures carry a levy of 2200dr per person and per car.

CHECKING IN If you have bought tickets in advance, or from a travel agent other than the official agent listed below, you must check in (to the appropriate agent's office, or at their booth in the departure hall) at least two hours before departure.

STOPOVERS Free if you specify them when booking, though you may have to pay re-embarkation taxes.

mer 8.30am–5pm, winter 8am–2.30pm; 400dr) on the corner of Mézonos and Arátou contains a number of exquisite objects from the province of Aháïa dating from the Mycenaean to the Roman eras.

Swimming near Pátra isn't really advisable, with the sea polluted for some kilometres to the southwest. Locals go to the **beaches** around Río (7km northeast; frequent bus #6 from the stop on Yerokostópoulou, near Zákynthos bus station) or to Kalográ (40km southwest, see above; 3 daily buses from KTEL station).

The Aháïa Clauss factory

The **Aháïa Clauss** factory (daily tours 9am–5pm) is an out-of-town time-filler, 8km southeast of Pátra; take the #7 bus. Tours show you around the wine-making process, and feature some treasured, century-old barrels of Mavrodhafni – a dark dessert wine named after the woman Clauss wanted to marry. You're given a glass of white wine to sample on reaching the factory's rather Teutonic bar, an echo of its founder's nationality. Along the walls are signed letters from celebrity recipients of Mavrodhafni. A shop sells all the factory's products, if you want a bottle for yourself.

COMPANIES, AGENTS AND DESTINATIONS

ANEK

United Ferries, Óthonos & Amalías 25 (☎061/226 053, fax 620 462).

Ancona: Tues, Fri direct (23hr); Wed, Sat & Sun via Igoumenítsa (32–33hr).

Trieste: Mon via Igoumenítsa (33hr); Wed & Thurs via Igoumenítsa and Corfu (32–34hr).

Adriatica

Cacouris, Óthonos & Amalías 8 (☎061/421 995). Shuttle coach runs Pátra–Athens in summer.

Brindisi: via Igoumenítsa and Corfu alternate days (19hr); direct daily in summer (14hr).

Hellenic Mediterranean Lines

Elmes Travel Services, Pénde Pigadhíon and Iróön Polytekhníou (☎061/452 521, fax 452 775).

Brindisi: daily via Kefalloniá, Igoumenítsa and Corfu (19hr 30min).

Marlines

Marlines, Athinón 16 (☎061/454 933).

Ancona: Mon, Tues & Thurs via Igoumenítsa (36hr).

MedLink Lines

Giannatos Travel, Óthonos & Amalías 15 (☎061/623 011, fax 623 320).

Brindisi: daily (13–14hr), in summer some via Kefalloniá and/or Igoumenítsa (15–16hrs).

Minoan Lines

Fotopoulos-Sotiropoulos, Athínon 2 (☎061/421 500, fax 420 800, *fspatra@ pat.forthnet.gr*).

Ancona: via Igoumenítsa Tues–Sun (21hr).

Venice: daily via Corfu and Igoumenítsa (33–37hr).

Strintzis

Telonis-Tsimaras Shipping, Óthonos & Amalías 14 (☎061/622 602, fax 623 110, *gtelonis@mail.otenet.gr*).

Ancona: Mon, Tues & Sun direct (22hr); Fri & Sat via Igoumenítsa and Corfu (30hr); otherwise direct.

Itháki: daily via Sámi on Kefalloniá (3hr 45min).

Venice: Mon–Thurs via Igoumenítsa and Corfu (32–36hr).

Superfast Ferries

Filopoulos-Parthenopoulos, Óthonos & Amalías 12 (☎061/622 500, fax 623 574).

Ancona: daily direct (18hr).

Bari: daily via Igoumenítsa (15hr).

Ventouris

Express Shipping Agencies Co, Óthonos & Amalías 81 (☎061/222 958).

Bari: direct alternate days (17hr 30min); via Kefalloniá alternate days (18hr).

Practicalities

If you are driving in or through Pátra, you will find the traffic and one-way system no less frustrating than Athens; an EOT map showing the direction of traffic, if not vital, will at least save time and probably maintain sanity. For **tourist information**, on week-days try the **EOT** office, at the entrance to the Italy ferry terminal (Mon–Fri 7am–9pm; ☎061/62 0353); otherwise the helpful **tourist police** (daily 7am–11pm; ☎061/45 1893) inside the same building.

For **money exchange**, there is an automatic machine outside the National Bank of Greece on the waterside Platía Tríon Symáhon, which also keeps special daily evening hours (6–8pm). Numerous other banks offer exchange during normal hours. For better exchange rates try the Kapa foreign exchange bureau at Óthonos & Amalías 5 (☎061/43 7261). The main **OTE** building (daily 7am–midnight) is on the corner of Goúnari and Kanakári and the main **post office** (Mon–Fri 7.30am–8pm) on the corner of Mézonos and Zaïmi.

Departures

The **ferry agents, train station** and main **KTEL bus terminal** could hardly be easier to find, grouped on the harbour road, Óthonos & Amalías. Full details of **ferry routes** are shown in the box above. **Buses** go almost everywhere from Pátra. From the **main KTEL** station, there are departures to Athens, Pýrgos and other towns in the Peloponnese, as well as to Ioánnina and Thessaloníki. From the **KTEL station** on **Faviérou**, the Étolo-Akarnanía service will take you to Messolóngi and Agrínio, where you can change for Lefkádha. You can pick up the Athens–Zákynthos and Athens–Kefalloniá buses (for information call ☎061/27 2246) at Óthonos & Amalías 58. Direct buses to Itéa, for Delphi (for information call ☎061/62 1200) leave (Mon–Sat) from Óthonos & Amalías 44.

Trains go from Pátra down the west coast of the Peloponnese, with changes at Alfiós (or Pýrgos) for Olympia, and at Kaló Neró (or Kyparissía) for routes inland to Kalamáta, Trípoli, Kórinthos and Athens. Trains go east along the southern shore of the Gulf of Kórinthos to Dhiakoftó, Kórinthos, Athens and Pireás. For train and bus frequencies see travel details at the end of this chapter on p.264.

Accommodation

Most of Pátra's **hotels** are on Ayíou Andhréou, one block back from Óthonos & Amalías, or on Ayíou Nikoláou, which runs back from the sea, near the train station and Platía Tríon Symáhon. Don't expect too much in the way of standards or value for money; most of the places cater for a very passing trade and don't make great efforts. Most of the older hotels nearer the waterfront have closed, or indeed collapsed. Of those still standing, choices include the following.

Adonis, Kapsáli (☎061/224 213, fax 226 971). On the junction with Kapsáli opposite the bus station. It's well furnished and maintained and includes a buffet-style breakfast; good value. ④.

Astir, Ayíou Andhréou 16 (☎061/277 502). Modern hotel with a swimming pool, sauna, roof garden and car parking, which still don't justify the price. ⑥.

Atlanta, Zaïmi 10 (☎061/220 098, fax 220 019). Central hotel, but still good value; out of season you should get a competitive price. ②.

El Greco, Ayíou Andhréou 145 (☎061/272 931). A good bargain hotel and top of its class; the manager is attentive and speaks English. ③.

Galaxy, Ayíou Nikoláou 9 (☎061/275 981). A well-placed hotel, if a touch pretentious; serves a good breakfast. ④.

Méditerranée, Ayíou Nikólaou 18 (☎061/279 602). Modern and adequate hotel, if undistinguished, with helpful staff. ④.

Rannia, Platía Ólgas & Ríga Feréou (☎061/220 114, fax 220 537). Very friendly, clean, faultless and well placed on the square, with a café and snack bar. ④.

Saint George Hotel, Ayíou Andhréou 73 (☎061/225 092). A good new clean and central hotel. ④.

Eating and drinking

Pátra's **restaurants** are fairly uninspiring, with countless fast-food places around Platía Tríon Symáhon, and along Ayíou Andhréou and Ayíou Nikoláou. But even here there are some reliable restaurants with character, and a mouth-watering patisserie-bakery at Kolokotróni 46. For fish, the best places are a couple of tavernas down by the fishing harbour, home to a somewhat half-hearted fleet, while for spit-roast specialities, several psistariés are grouped around Platía Omonías and Platía Konstantínou. **Nightlife** in town is largely concentrated around a noisy selection of bars at the steps of Ayíou Nikoláou.

If you're stuck for the night and feel the urge to escape to a quieter stretch of sea, hop on any #5 blue bus labelled "Tsoukaleíka" and alight at either **Monodhéndhri** or **Vrahnéïka**, 10km southwest of the city. There is now a practically unbroken chain of tavernas stretching 2km from Monodhéndhri to Vrahnéïka, of which *Thalassa Ouzeri* has the best selection of food. The others vary in price, range and quality but all share the seaside and sunset view. Real gourmets will want to check out the terrific cuisine at *Mesogeios/Mouragios*, in the suburb of **Boznítika**, 6km east of Pátra. Specialities include artichoke soufflé and seafood pasta served in a conch shell; the prices are reasonable. Choices in Pátra include the following.

Faros, cnr Othónos & Amalías and Sahtoúri. One of the best fish tavernas for quality and prices.

Hartofylakas, cnr Ríga Feréou/28-Oktovríou. A good-value estiatório, serving traditional food.

Krini, Pandokrátoros 57. An endearing place at the top of the old town, by the kástro. It has a limited but exemplary menu, and is a favourite with locals; it's possible to eat in the little garden at the back.

Majestic, Ayíou Nikoláou 2/4. Old-style estiatório, where you can choose from the day's hot dishes, which are tasty but expensive.

Nikolaras, Ayíou Nikoláou 50. Another old-style estiatório, serving good, traditional food on a cheap self-serve basis.

Listings

Airlines Air Greece, Ayíou Andhréou 6 (☎061/621 360); Olympic, Arátou 17–19 (☎061/222 901).

Books and newspapers Book's Corner, Ayíou Nikoláou 32, stocks useful maps and English-language newspapers. Lexis, Mézonos 38 and Patréos 90, stocks maps and a selection of Penguins. Romios on Kapsáli, behind the bus station, sells English-language books, and English-language papers are available from kiosks on the waterfront.

Car rental Major operators include: Avis, Kapsáli 11(☎061/275 547); Budget, Óthonos & Amalías 14 (☎061/623 200); Delta, Óthonos & Amalías 44 (☎061/272 764); Eurodollar, Albatros Travel, Óthonos & Amalías 48 (☎061/220 993); Hertz, 28-Oktovríou 2 (☎061/220 990); InterRent-EuropCar, Ayíou Andhréou 6 (☎061/621 360); and Thrifty, Óthonos & Amalías 14 (☎061/623 200).

Consulates Britain, Vótsi 2 (☎061/277 329); Germany, Mézonos 98 (☎061/221 943); Netherlands, Philopimónos 39 (☎061/271 846); Norway, 28-Oktovríou 85c (☎061/435 090); Sweden, Óthonos & Amalías 62 (☎061/271 702).

Poste restante Contact the main post office on the corner of Mézonos and Záïmi.

Travel agents These can help with information and reservations, and line Óthonos & Amalías: Albatros Travel (☎061/220 993); Marine Tours (☎061/621 166); Olympias Shipping and Travel Enterprises (☎061/275 495); Thomas Cook (☎061/226 053).

The north coast and the Kalávryta railway

From Pátra you can reach Kórinthos in two hours by **train** or **bus** along the national highway; the onward journey to Athens takes another ninety minutes. The resorts and villages lining the Gulf of Kórinthos are nothing very special, though none of them is overdeveloped. At most of them you find little more than a campsite, a few rooms for rent and a couple of seasonal tavernas. At both **Río** and **Éyio**, you can cross the gulf to the mainland by ferry. Beyond **Dhiakoftó**, if you're unhurried, it's worth taking the old **coast road** along the Gulf of Kórinthos; this runs below the national highway, often right by the sea.

However, to travel from Pátra to Kórinthos without taking the time to detour along the **Kalávryta railway** from Dhiakoftó would be to miss one of the best treats the Peloponnese has to offer – and certainly the finest train journey in Greece. Even if you have a car, this trip should still be part of your plans.

Río and Éyio

RÍO, connected by local bus #6 to Pátra (30min), signals the beginning of swimmable water, though most travellers stop here only to make use of the **ferry** across the gulf to Andírio – which will be replaced in a few years by a suspension bridge. This runs every fifteen minutes through the day and evening (half-hourly thereafter), shuttling cars (1500dr including driver) and passengers (150dr) across to the central mainland. It is a long-established crossing, testimony to which are the Turkish **forts** paired on either side of the gulf; the opening times of the squat Rio fortress with its marine moat are unreliable (officially Tues–Fri 8am–7pm, Sat–Sun 8am-2.30pm).

If you are crossing into the Peloponnese via Andírio, you might be tempted to stop by the sea here, rather than at Pátra. There are several **hotels**, including the inland *Georgios* (☎061/991 134; ③), in town towards the train station, or, both on the seafront south of the jetty, the *Rion Beach* (☎061/991 422, fax 991 390; ⑤) and the ultra-swish *Hotel Porto Rio* and casino (☎061/992 102, fax 992 115; ⑥). There are two **campsites**: the *Rio Mare* (☎061/990 762; May–Oct), just east of the jetty and fortress, and the *Rion* (☎061/991 585, fax 993 388; all year), south of the jetty but closer to the beach, which is poor just here but improves a little further south. The best of the restaurants is the *Tesseres Epohes* ("Four Seasons") with bargain prices in a romantic setting by the train station. Río seafront also boasts some of the most tub-thumping disco bars in the Pátra area – *Mojo* is particularly popular.

Moving east, there are better beaches, and a further **campsite**, the *Tsolis* (☎0691/31 469), at **ÉYIO**. Although not a place many people would choose to stay, there are a few hotels and rooms in Éyio. It's more likely you might want to eat there, though, and the main town, inland and uphill, has several decent psistariés, while just east of the harbour around Dhódheka Vrísses square are more eating establishments; the *Plessas Inomayirio* taverna is authentic and cheap – nearby stands an ancient plane tree supposedly from 200 AD and dedicated to the theoretically near-contemporaneous historian Pausanias. Nearby cliffs cut sharply into the hillside near the impressive Panayía Trypití church, marking the spot where local hero Miralis escaped from the Turks in 1821 by jumping over with his horse. A **ferry** crosses the gulf seven to nine times daily (7.30am–8.30pm; car and driver 3300dr, passengers 550dr) to Áyios Nikólaos, well placed for Delphi. Buses from Pátra stop at the bus station on the inland side of town, a considerable and inconvenient distance from the harbour or the rail station.

The best sands are at the village of **RHODHODHÁFNI**, 2km northwest of Éyio, the *Corali Beach* (☎0691/71 546; May–Sept) and the *Aeoli Beach* (☎0691/71 317; April–Oct) **campsites** are close to the beach.

Dhiakoftó and beyond

It is at **DHIAKOFTÓ** (Dhiakoptó) that the rack-and-pinion railway heads south up into the Vouraïkós gorge for Kalávryta (see following). If you arrive late in the day, it's worth spending the night here and making the train journey in daylight; the town can, in any case, be an attractive alternative to staying overnight in Pátra. The climate is very pleasant, less humid than Pátra and less furnace-like than Korinthía province to the east. There are four **hotels**: the pleasant, upmarket *Chris-Paul* (☎0691/41 715, fax 42 128; ④), which has a pool; the basic *Helmos* (☎0691/41 236; ②; closed in winter); the friendly *Lemonies* (☎0691/41 229; ②), opposite the school on the road to the beach, with a good restaurant and its own retsina; and the *Panorama* (☎0691/41 614; ④) 800m along the beach. The *Kohyli* on the corner of the beach road has decent food, as does the restaurant at the *Panorama*.

Travelling west beyond Dhiakoftó there is the final minor resort in Aháïa of Akráta, before the coastal strip of Korinthía province (see p.165). **AKRÁTA**, a small town with a beach annexe, is a little crowded, with three hotels and three campsites set along a drab, exposed stretch of beach.

Dhiakoftó to Kalávryta: the rack-and-pinion railway

Even if you have no interest in trains, the **rack-and-pinion railway** from Dhiakoftó to Kalávryta is a must. It's a crazy feat of Italian engineering, rising at gradients of up to one in seven as it cuts through the course of the **Vouraïkós gorge**. En route is a toy-train fantasy of tunnels, bridges and precipitous overhangs.

The railway was built between 1889 and 1896 to bring minerals from the mountains to the sea. Its steam locomotives were replaced some years ago – one remains by the line at Dhiakoftó with other relics, and another at Kalávryta – but the track itself retains all the charm of its period. The tunnels, for example, have delicately carved windows, and the narrow bridges zigzagging across the Vouraïkós seem engineered for sheer virtuosity.

It takes up to an hour to get from Dhiakoftó to Zakhloroú (confusingly listed on time-tables as Méga Spílio), and about another twenty minutes from there to Kalávryta. The best part of the trip is the stretch to **Zakhloroú**, along which the gorge narrows to a few feet at points, only to open out into brilliant, open shafts of light beside the Vouraïkós, clear and fast-running even in midsummer. In peak season the ride is very popular, so you'll probably need to buy tickets some hours before your preferred departure (including the return journey). Despite only covering some 22km, trains on this line can be subject to the same lengthy delays (or cancellations) as their grown-up counterparts on the main line below.

Zakhloroú and Méga Spílio

ZAKHLOROÚ is as perfect a train stop as could be imagined: a tiny hamlet echoing with the sound of the Vouraïkós River, which splits it into two neighbourhoods. It's a lovely, peaceful place with a gorgeous old wooden hotel, the very friendly and very reasonably priced *Romantzo* (☎0692/22 758; ②), which has a fine restaurant below. The only other hotel-restaurant is the adjacent *Messina* (☎0692/22 789; ②), sometimes closed during summer.

The eight-storey **Monastery of Méga Spílio** (Great Cave), built at a sixty-metre cave entrance under a 120-metre cliff, is a 45-minute walk from the village, up a rough donkey track along the cliff; this joins an access drive along the final stretch, which is often chock-a-block with tour buses. The monastery is reputedly the oldest in Greece, but it has been burned down and then rebuilt so many times that you'd hardly guess at its antiquity. The last major fire took place in 1934, after a keg of gunpowder left behind from the War of Independence exploded. In 1943, the Nazis killed many of the residents and looted seventy lorryloads of furniture and relics, much of it later recovered. Dress conduct for visitors is strict: skirts for women, and long sleeves and trousers for men. Only men are allowed to stay overnight, and the monks like visitors to arrive before 8pm, serving up a rough repast before closing the gates.

The view of the gorge from the monastery is for many the principal attraction. However, the cloister once had 450 monks and was among the richest in the Greek world, owning properties throughout the Peloponnese, in Macedonia, Constantinople and Asia Minor. In consequence, its treasury, arranged as a small **museum**, is outstanding. In the church, among its icons is a charred black wax and mastic image of the Virgin, one of three in Greece said to be by the hand of St Luke (but more probably from the tenth century). The monastery was founded by Sts Theodhoros and Simeon, after a vision by the shepherdess Euphrosyne in 362 AD led to the discovery of the icon in the cave behind the site of the later church.

Kalávryta and around

From Méga Spílio a new road has been hacked down to **KALÁVRYTA**. The train line is more in harmony with the surroundings, but coming from Zakhloroú the drama of the route is diminished as the gorge opens out. Kalávryta itself is beautifully positioned, with Mount Helmós as a backdrop, though it has a sad atmosphere. During World War II the Germans carried out one of their most brutal reprisal massacres, killing the entire male population – 1436 men and boys – and leaving the town in flames. Rebuilt, it is both depressing and poignant. The first and last sight is a mural, opposite the station, that reads: "Kalavryta, founder member of the Union of Martyred Towns, appeals to all to fight for world peace." The left clocktower on the central church stands fixed at 2.34pm – the hour of the massacre. Out in the countryside behind the town is a shrine to those massacred, with the single word "Peace" (*Iríni*).

The Nazis also burned the **monastery of Ayía Lávra**, 6km out of Kalávryta. As the site where Yermanos, Archbishop of Pátra, raised the flag to signal the War of Independence, the monastery is one of the great Greek national shrines. It, too, has been rebuilt, along with a small historical museum.

Staying at Kalávryta has a sense of pilgrimage about it for Greeks, and it's crowded with school parties during the week and with families at weekends. The general attitude to foreigners – perhaps understandably – is business-like rather than overtly friendly, and the town will probably not have the same appeal for the casual visitor. If you miss the last train back to Zakhloroú (currently at 7.30pm, but check on the day) there are several pleasant **hotels** whose rates drop outside of winter weekends. Among them are the hospitable *Polyxeni*, Lohagón Vassiléos Kapóta 13 (☎0692/22 141; ④); the friendly and luxurious *Filoxenia*, Ethaikís Ardistásis 20 (☎0692/22 422, fax 23 009, *filoxenia@otenet.gr*; ⑤); and the *Villa Kalavrita* (☎0692/22 712; ⑤) across the rail track from the station, which has comfortable, modern rooms with a fridge and TV. There are several adequate restaurants around the square – *To Tzaki* has a nice atmosphere and good, mostly grilled food. Kalávryta is also the main base for the **Helmos Ski Centre**, which is rapidly growing in popularity. There are a number of shops which can hire equipment, give information about the state of the slopes and maybe help with transport up to the centre.

A thirty-minute drive southeast of Kalávryta is the **Spílio Límnon** or Cave of the Lakes (summer daily 9am–6pm; winter Mon–Fri 9.30am–4.30pm, Sat & Sun 9.30am–6.30pm; 800dr; ☎0692/31 633). Mineral-saturated water trickling through a two-kilometre cavern system has precipitated natural dams, trapping a series of small underground lakes. Only the first 300m or so are as yet open to the public but the chambers are still well worth the trip.

The cave is on the same **bus** line from Kalávryta as the villages of Káto Loussí, Kastriá and Planitéro, and is 2km north of Kastriá. Buses also run from Kalávryta to Pátra four times daily.

Mount Helmós

The highest peaks of the imposing Helmós (Aroánia) range rear up a dozen or so kilometres to the southeast of Kalávryta. **Mount Helmós** itself, at 2355m, is only 50m short of the summit of Taïyetos to the south. However, the walk from Kalávryta is not an interesting approach, the trail having vanished under a paved road and the new ski centre (1900m) approached by it. To get the most from hiking on the mountain you need to climb up from the village of **Sólos**, on the west side – a five-hour-plus walk which takes you to the **Mavronéri waterfall**, source of the legendary Styx (Stýga, Stygós), the river which souls of the dead had to cross in order to enter Hades.

The hike from Sólos

To reach the path opening at Sólos, start at **Akráta** on the Pátra–Kórinthos road. From here it's a slow but beautiful 35km haul up a winding paved road. Buses run only three times a week, but hitching isn't too difficult in high summer.

SÓLOS is a tiny place, a cluster of stone cottages on a steep hillside just below the fir trees, and inhabited only in summer. Facing it across the valley is the larger but more scattered village of Peristéra, past which runs the easiest of the routes to Mavronéri.

Follow the **track** through Sólos, past the combined inn (all of ten beds) and *magazí* (café-store), where you can get a simple meal. Beyond the last houses the track curves around the head of a gully. On the right, going down its wooded flank, is a good path which leads to a bridge over the river at the bottom. Just beyond (15min; this and all subsequent times are from Sólos), you reach another track. There is a **chapel** on the left, and, on the wall of a house on the right, a sign saying "Pros Gounariánika" that points up a path to the left. Follow it past a **church** on a prominent knoll and on to the jeep track again, where, after 75 minutes, you turn left to the half-ruined hamlet of **Gounariánika**. From there continue steadily upwards along the west (right) flank of the valley through abandoned fields until you come to a stream-gully running down off the ridge above you on your right. On the far side of the stream the fir forest begins. It's an ideal camping place (2hr 30min; 1hr 30min going back down).

Once into the **woods**, the path is very clear. After about an hour (3hr 30min) you descend to a boulder-strewn **stream bed** with a rocky ravine to the right leading up to the foot of a huge bare crag, the east side of the Neraïdhórahi peak (2238m) visible from Kalávryta. Cross the stream and continue leftwards up the opposite bank. In June there are the most incredible wild flowers, including at least half a dozen different orchids, all the way up from here, plus rare blue butterflies.

After fifteen minutes' climb above the bank, you come out on top of a **grassy knoll** (3hr 30min), then dip back into the trees again. At the four-hour mark, you turn a corner into the mouth of the **Styx ravine**. Another five minutes' walk brings you to a **deep gully** where enormous banks of snow lie late into the spring. A few paces across a dividing rib of rock there is a second gully, where the path has been eroded and you have to cross some slippery scree.

Here you come to a wooded spur running down from the crag on the right. The trail winds up to a shoulder (4hr 20min), descends into another gully, and then winds up to a second shoulder of level rocky ground by some large black pines (4hr 30min), known as *To Dhiáselo toú Kynigoú* (the Hunter's Saddle). From there you can look into the

Styx ravine. Continue down the path towards the right until it dwindles at the foot of a vast crag (4hr 45min). You can now see the **Mavronéri waterfall**, a 200-metre-long, wavering plume of water pouring off the red cliffs up ahead.

To get to it, angle across the scree bank without losing altitude – the track is obliterated soon after the saddle – until you reach the base of the falls (5hr). There's a small **cave** under the fall, where a rare columbine grows. It is possible to continue up the valley, past some turf next to a seasonal pond where people camp, but the summit area proper is a bit of a let-down after the majesty of the Styx valley. Fairly clear and easy trails lead down from the south side of the watershed to join the E4 trail between the villages of Káto Loussí (12 km above Kalávryta) or Planitéro (8km from Klitoría); the appropriate *Korfes* or *YIS* maps have more details on these routes.

travel details

Trains

There are two types of train: **ordinary,** and **express** (Intercity or IC); the latter only stop at the larger stations and incur variable supplementary fares.

There are two main Peloponnesian lines:

Athens–Kórinthos–Dhiakoftó–Pátra–Pýrgos –Kyparissía–Kalamáta One train daily makes the full run in each direction. Another 8 daily run between Athens and Pátra, 7 continuing to Pýrgos, 5 as far as Kyparissía. Another 1 train daily covers the route between Pátra and Kalamáta, with a change at Kaló Neró or Kyparissía.

Approximate journey times are:
Athens–Kórinthos (1hr 30min–2hr)
Kórinthos–Dhiakoftó (1hr–1hr 30min)
Dhiakoftó–Pátra (45min–1hr 15min)
Pátra–Pýrgos (1hr 30min–2hr)
Pýrgos–Kyparissía (1hr–1hr 30min)
Kyparissía–Kalamáta (1hr 40min).

Athens (starts in Pireás)–Kórinthos–Mykínes (Mycenae)–Árgos–Trípoli–Kalamáta Five trains daily cover the full route, in each direction.

Approximate journey times are:
Athens–Kórinthos (1hr 30min–2hr)
Kórinthos–Mykínes (50min)
Mykínes–Árgos (10min)
Árgos–Trípoli (1hr 30min)
Trípoli–Kalamáta (2hr 20min).

In addition, there are the following branch lines:
Árgos–Náfplio 3–4 daily (18min).
Pýrgos–Olympia 5 trains daily (36min).
Pýrgos–Katákolo 1–2 daily (25min).
Dhiakoftó–Zakhloroú–Kalávryta 4 daily (Dhiakoftó–Zakhloroú 46min; Zakhloroú–Kalávryta 21min).

Buses

Buses detailed have similar frequency in each direction, so entries are given just once; for reference check under both starting-point and destination. Bus station timetables rarely indicate when there is a change of bus en route – this can involve a long wait.

Connections with Athens: Árgos (hourly; 2hr 15min); Kalamáta (8 daily; 4hr 30min); Kórinthos (hourly; 1hr); Mykínes (Mycenae) hourly; 2hr); Náfplio (hourly; 3hr); Olympia (4 daily; 5hr 30min); Pátra (28 daily from 2.30am to 9.30pm); Pýlos (2 daily; 7hr); Spárti (7–9 daily; 4hr 30min); Tíryns (hourly; 2hr 45min); Yeroliménas (2 daily in season only; 7hr).

Areópoli to: Kalamáta (4 daily changing at Ítylo; 2hr 30min); Láyia (daily; 1hr); Váthia (daily in season; 1hr 30min); Yeroliménas (2 daily in season only; 1hr).

Árgos to: Andhrítsena (1 daily; 3hr); Ástros (3 daily Mon–Fri; 1hr); Ayía Triádha (8 daily; 20min); Áyios Andhréas (3 daily Mon–Sat; 1hr 30min); Leonídhi (3 daily Mon–Fri; 3hr); Midhéa (3 daily; 40min); Mykínes (Mycenae; 5 daily; 30min); Mýli for Lerna (12 daily; 25min); Náfplio (15–17 daily; half-hourly; 30min); Neméa (2 daily; 1hr); Néo

Kíos (11 daily; 20min); Olympia (3 daily on weekdays; 4hr 30min); Spárti (8 daily; 3 hr); Tíryns (half hourly; 15 min); Trípoli (4 daily Mon–Fri, 3 daily Sat–Sun; 1hr 20min).

Kalamáta to: Areópoli (4 daily, changing at Ítylo; 1hr 30min to 2hr); Exohóri (2 daily; 1hr 30min); Finikoúnda (4 daily, changing at Pýlos; 2hr 15min; Hóra (5 daily, changing at Pýlos; 2hr); Kardhamýli (4 daily; 50 min); Koróni (8 daily; 1hr 20min); Megalópoli (8 daily; 1hr); Messíni (frequent except Sun; 25min); Pátra (2 daily; 4hr); Pýlos (9 daily; 1hr 20min); Saïdhóna (2 daily); Stoúpa (4 daily; 1hr); Trípoli (8 daily; 1hr 45min).

Kórinthos to: Árgos (hourly 1 hr); Kalamáta (7 daily; 4hr); Loutráki (half-hourly; 20min); Mykínes (Mycenae) (hourly; 30min); Náfplio (hourly; 1hr 30min); Neméa (5 daily; 45min); Spárti (8 daily; 4hr); Tíryns (hourly; 1hr 15min); Trípoli (9 daily; 1hr 30min).

Kyparissía to: Filiatrá (6 daily; 20min); Pýlos (5 daily changing at Hóra; 2hr); Pýrgos (4 daily; 1hr); Zaháro (4 daily; 25min).

Megalópoli to: Andhrítsena (2 daily; 1hr 15min); Pýrgos (2 daily; 4hr); Trípoli (8 daily; 40min).

Náfplio to: Arhéa Epídavros (3 daily; 1hr); Dhrépano (9 daily; 20min); Epidaurus (5 daily; 45min); Ermióni (3–4 daily; 2hr 15min); Galatás for Póros (2–3 daily; 2hr); Iría (2 daily); Karathónas beach (4 daily; 20min); Kóstas (3–4 daily; 2hr 15min); Kranídhi (3–4 daily; 1hr 50min); Lygourió (7 daily; 40min); Néo Kíos (11 daily; 20min); Pórto Héli (3–4 daily; 2hr); Toló (hourly; 25min); Tíryns (17 daily, half hourly; 15min); Trípoli (4 daily; 1hr 15min).

Pátra to: Ahaïa (26 daily); Itéa for Delphi (2 daily, Mon–Sat); Éyio (16–17 daily; 1hr); Ioánnina (4 daily; 5hr); Kalamáta (2 daily; 4hr); Kalávryta (4 daily; 2hr 15min); Kalogriá (3 daily; 1hr 15min); Pýrgos (7–10 daily; 2hr); Trípoli (2 daily; 4hr); Vólos (1 daily; 6hr); Zákynthos (4 daily; 2hr 30min including ferry from Kyllíni).

Pýlos to: Finikoúnda (4 daily; 45min); Hóra (7 daily; 40min); Kalamáta (9 daily; 1hr 20min); Kyparissía (6 daily, but none 1.15pm–7pm; 2hr); Methóni (6 daily; 20min).

Pýrgos to: Andhrítsena (2 daily; 2hr); Kalámata (2 daily; 2hr); Katákolo (9 daily; 30min); Kyparissía (2 daily; 1hr); Olympia (hourly, but none 12.30–3.30pm; 45–60min); Pátra (10–11 daily; 2hr).

Spárti to: Areópoli (2–3 daily; 2hr); Kalamáta (2 daily; 2hr 30min); Molái (6 daily; 2hr);

Monemvasiá (3 daily; 3hr); Mystra (11 daily, 6 on Sun; 15min); Monemvasiá (3 daily; 3hr); Neápoli (3 daily; 4hr); Yíthio (5 daily; 1hr).

Trípoli to: Andhrítsena (2 daily; 1hr 30min); Árgos (4 daily; 1hr 20min–1hr 50min); Ástros (2 daily Mon–Sat; 1hr 30min); Dhimitsána (1 daily; 1hr 30min); Kalamáta (6 daily; 2hr); Kalávryta (1 daily; 2hr 30min); Karýtena (2 daily; 1hr); (2 daily; 1hr 30min); Kyparissía (2 daily; 2hr); Megalópoli (9 daily Mon–Fri, 6 Sat–Sun; 40min); Náfplio (4 daily; 1hr 20min–1hr 50min); Spárti (2 daily; 1hr 20min); Olympia (2 daily Mon–Fri, 1–3 Sat–Sun; 5hr); Pátra (via Lámbia; 2 daily; 4hr); Pýlos (3 daily; 3hr); Pýrgos (3 daily; 3hr); Spárti (5–9 daily; 1hr 20min); Stemnítsa (1 daily; 1hr 15min); Tegéa (hourly; 20min); Trópea (4–5 daily; 2hr); Vytína 6 Mon–Fri, 4 Sat–Sun; 1hr 15min).

Yíthio to: Areópoli (4 daily; 50min); Láyia (daily; 1hr); Monemvasiá (2 daily; 2hr 30min).

Ferries

Across the Gulf of Kórinthos: Andírio–Río (every 15min, every 30min between 11pm and 7am; 10–20min); Éyio–Áyios Nikólaos (5.15am–8.30pm; 9 daily June–Oct, 7 daily Nov–May; 35–50min).

Galatás to: Póros (every 15min from dawn till past midnight; 5min).

Kósta to: Spétses (4 daily; 20min).

Kyllíni to: Zákynthos (daily 7–9 summer, 5 winter; 1hr 30min); Kefalloniá (5–6 summer, 2–4 winter; 1hr 45min to 2hr 15min).

Kýthira to: Kastélli, Crete (once weekly in season; 2hr 15min).

Pátra to: Igoumenítsa and Corfu (2–3 daily; 6–11hr/8–11hr); Kefalloniá and Itháki (1–2 daily; 2hr 30min/3hr 45min); also to Brindisi, Ancona, Bari, Trieste and Venice (Italy). See box on p.256 for details.

Yíthio to: Kýthira (5 days a week in high season; 2hr 30min); contact Rozaki (☎0733/22 207) for current information.

Hydrofoils

For details and frequencies of services, which vary drastically with season, contact local agents or the Minoan Flying Dolphins' main office in Pireás (Aktí Themistokléous 8; ☎01/412 8001).

Flying Dolphin hydrofoils run between the following ports:

Yérakas/Kyparíssi/Monemvasiá/Leonídhi/ Tyroú to Pórto Héli, Spétses, Ídhra and Pireás.

Neápoli (summer only) to Kýthira, Monemvasiá, Kyparíssi, Leonídhi and Pireás.

Kýthira to Monemvasiá, Kyparíssi, Leonídhi, Pórto Héli, Spétses, Ídhra and Pireás.

Méthana to Póros, Ídhra, Ermióni Éyina and Pireás.

Ermióni to Spétses, Pórto Héli, Ídhra, Póros, Méthana and Pireás.

Náfplio (midsummer only) to Monemvasiá, Toló, Spétses, Póros and Pireás.

Paleá Epídhavros (summer only) to Éyina and Pireás.

Summer-only excursion boats

Kósta and Pórto Héli: Water-taxis to Spétses according to demand (10–20min).

Flights

To/from **Athens–Kalamáta** (3 weekly; 50min); Kýthira (1–2 daily; 50min).

To/from **Pátra–Thessaloníki** (occasional flights on Air Greece from Áraxos airfield, near Kalogriá).

CHAPTER THREE

THESSALY AND CENTRAL GREECE

C entral Greece is a region of scattered highlights – above all the site of the ancient oracle at **Delphi** (modern *Dhelfí*), and, further to the north, the other-worldly rock monasteries of the **Metéora**. The area as a whole, dominated by the vast agricultural plain of Thessaly, is less exciting, with rather drab market and industrial towns. For scenic drama – and most of the historic sights – you have to head for the fringes.

The southern part of this region, below Thessaly proper, is known as **Stereá Elládha** – literally "Greek Continent", a name that reflects its nineteenth-century past as the only independent Greek mainland territory, along with Attica and the quasi-island of the Peloponnese. It corresponds to the ancient divisions of Boeotia and Phocis, the domains respectively of Thebes (modern *Thíva*) and Delphi. Most visitors head straight through these territories to Delphi, but if you have time there are some rewarding minor detours in the monastery of **Ósios Loukás** – with the finest Byzantine mosaics in the country – and **Gla**, the largest and most obscure of the Mycenaean sites. For hikers there is also the opportunity of climbing **Mount Parnassós**, the Muses' mountain.

The central plains of **Thessaly** (Thessalía) formed the bed of an ancient inland sea – rich agricultural land that was ceded reluctantly to the modern nation by the Turks in 1878. This region's attractions lie on its periphery, hemmed in by the mountain ranges of Ólymbos (Olympus), Píndhos (Pindus), Óssa and Pílion (Pelion). There are a number of routes to choose from. East from the major city and port of Vólos extends the slender peninsula of **Mount Pílion**, whose luxuriant woods and idyllic beaches are easily combined with island-hopping to the Sporades. To the west, **Kalambáka** gives access to the Metéora (not to be missed) and across the dramatic **Katára pass** over

---

ACCOMMODATION PRICE CODES

Throughout the book we've used the following **price codes** to denote the cheapest available double room in each establishment in high season. Out of season, rates can drop by more than fifty percent, especially if you are staying for three or more nights. Single rooms, where available, cost around seventy percent of the price of a double.

① Up to 6000dr	④ 12,000–16,000dr
② 6000–9000dr	⑤ 16,000–20,000dr
③ 9000–12,000dr	⑥ 20,000dr and upwards

Note: Youth hostels typically charge 2000–2500dr for a dormitory bed.
For more accommodation details, see pp.43–6.

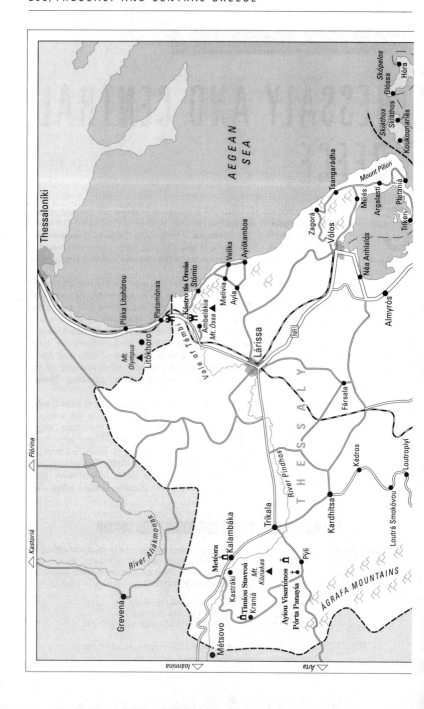

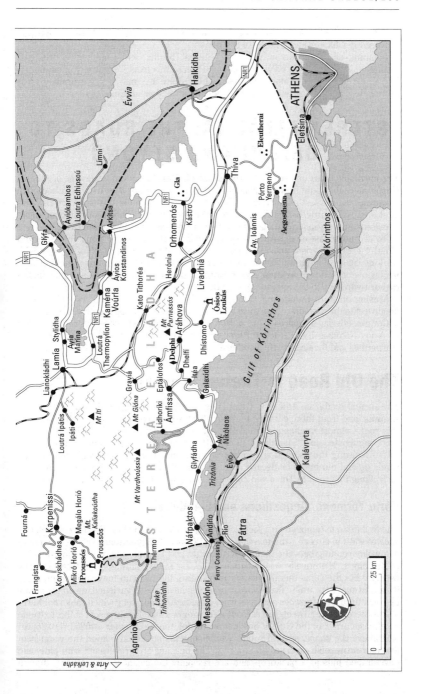

the Píndhos to Epirus. To the north, the horizon is dominated by **Mount Olympus** (covered in Chapter Five), home of the gods.

Looming across a narrow gulf from Štereá Elládha, and joined by a bridge at Halkídha, is the island of **Évvia** (Euboea). Though this feels – especially in summer – like an extension of the mainland (from where there are many ferry crossings), it is nonetheless a bona fide island and we detail its attractions in Chapter Eleven.

STEREÁ ELLÁDHA: THE ROADS TO DELPHI AND BEYOND

The inevitable focus of a visit to Stereá Elládha is **Delphi**, 150km northwest of Athens. Buses cover the route from the capital several times a day, or they can be picked up at **Livadhiá**, the nearest rail terminus. However, if you're in no hurry, there are rewards in slowing your progress: taking the "old road" to Thebes (Thíva), or detouring from Livadhiá to the Byzantine monastery of **Ósios Loukás** or to Mycenaean **Gla**.

To the northeast of the Athens–Delphi road, traffic thunders along the **National Road 1** towards Lárissa and Thessaloníki, skirting the coast for much of the way, with the long island of Évvia only a few kilometres across the gulf. Along this route there are ferries over to Évvia at **Arkítsa**, **Áyios Konstandínos** (where you can also pick up ferries or hydrofoils to the Sporades) and **Glýfa**.

Moving on from Delphi and Lamía, immediately north, two routes cross Thessaly: northwest to the Metéora, or northeast to Pílion. Another road leads southwest to the Gulf of Corinth, offering an approach to – or from – the **Peloponnese**, via ferries at Andírio–Río or Áyios Nikólaos–Éyio. A fourth, more remote route leads due west from Lamía to **Karpeníssi** and then across the southernmost extensions of the Píndhos mountains.

The Old Road to Thebes (Thíva)

The ancient road from Athens to Delphi began at the Parthenon as the **Sacred Way to Eleusis**, and from there climbed into the hills towards Thebes. It is possible to follow this route, almost unchanged since Oedipus supposedly trod it, by taking the minor road, signposted for "Mándhra", north off the motorway at modern Elefsína (see p.150). Leaving the polluted and industrial port, matters improve quickly, as the road winds up and out into a landscape of pines and grey stony hills. There are two buses daily along this road to Thíva and connections from there on to Livadhiá and Delphi.

Pórto Yermenó, Aegosthena and Eleutherai

The first thing to tempt you off the Sacred Way is a look at the best-preserved stretch of ancient walls in Greece – the fourth century BC fort of **Aegosthena** – above the mouth of a valley running between mounts Kytherónas and Patéras, and overlooking the Gulf of Kórinthos. Historically it is insignificant, being merely an outpost of Spartan's ally Megara, but the ruins themselves are impressive, the two end towers rising up more than 12m above the walls. The seaward ramparts have mostly vanished; up on the acropolis, a church with frescoes survives from a medieval monastery which took root here.

But there is little to keep you at **Pórto Yermenó**, a little family resort at this extreme northeast corner of the Gulf. It has just one **hotel**, the *Egosthenion* (☎0263/41 226; ③) well above the shore, several rooms establishments squeezed behind the waterfront and four or five fish tavernas all in a row. The beaches are gravel-sand with pine- and olive-draped hills as a backdrop, and are certainly the cleanest near Athens, though they can get very crowded in summer. But for those with transport (there is no bus service covering the 23km from the Elefsína–Thíva road) and a penchant for old walls, the twenty-five-minute drive along the side-road is worth it.

Back on the Thebes road, a kilometre north of the Pórto Yermenó turning, you pass another fortress – fourth-century BC **Eleutherai**. Signposted from the road, 400m to the east, the fort is again well preserved, with its northeast side almost intact and six of its circuit of towers surviving to varying degrees. The scant ruins of Eleutherai town itself lie down by the Aegosthena junction, while the fort defends a critical pass above; both sites have unlimited access.

Thíva (Thebes)

The modern town of **THÍVA** lies 20km north of Eleutherai, built right on the site of its mighty predecessor. For this very reason, there are almost no traces of the past: archeologists have had little success in excavating the crucial central areas, and the most interesting visit is to the excellent town **museum** (daily 8.30am–3pm; 600dr). This is to be found at the far (downhill) end of Pindhárou, the main street; look out for the Frankish tower in its forecourt. Among many fine exhibits is a unique collection of painted *larnakes* (Mycenaean sarcophagi) depicting, in bold expressionistic strokes, women lamenting their dead.

There are no direct **buses** from Thíva to Delphi, but services run frequently to Livadhiá (where there are better connections) and a couple of times a day to Halkídha, gateway to Évvia. If you get stranded between buses, there are two central if rather overpriced **hotels** opposite each other on Epaminónda: the *Niobe* at no. 63 (☎0262/27 949; ④) or the larger *Meletiou* at no. 58 (☎0262/27 333;④).

Livadhiá and around

Livadhiá lies at the edge of a great **agricultural plain**, much of it reclaimed lakebed, scattered with a few minor but enjoyable sites. It's a part of Greece that sees few tourists, most of whom are in a hurry to reach the glories of the Parnassós country just to the west.

Livadhiá

LIVADHIÁ is a pleasant town on the banks of the Herkína, a river of ancient fame which emerges from a dark gorge at the base of a fortress. It's an attractive place for a brief stop, with paired ancient and medieval sights, but bear in mind the last connection out, since overnighting here will prove costly.

The ancient curiosity is the site of the **Oracle of Trophonios**, a ten-minute walk from the main square, beside an old Turkish bridge. Here the waters of the Herkína rise from a series of springs, now channelled beside the (signposted) *Xenia* café. Above the springs, cut into the rock, are niches for votive offerings – in one of which, on a large chamber with a bench, the Turkish governor would sit for a quiet smoke. In antiquity, all who sought to consult the Oracle of Trophonios had first to bathe in the Springs of Memory and Forgetfulness. The oracle, a circular structure which gave entrance to caves deep in the gorge, has been tentatively identified at the top of the hill, near the remains of an unfinished temple of Zeus. It was visited by the Greek traveller-scholar Pausanias, who wrote that it left him "possessed with terror and hardly knowing himself or anything around him".

The **froúrio**, or castle, which overlooks the springs, provides the medieval interest; its entrance lies just around the corner up the hill to the west. An impressive and well-bastioned square structure, it was built in the fourteenth century and was a key early conquest in the War of Independence. But it's the medieval history that's most interesting. The castle was the stronghold of a small group of Catalan mercenaries, the Grand Company, who took control of central Greece in 1311 and – appointing a Sicilian prince as their ruler – held it for sixty years. They were a tiny, brutal band who had arrived in Greece from Spain in the wake of the Fourth Crusade. They wrested control from the Franks, who were then established in Athens and Thebes, in a cunning deviation from traditional rules of engagement. As the Frankish nobility approached Livadhiá, the vastly outnumbered Catalans diverted the river to flood the surrounding fields. The Frankish cavalry advanced into the unexpected marsh and were cut down to a man.

Practicalities

The town today is a minor provincial capital with a trade in milling cotton from the area. Though completely off the tourist route, recent landscaping along the springs is making it an even more enjoyable daytime pause before, or after, Delphi. Be warned that in season buses on towards Delphi often arrive and leave full, though two local ones start from Livadhiá around noon. Arriving by **bus**, you'll be dropped near the central square, **Platía Dhiákou**; the **train station** is a few kilometres out, but arrivals may be met by a shuttle bus (or more likely taxis) into town.

Staying overnight is highly problematic since virtually all of Livadhiá's budget hotels closed their doors in the early 1990s. If your budget doesn't run to the pricey *Livadhia* on Platía Kotsóni (☎0261/23 611; ⑥), or if you don't fancy the noisy *Philippos* (☎0261/24 931; ④), you'd be well advised to press on towards Aráhova and Delphi. There are a similarly limited number of **eating** options. Several tavernas and psistariés are scattered about town, the most obvious being the trio clustered at the T-junction five minutes west of the main square.

Orhomenos

Just 10km northeast of Livadhiá (10min; buses hourly) is the site of **ancient ORHOMENOS**, inhabited from Neolithic to Classical times. As the capital of the Minyans, a native Thessalian dynasty, it was one of the wealthiest Mycenaean cities.

Near the middle of the rather drab modern village of Orhomenós, along the road signposted for Dhiónysos village, is the **Treasury of Minyas** (Tues–Sat 9am–3pm, Sun 10am–2pm), a stone *tholos* similar to the tomb of Atreus at Mycenae. The roof has collapsed but it is otherwise complete, and its inner chamber, hewn from the rock, has an intricately carved marble ceiling. Much closer to the road are the remains of a fourth-century BC **theatre**, and behind, on the rocky hilltop, a tiny fortified acropolis from the same period.

Across the road from the theatre is the ninth-century Byzantine **Church of the Dormition**, built entirely of blocks from the theatre and column drums from a classical temple – as is the minute Byzantine church in the main village square. The larger triple-apsed church has some fine reliefs, including a sundial, with the remains of a monastery just to the south.

The citadel of Gla

Continuing east, in a highly worthwhile diversion, it's a further twenty minutes by bus (2 buses daily, 2.30pm & 7.15pm) to the village of Kástro, right next to the National Road towards Lárissa. If you walk through the village, cross the highway and then walk south (towards Athens) for about 100m you come to the signposted side-road which leads, within about 300m, to the Mycenaean **citadel of Gla**.

Athens street scene

Parliamentary guard in Athens

PETER WILSON

Detail on tomb, Eleusis

MICHAEL JENNER

Athens postcards

PETER WILSON

The Acropolis at night

Panorama of Athens

The Palaestra, Olympia, Peloponnese

Byzantine church, Mystra

Shepherd in the Zagorian mountains

The Tholos, Delphi

Acrocorinth: west curtain walls,
Peloponnese

Church in Miliés village, Pílion peninsula

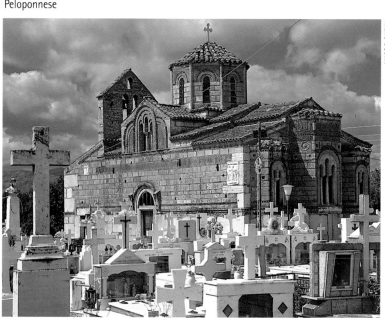

Twelfth-century church, Mérbaka, Argolid

An enormous and extraordinary site, **GLA** (unrestricted entrance) stands within a three-kilometre circuit of Cyclopean walls – a far larger citadel than either Tiryns or Mycenae. Almost nothing, however, is known about the site, save that it was once an island in Lake Kopaïs (which was drained in the last century) and that it may have been an outpost of the Minyans. The **walls** and **city gates** still stand to five metres in places, and are almost three kilometres in length, despite having been damaged when the city fell. Inside, on the higher ground, what is thought to have been a huge Mycenaean **palace** has been revealed; it appears to include a *megaron* (throne room) and various storerooms, though archeologists are puzzled by differences from the standard Mycenaean palace form. Further down, and currently being excavated, is a vast walled area believed to have been the **marketplace**.

Chaironeia

Directly north of Livadhiá, on the main road to Lamía, is **Chaironeia**, once the home of the writer Plutarch, but more famous as the site of one of the most **decisive battles** of ancient Greece. Here, in 338 BC, Philip of Macedon won a resounding victory over an alliance of Athenians, Thebans and Peloponnesians put together by Demosthenes. This defeat marked the death of the old city-states, from whom control passed forever into foreign hands: first Macedonian, later Roman.

Set beside the road, at modern Herónia, is a remarkable six-metre-high **stone lion**, originally part of the funerary monument to the Thebans (or, some say, to the Macedonians) killed in the battle. Adjacent is a small museum of local finds, and there are remains of ancient **acropolis** fortifications, with a theatre at their base, above the village.

The Oedipus crossroads, Ósios Loukás and Aráhova

West from Livadhiá, the landscape becomes ever more striking as Mount Parnassós and its attendant peaks loom high above the road. After 24km, about halfway to Delphi, you reach the so-called **Schist** (Split) or **Triodos** (Triple Way) **crossroads** – also known as the **Oedipus crossroads** – which was the intersection of the ancient roads from Delphi, Daulis (today Dávlia), Thebes (Thíva) and Ambrossos (Dhístomo). The old road actually lay in the gorge, below the modern one.

Pausanias identified this crossroads as the site of Oedipus's murder of his father, King Laius of Thebes, and his two attendants. According to the **myth**, Oedipus was returning on foot from Delphi while Laius was speeding towards him from the opposite direction on a chariot. Neither would give way, and in the altercation that followed Oedipus killed the trio, ignorant of who they were. It was to be, as Pausanias put it mildly, "the beginning of his troubles". Continuing to Thebes, Oedipus solved the riddle of the Sphinx, which had been ravaging the area, and was given the hand of widowed Queen Jocasta in marriage – unaware that he was marrying his own mother.

Getting to Ósios Loukás: Dhístomo

If you have transport, you can turn left at the crossroads and follow the minor road to Dhístomo, and thence 8km east to the **monastery of Ósios Loukás**. Travelling by bus, you may need to take a more roundabout route: first from Livadhiá to Dhístomo, then another bus on from there towards Stíri and Kyriáki – getting off at the fork to Ósios Loukás, leaving just a 2.5km walk. Alternatively, it's possible to hire a taxi in

DHÍSTOMO, which also has a couple of small **hotels** on the town square facing the church: the *America* (☎0267/22 079; ②) and *Koutriaris* (☎0267/22 268; ③).

Despite valiant attempts at beautification in its centre, Dhístomo remains a drab place, distinguished historically by one of the worst World War II **atrocities** in Greece: German occupying forces shot 232 of the inhabitants on June 10, 1944. The event is immortalized in a bleak grey and white memorial on a nearby hilltop – follow the signs to the marble-clad "mausoleum". On one plaque are the names of the victims; on two others apologetic sentiments from a German citizens' group and President Roman Herzog (1996).

Ósios Loukás monastery

The **monastery of Ósios Loukás** (daily: May to mid-Sept 8am–2pm & 4–7pm; winter 8am–5pm; 800dr) was a precursor of that last defiant flourish of **Byzantine art** that produced the great churches at Mystra in the Peloponnese. It is modest in scale, but from an architectural or decorative point of view ranks as one of the great buildings of medieval Greece. The setting, too, is exquisite – as beautiful as it is remote, especially in February when the many local almond trees are in bloom. As one approaches from Dhístomo, the monastery suddenly appears on its shady terrace, overlooking a spectacular sweep of the Elikónas peaks and an intervening valley.

The main structure comprises two domed churches, the larger **katholikón** of Ósios Loukás and the adjacent chapel of the **Theotókos**. They are joined by a common foundation wall but otherwise share few architectural features. Ten monks still live in the monastic buildings around the courtyard, but the monastery is essentially maintained as a museum, with snack and souvenir stalls in the grounds.

The katholikón

The **katholikón** (main church), built in the early eleventh century, is dedicated to a local beatified hermit, Luke of Stiri (not the Evangelist). Its design formed the basis of Byzantine octagonal-plan churches, and was later copied at Dhafní and at Mystra. Externally it is modest, with rough brick-and-stone walls surmounted by a well-proportioned dome. The interior, however, is startling. Built to a conventional cross-in-square plan, its atmosphere switches from austere to exultant as the eye moves along walls lined in red, grey and green marble to the gold-backed mosaics on the high ceiling. Light filtering through marble-encrusted windows reflects across the curved surfaces of the mosaics in the nave and bounces onto the marble walls, bringing out the subtlety of their shades.

The original **mosaics** were damaged by an earthquake in 1659, and in the dome and elsewhere have been replaced by unremarkable frescoes. But other surviving examples testify to their effect. On the right as you enter are a majestic *Resurrection*, rivalled only by the version at Néa Moní (Híos; see p.725), and *Thomas Probing Christ's Wound*. The mosaic of the *Niptir (Washing of the Apostles' Feet)* on the far left of the narthex is one of the finest here; its theme is an especially human one, the expressions of the apostles ranging between diffidence and surprise. This dynamic and richly humanized approach is again illustrated by the *Baptism*, high up on one of the curved squinch arches that support the dome. Here the naked Jesus reaches for the cross amidst a swirling mass of water, an illusion of depth created by the angle and curvature of the wall. The church's original **frescoes** are confined to the vaulted chambers at the corners of the cross plan and, though less imposing than the mosaics, employ subtle colours and shades, notably in *Christ Walking towards the Baptism*.

The Theotókos chapel and crypt

The chapel of the **Theotókos** (literally "God-Bearing", meaning the Virgin Mary) is a century older than the *katholikón*. From the outside it overshadows the main church with its elaborate brick decoration culminating in a highly Eastern-influenced, marble-panelled drum. The interior seems gloomy and cramped by comparison, highlighted only by a couple of fine Corinthian capitals and an original floor mosaic, now dimmed by the passage of time.

Finally, do not miss the vivid frescoes in the **crypt** of the *katholikón*, entered on the lower right-hand (south) side of the building. It's a good idea to bring a torch, since illumination is limited to three spotlights to preserve the colours of the frescoes.

Aráhova

Arriving at **ARÁHOVA**, the last town east of Delphi (just 11km further on), you are well and truly in Parnassós country. The peaks stand tiered above, sullied somewhat by the wide asphalt road cut to a ski-resort – the winter-weekend haunt of BMW-driving Athenians. If you want to **ski**, it's possible to hire equipment on a daily basis at the resort and even to get an all-in day package from Athens (see p.66). The resort's main problem is high winds, which often lead to the closure of its lifts, so check the forecast before you set off.

Skiing aside, the town is appealing, despite being split in two by the Livadhiá–Delphi road, and the après-ski commercialization. If you're not making for any other mountain areas, Aráhova is well worth an afternoon's pause before continuing to Delphi, and those with their own transport generally prefer staying here, as opposed to modern Dhelfí village. A number of houses in Aráhova retain their vernacular architecture, flanking narrow lanes twisting north up the slope or poised to the south on the edge of the olive-tree-choked Plistós gorge. The area is renowned for its strong purplish wines, honey, candied fruits and nuts, cheese, novelty noodles, *tsípouro* and woollen weavings; all are much in evidence in the roadside shops, though most of the woven goods are nowadays imported from Albania and northern Greece. Also of note is the local **festival of Áyios Yeóryios** (23 April, or the Tuesday after Easter if this date falls within Lent), centred on the church at the top of the hill, and one of the best opportunities to catch genuine folk-dancing during almost two days of continuous partying.

Practicalities

In the summer most people just stop for a meal and to shop, so finding **accommodation** is easy, even though several establishments close down. In winter, particularly at weekends, rooms are at a premium in all senses, with prices bumped up at least one category from the summer ranges cited below. At the cheaper end of the scale, there are two pleasant if modest, non-en-suite **hotels**, side by side at the Livadhiá end of town: the *Apollon* (☎0267/31 427; ①) and the *Parnassos* (☎0267/31 307; ②), both with good views. At the Delphi end of town, choose from among the plain but spacious *Apollon Inn* (☎0267/31 057, *Arachova-Inn@United-Hellas.com*; ① bathless rooms, ② with bath), an annexe of the *Apollon Hotel*; the *Pension Nostos* (☎0267/31 385, fax 31 765; ③), with balconies for most of the smallish rooms; or the recently refurbished *Xenia Hotel* (☎0267/31 230; ④), with its own parking, gorgeous views from all rooms and buffet breakfast included in the price.

During summer, a good fifty percent of Aráhova's eateries close down, but an amazing number of state-of-the-art bars and sweet shops continues to serve the local gilded youth. As testimony to the village's dual personality, the kafenío tables on the main fountain square remain packed out with their loudly discussing elders until late. Among the more durable and consistently open **tavernas** is the excellent *Karathanasi* on said square, with soups in the cooler months, bulk wine and assorted meat dishes; it has roof-terrace seating on summer nights. Next to the **post office**, near the Xenia Hotel, *Parnassos* is a recommended source of reasonably priced and tasty *mayireftá*.

Six **buses** daily go to Athens and seven to Delphi and Itéa, one or two of which go on to Pátra; bus timetables are displayed at the *Celena Cafeteria Bar*, open all day, right opposite the smaller square which doubles as a bus stop and taxi rank. Two **banks** with cash dispensers round out the list of essential amenities.

Delphi (Dhelfí)

With its site raised on the slopes of a high mountain terrace and dwarfed to either side by the massive, ominous crags of Parnassós, it's easy to see why the ancients believed **DELPHI** to be the centre of the earth. But more than the natural setting or even the occasional earthquake and avalanche were needed to confirm a divine presence. This, according to Plutarch, was achieved through the discovery of a rock chasm that exuded strange vapours and reduced all comers to frenzied, incoherent and undoubtedly **prophetic** mutterings.

The oracle: some history

The first **oracle** established on this spot was dedicated to **Gea** ("Mother Earth") and to **Poseidon** ("the Earth Shaker"). The serpent **Python**, son of Gea, was installed in a nearby cave, and communication made through the Pythian priestess. Python was subsequently slain by **Apollo**, whose cult had been imported from Crete (legend has it that he arrived in the form of a dolphin – hence the name *Delphoi*). The **Pythian Games** were established on an eight-year cycle to commemorate the feat, and perhaps also to placate the ancient deities.

The place was known to the **Mycenaeans**, whose votive offerings (tiny striped statues of goddesses and worshipping women) have been discovered near the site of Apollo's temple. Following the arrival of the **Dorians** in Greece at the beginning of the twelfth century BC, the sanctuary became the centre of the loose-knit association of Greek city-states known as the **Amphyctionic League**. The territory still belonged however, to the nearby city of Krissa, which, as the oracle gained in popularity, began to extort heavy dues from the pilgrims arriving at the port of Kirrha. In the sixth century BC the League was called on to intervene, and the first of a series of **Sacred Wars** broke out. The League wrested Delphi from the Krissaeans and made it an autonomous state. From then on Delphi experienced a rapid ascent to fame and respect, becoming within a few decades one of the major sanctuaries of Greece, with its tried and tested oracle generally thought to be the arbiter of truth.

For over a thousand years thereafter, a steady stream of **pilgrims** made its way up the dangerous mountain paths to seek divine direction in matters of war, worship, love or business. On arrival they would sacrifice a sheep or a goat and, depending on the omens, wait to submit questions inscribed on lead tablets. The Pythian priestess, a simple and devout village woman of fifty or more years, would chant her prophecies from a tripod positioned over the oracular chasm. Crucially, an attendant priest would then "interpret" her utterings and relay them to the enquirer in hexameter verse.

Many of the **oracular answers** were equivocal: Croesus, for example, was told that if he embarked on war against neighbouring Persia he would destroy a mighty empire; he did – and destroyed his own. But it's hard to imagine that the oracle would have retained its popularity and influence for so long without offering predominantly sound advice. Indeed, Strabo wrote that "of all oracles in the world, it had the reputation of being the most truthful." One explanation is that the Delphic priests were simply bet-

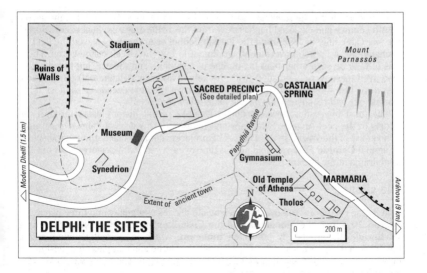

Map: DELPHI: THE SITES. Labels include: Stadium, Ruins of Walls, Mount Parnassós, SACRED PRECINCT (See detailed plan), CASTALIAN SPRING, Museum, Papadhiá Ravine, Gymnasium, Synedrion, Old Temple of Athena, MARMARIA, Extent of ancient town, Tholos, Modern Dhelfí (1.5 km), Aráhova (9 km), 0 — 200 m

ter informed than any other corporate body around at the time. Positioned at the centre of the Amphyctionic League, which became a kind of "United Nations" of the Greek city-states, they were in a position to amass a wealth of political, economic and social information, and, from the seventh century BC onwards, Delphi had its own network of informants throughout the Greek world.

The **influence** of the oracle spread abroad with the Classical age of colonization and its patronage grew, reaching a peak in the sixth century BC, with powerful benefactors such as Amasis, King of Egypt, and the unfortunate King Croesus of Lydia; many of the Greek city-states also dedicated treasuries at this time. Privileged position and enormous wealth, however, made Delphi vulnerable to Greek rivalries; the first Sacred Wars left it autonomous, but in the fifth century BC the oracle began to be too closely identified with individual states. Worse, it maintained a defeatist, almost treacherous attitude towards the Persian invasions – only partially mitigated when a Persian force, sent by Xerxes to raid Delphi, was crushed at the entrance to the sanctuary by a well-timed earthquake.

It never quite regained the same level of trust – and consequently of power – after these instances of bias and corruption. However, real **decline** did not set in until the fourth century BC, with the resumption of the Sacred Wars and the emergence of Macedonian control. Following prolonged squabbling among the Greek city-states, the sanctuary was seized by the Phocians in 356 BC, leading to Philip of Macedon's intervention to restore the Amphyctionic League to power. Seven years later, when the League again invited Philip to settle a dispute, this time provoked by the Amphissans, he responded by invading southern Greece. The independence of the city-states was brought to an end at the Battle of Chaironeia (see p.273), and Delphi's political intriguing was effectively over.

Under **Macedonian** and later **Roman** control, the oracle's role became increasingly domestic and insignificant, dispensing advice on marriages, loans, voyages and the like. The Romans thought little of its utterances, rather more of its treasure: Sulla plundered the sanctuary in 86 BC and Nero, outraged when the oracle pronounced judgement on the murder of his mother, carted away some five hundred bronze statues. Finally, with the demise of paganism under Theodosius late in the fourth century AD, the oracle became defunct.

In modern times, the sanctuary site was rediscovered towards the end of the seventeenth century and explored haphazardly from the 1840s onwards. Real **excavation** of the site came only in 1892 when the French School of Archeology leased the land, in exchange for a French government agreement to buy the Greek currant crop. There was little to be seen other than the outline of a stadium and theatre, but the villagers who lived there were persuaded (with the help of an army detachment) to move to a new town 1km west, and digging commenced. Over the next decade or so most of the excavations and reconstruction visible today were completed.

The most interesting development in Delphi's recent history came through the efforts of the poet Angelos Sikelianos and his American wife Eva Palmer to set up a "University of the World" in the 1920s. The project eventually failed, though it inspired an annual **Delphic Festival**, held now in June of each year, with performances of Classical drama in the ancient theatre.

The sites

Split by the road from Aráhova, the ancient site divides essentially into three parts: the **Sacred Precinct**, the **Marmaria** and the **Castalian spring**. In addition there is a worthwhile, though poorly presented **museum**, which is currently undergoing a much-needed expansion and facelift. All in all it's a large and complex ruin, best taken in two stages, with the sanctuary ideally at the beginning or end of the day, or (in winter) at lunchtime, to escape the crowds.

Make sure you have sturdy footwear as there's a lot of clambering up rough stone steps and paths, and take food and drink if you're planning a full day's visit; good picnicking spots are the theatre with its panorama of the sanctuary (its seats, alas, off-limits), or try the stadium for fewer interruptions.

The Sacred Precinct

The **Sacred Precinct** (summer daily 7.30am–7pm, winter daily 8am–5pm; 1200dr), or Temenos (Sanctuary) of Apollo, is entered, as in ancient times, by way of a small **agora** enclosed by ruins of Roman porticoes and shops for the sale of votive offerings. The paved **Sacred Way** begins after a few stairs, and zigzags uphill between the foundations of memorials and treasuries to the Temple of Apollo. Along each edge is a litter of statue bases where gold, bronze and painted-marble figures once stood; Pliny counted more than three thousand on his visit, and that was after Nero's infamous raid.

The choice and position of these **memorials** were dictated by more than religious zeal; many were used as a deliberate show of strength or as a direct insult against a rival Greek state. For instance, the **Offering of the Arcadians** on the right of the entrance (a line of bases that supported nine bronzes) was erected to commemorate their invasion of Laconia in 369 BC, and pointedly placed in front of the Lacedaemonians' own monument. Beside this, and following the same logic, the Spartans celebrated their victory over Athens by erecting their **Monument of the Admirals** – a large recessed structure, which once held 37 bronze statues of gods and generals – directly opposite the Athenians' **Offering of Marathon**.

Further up the path, past the Doric remains of the **Sikyonian Treasury** on the left, stretch the expansive foundations of the **Siphnian Treasury**, a grandiose Ionic temple erected in 525 BC. Siphnos had rich gold mines and intended the building to be an unrivalled show of opulence. Fragments of the caryatids that supported its west entrance, and the fine Parian marble frieze that adorned all four sides, are now in the museum. Above this is the **Treasury of the Athenians**, built, like the city's "Offering", after Marathon (490 BC). It was reconstructed in 1904–06 by matching the inscriptions that completely cover its blocks. These include honorific decrees in favour of Athens, lists

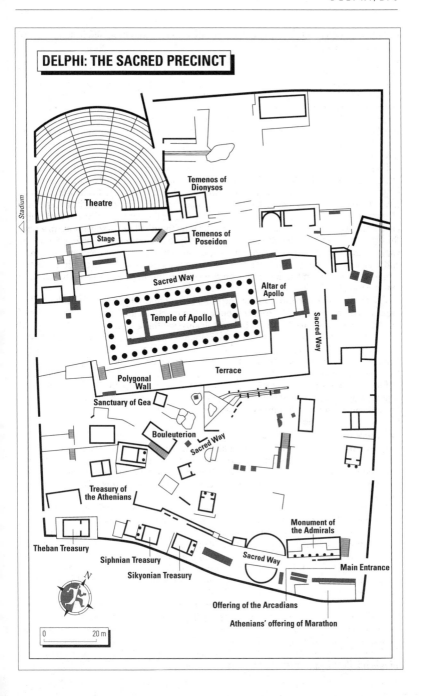

DELPHI: THE SACRED PRECINCT

Theatre

△ Stadium

Temenos of Dionysos

Stage

Temenos of Poseidon

Sacred Way

Temple of Apollo

Altar of Apollo

Sacred Way

Terrace

Polygonal Wall

Sanctuary of Gea

Bouleuterion

Sacred Way

Treasury of the Athenians

Theban Treasury

Siphnian Treasury

Sikyonian Treasury

Monument of the Admirals

Sacred Way

Main Entrance

Offering of the Arcadians

Athenians' offering of Marathon

N

0   20 m

of Athenian ambassadors to the Pythian Festival and a hymn to Apollo with its musical notation in Greek letters above the text.

Next to it are the foundations of the **Bouleuterion**, or council house, a reminder that Delphi needed administrators, and above sprawls the remarkable **Polygonal Wall** whose irregular interlocking blocks have withstood, intact, all earthquakes. It, too, is covered with inscriptions, but these almost universally refer to the emancipation of slaves; Delphi was one of the few places where such freedom could be made official and public by an inscribed register. An incongruous outcrop of rock between the wall and the treasuries marks the original **Sanctuary of Gea**. It was here, or more precisely on the recently built-up rock, that the Sibyl, an early itinerant priestess, was reputed to have uttered her prophecies.

Finally, the Sacred Way leads to the temple terrace where you are confronted with a large altar, erected by the island of Chios. Of the main body of the **Temple of Apollo**, only the foundations stood when it was uncovered by the French. Six Doric columns have since been re-erected, giving a vertical line to the ruins and providing some idea of the temple's former dominance over the whole of the sanctuary. In the innermost part of the temple was the *adyton*, a dark cell at the mouth of the oracular chasm where the Pythian priestess would officiate. No sign of cave or chasm has been found, nor any vapours that might have induced a trance, but it is likely that such a chasm did exist and was simply opened and closed by successive earthquakes. On the architrave of the temple – probably on the interior – were inscribed the maxims "Know Thyself" and "Moderation in All Things".

The theatre and stadium used for the main events of the Pythian Festival lie on terraces above the temple. The **theatre**, built in the fourth century BC with a capacity of five thousand, was closely connected with Dionysos, the god of ecstasy, the arts and wine, who reigned in Delphi over the winter months when the oracle was silent. A path leads up through cool pine groves to the **stadium**, a steep and longish walk which discourages many of the tour groups. Its site was artificially levelled in the fifth century BC, though it was banked with stone seats (giving a capacity of seven thousand) only in Roman times – the gift, like so many other public buildings in Greece, of Herodes Atticus. For even greater solitude, climb up above to the pine trees that have engulfed the remains of the fourth-century BC walls.

The museum

Delphi's **museum** (summer Mon noon–6.30pm & Tues–Sun 7.30am–7pm, winter earlier closure; 1200dr) contains a rare and exquisite collection of archaic sculpture, matched only by finds on the Acropolis. It features pottery, figures and friezes from the various treasuries, which, grouped together, give a good picture of the sanctuary's riches.

The most famous exhibit, placed at the far end of the central corridor, is the **Charioteer**, one of the few surviving bronzes of the fifth century BC. It was unearthed in 1896 along with other scant remains of the "Offering of Polyzalos", which probably toppled during the earthquake of 373 BC. The charioteer's eyes, made of onyx and set slightly askew, lend it a startling realism, while the demure expression sets the scene as a lap of honour. It is thought that the odd proportions of the body were designed by the sculptor (possibly Pythagoras of Samos) with perspective in mind; they would be "corrected" when the figure was viewed, as intended, from below.

Other major pieces include two huge **kouroi** (idealized archaic male figures) from the sixth century BC in the second room at the top of the stairs. To the right of this room, in the "Hall of the Siphnian Treasury", are large chunks of the beautiful and meticulously carved **Syphnian frieze**; they depict Zeus and other gods looking on as the Homeric heroes fight over the body of Patroclus, as well as the gods battling with the giants. In the same room is an elegant Ionic sculpture of the winged **Sphinx of the**

Naxians, dating from around 560 BC. Back along the main corridor is the **Athenian Treasury,** represented by fragments of the metopes, which depict the labours of Herakles, the adventures of Theseus and a battle with Amazons. Further on and to the right, the **Hall of the Monument of Daochos** is dominated by a group of three colossal dancing women, carved from Pentelic marble around an acanthus column. The figures, celebrating Dionysos, probably formed the stand for a tripod.

The Castalian spring

Following the road east of the sanctuary, towards Aráhova, you reach a sharp bend. To the left, marked by niches for votive offerings and by the remains of an archaic fountain house, the celebrated **Castalian spring** still flows from a cleft in the Phaedriades cliffs.

Visitors to Delphi (only men were allowed in the early centuries) were obliged to purify themselves in its waters, usually by washing their hair, though murderers had to take the full plunge. **Byron,** impressed by the legend that it succoured poetic inspiration, also jumped in. This is no longer possible, since the spring is fenced off owing to rock-falls from the Phaedriades cliffs.

The Marmaria

Across and below the road from the spring is the **Marmaria** (summer daily 8am–7pm, winter 8am–5pm; free), or Sanctuary of Athena, whom the Delphians worshipped as Athena Pronoia ("Guardian of the Temple"). The name Marmaria means "marble quarry" and derives from the medieval practice of filching the ancient blocks for private use.

The most conspicuous building in the precinct, and the first visible from the road, is the **Tholos,** a fourth-century BC rotunda. Three of its dome-columns and their entablature have been set up, but while these amply demonstrate the original beauty of the building (which is *the* postcard image of Delphi), its purpose remains a mystery.

At the entrance to the sanctuary stood the **Old Temple of Athena,** destroyed by the Persians and rebuilt in the Doric order during the fourth century BC; foundations of both can be traced. Outside the precinct on the northwest side (above the Marmaria) is a **gymnasium,** again built in the fourth century BC, but later enlarged by the Romans who added a running track on the now collapsed terrace; prominent among the ruins is a circular plunge bath which, filled with cold water, served to refresh the athletes after their exertions.

Practicalities: Modern Dhelfí

Modern Dhelfí is as inconsequential as its ancient namesake, 1500m to the east, is impressive. Entirely geared to tourism (including Greek skiers), its attraction lies in its mountain setting, proximity to the ruins and access to Mount Parnassós (see the following section).

There is a single **bus terminal,** located at the Itéa (west) end of town, where the upper and lower commercial streets link up. Westbound buses go to Ámfissa (whence you can pick up connections north), Itéa and (usually with a change) Náfpaktos, while eastbound services go only to Aráhova, Livadhiá or Athens. The main difficulty, since all coaches originate elsewhere, is that seats allocated for the Dhelfí ticket booth are limited and they sell out some hours in advance. If you're going to be stuck standing all the way to Athens, it's better to get off at Livadhiá and continue by train – there are four morning departures and five afternoon/early evening departures. Bus time-tables are available from the helpful **tourist office** (Mon–Fri 7.30am–2.30pm; ☎0265/82 900) in the town hall, done up in modern Neoclassical style. Other amenities include several **banks** (with cash dispensers) and a **post office,** all along the lower main street.

Accommodation

Accommodation is plentiful if not especially good value; like most Greek site villages, Dhelfí has a quick turnaround of visitors and, with over twenty hotels and pensions, finding an actual vacancy should present few problems. However, there is no set peak season – indeed winter weekends can see top rates charged, courtesy of the ski-trade spillover from Aráhova – so scope for bargaining depends on current traffic.

There are three **campsites** in the area: the closest is *Camping Apollon* (☎0265/82 762; open all year), alongside the road to Ámfissa/Itéa and less than 1km west of Dhelfí, with a pool and restaurant but more caravan than tent space. *Camping Delphi* (☎0265/82 475; open all year) lies 3km further along the same road, just after Khryssó, and *Camping Chrissa* (☎0265/82 050; April–Oct) is another 3km on, along the same road.

Athena, Vas. Pávlou ke Frederíkis 55 (☎0265/82 239). Near the bus station at the Itéa (west) end of town, this rather plain hotel has views of the gulf from back rooms. ③.

Hermes, Vas. Pávlou ke Frederíkis 27 (☎0265/82 318). Relatively new and quiet, with wonderful views. ⑤.

Odysseus Pension, Iséa 1, corner Filellínon, the street below and parallel to Vas. Pávlou ke Frederíkis (☎0265/82 235). Non-en-suite and spartan, but quiet, with a flowered terrace and unobstructed views. ③.

Olympic Hotel, Vas. Pávlou ke Frederíkis 59 (☎0265/82 793). Tasteful, pricey hotel, co-managed with the *Hermes*. Value for money though, and the price includes breakfast. ⑥.

Panorama, Osíou Louká 47 (☎0265/82 061). This peaceful hotel with lovely views is situated above most of the shops, in a residential area. Price includes breakfast. ④.

Panos/Pan, Vas. Pávlou ke Frederíkis 53 (☎0265/82 294). Adequate and comfortable with fine views of the gulf; the best, newest rooms, with small bathtubs, are in the attic. ④.

Pythia, Vas. Pávlou ke Frederíkis 68 (☎0265/82 328). Close to the site and museum; run as an annexe of the *Panos*, where you usually have to enquire first. ④.

Sun View Pension, Apóllonos 84, west end of street near Amalia Hotel (☎0265/82 349). Attractive, inexpensive en-suite rooms run by Loula Sotiriou. ③.

Varonos, Vas. Pávlou ke Frederíkis 25 (☎0265/82 345). Welcoming hotel, with private facilities in all rooms. Copious breakfasts are extra. ④.

Eating and drinking

Meals are most varied and appetizing at the long-running *Taverna Vachhos*, just below the main church on Apóllonos, the upper through road. The nearby *Lekaria*, Dhelfí's only "typical" taverna, has gone sharply downhill in recent years, so patronize it at your own risk; both establishments have views down to the gulf from their terraces. Otherwise, Dhelfí eateries are pretty much of a bland muchness, as you'd expect in a place that has to feed large coach parties.

Mount Parnassós

For a taste of the Greek alpine scene, **Parnassós** is probably the most convenient peak in the land, though its heights no longer rank as wilderness, having been disfigured by the ski-station above Aráhova and its accompanying paraphernalia of lifts, snack bars and access roads. The best routes for walkers are those up from Dhelfí to the **Corycian cave** (practicable from April to November), or the **Liákoura summit ascent** (May to October only). Those with their own transport can take advantage of sealed **roads** up the mountain from Aráhova on the south, or Lílea, Polýdhrosos or Amfília on the north slope, any of which could easily be combined with a walk. For extended explorations, Road Editions' 1:50,000 **map** no. 42, "Parnassos", is a wise investment; an attached booklet summarizes a slightly variant route to the Corycian cave.

Dhelfí to the Corycian cave

To reach the **trailhead** for this walk – and the initial path up the mountain – take the right-hand (approaching from Athens), uphill street through Dhelfí village, officially Apóllonos. At the top of the slope, by the church, turn right onto a road that doubles back to the **museum-house** (9am–3pm; closed Tues; 500dr) where the poet **Angelos Sikelianos** – he of the revived ancient festival (see p.278) – once lived. There is a bust of him outside.

Continue climbing from here, with more zigzags along a gravel surface, until reaching highest point of the fence enclosing the sanctuary ruins. Where the track ends at a gate, don't go into the site, but adopt a trail on your left, initially marked by a black-and-yellow rectangle on a white background. From the top of the hill the trail continues, well marked by more black-on-yellow metal diamonds: it's part of the E4 European long-distance trail. Initially steep, the way soon flattens out on a grassy knoll overlooking the stadium, and continues along a ridge next to a line of burned cypresses.

Soon after, you join up with an ancient cobbled trail coming from inside the fenced precinct, the **Kakí Skála**, which zigzags up the slope above you in broad arcs. The view from here is fantastic, stretching back over the Gulf of Kórinthos to the mountains of the Peloponnese. The cobbles end near two concrete inspection covers in the Dhelfí water supply, an hour plus above the village, at the top of the Phaedriades cliffs. Nearby stand some rock pinnacles, from one of which those guilty of sacrilege in ancient times were thrown to their deaths – a custom perhaps giving rise to the name *Kakí Skála* or "Evil Stairway".

E4 markers remain visible in the valley which opens out ahead of you. You can get simultaneous views south, and northeast towards the Parnassan summits, by detouring a little to the right to a wooden hut and a barn, then to a slight rise perhaps 150m further. The principal route becomes a gravel track bearing northeast; foresake the E4 diamonds and follow instead a metal sign pointing toward the cave, by taking the right fork near a spring and watering troughs, with some shepherds' huts scattered under the trees. This track passes a picnic ground and a chapel of Ayía Paraskeví within the next fifteen minutes, and acquires intermittent paved surface before skirting a sheepfold and another hut on the left. Some two-and-a-half hours above Dhelfí, you emerge from the fir woods with a view east and ahead to the rounded mass of the Yerondóvrahos peak (2367m) of the Parnassós massif.

Another fifteen minutes bring you to a spring, followed by another chapel (of Ayía Triádha) on the left, with a spring and picnic ground. To the left rises a steep ridge, on whose flank lies the ancient **Corycian cave**, in Greek the Korýkio Ándro. Ignore the Greek-only sign just behind the chapel, which indicates a dangerous and disused old trail, and persevere along the road about five more minutes to where a white bilingual sign points to a newer path, marked by orange paint splodges. After a twenty-minute scramble up the slope, you meet another dirt road; turn left and follow it to the end, about 10m below the conspicuous cave mouth.

This was sacred to Pan and the nymphs in ancient times, the presiding deities of Delphi during the winter months when Apollo was said to desert the oracle. Orgiastic rites were celebrated in November at the cave by women acting as the nymphs, who made the long hike up from Delphi on the Kakí Skála by torchlight. The cavern itself is chilly and forbidding, but if you look carefully with a torch you can find ancient inscriptions near the entrance; without artificial light you can't see more than a hundred metres inside. By the entrance you'll notice a rock with a man-made circular indentation – possibly an ancient altar to hold libations.

Descending to Dhelfí takes rather less than the three-and-half-hour ascent. The marked E4 route, on the other hand, continues almost due north – more on track than on path, it must be said – to the large village of **EPTÁLOFOS**, on the Arákhova–Lílea–

Graviá paved road. This, just below the forest with sweeping views north, is a popular Greek "hill station" and a prominent staging point on the E4; accordingly, there are a half-dozen places to **stay**, including the "*Hotel*" *Panorama* (☎0234/61 302, ③) or the *Mavrodhimos* rooms (☎0234/61 309,③), plus lots of **grills** around the plane-shaded platía.

The Liákoura summit

Liákoura is Parnassós's highest and finest peak (2457m) and can be approached either from the Dhelfí side or from the northeastern foothills of the mountain. The latter is the best walk, starting **from Áno Tithoréa**, but it involves taking a bus or train and then local taxi to the trailhead – plus camping out on the mountain. If you want a more casual look at Parnassós, it's probably better to walk up **from the Dhelfí side**, as a continuation of the Corycian cave outing, overnighting at the hamlet of **Kalývia** on the Livádhi plateau, some 45 minutes' walk beyond the cave. Here there are numerous chalet-hotels for skiers and a number of tavernas which operate all year.

For the energetic, it's possible to traverse the whole massif in around fifteen hours' walking time, starting from Dhelfí and descending at Áno Tithoréa, or vice versa. You will, however, need full camping equipment, as springs are poorly spaced, and the alpine shelters near the summit are either locked or very primitive.

Áno Tithoréa to Liákoura via the Velítsa ravine

The principal surviving wilderness route up Parnassós to Liákoura involves starting with a trip by train or bus as far as Káto Tithoréa, which is on the Livadhià–Amfíklia road and the Athens–Thessaloníki railway. You then need to get to the higher, twin village of **Áno Tithoréa**, a four-kilometre haul easiest accomplished by taxi (usually available, but bargain for the price beforehand). You should allow at least six hours for the ascent, and around four and a half hours for the descent, so it's best to arrive early in the day; come equipped for camping out on the mountain as lodging can be difficult to find.

From the platía in Áno Tithoréa, head southwest out of town until you reach some park benches overlooking the giant **Velítsa ravine**. Adjacent is a "waterfall" (in reality a leak in an aqueduct) which crosses the path beginning here a few minutes above the benches. A hundred metres further, bear left away from what seems to be the main track and descend towards the bed of the canyon. Once you're on the far side you can see the aqueduct again, now uncovered. Follow it until you reach the isolated chapel of Áyios Ioánnis (1hr from Áno Tithoréa).

Past the chapel, a fine alpine path heads off through the firs before you. The way is obvious for the next ninety minutes, with tremendous views of the crags filing up to the Liákoura summit, on your right across the valley. You emerge on a narrow neck of land, with a brief glimpse over the Ayía Marína valley and a monastery of Kímisis Theotókou to the east (left) – as well as a dirt track which nearly meets your route. The path, faint for an interval, heads slightly downhill and to the right to meet the floor of the Velítsa at the Tsáres spring (3hr 30min) – it's the last reliable water supply, so best fill up.

On the far bank of the river, head up a steep, scree-laden slope through the last of the trees to some sheep pens (4hr), then climb up to another pastoral hut (4hr 30min) at the base of the defile leading down from the main summit ridge. Beyond this point the going is gentler for much of the final ascent to the northwest (top right-hand) corner of this valley. A brief scramble up a rockfall to a gap in the ridge and you are at the base of Liákoura (5hr 30min). Orange paint-splashes – primarily orientated for those descending – stake out most of the approach from the Tsáres spring.

The **final ascent** is an easy twenty-minute scramble more or less up to the ridge line. On a clear morning, especially after rain, you're supposed to be able to see Mount

Olympus in the north, the Aegean to the east, the Ionian to the west and way down into the Peloponnese to the south. The best viewing is said to be in midsummer, but all too often you can see only cloud.

Along the gulf: Delphi to Náfpaktos

The train-less, almost beach-less north shore of the **Gulf of Kórinthos** is far less frequented than the south coast. The arid landscape, with harsh mountains inland, can be initially off-putting, but there are bits of cultivated valley and coastal plain, and attractive, low-key resorts in **Galaxídhi** and **Náfpaktos**, both reasonably well connected by bus. This coast also offers convenient access south to the Peloponnese, via the ferries at Áyios Nikólaos–Éyio or Andírio–Río. From both Éyio and Río, you can reach Pátra by rail or road. Alternatively, heading in the opposite direction, it is easy to reach Dhiakoftó and the Kalávryta rack-and-pinion railway (see p.261).

All buses heading southwest of Delphi towards the Gulf of Kórinthos stop first at Itéa, a gritty little town (literally, owing to the bauxite-ore dust hovering everywhere) where you may have to change buses for the next leg of the journey. (For the continuation of the route west from Andírio to Messolóngi and Agrínio, see p.367.)

Galaxídhi

GALAXÍDHI, 17km southwest of Itéa, is the first place you'd want to break a journey voluntarily, a quiet port rearing mirage-like out of an otherwise lifeless shore. The old town stands on a raised headland, crowned by the photogenic church of Áyios Nikólaos, patron saint of sailors. Two- and three- masted *kaïkia* and schooners were built alongside the old harbour of Hirólakkas, north of the headland, until the early 1900s; clusters of nineteenth-century shipowners' mansions, reminders of those prosperous days, have lately become the haunt of Athenian second-homers. Despite their restorations and a bit of a marina ethos down at the main southern harbour, the town still remains just the right side of tweeness, with an animated commercial high street and a variety of watering-holes. Just uphill from the new harbour, a small **maritime museum** (Sat–Sun 9.30am–2pm, Tues–Fri 9.30am–1pm; free) contains paintings and models of ships as well as old figureheads, while a modest **folk art museum** (daily except Tues 9.30am–1.30pm; 500dr), in an imposing tower-mansion just inland from Hirólakkas, has three rooms of turn-of-the-century embroideries and fashions.

There is no real beach, but if you stroll around the pine-covered headland flanking the new harbour, you'll find tiny pebbly **coves**, with chapel-crowned islets offshore. The only other local diversion is the four-kilometre drive up to the **monastery of Metamórfosis Sotíros**, well signposted under the flyover just west of town; the magnificent view is the thing, as the thirteenth-century *katholikón* is visibly unsound structurally and bare of frescoes – a single nun lives in the modern cloister alongside.

Practicalities

Accommodation is on the pricey side and hard to find in summer, or at weekends year-round, though all of it is en suite and usually with air-conditioning. The two least expensive places are the modern *Hotel Koukonas* (☎0265/41 179; ④), inland from the end of the new harbour, with clean if plain rooms, or the better-placed *Rooms Hirolakkas* (0265/41 170; ③), in a modernized old building beside the folk museum, where the sea breeze from Hirólakkas bay does duty for air-conditioning. Among several top-flight outfits, the clear winners are the *Hotel Galaxa* (☎0265/41 620, fax 42 053; ⑤), on the hillside beyond Hirólakkas, with a garden bar for views, and the delightful

Italian-run *Ganimede Hotel* (☎0265/41 328, fax 42 160; ④; closed Nov) in an old sea captain's house off the market street, with courtyard fountain garden plus good-value breakfasts.

Local consensus credits *To Porto* on the south harbour with being the best all-round **restaurant** for fish and *mayireftá*, though *Albatross*, inland on the street near Áyios Nikólaos, will also have very limited quantities of well-executed dishes from a similarly restricted menu. For a mix of authentic Italian and Greek specialities, look no further than the *Dhrosou*, on the same street as the *Ganimede*. Also worth mentioning as a simple grill is *O Dhionysos*, at the head of the south harbour, on Platía Máma. Galaxídhi is large enough to support a **post office** and a **bank** with a cash dispenser.

Áyios Nikólaos and Trizónia

West of Galaxídhi lies some of the sparsest scenery along the Greek shoreline; there are a few villages with scrappy beaches, none of them really warranting a stop. At **Áyios Nikólaos**, however, there's a year-round **ferry** across the gulf to the Peloponnese – an alternative to the crossing at Andírio–Río, 60km further west (see p.287). These ro-ro boats require forty minutes for the journey (9 times daily in summer, 6.30am–10pm, 550dr per passenger, 3300dr per car; ☎0266/31 854 or 0691/22 792). Westbound bus timings are perversely designed to just miss coinciding with ferry departures; if you miss the last sailing, **accommodation** possibilities include Theodore Katharakis's rooms (☎0266/31 177; ③), just east of the pebble beach. On a bluff, high above the coast road, sits the well-maintained campsite, *Doric Village* (☎0266/31 195), which also offers bungalows (④).

Trizónia

The Gulf of Kórinthos has about a dozen islets, but **Trizónia** – roughly halfway between Áyios Nikólaos and Náfpaktos, just across a narrow strait – is the largest and only inhabited one (permanent population circa 55). Green with vegetation and blissfully vehicle-free (except for a handful of service trucks), it has long been a favourite stopover for yachters, and makes an idyllic retreat for conventional travellers despite a lack of good beaches. To reach the island, follow signs from the main highway down to the settlement of Haniá (only its neighbour Glyfádha is shown on most maps), where a little boat shuttles across 11 times daily until about 9pm (200dr per person; more frequent in mid-summer). This calls at the appealing fishing harbour with its three fish **tavernas**, among which *Ta Dhyo Limania* and *Porto Trizonia* both prove reasonable and friendly. The sole **accommodation** is the modern but well-designed *Hotel Drymna* (☎0266/71 204, fax 71 304; ③), most of whose peaceful rooms overlook the yacht anchorage – and *Lizzie's Yacht Club* on the hillside opposite, a revered institution amongst the boating fraternity but open to all, constituting the island's main **nightlife**. The access track to it continues towards Trizónia's southeast tip, where the small, red-sand beach at Poúnda, a half-hour in total from the village, is the best of several swimming coves on the far side of the island.

Náfpaktos

The other place that stands out west of Galaxídhi, and indeed the largest settlement on the gulf's north shore, is **NÁFPAKTOS**, a lively market town and resort which straggles for some distance along the seafront, below its rambling Venetian castle. Some two hours' drive from Dhelfí, or an hour by buses and ferry from Pátra, it makes a convenient and attractive stopover, though diversion of the relentlessly heavy traffic through town would enhance its charm.

The pine-tufted **kástro** provides a picturesque backdrop, plus an enjoyable stroll through old houses to the top of its fortifications. The curtain walls plunge down to the sea, enclosing the oval-shaped old harbour and the westerly beach, with one of the original gates giving access to one end of the latter. The castle was long a formidable part of the Venetian Greek defences, and the **Battle of Lepanto** (Náfpaktos's medieval name) was fought just offshore from here in 1571. An allied Christian armada commanded by John of Austria devastated an Ottoman fleet – the first European naval victory over the Turks since the death of the dreaded pirate-admiral Barbarossa; Cervantes, author of *Don Quixote*, lost his left arm to a cannonball during the conflict. But Western supremacy on the high seas proved fleeting, since the Ottomans quickly replaced their shipping and wrested Cyprus from the Venetians the following year.

Practicalities

Buses run northwest to Agrínio (where you can pick up services to Ioánnina or Lefkádha), and east to Itéa and Ámfissa (for connections north into Thessaly). Local blue-and-white city buses go frequently to the ferry at Andírio, or you can sometimes get a seat on a long-distance bus heading to Pátra.

Despite a dozen hotels and a similar number of rooms or apartments, **accommodation** can be in short supply in summer, and noisy at any season. The westerly beach, with Navmahías as its frontage road, is both central and relatively quiet, and the place to go if your finances will stretch to the spotless *Plaza House* (☎0634/22 226, fax 23 174; ⑤) or the apartments *Regina*, run by two friendly young ladies (☎0634/21 555, fax 21 556; ④). Budget options include the shabby, non-en-suite *Hotel Amaryllis* (☎0634/27 237; ②), on Platía Liménos, just tolerable if you have a back room looking onto the castle walls; in the same price range, *Hotel Aegli* (☎0634/27 271; ③), at Ilárhou Kósta Tzavéla 75 (the westbound main thoroughfare), is also non-en-suite and even noisier. For another more tranquil setting, there's a cluster of comfortable hotels on the easterly beach, in Grímbovo district 2km out of the centre: the *Nafpaktos* (☎0634/29 551, fax 29 553; ⑤) is a modern place which promises an "American-style" breakfast, the *Akti* (☎0634/28 464, fax 24 171; ④) across the street is less pretentious, while the spanking clean *Hotel Afroditi* (☎0634/2992; ③) is closer to the shore. There's a good **campsite**, *Platanitis Beach* (☎0634/31 555; mid-May to Sept), 5km west of the town towards Andírio; to get there, catch a blue city bus from the main square – the last one leaves at 10pm.

There are few bona fide **restaurants**; the *Molos Taverna* and *Papoulis Ouzeri*, just east of the old port, are enjoyable and not too touristy. Otherwise, a local sweet tooth is attested to by an improbable number of **cafés** offering crepes, waffles and ice cream. One of the best, if not the most alluringly set, is the hygienic and friendly *Kreperi* at Mesolongíou 9, with a vast selection of fillings. The old port is completely ringed by cafés and bars which provide a fair proportion of Náfpaktos's **nightlife** and daytime dalliance as well.

The Andírio–Río ferry

The ferry at **Andírio** runs across the Gulf of Kórinthos to Río (see p.260) every fifteen minutes from 6.45am until 10.45pm, and less frequently during the night. The trip takes barely fifteen minutes, and fares are 120dr per passenger, 1500dr per car and driver. However, all this will be a thing of the past after 2002, when a giant, anti-seismic **suspension bridge** is completed by a French consortium.

Once across to Río, you can generally pick up a city bus immediately for Pátra, but as through bus services between the Dhelfí area and Pátra have improved in recent years, it might be worth getting one of these in Náfpaktos or even sooner. In summer, drivers should count on waiting for around thirty minutes to be loaded onto the ferry.

There are a few snack bars and – in the unlikely event you get stuck – the *Hotel Andirrion* (☎0634/31 450; ③) and the *Dounis Beach* campsite (☎0634/31 565; May–Oct) are on the Náfpaktos–Andírio road, 1km east of the ferry quay.

North to Lamía

Lamía is a half-day's journey north from Dhelfí, with a connection at Ámfissa: a slow but pleasant route skirting mounts Parnassós, Gióna and (to the northwest) Íti. At the historic pass of **Thermopylae**, the road joins the **coastal highway** from Athens.

Inland via Ámfissa

The inland road west from Dhelfí climbs slowly through a sea of groves, source of the acclaimed local green olives, to **ÁMFISSA**, a small town in the foothills of Mount Gióna. Its medieval name of Salona is still used conversationally; like Livadhiá, this strategic military location was a base for the Catalan Grand Company, who have left their mark on the **castle**. If you have time to kill between buses (the KTEL is on the main square), its ruins, which incorporate remnants of an ancient acropolis, make for a pleasant walk, if only to enjoy the shade of the pine trees and examine a few stretches of classical polygonal masonry. The **market** quarter of the town also repays a stroll: Ámfissa was once one of the major bell-making centres in the Balkans, and copper-alloy sheep bells are still produced and sold here. You would be unlucky to get stranded here, but if so, the *Apollon* at Gidhoyánnou 14, one block east of the platía (☎0265/72 261;③) is the best of three modest **hotels**. More likely you'll only patronize one of several café-bars on the partly pedestrianized square.

Serious **walkers** may want to use Ámfissa as a jumping-off point for the mountains west and north towards Karpeníssi: **Gióna**, **Vardhoússia** and **Íti**. There are bus routes, some only running once or twice weekly, to various trailhead villages in the foothills of these peaks, as well as to Lidhoríki, due west of Ámfissa, with better access to Vardhoússia and Gióna. Most travellers, however, continue north along the scenic **Lamía road**, dividing mounts Parnassós and Gióna, or along the **rail line** from Livadhiá to Lamía. This is one of the most dramatic stretches of railway in Europe, and has a history to match: it runs through the foothills of Gióna and Íti, and over the precipitous defile of the **Gorgopótamos River**, where in 1942 the Greek Resistance – all factions united for the first and last time, under the command of the British intelligence officer Brigadier Eddie Meyers – blew up a critical railway viaduct, cutting one of the Germans' vital supply lines to their army in North Africa for three months.

The coastal highway

The first 60km of the **Athens–Lamía** coastal highway are fast, efficient and generally dull. But as some patches beyond are being improved slowly, drivers should proceed with caution. Generally fairly flat, it runs a little inland, skirting various pockets of seasonal lakebed, like Límni Ilíki, north of Thíva, before reaching the coast. The most interesting stop, along with Thíva (see p.271) is the Mycenaean citadel of **Gla** (see p.272), near the village of Kástro.

There are also various links with the island of **Évvia**: first at Halkídha (where there's a causeway); then by ferry at **Arkítsa** to Loutrá Edhipsoú (every hour in season, every 2hr out of season, last at 9pm, 10.30pm July–Aug; 50min; passengers 530dr, cars 3300dr). Arkítsa itself is a rather upmarket resort, popular mainly with Greeks.

Áyios Konstandínos and Kaména Voúrla

Áyios Konstandínos is the closest port to Athens if you're heading for the islands of the Sporades. There are daily car **ferries**, usually just after midday, to Skiáthos and Skópelos, with an additional evening departure in season which continues on to Alónissos. In summer there are also at least three daily Flying Dolphin **hydrofoils** (passengers only) to Skiáthos, Skópelos and Alónissos; these are about twice as fast and twice as expensive as the ferry. For ferry information contact Alkyon Travel (☎0235/31 920); for hydrofoil information call the Flying Dolphin Office (☎0235/ 31 614), adjacent on the main square.

There should be no reason to stay in Áyios Konstandínos, but if you're stranded you can choose from among eight **hotels** – try the very simple *Hotel Poulia* (☎0235/31 663; ②) or the more pleasant *Amfitryon* (☎0235/31 702; ③) on the waterfront – and a **campsite**, *Camping Blue Bay* (☎0235/314 25). *O Faros Taverna* by the sea serves up a variety of fresh fishy delights.

Kaména Voúrla, 9km north, has a better beach; this is, however, very much a resort, used mainly by Greeks attracted by the spas here and at neighbouring Loutrá Thermopylíon (see below). Seafood aficionados are well looked after at the long line of decent fish tavernas along the promenade here, and there are dozens of acceptable hotels and rooms on the main street and shady backstreets.

Thermopylae and its spa

Just before joining the inland road, the highway enters the **Pass of Thermopylae**, where Leonidas and three hundred Spartans made a last stand against Xerxes's thirty-thousand-strong Persian army in 480 BC. The pass was much more defined in ancient times: a narrow defile with Mount Kalídhromo to the south and the sea – which has silted and retreated nearly 4km – to the north.

The tale of Spartan bravery is described at length by **Herodotus**. Leonidas, King of Sparta, stood guard over the pass with a mixed force of seven thousand Greeks, confident that it was the only approach an army could take to enter Greece from Thessaly. By night, however, Xerxes sent an advance party of his forces along a mountain trail and broke through the pass to attack the Greeks from the rear. Leonidas ordered a retreat of the main army, but remained in the pass himself, with his Spartan guard, to delay the Persians' progress. He and all but two of the guard fought to their deaths.

Loutrá Thermopylíon, midway through the pass, is named for the hot springs present here since antiquity. The grave mound of the fallen Spartans lies 500m away, opposite a gloriously heroic statue of Leonidas. The spa and restaurant facilities are intimidatingly built up, but there are a few cascades and drainage sluices where you can bathe undisturbed in the open air, if you can stomach the sulphurous stench.

Lamía and onward routes

LAMÍA is a busy provincial capital and an important transport junction for travellers. It sees few overnight visitors, but has a worthwhile sight in the Catalan castle, and abounds in excellent ouzeris and kafenía.

Heading **north from Lamía** there's a choice of three routes: to Tríkala and Kalambáka, to Lárissa, or around the coast to Vólos, but none is especially memorable. Fársala and Kardhítsa, on the routes to Lárissa and Tríkala respectively, are small, very ordinary country towns. The **Vólos road**, however, leading east along the coast, has a little more to delay your progress.

Lamía

The town centre is arranged around three main squares: Platía Párkou, Platía Eleftherías and Platía Laoú, the latter two good venues for sipping a drink and watching Greek life go by. **Platía Eleftherías** is the town's social hub and scene of the evening vólta, with outdoor café tables and a little bandstand-gazebo. The cathedral and Neoclassical provincial government building flank the square on the north, with the Galaxias two-plex winter cinema tucked into the southwest corner. Just east and downhill from Eleftherías is the atmospheric **Platía Laoú**, shaded by plane trees crowded in autumn with migratory birds. The third square, **Platía Párkou,** lies amidst the main shopping area, with several **banks** (with cash dispensers) grouped around it, and blue city buses flocking here to spawn, as it were. On Saturdays, the streets below Párkou turn into a lively **market**, with everything from rheumatism cures to plastic combs on sale.

Looking down on the city from the north is the fourteenth-century Catalan castle, which boasts superb views and also houses an archeological **museum** (Tues–Sun 8.30am–2.30pm; 500dr) exhibiting a variety of finds – Neolithic, Mycenaean, Classical, Hellenistic and Roman – in a Neoclassical building dating from the 1850s. Other diversions in Lamía include a state **theatre** on Ipsilándou (which leads northwest from Laoú), used for art exhibitions and in winter as an art-film cinema.

Practicalities

Buses, including a local service from the train station (6km out), arrive at terminals scattered throughout the town, though none is much further than ten minutes' walk away from Platía Párkou. Karpeníssi services use a terminal on Márkou Bótsari; those for Ámfissa, Lárissa, Tríkala and the north, a terminal (the remotest) out on Thermopýlon, past the train tracks; those for Vólos, the stop at the corner of Livadhítou and Rozáki-Ángeli; while buses for Athens and Thessaloníki go from the corner of Papakyriazí and Satovriándou, near the Karpeníssi station. The most convenient **taxi** rank is at the top end of Andhroútsou, behind the cathedral.

Accommodation prospects are vastly overpriced and poorly sited in Lamía. There are a couple of drab hotels on Ódhos Rozáki-Ángeli, convenient to the nearby meat-and-fish market: the dire *Thermopylae* (☎0231/21 366; ④) at no. 36, and the slightly better *Athina* (☎0231/20 700; ④) across the way at no. 41. The *Samaras* (☎0231/42 701; ⑥) opposite the **post office** on pretty Platía Dhiákou, south of Eleftherías, is a more attractive alternative, but disinclined to bargain much; the *Apollonio* at one corner of Párkou (entrance on Vasakári; ☎0231/22 668; ⑤) makes a reasonable compromise.

By contrast, you're spoilt for choice in the matter of **food and drink**, making Lamía a good lunch halt. On Laoú you'll find two decent *mayireftá* tavernas, the *Megalexandhros* and (actually around the corner on Kalyvá Bakoyánni) the *Ilysia*, the latter in particular offers a wide variety of reasonably priced casserole specialities. Leading off from one corner of this platía is Karaïskáki, a vegetarian's nightmare of a street, with whole sheep roasting on spits and the smell of *patsás* (tripe-and-trotter soup) wafting though the air. Andhroútsou, a mostly pedestrianized lane threading between platías Laoú and Eleftherías, is crammed full of attractive ouzeris, of which *Aman Aman* and *Allo Skedhio* are reckoned the best; the former (evenings only) beyond the cathedral, the latter one of three clustered in a nameless tiny plaza just down some steps from Eleftherías. The most durable cafés in Platía Eleftherías are the *Viva*, *Remezzo* and *Contratto*.

Lamía to Vólos

The first temptation on the coast road to Vólos is **Ayía Marína**, 12km east of Lamía, where the seafood tavernas – a popular weekend jaunt for Lamian families – are much better than the rather pathetic beach.

A couple of kilometres further, **STYLÍDHA** was once one of the major ports of the Aegean; it was at the opera house here that Maria Callas's grandfather outsang a visiting Italian star and started a dynasty. Today the unsightly town is chiefly concerned with olive-oil bottling and cement – not an inspiring prospect, and there is no longer any hydrofoil service from here to the Sporades to prompt a stop. At Karavómylos and Akhládhi, 8km and 19km east of Stylídha respectively, the fish tavernas are again more inviting than the beaches, though you'll need your own transport.

The best beaches along this route are near **Glýfa** 30km further north, though it is 11km off the highway and served only by one afternoon bus from Lamía. It has the mainland's northernmost ferry crossing to **Évvia**: eight times daily in July and August to Áyiokambos (last ferry at 8.30–9.30pm summer, 5.30pm winter; 30min; passengers 350dr, cars 2700dr). **Rooms** are on offer in private houses and at several hotels, the cheapest of which is the *Oassis* (☎0238/61 353; ②).

Finally, rounding the Pagasitic Gulf towards Vólos, car drivers might want to stop at **Néa Anhíalos**, where five early Christian basilicas have been uncovered. Their mosaics and the small site museum are interesting, though perhaps not enough to make it worth risking a three-hour wait between buses.

West to Karpeníssi – and beyond

The road west from Lamía climbs out of the Sperhiós valley, with glimpses on the way of mounts Íti, Gióna and Vardhoússia, 10km to the south. If you want to do some **hiking**, there are satisfying routes on Mount Íti (the classical Oeta), easiest approached from the village of Ipáti. The **Karpeníssi valley**, too, lends itself to walking trips amid a countryside of dark fir forest and snow-fringed mountains, which the EOT promotes (with some justice) as "the Greek Switzerland". Since the mid-1990s, both summer and winter tourism, mostly domestic, has really taken off here, such that accommodation prices in the Karpeníssi area are also authentically Swiss. Besides walking, skiing on Mount Tymfristós and summertime rafting on the local rivers are the main outdoor activities.

Ipáti and Mount Íti

Mount Íti is one of the most beautiful of Greek mountains, its green northeast slopes constituting a national park, and also unusually accessible by Greek standards. There are buses almost hourly from Lamía to Ipáti, the usual trailhead; if you arrive by train, these can be picked up en route at Lamía's "local" station, Lianokládhi, 6km from the town. Be sure not to get off the bus at the sulphurous spa of Loutrá Ipátis, 5km north of and below Ipáti proper.

IPÁTI is a medium-sized village, clustered below a castle, with two modest **hotels**, catering mainly for Greek families: the courteous *Panorama* (☎0231/98 222; ②), just above the square and open most of the year, or the more basic and noisy *Panhellinion* (☎0231/98 340; ②) right on the platía, open in high summer only. There are also a couple of reasonable **tavernas**, such as *To Hani* on the road into town.

Route-finding on Mount Íti has been eased recently by the availability of a decent topographic map published by Road Editions (no. 43, 1:50,000, with route summaries in English). The classic full traverse of the range from Ipáti to Pávliani, taking in the 2150m summit of Pýrgos, is an ambitious undertaking of between ten and eleven hours, best spread over two days; a limited day outing, however, should be feasible if you've reasonable orientation skills. The way out of Ipáti, starting from the square, is marked with red paint splodges or square placards; the actual path starting at the top of the village leads in around four hours to an EOS refuge known as **Trápeza** (usually locked, but with a spring and camping space nearby). This is a steep but rewarding walk, giving a good idea of Íti's sheer rock ramparts and lush meadows. From there you could return on a different path via Zapandólakka to Ipáti for a full-day loop hike, overnighting twice in the village. Otherwise, continue more or less due south to the flat-topped peak, where in legend Herakles (Hercules) killed himself to escape the agony of the poisoned tunic which his wife Deinaneira had given him. From there, proceed southwest via the Piyés and Katavóthra plateaus, on a mixture of track, path and cross-country surface, to the village of Pávliani where there are food, lodging and uncertain connections back to Lamía.

Karpeníssi

The main road west from Lamía and Ipáti, after scaling a spur of Mount Tymfristós (an all-year tunnel below the snowline is set to open in late 2000), drops down to the town of **KARPENÍSSI**. Its site is spectacular – huddled at the base of the peak and head of the Karpenisiótis valley, which extends south all the way to the wall-like Mount Panetolikó – though the town itself is entirely nondescript, having been destroyed in World War II by the Germans and again during the civil war. During the latter, it was captured and held for a week by Communist guerrillas in January 1949. In the course of the fighting, an American pilot was shot down – thereby gaining, as C.M.Woodhouse observes in *Modern Greece*, "probably the unenviable distinction of being the first American serviceman to be killed in action by Communist arms".

Except on summer weekends or during the skiing season, **accommodation** is easily found, if not that appealing; most of the eight hotels are noisy or overpriced, though bargaining at midweek is always productive. Best value and quietest are the *Galini* (☎0237/22 914;④) on Ríga Feréou 3, a lane in the bazaar, followed by *Elvetia* at Zinopoúlou 17 (☎0237/22 465, fax 80 112; ③ no bath, ④ en suite) and the plush *Anesis* (☎0237/80 700; ⑥) at Zinopoúlou 50. Zinopoúlou leads into town from the east, winding up at the leafy central square and adjacent **KTEL terminal**. The friendly municipal **tourist office** (☎0237/21016), opposite the **bus** and **taxi** stations, is a mine of information on the whole area, dispensing useful free maps. They also keep lists of accommodation (typically ②–③), the most obvious of which, central yet quiet, are Kostas Koutsikos' *Dhomátia*, up some steps opposite the *dhimarhío* (☎0237/21 400; ②). For the desperate, there's always the seedy *Lefkon Oros/Mont Blanc Hotel* (☎0237/21 341; ②), festooned with the washing of seasonal workers renting long-term.

Eating options are similarly limited; central exceptions to the plethora of fast-food outlets and après-ski *barákia* are the *Psistaria Spitiko Poniras*, opposite the bus station, or *Adherfi Triandafylli*, a good all-rounder opposite the OTE, just southwest of the square. For a bit more, locals prefer *Esy Oti Pis*, past the police station, at the start of the road to Agrínio, or (going a bit further, then left) the garden-seating *Panorama*, just below an unmissable unfinished hotel.

Finally, if you want to join an organized rafting or hiking expedition in the nearby mountains, contact the local branch of Trekking Hellas (☎0237/25 940 or 094/42 06 308) or in Athens.

Around Karpeníssi

Your first conceivable halt in the Karpenissiótis valley, 5km by road south of town, is the museum-village of **KORYSKHÁDES**, whose stone houses are famous for their ornate wooden balconies with views across the valley to Mount Kaliakoúdha. All but three of the permanent population have decamped, selling up to an enterprise which has meticulously restored several mansions as premier **accommodation** – rooms, suites, family apartments – priced in Swiss fashion (☎0237/25 102, fax 23 456; ⑤ buffet breakfast included). The only place to **eat or drink** is the combination kafenío-restaurant, also the scheme's contact office, on the repaved platía.

Megálo Horió and Mikró Horió

For villages with more of a lived-in feel to them, and more of this stunning countryside, head 16km downriver, again on the main valley-floor, to **MEGÁLO HORIÓ** and **MIKRÓ HORIÓ** ("Big Village" and "Little Village"); buses make the trip twice daily. Megálo, on the left-hand (east) side of the valley, has slightly more choice in places to stay and eat, but again no bargains. The friendliest, best sited and least expensive **accommodation** is the *Agnandi* (☎0237/41 303; ③), to your left on the approach road, being modern but tasteful rooms with knockout views across the village to the mountains, and a communal ground-floor kitchen. Otherwise try the garden-set *Anerada Pension* (☎0237/41 535, ⑤) or, right in the heart of things, the "high-rise" *Antigone Hotel* (☎0237/41 395; ④) which doubles as the main bar. There's a small **restaurant** adjacent, near which red-paint waymarks stake out the start of the three-and-a-half-hour one way trek up Mount Kaliakoúdha (2098m) which dominates the village.

Mikró, visible across the valley at the foot of Mount Helidhóna, has a turbulent history; it was a major centre for the World War II Resistance, with a clandestine printing press, and in January 1963 an avalanche effectively wiped out the western tip of the village, killing thirteen. The place was already in bad official odour because of its wartime stance, and every goverment since the disaster has exerted pressure in various ways to move the survivors 4km downhill to the replacement Néo (New) Mikró Horió. Here "Swiss" silliness reaches its apotheosis in the pretentious *Country Club Hellas Hotel* (☎0273/41 570, fax 41 577), where you can drop over 30,000dr a night if you're so inclined. There are a few other, more reasonable options in the village, but it's best to continue to road's end at Paleó (Old) Mikró Horió, where the en-suite *Helidhona Hotel* (☎0237/41 221, mobile ☎094/5368945; ④) by the fountain and plane tree is about the most reasonable lodging in the valley, with rare single rates and knockout views out back towards Mount Tymfristós. Cooking at the ground-floor restaurant is only average but cheap and sustaining; there are no shops in the moribund village, so come equipped for the three-hour hike up Mount Helidhóna (1978m), indicated by blue or yellow waymarks.

Proussós and beyond

Beyond these villages, the valley narrows to a spectacular **gorge** with two narrows at Klidhí and Patímata tis Panayías before emerging at the junction of the Karpenisiótis and Trikeriótis rivers at Dhípotama, where rafting outfitters begin their expeditions. A paved if steep road through the canyon has made a visit to the monastery and village of **PROUSSÓS** (33km out of Karpeníssi) easier than before, though only three afternoon buses a week do the trip. The **monastery**, amazingly set on a cliff in a bend of a Trikeriótis tributary, opposite two rock pinnacles, flanked by two eighteenth-century defensive towers associated with Yeóryios Karaïskakis, the revolutionary war figure who used the place as a stronghold. Massive and much rebuilt after a succession of fires (started by candles), Proussoú (the official nomenclature) is presently inhabited by just two monks plus some layworkers. Coachloads of pilgrims pay reverence to the icon of the Panayía Proussiótissa in the ninth-century *katholikón*. Here, or in the treasury (*skevofylakíon*), you can see curiosities such as paper made from the skin of an embryo goat and an icon of the Panayía with its eyes gouged out. (According to the locals, the Communist rebels of the 1940s were responsible for this, though the Turks were wont to perform the same sacrilege, and credulous villagers attributed magical powers to the dust thus obtained.)

The **village**, a kilometre further on, has a drab community **hotel**, the *Agathidis* (☎0237/80 813; ④) and several meat-orientated, evening-only tavernas around the central square; more reliably open, and with good, cheap *mayireftá*, is the *Proussiotissa Taverna* just off the side-drive to the monastery.

Routes out of Karpeníssi

Roads southwest or north from Karpeníssi climb high into the mountains of **Ágrafa**, the southernmost extension of the Píndhos. In winter critical passes are generally closed, but through the summer they're generally serviceable.

The most remote and dramatic route, with no bus service, is on **south from Proussós** (see above), but you'll need a jeep or vehicle with high clearance, as there's 12km of incredibly rough dirt track over Panetolikó until pavement resumes at Lambíri, where a narrow but paved road brings you out after 21km more at **Thérmo**, on the shores of Lake Trihonídha. There you are within striking distance (and a daily bus ride) of Agrínio, with its connections to Patrá and Ioánnina (see p.254 and p.329 respectively).

The direct **Karpeníssi–Agrínio** road is paved, but extremely sinuous, so it still takes the one morning bus a good three and a half hours to cover the 115km. The beauty of the first half of the journey cannot be overemphasized; it's largely empty country, with the only place of any size (having a filling station and a taverna) being the village of **Frangísta**, which straddles a valley, 41km from Karpeníssi. Beyond Frangísta, the bus trundles past the giant **Kremastón dam** on the Tavropós, Trikeriótis and Aheлóös rivers, skirts Panetolikó, then winds down through tobacco-planted hills to Agrínio. If you wish to explore the Ágrafa wilderness to the north, leave the bus at the turnoff for Kerasohóri, 27km out of Karpeníssi.

With your own transport, one of the best options – giving direct access to the Metéora (see p.315) – is the **route north to Kardhítsa**, which takes off from the top of the pass east of Karpeníssi, directly above the soon-to-be-completed tunnel. Except for a few short dirt patches – being repaired – the way is paved and wide, a beautiful drive where sweeping vistas over central Greece alternate with fir forest. It's 28km around Mount Tymfristós to the turning for **Fourná** village, with a hotel (*Wild Beauty* ☎0237/51 223; ③) if needed; then 64km more to Kardhítsa, with little in between other than **Loutropiyí**, where you can munch on *souvláki*; **Loutrá Smokóvou**, where you can drown any sorrows in the little spa; and Kédhros, with the first fuel since Karpeníssi, and where the road straightens out for the final flat and straight approach to Kardhítsa. Allow just over two hours from Karpeníssi – a considerable saving in time and mileage versus going all the way back to Lamía, and then northwest across the dull Thessalian plains.

THESSALY

The highlights of travelling through **Thessaly** are easily summarized. Over to the east, curling down from the industrial port-city of Vólos, is the **Pílion** (Pelion) mountain peninsula. The villages on its lush, orchard-covered slopes are among the most beautiful in the country – a long-established resort area for Greeks and numerous foreign camper-van tourists, though still with many unspoiled corners. To the west is a sight not to be missed on any mainland exploration: the extraordinary "monasteries in the air" of the **Metéora**.

The **central plains** are to be passed through, rather than visited. That said, **Lárissa**, the region's capital, is making itself into a relatively pleasant city, besides providing efficient connections by bus to Vólos and to Kalambáka (via Tríkala).

Heading north or west from Lárissa, you'll find yourself in one mountain range or another. The dramatic route over the Píndhos, from Kalambáka to Ioánnina, is covered in the following chapter. North from Kalambáka there are reasonable roads, though few buses, into western Macedonia, with the lakeside town of Kastoriá an obvious focus. Most travellers, however, head north from Lárissa towards Thessaloníki, a very beautiful route in the shadow of Mount Olympus (see Chapter Five).

Vólos

Arriving at the city of **VÓLOS** gives little hint of Pílion's promise. It's hard to imagine the mythological past of this busy modern port, but this is the site of ancient Iolkos, from where Jason and the Argonauts set off on their quest for the Golden Fleece. Greece's fastest-growing industrial centre and a major depot for long-distance truck drivers, Vólos was rebuilt in utilitarian style after a series of devastating earthquakes between 1947 and 1957, and is now edging to its natural limits against the Pílion foothills behind. This admitted, it's a lively place with a large university-student population, beginning to revel in recently acquired prosperity, and you could do worse than spend a few hours or even a night here while waiting for a bus up the mountain or a boat to Skiáthos, Skópelos or Alónissos, for which Vólos is the **main port**.

The most attractive place to linger is along the eastern waterfront esplanade, between the landscaped **Platía Yeoryíou** and the archeological museum, which is itself a highly recommended diversion. Imaginatively laid out and clearly labelled in English, the **Archeological Museum** (daily except Mon 8.30am–3pm; 500dr) features a unique collection of painted grave *stelai* depicting, in now-faded colours, the everyday scenarios of fifth-century BC life, as well as a variety of graves complete with skeletons. It also has one of the best European collections of Neolithic pottery, tools and figurines, from the local sites of Sesklo and Dimini (both of which – respectively 15km and 3km west of Vólos – can be visited, though they are of essentially specialist interest).

Along with Lárissa, Halkídha and Ioánnina, Vólos was historically home to one of the larger **Jewish communities** of central Greece. Local Jews were well integrated into the social and political life of the town, such that during World War II only 155 out of the thousand-strong community were caught and killed by the Nazis; the rest joined the Resistance or were otherwise sheltered on Mount Pílion. The victims have a prominent, sculpted memorial in one corner of Platía Ríga Feréou, donated by one of the survivors.

Practicalities

Ferries and hydrofoils call at the port's **main quay**, and most other services are found within a couple of blocks. An exception is the **bus station** on Grigoríou Lambráki, ten minutes' walk southwest of the main square, **Platía Ríga Feréou**. Arrayed around the latter are the **train station** and the fairly helpful **EOT** office (Mon–Fri 7.30am–2pm ☎0421/23 500 or 37 417), which provides information on bus and ferry services as well as accommodation. Better maps, and a selection of foreign-language books and periodicals, can be found at Tsekouras, Venizélou 1, just by the quay. Like Áyios Konstandínos, Vólos has regular ferries and, in summer, quicker hydrofoils to the Sporades. **Ferries** leave two to three times daily for Skiáthos, Skópelos and Alónissos; the last departure is generally 5pm (except on Sat). **Hydrofoils** (Minoan Flying Dolphins, ☎0421/39 786) run four or five times daily to Skiáthos, Skópelos and Alónissos, continuing five times a week to Skýros. In midsummer there are also regular hydrofoils to the islands from **Tríkeri** and **Plataniá** at the foot of Mount Pílion (see p.309). The most convenient and switched-on agent for both types of craft to the Sporades is Falcon Tours, at Argonaftón 34 (☎0421/21 626); for the occasional sailings

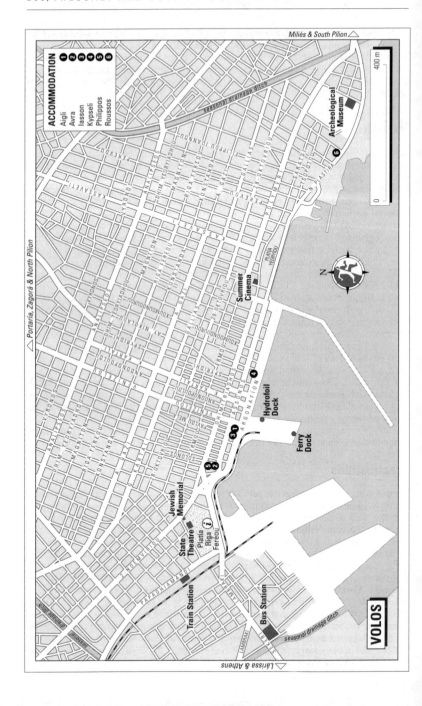

Miliés & South Pílion △

ACCOMMODATION
1 Aigli
2 Avra
3 Iasson
4 Kypseli
5 Philippos
6 Roussos

seasonal drainage ditch

△ Portaria, Zagorá & North Pílion

Archeological Museum

Summer Cinema

Hydrofoil Dock

Ferry Dock

Jewish Memorial

State Theatre

Platía Ríga Feréou

Train Station

Bus Station

seasonal drainage ditch

Lárissa & Athens ▽

N

VOLOS

0   400 m

to the Cyclades and Crete, ring Vis Travel on ☎0421/31 959. For information after-hours phone the port police at ☎0421/38 888.

If you want to **rent a car** to explore Mount Pílion, try European Cars (☎0421/36 238) at Iássonos 83, one block inland and parallel to the waterfront.

Accommodation

Hotels are fairly plentiful, with a concentration of acceptable ones in the grid of streets behind the port. Budget options include the humble *Avra* at Sólonos 3 (☎0421/25 370; ②); the more comfortable, double-glazed *Iasson/Jason* (☎0421/26 075; ③), partly facing the port at Pávlou Melá 1; and the seaside *Kypseli* at Ayíou Nikoláou 1 (☎0421/24 420; ③ shared bathroom, ④ en-suite). Further out at Iatrou Tzánou 1, the E-class but en-suite *Roussas* (☎0421/21 732; ③) is perhaps the best value, with relatively easy parking, convenience to the museum and ouzeris, and helpful staff. The *Philippos* (☎0421/37 607; ⑤), inland at Sólonos 9, rates as mid-range, while the *Aigli* (☎0421/24 471; ⑥) at Argonaftón 24–26, an Art Deco hotel on the quayside, is strictly for splurging.

Restaurants and nightlife

Vólos specializes in one of Greece's most endearing institutions – the authentic **ouzerí**, serving a huge variety of *mezédhes* washed down, not necessarily with ouzo but with *tsípouro*, the favoured spirit of the northern mainland. Among the ouzeris strung out along the waterfront street of Argonaftón, *O Yiorgos* at no. 15 has good seafood if slack service (Greek-only menu); *Naftilia* at no. 1 and *Iolkos* also get good marks. More pricey, but excellent, **tavernas** are on Nikifórou Plastíra, near the museum, interspersed with cafés and *barákia*; these include *Pagasitiko*, *Monosandalon*, and *Akti Tselepi*, all specializing in seafood and mostly open in the evenings only. About the last surviving traditional *mayireftá* taverna is *Harama* at Dhimitriádhos 49.

As for **nightlife**, concerts and plays are frequently performed in the open-air theatre (tickets can be bought at Kehaïdis music store at the corner of Iássonos and Kartáli streets, one block in from the waterfront), while the summer cinema Exoraïstiki occupies one corner of Platía Yeoryíou. There are dozens of discos on the eastern outskirts of town, and a few casual spots where local musicians take the floor – some programmed, some spontaneously – for example at *Iy Skala tou Milanou*, on the corner of Venizélou and Analípseos.

Mount Pílion (Pelion)

The **Mount Pílion peninsula**, with its lush orchards of apple, pear and nut trees and dense forests of beech and oak, seems designed to confound stereotypical images of Greece. Scarcely a rock is visible along the slopes, and the sound of water comes gurgling up from crevices or aqueducts beside every track; summer temperatures here are a good 15°F cooler than the rest of Thessaly. Pílion is reputed to be the land of the mythical centaurs, and the site of revelries by ancient gods – thus the name *Kentavros* (Centaur) for various hotels and bars.

Pílion **villages** are equally idiosyncratic, often spread out over wide areas due to easy availability of water, their various quarters linked by winding cobbled paths. They formed a semi-autonomous district throughout the Ottoman occupation, and during the eighteenth century became something of a nursery for Greek Orthodox culture, fostered by semi-underground education and a revival of **folk art** and **traditional architecture**. By Greek standards, there is also a strong regional **cuisine**, with specialities such as *spedzofaí* (sausage and pepper casserole), *kounéli kokkinistó* (rabbit stew) and *gída stó foúrno* (baked goat). Herbs, a wide range of fruit, homemade preserves or "spoon sweets" and honey are important local products.

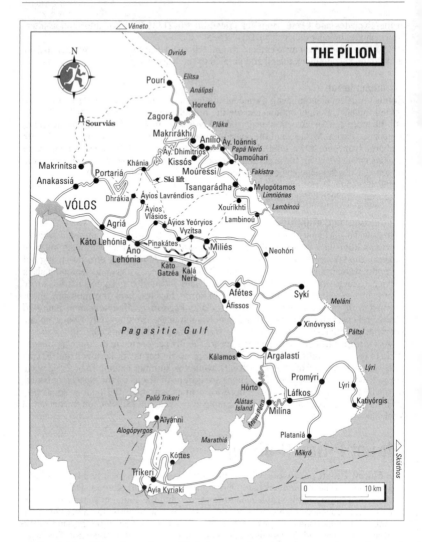

THE PÍLION

Many of the villages have changed little in appearance over the centuries, and reward visits with their ornate mansions, churches and sprawling platías – invariably shaded by several vast plane trees, sheltering the local cafés. The slate-roofed **churches** are highly distinctive, built in a low, wide style, often with a detached bell-tower, marble reliefs on the apse and always ornamented inside with carved wood. Two communities, **Makrinítsa** and **Vyzítsa**, have been designated by the EOT as protected showpieces of the region, but almost every hamlet offers its own unique attractions.

Add to the above the delights of a dozen or so excellent **beaches**, plus a growing number of maintained **hiking** routes (see box opposite), and you have a recipe for an instant holiday idyll – or disaster, if your timing is wrong. Lying conveniently between

Athens and Thessaloníki, Pílion is a long-established favourite with Greek vacationers, who inundate the place at Eastertime, from mid-July to mid-August and during any three-day weekend year-round. At such times you'd be pushing your luck more than usual to show up without a reservation, when in any case prices are the highest on the mainland.

Getting around Pílion
The peninsula is divided into three regions, with the best concentration of distinctive communities just **north and east** of Vólos and along the **northeast coast**. The **southwest** coast is less scenically interesting, with concentrated development along the Pagasitic Gulf, despite its lack of decent beaches. The far **south**, relatively low-lying and sparsely populated, has just one major resort, Plataniá, and a few scattered inland villages.

Travelling between the villages can be tricky without your own transport. **Buses** to the east cover two main routes: Vólos–Hánia–Zagorá (2–5 daily) and Vólos–Tsangarádha–Áyios Ioánnis via Miliés (2 daily), with just one daily service linking Zagorá and Tsangarádha to complete the loop. The far south is equally sparsely served, with just two or three departures a day to Plataniá and Tríkeri, though the respective northern and western highlights of Makrinítsa and Vyzítza both have more frequent connections.

Alternatives include **renting a car** in Vólos (essential if you're pushed for time), some very uncertain hitching or walking. Any mode of transport means slow progress, since grades are sharp, and perilously narrow roads snake around ravine contours, seemingly never getting closer to villages just across the way.

Leaving Pílion, you needn't necessarily return to Vólos but can take advantage of regular summer **hydrofoils** from Plataniá, Tríkeri or Áyios Ioánnis to the Sporades

---

WALKING ON MOUNT PÍLION

Until the mid-twentieth century, the Pílion villages were linked exclusively by an unusually dense network of **kalderímia** (old cobbled paths). The automobile age either bulldozed many or consigned others to disuse, and in the local hothouse climate, neglected trails were blocked by vegetation within a few years. Since the early 1990s, however, committed local residents and village councils have mounted various campaigns to clean, restore, mark and document these superb walking routes, and it can now be said that, along with Ípiros, the Pílion is the only region of Greece where the number of hiking opportunities is growing rather than dwindling. Even if you are not a hard-core trekker, the refurbished paths provide essential shortcuts between villages or down to the beaches.

The preferred walking seasons are May through early June, and early September through October; summer is hot and humid, and the winter mist- and snowline in the north can dip well below the villages. If you're serious about hikng here, a number of individuals (noted in the text) offer guided walks. Otherwise, you may want to equip yourself with some or all of the following: Road Editions' 1:60,000 map no. 33 "Pilio", which is also by far the best touring map, and sold locally; the now out-of print *Trekking in Greece* (see "Books" in Contexts); and (if you can read Greek) Nikos Haratsis' *Odhigos Piliou Yia Peripatites* (Guide to Pílion for Walkers), Grafi Editions, Vólos. These each have their virtues and defects, and do not solve all problems. The Road map does not trace walking routes or some minor roads exactly, despite using Ordnance-Survey-type contours. The Haratsis book has non-scale, hand-drawn maps with crabbed Greek script, and often imprecise text directions. In the accounts below, we have indicated the best and most useful routes, with elapsed times, start points and brief summaries; doubtless you will find your own.

islands. Arriving fairly directly in Pílion from overseas is now possible, using summer-only charter flights to either Skiáthos (frequent) or Anhiálos, near Vólos (weekly only), followed by a short transfer, though seats for flight-only or fly-drive packages are in short supply.

The north

Before crossing over to the popular east coast on the main Vólos–Zagorá route, consider pausing at either **Portariá** or **Makrinítsa**. Both villages have intrinsic attractions and make good first or last stops on any touring circuit.

Anakassiá and Portariá

The first encountered Pílion village, **ANAKASSIÁ** is just 4km out of town, and few casual visitors give more than a passing glance to what is essentially a suburb of Vólos. What they miss is a small but very beautiful museum (signposted) dedicated to the "naive" painter **Theophilos** (1873–1934). A great eccentric, originally from Lésvos, Theophilos lived for long periods in both Athens and Vólos, where he wandered around, often dressed in traditional costumes, painting frescoes for anyone prepared either to pay or feed him. In Pílion you find his work in the most unlikely places, mostly unheralded, including a number of village tavernas and kafenía. Here, the **museum** (daily 9am–3pm) occupies the **Arhondikó Kóndos**, an eighteenth-century mansion whose first floor Theophilos entirely frescoed with scenes from the Greek War of Independence – one of his favourite themes.

PORTARIÁ, 14km east of Vólos, has a more mountainous feel with a soundtrack of running streams. Regrettably, the areas closest to the busy road have become tacky and commercialized, but the back streets are still rewarding. The chief glory, as so often in Pílion, is the main square, shaded by tremendous plane trees, one planted in 1220. If you decide to stay, you can pick from among more than a dozen traditional inns and **hotels**; the obvious, modern (and noisy) *Filoxenia* and *Pelias* just off the main square are worth shunning in favour of restored pensions such as the *Arhondiko Athanasaki* (☎0428/99 235, fax 90 091; ④) just above the road but quiet, with private parking and plain but large rooms, or the smaller, more secluded *Arhondiko Klitsa* (☎0428/99 418, fax 27 551; ④). For those on a budget, the less characterful *Viky's* (☎0428/99 520; ③) just outside Portariá on the road to Makrinítsa, is the main choice.

Makrinítsa

From Portariá many buses detour 2km northwest to **MAKRINÍTSA**, 17km from Vólos, where stone houses straggle picturesquely down the mountainside. Founded in 1204 by refugees from the first sacking of Constantinople, it offers six outstanding churches plus a monastery, and a group of **traditional mansions** – many restored as accommodation. If your time in Pílion is limited, Makrinítsa is perhaps the best single target, since the village ranks as one of Greece's prettiest. Inevitably, there is blight on the main lane into the centre from tatty souvenir shops, and plenty of (Greek) day-trippers, but both are easy to escape, and the views over the Pagasitic Gulf are splendid.

There's a two hundred-metre altitude difference between the upper and lower quarters of Makrinítsa, so to get a full sense of the village takes a half-day's rambling. Most impressive of the churches are **Áyios Ioánnis**, next to the fountain on the shady main platía, and the beautiful eighteenth-century **monastery of Panayía Makrinítissa**, right under the clocktower. Many of the sanctuaries and frescoes here are only a few centuries old, but the marble relief work on some of the apses (the curvature behind the altar) is the best of its type in Greece. A few metres on from the Áyios Ioánnis square there are **Theóphilos frescoes** (see above) in a café.

If you are looking for a **challenging walk** in Pílion, the village is also the starting point for the five-hour-long trek to the deserted, frescoed **monastery of Sourviás**. This begins at the little plaza known as Bráni, and sticks largely to *kalderími* and path surface. There is another route via the chapel of Panayía Leskhianí which takes only three-and-a-half hours one way, and which also starts at Platía Bránis, but in this case you begin on a steep cement track west past the monastery of Ayíou Yerasímou, though trail resumes for most of the way once Makrinítsa is out of sight.

Accommodation in Makrinítsa is abundant but, as everywhere on Pílion, not cheap. Three of the "traditional inns" (*Xiradhaki* to the east of the main square, and the more remote *Mousli* and *Sissilianou*) are beginning to show their age, and are not necessarily the best choices here. They are co-managed (☎0428/99 250 or 99 256; ④), and almost uniquely offer singles, but are often noisy and very spartanly furnished. Better, privately run options include the atmospheric, slightly funky *Arkhondiko Diomidi* (☎0428/99 430, fax 99 114; ④), directly overhead, gazing from the platía church; the *Theophilos* (☎0428/99 435; ④), with contemporary furnishings; and the cosy *Rooms Routsou* (☎0428/99 090; ④), in an older building on the way to the platía. There are a few rather commercialized **tavernas** right on the platía, but the series of three tucked behind the church are the most atmospheric and most locally patronized.

Hánia

Travelling on over the mountain, beyond Portariá, the road hairpins up to the **Hánia pass**, and the eponymous village, a stark cluster of modern houses and a smattering of hotels which you shouldn't need to use. Its **tavernas**, however, may come in handy as a lunch stop for hikers **trekking** between Portariá or Dhrákia and Zagorá, five- to six-hour undertakings, mostly on path. A minor road leads 4km southeast to the small Agriólefkes **ski resort** (open Jan–March). Once past Hánia, the view suddenly opens to take in the whole northeast coast of the peninsula as you spiral down to a fork: the left turning leads to Zagorá, the right towards Tsangarádha.

The northeast coast

Pílion's best (and most popular) beaches, plus its lushest scenery, are found on the Aegean-facing **northeast coast**, which bears the brunt of winter storms. A relatively humid climate and shady dells nurture exotic flowers, locally bred and sold at the roadside. The "county town" of the region and major producer and packer of fruit is **Zagorá**, the apple capital of Greece.

Zagorá and Pourí

The largest Pílion village, **ZAGORÁ** has a life more independent of tourism than its neighbours, though government studies give the fruit orchards only until the year 2020 to survive, owing to depleted soil and overuse of pesticides. Raspberries are currently being proposed as a breakaway from apple monoculture; most of the residents are opposed to tourism, and wish to continue somehow as farmers.

Visitors often jump to unfavourable conclusions from the workaday, concrete main street where the bus calls; in fact there are four well-preserved and architecturally more varied areas, based around the squares of **Ayía Paraskeví, Ayía Kyriakí, Áyios Yeóryios** and **Metamórfosis (Sotíra)**, strung out over five kilometres. Coming from Vólos, turn left at the first filling station to find Ayía Paraskeví (Perahóra) up the hillside. Ayía Kyriakí is effectively the centre of Zagorá. Bearing left away from the turning for Horeftó will bring you to the broad platía of Áyios Yeóryios, in the shadow of its lovely plane tree and beautiful eighteenth-century church, while Sotíra lies beyond this, above the road to Pourí. At the second bend of the road down to Horeftó beach stands the **Ríga Feréou "secret" school**, now a gallery/folk museum, kept open in July and August.

The prime **accommodation** choice in Zagorá is the *Villa Horizonte* (☎0426/23 342, fax 23 176, *www.villa-horizonte.com*; ④–⑤), 400m down a signposted, narrow dirt track heading east from the "secret" school. It's essentially a cultural centre which organizes and hosts concerts, seminars, craft exhibitions and walking holidays. At slow times Wolf and Ingrid offer just accommodation in designer-decor, themed rooms, with generous, healthy buffet breakfast included. Other, more conventional lodging in Zagorá is often more reasonably priced than elsewhere in the region. There are a few rooms places, such as *Marika Vlahou* (☎0426/22 153; ②), above a metal shop in Ayía Kyriakí, or the simple but warmly welcoming *Yiannis Halkias* (☎0426/22 159; ③), near the turn for Horeftó, as well as an impeccably restored mansion, the *Arhontiko Konstantinidi* (☎0426/23 391; ⑥) with a beautiful garden and breakfasts of *Villa Horizonte* standard. All four parish squares host grill-tavernas: *O Takis* in Ayía Kyriakí is reasonable, *Kyriazis* in Sotíra is best for mezédhes, while *O Petros* (aka *Fani's*) at Áyios Yeóryios is a good all-rounder. There's also a **post office** and **bank** in Ayía Kyriakí, which changes only travellers' cheques or cash – no Eurocheques or plastic.

The road from Zagorá to **POURÍ**, one of the northernmost communities on Pílion, is a spectacular approach to a regally situated village. Theoharis Hiotis rents rooms (☎0426/23 168; ③) here in his modern pension 250m beyond the square, though eating options are limited to a kafenío doing simple mezédhes below the platía. Also worth a stop are a carpet-weaving shop with hand-knotted carpets, and a sculpture/pottery gallery. The two dazzling, usually deserted beaches of **Elítsa** and **Ovriós** below the village give you an idea of what Horeftó and Áyios Ioánnis looked like twenty years ago. Pourí is also a major trailhead for **ambitious treks** such as the five-and-a-half hour hike to Sourviás monastery, initially track but then trail, or the eight-hour expedition to Véneto, northernmost village in Pílion, via the abandoned hamlet of Paleá Mintzéla. Either requires more stamina and orientation skills than the usual Pílion outing; if you're not confident, Wolf at *Villa Horizonte* organizes regular group treks at the right time of year.

Horeftó

Eight twisting kilometres down the mountain, **HOREFTÓ** (5 buses daily in summer, 2 off season) makes an excellent coastal base. There is a choice of beaches here: the long, decent one in front of the former fishing village, and another smaller bay (used by nude bathers) around the headland at the north end, five minutes beyond where the frontage road stops. Determined explorers can follow a coastal path for twenty minutes more to the coves of **Análipsi** – the southerly one a little paradise with a spring, popular with freelance campers, the further road-accessible and rockier. There are also two hour-plus *kalderímia* up to Zagorá, one of them passing by the Ríga Feréou school, which can be combined to make an enjoyable loop.

Horeftó supports half a dozen hotels and lots of rooms for rent. The best-value and best-located **hotels** are the *Hayiati* (☎0426/22 405; ④) and *Erato* (☎0426/22 445; ③), both at the quiet, southern end of the coast road. Other attractive possibilities include the spacious *Flamingo Apartments* (☎0426/22 579, fax 22 815; ⑤), on a dirt road very near the beach, and Kosta Kapaniri's simple but spotless little apartments (☎0426/63 779; ④), among the trees. If you show up without booking during mid-summer you'll likely end up at the **campsite** (☎0426/22 180), at the extreme south end of the main beach.

Eating options in Horeftó have improved of late, with *O Petros* (a branch of the one in Zagorá) being an excellent all-rounder, while *Ta Dhelfínia* proves a competent ouzerí. *To Milo tis Eridhos*, run by the Apple Growers Cooperative, gets highly mixed reviews – patronize at your own risk; two or three **bars** provide evening distraction.

Kissós

The easterly turning at the junction below Hánia leads through or past Makriráhi, resolutely non-touristy, Anílio (meaning "without sun") and Áyios Dhimítrios towards the side road for **KISSÓS**. This unspoilt corner of Pílion lies 1km off the main road, virtually buried in foliage, with sleepy residential quarters ascending in terraces either side of eighteenth-century **Ayía Marína**, one of the finest churches on the peninsula. The *Xenonas Kissos* (☎0426/31 214; ③) opposite the church ranks among the best-value **accommodation** in Pílion, and the welcoming Garoufalias family dish out an appetizing line of *mayireftá* at the downstairs taverna, though the more prosaically set *Makis* across the street is as good or better. There are several other places to stay should the *Kissos* be full.

Áyios Ioánnis to Damoúhari

Heading for the coast via Áyios Dhimítrios, you tackle 6km of twisting paved road down to **ÁYIOS IOÁNNIS**, eastern Pílion's major resort. Despite a score of hotels and private rooms, finding a bed here is as problematic as anywhere on the peninsula in peak season, with significant package presence. Budget **accommodation** options include *Rooms Armonia* (☎0426/31 242; ③) at mid-esplanade, with a decent taverna, or the very basic but clean *Evripidis* (☎0426/31 338; ③). With a bit more to spend, try the civilized, good-taste *Anessis* (☎0426/31 123; ④), which welcomes walk-ins to its pastel-decor rooms; the kitschly furnished *Zephyros* (☎0426/31 335; ④) at the quieter, south end of the strip; and the somewhat impersonal but good-value *Aloe* (☎0426/31 240; ④), sprawling behind its lawn-garden. As for **eating**, *Akroyiali*, *Poseidon* and *To Kyma* come recommended, in addition to *Armonia*. For a splurge meal, try the elegant *Ostria* taverna inland, which features *nouvelle Greque* cuisine at a modest markup.

The **beach** at Áyios Ioánnis is popular and commercialized, with windsurfing boards and waterskis for rent. For more ambitious activities, such as sea-kayaking, mountainbiking and horse-riding, contact local **travel agency** Les Hirondelles (☎0426/31 181, *www.les-hirondelles.gr*), which also sells hydrofoil tickets, changes money and arranges accommodation if necessary. For a quieter time and finer sand, walk either ten minutes north to **Pláka** beach, with its mostly young, Greek clientele, or fifteen minutes south (past the **campsite**) to **Papa Neró** beach, the best bronzing spot in the vicinity. At present it's fronted by just a few rooms for rent – try *Iy Orea Ammoudhia* (☎0426/31 219; ③) – and two good tavernas, though a mass of building sites on the slope above suggest its peaceful days are numbered.

South from the campsite, a narrow paved road leads to **DAMOÚHARI**, a hamlet set amid olive trees and fringing a secluded port. The construction of another road down from Moúressi has put an end to its seclusion, and villas are springing up fast amongst the olive trees. However, there is a large pebble beach, two pleasant tavernas and the overgrown ruins of a Venetian castle. Top **accommodation** choice here is the *Hotel Damouhari* (☎0426/49 840; ④–⑤) in bungalow and apartment format, with antiques in the rooms and fine decor in the bar which is better known as *Kleopatra Miramare*. If they're full with Dutch tours – likely in mid-summer – the alternatives are the comparatively modest *Rooms Kastro* (☎0426/49 475; ④) and Thomas Olkas's rooms, both nearby.

From Damoúhari, it's possible to walk to **Tsangarádha** (see below) in a little over an hour, a popular and rewarding trip (though most folk do it downhill). At the mouth of the ravine leading down to the larger bay, a spectacular *kalderími* begins its steep ascent, allowing glimpses of up to six villages simultaneously, and even the Sporades on a clear day, from points along the way. Subsequently there is deep shade, and springwater approaching Ayía Kyriakí; the path emerges in the Ayía Paraskeví quarter of Tsangarádha, just downhill from the post office.

Tsangarádha and Moúressi

TSANGARÁDHA is the largest northeastern village after Zagorá, though it may not seem so at first since it's divided into four distinct quarters – **Taxiárhes**, **Ayía Paraskeví**, **Ayía Kyriakí** and **Áyios Stéfanos** – strung along several kilometres of road. Each of these is scattered around a namesake church and platía, the finest of which is **Ayía Paraskeví**, shaded by reputedly the heftiest plane tree in Greece – pushing a thousand years in age, and requiring eighteen men to encircle.

Most **accommodation** in this area is pricey, and on the noisy main road. Exceptions in one respect or another include the friendly, en-suite *Villa ton Rodhon* (☎0426/49 340; ④), right by the cobbled path to Damoúhari, a 1970s construction where most plain rooms have sea views and balconies; and the *Konaki Hotel* (☎0426/49 481; ④), just south of the Ayía Paraskeví square but set back from the road. There are also some inexpensive rooms for rent in the southern parish of **Taxiárhes** (linked by a *kalderími* with Ayía Paraskeví). With deeper pockets, you can opt for the *Thymeli Inn*, a restoration project at Sfetseïka Ayíou Yeoryíou district (☎0426/49 595; ⑤) or the antiques-furnished, British/American-run *Lost Unicorn* (☎0426/49 930, fax 49 931; ⑥), just off Ayía Paraskeví square, its common areas set up like a British club. Local **eating** options are not brilliant, though honourable exceptions are *To Kalyvi* in Taxiárhes, and (even better) *Aleka's* on the main road at Ayía Paraskeví, which also runs an inn at pricey mock-traditional units (☎0426/49 380, fax 49 189, *helen@oceanisgr.com*; ⑤).

In general, better **meals** are to be had at **MOÚRESSI**, 3km northwest on the road. At either *To Tavernaki* or the more jolly *Iy Dhrosia* up on the main highway here, you can get specialities like *fasólies hándres* (delicately flavoured pinto beans) and assorted offal on a spit. Down in the village centre, there's a prime local **accommodation** choice: *The Old Silk Store* (☎0426/49 086 or 01822/832309 in UK; ③, or ④ with breakfast), a nineteenth-century mansion with a breakfast garden, barbecue area and high-ceilinged, en-suite rooms (including one self-catering studio). English proprietress Jill Sleeman can help with travel arrangements and also leads walking tours in the area.

The coast: Mylopótamos to Lambinoú

From Tsangarádha, ninety-minute paths from both Taxiárhes and Ayía Paraskeví, or a seven-kilometre hairpin road (with a daily bus) snake down to **MYLOPÓTAMOS**, a collection of attractive pebble coves. The two largest are separated by a naturally tunnelled rock wall, with a pair of serviceable tavernas just above. They attract a multinational summer crowd, who pack into a cluster of **accommodation** lining the approach road; the nearest is the rundown *Diakoumis* (☎0423/49 203; ④), with spectacular views from precarious wooden terraces. The *Christos-Marina* bungalows (☎0423/49 400; ⑤), about halfway along the approach road, offer mock-traditional units with balconies.

If you want more solitude, try **Fakístra beach**, the next swimmable cove to the north. It's most satisfyingly reached on foot from Damoúhari, via a coastal corniche trail which takes off between two prominent stakes, fifteen minutes uphill from the latter beach. Green-dot waymarks lead you down towards sea level through olive groves. After about half an hour, you cross Makrolítharo bay with its rocky shore and striking promontory; the path, unmarked now, continues from the far side, climbing gradually through more olives to a spectacular viewpoint taking in a cliff-cave which was purportedly another "secret school" in bygone times. Some thirty minutes past Makrolítharo, you pass the marked side-trail accessing the school, and then almost immediately the end of the road-for-the-lazy down from Ayía Kyriakí; it's unpaved the last 3km, with a tiny parking area, from which it's a few minutes more (total 80min from Damoúhari) to the cliff-girt, pea-gravel-and-sand bay with a shattered castle atop the southerly palisade.

Southeast of Mylopótamos lie two more attractive **beaches**: Limniónas and Lambinoú. Both can be reached along the coast by rough dirt track, but most people arrive via the inland village of Lambinoú, whence a paved road leads 3km down past the abandoned monastery of Lambidhónas. **Lambinoú** cove, with a snack bar, is a narrow, deep square of sand where three parties would constitute a crowd. **Limniónas** is reached via a separate track system from the monastery.

Just above the main road en route from Tsangarádha to Lambinoú, the nondescript village of Xouríkhti is the eastern trailhead for an enjoyable three-hour **hike to Miliés**. The path, which wends its way through a mix of open hillside and shady dell, is marked all along its length. Before the road around the hill via Lambinoú and Kalamáki was opened in 1938, this was the principal thoroughfare between the railhead at Miliés and the Tsangarádha area. It is quite feasible to do this walk one-way and then, with an eye to bus schedules, take an afternoon KTEL back to your starting point.

The west

Lying in the "rain shadow" of the mountain, the western Pílion villages and coast have a drier, more Mediterranean climate, with olives and arbutus shrubs predominating, except in shady, well-watered ravines. The beaches, at least until you get past Kalá Nerá, are far more developed than their natural endowments merit and lack the character of those on the east side. Inland it is a different story, with pleasant foothill villages and – for a change – decent bus services. **Miliés** and **Vyzítsa** in particular both make good bases for car-touring or hiking.

Miliés

Like Tsangarádha, the sizable village of **MILIÉS** (sometimes Miléës or Mileai on signs) was an important centre of culture during the eighteenth century. It retains a number of imposing mansions and an interesting church, the **Taxiárhis**, whose narthex (usually open) is decorated with brilliant frescoes. There is also a small **folk museum** (Tues–Sun 10am–2pm; free), which displays local artefacts and sponsors a crafts festival in early July.

Accommodation is somewhat limited, since most people stay nearby at Vyzítsa; the choice boils down to either a couple of traditional EOT-run mansions – the *Filippidi* and *Evangelinaki* (☎0423/86 714, ④) – or *O Paleos Stathmos* (☎0423/86 425; ④), accessible by *kaldherími* from the main square, whose very plain rooms are only worth it if you get a balconied front unit. **Eating and drinking** options include a simple grill, *Panorama*, just above the platía, plus a few kafenía-with-snacks on the square. The famous restaurant attached to *O Palios Stathmos* has, alas, taken a sharp dive in quality of late and can no longer be wholeheartedly recommended. The most distinctive food in town comes from the excellent *Korbas* bakery down by the Vólos road junction by the bus stop, which cranks out every kind of Pílion bread, pie, turnover and cake imaginable.

Vyzítsa

VYZÍTSA, 3km further up the mountain from Miliés and alive with water in streams and aqueducts, has been designated as a "traditional settlement" by the EOT. It has a more open and less lived-in feel than either Makrinítsa or Miliés, though it draws surprisingly large crowds of day-trippers in summer. Nonetheless it's an excellent base, with several privatized, ex-EOT lodges in converted mansions. Pick of this **accommodation**, from the standpoint of decor and quiet, would be the *Arhondiko Vafiadi* (☎0423/86 765, fax 86 045; ⑤ with breakfast), two floors of very plush rooms and original art in the common areas; or the slightly plainer but airy *Arhondiko Kondou* (☎0423/86 793; ⑤ with breakfast), both a five-minute walk up-slope from the car-park platía. About the best value here, with the feel of staying in an *arhondikó* without the expense, is the *Thetis* (☎0423/86 111; ③), conveniently just west of the car park but

THE PÍLION TRENÁKI

A prime attraction in the western Pílion is the old *trenáki* or **narrow-gauge railway** which originally ran between Vólos and Miliés. The 60km line, in service until 1971, was laid out between 1894 and 1903 by an Italian consortium under the supervision of engineer Evaristo de Chirico, father of the famous artist Giorgio de Chirico. The boy, born in Vólos in 1888, spent his formative years with his father on the job-site, which accounts for the little trains which chug across several of his paintings (such as *The Hour of Silence* and *The Seer's Reward*, both 1913). To conquer the maximum 2.8 percent grade and numerous ravines between Lehónia and Miliés, the elder de Chirico designed six multiple-span stone viaducts, buttressing with blind arches, tunnels and a riveted iron trestle bridge, all justly considered masterpieces of form and function. The bridge, some 700m west of the terminus in Miliés, spans a particularly deep gorge and can be crossed on a **pedestrian catwalk**; indeed, followed the entire route down to Áno Lehónia is a popular three-hour walk, with occasional springs and picnic spots en route.

In 1997, after seven years of rumours, an excursion service, using one of the original Belgian **steam locomotives**, was resumed as a tourist attraction on weekends and holidays year-round, and several of the Belle Époque stations restored. The train leaves Áno Lehónia on the coast at 11am, taking 90 minutes to reach Miliés, from where it returns at 5pm. Tickets are currently a hefty 4000dr, whether you go one-way or round trip, and go on sale at 9–9.30am. However, groups often book out the handful of carriages, so you're well advised to make enquiries at Vólos station a few days in advance. There is talk of extending the run from Lehónia to Vólos, but this would involve expensive re-routing of the track or at least prising it free from the asphalt road in which it's embedded from Káto Lehónia to Vólos.

calm enough, with good breakfasts included at the adjacent stone-built café. The approach road to the village is lined with more prosaically set inns, best of which is the *Hotel Stoïkos* (☎0423/86 406; ④), most of whose well-executed modern rooms appointed in "traditional" style have views. The least expensive option, and probably the last to fill at busy times, are the modern *Rooms Afroditi* (☎0423/86 484; ②), some 200m past the upper platía. The tiered, upper platía with its fountains and three plane trees, each larger than the last, offers three **tavernas**, of which *To Balkonaki* is acceptable though nothing extraordinary; probably the best eating is available at *O Yiorgaras*, out on the main road.

Vyzítsa sits at the nexus of a number of trails down to the coast at Kalá Nerá, which can be combined into **loop-hikes** of half-day duration. From the chapel of Zoödhóhou Piyí in Vyzítsa, a sporadically marked route takes you around a vast landslip zone, and then across two ravines (bridges) and a brief stretch of farm track until dropping to Kalá Nerá, via Aryireïka hamlet, just under two hours later. Once down on the main highway, you can bear left (east) and adopt the oblique cemetery track (actually signposted for two monasteries and Aryiraïka) which begins the ninety-minute hike up to Miliés. Alternatively, and preferably perhaps, turn right (west) and complete a circuit by turning onto the inconspicuously indicated *kalderími* taking off just before the filling station, opposite the OTE circuit building. This climbs, in just over ninety minutes, to Pinakátes, almost entirely along a cleaned and meticulously restored *kalderími*, with superb views over the ravine separating Olgá hamlet from Aryireïka, and de Chirico's five-arched rail bridge therein. Once in Miliés or Pinakátes, the final link back to Vyzítsa may be tricky; there is a signposted *kalderími* from Miliés, but the nominally half-hour path from the edge of Pinakátes to Vyzítsa's upper square is so overgrown it will probably take you close to an hour.

Pinakátes to Dhrákia

PINAKÁTES, tucked at the top of a densely forested ravine, was long among the least visited and most desolate of the west Pílion villages, despite being the terminus of a bus line from Vólos. No longer: the sealing of the road in from Vyzítsa, and trendy Greeks buying up crumbling mansions for restoration, have seen to that. For the moment it remains a superbly atmospheric spot, with a pricey mansion-**inn**, *Xiradhakis* (☎0423/86 376; ⑤), a single **taverna** on the shaded square and a little kafenío by the metal church belfry where you can sample twenty flavours of *glyká koutalioú* or "spoon sweets".

The next village on the road (and bus route) west to Vólos, **ÁYIOS YEÓRYIOS NILÍAS**, should be a major walkers' mecca – except that amenities are limited to a lone platía-**taverna** and two pricier-than-usual traditional mansion **inns**: the eighteenth-century *Arhondiko Dereli* (☎0428/93 163; ⑤) and the nineteenth-century *Arhondiko Tzortzis* (☎0428/94 923; ⑥). The long hikes from here, however, are superb: an eminently scenic, four-hour traverse to Tsangarádha, mostly on path and with plenty of stream bed and beech forest en route; and the three-hour trek up to the Agriólefkes ski centre, again mostly through beech woods with path underfoot. Another brief *kalderími* links Áyios Yeóryios with Áyios Vlásios, the next village downhill – no accommodation, just a taverna-café for a halt before continuing ninety minutes north on foot over a *kalderími* to **ÁYIOS LAVRÉNDIOS**, a quietly homogenous village with **accommodation**: the *Hotel Kentavros* (☎0421/96 224; ④–⑤). This has no public transport from Vólos; nor does **DHRÁKIA**, just across the top of the valley here and an hour's distant on foot (mostly by dirt track). At Dhrákia there are no formal amenities, but you're poised for hikes onward to Hánia (90min) or Portariá (2hr 30min).

The coast

Most of the coast between Vólos and Koropí (below Miliés) is unenticing, and for much of its course the road runs well inland. At Agriá, for example, a giant facility of Hercules Cement casts its shadow over rashes of hotels and neon-garish tavernas, while spilling a horrid brown sludge into the Pagasitic Gulf. The little settlements beyond are very much suburbs of Vólos, with city bus #5 plying as far as Áno Lehónia, handy for catching the weekend *trenáki* (see box opposite). Heading southeast, things improve slightly at the little resort and narrow beach of Maláki, the first place anyone gets in the water. Olive groves line the road at Káto Gatzéa, where there are three **campsites**, of which *Hellas* and *Sikia* (also with bungalows), almost in Kalá Nerá, have the edge over the *Marina*. The next place, Kalá Nerá, is as noted above an important trailhead for some of the best Pílion walks, but otherwise of little intrinsic interest.

The south

Once **south** of the road linking Kalá Nerá, Miliés and Tsangarádha, Pílion becomes drier, lower and more stereotypically Mediterranean, the terrain less dramatic, the villages more scattered. There are, however, some interesting pockets, and considerably less tourism inland, though a number of busy coastal resorts attract a mixed clientele of foreigners and locals.

The area can be reached a little tortuously by bus, but much more comfortably by sea. In summer, **hydrofoils** from Vólos call at least daily at the port of Ayía Kyriakí (Tríkeri) after first pausing at the little island of Paleó Tríkeri, and frequently continue to the resort of Plataniá.

Argalastí and around

AFÉTES is the first village encountered on the land approach, and worth the brief detour for its vast platía with five plane trees, ornate church, supper-only taverna and single-arch bridge below the car park. A few kilometres downhill lies Áfyssos, a busy resort bulging with weekend apartments for Greeks.

ARGALASTÍ, 12km southeast, is much the biggest place in the south; you can **stay** well away from the main through road at the *Agamemnon* (☎0423/54 557), a restored nineteenth-century mansion hotel with a pool, and eat at one of three **tavernas** on the platía, admittedly not as attractive as some others on the mountain; *Sfindeo* is well attended at lunchtime.

You can reach the Pagasitic Gulf at Kálamos, an hour's path-walk west, but by far the best beach – and amenities to go with it – are at **Páltsi**, 12km away on the east coast and officially signposted as "Áyios Konstandínos". Just inland from the sandy, boulder-studded bay are three decent tavernas and a unique **hotel**, *Erovios* (summer ☎0423/54 203 or 01/64 67 181 winter; ③), genially run by California-educated Stelios Kaloyirou. During July and August the premises are completely given over to New Age seminars, but in spring or fall the simple, 1970s units – some with kitchens, all with large balconies – are open to independent travellers.

Hórto to Marathiá: the coast

Continuing due south from Argalastí, you reach the sea again after 7km at **HÓRTO**, a quiet little resort attended mostly by Greeks and largely protected from exploitation by its mediocre beaches. The best **taverna** of three is the *Perigiali*, just behind the most secluded of the trio of coves here.

Just 3km further, **MILÍNA** is far more commercialized, with a half-dozen **accommodation** establishments on the water (such as *Xenon Athina* ☎0423/65 473; ③), many more in the backstreets and four or five bona fide **tavernas**, none really standing out. There's also a hillside olive-grove **campsite**, the *Olizon*. The beach, however, is the scanty Pagasitic norm; Milína is mostly a place to watch magnificent sunsets over the offshore islets and distant mainland ridges.

Milína is also one terminus of a pair of hour-long *kalderímia* linking the coast with the inland village of Láfkos, which can be combined for an enjoyable circuit. Beginning from the church on the shore road in Milína, head ten minutes inland along the side road until you see the recently restored *kalderími* erupting in an olive grove; from Láfkos, the return route starts at the far end of its platía, exiting the village from its lowest houses.

LÁFKOS itself is a handsome, ridgetop village graced by another respectable, car-free platía with a record number of plane trees in residence and several places to **eat**, such as *O Sakis*. The local herb-gathering industry gets a look-in at a small retail outlet, Violeta, at one corner. Just off the start of the path down to Milína, there's an **inn** restoration, the *Xenon Lafkos* (☎0423/65 017; ④).

Beyond Milína, there are no more real villages and the landscape becomes increasingly bleak, with only the occasional weekend villa or moored boat to vary the horizon. Some 4km along, at landlocked **Mávri Pétra** bay, yachts anchored in the lee of Alátas islet (Sunsail has an office here) are beginning to outnumber fishing boats, but the roadside *Favios* taverna is still a reliable venue for retsina and fresh fish. People tend to play on the water rather than in it, as the gulf here is apt to be warm, with plenty of flotsam and garbage washed down from Vólos. About the best swimming beach hereabouts is at **Marathiá**, 7km further, where each of two rival tavernas maintains its own access drive and parking area. Better beaches near Láfkos, again on the east-facing Aegean coast, are relatively unspoilt Lýri and Katiyiórgis, both reach via the inland villages of Promýri and Lýri.

Plataniá

Láfkos is also the junction point for the most popular local beach, **PLATANIÁ** (sometimes spelled "Plataniás"), a small resort near the end of the Pílion peninsula with three daily buses from Vólos. The beach is excellent, though the resort is often a bit crowded with Greek holidaymakers: walk to the westerly beach of **Mikró** for more seclusion.

Among the half-dozen **hotels**, the most economical are the waterfront *Kyma* (☎0423/71 269; ②) and *Platania* (☎0423/71 266; ②), though the *Drossero Akroyiali* (☎0423/71 210; ③) is of a higher standard; there is also a **campsite**, the *Louisa*. Most of the half-dozen waterside **restaurants** serve tasty seafood, but none really stands out. Les Hirondelles **travel agency** has a branch here as well (☎0423/71 231), offering the usual activities and selling tickets for the several weekly hydrofoils (see "Travel Details" on p.322).

Tríkeri

Forming a "crab claw" at the extreme southeast end of Pílion, the semi-peninsula of **Tríkeri** still feels very remote. It was used after the 1946–49 civil war as a place of exile for political prisoners (along with the island of Paleó Tríkeri), and until a few years ago there was no real road connecting it with the rest of Pílion. It now boasts the best road in Pílion, connecting it with Milína in less than thirty minutes. There are a couple of daily buses from Vólos, but the area can also be reached by hydrofoil from Vólos or the Sporades (daily from April to October, going up to twice daily between June and mid-September).

The hilltop village of **TRÍKERI** (called simply "Horió" in local parlance) has few amenities for outsiders other than some simple, evening-only kafenía and grills on the little square, shaded here by pea-family trees rather than the usual planes. The new road has prompted a spate of cement construction and re-roofing, and donkeys as a mode of transport are on the wane, but the half-hour *kalderími* down to the port of **AYÍA KYRIAKÍ** is still well used (drivers face a winding, 6km road). This is principally a working fishing village, something of a rarity in modern Greece, and much the most attractive spot on this coast. In the local boatyard, large kaïkia and occasionally yachts, are built in much the same way they have been for the last hundred years. There are a few **rooms** to rent in the backstreets and at Mýlos cove, 1km west (*O Lambis* ☎0423/91 587; ③), but otherwise minimal concessions to tourism, perhaps because there's no good beach close by. However, multicoloured fishing boats, views across the straits to Évvia, cheap petrol for the trip out and excellent seafood combine to make it a captivating, unspoilt little spot. Facing east from the car park and bus turn-around area, one sees three **tavernas**, best being the easternmost, *Mouragio*; the fish is reliably fresh and wild (not farmed), though not as cheap as it used to be.

Paleó Tríkeri islet

"Horió" is something of a walkers' focus, with intact if shadeless paths 45 minutes northeast to Kóttes, the winter port, and two hours north to Alogópyrgos, a pebble beach and informal crossing point for **Paleó Tríkeri** (or Nisí Tríkeri – Tríkeri island). This has a village, two places to stay, a couple of tavernas and sand – which perhaps makes it the smallest Greek island with everything you really need. Little more than 2.5km from end to end, it consists of a few olive-covered hills and a fringe of small, rocky beaches.

The port and lone village of **Aïyánni**, is tiny, with a single shop and a good taverna by the harbour. Following a track up from the village for around ten minutes, you reach the nineteenth-century **Evangelistrías monastery** (daily 8am–3pm & 6–8pm), venue for a work-holiday camp for European teenagers, at the centre of the island. Past here, you reach a large bay and the island **hotel**: the *Palio Trikeri* (☎0423/91 432; ③), with a restaurant overlooking the beach. The *Galatia* also offers studios (☎0423/91 031 or 55 505; ④) and meals, and there's generally no problem camping under the olive trees nearby.

The island is connected with Ayía Kyriakí and Vólos by regular **hydrofoil**; otherwise, you can try getting to Alogópyrgos via the newish dirt track from just north of "Horió" – which cuts across the path – and hailing a small boat to come fetch you from the far side of the narrow strait here.

Lárissa

LÁRISSA stands at the heart of the Thessalian plain: a large market centre approached across a prosperous but dull landscape of wheat and corn fields. It is also a major garrison town: the airport remains reserved for military use, and the Thessalonian writer Yorgos Ioannou, rusticated here in 1958 as a teacher, slammed it as an "arrogant, nouveau-riche provincial town full of horrific army officers and their majestic wives". Though undeniably modern and unremarkable, Lárissa has improved a bit since, while retaining a few old streets that hint at its recent past as a Turkish provincial capital.

The highest point of the town – the ancient acropolis of Áyios Ahíllios – is dominated by the remains of a medieval fortress, which is closed to the public. Down below, the centre is being made into a series of landscaped squares, connected by pedestrian streets lined with the usual upmarket boutiques. Life focuses on **Platía Makaríou**, which features several fountains, flowerbeds and statues, and rows of trendy cafés shaded by smart white umbrellas. Save at least an hour for the newly renovated **archeological museum**, 31-Avgoústou 2 (Tues–Sun 8.30am–3pm; free), with its fascinating collection of Neolithic finds. The modern Greek paintings in the Lárissa **Pinakothiki** (Tues–Sun 11am–2.30pm & 6.30–10pm; 100dr), at Roosevelt 59, are considered second only to those in the National Gallery in Athens. Otherwise, the **Alcazar** park, beside the Piniós, Thessaly's major river, remains a pleasant place to spend a few hours. As a major **road and rail junction**, the town has efficient connections with most places you'd want to reach: Vólos to the east; Tríkala and Kalambáka to the west; Lamía to the south; the Vale of Témbi (see below), Mount Olympus and Thessaloníki along the national highway to the northeast.

You probably won't choose to stay in Lárissa, but if you need to, there are numerous **hotels**. The cheapest are a trio of places in the square by the train station: the *Diethnes* (☎041/234 210; ②), the last resort, non-en-suite *Neon* (☎041/236 268; ②) and the renovated *Pantheon* (☎041/236 726; ③). More savoury options include the *Atlantic* at Panagoúli 1 (☎041/287 711; ④) or the Adonis at Panagoúli 8 (☎041/534 648; ③). *Ellas*, at Roosevelt 28, serves inexpensive **meals** and is always packed with locals, while *Filoxenia*, a few doors up on the aforementioned square itself, is also good value if slightly fancier.

North towards Mount Olympus: the Vale of Témbi and the coast

Travelling north from Lárissa, the National Highway heads towards Thessaloníki, a highly scenic route through the **Vale of Témbi**, between mounts Olympus and Óssa, before emerging on the coast. Accounts of the valley and the best of the **beaches** east of Mount Óssa follow; for details on Mount Olympus, see p.399. If you are driving, be aware that the road upgrading programme for the National Highway has now progressed to this stretch, which means highly dangerous, two-lane conditions between Lárissa and Kateríni for the next few years.

Ambelákia

If you have time, or a vehicle, a worthwhile first stop in the Témbi region is **AMBELÁKIA**, a large village in the foothills of Mount Óssa. In the eighteenth century, this community supported the world's first **industrial co-operative**, producing, dyeing and exporting textiles, and maintaining its own branch offices as far afield as London. With the co-operative came a rare and enlightened prosperity. At a time when most of Greece lay stagnant under Turkish rule, Ambelákia was largely autonomous; it held democratic assemblies, offered free education and medical care and even subsidized weekly performances of ancient drama. The brave experiment lasted over a century, eventually succumbing to the triple ravages of war, economics and the industrial revolution. In 1811 Ali Pasha raided the town, and a decade later any chance of recovery was lost with the collapse of the Viennese bank in which the town's wealth was deposited.

Until World War II, however, over six hundred mansions survived in the town. Today there are just 36, many in poor condition but some finally benefiting from renovation. You can still get some idea of the former prosperity by visiting the **Mansion of George Schwarz**. The home of the co-operative's last president, this *arhondikó* (Tues–Sat 8.45am–3pm, Sun 9.30am–2.30pm; 600dr) is built in grand, old-Constantinople style. The exterior has been admirably restored, and the charming Ottoman-rococo interior is also currently undergoing conservation works. Schwarz, incidentally, was a Greek, despite the German-sounding name, which was merely the Austrian bank's translation of his real surname, Mavros (Black).

Without being twee, Ambelákia is an attractive, un-self-conscious place, with a cobbled high street, a couple of old fashioned bakeries and three psistariés on the plane-and-mulberry-shaded square. The middle one, *O Platanos*, also offers simple **rooms** in a quiet house (☎0495/93 130; ②); there are more available through the Women's Agrotourism Co-operative (☎0495/93 401; ②), visitable in person at their café, *To Rodi*. There's also a mock-traditional **hotel**, the *Ennea Mousses* (☎0495/93 405; ④), on the left entering town just before the square, but this seems to operate on demand only and if you're intent on staying there, ring the owner first in Lárissa (☎041/550 744).

The town is connected by bus with Lárissa (3 daily); or you can walk up a cobbled way in about an hour from the Témbi train station, part of the recently designated **O2 long-distance trail**. This continues within three hours to Spília village, high up on Mount Óssa, and thence over the top to Stómio or Karítsa.

The Vale of Témbi

Two kilometres beyond the Ambelákia turnoff, you enter the **Vale of Témbi**, a valley cut over the eons by the Piniós, which runs for nearly ten kilometres between the steep cliffs of the Olympus (Ólymbos) and Óssa ranges. In antiquity it was sacred to Apollo and constituted one of the few possible approaches into Greece – being the path taken by both Xerxes and Alexander the Great – and it remained an important passage during the Middle Ages. Walkers might consider a hike along the valley, which can also be traversed by canoe on the Piniós. However, both National Road 1 and the railway forge through Témbi, impinging considerably on its beauties. One of the most popular stops is the **Spring of Venus**. Halfway through the vale (on the right, coming from Lárissa) are the ruins of the **Kástro tís Oreás** (Castle of the Beautiful Maiden), one of four Frankish guardposts here, while marking the northern end of the pass is a second **medieval fortress** at Platamónas (summer Tues–Fri 8am–7pm, winter Tues–Sun 8.30am–5pm, all year Sat & Sun 8.30am–3pm), also crusader-built. An impressive citadel, it's currently being restored for use in the Olympos Festival (July–Aug), while a new rail tunnel has been bored right under it. A steep dirt track leads to it from the busy main highway, for the expected views.

Platamónas marks the beginning of **Macedonia** and heralds a rather grim succession of dull resorts fronting the narrow, pebbly beaches of the Thermaïkós Gulf. The coast south of the castles is a better bet (see below). Inland, the mountain spectacle continues, with **Mount Olympus** (Óros Ólymbos) casting ever-longer shadows; the trailhead for climbing it is Litóhoro (see p.401).

Stómio and the Óssa Coast

A side-road, close by the Kástro tís Oreás, takes you the 12km to **STÓMIO**, an unexceptional seaside village near the mouth of the river Piniós. The beach here is a relatively new phenomenon – a 1950s flood changed the river's course, creating a vast sandspit behind the abandoned riverbed. The dense beech trees of Óssa march down almost to the shore, masking some of Stómio's more uninspired recent construction; the place is cheerfully downmarket and resolutely Greek working-class, though an influx of EU money is resulting in cosmetic "improvements". The marshes flanking the old river-branch make the beach a fine spot for birdwatchers, and swimmers can bathe in clear waters, while gazing at Mount Olympus.

Outside July and August – when Stómio draws big crowds from the hinterland – you shouldn't have any trouble finding **accommodation**, though rooms closest to the waterfront are apt to be noisy. Much the best choice is the ebulliently welcoming *Hotel Panorama* (☎0495/91 345 or mobile 094/4288581; ③), in a calm uphill setting; all rooms have orthopedic beds, veranda access and ceiling fans, while some allow self-catering. The municipal beachside **campsite** divides into two zones: one fenced with showers and power hook-ups for caravans, the other free, with cold taps and toilets only, squalid and used mostly by impecunious tenters and the occasional gypsy party. Of the four tavernas on the seafront road leading to the fishing port, the furthest – *To Tsayezi* – has squirmingly fresh fare, *krítamo* (samphire) garnish and normal prices; *Iy Gorgona* is a likely alternative. A few bars, like *O Faros* just below the Panorama, offer a semblance of nightlife.

Down the coast towards Pílion, towards which the road is entirely paved, Koutsupiá and Kókkino Neró have smaller beaches and serve as rather scruffy resorts for Larissans and Trikalans. **Ayiókambos** and **Velíka**, east and southeast of the attractive Óssa hill villages of **Ayiá** and **Melívia**, have long sandy beaches and get a more international crowd. All four villages are served by bus from Lárissa; for **accommodation** try the *Golden Beach* (☎0494/51 222; ⑤) at Ayiókambos, which has a pool and tennis courts, or the modest eight-room *Melivia Beach* (☎0494/51 128; ③) on the shore at Velíka. There are also plenty of campsites in the area.

West from Lárissa: Tríkala and the Pýli region

West from Lárissa, the road trails the river Piniós to **Tríkala**, an enjoyable provincial town with a scattering of Byzantine monuments nearby. For most travellers, it's simply a staging post en route to Kalambáka and the Metéora; frequent buses join it with Lárissa, and there are connections north and west as well. The narrow-gauge railway which used to arc between Lárissa, Tríkala and Kalambáka was dug up in 1998, and services will not resume until or unless a standard-gauge line is fitted across the Píndhos mountains via the Katára tunnel, as part of a projected high-speed train link from Vólos to Igoumenítsa.

Tríkala

TRÍKALA is quite an attractive metropolis after the scruffy agricultural depot-towns of central Thessaly, spread out along the banks of the Lethéos, a tributary of the Piniós, and backed by the mountains of the Kóziakas range. It was the capital of the nineteenth-century Ottoman province and retains quite a few houses from that era, in the Varoúsi district below the fortress clocktower at the north end of town. Downriver from the bus station on the same bank, a minaret-less yet very stately and recently restored Turkish mosque, the **Koursoum Tzami** also survives, a graceful accompaniment to the town's numerous stone churches.

The town's inner **fortress**, a Turkish and Byzantine adaptation of a claimed fourth-century BC foundation, is closed to the public except for special events, but the outer walls host attractive gardens and a pleasantly shaded terrace café. Down in the flat-lands, on busy Saráfi, lie the meagre, half-excavated remains of a **sanctuary of Asklepios**; according to some accounts, the cult of the healing god originated here in ancient Trikke (see p.179). The liveliest part of town, encompassing what's left of the old **bazaar**, is in the streets around the central Platía Iróön Polytekhníou on the river-side, with a statue of local hero Stefanos Sarafis, commander of ELAS during the civil war.

Practicalities

The **post office** is situated off Platía Iróön Polytekhníou, as are several **banks** with cash dispensers. The **bus station** is on the west bank of the river, 300m southeast of the square; the main **taxi** ranks are on Iróön Polytekhníou and its continuation across the river, Platía Ríga Feréou. As ever, drivers should be mindful of the pay-and-display **parking** scheme, easily enough avoided by parking slightly out of the centre.

Accommodation, as usual for untouristed mainland towns, is problematic; the cheapest, non-en-suite hotel, the *Palladion* (☎0431/28 091; ③), still overpriced, lies within sight of the two squares at Výronos 4. Affordable mid-range alternatives include the *Lithaeon*, Óthonos 18, directly above the bus station (☎0431/20 690; ④), and the slightly cushier, quieter *Hotel Dina*, on the corner of Asklipíou and Karanasíou, near Platía Ríga Feréou (☎0431/74 777; ⑤).

Restaurants are scattered throughout the town, mostly on the west bank of the river. A good, cheap lunch of *mayireftá* can be had between bus connections at *Katarahias*, Óthonos 10, while *Taverna O Babis*, next to the *Hotel Dina* at Karnasíou 3, is well regarded by the locals for both oven food and grills. Another nearby possibility is *Pliatsikas* on Iouliéttas Adhám, which runs perpendicular to Karnasíou and roughly parallel to Asklipíou. Pedestrianized Asklipíou itself, forging southwest from Ríga Feréou towards the now-disused train station, is the town's daytime social hub, with plenty of somewhat pricey cafés and zaharoplastía to choose from. Like Lárissa, Tríkala has been well gentrified in the last few years – there are the typical outlets of The Body Shop and Marks and Spencer – but rural life gets a look-in at the traditional Thessalian cheese shop *Galaktos Batayanni*, Iouliéttas Adhám 10 – identifiable by the range of goatbells hanging inside.

Pýli

It takes some effort of will to delay immediate progress to Kalambáka and the Metéora. Byzantine aficionados, however, may be tempted by a detour to **PÝLI**, 19km southwest of Tríkala, for the thirteenth-century church of **Pórta Panayía**, one of the unsung beauties of Thessaly, in a superb setting at the beginning of a gorge. Nearby, there is an outstanding cycle of frescoes at the monastery of **Ayíou Visaríonos Dousíkou** (men only admitted), which would be a major tourist attraction were it not overshadowed by its spectacular neighbour, Metéora.

Regular **buses** run to Pýli from Tríkala, almost hourly during the day. Near Pórta Panayía and beside a fountain-fed oasis there are two simple **grills** – a far nicer lunch stop than Tríkala; in the village across the river there is a rather drab **hotel**, the *Babanara* (☎0431/22 325; ④), plus an even pricier one near the church-oasis, the *Pyli* (☎0431/23 510; ⑤).

Pórta Panayía

The church of **Pórta Panayía** (daily: summer 8am–noon & 4–8pm; winter 9am–noon & 3–5pm; donation) is a ten-minute walk uphill from the bus stop in Pýli village. Cross the Portaïkós River on the footbridge, then bear left on the far bank until you see its dome in a clump of trees below the north-bank frontage road; cars must use a slightly longer route via a one-lane vehicle bridge. The caretaker lives in a white house below the nearby tavernas.

Much of the church was completed in 1283 by one Ioannis Doukas, a prince of the Despotate of Epirus. Its architecture is somewhat bizarre, in that the current narthex is probably a fourteenth-century Serbian remodelling of the original dome and transept. The original nave on its west side collapsed in an earthquake, and its replacement to the east gives the whole a "backwards" orientation. In the Doukas section, perpendicular barrel vaults over a narrow transept and more generous nave lend antiseismic properties, with further support from six columns. The highlights of the interior are a pair of **mosaic icons** depicting Joseph, Mary and the Child, and a marble iconostasis. The **frescoes** have fared less well, with many of the figures blackened by fire and barely discernible. The most interesting image is next to the tiny font, over Ioannis Doukas's tomb, where a lunette shows the Archangel Michael leading a realistically portrayed Doukas by the hand to the enthroned Virgin with Child.

A kilometre upstream, easiest reached along the Pýli bank of the river, a graceful **medieval bridge** (currently scaffolded) spans the Portaïkós at the point where it exits a narrow mountain gorge. A couple of cafés and snack bars take advantage of the setting; the whole area being a very popular weekend outing venue for the locals, so that its tranquil beauty is best appreciated on a weekday. You can cross the bridge to follow paths some distance along the gorge on the opposite side; the EU Leader II programme is currently cleaning and marking more to make long traverses possible on Mount Kóziakas.

Ayíou Visaríonos Dousíkou

The monastery of **Ayíou Visaríonos Dousíkou** – known locally as Aï Vissáris – has a stunning setting, 500m up a flank of Mount Kóziakas, looking out over most of Thessaly. The small community of monks is keen to maintain its isolation, excluding women from visits and admitting men only with suspicion. In theory, visits are allowed from 8am to noon and 3.30pm to 7pm (3–6.30pm in winter), with preference given to Orthodox visitors and/or Greek speakers. To reach the monastery, cross the single-lane road bridge over the Portaïkós as for Pórta Panayía, but turn right instead, then left almost instantly onto a signed dirt track which leads up for 4.5km. This is slowly being paved from the top down; in theory walkers will soon be able to reach the place directly from the old bridge on one of the Leader paths.

The monastery was founded in 1530 by Visarionos (Bessarion), a native of Pýli, and contains a perfect **cycle of frescoes** by Tzortzis – one of the major painters of Mount

Athos – executed between 1550 and 1558 and recently restored to brilliance. These, and the institution as a whole, miraculously escaped damage in 1940, when two Italian bombs fell in the courtyard but failed to explode.

Originally, the monastery perched on a cliff as steep as any at Metéora, but in 1962 the abyss was largely filled in with kitchen gardens, and a new road and gate opened. This rendered ornamental the pulleys and ladder on the east wall, which like much of the place had survived intact since its foundation. In its heyday, nearly three hundred monks lived at the monastery; currently there are around ten.

The Monasteries of Metéora

The **monasteries of Metéora** are indisputably one of the great sights of mainland Greece. These extraordinary buildings, perched on seemingly inaccessible pinnacles of rock, occupy a valley just to the north of **Kalambáka**; the name *metéora* means literally "rocks in the air". Arriving at the town, your eye is drawn inexorably towards the outermost of these weird grey cylinders. Overhead to the right you can make out the closest of the monasteries, Ayíou Stefánou, firmly ensconced on a massive pedestal; beyond stretches a chaotic confusion of pinnacles, cones and stubbier, rounded cliffs – beaten into bizarre and otherworldly shapes by the action of the prehistoric sea that covered the plain of Thessaly around thirty million years ago.

Some history

The Meteorite monasteries are as enigmatic as they are spectacular. Legend has it that **St Athanasios**, who founded Megálou Meteórou (the Great Meteoron) – the earliest of the buildings – flew up to the rocks on the back of an eagle. A more prosaic version suggests that the villagers of Stáyi, the medieval precursor of Kalambáka, may have become adept at climbing, and helped the original monks up. The difficulties of access and building are hard to overstate; a German guide published for rock climbers grades almost all the Metéora routes as "advanced", even with modern high-tech climbing gear.

The earliest religious communities here appeared in the late tenth century, when groups of **hermits** made their homes in the caves that score many of the rocks. In 1336 they were joined by two monks from Mount Athos, **Gregorios**, Abbot of Magoula, and his companion, **Athanasios**. Gregorios returned shortly to Athos but he left Athanasios behind, ordering him to establish a monastery. This Athanasios did, whether supernaturally assisted or not, imposing a particularly austere and ascetic rule. He was quickly joined by many brothers, including, in 1371, **John Paleologos**, who refused the throne of Serbia to become the monk Ioasaph.

The royal presence was an important aid to the **endowment** of the monasteries, which followed swiftly on all the accessible, and many of the inaccessible rocks. They reached their zenith during the reign of the Ottoman sultan Süleyman the Magnificent (1520–66), by which time 24 of the rocks had been surmounted by monasteries and hermitages. The major establishments accumulated great wealth, flourishing on revenues of estates granted them in distant Wallachia and Moldavia, as well as in Thessaly itself. They retained these estates, more or less intact, until the eighteenth century, at which time monasticism here, as elsewhere in Greece, began to decline.

During the intervening centuries, numerous disputes arose over power and precedence among the monasteries. However, the principal factors in the Metéora's fall from glory were physical and economic. Many of the buildings, especially the smaller hermitages, were just not built to withstand centuries of use and, perhaps neglected or unoccupied, gradually disintegrated. The grander monasteries suffered **depopulation**, conspicuously so in the nineteenth century as a modern Greek state was established to

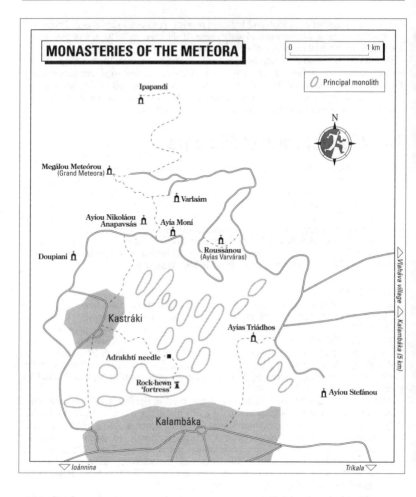

MONASTERIES OF THE METÉORA

0   1 km

⌀ Principal monolith

N

Ipapandí

Megálou Meteórou
(Grand Meteora)

Varlaám

Ayíou Nikoláou
Anapavsás

Ayía Moní

Doupianí

Roussánou
(Ayías Varváras)

▷ Vlahává village ▷ Kalambáka (5 km)

Kastráki

Ayías Triádhos

Adrakhtí needle ■

Rock-hewn
'fortress'

Ayíou Stefánou

Kalambáka

▽ *Ioánnina*   *Trikala* ▽

the south – with Thessaly itself initially excluded – and monasticism lost its exclusive identification with Greek nationalism and resistance to Turkish rule.

During the twentieth century the crisis accelerated after the monastic lands and revenues, already much reduced from their heyday, were taken over by the state for use by Greek refugees from Asia Minor, after the Greco-Turkish war of 1919–22. By the 1950s, there were just five active monasteries, struggling along with little more than a dozen monks between them – an era superbly chronicled in Patrick Leigh Fermor's *Roumeli*. Ironically, before their expropriation for **tourism** over the last three decades, the monasteries had begun to revive a little, attracting a number of young and intellectually rigorous brothers. Today, put firmly on the map by appearances in such films as James Bond's *For Your Eyes Only*, the four most accessible monasteries and convents are essentially showcase monuments. Only two, **Ayías Triádhos** (the Holy Trinity) and **Ayíou Stefánou**, continue to function with a primarily religious purpose.

Practicalities: Kalambáka and Kastráki

Visiting the Metéora demands a full day, which means staying at least one night in **Kalambáka** or at the village of **Kastráki**, 2km to the northwest. If at all possible, opt for Kastráki; it wins hands down on atmosphere and situation, set as it is right in the shadow of the rocks. The older, upper quarters of the village make for pleasant strolls, and have recently had their lanes repaved thanks to EU funding. Kastráki also offers much better value for money lodging-wise, and has two of the best local campsites.

One slightly advanced "stroll" – though still not up to abseiling standard – is the steep scramble from the edge of Kastráki up to the rock-hewn, scarcely visible **"fortress" of Kalambáka**, on the 630m Ayiá monolith. Pass the cemetery, skirt the obvious "needle" of Adrakhtí and test your susceptibility to vertigo and Darwinian descent from the apes by heading up the steep gully to the right, keeping to its left side. After five minutes on all fours, you reach a proper path leading to stairs and cistern – the very edge of the citadel. Few will prudently go much further.

Kalambáka

KALAMBÁKA has no particular allure, save for its position near the rocks. The town was burned by the Germans during World War II and very few pre-war buildings remain, save for the old cathedral. This, the **Mitrópolis** (daily late afternoons; 200dr) stands a couple of streets above its modern successor, at the top end of the town. It was founded in the seventh century on the site of a temple to Apollo and incorporates various classical drums and fragments in its erratically designed walls. Inside there are fourteenth-century Byzantine frescoes and, most unusually in a Greek church, a great double marble pulpit in the central aisle.

Arriving by **bus** in season (there's no train service), you're likely to be offered a **room** by waiting proprietors. Unfortunately, not all of them are reputable, so preferably hunt for accommodation independently, to avoid being cheated. This should not be difficult, as there are numerous signs on the road into town from the bus station and plenty of rather undistinguished **hotels**, most of them prone to road noise, with minimal views or character and above-average rates, reflecting the commercialization of the Metéora. The best budget choice is the welcoming *Hotel Meteora* (☎0432/22 367; ③) at Ploutárhou 13, a side-street up to the right as you leave Kalambáka for Kastráki, at the foot of the extraordinary rocks. Also in the upper, quieter part of town, some 700m up from the main square, near the start/end of the trail to Ayías Triádhos at Kanári 21, are the *Koka Roka Rooms* (☎0432/24 554; ③), with a decent attached restaurant. Mid-range options include the *Odyssion* (☎0432/22 320; ③) on the main through road at the Kastráki end of things, while en-suite rooms at the *Helvetia* more or less opposite (☎0432/23 041; ④) are better than the building's exterior would suggest.

Kastráki

KASTRÁKI is twenty minutes' walk out of Kalambáka; there's a short cut if you follow a footpath out of the northwest corner of the town. In season there are regular buses throughout the day.

Entering the downhill end of the village, you pass the first of two **campsites** here, *Camping Vrahos* (☎0432/22 293, fax 23 134), which offers **rock-climbing** and **hang-gliding** lessons in English: sign up on the premises. The other, *Camping Boufidhis/The Cave* (☎0432/24 802) at the top end of the through road, is a bit more cramped but wonderfully grassy and shady for tents, incomparably set on the far side of the village with the monasteries of Ayíou Nikoláou and Roussánou rearing above. Both have swimming pools, as do the other more distant sites out on the Tríkala and Ioánnina roads – the best placed of which is probably the *Meteora Garden*, 1km southwest of Kastráki.

The village has hundreds of **rooms** for rent, mostly of a very high standard, as well as a handful of small, bona fide hotels. It's vital, however, to get off the main through road up to the monasteries, which has coaches rumbling through much of the day. Meeting this criterion is *Doupiani House* (☎0432/77 555, fax 75 326; ④), well signposted left of the road near *The Cave*, with fine views from most of the air-conditioned rooms. *Ziogas Rooms* (☎0432/24 037; ③), further downhill and set well back from the road, offers large, balconied units, most with superb views and heating for winter. *The Cave* also offers the remote *Villa San Giorgio* (④), in a calm lane at the top of the village, plus noisier rooms (③) by the campsite, with swimming-pool privileges for both. In the village centre itself, by the church, the simple *Bataloyiannis Asterios* (☎0432/23 253; ③) is fine if you get a rear-facing room. Among more than a dozen **places to eat**, those with a local clientele and reasonable prices include the *Plakia Gardhenia*, just below the church; the *Bataloyiannis*, across the way, with a lovely terrace and a good range of *mayireftá* (grilled items predominate elsewhere); and the *Zioga* next to the eponymous rooms. One pub-gelateria, *Alpha Beta Gamma* on the through road, provides formal **nightlife** and sweets.

Visiting the monasteries

There are six Metéora monasteries, each open to visits at slightly different hours and days (see below). To see them all in a day, start early to take in Ayíou Nikoláou, Varlaám and Megálou Meteórou before 1pm, leaving the afternoon for Roussánou, Ayías Triádhos and Ayíou Stefánou.

The road route from **Kastráki to Ayíou Stefánou** is just under 10km. Walking, you can veer off the tarmac occasionally onto a few short-cut paths; at Ayíou Stefánou the "circuit" stops (the road signposted Kalambáka just before Ayías Triádhos is a highly indirect 5km). In season there are a number of daily buses (most reliably at about 9am and 1pm) from Kalambáka up the road as far as Megálou Meteórou/Varlaám; even taken just part of the way they will give you the necessary head start to make a hiking day manageable. Hitching is also pretty straightforward.

Before setting out it is worth buying **food and drink** to last the day; there are only a couple of drinks/fruit stands on the circuit, by Varlaám and Megálou Meteórou. And finally, don't forget to carry money with you: each monastery levies an admission charge – currently 500dr, with students half price except at Ayías Triádhos.

For visits to all the monasteries, **dress code** is strict. For women this means wearing a skirt – not trousers; for men, long trousers. Both sexes must cover their shoulders. Skirts are often lent to female visitors, but it's best not to count on this.

Doupianí and Ayíou Nikoláou Anapavsás

North from Kastráki the road loops around between huge outcrops of rock, passing below the chapel-hermitage of **Doupianí**, the first communal church of the early monastic settlements. This stretch takes around twenty minutes to walk from the centre of Kastráki. A further ten minutes and you reach a stepped path to the left, which winds around and up a low rock, on which is sited **Ayíou Nikoláou Anapavsás** (daily: July–Aug 9am–6pm; Sept–June 9–5pm). A small, recently restored monastery, this has some superb sixteenth-century frescoes in its *katholikón* (main chapel) by the Cretan painter Theophanes. Oddly, the *katholikón* faces almost due north rather than east because of the rock's shape. As well as the Theophanes paintings there are later, naive images that show Adam naming the animals, including a basilisk – the legendary lizard-like beast that could kill by a breath or glance. Ayíou Nikoláou is also accessible, more directly, by dirt track and path, directly from the platía of Kastráki in fifteen minutes.

Next to Ayíou Nikoláou, on a needle-thin shaft, sits abandoned **Ayía Moní**, ruined by an earthquake in 1858.

Roussánou

Bearing off to the right, fifteen minutes or so further on from Ayíou Nikoláou, a well-signed and cobbled path ascends to the tiny and compact convent of **Roussánou** (daily: summer 9am–6pm; winter 9am–1pm & 3.30–6pm), also known as Ayías Varváras; from another descending trail off a higher loop of road, the final approach is across a dizzying bridge from an adjacent rock. Roussánou has perhaps the most extraordinary site of all the monasteries, its walls edging right up to sheer drops all around. Inside, the narthex of its main chapel has particularly gruesome seventeenth-century frescoes of martyrdom and judgement, the only respite from sundry beheadings, spearings and mutilations being the lions licking Daniel's feet in his imprisonment (near the window).

A short way beyond Roussánou the road divides, the left fork heading towards Varlaám and the Megálou Meteórou. Both of these monasteries are also more directly accessible on foot via a partly cobbled and shaded path leading off the road, 250m past Ayíou Nikoláou; twenty minutes up this path bear right at a T-junction to reach Varlaám in ten minutes, or left for Megálou Meteórou within twenty steeper minutes.

Varlaám (Barlaam)

Varlaám (daily except Fri, 9am–1pm & 3–6pm) is one of the earliest established monasteries, standing on the site of a hermitage established by St Varlaam – a key figure in Meteorite history – shortly after Athanasios's arrival. The present building was founded by two brothers from Ioánnina in 1517 and is one of the most beautiful in the valley.

The monastery's *katholikón*, dedicated to Ayíon Pándon (All Saints), is small but glorious, supported by painted beams and with walls and pillars totally covered by frescoes. A dominant theme, well suited to the Metéora, are the desert ascetics, and there are many scenes of martyrdom. The highly vivid *Last Judgement* (1548), has a gaping Leviathan swallowing the damned, and, dominating the hierarchy of paintings, a great *Pandokrátor* (Christ in Majesty) in the inner of two domes (1566). In the refectory is a small museum of icons, inlaid furniture and textiles; elsewhere the monks' original water barrel is displayed.

Varlaám also retains intact its old **ascent tower**, with a precipitous reception platform and dubious windlass mechanism. Until the 1920s the only way of reaching most of the Meteorite monasteries was by being hauled up in a net drawn by rope and windlass, or by the equally perilous retractable ladders. Patrick Leigh Fermor, who stayed at Varlaám in the 1950s, reported a macabre anecdote about a former abbot: asked how often the rope was changed, he replied, "When it breaks."

Steps were eventually cut to all of the monasteries on the orders of the Bishop of Tríkala, doubtless unnerved by the vulnerability of his authority on visits. Today the ropes are used only for carrying up supplies and building materials.

Megálou Meteórou (Great Meteora)

The **Megálou Meteórou** (daily except Tues, 9am–1pm & 3–6pm) is the grandest and highest of the monasteries, built on the "Broad Rock" some 600m above sea level. It had extensive privileges and held sway over the area for several centuries: in an eighteenth-century engraving (displayed in the museum) it is depicted literally towering above the others. How Athanasios got onto this rock is a wonder.

The monastery's **katholikón**, dedicated to the *Metamórfosis* (Transfiguration), is the most magnificent in Metéora, a beautiful cross-in-square church, its columns and beams supporting a lofty dome with another *Pandokrátor*. It was rebuilt in the sixteenth century, with the original chapel, constructed by Athanasios and Ioasaph, forming just the *ierón*, the sanctuary behind the intricately carved *témblon*, or altar screen. Frescoes, however, are much later than those of the preceding monasteries and not as significant artistically; those in the narthex concentrate almost exclusively on grisly martyrdoms. The other monastery rooms comprise a vast, arcaded cluster of buildings. The *kellari*, or storage cellar, holds an exhibit of rural impedimenta, including a stuffed wolf; in the domed and vaulted refectory is a **museum**, featuring a number of exquisite carved-wood crosses, rare icons and an incense-burner made from a conch shell, as well as a wooden calendar of saints. You can also visit the ancient domed and smoke-blackened kitchen.

Ipapandí, Ayías Triádhos and Ayíou Stefánou

If you are visiting the valley in midsummer, you may by this point be impressed by the buildings but depressed by the crowds, which detract from the wild, spiritual romance of the valley. The remaining monasteries on the "east loop" are less visited, and for a real escape, you can take a short walk north to the tiny hermitage of Ipapandí.

From the car park for Megálou Meteórou, head northeast along multiple traces visible beside a downed metal fence; after about five minutes, you'll reach a prominent pass in the ridge where several trails cross and the main, wide path begins descending, still northeast, through oak woods. This arcs twice around the tops of ravines, until some thirty minutes along you hit the rough service track going ten more minutes west towards **Ipapandí**, now visible wedged into its cliff-face. It's closed for a lengthy restoration which should be complete by late 2000, after which a resident monk or two will receive visitors come to admire the fine frescoes in the fourteenth-century chapel here. Until then, the best view is from the next round-topped monolith along, with a statue of an heroic monk, a crucifix and a circular area with a flagpole.

Following the main road, it's about thirty minutes' walk from the Varlaám/Megálou Meteórou fork to **Ayías Triádhos** (daily except Thurs, 9am–12.30pm & 3–5pm), whose final approach consists of 130 steps carved into a tunnel in the rock. You emerge into a light and airy compound, recently renovated. There's a small folk museum of weavings and kitchen/farm implements, but in general less to be seen than elsewhere – many of the frescoes in the *katholikón* are black with soot and damp, a project to clean and restore them having stalled at an early stage. Most tour buses, mercifully, do not stop here, and the life of the place remains essentially monastic – even if there are only three brothers to maintain it.

Ayíou Stefánou (Tues–Sun 9am–1pm and 3.20–6pm), the last and easternmost of the monasteries, is fifteen minutes' walk beyond here, appearing suddenly at a bend in the road. Again it is active, occupied this time by nuns, but despite ongoing extensive works the buildings are a little disappointing, having been bombed during the war, and it's the obvious one to miss if you're short of time. That said, one small undamaged chapel contains fine original frescoes, and the museum is worthwhile. As at every turn and twist of this valley, the view is amazing, and many visitors leave the convent refreshed by its relative absence of commerciality – though the nuns aren't above peddling a trinket or two.

Although Ayías Triádhos teeters above a deep ravine and the little garden ends in a precipitous drop, there is an obvious, well-signposted **path** from the bottom of the monastery's access steps which leads back to **Kalambáka**. This is about 3km in length, saving a long trudge back around the circuit; it's a partly cobbled, all-weather surface in decent shape. By contrast, the old trail to Kalambáka from Ayíou Stefánou is said to be disused and dangerous

On from Kalambáka

West from Kalambáka runs one of the most dramatic roads in Greece, negotiating the **Katára pass** across the Píndhos mountains to Métsovo and Ioánnina. This route, taking you into northern Epirus, is covered at the beginning of the next chapter.

North from Kalambáka a road leads through Grevená into Macedonia, and then forks: northwest to Kastoriá, or northeast to Siátista, Kozáni, Véria and Thessaloníki (see Chapter Five). The **Grevená road** is scenic, well graded and little travelled; its only drawback is that there are just two daily buses to ghastly Grevená itself, and not a lot of other transport. Finally, there's a possible side-trip into the mountains west of Metéora to visit one of Greece's most peculiar churches.

The church of Timíou Stavroú

If you have your own transport, the flamboyant medieval **church of Timíou Stavroú**, 42km northwest from Kalambáka, between the villages of Kranía (Kranéa on some maps) and Dholianá, is well worth a visit. The church itself, originally eighteenth century but seeming far older, is a masterpiece of whimsy, matched in concept only by two specimens in Romania and Russia. It sports no fewer than twelve turret-like cupolas, higher than they are wide: three are over the nave, one over each of the three apses, and six over the ends of the triple transept. The church is in perfect repair, despite some hasty postwar restoration (it was badly damaged in 1943) and bulldozing, and a terrace below with a fountain makes an ideal picnic spot.

To reach the church, head 10km north of Kalambáka and instead of taking the Métsovo/Ioánnina-bound highway, bear left into a narrower road with multiple signposts for high villages. Climb steadily over a pass on the shoulder of Mount Tringía and then drop sharply into the densely forested valley of the Aspropótamos River, one of the loveliest in the Píndhos. From the *Aspropotamos* taverna, continue 1500m further south to a tiny bridge and a signposted track on the left which leads after 500m to the church, at a height of 1150m. There's a bus from Tríkala to Kranía most days in the summer; a small hotel, the *Aspropotomos* (☎0432/87 277; ③) is open from June to September only.

travel details

Trains

Athens–Thíva–Livadhiá–Lianokládhi (Lamía)–Lárissa

Thirteen trains daily, in each direction: about five of these are expresses (marked IC on schedules) which may skip Thíva or Livadhiá, and take only four hours to reach Lárissa.

Approximate non-express journey times:
Athens–Thíva (1hr 15min)
Thíva–Livadhiá (30min)
Livadhiá–Lianokládhi (1hr 30min–2hr)
Lianokládhi–Lárissa (1hr 30min–2hr 30min)

Lárissa–Platamónas–Kateríni–Thessaloníki
Eleven daily in each direction.

Approximate journey times:
Lárissa–Platamónas (50min)
Lárissa–Kateríni (1hr 10min)
Kateríni–Thessaloníki (1hr 10min).
Lárissa–Thessaloníki (express intercity; 2hr)

Vólos–Lárissa
Twelve daily in each direction (1hr 5min).
NB All onward service between Lárissa and Kalambáka is suspended until further notice.

Vólos–Athens
Three daily in each direction (5hr); through service without changing.

Vólos–Lárissa–Thessaloníki
One daily only in each direction (4hr); through service without changing.

Buses

Buses detailed have similar frequency in each direction, so entries are given just once; for reference check under both starting-point and destination.

Connections with Athens Dhelfí (6–7 daily; 3hr); Karpeníssi (2 daily; 6hr); Lamía (hourly; 3hr 15min); Lárissa (6 daily; 5hr); Thíva/Livadhiá (hourly; 1hr 30min/2hr 10min); Tríkala (7 daily; 5hr 30min); Vólos (9 daily; 4hr 30min).

Ámfissa to: Lamía (3 daily; 2hr 30min); Náfpaktos (4–5 daily; 2hr).

Andírio to: Messolóngi/Agrínio (12 daily; 1hr 30min).

Dhelfí to: Ámfissa (7 daily; 40min); Itéa (5–6 daily; 30min); Pátra (3 daily; 3hr).

Elefsína to: Thíva (Thebes) (2 daily; 1hr 30min).

Itéa to: Galaxídhi/Náfpaktos (4–5 daily Mon–Sat, 3 Sun; 30min/1hr 30min).

Kalambáka to: Grevená (2 daily; 1hr 30min); Métsovo/Ioánnina (2 daily; 1hr 30min/3hr 30min); Vólos (4 daily; 2hr 30 min).

Karpeníssi to: Agrínio (1 most days, 2 Fri; 3hr 30min); Megálo/Mikró Horió (2 daily); Proussós (Mon, Wed & Fri at 1pm).

Lamía to: Karpeníssi (4 daily; 2hr); Lárissa (4 daily; 3hr 30min); Thessaloníki (2 daily; 4hr 30min); Tríkala, via Kardhítsa (4 daily; 3hr); Vólos (2 daily; 3hr).

Lárissa to: Kalambáka (hourly; 2hr); Litóhoro junction (almost hourly; 1hr 45min); Stómio (4 daily Mon–Fri, 5 daily weekends/hols; 1hr 25min); Tríkala (every half-hour; 1hr).

Livadhiá to: Aráhova/Dhelfí (6 daily; 40min/1hr); Dhístomo, for Ósios Loukás (10 daily; 45min); Ósios Loukás, direct (daily at 1pm; 1hr).

Náfpaktos: Frequent blue city bus to Andírio for most connections.

Thíva to: Halkídha (2 daily; 1hr 20min); Livadhiá (hourly; 1hr).

Tríkala to: Kalambáka (hourly; 30min); Kalambáka–Métsovo–Ioánnina (2 daily; 30min/2hr/4hr); Kalambáka–Grevená (2 daily; 30min/2hr); Pýli (13 daily).

Vólos to: Lárissa (hourly; 1hr 15min); Miliés/Vyzítsa (6 daily; 1hr/1hr 10min); Plataniá (3 daily; 2hr); Portariá/Makrinítsa (10 daily; 40min/50min); Thessaloníki (5 daily; 3hr 20min); Tríkala (4 daily; 2hr 30min); Tríkeri (2 daily; 2hr); Tsangarádha/Áyios Ioánnis (2 daily; 2hr/2hr 30min); Zagorá (4 daily; 2hr).

Ferries

Áyios Konstandínos to: Skiáthos (1–2 daily; 2hr 30min); Skópelos (1–2 daily; 3hr 30min);

Alónissos (1–2 daily; 4hr 40min). ☎0235/31 759 for port police, 31 614 for current agent.

Vólos to: Skiáthos (2–4 daily; 2hr 30min–3hr) and Skópelos (2–4 daily; 4–5hr), at least one continuing to Alónissos (5–6hr). Also one weekly service to select Cyclades and Crete (Iráklio). Call port police on ☎0421/24 758 for information.

To Évvia Arkítsa–Loutrá Edhípsou (hourly, every 2hr in winter, last at 11pm/8pm; 50min); Glyfá–Ayiókambos (8 daily, 4 in winter; last at 8.15pm/5pm; 30min).

Haniá–Trizónia (11 daily spring/fall 7am–9pm, more in summer; 5min journey; no cars taken).

Across the Gulf of Kórinthos Andírio–Río (every 15min, much less often after midnight; 15min journey); Áyios Nikólaos–Éyio (9 times daily in summer; 35–40min journey).

Hydrofoils

Flying Dolphins run from the following ports. "In season" means June to mid-September.

Áyios Ioánnis 3–4 weekly in season to Skiáthos, Skópelos and Alónissos.

Áyios Konstandínos At least 3 daily in season to Skiáthos, Skópelos and Alónissos, some stopping at Tríkeri, Paleó Tríkeri and Plataniá in the southern Pílion.

Plataniá 5–6 weekly in season to Skiáthos, Skópelos and Alónissos.

Tríkeri/Paleó Tríkeri 2 daily in season to Skiáthos, Skópelos, Alónissos and Vólos.

Vólos 4–5 daily in season to Skiáthos, Skópelos and Alónissos, with 5 weekly continuing to Skýros; last reliable departure 3pm; at least one daily calls at Tríkeri/Paleó Tríkeri, 4–5 weekly at Plataniá.

For details of services, which vary drastically with the seasons, you are advised to contact local agents (in Áyios Ioánnis ☎0426/31 181; in Áyios Konstandínos ☎0235/31 614; in Vólos ☎0421/39 786; in Plataniá ☎0423/71 231; in Tríkeri ☎0423/91 556); or call ☎01/32 44 600 for information on any route.

CHAPTER FOUR

EPIRUS AND THE WEST

Epirus (Ípiros in modern Greek) has the strongest regional identity in mainland Greece. It owes this character to its mountains: the rugged peaks and passes, forested ravines and turbulent rivers of the **Píndhos** (Pindus) **range**. They have protected and isolated Epirus from outside interference, securing it a large measure of autonomy even under Turkish rule.

Because of this remoteness, the region's role in Greek affairs was peripheral in ancient times. There are just four archeological sites of importance, two of them oracles chosen for their isolation. At **Dodona**, the sanctuary includes a spectacular Classical theatre; at **Ephyra**, the weird remains of a Necromanteion (Oracle of the Dead) was touted by the ancients as the gateway to Hades. **Kassopi** and **Nikopolis**, both near Préveza, are more conventional ancient cities.

In more recent times, **Lord Byron** has been the region's greatest publicist. He visited in 1809 when the tyrannical ruler Ali Pasha was at the height of his power, and the poet's tales of passionate intrigue, fierce-eyed brigandage and braggadocio sent a frisson of horror down romantic Western spines. Byron went on to distinguish himself in the southern province of **Étolo-Akarnanía** by supplying and training troops for the Greek War of Independence, and of course dying at **Messolóngi**.

Despite eventual Greek victory in the War of Independence, the Ottomans remained in Epirus, and were not finally ousted until February 1913. A disputed frontier territory throughout the nineteenth century, the region never recovered its medieval prosperity. When the Italians invaded in 1940, followed by the Germans in 1941, its mountains became first the stronghold of the Resistance, then a battleground for rival political factions and finally, after 1946, the chief bastion of the Communist Democratic Army in the **civil war**. The events of this period (see the box on p.325) are among the saddest of modern Greek history, and continue to reverberate today, not least in Epirus's consistent ranking in EU studies as one of the poorest parts of western Europe.

However, the **mountains** are still the place to head for in Epirus. The people are friendly and hospitable, and certain aspects of their traditional way of life are still in force. Latinate-speaking Vlach and Doric-speaking Sarakatsan shepherds (see "Greek Minorities" in Contexts, p.860) still bring their flocks to the high mountain pastures in

---

ACCOMMODATION PRICE CODES

Throughout the book we've used the following **price codes** to denote the cheapest available double room in each establishment in high season. Out of season, rates can drop by more than fifty percent, especially if you are staying for three or more nights. Single rooms, where available, cost around seventy percent of the price of a double.

① Up to 6000dr	④ 12,000–16,000dr
② 6000–9000dr	⑤ 16,000–20,000dr
③ 9000–12,000dr	⑥ 20,000dr and upwards

Note: Youth hostels typically charge 2000–2500dr for a dormitory bed.
For more accommodation details, see pp.43–6.

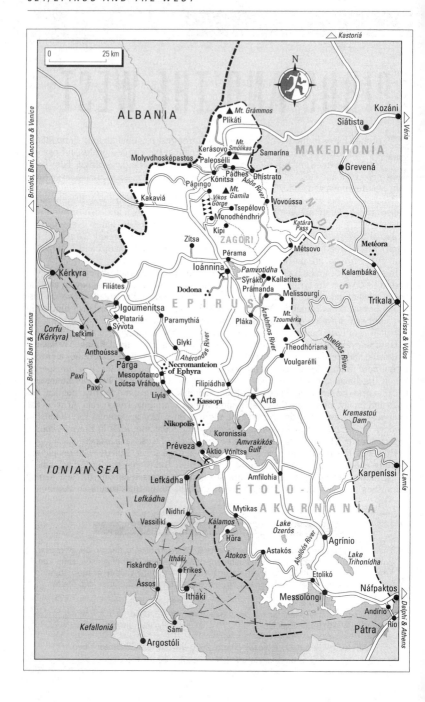

summer. Bears leave footprints on riverbanks or raid beehives, risking an (illegal) bullet in the head, while wolves keep a hungry eye out for stray ewes and goats.

The best single area to visit is around **mounts Gamíla** and **Smólikas**, with the **Aóös** and **Víkos gorges** to walk through and the splendid **villages of Zagóri** to stay in. You have to explore on foot to get a full flavour of the place, and not surprisingly the Píndhos has become a popular hiking venue.

Some of the road routes offer less strenuous travelling highlights – above all the Kalambáka–Ioánnina highway as it negotiates the **Katára pass**. En route is **Métsovo**, perhaps the easiest location for a taste of mountain life, though increasingly commercialized of late. **Ioánnina**, Ali Pasha's capital, is a town of some character, with its island and lake, and the main transport hub for trips into Zagóri. Other than **Árta**, prettily set and with some fine Byzantine churches, there are few other urban attractions.

WORLD WAR II AND THE CIVIL WAR IN EPIRUS

In **November 1940**, the **Italians** invaded Epirus, pushing down from Albania as far as Kalpáki, just south of Kónitsa. United as a nation for the first time in decades, the Greeks repulsed the attack and humiliated Mussolini. However, the euphoria was short-lived as the following April the Germans attacked and rapidly overran Greece.

When parcelling out various portions of the country to their allies for administration, the Germans initially assigned Epirus to the Italians, who trod lightly in the province where they had just been so soundly beaten. After Mussolini's capitulation in September 1943 the Germans assumed direct responsibility for Epirus, and conditions worsened. Together with the mountains of central Greece to the south, the Epirot Píndhos was the main staging point for various **guerrilla bands**, foremost among them the Communist-dominated **ELAS**. Resistance harassment and ambush of the occupying forces incurred harsh reprisals, including the burning in early 1944 of virtually every Vlach village along the Aóös River.

The wartime flight to the cities from the mountains dates more or less from these atrocities, and the vicissitudes of the subsequent **civil war** (1946–49) dashed any lingering hope of a reasonable existence in the mountains. Victims of reprisals by either the Communists or the Royalist/Nationalist central government, villagers fled to safety in the cities, and many never returned. Wherever you go in the back country you'll hear people talk of these times. Some blame the Communists, some blame the Nationalists and all blame the British: "They set us at each other's throats," many will say, and with much justice.

Since 1975, many men (and a few women) who fought in ELAS, either as volunteers or conscripts, have returned to their villages – some of them after thirty years of exile in the USSR and other Eastern Bloc countries. Numerous others had been carried off as children to Albania, and made to work in labour camps before being distributed to various East European states. The political Right claims that this *pedhomázema* – the roundup of children – was a cynical and merciless ploy to train up an army of dedicated revolutionaries for the future. The Left retorts that it was a prudent evacuation of noncombatants from a war zone.

One thing, however, is certain. The Right won, with the backing of the British and, more significantly, the Americans, and they used that victory to maintain an undemocratic and vengeful regime for the best part of the following quarter-century. Many Epirot villagers, regardless of political conviction, believe that the poverty and backwardness in which their communities have remained was a deliberate punishment for being part of Communist-held territory during the civil war. For decades they were constantly harassed by the police, who controlled the issue of all sorts of licences and certificates needed to find public-sector work, to travel, to put children in better schools, to run one's own business and so forth. Only since the 1980s have things really changed, and the past finally treated as another, and separate, age.

The **coast**, in both Epirus and Étolo-Akarnanía, is in general disappointing. **Igoumenítsa** is a useful ferry terminal for Corfu and Italy, but otherwise will win few admirers. **Párga**, *the* major Epirot resort, has been developed beyond its capacity, though **Préveza** has retained some character against the odds and is now a major gateway and nightspot for charter-package patrons. Between these two towns is a string of functional beaches and, just inland, a scenic highlight – the **gorge of the Aheróndas River**.

South of Préveza, you enter a low, marshy landscape of lakes and land-locked gulfs hemmed in by bare hills – of interest mainly to the birdwatcher and fish-dinner enthusiast. For better beach escapes in this part of the world you need islands, fortunately close at hand in the Ionian group – **Lefkádha** (see p.812) is actually connected to the mainland by a movable bridge.

THE PÍNDHOS MOUNTAINS

Even if you have no plans to go hiking, the **Píndhos range** deserves a few days' detour. The remoteness and traditional architecture, the air, the peaks, all constitute a very different Greece to the popular tourist image and, despite increasing popularity as a trekking destination, the area remains relatively unspoilt.

If you are coming from central Greece, the best of the main routes is **Kalambáka–Métsovo–Ioánnina**, which divides the **north Píndhos** from the **south Píndhos**. If you are arriving by ferry at Igoumenítsa, getting up to **Ioánnina** enables you to reverse this itinerary, which is quite the most attractive route into the central mainland. **Walkers** will want to make directly for the **Zagóri**, north of Ioánnina, where trekking excitements beckon.

A number of **hiking routes** are detailed in the text; others can be found in specialist guides (see "Books" in Contexts, p.910). Most of the routes are arduous and lonesome, rather than dangerous. But all the same, this is high-mountain country, with rather unpredictable microclimates, and it's inadvisable to set off on the longer, more ambitious itineraries unless you are already familiar with basic trekking routines.

Kalambáka to Ioánnina

West of Kalambáka (see p.317), the 1694-metre **Katára pass** cuts across the central range of the Píndhos to link Thessaly and Epirus. This route, the only motor road across these mountains that is kept open in winter (except during blizzards), is one of the most spectacular in the country and worth taking for the journey alone. It is the shortest east–west crossing in Greece, though distances here are deceptive. The road switchbacks and zigzags through folds in the enormous peaks, which rise to more than 2300m around Métsovo, and from November to April the snowline must be crossed. All this, however, will soon be a bygone thing, as an enormous tunnel has been bored through the ridge here to spare drivers the dangerously curvy present highway. However the actual road works (plus a projected high-speed rail-line) through it are delayed, so don't expect to be able to use this time-saving route until 2001 at least.

Just two **buses** daily cover the entire route, running between Tríkala and Ioánnina, with stops at Kalambáka and Métsovo. If you're **driving**, allow half a day for the journey from Kalambáka to Ioánnina (114km), and in winter check on conditions before setting out. Anyone planning on **hitching** from Kalambáka should take a lift only if it's going through to Ioánnina or Métsovo, for there's nothing but forest in between, plus several small villages without any facilities.

Métsovo

MÉTSOVO spreads just west of the Katára pass, and just off the Kalambáka–Ioánnina highway. It is a small, often rainy alpine town built on two sides of a ravine and guarded by a forbidding range of peaks to the south and east. This startling site is matched by a traditional architecture and way of life. Immediately below the highway begin tiers of eighteenth- and nineteenth-century stone houses with wooden balconies. These dwellings spill down the slope to and past the main platía, where a dwindling number of old men still loiter, especially after Sunday mass, magnificent in their full traditional dress, from flat black caps to pompommed shoes; the women, enveloped in rich blue weave and a kerchief over a pair of braids, have a more subdued appearance but are more regularly seen in such garb.

If you arrive outside of the two high seasons, stay overnight and take the time to walk in the valley below, the place can seem magical. During the summer, however, your experience may not be so positive. Métsovo has become a favourite target for bus tours full of Greeks, and its beauty veers perilously close to the artificially quaint. Souvenir shops selling kitsch wooden artefacts and "traditional" weavings (often imported from Albania these days) have proliferated, while the stone roofs of the mansions have been completely replaced by ugly pantiles (it's claimed the slates cracked too readily under the weight of the yearly snowfall).

Nonetheless, it would be a shame to pass through Métsovo too speedily, for its history and status as the Vlach "capital" (see "Greek Minorities" in Contexts, p.860) are unique. Positioned on the only commercially and militarily viable route across the Píndhos, it won a measure of independence, both political and economic, in the earliest days of Ottoman rule. These privileges were greatly extended in 1659 by a grateful Turkish vizier who, restored to the sultan's favour, wanted to say a proper thank you to the Metsovite shepherd who had protected him during his disgrace.

Métsovo's continued prosperity, and the preservation of some of its traditions, are largely due to Baron Tositsas, banker scion of a Metsovite family living in Switzerland, who left his colossal fortune to an endowment that benefits industries and crafts in and around the town.

The town and around

The Métsovo **museum** occupies the eighteenth-century **Arhondikó Tosítsa** (daily except Thurs 9am–1.30pm & 4–6pm; group tours only every half-hour; 500dr), the old Tosítsa mansion just off the main thoroughfare. This has been restored to its full glory, and with its panelled rooms, rugs and fine collection of Epirot crafts and costumes, gives a real sense of the town's wealth and grandeur in that era.

The other major Métsovo attraction is the relatively remote monastery of **Áyios Nikólaos**, signposted from the main platía but in fact twenty minutes' walk below town, just off the half-cemented-over *kalderími* headed for Anílio, the village across the ravine. The *katholikón* was built in the fourteenth century to a bizarre plan. It is topped by a simple barrel vault, and what might once have been the narthex became over time a *yinaikonítis* or women's gallery, something seen rarely elsewhere in Greece, except Kastoriá (see p.416). The brilliant **frescoes**, mostly scenes from Christ's life and assorted martyrdoms, exhibit a highly unusual style dating from the eighteenth century, and were cleaned and illuminated during the 1980s, courtesy of the Tositsa Foundation. Since there is no dome, the Four Evangelists are painted on four partly recessed columns rather than on pendentives, as is the norm. The barrel vault features three medallions – the Virgin and Child, an Archangel and a *Pandokrátor* (Christ in Majesty) – forming an unusual series of iconographies. A warden couple live on the premises and receive visitors until 7.30pm. You'll be shown the monks' former cells, with insulating walls of mud and straw, and the abbot's more sumptuous quarters; a donation or purchase of postcards is expected.

The village of **ANÍLIO** (Sunless) is a further half-hour down, then up, and you'll have to make the gruelling trek back the same way. Like Métsovo, its population is Vlach-speaking, and its architecture more genuinely traditional. There are no pretensions to tourist appeal, with its architecture executed in dull cement. You can, however, get an excellent, reasonably priced lunch at the platía before starting back.

For more advanced hikes over tracks or trails, ranging in length from a few hours to a few days, consult the folding map which the "Development Enterprise of Métsovo Municipality" has prepared (available free locally, but labelled and described in Greek only).

Practicalities

The **bus stop** is in the town centre; the **post office** is on the main street, as are three **banks** with cash dispensers.

Métsovo has a wide range of **accommodation**, with thirteen hotels plus quite a few rooms and apartments for rent, virtually all of it en suite. Outside of the ski season, the town's festival (July 26) or late August, you should have little trouble in getting a bed or bargaining posted rates down a category. Mid-range **hotels** include the rustic-style *Flokas* (☎0656/41 309, fax 41 547; ③), on the street leading south from the square, with views from the top-floor rooms; or the much larger *Bitounis* (☎0656/41 217, fax 41 545; ④), at the top of the main street, whose affable proprietor Tolis lived in London for eight years. Cousins of his run the friendly *Athens/Athenai*, just off the main platía (☎0656/41 332; ②), a budget option offering clean rooms and en-suite showers, which was one of the first hotels in Epirus (1925), with the feel of a good French country inn. It has a slightly fancier annexe with full bathrooms called the *Filoxenia* (☎0656/41 021, fax 42 009; ③), just behind the grassy hillock of the central park; never mind the gruff proprietor, it's excellent value, with valley views out the back rooms. The *Kassaros* (☎0656/41 346; ⑤), a few steps south, is comfortable, compact and quiet, though like the *Bitounis* it occasionally fills with tours; all rooms have views over to Anílio. The *Andonis* (ex-Tolis), quietly sited just above the main square (☎0656/42 300, fax 42 298; ⑤, ③ low season), has the largest, most plushly appointed rooms in town, which it ought to for the price.

Meals are overwhelmingly meat-orientated, as befits a pastoral centre. Three of the simpler grills are *Kryfi Folia* on the main platía, *To Tzaki* next door, and *To Koutouki tou Nikola*, also with some non-meat dishes, directly below and behind the post office; all function principally in the evening. The main vegetarian and lunchtime option, with the fullest menu, is the restaurant attached to the *Athens*, which does good, reasonably priced casserole food, accompanied by decent house wine. Wine buffs may want to try the fabled *katóyi*, available in some of these restaurants and in local shops – a moderately expensive limited bottling from tiny vineyards down on the Árakhthos River. This, and other local specialities such as *trahanádhes* (sweet- and sour- dough grain-soup base), the smoked *metsovóne* cheese and *hilópites* (like tagliatelli, long or chopped into cubes) can be obtained at local shops such as Iy Piyi or O Vlahos, just downhill from the *Bitounis*.

Nightlife takes the form of a few conspicuously noisy pubs, cafés and discos uphill from the post office on the main street.

Villages of eastern Zagóri

For a taste of wilder, remoter scenery, and a truer, grittier picture of contemporary mountain life, follow the paved road up into the Píndhos from the Baldhoúma junction on the Métsovo–Ioánnina highway. This precipitous route snakes its way north along the valley of the Várdhas River, through a lush landscape of broad-leafed trees and scrub. At **GREVENÍTI**, the first of a series of predominantly Vlach villages, a black pine forest takes over and continues virtually all the way to Albania; you can stay here at **rooms** run by Anastasia Panayiotopoulou (☎0656/31 212; ③).

Greveníti and the neighbouring villages of **Flambourári** and **Elatohóri** have basic *xenónes* (inns) and places to eat, plus bus services from Ioánnina three days weekly in common with Vovoússa (see below), though the villages are badly depopulated, having failed to recover from wartime destruction inflicted by the Germans in pursuit of Resistance fighters. What remains, however, is very attractive: stone-roofed churches, vine-shaded terraces and courtyards full of flowers and logs stacked for winter. Best of all is the beautiful village of **Makrinó** and its fine monastery, an hour's glorious walk across the ravine from Elatohóri (or a more circuitous twenty-minute drive by car).

The main road continues, winding northeast to **VOVOÚSSA**, which lies right on the Aóös River, its milky green waters spanned here by a high-arched, eighteenth-century bridge. On either side, wooded ridges rise steeply to the skyline, culminating in 2177m Avgó peak just east. The village has a couple of psistariés, and a single (poorly stocked) shop, all of which are open more or less year-round. The large riverside **hotel**, the *Perivoli* (no telephone; 8000dr), is worth a look just for its rambling, slightly spooky lay-out; there are also a very few **rooms** available in peak season, such as those of Evvangelia Dhrouyia (☎0656/31 364; ③) or Athanasios Stangoyiannis (☎0656/31 365; ③). If you prefer to camp, turn left off the road onto the old path just past the Vovoússa road-sign, and walk for about fifteen minutes downstream to where a stretch of river-bank meadow makes an idyllic site. Fresh paw-prints are often seen in the riverside mud here, but the locals swear bears are timid creatures who avoid contact with humans.

There is a sporadic **bus service** to Vovoússa from Ioánnina at 1.15pm on Monday and Friday, returning to Ioánnina the next morning at 6am; Sundays they leave from Ioánnina at 7.45am, returning at 2pm. Alternatively, you could hike along a marked long-distance route down the Aóös River valley to Dhístrato on Mount Smólikas, where there's an inn and early morning bus service (Tues, Thurs & Sat am, plus Sunday pm) to Kónitsa (see p.347). The trek, partly along trail and partly on abandoned forestry track, keeps to the east bank of the Aóös, is shown more or less correctly on the Métsovo municipality's map, and takes a full day to accomplish.

Ioánnina and around

Descending from Métsovo, you approach **IOÁNNINA** through more spectacular folds of the Píndhos, emerging high above the great lake of **Pamvotídha** (Pamvotis). The old town stands on a rocky promontory jutting out into the water, its fortifications punctuated by towers and minarets. From this base, Ali Pasha wrested from Ottoman authority a fiefdom that encompassed much of western Greece – an act of contemptuous rebellion that portended wider defiance in the Greeks' own War of Independence.

Disappointingly, most of the city is modern and undistinguished – a testimony not so much to Ali Pasha, although he did raze much of it to the ground while under siege in 1820, as to developers in the 1950s and 1960s. However, there are several stone **mosques** to evoke the Ottoman era, and the fortifications of Ali Pasha's citadel, the **Froúrio**, survive more or less intact.

Ioánnina is also the jump-off point for visits to the **caves of Pérama**, some of Greece's largest, on the west shore of the lake, and the longer excursion to the mysterious and remote Oracle of Zeus at **Dodona**, as well as to Epirus's most rewarding corner, **Zagóri** (see p.337).

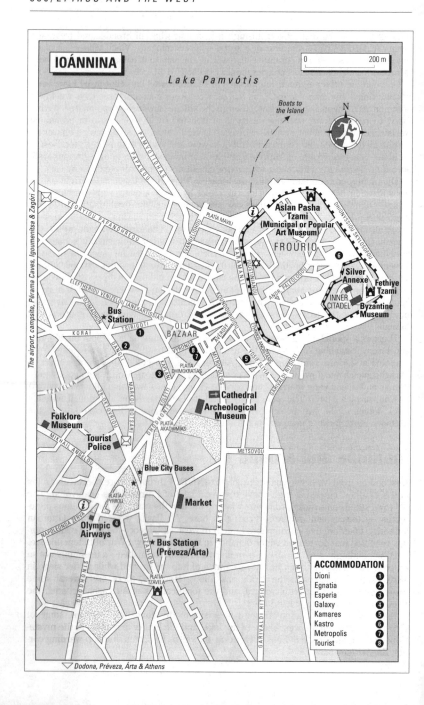

IOÁNNINA

0   200 m

Lake Pamvótis

Boats to
the Island

N

PAPAGOU

PAMVOTIDHAS

YEORYIOU PAPANDHREOU

PLATÍA MAVILI

EVANGELIDHOU

The airport, campsite, Pérama Caves, Igoumenitsa & Zagóri

ELEFTHERIOU VENIZELOU (ANEKASTISTASIS)

KARAMANLI

ANDR. PALEOLOGOU

DHIONYSSIOU-SKYLOSOFOU

Aslan Pasha
Tzami
(Municipal or Popular
Art Museum)

FROÚRIO

Silver
Annexe

INNER
CITADEL

Fethiye
Tzami

Byzantine
Museum

KOUNDOURIOTOU

PLATÍA DIMARATOU

**Bus
Station**

KORAÍ

TSIRIGOTI

**OLD
BAZAAR**

VYRONOS

AVEROFF

ETHN. ANDISTASIS

IOSIF ELIYIA

GARIVALDI RITSOTI

PLATÍA
DHIMOKRATÍAS

MITROPOLEOS

BYZANTIOU

TZAVELLA

MARKOU BOTSARI

28 OKTOVRIOU

OKTO MONIS

MIKHAÍL ANGELOU

NAPOLEONOS ZERVA

**Folklore
Museum**

**Tourist
Police**

Blue City Buses

PLATÍA
AKADHIMÍAS

Cathedral

**Archeological
Museum**

METSOVOU

PLATÍA
PYRROU

Market

H. KATSARI

**Olympic
Airways**

**Bus Station
(Préveza/Árta)**

DHODHONIS

BIZANIOU

PLATÍA
TZAVELA

GARIVALDI RITSOTI

AKTÍ MIAOULI

ACCOMMODATION

Dioni	❶
Egnatia	❷
Esperia	❸
Galaxy	❹
Kamares	❺
Kastro	❻
Metropolis	❼
Tourist	❽

Dodona, Préveza, Árta & Athens

Arrival, orientation and information

Ioánnina **airport** is on the road out to the Pérama caves, 5km from the centre. It's connected to town by city bus #7 (the most frequent); #1 and #13 also pass by. All such blue-and-white buses leave Ioánnina from a series of stops below the central **Platía Pýrrou**.

KTEL buses arrive at one of two terminals. The main station is at **Zozimádhon 4**, north of Platía Pýrrou; this serves most points north and west, including Métsovo, Kalambáka, Igoumenítsa, Kónitsa and the Zagóri villages. A smaller terminal at **Bizaníou 19** connects Árta, Préveza, Dodona and all villages in the south or east parts of Epirus. It is advisable, especially on summer weekends, to buy tickets for both coast and mountains the day before. For more efficient explorations of the poorly served Zagóri area, consider **car rental** from the likes of Avis at Dhodhónis 96 (☎0651/46 333), Budget at Dhodhónis 109 (☎0651/43 901), European at Koundourióti 2 (☎0651/67 715), Hertz at Dhodhónis 105 (☎0651/48 990), Pier 1 at Spýrou Lámbrou 17 (☎0651/64 360) or Tomaso at Dhodhónis 42 (☎0651/66 900). Despite this multiplicity of outlets, expect to pay at least 12,000dr a day for short hire periods.

The axis of the town centre is the confusing, oddly angled jumble of streets between Platía Pýrrou and the **Froúrio**, Ali Pasha's old citadel. Near the latter is the old bazaar area – still in part an artesans' marketplace. Within sight of Platía Pýrrou are all the

---

ALI PASHA

Ali Pasha, a highly ambivalent "heroic rebel", is the major figure in Ioanninan and Epirot history. The so-called "Lion of Ioánnina", on balance a highly talented sociopath, pursued a policy that was consistent only in its ambition and self-interest. His attacks on the Ottoman imperial government were matched by acts of appalling and vindictive **savagery** against his largely Greek Orthodox subjects. Despite all this, he is still held in some regard by locals, the rationale being "a son of a bitch, but at least *our* son of a bitch"; a platía in the citadel is even named for him.

Ali was born in 1741 in Tepelene, Albania, and rose to power under Turkish patronage, being made pasha of Tríkala in reward for his efforts in the sultan's war against Austria. His ambitions, however, were of a grander order and that same year he **seized Ioánnina**, an important town since the thirteenth century, with a population of 30,000 – probably the largest in Greece at the time. Paying sporadic tribute to the sultan, he operated from this power base for the next 33 years, allying himself in turn, and as the moment suited him, with the British, French or Ottomans.

In 1809, when his dependence upon the sultan was nominal, Ali was visited by the young **Lord Byron**, whom he overwhelmed with hospitality and attention. (The tyrant's sexual tastes were famously omnivorous, and it is recorded that he was particularly taken with the poet's "small ears", a purported mark of good breeding.) Byron, impressed for his part with the renegade's daring and stature, and the lively **revival of Greek culture** in Ioánnina (which, he wrote, was "superior in wealth, refinement and learning" to any town in Greece), commemorated the meeting in *Childe Harold*. The portrait that he draws, however, is an ambiguous one, since he was well aware that beneath the Pasha's splendid court and deceptively mild countenance there were "deeds that lurk" and "stain him with disgrace".

In a letter to his mother Byron was more explicit, concluding that "His highness is a remorseless tyrant, guilty of the most horrible cruelties, very brave, so good a general that they call him the Mahometan Buonaparte . . . but as barbarous as he is successful, roasting rebels, etc, etc". Of the rebels, the most illustrious was Katsandonis the klepht who, wracked by smallpox, was captured by Ali in a cave in the Ágrafa mountains. He imprisoned the unfortunate wretch in a waterlogged lakeside dungeon and finally executed him in public by breaking his bones with a sledgehammer.

essential services: most of the **banks** (all with cash dispensers) and the central **post office** (Mon–Fri 7.30am–8pm), the latter on 28-Oktovríou. There's a second post office closer to the lake on Yeoryíou Papandhréou, keeping the same hours, that's particularly handy for the campsite. **Information** on current bus timetables is most easily obtained at the friendly **EOT** (Sept–June Mon–Fri 7.30am–2.30pm; additional hours July–Aug Mon–Fri 5.30–8.30pm & Sat 9am–1pm); when they're shut, refer to the **tourist police** on 28-Oktovríou, opposite the post office.

Accommodation

Most Ioánnina **hotels** are noisy or otherwise badly placed, and expensive for what's on offer, though at slow times they may cut prices by a category. High season, such as it is, tends to be winter, not summer. The town's pay-and-display parking scheme is pretty comprehensive, with punch-out cards permitting only two hours at a time; thus hotels with their own parking or garages are indicated. If you arrive early enough in the day, and value tranquillity above luxury, it's worth heading straight out to Nissí island (see p.333), where the **inn** run by the Dellas family offers about the cheapest, most attractive accommodation available. You will also find dozens of **rooms** in Pérama village as you walk to the caves.

Camping, unusually for a town, is an attractive option and *Camping Limnopoula*, 2km out of town on the Pérama road (city bus #2 or a 20-min walk from Platía Mavíli), is a pleasant, well-equipped, mosquito-free site, though a bit cramped and more geared towards camper vans than tents.

Dioni, Tsirigóti 10 (☎0651/27 032). The most pleasant of several hotels on this street leading away from the Zozimádhon bus station; has a car park. ④.

Egnatia, Danglí 2, corner Aravandinoú (☎0651/32 071). Another decent hotel near Zozimádhon bus station, especially if you get a side room, though favoured by trekking groups and sometimes block-booked. Has a garage. ④.

Esperia, Kapláni 3 (☎0651/24 111). One of the few savoury, quiet cheapies in town, with large, balconied, en-suite rooms (though furnishings are distressed 1970s vintage). ③.

Galaxy, Platía Pýrrou, south corner (☎0651/25 056, fax 30 724). Comfortable, quiet, refurbished in 1997, with spectacular mountain/lake views from the balconies, air con and small tubs in the baths. You don't get much more central; limited parking. ⑤.

Kamares, Zalakósta 74 (☎0651/79 348); a bit hard to find, look for the dirt-lane continuation of the named street (which has fee-free parking). Rooms in a restored Turkish mansion in a quietish neighbourhood near the citadel; the wood-decor attic rooms with air con are best, but ring first as many are occupied long-term by corporate or army personnel. ④.

Kastro, Andhroníkou Paleológou 57, inside the Froúrio (☎ & fax 0651/22 866). A newish (1998), tastefully restored inn on the way to the Fethiye Tzami, whose seven unique rooms feature lots of double beds. Limited street parking. Rates, including breakfast, from ④ (low season) to ⑥ for the best upstairs units.

Metropolis/Metropole, Krystálli 2, cnr Avéroff (☎0651/26 207). Pretty basic (non-en-suite) and noisy, but clean enough budget hotel. ③.

Sotiris Dellas (☎0651/81 494). A good if simple pension on Nissí with eight non-en-suite rooms; you'll find the owners at the house right next to the school, or adjacent the inn at their *Snak-Bar Seraï*. ②.

Tourist, Kolétti 18, corner Krystálli (☎0651/26 443). Around the corner from the *Metropolis*, but quieter and more comfortable; 1995-redone rooms all have baths. ④.

The town

The **Froúrio** is an obvious point to direct your explorations. In its heyday the walls dropped abruptly to the lake, and were moated on their (southwest) landward side. The moat has been filled in, and a quay-esplanade now extends below the lakeside ramparts, but there is still the feel of a citadel; inside nestles a quiet residental zone with narrow alleys and its own shops.

Signs inside direct you to the **Municipal (Popular Art) Museum** (daily Mon–Fri 8.30am–2.30pm, Sat–Sun 9am–3pm; 700dr), an elegantly arranged collection of Epirot costumes, guns and jewellery. More poignant is a section devoted to synagogue rugs and tapestries recently donated by the dwindling Jewish community of 35; their *hávra* or **synagogue** at Ioustiniánou 16 can be visited on application to the community office at Iosif Eliyía 18 (the unmarked, ground-floor storefront – only Greek or Hebrew spoken). The so-called Muslim wing features a mother-of-pearl suite, with the pipe of Esat Pasha, last Ottoman governor here. The museum is housed in the well-preserved, nocturnally illuminated **Aslan Pasha Tzami**, allowing a rare glimpse of the interior of a Greek mosque; it retains the decoration on its dome and the recesses in the vestibule for worshippers' shoes. In the adjacent quarters, tradition places Ali's attempted rape in 1801 of Kyra Phrosyne, the mistress of his eldest son. Her "provocation" had been to refuse the 62-year-old tyrant's sexual advances; together with seventeen of her companions, she was bound, weighted and thrown alive into Lake Pamvotis. The incident gave rise to several folk songs, and her ghost is still said to hover over the water on moonlit nights.

To the east of the Aslan Pasha Tzami lies the **inner citadel** or acropolis of the fortress (daily 7am–10pm; free). This was used for some years by the Greek military and most of its buildings – including Ali's palace where Byron was entertained – have unfortunately been adapted or restored to a point at which they can no longer be recognized as eighteenth-century structures. Ali Pasha's tomb is purported to be close by the old **Fethiye Tzami** (Victory Mosque), though no identifiable trace of it remains. The tyrant's former palace has been pressed into service as the **Byzantine Museum** (Tues–Sat 8.30am–3pm; 500dr), a remarkably thin collection which can be skipped without regret if time is short: six rooms containing masonry from assorted collapsed Epirot basilicas, troves of coins, medieval pottery and post-Byzantine icons, mostly sixteenth- and seventeenth-century. The only genuinely Byzantine painting is a fresco fragment of *The Betrayal*, from a damaged church in Voulgarélli. A few paces away, in the purported treasury of Ali Pasha's seraglio, is a marginally better auxiliary exhibit devoted to Ioánnina's long-running silver industry, featuring both secular and ecclesiastical work from the nineteenth century, and an explanatory mock-up of a smith's workbench.

Apart from the Froúrio, the town's most enjoyable quarter is that of the old **bazaar**, a roughly semicircular area focused on the citadel's main gate. This retains a cluster of Ottoman-era buildings (including some imposing houses with ornate window grilles), as well as a scattering of copper- and tin-smiths, plus the silver-smiths that were for centuries a mainstay of the town's economy.

Just off the central Platía Dhimokratías, set beside a small park behind the National Bank, is the well-lit and well-labelled **archeological museum** (Tues–Sun 8.30am–2.30pm; 500dr). It's certainly a must if you're planning a visit to the theatre and oracle of Dodona, for on display here – along with some exceptionally well-crafted bronze seals – is a fascinating collection of lead tablets inscribed with questions to the oracle. There are ornate relief-carved Roman sarcophagi from Paramythiá and Igoumenítsa and, among numerous bronze statuettes, two Hellenistic children, one throwing a ball and one holding a dove. The ancient collection is rounded off by burial finds and pottery from Ambracia (Árta), Acheron (the Necromanteion of Ephyra) and Vítsa; an incogruous modern-art collection at the rear is of minimal interest.

Nissí island

The island of **Nissí** in Lake Pamvotídha is connected by motor-launches (half-hourly in summer, hourly otherwise, 8am–11pm; 200dr) from the quay northwest of the Froúrio on Platía Mavíli. The beautiful island village, founded in the sixteenth century by refugees from the Máni in the Peloponnese, is flanked by several **monasteries**, providing a perfect focus for an afternoon's visit. By day the main lane leading up from the boat dock is crammed with stalls selling jewellery and kitsch souvenirs. Quiet descends with the sun as it sets superbly over the reedbeds that fringe the island, except at the pair of restaurants on the waterfront and another cluster by Pandelímonos; outside cars are not allowed, and the islanders have just a few vehicles which they haul across on a chain-barge to the mainland opposite.

The **monastery of Pandelímonos**, just to the east of the village, is perhaps the most dramatic of Ioánnina's Ali Pasha sites, though it is in fact a complete reconstruction, as the original building was smashed some years ago by a falling tree. In January 1822 Ali was assassinated here, his hiding place having been revealed to the Turks, who had finally lost patience with his intrigues. Trapped in his rooms on the upper storey, he was shot from the floor below, then decapitated (supposedly on the second step from the top), with his head sent to the sultan as a trophy. The fateful bullet holes in the floorboards form the centrepiece of a small **museum** (summer daily; 150dr) devoted to the tyrant, along with numerous wonderful period prints and knick-knacks like Ali's splendid hubble-bubble on the fireplace.

Three other **monasteries** – **Filanthropinón**, **Ayíou Nikoláou Stratigopoúlou** or **Dilíou**, and **Eleoússas** (closed indefinitely for extensive restoration) – lie south of the village in the order cited. They are quite clearly signposted and stand within a few hundred yards of one another along a lovely tree-lined lane; the first two are maintained by resident families, who allow brief visits except during siesta hours (knock for admission if the doors are shut). Both monasteries are attractively situated, with pleasant courtyards, though visits essentially consist of being shown their main chapel, or *katholikón*. These feature late and post-Byzantine **frescoes**, in various states of preservation.

The finest are those of Filanthropinón, a simple barrel-vaulted structure with a blind narthex and two *pareklísia* (side chapels). A complete cycle of Christ's life in the inner nave dates from just after the monastery's foundation in 1292; there are plenty of episodes on boats in the Sea of Galilee, as befits a lake-island church. Lower down, throughout the building, are the saints, including (just east of the door to the south *pareklísion*) the apocryphal Khristóforos (Christopher). Higher up, in the outer nave and north *pareklísion*, graphic martyrdoms predominate: sundry beheadings, drag-

---

LAKE PAMVOTÍDHA AND ITS ECOLOGY

Murkily green and visibly dirty, **Lake Pamvotídha** is not simply polluted but also slowly shrinking. The springs which historically fed it along its north shore suddenly dried up in the early 1980s, and shortly thereafter the lake stopped draining towards the Adriatic. Contaminated runoff from Ioánnina and surrounding farmland began to accumulate, a problem exacerbated by four dry years between 1989 and 1992, which lowered the water level almost 2m in a lake that's at best 15m deep (though after a few wet winters, it has risen again). Swimming is forbidden, though few would want to under present circumstances.

In the face of all this, the inhabitants of the island struggle to continue **fishing**. The lake was stocked with three species from Hungary in 1986, though all but one of these, the hardy, carp-like *kyprínos*, have been fished out as they failed to reproduce. Ioánnina inhabitants generally refuse to eat anything out of the lake, so the islanders are forced to sell their catch at a pittance for shipment to Thessaloníki, where it retails for ten times the price. Given such dire economics, fishing continues mainly to pass the time and supplement local diets. The only lake items on Nissí restaurant menus are the legs of frogs caught in the surrounding reedbeds, some of the eels and the *kyprínos*.

gings, impalings and boilings. At the east end of the north chapel, Adam names the beasts in the Garden of Eden, while the ceiling of the narthex holds a fine *Transfiguration*. In the south chapel, just west of the door, ancient Greek sages (Solon, Aristotle, Plutarch) make a rare appearance, indicating that this may have been a school for Hellenic culture during the Turkish period.

The frescoes in Dilíou are being slowly cleaned, and should eventually equal Filanthropinón's in interest. Currently the narthex offers, from the Life of the Virgin, a fine *Adoration of the Magi* and a *Flight into Egypt* on the west wall, plus a typically sur- real *Apocalypse* over the door to the naos. There's a fine touch to the *Nativity*, where an angel sternly awakens Joseph with a wagging finger.

Beyond these three monasteries the track loops anticlockwise around the island until you emerge by a fourth monastery, **Ioánnou Prodhrómou**, right behind Pandelímonos, which holds the keys. However the interior is of less interest than the exterior's three-windowed gables and brickwork.

Eating, nightlife and entertainment

For **eating, the island** is the most atmospheric location with its slightly expensive tav- ernas by the boat dock featuring freshwater specialities like eel (*héli*), crayfish (*kar- avídhes*) and frogs' legs, as well as lake carp (*kyprínos*). The remoter, lakefront Seraï by the Dellas inn is a friendly local hangout purveying less expensive meals. If you'd rather not sample anything fished from those murky waters, the farmed trout (*péstro- fa*) is cheaper and possibly safer. In winter the tavernas provide lunch only.

In town, more standard fare can be found around the bazaar near the Froúrio gate; try the *Ivi* restaurant for basic *mayireftá*, or, for grills, the worthy rivals *To Kourmanio* and *To Manteio*, both exactly opposite the gate. inexpensive and with sizable good por- tions. For lakeside dining, head northwest along Odhós Pamvotídhas, where a half- dozen psistariés and ouzeris beckon. Of these, *Filippos* and *Stin Ithaki* (strong on fish) are well attended, but the furthest one, *Mezedhadhiko Syn 2* (pronounced "Sýn Dhýo"), rates highly for an imaginative and lengthy menu, reasonable prices and a loyal local clientele. It's part of a small chain: *Syn 1* is at Dhodhónis 79, while *Syn 3* – grills only – perches on the hillside across the lake at Amfithéa village.

For **snacks**, recall that Ioánnina is the original home of the *bougátsa* (custard-tart), fresh at breakfast time with sweet or savoury fillings from *Select* at Platía Dhimokratías 2, whose decor has seemingly remained unchanged for thirty years. For a more con- temporary environment, the patisserie *Vrettania*, under the eponymous hotel at Platía Dhimodratías 11/A, also has excellent own-made ice cream.

Nightlife oscillates between the calmer **cafés** on and around Platía Pýrrou (includ- ing *The Old Post*, the former mail office, with its Baroque fittings) and the **bars** and (generally mediocre) tavernas on Platía Mavíli, heart of the Mólos or lakefront. The bars, especially *Yperokeanios* and *Gallery*, are more fun, in conjunction with the pre- vailing, gas-lantern carnival atmosphere outside, enlivened by sellers of *halvás* (sweet- meat) and roast corn. About 100m beyond *Syn 2* is *Kyknos*, a music bar aimed at the stu- dent crowd which only really gets going after 11pm. There are more theme bars, creperies and kafenía scattered across the approaches to the castle, along completely gentrified Karamanlí, and at the far end of Ethnikís Andistásis, at the southern corner of the citadel, though several failed operations suggest excess capacity.

Back up on Platía Pýrrou, there are also three **cinemas**, which – thanks to the univer- sity students – usually host quite a decent programme of first-run films. From mid-July to mid-August, the biggest formal events are part of the *Politistikó Kalokéri* (Cultural Summer), music and theatre performances, plus the odd cultural exhibition. Most of the events take place in the hillside **Fróntzos theatre**, just outside the town (there is also a pleasant summer restaurant here, with fine views down to the town and lake). Tickets are available from the Folklore Museum (Mon 5.30–8pm & Wed 10am–1pm) at Miha**ï**l Angélou 42 or the EOT office. Some years there are a few performances of Classical drama and contemporary music at the ancient **theatre of Dodona** (see below).

North to the Pérama caves

Five kilometres north of Ioánnina, the village of **PÉRAMA** boasts what are reputed to be Greece's largest system of **caves** (daily: summer 8am–8pm; winter 8am–sunset; 1500dr, students half price), which extend and echo for kilometres beneath a low hill. They were discovered during the last war by a guerrilla in hiding from the Germans. The half-hour mandatory tours of the complex are Greek-only, save a brief printed summary in English, and a little perfunctory (consisting in the main of a student reeling off the names of various suggestively shaped formations), but not enough to spoil the experience, though the same might not be said for the ugly concrete path which has been threaded through the caverns.

To reach the caves, take a #8 blue city bus (buy your ticket in advance from a kiosk) from the terminal below Platía Pýrrou to Pérama village; the caves are a ten-minute walk inland from the bus stop, past tacky souvenir shops. If you are driving, you can make a circuit of it. The road splits shortly after Pérama: one fork leading up towards Métsovo, with superb views down over Ioánnina and the lake; the other running around the lake, with a shoreline café midway.

South to Dodona: the Oracle of Zeus

At **DODONA**, 22km southwest of Ioánnina, in a wildly mountainous and once-isolated region, lie the ruins of the **Oracle of Zeus** dominated by a vast and elegant theatre. The oracle is a very ancient site indeed. "Wintry Dodona" is mentioned in Homer, and the worship here of Zeus and of the sacred oak tree seems to have been connected with the first Hellenic tribes who arrived in Epirus around 1900 BC.

The origins of the oracle – the oldest in Greece – are shadowy. Herodotus gives an enigmatic story about the arrival of a *peleiae* or dove from Egyptian Thebes which settled in an oak tree and ordered a place of divination to be made. The word *peleiae* in fact meant both dove and old woman, so it's possible that the legend he heard refers to an original priestess – perhaps captured from the Middle East and having some knowledge of divination. The **oak tree**, stamped on the ancient coins of the area, was central to the cult. Herodotus recorded that the oracle spoke through the rustling of the oak's leaves in sounds amplified by copper vessels suspended from its branches. These would then be interpreted by frenzied priestesses and strange priests who slept on the ground and never washed their feet. Legend also asserts that the Argonauts used this oak to build their ship, with the presumably charmed properties of the wood enabling them to get out of numerous tight spots.

The site

Mon–Fri 8am–7pm (winter 8am–5pm), Sat & Sun 8.30am–3pm; 500dr.

Entering the site past a few seat-tiers of a third-century BC **stadium**, you are immediately confronted by the massive western retaining wall of the **theatre**. Built during the time of Pyrrhus (297–272 BC), this was one of the largest on the Greek mainland, rivalled only by those at Argos and Megalopolis. Later, the Romans made adaptations necessary for their blood sports, adding a protective wall over the lower seating and also a drainage channel, cut in a horseshoe shape around the orchestra. What you see today is a meticulous reconstruction of the late nineteenth century, since until then the theatre had been an almost incomprehensible jumble of stones.

The theatre is used occasionally, to marvellous effect, for weekend ancient drama and music performances during Ioánnina's summer cultural festival (see p.335). This is one of the most glorious settings in Greece, facing out across a green, silent valley to the slopes of Mount Tómaros. At the top of the *cavea*, or seating curve, a grand entrance gate leads into the **acropolis**, an overgrown and largely unexcavated area. The foundations of its walls, mostly Hellenistic, are a remarkable four to five metres wide.

Beside the theatre, and tiered uncharacteristically against the same slope, are the foundations of a *bouleuterion*, beyond which lie the complex ruins of the **Sanctuary of Zeus**, site of the oracle itself. There was no temple as such until the end of the fifth century BC; until then, worship had centred upon the sacred oak, which stood alone within a circle of votive tripods and cauldrons. Building began modestly with a small stone temple-precinct, and in the time of Pyrrhus the precinct was enclosed with Ionic colonnades. In 219 BC the sacred house was sacked by the Aetolians and a larger temple was built with a monumental *propylaion*. This survived until the fourth century AD, when the oak tree was hacked down by Christian reformists. It is remains of the later precinct that can be seen today, distinguishable by a modern oak planted at the centre by a helpfully reverent archeologist. Ruins of an early Christian **basilica**, constructed on a sanctuary of Hercules (Herakles), are also prominent nearby – distinguished by rounded column stumps.

Many **oracular inscriptions** were found scattered around the site when it was systematically excavated in 1952. Now displayed in Ioánnina's archeological museum, they give you a good idea of the personal realm of the oracle's influence in the years after it had been eclipsed by Delphi. More interestingly, they also offer a glimpse of the fears and inadequacies that motivated the pilgrims of the age to journey here, asking such domestic questions as: "Am I her children's father?" and, memorably, "Has Pleistos stolen the wool from my mattress?"

Practicalities

Relatively few people make the detour to Dodona, so the site and **DHODHÓNI** – the little village to the west of it – are completely unspoilt. **Transport** is accordingly sparse, with only two buses a day direct from Ioánnina (Mon–Wed, Fri & Sat 6.30am & 4pm, Sun 4pm only) to Melingí village, via the site. Alternatively, buses for the village of Zotikó (Mon, Wed & Fri at 2pm) pass within 2km of the site; the bus conductor will point out the kafenío where you should alight for the final, downhill walk, and the "real" return bus calls at the site car park at about 5pm, giving you a clear three hours to look around. Hitching to the site from the junction 7km south of Ioánnina should be feasible in summer, or a round trip by taxi from Ioánnina with an hour at the site can be negotiated for a reasonable amount – say 5000dr per carload.

Alternatively, you could always stay the night here. There are some lovely spots to **camp**, a friendly if basic **taverna** in the village, which has **rooms** run by Stefanos Nastos (☎0651/71 106, ②) and a small, less welcoming **hotel** at the site, the *Andromachi* (☎0651/82 296; ④), which fills only at festival time.

Zagóri

Few parts of Greece are more surprising, or more beguiling, than **Zagóri**. A wild, infertile region, it lies to the north of Ioánnina, bounded by the roads to Kónitsa and Métsovo on the west and south, and the Aóös River valley to the northeast. The beauty of its landscape is unquestionable: miles of forest, barren limestone wastes, rugged mountains deeply furrowed by foaming rivers and partly subterranean streams. But there is hardly an arable inch anywhere, and scarcely a job for any of its few remaining

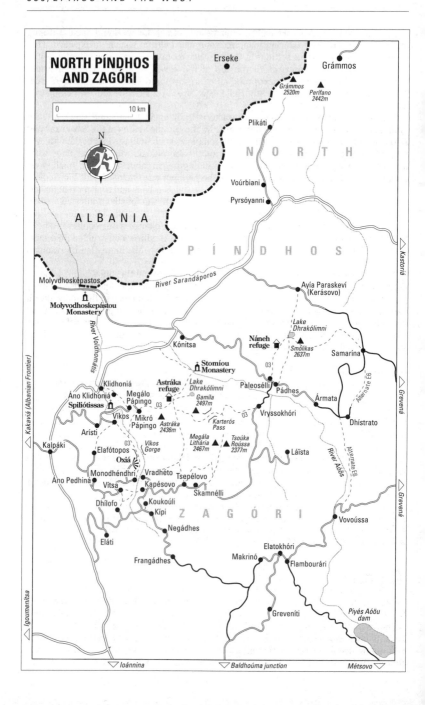

inhabitants. The last place, in fact, that one would expect to find some of the most imposing architecture in Greece.

Yet the **Zagorohória**, as the 46 villages of Zagóri are called, are full of grand stone *arhondiká* (mansions) enclosed by semi-fortified walls, with deep-eaved gateways opening onto immaculately cobbled streets. Though they look older, the *arhondiká* are mostly late eighteenth or early nineteenth century. By the 1960s, many had fallen into disrepair or been insensitively restored, but the government now ensures (in several listed villages, anyway) that repairs are carried out in the proper materials, rather than cheap brick and sheet metal; new structures are required to have local stone cladding. Inside, if you are lucky enough to get a glimpse, the living quarters are upstairs, arranged on an **Ottoman** model. Instead of furniture, low platforms line the rooms on either side of an often elaborately hooded fireplace; strewn with rugs and cushions, they serve as couches for sitting during the day and sleeping at night. The wall facing the fire is usually lined with panelled and sometimes painted storage cupboards called *misándres*. In the grander houses the intricately fretted wooden ceilings are often painted as well. Additionally, most houses have a *bímsa* (secret, fireproof bunker) for hiding the family gold and perhaps a wife and child or two whenever Albanian or other Muslim marauders threatened; even if the house was torched, the survivors could dig out their wealth and start over again.

As for the countryside, much the best way of savouring it is on foot, **hiking** the dozens of paths which, gliding through forest and sheepfold or slipping over passes and hogbacks, connect the outlying villages. The most popular outing – now very much part of the holiday trekking-company circuit – is along the awesome **Víkos gorge**. It's not to be missed, though for more of a feel of the back country, you may want to continue northeast, over towards **Mount Gamíla** and the remoter Vlach villages at the base of **Mount Smólikas** (see p.348).

If you would rather have things organized for you, Kostas Vasiliou at Robinson Expeditions, Ogdhóïs Merarkhías 10, Ioánnina (☎0651/29 402, best to fax or email from abroad: ☎25 071 or *robinson@compulink.gr*), near the campsite by a BP filling station, runs **group treks** for a number of overseas hiking companies but welcomes walk-in custom. If you arrange things in advance, or are prepared to wait a few days, he will do his best to fit you in.

The Víkos gorge and western Zagóri

The walls of the **Víkos gorge** are nearly 1000m high in places, cutting right through the limestone tablelands of Mount Gamíla, and separating the villages of the western and central Zagóri. It is quite the equal of the famous Samarian gorge in Crete, and a **hike** through or around it – depending on your abilities and time – is likely to be the highlight of a visit to the Zagóri. Since 1975 a national park has encompassed both Víkos and the equally gorgeous Aóös River canyon to the north and, to date at least, various plans for ski centres, téléfériques and dams have been fought off.

Touristic development, however, has proceeded apace since the early 1980s, when British and French trekking companies first began coming here, and today almost every hamlet within spitting distance of the canyon (and indeed any sizable village elsewhere in Zagóri) has some form of accommodation and tavernas. Be warned, though, that the area's popularity is such that you won't get a room to save your life from mid-July through late August, when a tent provides an essential fallback. During the rest of the year, weekends and three-day holidays are also unwise times to show up without advance reservations. Moreover, you may have to settle for staying in some of the outlying villages, away from the immediate environs of the gorge – though this will work out slightly less expensive, and the "second choice" village may have a more genuine community feel.

HIKING WARNINGS

Despite the Víkos Gorge's popularity and recent improvements in local trail maintenance, mapping and waymarking, it is worth emphasizing that the traverse is not a Sunday stroll and that there is still plenty of scope for getting lost or worse. During April or early May, snowmelt often makes the Monodhéndhri end impassable due to high run-off, and in a rainstorm the sides of the gorge can become an oozing mass of mud, tree-trunks and scree.

At the best of times it's not really a hike to be attempted with low-cut trainers and PVC water bottles, as so many do. It is also strongly recommended that walkers go in parties of four or more, since isolated hikers are more vulnerable to attack by desperate, possibly armed Albanians living rough in the bushes. A stout stick for warding off snakes and belligerent livestock, and for purchase when traversing bald or scree-laden slopes, would not go amiss either. Finally, owing partly to the decrease in grazing and the gradual re-afforestation of the area, the local **bear population** is on the increase; sightings of tracks and actual individuals are becoming commonplace, especially around Kípi and Pápingo, though they are shy and (except for females with cubs) flee humans who stumble on them.

The Ioánnina EOT hands out photocopies of the *Korfes* magazine's **topographical map** of the Víkos gorge area, but this is old (1984–85) and full of dangerous errors. If you are going beyond the gorge, the collection of maps which the EOS reps in Megálo and Mikró Pápingo keep on hand are more authoritative and should at least be glanced at. In 1995, the EU-funded **"Life" programme** signposted some thirty "Z"-prefixed trails in western and central Zagóri, but elapsed times given are often unreliable, waymarking en route – often vandalized by hunters and other interested parties – can be haphazard and trail maintenance since then has been spotty. A folding map-booklet, *Orivatikos Odhoiporikos Hartis Zagoriou* (1:100,000; 950dr) is sold locally, but the text is in Greek only, and the actual map, with its blurry ink and faint contour lines, is virtually useless. You really do need access to a specialist guide – for example, photocopies of pp. 167–85 of the out-of-print *Trekking in Greece* (see "Books" in *Contexts*, p.910) – and some trekking nous if you plan to venture off the most trodden routes.

Monodhéndhri is the most popular starting point for a traverse of the gorge, but is by no means the only one; explorations in the area generally lend themselves to linear or loop trips of some days' length, rather than basing yourself somewhere for a week.

Monodhéndhri

Near the south end of the gorge, perched right on the rim, stands the handsome village of **MONODHÉNDHRI**. It is one of the best preserved of the western Zagóri communities, all of which escaped the wartime devastation suffered by their eastern cousins. The wide, rather tasteless modern *kalderími* leading off from the far end of the lower platía leads to the eagle's nest monastery of **Áyia Paraskeví**, teetering on the very brink of the gorge and now uninhabited. If you have a good head for heights, continue on around the adjacent cliff-face and the path eventually comes to a dead end near **Megáli Spiliá**, a well-hidden cave where the villagers used to barricade themselves in times of danger. In all, count on just under an hour for visiting these sites. For an even more spectacular view of the gorge, follow signs towards **Oxiá** (7km by car, slightly shorter by the Z8 path), where a short *kalderími* leads out from road's end onto a natural balcony where all of Víkos is spread vertiginously at your feet.

On weekdays there are two daily **buses** here from Ioánnina, at 6am and 4.15pm; those with their own transport should leave vehicles at the car park by the lower, cobbled platía. If you take the later bus, be advised that the handful of inns by the upper, asphalt platía where the bus calls are relatively pricey (for example, *Arhondiko Kalderími*, ☎0653/71 510; *Arhondiko Zarkadas*, ☎0653/71 305, both ④), while the *Hotel Víkos* near the lower square is even fancier (☎0653/71 332; ⑤); the only real budget option is the *Monodendri*, aka *Katerina's* (☎0653/71 300; ③), with plain but adequate rooms both en suite and not, as well as an attached snack bar. For other **meals**, best options are either *O Dhionysos* near the upper plaza or *Kikitsas' Pie* (sic) near the lower one, both featuring local recipes such as *alevrópitta* (an egg, flour and milk fry-up); however, there is no shop, so come supplied for your gorge trek.

Alternative bases and walks

During busy times of the year, you may choose – or be forced – to stay in other villages near this end of the gorge. At nearby **VÍTSA**, 2km below Monodhendhri, additional en-suite accommodation is available at *Arhondiko Dhanou* (☎0653/71 371; ④), in the upper quarter, and at *Selíni* (☎0653/71 471, fax 71 350; ⑤) in the lower of the two ridgeline neighbourhoods, with its own access drive well marked. To some tastes Vítsa is a less claustrophobic, more attractive village than Monodhéndhri, with a few **tavernas**, a fine platía and alternative access to the gorge. This is via the signposted Skála Vítsas, a half-hour's gentle descent along the Z9 path, partly on engineered stair-path, to the handsome single-arched Mitsíou bridge; from there it's possible to continue upstream to Kípi village via the O3 path (see p.346), or veer downstream along the heart of the gorge.

From either Vítsa or the bridge, the Z15 trail leads south to Dhílofo; the start of the path in Vítsa is trickier to find than the branch leading from the bridge, but once accomplished you've twenty minutes' descent to a streambed (ford, no bridge), where the Mitsíou branch joins you, then a climb along a crumbled *kalderími* which peters out in schist badlands. After another stream crossing with no waymarks to help, the path resumes before becoming a track system leaving you at the outskirts of **DHÍLOFO**, just over an hour along. One of the most handsome of the Zagorian villages, formerly called **Sopetséli**, it also has road access (though cars must be left at the outskirts) and has been "discovered" since the mid-1990s; you may **stay** at the non-en-suite *Aithrio Inn*, on the plane-tree platía, run by the *Lithos Bar Restaurant* at the village entrance (☎0653/61 362 or mobile 094/4153644; ③). The *Lithos* hosts special events on summer weekends, though the *Tzimoyiannis* **taverna**, actually nearer the inn, is more traditional.

From Dhílofo walkers can continue down to the chapel of Áyios Minás on the main valley-floor road. From this point, the Z24 path gives access to Eláti village, but nearly half of the one-hour time course is along asphalt or bulldozer track, with path only near the end, so you may as well visit **ELÁTI** by car. You're rather distant here from the gorge country, but there are fine views north to the peaks of Gamíla, plus a good but seldom full **hotel-restaurant**, the *Elati* (☎0653/71 180, fax 71 181; ④), run by an engaging Canadian Greek.

If you still have no luck with vacancies in any of the foregoing spots, **ÁNO PED-HINÁ**, 4km west of Vítsa and Monodhéndhri, offers several places to **stay**, of which the favourite is the long-running, Dutch co-managed *Spiti tou Oresti* (☎0653/71 202; ④) and some **tavernas**. This village is served by the same bus going to Vítsa and Monodhéndhri, and has recently acquired an extra attraction in the form of an old convent which has been restored and reinhabited since 1997 by four nuns who welcome visitors. From Áno Pedhiná, the Z5 and Z4 routes, via Elafótopos (no accommodation), take you around most of the Víkos Gorge at problematic times of the year, ending up at Víkos village (see p.342) after three-plus hours.

Monodhéndhri to Pápingo: through the gorge

All of the above notwithstanding, the most-used **path down to the gorge** begins beside the arcaded church of Áyios Athanásios in Monodhéndhri's lower platía. Having first passed the village's municipal amphitheatre, the path is paved for most of the way down to the riverbed, whose stony course you can quite easily parallel for the first hour or so of the walk. The walk along the gorge is not difficult to follow, since the entire route is waymarked, in parts a bit faintly, by red-paint dots and white-on-red stencilled metal diamonds with the legend O3. This refers to a long-distance path, which begins south of Kípi and as of writing can be followed across Mount Gamíla all the way to Mount Smólikas. In the near future, trail maintenance works are planned to prepare a route well up on the wooded, true left bank; until then expect a certain amount of boulder-hopping in the gorge bed, and slippery, land-slid patches on the sides.

About two and a half hours out of Monodhéndhri you draw even with the mouth of the **Mégas Lákkos ravine**, the only major breach in the eastern wall of the gorge; a spring here has been improved with piping to make it more reliable later in the year. Another forty minutes' level tramping brings you past the small, white shrine of **Ayía Triádha** with a recessed well opposite. A further hour yet (around 4hr 30min from Monodhéndhri) sees the gorge begin to open out and the sheer walls recede.

As the gorge widens you are faced with a choice. Continuing straight, on the best-defined path, takes you close to a beautifully set eighteenth-century chapel of the Panayía, past which the route becomes a well-paved *kalderími*, climbing up and left to the hamlet of **VÍKOS** (alias Vitsikó). This section has been kept in good repair by the locals and takes half an hour to walk. The hamlet has two small affiliated **inns** (☎0653/41 176; ③), run by the Karpouzis family.

Most walkers, however, prefer to follow the marked O3 route to the two **Pápingo villages**, crossing the gorge bed at the **Voïdhomátis springs**, some five hours from Monodhéndhri. This trail was regraded and rerouted in 1985 and is fairly straightforward to follow. It's about two hours' walk to Mikró Pápingo, slightly less to Megálo, with the divide in the trail nearly ninety minutes above the riverbed crossing. Midway, after an initial steep climb, there's a fine view down into the north end of the gorge in the vicinity of some weathered, tooth-like pinnacles, before the trail traverses a stable rock slide to the fork. Should you be taking the same route, but in reverse, the start of the path in each Pápingo village is currently signposted in Greek only.

The Pápingo villages and around

MEGÁLO PÁPINGO is, as its name suggests, the larger of these paired villages: two distinct quarters comprising fifty or so houses along a tributary of the Voïdhomátis River, which served as the location for the filming of *Signs and Wonders*, starring Charlotte Rampling, in March 1999. Even before this, it had long been a haunt of wealthy, trendy Greeks, making it a poor choice of base in peak season, though it is still delightful at other times, when most **accommodation** proprietors will knock a few thousand drachmas off room rates. Behind the central café is the refurbished eighteen-bed *Pension Koulis* (☎0653/41 138 or 41 115; ④) with en-suite rooms, the historic original inn run by the Khristodhoulou family, who are also the local EOS representatives. As such, they can advise on space in the Astráka hut and walks towards Mount Gamíla (see below), and the managers, Nikos and Vangelis, speak English. On the south side of the village, a second inn, *Xenonas Kalliopi* (☎0653/41 081; ③), offers en-suite rooms with views and good home-style meals at the only year-round-reliable taverna, and there are cheaper *dhomátia* at no. 5 of the lane leading there. If money is no object, Nikos and Poli's *Ta Spitia tou Saxoni* (☎0653/41 615, fax 41 891; ⑥) an immaculate, eighteen-bed pension on the lane leading to the Klidhoniá path (see below) is one place to part with it; another, way at the far end of the village, is the *Xenonas Papaevangelou* (☎0653/41 135, fax 41 988; ⑤), with large, varying rooms, inviting common areas and genial, multilingual manager George. The best of five independent **tavernas** in the village is the *Ouzerí Nikos Tsoumanis*, with many regional dishes; by contrast, avoid the vastly overpriced *Yiorgos*, opposite the *Koulis*.

MIKRÓ PÁPINGO, around half the size of its neighbour, crouches below an outcrop of grey limestone rocks known as the *Pýrgi* (Towers). The village has one main **inn**, *Xenon O Dhias* (☎0653/41 257, fax 41 892; ③–④), up to Megálo Pápingo standards, whose proprietor Kostas Tsoumanis is sympathetic to trekkers; he can arrange shuttles back to cars left in Monodhéndhri, and often gives discounts to those with backpacks. There is also a resident mountain guide, Panos Sotiropoulos. Slightly less pricey are various rented **rooms** around the inn, for example those of Evangelia Pantazi (☎0653/41 110; ③).

Bus journeys from Pápingo back to Ioánnina can be rather haphazard affairs since the service is erratic. Scheduled departures from Ioánnina (Mon, Wed & Fri at 6am & 3pm) turn around for the return trip immediately upon arrival at Megálo Pápingo, an hour or so later; in mid-summer there is also a service on Sunday, leaving Ioánnina at 9.30am and getting back to town in the late afternoon. If you miss the departure, the best course is to walk to the village of Klidhoniá on the Kónitsa–Ioánnina highway, which has regular buses. It's around a two-and-a-half-hour walk west from Megálo Pápingo, via the nearly abandoned hamlet of Áno Klidhoniá, on a better-than-average, marked path, and certainly quicker than the dreary 23-kilometre haul to the highway along the paved road which passes through Arísti.

The lower Voïdhomátis River valley

There are almost always **accommodation** vacancies in **ARÍSTI**, west of the Voïdhomátis River; best of a handful here is the *Zissis* (☎0653/41 147, fax 42 148; ④), with small but appealing rooms in mock-trad style, and a good attached restaurant; it's near the bottom of the village en route to the Pápingos.

Roughly halfway between the Kónitsa–Ioánnina highway and Megálo Pápingo, the paved side-road descends sharply from Arísti to cross the Voïdhomátis as it flows out of the Víkos gorge. The immediate environs of the bridge are a popular picnic area in summer (no camping allowed), but riverbank trails allow you to hike to more peaceful, tree-shaded spots upstream before the gorge blocks further progress. **Kayaking** and **rafting** are the only ways to visit these narrows; swimming in the Voïdhomátis is a privilege enjoyed only by the (not to be fished) trout, though anyone ignoring the ban would probably perish anyway in the icy waters. Downstream lies the restored, cliff-clinging monastery of **Spiliótissas**; a track (closed to cars) leads to it through a plane grove, west of the road, about 400m before the bridge. It must be said, though, that the best views of the monastery are from the road as it begins ascending to Pápingo.

Hikes across the Gamíla range

For walkers keen on further, fairly arduous hiking, there are a number of routes on from the Pápingo villages, up and across the **Gamíla** range into the central Zagóri. These are linked by the aforementioned O3 long-distance trail.

Pápingo to the Astráka refuge

All onward hikes east into Gamíla begin with the steep but straightforward ascent to the **refuge** on **Astráka col**. Though the refuge is clearly visible from Megálo Pápingo, the trail essentially starts at Mikró Pápingo. The two villages are linked by a three-kilometre asphalt road, which takes 45 minutes to walk; it's better to take the marked, short-cutting, restored *kalderími* off the road, via a historic bridge, which reduces the journey time to half an hour. If you do take the road, just before the bend – at a spot graced by a masoned mock-arch – you can detour to the **kolymvitíria** or natural swimming pools, a few paces up the stream bed.

PACKHORSE BRIDGES

A perennial pleasure as you stumble down boulder-strewn ravine beds that are bone dry an hour after a thunderstorm is coming upon one of the many fine stone "**packhorse**" bridges that abound in the Zagóri. One-, two- or even three-arched, these bridges, and the old cobbled paths serving them, were the only link with the outside world for these remote communities until motor roads were opened up in the 1950s. They were erected mainly in the nineteenth century by gangs of itinerant craftsmen and financed by local worthies.

Like the semi-nomadic Vlach and Sarakatsan shepherds of Epirus, these wandering construction gangs or *bouloúkia* were away from home between the feasts of Áyios Yeóryios (St George's Day) in April and Áyios Dhimítrios in October. As in other mountainous regions of Europe they came from remote and poor communities, Pyrsóyianni and Voúrbiani in particular in the Kónitsa area, and Ágnanda, Prámanda and Houliarádhes southeast of Ioánnina. Closely guarding the secrets of their trade with their own invented argot, they travelled the length and breadth of Greece and the Balkans, right up to World War II.

While you're in the Zagóri region, a good side-trip, easiest done from Vítsa, Dhílofo, Kípi or Koukoúli, would be to take a look at the half-dozen fantastic bridges in the vicinity. One is below Vítsa; one right beside the main valley road; one between Kípi and Koukoúli; and the remainder to either side of Kípi: one spectacular triple span downstream, three more upstream from the village. These bridges span the upper reaches of the Víkos gorge and its tributaries, and constitute the most representative and accessible examples of the vanished craft of packhorse-bridge building.

At the top of Mikró Pápingo, the well-signposted, maintained O3 trail resumes. Ten minutes out, you pass a chapel of Áyios Pandelímon, then head through forest to the Antálki spring (about 40min from Mikró Pápingo). From here the forest thins as you climb towards the Tráfos spring (1hr 40min from Mikró). Twenty minutes beyond Tráfos, a signposted trail branches right towards the **Astráka summit** (2436m), which is a three-hour round-trip from this point. If you ignore this trail, and keep straight with the O3 markers, in around 35 minutes you will reach the **EOS refuge**, perched on the saddle joining Astráka with Mount Lápatos (2hr 45min from Mikró Pápingo).

The hut is open and permanently staffed from mid-May to mid-October, but until an expansion to sixty bunks is completed, space is at a premium; fees are the refuge standard of 2500dr (20 percent discount for affiliated European alpine club members), and meals are also relatively expensive. If you want to squeeze in amongst the Greek and foreign trekking/climbing groups, phone direct on mobile ☎094/5794748, or have either the *Pension Koulis* or *Xenon O Dhias* (who are in radio contact with the hut) make the necessary arrangements.

East of Astráka

Northeast of the refuge, on the far side of the boggy Lákka Tsoumáni valley below, the gleaming **lake of Dhrakólimni**, alive with newts, is tucked away on the very edge of the Gamíla range. This lies about an hour from the refuge, along a well-grooved-in and waymarked path.

East of the refuge, the O3 route takes you on a strenuous nine-hour hike to the village of Vryssohóri via the **Karterós pass**. Despite waymarking, the casual walker may find this an intimidating hike; it's best attempted only if you're an experienced trekker and equipped with the appropriate maps. At first, the path heads towards **Mount Gamíla** (2497m), itself a good two-and-a-half-hour climb from the refuge, but then veers off south from the final summit approach to negotiate the pass between the

Karterós and Gamíla peaks, with a nasty scree slide on the far side. Near the usually empty sheepfold of Kátsanos, this route eventually joins an easier, unmarked trail coming over from the village of Skamnélli in the south, before the final descent to Vryssohóri (see p.346 for details).

South to central Zagóri

A more obvious, less demanding onward trek from Astráka col is the six-hour route, on an often-faint trail – now designated as the Z1 – south across the Gamíla uplands, via the Mirioúli sheepfold and the head of the Mégas Lákkos gorge, to the villages of central Zagóri. Besides water at Mirioúli, there is only one other tiny spring en route, and for the most part the scenery consists of forbidding limestone-dell-scape, but **TSEPÉLOVO**, the main destination, is among the finest of the Zagorohória. New pensions and hotels seem to open here all the time, making it the biggest tourist centre in Zagóri after the Pápingo villages. English-speaking Nikoletta Gouri has assumed management of the 1996-renovated *Hotel Gouris* (☎0653/81 214 or 81 288; ③). There is also a good-value inn restoration, the *Fanis* (☎0653/81 271; ③), higher in the village, as well as independent tavernas on the platía and out on the road by the school. A relatively recent entry on the scene is *To Palio Arhondiko* (☎0653/81 216; ④), which provides rooms with or without a bath in another restored mansion. Three pairs of weekly **buses** (Mon, Wed & Fri) connect the village with Ioánnina; they leave Ioánnina at 7am (6am in summer) and at 3.15pm, ending their run in Skamnélli (see below) and then returning via Tsepélovo an hour or so later.

The adjacent village of **SKAMNÉLLI**, 3.5km along, isn't the most prepossessing place with its tin-and-tile roofs, but it's a useful base in its own right, as the start of a schematically marked hiking route to Stomíou monastery in the Aóös valley, via the Goúra plateau and Karterós. The *Hotel Pindhos* down by the road (☎0653/81 280; ④) is institutional and on the modern side, though it has the biggest restaurant for miles around; *Paradhisos* rooms, at the very top of the village (☎0653/81 378; ③), are quieter and more traditionally built.

Descending 12km by road from Tsepélovo towards Ioánnina brings you to the celebrated cluster of **old bridges** (see box opposite) around Kípi, plus the amazing coiled-spring *kalderími* linking Kapésovo and Vradhéto. The bridges span the very upper reaches of the Víkos gorge, which can be reached nearly as easily from here as it can from Monodhéndhri or Vítsa. If you haven't a vehicle, by far the best way of heading down-valley is via two 'Z' trails, considered together to offer the best walking in central Zagóri. The **Z13** first heads southeast out of Tsepélovo, over the Vikákis ravine and through oak forest, to reach Negádhes (basic kafenío) within just over two hours; shortly before arrival, you can veer west onto the **Z12** for just under two hours to Kípi.

Kapésovo, Koukoúli and Kípi

Of the three villages closest to the bridges, **KAPÉSOVO** is the highest, an attractive place, mostly invisible from the road and offering yet another possible access to the Víkos gorge. The gigantic former schoolhouse, dating from 1861, is now home to an informal ethnographic collection, including wolf-traps, and also hosts special events. The local **inn**, *To Kapesovo* (☎0653/71 723; ④), though well appointed, is alas neurotically managed, with more rules than a Victorian orphanage; the **café-taverna** on the platía does evening meals. Besides the famous *kalderími* up to Vradhéto, there's a brief corniche route (the "Katafí") to an overlook of the Mezariá ravine. The conventional trail down to Víkos, though a bit weedy, is well marked through oak forest.

Some 4km downhill from Kapésovo, **KOUKOÚLI** is another barely commercialized, atmospheric village, with cars banned from the village proper. For the moment, the sole **accommodation** option is the professionally managed *Xenon Koukouli* (☎0653/71 627;

④–⑤ with breakfast), occupying two separate buildings – enquire at the central **kafenío-snack bar**, which also does creditable meals. However by mid-2000, resident Brits Roy and Effi Hounsell (☎0753/71 743) should have their smaller, less expensive inn up and running. Koukoúli, too, has relatively direct access to the gorge: an unmarked but still usable path leads from the southwest entrance of the village down to the O3 threading between Kípi and the Mitsíou bridge.

KÍPI, 2km up a side turning 6km below Kapésovo, is another handsome village with **accommodation** at rooms run by Mina Vlahopoulou (☎0653/51 262; ③) and Evangelia Dherva (☎0653/51 280; ③), though note that these phone numbers are set to change. Down on the main road stands what's considered the best **taverna** in the area, *Stou Mihali*, serving local dishes plus the usual standards. Also on the through road is an **activity centre** run by Robinson Expeditions (☎0653/71 041, mobile ☎094/4525324), which in addition to offering regular guided walks on some of the many Z trails passing nearby, will also organize canyoning, mountain-biking, rock-climbing and paragliding outings. The regular **bus** (Mon, Wed & Fri), the same one serving Tsepélovo and Skamnélli, leaves for Ioánnina at 7am and 5pm on the days indicated.

North to the Aóös valley and north Píndhos

Beyond Skamnélli, forest appears, extending north to the **Aóös valley**. Fourteen kilometres or so out of the village, the road branches north towards Vryssohóri, which has buses from Ioánnina only on Tuesday and Thursday, at 8.45am. Rather than follow this relatively dull road on foot, you can get there in seven hours from Skamnélli by walking over a pass between the peaks of **Megála Lithária** (2467m) and **Tsoúka Roússa** (2377m). This is a rather easier hike than that through the Karterós pass previously described, and covered by many of the organized trekking groups. An added bonus is the unrivalled display of mountain wildflowers in the **Goúra valley**, directly below Tsoúka Roússa.

After the approach, **VRYSSOHÓRI** is a little anticlimactic, being almost swallowed by the dense woods at the base of Tsoúka Roússa peak. Tiny and ramshackle (this was one of the settlements burned by the Germans in the war), the village has just one small **inn** run by Stamatia Tsoumani (☎0653/81 497; ②), but no proper taverna or even a store. If necessary, you can camp at the edge of town by one of two springs on either side of the O3 coming down from Karterós.

The O3 used to continue as a trail across the Aóös from Vryssohóri to **Paleosélli** in the north Píndhos, but the path was bulldozed into a dirt track in 1989. If you are purist about avoiding road-tramping, you will have to follow a slightly longer, pretty, but as yet unmarked trail from Vryssohóri via Áyios Minás chapel down to the Aóös. Ford the river (at low water only), and bushwhack a bit on the other side up to Paleosélli. You would need to allow about three and a half hours for this stretch, which permits direct access to the villages of Paleosélli and Pádhes on the southern slopes of Mount Smólikas (see p.348). Alternatively, the O3 resumes after a fashion on the far side of the bridge, cutting across the curves of the new road en route to Pádhes.

The north Píndhos

The region **north of the Aóös River** is far less visited than Zagóri. Its landscape is just as scenic but its villages are very poor relatives – virtually all those within sight of the river were burned in the war, accounting for their present haphazard appearance. The villagers claim that before this disaster their houses exceeded in splendour those of Zagóri, since they had ample timber to span huge widths and for carved interiors.

The region is dominated by mounts **Smólikas** and **Grámmos**, two of the highest peaks in Greece. The former can be approached on foot from **Mount Gamíla** (see p.344) or by vehicle from **Kónitsa**, the largest settlement in these parts, just off the Ioánnina–Kastoriá highway.

Kónitsa and around

KÓNITSA is a sleepy little town whose most memorable features are a famous bridge and a view. The **bridge**, over the Aóös, is a giant, built around 1870 but looking far older. The **view** comes from the town's amphitheatre-like setting on the slopes of Mount Trapezítsa, above a broad flood plain where the Aóös and Voïdhomátis rivers mingle with the Sarandáporos before flowing through Albania to the sea.

The town was besieged by the Communist Democratic Army over New Year 1948, in their last, unsuccessful bid to establish a provisional capital. Much was destroyed in the fighting, though parts of the old bazaar and a tiny Turkish neighbourhood near the river survive, as well as (near the top of town) a very dilapidated mansion which was apparently the birthplace of Hamko Hanim, mother of Ali Pasha (see p.331). However, in July 1996 a severe earthquake damaged numerous structures in the lower quarters; many families and businesses will be housed in temporary pre-fab structures for the immediate future.

The **bus terminal** (six buses daily to Ioánnina and connections to most villages in this section) is on the central platía; the **bank** (cash dispenser) and **post office** are just to the south. Kónitsa has recently acquired some importance as a kayakers' and walkers' centre; *Paddlers* (☎0655/23 777), down at the main-highway river-bridge (not the old one), is one outfit organizing river trips. Accordingly, *dhomátia* have sprung up like mushrooms on the serpentine approach road up from the main highway, and along the minor lane to the historic bridge. Longest established, and one of the best, is *To Dhendro* (☎0655/23 982, fax 22 055; ③), whose English-speaking proprietor Ioannis, one of the characters of Epirus, is a mine of local information; cooking at the attached restaurant is good too, with unusual pepper-based dishes. Amongst other rooms, best choice from the standpoint of calm is *Yerakofolia* (☎0655/22 168; ②), 300m along the road to Pádhes. The *Kouyias*, up on the main street near the **post office** (☎0655/23 830; ④) is the only bona fide hotel in the town centre and a rather less inspiring choice. The only really fancy spot is the *Gefyri*, down by the old bridge (☎0655/23 780; ⑤), and while the rooms (one or two with river view) are decent enough, noise from the adjacent nightclub may mean you don't get your money's worth. Apart from *To Dhendro*, *To Steki* on the central platía is a good, inexpensive taverna offering *mayireftá*.

The Aóös gorge

Kónitsa can serve as a base for a fine afternoon's walking. Beginning at the old bridge over the Aóös, either of two interweaving paths on the south bank leads within an hour and a half to the eighteenth-century **monastery of Stomíou**, perched on a bluff overlooking the narrowest part of the Aóös gorge. The *katholikón* here is of minimal interest, and the premises have been rather brutally restored, but the setting is sublime. There are two springs to drink from, and many visitors camp in the surroundings, after bathing in the river below.

Beyond Stomíou the slopes are shaggy with vegetation constituting one of the last pristine habitats for lynx, roe deer and birds of prey. A minimally waymarked path climbs from the monastery gate up to the **Astráka area** (see p.343). This is a five-hour uphill walk, rather less in reverse, and a very useful trekkers' link between the Gamíla and the Smólikas regions, provided you have a good map. It is less arduous than the Astráka–Vryssohóri route and allows all sorts of loops through both Gamíla and the north Píndhos.

Molyvdhosképastos: village and monastery

The tiny hillside village of **MOLYVDHOSKÉPASTOS** hugs the Albanian border 23km west of Kónitsa. The place was once a haunt of the seventh-century emperor Constantine IV Pogonatos, though only a few of his monuments survive intact. One of these is the tiny chapel of **Ayía Triádha**, on a crag below; another is the present parish church of **Áyii Apóstoli**, right on the frontier. If you can get in, the church has fine frescoes, and the view from its terrace – into Albania, over the Aóös valley, and east to Smólikas and Gamíla – is among the finest in Epirus. Unfortunately, photography is forbidden locally and you may need to present ID at a military checkpoint back at the Aóös bridge.

A weekday **bus** comes out to Molyvdhosképastos at 2.45pm from Kónitsa, but does not return until the next morning, in which case the only **place to stay** is at the posh *Hotel Bourazani* (☎0655/61 283, fax 61 321; ⑤), set in its own deer park by the river bridge 10km before Molyvdhosképastos. On June 29, the village itself comes to life for the **festival** of its patron saints, Peter and Paul, with music and feasting until dawn.

Five kilometres below the village is the **monastery of Molyvdhoskepástou**, the most important of the emperor's surviving monuments. Repopulated early in the 1990s and attractively restored by its half-dozen monks, it enjoys a bucolic setting on the bank of the Aóös. The curiously long and narrow church, with a precariously high Serbian-type dome, is thirteenth century. The nave ceiling is supported by arches and vaults; the airier exonarthex was a later addition, and the frescoes throughout are in a poor state. This is a working monastery, so don't visit between 3pm and 5pm; the monks are also quite fanatical, not uncommon in cases of monastic revival, and if you admit to Christian sentiments, you'll be encouraged to visit a confessional chapel to account for your sins.

East of Kónitsa: Mount Smólikas

Mount Smólikas (2637m) is the second highest peak in Greece. It dominates a beautiful and very extensive range, covering a hundred square kilometres of mountain territory above 1700m in elevation, and including a lovely mountain lake, **Dhrakólimni** (not to be confused with its namesake on Mount Gamíla). The region is also one of the last heartlands of traditional shepherd life, which is best witnessed in summer at the Vlach village of **Samarína**.

Kónitsa–Dhístrato **buses** (Mon, Wed & Fri 2.30pm, Sun 3pm) roll through the mountains, stopping en route at Paleosélli and Pádhes, the two best trailheads on the mountain's southern flank. **PALEOSÉLLI** is much more of a going concern, with two simple stores, a pair of kafenía and an **inn-taverna** on the post-office plaza run by Yiorgos Tzimas. **PÁDHES**, 3km further along, has rather less to offer: a single, stone-built building in the centre, the former school, which triples as the shop, **taverna** and **inn** (① for each of 17 beds) – the catch being that it operates only in the early morning and after 6pm, when someone motorbikes in from the nearby village of Ármata to unlock the premises.

Asphalt road surfacing is being extended the 20km from Pádhes to **DHÍSTRATO** at the end of the bus line; this large, relatively thriving village has no fewer than four licensed conventional **rooms** establishments, thanks to the ski centre nearby just over the provincial border on Mount Vassilítsa. From just before Dhístrato it's possible to drive north to Samarína (see opposite), but it's nineteen pretty rutted kilometres, passable only from May until the first snows, and needing a jeep or high-clearance vehicle even then.

Hiking from Paleosélli

There is a fine trail from Paleosélli up to **Dhrakólimni** (a little over 4hr), and from there you can make an ascent of **Mount Smólikas** (another 90min). There is also a marked path to the lake from Pádhes, though a dirt road cuts across it at several points.

The Paleosélli–Dhrakólimni route has been waymarked as part of the O3 and a **refuge** established midway, at a spring and sheepfold known as Náneh, an idyllic little spot 1600m up with camping space, an external water supply and a toilet. Keys for this shelter are available from the Paleosélli inn. Beyond the refuge, the trail becomes less distinct but waymarks lead you up onto a ridge aiming for the summit of Mount Smólikas, though the path markings disappear at the treeline. Just over two walking hours from the refuge you should emerge into the little depression containing the **lake**. You can camp here, but level space is at a premium, the lake itself isn't potable (use sheep-free springs nearby) and you'll need a tent to protect against the cold and damp. Moving along the ridge above the lake, you can reach the **summit of Smólikas**, by tackling a rather steep, pathless slope with grass and stone underfoot. It is not unusual to see chamoix near the top.

The easiest way down from Smólikas is a scenic and well-trodden two-and-a-half-hour path to the hamlet of **AYÍA PARASKEVÍ** (also known as Kerásovo). The path leads off at a sheepfold in the vale between the lake and the summit. There are a couple of basic **tavernas** in the village, including one on the ground floor of the central *Smolikas* hotel (☎0655/41 215; ③), open all year; if it's full, camping near the village is tolerated. Four days weekly, currently Monday, Tuesday, Thursday and Friday, there's a **bus** service to Kónitsa, with the return the same day at 2.30 or 3pm.

Hiking from Dhrakólimni to Samarína

If you have a good head for heights, and you're not carrying too heavy a pack, the best hiking route from **Dhrakólimni to Samarína** involves tracing the ridge east from the summit, the start of a seven-hour walking day. After an hour-plus of cross-country progress, you'll reach a small, bleak pass in the watershed, where you link up with a real path coming up from the village of Pádhes, hereabouts marked by faint yellow paint splodges on the rocks. Once through this gap, you descend into the rather lunar, northwest-facing cirque which eventually drains down to the hamlet of Ayía Paraskeví.

Next you traverse the base of one of Smólikas's secondary peaks as a prelude to creeping up a scree-laden rock "stair". From the top of this waymarks change from yellow to red, and a line of cairns guides you across a broad, flat-topped ridge. The path soon levels out on another neck of land. To the left yawns a dry gully (to be avoided) and way off to the right (south) can be glimpsed the other of Smólikas's lakes, as large as Dhrakólimni but difficult to reach. Try not to stray in either direction in poor visibility, as there are steep drops to either side.

Beyond, you encounter the leading edge of the black pine forest, at the foot of a peak, which is capped by a wooden altimeter. The trail threads between this knoll and another, at the foot of which lies Samarína. Twenty minutes or so beyond this pass, a spring oozes from serpentine strata, some six hours from Smólikas summit. There follows a sharper descent through thick forest, with a second spring gurgling into a log trough set in a beautiful mountain clearing, to which there is now a direct road. Below this, the woods end abruptly and you'll emerge on a bare slope directly above Samarína.

Samarína

At 1450m, just over the border in Grevená province, **SAMARÍNA** is claimed to be the highest village in Greece. It's principally inhabited in the summer when it fills up with Vlachs from the plains of Thessaly, and their sheep – some 50,000 of them. The village was burned during both World War II and the civil war, and was rebuilt in brutalist, cheap-and-easy style, with no concessions to Olde Worlde town planning. Thus, while Samarína may seem like the Bright Lights after several days' trekking, it's emphatically not somewhere you'd go out of your way to visit. This acknowledged, it's a thriving and friendly place, very proud of its Vlach traditions. The high point of the year is the **Feast of the Assumption** on August 15, when there is much music and merry-making and the place is swamped by nostalgic Vlachs from Athens and all over the country.

The interior of the main church, the **Panayía**, is superb, with frescoes and painted ceilings and an intricately carved *témblon*, where the angels, soldiers and biblical fig-ures are dressed in mustachios and *fustanélles* (the Greek kilt). Though it looks a lot older, like many other churches in the region it dates from around 1800. Its special hallmark is an adult black pine growing out of the roof of the apse, and no one can remember a time without it. The keys are with the priest, who lives opposite the main gate.

The improbably large stone building that confronts you at the top of the village is a **hotel** (☎0462/95 216; ④), now open all year, with winter sports to hand and for whose sake an improved, all-weather road is being graded in from Grévena. There are less pricey en-suite **rooms** on or just off the stone-paving: those of Ioannis Parlitis (☎0462/95 279; ②), some with cooking facilities, or noisier ones above *O Yeros Smolikas*, one of six **grills** here. Yet more basic are the breeze-block rooms in the "Hotel" *Kyparissi* (☎0462/95 253; ②), out on the east edge of the village, though these tend to operate only in July and August. Failing all of these, no one will mind if you camp in the pastures beyond the village itself

Leaving Samarína, you have two choices. There is a bus to **Grevená**, 40km distant on the Kalambáka–Kastoriá road from June to September, but not every day, though a lift is not too hard to get if you ask around. If you are committed to staying in Epirus, follow the E6 trail via the monastery of Ayía Paraskeví and Goúrna ridge to **Dhístrato** (p.348), which has lodging and where you might coincide with an early-morning bus back to Kónitsa, or keep going to Vovoússa on the east bank of the Aóös, with its less frequent buses to Ioánnina.

North of Kónitsa: Mount Grámmos

It was on **Mount Grámmos** that the Democratic Communist Army made its last stand in the civil war. Its eventual retreat into Albania followed a bitter campaign which saw tens of thousands of deaths and the world's first use of napalm (supplied by the United States). The upper slopes of the mountain remain totally bare, and as you walk the high ridges you still see rusting cartridges and trenches from the fighting.

If you want to visit the range, and peer down into the wilds of Albania, the most use-ful base is the village of Plikáti. The simplest way here is from Kónitsa by **bus** (Mon, Wed & Fri 2pm). Coming here from the Smólikas area, you're best off walking out to **Ayía Paraskeví**, where there are **buses** to Kónitsa (see p.349); if you're too impatient to wait for the afternoon bus to Plikáti, the turnoff to that village is just 10km north of the Ayía Paraskeví side-road, and you could always try your luck hitching.

Plikáti and a hike up Mount Grámmos

There's a singularly end-of-the-world feel to **PLIKÁTI** – it's the closest Greek village to the Albanian frontier, and trailhead for Greece's remotest, least frequented mountain, Grámmos. Some eighteen paved kilometres off the main highway, it's a traditional-looking place, with stone houses, the usual tiny permanent population, a couple of exceedingly basic **inns** (one merely two rooms rented by Angeliki Theologou) and a combination taverna/general store. Brace yourself to be stared at, as relatively few for-eigners make it up here nowadays.

Mount Grámmos (2520m) is the fourth loftiest Greek peak, and in making the ascent you should plan on a round trip of eight hours from Plikáti. The easiest strat-egy is to angle northeast up the gentler slopes leading to Perífano (2442m), second highest point in the range, rather than tackling head-on the badly eroded and steep incline immediately below the main peak. The route in the indicated direction is clear for the first two hours out of the village, crossing the river and switchbacking up through bushes and then beech trees before it peters out at a sheepfold. Just above this are the last water sources on this side of the ridge: various trickles feeding a pond. Bearing west along a plain trail, you can thread along the crest for roughly an hour to the **summit**, its cairn covered in a babel of initials and multilingual graffiti. Below, to the west, a cultivated Albanian valley stretches to the barns of Erseke, 5km distant.

In the opposite direction from the summit, you can follow the watershed to the lower **Aréna massif**, which is garnished with a trio of small lakes and clumps of beech trees. The summer-only village of Grámmos is visible from the summit ridge, and though a clear trail leads to the place (which is in Kastoriá province), there is no onward means of transport.

The south Píndhos

Most hikers arriving at Ioánnina have their sights firmly set northwards, especially on the Víkos gorge and the Zagóri villages. If you're feeling adventurous, however, and are not too particular about where you sleep or what you eat, the **remote villages** of the south Píndhos provide an interesting alternative. They perch on the beetling flanks of **mounts Tzoumérka** and **Kakardhítsa**, two overlapping ridges of bare mountains linked by a high plateau, plainly visible from Ioánnina. There are few special sights, but you'll get a solid, undiluted experience of Epirot life.

On weekdays **buses** leave from Ioánnina's southern station at 5am and 3.15pm for Ágnanda and Prámanda, with an additional Saturday service at 3.15pm and on Sundays at 2.30pm; there is also service from Árta to Prámanda and beyond. Buses run a couple of times daily in either direction along the secondary road between Árta and Ioánnina, stopping at **Pláka**, which has an eighteenth-century bridge over the Arahthós amid stunning scenery. Here you can flag down one of the twice-daily Árta-based buses continuing along the side-road east as far as Melissouryí.

Ágnanda to Melissouryí

The first village of any size is 12km above Pláka at **ÁGNANDA**, heavily damaged in the last war and not particularly attractive, though it does have one **inn** (☎0685/31 332; ③). It's better to continue on to **PRÁMANDA**, which is no more distinguished architecturally than Ágnanda, but enjoys a wonderful setting strewn across several ridges. The village is dominated by Mount Kakardhítsa behind and commands fine views of the Kallaritikós valley. Nearby there is a huge cave, inhabited in Neolithic times, to which any villager will give you directions if you ask for the *spília*. The enormous church of **Ayía Paraskeví** almost uniquely escaped wartime devastation, and as an example of nineteenth-century kitsch it is hard to beat. The village has a **post office**, a rather primitive *xenónas* (inn), plus a handful of **tavernas** and psistariés, though there is a more comfortable **hotel**, the *Tzoumerka* (☎0659/61 590; ④) in the tiny hamlet of **TSÓPELAS**, 2km out on the road to Melissouryí.

MELISSOURYÍ, 5km to the southeast of Prámanda, is more rewarding. The village escaped destruction during the war, though most buildings – including the historic church – have lost their slate roofs in favour of ugly pantiles. There is a **taverna** and one large **inn** (☎0659/61 357; ③), run by a Mr Karadhimas, though it is not to be counted on in midsummer, when all accommodation is likely to be booked by holidaying relatives from the cities. There are two daily weekday **buses** to Árta from Melissouryí, at 6am and 5pm.

Hikes from Melissouryí

Melissourgí is a good base for rambles on the **Kostelláta plateau** to the south. This upland separates Mount Kakardhítsa (2429m), which looms sheer above the village, from the more pyramidal Mount Tzoumérka (2399m). Heading south, you can cross these high pastures in a day and a half. The initial stretch of path from Melissouryí is very faintly waymarked with red-paint arrows, and there are intermittent *stánes* (summer sheepfolds) if you need water or directions. You can descend to the villages of **THEODHÓRIANA** or **VOULGARÉLLI** (officially Dhrossopiyí), at the edge of the Ahelóös river basin; both have daily early-morning buses to Árta, as well as modest **inns** and **tavernas**. In Voulgarélli, the not-so-modest *Arhondiko Villa Sofia* beckons (☎0685/22 713; ⑤); however, it's car-inaccessible at the top of a slope and overpriced, so luckily two more reasonable, less publicized outfits, including the *Galini* (☎0685/22 135; ③) are available lower down the hill.

Prámanda to Syráko

Some days the **bus** from Ioánnina continues to **Matsoúki**, the last village on the provincial route, beautifully set near the head of a partly forested valley and offering easy access to Mount Kakardhítsa, as well as a few beds. On days when the bus doesn't serve Matsoúki, it runs instead as far as the hamlet of **Kipína**. A famous namesake **monastery**, founded in 1381 but uninhabited today, hangs like a martin's nest from the cliff-face a half-hour's walk beyond the hamlet.

Kallarítes

Beyond this point, you can follow the road upstream for around half an hour through a tunnel and past a road bridge to join the remnant of a wonderful *kalderími* climbing up to the village of **KALLARÍTES**, perched superbly above the upper reaches of the Kallaritikós River. This depleted village, one of the southernmost Vlach settlements in the Píndhos, was a veritable eldorado until the close of the nineteenth century. Fame and fortune were based on its specialization in gold- and silver-smithing, and even today the craftsmen of Ioánnina are mostly of Kallaritiot descent – as in fact is Vulgari, one of the world's most celebrated contemporary jewellers. Though the village is all but deserted except during summer holidays, the grand houses of the departed rich are kept in excellent repair by their descendants. The flagstoned platía has probably remained unchanged for a century, with its old-fashioned stores and *stele* commemorating local emigré Kallaritiots, who helped finance the Greek revolution. There are two **café-grills** on the platía, but the municipal **inn** has not operated for some years, so you should plan on camping.

Khroússias gorge and Syráko

Just beyond Kallarítes, the awesome **Khroússias gorge** separates the village from its neighbour Syráko, visible high up on the west bank but a good hour's walk away. The trail is spectacular, including a near-vertical "ladder" hewn out of the rockface. Down on the bridge over the river you can peer upstream at a pair of abandoned watermills. The canyon walls are steep and the sun shines down here for only a few hours a day, even in summer.

SYRÁKO, hugging a steep-sloped ravine, is even more strikingly set than Kallarítes, with well-preserved *arhondiká*, archways and churches more reminiscent of those in the Zagóri. Not to be upstaged by Kallarítes, the village has also erected a number of monuments to various national figures (including the poet Krystallis) who hailed from here. There is a **taverna** (summer only), a kafenío and a very few **rooms**; if these are unavailable, you can beg a mattress on the floor in the school during the summer. Bus service is nonexistent, so if you've hiked here you should plan on hitching or walking out.

THE COAST AND THE SOUTH

The **Epirot coast** is nothing special, with **Igoumenítsa** a purely functional ferry port and **Párga**, the most attractive resort, overdeveloped and best left for out-of-season visiting. Head a little inland, however, and things start looking up. Close by Párga, the **Necromanteion of Ephyra** (the legendary gate of Hades) is an intriguing detour; the **gorge of the Ahérondas River** offers fine hiking; and the imposing ruins of **Kassopi** and **Nikopolis** break the journey to Préveza. Best of all is **Árta**, an interesting little provincial town surrounded by Byzantine churches, approached either around the Amvrakikós gulf, or more impressively along the plane-shaded Loúros river gorge from Ioánnina.

Moving south into **Étolo-Akarnanía**, the landscape becomes increasingly desolate with little to delay your progress to the island of Lefkádha (see p.812) or to Andírio, for the ferry to the Peloponnese. Committed isolates might hole up on **Kálamos** island, south of Vónitsa. Byron's heart is buried at **Messolóngi**, though it's otherwise an unglamorous town.

Igoumenítsa and around

IGOUMENÍTSA is Greece's third passenger port, after Pireás and Pátra, with almost hourly ferries to Corfu and several daily to Italy. As land travel through most of ex-Yugoslavia remains a dodgy option, sea traffic between Greece and Italy has increased significantly.

These ferry functions and a lively waterfront apart, the town is pretty unappealing; it was levelled during the last war and rebuilt in a sprawling, utilitarian style. If you can arrange it, try to get a ferry out on the day you arrive; virtually every day in season there will be both morning and evening sailings to Italy. To take a vehicle, or get a cabin berth on afternoon or evening sailings (see box overleaf), it's best to make reservations in advance. If you find yourself stuck for the day, you are better off taking one of the limited range of **excursions** from Igoumenítsa than hanging around town.

Practicalities

All **boats**, both local ferries to Corfu and international liners, now use the so-called "new" port, some 500m south of the old dock in the central part of the quay, where you'll still find the **EOT office** (daily 7am–2pm; ☎0665/22 227), next to the customs house. The **bus station** is five minutes away at Kýprou 47. Driving your own car, beware of Igoumenítsa's **fee-parking** scheme, nominally in effect 8am–8pm (though enforcement in 1999 was lax): you buy tickets at kiosks, not at pay-and-display machines.

The town is not large but **hotels** are plentiful, if rather lugubrious and overpriced; most are to be found either along or just back from the waterfront. The nearest budget hotel to the port, at Ethnikís Andistásis 58A, is the *Acropolis* (☎0665/22 342; ②), non-en-suite but with sea views. Inland, at the southeast corner of the main platía, stands the more comfortable *Egnatia*, at Eleftherías 1 (☎0665/23 648; ③); ask for a rear room facing the pine grove. Perhaps the best budget choice is the non-en-suite *Stavrodhromi*, Soulíou 14, the street leading diagonally uphill and northeast from the square (☎0665/22 343; ②), with a pleasant atmosphere and a restaurant that makes its own wine. The closest **campsite** is the *Kalami Beach* (☎0665/71 211), just before Platariá, a nine-kilometre bus ride away.

Ferries leave for Italy between 6am and 11am, with another cluster of evening departures between 8.30pm and midnight. Ticket agencies tend to stay open until the last boat which they handle has departed.

Except where noted, frequencies of ferry crossings detailed below are for the **high season**, the definition of which varies slightly between companies. Broadly, for crossings from Italy to Greece, high season is between early July and mid-August, especially at weekends; from Greece to Italy, it is between early August and early September. Out of season, most services are reduced to two or three weekly on many lines.

Most **ticket agencies** for international ferries are found along Ethnikís Andistásis, which lines the waterfront. Tickets for domestic services are purchased at little booths on the domestic ferry quay, at the southerly "new" port. All companies offer a variety of **fares** for cabin, "airplane" seats and deck passage, as well as reductions for student or railcard holders, as well as hefty discounts on return tickets. High-season fares to Bari, for example, range from 12,000–16,000dr for the cheapest deck seats to 32,000–44,000dr for two-berth cabins with baths. Cars are carried on all ferries; as a guideline count on 13,500–16,000dr for a small sedan to Bari. Many companies allow you to sleep in a camper or van on deck, sparing you the cost of a cabin, or even upgrade you free to a cabin for the basic seat fare. It pays to shop around, as fares vary significantly from company to company, often a function of boat quality and speed. Brindisi tends to be marginally less expensive as a destination than Bari, Ancona rather more; Venice and Trieste are vastly more costly destinations, but many drivers reckon it worth the extra money in terms of savings on expensive Italian fuel and skipping hazardous motorway travel.

All international departures carry an **embarkation tax** of 1500–2200dr per person and per car; this figure is sometimes not included in quoted prices, beware. If you have bought tickets in advance, or from a travel agent other than the local authorized agent – and most agencies sell for several companies – you must **check in** (to the appropriate *official* agent as listed below, or at their booth in the port) at least two hours before departure. Unlike sailings from Pátra, ferries from Igoumenítsa to Italy are not allowed to sell tickets with a **stopover** on Corfu. You can, however, take the regular Corfu ferry over and then pick up most ferry routes on from there.

INTERNATIONAL FERRY COMPANIES, DESTINATIONS AND AGENTS

Adriatica Brindisi (11hr) via Corfu, daily 7am, year-round. Oscar Travel, Ayíon Apostólon 149 (☎0665/26 410).

Agoudimos Brindisi (10hr), daily at 11am (mid-June to mid-Aug), or 11pm (mid-Aug to mid-Sept), less often till Christmas.

Not surprisingly, **restaurants** and **cafés** are generally pretty uninspiring and thin on the ground; for lunch, try *Martinis Sotiriou* inland at Grigoríou Lambráki 32, or *To Astron* at Venizélou 9 for cheap oven food. After dark several fish tavernas and ouzerís at the very north end of the front, near the Dhrépano turning, come to life, as does the *Psarotaverna O Timios*, just south of the new port. Several **banks** with cash dispensers are scattered along the south end of the front; at the north end, actually just inland on Evangelistrías, is the short-hours **post office**.

Around Igoumenítsa

The best brief escapes are probably to the **beach**. The closest strand lies 5km west at **Dhrépano**, a crescent-shaped sand spit (the name means "sickle") shaded by myrtle and closing off a lagoon. Local city buses serve it, and there are a few simple snack bars along its two-kilometre length.

Roussanoglou Shipping, Ethnikís Andistásis 46 (☎0665/23 630).

ANEK Ancona (22hr 30min), direct Thurs, Sun & Mon 10.30am; Trieste (24–26hr), direct Mon, Tues, Thurs, Fri & Sat variable 7am–4pm. Revis Brothers, Ethnikís Andistásis 34 (☎0665/22 104).

Diler Lines Brindisi direct (10hr) or via Corfu (10hr 30min), usually 11pm (late June to early Sept only). Thalassa Travel, Ethnikís Andistásis 20 (☎0655/22 001).

European Seaways Brindisi (11hr), daily except Tues via Corfu, usually at 10am (late June to early Aug), but 11pm (early Aug to early Sept). Katsios Brothers, Ethnikís Andistásis 54 (☎0655/22 877).

Fragline Brindisi (10hr) via Corfu, 6–7 days weekly at 7am; occasional direct sailings 10am (9hr) or via Corfu at 10.30pm. Revis Brothers, Ethnikís Andistásis 34 (☎0665/22 158).

Hellenic Mediterranean Lines Brindisi (10hr) via Corfu, daily (mid-June to early Sept) at either 12.30am or 7.30am. Hellenic Mediterranean Lines, Ethnikís Andistásis 30 (☎0665/25 682).

Jadrolinija Bari (11hr 30min), Thur at 8pm (July–Aug), Sun at 8pm (late June & late Sept). Katsios Brothers, Ethnikís Andistásis 54 (☎0665/22 877).

Marlines Bari (11hr), Sun, Tues, Thurs at 10pm, Sat at 8am (late June to early Sept only). Marlines, Ethnikís Andistásis 42 (☎0665/23 301).

Med Link Lines, Brindisi (10hr), sporadic days in August at 2am. Eleni Pantazi, 8-Dhekemvríou 27 (☎0655/26 833).

Minoan Lines Ancona direct all year (16hr), Tue–Fri at 9–11pm, Sat–Sun 2am; Venice direct (23hr 30min) March-Oct daily at 7.30-10.30am. Minoan Lines, Ethnikís Andistásis 58A (☎0665/22 952).

Strintzis Ancona (23hr), Sat & a few Mon 8.30–9pm, Nov–March only; Venice (30hr), Wed, Fri & a few Thur at 5–6am, Nov–March only; check-in at Yoyakis Travel, Ethnikís Andistásis 44 (☎0665/28 259); Brindisi (8hr 30min) via Corfu, daily April–Oct except Mon at 11.30pm, separate check-in at Ferry Travel, Kostí Palamá 1 (☎0665/27 358).

Superfast, Bari (9hr 30min), daily at midnight except Feb. Pitoulis, Ayíon Apostólon 61 (☎0655/28 150).

Ventouris Bari (12hr 30min–13hr 30min), via Corfu high season only, direct otherwise; roughly, every other day at 9.30pm, except Sun at 8am; Brindisi (9hr), daily late June to early Sept at 10pm, except Fri at 11am & Sat at 10am. Milano Travel, Ayíon Apostólon 11B (☎0665/24 237).

DOMESTIC FERRIES

Corfu (Town) Hourly ferries in season from 4.30am to 10pm (1hr–1hr 15min).

Corfu (Lefkímmi) 6 daily, 7.30am–9pm (2hr).

Inland, few destinations reward the effort expended to get to them, despite earnest promotion in EOT brochures. There is a regular bus to the "traditional village" of **Filiátes**, 19km north of Igoumenítsa, but it proves to be a drab place, with a paltry number of old Epirot houses and little else, not even a taverna, to redeem it. The old hill town of **Paramythiá**, 38km to the southeast (2 buses daily), is another disappointment. A castle is scarcely in evidence, the Byzantine cemetery church of Kímisis Theotókou on the outskirts has little of note inside or out, and despite its being touted as a centre for copper-working, just two mediocre metal shops remain in a tiny bazaar much encroached on by 1960s architecture – nothing comparable to what you'd more easily and conveniently see in Ioánnina. For an inland excursion, your time would be much better spent at the remarkable **Necromanteion of Ephyra** or the **Aheróndas gorge** (see p.358).

South along the coast, other beaches flank the campsites at Kalámi (9km) and Platariá (12km), but Sývota (23km) is by far the most attractive option in this direction.

Sývota

The sleepy resort of **SÝVOTA**, surrounded by olive groves, drapes itself over some evocative coastal topography while gazing out to Corfu and Paxí. It's a place Greeks favour for their holidays, so summer apartments predominate, though foreign package companies have discovered Sývota of late. The north bay and its small port has been developed and prettified with pedestrianization; it's a popular berthing for yachts, despite fierce afternoon winds, and renting a small boat is the most practical way of exploring the convoluted coast. The village centre – such as it is – lies a kilometre inland, with smaller, sandier bays found just off the road south to Pérdhika (and eventually, Párga, a link not shown on many maps). In order of occurrence, there's small, shady **Závia**, bigger, sunnier **Méga Ámmos**, **Mikrí Ámmos** (now rechristened "BB Beach"), **Méga Tráfos** and **Ayía Paraskeví**, with an islet to swim to, as well as the island of **Mávro Óros**, joined to the mainland by the sandspit of **Bélla Vráka**. A potential problem here is the distance to be covered: the beaches are spread out along more than 6km, there's limited local transport hire, and only a rudimentary **bus** service through here (3 Mon–Fri, 2 Sat).

Among **hotels** taking walk-in trade, there's the basic, tree-shrouded *Hellas* (☎0665/93 227; ③) in the village centre, the studio apartments *Long Summer* (☎0655/93 260), further towards the beach but still inland, or – best of all – the well-maintained *Villa Anneta* gallery apartments (☎0665/93 457 or 27 386; ④) for up to four people, in a lovely garden setting 250m from the harbour roundabout – the friendly managing family has some tours but keeps a few units for walk-ins. You'll pay more to be out near the beaches, and get more facilities: at Méga Ámmos by far the better of two spots is the *Mikros Paradisos* (☎0665/93 281, fax 93 501; ④), also with pricier air-con bungalows and family units scattered across lovely grounds with a tennis court. There are some packages here, including UK's Sunvil; advantageous half-board rates include homemade wine. There's also a **campsite** (☎0655/93 375) just north of the harbour, open May to October.

The beaches all have grills or simple snack bars, but for relatively haute cuisine the harbour is the place, where about ten comparable **tavernas** vie for your custom. Here also you can catch the seasonal **ferry** to Paxí, less reliable and pricier (4900dr one way) than Parga's; contact Isabella Travel (☎0665/93 317 or 93 050) for current details – they also **rent cars and bikes**.

Párga and around

PÁRGA is a photogenic and popular coastal town, approximately 50km south of Igoumenítsa on the Epirot shoreline. Its arc of tiered houses, set below a Norman-Venetian **kástro**, and its superb **beaches**, with a string of rocky islets offshore, constitute as enticing a resort as any in western Greece. However, since the late 1980s this has been swamped by concrete apartments at the outskirts, and package tourism has even engulfed the next village, Anthoússa, 3km west, where numerous tavernas and accommodation places nestle under a tiny, hatbox castle nocturnally illuminated for tourists' benefit. In peak season, it's hard to recommend more than a brief stopover in Párga (if you can find a room) before taking the local **ferry to Paxí**, which in July and August must also be reserved a day ahead. The Corfu model, presumably, was just too close to ignore, though plans to enlarge the harbour to accommodate cruise liners have fortunately been suspended.

Párga's fate is all the more poignant given its idiosyncratic **history**. From the fourteenth to the eighteenth centuries Párga was a lone Venetian toehold in Epirus, complementing the Serene Republic's offshore possessions in the Ionian islands. The Lion of St Mark – symbol of Venice – is still visible on the kástro keep. Under Venetian rule, a small community of Jews prospered here from the export of citrons to western Europe for liturgical use; they are long gone but lemon groves, descendants of the original orchards, remain at Anthoússa. Later, the Napoleonic French took the town for a brief period, leaving additional fortifications on the largest **islet**, a 200-metre swim from the harbour beach.

At the start of the nineteenth century, the town enjoyed a stint of independence, being self-sufficient through the export of olives, still a mainstay of the region's agriculture. After that, the British acquired Párga and subsequently sold it to Ali Pasha. The townspeople, knowing his reputation, decamped to the Ionian islands, the area being resettled by Muslims who remained until the exchange of populations in 1923, when they were replaced in part by Orthodox Greeks from the area around Constantinople.

The town and its beaches

The town is dominated by the bluff-top **Kástro** (open all day; free), a haven from Párga's bustle. A long stair-street leads up to the ruined, cypress-tufted ramparts, which offer excellent views of the town, its waterfront and a mountainous backdrop. Párga's fine **beaches** line three consecutive bays, split by the fortress headland, and get very crowded in midsummer. The small bay of **Kryonéri** lies opposite the church-studded islet, an easy swim away (or reachable by self-drive motorboat, a popular option). Immediately beyond the kástro (and on foot easiest reached by the long ramp from the kástro gate; also water-taxis in season) lies **Váltos beach**, more than a kilometre in length as it sprawls around to the hamlet of the same name. **Lýkhnos**, 3km in the opposite (southeast) direction, is a similarly huge beach; a shaded path through the olive groves shortcuts the winding road in.

Practicalities

Buses link Párga with Igoumenítsa and Préveza four or five times daily, less on Sunday; the stop is just north of the junction of Alexándhrou Bánga and Spýrou Livadhá, across from a small café that doubles as a ticket office. The **post office** is just a few paces away along Bánga, start of the main market street, which also has two **banks** with cash dispensers. The half-dozen local travel agencies, concentrated on the waterfront, cater mostly to package tourists, but they also rent motorbikes and cars (fronting for EuroHire ☎0684/32 583 and Avis ☎0684/26 632), sell tickets for the seasonal morning passenger **ferry** to Paxí (about 3000dr one way), and also run **boat tours** up the Aheróndas River to the Necromanteion of Ephyra, allowing good views of the delta birdlife en route.

From late June to early September package tourists monopolize most of the hotels and better rooms places; in the UK, Direct Greece and Sunvil offer some of the better-sited and -appointed properties. This leaves the remainder, often reserved by Italians for weeks in advance; only during May and October will you more or less have the run of the place. Just three **hotels** remain which are not block-booked by companies: the *Ayios Nektarios* (☎0684/31 324, fax 32 150; ③), on the edge of town at the corner of Livadhá and the road in, which has a small self-catering kitchen and fair-sized rooms, with those facing the rear the best; the mostly German-patronized *Galini* (☎0684/31 581, fax 32 221; ③), set nearby in an orchard and quiet as the name ("Serenity") implies, whose enormous rooms were refurbished in 1990; and the *Paradise* on Spýrou Livadhá opposite the school (☎0684/31 229, fax 31 266; ④), noisy and worthwhile only if you snag a rear room. Better, however, than any of these is the *Magda Apartments* (☎0684/31 332, fax 31 690), on the road to Anthoússa before the Váltos turning. Two-person (④) to four-person (⑤) units enjoy a fine hillside garden environment with mountain views; proprietor Ilias promises breakfast at any hour, plays non-Zorba music in the bar with his sons and presides generally over a civilized setup from March to November.

Rooms are theoretically plentiful, but the plushest are block-booked and the rest are rarely flogged at quayside or bus stop. The best hunting strategy is to take the stair-street up to the castle entrance, where the lane leading perpendicularly away along the ridge – officially Patatoúka, popularly Tourkopázaro – is one solid line of rooms, many with unbeatable views over Váltos beach. Representative of ones left for on-spec tourists are the incredibly friendly and resolutely basic ones of Kostas and Katerina Pappas at no. 36 (☎0684/31 301; ③), with a roof terrace and mixed bathless and en-suite rooms.

There are **campsites** just behind Kryonéri beach at *Parga Camping* (☎0684/31 161) and *Elaia Camping* (☎0684/31 130), among olive groves 600m inland. Váltos beach also has a newer, unobtrusive site, *Valtos* (☎31 287), at the far end by the new yacht harbour, but the enormous *Enjoy Lyhnos Camping* (☎0684/31 171) straddles the road access to Lykhnos beach, making you feel compelled to use their facilities.

For **meals**, there are easily two dozen full-service tavernas aroud the town, though most have had their menus predictably warped by the mass-tourist trade. Exceptions include long-running *To Kantouni*, at the rear of the market on Platía Ayíou Dhimitríou, which seems to have maintained high standards since a 1997 change in management. On the west waterfront of Kamíni, *Psarotaverna Zorbas* (aka *Triadha's* after the proprietress) is a good venue for fish, with fair portions and decent service. On the busier east quay, where you'll see quite a few Greek holidaymakers eating, *To Kyma* is the best of roughly half a dozen here, with reasonably priced, non-greasy if standard fare; *To Souli* ranks as runner-up. Up on Patatoúka leading off the castle gate, none of several establishments really stands out, though *Three Plane Trees* seems reasonable and well placed. Lastly, *Creperie Eden/Edem* on Platía Ayíou Dhimitríou can be recommended for breakfast and desserts. Incidentally, most Párga tavernas offer local wine from the barrel; the red is generally excellent. For more extended drinking, **nightlife** centres around a half-dozen noisy but well-behaved bars on the main quay: choose according to crowd and musical format.

Southeast to the Necromanteion of Ephyra

The **Necromanteion of Ephyra** (or Sanctuary of Persephone and Hades) stands just above the village of Mesopótamo, 22km southeast of Párga. Compared with Greece's other ancient remains, the site has few visitors, and this, coupled with its obscure location, makes it a worthwhile and slightly unusual excursion. The sanctuary is sited on a low, rocky hill, above what in ancient times was the mouth of the Acheron (Ahérondas in modern Greek), associated with the mythical Styx, river of the underworld. According to mythology, this was the spot from where Charon rowed the dead across to Hades, and from Mycenaean to Roman times it maintained an elaborate oracle of the dead. Ephyra never achieved the stature of Delphi or Dodona, but its fame was sufficient for Homer, writing (it is assumed) in the ninth century BC, to use it as the setting for Odysseus's visit to Hades. This he does explicitly, with Circe advising Odysseus:

> *You will come to a wild coast and to Persephone's grove, where the hill poplars grow and the willows that so quickly lose their seeds. Beach your boat there by Ocean's swirling stream and march on into Hades' Kingdom of Decay. There the River of Flaming Fire and the River of Lamentation, which is a branch of the Waters of the Styx, unite around a pinnacle of rock to pour their thundering streams into Acheron. This is the spot, my lord, that I bid you seek out . . . then the souls of the dead and departed will come up in their multitudes.*

The sanctuary

Trees still mark the sanctuary's site (daily 8am–3pm, possibly later in peak season; 500dr; site booklet 1500dr extra), though today they are primarily cypresses, emblems of the dead throughout the Mediterranean. The lake, which once enclosed the island-oracle, has receded to the vague line of the Ahérondas skirting the plain: from the sanctuary you can pick out its course from a fringe of Homer's willows. As for the sanctuary itself, its **ruins**, flanked by an early **Christian basilica**, offer a fascinating exposé of the confidence tricks pulled by its priestly initiates.

According to contemporary accounts, **pilgrims** arriving on the oracle-island were accommodated for a night in windowless rooms. Impressed by the atmosphere, and by their mission to consult with the souls of the dead, they would then be relieved of their votive offerings, while awaiting their consultation with the dead. When their turn came, they would be sent groping along labyrinthine corridors into the heart of the sanctuary, where, further disorientated by hallucinogenic vapours, they would be lowered into the antechamber of "Hades" itself to witness whatever spiritual visitation the priests might have devised.

The remains of the sanctuary – walls of Cyclopean masonry standing up to head height – allowed excavators to identify the function of each room, and there is a rudimentary plan at the entrance. At the very top, visible from a considerable distance, sits a **medieval chapel** retaining eighteenth-century fresco fragments; just below, *pithária* or giant storage urns have been left in situ. At the centre of the site is a long room with high walls, flanked by chambers used for votive offerings. From here metal steps lead to the damp, vaulted underground chamber where the necromantic audiences took place. Originally this descent was by means of a precarious windlass mechanism – which was found on the site.

Practicalities

The Necromanteion is most easily reached by boat **tour** (or rented motorbike) from Párga. Puny mopeds will not cope well with the grades and speeds of the improved main highway between the two points; you'll need at least an 80cc bike. Buses from Párga stop at Kastrí (2km before Kanalláki), 5km from the site, and since the improvement and re-routing of the coast road should call at Mesopótamo as well – ask before alighting.

Buses from Párga and Préveza also pass through **KANALLÁKI**, where scooters (a more feasible mode of transport from here) can be rented in summer. There are two basic **hotels** in Kanalláki, the *Ephyra* (☎0684/22 128; ②) and *Akheron* (☎0684/22 241; ②), beside each other near the main platía, plus a few psistariés. In theory, the village could make a useful base for leisurely exploration of both the Necromanteion and the Soúli area (see below), but in act it's an ugly, dusty place bearing all the hallmarks of massive wartime destruction and/or hasty refugee settlement.

East into Souliot country

The highland region east of Párga was the traditional heartland of the **Souliots**, an independent-spirited tribe of Orthodox Christians and great mountain-warriors. During the last decades of the eighteenth century and the first decade of the nineteenth, the Souliots conducted a perennial rebellion against Ali Pasha and his Albanians from their village strongholds above the **Ahérondas gorge** and the mountains to the south. Although it seems hard today to think of the placid Ahérondas near the Necromanteion of Ephyra as the way to hell, only a few kilometres to the east its waters cut deep into rock strata and swirl in unnavigable eddies as the river saws a course through its gorge. While not in quite the same league as the Víkos (see p.339), it is certainly a respectable wilderness, and if you're looking for a solitary adventure inland from Párga you won't find better (except on weekends, when locals will be out in force).

Hikes up the gorge starts at **GLYKÍ**, 12km from Kanalláki on a side road between Préveza and Paramythiá (one daily bus from the former). The river, still relatively calm here, is flanked on one bank by a mediocre, overpriced *exóhiko kéndro* (see below for a better alternative) and on the other (the south or true-left bank) by a sign reading "Skála Tzavélainas", pointing up a paved road. Following this, you can bear left after 700m towards the signposted *Piyes Aheronda* **taverna** (1300m in total from the main road), much better and cheaper than its rival, with shaded seating in the river sand and good wading for kids.

Continue another 100m on the road and bear left towards a modern chapel, 1km from the bridge; this side track deteriorates and ends 1700m from Glykí at a laboriously wrought tunnel which often has cars parked inside, as well as beside, it. The *skála* (a well-constructed path) begins just to its left; ignore, after 100m, a trail plunging down towards the river, since it's dangerously washed out within minutes. Below, the canyon walls squeeze together, and upstream a carpet of greenery covers a wilderness, rolling up to the plainly visible castle of Kiáfa.

The main trail, waymarked sporadically with blue arrows and yellow rectangles, descends to the Ahérondas and crosses a relatively modern bridge after twenty minutes' hiking. It then immediately takes a much older bridge over a tributary, the outflow of the Tsangariótiko River, known locally as the **Piyés Soulíou** (Souliot Springs). Beyond here the marked route climbs up through the oaks out of the Ahérondas valley. After paralleling the Tsangariótiko, the trail turns up yet another side ravine to reach the tiny, poor hamlet of **SAMONÍDHA** (*Samoníva* in dialect) – around two hours' walk from Glykí, ninety minutes from the tunnel – where there's a well behind the community office; the nearest kafenío/taverna is in the village of **SOÚLI**, 3km to the north.

From Samonídha a bulldozed track leads up within another half-hour to **Kiáfa castle**, one of several the local Souliots erected in their many and protracted wars with the Turks.

South to Préveza

Approaches to Préveza (see p.362) from the Necromanteion and Aheróndas area feature a few more minor sites and resorts before edging out onto the landlocked **Amvrakikós (Ambracian) Gulf**, where in 31 BC Octavian defeated Antony and Cleopatra at the Battle of Actium. Suitably enough, the most substantial of the ruins is Octavian's "Victory City" of **Nikopolis,** just south of the point where the Igoumenítsa–Préveza and the Árta–Préveza highways meet.

Two local **buses** cover the coastal route to Préveza from **AMMOUDHIÁ**, a surprisingly unspoilt little beach resort 5km due west of the Necromanteion at the mouth of the Ahérondas. As with most of the spots along this coast, Germans and Italians equipped with camper vans occupy the eucalyptus grove separating the rather scrappy village (two hotels, rooms, a few tavernas) from the 700-metre sandy beach. Compared with other nearby beaches, however, it's not the most scenic or practical: plenty of litter washes up, and the river – which bounds the village to one side – can make for cold swimming.

Other, better places to break your journey, if you take this route with your own vehicle, are at **Liyiá**, unmarked on many maps, and **Loútsa Vráhou** immediately north (same exit from the newish main highway). At the former there are **rooms** to rent, an impromptu campsite, several tavernas and an enormous, boulder-strewn beach, all overlooked by a crumbling castle in the distance; Loútsa Vráhou's beach is longer and sandier, with a similar range of amenities behind. The long-distance buses to and from Párga or Igoumenítsa don't pass this way, but head inland at Mesopótamo, before joining the coastal road near Nikopolis.

Inland: Zálongo and ancient Kassopi

Some 28km on the inland route from Mesopótamo, you pass a turning east to the village of **Kamarína** (3km along, 1 taverna), overlooked by the monastery and monument of Zálongo and the ruins of ancient Kassopi. These are a steep, shadeless six-kilometre climb from the main highway, though a daily **bus** from Préveza goes direct to the site each morning at 6am and at 2pm. An early start does have its rewards, since both places are glorious vantage points from which to watch the sunrise. Otherwise a taxi or your own transport is a good idea; there's also an approach (unsignposted) through the village of Kryopiyí, also 3km off the main road, somewhat quicker if you're coming from Glykí.

The **monastery of Zálongo** is a staple of Greek schoolbook history, immortalized by the defiant mass suicide of a group of Souliot women. In 1806, Albanian troops cornered a large band of Souliots in the monastery. As this refuge was overrun, about sixty Souliot women and children fled to the top of the cliff above and, to the amazement of the approaching Muslim troops, the mothers danced one by one, with their children in their arms, over the edge of the precipice. This act is commemorated by a truly hideous modern cement-and-stone **sculpture**, approached by several hundred steps. Along with the monastery just below (shut 2–4pm & Thurs; no intrinsic interest), the monument attracts regular coach tours of Greek schoolchildren and (on weekends) adults.

Slightly to the west of the monastery, on a natural balcony just below the summit of a similar bluff, are the remains of **ancient Kassopi**, a minor Thesprotian city-state today approached via a long path through a pine grove. Theoretically the site is open daily 8am to 3pm and is free; in practice the warden tries to sell you a ticket and leaves the gate open after-hours. The ruins date mainly from the fourth century BC, with extensive second-century rebuilding after the city was sacked by the Romans; the place was definitively abandoned in 31 BC when its citizens were commanded to inhabit Nikopolis (see below). An excellent site plan affixed to the warden's hut helps to locate highlights, including the central *agora*, a tiny, eroded odeion and (most impressive) a *katagoyeion* or hostelry for representatives of the Kassopian federation. Principally, though, Kassopi is memorable for its superb location – some 600m above sea level, with the Ionian Sea coastline and Lefkádha laid out below.

Nikopolis

The "Victory City" of **NIKOPOLIS** was founded by Octavian on the site where his army had camped prior to the Battle of Actium. An arrogant and ill-considered gesture, it made little geographical sense. The settlement was on unfirm ground, water had to be transported by aqueduct from the distant springs of the Loúros, and a population had to be forcibly imported from towns as far afield as the Gulf of Corinth. However, such delusionary posturing was perhaps understandable. At **Actium**, Octavian had first blockaded and then largely annihilated the combined fleets of Antony and Cleopatra, gathered there for the invasion of Italy. The rewards were sweet, subsequently transforming Octavian from military commander to emperor of Rome, with the adopted title Augustus.

The history of Nikopolis is undistinguished, with much of its original population drifting back to their homes. As the Roman empire declined, the city suffered sacking by Vandals and Goths. Later, in the sixth century AD, it was restored by Justininan and flourished for a while as a Byzantine city, but within four centuries it had sunk again into the earth, devastated by the combined effect of earthquakes and Bulgar raids.

The site and museum

The far-flung and overgrown ruins begin 7km north of Préveza, on either side of the main road. Travelling by **bus**, you could just ask to be set down here, though it's a long walk back to town. It would be better to hire a taxi in Préveza for a couple of hours, or visit with a rental car, as the site is really too scattered to tour on foot.

The ruins (access unrestricted) looks impressive from the road. A great **theatre** stands to the east and as you approach the site museum, past remnants of the **baths**, there is a formidable stretch of sixth-century Byzantine **fortified walls**. But as you walk around, the promise of this enormous site is unfulfilled; few other remains reward close inspection. The ruins are also a home to snakes, butterflies, the odd tortoise and, in spring, numerous wildflowers.

From the scant foundations of the sixth-century **basilica of Alkysonos**, it's a two-kilometre walk to the main **theatre**, whose arches stand amidst dangerously crumbling masonry. To the left of this you can just make out the sunken outline of the **stadium**, below the modern village of Smyrtoúna. Octavian's own tent was pitched upon the hill above the village, and a massive **podium** remains from the commemorative monument that he erected. On a terrace alongside, excavations have revealed the remains of "beaks" (ramming protuberances) of some of the captured warships, which he dedicated to the gods.

The dull **museum** (daily except Mon 8.30am–2.30pm; 500dr) consists of two rooms containing a rather uninspiring collection of Roman sarcophagi and coins. Its caretaker's main function used to be wardenship of the Roman and Byzantine mosaics unearthed amidst the foundations of the sixth-century **basilica of Doumetios** nearby, but these have recently been covered by a protective layer of sand and polythene. If available, the caretaker will escort you to the Roman **odeion**, for which he has the keys. This dates from the original construction of the city and has been well restored for use in a summer music festival (see "Préveza" below).

Préveza

Modern **PRÉVEZA**, at the tip of the Amvrakikós Gulf, is a relatively insignificant successor to Nikopolis, but not without its charm. Numerous **cafés** and **tavernas** line the waterfront, facing Actium (modern Áktio) where the forces of Antony and Cleopatra were defeated. With the advent of charter traffic to nearby Áktio airport since the 1980s, this provincial capital has had a facelift of sorts, and more character remains in the pedestrianized old quarter than at Párga. Préveza merits a brief stopover, not only for Nikopolis, but also for its lively evenings and particularly the delicious fish on offer at the *psarotavérnes*.

Charter flights arriving at the **airport** generally have transport laid on to Lefkádha or Párga; otherwise there are taxis for the seven-kilometre trip to town. The **bus station** in Préveza is on Leofóros Irínis, 1km southwest of the new ferry dock at the north end of the quay, with the massive castle of Ayíou Andhróu interposed between the two. **Ferries** across the gulf ply across to Áktio jetty, where you can pick up buses (four or five daily) to Vónitsa and Lefkádha (times are displayed on the quayside ticket office). The post office and tourist office share a building on the north quay, on the way to the new ferry dock which has much calmed traffic through the town centre; Olympic Airways is nearby at the corner of Spiliádhou and Vasilíou Bálkou.

Accommodation

The four in-town **hotels** are neither especially inviting nor geared to budget travellers; it's assumed that any clued-up tourist will be staying at beachfront resort hotels to the north, and only coming to town after dark for the lively nightlife. Most obvious, and most expensive, is the noisy *Preveza City* on Odhós Irínis 200m south of the KTEL (☎0682/27 365; ④), which seems to specialize in hosting Greek conventions; much better is the *Dioni* on Platía Papayeoryíou, a quiet pedestrian zone more or less just behind (☎0682/27 381, fax 27 384; ③). The *Minos*, a bit south on 21-Oktovríou (☎0682/28 424; ③) is bargainable from the posted rates but has awkward management; the only seafront establishment is the 1998-renovated *Avra* at Venizélou 19 (☎0682/21 230; ④). Failing these, there are a few rooms on the shore road on the far side of the peninsula; follow this road south out of town about 2km, curling around the **Pandokrátoras** castle at the peninsula tip. The nearest **campsite** is *Camping Kalamitsi* (☎0682/22 368), around 4km north of town on the broad highway which skims along a few hundred metres back from the coast. Any bus running towards Kanáli (15km out, and not to be confused with Kanalláki) will pass the summer-only sites of *Monolithi* (☎0682/51 755) and *Kanali* (☎0682/22 741), on either side of the road at **Monolíthi** beach, a fine stretch of sand beginning 11km from Préveza.

Eating, drinking and nightlife

There are at least a dozen **tavernas** scattered around the inland market lanes in central Préveza, with cafés and bars on the pedestrianized portion of waterfront boulevard Venizélou. Good inland choices include *Psatha*, Dhardhanellíou 2 (west of the main shopping thoroughfare), for standard oven fare, and the long-running *Amvrosios*, specializing in grilled sardines and barrel wine at budget prices, on the lane leading seaward from the Venetian clocktower. If this is shut for any reason, try its adjacent competitors *Stavraka* or *Iy Trata*, or (even more down-to-earth) *Ouzeri Ousies*, on a nameless lane one block inland and parallel to the front. By night, these bazaar alleys, particularly within a 100-metre radius of the fish-market building and the clocktower, come alive with an assortment of bars, ouzeris, cafés (including an Internet one at Vasilíou Bálkou 6–8) and shops, patronized by a mixture of locals and guests from the surrounding resorts. In terms of organized culture, July and August see a range of musical and theatrical events as part of the **Nikopolia festival**, held at Nikopolis.

Árta and around

Fifty kilometres northeast of Préveza lies **ÁRTA**, finely situated in a loop of the broad Árakhthos River as it meanders towards the **Amvrakikós Gulf**, 20km to the south. It is one of the more pleasant Greek towns: a quiet place, very much the provincial capital, with an old centre that retains much of its Ottoman-bazaar aspect (including a covered market on Pýrrou), and some celebrated medieval monuments.

From the west, you enter town by the 1993-restored packhorse **bridge**, subject of song and poetry throughout the mainland. A grisly legend – found elsewhere in the Balkans – maintains that the bridge builder, continually thwarted by the current washing his foundations away, took the advice of a bird and sealed up his wife in the central pier; the bridge finally held but the woman's voice haunted the place thereafter.

The town

Árta was known anciently as Ambracia and had a brief period of fame as the capital of Pyrrhus, king of Epirus; it was the base for the king's hard-won campaigns ("Another such victory and I am lost") in Italy – the original Pyrrhic victories. The foundations of a **temple of Apollo** and an **odeion** lie on either side of Odhós Pýrrou, but otherwise there are very few remains from this period. At the northeast end of the street is the **Froúrio**, the ancient acropolis and the citadel in every subsequent era; regrettably, it is now locked, seemingly indefinitely.

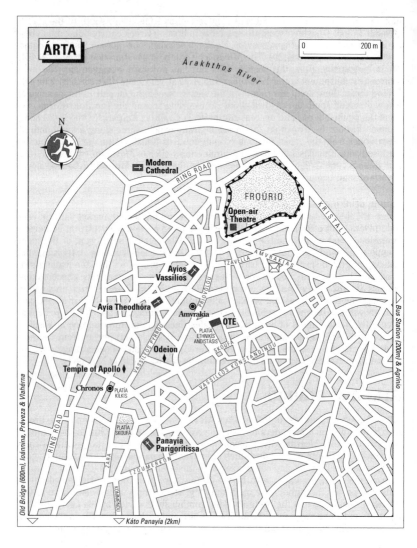

More substantial monuments date from Árta's second burst of glory, following the 1204 fall of Constantinople, when the town was the centre of **Despotate of Epirus**, an autonomous Byzantine state. The despotate, which stretched from Corfu to Thessaloníki, was governed by the Angelos dynasty (the imperial family expelled from Constantinople) and survived until 1449, when the garrison surrendered to the Turks.

Most striking and certainly the most bizarre of the Byzantine monuments is the **Panayía Parigorítissa** (sometimes rendered Parigorítria; Tues–Sun 8.30am–2.30pm; 500dr includes useful pamphlet), a grandiose, five-domed cube that rears above Platía Skoufá, at the southwest end of that street. The interior is almost Gothic in appearance, the main dome being supported by an extraordinary cantilevered-pilaster system that looks unwieldy and unsafe. Up top, this insecurity is accentuated by a looming *Pandokrátor* (Christ in Majesty) mosaic in excellent condition, overshadowing the sixteenth- and seventeenth-century frescoes in the sanctuary and nave. The church, flanked by two side chapels, was built in 1283–96 by Despot Nikiforos I as part of a monastic complex; of this, sixteen cells and the refectory remain east and south of the church, along with the excavated foundations of an early shrine, and there are plans to restore them as an archeological museum.

Two smaller Byzantine churches from the same period also survive in the town. Both have a more conventional structure but are enlivened by highly elaborate brick and tile decorations on the outside walls. They're usually locked, but this is no tragedy since the exteriors are the main interest. **Ayía Theódhora**, containing the fine marble tomb of the wife of the Epirot ruler Michael II, stands in its own courtyard halfway down Pýrrou. A little further north, opposite the produce market, is thirteenth-century **Áyios Vasílios**, a gem ornamented with glazed polychrome tiles and bas-reliefs.

Nearby monasteries and churches

Amid the orange groves surrounding Árta, a number of **monasteries and churches** were built during the despotate, many of them by members of the imperial Angelos dynasty; all are well signposted with yellow-on-brown placards.

Within easy walking distance (2km along Odhós Komméno) stands the **monastery of Káto Panayía** (daily May–Sept 7am–1pm & 4.30–7.30pm; Oct–Apr 8am–1pm & 3–6pm), erected by Michael II between 1231 and 1271. This is now a working convent occupied by a dozen nuns, and in one corner of the garden, several caged peacocks. The *katholikón* in a shaded courtyard has extravagant exterior decoration, and frescoes inside showing Christ in three guises. The gabled roof of the triple-aisled nave is supported by six columns; one of the two cross-vaults serves as a narthex. Many of the frescoes are badly smudged, but the highlight is an undamaged version of Christ as Emmanuel in the front vault. The west outer wall sports a graphic *Last Judgement*, but this is definitely a case where the interior is more compelling than the exterior.

Further out of Árta, 6km north by a circuitous route (11–12 buses daily from the ring-road stop), the monastic church of **Panayía Vlahernón** in Vlahérna village is engaging both inside and out. To the basic three-aisled twelfth-century plan, Michael II added the trio of domes in the following century, as well as the narthex; one of the two tombs inside is thought to be his. Having found the key custodian at the nearby kafenío, you enter the south narthex door under a fine **relief** of the Archangel Michael. Dissimilar columns support the added cupolas, but the church is more remarkable for what is hidden from view. The warden will lift a section of carpet to reveal a magnificent **mosaic**, just one portion of a vast marble floor punctuated with such tessellations. Only a few of numerous **frescoes** thought to be under plaster are exposed. This is the most beautiful of Árta's churches, worth contemplating at length from the kafenío.

If you get hooked, there are three more churches within easy reach of Árta, all signposted after a fashion; these have apparently never been associated with a monastery, and today serve as the graveyard chapels for the nearest village. **Panayía tís Bryónis** lies 800m up the side road towards Megárhi, the turning 6km out of Árta en route to Amfilohía; dating from 1232, with some fine brickwork, it unhappily got hideous new roof tiles in 1998. By taking the road for Kostákio and Anéza from the historic bridge, and then turning west towards Plisí, you should reach **Áyios Dhimítrios Katsoúris** after 5km, partly eleventh century in vintage, with a free-standing belfry. If the priest is in at the neighbouring cottage, you'll get to see a frescoed interior. Some 2km further north, at the edge of Kirkizátes village, stands **Áyios Nikólaos tís Rodhiás**, a thirteenth-century, single-apsed chapel with contemporary frescoes in fair condition.

Practicalities

Arriving by **bus**, you'll be dropped at a terminus on the riverbank, on the northern out-skirts of town, though there is a discretional stop on the ring road east of both the mod-ern and the Byzantine bridges. From the main station it's a ten-minute walk along **Odhós Skoufá**, the main thoroughfare, to the central **Platía Ethnikís Andistásis**. Skoufá, which is the town's main commercial street and wholly pedestrianized (as are most of its narrower perpendiculars), and its parallel streets, Pýrrou and Konstandínou, wind through the oldest part of town. If you come by car, beware of the fee-parking scheme in effect during business hours: a red strip on the sign means free parking up to two hours, but a green strip means you must seek out a coin-op machine for a windscreen ticket.

There are just two **hotels**, normally enough for the trickle of tourists and business visitors, though as at Préveza none constitutes great value. The *Amvrakia*, Priovólou 13 (☎0681/28 311; fax 78 544; ③ bathless, ④ en suite), is the best choice, a comfortable hotel with a good position on a pedestrian way, just off Platía Ethnikís Andistásis. The *Cronos* (☎0681/22 211; ④) on Platía Kílkis is noisy and vastly overpriced; the *Xenia* up in the castle, despite profuse signposting around town, has closed.

Árta **restaurants**, what few there are, can be excellent value, catering for locals rather than tourists. Best in the centre is the *Skalinon*, just next to the *Amvrakia* hotel, open lunch only Monday to Saturday; run by a woman, with more than usual attention to decor, it provides ample choice for vegetarians. A more ordinary option for *mayireftá* is the *Ellinikon* at Skoufá 5. Most visitors, however, will gravitate towards the old bridge, where you can admire the structure at leisure over a coffee or a meal. *O Protomastoras* offers adequate, inexpensive fare to a young crowd under a shady plane, as does adjacent *Yefira*; the *Cafe Mylos* at the far end of the pedestrianized span is an after-hours *baráki*. In the evenings, people tend to perform their vólta around Platía Ethnikís Andistásis or congregate in its cafés; a remoter, pleasant one, within sight of Panayía Paregorítissa, is *En Arta*, with seating by a fountain and plane tree.

The Amvrakikós Gulf

Árta is the exceptional bright spot close to the **Amvrakikós Gulf**. Further around, and in fact all the way south to the open sea, there is little to prompt a stop. Locals from Árta head at weekends for seafood meals at the fishing villages of **MENÍDHI** (21km) or **KORONÍSSIA** (25km), whose final approach lies along a wave-lashed causeway flanked by a scrappy beach popular with windsurfers. Today the village, once an island, offers a few fish tavernas, some rooms and, up on the hill, yet another Byzantine church, the rather lopsided, tenth-century **Yénnisis tis Theotókou**, surveying the gulf and lagoons below.

AMFILOHÍA is promisingly situated at the head of the gulf, but in reality proves a very dull, small town. The chance for a swim would also seem from the map to be a redeeming feature, but the water here is at its most stagnant, with only a miniature, fenced-in municipal beach as a way in. If you're marooned here, best emergency fall-back **hotel** is probably the *Oscar* (☎0642/22 155; ④) at the west end of the quay.

If you need to stay the night on this coastline, **VÓNITSA**, 35km west of Amfilóhia, would be a more convenient and pleasant choice. Again it's not an exciting place, and frustratingly distant from real sea, but represents a definite improvement on Amfilohía with its lively waterside, tree-lined squares and a substantial Byzantine **castle** above. Among five **hotels**, pick of the litter is the comfortable enough *Bel Mare* (☎0643/22 394; ④) on the castle end of the *paralía*; the *Leto* just inland on Platía Anaktoríou has castle views but is considerably more basic (☎0643/22 246; ②). As at Préveza across the gulf, sardines figure prominently on the menus of a half-dozen waterfront **tavernas**. Infrequent local **buses** cover the 14km to **ÁKTIO**, the south ferry terminal across the gulf from Préveza, passing Áktio airport.

The coast south to Messolóngi

Heading south for Messolóngi and the Gulf of Kórinthos, there is not much more of interest, at least on the direct **inland route**. From Amfilohía, you pass a few swampy patches of lake pumped for irrigating the local tobacco. Midway down the Amfilohía–Messolóngi road, **AGRÍNIO** is little more than a transport link for this area, with buses to Árta/Ioánnina, Karpeníssi and south to Andírio, where there are local buses to Náfpaktos, as well as the ferry across the Gulf of Kórinthos to the Peloponnese.

Mýtikas and Kálamos island

The **coast south from Vónitsa** is bleakly impressive, with a quiet stretch of road that skirts the shoreline with nothing but an arid wilderness inland. However, if you have transport there are great opportunities for finding tiny deserted beaches. There is just one sleepy but pleasant settlement, **MÝTIKAS**, whose rows of old-fashioned houses strung along a pebbly shore look out onto the island of Kálamos. As yet development is minimal, consisting of three **hotels** – best of these the *Kymata* (0646/81 258 or 81 311; ③) – and rooms or studios, representative ones being those of *Alekos Lekatsas* (☎0646/81 097; ③) with cooking facilities and sea view. Of several **tavernas** pitched mostly at locals, *Ouzeri Stou Thoma* is the most elaborate but still very reasonable. It's a pleasant place to break a journey or wait for a boat across to the island of Kálamos (see below).Two kilometres of uncommercialized beach leads east from the village, getting better as you proceed, all with a backdrop of sheer, amphitheatric mountainsides.

The island of **Kálamos,** the largest of a mini-archipelago west of Astakós, is essentially a partly wooded mountain rising abruptly from the sea. Though officially part of Lefkádha in the Ionian group, all utility and transport links are to the mainland opposite. In summer there are usually a few yachts moored in the small harbour below the main village, Hóra, but otherwise the island, with a permanent population of about three hundred, sees few visitors and is ill equipped to host them. The only regular connection is a daily kaïki from Mýtikas, which leaves the mainland at noon and returns from the island at 7.30am the next day; in summer the same craft may do group daytrips, but otherwise you must charter the entire boat for 6000dr. At time of writing there is **no reliable accommodation** available in Hóra (except perhaps in August, when it will be full anyway), so come with camping gear if you intend to stay the night – though even this is difficult, given the lack of flat ground.

HÓRA, spread out among gardens and olive groves on the south coast, largely survived the 1953 earthquake which devastated so many of the Ionian islands, though there's been no lack of insensitive building since. There are two basic kafenía/tavernas and a "supermarket" by the harbour, plus a bakery and sweetshop higher up, next to a **post office**. The gravelly village **beach**, 15 minutes southwest (follow the seaward lane from the quay, bearing left at every option) has no reliable facilities; the much better beach of **Merithiá** lies twenty minutes northeast of the port, via a rough scramble along the shore. Your reward will be 500m of sand and fine gravel which could easily fit in all the tourists Kálamos is ever likely to get, and this could be one of the better places to camp, though there's no shade or fresh water.

KÁSTRO, an old fortified settlement at the north tip of the island facing Mýtikas, is linked to the port by a seven-kilometre asphalt road; the ninety-minute walk is drudgery, despite pine-shade and views, so try and hitch the sparse traffic. The small, five-bastioned castle here may possibly be Byzantine, and surveyed the straits between here and Mýtikas, as suggested by the name of the road's-end hamlet 2km beyond,

Episkopí (Overlook). Its walls are surrounded by a dozen or so houses, mostly roofless and abandoned, and the overgrown bailey is now used by villagers to keep their hens and sheep. A spring just above the road provides water, and a damp church of Áyios Nikólaos huddles beside the fortifications. Down towards Kástro's harbour, a few more houses are still inhabited, though there's no shop or café. Small, exquisite beaches dot the coast between Hóra and Kástro, though they can only be seen and reached by sea, not from the road.

Southwest of Hóra, a broad mule-and-tractor track leads to **Kefáli (Pórto Leóne)**, near the island's southern tip, which shelters a deep bay protected in all weathers and thus beloved of Ionian yacht flotillas. The lower village has been deserted since the 1953 earthquake; a higher, pirate-proof settlement, nearly invisible now in its dereliction, was abandoned a few centuries ago. It's a shadeless, two-hour walk across scrub-covered mountainside from Hóra, with only views across to the neighbouring island of Kástos to compensate; as ever in this region, you're best off going by boat.

Astakós and Etolikó

South from here, the coast road loops around to **ASTAKÓS**, a place whose name means "lobster". Patrick Leigh Fermor, in *Roumeli*, fantasizes about arriving at this gastronomic-sounding place and ordering its namesake for supper; it turned out to be a crashing non-event, and you still won't get lobster at any of the half-dozen tavernas which line its quay on the north flank of the gulf here. Like Amfilohía, the location of the village is its most attractive attribute, though yacht flotillas call to take on water, and many of the older buildings have been preserved.

Arriving by land, the KTEL (two through connections with Athens daily, five via Agrínio) is at one end of the quay, while the single hotel, *Stratos* (☎0646/41 911, fax 41 227; ④), sprawls at the other, overlooking the tiny, gravelly town beach; in peak season some studio-type rooms are on offer elsewhere. Buses dovetail fairly well with the **ferries across to Itháki and Kefalloniá**, which leave twice daily much of the year: roughly at 1 and 9pm in summer, noon and 6pm in the off-season.

Beyond here the scenery becomes greenery as the road winds 26km over oak-covered hills to **ETOLIKÓ**, built on an island in the eponymous, rather sumpy lagoon and reached by two causeways. The town is visibly less prosperous than Messolóngi (see below), of which it seems a miniature version – there's a prominent gypsy presence – but it could make a good emergency halt with a perfectly acceptable en-suite **hotel** on the west-facing quay: the *Alexandra* (☎0632/23 019; ③). Next door is the town's fanciest **restaurant**, *To Stafnokari*, specializing in local seafood, and there's the usual complement of bars and kafenía in the centre, plus a bank and post office. Occasional buses ply to Messolóngi, just 10km southeast, past the salt factories that are today the area's mainstay.

Messolóngi

MESSOLÓNGI (Missolongi), for most visitors, is irrevocably bound with the name of **Lord Byron**, who died in the town, to dramatic world effect, while organizer of the local Greek forces during the War of Independence (see box opposite). The town has an obvious interest in this literary past, but as in Byron's time, it's a fairly shabby and desperately unromantic place: wet through autumn and spring, and comprised mostly of drab, modern buildings. To be fair, the town has been spruced up of late, especially around the centre, but if you come here on a pilgrimage, it's still best to plan on moving on within the day.

The town

You enter the town from the northeast by the **Gate of the Exodus**, whose name recalls an attempt by nine thousand men, women and children to break out during the Turks' year-long siege in 1826. In one wild dash they managed to get free of the town, leaving a group of defenders to destroy it in their wake. But they were betrayed and in the supposed safety of nearby Mount Zygós were ambushed and massacred by a large Albanian mercenary force.

Just inside this gate, on the right, partly bounded by the remains of the fortifications, is the **Kípos Iróön**, or **Garden of Heroes** (summer 9am–8pm; winter 9am–5pm) – though it is signposted in English as "Heroes' Tombs" – where a tumulus covers the bodies of the town's unnamed defenders. Beside the tomb of the Greek Souliot commander, Markos Botsaris, is a **statue of Byron**, erected in 1881, under which is buried the poet's heart. The rest of Byron's remains were taken back to his family home, Newstead Abbey, despite his dying request: "Here let my bones moulder; lay me in the first corner without pomp or nonsense." Perhaps he knew this would be disregarded. There is certainly a touch of pomp in the carving of Byron's coat of arms with a royal crown above; there had been speculation that Byron would be

---

O LÓRDHOS VÝRONOS: BYRON IN MESSOLÓNGI

Byron arrived at Messolóngi, a squalid and inhospitable town surrounded by marshland, in January 1824. The town, with its small port allowing access to the Ionian islands, was the western centre of **resistance** against the Turks. The poet, who had contributed much of his personal fortune to the war effort, as well as his own fame, was enthusiastically greeted with a 21-gun salute.

On landing, he was made **commander-in-chief** of the five thousand soldiers gathered at the garrison, a role that was as much political as military. The Greek forces, led by klephtic brigand-generals, were divided among themselves and each faction separately and persistently petitioned him for money. He had already wasted months on the island of Kefalloniá, trying to assess their claims and quarrels before finalizing his own military plan – to march full force on Náfpaktos and from there take control of the Gulf of Corinth – but in Messolóngi he was again forced to delay.

Occasionally Byron despaired: "Here we sit in this realm of mud and discord", he wrote in his journal. But while other Philhellenes were returning home, disillusioned by the squabbles and larceny of the Greeks, or appalled by the conditions in this damp, stagnant town, he stayed, campaigning eloquently and profitably for the cause. Outside his house, he drilled soldiers; in the lagoon he rowed, and shot, and caught a fever. On April 19, 1824, Byron died, pronouncing a few days earlier, in a moment of resignation, "My wealth, my abilities, I devoted to the cause of Greece – well, here is my life to her!" It was, bathetically, the most important contribution he could have made to the struggle.

The news of the poet's death reverberated across northern Europe, swelled to heroic proportions by his admirers. Arguably it changed the course of the war in Greece. When Messolóngi fell again to the Ottomans, in 1826, there was outcry in the European press, and the French and English forces were finally galvanized into action, sending a joint naval force for protection. It was this force that accidentally engaged an Egyptian fleet at Navarino Bay (see p.240), striking a fatal blow against the Ottoman navy.

Byron, ever since independence, has been a Greek national hero. Almost every town in the country has a street – Výronos – named after him; not a few men still answer to "Vyron" as a first name; there was once an eponymous brand of cigarettes (perhaps the ultimate Greek tribute); and, most importantly, the respect he inspired was for many years generalized to his fellow countrymen – before being dissipated in this century by British interference in the civil war and bungling in Cyprus.

offered the crown of an independent Greece. Among the palm trees and rusty cannons there are other monuments – busts, obelisks, cenotaphs – to American, German and French Philhellenes.

Elsewhere in the town, traces of Byron are sparse. The **house** in which he lived and died was destroyed during World War II and its site is marked by a clumsy memorial garden. It's on Odhós Levídhou, reached from the central platía by walking down to the end of Hariláou Trikoúpi and turning left.

Back in the central Platía Bótsari, the mock-Neoclassical town hall houses a small **museum** devoted to the revolution (Mon–Fri 9am–1.30pm & 4–7pm, weekends 9am–1pm & 4–7pm; free), with some emotive paintings of the independence struggle on the upper floor (including a reproduction of Delacroix's *Gate of the Sortie*), reproductions of period lithographs and a rather desperate collection of Byronia on the ground floor, padded out with a brass souvenir plaque of Newstead Abbey. The credibility of the museum is further overreached by a central display of ephemera from the Nottinghamshire town of Gedling, which is twinned with Messolóngi. Pride of place, by the entrance, goes to an original edition of Solomos's poem "Hymn to Liberty", now the national anthem. Despite the evident thinness of the exhibits, ground has now been broken west of town for a new "Lord Byron Museum" to be filled with who knows what.

Perhaps more interesting and enjoyable than any of this is a walk across the **lagoon**, past the **forts** of Vassiládhi and Kleissoúra, which were vital defences against the Turkish navy. The lagoon, with its salt-pans and fish farms, attracts coastal birds. Migrant waders pass through and, in spring, avocets and black-winged stilts nest here. A causeway extends for about 5km and reaches the open sea at **TOURLÍDHA**, a hamlet of pre-fab summer cottages on stilts, and a taverna, the *Alikes*, haunted by coach tours; its rival, *To Iliovasilema*, appears to function only at high season.

Practicalities

Long-distance **buses** arrive at the KTEL on Mavrokordháto 5, next to the central Platía Bótsari, and the local blue-and-white ones park just a few paces away. You can **rent bicycles** from the *Theoxenia* hotel should you wish to explore the lagoon; they are a popular option among locals, given the town's unrelenting flatness. The **post office** stands just a block east of the square; the big telecoms antenna marks the spot.

Hotels in Messolóngi are a bit cheerless, expensive and often block-booked by tour groups. Etolikó (see p.368), 10km to the west, could be a cheaper, less crowded alternative for the night. If you need or want to stay in the town, a good option is the *Avra*, Hariláou Trikoúpi 5 (☎0631/22 284; ②); it's adjacent to the central platía and close to the best of the Messolóngi's eating and drinking venues. More upmarket and impersonal choices include the massive *Liberty*, Iróön Polytekhníou 41 (☎0631/28 050; ④), overpriced though with park views from most rooms, one block from the Heroes' Garden, or the *Theoxenia* (☎0631/22 493; ④), a small complex amidst landscaping just south of town on the lagoon shore.

Of late, the prevailing Greek craze for innovative ouzeris and *barákia* has swept through Messolóngi, resulting in a vastly improved **eating and drinking** scene, making a lunch stop here something to plan rather than dread. The place is especially famous for its eels, hunted with tridents in the lagoon. The main concentration of establishments is along Athanasíou Razikotsíka, a street one block south of Hariláou Trikoúpi. *O Nikos* at no.7 has been tried and passed muster, but there is also *Fagadhiko* and *Poseidhon* at no.4, and *Marokia* at no.8. In the narrow alleys linking these two broader streets are more bars, kafenía and ouzeris, for example the *Rodhon* which has an impressive range of imported beers.

travel details

Buses

Buses detailed have similar frequency in each direction, so entries are given just once; for reference check under both starting-point and destination.

Agrínio to: Corfu (bus/ferry, 2 daily in season; 4hr); Ioánnina (6 daily); Karpeníssi (1 daily, 2 Fri; 3hr 30min); Lefkádha (5 daily; 2hr); Messolóngi–Andírio (12 daily; 1hr/1hr 30min).

Áktio to: Lefkádha (5 daily; 45 min).

Árta to: Ioánnina (10 Mon–Fri, 6 Sat/Sun; 2hr 30min); Prámanda and Melissouryí (2 daily 5am/2pm; 1hr 30min); Préveza (5 Mon–Fri, 2 Sat/Sun; 1hr); Theodhóriana (daily Mon–Fri at 2pm; 1hr 15min).

Igoumenítsa to: Athens (4 daily; 8hr); Párga (4 daily, 3 Sat, 1 Sun; 1hr 30min); Préveza (2 daily; 3hr); Sývota (bus marked Pérdhika, 3 daily, 2 Saturday, 30min); Thessaloníki (1 daily; 8hr 30min).

Ioánnina to: Athens (9 daily; 7hr 30min); Dodona (Mon–Sat except Thurs 6.30am & 4pm; Sun 7.30pm only; 40min); Igoumenítsa (9 daily; 2hr); Kastoriá, via Kónitsa (2 daily, change at Neápoli; 6hr); Kónitsa (6 daily; 1hr 30min); Métsovo (3 daily, 2 Sun; 1hr 30min); Monodhéndhri (2 daily Mon–Fri 6am/4.15pm; 45min); Pápingo (Mon, Wed & Fri 6am/3pm; 1hr); Paramythiá/Párga (1 daily; 2hr/3hr); Patra via Agrínio (4 daily; 4hr 30min); Prámanda (2 daily Mon–Fri 5am/3.15pm, Sat–Sun 3.15pm only; 2hr); Préveza (10 daily, 8 Sun; 2hr 30min); Thessaloníki (6 daily; 8hr); Tríkala, via Métsovo and Kalambáka (3 daily; 1hr 30min/3hr); Tsepélovo (2 daily Mon, Wed & Fri 6am & 3.15pm; 1hr); Vovoússa (Mon & Fri 1.15pm, Sun 7.45am; 1hr 30min).

Messolóngi to: Astakós (2 daily; 1hr 15min); Athens (8 daily; 4hr); Ioánnina (6 daily, 2hr 30min); Pátra (8 daily, 1hr 30min).

Préveza to: Glykí (1 daily; 1hr); Lefkádha (4 daily, 45min); Párga (4 Mon–Sat, 3 Sun; 1hr 30min).

Vónitsa to: Áktio (3 daily; 30 min); Lefkádha (5 daily; 30min).

Ferries

Astakós to: Itháki & Kefalloniá (2 daily most of the year).

Igoumenítsa to: Corfu Town (hourly, 4.30am–10pm; 1hr–1hr 15min); Lefkímmi in southern Corfu, (6 daily, 7.30am–9pm; 2hr). Also to Ancona, Bari, Trieste, Venice and Brindisi (Italy). See box on p.354 for details.

Párga to: Paxí (daily 9.30am May–Sept; 2hr).

Préveza to: Áktio (every 20min 9am–9pm, every half-hour 6am–9am & 9pm–midnight, every hour midnight–6am; 10min).

Sývota to: Paxí (1–2 weekly, in season; 2hr).

Flights

Ioánnina to: Athens (2–3 daily, 1hr 5min); Thessaloníki (1 daily; 45min).

Préveza to: Athens (3–4 weekly; 55min).

Also regular international charters between Préveza (Áktio) and Britain.

CHAPTER FIVE

THE NORTH: MACEDONIA AND THRACE

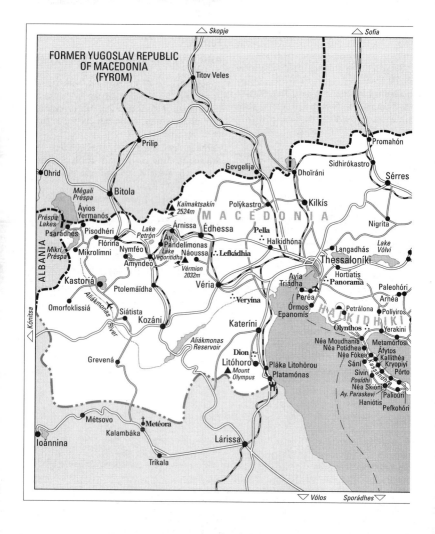

T he two northern regions of **Macedonia** and **Thrace** have been part of the Greek state for just less than three generations. Macedonia (*Makedhonía*) was surrendered by the Turks after the Balkan wars in 1913; Greek sovereignty over Thrace (*Thráki*) was only confirmed in 1923. As such, the region stands slightly apart from the rest of the nation, an impression reinforced for visitors by scenery and climate that are essentially Balkan. Macedonia is characterized by an abundance of lakes to the west, and in the east by heavily cultivated flood plains and the deltas of rivers with sources in former Yugoslavia or Bulgaria. The climate can be harsh, with steamy summers and bitterly cold winters, especially up in the Rhodópi mountains that form a natural frontier with Bulgaria.

These factors, along with a dearth of good beaches and thus direct charter flights from abroad, plus often overpriced accommodation, may explain why northern

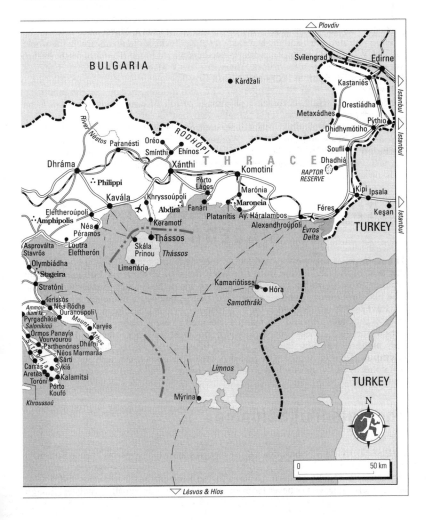

Greece is so little known to outsiders, even those who have travelled widely through-out the rest of the mainland and the islands. The only areas to draw more than a scat-tering of visitors, even at the height of the summer, are Halkidhikí and Mount Olympus. **Halkidhikí**, the three-pronged peninsula-province trailing below Thessaloníki, serves as a beach-playground for that city – and growing numbers of foreigners – in the often overblown resort areas of Kassándhra and Sithonía. More hard-won pleasures – and stunning views – are available on the slopes of **Mount Olympus**, the mythical abode of the gods and a mecca for walkers in the south of the region. As for the rest, few travellers look beyond the dull trunk routes to Turkey and Bulgaria, along which only **Xánthi** or the **Dhadhiá Forest** really merit more than just a meal stop.

With a more prolonged acquaintance, the north may well grow on you. Part of its appeal lies in its vigorous day-to-day life, independent of tourism, at its most evident in the sybaritic Macedonian capital of **Thessaloníki** (Salonica) and the north's second port-city, **Kavála**. Other attractions lie in rugged western Macedonia, around the **Préspa national park** and the lakeside city of **Kastoriá**. Monuments are on the whole modest, with the exception of ancient Macedonian king Philip II's tomb, discovered at **Veryína** and now open to visitors. There are lesser Macedonian and Roman sites at **Pella** and at **Philippi**, St Paul's first stop in Greece.

If you are male, over 18 and interested enough in monasticism – or Byzantine art, music and architecture – to obtain a pilgrimage permit, **Mount Áthos** may prove to be a highlight of a Greek stay. This "Monks' Republic" occupies the mountainous east-ernmost prong of Halkidhikí, maintaining control over twenty monasteries and numer-ous dependencies and hermitages. **Women** (and most female animals) have been **excluded** from the peninsula since a decree of 1060, although it is possible for both sexes to view the monasteries from the sea by taking a boat tour from the resorts of Ierissós and Ouranoúpoli in the "secular" part of Athos.

THESSALONÍKI AND WESTERN MACEDONIA

Thessaloníki is the fulcrum, and focus, to Macedonian travel. If you are heading for the west of the region, the train ride from there to **Flórina** via **Édhessa**, edging around Lake Vegoritídha, is one of the most scenic in the country. **Kastoriá**, for those who like their towns remote and speckled with Byzantine monuments, is also highly worthwhile, though reached in the final instance by bus from the important junction-town of Amýndeo. Beyond Flórina, the secluded **Préspa lakes**, straddling the fron-tiers of three countries, constitute one of the finest wildlife refuges in the Balkans. The biggest attraction in this part of Macedonia, however, has to be **Mount Olympus** (Óros Ólymbos). The fabled home of the gods soars high above the town of Litóhoro, easily approached from the highway or rail line between Lárissa and Thessaloníki.

Thessaloníki (Salonica)

The second city of Greece and administrative centre for the two northern regions, **THESSALONÍKI** – or Salonica, as the city was known in western Europe until well into this century – has a very different feel to Athens: more Balkan-European and modern, less Middle Eastern. Situated at the head of the Thermaïkos gulf, it also seems more open; you're never far from the sea, and the air actually circulates, though this is a bit of mixed blessing since the bay, anywhere near town, is pretty much a sump.

The "modern" quality of Thessaloníki is due largely to a disastrous **1917 fire** which levelled most of the old plaster houses along a labyrinth of Ottoman lanes, including the entire Jewish quarter with its 32 synagogues (see below), rendering 70,000 (nearly half the population) homeless. The city was rebuilt over the next eight years on a grid plan prepared under the supervision of French architect and archeologist Ernest Hébrard, with long central avenues running parallel to the seafront, and cross-streets densely planted with shade trees. Hébrard's prohibition of high-rises was blithely disregarded within two decades, but Thessaloníki is still a more livable, though arguably less interesting, city than Athens, with a more cosmopolitan, wealthy aspect, stimulated by its major university, international trade fair and famously avant-garde live music and entertainment scene. But this opulence – epitomized best in the local women, regarded as the best dressed in Greece – has served as a magnet for a permanent floating underclass. Pontian (Russian Black Sea) Greeks flog substandard Soviet goods at the street markets, unemployed Albanian or east European refuges congregate on park lawns, and assertive beggars and buskers – not all of them gypsies – make the rounds of the outdoor tavernas.

Even before this influx, Athenians loved to disparage the city as "Bulgaria", but they would be more accurate to call it "Anatolia", for Thessaloníki is the 1923 refugees' metropolis par excellence, most obvious in the baldly Turkish surnames (such as Dereli, Mumtzi and Aslanoglu) of the locals and the spicy Anatolian recipes and snacks seen nowhere else in Greece. In absolute numbers, Athens may have received more Asia Minor Greeks, but proportionately Thessaloníki is the most purely Anatolian – especially Pontian – city in the land. Its own self-deprecating nicknames are *Iy Protévoussa ton Prosfigón* ("The Refugee Capital", after the ring of 1920s settlements, all prefixed by "Nea", around it) and *Ftohómana* (Mother of the Poor) – monikers duly appropriated by native writers such as Yiorgos Ioannou and Nikos Pentzikis (see "Books" in Contexts, p.901).

However, before 1923, the population was as mixed as any in the Balkans, with Greek Orthodox Christians in a distinct minority. Besides Ottoman Muslims, who had called the city "Selanı" since their arrival in 1430, there were Slavs (who knew it as "Solun"), Albanians and the largest European **Jewish** community of the age: 80,000, or nearly half of the inhabitants, for whom "Salonica" ranked as a "Mother of Israel", before the first waves of emigration to Palestine began after World War I. Numbers had dropped to fewer than 60,000 at the onset of World War II, when all but a tiny fraction were deported from Platía Eleftherías to the concentration camps, in one of the worst atrocities committed in the Balkans. It was this operation in which former Austrian president Kurt Waldheim has been implicated. The vast Jewish cemeteries east of the city centre were desecrated, and later covered over by the new university and expanded trade fair grounds in 1948.

You can catch glimpses of "Old Salonica" today in the walled **Kástra** quarter, on the hillside beyond the modern grid of streets. Even amidst the post-1917 flatlands below, there are pockets of Ottoman buildings which miraculously survived the fire, and slightly later Greek Art Deco piles which escaped 1950s developers. For most visitors, however, it is Thessaloníki's excellent **archeological museum**, albeit depleted of late since the transfer of most Philip II-related exhibits back to Veryína, which stands out. Additionally, if you have developed a taste for Byzantine monuments, a unique array of **churches** dating from Roman times to the fifteenth century constitutes a showcase of the changing styles of Orthodox religious architecture, while a smaller number of **Islamic monuments** – virtually all of them from the fifteenth century – attests to Thessaloníki's status as the first Ottoman Balkan city, when Athens was still a village.

A NOTE ON MACEDONIA

The name **Macedonia** is a geographical term of long standing, applied to an area that has always been populated by a variety of races and cultures. It is today divided unequally between the modern states of Greece, Bulgaria, the Former Yugoslav Republic of Macedonia (FYROM) and Albania, with Greece retaining by far the greatest extent.

The original **Kingdom of Macedonia**, which gained pre-eminence under Philip II and Alexander the Great, was a Greek affair – governed by Greek kings and inhabited by a predominantly Greek population. Its early borders spread south to Mount Olympus, west to present-day Kastoriá, east to Kavála and north into parts of what was Yugoslavia. It lasted, however, for little more than two centuries. In subsequent years the region fell under the successive control of Romans, Slavs, Byzantines, Saracens and Bulgars, before eventual subjugation, along with southern Greece, under Ottoman Turkish rule.

In the late nineteenth century, when the disintegration of the **Ottoman empire** began to raise the issue of future national territories, the name Macedonia denoted simply the geographical region. Its heterogeneous population included Greeks, Slavs and Bulgarians – who referred to themselves and their language as "Macedonian" – as well as large numbers of Jews, Serbs, Vlachs, Albanians and Turks. No one ethnic group predominated overall, and Greek Orthodox were often in a distinct minority, particularly in Thessaloníki. The first nationalist struggles for the territory began in the 1870s, when small armies of Greek *andartes*, Serbian *chetniks* and Bulgarian *comitadjis* took root in the mountain areas, battling each other ferociously before uniting briefly against the Ottomans in the first Balkan War.

Following Turkish defeat, things swiftly became more complex. The **Bulgarians** laid sole claim to Macedonia in the second Balkan War, but were defeated, and a 1912 Greco-Serbian agreement divided the bulk of Macedonian territory between the two states along approximate linguistic/ethnic lines. During World War I, however, the Bulgarians occupied much of Macedonia and Thrace, until their capitulation in 1917. After the Versailles peace conference, a small part of Slavophone Macedonia remained in Bulgaria, and there were population exchanges of Greek-speakers living in Bulgaria and "Bulgarians" in Greece. This was followed, in 1923, by the arrival and settlement of hundreds of thousands of Greek refugees from Asia Minor, who – settling throughout Greek Macedonia – effectively swamped any remaining Slavophone population. During World War II the Bulgarians again occupied all of eastern Macedonia and Thrace (beyond the River Strýmon), as allies of Nazi Germany. Their defeat by the Allies led to withdrawal and seems to have vanquished ambitions; recent Bulgarian leaders, both Communist and post-Communist, have renounced all territorial claims and "minority rights" for "Greek-Bulgarians".

The position of Yugoslavia, though, which under Tito established the **Socialist Republic of Macedonia** in its share of the historical territory, was more ambiguous. During the decades of its unity there were Yugoslav propaganda attempts to suggest Slav affinities with the ancient Macedonian kingdom, and, by extension, with the present Greek population. When the Yugoslav federation fell apart violently in mid-1991, the issue resurfaced at the top of the Greeks' political agenda, after the population of Yugoslav Macedonia voted overwhelmingly for an independent nation of Macedonia.

The downside, for visitors as well as residents, is a complex of **problems** all too reminiscent of Athens. Industries and residences alike discharge their waste, untreated, into the gulf (with slight improvements of late), and traffic on the main avenues, despite a comprehensive one-way system, is often at a standstill. After years of planning and sporadic discussion, contracts to dig a metro system have finally been tendered, with work to start in 2001. Additionally, the punishing 1991–95 blockade of the FYROM hoisted Greece on its own petard, bringing activity at Thessaloníki's busy port – the natural gateway to the landlocked republic – to a near-standstill.

Greek reaction was vitriolic, and all the more so when the fledgling nation adopted the star of Veryína (the symbol of the ancient Macedonian dynasty) on its flag and coinage. Had the new state opted for a different name and logo, the Greeks undoubtedly would have had no quarrel: an impoverished nation of two million, after all, posed little strategic threat. But its adoption of the Macedonian name and symbol was too much: Greeks claimed a cultural and historical copyright over both, and felt their "expropriation" as an act of aggression. Far-Right nationalists even called for invasion.

The Mitsotakis government, ensnared in this nightmare, managed to resist military action, but spared no effort to thwart the Yugoslav-Macedonian aspirations, spurred along by huge popular demonstrations in Thessaloníki and Athens. Ministers were sent on interminable rounds of EU capitals, imploring their allies not to recognize any state assuming the name of "Macedonia"; increasingly rebuffed by the international community, the Greeks instigated an **economic boycott** of the fledgling state, only lifted in late 1995.

These moves severely destabilized the new country but did nothing to halt its recognition by the UN and EU – albeit under a convoluted (and presumably interim) title, the **Former Yugoslav Republic of Macedonia** (FYROM). Greeks have had to accept this *de facto* situation, but many still refuse to use the name, referring to the territory informally and derogatorily as *Ta Skópia*, after the capital, and its people as **Skopianá**. References in the popular press tend to use the phrase the "rump Skopje republic" in terms scarcely less disparaging than those reserved for the "Turkish pseudo-state of Northern Cyprus"; indeed it is prohibited to refer in print to Yugoslav "Macedonia" except in inverted commas, the official acronym being PYDM (Proín Yugoslavikí Dhimokratías Makedhonías), the Greek rendition of FYROM. Official posters throughout Greece proclaim that "Macedonia was, is and always will be Greek and only Greek", for "three thousand years" no less, and further exhort viewers to "read history".

This war of words is probably louder than any likely deeds but it is bad news for the beleaguered, landlocked republic, and for those approximately 40,000 Slavophones remaining in Greek Macedonia and Thrace, whose existence Greece adamantly refuses to admit. Activists leafleting for recognition of this minority – who were long accused of plotting to dismember the country during the civil war – have been arrested; moreover, a respected professor, **Anastasia Karakasidou**, received death threats while resident in Thessaloníki during 1994 for presenting research establishing that Macedonia had only become "Greek" politically and ethnically since the turn of the century, by means of a deliberate process of Hellenization which hadn't sufficed to completely erase memory of more heterogeneous personal identities among villagers in the North. Worse was to come in February 1996, when her manuscript detailing these decades of assimilative pressure, *Fields of Wheat, Hills of Blood*, was declined for publication by Cambridge University Press, despite a ringing endorsement from its editorial review board; the reasons given were concern for the safety of CUP personnel in Greece and, more crassly, the endangering of CUP's lucrative sale of TEFL materials within Greece. Karakasidou, who now teaches at SUNY Stony Brook in the US, eventually had her work published by the University of Chicago (see "Books" in *Contexts*), but the foregoing highlights the sadly narrow permitted limits of public discussion on this issue, both in Greece and in the Greek diaspora communities.

Under the circumstances, the city's designation as **European Cultural Capital for 1997** came as water to the desert, with a huge boost in prestige and visitor numbers which was not entirely transient. The year's most tangible legacy – thanks to EU funds – was extensive signposting and sprucing up of long-neglected medieval buildings, though the refurbishing of various events venues was less successful, with some still shut for works. At the same time came an equally overdue recognition of the nearly vanished Jewish community's role in making the city what it is, in the form of a museum or two and a memorial to the victims of the 1943 deportations.

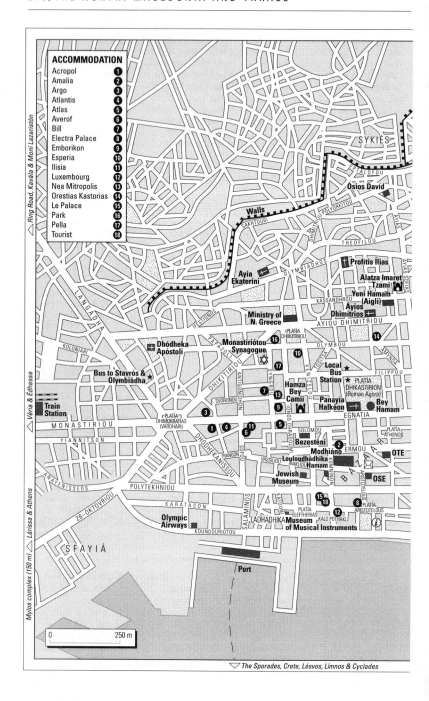

ACCOMMODATION

Acropol ❶
Amalia ❷
Argo ❸
Atlantis ❹
Atlas ❺
Averof ❻
Bill ❼
Electra Palace ❽
Emborikon ❾
Esperia ❿
Ilisia ⓫
Luxembourg ⓬
Nea Mitropolis ⓭
Orestias Kastorias ⓮
Le Palace ⓯
Park ⓰
Pella ⓱
Tourist ⓲

Ring Road, Kavála & Moní Lazaristón

SYKIÉS

Ósios David

Walls

Profítis Ilías

Ayía Ekateríni

Alatza Imaret Tzami

Yeni Hamam (Aigli)

Ministry of N. Greece

Áyios Dhimítrios

Monastiriótou Synagogue

Dhódheka Apóstoli

Bus to Stavrós & Olymbiádha

Hamza Bey Camii

Local Bus Station

PLATÍA DHIKASTIRÍON (Roman Agorá)

Panayía Halkéon

Bey Hamam

Train Station

Véria & Édhessa

MONASTIRÍOU

YIANNITSON

PLATÍA DHIMOKRATÍAS (VARDHÁRI)

EGNATÍA

PLATÍA ATHONOS

Bezesténi

Modhiáno

Louloudhádhika Hamam

OTE

Jewish Museum

OSE

Lárissa & Athens

ANATENÍSSEOS

26-OKTOVRÍOU

KARATÁSON

PLATÍA ELEFTHERÍAS

PLATÍA ARISTOTÉLOUS

POLYTEKHNÍOU

Olympic Airways

LADHÁDHIKA

Museum of Musical Instruments

Mýlos complex (150 m)

SFAYIÁ

KOUNDOURIÓTOU

Port

0   250 m

▽ The Sporades, Crete, Lésvos, Límnos & Cyclades

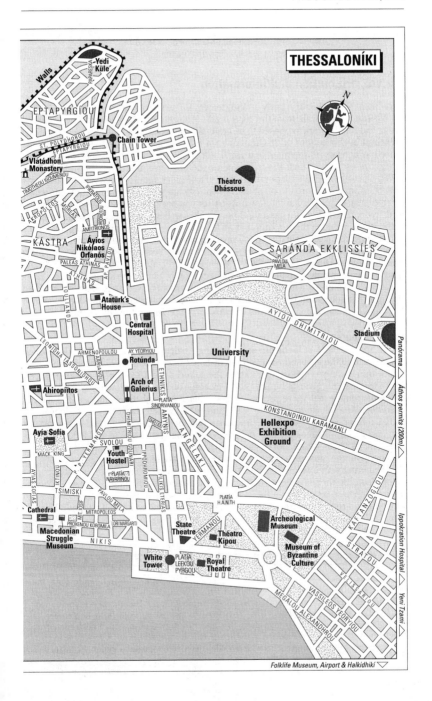

The Thessaloníki phone code is ☎031

Arrival, orientation and information

Arriving in Thessaloníki is fairly straightforward. The **train station** on the west side of town is just a short walk from the central grid of streets and the harbour. The scattered provincial KTELs were supposed to be gradually gathered after 1992 into one giant **bus terminal** at the bottom of 26-Oktovríou, in the Sfayiá district, but resistance to the move has been overwhelming, and you'll still arrive at a variety of points, mostly within sight of each other near the train station; the most useful are detailed in "Listings", p.394. Coming from the **airport**, city bus #78 (135dr) shuttles back and forth hourly between 6am and 11pm; the most convenient city stops are the train station and Platía Aristotélous, though a taxi into town won't set you back more than 2000dr. All **ferries and hydrofoils** call at the passenger port, within walking distance of the train station, at the western end of the seafront. For all ferry agencies, see "Listings"; Aegean routes and frequencies are detailed in the "Travel details" at the end of the chapter.

Once within the grid, **orientation** is made relatively straightforward by several main avenues: Ayíou Dhimitríou, Egnatía, Tsimiskí and Mitropóleos. All run parallel to the quay, but confusingly change their names repeatedly as they head east into the city's post-medieval annexe. The divide between the older and newer parts of town is marked by the exhibition grounds and the start of the seaside park strip, known locally as Zoo Park and dominated by the **Lefkós Pýrgos** or White Tower, the city's symbol.

City transport

There are two types of **local buses**: the orange articulated "caterpillar" models which operate within the city, and the deep red or blue buses which travel further afield. The fare within the city is 100dr; it's 135dr to the suburbs and 150dr out to nearby villages. In most cases, there's an automatic ticket machine on the bus – which may *not* take 100-drachma coins – but there are still a few where you pay the conductor at the rear entrance. Useful lines include #10 and #11, which both ply the length of Egnatía/Karamanlí. From Platía Eleftherías (just behind the sea front), buses initially run east along Mitropóleos; line #5 takes you to the archeological and folklore museums, and #22/28 heads north through Kástra to the highest quarter, known as Eptapyrgíou, the most pleasant part of town. **Taxis** are blue, with white tops.

If you bring your own **car**, it's best to use the attended fee parking area that occupies all of Platía Eleftherías, where you pay on exit. Otherwise, finding a kerbside space is a fairly hopeless task, even in the suburbs; you must then usually go to a *períptero* to buy blue-and-red strip cards which you cancel yourself for an hour at a time (300dr per hour) – buy as many as you need in advance for display in the windscreen. Fees are

---

THESSALONÍKI'S FESTIVALS – AND HOTEL RATES

The city's festival season begins in September with the **International Trade Fair**, the major event of the year. This is followed almost immediately by a **Festival of Greek Song**, and finally, for much of October and November, by the **Dhimitría** celebrations for the city's patron saint. The **Film Festival** was moved in 1992 from September to November, merely helping to prolong the hoteliers' high season, which here runs from September to March. The period of the Trade Fair, particularly, is not a good time to visit. **Hotels** are full, and proprietors who would otherwise be happy to knock a category or two off prices will instead add a twenty-percent surcharge.

payable 8am to 8pm Monday to Friday, 8am to 3pm on Saturday. If you intend to drive around the city, arm yourself with a map showing the one-way system (such as the one published by EOT), which otherwise can be infuriating.

Information

The main **EOT** office is at completely pedestrianized Platía Aristotélous 8 (Mon–Fri 9am–9pm, Sat 10am–6pm, Sun 10am–5pm; ☎271 888); it also has a booth at the airport. When these are closed, try the **tourist police** post (daily 8am–2pm, and Tues, Thurs & Fri 5–9pm; ☎254 871) at Dhodhekanísou 4.

Maps can be problematic; free handouts at the tourist office are often out of stock, and there's no commercially available product overseas. The bound A-to-Z-type atlas published by Malliaris, *Polyodhigos tis Thessalonikis*, is heavy, expensive and not very good. A more useful **book**, with a large-scale folding map, is *Monuments of Thessaloníki* by Apostolos Papayiannopoulos (1500dr), technically out of print but still possibly available at Áyios Dhimítrios church. Other recommended regional archeological guides, *Wandering in Byzantine Thessaloniki* and *Monuments of Thessaloniki* (see box, p.387), are easier to find locally but have rudimentary street plans.

Listings magazines are thin on the ground, with no equivalent of Athens' *Athinorama*; the closest you'll get (if you can read Greek) is the biweekly free broadsheet *Politismika*, available at some record stores and art galleries.

Accommodation

Outside of the festival season, reasonably priced hotel rooms are fairly easy to find, if not always very attractively situated. You will, however, find accommodation relatively expensive – fifteen percent more than Athens or the Peloponnese for equivalent facilities. Modest to comfortable hotels tend to cluster in two areas: around the beginning of Egnatía – although many of the establishments here are plagued by street noise – or in the more agreeable zone between Eleftherías and Aristotélous squares. There are also some good bets between Egnatía and Ayíou Dhimitríou, also a relatively quiet area. Of late there has been a general rise in standards by low-class hotels striving to remain competitive, through a wave of conversions of older buildings to en-suite facilities – often nothing more than partitioning off a room corner to make an en-suite bathroom. TVs and double glazing are also all the rage, the latter absolutely vital on the busiest boulevards.

The now-decertified **Youth Hostel** at Svólou 44 (☎225 946; 2000dr per person) is well located; take bus #10 from the train station to the Kamára stop. However, this particular outfit has generated numerous complaints about filth and generally poor management; if you're still keen, the office is closed from 11am to 7pm, plus there's a strict midnight curfew.

ACCOMMODATION PRICE CODES

Throughout the book we've used the following **price codes** to denote the cheapest available double room in each establishment in high season. Out of season, rates can drop by more than fifty percent, especially if you are staying for three or more nights. Single rooms, where available, cost around seventy percent of the price of a double.

① Up to 6000dr	④ 12,000–16,000dr
② 6000–9000dr	⑤ 16,000–20,000dr
③ 9000–12,000dr	⑥ 20,000dr and upwards

Note: Youth hostels typically charge 2000–2500dr for a dormitory bed.
For more accommodation details, see pp.43–6.

The closest **campsites** are at the small resorts of Ayía Triádha and Órmos Epanomís, 24km and 33km away respectively; see p.397 for more information. Both are EOT sites and, of the two, the further is the better – as is the beach there. Take bus #73 from Platía Dhikastiríon for Ayía Triádha; bus #69 for Órmos Epanomís.

Lower Egnatía

Acropol, Egnatía 10, cnr of Tandalídhou 4 (☎536 170). Quiet and clean, this is a good option with toilet and shower down the corridor. No breakfast. ③.

Argo, Egnatía 11 (☎519 770). An old affair with basic, but acceptable, rooms, some of which have private facilities. ③ shared bathrooms, ④ en-suite.

Atlantis Egnatía 14 (☎540 131). All non-en-suite, with the better rooms facing a side-street. ③.

Atlas, Egnatía 40 (☎537 046; 9000dr). Centrally located, furthest from the train station of the Egnatía hotels. Rooms at the front are noisy. ③ shared bathrooms, ④ en-suite.

Averof, Sófou 24, south of Egnatía (☎538 840, fax 543 194). A good, friendly cheapie, not too noisy and used to foreigners' needs. Some rooms converted to en-suite in 1998. ③ shared bathrooms, ④ en-suite.

Emborikon, Syngrou 14, cnr Egnatia (☎514 431). Good value, despite the shared bathrooms, and with helpful staff. ④

Ilisia, Egnatía 24 (☎528 492). A good deal, this hotel has originally en-suite facilities and a courteous welcome. ④–⑤.

Between Eleftherías and Aristotélous

Amalia, Ermoú 33 (☎268 321, fax 233 356). A decent, if slightly overpriced hotel, quiet enough at night, and well placed near the market. ⑥.

Electra Palace, Platía Aristotélous 5/A (☎232 221, fax 235 947). One of the most expensive hotels in town, and in the most prestigious position – but it can get noise from events in the square. ⑥.

Le Palace, Tsimiskí 12 (☎257 400, fax 256 689, *qcas@otenet.gr*). Completely refurbished in 1998, this Art Deco hotel is good value: wood-floor rooms with designer baths and double glazing. Characterful common areas comprise mezzanine lounge, a ground-floor café, businessmen's restaurant. Buffet breakfast included in rates. ⑤–⑥.

Luxembourg, Komninón 6 (☎278 449; 10,000dr en-suite). A well-priced Neoclassical pile that's clean enough, with real bathrooms, phones and TVs, but a bit gloomy and ripe for an overhaul. ④–⑤.

Tourist, Mitropóleos 21 (☎276 335, fax 226 865). A rambling Belle Epoque palace with parquet-floored lounges and breakfast salon; 1990s-refurbished rooms all en suite; just two singles. Popular with the trendy set, so must be booked in advance. Rates include breakfast. ④.

Between Egnatía and Ayíou Dhimitríou

Bill, Syngroú 29, cnr of Amvrossíou (☎537 666). In a quiet, tree-lined side street, this is a good find, if getting a bit well worn; balconies, and original bathrooms in en-suite units (avoid the bathless rooms). ④ shared bathrooms, ⑤ en-suite.

Esperia, Olýmbou 58 (☎269 321, fax 269 457). Refurbished in 1995, though slightly overpriced, with double-glazed views north to the hills. ⑥.

Nea Mitropolis, Syngroú 22 (☎525 540, fax 539 910). Clean, good value and well maintained, not too noisy despite its proximity to Egnatía. ③ shared bathrooms, ④ en-suite

Orestias Kastorias, Agnóstou Stratiótou 14, corner of Olýmbou (☎276 517, fax 276 572). With most rooms of this 1920s building recently converted to en suite, this is a prime, friendly choice and one of the quieter hotels in the city; reservations suggested. ③ shared bathrooms, ④ en suite.

Park, Íonos Dhragoúmi 81 (524 121, fax 524 193). Modern and sterile, but comfortable, spotless, double-glazed rooms with limited sea views. ⑥.

Pella, Íonos Dhragoúmi 63 (☎524 221, fax 524 223). A tall, narrow, modern hotel on a moderately quiet street; popular with wealthy tourists and frugal businessmen. ⑤–⑥.

Central Thessaloníki

Although scholarly opinion now holds that the main Via Egnatia skirted the ancient city walls, there is no doubt that the modern **Odhós Egnatía** follows the course of an important Roman street or processional way. At some point during your time in town you are certain to ride or walk down it, catching glimpses of various monuments that line it.

Near the eastern corner of Platía Dhikastiríon stands the disused fifteenth-century **Bey Hamam** or Turkish **bath**, its doorway surmounted by elaborate stalactite ornamentation. It functioned as a public baths until 1968, and should it ever be open there is more fine stalactite vaulting inside. Other nearby **Ottoman monuments** include the six-domed **Bezestέni** or covered valuables market at the corner of Venizélou and Egnatía, given a facelift as part of the 1997 works and once again home to plush shops. Directly opposite, on the north side of Egnatía, squats another prominent mosque, the fifteenth-century purpose-built **Hamza Bey Camii** (most mosques in Ottoman Thessaloníki were converted churches); today, also home to more modest shops, it bears the sign "Alcazar" from its days as a cinema of that name.

Back up on the southwestern corner of the platía, the eleventh-century **Panayía Halkéon** church is a classic though rather unimaginative example of the cross-in-square form (see box on Roman and Byzantine Salonica, p.386). Until its restoration is complete there is effectively no entry, but you should be able to make out the founder's dedicatory inscription over one door. As the name indicates, it served during the Ottoman occupation as the copperworkers' guild mosque; the only remnant of this tradition are the handful of kitsch-copper-souvenir shops which operate just across the street. For real antiques – mostly old lamps, bedsteads and wooden furniture, and not particularly cheap – you're best off heading uphill two blocks to Tossítsa, home (along with a courtyard just west) to the city's **flea market**.

Across the way from Panayía Halkéon lies the **main bazaar** area, bounded roughly by Egnatía on the northwest, Dhragoúmi on the southwest, Ayías Sofías on the northeast, and Tsimiskí to the southeast. Much the most interesting bit, and a quiet mid-town oasis, is a grid of lanes in the northeastern quadrant, northeast between Ayías Sofías and Aristotélous, devoted to selling live animals, wood and cane furniture, chair-seat-reweavers, and crafts shops.

At the very heart of the larger area sprawls the **Modhiáno**, the central meat, fish and produce market, named after the wealthy **Jewish** Modiano family which long owned it. Unfortunately it is now in decline, with many stalls vacant, but still makes an atmospheric and authentic destination for a meal (see "Eating", p.390). It is said that until the 1930s, Ladino (Judeo-Spanish) was the principal language of commerce here and in the nearby harbour, where all work ceased for the Jewish Sabbath.

Thessaloníki's only surviving pre-1943 **synagogue** is the Monastiriótou at Syngroú 35, with an imposing facade, open normally for Friday evening and Saturday morning worship. Yet another by-product of 1997 was the establishment of the **Museum of the Jewish Presence** at Ayíou Miná 13, southwest of the Modhiáno. However, this has not officially opened yet and for the moment one must be content with the nearby **Simon Marks Museum** at Vassilíou Iraklíou 26, First Floor (Mon–Fri 10am–1.30pm; free). Most of it obsessively documents the rise of Nazism in Germany from the ashes of World War I. Thessaloníki gets covered only in the tiny right-hand gallery, which traces the history of the local Jewry at a gallop, focusing mostly on post-1917 events and barely hinting at the yawning rifts in the community between Zionists, socialists and traditionalists.

Remains of Salonica's formative years in the eastern Roman empire are thin on the ground; those that survive are concentrated to either side of Egnatía. Ruins of the **Roman agora** were unearthed in the 1970s in the vast Platía Dhikastiríon, behind

Panayía Halkéon; they have yielded little in the way of structures, though they're still being excavated. Rather more prominent is a reconstructed **odeion** at the north corner of the square.

Tucked just out of sight north of the boulevard, the fifth-century, three-aisled basilica of **Panayía Ahiropíïtos** (now under scaffolding) is the oldest in the city, featuring arcades, monolithic columns and often highly elaborate capitals – a popular development begun under Theodosius. Only the mosaics beneath the arches survive, depicting birds, fruits and vegetation in a rich Alexandrian style.

The Rotunda and the Arch of Galerius

Further along on the same side of Egnatía, the **Rotunda**, later converted rather strangely to the church of **Áyios Yeóryios**, is the most striking single Roman monument – designed, but never used, as an imperial mausoleum (possibly for Galerius) and consecrated for Christian use in the late fourth century by adding a sanctuary, an apse, a narthex and rich mosaics. Later it became one of the city's major mosques, from which period the minaret remains. Following lengthy repairs in the wake of the 1978 earthquake, Áyios Yeóryios is once again open to the public (Mon–Fri 8.30am–5pm; free) and ranks as a must-see for the sake of its superb mosaics, the finest of their era outside Constantinople or Ravenna. Ones already visible include a miscellaneous aviary of birds in the south vault; ducks, partridge and woodcock in the southeast vault; while up in the damaged dome the head of a mythical phoenix is visible with angels just outside a circular rainbow. Shortly to emerge from scaffolding, just down from the dome, are fifteen naturalistically portrayed saints, many Roman soldier-martyrs, all sheltering under a fantastic structure where peacocks and birds of paradise perch, meant to symbolize the City of Heaven.

The Rotunda originally formed part of a larger complex which included the **Arch of Galerius**, Roman palaces and a hippodrome. Now swathed in scaffolding to prevent its collapse from pollution damage, the arch is the surviving span of a dome-surmounted arcade leading towards the palaces. Built to commemorate the emperor's victories over the Persians in 297 AD, its piers contain reliefs of the battle scenes interspersed with glorified poses of Galerius himself. The scant remains of **Galerius's palace** can be viewed, below the modern street level, along pedestrianized Dhimitríou Goúnari and its extension, Platía Navarínou.

Ayía Sofía

Between Egnatía and Navarínou, and not to be confused with the city's undistinguished modern cathedral on Mitropóleos, the eighth-century church of **Ayía Sofía** was consciously modelled on its more illustrious namesake in Constantinople. It replaced an older basilica, the only trace of which remains a few paces south, as the below-street-level *ayíasma* or holy well of John the Baptist, itself originally a Roman nymphaeum. Ayía Sofía's dome, ten metres in diameter, bears a splendid mosaic of the *Ascension*, for which you'll need opera glasses. Christ, borne up to the heavens by two angels, sits resplendent on a rainbow throne, right hand extended in blessing; below a wry inscription quotes Acts 1:11: "Ye men of Galilee, why stand ye gazing up into heaven?" The whole is ringed by fifteen figures: the Virgin, attended by two angels, and the twelve apostles shown reacting variously to the miracle above. The dome was restored late in the 1980s; the rest of the interior decoration was plastered over after the 1917 fire. Another fine mosaic of the Virgin Enthroned, in the apse, is currently hidden by the *iconostasis*, and scaffolding; it apparently replaced a cross, of which traces are visible, dating from the Iconoclast period. Outside, on the north flank of the building, is a curious Ottoman tower, not the minaret pulled down from the south flank after 1912; the tower lost its dome at the same time as a Byzantine portico on the west side was demolished.

The White Tower

The most prominent central post-Byzantine monument is a short walk southeast of here on the seafront: the **White Tower (Lefkós Pýrgos)**, which formed the southeast corner of the city's Byzantine and Turkish defences before most of the walls were demolished late in the nineteenth century. Prior to this, it was the "Bloody Tower", a place of imprisonment and (in 1826) execution of the janissaries, until the Greeks whitewashed both the building and its image after World War I, removing at the same time a polygonal outer enclosure built by the Ottomans in 1875. Today, stripped of white pigment, it looks a little stagey in its isolation, but is a graceful symbol nonetheless, which for years appeared as the background logo on the evening TV news. It was restored in 1985 for Salonica's 2300th birthday celebrations and now houses a small but well-presented **museum** of Byzantine secular and sacred art – icons, jewellery, pottery, metalwork, coins – plus several displays on the history of Thessaloníki (daily except Mon, 8am–2pm; free). You can climb to the top for the views and a very pleasant, normally priced **café**.

The Archeological Museum

Despite recent depletions, it's still worth finding time for the **Archeological Museum** (summer Mon 12.30–7pm, Tues–Sun 8am–7pm; winter Mon 10.30am–5pm, Tues–Sun 8am–5pm; 1500dr) on the oddly named Platía H.A.N.T.H (YMCA), just a few minutes' walk from the White Tower. The central gallery, opposite as you enter, is devoted to rich grave finds from ancient Sindos, a few kilometres north of the modern city, while the left-hand wing is taken up by Hellenistic and Roman art, in particular some exquisite blown-glass birds, found in the tumuli or *toúmbes* which stud the plain around Thessaloníki.

But these are all just appetizers for – or anticlimaxes after – the **Veryína exhibition** in the south hall, which displays – and clearly labels in both English and Greek – many of the finds from the Royal Tombs of Philip II of Macedon (father of Alexander the Great) and others at the ancient Macedonian capital of Aigai (at modern Veryína, see p.406). They include startling amounts of gold and silver – masks, crowns, necklaces, earrings and bracelets – all of extraordinarily imaginative craftsmanship, both beautiful and practical, as well as pieces in ivory and bronze. Examples include a silver wine strainer with goose-head handles, a perforated bronze lampshade and the enormous bronze *kratir* from the small site of Dhervéni, which, in its richly ornate rendition of the life of the god Dionysos, prefigures Baroque art. However, the long-running star exhibits – the *larnax* or gold ossuary casket of Philip II, plus that of a consort of his, and assorted gold wreaths, have been transferred back to Veryína itself, and the bones of the king are no longer on view.

Through these finds, here and elsewhere, the history of the Macedonian dynasty and empire is traced: at first impression a surprisingly political act, but the discoveries at Veryína have been used by Greece to emphasize the fundamental "Greekness" of the modern provinces of Makedhonía and Thráki. Although these territories might seem to an outsider an accepted and inviolable part of Greece, their recent occupation by Turks and Bulgarians is still very much part of Greek political memory. The ancient sites themselves are a significant part of the debate; during the Bulgarian occupation of the north during World War II, for example, there was a deliberate policy of vandalism towards "Greek Macedonian" and "Greek Thracian" remains. Thus archeology in northern Greece has always been a nationalist as well as an academic issue, and the museum itself is a brilliantly executed "educational" endeavour.

Folklife (Ethnological) Museum of Macedonia

The **Folklife Museum** at Vasilíssis Ólgas 68 (closed indefinitely for works) is the best of its kind in Greece, with well-written commentaries (English and Greek) accompanying displays on housing, costumes, day-to-day work and crafts. The exhibits, on weaving and spinning especially, are beautiful. And there is a sharp, highly un-folkloric emphasis on context: on the role of women in the community, the clash between tradition and progress, and the yearly cycle of agricultural and religious festivals. Even the traditional costumes are presented in a manner that goes beyond the mere picturesque.

The collection is housed in the elegant turn-of-the-century mansion of the **Modiano** family, they of the meat market, and one of several Jewish-built villas hereabouts. The museum is just a twenty-minute walk (or short bus ride) from the archeological museum; catch the #5 bus as it runs east along Mitropóleos.

The Dönme and the Yeni Cami

The **Dönme**, or more properly **Ma'min**, were an offshoot of Judaism elaborated by followers of the seventeenth-century "False Messiah" Sabbatai Zvi; outwardly they embraced Islam after his forced conversion, and were counted as part of the Ottoman Muslim population, but secretly continued certain aspects of Jewish worship and married only among themselves. Numbering about 15,000 of the city's wealthier citizens, they were disproportionately important in the commerce of pre-fire Salonica, and later – following their voluntary emigration or expulsion – that of republican Turkey.

ROMAN AND BYZANTINE SALONICA AND ITS CHURCHES

Macedonia became a **Roman province** in 146 BC, and Salonica, with its strategic position allowing both land and sea access, was the natural and immediate choice of capital. Its fortunes and significance were boosted by the building of the Via Egnatia, the great road linking Rome (via Brindisi) with Byzantium and the East, along whose course Amphipolis, Philippi and Neapolis (now Kavála) were also to develop.

Christianity had slow beginnings in the city. St Paul visited twice, being driven out on the first occasion after provoking the Jewish community. On the second, in the year 56, he stayed long enough to found a church, later writing the two Epistles to the Thessalonians, his congregation there. It was another three centuries, however, before the new religion took full root. Galerius, who acceded as eastern emperor upon Byzantium's break with Rome, provided the city with virtually all its surviving late Roman monuments – and its patron saint, Demetrius (Dhimítrios), whom he martyred. The first resident Christian emperor was **Theodosius** (reigned 379–95), who after his conversion issued here the Edict of Salonica, officially ending paganism.

Under Justinian's rule (527–65) Salonica became the second city of Byzantium after Constantinople, which it remained – under constant pressure from Goths and Slavs – until its sacking by Saracens in 904. The storming and sacking continued under the Normans of Sicily (1185) and with the Fourth Crusade (1204), when the city became for a time capital of the Latin Kingdom of Salonica. It was, however, restored to the Byzantine Empire of Nicea in 1246, reaching a cultural **"Golden Age"** amidst the theological conflict and political rebellion of the next two centuries, until Turkish conquest and occupation in 1430.

The most prominent of Roman public buildings had been the **basilica**: a large wooden-roofed hall, with aisles split by rows of columns. It was ideally suited for conversion to Christian congregational worship, a process achieved simply by placing a canopied altar at what became the apse, and dividing it from the main body of the church (the nave) by a screen (a forerunner to the *témblon*). The baptistery, a smaller, distinct building, was then added to one side. The upper reaches of wall were adorned with mosaics illustrating Christ's incarnation and man's redemption, while at eye level stood a blank lining of marble. (Frescoes, a far more economical medium, did not become fashionable until much later – during the thirteenth and fourteenth centuries – when their scope for expression and movement was fully realized.)

Concentrated in the wealthy eastern annexe, they were also responsible for numerous sumptuous villas in the same area as the Modiano, many still standing, but their enduring civic contribution is the orientalized Art Nouveau **Yeni Cami**, built in 1904, the last mosque built in the city. Designed by an Italian architect, it is an engaging folly, often open for special exhibitions; in fact it long served as Thessaloníki's archeological museum after 1923. The interior, if you gain admission, is nothing other than an Iberian synagogue in disguise, its decor likely to overshadow any displays. This mosque is easy to find, well signposted about a kilometre northwest up Vasilíssis Olgás from the Folklife Museum, then 100m up a side-street.

Museum of Macedonian Struggle

If the archeological museum helps you understand better the present-day importance to Greeks of the Royal Tombs at Veryína, the **Museum of Macedonian Struggle** at the corner of Proxénou Koromilá and Ayías Sofías (Tues–Fri 9am–2pm, plus Wed 6–8pm, Sat–Sun 11am–2.30pm; free) helps to explain their ongoing concern about FYROM or Bulgarian claims to "Greek" Macedonia. The museum illustrates, by means of photographs, posters, pamphlets and dioramas, the struggle to liberate northern Greece, from the 1870s onwards. In a primary role as an educational endeavour for

By the sixth century architects had succumbed to eastern influence and set about improving their basilicas with the addition of a dome. For inspiration they turned to the highly effective Ayía Sofía in Constantinople – the most striking of all Justinian's churches. Aesthetic effect, however, was not the only accomplishment, for the structure lent itself perfectly to the prevailing representational art. The mosaics and frescoes adorning its surfaces became physically interrelated or counterposed, creating a powerful spiritual aid. The eye would be uplifted at once to meet the gaze of the *Pandokrátor* (Christ in Majesty) in the dome, illuminated by the windows of the drum. Between these windows the prophets and apostles would be depicted, and as the lower levels were scanned the liturgy would unfold amid a hierarchy of saints.

The most successful shape to emerge during later experiments with the dome was the "Greek cross-in-square" – four equal arms that efficiently absorb the weight of the dome, passing it from high barrel vaults to lower vaulted chambers fitted inside its angles. Architecturally it was a perfect solution; a square ground plan was produced inside the church with an aesthetically pleasing cruciform shape evident in the superstructure. Best of all, it was entirely self-supporting.

By the mid-tenth century it had become the conventional form. Architects, no longer interested in new designs, exploited the old, which proved remarkably flexible; subsidiary drums were introduced above corners of the square, proportions were stretched ever taller, and the outer walls became masoned with elaborate brick and stone patterning.

Almost all the main Byzantine churches can be found in central Thessaloníki. Under the Turks most of the buildings were converted for use as mosques, a process that obscured many of their original features and destroyed (by whitewashing) the majority of their frescoes and mosaics. Further damage came with the 1917 fire and more recently with the earthquake of 1978. Restoration seems a glacially slow process, guaranteeing that many of the sanctuaries are locked, or shrouded in scaffolding, or both, at any given moment. But these disappointments acknowledged, the churches of Thessaloníki remain an impressive and illuminating group.

If you develop a consuming interest in the subject, there are two locally available stone-by-stone **guides** worth having: the inexpensive, succinct *Monuments of Thessaloniki* (Molho Editions), with coverage only of Roman and Christian sites but better site plans, or the more comprehensive but pricier and rather densely written *Wandering in Byzantine Thessaloniki* (Kapon Editions), which includes Ottoman monuments and has better reproductions.

schoolkids, it's (understandably) all in Greek, but you can borrow an English-language commentary and appreciate the significance of the building in which the museum is housed – the former Greek consulate, from which fifth-columnist Consul Koromilas himself masterminded the struggle.

The Byzantine museums

Besides the gallery in the White Tower, there are two other recently inaugurated museums which, with varying degrees of success, attempt to do justice to Byzantine civilisation.

The first, in Ladhádhika district at Katoúni 12–14, is the heavily promoted, privately run **Museum of Ancient, Byzantine and Post-Byzantine Musical Instruments** (Tues–Sun 9am–3pm & 5–10pm; 1500dr) occupying three floors of a purpose-built block. Put charitably, this is a triumph of style over substance – you're paying to see reproductions of artistic presentations of ancient instruments on walls, vases, drinking cups and so forth. Though each type (such as bagpipes or harps) is given a wing to itself, there's nothing in the way of interpretation or placing the instruments in social or musical context. It comes as little surprise, then, to learn that the museum is largely the brainchild of widely discredited Byzantine music "reconstructor" Khristodhoulos Halaris.

The state-run **Museum of Byzantine Culture** at Stratou 2, just past the Archeological Museum (Mon noon–7pm, Tues–Sun 8am–7pm; 1500dr), makes a rather better fist of the early Christian tombs and graves excavated in the city, featuring rescued wall paintings depicting Susannah and the Elders, and a naked rower surrounded by sea creatures.

Kástra and Eptapyrgíou

Above Odhós Kassándhrou, hillside **Kástra** is the main surviving quarter of Ottoman Thessaloníki. Although they are gradually becoming swamped by new apartment buildings, the streets here remain ramshackle and atmospheric, a labyrinth of timber-framed houses and winding steps. In the past few years the stigma of the district's "Turkishness" has been overcome as the older houses are bought up and restored, and it is justifiably one of the city's favourite after-dark destinations. Along the least confusing walking route up, from the intersection of Ayíou Nikoláou and Ayíou Dhimitríou, spare a glance for the fifteenth-centuury **Altaza Imaret Tzami** on the right, with a handsome portico and multiple domes, used for special events, and the seventeenth-century **Yeni Hamam** diagonally opposite, now a summer cinema and music venue.

Áyios Dhimítrios and other churches

At the very foot of the slope, just below the two Ottoman monuments preceding, is a massive yet simple church, **Áyios Dhimítrios** (Mon 1.30–7.30pm; Tues–Sun 8am–7.30pm; free), conceived in the fifth century though heavily restored since. The *de facto* cathedral of the city, with pride of place in Thessalonian hearts, it was almost entirely rebuilt after the 1917 fire, which destroyed all but the apse and colonnades. The church is dedicated to the city's patron saint and stands on the site of his martyrdom, and even if you know beforehand that it is the largest basilica in Greece, its immense interior comes as a surprise.

Amid the multicoloured marble columns and vast extents of white plaster, six small surviving **mosaics**, mostly on the columns flanking the altar, make an easy focal point; of these, four date back to the church's second reconstruction after the fire of 620. The seventh-century mosaic of *Áyios Dhimítrios Flanked by the Church's Two Founders*, on the south pier beside the steps to the crypt, was described by Osbert Lancaster as "the

greatest remaining masterpiece of pictorial art of the pre-Iconoclastic era in Greece";
this, and the adjacent mosaics of *Áyios Sérgios* and *Áyios Dhimítrios with a Deacon*, contrast well with their contemporary on the north column, a warm and humane mosaic of
the saint with two young children. The fifth-century mosaics are a *Deisis* with the Virgin
and Áyios Theódhoros on the north pier, and, high on the west wall of the inner south
aisle, a child being presented or dedicated to the saint.

The **crypt** (same hours; free), unearthed after the great fire, contains the *martyrion*
of the saint – probably an adaptation of the Roman baths in which he was imprisoned –
and a whole exhibit of beautifully carved column-capitals, labelled in Greek only and
arrayed around a seven-columned fountain and collecting basin.

Around Áyios Dhimítrios are several more churches, utterly different in feel. West
along Ayíou Dhimitríou is the somewhat remote church of **Dhódheka Apóstoli**, built
with seven more centuries of experience and the bold Renaissance influence of Mystra
(see p.214). Its five domes rise in perfect symmetry above walls of fine brickwork, while
inside are glorious fourteenth-century mosaics, virtually the last executed in the
Byzantine empire, in particular a *Nativity*, an *Entry into Jerusalem*, a *Resurrection* and a
Transfiguration.

To the west, **Ayía Ekateríni**, built just before Dhódheka Apóstoli, has fine brickwork, exploiting all the natural colours of the stones, though its interior frescoes are
now fragmentary. **Profítis Ilías**, between Ayía Ekateríni and Áyios Dhimítrios, is in the
same vein as Dhódheka Apóstoli, though less imposing, and with negligible surviving
interior frescoes.

Áyios Nikólaos Orfanós

Fourteenth-century **Áyios Nikólaos Orfanós** (Tues–Sun 9am–2.30 pm; entrance from
Irodhótou, warden at no.17) is a diminutive, much-altered basilica to the north of Áyios
Dhimítrios, whose imaginative and well-preserved frescoes are the most accessible and
expressive in the city. In the south aisle, Áyios Yerásimos of Jordan is seen with anthro-
pomorphic lions, with Christ's miracles set forth in a row above. The naos is devoted to
episodes from the Passion, in particular the rarely depicted *Christ Mounting the Cross*
and *Pilate Seated in Judgment* at a wooden desk, just like a Byzantine scribe of the era.
Above the Virgin Platytera in the apse conch looms the equally unusual *Áyion
Mandílion*, an image of Christ's head superimposed on a legendary veil sent to an
ancient king of Anatolian Edessa. Around the apse is a wonderful *Niptir* (Christ
Washing the Disciple's Feet), in which it is thought the painter inserted (in lieu of a sig-
nature) an image of himself at the top right above the conch, riding a horse and wearing a white turban. Frescoes of the north aisle, illustrating the Akathistos hymn glori-
fying the Virgin, are less intact, but do feature a wonderful *Dream of Joseph* on one column capital.

Ósios Davíd

A long, angled walk from Áyios Nikólaos, or a shorter, stiffer direct climb up from the
Yeni Hamam, **Ósios Davíd** (Mon–Sat daily 8am–noon & 5–6pm, Sun 8–10.30am), a
tiny fifth-century church on Odhós Timothéou, does not really fit into any architectural progression, since the Ottomans demolished much of the building when converting
it to a mosque. However, it has arguably the finest mosaic in the city, depicting a clean-
shaven Christ Emmanuel appearing in a vision, surrounded by the Tetramorphs or
symbols of the four Gospels. The four Rivers of Paradise, replete with fish, flow from
beneath Christ, lapping the feet of the prophets Ezekiel and Habakkuk, who respectively cringe in terror and ponder reflectively at the revelation. Ask the curator to
switch on the floodlights for a better view. Nearby, the still-functioning **monastery of
Vlatádhon** is most noteworthy for its peaceful, tree-shaded courtyard, a perfect place

to complete a tour; you may gain access to the much-restored *katholikón*, which has just a very few fourteenth-century frescoes inside.

The ramparts and Eptapyrgíou
Sections of the fourteenth-century **Byzantine ramparts**, constructed with brick and rubble on top of old Roman foundations, crop up all around the northern part of town. The best-preserved portion begins at a large circular keep, known as the Trigónion or "Chain Tower" (after its encircling ornamental moulding), in the northeast angle where the easterly city walls change direction. A much smaller circuit of walls rambles around the district of **Eptapyrgíou**, enclosing the old eponymous acropolis at the top end. For centuries it served as the city's prison – described as a sort of Greek Devil's Island in a number of plaintive old songs entitled "Yediküle" (Turkish for "Eptapyrgíou" or "Seven Towers") – until abandoned as too inhumane in 1989; it is now being restored, supposedly as a museum commemorating its inmates, who included many political prisoners. On its south side, the wall is followed by Odhós Eptapyrgíou and edged by a small strip of park – a good place to sit and scan Thessaloníki. Nearby, various tavernas come alive in the late afternoon and evening.

Ataturk's house
If you approach or leave Kástra on its east side, it's worth casting an eye at the Turkish consulate at the bottom of Apostólou Pávlou. In the pink, nineteenth-century building beside it at no.17, **Kemal Ataturk**, first president and creator of the modern state of Turkey, was born. The consulate maintains the house as a small museum, with its original fixtures. To visit you must apply for admission at the main building, with your passport (Mon–Fri 9am–1pm & 2–6pm). Security is tight, and for good reason – Ataturk has been held largely responsible for the traumatic exchange of Greek and Turkish populations in 1923. In 1981 a Turkish celebration of the centenary of his birth had to be called off after a Greek stunt pilot threatened a kamikaze dive at the house.

Eating

Since the early 1990s there has been an explosion of interesting places to eat and drink in Thessaloníki, parallelling the increasing prosperity of the city, so there's little excuse for frequenting the fast-food outlets which, on first impression, seem to dominate the centre. Most of the listings below, categorized both by district and price per person, are within walking distance of Platía Aristotélous, and for those that aren't we've given the appropriate transport connections. Most of the city's ouzeris will provide some sort of sweet on the house, often semolina *halvás* or watermelon. Thessalonians take their summer holidays a bit earlier than Athenians, so the notation "closed in midsummer" means mid-July to mid-August.

Scattered across town are several honourable exceptions to the stricture on fast food, suitable for **breakfast** or a **quick snack**. Perhaps the best all-rounder is *Hotpot* at Komninón 15, open 24 hours, with full omelette-based breakfasts, pizzas, salads and pasta dishes. *Family* at Mitropóleos 67, corner Ayías Sofías, offers pastries, turnovers, sandwiches and good coffee or juice for breakfast, plus pizzas and pasta after noon. There's cheaper self-service at the window stools, or pay extra to be waited on at the sidewalk tables. *Vavel/Babel* at Komninón 20 uniquely offers crepes, plus a salad bar, fresh juices and coffee in a pleasant indoor/outdoor environment. Quality biscuit junkies will be in heaven at either *Armenaki*, Venizélou 10, or *Cookie Man*, Mackenzie King 8 (by Ayía Sofía church), both purveying myriad varieties of fresh-baked cookies by weight.

Downtown: between the sea and Odhós Ayíou Dhimitríou

UNDER 4000DR

Ta Adhelfia tis Pixarias, Platía Navarínou 7. Best of several similar places on this archeological site/square, with delicacies such as *tzigerosárma* (lamb liver in cabbage) and *mýdhia saganáki*, plus real tablecloths – though often haphazard service and smallish portions as well. Often packed, so go early; indoor mezzanine seating in winter.

Iy Gonia tou Merakli, Avyerinoú, alley off Platía Áthonos. Inexpensive sea food and bulk wine make this about the best of several ouzeris in these lanes between this plaza and Aristotélous, which by day preserve their old commercial character.

Iridha, Olýmbou 83. A normal-priced taverna under the hotel *Orestias Kastorias*, offering a wide-ranging menu of *mayireftá*, mezédhes and grills. The speciality *soutzoukákia* bear little relation to the usual Greek version, being more like Turkish *inegöl köfte*. Attentive service and real table napery. Seating indoors or outdoors under some of the city's famous acacias; open all year.

Kamares, Ayíou Yeoryíou 11, Platía Rotóndas. Excellent seafood, salads and grilled meat at this year-round place, washed down by bulk wine from Límnos. Summer outdoor seating beside the park, just behind the Rotonda apse.

Koumbarakia, Egnatía 140. Tucked behind the little Byzantine chapel of the Transfiguration, the outdoor tables of this durable ouzerí groan with Macedonian-style grills, seafood and salads, including *túrsi* (pickled vegetables). Closed Sun and midsummer.

Loutros, Komninón 15. Partly housed in the men's section of the former Yehuda (Jews') or Loulouládhika (Flower-Mart) Baths, with outdoor seating on the adjacent pavement next to the modern flower market. Good fried seafood, simple *orektiká* and excellent retsina, compensating somewhat for the rough-and-ready surroundings (currently under restoration). Closed in summer.

O Myrovolos tis Smyrnis, in arcade in the Modiano off Komninón 32. Friendly, crowded ouzerí, also known as *Tou Thanassi* and reckoned the best (and marginally most expensive) of several clustered here. Typical fare includes cheese-stuffed squid, Smyrna-style meatballs, stuffed potatoes and grilled baby fish. Attracts a crowd of locals happy to empty several pitchers of tsípouro or Límnos bulk wine of an afternoon in the company of gypsy buskers. Open all year, air-conditioned in summer; despite ample seating, reservations recommended on ☎274 170.

Nea Ilyssia, Sófou 17. Opposite the *Averof* hotel, this popular travellers' restaurant is open long hours (8.30am–2am) and serves highly regarded *mayireftá*.

Platía Athonos, Dhragoúmi, alley off said platía. Another good choice in this popular area, and one that's open for lunch.

OVER 4000DR

Aproöpto, Zefxídhos 6, a pedestrian lane between Iktínou and Pávlou Melá. A somewhat snooty ouzerí with outdoor seating and rather westernized fare (stuffed mushrooms, blue-cheese sauces everywhere). Open all year round, but closed Sun.

Aristotelous, Aristotélous 8. Tucked into a courtyard off Odhós Aristotélous (enter next to Blow Up Records), this upmarket ouzerí with its fine arcaded interior and courtyard gets crowded for the sake of standard but well-executed mezédhes. Open daily except July–Aug and Sun pm.

Pazar Hamam, Komninón 15a. Newer rival to *O Loutros*, housed in the women's section of the same baths. Imaginative recipes from the inconsistently available menu are offset by slipshod service and small portions. Still, worth a try, especially in winter when you can sit inside under the skylit dome.

Tottis, Platía Aristotélous 2–3. Café, gelateria and (pricey) adjacent restaurant, that's as much a meeting place as a dining spot.

Tsarouhas, Olýmbou 78, near Platía Dhikastiríon. Reputedly the best, and certainly the most famous, of the city's *patsatzídhika* – kitchens devoted to tripe-and-trotter soup. Lots of other *mayiréfta*, and Anatolian puddings such as *kazandibí*. Closed midsummer; otherwise open all hours, and thus prices bumped up for the convenience (and full staffing).

Kástra and Eptapyrgíou

Most of the places listed below cling to either side of the walls encircling Eptapyrgíou district; bus #22 or #28 from Platía Eleftherías spares you the climb. Numbers of garish, neon-lit joints near the Chain Tower are worth avoiding.

UNDER 4000DR

Iy Kamara, Steryíou Polidhórou 15. Inside the main Portára gate of the Kástra. Smallish portions of good Anatolian/Cypriot food, served alongside the park strip inside the walls. On the #22 route, Plátanos stop.

To Makedhoniko, Sykiés district. From the main Portára gate, head west, keeping to the walls as much as practicable, until you reach the taverna at the west end of the walls, near a third minor gate; alternatively, bus #28 goes right through this gateway. Very limited menu of *tís óras*, dips, salad and retsina, but also very cheap and popular with the trendy set.

OVER 4000DR

Hiotis, Graviás 2. Just inside the second (eastern) castle gate, near the Chain Tower. Mussels, kebabs and *kokorétsi* served on the terrace under the ramparts, weather permitting. Dinner only in summer, lunch and dinner rest of the year.

To Ye(n)di, Paparéska 13, at the very top of Kástra, opposite the Yedi Küle citadel. Daily-variable ouzeri-type menu dished up in largish portions, to accompany tsípouro, oúzo or house wine. Ample indoor or terrace seating under trees opposite the gate of Yedi Küle, but service can get overstretched owing to popularity. Supper only.

The eastern suburbs

The establishments below cater primarily to the well-heeled residents of the "better" part of town, so food can therefore be more elegant – and routinely more than 4000dr per person, plus any taxi fares required.

Archipelagos, Kanári 1, corner Platía Eleftherías Néa Kríni. A fancy seafood place and one of the best in the area. Take bus #5 or a taxi. Open daily 1pm–midnight.

Batis, Platía Eleftherías 2, Néa Kríni, opposite the preceding. Much homier and almost normal priced compared to *Archipelagos*. Grilled octopus and other fish dishes served on the open-air seaview terrace.

Krikelas, Ethnikís Andistásis 32, in Byzándio district, on the way to the airport. A somewhat touristy venue marooned in a desert of private medical clinics and car showrooms, but the chef here is one of the best in Greece, drawing on half a century of experience. Indoor seating only, thus closed July–Sept.

Ta Pringiponissia, Krítis 60, east of 25-Martíou, 600m beyond the ethnological museum. Delicious Constantinopolitan-Greek food served in a pleasant three-level designer building; you select from proferred trays of hot and cold mezédhes. Open all year; closed Sun.

Drinking, nightlife and entertainment

Ladhádhika, the tough former warehouse, red-light and commercial district behind the harbour, has since the early 1990s been gentrified to become the trendiest district for **nightlife**, particularly pedestrianized Katoúni, Éyiptou and Platía Morihóvou. These and nearby streets are lined by a bewildering mix of cafés, windowless techno-*barákia* (complete with bouncers and sunglass-clad patrons), gelaterie, numerous ouzeris and even a few full-on tavernas, including a Chinese eatery. Establishments have a high turnover rate, so singling them out is fairly pointless: just stroll by and choose according to crowd and noise level. During the warmer months, action shifts to various glitzy, barn-like establishments lining the coast road out to Kalamariá, and to the nightly vólta (promenade) that takes place between the Arch of Galerius and the seafront along pedestrianized Dhimitríou Goúnari, which bulges out halfway down to include Platía Navarínou.

Bars, cafés, music clubs

Alambra, Níkis 19. An "in" waterfront hangout, most pleasant of several here, with pricey coffees and alcohol at indoor or sidewalk seating. Purports to be a reincarnation of a pre-fire kafenío at roughly this location.

Kourdhisto Gourouni, Ayías Sofías 31. Ten different foreign brews on tap, more than sixty bottled varieties at this stylish bar with indoor and outdoor seating; expensive food menu also.

Mandragoras, Mitropóleos 98. A large and elegant upstairs wine-and-mezédhes bar, run by a man who twice won the state lottery. Closed in summer.

Ntore (Doré) Zythos, Tsiroyiánni 7, opposite the White Tower. New branch of the original *Zythos* (see below), with food claimed as good or better than at its parent.

Yeni Hamam, cnr Ayíou Nikoláou and Kassándhrou, behind Áyios Dhimítrios church. Predating the 1997 wave of renovations, this classy bar-ouzerí with Anatolian decor occupies part of this dependency of the nearby Alatza Imaret Camii nearby on Kassándhrou. A small events hall takes up the double-domed main chamber of the baths, with bar seating outside in summer, when the garden becomes an outdoor cinema.

Zythos, Platía Katoúni 5. The first bar established in Ladhádhika, still one of the best and the only one active at lunch time, when food is served along with two dozen varieties of foreign beer – *zýthos* means "beer" in *katharévoussa* Greek.

Events

Winter **dance**, **concert** and **theatre** events tend to take place in the 1997-redone *Kratikó Théatro* (State Theatre) or the *Vassilikó Théatro* (Royal Theatre; still shut for works), within sight of each other behind the White Tower. In summer things move to one of a number of outdoor venues: the *Théatro Kípou* (Garden Theatre), near the Archeological Museum; well up the hill at the *Théatro Dhássous* (Forest Theatre), in the pines southeast of the upper town, with events from late June to mid-September; or the *Théatro Damari*, above the Kaftantzoglio Stadium in Triandhría district, which hosts big Greek or international stars like Marinella, James Brown or Tito Puente. In the absence of a reliable city listings magazine, watch for posters in the windows of the usual ticket vendors: the record stores Blow Up (Aristotélous 8), Albandis (Mitropóleos 14–16), Patsis (Tsimiskí 41) and Virgin (shopping mall at Tsimiskí 43), as well as at Zythos/Ntore (Doré) Zythos (as above).

For more cutting-edge events (occasional monthly programmes from Blow Up Records, Aristotélous 8), *Mylos* at Andhréou Yeoryíou 56 is a multi-functional cultural complex housed in an old flour mill 2km southeast of the centre, founded in 1991 by one Nikos Stefanidhis. Here you'll find a couple of bars, a live jazz café, a popular *tsipourádhiko* (open for lunch), a summer cinema, concert halls and exhibition galleries of various sizes, plus a theatre. It has spawned various smaller imitators near and far in Greece, including (in Thessaloníki) *Moní Lazaristón* in Stavroúpoli at Kolokotróni 25, a deconsecrated Catholic monastery 2km out from the centre along Langadhá, which also hosts regular concerts, mostly by top Greek performers, as well as exhibitions.

Cinema

Indoor cinemas, shut in summer unless otherwise indicated, tend to cluster between the White Tower and the Galerius arch; those known to concentrate on quality first-run material include *Alexandhros*, Ethnikís Amýnis 1 (open in summer); *Egnatia*, Patriárhou Ioakím 1, corner Keramopoúlou, by Ayía Sofía; *Esperos*, Svólou 22 (open in summer); *Makedhonikon*, Filikís Eterías, corner Dhimitríou Margaríti; *Navarinon*, on the namesake plaza; and *Vakoura*, Ioánnou Miháïl 10. **Summer cinemas** have all but vanished from downtown Thessaloníki, owing to spiralling property values; the only ones left are the *Alex*, at Olýmbou 106; the nearby *Aigli* outside the Yeni Hamam; *Ellinis*, the summer branch of the *Egnatia*, on Platía H.A.N.T.H.; and the comparatively remote *Natali*, at the start of Megálou Alexándhrou by the *Macedonia Palace* hotel.

You'll have to stroll by to see what's playing unless you can read the daily Greek papers.

Listings

Airlines Air Greece, Tsimiskí 17 (☎236 946); Britannia, c/o Doucas Tours, Venizélou 8 (☎269 984); Cronus, Vas. Yeoryíou 18 (☎870555); Olympic, Koundourióti 3 (☎230240). Most other airlines are represented by general sales agents or bucket shops (see below).

Airport At Mikrá, 16km out and served by bus #78; ☎411 977 for flight information.

Books and papers Molho, Tsimiskí 10, is far and away the best shop in the city, with an excellent stock of English-language books (in particular related to Thessaloníki), magazines and newspapers. Promithevs, at Ermoú 75, is your only alternative.

Bus terminals The unified terminal on 26-Oktovríou has effectively flopped, except for a few Athens services; most KTELs are still scattered all over town, mostly opposite the train station, and locations should be checked with EOT. Currently, the most useful ones include: Alexandhroúpoli, Koloniári 31; Édhessa/Véria, Monastiríou 75; Flórina, Anayenníseos 42; Halkidhikí, Karakássi 68, in the east of town (#10 bus to Bótsari stop); Ioánnina, Khrístou Pípsou 19; Kastoriá, Anayenníseos 4; Kavála, Langadhá 59; Komotiní, cnr Olympíou Yeorgáki and Irínis; Litóhoro, Sapfoús 10; Pélla, Anayenníseos 22; Tríkala, Monastiríou 65; Vólos, Anayenníseos 22; Xánthi, Ayíou Nestóros 22.

Camping gear Petridhis, Vas. Iraklíou 43; or World Jamboree, at Íonos Dhelíou 6, off Ethnikís Amýnis.

Car rental Many are clustered near the fairgrounds and Archeological Museum on Angeláki, which is a good place to comparison-shop.The leading agencies have kiosks at the airport, too. Specific outfits include *Avis*, Níkis 3 (☎227 126); *Budget*, Angeláki 15 (☎274 272); Eurodollar, Ethnikís Andistásis 157 (☎456 630); *Europcar/Inter Rent*, Papandhréou 5 (☎826 333); *European*, Angeláki 15 (☎281 603); *Eurorent*, Angeláki 3 (☎286 327); *Hertz*, Venizélou 5 (☎224 906); *Thrifty*, Angeláki 5 (☎241 241).

Consulates Important for onward travel in the Balkans, but no longer needed for introductory letters to Áthos (see below). *Bulgaria*, Mánou 12 (☎829 210); *Canada*, Tsimiskí 17 (☎256 350); *Denmark*, Komminón 26 (☎284 065); *Netherlands*, Komninón 26 (☎227 477); *Romania*, Níkis 13, 4th Floor (☎225 481); South Africa, Tsimiskí 51 (☎274 393); *UK/Commonwealth*: honorary consul is at Venizélou 8, 8th floor (Mon–Fri 8am–1pm; ☎278 006); *US*, Tsimiskí 43, Bldg A, 7th Floor (Mon–Fri 9am–noon; ☎242 905). Note that there is no full consulate for the FYROM in Thessaloníki; visas, if required, should be obtained in Athens rather than chancing the frontier.

Cultural institutes British Council, Ethnikís Amýnis 9, cnr Tsimiskí; free library and reading room, plus various events in the winter months. USIS Library, Mitropóleos 34, 2nd Floor (closed summer).

Exchange For changing notes, use the 24hr automatic exchange machine at the National Bank on Platía Aristotélous 6. Thessaloníki has plenty of cash dispensers accepting a variety of foreign plastic.

Ferry ticket agents The main agent for the DANE ferry to Sámos and the Dodecanese, plus G&A sailings to the Dodecanese, is Omikron Travel, Salamínos 4 (☎555 995). Minoan Line or G&A sailings to the Sporádhes, Cyclades and Crete, as well as all hydrofoils to the Sporádhes, are best obtained from Kriti/Crete Air Travel, Íonos Dhragoúmi 1, cnr Koundouriótou (☎534 376). Karacharisis at Koundourióti 8 (☎524 544) is the main NEL agent, and also deals in all G&A sailings and Minoan Lines. For routes and frequencies, see "Travel details", pp.458–9.

Football Thessaloníki's main team is PAOK, whose stadium is in the east of the city at Toúmba – off our map, though visible in square A5 of the EOT "Thessaloniki/Halkidhiki" handout or box 46 of the *Polyodhigos*/National Bank folding map.

Hospitals For minor trauma, use the *Yenniko Kendriko* at Ethnikís Amýnis 41; otherwise, head for the *Ippokration* at Konstandinopóleos 49, in the eastern part of town.

Internet café Most central is Globus, Amýnda 12, near the *Orestias Kastorias* hotel.

Laundries There are several coin-ops where you can leave your clothes to be washed, and collect them later, including Bianca, Antoniádhou 3, near the Arch of Galerius (open all day), and Freskadha, Filíppou 105, beside the Rotunda.

Mt Áthos permits Regardless of what you may read in other sources, prospective foreign pilgrims no longer need visit either their own consulate for recommendation letters, nor the Ministry of

Northern Greece. Proceed directly to the *Grafío Proskynitón Ayíou Órous* (Pilgrims' Office for Mt Áthos), Konstandínou Karamanlí 14 (formerly Egnatía 14), 1st Floor, 546 38 Thessaloníki. Walk-in hours – bring your passport – are Mon–Sat 8.30am–1.30pm, plus Mon, Tue, Thur & Fri 6–8pm. Telephone bookings (English spoken) are accepted on the days indicated 11am–1pm & 6.30–7.30pm, but you will still have to post a copy of your passport front pages, and reconfirm the reservation closer to the intended date. Ten permits per day are issued to foreign non-Orthodox, one hundred daily to Greek Orthodox of whatever nationality. Foreigners should ring ☎861 611; Greek Orthodox ☎833 733.

OTE Ermoú 40, at junction with Karólou Díehl. Open daily 24hr, but only card-phones available.

Post office Main branch (for poste restante and complicated parcel services) is at Aristotélous 26 (Mon–Fri 7.30am–8pm, Sat 7.30am–2.15pm, Sun 9am–1.30pm). There are other post offices around the city: the most useful ones are at Tsimiskí 5, Ethnikís Amýnis 9a and Ayíou Dhimitríou 98.

Records Best of Thessaloníki's various record stores for Greek music are Studio 52, Dhimitríou Goúnari 46, basement, with lots of out-of-print vinyl and cassettes plus well-sorted CDs, and En Chordais, Ippodhromíou 3–4, a traditional music school and instrument shop which also has a well-selected stock of folk and innovative CDs.

Train tickets All services depart from the giant station down on Monastiríou, the southwestern continuation of Egnatía, well served by buses. If you want to buy tickets or make reservations in advance, the OSE office at Aristotélous 18 (Tues–Fri 8am–9pm, Mon & Sat 8am–3pm) is far more central and helpful than the station ticket-windows.

Travel agents Flights out of Thessaloníki are not cheap, but for what they're worth most general sales agents and consolidators cluster around Platía Eleftherías, especially on Kalapotháki, Komninón, Níkis and Mitropóleos. Students and youth travellers should try Nouvelles Frontières at Kalopotháki 8 (☎237 700), Etos at Svólou 44, under the youth hostel (☎263 814), or Sunflight – not just for under-30s – at Tsimiskí 114 (☎280 500). For cheap buses to Turkey, try Bus and Atlantic Tours, Aristotélous 10, 4th Floor (☎226 036). Mountain trekking and other outdoor expeditions are offered by Trekking Hellas, Mitropóleos 60 (☎264 082).

Wine Northern Greece nurtures some fine vineyards, and accordingly Thessaloníki has some excellent bottle-shops affordably selling vintages superior to your average taverna plonk: Iy Tsaritsani, Avyerinoú 9, off Platía Áthonos; Aneroto, Dhimitríou Goúnari 42; and Reklos, Ayíou Dhimitríou 118, cnr Ayías Sofías.

Out from the city

The main weekend escape from Thessaloníki is to the three-pronged Halkidhikí peninsula, but to get to its better beaches requires more than a day-trip. If you just want a respite from the city, or a walk in the hills, consider instead Thessaloníki's own local villages and suburbs. Further out, drivers en route to Néa Moudhaniá can take in the extraordinary cave near Petrálona – though half-day trips with a local tour operator make this a possibility for those without their own transport, too.

Panórama and Hortiátis

On the hillside 11km east of town, **PANÓRAMA**, the closest escape from the city, is exactly what its name suggests: a high, hillside viewpoint looking down over Thessaloníki and the gulf. The original village was razed to the ground by the Germans in retaliation for partisan sabotage during World War II – there's a monument to those burnt alive in the action – and Panórama has been rebuilt with smart villas, coffee shops and a large, modern shopping mall. Of more appeal are a number of cafés, tavernas and zaharoplastía. The best-known of these is *Elenidhi-To Ariston*, which serves up the premier local speciality, *trígona* (custard-filled triangular confections), wonderful *dondurma* (Turkish-style ice cream) and *salépi* (a beverage made from the ground-up root of *Orchis mascula*). The village can be reached by #58 bus from Platía Dhikastiríon, or by taxi (around 1100dr one way).

ANASTENARIÁ: THE FIRE WALKERS OF LANGADHÁS

On May 21, the feast day of Sts Constantine and Helen, villagers at **LANGADHÁS**, 20km north of Thessaloníki, perform a ritual barefoot **dance across a bed of burning coals**. The festival rites are of unknown and strongly disputed origin. It has been suggested that they are remnants of a Dionysiac cult, though devotees assert a purely Christian tradition. This seems to relate to a fire, around 1250, in the Thracian village of Kósti. Holy icons were heard groaning from the flames and were rescued by villagers, who emerged miraculously unburnt from the blazing church. The icons, passed down by their families, are believed to ensure protection during the fire-walking. Equally important is piety and purity of heart: it is said that no one with any harboured grudges or unconfessed sins can pass through the coals unscathed. The Greek Church authorities, however, refuse to sanction any service on the day of the ritual; it has even been accused of planting glass among the coals to try and discredit this "devil's gift".

Whatever the origin, the rite is still performed most years – lately as something of a tourist attraction, with an admission charge and repeat performances over the next two days. It is nevertheless eerie and impressive, beginning around 7pm with the lighting of a cone of hardwood logs. A couple of hours later their embers are raked into a circle and, just before complete darkness, a traditional Macedonian *daoúli* **drummer** and two **lyra players** precede about sixteen women and men into the arena. These *anastenarídhes* (literally "groaners"), in partial trance, then shuffle across the coals for about a quarter of an hour.

During the 1980s, cult members were subjected to various **scientific tests**. The only established clues were that the dancers' brain waves indicate some altered state – when brain activity returns to normal they instinctively left the embers – and that their rhythmical steps maintain minimum skin contact with the fires. There was no suggestion of fraud, however. In 1981 an Englishman jumped into the arena, was badly burnt and had to be rescued by the police from irate devotees and dancers. Between 1991 and 1994, however, the rites failed to take place, owing to continued pressure from the Church and the *anastenarídhes'* own ire at being viewed merely as freak-show attractions. By 1998, however, the event had resumed in public, and if you decide to go, arrive early at Langadhás – by 5.30pm at the latest – in order to get a good seat. Frequent buses ply from a dedicated terminal on Odhós Langadhás in Thessaloníki. Be prepared, too, for the circus-like commercialism, though this in itself can be quite fun.

Other *anastenarídhes* used to "perform" at **Melíki**, near Véria, and at the villages of **Ayía Eléni** and **Áyios Pétros** near Sérres. Crowds, though, were reputed to be just as large and fire-walkers fewer. If you're in Greece, anywhere, and moderately interested, you can catch the show on the ET TV news at 9pm. Their cameramen are at Langadhás, too.

Still more of a retreat is **HORTIÁTIS**, 11km further on (or 16km direct from Thessaloníki), set in an area known as *Hília Dhéndhra* (Thousand Trees), which since ancient times has supplied Thessaloníki with water – you can still see the ruined aqueduct to one side of the road. Hortiátis is accessible on the #61 bus, which meets passengers alighting the #58 at the crossroads where those buses head up to Panoráma. Again, it offers sweeping views over the city, good walking among the pines and some popular places to eat; the *Tsakis* taverna has a well-deserved reputation, so in summer you should reserve tables in advance (☎349 874) to avoid disappointment.

Beaches

To swim near Thessaloníki you need to get well clear of the gulf, where the pollution is all too visible – and odorous. This means heading southwest towards Kateríni and the beaches below Mount Olympus (along the fast, four-land National Road), or southeast towards Halkidhikí.

If all you want is a meal by the sea, then you can take local buses around the gulf. Bus #75 runs to **PERÉA**, 20km from Thessaloníki, a medium-sized weekender resort with good seafront tavernas but brutalist architecture and a rather unpleasant beach. If you fancied a final ocean-view overnight before a flight home, the nominally B-class *Xenia-Ilios* (☎0392/25 551; ④) is the least pricey of three beachfront hotels, and might represent good value – except that it's the training ground for the official tourism academy, so expect haphazard if willing service. Bus #73 serves **AYÍA TRIÁDHA**, 2.5km further west, where there is an EOT **campsite**, the *Akti Thermaïkou* (☎0392/51 360; open all year), rooms to rent and a few more **hotels**, most economical of these the shoreline *Aegean* (☎0392/51 236; ③), though for more comfort go for the *Galaxias* (☎0392/22 291; ⑥), 1km before the centre, which was renovated in 1995.

Bus #69 veers south, via inland Epanomís, to the better strand of **ÓRMOS EPANOMÍS**, 33km from Thessaloníki, although some people prefer to travel on to Néa Kalikrátia before taking to the water. There is a second EOT **campsite** at Órmos Epanomís (☎0392/41 378; April–Oct), more attractive and with more shade than the one at Ayía Triádha.

Petrálona

Fifty kilometres southeast of Thessaloníki is the **cave of Kókkines Pétres** (Red Stones), discovered in 1959 by villagers from nearby **PETRÁLONA** looking for water. Besides an impressive display of stalagmites and stalactites, the villagers – and, later, academics – found the fossilized remains of prehistoric animals and, most dramatic of all, a Neanderthal skull.

The cave, kitted out with dioramas of prehistoric activities and well worth a visit, makes an interesting diversion on the way to or from the Kassándhra peninsula; you'll find the village of Petrálona itself roughly 4km north of Eleohória, on the old road running from Thessaloníki to Néa Moudhaniá at the neck of the peninsula. It's open every day (9am–7pm; may close 5pm in winter; 1500dr) and there's a small café on site, though the museum there is shut indefinitely. *Doucas Tours* in Thessaloníki (Venizélou 8, under the UK consulate) operates a half-day trip.

Pella

PELLA was the capital of Macedonia throughout its greatest period, and the first real capital of Greece after Philip II forcibly unified the country around 338 BC. It was founded some sixty years earlier by King Archelaos, who transferred the royal Macedonian court here from Aigai (see "Veryína", p.406), and from its beginnings it was a major centre of culture. The royal palace was decorated by Zeuxis and said to be the greatest artistic showplace since the time of Classical Athens. Euripides wrote and produced his last plays at the court, and here, too, Aristotle was to tutor the young Alexander the Great – born, like his father Philip II, in the city.

The site today, fringed by the road to Édhessa, is an easy and rewarding day-trip from Thessaloníki. Its main treasures are a series of pebble mosaics, some in the museum, others in situ. For an understanding of the context, it is best to visit after looking around the Archeological Museum at Thessaloníki.

The site

Summer Mon noon–7pm, Tues–Sun 8am–7pm; closes 3pm winter; 1000dr.

When Archelaos founded Pella, it lay at the head of a broad lake, connected to the Thermaïkós Gulf by a navigable river. By the second century BC the river had begun to silt up and the city fell into decline. It was destroyed by the Romans in 146 BC and never rebuilt. Today its **ruins** stand in the middle of a broad expanse of plain, 40km from Thessaloníki and the sea.

Pella was located by chance finds in 1957; preliminary excavations have revealed a vast site covering over 485 hectares. As yet, only a few blocks of the city have been fully excavated but they have proved exciting, and investigations are continuing. The **acropolis** at Pella is a low hill to the west of the modern village of Pélla. Excavation is in progress on a sizable building, probably a palace, but at present it's illuminating mainly for the idea it gives you of the size and scope of the site. To the north of the road, at the main site, stand the low remains of a grand official building, probably a government office; it is divided into three large open courts, each enclosed by a *peristyle*, or portico (the columns of the central one have been re-erected), and bordered by wide streets with a sophisticated drainage system.

The three main rooms of the first court have patterned geometric floors, in the centre of which were found intricate **pebble mosaics** depicting scenes of a lion hunt, a griffin attacking a deer and Dionysos riding a panther. These are now in the **museum** across the road (same hours as site; separate 1000dr admission). But in the third court three late fourth-century BC mosaics have been left in situ under sheltering canopies; one, a stag hunt, is complete, and astounding in its dynamism and use of perspective. The others represent, respectively, the rape of Helen by Paris and his friends Forvas and Theseus, and a fight between a Greek and an Amazon.

It is the graceful and fluid quality of these compositions that sets them apart from later Roman and Byzantine mosaics, and which more than justifies a visit. The uncut pebbles, carefully chosen for their soft shades, blend so naturally that the shapes and movements of the subjects seem gradated rather than fixed, especially in the action of the hunting scenes and the rippling movement of the leopard with Dionysos. Strips of lead or clay are used to outline special features; the eyes, all now missing, were probably semiprecious stones.

The mosaics are inevitably a hard act to follow, but the museum merits another half-hour of perusal for the sake of its other well-presented exhibits. Highlights include rich grave finds from the two local necropolises, delicately worked terracotta figurines from a sanctuary of Aphrodite and Cybele, a large horde of late Classical/early Hellenistic coins, and – on the rarely seen domestic level – metal door fittings: pivots, knocker plates and crude keys.

Getting there

Pella is easiest reached from Thessaloníki. Just take any of the Édhessa **buses**, which run more or less half-hourly through the day and stop by the Pella museum. If you arrive late and want to stay, the nearest **hotel** is at Halkidhóna, 8km east on the road back to Thessaloníki: the *Kornílios* (☎0391/23 888; ②).

Continuing **to Aigai/Veryína** by public transport, you'll need to get a bus, or walk, back down the Thessaloníki road to the junction at Halkidhóna. From here you can pick up Thessaloníki–Véria buses.

Dion

Ancient **DION**, in the foothills of Mount Olympus, was the Macedonians' sacred city. At this site – a harbour before the river mouth silted up – the kingdom maintained its principal sanctuaries: to Zeus (from which the name *Dion*, or *Dios*, is derived) above all, but also to Demeter, Artemis, Asclepius and, later, to foreign gods such as the Egyptians Isis and Serapis. Philip II and Alexander both came to sacrifice to Zeus here before their expeditions. Inscriptions found at the sanctuaries referring to boundary

disputes, treaties and other affairs of state suggest that the political and social importance of the city's festivals exceeded a purely Macedonian domain.

Most exciting for visitors, however, are the finds of mosaics, temples and baths that
have been excavated since 1990 – work that remains in progress whenever funds allow.
These are not quite on a par with the Veryína tombs, but still rank among the major discoveries of ancient Macedonian history and culture. If you are heading for Mount
Olympus, they are certainly worth a half-day detour. At the village of **DHIÓN** (formerly
Malathiriá), 7km inland from Litóhoro beach or reached by #14 bus from Kateríni, take
a side-road 400m east from the *Hotel Dion*, past the remains of a **theatre**, put to good
use during the summer Olympus Festival. The main **site** lies ahead (summer daily
8am–7pm; winter closes 5pm; 1600dr). The integrity of the site and its finds is due to
the nature of the city's demise. At some point in the fifth century AD, a series of earthquakes prompted an evacuation of Dion, which was then swallowed up by a mudslide
from the mountain. The place is still quite waterlogged, and constant pumping against
the local aquifer is necessary. The main visible excavations are of the vast **public baths**
complex and, outside the city **walls**, the **sanctuaries** of Demeter and Aphrodite-Isis. In
the latter a small temple has been unearthed, along with its cult statue – a copy of which
remains in situ. The finest mosaics so far discovered lie in a former banquet room; they
depict the god Dionysos on a chariot, but owing to a badly designed protective canopy
and walkways are scarcely visible. Two Christian **basilicas** attest to the town's later
years as a Byzantine bishopric in the fourth and fifth centuries AD. An observation platform allows you to view the layout of the site more clearly.

Back in the village, a large but badly labelled **museum** (Mon 12.30–7pm, Tues–Fri
8am–2pm, Sat–Sun 8am–2.30pm; winter Mon–Fri closes at 5pm; 1600dr) houses most
of the finds. The sculpture, perfectly preserved by the mud, is impressive, and accompanied by various tombstones and altars. In the basement sprawls a fine mosaic of
Medusa, off-limits but adequately viewed down through the stairwell. Upstairs, along
with extensive displays of pottery and coinage, is a collection of everyday items, including surgical and dental tools perhaps connected with the sanctuary of Asclepius, the
healing god. Pride of place, however, goes to the remains of a first-century BC pipe
organ, discovered in 1992 and exhibited on the upper storey.

There is now a direct, signposted, paved road between Dion and Litóhoro (see
below), crossing a formerly out-of-bounds army firing range; in Litóhoro, this diverges
from the road heading up the mountain. If you want to **stay overnight**, the *Hotel Dion*
stands at the crossroads by the bus stop (☎0351/53 682; ④), 100m below the museum;
on the pedestrian street linking the two are a few tavernas firmly pitched at the tourist
trade. The nearest campsites are on the beach at Varikó, 11km away: *Stani* (☎0352/61
277) and *Niteas* (☎0352/61 290), both open all year round.

Mount Olympus (Óros Ólymbos)

The highest, most magical and most dramatic of all Greek mountains, **Mount
Olympus** – *Ólymbos* in Greek – rears straight up nearly 3000 metres from the shores
of the Thermaïkos Gulf. Dense forests cover its lower slopes, and its **wildflowers** are
without parallel even by Greek standards. To make the most of it, you need to allow two
to three days' hiking.

Equipped with decent boots and warm clothing, no special expertise is necessary to
get to the top in summer (mid-June – Oct), though it's a long hard pull requiring a good
deal of stamina; winter climbs, of course, are another matter. At any time of year
Olympus is a mountain to be treated with respect: its weather is notoriously fickle and
it regularly claims lives.

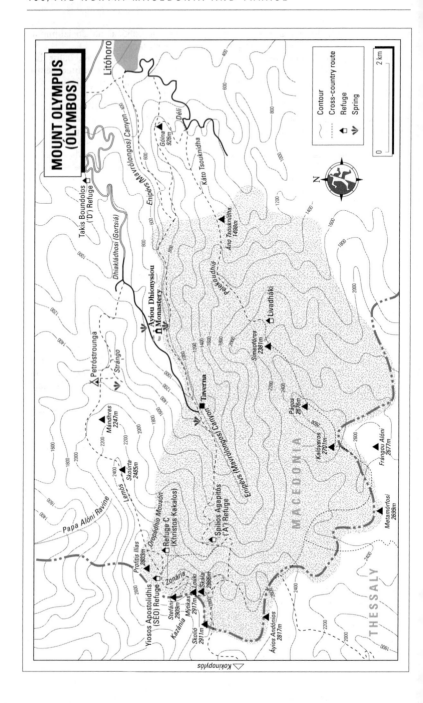

MOUNT OLYMPUS
(ÓLYMBOS)

Contour
Cross-country route
Refuge
Spring

2 km

N

MACEDONIA

THESSALY

Litóhoro

Gólna 926m

Káto Tsouknidha

Déli

Enipévs (Mavrólongos) Canyon

Ano Tsouknídha 1498m

Takis Boundolos ('D') Refuge

Dhiakládhosi (Gortsiá)

Ayíou Dhionysíou Monastery

Palea Loudhiá

Livadháki

Petróstrounga

Strángo

Taverna

Simandíros 2381m

Mandhres 2247m

Skoúrta 2485m

Págos 2676m

Lemós

Kalóyeros 2701m

Dhromého Mousón

Papa Alóni Ravine

Refuge C (Khrístos Kakálos)

Spílios Agapitós ('A') Refuge

Enipévs (Mavrólongos) Canyon

Frángou Alóni 2677m

Metamórfosi 2699m

Profítis Ilías 2800m

Yíosos Apostolídhis (SEO) Refuge

Zonária

Loúki

Stefáni 2909m

Skála 2866m

Kazánia Mýtikas 2917m

Skolió 2911m

Ayios Andónios 2817m

Kokinopilós

Litóhoro and Olympus practicalities

The best base for a walk up the mountain is the deceptively large village of **LITÓHORO** on the eastern side. An intrinsically dull garrison town with two huge army camps on the approach road, its setting in good weather affords intoxicating dawn-of-climb views into the heart of the range. Reaching Litóhoro is fairly easy. There's a train station 9km distant on the coast, from where there are more or less hourly buses (or taxis late at night); you can get the same bus direct from Thessaloníki or the market town of Kateríni.

The Litóhoro youth hostel has closed down, its old niche occupied either by *dhomátia* (①) available through the management of the *Psistaria Olympos* on the main square, those of Papanikolaou (☎0352/81 236; ②) or the exceedingly plain but converted-to-ensuite *Park* at Ayíou Nikoláou 23 (☎0352/81 252; ②), near the bottom of town. It's worth a bit extra for better, quieter **hotels**. The *Markissia* at Dhionýsou 5 (☎0352/81 831; ②), just down from 28-Oktovríou, is good value, though singles are tiny; if it's unattended, enquire at the novelty shop nearby. At the newish, spotless *Enipeís* (☎0352/81 328; ③), on the main square near the National Bank, first-floor rear rooms have the best views in town; attic rooms with skylight only are cheaper. Immediately opposite stands the *Aphrodite* (☎0352/81 415; ③) with only averagely clean rooms, few of which have any view. During spring or autumn, there's little price difference between Litóhoro hotels, so you may as well plump for the *Myrto* on Ayíou Nikoláou, just downhill from the main square (☎0352/81 398, fax 82 298; ③), open all year and considered the best accommodation here.

As for **eating**, there's a rash of fast-food places in the square and down Ayíou Nikoláou, but along the uphill side streets, there are more attractive possibilities, such as the *Ouzeri Manos* at 28-Oktovríou 3, just down from the **post office** at no. 11, with a limited menu of seafood titbits; or the *Dhamaskinia*, on Vasiléos Konstandínou. At the start of the road up the mountain, literally above the SEO office, are two cheap-and-cheerful, sit-down grill houses – the *Zeus* in particular has passed muster. For sustenance while walking, you'll need to buy food in Litóhoro, though water can wait until you're at the vicinity of either of two trailheads (see below).

Accommodation **on Olympus** itself is better organized than on any other mountain in Greece. There are two staffed **refuges**: the EOS-run *Spilios Agapitos* at 2100m (open May 15–Oct 15; ☎0352/81 800, reservations recommended in summer), commonly known as Refuge "A", and the SEO-managed *Yiosos Apostolidhis* hut at 2700m (open only July–Sept, though its glassed-in porch is always available for climbers in need). There is no set phone number for this refuge, since the wardenship is often in a state of flux; contact the SEO information office in Litóhoro at ☎0352/82 300 (evenings only). Both currently charge around 2500dr for a bunk (you can camp at Refuge "A" for 700dr, using their bathroom), with lights out and outer door locked at 10pm. Meals at either shelter are relatively expensive, and mandatory since no cooking is allowed inside; bring more money than you think you'll require, as bad weather can ground you a day or two longer than planned. Both the *Ethniki/National* and *Emboriki/Commercial* **banks** in Litóhoro have cash dispensers.

This guide contains all the intelligence you need to head up the mountain immediately on arrival if you so desire, since **information** sources in Litóhoro can be patchy. EOS (summer only Mon–Fri 9.30am–12.30pm & 6.30–8.30pm, Sat 9am–noon) maintains a well-signposted office 200m west of the *Hotel Myrto*, but they've no set hours off-season, and their free leaflet is quite useless. Rival club SEO is tucked away along the road to the national park, just 50m along, behind and below the grills cited above, and opens only in the evenings. The best, most easily available commercial **trekking map** is Road Editions' no. 31 "Olymbos" at 1:50,000, available from specialist map shops abroad or in Athens or Thessaloníki; a good alternative is one of the same scale that is co-produced by *Korfes* magazine and EOS. One or other is occasionally available at a shop on Ayíou Nikólaou opposite the start of the Ólymbos road, but best not count on this.

The mountain

To reach alpine Olympus, you've a choice of road or foot routes. With your own vehicle, you can **drive** deep into the mountain along a fairly decent road, the first 11km of which is now paved – with the same treatment planned soon for the remainder. There is an information booth at Km3, where (in high season anyway) your nationality is recorded and you're given some literature advising you of the park rules, but so far there's no admission charge. Conservationists have agitated for a total ban on private vehicles within the park, and all told it is much better to **walk** in from Litóhoro, as far as the monastery of Ayíou Dhionysíou, and beyond to the two trailheads following.

As for the final **ascent routes**, there are two main paths: one beginning at Priónia, just under 18km up the mountain at the road's end, where a primitive, summer-only taverna operates by toilets, and the spring; the other at a spot called Dhiakládhosi or Gortsiá (13km along), marked by a signboard displaying a map of the range. The Priónia path is more frequented and more convenient, the Dhiakládhosi trail longer but more beautiful. A 1800-metre driveway, appearing on the main road at 15.5km (about halfway between the two trailheads), leads down to Ayíou Dhionysíou. At the spot called Stavrós, 9km above Litóhoro, there's a third **refuge** (really a roadhouse, officially called *Takis Boundolos*; ☎0352/84 519), but it's not conspicuously welcoming and usually booked up, though it does have the highest card-phone on the mountain.

The Mavrólongos canyon and Ayíou Dhionysíou monastery

Some years ago the Greek overland-trail committee rehabilitated old paths in the superlatively beautiful Mavrólongos (Enipévs) river canyon to make a fine section of the **E4 overland trail**, thus sparing hikers the drudgery of walking up the road or the expense of a taxi. Black-on-yellow diamond markers begin near Litóhoro's central platía; follow road signs for Mýli and bear down and right at the cemetery. Once out of town, waymarks lead you along a rollercoaster course by the river for four hours to Ayíou Dhionysíou. It's a delightful route, but you'll need basic hiking skills as there are some scrambles over steep terrain, and a few water crossings.

The **monastery** itself was burned by the Germans in 1943 for allegedly harbouring anti-occupation guerrillas, and the surviving monks, rather than rebuilding, relocated to new premises near Litóhoro. After years of dereliction and vandalism, Ayíou Dhionysíou is undergoing a snail's-pace restoration; so far the *katholikón* has been re-erected, though 1.5 billion drachmas more are needed for the rest. If you ask the resident warden, Father Anthimios, nicely and contribute your mite to the deficit, you may stay in any vacant ground-floor cells (iron bedsteads). There's potable water just outside, much used by people camping along the riverbanks below the perimeter wall (tolerated despite falling within national park territory), though you may have to contend with wild boar, reintroduced locally by Greek ecologists.

From Ayíou Dhionysíou it's just under an hour more upstream along the riverside E4 to Priónia, or slightly less up the driveway and then east to the Dhiakládhosi trailhead.

The ascent from Priónia

The E4 carries on just uphill from the taverna, by an EOS signpost giving the time to the refuge as two hours thirty minutes (allow 3hr). You cross a stream (last water before the *Spilios Agapitos* refuge, purification advisable) and start to climb steeply up through woods of beech and black pine. This path, the continuation of the E4, is well trodden and marked, so there is no danger of getting lost. As you gain height there are majestic views across the Mavrólongos ravine to your left and to the peaks towering above you.

The *Spilios Agapitos* **refuge** perches on the edge of an abrupt spur, surrounded by huge storm-beaten trees. The resident warden runs a tight ship, and you need to let him know in good time if you want a meal and a bed. It's best to stay overnight here, as you should make an early start for the three-hour ascent to Mýtikas, the highest peak at 2917m. The peaks frequently cloud up by midday and you lose the view, to say nothing of the danger of catching one of Zeus's thunderbolts, for this was the mythical seat of the gods. Besides, nights at the refuge are fantastic: a log fire blazes; you watch the sun set on the peaks, and dawn break over the Aegean; there are billions of stars.

The summit area

The E4 path continues behind the refuge (the last water source on the mountain), climbing to the left up a steep spur among the last of the trees. Having ignored an initial right fork towards the usually unstaffed *Khristos Kakalos* hut (Refuge "C"), within an hour you reach a signposted **fork** above the treeline. Straight on takes you across the range to Kokkinopylós village with the E4 waymarks, or with a slight deviation right to Mýtikas, via the ridge known as Kakí Skála (1hr 30min). An immediate right turn leads to the *Yiosos Apostolidhis* hut in one hour along the so-called Zonária trail, with the option after forty minutes of taking the very steep Loúki couloir left up to Mýtikas; if you do this, be wary of rockfalls.

For the safer **Kakí Skála route**, continue up the right flank of the stony featureless valley in front of you, with the Áyios Andónios peak up to your left. An hour's dull climb brings you to the summit ridge between the peaks of Skolió on the left and Skála on the right. You know you're there when one more step would tip you over a 500-metre sheer drop into the Kazánia chasm; take great care. The Kakí Skála (Evil Stairway) begins in a narrow cleft on the right just short of the ridge; paint splashes mark the way. The route keeps just below the ridge, so you are protected from the drop into Kázania. Even so, those who don't like heights are likely to be reduced to a whimpering crouch.

You start with a slightly descending rightward traverse to a narrow nick in the ridge revealing the drop to Kazánia – easily negotiated. Continue traversing right, skirting the base of the Skála peak, then climb leftwards up a steepish gully made a little awkward by loose rock on sloping footholds. Bear right at the top over steep but reassuringly solid rock, and across a narrow neck. Step left around an awkward corner and there in front of you, scarcely a hundred metres away, is **Mýtikas summit**, an airy, boulder-strewn platform with a trigonometric point, tin Greek flag and visitors' book. In reasonable conditions it's about forty minutes to the summit from the start of Káki Skála; three hours from the refuge; five and a half hours from Prióna.

A stone's throw to the north of Mýtikas is the **Stefáni peak**, also known as the Throne of Zeus, a bristling hog's back of rock with a couple of nastily exposed moves to scale the last few feet.

Descending from Mýtikas, you can either go back the way you came, with the option of turning left at the signpost (see above) for the *Yiosos Apostolidhis* hut (2hr 30min from Mýtikas by this route), or you can step out, apparently into space, in the direction of Stefáni and turn immediately down to the right into the mouth of the Loúki couloir. It takes about forty minutes of downward scrambling to reach the main path where you turn left for the hut, skirting the impressive northeast face of Stefáni (1hr), or go right, back to the familiar signpost and down the E4 to *Spilios Agapitos* (2hr altogether).

The ascent from Dhiakládhosi (Gortsiá)

Starting from the small parking area beyond the information placard, take the narrow path going up and left via faint steps – with a wood railing and wooden awning – not the forest track heading down and right. An hour along, you reach the meadow of **Bárba**, and two hours out you'll arrive at a messy junction with a modern water tank and various placards – take left forks en route when given the choice. The signs point hard left to the spring at **Strángo**; right for the direct path to Petróstrounga; and straight on for the old, more scenic way to **Petróstrounga**, passed some two and a half hours along.

Beyond this summer pastoral colony, there's an indicated right, then the trail wanders up to the base of **Skoúrta** knoll (4hr 15min), above the treeline. After crossing the Lemós (Neck) ridge dividing the Papá Alóni and Mavrólongos ravines, with spectacular views into both, five and a quarter hours should see you up on the Oropédhio Musón (Plateau of the Muses), five and a half hours to the *Apostolidhis* refuge, visible the last fifteen minutes. But you should count on seven hours, including rests, for this route; going down takes about four and a half hours, a highly recommended descent if you've come up from Priónia.

It takes about an hour, losing altitude, to traverse the onward Zonária path linking *Apostolidhis* and the E4, skimming the base of the peaks – about the same time as coming the other way as described above.

The southern ridge route

To experience complete solitude on Olympus, continue past Áyios Andónios, the peak just south of Skála and the E4 trail, and begin to ridge-walk the line of peaks that bounds the Mavrólongos to the south. Much of this trek past Metamórfosi, Kalóyeros, and Págos summits is cross-country, but with the recommended map, route-finding is easy on a clear day. It's six and a half walking hours from the *Apostolidhis* hut to the dilapidated but serviceable, unstaffed shelter at **Livadháki**, with unreliable cistern water only – you'll need to carry at least a couple litres in with you. From Livadháki a good trail descends via the ridges of Pelekoudhiá and Tsouknídha, coming out three and a quarter hours on at the meadow of **Déli**, where you're just above a forest road which leads 7km down to Litóhoro.

Alternatively, a faint but followable trail at Déli (on our map, but not on the Road Editions or EOS products) dips down into a ravine and up onto **Gólna** knoll, intersecting another, sporadically marked path up from Litóhoro that leads over into the Mavrólongos watershed to join up with the E4. Just above the junction woodcutters have rather messed up the path, but persevere, and you'll suddenly drop down on to the E4 about halfway along its course, some ninety minutes out of Déli. This last section makes a beautiful, if challenging walk.

Véria and Veryína

The broad agricultural plain extending west from Thessaloníki eventually collides with an abrupt, wooded escarpment, at the panoramic edge of which several towns have grown up. The largest of these, **Véria**, has few particular sites or monuments, but it is one of the more interesting northern Greek communities and lies within twenty minutes' drive of the excavations of ancient Aigai at **Veryína**.

Véria

Visitors to **VÉRIA** arriving by bus (the **train station** is hopelessly inconvenient, 3km east of the centre) will traipse south along Odhós Venizélou from the main **KTEL** to the point where the street splits. Odhós Elías, a short but fashionable thoroughfare, leads briefly south from this point to the Belvedere, the escarpment view-park to reintersect Venizélou, where Odhós Anixéos snakes north along the cliff edge, past Véria's most prestigious district. En route Anixéos passes the **archeological museum** (daily except Mon

8.30am–3pm; 500dr), which has no finds from Veryína (see below), but contains mostly Roman oddments from the immediate area. Partly pedestrianized, one-way **Mitropóleos** heads west from the triple junction towards the central Platía Konstandínou Ráktivan – universally called **Platía Oroloyíou**, after a long-vanished clocktower – passing on its way the **post office** on side-street Dhionysíou Solomoú, various banks (with cash dispensers) and the new cathedral. On the far western side of Platía Oroloyíou is a separate, small KTEL terminal for Kozáni and Thessaloníki services.

The twelfth-century **old cathedral**, opposite a gnarled plane tree from which the conquering Turks hanged the town's archbishop in 1430, is just off Odhós Vassiléos Konstandínou (better known as Odhós **Kendrikís**), which links Venizélou and Platía Ráktivan. Near the tree, what remains of the old **bazaar** straddles Kendrikís; downhill and to the northwest tumbles the riverside Ottoman quarter of **Barboúta** or Barboúti. Largely **Jewish** before the 1943 deportations annihilated the 850-strong community, it is today largely abandoned, though EU-funded restoration of the crumbling houses – many bearing Hebrew inscriptions – is proceeding apace. The disused **synagogue** here can be reached either along pedestrianized Odhós Sófou, or via Odhós Dhekátis Merarhías, another stepped lane taking off from behind the yellow officers' club up on Platía Oroloyíou. When you reach a plaza with a small amphitheatre, look for a long stone building, partly ochre-painted with an awning over the door, which is usually ajar to permit a look at the rambling, arcaded interior. Survivals of the **Muslim** presence in Véria are more numerous and more conspicuous: a wonderful *hamam* complex on Loutroú, west of Mitropóleos; a minaret tacked onto the old cathedral; a small mosque on Kendrikís; and a larger one on Márkou Bótsari, just south of Platía Oroloyíou.

Christianity has a venerably long history here: St Paul preached in Véria (Acts 17:1–13) on two occasions, and a gaudy alcove shrine at the base of Mavromiháli marks the supposed spot of his sermons. But the town is more famous for sixty or so small medieval **churches**, mostly dating from the sixteenth to eighteenth century. In order to avoid offending Muslim sensibilities, they were once disguised as barns or warehouses, with little dormer windows rather than domes to admit light; but today, often surrounded by cleared spaces and well labelled, they are not hard to find. They are, however, generally locked, only viewable (with a good scholarly reason) by application to the 11th Ephorate of Byzantine Antiquities. The only church regularly open is **Khristós** (daily except Mon 8.30am–3pm; free), with cleaned fourteenth-century frescoes, near the lower end of Mitropóleos. The most striking images here are a *Dormition/Assumption* over the west door; a *Metamórfosis (Transfiguration)* on the south wall, with one disciple somersaulting backwards in fear; and on the north wall a rare image of Christ mounting the Cross on a ladder. The key-keeper may offer to show you the nearby tenth-century chapel of **Kýrikos and Ioulíta**, but its frescoes are alas uncleaned and likely to remain so, since churches in Kastoriá and Kozáni provinces seem to have priority in this respect.

Practicalities

There are just a bare handful of **hotels** scattered across Véria, generally overpriced and/or noisy in typical mainland fashion. The least expensive is the en-suite *Veroi* at Kendrikís 4, just off Platía Oroloyíou (☎0331/22 866; ④), adequate and clean. Your two upmarket choices are the *Villa Elia*, Elías 16 (☎0331/26 800, fax 21 880; ⑤), but prone to street noise, and the *Makedonia*, Kondoyeorgáki 50 (☎ & fax 0331/66 902; ⑤), far enough past the bars (see below) for nocturnal peace, with a roof garden and substantial breakfasts.

Restaurants in Véria are rather better than its accommodation, and constitute ample excuse for a meal stop. An excellent lunch choice is *Sarafopoulos* at Kendrikís 16, with cheap but hygienic *mayireftá*; more elaborate are a pair of ouzeris, *Skholarhio/To Steki tou Goulara* and *Nikos*, opposite each other on pedestrianized

Patriárhou Ioakeím, 100m downhill from Mitropóleos. *Skholarhio* in particular is friendly and appetizing, with grilled quail and vegetarian *mezédhes* on offer from Mr Goularas. This lane is the focus of another old quarter finally getting the attention it deserves, most conspicuously in the form of nocturnal café/bars installed in the old Ottoman houses. For supper, an enduring favourite is *Kostalar* (shut Mon) in Papákia district at Afrodhítis 2/D, reached by following Mavromiháli uphill from the St Paul shrine to a plane-tree-shaded square with rivulets; this place has been going since 1939, offering clay-pot oven dishes and grills. Another popular nocturnal venue is the *Ouzeri Yiaze stin Petra*, on Anixéos as it heads downhill from the tourist pavilion, corner Koundourióti; not the most inspired location, but consistently good grills and appetizers since the late 1980s.

By day, by far the most pleasant place for a coffee is the normally priced tourist pavilion at the edge of the Belvedere, with its shady terrace overlooking the plain (though meals here are not recommended). In the same area, *Kamelot* on Anixéos, opposite the church near Odhós Pastér, is a quiet café/bar, popular with a broad spectrum of Veriots, with a shady courtyard and upstairs rooms for playing *távli*. If you crave more action **after dark**, a pedestrianized area west of Mitropóleos, crammed full with noisy *barákia* installed in restored Ottoman houses, comes into its own. Most of these clubs are on Kondoyeorgáki, heading downhill from the Khristós church, and its perpendicular Éllis. Obviously you'll choose on the basis of crowd, decor, music and simply where you can squeeze in, as management and format change regularly; at any given time several claim to be Internet cafés.

Veryína: ancient Aigai

Excavations at **VERYÍNA**, 13km southeast of Véria, have revolutionized Macedonian archeology since the 1970s. A series of chamber tombs, unearthed here by Professor Manolis Andronikos (1919–92), are now unequivocally accepted as those of Philip II and other members of the Macedonian royal family. This means that the site itself must be that of **Aigai**, the original Macedonian royal capital before the shift to Pella, and later its necropolis. Finds from the site and tombs, the richest Greek trove since the discovery of Mycenae, are exhibited on the spot, as well as (to a diminished extent) at Thessaloníki's archeological museum. The main tombs are displayed in situ; visitors walk down narrow underground passages into a climate-controlled bunker which allows them to see the ornamental facades and the empty chambers beyond. Overhead, the earth of the tumulus has been replaced.

Until recently the modern village of Veryína had limited facilities, but with the advent of tourism two reasonable **tavernas** have opened in the village centre, as has a **cash dispenser** booth and foreign-note changer. There's also decent **accommodation** on the northeast edge of things, conveniently near the stop for Véria-bound buses: *Pension Sofia Hatziagapidou* (☎0331/92 510 or 25 703; ④), en-suite rooms with fans and balconies, plus copious breakfast included in the price.

The sites

Tues–Sun 8am–7pm, Mon 12.30–7pm; closes 5pm winter; 1500dr includes excellent handout.

Ancient Aigai is documented as the sanctuary and royal burial place of the Macedonian kings. It was here that Philip II was assassinated and buried – and tradition maintained that the dynasty would be destroyed if any king were buried elsewhere, as indeed happened after the death of Alexander the Great in Asia. Until Andronikos's finds in November 1977 – the culmination of decades of work on the site – Aigai had long been assumed to be lost beneath modern Édhessa, a theory now completely discarded.

THE ROYAL TOMBS

What Andronikos discovered, under a tumulus just outside modern Veryína, were several large and indisputably Macedonian chamber tombs, identified as the **Royal Tombs**. From outside, all that's visible is a low hillock with skylights and long ramps leading inside, but once underground the facades and doorways of the several tombs are well illuminated, behind glass.

You're meant to tour the four tombs in the order IV-I-II-III. Tomb IV, the so-called "Doric", was looted in antiquity; so too was **Tomb I**, that of **"Persephone"**, but it retained a delicate and exquisitely crafted mural of the rape of Persephone by Hades, the only complete example of an ancient Greek painting that has yet been found. **Tomb II**, confidently identified as that of **Philip II**, is a much grander vaulted tomb with a Doric facade adorned by a sumptuous painted frieze of Philip, Alexander and their retinue on a lion hunt. This – incredibly – was intact, having been deliberately disguised with rubble from later tomb pillagings. Among the treasures to emerge – now displayed in the dimly lit but well-labelled hall here – were a marble sarcophagus containing a gold *larnax* or ossuary, its cover embossed with the exploding, eight-point-star symbol of the royal line on its lid, a symbol now harnessed irrevocably to the Greek-nationalist juggernaut. Still more significantly, five small ivory heads were found, among them representations of both Philip II and Alexander. It was this clue, as well as the fact that the skull bore marks of a disfiguring facial wound Philip was known to have sustained, that led to the identification of the tomb as his. Also on view is the famous gold oak-leaf wreath, and a more modest companion *larnax* found in the antechamber, presumed to contain the carefully wrapped bones and ashes of a legitimate queen or concubine.

Tomb III is thought to be that of Alexander IV, "the Great's" son, murdered in adolescence – thus the moniker **"Prince's Tomb"**. His bones were discovered in a silver vase. From the tomb frieze, a superb miniature of Dionysos and his consort is highlighted.

MACEDONIAN TOMB AND PALATÍTSA PALACE

The so-called **"Macedonian Tomb"**, actually five adjacent tombs, can also be visited after a fashion (same times as above; same admission ticket). They are about 500m uphill and south of the village and, like the Royal Tombs, lie well below the modern ground level, protected by a vast tin roof. When he's around, the guard will let you into the dig, though not into the tombs themselves. Excavated by the French in 1861, the most prominent one, thought to be that of Philip's mother Eurydike, has the form of a temple, with an Ionic facade of half-columns breached by two successive marble portals opening onto ante- and main chambers. Inside you can just make out an imposing marble throne with sphinxes carved on the sides, armrests and footstool. The neighbouring two pairs of tombs, still under slow-motion excavation, are said to be similar in design.

On a slope southeast of the village, across a ravine and 1km by road beyond the main village crossroads and a vast new car park, the ruins of the **Palace of Palatítsa** (daily summer 8am–7pm; 500dr) occupy a low hill. This complex was probably built during the third century BC as a summer residence for the last great Macedonian king, Antigonus Gonatus. It is now little more than foundations, but amidst the confusing litter of column drums and capitals you can make out a triple *propylaion* (entrance gate) opening onto a central courtyard. This is framed by broad porticoes and colonnades which, on the south side, preserve a well-executed mosaic now, alas, invisible under protective sand and gravel following frost damage. Despite its lack of substance Palatítsa is an attractive site, dominated by a grand old oak tree looking out across the plains, scattered with Iron Age (tenth- to seventh-century BC) tumuli and who knows what else. The only substantial items dug up to date are the first two tiers of the **theatre** just below, where Philip II was assassinated in 336 BC, some say at the wedding of his daughter.

Édhessa, Lefkádhia and Náoussa

With your own vehicle, the other two escarpment towns can be easily and enjoyably toured in a day or less, with an unspoilt archeological site – Lefkádhia – in between. Travelling by public transport, however, especially by train, stopping off is time-consuming and probably more trouble than it's worth – in which case Édhessa, astride the main route between Thessaloníki and the far west of Macedonia, is the place you're most likely to halt.

Édhessa

ÉDHESSA, like Véria, makes a pleasant brief stopover, its modest fame attributed to the waters that flow through the town. Descending from the mountains to the north, they flow swiftly through the middle of town in several courses and then, just to the east, cascade down a dramatic ravine, luxuriant with vegetation, to the plain below. From the train station, walk straight for 400m until you see the main branch of the walled-in river, paralleled by Tsimiskí street. Turn left and you will come to the **water-falls**, focus of a park with a couple of cafés. For the **Byzantine bridge**, turn right from here and follow the river for about 600 metres. Paths also lead down the ravine, providing access to caves below the waterfalls.

The town itself is a little ordinary, but the various streamside parks and wide pedestrian pavements are a rare pleasure in a country where the car is tyrant – indeed, Édhessa was the pioneering town in Greece for pedestrianization – and the train and bus stations are both well placed for breaking a journey. The **train station** is at the north end of 18-Oktovríou. The main **KTEL** is on the corner of Filíppou and Pávlou Melá (you follow Filíppou north into the centre); there's a second, smaller terminal for Flórina/Kastória services only, nearby at the corner of Egnatía and Pávlou Melá. Map placards placed at critical intersections facilitate navigation; the **post office** is on Dhimokratías, while three **banks** – Ethniki/National, Emboriki/Commercial and Alpha Pisteos/Credit – sport cash dispensers.

For **accommodation**, choose between the slightly shabby but adequate and friendly *Pella*, Egnatia 26–30 (☎0381/23 541, ③ en-suite, ② not), or the more comfortable and air-conditioned *Alfa*, virtually next door at no. 36 (☎0381/22 221; ④); quieter but less friendly is the air-conditioned *Elena* on Dhimitríou Rízou 4, corner Platía Timenídhon (☎0381/23 218; ④), whose management (unlike the others) may refuse to bargain at slack times. All three hotels are a five-minute walk from the two KTEL terminals. Closer to the train station, and best of the town's hotels, is *Katarraktes* (☎0381/22 300, fax 27 237; ⑤), perched as the name suggests near the waterfalls. **Restaurants** aren't numerous, but there's enough choice for a short stay; very close to the more modest hotels are *To Roloï* Ayíos Dhimitríou 5, good for *mayireftá*, and *O Pavlos* beyond the clocktower at Péllis 8, fine for grills and mezédhes. **Café** and **bar** life happens on the pedestrian zones flanking the rivulets, especially on Angelí Gátsou. The *Ilektra*, opposite the *Pella* and *Alfa* hotels, is one of the few places offering a sit-down **breakfast** of both coffee and pastries.

Lefkádhia

Thirty kilometres south of Édhessa on the road to Véria, Lefkádhia has not been positively identified with any Macedonian city, but it is thought possibly to have been Mieza, where Aristotle taught. The modern village of **LEFKÁDHIA** lies just west of the main road, but you should turn off east at a sign reading "To the Macedonian Tombs". There are, in fact, four subterranean tombs in all – though only one has a guard, who keeps the keys to the other three.

The staffed one, the so-called **Great Tomb** or **Tomb of Judgement** (closed for restoration), east of the main road just past the train tracks, is the largest Macedonian temple-tomb yet discovered. Despite extensive cement protection, it has been so badly damaged by creeping damp from the very high local water table that extensive consolidation works are underway, probably involving its complete dismantling and reconstruction. It dates from the third century BC, and was probably built for a general, depicted on the left, in one of the barely surviving frescoes, being led by Hermes in his role of conductor of souls. Other faded frescoes on the right represent the judges of Hades – hence the tomb's alias. A once-elaborate double-storeyed facade, half Doric and half Ionic, has almost completely crumbled away; on the entablature frieze you can barely make out a battle between Persians and Macedonians.

The **Anthimíon Tomb**, 150m further along the same country road, is more impressive, with its four Ionic facade columns, two marble interior sarcophagi with inscribed lids, and well-preserved frescoes. The tympanum bears portraits of a couple, presumably the tomb occupants, though the man's face has been rubbed out. Ornamental designs and three giant *akrokerámata* (cornice ornaments) complete the pediment decoration. Between the double set of portals, the ceiling frescoes are perhaps stylized representations of octopuses and other water creatures.

The other two local tombs are of essentially specialist interest. The one signposted "Kinch's Macedonian Tomb", after the Dane who discovered it, is on the east side of the main road, on the way back towards the village. The tomb of **Lyson-Kallikles** is signposted west of the main road, before the turning to the village, at the end of a one-kilometre dirt track through peach orchards; to visit, you have lower yourself through a usually locked grating in the ceiling, the original entrance having been long since buried.

Náoussa

Four kilometres south of the tombs is a turning west, off the main road, to **NÁOUSSA**, a small country town whose vintners, the **Boutari** company, produce some of Greece's best wines, and whose mills turn out vast numbers of brightly coloured acrylic blankets for the nation's hotels. Along with Véria, the town is also at the heart of the country's main peach-growing region – excuse enough for at least a stop in July – and hosts one of Macedonia's most elaborate pre-Lenten carnivals. That said, Náoussa is generally the least distinguished of the three escarpment towns – a pleasant enough place to live but not necessarily to holiday at. In winter, however, Náoussa is very busy with Greeks enjoying the two excellent ski centres overhead on Mount Vérmion.

If you do drop in, the big attraction is the parkland of **Áyios Nikólaos**, 4km beyond town (itself 6km west of the main road), an oasis of giant plane trees nourished by the streams that bubble from the earth here. Most of the space is filled by a fun-fair and go-kart track, such attractions swarmed over by school-groups during the week, all and sundry at weekends. The riverbanks are additionally lined with several more or less identically priced tavernas featuring farm-raised trout (the *Nisaki* is the most pleasantly set). Just upstream, the *Hotel Vermion* (☎0332/29 311; ⑤) is open year-round and has a decent restaurant. The torrents eventually cut through the town below, lending it some definition and a green vegetation belt, but it's a distinct miniature of Édhessa.

South of the large belfried church, which you pass as you wind up from the main road, there's a small park strip, lined with the bulk of Náoussa's **restaurants** and bars. The only **accommodation** in town is the well-priced, en-suite *Hellas* at Megálou Alexándhrou 16 (☎0332/22 006; ④). The **KTEL** is at the lower end of town, while the **train station** is a good 7km distant.

West from Édhessa: Flórina and the lakes

West of Édhessa lies **Límni Vegoritídha**, the first of a series of lakes that punctuate the landscape towards Kastoriá, and up to and across the border with the Former Yugoslav Republic of Macedonia (FYROM). The rail line between Édhessa and Flórina traces the lake's west shore: a fine journey which could be broken at either of the two village train stops, Árnissa and Áyios Pandelímonas.

ÁRNISSA has perhaps the better setting, opposite an islet and amidst apple orchards; for a swim, head for the water, then walk right for a quarter of an hour until you find a break in the shoreline reedbeds. The one-street village itself is a little drab, and its rock-bottom *Megali Hellas* hotel has closed down, but it does come alive on Tuesdays when the weekly market attracts families from miles around, using their tractors as taxis. To the north of the village rises **Mount Kaïmaktsalán**, scene of one of the bloodiest and more important battles of World War I, which raged intermittently from 1916 to 1918 until a Serbian–Greek force managed to break through the German–Bulgarian lines. The 2524-metre summit marks the Greek–"Yugoslav" frontier and bears a small memorial chapel to the fallen. If you can get a lift to the end of the road at Kalývia, it's a beautiful walk beyond, though it's as well to remember that much of the area has been developed as the Vórras ski resort, one of the highest and best in northern Greece.

The more attractive of the lakeside villages, however, is **ÁYIOS PANDELÍMONAS**, with its red-roofed houses crowned by a ruined windmill, and a small beach if you're prepared to swim in the slightly algae-ridden waters. The lakeside *Epiheirisi* **restaurant** has no rooms available, but keeps watch over the basic, informal **campsite** alongside. Rail and road then pass through Amýndeo (no reputable accommodation, and a dire place to get stuck) before turning north towards Flórina. Some 1500m west of Amýndeo, a short diversion to the right brings you to the smaller lake of **Petrón** and the hillside ruins of Hellenistic Petres on the west shore, excavated during the early 1990s and the subject of an interesting display on the first floor of the museum at Flórina (see below).

Flórina

FLÓRINA, surrounded by hills densely wooded in beech, is the last town before the FYROM border 13km to the north and as such, is quite a lively market centre. Cars can cross the border but at present there are no through trains. There is little of intrinsic interest in the town itself, other than the **archeological museum** 150m from the train station (Tues–Fri 8.30am–3pm; 500dr), and the main reason for a visit is to see the Préspa lakes, 40km west (see opposite). The town is mostly known for being the seat of an egregiously reactionary archbishop, an appointee of the colonels' junta, who despite his various misdemeanours (including the destruction of "Slavic" medieval church frescoes) and inflammatory rantings has died in bed in the odour of sanctity. He and others of his ilk made life difficult for Greek film-maker Theo Angelopoulos when the latter was using Flórina for locations, such as in *Odysseus' Gaze*.

The local economy has been hard hit by the collapse of Yugoslavia, mainly because FYROM-ers no longer come here to shop, and Germans and Austrians no longer pass through on their way to the Peloponnese beaches, hard facts only slightly offset by visits of Mercedes-propelled Albanian mafiosi from Körçe (there's a border crossing 51km distant at Krystallopiyí). This hasn't had a salutory effect on **hotel** prices, which remain exorbitant; cheapest (relatively), near the train station, is the *Ellinis* at Pávlou Melá 31 (☎0385/22 671; ③). Further up pedestrianized Pávlou Melá, across the central square and onto the continuation Megálou Alexándhrou, stands the more comfortable and quieter *Lyngos* (☎0385/28 322, fax 29 643; ⑥) at Tagmatárhou Naoúm 1, with large bal-conied, hi-tech rooms renovated in 1996. The *Antigoni* (☎0385/23 180; ⑤), at Ariánou 1, corner Stefánou Dhragoúmi, diagonally opposite the **KTEL**, is noisy and a definite third choice. Three full-on **restaurants**, as opposed to the numerous cafés and bars on Pávlou Melá, are found on 25-Martíou, running west from the central platía towards the river bisecting the town; there's another excellent one, *Iy Prespa*, on a side-street off Pávlou Melá.

Given the expense of hotels here, and the dearth of local attractions, it's well worth planning to arrive before 1pm if possible, as moving on will likely be your main priori-ty. There's no longer any direct bus from **Flórina to Kastoriá**, and it's easy to see why, as there's little in between other than dense forest and a few crumbling villages, half-deserted since the civil war. The road is paved, however, climbing sharply and snaking out of Flórina to the 1600-metre Pisodhéri saddle, site of one of the livelier villages and the Vígla ski lift. **PISODHÉRI** village offers the *Xenonas Modestios* (☎0385/45 928, fax 45 801; ④), an **inn** restoration that's rather better value than anything in Flórina; eat nearby at *Kyra Panayiota's* simple streamside **diner**. Since its resurfacing, this road is kept snow-ploughed in winter; it follows the headwaters of the Aliákmonas River, the longest in Greece, most of the way to Kastoriá.

There are, however, two daily buses (currently 6.45am and 2.30pm) to **Áyios Yermanós** in the **Préspa** basin, and if Kastoriá-bound you could conceivably take these to the Préspa turnoff and hitch the remaining 35km to Kastoriá, rather than going all the way around via dreary Amýndeo.

The Préspa lakes

Rising west out of the Aliákmonas valley on the paved side road towards Préspa, you have little hint of what's ahead until suddenly you top a pass, and a shimmering expanse of water riven by islets and ridges appears. It is not, at first glance, postcard-pretty, but the basin has an eerie, back-of-beyond quality that grows on you with further acquain-tance – and a turbulent recent history that belies its current role as one of the Balkans' most important wildlife sanctuaries.

During the Byzantine era, Préspa became a prominent place of exile for troublesome noblemen, thus accounting for the surprising number of **ecclesiastical monuments** in this backwater. In the tenth century it briefly hosted the court of the Bulgarian Tsar Samuel before his defeat by Byzantine Emperor Basil II. Under the Ottomans the area again lapsed into obscurity, only to regain the dubious benefits of strategic importance in just about every European war of this century, culminating in vicious local battles during the 1947–49 Greek civil war. In 1988 a forest fire on the eastern ridge treated observers to a dangerous fireworks display, as dozens of unexploded artillery shells were touched off by the heat. After World War II Préspa lay desolate and largely depop-ulated, as the locals fled abroad to Eastern Europe, North America and Australia, in response to a punitive government policy of forced assimilation operating against Macedonian-speakers – as all the lake-dwellers are. It is only since the late 1970s that the villages, still comparatively primitive and neglected, have begun to refill during the summer, when beans and hay are grown as close to the two lakes as the national park authorities allow – ecologists, self-styled or bona fide, are not popular here, as farmers resent proposed restrictions on land use, pesticides and chemical fertilizers. A common sight everywhere are lake-reeds, cut and stacked for use as bean-poles.

Mikrí Préspa, the southerly lake, is mostly shallow (9m maximum depth) and reedy, with a narrow fjord curling west to just penetrate Albania. The borders of Greece, Albania and FYROM meet in the middle of deeper **Megáli Préspa**, dividing its waters unequally, making the area doomed to play some role in whatever Balkan uproars lie in the future. During the past few years a steady stream of Albanian refugees have used the basin as an exit corridor into Greece. Though they used to be routinely caught and returned to Albania by the army, their presence as illegal agricultural workers is now tolerated, as farms in the area are perennially short-handed. Considering that for years you needed an official permit to visit Préspa, and given the uncertain future, the Greek military presence is surprisingly unobtrusive and sovereignty lightly **exercised**. As indicated above, the border here is extremely porous – though free-lance forays into Albania are emphatically unrecommended – and a certain amount of smuggling in duty-free goods occurs.

The core of the **national park**, established in 1971, barely encompasses Mikrí Préspa and its shores, but the peripheral zone extends well into the surrounding mountains, affording protection of sorts to a variety of land mammals. You'll almost certainly see foxes crossing the road, though the wolves and bears up on the ridges are considerably shyer. The lakes have a dozen resident fish species, including *tsiróni* – a sort of freshwater sardine – and *grivádhi*, a kind of carp. But it's **bird life** for which the Préspa basin, particularly the smaller lake, is most famous. There are few birds of prey, but you should see a fair number of egrets, cormorants, crested grebes and pelicans, which nest in the spring, with the chicks out and about by summer. They feed partly on the large numbers of snakes, which include vipers, whip snakes and harmless water snakes which you may encounter while swimming. Observation towers are available at Vromolímni and near Áyios Ahíllios, but dawn spent anywhere at the edge of the reedbeds with a pair of binoculars will be immensely rewarding (though bear in mind that you are not allowed to boat or wade into the reeds). There are **park information centres** in the villages of Áyios Yermanós and Psarádhes (see below).

While you may arrive from Flórina by bus, you really can't hope to tour the area without some **means of transport** – either a mountain bike or a car. Similarly, in view of the area's past under-development, don't expect much in the way of **facilities**: food is adequate and inexpensive, but exceedingly simple; the same might be said of local accommodation, though this has improved since the early 1990s. Préspa is an increasingly popular target for holidaying Greeks and (for some reason) Dutch, and you'd be wise to reserve the few accommodations listed during mid-summer, especially at weekends.

The way in: Mikrolímni

MIKROLÍMNI, 5km up a side road off the main route into the valley, would be your first conceivable stop. The small shop and fish taverna owned by Yiorgos Hassou, on the shore square, has three **rooms** to let (☎0385/61 221 or 45 931; ②). In the evening, you can look towards sunsets over reedbeds and the snake-infested Vidhronísi (Vitrinítsi) islet, though swimming isn't good here, or anywhere else on Mikrí Préspa for that matter. At the far end of the hamlet is a sporadically used biological observation station, literally the last house in Greece, and beyond that the lake narrows between sheer hillsides on its way to Albania. A prominent trail, much used by fleeing Albanians, leads there, paralleling the long inlet, but it would be unwise to walk its full length.

Regain the main road, which reaches a T-junction 16km from the main Flórina–Kastoriá highway, on the spit which separates the larger and smaller lakes. It's probable that at one time there was just one lake here, but now there's a four-metre elevation difference. Bearing right at the junction leads within 4km to Áyios Yermanós; the left option splits again at the west end of the spit, bearing south toward the islet of Áyios Ahíllios or northwest toward the hamlet of Psarádhes (see opposite).

Áyios Yermanós

ÁYIOS YERMANÓS proves a surprisingly large village of tile-roofed houses, very much the district "town", overlooking a patch of Megáli Préspa in the distance. It's worth making the trip up just to see two tiny late Byzantine churches, whose frescoes, dating from the time when the place belonged to the bishopric of Ohrid, display a marked Macedonian influence. The lower church, Áyios Athanásios, was renovated in 1995 but if it's open (a rare event) you can glimpse a dog-faced *St Christopher* among a line of saints opposite the door.

The main thing to see, however, is the tiny, eleventh-century parish church of Áyios Yermanós up on the square, hidden behind a new monster awkwardly tacked onto it in 1882. The Byzantine structure (may be shut for repairs) has its own entrance, and the frescoes, skilfully retouched in 1743, can be lit; the switch is hidden in the narthex. There are more hagiographies and martyrdoms than possible to list here, but there's a complete catalogue of them (in Greek) by the door. Among the best are the dome's *Pandokrátor*, a *Nativity* and *Baptism* right of the dome; a *Crucifixion* and *Resurrection* to the left; plus the saints *Peter and Paul, Kosmas and Damian, Tryphon and Pandelimon* by the door. Less conventional scenes include the *Entry into Jerusalem* and *Simon Helping Christ with the Cross*, opposite the door, and the *Apocalypse*, with the *Succouring of Mary the Beatified by Zozimas*, in the narthex. Mary was an Alexandrine courtesan who, repenting of her ways, retired to the desert for forty years. She was found, a withered crone on the point of death, by Zozimas, abbot of a desert monastery, and is traditionally shown being spoon-fed like an infant.

The village has the excellent **Préspa information centre** (mid–June to mid–Sept daily 9.30am–1.30pm & 5–7.30pm; mid-Sept to mid-June daily 10am–2pm), focusing on the wildlife of the national park; given sufficient warning the centre can arrange guides for trips into the park. It also sells locally farmed organic products. In addition to a **post office** – the only one in the Préspa basin – the village has two places to **stay**: Makis Arabatzis' *Les Pelicans* (☎0385/51 442; ②), across from Áyios Athanásios and with a bit of lake view from its terrace, or three more pleasant, renovated old houses at the very top of the village, run by the local *Women's Cooperative* and heated by wood stoves in winter. Reservations (☎0385/51 320 or 51 355; ③) are strongly advised, especially in August when a folk-dance seminar takes place here. These premises – plus a larger, centrally heated building at the bottom of the village – are open year-round. The only **taverna** in Áyios Yermanós is *Lefteris*, up by the women's inn, though there is another in Lemós, the village 1km below.

Across the spit: Koúla and Psarádhes

At the far end of the causeway dividing the two lakes, 4km from the T-junction, is **Koúla beach**, and a cluster of what passes for touristic development hereabouts: a patch of reed-free sand from where you can swim in Megáli Préspa, a free but basic camping area, now bereft of its water tap, and an army post. Tents and vans sprout by the "sailing club", actually a seemingly defunct taverna; *Iy Koula*, up by the army guard-post, is the only other (not very good, and overpriced) alternative. Just below it, you can see where Mikrí Préspa drains into Mégali Préspa.

If you don't intend to camp, it's best to bear right just above the army post, reaching after 6km the rickety village of **PSARÁDHES** (*Nivítsa* in Slavic dialect), whose lanes make for an hour's stroll. Unfortunately the wonderful old houses lining them are increasingly derelict, with nothing being done either to preserve them, or check the spread of unsightly modern construction. A good example of that, across the rather stagnant inlet here, is the bunker-style *Hotel Psaradhes* (☎0385/46 015; ③), an ugly necessity given the number of summer and weekend visitors here. Best of the few **rooms** in the village itself – and very sparsely furnished at that – are those above the *Taverna Syndrofia* (☎0385/46 107; ②), which is a good spot to sample lake fish and the proprietor Lazaros Khristianopoulos' wine. You won't see the fish fried here anywhere else in Greece; similarly, the cows ambling through Psarádhes are a locally adapted dwarf variety. Of the other three **tavernas**, *Paradhosi* seems the best of the bunch, and the most reliably open.

The village elders who used to gabble away in mixed Macedonian and Greek at the inland-platía kafenío have been turfed out and the place refurbished as a youth *baráki*, *Mythos*, which does creditable coffees; similarly, the waterfront has been paved and land-scaped, with parking provided for tour coaches. Exhibits at Psarádhes' **visitors' centre** (same hours as at Áyios Yermanós) on the basin's wildlife and agricultural economy, as well as literature for sale, are in Greek only, but you'll get the gist anyway, and the fold-ing pamphlet on sale contains the most detailed map of the area available.

Although there are white-rock swimming beaches below the hotel, the best outing from Psarádhes is a **boat excursion** to (and past) various medieval shrines and *ask-itíria* (hermitages) tucked into the shore leading around the promontory to Albania. The going rate per boat (ask, for example, at *Taverna Syndrofía*) is 6000dr, so you'll want to assemble a party of four. Even if you have no particular interest in churches, the ride alone is well worth it, as cormorants, gulls and pelicans skim the limpid waters of Megáli Préspa reflecting the mountains of Albania. Your guide will point out a fifteenth-century icon of the Virgin painted onto the rock opposite the village, and (on the far side of the peninsula) the thirteenth-century hermitage of Metamórfosis, whose icons have either been stolen or taken to the safety of the Flórina museum. Usually, your only landfall is the spectacular fifteenth-century rock-church of **Panayía Eleoússas**, concealed at the top of a deep chasm some 500m before the frontier. From the top of the long stairway up, you've a fantastic framed view of the lake and Albania; the deceptively simple vaulted chapel contains a plethora of expressive, naive frescoes. They commemorate critical episodes from the life of Christ: to the right of the door, Mary Magdalene washes Christ's feet, with the *Transfiguration* just above, while oppo-site are a moving *Lamentation*, the *Myrrofóri* at the sepulchre and an unusual *Resurrection* showing only Adam.

Áyios Ahíllios

The leftward option at the end of the causeway takes you, after 1500m, to the jetty for the islet of **Áyios Ahíllios**, with an impoverished hamlet of the same name. Five families totalling under thirty inhabitants still live there, whose members (incuding small boys) keep watch for potential visitors, with a boat usually appearing as if by magic within moments of your arrival. If necessary, ring ☎0385/46 111 to summon a boat (1500dr for 1–2 persons, 2000dr for more), though a simple footbridge is planned in the near future – as is, surprisingly, a small rooms place. Once on the island, you can climb its cross-spiked summit for unrivalled views of Mikrí Préspa, or take the ten-minute walk to the ruined Byzantine basilica of **Áyios Ahíllios**, This used to have an egret mosaic on the south side of the sanctuary, but it was either stolen or crumbled away in the early 1990s. There is also a ruined sixteenth-century monastery of Panayía Porfýras near the south end of the islet, but boatmen often tend not to include this unless specifically asked.

Kastoriá and around

Set on a peninsula extending deep into a slate-coloured lake, **KASTORIÁ** is one of the most interesting and attractive towns of mainland Greece. It is a relatively wealthy place and has been so for centuries as the centre of the Greek (and Balkan) fur trade; although the local beavers (*kastóri* in Greek) of the name had been trapped to extinc-tion by the nineteenth century, Kastoriá still supports a considerable industry of furri-ers who make up coats, gloves and other items from fur scraps imported from Canada and Scandinavia. Animal-rights activists will find the place heavy going, as the industry is well-nigh ubiquitous: you'll see scraps drying on racks, and mega-stores line all the approach highways, pitched at Russian mafiosi buying mink coats for their womenfolk, judging from the profuse Cyrillic signposting.

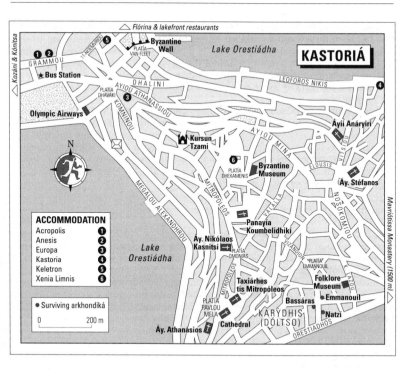

For most visitors, however, the main appeal lies in traces of the town's former prosperity: half a dozen splendid *arhondiká* – **mansions** of the old fur families – dating from the seventeenth to nineteenth centuries, plus some fifty Byzantine and medieval **churches**, though only a handful are visitable and of compelling interest. Of Muslim settlement the main reminder is the minaretless Kursun Tzami marooned in a ridgetop car park; there's also a patch of originally Byzantine fortification wall down on the neck of the peninsula.

Kastoriá suffered heavy damage during both World War II and the civil war which followed it. Platía Van Fleet, by the lakeside at the neck of the promontory, commemorates the US general who supervised the Greek Nationalist Army's operations against the Communist Democratic Army in the final campaigns of 1948–49. The town was nearly captured by the Communists in 1948, and Vítsi, the mountain dominating the eastern shore of the lake, was, together with Mount Grámmos, the scene of their last stand in August 1949. However, most of the destruction of Kastoriá's architectural heritage is not due so much to munitions as to 1950s neglect and 1960s development. It is miraculous that so many isolated specimens of humble Balkan vernacular and Neoclassical townhouses survive, mostly higher up on the peninsula where the steep grades have frustrated cement mixers.

Town museums

For a sense of what Kastoriá must once have been during its heyday, the best quarter of town is the former lakeside quarter of **Karýdhis** (also Dóltso), around Platía

Emmanouíl. Nearby at Kapetán Lázou 10, the seventeenth-century Aïvazís family mansion has been turned into a **Folklore Museum** (daily 10am–noon & 3–6pm; 400dr). The house was inhabited until 1972 and its furnishings and ceilings are in excellent repair. The caretaker, on request, will show you some of the other surviving *arhondiká*. The most notable – the nearby **Bassáras**, **Natzís**, and **Emmanouíl**, close together on Vyzandíon – are marked on the map, with the latter two having been restored during the 1990s.

The **Byzantine museum** up on Platía Dhexamenís, opposite the *Xenia Limnis* hotel (Tues–Sun 8.30am–3pm; 500dr) is rather more rewarding than Ioannina's (see p.333), wisely going for quality over quantity in this well-lit collection spanning the twelfth to the sixteenth centuries. Highlights include an unusually expressive thirteenth-century one of Áyios Nikólaos and a fourteenth-century *Ayii Anaryiri*, plus a later one depicting the life of Áyios Yeóryios. There are also a few double-sided icons, including a rare *Deposition*, intended for use in religious processions.

Byzantine churches

Kastoriá's noteworthy Byzantine **churches** can only be visited by application to the key-keeper, found at the museum up on Platía Dhexamení; while friendly and knowledgeable, he speaks only Greek. Shown on the map, they are small structures which almost certainly began life as private chapels founded by wealthy donors from amongst the mansion owners. **Áyii Anáryiri** dates from the eleventh century, with three layers of frescoes spanning the following two hundred years. It is currently shut for further works, and only one of the frescoes, the soldier-saints *Áyios Yeóryios with Áyios Dhimítrios*, has thus far been cleared of grime. Nearby **Áyios Stéfanos**, also closed at present, is of the tenth century and has been little changed over the years. Its frescoes are insignificant but it does have an unusual women's gallery or *yinaikonítis*.

The excellent frescoes of twelfth-century **Áyios Nikólaos Kasnítsi** were returned to their former glory during the late 1980s. The unusual epithet stems from the donor, who is shown with his wife on the narthex wall presenting a model of the church to Christ. Lower down are ranks of exclusively female saints, to console the women congregated in the narthex which long served as a women's gallery. High up on the west wall of the nave, the *Dormition* and the *Transfiguration* are in good condition, the former inexplicably backwards (the Virgin's head is usually to the left). **Taxiárhes tís Mitropóleos**, the oldest (ninth-century) church, was built on the foundations of an earlier pagan temple, of which recycled columns and capitals are visible. Its more prominent frescoes, such as that of the *Virgin Platytera and Adoring Archangels* in the conch of the apse, and a conventional *Dormition* on the west wall, are fourteenth century. In the north aisle is the tomb of Greek Macedonian nationalist Pavlos Melas, assassinated by Bulgarians at a nearby village in 1906, and commemorated by street-names across northern Greece; his widow, who survived to the age of 101 (she died in 1974), is interred with him. Lastly, the **Panayía Koumbelidhikí**, so named because of its unusual dome (*kübe* in Turkish), is currently undergoing much-needed repairs, but it still retains one startling and well-illuminated fresco: a portrayal – almost unique in Greece – of God the Father in a ceiling mural of the *Holy Trinity*. The building was constructed in stages, with the apse completed in the tenth century and the narthex in the fifteenth. The dome was meticulously restored after being destroyed by Italian bombing in 1940.

If tracking down buildings seems too frustrating a pursuit, perhaps the most pleasant thing to do in Kastoriá is to follow the narrow but paved track which runs all around the **lake shore** to the east of town; vehicles must circulate anticlockwise. Although the lake itself is visibly polluted, wildlife still abounds – frogs, tortoises and water snakes especially, and on a spring day numerous fish break water. Near the southeastern tip of the peninsula, 2500m from the cluster of mansions or 3500m from the *Hotel Kastoria*,

Ancient Kassopi, Epirus

Metéora, Northern Greece

Dhohiaríou monastery, Mount Athos

Ayíou Pávlou seen from its bay

MARC S. DUBIN

Ayíos Ahillíos basilica, Mikrí Préspa

PETER WILSON

Goats on a cliff, Northern Greece

Triple-arched bridge near Kípi

Mansion with bougainvillea, Ídhra

Port of Ídhra

Riverbed in Víkos gorge, Zagória

Harbour in Éyina

Bay in Párga

stands the **Mavriótissa monastery**, flanked by peacocks and a fair-value restaurant highly popular with Greek tours. Two churches are all that remains of the monastery: a smaller fourteenth-century chapel, with fine frescoes of scenes from Christ's life, abutting the larger, wood-roofed eleventh-century *katholikón* on whose outer wall looms a well-preserved *Tree of Jesse*, showing the genealogy of the Saviour. The warden-priest runs a very basic **campsite** a few paces away, if none of the town hotels (see below) appeals.

Practicalities

In the unlikely event that you fly in on Olympic Airways, the airport is 10km south of town; the in-town air terminal is at Megálou Alexándhrou 15. Arriving at the **bus station**, you'll find yourself at the western edge of the peninsula. Coming **by car**, beware of the fee-parking scheme in effect across much of the city centre; only the two top hotels have free or off-street parking. Kastoriá has at least one **car rental** outfit, if you'd like your own transport to the Préspa region: Tomaso at Grammou 147 (☎0467/84 000).

Most of Kastoriá's **hotels**, especially those within easy walking distance of the bus station, are noisy and overpriced; moreover, despite this, they are likely to be full pretty much year-round with people on fur-buying sprees, so try to phone ahead for reservations. Uninspiring choices closest to the bus station on Grámmou include the en-suite *Anessis* at no. 10 (☎0467/83 908; ④) and the *Acropolis* at no. 16 (☎0467/83 737; ②–③), the latter having rooms with and without private facilities. Next notch up is occupied by the *Keletron*, 11-Noemvríou 52 (☎0467/22 676; ③), with entrance on a side-street and some rooms overlooking leafy Platía Van Fleet; the *Europa*, Ayíou Athanasíou 12 (☎0467/23 826, fax 25 154; ④) is more comfortable but still plagued by traffic noise. Frankly, if you have the extra cash and/or a car, you're best off at one or other of the top town hotels. The fairly quiet *Kastoria*, Nikís 122 (☎0467/29 453, fax 29 608; ⑤), at the far end of the northern waterfront, was renovated and upgraded in 1998, offering lake views from its balconied, air-conditioned front rooms, plus free parking. The *Xenia Limnis/Xenia du Lac* (☎0467/22 565, fax 26 391; ⑤), peacefully set near the top of town by the museum, has private parking, and its wood-floored rooms are comfortable enough, if 1970s vintage.

The best venue for **restaurants** is Platía Omonías, where the *Omonoia* and the *Mantziaris* (officially oppposite at Valallá 8) are both excellent for *mayireftá* and more or less identically priced, with tables on the square. Lakeside dining is pretty much restricted to either the restaurant at Mavriótissas (see above); *Ta Balkania* at Orestíon 37 (the northwest quay), with good grills and outdoor seating under plane trees; or *Katergo* nearby at no. 19, a trendier, more recent ouzerí featuring specialities such as aubergines stuffed with bacon and cheese. **Nightlife**, such as it is, takes place at a half-dozen *barákia* between *Ta Balkania* and Platía Van Fleet.

Around Kastoriá

If you have your own transport, you might make a trip 14km southwest to **OMORFOKLISSIÁ**, an eerie village of mudbrick houses inherited post-1923 from Muslim peasants. It has a fourteenth-century Byzantine church with a lofty cupola, attached belfry and, inside, a huge, primitive carved-relief wooden **icon of St George** thought to date from the eleventh century.

SIÁTISTA, draped along a single ridge in a forbiddingly bare landscape 70km south of Kastoriá, is also a worthy destination. Located just above the point where the road splits for Kozáni or Kastoriá, it too was an important fur centre, and also boasts a handful of eighteenth-century mansions or *arhondiká*, which you can visit. The eighteenth-century house of **Hatzimihaïl Kanatsoúli** at Mitropóleos 1, near the police station, is still lived in but you can ring to be shown around. The first two floors are occupied; upstairs, a corner room has naive murals of mythological scenes (including Kronos's castration of Ouranos). The dilapidated **Nerantzópoulos mansion** (Mon–Sat 8.30am–3pm, Sun 9.30am–2.30pm) is on the upper square, by the Ethniki Trapeza/National Bank; the warden here has the keys for several other houses, of which the largest and most elaborate is the **Manoússi mansion**, dating from 1763, in a vale below the Kanatsoúli along with various other surviving *arhondiká*. Ceiling medallions often sport a carved cluster of fruit or a melon with a slice missing, where you'd expect a chandelier attachment point; there are more three-dimensional floral and fruit carvings up at the tops of the walls, which are adorned with stylized murals of pastoral and fictitious urban scenes. The church of **Áyia Paraskeví**, on the lowest platía, has soot-blackened seventeenth-century frescoes inside; until the scheduled cleaning occurs, you're better off glancing at the exterior ones.

Almost everything you need in Siátista – **banks** with cash dispensers, the **post office** – are found along the single, long main street, including the impressive *Archontikon* **hotel** (☎0465/21 298, fax 22 835; ④), which has a reasonable restaurant and café on the ground floor; it often fills with Greek tours, so if you've your heart set on staying here, check for space in advance. Other options for **eating** out are limited; the *Psistaria Ouzeri O Platanos*, just below Áyia Paraskeví, has acceptable food but a rather boozy male environment – the hotel is more genteel. The easiest bus connections are with Kozáni, 28km distant.

The mountain village of **NYMFÉO** lies 60km northeast of Kastoriá, the last 9km via an incredibly steep hairpin side road. Perched halfway up the eastern flank of Vérno/Vítsi, this much-publicized spot essentially functions as a "hill station" for wealthy Thessaloníki yuppies, the Himalayan-foothills analogy being reinforced by snow-shedding lead roofs on the squat stone houses and the idiosyncratic tower of the nineteenth-century school. Facilities are priced accordingly, there are few signs in any language but Greek, and the gruff villagers seem positively put out at the prospect of having to accommodate foreigners. The only inexpensive lodging is the central, ugly, non-en-suite **hotel** *Iy Neveska* (the old Slavic name for the place; no phone; ②); anything else – for example, **rooms** *Eterne* with self-catering facilities (☎0386/31 230), is at least ④. One of the few establishments run with any degree of professionalism – and a reliable source of decent, if pricey, food – is an **inn** at the outskirts, *Ta Linouryia* (☎0386/31 133 or ☎031/241 334), but most of its beds are arranged as quads or even octuples (price ⑥ for 4 sharing). If money is no object, then part with it to the tune of £100-plus per night at mansion-like *La Moare* just uphill (☎031/287 626, fax 287 401; ⑥), run by the Boutari vintner family and one of the most exclusive hotels in Greece. *Kyria Neratza's*, back in the centre, is the main **eating** alternative, purveying such treats as aubergine "caviar" and spiced beef stew. If you surmount the logistic obstacles presented, Nymféo could be a good base for an active weekend, given that it straddles the E4 long-distance trail, and that horse-riding at an English-run stables and winter sports are easily to hand.

HALKIDHIKÍ AND EASTERN MACEDONIA

Halkidhikí, easily reached by bus from Thessaloníki, is the clear highlight of Macedonia's eastern half. Its first two peninsulas, Kassándra and Sithonía, shelter the north's main concentration of beaches; the third, Áthos, the country's finest, though most secretive, monasteries.

Moving east, there are a few more good beaches en route to **Kavála**, but little of interest inland, with a scattering of small market towns serving a population that – as in neighbouring Thrace – produces the main Greek tobacco crop.

Kassándhra, Sithonía and secular Áthos

The squid-shaped peninsula of **Halkidhikí** begins at a perforated edge of shallow lakes east of Thessaloníki, then extends into three prongs of land – Kassándhra, Sithonía and Áthos – trailing like tentacles into the Aegean sea.

Mount Áthos, the easternmost peninsula, is in all ways separate, a "Holy Mountain" whose monastic population, semi-autonomous within the Greek state, excludes all women – even as visitors. For men who wish to experience Athonite life, a visit involves recently simplified procedures which are detailed, with the monastic sights, in the section beginning on p.427. The most that women can do is to glimpse the buildings from offshore cruise *kaíkia* sailing from the two small resorts on the periphery of the peninsula – Ierissós and Ouranoúpoli – on the "secular" part of the Áthos peninsula.

Kassándhra and **Sithonía**, by contrast, host some of the most overblown holiday resorts in Greece. Up until the late 1980s these were popular mainly with Greeks, but they've since been fairly comprehensively developed, with most European package-tour companies maintaining a presence at often monstrously huge complexes. On Kassándhra especially, almost any reasonable beach is accompanied by a crop of villas or several hotel developments, while huge billboards advertise campsite complexes miles in advance. Still larger signs at the entrance to each peninsula of Halkidhikí remind you that camping outside authorized sites is strictly prohibited, although in theory it's possible, as most beaches here are equipped with free freshwater showers. Of late, vacancies have been the norm except mid-July to mid-August; roadside hotels will hang out signs to that effect, with a going rate of ③–④ before July 15. The beaches themselves consist of white sand, ranging in consistency from powder to coarse-grained; less appealing are the fortunately stingless jellyfish which drift about nearly everywhere.

Both Kassándhra and Sithonía are connected to Thessaloníki by a four-lane express-way which ends at Néa Moudhaniá, from where a network of fast two-lane roads extend around their coastlines. Buses run frequently to all the larger resorts. In spite of this, neither peninsula is that easy to travel around if you are dependent on **public transport**. You really have to pick a place and stay there, perhaps **renting a motorbike** or **car** for local excursions.

Kassándhra

Kassándhra, the nearest, boot-shaped prong to Thessaloníki, is also by far the most developed, though once past the grain fields around Kallithéa, extensive forest survives unscathed along the hilly spine of the peninsula. Its population took part in the independence uprising of 1821, but was defeated and massacred; the handful of attractive villages, mostly inland, essentially date from just after, though often built atop ancient or medieval foundations. On the coast, there were only a few small fishing hamlets here until after 1923, when the peninsula was resettled by refugees from around the Sea of Marmara – these have since burgeoned into holiday venues. Unless very pushed for time, most travellers choose to keep going to Sithonía or the top end of Áthos.

Néa Moudhaniá

On the peninsula's west coast, the first resort, **NÉA MOUDHANIÁ**, is really a sizable town, complete with several **banks** (cash dispensers) and a **post office**, also serving as a minor hydrofoil port. They sail from here to Skiáthos, Skópelos and Alónissos daily in the morning from June to early September only. If you need to stay, there's a campsite on a sandy beach 3km southeast – the *Ouzouni Beach* (☎0373/42 100; May–Sept) – and five mid-range **hotels**, of which the *Philippos* (☎0373/24 429; ④), inland opposite the school, is preferable to the non-bargaining *Thalia* (☎0373/23 106; ④). Best waterfront **eating** is at *Taverna Ouzeri Maïstrali*, at the far left end of the quay as you face the sea.

Néa Potídhea, Néa Fókea and Sáni

NÉA POTÍDHEA, some 6km past Néa Moudhaniá by the canal which severs the narrow neck of Kassándhra, is a bit of an eyesore like all of the coastal refugee settlements, its seafront promenade a mini-Coney Island/Blackpool with its mechanical animals, and fast-food joints alternating with bars. This accepted, the front is in fact pedestrianized and well landscaped, and the beach itself broad, sandy and reef-free. Greek families rent summer apartments here long-term, making it a poor bet for a quick overnight, while an otherwise fairly young crowd lends a laidback feel. The way to the fishing port at the west end of the canal is flanked by the ruined fortifications of ancient Potidaia; at the end you'll find two worthy **fish tavernas**, *Ta Kastra* (perched amidst bits of wall) and *Marina*, overlooking the sea and another, half-submerged bit of antiquity.

The next resort, **NÉA FÓKEA**, seems a relatively modest place overlooked by a Byzantine watchtower. There are three **tavernas** on the little fishing port, from where a long beach heads north under cliffs, improving as you distance yourself from the tower. As at Néa Potídhea, apartments predominate, many occupied by Scandinavian package tourists.

From Néa Fókea, an eight-kilometre paved side road takes you to the western shore of the peninsula, where SÁNI offers the *Blue Dream* campsite (☎0374/31 435; May–Sept); it's operated by the village and is more relaxed than most. Otherwise there are only several luxury mega-complexes, indicative of the clientele attracted here, for whose benefit the summer **Sáni Festival** is staged: principally musical events, with a cosmopolitan billing of world music, salsa, jazz and cutting-edge Greek stars.

Áfytos to Kryopiyí

Some 5km south of Néa Fókea, you reach the turning east for **ÁFYTOS** (Áthytos), by far the most attractive spot on Kassándhra, if a bit self-consciously so. This large village of tiled-roofed, traditional houses spreads over a series of ravines furrowing the bluff here, which ends in a sharp drop to the sea. Near the cliff bottom a series of springs oozes from a rock overhang, nurturing a little oasis – and doubtless a spur in founding of ancient Aphytis, the village's predecessor. The beach here is poor by Halkidhikí standards, marred by rock sills with lots of sea urchins, a fact which (along with a local preservation order) has probably kept Áfytos from going the way of most coastal resorts here. On the square, focus of a mesh of slightly twee cobbled lanes closed to traffic for the nightly *vólta*, stands a handsome church in post-Byzantine style, dating only from 1850 but seeming much older.

There is inevitably a strong package presence, but there are still numbers of **rooms** for independent travellers, best sited for sea views at the cliff-edge (though you'll get mosquitos from the oasis) and priced at ③, often with some sort of self-catering facility. If you wanted a bona fide **hotel**, try the *Stamos* (☎0374/91 520, fax 91 234; ④ includes breakfast) on the minor road leading to the cliff-edge; with its courtyard pool and studios for three or four, it's good for families. Down on the shore, the medium-sized *Blue Bay* (☎0374/91 644, fax 91 646; ⑤) dominates one of the most usable patches of beach, but tends to fill in peak season with Czech tour groups.

Eating out is best just off the church square at *Estia*, aka *Voula's* after the genial proprietress, open most of the year and offering very rich, creative if slightly pricey meat-and-vegetable-based baked creations, plus good bulk wine. Closest alternative, by the church, is the *Inomayerio Koutouki*, the old boys' hangout: copious drink, salads and one dish of the day only. For full **buffet breakfast** at a fair price, look no further than *Gastronomia*, near the *Stamos* (no relation to the namesake in the centre) – probably worth trying their Italian fare by night as well. **Nightlife** is fairly lively and not entirely tourist-pitched, with Greek musicians often playing the bars at summer weekends, sometimes under the aegis of the **Kassándhra Festival** which Áfytos shares with nearby Síviri: Shakespearean and ancient Greek plays, blues, soul, classical and Greek music.

Within 4km more you reach the horrrible roadside strip-development of **KALLITHÉA**, a complete contrast to Áfytos and with only **banks** (cash dispensers) and **motorbike/windsurfer rental** to its credit. There are half-a-dozen mammoth hotels (⑥) on the beach, plus a like number of apartments in the ④ category that may have vacancies on spec. **KRYOPIYÍ**, just under 6km further, means more of the same down by the water, where there's a steeply shelving beach, but it has preserved its old village core 1500m inland and up the hill. By the somewhat gentrified platía are two **tavernas**, of which the *Platia* has a slight edge over its rival. There's a regular **shuttle bus** from the beach area that stops by the church.

The far southeast

Beyond Kryopiyí, you head towards the "toe" of the Kassandhrian boot via three consecutive coastal resorts – Polýhrono, Haniótis and Pefkohóri – lining the "lace-up". Each vies to exceed its neighbour in tackiness and excess capacity (signs tempt you with offers of vacant rooms); at **HANIÓTIS** in particular, you have to wend your way through some fairly downmarket if low-rise development – three dozen hotels and apartment units of it – to reach the long but narrow beach (standing room only from the day school lets out). Just southeast of **PEFKOHÓRI**, which has an official **campsite**, a lagoon enclosed by a pine-tufted spit is just about the only spot on the peninsula where rough camping seems to be winked at. At the bay of **Khroussoú**, there are two more recognized **campsites** and rather more low-key development than the preceding. From here, rather than visit the "toe"-cape, the main road climbs inland and west to the ridge-top village of **PALIOÚRI**, also full of lodging – a testimony to the high-season coastal mobbing.

The west coast

The west coast of Kassándhra is in general developed more for Greek weekenders rather than foreigners, with plenty of *ikismí* (garden-villa or apartment clusters) pitched at Thessalonians. Some 6km beyond hilltop Palioúri you emerge at **AYÍA PARASKEVÍ**, a very attractive and village with sea views, untouched save for a pair of simple **tavernas** and a fancy-paved central roundabout. However a 1998 fire did for most of the pine forest from here down to **LOUTRÁ** on the coast, with its thermal spa and handful of Greek-pitched hotels. **NÉA SKIÓNI**, 6km northwest, makes a better conventional base, with its unburnt backdrop, good beach and a couple of tavernas supplied by a tiny fleet in the fishing port. Amongst the apartments there's just one bona fide **hotel**: *Cavos* (☎0374/71 463; ④). **Mála**, nominally 8km northwest, is not really a village but a string of weekend real-estate which blocks access to most of the coast from just outside Néa Skióni. **Kalándhra**, up on the cape here out of sight of bygone pirates, is another attractive, "real" village just off the route to **Posídhi beach**, which isn't wonderful, though beyond the lively beach bar, at the lighthouse cape, the rock reef abates and you can skinny-dip. The campsite in the nearby pine grove is for University of Thessaloníki students only, and the access road dead-ends rather than continuing along the coast to **SÍVIRI**. This, reached by backtracking via Kalándhra, has a more pleasant beach and seems a larger, busier version of Néa Skióni. From here there's again no direct coastal access to Sáni; you must first use the trans-peninsular road back to Kallithéa.

Sithonía

As you move east across Halkidhikí and away from the frontline of tourism, the landscape becomes increasingly green and hilly, culminating in the isolated and spectacular scenery of the Holy Mountain, looming across the gulf lapping Sithonía's east coast. The **Sithonía** peninsula is more rugged but better cultivated than Kassándhra, though here there are even fewer true villages, and those that do exist mostly date from the 1920s resettlement era. Pine forests cover many of the slopes, particularly in the south, giving way to olive groves on the coast. Small sandy inlets with relatively discreet pockets of campsites and tavernas make a welcome change from sprawling mega-resorts, though as on Kassándhra plenty of real estate is being sold off to weekending Greeks.

If you're under your own steam, some 6km past the last motorway exit at Néa Moudhaniá en route to Sithonía, it's worth making the slight detour to **ancient Olynthos** (Tues–Sun 8.30am–2pm; 800dr). This is a rare example of an unmodified Classical town laid out to the grid plan of Hippodamus. There's an initially off-putting walk of 700m from the ticket booth, but well-excavated streets, houses and even some mosaics to see once you arrive. The modern village of **ÓLYNTHOS**, 1km west across the riverbed here, has **food** and a **hotel**, the central *Olynthos* (☎0379/91 666; ③).

Metamórfosi

Suitably enough, **METAMÓRFOSI** ("Transfiguration"), at the western base of Sithonía, signals the transformation. Its beach is only adequate but there's good swimming, and the village, while relentlessly modern, has an easy-going air. In addition to the friendly *Hotel Golden Beach* (☎0375/22 063; ⑤), with its cool courtyard and café backing onto the village square, there are two **campsites**: *Sithon*, 5km west (☎0375/22 414; May–Sept), and the preferable *Mylos*, 3km east, on the beach side of the road. In high season, both campsites and village can be a little crowded, but there are a fair number of **tavernas** clustered in and around the village square which seem to soak up business.

Moving on to Sithonía proper, it's best to follow the loop road clockwise around the east coast, so that the peak of Áthos is always before you. **Bus services** are sparse, however: there are up to five buses daily around the west coast to Sárti, and up to three a day direct to Vourvouroú, but there's no KTEL connection between these two endpoints. A complete circuit is only really possible with your own transport.

Órmos Panayía to Vourvouroú

ÓRMOS PANAYÍA, first of the east coast resorts, is nowadays well developed; ranks of villas dwarf the picturesque hamlet and tiny harbour, and the nearest decent beaches lie 4km north en route to Pyrgadhíkia, below the inland village of Áyios Nikólaos. The only conceivable reason to stop at Órmos would be to catch the excursion boats that sail around Áthos from here, but these are expensive and often pre-reserved for tourists bused in from the big Halkidhikí resorts.

VOURVOUROÚ, 8km downcoast from Órmos, is not a typical resort, since it's essentially a vacation-villa project for Thessaloníki professors, established in the late 1950s on land expropriated from Vatopedhíou monastery on Áthos. There is a fair amount of short-term **accommodation**: as well as numbers of **rooms**, there's the seafront **hotel** *Dhiaporos* (☎0375/91 313; ⑤; half-board may be obligatory), with its cool rooftop restaurant, and the plain but en-suite *Vourvourou* (☎0375/91 261; ③), open June–Sept only, plus the 1997-built, rather sterile *Rema* just inland (☎0375/91 142, fax 91 071; ⑤ half-board), which often has low-season specials. The strange feel of the place is accentuated by those plot owners who haven't bothered to build villas (so far very scattered) and merely tent down, making it hard to tell which are the real campsites. Islets astride the mouth of the bay make for a fine setting, but the beach, while sandy, is extremely narrow, and Vourvouroú is really more of a yachters' haven. **Tavernas** are relatively inexpensive because they're banking on a return clientele (which includes lots of Germans); the *Itamos*, inland from the road, is the best; the *Gorgona/Pullman*, while the nicest positioned, gets coach tours as the alias implies. There are two **campsites**: *Dionysos* (☎0375/91 214; April–Oct), simple but adequate, part of which faces the beach, and *Glaros* (no phone; mostly caravans), facing Karýdhi beach at the eastern end of things.

Some of Sithonía's best **beaches** line the thirty kilometres of road between Vourvouroú and Sárti: five signposted sandy coves, each with a **campsite** and little else. The names of the bays reflect the fact that most of the land here belonged to various Athonite monasteries until confiscated by the Greek government to resettle Anatolian refugees.

Sárti

Concrete-grid **SÁRTI** itself, rising to a ridge on the north, is set slightly back from its broad, two-kilometre-long beach, with only the scale of the bay protecting it from being utterly overrun in summer by Germans (plus growing numbers of Hungarians and Czechs). There are hundreds of **rooms** (though often not enough to go around), the choicest being in the southerly part of town, and not all of these block-booked by foreign companies. At the south end of the beach is another cluster of development, including a **hotel**, the *Sarti Beach* (☎0375/94 250; ④) and the shady *Camping Sarti Beach* (☎0375/94 629; May–Sept), the campsite laid out between the road and the hotel grounds. *Iy Neraïda* and *O Stavros* are two of the less expensive **tavernas** lining the landscaped shore esplanade, but the perennial (if pricey) favourite amongst Greeks, *Ta Vrahakia* (no sign), stands at the far north end of the beach, overlooking the "little rocks" of the name, and dishing up rich *mayireftá*. Inland you'll find a short-hours **bank** and a rather tattily commercialized square ringed by forgettable fast-food joints – plus the big local travel agency, Sithon Travel (☎0375/94 066), which does **car rental**.

Paralía Sykiás and Kalamítsi

PARALÍA SYKIÁS, 8km further along, has a beach somewhat inferior to Sárti's and thus less developed so far. What there is, however, seems not very user-friendly: just a few tavernas well back from the sea along 2km of coastal highway, with much of the intervening space fenced off for some unaesthetic incipient development. At the north end of the beach a **campsite**, *Melissi* (☎0375/41 631), shelters in some trees. Best strategy here is to follow the side road at the south end of the beach towards the more scenic coves at **Linaráki**, where *Pende Vimata stin Ammo* is the most noteworthy of three **tavernas** here, or beyond to Pigadháki. "Town" for these parts, with a **post office** and shops, is **SYKIÁ**, 2km inland, a surprisingly large place hemmed in by a bowl of rocky hills and thus invisible to pirates.

KALAMÍTSI, another 8km south of Paralía Sykiás, consists of a beautiful double bay sheltered by islets, with relatively little commercialization to date. At the north bay of Pórto, there's a basic **campsite** (☎0375/41 346) containing the North Aegean scuba centre (☎0375/41 148), though staff are none too friendly and all literature and pricing is in German. More worthwhile is the **taverna** *O Yiorgakis* next door, with varied, reasonably priced food, and good **rooms** behind (☎0375/41 338; ③ simple rooms, ④ self-catering). The small beach just out front can get cramped in mid-summer, at which time you can easily swim out to the main islet for less company. The equally sandy south bay is rather monopolized by the fancier *Camping Kalamitsi* (☎0375/41 411; May–Sept).

Pórto Koufó, Toróni, Tristeníka

Sithonía's forest cover has been diminishing since Sárti, and as you round the tip of the peninsula it vanishes completely, with bare hills spilling into the sea to create a handful of deep bays. **PÓRTO KOUFÓ**, just northwest of the cape, is the most dramatic of these, almost completely cut off from the open sea by high cliffs. The name Koufó ("deaf" in Greek) is said to come from one's inability to hear the sea within the confines of this inlet, which served as an Axis submarine shelter during World War II. There's a decent beach near where the road drops down from the east, as well as a small, stark, pricey **hotel** and a few **rooms**. The north end of the inlet, a kilometre from the beach area, is a yacht and fishing harbour with a string of five somewhat expensive seafood **tavernas**; *O Pefkos* is the least expensive, though not very inspired, alternative.

TORÓNI, 3km north, is the antithesis of this, an exposed, two-kilometre-long crescent of sand with wooded hills behind. It's probably your best Sithonian bet as a base if you just want to flop on a beach for a few days; for more stimulation there is a minimal **archeological site** (currently off-limits) on the southern cape, sporting the remains of an ancient fortress and early Christian basilica. After being overlooked until the late 1990s, it has "arrived" touristically in a modest way, especially amongst Germans and Czechs. Open spaces are slowly filling, too, with apartments for Greek weekenders, though the Sykiá municipality has banned beachfront building. The half-dozen combination **taverna-studio rooms** scattered the length of the beach are all pre- or suffixed "*Haus*", for example *Haus Sakis* (☎0375/51 261; ③), with comfortable rooms upstairs and good food plus German beer on tap at street level.

Just 2km north is the turning for **TRISTENÍKA (ARETÉS)**, now much as Toróni must have been in the 1980s: another outstanding two-kilometre beach, reached by a bumpy, 1800-metre sand and dirt track past the first hopeful taverna and rooms outfit, with a tiny hamlet 1km off the main road. At the south end of the sand, served by its own access drive, is *Camping Isa* (☎0375/51 235; May–Sept).

Some 5km further north along the main road, there's a turning for the recommended, friendly *Camping Areti* (0375/71 430, fax 71 573) nestled between Cape Papadhiá and Lýkithos hamlet, with views of three islets over its private beach. Besides tent space in well-landscaped olive groves, there are also wood chalets with all amenities at ③ rates.

Pórto Carrás to Parthenónas

Beyond Tristeníka, you edge back into high-tech resort territory, epitomized by Greece's largest planned holiday complex, **PÓRTO CARRÁS**. Established by the Carras wine and shipping dynasty, it features an in-house shopping centre, golf course and vineyards, while from the ten-kilometre private beach in front, you can indulge in every imaginable watersport. Since the death of founder John Carras, the complex has been sold off and split into three futuristic luxury hotels: *Meliton Beach*, *Village Inn* and *Sithonia Beach*.

The nearest proper town to all this, with **banks** (cash dispensers) and a **post office**, is **NÉOS MARMARÁS**, a once-attractive fishing port with a small beach. Nowadays, it's popular with Greeks who stay in a score of modest hotels and a like number of apartment developments. Failing that, the last **campsite** in Sithonía is 3km to the north – *Castello* (☎0375/71 095; May–Sept) – at which point the beach is sandy, and there's tennis, volleyball and a restaurant. There is exceptionally good *yíros* at *Fast Food O Dhimitris*, between the church and the bus stop.

If you're curious as to what Sithonía looked like before all this happened, a road leads 5km from Néos Marmarás to **PARTHENÓNAS**, the lone "traditional" village on Sithonía, crouched at the base of 808-metre Mount Ítamos. The place was abandoned in the 1960s in favour of the shore, and never even provided with mains electricity; its dilapidated but appealing houses are now slowly being sold off to wealthy Greeks and

Germans. The *Pension Parthenon* (☎0375/71 445) in one such dwelling has apparently folded, but you might find it operating under new management. *Paul's Taverna* here remains a lively venue where Greek dancing sessions punctuate the fare.

East to secular Áthos

From Órmos Panayía a mostly paved road winds around the coast to Ierissós at the head of the Áthos peninsula – the final ten-kilometre stretch between Gomáti and Ierissós has been regraded, and should be sealed by the year 2000. The principal place you'd think to stop is **PYRGADHÍKIA**, a ravine-set fishing village taken over by German and Greek holidaymakers during July, but otherwise peaceful. There are a few basic, unenticingly placed **hotels**, such as the *Possidon* (☎0375/93 357; ②), but you still might lunch here at one of four waterfront tavernas. There's little beach to speak of, though good ones pop up intermittently along the 6km southwest to **SALONIKIOÚ**, where there are **studio-rooms** and **tavernas**.

No buses cover the above route, however, and if you're dependent on public transport you'll have to backtrack as far as Yerakiní and then inland to Halkidhikí's capital, **POLÝIROS**, a drab market town with an unexciting archeological museum. At Áyios Pródhromos, 20km north, you can pick up buses heading for Áthos via **ARNÉA**, which has some fine old quarters and a reputation for (somewhat touristy) carpets and other colourful handwoven goods. This could merit a brief stopover, as the municipal corporation has restored an old mansion as high-quality **accommodation**: *Archontiko Mitsiou* (☎0372/22 744, fax 22 988; ④ with breakfast), with large, wood-decor rooms. There's more accommodation at **PALEOHÓRI**, 5km further east towards Stáyira, where the genial *Park Hotel Tasos* (☎0372/41 722, fax 41 858; ④), on the westerly outskirts, has exceptionally quiet, if 1970s-vintage, rooms. The ground-floor lounge is a veritable museum of good-natured kitsch; none of the several tavernas on the road through town are up to much, so if the hotel restaurant is open, take advantage. From the high, partly forested plateau here, the road drops down to the sea again at Stratóni, then veers south to Ierissós.

Ierissós and Néa Ródha

IERISSÓS, with a good, long beach and a vast, promontory-flanked gulf, is the most Greek-patronized of the "secular Áthos" resorts, although the sizable town itself, built well back from the shore and with room to expand, is a sterile concrete grid dating from after a devastating 1932 earthquake. The only hint of pre-touristic life is the vast caique-building dry dock to the south.

There are numerous **rooms**, an inexpensive **hotel** – the en-suite, friendly if sometimes noisy *Marcos* (☎0377/22 518; ②) overlooking its own garden and car park at the south end of town – and two basic **campsites** (one, at the north edge of town; the other, *Delfini* (☎0377/22 208), on the way to Néa Ródha). The beach is surprisingly uncluttered – if rather straight-arrow dull – with just a handful of **bars** behind the landscaped promenade. Currently the best of several mediocre **tavernas** is *O Iosif*, just inland on the main drag, with decent mezédhes, but establish prices before ordering. Rounding off the list of amenities, there's a **post office**, two **banks** and a summer **cinema** by the campsite. Ierissós is also the main port for the northeast shore of Áthos; sailings take place three times weekly (typically Mon, Thur & Sat) year-round at 8am, as weather – which can turn very stormy on this side – allows.

The road beyond Ierissós passes through the resort of **NÉA RÓDHA**, with a small beach and no more claim to architectural distinction than its neighbour, but worth knowing about as an alternative point for picking up the morning boat from Ierissós. Just beyond here your route veers inland to follow a boggy depression that's the remaining stretch of **Xerxes' canal**, cut by the Persian invader in 480 BC to spare his fleet the shipwreck at the tip of Áthos that had befallen the previous expedition eleven years before.

Ammoulianí

You emerge on the southwest-facing coast at **Trypití** ("Perforated"), not a settlement but merely the western exit of Xerxes' canal and now also the ferry jetty for the small island of **AMMOULIANÍ** (up to 7 daily crossings in summer, cars carried). This is Macedonia's only inhabited Aegean island apart from Thássos, and after decades of eking out an existence as a fishing community of refugees from the Sea of Marmara, has in recent years had to adjust to a new role as a popular target for Thessalonian weekenders and (to a lesser extent) surplus Germanophone holidaymakers from Ouranoúpoli (see below). Like anywhere else in Halkidikí, it's impossibly oversubscribed in July and August, but in spring or autumn this low-lying, scrub and olive-covered islet can make an idyllic hideaway.

The only town, where the ferries dock, is another unprepossessing grid of concrete slung over a ridge, with few pre-1960s buildings remaining; it is, however, chock-a-block with **rooms**, many self-catering, and two **hotels** plainly visible on the left as you sail in. The better of these is the *Sunrise* (☎0377/51 273, fax 51 174; ④ including buffet breakfast), with its own swimming jetty and reliable hot water. Of the village's half-dozen **tavernas**, *Alekos* (on the front), *Iy Klimataria* (on the road out) and *Yannis* (facing the rear Limanáki port) get high marks for hygiene and good value. There are a few shops for self-caterers, but **no bank or post office**. As for **nightlif**e, you've two bars (one, *Barka*, does breakfasts) and two discos a few hundred metres out of town on the main island road.

This leads southwest, after two paved kilometres, to **Alykés**, the islet's most famous beach, with a namesake salt-marsh inland, a taverna and separate café behind the sand, and a rather parched campsite. Ammoulianí's best beaches however, lie in the far southeast, facing the straits with the Áthos peninsula. To reach them, bear left off the pavement 1500m out of town where the *Agionissi* luxury resort is signposted, onto a smooth, sand-dirt track. Some 2km along this, you pass the tiny chapel and cistern of **Áyios Yeóryios** overlooking the excellent eponymous beach. Just beyond stands the popular lunchtime-only *Sarandis*, but it's pricier than the exceedingly simple fare warrants, and you might prefer to continue to the far end of the beach and the *Gripos Ouzeri*, which is better value. This also offers a half-dozen upstairs rooms of considerable charm (☎0377/51 049; ②), with copper antiques, beam ceilings, terracotta floor tiles and large balconies. Nikos, the affable owner, keeps pheasants and other exotic fowl, whose squawkings vie with those of the gulls nesting on the rock slets of the Dhrénia archipelago just offshore. You can continue a final 500m to even more idyllically set **Megáli Ámmos** beach, where there's a café with seats in the sand, a seasonal taverna and a pleasant, olive-shaded campsite. Still other, less accessible beaches beckon in the northwest of the island, served in season by excursion boats from the town; a popular map-postcard on sale will give necessary hints if you'd like to reach them on foot or (better) rented bicycle.

Ouranoúpoli

Fifteen kilometres beyond Ierissós, **OURANOÚPOLI** is the last community before the restricted monastic domains, with a centre that's downright tatty, showing the effects of too much Greek-weekender and German-package tourism. Somewhat mysteriously, it has become a major resort aside from its function as the main gateway to Mount Áthos; local beaches, stretching intermittently for several kilometres to the north, are sandy enough but narrow and cramped – certainly not the best Halkidikí has to offer. If you're compelled to stay the night while waiting for passage to Áthos, the best temporary escape would be either to take a cruise, or to **rent a motor boat**, to the mini-archipelago of **Dhrénia** just opposite, with almost tropical sandy bays and tavernas on the larger islets.

The only other diversion in Ouranoúpoli is the Byzantine **Phosphori tower** by the bus stop, visible from some distance. Here for nearly thirty years lived Sydney Loch, author of *Athos: the Holy Mountain*, published posthumously in 1957 and still an excellent, if now rather nostalgic, guide to the monasteries. Loch and his wife Joyce, who died in the tower in 1982, were a Scots-Australian missionary couple who devoted most of their lives to the refugees of Halkidhikí. The cottage industry of carpet-weaving, which they taught the local villagers, is increasingly less in evidence.

Two **ferries** – the *Ayios Nikolaos* and the *Axion Esti* – take turns calling along the southwest shore of Áthos, and they're probably the main reason you're here. Throughout the year there's just one daily departure, at around 9.45am; tickets, whose price depends on destination, should be purchased before boarding from the *Athoniki* agency, near the medieval tower. One of these, or perhaps another craft, also offers co-ed half-day **cruises** in season (4000dr a head; departs 10.30am), which skim along the Athonite coast, keeping their contaminating female presence 500m offshore as required by the monastic authorities.

If you need to **stay** – and fortunately proprietors are fairly used to one-night stands, en route to or from Áthos – there are a fair number of rooms and a similar quantity of hotels, virtually all of them en suite. Less expensive ones include the *Diana* (☎0377/71 052; ②) and the adjacent *Rooms Lazaros Antonakis* (☎0377/71 366; ②), both on the road leading down from the pilgrims' office. On the southerly seafront there's the *Akroyali* (☎0377/71 201, fax 71 395; ③), which shares management with the *Makedonia*, slightly uphill and inland (☎0377/71 085, fax 71 395; ③), a pleasantly quiet spot with a small package presence. About 300m out of town towards the monastic border, the *Avra* (☎0377/71 189, fax 71 095; ④ with breakfast) isn't wildly friendly but the seaview rooms are clean and spacious. If money's no object, the closest high-grade hotel to town that isn't utterly dominated by packages is the *Xenia*, on the beach (☎0377/71 412, fax 71 362; ⑥), with substantial bargains outside peak season. A **campsite**, better appointed than those in Ierissós, lies 2km north of the village, amidst a crop of luxury hotel complexes which have sprouted where there's more space to spread out. The half-dozen obvious waterfront **tavernas** all tout identical rip-off menus, though you're unlikely to care much about value for money before (or especially after) several lean days on Áthos. On the south waterfront, respectively just before and after the town limits sign, are two more appealing alternatives: *Mantho*, a traditional-format estiatório with plenty of *mayireftá*, and the fancier *Athos*, next to the hotel *Avra*, with a huge menu featuring grilled vegetables, soups and (unusually) sweets. Ouranoúpoli has a **post office**, but no bank.

Mount Áthos: the monks' republic

The population of the **Mount Áthos** peninsula has been exclusively male – farm animals included – since the *ávaton* edict, banning females permanent or transient, was promulgated by the Byzantine emperor Constantine Monomachos in 1060. Known in Greek as the **Áyion Óros** (Holy Mountain), it is an administratively autonomous province of the country – a "monks' republic" – on whose slopes are gathered twenty monasteries, plus a number of smaller dependencies and hermitages.

Most of the **monasteries** were founded in the tenth and eleventh centuries; today, all survive in a state of comparative decline but they remain unsurpassed in their general and architectural interest, and for the art treasures they contain. If you are male, over 18 years old and have a genuine interest in monasticism or Greek Orthodoxy,

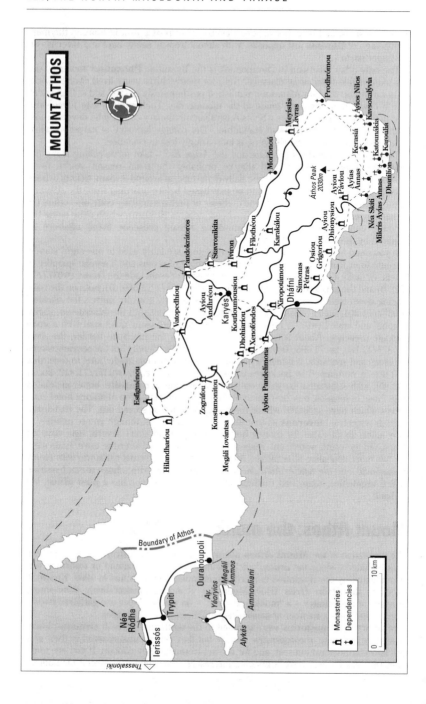

sacred music or simply in Byzantine and medieval architecture, a visit is strongly rec-ommended. It takes less than an hour to arrange, either in Thessaloníki or Athens (see p.431 for details), and the rewards more than justify any efforts. In addition to the reli-gious and architectural aspects of Áthos, it should be added that the peninsula, despite some horrific fires and heavy logging in recent years, remains one of the most beauti-ful parts of Greece. With only the occasional service vehicle, two buses and sporadic coastal boats, a visit necessarily involves walking between settlements – preferably on paths through dense woods, up the main peak or above what is perhaps the Mediterranean's last undeveloped coastline. For many visitors, this – as much as the experience of monasticism – is the highlight of time spent on the Holy Mountain.

The Theocratic Republic: some history

By a legislative decree of 1926, Áthos has the status of **Theocratic Republic**. It is gov-erned from the small town and capital of Karyés by the *Ayía Epistasía* (Holy Superintendency), a council of twenty representatives elected for one-year terms by each of the monasteries. At the same time Áthos remains a part of Greece. All foreign monks must adopt Greek citizenship and the Greek civil government is represented by an appointed governor and a small police force.

Each monastery has a distinct place in the **Athonite hierarchy**: Meyístis Lávras holds the prestigious first place, Kastamonítou ranks twentieth. All other settlements are attached to one or other of the twenty "ruling" monasteries; the dependencies range from a *skíti* (either a group of houses, or a cloister-like compound scarcely dis-tinguishable from a monastery) through a *kellí* (a sort of farmhouse) to an *isihastírio* (a solitary hermitage, often a cave). Numerous laymen – including many Muslim Albanians of late – also live on Áthos, mostly employed as agricultural or manual labour-ers by the monasteries.

The **development of monasticism** on Áthos is a matter of some controversy, and foundation legends abound. The most popular asserts that the Virgin Mary was blown ashore here on her way to Cyprus; she was overcome by the great beauty of the moun-tain and a celestial voice consecrated the place in her name. Another tradition relates that Constantine the Great founded the first monastery in the fourth century, but this is certainly far too early. The earliest historical reference to Athonite monks is to their attendance at a council of the Empress Theodora in 843; probably there were some monks here by the end of the seventh century. Áthos was particularly appropriate for early Christian monasticism, its deserted and isolated slopes providing a natural refuge from the outside world – especially from the Arab conquests in the east, and during the Iconoclastic phase of the Byzantine empire (eighth to ninth centuries). Moreover its awesome beauty, which so impressed the Virgin, facilitated communion with God.

The most famous of the **early monks** were Peter the Athonite and St Euthymios of Salonica, both of whom lived in cave-hermitages on the slopes during the mid-ninth century. In 885 an edict of Emperor Basil I recognized Áthos as the sole preserve of monks, and gradually hermits came together to form communities known in church Greek as *koinobia* (literally "life in common"). The year 963 is the traditional date for the **foundation of the first monastery**, Meyístis Lávras, by Athanasios the Athonite; Emperor Nikiforos Fokas provided considerable financial assistance. Over the next two centuries, with the protection of other Byzantine emperors, foundations were frequent, the monasteries reaching forty in number (reputedly with a thousand monks in each), alongside many smaller communities.

Troubles for Áthos began at the end of the eleventh century. The monasteries suf-fered sporadically from pirate raids and from the settlement of three hundred Vlach shepherd families on the mountain. After a reputedly scandalous episode between the monks and the shepherdesses, the Vlachs were ejected and a new imperial *chryssobull* ("golden" edict) was issued, confirming that no female mammal, human or animal, be allowed to set foot on Áthos. This edict, called the *ávaton*, remains in force today, excepting various cats to control rodents.

During the twelfth century, the monasteries gained an international – or at least, a **pan-Orthodox** – aspect, as Romanian, Russian and Serbian monks flocked to the mountain in retreat from the turbulence of the age. Áthos itself was subjected to Frankish raids during the Latin occupation of Constantinople (1204–61) and, even after this, faced great pressure from the Unionists of Latin Salonica to unite with western Catholics; in the courtyard of Zográfou there is still a monument to the monks who were martyred at this time while attempting to preserve the independence of Orthodox Christianity. In the early fourteenth century the monasteries suffered two disastrous years of pillage by Catalan mercenaries but they recovered, primarily through Serbian benefactors, to enjoy a period of great prosperity in the fifteenth and sixteenth centuries.

After the fall of the Byzantine empire to the Ottomans, the fathers wisely declined to resist, maintaining good relations with the early sultans, one of whom paid a state visit. The later Middle Ages brought **economic problems**, with heavy taxes and confiscations, and as a defence many of the monasteries dissolved their common holdings and reverted to an idiorrhythmic system, a self-regulating form of monasticism where monks live and worship in a loosely bound community but work and eat individually. However, Áthos remained the spiritual centre of Orthodoxy, and during the seventeenth and eighteenth centuries even built and maintained its own schools.

The mountain's real decline came after the **War of Independence**, in which many of the monks fought alongside the Greek revolutionary forces. In Macedonia the insurrectionists were easily subdued, the region remaining under Ottoman control, and the monks paid the price. A permanent Turkish garrison was established on the mountain and monastery populations fell sharply as, in the wake of independence for southern Greece, monasticism became less of a focus for Greek Orthodox Christianity.

At the end of the last century and the beginning of this one **foreign Orthodox** monks, particularly Russian ones, tried to step in and fill the vacuum. But the Athonite fathers have always resisted any move that might dilute the Greek character of the Holy Mountain, even – until recently – at the expense of its material prosperity. During the early 1960s, numbers were at their lowest ever, barely a thousand, compared to 20,000 in Áthos's heyday. Today, however, the monastic population has climbed to about two thousand, its average age has dropped significantly, and the number of well-educated monks increased markedly.

This revival is due partly to the increasing appeal of the contemplative life in a blatantly materialistic and morally relativistic age, but more importantly to a wave of rather militant sectarian sentiment, which has swept both the Holy Mountain and world Orthodoxy at large. Active recruitment and evangelizing has produced a large crop of novices from every continent, particularly visible in such monasteries as Símonos Pétras, Filothéou and Vatopedhíou. On the negative side, some less picturesque manifestations of worldliness have appeared at the monasteries: supposed "pilgrims" are glued to their mobile phones come evening (card-phones are available for the rest of us), many of the monasteries have faxes, and much of the Mountain resembles a building site, with massive, ongoing restoration or new building works underway at every monastery or *skíti*, usually with little regard for traditional architecture. The ro-ro ferries from "the world" bring massive, clanking trucks carrying building materials on the trip in, exchanging these for partially milled lumber on the way out. Jet fighters roar overhead on regular sorties from nearby Límnos, and there are even two helipads on Áthos, though the jets at least cannot be blamed on the Church. Some of the monks (and not a few foreigners, including the late Byzantine specialist Philip Sherrard) feel that this modernization has got out of hand, and there is already something of a murmuring backlash against it; one beneficial effect of this will hopefully be to preserve what remains of Athos's rapidly dwindling trail system from the road-builders.

ATHONITE TERMS

Arhondáris Guestmaster of a monastery or *skíti*, responsible for all visitors; similarly, *arhondaríki*, the guest quarters themselves.

Arsanás Harbour annexe of each monastery or *skíti*, where ro-ro ferries or *kaïkia* anchor; they can be a considerable distance from the institution in question.

Cenobitic/Idiorrythmic Historically, this is (increasingly, was) the major distinction between religious foundations on the Mountain. At cenobite establishments the monks eat all meals together, hold all property in common and have rigidly scheduled days. Those remaining foundations that are idiorrhythmic are more individualistic: the monks eat in their own quarters and study or worship when and as they wish. Beginning in the mid-1980s, all of the remaining idiorrhythmic monasteries reverted to cenobitic status, with Pandokrátoros the last hold-out until 1992. Currently monks wishing to follow a more independent path must take up residence in an idiorrhythmic *skíti* (most of them are) or a *kellí*.

Dhíkeos The "righteous one" – head of an idiorrhythmic foundation.

Dhókimos A novice monk.

Fiáli The covered font for holy water in some monastery courtyards; often very ornate.

Igoúmenos Abbot, the head of a monastery.

Katholikón Main church of a monastery.

Kyriakón Central chapel of a *skíti*, where the residents worship together once weekly.

Trapezaría Refectory, or dining room.

Yérondas A novice's spiritual elder and supervisor, not necessarily the abbot; akin to the *staretz* of the Russian Orthodox tradition.

Critics also assert that the "renaissance" has transformed religious life on Áthos with little tact, compelling many supposedly lax idiorrhythmic houses to become cenobitic as the price of their revitalization. In an echo of the conflicts earlier this century, there has also allegedly been interference with the efforts of the non-Greek foundations to recruit brothers and receive pilgrims from their home country, and in general a confusion of the aims of Orthodoxy and Hellenism. Specifically, there have been consistent complaints that Orthodox pilgrims from Slavic countries are routinely subject to petty harassment from the Greek authorities, and that clerics and novices from Serbia, Russia, Romania and Bulgaria must be approved for entry by the Ecumenical Patriarchate in Istanbul, unlike Greek priests.

If these tensions appear unseemly in a commonwealth devoted to spiritual perfection, it's worth remembering that doctrinal strife has always been part of Athonite history; that most of the monks still are Greek; and that donning the habit doesn't quell their inborn love of intrigue. Also, in a perverse way, the ongoing controversies demonstrate a renewed vitality, inasmuch as Mount Athos, and who controls it, are seen once again as having some global importance.

Permits and entry

Until a few decades ago foreigners could visit Áthos quite easily, but during the early 1970s the number of tourists grew so great that the monasteries could no longer cope. Since then a permit system has been instituted, and only Greeks – and to a lesser extent foreign Greek Orthodox, who automatically rank as religious pilgrims – are exempt from it. There have, incidentally, been recent mutterings in the foreign press that Áthos, as a sub-province of Greece, must cease controlling its own borders, even to the extent of admitting women, but the Mountain and its foreign sympathizers promise to fight any such changes, and the permit system is likely to remain in place for some years yet.

The first step in **acquiring a permit** to visit and stay on Áthos is to call at the pilgrims' office for Mount Áthos (*Grafío Proskynitón Ayíou Órous*) in Thessaloníki, located at Konstandínou Karamanlí 14 (formerly Néa Egnatía 172), First Floor. This is open Mon–Sat 8.30am–1.30pm & Mon, Tues, Thurs & Fri 6–8pm. Telephone enquiries are taken daily Mon–Sat 11am–1pm and on the days indicated above, 6.30–7.30pm. Heterodox foreigners, who are allotted just ten entry permits per day, should ring ☎031/861 611; Greek Orthodox foreigners, who are allowed one hundred entry permits daily, should ring ☎031/833 733. You will need to bring your passport if calling in person; if making a phone booking, fax the vital pages to ☎031/861 811. Staff are helpful and speak English; after consultation, you will be issued a reservation confirmation slip valid for four days' residence on Áthos, which will have a date specified for initial entry to the monastic republic. This may not be the date of your choice from May to September, or at Orthodox Easter time, when it's all but mandatory to apply for permission several weeks in advance. Greek Orthodox of whatever nationality are entitled to a two-week sojourn.

To get to Áthos, take a Halkidhikí KTEL bus from its terminal at Karakássi 68 to Ouranoúpoli or Ierissós (see "East to secular Áthos", p.425). From Ouranoúpoli just one **boat** daily throughout the year sails at 9.45am as far as **Dháfni**, the main port on the southwestern coast of Áthos, stopping at each *arsanás* or coastal monastery on route; from Dháfni, there's a connecting service onward to the *skíti* of Ayías Ánnas. If you're setting out on the day your permit starts, you'll have to take the earliest (6am) KTEL departure to connect with the boat. At Ierissós, the boat leaves at 8.30am (year round on Mon, Thurs & Sat), earlier in the morning than the first bus will pass through, entailing an overnight stop here – and a chance to see if bad weather will force a cancellation. This service along the northeast shore goes as far as the monastery of **Ivíron**, but it may not stop at every *arsanás* on the way, and there's no longer any boat service up to Meyístis Lávras. Ouranoúpoli–Dháfni takes about ninety minutes, Ierissós–Ivíron more than two hours; the boats turn around for the return trip more or less immediately upon arrival. Fares are inexpensive, for example about 1000dr from Ouranoúpoli to Dháfni, or just a few hundred drachmes from one of the southwest coastal monasteries back to Dháfni.

In Ouranoúpoli, you must call at the **Grafío Proskyníton** (pilgrims' bureau, daily 8.10am–2pm), at the entry to the town, behind the Jet Oil filling station. If you've stayed overnight, it's suggested that you arrive well before opening time, as the little office is mobbed once the 6am bus from Thessaloníki arrives. Here you exchange your reservations confirmation slip for a document called the **dhiamonitírion** (8000dr, or 4000dr for card-carrying students under 27), which entitles you to stay at any of the main monasteries or *skítes*. Armed with this, you may get off the boat at the *arsanás* of any of the southwest coastal monasteries. Starting from Ierissós or Néa Rodha, passengers will be granted this permit from a police post at the *arsanás* of Hilandharíou, the first monastery on the northeast coast; they are then free to disembark or continue with the boat to a dock of another monastery of their choice.

As of writing, ten of the monasteries require **advance reservations** by phone or fax throughout the year; those showing up on spec will, in theory, be turned away, though experience suggests that the *arhondáres* are not consistently strict on this point. These **problematic monasteries** are identified in the text, and phone numbers given for all of them – though phones often go unanswered for much of the day, especially on religious holidays, so be persistent.

Many visitors wish to arrange for an **extension** of the basic four-day period. This can theoretically be done at the *Ayía Epistasía* (Holy Superintendancy) in Karyés, though you should have a good reason; two or three extra days are normally granted, and your chances are much better out of season. If you and a particular monastery are particularly taken with each other, and you intend to become a novice, an *idhikó dhiamonitírio* (special sojourning permit) can be arranged. In the past nobody was terribly bothered if you stayed five days or even a week on the mountain, except in summer when monastic accommodation gets quite crowded; the four-day limit was originally enforced to discourage gawkers and others with frivolous motives for visiting. Nowadays, however, most guestmasters ask to see your *dhiamonitírion*, and if you strike the monks as behaving presumptuously or inappropriately, no amount of time remaining on your permit will persuade them to host you. As signs on walls repeatedly remind you, "Hospitality is not obligatory."

The way of life

With *dhiamonitírion* in hand, you will be admitted to stay and eat in the main monasteries – and certain *skítes* – free of charge. If you offer money it will be refused, though Orthodox pilgrims are encouraged to buy candles, incense, CDs of liturgical music and icon reproductions of varying quality at those *skítes* which specialize in their production, or at monastery shops supplied by them. **Accommodation** is usually in dormitories, and fairly spartan, but there's usually a shower down the hall (sometimes hot) and you're always given sheets and blankets, so you don't need to lug a sleeping bag around. Áthos grows much of its own **food**, and the monastic diet is based on tomatoes, beans, olives, green vegetables, coarse bread, cheese and pasta, with occasional treats like *halvás* and fruit included. After Sunday morning service, wine often accompanies fish (fresh or tinned) in the heartiest meal of the week. Normally only two meals a day are served, the first at mid-morning, the latter about an hour and a half to two hours before sunset. You will need to be partly self-sufficient in provisions – especially dried fruits, nuts, sweets – both for the times when you fail to coincide with meals and for the long walks between monasteries. (If you arrive after the morning or evening meal you will generally be served leftovers set aside for latecomers.) There are a few shops in Karyés, but for better selection and to save valuable time you should stock up before coming to Áthos.

If you're planning to **walk between monasteries**, you should get hold of one of two **maps**: the first simply entitled "Athos", produced in Austria at a scale of 1:50,000 by Reinhold Zwerger (Wohlmutstr 8, A 1020 Wien; ☎43/222/262205 or 43/2641/67212), is no longer available in Greece but may still be stocked by specialist map shops like Stanford's in London. The other, a simple sketch map of all the roads and trails on Mount Áthos, was prepared by Theodhoros Tsiropoulos of Thessaloníki (☎031/430 196), who has marked most of the surviving Athonite trails with white-lettering-on-red-field wooden signposts. The map provided by *Korfes* magazine is now obsolete and contains potentially dangerous errors, but it's still more useful than any of the fanciful touristic productions sold in Ouranoúpoli. Even equipped with the better maps, you'll still need to be pointed to the start of trails at each monastery, and confirm walking times and path conditions. New roads are constantly being built, and trails accordingly abandoned, and in the humid local climate they become completely overgrown within two years if not used.

If need be, you can supplement walking with the regular **kaïki** service provided by the little *Ayia Anna* on the southwest coast only. This departs from the *skíti* of Kavsokalývia, near the southern tip of the peninsula, via all intervening *arsanádhes*, to Dháfni at about 9.15am in summer, with onward connections towards the "border" just after noon. There is no longer any regular linking service between Kavsokalývia and Meyístis Lávras, nor between the latter and Ivíron. The decrepit, cast-off school buses of yore which plied between Dháfni and Ivíron via Karyés have been replaced by sleek Landrover minibuses scheduled (in theory) to coincide with the arrival times of the larger ferries; they can be expensive, and especially if driven by lay-workers you should establish a price beforehand

However you move around, you must reach your destination **before dark**, since all monasteries and many *skítes* lock their front gates at sunset – leaving you outside with the wild boars and (it is claimed) a handful of wolves. Upon arrival you should ask for the *arhondáris* (**guestmaster**), who will proffer the traditional welcome of a *tsípouro* (distilled spirits) and *loukoúmi* (Turkish delight) before showing you to your bed. These days guestmasters tend to speak good English, a reflection of the increasing numbers of Cypriot, Australian or educated Greek novices on Áthos.

You will find the monastic **daily schedule** somewhat disorientating, and adapted according to the seasonal time of sunrise and sunset. On the northeast side of the peninsula 12 o'clock is reckoned from the hour of sunrise, and on the opposite side clocktowers show both hands up at sunset, in the traditional Byzantine manner. Yet Vatopedhíou keeps "worldly" time, as do most monks' wrist-watches, and in most monasteries two wall-clocks are mounted side-by-side: one showing secular time, including daylight savings, the other "Byzantine" time. However the **Julian calendar**, two weeks behind the outside world, is universally observed, in particular for the observation of the frequent holy days. Most monasteries have electric power from generators – though this may be switched on for just a few hours at dusk, powering feeble bulbs – and all now have phones, sometimes faxes as well. But these have affected the round of life very little; both you and the monks will go to bed early, shortly after sunset. Sometimes in the small hours your hosts will awake for solitary meditation and study, followed by *órthros*, or matins. Around sunrise there is another quiet period, just before the *akolouthía*, or main liturgy. Next comes the morning meal, anywhere from 9.30am to 11.30am depending on the time of year and day of week. The afternoon is devoted to manual labour until the *esperinós*, or vespers, often announced by a carillon "concert" of some musicality, and actually almost three hours before sunset in summer (much less in winter). This is followed immediately by the evening meal and the short *apódhipno*, or compline service.

A few words about **attitudes and behaviour** towards your hosts (and vice versa) are in order, as many misunderstandings arise from mutual perceptions of disrespect, real or imagined. For your part, you should be fully clad at all times, even when going from dormitory to bathroom; this in effect means no shorts, no hats inside monasteries and sleeves that come down to the middle of the biceps. If you swim, do so where nobody can see you, and don't do it naked. Smoking in most foundations is forbidden, though a few allow you to indulge out on the balconies. It would be criminal to do so on the trail, given the chronic fire danger; you might just want to give it up as a penance for the duration of your stay. Singing, whistling and raised voices are taboo; so is standing with your hands behind your back or crossing your legs when seated, both considered overbearing stances. If you want to photograph monks you should always ask permission, though photography is forbidden altogether in many monasteries, and video cameras are completely banned from the mountain. It's best not to go poking around corners of the buildings where you're not specifically invited, even if they seem open to the public.

Monasteries, and their tenants, tend to vary a good deal in their handling of visitors, and their reputations, deserved or otherwise, tend to precede them as a favourite subject of trail gossip among foreigners. You will find that as a non-Orthodox you may be politely ignored, or worse, with signs at some institutions specifically forbidding you from attending services or sharing meals with the monks. Other monasteries are by contrast quite engaging, putting themselves at the disposal of visitors of whatever creed. It is not unknown to be treated to ferocious bigotry and disarming gentility at the same place within the space of ten minutes, making it tricky to draw conclusions about Áthos in general and monasteries in particular. If you are non-Orthodox, and seem to understand enough Greek to get the message, you'll probably be told at some point, subtly or less so, that you're bound for Hell unless you convert to the True Faith. While this may seem offensive, it pays to remember that the monks are expecting religious pilgrims, not tourists, and that their role is to be committed, not tolerant. On average, expect those monks with some level of education or smattering of foreign languages to be benignly interested in you, and a very soft-sell in the form of a reading library of pamphlets and books left at your disposal. Incidentally, idiorrhythmic *skítes* (see below) tend to provide exceedingly basic accommodation and food, even by austere monastic standards, and *kelliá* are not bound by the monastic rule of hospitality, so you really need to know someone at a *kellí* in order to stay the night.

The monasteries

Obviously you can't hope to visit all twenty monasteries during a short stay, though if you're able to extend the basic four-day period for a few days you can fairly easily see the peninsula's most prominent foundations. The dirt road linking the southwestern port of Dháfni with the northeastern coastal monastery of Ivíron by way of Karyés, the capital, not only cuts the peninsula roughly in two but also separates the monasteries into equal southeastern and northwestern groups; the division is not so arbitrary as it seems, since the remaining path system seems to reflect it and the feel of the two halves is very different.

The southeastern group

IVÍRON

The vast **IVÍRON** monastery (☎0377/23 643; booking required noon–2pm) is not a bad introduction to Áthos, and is well poised for walks or rides in various directions. Although founded late in the tenth century by Iberian (Georgian) monks, the last Georgian died in the 1950s and today it is a cenobitic house of forty monks, many of whom moved here from nearby Stavronikíta, under the tutelage of the abbot Vasilios, one of the luminaries of the monastic revival, who to his credit has also spoken out on occasion against the unseemly modernization of life on the Mountain. The focus of pilgrimage is the miraculous **icon** of the *Portaḯtissa*, the Virgin Guarding the Gate, housed in a special chapel to the left of the entrance. It is believed that if this protecting image ever leaves Áthos, then great misfortune will befall the monks. The **katholikón** is among the largest on the mountain, with an elaborate mosaic floor dating from 1030. The frescoes are recent and of limited interest, but not so various pagan touches such as the Persian-influenced gold crown around the chandelier, and two Hellenistic columns from a temple of Poseidon with rams-head capitals which once stood here. There's also a silver-leaf lemon tree crafted in Moscow; because of the Georgian connection, Russians were lavish donors to this monastery. The bare-white refectory is, unusually, unadorned except for a pulpit on the south wall, formerly used to deliver the mealtime homily. There is also an immensely rich library and treasury-museum, presided over by the kindly Father Iakovos, who speaks excellent French and English, and sells copies of the abbot's monographs.

KARYÉS AND AROUND: MINOR MONASTERIES

Though you no longer have to call in here except for extensions of the *dhiamontírion*, a look around **KARYÉS** is rewarding: the main church of the Protáton, dating from 965, contains exceptional fourteenth-century **frescoes** of the Macedonian school. Karyés also has a few **restaurants**, where you may be able to get heartier fare than is typical in the monasteries, and a simple inn – though there seems little reason to patronize it. At the northern edge of "town" sprawls the enormous cloister-like *skíti* of **Ayíou Andhréou**, a Russian dependency of the great Vatopedhíou monastery, erected hurriedly last century but today virtually deserted.

A signposted trail leads up and west within an hour to small but tidy **KOUTLOU-MOUSÍOU** (☎0377/23 226; booking required noon–2pm), at the very edge of Karyés. Much the most interesting thing about it is its name, which appears to be that of a Selçuk chieftain converted to Christianity.

From Ivíron another path stumbles south uphill, tangling with roads, to reach **FILOTHÉOU** (☎0377/23 256, fax 23 674), which was at the forefront of the monastic revival in the early 1980s, courtesy of its abbot Ephraim, and hence one of the more vital monasteries. It is not, however, one of the more impressive foundations from an architectural or artistic point of view – though the lawn surfacing the entire courtyard is an interesting touch – and it's one of those houses where the non-Orthodox are forbidden from attending church or eating with the monks.

The same is true at **KARAKÁLOU** (☎0377/23 225; booking required noon–2pm), 45 minutes' walk (mostly on paths) below Filothéou, also accessible via a short trail up from its *arsanás*. The lofty keep is typical of the fortress-monasteries built close enough to the shore to be victimized by pirates. Between here and Meyístis Lávras the trail system has been destroyed, replaced by a road that makes for six hours of dreary tramping, so it's advisable to arranging a lift with a service vehicle. Fairly regular transfers are provided by Landrover minibus from the boat jetty at Ivíron; such vehicles tend to show up between 12.30 and 1pm, and you should pay no more than 2000dr to get to Meyístis Lávras or the *skíti* or Prodhrómou just beyond. If a monk is driving, you may just get a lift for free; the drive takes just over an hour to Meyístis Lávras, nearly ninety minutes to Prodhrómou.

MEYÍSTIS LÁVRAS AND THE ATHONITE WILDERNESS

MEYÍSTIS LÁVRAS (the "Great Lavra" ☎0377/23 758) is the oldest and foremost of the ruling monasteries, and physically the most imposing establishment on Áthos, with no fewer than fifteen chapels within its walls. Although there are a fair number of additions from the last century, it has (uniquely among the twenty) never suffered from fire. The treasury and library are both predictably rich, the latter containing over two thousand precious manuscripts, though the ordinary traveller is unlikely to view them; as is usual, several monks (out of the 25 here) have complementary keys which must be operated together to gain entrance. What you will see at mealtime are the superior **frescoes** in the **trapezaría**, executed by Theophanes the Cretan in 1535. Hagiographies and grisly martyrdoms line the apse, while there's a *Tree of Jesse* (the genealogy of Jesus) in the south transept, the *Death of Athanasios* (the founder) opposite and an *Apocalypse* to the left of the main entry. In the western apse is a *Last Supper*, not surprisingly a popular theme in refectories. Just outside the door stands a huge **fiáli**, largest on the mountain, with recycled columns from a pagan temple supporting the canopy. The **katholikón**, near the rear of the large but cluttered courtyard, contains more frescoes by Theophanes.

Beyond Meyístis Lávras lies some of the most beautiful and deserted wilderness on the peninsula – the so-called Athonite "desert", beloved of ascetics – now partly compromised by a track bulldozed over the most direct path south to one of Meyístis Lávras's many dependencies, **Skíti Prodhrómou**. Under the aegis of the saintly elder Petronios, it is now full of young Romanian monks who keep the place immaculate. Just ten minutes away by marked path there's the **hermitage-cave of St Athanasios**, watched over by five skulls.

Most first-time visitors will, however, proceed without delay from Meyístis Lávras on a traverse of up to six hours across the tip of Áthos, through incomparably rugged territory along paths unlikely to be destroyed in the future – the local monks intend to keep it this way, and this is the only place on Áthos where trails are at all maintained. A few minutes past the point where the ascending paths from Meyístis Lávras and Prodhrómou link up, there's a turning down and left towards the *kellí* of **Áyios Nílos**, reached by crossing an intimidating but stablized rockfall. There's a welcome **spring** here – many on Áthos are neglected and dried up – and you can visit the cave of the medieval hermit Nilos on the far side of the prominent crag here. Otherwise, it's plainly visible after you descend through a fearsome ravine and climb up the far side; his tomb, towards the base of the same cliff, is difficult to reach.

About an hour past Áyios Nílos, or nearly three from Meyístis Lávras, you come to the sizable *skíti* of **Kavsokalývia (Ayías Triádhas)**, where donkeys are much in evidence toiling up between the tiered cottages. The community took root around the tombs of the saints Maximios and Akakios, and there's a surprisingly large and comprehensively frescoed *kyriakón* beside the small and rather plain guest quarters.

To rejoin the main trail from here involves a punishing climb over a 500-metre altitude difference, which can be avoided by taking the daily morning kaïki from Kavsokalývia's *arsanás*, a half-hour below. Disembark at the next port for the hermitages of Karoúlia and Katounákia, where you face a much more manageable climb of 200m (45min) up to the **Dhanilíon** academy, where monks and laymen perfect their technique of Byzantine chanting. From here it's an hour-plus walking on a gentle contour path to the *skíti* of Ayías Ánnas, via incongruously modernized Mikrís Ayías Ánnas, whose helipad and solar-powered villas would not disgrace a trendy Greek island.

However, the commonest strategy involves heading directly west from Prodhrómou, via the only water at the Krýa Nerá stream, to **Skíti Ayías Ánnas**, whose buildings tumble downslope to a perennial-summer patch of coast capable of ripening lemons. This, with its 1999-renovated *arhondaríki*, is the usual "base camp" for the climb of **Áthos peak** itself (2030m) – best left for the next morning, and the months May–June and September.

With a (pre-)dawn start, you gain the necessary mercy of a little shade and can expect to be up top just over four walking hours from Ayías Ánnas, with the combination refuge-church of **Panayía** passed a little over an hour before reaching the summit. Some hikers plan an overnight stop at this shelter, to watch the sunrise from the peak, but for this you must be self-sufficient in **food**. There's no spring **water** en route – you drink from cisterns at Panayía or at **Metamórfosis**, the tiny chapel atop the peak.

Returning from the peak before noon, you'll still have time to reach one of the monasteries north of Ayías Ánnas; the path continues to be delightful, and affords a sudden, breathtaking view of **AYÍOU PÁVLOU** (☎0377/23 250) as you round a bend. Except for the ugly scar of the new access road off to the left, which continues down to its *arsanás*, little can have changed in the perspective since Edward Lear painted it in the 1850s. Up close, the monastery, about ninety minutes from Ayías Ánnas, does not fulfil the promise of first sight; the courtyard lacks charm, as do the echoing, hospital-like guest area. Traditionally home to monks from the island of Kefalloniá, Ayíou Pávlou now has far more Cypriot brothers.

THE "HANGING" MONASTERIES

From Ayíou Pávlou it's another hour to **DHIONYSÍOU** (☎0377/23 687, fax 23 686), a fortified structure perched spectacularly on a coastal cliff, and among the most richly endowed monasteries. It is one of those houses where the non-Orthodox must eat separately from the monks, though there's a neat and airy *arkhondaríki* that come as a relief after so many claustrophobic facilities. Sadly, it is difficult to make out the sixteenth-century **frescoes** by the Cretan Tzortzis in the hopelessly dim *katholikón*, likewise an icon attributed to the Evangelist Luke; however, those of Theophanes on the inside and out of the **trapezaría** are another story. The interior features *The Entry of* *the Saints into Paradise* and *The Ladder to Heaven*; the exterior wall bears a version of the *Apocalypse*, complete with what looks suspiciously like a nuclear mushroom cloud. Unusually, the Cypriot warden may offer a tour of the **library** with its illuminated gospels on silk-fortified paper, wooden carved miniature of the Passion week and ivory crucifixes. You've little chance, however, of seeing Dhionysíou's great treasure, the three-metre-long **chryssobull** of the Trapezuntine emperor Alexios III Komnenos. Extensive modernization has been carried out here, with mixed results: clean electric power is supplied by a water turbine up-canyon, but the old half-timbered facade has been replaced with a rather brutal concrete-stucco one.

The onward path to **OSÍOU GRIGORÍOU** (☎0377/23 668, booking required 11am–1pm) is a bit neglected but spectacular and still usable, depositing you at the front door within an hour and a quarter of leaving Dhionysíou. Of all the monasteries and *skítes* it has the most intimate relation with the sea, though every building dates from after a devastating fire in 1761. It also – uniquely among the monasteries – has no road access as yet, making it nearly as peaceful as the *skítes* of the "desert". Owing to yet another charismatic abbot, some forty monks live here, usually vastly outnumbered by Greek pilgrims attracted by the place's reputation and calibre of chanting. In the old guest quarters there's an attractive "common room"-library with literature on Orthodoxy; the guest overflow stays in a new, wood-trimmed hostel outside the gate, by the boat dock.

The southwest coastal trail system ends ninety minutes later at **SÍMONOS PÉTRAS** (abbreviated **Simópetra**; ☎0377/23 254, fax 23 707, reservations required 1–3pm) or "The Rock of Simon", after the foundation legend asserting that the hermit Simon was directed to build a monastery here by a mysterious light hovering over the sheer pinnacle. Though entirely rebuilt in the wake of a fire a century ago, Simópetra is perhaps the most visually striking monastery on Áthos. With its multiple storeys, ringed by wooden balconies overhanging sheer 300-metre drops, it resembles nothing so much as a Tibetan lamasery. As at Dhionysíou, of which it seems an exaggerated rendition, the courtyard is quite narrow. Thanks to the fire there are no material treasures worth mentioning, though the monastery rivals Filothéou in vigour, with sixty monks from a dozen countries around the world, and the choir is generally acknowledged to be the best on Áthos. Unfortunately, because of the spectacle it presents, and its feasibility as an easy first stop out of Dháfni, Simópetra is always crowded with foreigners and Orthodox alike, and might be better admired from a distance, especially during summer.

Further walking is inadvisable and it's best to arrange a lift northwest up the peninsula, or catch the morning boat in the same direction.

The northwestern group

DHÁFNI PORT AND THE RUSSIAN MONASTERY

Though you may not ever pass through Karyés, at some point you'll make the acquaintance of **DHÁFNI**, if only to change boats, since the service on this coast is not continuous. There's a **post office**, some rather tacky souvenir shops and a **customs** post – much more vigilant when you leave than upon entry; all passengers' baggage is inspected to check traffic in smuggled-out treasures. A number of eagle-brooch-capped Athonite police skulk about as well, ever ready to pounce on real or imagined violations of the Athonite dress and behaviour codes. There's a **taverna** where you can get a beer and bean soup, but no shops adequate for restocking on food and drink.

The kaïki usually has an hour's layover here before heading back towards Ayías Ánnas, during which time the captain can often be persuaded (for a reasonable fee) to take groups as far as the Russian monastery of **AYÍOU PANDELÍMONA** (alias **Roussikó**; ☎0377/23 252), sparing you a dull forty-minute walk from the port. Most of the monks are Russian, an ethnic predominance strongly reflected in onion-shaped **domes** and the softer faces of the frescoes. The majority of the buildings were erected at speed just after the mid-1800s, as part of Tsarist Russia's campaign for eminence on the Mountain, and have a utilitarian, barracks-like quality. The sole unique features are the corrosion-green lead roofs and the enormous **bell** over the refectory, the second largest in the world, which always prompts speculation as to how it got there. Otherwise, the small population fairly rattles around the echoing halls, the effect of desolation increased by ranks of outer dormitories gutted by a fire in 1968. If you're an architecture buff, Roussikó can probably be omitted without a twinge of conscience; students of turn-of-the-century kitsch will be delighted, however, with mass-produced saints' calendars, gaudy reliquaries and a torrent of gold (or at least gilt) fixtures in the seldom-used *katholikón*. If you are permitted to attend service in the top-storey chapel north of the belfry, do so for the sake of the Slavonic chanting, though it must be said that the residents don't exactly put themselves out for non-Slavs. However, since the collapse of the Soviet Union, Ayíou Pandelímona anticipates a material and spiritual renaissance of sorts, and ongoing works are doubtless intended to accommodate the growing flood of Russian Orthodox pilgrims.

Actually closer to Dháfni, a bit inland on what remains of the old path towards Karyés, stands the square compound of **XIROPOTÁMOU** (reservations required 1–3pm; ☎0377/23 251), with most of its construction and church frescoes dating from the eighteenth century, except for two wings that were fire-damaged in 1952. Like Filothéou, this monastery was at the forefront of the 1980s "renaissance"; here again non-Orthodox are kept segregated from the faithful at meal times.

GREEK COASTAL MONASTERIES
From the vicinity of Dháfni or Roussikó, most pilgrims continue along the coast, reaching **XENOFÓNDOS** (☎0377/23 249) along a mix of trail and tractor track an hour after quitting the Russian monastery. Approached from this direction, Xenofóndos's busy sawmill gives it a vaguely industrial air. The enormous, sloping, irregularly shaped court, expanded upward last century, is unique in possessing two *katholiká*. The small, older one – with exterior frescoes of the Cretan school – was outgrown and replaced during the 1830s by the huge upper one. Among its many icons are two fine **mosaic** ones of saints Yeóryios and Dhimítrios. The guest quarters occupy a modern wing overlooking the sea at the extreme south end of the perimeter.

A half-hour's walk separates Xenofóndos from **DHOHIARÍOU** (☎0377/23 245), one of the more picturesque monasteries on this coast but not conspicuously friendly to the non-Orthodox. Early 1990s renovations left untouched the spare but clean *arhondaríki*, which sees few foreigners. An exceptionally lofty, large **katholikón** nearly fills the court, though its Cretan-school frescoes, possibly by Tzortzis, were clumsily retouched in 1855. Much better are the late seventeenth-century ones in the long, narrow **refectory**, with its sea views some of the nicest on Áthos. Even Orthodox pilgrims have trouble getting to see the wonder-working icon of *Gorgoipikóöu* (She Who is Quick to Hear), housed in a chapel between church and *trapezaría*.

THE FAR NORTHERN MONASTERIES
The direct trail inland and up to Konstamonítou has been reclaimed by the forest, so to get there you have to go in a roundabout fashion 45 minutes along the coast to its *arsanás*, and then as much time again sharply up on a track which has regrettably buried the old cobbled way. **KONSTAMONÍTOU** (☎0377/23 228), hidden up in a thickly wooded valley, seems as humble, bare and poor as you'd expect from the last-ranking monastery; the *katholikón* nearly fills the quadrangular court where the grass is literally growing up through the cracks. Non-Orthodox and believers are segregated, not that many foreigners make it this far.

From here you can continue on foot for ninety minutes to Zográfou, more usually reached directly from its *arsanás* (second stop on the boat route from Ouranoúpoli) within an hour by a track which has obliterated eighty percent of the old path. **ZOGRÁFOU** (☎0377/23 247), the furthest inland of the monasteries, is populated by a handful of elderly Bulgarian monks whose numbers are not being replenished, owing to long-standing indifference by both the Greek and Bulgarian governments. A stroll down the empty, rambling corridors past the scarcely maintained seventeenth- and eighteenth-century cells lends an appreciation of the enormous workload that falls on so few shoulders, yet even here building materials are piled high for the imminent makeover. "Zográfou" means "of the Painter", in reference to a tenth-century legend: the Slavs who founded the monastery couldn't decide on a patron saint, so they put a wooden panel by the altar, and after lengthy prayer a painting of Áyios Yeóryios – henceforth the institution's protector – appeared.

From Zográfou the direct trails to Esfigmenoú and Vatopedhíou have been bull-dozed, so the best option if you're crossing the peninsula is to follow the one surviving path which begins as a shaded *kalderími* and is only sullied by tracks for about twenty minutes near the high point. After some three hours on this high-quality route, you suddenly drop down to **HILANDHARÍOU (Hilandar** in Serbian; ☎0377/23 797), hidden in a shady glen and fringed by vast, mechanically tilled gardens and orchards. This enormous, irregularly shaped monastery has been hard hit by the recent Balkan wars which has pretty much cut off the flow of Serbian pilgrims, and all things considered the twenty, mostly young monks who come in rota from Serbia are amazingly civil and hospitable to English visitors. Hilandharíou has been Serbian since its thirteenth-century patronization by Serbian kings, and as you'd expect for a beacon of medieval Serbian culture, the library and treasury are well endowed. More recently it has allegedly served as a hotbed of Serbian nationalism, and the floating population of tatooed Serbian lay-workers may or may not be fugitive Bosnian Serbs accused of war crimes, a dubious revival of the Holy Mountain's historic role as a no-questions-asked place of asylum. The **katholikón**, at the bottom end of the sloping, triangular court-yard, dates from the fourteenth century, but its frescoes, similar in style to those in the Protáton at Karyés, have been retouched. On the south side of the church, an allegedly 800-year-old grapevine has sprouted miraculously of its own accord from a holy tomb; the monks make raisins of its grapes, to which are ascribed various miraculous properties. Opposite the door of the **refectory**, there's a fresco of the *Ouranóskala* or Stairway to Heaven, in which righteous monks are being assisted upwards by angels, while a few wicked ones are being yanked down by demons to the mouth of Hell. Last but perhaps not least, the reception area is the most sumptuous and tasteful on the Mountain, more like the lobby of a Spanish parador, and the *arhondaríki* is also among the most salubrious.

NORTHEAST COAST MONASTERIES

From Hilandharioú purists can follow a path east, then north, with considerable elevation change, to **ESFIGMENOÚ** monastery (☎0377/23 796), though most will opt for the easier, though duller hour-long track walk north, then east. Built directly at sea level in fortress style, it is the strictest foundation on Áthos, such that it does not recognize the authority of current Patriarch Vartholomeos and in its schismatic state has little to do with the other nineteen monasteries. Some of its ninety monks have erected a sign facing the sea, reading "Orthodoxy or Death", which does not encourage a casual visit; the premises, lit by oil lamp, have an accordingly harsh feel despite a courtyard full of citrus and banana trees.

Nonetheless, Esfigmenoú marks the start of one of the more wonderful surviving Áthos treks, the three-and-a-half hour coastal trek to Vatopedhíou (which, incidentally, tends to close an hour *before* sunset). There's track for the initial twenty minutes, then a path heads off left (seaward); shortly after the high point of the route, an hour along the path, a well-preserved *kalderími* kicks in for the long descent through the thick Dhafnára laurel groves to emerge briefly on the coast, about two-and-a-half hours along, before heading slightly inland again as a *kalderími* on the final approach.

VATOPEDHÍOU (☎23 219; booking required 10am–4pm) exceeds Meyístis Lávras in size, nearly matches it in importance and wealth, and makes a good beginning or farewell to Áthos. The cobbled, slanting court with its freestanding belfry seems more like a town plaza, ringed by stairways and stacks of cells – in the throes of renovation until 2001 – for more than three hundred monks. The **katholikón**, one of the oldest on the mountain, has the usual array of frescoes painted over for better or worse, but more uniquely three **mosaics** flanking the door of the inner narthex: Gabriel (left) and the Virgin (right) comprising an *Annunciation*, with the *Deisis* (the Virgin, Christ and John the Baptist) above. The growing population of about 75 welcoming monks, mostly young and mostly Cypriot or Australian in background, makes this a good place to get to grips with Orthodoxy, with plenty of English-speakers to talk to and reading material provided in the *arhondaríki*. Even if you're not staying, it's possible to have a small snack here and retire from the heat of midday before resuming progress to other monasteries.

Continuing southeast, you can initially short-cut dust-tracks on the *kalderími* for the first hour-plus up to the ridge, but the ninety-minute trail from there to Pandokrátoros was chewed up by bulldozers in 1998 and is now all but impossible to find going in this direction. Allow nearly three hours to reach **PANDOKRÁTOROS** (☎0377/23 226; booking required noon–2pm). Other than a hilltop setting overlooking its own picturesque fishing harbour, and the courtyard with its eight Valencia orange trees, there is little of artistic note – perhaps still less given ambitious renovations – though the 35 young monks are welcoming, and the guest wing overlooks the sea. In a valley above looms its dependent *skíti* of **Profítis Ilías**, a relic of the Russian expansion drive and today home to a handful of monks from several different countries.

Continuing on the now-shady, roller-coasting shoreline trail, it's under an hour door-to-door to tiny **STAVRONIKÍTA** (☎0377/23 255; booking required 1–3pm). With some of the best views of Áthos peak available, it's also the best example of an Athonite coastal fortress-monastery and distinctly vertical in orientation on its surf-lashed promontory. Long one of the poorest houses, Stavronikíta was completely revitalized under the abbot Vasilios before his move to Ivíron, and, surrounded by aqueduct-fed kitchen gardens, remains pin-neat. The narrow **katholikón** occupies virtually all of the gloomy courtyard, and the **refectory**, normally opposite, had to be shifted upstairs to the south wing; it's a spartan room with a single window on the water, and fresco fragments by Theophanes of the *Death of Áyios Nikólaos* (the patron) and the *Last Supper*. Many Australians, including the most recent abbot, number among the 25 monks, who really are strict about bookings for the small, oil-lamp-lit guest quarters and who will roust all, Orthodox and infidel alike, for 3.30am matins. All non-Orthodox guests will be sent on their way an hour or so after sunrise, after coffee and biscuits. Despite (or because of) the foregoing, this is a popular monastery with young, educated city Greeks. From here an hour's walk, mostly on path, separates you from Ivíron.

The coast to Kavála

Heading towards Kavála from Sithonía or Áthos by public transport is surprisingly tricky, since buses from either peninsula run only back to Thessaloníki. However, the gap between the Thessaloníki–Halkidhikí and Thessaloníki–Kavála services is only 16km wide at one point, with a couple of places you wouldn't mind getting stuck at along the way, so if you don't have your own transport, you could always walk.

To begin, you should get off the Ouranoúpoli–Thessaloníki bus at the drab coastal village of **STRATÓNI**. The bay here is dominated by the local mine workings, and there is little incentive to stay, though there are several tavernas on the grey-black beach and even one basic hotel, the *Angelika* (☎0376/22 075; ③). From Stratóni, the scenic road glides over the forested ridge north 15km to the beach resort of Olymbiádha and regular buses to the Thessaloníki–Kavála highway; these orange vehicles end up in Thessaloníki at a special terminal at Irínis 17, behind Langadhás 16, and ply four times daily Monday to Friday, three times on Saturday and twice on Sunday.

OLYMBIÁDHA itself is still very low-key, though a considerable shadow hangs over the immediate future. The Athens-based mining company TVX wants to establish a highly polluting gold-processing plant here, and the locals are understandably up in arms at the prospect of losing their pristine environment; during 1999 there were demonstrations and criminal prosecutions for sabotage of company equipment. At quieter times you may stay in **rooms,** a pair of shaded, streamside campsites – *Olympias* and *Corali* (☎0376/51 304) – 1km north and 500km inland respectively, and a pair of co-managed hotels: the quieter *Liotopi* at the south edge of town, with breakfast served in a lush garden, and the central *Germany* with a ground-floor taverna (both ☎0376/51 362, fax 51 255; ⑤). There are three other **tavernas** on the southern bay, cheapest and most characterful being the *Kapetan Manolis/Platanos* by the concrete jetty. All along this shore the local speciality is **mussels** (*mýdhia*), farmed in floating nursery beds and typically served in a spicy cheese sauce, or sold raw for home use at roadside stalls.

The small town **beaches** are fine, but there are other ones – such as Próti Ammoudhiá, where the water can be murky – 2km back towards Stratóni, behind the promontory containing **ancient Stageira**, birthplace of Aristotle. This covers two hilltops joined by a saddle, and is under continuous summer excavation; it's now completely fenced off, but when the gates are open you're free to have a wander around, though there's not much on view yet apart from the western wall and towers guarding the landward approach, a few paved streets and house foundations. It is, however perhaps unique in Greece for having been a city built of granite rather than marble or limestone.

STAVRÓS, 12km north of Olymbiádha – the interval dotted with semi-accessible coves – is a much bigger, busier place than Olymbiádha: a neon-lit, fun-faired vulgarity for the Thessaloníki working classes. It does, though, have a beautiful seafront of plane trees, and up to ten daily orange buses to the Irínis 17 terminal, off Langadhás in Thessaloníki. Among five modest **hotels**, the *Athos* (☎0397/61 353; ③) is the best placed and represents best value; **tavernas** such as *Iy Amalthia* or *Iy Platania*, at the far south end of town, are the most authentic and least fast-foody.

From here you're just 4km from the main E90 highway, where just east of the junction the first coastal place of any size – **ASPROVÁLTA** – will come as a jolt after the relative calm of Halkidhikí. Minimally attractive, it's essentially a summer suburb of Sérres and Thessaloníki, with frequent bus service from the Irínis 17 terminal.

Fourteen kilometres east of Asproválta, the road to Kavála crosses the **River Strymónas**, recorded as one of the most polluted in Europe owing to dumping of toxic substances near its sources in Bulgaria. If you bear onto a minor road signposted for Nigríta, rather continuing over the river bridge, after less than a kilometre you'll find on your left the colossal marble **Lion of Amphipolis**. This was reconstructed in 1937 from fragments found when excavating the nearby ancient city of Amphipolis, and is thought to date from the end of the fourth century BC. **Ancient Amphipolis** itself, some 3km further on (Tues–Sun 8.30am–3pm), figured largely in Thucydides' *Peloponnesian Wars*. It's well worth the extra detour, preserving considerable chunks of fortification wall, foundations of a fifth-century BC river bridge and an early Christian basilica with mosaic floors.

Beyond the Strymónas, there's a choice of routes east: the shorter, but slower inland road via the villages at the base of Mount Pangéo, or the slightly longer but quicker coast highway, which is the one long-distance buses to Kavála tend to use. This is being upgraded to motorway status as part of the "Via Egnatia" project, though there's not a great deal along the way other than some vineyards, an occasional crumbled medieval watchtower and duney, white-sand **beaches**, the best in eastern Macedonia, scarcely developed and relatively free from river-borne pollution. The first place of any size **NÉA PÉRAMOS**, 14km before Kavála, which sports an unheralded **castle** at one corner of its sandy, sheltered bay. This isn't a bad place to spend a couple of hours, especially before taking one of the several daily **ro-ro ferries** to the island of Thássos. *Camping Anatoli* (☎0594/21 027; May–Sept) at the west end of things, with a saltwater swimming pool, can be recommended if you want to spend the night. The only other **campsites** between here and Kavála are the *Estella*, 5km east, or the pricier *Batis*, 10km along and already hedged by Kavála's sprawl.

Kavála

KAVÁLA, backing onto the easterly foothills of Mount Sýmvolo, is the second largest city of Macedonia and the second port for northern Greece. Coming in through the suburbs, there seems little to recommend a stay. But the centre is fairly pleasant and characterful, grouped about the nineteenth-century harbour area and its old tobacco

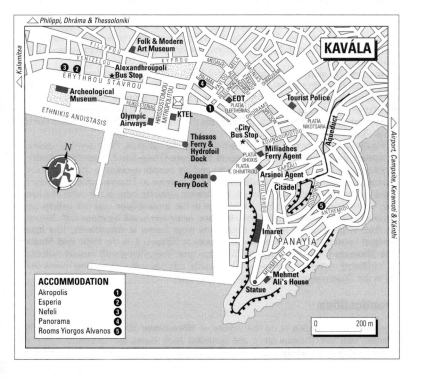

warehouses. A citadel looks down from a rocky promontory to the east, and an elegant Turkish aqueduct leaps over modern buildings into the old quarter on the bluff.

The town was known anciently as Neapolis, and as such served for two centuries or more as a terminus of the Via Egnatía and the first European port of call for merchants and travellers from the Middle East. It was here that St Paul landed en route to Philippi (see p.446), on his initial mission to Europe. In later years, the port and citadel took on considerable military significance, being occupied in turn by Byzantines, Normans, Franks, Venetians, Ottomans and (during both world wars) Bulgarians.

The town

Although the remnants of Kavála's Turkish past are mostly neglected, the wedge-shaped **Panayía** quarter to the east of the port preserves a scattering of eighteenth- and nineteenth-century buildings and considerable atmosphere. It is by far the most attractive part of town to explore, with twisting lanes wandering up towards the citadel.

The most conspicuous and interesting of its buildings is the **Imaret**, overlooking the harbour on Poulidhoú. An elongated, multi-domed structure with Arabic inscriptions over many doorways, it was originally a combination soup kitchen-cum-hostel, housing three hundred *softas*, or theological students. After many decades of dereliction it was refurbished during the early 1990s, appropriately enough, as a restaurant-bar (see "Eating and drinking", opposite). Claimed to be the largest Islamic public building in Europe, it was endowed by **Mehmet Ali**, pasha of Egypt and founder of the dynasty which ended with King Farouk. The house where Mehmet Ali was born to an Albanian family in 1769, near the corner of Pavlídhou and Méhmet Alí, is maintained as a monument. It provides an opportunity – rare in Greece – to look over a prestigious Islamic house, with its wood-panelled reception rooms, ground-floor stables and first-floor harem (daily except Mon 10am–2pm; officially free but easiest in a group; tip the non-English-speaking guide). Nearby rears an equestrian statue of the great man – a useful landmark.

You can also visit the Byzantine **citadel** (daily 10am–7pm; free) to explore the ramparts, towers, dungeon and cistern; in season it co-hosts the rather misnamed Philippi-Thássos Festival of drama and music in its main court. From here, down towards the middle of town, north of Panayía's narrow maze of streets, the **aqueduct**, built on a Roman model during the reign of Süleyman the Magnificent (1520–66), spans the traffic in Platía Nikotsára.

Finally, on the other side of the harbour from the old town, there are two museums of moderate interest. The **Archeological Museum** (Tues–Sun 8.30am–6pm; 500dr) on Erythroú Stavroú contains a fine dolphin and lily mosaic upstairs in the Abdira room, plus painted sarcophagi in the adjacent section devoted to Thasian colonies. By far the most intriguing object here, though, is a bronze statuette-lamp in the form of a kneeling, bound barbarian prisoner. Downstairs in the ground-floor rear left gallery are a reconstructed Macedonian funeral chamber, many terracotta figurines still decorated in their original paint and gold ornaments from tombs at Amphipolis. Just inland, wedged between former tobacco warehouses at Filíppou 4, is the **Folk and Modern Art Museum** (Mon–Fri 8am–2pm, Sat 9am–1pm; free). Along with various collections of traditional costumes and household utensils, this has some interesting rooms devoted to the Thássos-born sculptor Polygnotos Vayis.

Practicalities

The main **bus station** is on the corner of Mitropolítou Khrysosstómou and Filikís Eterías, near the Thássos ferry and hydrofoil dock; buses for Alexandhroúpoli stop some blocks away on Erythroú Stavroú, in front of the *Hotel Oceanis*. **Taxis** are coloured deep orange; if you're **driving** in, you can usually (just) find a space on the quay car park near the Thássos dock. In the main square, Platía Eleftherías, you'll find an **EOT** office, which can provide details (and sell tickets) for the summer Philippi-Thássos Festival. Right next door is a long-hours money **exchange** booth, Midas, and the Ionian Bank has erected an automatic note-changer on the fishing wharf, though the square is ringed by several banks with cash dispensers. Kavála's "international" **airport**, used by package holidaymakers en route to Thássos, lies 29km southeast in coastal marshland between the town and Keramotí.

Accommodation

Abundant, good-value **hotel** rooms are not the order of the day in Kavála, though proprietors can often be bargained down a category or two in the off-season. Especially if you're arriving on an afternoon charter in summer, you might well prefer to transfer from the airport to Keramotí for a ferry to Thássos with its wide choice of accommodation (see p.754), reserving Kavála for a day-trip.

While there are some dosshouses on the pedestrian streets just off Platía Eleftherías, suitable for those with a consuming interest in the underbelly of Balkan culture, for most travellers the cheapest acceptable outfits will be the *Panorama* at Venizélou 26–32/C (☎051/224 205; ④ en-suite, ③ not) or the *Akropolis* (☎051/223 543, fax 830 752; ④ en-suite, ③ not) at Eleftheríou Venizélou 29, west of Platía Eleftherías, with English-speaking management and large, eccentric rooms in a variety of formats. Of two nearly adjacent hotels out on Erythroú Stavroú opposite the archeological museum, the *Esperia* (☎051/229 621, fax 220 621; ⑥) at no. 42–44 is far preferable to the C-class *Nefeli* (☎051/227 441, fax 227 440; ⑤) at no. 50, by virtue of air-conditioning, double-glazing, good breakfasts on a terrace and availability of side or back rooms. The only private **rooms** in the centre are those of *Yiorgos Alvanos* at Anthemíou 35 (☎051/228 412; b), in an old house at the heart of the old Panayía quarter – worth trying if you arrive early in the day. An alternative place to stay, frequented by many Greek tourists, is the beach-suburb of Kalamítsa, to the west of town, served by the #8 city bus. The closest **campsite** is *Irini* (☎051/229 785; open all year), on the shore 3km east of the port; city bus #2 goes there.

Eating and drinking

Eating out in Kavála is a more cheerful prospect than staying the night; ignore the tourist-traps along the waterfront and walk instead up into the Panayía district, where a cluster of tavernas with outdoor seating on Poulídhou, interspersed with café-bars, tempts you with good and reasonably priced grills and seafood. Starting opposite the lower end of the Imaret, you have as you proceed uphill *O Kanadhos*, *Antonia* and *To Koutoukaki*, all of them with their loyalists and perfectly adequate. Beyond the main entrance to the Imaret lies one more potential eatery, *To Steki tou Iordan*, but if you've made it this far, you may as well plump for the Imaret itself, certainly the most atmospheric premises in the province. The courtyard floor is a café-bar; somewhat limited-menu meals are served on the upper gallery overlooking whitewashed arcades and the harbour.

Ferry services

Car ferries sail from Kavála to **Thássos** almost hourly from 6am to 9pm in season; virtually all run to the port of Skála Prínou (1hr 15min). From September to April, when services drop to just a handful of boats daily, you may be better off taking the bus or driving to Keramotí, 46km southwest, and then using the car ferry from there to Thássos. **KERAMOTÍ** itself provides an alternative, though unexciting, stopover. It's a small, rather drab village amidst corn fields in the Néstos delta, with a decent beach backed by pines, a few rooms and a half-dozen hotels which you shouldn't have to patronize, as the last ferry leaves for Thássos at about 10pm.

Other ferry services from Kavála are fairly predictable as to weekly pattern, though not to specific days. From late July until late August, there have historically been five weekly departures to **Samothráki** (typically Mon, Tues, Wed, Fri & Sat; 4hr), though these didn't run in 1999. There are four boats to **Límnos** (Tues, Thurs, Sat & Sun), dwindling to two off-season. Two or three of these continue to various islands and mainland ports, among them Áyios Efstrátios, Lésvos, Híos and Rafína/Pireás. Details for Límnos and beyond are available from *Nikos Miliadhes*, tucked away behind Platía Karaolí Dhimitríou (☎051/226 147 or 223 421), while the Samothráki services, if they've resumed, can be checked at the nearby agency *Arsinoi-Saos* (☎051/835 671).

Philippi

As you might expect, **PHILIPPI** (*Filippoi* on some maps) was named after Philip II of Macedon, who wrested the town from the Thracians in 356 BC for the sake of nearby gold mines on Mount Pangéo. However, it owed its later importance and prosperity to the Roman building of the Via Egnatia, which ran from the Adriatic to Byzantium. With Kavála/Neápolis as its port, Philippi was essentially the easternmost town of Roman-occupied Europe.

Here also, as at Actium, the fate of the Roman empire was decided on Greek soil, at the **Battle of Philippi** in 42 BC. After assassinating Julius Caesar, Brutus and Cassius had fled east of the Adriatic and, against their better judgement, were forced into confrontation on the Philippi plains with the pursuing armies of Antony and Octavian. The "honourable conspirators", who could have successfully exhausted the enemy by avoiding action, were decimated by Octavian in two successive battles, and, as defeat became imminent, first Cassius, then Brutus killed himself – the latter running on his comrade's sword with the purported Shakespearian sentiment, "Caesar now be still, I killed thee not with half so good a will."

St Paul landed at Kavála and visited Philippi in 49 AD and so began his mission in Europe. Despite being cast into prison he retained a special affection for the Philippians, his first converts, and the congregation that he established was one of the earliest to flourish in Greece. It has furnished the principal remains of the site: several impressive, although ruined, basilican churches.

Philippi is easily reached from Kavála, just 14km distant; buses (which continue to the dull market town of Dhráma) leave every half-hour, and drop you by the road that now splits the site.

The site

Tues–Sun 8.30am–6pm; 800dr.

The most conspicuous of the churches is the **Direkler** (Turkish for "columns" or "piers"), to the south of the modern road which here follows the line of the Via Egnatia. Also known as Basilica B, this was an unsuccessful attempt by its sixth-century architect to improve the basilica design by adding a dome. In this instance the entire east wall collapsed under the weight, leaving only the narthex convertible for worship during the tenth century. The central arch of its west wall and a few pillars of reused antique drums stand amid remains of the Roman **forum**. A line of second-century porticoes spreads outwards in front of the church, and on their east side are the foundations of a colonnaded octagonal church which was approached from the Via Egnatia by a great gate. Behind the Direkler and, perversely, the most interesting and best-preserved building of the site, is a huge monumental **public latrine** with nearly fifty of its original marble seats still intact.

Across the road on the northern side, stone steps climb up to a terrace, passing on the right a Roman crypt, reputed to have been the **prison of St Paul** and appropriately frescoed. The terrace flattens out onto a huge paved atrium that extends to the foundations of another extremely large basilica, the so-called Basilica A. Continuing in the same direction around the base of a hill you emerge above a **theatre** cut into its side. Though dating from the original town it was heavily remodelled as an amphitheatre by the Romans – the bas-reliefs of Nemesis, Mars and Victory (on the left of the stage) all belong to this period. It is now used for performances during the annual summer Philippi-Thássos Festival. The **museum** (currently closed for renovation), above the road at the far end of the site, is rather dreary.

The best general impression of the site – which is very extensive despite a lack of obviously notable buildings – and of the battlefield behind it can be gained from the **acropolis**, a steep climb along a path from the museum. Its own remains are predominantly medieval.

THRACE (THRÁKI)

Separated from Macedonia to the west by the Néstos River and from (Turkish) Eastern Thrace by the Évros river delta, **Western Thrace** is the Greek state's most recent acquisition. The area was under effective Greek control from 1920, the Treaty of Lausanne (1923) confirming Greek sovereignty and also sanctioning the exchange of 390,000 Muslims, principally from Macedonia and Epirus, for more than a million ethnic Greeks from Eastern Thrace and Asia Minor. But the Muslims of Western Thrace, in reciprocity for a continued Greek presence in and around Constantinople, were exempt from the exchanges and continue to live in the region.

Thrace was originally inhabited by a people with their own, non-Hellenic, language and religion. From the seventh century BC onwards it was colonized by Greeks, and after Alexander's time the area took on a strategic significance as the land route between Greece and Byzantium. It was later controlled by the Roman and Byzantine empires, and after 1361 by the Ottoman Turks.

Nowadays, out of a total population of 360,000, there are around 120,000 Muslims, made up (approximately) of 60,000 **Turkish-speakers**, 40,000 **Pomaks** and 20,000 **gypsies**. These figures are disputed by Turkish Muslims who put their numbers alone at something between 100,000 and 120,000. The Greek government lumps all three groups together as "a Muslim minority" principally of Turkish descent, and provides Turkish-language education for all the Muslim minorities (despite the fact that the Pomaks speak a language very similar to Bulgarian). Greek authorities also point to the hundreds of functioning mosques, the Turkish-language newspapers and a Turkish-language radio station in Komotiní as evidence of their goodwill. However, since 1968 only graduates from a special Academy in Thessaloníki have been allowed to teach in the Turkish-language schools here – thus (deliberately) isolating Thracian Turks from mainstream Turkish culture – and on various occasions the Greek authorities have interfered with Muslim religious appointments. In 1985, when the mufti of Komotiní died, he was replaced by a government appointee. When he resigned, another mufti was appointed by the authorities. In August 1991, the Greeks appointed a new Muslim leader in Xánthi, again without consulting the Muslim community.

There is no doubt in the minds of local Turks and Pomaks that in secular matters, too, they are the victims of **discrimination**. Muslim villages, they say, receive less help from the state than Greek villages; until the late 1990s a few were still without electricity, and many lacked proper roads. Muslim schools are underfunded; Muslims are unable to join the police force; and it is extremely difficult for them to buy property or get bank loans – although most ethnic Turks do also acknowledge that they are still materially better off than their counterparts in Turkey.

There have been occasional explosions of intercommunal violence, and matters have only worsened since the reincorporation, in neighbouring Bulgaria, of the Turkish minority into the commercial and political life of that country, with the Greeks becoming increasingly aware of the potential for unrest. In July 1991 the Greek government put forward a plan to demilitarize the whole of Thrace, including Bulgarian and Turkish sectors. The plan received a positive reply from the Bulgarian government, but, ominously, Turkey reserved its position, and Greece remains fearful of Turkish agitation in Western Thrace that might lead to a Cyprus-type military operation where Turkish forces "come to the assistance" of an "oppressed" minority. The Turkish consulate at Komotiní has long been considered a conduit for fifth-column activities, with incumbent consuls regularly expelled by Greece for "activities incompatible with diplomatic status". These activities constitute not espionage, but alleged attempts to foment local disturbances. Occasionally the Greek secret service has been accused of playing rougher, as in the case of the outspoken former MP for Thrace, Ahmet Sadiq, who was killed in an allegedly "manufactured" road accident in July 1995.

As an outsider you will probably not notice the intercommunal tensions, but you will not be able to avoid the many military installations in the border zones of the province. However, there are mixed villages where Muslims and Greeks appear to coexist quite amicably, and Thracians, both Muslim and Orthodox, have a deserved reputation for hospitality.

Compared to the rest of the mainland, there is little tangible to see, and most travellers take a bus straight through to **Alexandhroúpoli**, for the ferry to Samothráki, or head straight on to **Istanbul**. But Thrace's many rulers left some mark on the area, and there are a few well-preserved monuments, most significantly the remains of the coastal cities of Abdira, south of Xánthi, and Maroneia, southeast of Komotiní – Greek colonies in the seventh century BC that were abandoned in Byzantine times when the inhabitants moved inland to escape pirate raids. Otherwise, the landscape itself holds most appeal, with the train line forging a circuitous but scenic route below the foothills of the Rodhópi mountains that's at its best in the **Néstos valley** between Paranésti and Xánthi. If you make time to explore the backstreets of the towns, or venture up the myriad tracks to tiny, isolated villages in the Rodhópi mountains, you'll find an atmosphere quite unlike any other part of Greece.

Xánthi and around

Coming from Kavála, after the turning to the airport and shortly after the turning to Keramotí you cross the Néstos River, which with the **Rhodópi mountains** forms the border of Greek Thrace. The Greek/Turkish, Christian/Muslim demographics are almost immediately apparent in the villages: the Turkish settlements, long established, with their tiled, whitewashed houses and pencil-thin minarets; the Greek ones, often adjacent, built in drab modern style for the refugees of the 1920s.

Xánthi

XÁNTHI (*Iskeçe* to the Turks), the first town of any size, is perhaps the most interesting point to break a journey. There is a busy market area, good food, and – up the hill to the north of the main café-lined square – a very attractive old quarter. The town is also home to the University of Thrace, which lends a lively air to the place, particularly in the area between the bazaar and the campus, where bars, cinemas and bistros are busy in term time. Try if you can to visit on Saturday, the day of Xánthi's **street fair** –

a huge affair, attended equally by Greeks, Pomaks and Turks, held in a large open space near the fire station on the eastern side of the town.

The narrow, cobbled streets of the **old town** are home to a number of very fine mansions – some restored, some derelict – with highly coloured exteriors, bay windows and wrought-iron balconies; most date from the mid-nineteenth century when Xánthi's tobacco merchants made their fortunes. One of them has been turned into a **folk museum** (daily 11am–1pm; Mon, Wed, Fri, Sat extra hours 7–9.30pm; 300dr), at Antiká 7, at the bottom of the grade up into the right-bank quarter of the old town. A Siamese-twin dwelling originally built for two tobacco magnate brothers, it has been lovingly restored with painted wooden panels and decorated plaster and floral designs on the walls and ceilings, as well as displays of Thracian clothes and jewellery, a postcard collection and cakes of tobacco.

Further up, the roads become increasingly narrow and steep, and the Turkish presence (about fifteen percent of the total urban population) is more noticeable: most of the women have their heads covered, and the more religious ones wear full-length cloaks. Churches and mosques hide behind whitewashed houses with tiled roofs, and orange-brown tobacco leaves are strung along drying frames. Numerous houses, no matter how modest, sport a dish for tuning into Turkish satellite television.

To the north, overlooking the town from on high, is the **Panayía convent**, while beyond stands the **Áyios Nikólaos monastery**, from which there are fine views north into the forested Rhodópi mountains. To reach them by car from the river bridge, follow road signs for "*Monastíria*"; on foot, walk fifteen minutes up through the left-bank neighbourhood of Samakóv.

Practicalities

Arriving, you'll be either at the **train station**, 2km south of the centre, just off the Kavála road (taxis to hand), or at the very central main **KTEL**, just off Platía Eleftherías, on the northeast corner of the central market hall; there's a separate terminal for Kavála services opposite the south end of the market, on Sarándon Ekklissíon. 28-Oktovríou is the main south–north thoroughfare, passing just east of Platía Eleftherías and terminating at the central platía with its prominent clocktower. From there traffic is funnelled out of town, towards Komotiní, on Mihaïl Karaolí. Xánthi's pay-and-display **parking** scheme is pretty comprehensive, with fees payable from 8.30am to 9pm, Monday to Saturday. **Taxis**, unusually, are avocado green with white tops. The **post office** and Olympic Airways both lie within sight of the central platía, on its uphill side.

Downtown **hotel** choices are limited, often noisy and typically overpriced; the central *Xenia*, despite its continued appearance in assorted tourism literature, has shut down. Least expensive is the *Dimokritos*, 28-Oktovríou 41 (☎0541/25 111; ④), near the KTEL, whose well-worn but en-suite rooms (quieter rear ones refurbished 1998) are a bit better than the gloomy lobby and halls promise. More or less around the corner at Mihaïl Karaolí 40, the *Orfeas* (☎0541/20 121, fax 20 998; ④) is 1996-vintage and worth the extra 2000dr or so. The *Xanthippion*, 28-Oktovríou 212–214 (☎0541/77 061; ⑤), slightly out of the centre, is probably the quietest of the three.

Choices in **restaurants** are somewhat better; just off the main square at pedestrianized Yeoryíou Stavroú 18, installed in the defunct Lux Hotel, is the eminently reasonable *Midhos Kafe Psistaria* (actually an ouzerí), with a large summer garden out back, quick service and a mix of mezédhes and *mayireftá*. At the upper end of cobbled Paleológou, essentially the entrance to the old town, are a trio of ouzeris – *Arhondissa*, *Kyvotos* and *Haradhra* (reached from a side-street) – all with similar menus and prices, though be aware that they all shut at lunch and during high summer. For a good-value summertime grilled supper from a limited menu but in a superb setting, look no further than the *Nisaki* on the banks of the Podhonífi River dividing the town. To find it, follow Odhós Pindhárou upstream from behind the abandoned *Xenia* hotel, to this street's end at the base of the old town. Odhós Vasilíssis Sofías, leading down off Paleológou from the little park with a bust of Mr Antikas to the river, is the focus of Xánthi's **nightlife**. Doyen of the various bars here is the enormous *Kyverneío*, opposite the university's engineering faculty. The quality cinema is *Olympia*, at the bottom of the old town behind the municipal library, or in summer premises by the town hall, 200m downhill.

North of Xánthi

Much of the countryside north of Xánthi, towards the Bulgarian border, is a military "controlled area", dotted with signs denoting the fact. Greeks will tell you that access is restricted because of the sensitivity of the frontier with Bulgaria; ethnic Pomaks claim the army uses the border as an excuse to keep tabs on them, and until the early 1990s foreigners needed a special pass to visit the area.

If you do venture up into the western Rodhópi range here, the main reward is some magnificent scenery; there's not much arable land amidst the wild, pine-forested hills, and what there is – down in the river valleys – is devoted entirely to tobacco, hand-tilled by the blonde, fair-haired Pomaks who, claims of Greek nationalists to the contrary, are about as close as you'll find to the original ancestral Thracians. They were Bogomil-Christian Slavs forcibly converted to Islam in the sixteenth century, who still speak a corrupt dialect of Bulgarian with generous mixtures of Greek and Turkish.

There are a number of Muslim villages, though with a modest increase in material prosperity since the 1980s, they have mostly lost their traditional architecture to concrete multistorey apartments. **SMÍNTHI**, a large and dispersed Pomak settlement with a mosque and tall minaret, has two psistariés on the through road, the only thing remotely resembling tourist facilities in the region. **EHÍNOS**, encroached on by oak and beech woods, no longer has much appeal but remains the main market town for the region. **ORÉO**, 6km up a side road northwest of Smínthi, is dramatically set on a steep hillside with cloud-covered peaks behind and terraces falling away to the riverbed, and retains the picturesqueness of lingering poverty. The ground floors of the houses are used for corralling animals or storing farm produce, but it has no coffeehouse, at least not for visitors. Because of the hard time they've had, Pomaks tend to keep themselves to themselves.

South of Xánthi: along the coast

South of Xánthi, the coastal plain, bright with cotton, tobacco and cereals, stretches to the sea. Heading towards modern Ávdira, you'll pass through **Yenisséa** (Yeniçe), an unspectacular farming village with one of the oldest **mosques** in Thrace, dating from the sixteenth century. Now derelict, it's a low whitewashed building with a tiled roof, crumbled wooden portico and truncated minaret.

Regular buses serve the village of **ÁVDHIRA**, 10km further on, and, in summer, run on to the **beach** of Paralía Avdhíron, 7km beyond, passing through the site of **ancient Abdira** (daily 9am–3pm; free). The walls of the ancient acropolis are visible on a low headland above the sea, and there are traces of Roman baths, a theatre and an ancient acropolis. However, the best finds have been taken off to museums in Kavála and Komotiní, the remains are unspectacular, and the setting not particularly attractive. If you have time only for one site, you're better off going to Marónia (see below).

For the most part, the coast east from here is flat and dull. At the southern end of brackish Lake Vistonídha stands **PÓRTO LÁGOS**, a semi-derelict harbour partly redeemed by the nearby monastery of **Áyios Nikólaos** (open reasonable hours except 1–5pm) built on two islets in the lagoon – though the structure itself is modern and undistinguished. The surrounding marshland is an important site for birdlife, and is more accessible than the Évros delta (see p.454); a few observation towers have been provided along the reedy shoreline.

Nearby, 7km southeast and 32km from Xánthi, the small resort of **FANÁRI** has a long, sandy beach (good for Thrace, average for Greece) backed by two co-managed **places to stay**: the all-white, modern *Fanari Hotel* (☎0535/31 300, fax 31 388; ④), set well back from the beach at the eastern edge of the village, and the smaller, potentially noisier *Pension Theodora* (☎ & fax 0535/31 242; ③), out on the village promontory by the fishing port. Given the cost and unattractiveness of accommodation in both Xánthi and Komotiní, one or the other might be a good compromise for overnighting and visiting each town on day trips. The *Fanari* has a restaurant and there are a number of other fish **tavernas**. There's also an EOT campsite, the *Fanari* (☎0535/31 270; May–Oct), 500m east of the *Fanari Hotel*, just before the the the public beach. Fanári village is popular with Komotiniots in the evenings and at weekends, and its beach gets busy in the high summer, but there are less crowded spots a few kilometres east.

Marónia and further east

Further along the coast, **ancient Maroneia** has little more to see than Abdira, but the site is altogether more attractive. Most of it is still unexcavated, and the visible remains are scattered among the olive trees and undergrowth at the foot of Mount Ísmaros, now anachronistically crowned with the large, white "golf balls" of a radar station. The founder of the city is reckoned to be Maron, the son of the god of wine, Dionysos (Ísmaros is known locally as the Mountain of Dionysos), and the city became one of the most powerful in all of ancient Thrace. The site, which can be explored at will, is badly signposted, but you should be able to track down traces of a theatre, a sanctuary of Dionysos and various buildings including a house with a well-preserved mosaic floor. The land walls of the city are preserved to a height of two metres, together with a Roman tower above the harbour. Over time, the sea has done its own excavation, eroding the crumbling cliffs, revealing shards of pottery and ancient walls.

The pleasant, modern village of **MARÓNIA**, 4km inland with six daily buses from Komotiní, has a few surviving old Thracian mansions with jutting balconies, and some **rooms** (☎0533/41 158; ②) offered through a women's co-operative, though eating options around the shady square aren't brilliant. The women's co-operative will supply daily meals during July and August, but only at weekends otherwise.

Marónia's harbour of **Áyios Harálambos**, below the edge of the archeological site and 4km south of modern Marónia, was (along with the road down) "improved" during the 1990s in anticipation of a tourism boom that never happened; it's frankly a miserable place, baking in the heat of the surrounding cliffs, with no usable beach and two overpriced, overstretched tavernas. By contrast **Platanítis**, 4km west of Marónia by another paved but unsigned road, has a small but adequate gravel and sand beach – essentially a gap in the red cliffs – and a good, reasonably priced fish taverna, *O Yerasimos*.

Komotiní

KOMOTINÍ, 48km east of Xánthi along the direct road skirting the Rodhópi foothills, is larger and less attractive, with ranks of apartment buildings and gridded suburbs to the south and west, their dusty, noisy streets clogged with traffic. Markedly more Turkish than Xánthi, it has fourteen functioning mosques, and social mixing between the different ethnic groups – roughly at parity population-wise – is even less common, although Orthodox and Muslim continue to live in the same neighbourhoods. Of late the town has become even more polyglot, with an influx of Greek, Armenian and Georgian Christians from the Caucasus.

During the thirteenth century, the city gained importance and wealth due to its position on the Via Egnatia. When the Ottomans took the city in 1361, they changed its name to Gümülçine, as it's still known to its ethnic Turks. In 1912, at the outbreak of the First Balkan War, Komotiní fell to the Bulgarians; it was liberated by Greek forces in the following year, only to be taken once more by the Bulgarians during World War I. It was finally and definitively joined to Greece on May 14, 1920.

The old **bazaar**, to the north of central Platía Irínis and the through boulevard Orféos, is very pleasant, lodged between mosques and a fine Ottoman-era clocktower. Shady cafés and tiny shops sell everything from carpets to iron buckets, and it's especially busy on Tuesdays when the villagers from the surrounding area come into town to sell their wares. Behind this old quarter, you can see the modern **cathedral** and the remains of Komotiní's **Byzantine walls**, in one corner of which once stood a fine **synagogue**, demolished after its dome collapsed in the late 1980s.

Traditionally a city with both Greek and Turkish inhabitants, Komotiní began to be dominated by Greek influence in the waning years of the Ottoman empire, when rich Greeks funded schools in the city to develop Greek culture and ideals. Some of these educational foundations still survive: one, the **Hellenic Civic School of Nestor Tsanakali**, a Neoclassical structure on Dhimokrítou, is now the official residence of the dean of the University of Thrace, whose faculties Komotiní shares with Xánthi. Another, at Ayíou Yeoryíou 13, on the other side of the park, has become Komotiní's **Folk Life Museum** (daily except Sun 10am–1pm; free), displaying examples of Thracian embroidery, traditional Thracian dress, silverware, copperware and a collection of religious seals. The **Archeological Museum** at Simeonídhi 4 (daily 9am–5pm; free), just to the right of the main road from Xánthi and well signposted, is also worth a visit, giving a lucid overview of Thracian history, by means of plans and finds from local sites, from its beginnings up to the Byzantine era. On display are a number of statues, busts, bas-reliefs, jewellery and artefacts from the archeological sites around Komotiní.

Practicalities

If you need to stay, be aware that the **hotel** situation is nearly as unpromising as Xánthi's. Rock-bottom is the spartan *Hellas* at Dhimokrítou 31 (☎0531/22 055; ②), with shared showers and toilets, at a noisy intersection in the west of town. The more central, air-conditioned *Olympos*, at Orféos 37, is a much better choice (☎0531/37 690; ⑤ en-suite, ④ not), though it tends to fill with business types. Marginally quieter, but ridiculously overpriced, is the *Astoria*, a Neoclassical inn restoration at Platía Irínis 28 (☎0531/35 054; ⑥); for that sort of money you'd be better off at the *Anatolia*, Anhiálou 53 (☎0531/36 242; ⑤). The best **eating** is to be found in the narrowest lanes of the bazaar just north of Orféos, where the *Yiaxis* and *Apolavsis* ouzeris put out tables under arbours; there's also a good, Turkish-run psistariá opposite the clocktower, behind the main mosque, run by Mumin Mehmet Muhsin.

Alexandhroúpoli

A modern city, designed by Russian military architects during the Russian-Turkish war of 1878, **ALEXANDHROÚPOLI** – Dedeağaç to the Turks and Bulgars – does not, on first acquaintance, have much to recommend it: a border town and military garrison, with overland travellers in transit and Greek holidaymakers competing in summer for limited space in the few hotels and the campsite.

The town became Greek in 1920, when it was renamed Alexandhroúpoli after a visit from Greece's King Alexander. There are no obvious sights and the heavy military presence can be oppressive. The Turkish quarter, literally on the wrong side of the tracks, may or may not whet the appetite for the unadulterated article across the border. Otherwise it's the seafront that best characterizes the town; dominated by a huge

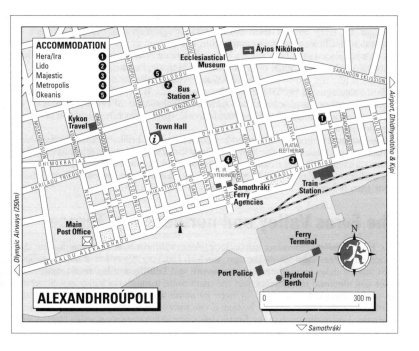

ACCOMMODATION
Hera/Ira ❶
Lido ❷
Majestic ❸
Metropolis ❹
Okeanis ❺

Áyios Nikólaos
Ecclesiastical Museum
Bus Station ★
Kykon Travel
Town Hall ℹ
SARANDON EKLISSION
Airport, Dhidhymótiho & Kípi
PLATIA ELEFTHERIAS
Samothráki Ferry Agencies
Train Station
Main Post Office
Olympic Airways (250m)
Ferry Terminal
N
Port Police
Hydrofoil Berth
0   300 m

ALEXANDHROÚPOLI

▽ Samothráki

lighthouse built in 1880 (and adopted as the town's symbol), it comes alive at dusk when the locals begin their evening vólta. Traffic is diverted and café tables spill out onto the road and around the lighthouse; makeshift stalls along the pavements sell salted seeds, pirate cassettes and grilled sweetcorn. On summer evenings, there are events at the makeshift amphitheatre in the municipal gardens beyond the western end of the seafront.

Practicalities

Arriving by **train**, you'll be deposited conveniently next to the port; the **KTEL** is at Venizélou 36, several blocks inland. **Drivers** will find it prudent to enter town from the west along coastal Megálou Alexándhrou, signposted for the ferries and restaurants, since the prevailing craze for pedestrianization, one-way systems and fee parking effectively block movement between Dhimokratías – local name for the Via Egnatia – and the sea.

For the island of **Samothráki** (see p.750), there is at least one daily **ferry** year-round and, in July and August, two a day – often three on Fridays, Saturdays and Sundays. Tickets can be bought from either the Vatsis agency Kýprou 5 (☎0551/26 721) or the agent for the *Arsinoi/Saos* across the way (☎0551/22 215). Drivers should be aware that this is a grotesquely expensive monopoly sailing: 11,000dr for a small car on the one-way, two-hour journey, a price that would normally get you several hours of travel. **Hydrofoil** departures to Samothráki and occasionally beyond are handled by either Arsinoi or Caravettis Shipping (☎0551/37 074). Occasional NEL sailings for north Aegean islands, as well as the once-weekly G&A ferry to Rhodes and several intervening islands, are represented by Kykon Tours at Venizélou 68 (☎0551/25 455).

The **hotels** nearest the port and train station cater for those just passing through, whether by ferry to and from Samothráki or by train into Turkey or back to Thessaloníki. Choices get more comfortable, and quieter, as you move inland. The closest en-suite place to the train station is the overpriced *Metropolis*, Athanasíou Dhiákou 11 (☎0551/26 443; ③), while even closer is the *Majestic*, Platía Eleftherías 7 (☎0551/26 444; ②), a friendly, old-fashioned, non-en-suite cheapie. Better value than either is the *Lido* at Paleológou 15 (☎0551/28 808; ②), a bargain for large, bathed rooms. More luxury means either the air-conditioned *Okeanis* at Paleológou 20 (☎0551/28 830; ⑤) or the *Ira/Hera* at Dhimokratías 179 (☎0551/23 941; ⑤), worthwhile only if you get a quieter side room.

Restaurants are relatively limited in number, and not brilliant. *Psarotaverna Anesti* at Athanasíou Dhiákou 5 is the best, especially for supper. Of two overpriced establishments on Platía Iróön Polytekhníou, which have had lengthy acquaintance with a captive audience awaiting ferries to Samothráki, *Iy Klimatariá* is somewhat more wholesome than *Iy Neraïda*.

The Évros Valley and northeastern Thrace

The **Évros Valley**, extending northeast of Alexandhroúpoli, is a prosperous but dull agricultural area. Most towns are ugly, modern concrete affairs full of bored soldiers, with little to delay you; others, such as **Souflí** and **Dhidhymótiho**, retain some character and medieval monuments, and the main route through the valley is well served by public transport. The standout here by some way is the **Dhadhiá Forest** and wildlife reserve, also reachable by bus; if you have your own transport, you can head east from Alexandhroúpoli to the **Évros delta**, one of Europe's most important wetland areas for birds – and one of Greece's most sensitive military areas.

The Évros delta

To the southeast, the **Évros Delta** is home to more than 250 different species of birds, including sea eagles. The easiest way to get there (if you have a car) is to leave Alexandhroúpoli on the main road (E90/E85) towards Turkey and Bulgaria. After passing the airport on the right after 7km, continue to **Loutrá Traianópolis**, 13km away, the site of an ancient Roman spa and its modern continuation. There are three modest hotels (all ②–③) in the vicinity, any of which would make a good base for exploring the delta, best approached by turning right off the main road and taking the dirt track that runs alongside the *Hotel Isidora*. The delta is crisscrossed with tracks along the dykes used by farmers taking advantage of the plentiful water supply for growing sweet corn and cotton. The south is the most inspiring part, well away from the army installations to the north; as you go further into the wetlands, the landscape becomes utterly desolate, with decrepit clusters of fishing huts among the sandbars and inlets. At the mouth of the delta sprawls a huge saltwater lake called **Límni Dhrakónda**. Obviously what you see depends on the time of year, but even if birdlife is a bit thin on the ground, the atmosphere of the place is worth experiencing.

Féres: Panayía Kosmosótira

Northeast into the valley proper, 28km from Alexandhroúpoli, the otherwise unremarkable town of **FÉRES**, draped over several hills and ravines, offers the imposing twelfth-century Byzantine church of **Panayía Kosmosótira**. Though rather vaguely signposted, it's recognizable from afar by its broad, lead-sheathed dome and commanding hilltop position. Founded by a member of the Komnenos dynasty, it was originally part of a fortified monastery, of which only two ruined towers on the south remain. The church's exterior seems a bit unpromising, with the original masonry covered by many layers of rendering, and the frescoes inside have been obliterated except for some saints at the transept ends. Mostly what impresses are the huge capitals of the paired pier-columns, and the lofty airiness of the twelve-windowed cupola, surrounded by four subsidiary domes – a design rare in Greece outside of Thessaloníki.

If you have to change buses en route to the border post at Kípi, as sometimes happens, and have some time to wait, the church is well worth seeking out; it's just a few paces east of the main commercial street. With your own car, it's an easy five-minute detour from the main highway. There's an overpriced hotel in Féres, the *Anthi* (☎0555/24 201; ④), on the way into town as you approach from the south.

The Dhadhiá Forest

Continuing north, the next attraction is the **Dhadhiá Forest Reserve**, reached by a road off to the left 1km after passing Likófi (Likófos). After a seven-kilometre drive through the rolling, forested hills, you reach the reserve **information centre** (daily 9am–8pm; ☎0554/32 290), at the heart of 35,200 hectares of protected oak and pine forest covering volcanic ridges. The diversity of landscape and vegetation and the proximity of important migration routes make for an extremely diverse flora and fauna, but raptors are the star attraction, and main impetus for this WWF project. All cars – except for a special tour van which makes sorties several times daily (500dr) – are banned from core areas totalling 7200 hectares, and foot access is restricted to two marked trails: a two-hour route up to the reserve's highest point, 520-metre **Gíbrena** with its ruined Byzantine castle, and another ninety-minute loop-route to an observation hide overlooking **Mavrórema** canyon. The region is claimed to be the last European home of the **black vulture**, outside of Spain; they, and griffon vultures, make up the bulk of sightings from this post. You'll need a comprisive bird manual, as rudimentary keying posters at the hide are in Greek only.

If you're a keen birder, you'll want to stay the night, as the best raptor viewing is before 9am or after 6pm in summer (they can be seen all day Oct–March). Next to the visitors' centre stands a very clean **"ecotourism hostel"** run by Dhadhiá village (☎0554/32 263; ③), where the en-suite rooms have been given bird names instead of numbers (keys from the café across the car park, until 11pm). The café supplies breakfast, but for other **meals** you'll retire to **DHADHIÁ** village, 1km back on the route in, which can offer the inexpensive *Psistaria tou Yiorgou* near the Mobil station, plus a surprisingly active nightlife at a handful of **bars**.

Soufí and Dhidhymótiho

The nearest town to Dhadhiá, 7km north of the side-turning, is **SOUFLÍ**, renowned for a now all-but-vanished silk industry. This is commemorated in a wel-signposted museum (Mon–Fri 8am–3.30pm, Sat–Sun 9am–2pm), a few hundred metres uphill and west of the main through road. It's lodged in a fine old ochre-tinted mansion, one of a number of surviving vernacular houses which lend Soufí some distinction. If you want or need to stay, there's just two **hotels**, both on the noisy main highway: the basic, non-en-suite *Egnatia* (☎0554/24 124; ②) at no. 225, or the overpriced *Orfeas/Orpheus* (☎0554/22 922; ④), at no. 172. **Eating** and **drinking** options aren't great either, consisting mostly of pizzerias, *souvladzídhika* and *barákia* for the lads in the armed forces.

DHIDHYMÓTIHO, 30km further northeast by the border, is the only other stop along the trunk route of any interest. The old part of town is still partially enclosed by the remains of double Byzantine fortifications (hence the name, which means "double wall"), and some old houses and churches survive, but the area has a feeling of decay despite continuing efforts at restoration. Like Komotiní, the town once had a fine **syn-agogue** for its thousand-strong Jewish community, but this was sold and demolished in 1985, after having been ransacked during World War II at the instigation of the Nazis – who had spread about the (false) rumour that treasure was secreted in its walls. Below the fortified hill, on the central platía, stands the most important surviving monument, a fourteenth-century **mosque**, the oldest and second largest in the Balkans. A great square box of a building with a pyramidal metal roof, its design harks back to Seljuk and other pre-Ottoman prototypes in central Anatolia, and you'll see nothing else like it between here and Divriği or Erzurum in Turkey. Unfortunately, the interior is closed indefinitely for restoration, though you can still admire the ornate north portal.

Staying presents a problem, as neither **hotel** is wonderful. The less expensive and more central is the none-too-welcoming *Anesis* (☎0553/24 850; ③), 250m northwest of the mosque on Vassiléos Alexándhrou. Your other choice is the *Plotini* (☎0553/23 400; ⑤) a rather gaudy building inconveniently set 1km south of town across the river, on the west side of the road. For a **meal**, try the *Zythestiatorio Kypselaki* (lunch only), in the central market hall just above the mosque.

Metaxádhes and Orestiádha

Further north still, smaller roads take you through isolated villages and beautiful countryside. **Metaxádhes**, 31km west of Dhidhymótiho, is one of the most handsome villages in the area, sited on a steep hill, its large houses built traditionally of stone and wood with tiled roofs and lush gardens. Fought over by Bulgars and Turks, Metaxádhes used to support a Turkish community but now its population is exclusively Greek. Beyond Metaxádhes, you descend north into the vast, fertile **Árdhas River plain** that dominates the northeastern tip of Greek Thrace. Rich farmland – the main crops are sunflowers, sweet corn and (increasingly) sugar beet – supports a large number of modern villages, many of them populated by settlers from Asia Minor.

Hemmed in on three sides by Bulgaria and Turkey, it has been a Greek priority to establish a Greek population in this extremely sensitive and strategic corner of Thrace; lately the process continues with Pontic Greeks repatriated from the Caucasus and elsewhere in the ex-USSR. Military barracks are liberally scattered through the hinterland and along the eastern border with Turkey; there are numerous surveillance posts, all flying Greek flags, looking over to the minarets of Turkey across the Évros river valley.

The main town beyond Dhidhymótiho is **ORESTIÁDHA**, a post-1923 market centre with restaurants, bars and lots of cake shops in its main square. It also has at least one bank, something worth bearing in mind when returning from Bulgaria or Turkey, though you'll get a poor rate exchanging the currencies of those countries. You could spend a fairly expensive night here before or after crossing the border; **hotels** include the *Alexandros* (☎0552/27 000; ⑤), the older *Elektra* (☎0552/23 540; ④) at Pandazídhou 50, with the *Iridanos* **restaurant** alongside, and the rather elderly C-class *Vienni/Vienna* at Oréstou 64 (☎0552/22 578; ④ en-suite, ③ not).

On to Turkey or Bulgaria

Crossing into Turkey from Alexandhroúpoli, you are presented with a bewildering choice of routes; currently there's only one daily rail link to Bulgaria. Current times for rail departures should be confirmed locally.

British passport holders need a **Turkish visa**, which costs £10 at the border, Americans also require a visa, costing $45. Border guards can be very exigent about linking currencies to nationalities – Brits for example, can only pay with sterling, not any other hard currency – and will often only accept other denominations with ruinous surcharges, so come prepared. **Bulgarian visas** are required for all nationals and are expensive; prices fluctuate, but count on $70 (have US currency ready) for a transit pass at the border, somewhat less if you obtain it at a consulate beforehand.

By bus to Turkey

The simplest way to travel from northern Greece to Turkey, if you can get a ticket, is to go **by bus** direct to Istanbul. There is currently just one departure daily, run by OSE (tickets from the main train stations); the problem is that this starts in Thessaloníki, and by this stage will probably be full. There used to be a few private coaches, but service is currently suspended; ask for current details at travel agents in Xánthi, Komotiní or Alexandhroúpoli.

An alternative is to take a local bus to the border at **KÍPI** (6 daily). You are not allowed to cross the frontier here on foot, but it is generally no problem to get a driver to shuttle you the 500m across to the Turkish post, and perhaps even to give you a lift beyond. The nearest town is Ipsala (5km further on), but if possible get as far as Keşan, (30km), from where buses to Istanbul are much more frequent.

By train to Turkey

Travelling by **train** to Istanbul should in theory be simpler. However, the only through connection leaves Alexandhroúpoli just after noon, crossing the border at Pýthio two hours later and taking (in theory) nine more hours (including a long halt at the frontier) to reach Istanbul. On the Greek side this service theoretically has express status, but don't be surprised if the train – which originates in Thessaloníki – shows up late.

You might prefer to take a more frequent local train through Pýthio and on to **KASTANIÉS**, opposite Turkish Edirne. You must use a departure from Alexandhroúpoli prior to 9.45am; later ones arrive after the border post (daily 9am–1pm) has closed. There's no accommodation in Kastaniés, but unlike at Kípi you are allowed to walk across the border (under army escort). Once on the Turkish side, there's bus service to the first Turkish village, 2km beyond the frontier; it's 7km in total from the border to Edirne (Adhrianoúpoli to the Greeks) – an attractive and historic city with some important Ottoman monuments and frequent buses making the three-hour trip to Istanbul. For more information, see the *Rough Guide to Turkey*.

Into Bulgaria

To Bulgaria from Alexandhroúpoli there is just one connecting **train** daily, leaving at about 5am and reaching Greek Orménio some three hours later, where you may have to change trains for the fifteen-minute journey to Svilengrad inside Bulgaria. This turns around less than an hour later for a service back to Alexandhroúpoli. From Svilengrad (which has just one expensive hotel), it is best to plan on moving on the same day towards Plovdiv. For further details, see the *Rough Guide to Bulgaria*.

travel details

Note: *Onward services in the states of the former Yugoslavia are currently sharply reduced, and with the exception of trains into the FYROM from Thessaloníki it is impossible to obtain reliable information on schedules; in the wake of the 1999 war these routes are, in any case, inadvisable for independent travellers.*

International Trains

Alexandhroúpoli–Istanbul (Turkey) Semi-direct (change cars at Pýthio or in Turkey at Uzunköprü) "express", arriving Istanbul after 9hr minimum, including an hour or longer wait at the border.

Alexandhroúpoli–Dhidhymótiho–Orestiádha –Kastaniés (for Edirne) 6 daily, but only 3 departures reach frontier post while open; 2hr 45min for whole journey.

Alexandhroúpoli–Svilengrad (Bulgaria) 1 daily; 3hr.

Thessaloníki–Gevgeli (FYROM) 1 daily; 1hr 30min–2hr.

Thessaloníki–Promahón/Koulata, Bulgarian frontier (1 daily; 2hr 30min).

Domestic Trains

Thessaloníki–Kateríni/Lárissa/Athens 4 express, 5 slower trains daily in each direction (6–7hr 30min for entire journey).

Thessaloníki–Lárissa 3 daily in each direction (2hr 45min), 1 continuing to **Vólos** (4hr total).

Thessaloníki–Véria/Édhessa/Amýndeo/ Flórina 4 daily to Flórina (3hr 30min), changing as necessary at Amýndeo; connections between Amýndeo and Kozáni (3hr 30min) 6 times daily; 1 daily only up to Édhessa (2hr).

Thessaloníki–Sérres/Dhráma/Xánthi/ Komotiní/Alexandhroúpoli 2 daily expresses, well spaced, plus 3 slower trains (Thessaloníki–Xánthi 4hr–5hr; Xánthi–Alexandhroúpoli 1hr 30min–2hr).

Buses

Alexandhroúpoli to: Dhadhiá (2 daily; 1hr 20min); Dhidhymótiho (17 daily Mon–Fri, 14 daily Sat–Sun; 2hr); Istanbul (daily OSE bus; 8hr); Kípi (5 daily; 45min); Komotiní (14 daily; 1hr).

Édhessa to: Flórina (4 daily; 2hr); Kastoriá (4 daily; 2hr 30min, change at Amýndeo); Véria (6 Mon–Sat, 2 Sun; 50min).

Flórina to: Préspa basin, 2 daily (1 hr).

Kastoriá to: Flórina (4 daily indirect services via Amýndeo; 3hr including layover).

Kateríni to: Dhión (12 daily; 20min); to Litóhoro, for Mt Olympus (18 Mon–Sat, 12 Sun; 30min).

Kavála to: Keramotí (12 daily; 1hr); Philippi (half-hourly 6am–8.30pm; 20min); Xánthi/Komotiní (half-hourly 6am–9pm; 1hr/2hr); Alexandhroúpoli (5 daily; 3hr).

Komotiní to: Fanári (7 daily Mon–Fri, 6 Sat, 5 Sun)

Kozáni to: Grevená (8 daily; 1hr); Siátista (4 daily; 30min).

Thessaloníki to: Alexandhroúpoli (5 daily; 6hr); Arnéa–Ierissós/Ouranoúpoli (5–7 daily; 2hr/3hr 30min); Athens (16 daily; 7hr); Flórina (6 daily; 3hr 30min); Istanbul (almost daily with OSE, occasional privately operated; 14hr); Kalambáka (7 daily; 4hr 30min); Ioánnina (5 daily; 7hr); Kastoriá (5 daily; 4hr); Litóhoro, for Mt Olympus (7 daily; 1hr 30min); Kavála (hourly 6am–10pm; 3hr); Pélla/Édhessa (hourly; 1hr/1hr 15min); Sárti, via Polýiros (3 daily; 4hr 30min); Sofia (daily with OSE; 7hr 30min); Véria (half-hourly; 1hr 15min); Vólos (4 daily; 4hr); Vourvouroú, via Polýiros (3 daily; 3hr).

Véria to: Édhessa, via Náoussa (6 daily; 1hr 15min); Kozáni (8 daily; 1hr).

Xánthi to: Kavála (half-hourly, 6am–9pm; 1hr); Komotiní (17–18 daily, via coast or inland; 50min); Thessaloníki (6–7 daily; 4hr).

Ferries

Alexandhroúpoli to: Límnos, Lésvos, Híos, Sámos, Kós or Kálymnos, Rhodes (1 weekly); Samothráki (1–3 daily in season, 4 weekly out of season).

Kavála to: Thássos (Skála Prínou) (4–15 daily, average 8, depending on season); Samothráki (2–5 weekly Apr–Sept); Límnos and Áyios Efstrátios (2–4 weekly); Lésvos and Híos (2–3 weekly).

Keramotí to: Thássos (Liménas) (10 daily, year-round).

Thessaloníki to: Límnos, Lésvos and Híos (1–2 weekly June–Sept); Sámos, Léros or Kálymnos,

Kós, Rhodes (1 weekly May–Oct); Iráklion (Crete) via Skiáthos, Tínos, Sýros, Mýkonos, Páros, Náxos and Thíra (2–5 weekly March–Oct).

Hydrofoils

Alexandhroúpoli to: Samothráki, (1–2 daily July–Aug).

Kavála to: Thássos (Liménas) (8–15 daily); Thássos (west coast resorts) (1–3 daily).

Thessaloníki to: Skiáthos, Skópelos and Alónissos (June–mid-Sept, at least daily); Skýros and Áyios Ioánnis (Pílion) (2–4 weekly early July to mid-Sept).

Flights

All flights are on Olympic unless specified.

Alexandhroúpoli to: Athens (2 daily; 1hr).

Kastoriá to: Athens (3–4 weekly; 1hr 15min).

Kavála to: Athens (1–2 daily; 1hr).

Kozáni to: Athens (3–4 weekly; 1hr 10min).

Thessaloníki to: Athens (8–10; 50min); Corfu (2–5 weekly; 1hr); Haniá, Crete (2 weekly; 2hr); Híos (2 weekly; 1hr 50min); Ioánnina (5–7 weekly; 50min); Iráklion, Crete (2–3 weekly on Olympic, at least daily on Air Greece; 2hr); Lésvos (6–8 weekly; 1–2hr); Límnos (4–7 weekly; 50min); Sámos (2 weekly on Olympic, 2 weekly on Air Manos; 1hr 40min); Thíra (3 weekly summer only; 1hr 30min).

PART THREE

THE

ISLANDS

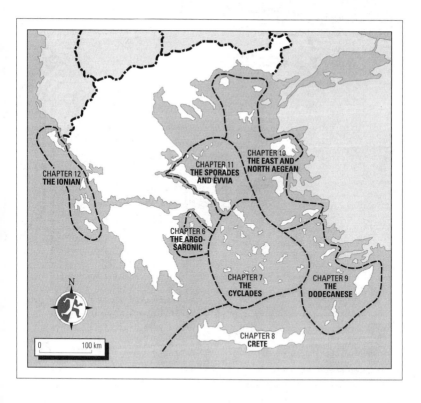

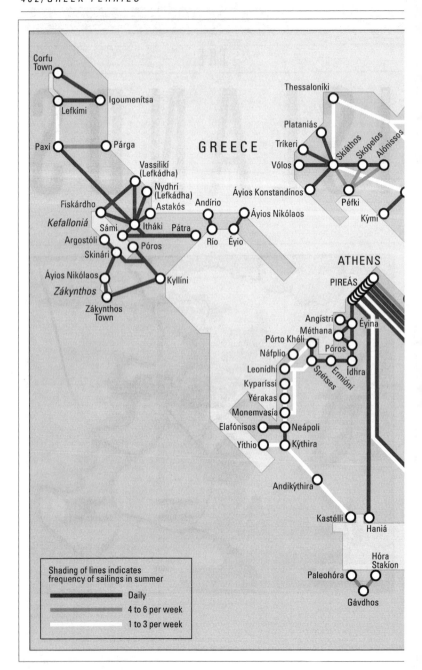

Shading of lines indicates
frequency of sailings in summer

Daily
4 to 6 per week
1 to 3 per week

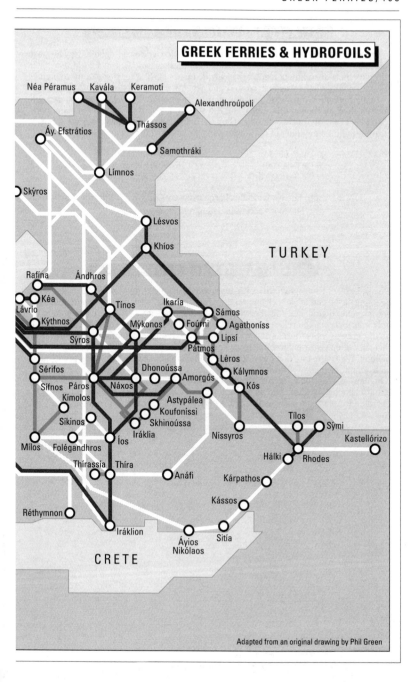

GREEK FERRIES & HYDROFOILS

Néa Péramus
Kavála
Keramotí
Alexandhroúpoli
Thássos
Áy. Efstrátios
Samothráki
Límnos
Skýros
Lésvos
Khíos
TURKEY
Rafína
Ándhros
Kéa
Lávrio
Tínos
Ikaría
Sámos
Kýthnos
Mýkonos
Foúrni
Agathoníss
Sýros
Lipsí
Pátmos
Léros
Sérifos
Dhonoússa
Kálymnos
Sífnos
Páros
Náxos
Amorgós
Kós
Kímolos
Astypálea
Koufoníssi
Tílos
Síkinos
Skhinoússa
Sými
Iráklia
Níssyros
Kastellórizo
Mílos
Folégandhros
Hálki
Rhodes
Thírassía
Thíra
Anáfi
Kárpathos
Réthymnon
Kássos
Iráklion
Áyios
Sitía
Nikólaos
CRETE

Adapted from an original drawing by Phil Green

ACCOMMODATION PRICE CODES

Throughout the book we've used the following **price codes** to denote the cheapest available double room in each establishment in high season. Out of season, rates can drop by more than fifty percent, especially if you are staying for three or more nights. Single rooms, where available, cost around seventy percent of the price of a double.

Rented private rooms on the islands usually fall into the ② or ③ categories, depending on their location and facilities, and the season; a few in the ④ category are more like plush self-catering apartments. They are not generally available from late October through to the beginning of April, when only hotels tend to remain open.

① Up to 6000dr	④ 12,000–16,000dr
② 6000–9000dr	⑤ 16,000–20,000dr
③ 9000–12,000dr	⑥ 20,000dr and upwards

Note: Youth hostels typically charge 2000–2500dr for a dormitory bed.
For more accommodation details, see pp.43–6.

FERRY ROUTES AND SCHEDULES

Details of ferry routes, together with approximate journey times and frequencies, are to be found at the end of each chapter in the "Travel details" section. Please note that these are for general guidance only. Ferry schedules change with alarming regularity and the only information to be relied upon is that provided by the port police in each island harbour. Ferry agents in Pireás and on the islands are helpful, of course, but keep in mind that they often represent just one ferry line and won't necessarily inform you of the competition. Be aware, too, that ferry services to the smaller islands tend to be pretty skeletal from mid-September through to April.

In many island groups, ferries are supplemented by Flying Dolphin hydrofoils – which tend to take half the time and be twice the price. Most of the major hydrofoil routes are operated from May to early September, with lesser ones sometimes running in July and August only.

CHAPTER SIX

THE ARGO-SARONIC

T he rocky, volcanic chain of **Argo-Saronic** islands, most of them barely an olive's throw from the Argolid, differs to a surprising extent not just from the mainland but from one another. Less surprising is their massive popularity, with Éyina (Aegina) almost becoming an Athenian suburb at weekends. Ídhra (Hydra),

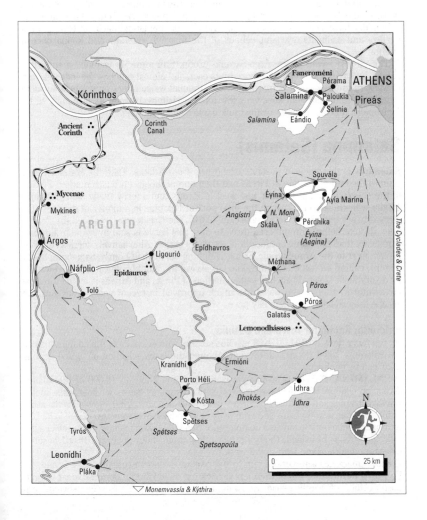

Póros and Spétses (Spetsai) are not far behind in summer, though their visitors tend to be predominantly cruise- and package-tourists. More than any other group, these islands are at their best out of season, when populations fall dramatically and the port towns return to a quieter, more provincial life.

Éyina, important in antiquity and more or less continually inhabited since then, is the most fertile of the group, famous for its pistachio nuts, as well as for one of the finest ancient temples in Greece. Its main problem – the crowds – can be escaped by avoiding weekends, or taking the time to explore its satellite isle, **Angístri**.

The three southerly islands, **Spétses**, **Ídhra** and **Póros**, are pine-cloaked and comparatively infertile. They were not extensively settled until medieval times, when refugees from the mainland – principally Albanian Christians – established themselves here. In response to the barrenness of their new homes the islanders adopted piracy as a livelihood. The seamanship and huge fleets thus acquired were placed at the disposal of the Greek nation during the War of Independence. Today, foreigners and Athenians have replaced locals in the rapidly depopulating harbour towns; windsurfers and sailboats are faint echoes of the massed warships and kaïkia once at anchor.

The closest island of the Argo-Saronic group, **Salamína**, is virtually a suburb of Pireás, just over a kilometre offshore to its east, and almost touches the industrial city of Mégara to the west. It is frequented by Athenian weekenders or is a base for commuting to the capital, but sees very few foreign visitors. Despite its proximity to the metropolis, it is noted for its distinct folk dances and costumes.

Salamína (Salamis)

Salamína is the quickest possible island hop from Athens. Take the Kifissiá–Pireás train to the end of the line in Pireás and then one of the green buses marked Pérama to the shipyard port of Pérama, just west of Pireás, and a ferry (daily 5am–midnight; 140dr) will whisk you across to the little port of Paloukía in a matter of minutes. The ferry crosses the narrow strait where, in 480BC, the Greek navy trounced the Persian fleet, despite being outnumbered three to one; this battle is said by some to be more significant than the Battle of Marathon, ten years earlier. Alternatively, ferries run from Pireás, next to the Argo-Saronic Flying Dolphins berth (half-hourly, 8am–5pm; 360dr; 45min), calling en route at Ambelákia. On arrival in Paloukía, you won't be rewarded by desirable or isolated beaches – the pollution of Pireás and Athens is a little too close for comfort, although the water has much improved in recent years – but you may escape the capital's smog and city pace.

Paloukía, Salamína Town and Selínia

By the ferry dock in **PALOUKÍA** is a bus station, with services to the contiguous capital Salamína Town (3km), and beyond, though the large selection of signed destinations can be confusing.

SALAMÍNA TOWN (also known as Kouloúri) is home to 18,000 of the island's 23,000 population. It's a depressing place, with a couple of banks, a fish market, motorway-like traffic, and an over-optimistic (and long-closed) tourist office. Pretty much uniquely for an island town – and emphasizing the absence of tourists – there is no bike or moped rental outlet, and also no hotel (not that you'd want to stay). Bus services link most points on the island, though information about them is scanty. Iliaktí beach is pleasant enough, some 5km to the west.

Buses marked **Faneroméni** run to the port at the northwest tip of the island, the **Voudóro peninsula**, where there are ferries across to Lákki Kalomírou, near Mégara on the Athens–Kórinthos road. En route it passes close by the frescoed seventeenth-century **monastery of Faneroméni** (6km from Salamína), rather majestically sited above the gulf.

Around 6km to the south of Paloukía is a third island port, **SELÍNIA**, which has connections direct to the Pireás ferry dock (winter 9.30am, summer five crossings daily between 8am–2.30pm; 380dr; 30min). It can also be reached direct by bus from Paloukía. This is the main summer resort, with a pleasant waterfront, a bank, several tavernas and two inexpensive hotels, the *Akroyali* (☎01/46 73 263; ③) and *Votsalakia* (☎01/46 71 334; ③).

Eándio and the south

South from Salamína Town, the road edges the coast towards Eándio (6km; regular buses). There are a few tavernas along the way, but the sea vistas are not inspiring. **EÁNDIO**, however, is quite a pleasant village, with a little pebble beach and the island's best **hotel**, the *Gabriel* (☎01/46 62 275; ④), owned by poet and journalist Giorgos Tzimas, who can be prevailed upon to recite a poem or two. The hotel overlooks the bay, whose waters are said to be returning to health, although the Salamína waterfront opposite can be less than sweet-smelling.

Two roads continue from Eándio. The one to the southeast runs to the unassuming village resorts of Peráni and Paralía (both around 4km from Eándio). The more interesting route is southeast towards Kanákia (8km from Eándio; no buses), over the island's pine-covered mountain, and passing (at around 5km) a monastery – dedicated, like most Salamína churches, to Áyios Nikólaos. At the monastery, turn off left to the harbour and small-scale resort of Peristéria (5km). This is a much more attractive settlement than the littered beach and scruffy huts of Kanákia itself.

Éyina (Aegina)

Given its current population of a little over 10,000, it seems incredible that **Éyina** (Aegina, Aigina) was a major power in Classical times, rivalling Athens. It carried trade to the limits of the known world, maintained a sophisticated silver coinage system (the first in Greece) and had prominent athletes and craftsmen. During the fifth century BC, however, the islanders made the political mistake of siding with their fellow Dorians, the Spartans. Athens seized on this as an excuse to act on a long-standing jealousy; her fleets defeated those of the islanders in two separate sea battles and, after the second, the population was expelled and replaced by more tractable colonists.

Subsequent history was less distinguished, with the pattern of occupation familiar to central Greece – by Romans, Franks, Venetians, Catalans and Turks – before the War of Independence brought a brief period as seat of government for the fledgling Greek nation. For a time it was, like Salamína, a prison island; only comparatively recently has it shaken off the consequent unfavourable reputation. The grim Éyina prison still stands, behind the stadium, but is currently used as a stray-dog shelter. These days, the island is most famous for its **pistachio orchards**, whose thirsty trees lower the water table several feet annually – hence the notices warning you of the perennial water crisis.

Athenians regard Éyina as a beach annexe for their city, being the closest place to the capital most of them would swim at, though for tourists it has a monument as fine as any in the Aegean in its beautiful fifth-century BC **Temple of Afaia**. This is located on the east coast, close to the port of **Ayía Marína**, and if it is your primary goal, you'd do best to take one of the ferries or hydrofoils which run directly to that port in season. If you plan to stay, then make sure your boat will dock at **Éyina Town**, the island capital. Ferries and hydrofoils also stop at **Souvála**, a Greek weekend retreat between the two ports devoid of interest to outsiders. Hydrofoils are far more frequent than ferries,

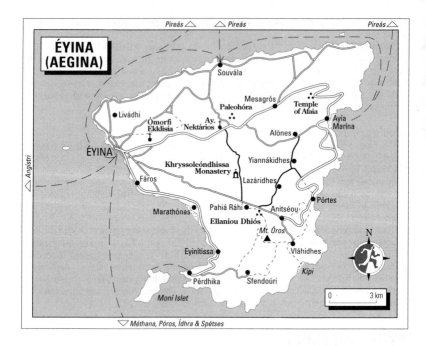

ÉYINA (AEGINA)

Pireás △   △ Pireás   Pireás △

Souvála

Mesagrós
Paleohóra   Temple
of Afaia

● Livádhi   Ayía
Ómorfi   Ay.   Marína
Ekklisía   Nektários
Alónes ●

ÉYINA

Yiannákidhes ●
Khryssoleóndhissa
Monastery
Fáros ●   Lazáridhes ●

● Pórtes
Pahiá Ráhi ●   Anitséou ●
Marathónas
Ellaníou Dhiós
Mt. Óros
▲
Eyinítissa ●   ● Vláhidhes

Kípi
N
Pérdhika ●   Sfendoúri

Moní Islet   0   3 km

△ Angístri

▽ Méthana, Póros, Ídhra & Spétses

run from the same quay in Pireás as the conventional boats, and cost hardly any more for this particular destination.

Éyina Town

A solitary column of the Temple of Apollo beckons as your ferry or hydrofoil steams around the point into the harbour at **ÉYINA TOWN**. The island's capital, it makes an attractive base, with some grand old buildings from the time (1826–28) when it served as the first capital of Greece during the War of Independence. And for somewhere so close to Athens, it isn't especially overrun by foreign tourists, although accommodation prices are high, particularly at weekends.

The **long harbour** waterfront combines the workaday with the picturesque, but is nonetheless appealing: fishermen talk and tend their nets, and kaïkia selling produce from the mainland bob at anchor. North of the port, behind the small town beach, the rather weather-beaten Apollo temple column stands on a low hill that was the ancient acropolis and is known, logically enough, as **Kolóna** (Column). Around the temple are **ruins** (daily 8.30am–3pm; 500dr), but unlike at Afaia (see below), extensive excavation has been possible, revealing five thousand years of settlement and ten layers of city life. There is a small museum in the grounds. On the north flank of Kolóna hill there's an attractive bay with a very small, sandy **beach** – the best spot for swimming in the immediate vicinity of the town.

The town's other sights, such as they are, are the frescoed thirteenth-century church of **Ómorfi Ekklisía**, fifteen minutes' walk east of the port, and a house in the suburb of Livádhi, just to the north, where a plaque recalls the residence of **Nikos Kazantzakis**, when he was writing his most celebrated book, *Zorba the Greek*.

Arrival and accommodation

The **bus station** is on the over-ambitiously refurbished Platía Ethneyersías, just north of the ferry arrival point, with excellent services to most villages; buy your tickets before you get on the bus. Horse buggies and taxis go from nearby, the **post office** is here, and most accommodation is in the area immediately behind the square. Several offices on and behind the main waterfront rent cars, mopeds, motorbikes and mountain bikes, though Éyina is large and hilly enough to make a motor worthwhile for anything other than a pedal to the beaches towards Pérdhika. Four **banks** line the main water-front. There's a **tourist police** post (☎0297/23 333) in the same building as the regular police, immediately behind the post office but reached from Leonárdhou Ladhá. Aegina Island Holidays (☎0297/26 430) on the waterfront, offers excursions to the Epidaurus theatre festival (see p.177) and handles tickets for the Sea Falcon Hydrofoils to Souvála and Ayía Marína.

Good inexpensive **accommodation** can be found in the *Electra* rooms (☎0297/23 360, fax 26 715; ③) on Leonárdhou Ladhá. The Scottish-run *House of Peace* (☎0297/28 726, fax 24 742; *houseofpeace@aig.forthnet.gr*, ③) is an old villa with charming, inexpensive self-catering rooms set in a large, quiet garden behind the bus station. Computer and email links are available, and the owner acts as an agent for other accommodation on Éyina and Angístri. On the seafront between Platía Ethneyersías and Kolóna are the *Areti* (☎0297/23 593; ⑤) and *Avra* (☎0297/22 303, fax 23 917; ⑤) hotels, where sea views for both of them compensate for the traffic noise. Next to the *Avra* is the friendly *Plaza Hotel* (☎0297/25 600; ④), while inland, near the cathedral, is the attractively restored *Traditional Pension* (*Eyinitiko Arhondiko*; ☎0297/24 968, fax 24 156; ④).

Eating and entertainment

Directly behind the fish market on P. Irióti is a particularly good and inexpensive seafood **taverna**, the *Psarotaverna Agora*, with outdoor seating on the cobbles in summer. Next to the *Areti* hotel, the small *Lekkas* is excellent for no-nonsense meat grills by the waterside, and near the *Plaza Hotel* is *Floisvos*, also offering charcoal-grilled food by the sea. Further south along the main quay, near the Ionian Bank, the *Economou* fish taverna-ouzeri serves good traditional food, while a couple of kilometres south, in the suburbs, the *Stratigos* serves straightforward but well-prepared food overlooking the little harbour at Fáros. Self-caterers will find good prices at the Kritikou supermarket on the Ayía Marína road, just beyond the stadium and prison.

In terms of **nightlife**, Éyina Town boasts two summer **cinemas**: the Olympia near the football grounds before the *Miranda* hotel and the new Akroyiali at the end of Eyina harbour on the Pérdhika road, which shows quality foreign films; the winter cinema, the Titina, is by the park of the medieval tower-house, a block below the OTE. The young and lively might try the *Apocalypse* or *Perdiotika* bars, or Petros' *Tropic* all-night café. The well-heeled can sample genuine live *bouzoúki* at Athenian prices at *Kanellas*, also on the waterfront. Most discos are across the island in Ayía Marína, but the vast *Vareladiko* disco is in Fáros, just beyond the *Stratigos* taverna.

The free *Essential Aegina* is a useful **listings** booklet, updated regularly during the summer season.

The Temple of Afaia

The Doric **Temple of Afaia** (Mon–Fri 8.00am–7pm, Sat & Sun 8.00am–3pm; 800dr) lies 12km east of Éyina Town, among pines that are tapped to flavour the local retsina, and beside a less aesthetic radio mast. It is one of the most complete and visually complex ancient buildings in Greece, its superimposed arrays of columns and lintels evocative of an Escher drawing. Built in the fifth century BC to replace a destroyed sixth century original, it slightly predates the Parthenon. The dedication is unusual: Afaia was a Cretan nymph who had fled from the lust of King Minos, and seems to have been worshipped almost exclusively on Éyina. As recently as two centuries ago the temple's pediments were intact and virtually perfect, depicting two battles at Troy. However, like the Elgin marbles they were "purchased" from the Turks – this time by Ludwig I of Bavaria, which explains their current residence in the Munich Glyptothek museum.

Buses from Éyina Town to Ayía Marína stop at the temple, or you could walk from Ayía Marína along the path that takes up where Kolokotróni leaves off, but rented transport allows you to stop at the monastery of Áyios Nektários and at the island's former capital of Paleohóra.

Áyios Nektários and Paleohóra

Áyios Nektários, a whitewashed modern convent situated around halfway to the Temple of Afaia, was named in honour of the Greek Orthodox Church's most recent and controversial saint, Anastasios Kefalas, a rather high-living monk who died in 1920 and was canonized in 1962. An oversized church – the largest in Greece – was recently completed on the main road below. Opposite the convent car park a partly paved road leads up into the hills towards the seventeenth-century convent of Khryssoleóndissa – primarily worth seeing for its views.

Paleohóra, a kilometre or so further east, was built in the ninth century as protection against piracy, but failed singularly in this capacity during Barbarossa's 1537 raid. Abandoned in 1827 following Greek independence, Paleohóra is now utterly deserted, but possesses the romantic appeal of a ghost village. You can drive right up to the site: take the turning left after passing the new large church and keep going about 400m. Some twenty of Paleohóra's reputed 365 churches and monasteries – one for every saint's day – remain in recognizable state, and can be visited, but only those of Episkopí (locked), Áyios Yeóryios and Metamórfosis (on the lower of the two trails) retain frescoes of any merit or in any state of preservation. Little remains of the town itself; when the islanders left, they simply abandoned their houses and moved to Éyina Town.

The East: Ayía Marína and Pórtes

The island's major package resort of **AYÍA MARÍNA**, 15km from Éyina Town, lies on the east coast of the island, south of the Afaia temple ridge. The concentrated tackiness of its jam-packed high street is something rarely seen this side of Corfu: signs abound for Guinness and cider, burger bars, and salaciously named cocktails. The beach is packed and overlooked by constantly sprouting, half-built hotels, and the water is not clean. It's really only worth coming here for connections to Pireás. There are some five ferries a day in season, with departures in the morning and late in the afternoon, and the Sea Falcon Line hydrofoils (☎0297/26 430) link both Ayía Marína and Souvála with Pireás.

Beyond the resort, the paved road continues south 8km to **PÓRTES**, a low-key shore hamlet. Among the uneasy mix of new summer villas-in-progress (no short-term accommodation) and old basalt cottages are scattered a few tiny fish **tavernas** and snack bars, with a functional beach between the two fishing anchorages. The road climbs to the village of Anitséou, just below a major saddle on the flank of Mount Óros, and then forges west towards the scenic village of **Pahiá Ráhi**, almost entirely rebuilt in traditional style by foreign owners. From here, a sharp, winding descent leads to the main west-coast road at Marathónas (for which see opposite), or a longer, paved and tree-lined route back to Éyina Town.

Mount Óros

Just south of the saddle between Pahiá Ráhi and Anitséou, mentioned above, are the foundations of the shrine of **Ellaníou Dhiós**, with the monastery of Taxiárhis squatting amid the massive masonry. The 532-metre summit cone of **Mount Óros**, an hour's walk from the highest point of the road, is capped by the modern chapel of Análipsi (the Ascension) and has views across the entire island and much of the Argo-Saronic Gulf.

A few other **paths** cross the largely roadless, volcanic flanks of Óros from Vláhidhes. Amazingly in this bulldozer-mad country, one to **Sfendoúri** hamlet still mostly survives, spasmodically marked by white paint blobs. The unmarked but well-used path, down to the sea at Kípi, may look tempting, but the litter-strewn boulder beach is far less appealing close to. Gerald Thompson's *A Walking Guide to Aegina*, available locally, describes in detail a series of walks across the range of mountains and wooded valleys between Mount Óros and the Afaia temple and down to the port of Souvála, all avoiding main roads.

The West: Marathónas, Pérdhika and Moní islet

The road due south of Éyina Town running along the west coast of the island is served by regular buses (8–10 daily). Small but sprawling **MARATHÓNAS**, 5km from Éyina, has the biggest of the west coast's small and rather scruffy sand beaches, and is tolerable enough, with a scattering of rooms, tavernas and cafés along the shore.

PÉRDHIKA, 9km along and the end of the coastal line, is more scenically set on its little bay and certainly has the best range of non-packaged accommodation on the island, outside Éyina Town. There are **rooms** on the main road, and just off it, immediately before the waterfront, the well-priced *Hotel Hippocampus* (☎0297/61 363; ②). On first sight the elongated village can appear characterless; however, further exploration reveals a relaxed, seaside-holiday atmosphere, very different from the rest of the island. On the attractive, pedestrianized waterfront esplanade, overlooking a panorama of Moní islet and the Peloponnese, are a dozen **tavernas** and cafés; probably the best food is at the first, *Nondas*.

The only other diversion at Pérdhika is a trip to the pale limestone offshore islet of **Moní** (500dr one way; 10min; several departures daily). There was once an EOT-run campsite on Moní, but this is now abandoned and derelict. There are no facilities on the island and most of it is fenced off as a nature conservation area. It's really only worth the trip for a swim in wonderfully clear water, as Pérdhika bay itself is of questionable cleanliness and has very small beach areas.

Angístri

Angístri, a quarter-hour by catamaran from Éyina, is small enough to be overlooked by most island-hoppers, though it is now in many foreign holiday brochures. The island fosters an uneasy coexistence between Athenian and German old-timers, who bought property here years ago, and British newcomers on package trips. Beaches, however, remain better and less crowded than on Éyina, and out of season the pine-covered island succumbs to a leisurely village pace, with many islanders still making a living from fishing and farming. Headscarves worn by the old women indicate the islanders' Albanian ancestry, and until recently they still spoke Arvanítika – a dialect of medieval Albanian with Greek accretions – amongst themselves.

The Angístri dock in Éyina Town is immediately south of the main harbour. **Boats and catamarans** from Éyina and Pireás call at Skála, and possibly at Mýlos. **From Pireás**, a direct ferry runs at least twice daily in season, once a day out of season, tak-

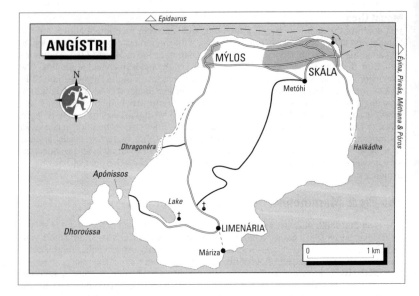

ing two hours; the fast catamaran three times a day, via Éyina, takes one hour. A water taxi is based in Angístri, but will be more expensive.

Skála and Mýlos

The essentially modern resort of **SKÁLA** is dominated by many new apartment buildings and hotels with little to distinguish them; they tend to face either inland or the windswept northeast corner of the island, over which Skála is rapidly spreading. The popular town beach, Angístri's only sandy one, nestles against the protected south shore of this headland, below an enormous church that is the local landmark. Just inland of the ferry dock is the attractive hotel *Yanna* (☎0297/91 228; ③), sharing a pool with the *Alter Ego* self-catering apartments; both are run by the helpful Nektarios Panou of Skala Travel (☎0297/91 356, fax 91 342; *nik.panou@otenet.gr*), who can arrange reservations for other accommodation. On summer weekends you would be well advised to reserve ahead. The *Neptune* taverna in Skála and the *Sailor* and *Konaki* in Mýlos are recommended.

Both **mopeds** and **mountain bikes** are available for rent; Limenária, near the end of the trans-island road, is less than 8km distant, so in cooler weather you can comfortably cross Angístri on foot or by bike. A road to the left of the harbour leads within fifteen minutes to the *Angistri Club*, with a disco-bar on the rocks above the sea, and the nearby *Alkyoni* taverna. From there, it's another ten minutes' walk to the secluded **Halikádha** pebble beach backed by crumbling cliffs and pine-covered hills; along with Dhragonéra (see opposite), this is the best that the island has to offer, and is clothing-optional.

Metóhi, the hillside hamlet just above Skála, was once the main village, and in recent years has been completely bought up and restored by foreigners and Athenians; there are no facilities.

Ever-spreading Skála threatens in the future to merge with **MÝLOS** (Megalohóri), just 1500m west along the north coast. Once you penetrate a husk of new construction, you find an attractive, traditional Argo-Saronic-style village centre. Although there's no decent beach nearby, it makes an alternative base to Skála, with plenty of rented **rooms** and some **hotels**. The *Milos Hotel* (☎0297/91 241; ③) is a good, well-positioned choice.

The rest of the island
A regular bus service, designed to dovetail with the ferry schedule, connects Skála and Mýlos with Limenária on the far side of the island – or you could hike from Metóhi along a winding dirt road through the pine forest, with views across to Éyina and the Peloponnese. The paved west-coast road takes you past the turning for **Dhragonéra**, a broad pebble beach with a dramatic panorama across to the mainland.

 LIMENÁRIA is a small farming community set at the edge of a fertile plateau in the southeast corner of the island, and still largely unaffected by tourism. There are two tavernas – *Tasos* is very good – and a few rooms. A sign points to a misleadingly named "beach", really just a spot, often monopolized by male naturists, where you can swim off the rocks. A half-hour walk west of Limenária, on the old path which parallels the road, will bring you past a shallow salt lake, to a seasonal taverna overlooking the tiny islet of Apónissos and larger Dhoroússa beyond.

Póros

Separated from the mainland by a 450-metre strait, **Póros** ("the ford") only just counts as an island – but qualify it does, and far more than any other Argo-Saronic islands it is package-tour territory – its proximity to Pireás also means a weekend Athenian invasion. The island town has character though, and the topography is interesting. Póros is in fact two islands, **Sferiá** (Póros Town) and the much more extensive **Kalávria**, separated from each other by a shallow engineered canal, which is now silting up.

 In addition to its regular ferry and hydrofoil connections with Pireás and the other Argo-Saronics, Póros has frequent boats shuttling across from the workaday mainland port of **Galatás** in the Peloponnese, and there's a car ferry every twenty minutes from near the Naval Academy. These allow for some interesting excursions – locally to the lemon groves of Lemonodhássos, ancient Troezen near Trizína, and the nearby Devil's Bridge (see p.182). Further afield, day-trips to Náfplio or to performances of ancient drama at the great theatre of Epidaurus are possible by car, or by taking an excursion, available through travel agents in Póros Town (see below).

Póros Town

Ferries from the Argo-Saronics or from Galatás drop you at **PÓROS**, the main town on the island, which rises steeply on three sides of the tiny volcanic Sferiá. The harbour and town are picturesque, and the cafés and waterfront lively. Fishermen sell their catches direct from the boat and it is possible to arrange fishing trips. Particular sights are the hill-top clocktower and a small, well-labelled **archeological museum** (Mon–Sat 9am–3pm; free), with items from the mainland site of Troezen and elsewhere.

 Near the main ferry dock is the helpful Family Tours (☎0298/23 743, fax 24 480) which has a variety of rooms available. Also on the waterfront are three other **travel agents**: Marinos Tours (☎0298/23 423), sole agents for the Flying Dolphin hydrofoils and with well-priced local maps, Hellenic Sun Travel (☎0298/25 901) and Saronic Gulf Travel (☎0298/24 555). All these agencies **exchange** money, arrange **accommodation** in rented rooms and handle **tours** off the island. If you want to look around on your own, the quieter places are up on the hill behind the clocktower, although prices are generally on the high side. To the right of the road to Kalávria

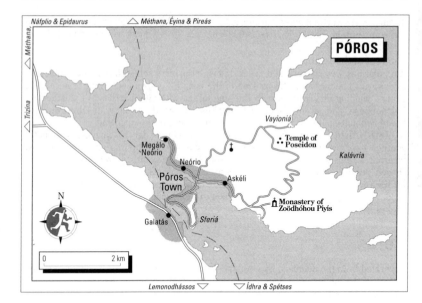

you'll find two reasonable hotels: *Dimitra* (☎0298/25 902, fax 25 653; ③) and *Latsi* (☎0298/22 392; ③). Most of the other hotels are across the canal. Camping is not encouraged anywhere on the island and the nearest official campsite, *Kyrayelo*, is just west of Galatás.

Down on the quayside, among the cafés, bars, creperies and souvenir shops facing Galatás, good-value **restaurants** include *Grill Oasis* and *Mouragio*, at the far end away from the ferry dock. *Moskhoyiannis* has traditional Greek food in the souvenir lane which runs between the Alpha Pistos (Alpha Credit) bank and the post office square. A well-signed lane, between the *Latsi* and the school, leads gently up, past the police station and Ergani weaving shop, to the upper square. Here, by the Áyios Yeóryios cathedral are a cluster of good tavernas: *Platanos, Perasma, Dimitris* – the last run by a local butcher, so excellent meat – and, just beyond, the *Kipos (Garden)*. The *Lithos* bar is nearby. The *Korali* and *Sirocco* **discos** provide nightlife, with both Greek and foreign music.

Additional facilities around the waterfront include **moped** and **bicycle** rental outlets (you can take either across on boats to the mainland), four **banks**, the **post office**, the summer-only Diana **cinema** and the helpful **tourist police** (☎0298/22 462; mid-May to Sept).

Kalávria

Most of Póros's **hotels** are to be found on Kalávria, the main body of the island, just across the canal beyond the Naval Cadets' Training School. They stretch for a couple of kilometres on either side of the bridge, with some of those to the west in Neório ideally situated to catch the dawn chorus – the Navy's marching band. If you'd rather sleep on, head beyond the first bay where the fishing boats tie up. Two kilometres from the bridge, in **Megálo Neório**, is the pleasant *Pavlou* hotel (☎0298/22 734, fax 22 735; ⑤), a larger beach and a watersports centre.

Alternatively, turn right through **Askéli**, where posh hotels and villas face good clear water. Two **bus** routes run half-hourly from Poros Town waterfront to Askéli and Zoödhóhou Piyís, and to Neório.

The monastery of Zoödhóhou Piyís and Temple of Poseidon

At the end of the four-kilometre stretch of road through Askéli lies the eighteenth-century **monastery of Zoödhóhou Piyís**, whose monks have fled the tourists and been replaced by a caretaker. It's a pretty spot, with a couple of summer tavernas at the beach below.

From here you can either walk up across to the northern side of the island through the pines, or bike along the road. Initially, Kalávria appears to be mostly pine forest, but the far side has fertile plateaus, olive terraces, small deserted beaches in narrow inlets and magnificent panoramic views. Foot or bike routes should lead you to a saddle in the hills and the few columns and ruins that make up the sixth-century BC **Temple of Poseidon** – though keep your eyes open or you may miss them; look for a small blue caretaker's hut. It was here that Demosthenes, fleeing from the Macedonians after taking part in the last-ditch resistance of the Athenians, took poison rather than surrender. The road leads on, back down in a circular route to the canal and Sferiá.

Ídhra (Hydra)

The port and town of **Ídhra**, with tiers of substantial greystone mansions and white-walled, red-tiled houses climbing up from a perfect horseshoe harbour, are a beautiful spectacle. Unfortunately, thousands of others think so too, and from Easter until September it's packed to the gills. The front becomes one long outdoor café and souvenir stall, the hotels are full and the discos flourish. Once a fashionable artists' colony, established in the 1960s as people restored the grand old houses, it has experienced a predictable metamorphosis into one of the more popular (and expensive) resorts in Greece. But this acknowledged, a visit is still recommended, especially out of peak season.

Ídhra Town

The waterfront of **ÍDHRA TOWN** is lined with mansions, most of them built during the eighteenth century, on the accumulated wealth of a remarkable merchant fleet of 160 ships which traded as far afield as America and, during the Napoleonic Wars, broke the British blockade to sell grain to France. Fortunes were made and the island also enjoyed a special relationship with the Turkish Porte, governing itself and paying no tax, but providing sailors for the sultan's navy. These conditions naturally attracted Greek immigrants from the less-privileged mainland, and by the 1820s the town's population was nearly 20,000 – an incredible figure when you reflect that today it is under

---

ÍDHRA FESTIVALS

On the second or third weekend in June, Ídhra Town celebrates the **Miaoulia**, in honour of Admiral Andreas Miaoulis whose **fire boats**, packed with explosives, were set adrift upwind of the Turkish fleet during the War of Independence. The highlight of the celebrations is the burning of a boat at sea as a tribute to the sailors who risked their lives in this dangerous enterprise.

On an altogether more peaceful note, the **International Puppet Theatre Festival** takes place here at the end of July and appeals to children of all ages.

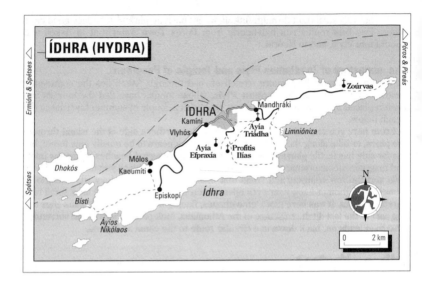

3000. During the War of Independence, Hydriot merchants provided many of the ships for the Greek forces and consequently many of the commanders.

The **mansions** (*arhóndika*) of these merchant families, designed by Venetian and Genoese architects, are still the great monuments of the town. A town map is available locally, if you are interested in seeking them out – some are labelled at the entrance with "*Oikía*" (home) and the family name. On the western waterfront, and the hill behind, are the **Voulgaris** mansion, with its interesting interior, and the **Tombazis** mansion, used as a holiday hostel for arts students. Set among pines above the restored windmill on the western point, the **Koundouriotis** mansion was the home of George Koundouriotis, a wealthy shipowner who fought in the War of Independence and whose great grandson, Pavlos Koundouriotis, was president of republican Greece in the 1920s. It is being refurbished as a museum with EU funding. On the eastern waterfront are the **Kriezis** mansion, the **Spiliopoulos** mansion and the **Tsamados** mansion – now the national merchant navy college which you can sometimes visit between lectures. The **historical archives museum** is also on the eastern waterfront (Tues–Sun 9am–2.30pm; 500dr).

Ídhra is also reputedly hallowed by no fewer than 365 churches – a total claimed by many a Greek island, but here with some justice. The most important is the church of **Panayía Mitropóleos**, set in a monastic courtyard by the port, with a distinctive clock-tower and a **Byzantine museum** of uncertain opening hours.

Practicalities

The town is small and compact, but away from the waterfront the streets and alleyways are steep and maps slightly ambiguous, so finding your way around can be difficult. There are several **banks** along the waterfront, and the **tourist police** (daily mid-May to mid-Oct, 9am–10pm; ☎0298/52 205) are on Vótsi. The **post office** and a **laundry** are on the small market square, behind the National Bank. The ferry office, Hydreoniki Travel (☎0298/54 007) is upstairs on a side-street to the left of the Bank, while the new Minoan hydrofoil office is through a doorway on the eastern waterfront, about 10m beyond the Studio Hydra shop.

There are a number of **pensions** and **hotels** along, or just behind, the waterfront in Ídhra Town, often charging up to a third more than usual island rates. Some of the restaurants along the waterfront act as agents for the outlying pensions and hotels, which could save you time and footwork; better still, phone ahead and book – certainly for any weekend. The *Amarillis* at Tombázi 15 (☎0298/53 611; ③) is a small hotel with comfortable rooms and private facilities; or there are a couple of old mansions beautifully converted into hotels, *Angelika*, Miaoúli 42 (☎0298/53 202; ⑥), and *Hydra*, steeply uphill at Voulgari 8 (☎0298/52 102; ③–④). Of the pensions, try the *Theresia*, further up Tombázi (☎0298/53 984; ③).

There's no shortage of **restaurants** and cafés around the waterfront, but for good tavernas you would do well to head a little inland. The *Garden* taverna, known for good meat, is on the road heading up from the hydrofoil dock, with the equally good *Xeri Elia* down the narrow street outside The *Garden*'s wall. Above the *Amarillis Hotel* is the small *Barba Dimas* taverna, which has wonderful mezédhes, snails and fish. Farther up on the same road, *To Kryfo Limani* is a pleasant taverna in a small garden, while farther yet will bring you good home cooking at the *Yeitoniko* (also known as *Manolis & Christina's*), which has tables on its small veranda. For light snacks and refreshments, try the small and friendly *Pigadi* café, below the *Amarillis*.

For **nightlife** go west; the long-established *Kavos* above the harbour is the best disco, while *Heaven* has impressive views from its hillside site. *Hydronetta*, above the sea at the edge of town, towards Kamíni, is lively and plays foreign music.

Beaches around Ídhra Town

The town's only sandy beach is at **MANDHRÁKI**, 1.5km east of the harbour along a concrete track; it's the private domain of the *Miramare Hotel* (☎0298/52 300; ⑤), although the windsurfing centre is open to all.

On the opposite side of the harbour, to the southwest, a broad coastal path leads around to **KAMÍNI**, about a twenty-minute walk. Just as you reach Kamíni on the right is a small pension, *Antonia* (☎0298/52 481; ③) On the left, across the street, Eléni Petrolékka has a popular rival pension and apartments (☎0298/52 701; ③). Also on the left is the *Kodylenia* restaurant, with fresh fish and wonderful views of the sunset. About 100m up the dry, paved streambed to the left is *Christina's*, a fine traditional Greek fish taverna.

Thirty minutes' walk beyond Kamíni (or a boat ride from the port) will bring you to **VLYHÓS**, a small hamlet with three tavernas, rooms, a small **beach** and a restored nineteenth-century bridge. The *Iliovasilema* taverna enjoys sunset views from the water's edge, near the small jetty, while just beyond are the attractive *Antigone* rooms (☎0298/53 228, fax 53 042; ⑤) and café. Any of these establishments can call a water taxi to whisk you back to town. **Camping** is tolerated here (though nowhere else closer to town) and the swimming in the lee of an offshore islet is good. Further out is the steep-sided island of **Dhokós**, large but only seasonally inhabited by goatherds and people tending their olives.

The interior and south coast

There are no motor vehicles on Ídhra, except for a few lorries to cart away rubble and rubbish, and no surfaced roads away from the port: the island is mountainous and its interior accessible only by foot or hoof. The net result is that most tourists don't venture beyond the town, so by a little walking you can find yourself in a dramatically different kind of island. The pines devastated by forest fires in 1985 are now regenerating.

Following the streets of the town upwards and inland behind the *Angelica* you reach a path which winds up the mountain, in about an hour's walk, to the **monastery of Profítis Ilías** and the **convent of Ayía Efpraxía**. Both are beautifully situated; the nuns at the convent (the lower of the two) offer hand-woven fabrics for sale. A path continues behind Profítis Ilías to a saddle overlooking the south coast and a steeply descending *kalderími* onwards to scattered houses and chapels near the sea. From the saddle, a faint path climbs to the right in twenty minutes to the 588-metre summit of Mount Éros, the Argo-Saronic islands' highest viewpoint. To the east of Profítis Ilías are three more monasteries, the nearest to town being **Ayía Triádha**, occupied by a few monks (no women admitted). From here a path continues east for two more hours to the cloister of **Zourvás** in the extreme east of the island.

A dirt road continues west of Vlyhós, past a busy boat repair yard, to **Episkopí**, a high plateau planted with olives and vineyards and dotted by a scattering of homes (no facilities), and then climbs above Mólos Bay, the property of an Athenian hospital owner, and closed to the public. From Episkopí itself, vague tracks lead to the southwestern extreme of the island, on either side of which the bays of **Bísti** and **Áyios Nikólaos** offer solitude and good swimming. Bísti has a pebble beach with good rocks for swimming off at one side; Ayios Nikólaos has a small sand beach. Points on the coast can be reached much more easily by water taxis, which will drop you off and then pick you up again at any time you arrange.

The best cove of the many on the south coast is **Limnióniza** (beyond Ayía Triádha), with a pebble beach and pine trees – though the overland access path is long (a half hour plus from town) and rough, and arrival by sea is recommended.

Spétses (Spetsai)

Spétses was the island where John Fowles once lived and which he used, thinly disguised as Phraxos, as the setting for *The Magus*. It is today very popular with well-to-do Athenians and with foreigners, and seems to have risen above the bad 1980s reputation earned by an unhealthy proportion of cheap package tours and lager louts. The architecture of Spétses Town is distinct and distinguished, though less photogenic than that

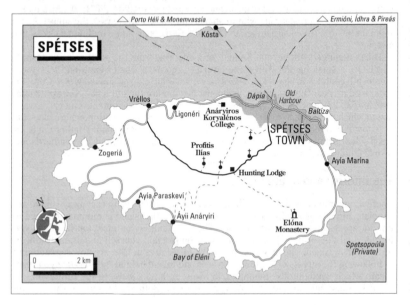

of Ídhra. Lacking any dramatic topography, and despite a bout of forest-fire devastation in 1990, hints of the landscape described by Fowles are still to be seen: "away from its inhabited corner [it is] truly haunted . . . its pine forests uncanny". Remarkably, at Áyii Anáryiri, Spétses' best beach, development has been restrained to a scattering of holiday villas.

Spétses Town

SPÉTSES TOWN is the island's port – and its only settlement. It shares with Ídhra the same history of late eighteenth-century mercantile adventure and prosperity, and the same leading role in the War of Independence, which made its foremost citizens the aristocrats of the newly independent Greek state. Pebble-mosaic courtyards and streets sprawl between 200-year-old mansions, whose architecture is quite distinct from the Peloponnesian styles across the water. Though homeowners may bring private cars onto the island, their movement inside the town limits is prohibited. A few taxis supplement the horse-drawn buggies, whose bells ring cheerfully night and day along the long waterfront, though animal welfare activists are justifiably worried by the condition of some of the horses by summer's end. Motorbikes, mopeds and noisy three-wheel mini-trucks are the preferred mode of transport, and career continuously through the town streets, making life almost as difficult for pedestrians as if cars had been allowed.

The sights are principally the majestic old houses and gardens, the grandest of which is the magnificent Mexis family mansion, built in 1795 and now used as the **local museum** (Tues–Sun 8.30am–2.15pm; 500dr), housing displays of relics from the War of Independence that include the bones of the Spetsiot admiral-heroine **Laskarina Bouboulina**. One of Bouboulina's homes, to the rear of the cannon-studded main harbour known as the **Dápia**, has been made into a **museum** (daily morning & late afternoon; 1000dr) by her descendants and is well worth visiting. Guided tours (30min) are given in English several times a day.

Just outside the town, Fowles aficionados will notice **Anáryiros Koryalénos College**, a curious Greek re-creation of an English public school where the author was employed and set part of his tale; it is now vacant, save for the occasional conference or kids' holiday programme. Like the massive waterfront **Hotel Posidonion** – now no longer a hotel – where kings and presidents once slept, the college was endowed by Sotirios Anaryiros, the island's great nineteenth-century benefactor. An enormously rich self-made man, he was also responsible for replanting the pine forest that now covers the island. His former residence, behind the *Hotel Roumani*, is a Pharaonic monument to bad taste.

Walking east from the Dápia, you pass the **Old Harbour** inlet, still a well-protected mooring, and the church of **Áyios Nikólaos** – with its graceful belfry, *"Freedom or Death"* memorial and some giant pebble mosaics. At the end of the road you reach the **Baltíza** inlet where, among the sardine-packed yachts, half a dozen boatyards continue to build kaïkia in the traditional manner; it was one of these that recreated the *Argo* for Tim Severin's re-enactment of the "Jason Voyage". An extensive new housing development behind Baltíza will probably edge local prices even higher.

Practicalities
A good way to get around the island is by bike, and, despite the hills, you can reach most points or make the 25km circuit without too much exertion. Several reliable **bike** and **moped** rental outlets are scattered through town.

All kinds of **accommodation** are available in Spétses Town, but be warned that prices are inflated in high season, although the town is smaller and less steep than Ídhra, so hunting around for a good deal is not such hard work. If you don't fancy pounding the streets yourself, try Alasia Travel (☎0298/74 098) or Melédon Tourist and Travel Agency (☎0298/74 497), both by the Dápia. Two simple but comfortable hotels are *Faros* (☎0298/72 613, fax 72 614; ④) on Platía Oroloyíou ("Clocktower Square") and *Stelios* (☎0298/72 971; ③) on the waterfront. A few hotels – the *Faros*, the *Alexandris* (☎0298/72 211; ④), above the petrol station, and the waterfront *Klimis* (☎0298/72 334; ④) stay open all winter. Inland and uphill from the centre, near the *Lazaros* taverna, rooms at the *Villa Orizontes* (☎0298/72 509; ③) have a fridge and extensive sea views.

In Spétses Town, **food** and **drink** tend to be overpriced. Among the better options are *Roussos*, 300m east of the Dápia, just beyond the *Klimis*; or the *Lazaros* taverna, about 400m up from the Dápia. For fish, go to the *Bouboulina* ouzerí opposite the fish market, which is before *Klimis*, or the long-established *Patralis* near the water in Kounoupítsa, west towards the *Spetses* hotel. The ouzerí *Byzantino* is popular, characterful, but expensive, as are many other places around the Old Harbour.

By day, *To Kafenio*, near the Flying Dolphin office at the Dápia, remains steadfastly traditional, with drinks and lunchtime mezedhes – a good place to watch and wait for your ferry. By night, clubbers head for *Figaro*, in the Old Harbour, and the places at the other end of town around Kounoupítsa. Few of these places shut until the fishermen are setting out.

The **post office** is near the *Roussos* taverna, while a couple of **banks** are behind the Dápia, near the *Roumani* hotel. There is a **laundry** behind Platía Oroloyíou.

Around the island

For **swimming** you need to get clear of the town. Beaches within walking distance are at **Ayía Marína** (twenty minutes east, with the very pleasant *Paradise* restaurant), at various spots beyond the **Old Harbour**, and several other spots half an hour away in either direction. The tempting smaller isle of **Spetsopoúla**, just offshore from Ayía Marína, is off-limits: it's the private property of the heirs of shipping magnate Stavros Niarchos.

For heading further afield, you'll need to hire a **bike** or **moped**, or use the **kaïkia** rides from the Dápia, which run to beaches around the island in summer. A very expensive alternative are **water taxis**, though they can take up to ten people. **Walkers** might want to go over the top of the island to Áyii Anáryiri; forest fire has ravaged much of the southern side's pines between Ayía Marína and Áyii Anáryiri, though happily they are growing back. Routes out of town start from beyond the *Lazaros* taverna, and pass the forest service firewatch tower. Brave the precariously attached steps and you're rewarded with the island's highest and best viewpoint.

West from Spétses Town

Heading west from the Dápia around the coast, the road is paved or in good condition almost all around the island. The forest that survived the fires stretches from the central hills right down to the western shores and makes for a beautiful coastline with little coves and rocky promontories, all shaded by trees. *Panas Taverna* at Ligonéri, run by a Greek-American woman, provides wonderful respite from the bustle of town. You can swim below and then have lunch or dinner under the pines. A regular bus service runs to Ligonéri in season, from in front of the *Hotel Posidonion*.

Vréllos is the next place you come to, at the mouth of a wooded valley known locally as "Paradise", which would be a fairly apt description, except that, like so many of the beaches, it becomes littered every year with windblown rubbish. However, the entire shore is dotted with coves and in a few places there are small, seasonal tavernas – there's a good one at **Zogeriá**, for instance, where the scenery and rocks more than make up for the small beach.

Working your way anti-clockwise around the coast towards Áyii Anáryiri you reach **Áyia Paraskeví** with its small church and beach – one of the most beautiful coves on

Spétses and an alternate stop on some of the kaïki runs. There's a basic beach café and watersports here in summer. On the hill behind is the house John Fowles used as the setting for *The Magus*, the **Villa Yasemiá**. It was owned by the late Alkis Botassis, who claimed to be the model for the *Magus* character – though Fowles denies "appropriating" anything more than his "outward appearance" and the "superb site" of his house.

Áyii Anáryiri

Áyii Anáryiri, on the south side of the island, is the best, if also the most popular, beach: a beautiful, long, sheltered bay of fine sand. Gorgeous first thing in the morning, it fills up later in the day, with bathers, windsurfers and, at one corner, speedboat-driving waterski instructors. On the right-hand side of the bay, looking out to sea, there's a sea cave, which you can walk or swim to and explore, if you're not discouraged by the ominous rockfall on the access steps. There's a good seafront taverna and another just behind, *Tassos*, run by one of the island's great eccentrics.

travel details

Ferries

From the central harbour at **Pireás** at least 4 boats daily run to Ayía Marína (1hr) and 11 to Éyina (1hr 30min); 1–2 daily to Skála and Mýlos (2hr); 4 daily to Póros (3hr 30min); 1–2 daily to Ídhra (4hr 30min) and Spétses (5hr 30min). About 4 connections daily between Éyina and Póros; 4–5 daily between Éyina and Angístri; from Angístri about 4 weekly to Paleá Epídhavros, far less frequently to Póros and Méthana.

Most of the ferries stop on the Peloponnesian mainland at Méthana (between Éyina and Póros) and Ermióni (between Ídhra and Spétses); it is possible to board them here. Some continue from Spétses to Pórto Héli. There are also constant boats between Póros and Galatás (10min) from dawn until late at night, boat-taxis between Spétses and Pórto Héli, and 4 daily ferries between Spétses and Kósta.

NB There are more ferries at weekends and fewer out of season (although the service remains good); for Éyina and Póros they leave Pireás most frequently between 7.30am and 9am, and 2pm and 4pm. Do not buy a return ticket as it saves no money and limits you to one specific boat. The general information number for the Argo-Saronic ferries is ☎01/41 75 382.

Flying Dolphin hydrofoils

Approximately hourly services from the central harbour at Pireás to **Éyina** only 6am–8pm in season, 7am–7pm out of season (40min).

All hydrofoils going beyond Éyina leave from the **Zéa Marina**: 4–15 times daily to Póros (1hr), Ídhra (1hr 40min) and Spétses (2hr–2hr 30min). All these times depend upon the stops en route, and frequencies vary with the season.

Éyina is connected with Méthana and Póros 1–3 times a day; Póros, Ídhra and Spétses with each other 5–7 times daily. Some hydrofoils also stop at Méthana and Ermióni and most of those to Spétses continue to Porto Héli (15min more). This is a junction of the hydrofoil route – in season there is usually one a day onwards to Toló and Náfplio (and vice versa; 30 and 45min) and another to Monemvassía (2hr). The Monemvassía hydrofoil continues 2–4 days a week (Friday to Sunday) to the island of Kýthira.

NB Services are heavily reduced out of season, though all the routes between Pórto Héli and Pireás still run. Hydrofoils are usually twice as fast and twice as expensive as ordinary boats, though to Éyina the price is little different. You can now buy round-trip tickets to destinations in the Argo-Saronic Gulf. In season, it's not unusual for departures to be fully booked for a day or so at a time.

Details and tickets available from the Minoan Pireás Flying Dolphins office at Ákti Themistokléous 8 (☎01/42 80 001, number perennially engaged). Their Ceres Athens office at Filellínon 3 (☎01/32 44 600) is more convenient if you are in Athens. Tickets can also be bought at the departure quays on Aktí Tselépi in Pireás and at Zéa.

CHAPTER SEVEN

THE CYCLADES

Named after the circle they form around the sacred island of Delos, the **Cyclades** (Kykládhes) is the most satisfying Greek archipelago for island-hopping. On no other group do you get quite such a strong feeling of each island as a microcosm, each with its own distinct traditions, customs and path of modern development. Most of these self-contained realms are compact enough to walk around in a few days, giving you a sense of completeness and identity impossible on, say, Crete or most of the Ionian islands.

The islands do share some features however, the majority of them (Ándhros, Náxos, Sérifos and Kéa excepted) being arid and rocky; most also share the "Cycladic" style of brilliant white, cubist architecture. The extent and impact of tourism, though, is markedly haphazard, so that although some English is spoken on most islands, a slight detour from the beaten track – from Íos to Síkinos, for example – can have you groping for your Greek phrasebook.

But whatever the level of tourist development, there are only two islands where it has come completely to dominate their character: **Íos**, the original hippie-island and still a paradise for hard-drinking backpackers, and **Mýkonos**, by far the most popular of the group, with its teeming old town, selection of nude beaches and sophisticated clubs and gay bars. After these two, **Páros**, **Sífnos**, **Náxos**, and **Thíra** (Santoríni) are currently the most popular, with their beaches and main towns drastically overcrowded at the height of the season. To avoid the hordes altogether – except in August, when nearly everywhere is overrun and escape is impossible – the most promising islands are **Síkinos**, **Kímolos** or **Anáfi**, or the minor islets around Náxos. For a different view of the Cyclades, visit **Tínos** and its imposing pilgrimage church, a major spiritual centre of Greek Orthodoxy, or **Sýros** with its elegant townscape, and (like Tínos), large Catholic minority. Due to their closeness to Athens, adjacent **Kýthnos** and **Kéa** are predictably popular – and relatively expensive – weekend havens for Greeks. The one major ancient

ACCOMMODATION PRICE CODES

Throughout the book we've used the following **price codes** to denote the cheapest available double room in each establishment in high season. Out of season, rates can drop by more than fifty percent, especially if you are staying for three or more nights. Single rooms, where available, cost around seventy percent of the price of a double.

Rented private rooms on the islands usually fall into the ② or ③ categories, depending on their location and facilities, and the season; a few in the ④ category are more like plush self-catering apartments. They are not generally available from late October through to the beginning of April, when only hotels tend to remain open.

① Up to 6000dr	④ 12,000–16,000dr
② 6000–9000dr	⑤ 16,000–20,000dr
③ 9000–12,000dr	⑥ 20,000dr and upwards

Note: Youth hostels typically charge 2000–2500dr for a dormitory bed.
For more accommodation details, see pp.43–6.

site is **Delos** (Dhílos), certainly worth making time for; the commercial and religious centre of the Classical Greek world, it's visited most easily on a day-trip, by kaïki or jet boat from Mýkonos.

When it comes to **moving on**, many of the islands – in particular Mílos, Páros, Náxos and Thíra – are handily connected with Crete (easier in season), while from Tínos, Mýkonos, Sýros, Páros, Náxos, Thíra or Amorgós you can reach many of the Dodecanese by direct boat. Similarly, you can regularly get from Mýkonos, Náxos, Sýros and Páros to Ikaría and Sámos (in the eastern Aegean – see p.715 and p.703).

One consideration for the timing of your visit is that the Cyclades often get frustratingly **stormy**, particularly in early spring or late autumn, and it's also the group worst affected by the *meltémi*, which blows sand and tables about with ease throughout much of July and August. Delayed or cancelled ferries are not uncommon, so if you're heading back to Athens to catch a flight leave yourself a day or two's leeway.

Kéa (Tziá)

Kéa is the closest of the Cyclades to the mainland and is extremely popular in summer, and at weekends year-round, with Athenians. Their impact is mostly confined to certain small coastal resorts, leaving most of the interior quiet, although there is a preponderance of expensive apartments and villas and not as many good tavernas as you might expect because so many visitors self-cater. Midweek, or outside peak season, Kéa is a more enticing destination, with its rocky, forbidding perimeter and inland oak and almond groves.

As ancient Keos, the island and its strategic, well-placed harbour supported four cities – a pre-eminence that continued until the nineteenth century when Sýros became the main Greek port. Today, tourists account for the sea traffic: regular (in season) ferry connections with Lávrio on the mainland (only a ninety-minute bus ride from Athens), plus useful hydrofoils and ferries to and from Pireás, Sýros, and Kýthnos.

The northwest coast: Korissía to Otziás

The small northern ferry and hydrofoil port of **KORISSÍA** has fallen victim to uneven expansion and has little beauty to lose; if you don't like its looks upon disembarking, try to get a bus to Písses (16km), Otziás (6km) or Ioulídha (6km). Buses usually meet the boats; from July until August there's a regular fixed schedule around the island, but at other times they can be very elusive. There are just four **taxis** on Kéa, and two motorbike rental outfits: Antonis (☎0288/21 097), close to the *Karthea* hotel, and Moto Center (☎0288/21 844), a little inland near the **OTE**, both of them being more expensive than on most islands.

There's a list of rooms in the seafront tourist information office, and the kindly agents for the Flying Dolphin hydrofoils (To Stegadhi bookshop) sell maps and guides, and can phone around in search of **accommodation**. The best choices are the *Nikitas* pension (☎0288/21 193; ③), open all year and very friendly; *Hotel Korissia* (☎0288/21 484; ④), well inland along the stream bed; *Hotel Tzia* (☎0288/21 305; ④), right behind the best end of the otherwise uninspiring port beach; and the somewhat noisy *Karthea* (☎0288/21 204; ④), which does, however, boast single rooms and year-round operation – and a cameo appearance in recent Greek history. When the junta fell in July 1974, the colonels were initially imprisoned for some weeks in the then-new hotel, while the recently restored civilian government pondered what to do with them; Kéa was then so remote and unvisited that the erstwhile tyrants were safely out of reach of a vengeful populace. For **eating**, *Iy Akri* and *Angyrovoli* near the *Karthea* hotel have standard fare, while near the jetty *Apothiki* seems more popular than its smarter neighbour,

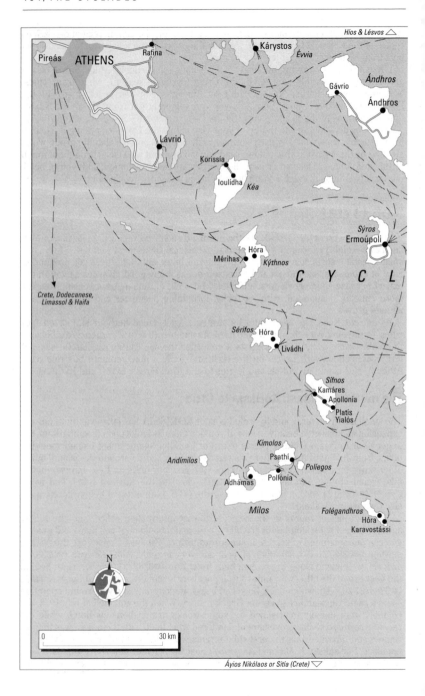

Híos & Lésvos △

Pireás
ATHENS
Rafina
Kárystos
Évvia

Gávrio
Ándhros
Ándhros

Lávrio

Korissía
Ioulídha
Kéa

Sýros
Ermoúpoli

Mérihas
Hóra
Kýthnos

C Y C L

Crete, Dodecanese,
Limassol & Haifa

Sérifos
Hóra
Livádhi

Sífnos
Kamáres
Apollonía
Platis
Yialós

Kímolos
Andímilos
Psathí
Políegos
Adhámas
Pollónia

Folégandhros
Hóra
Karavostássi

Mílos

N

0   30 km

Áyios Nikólaos or Sitía (Crete) ▽

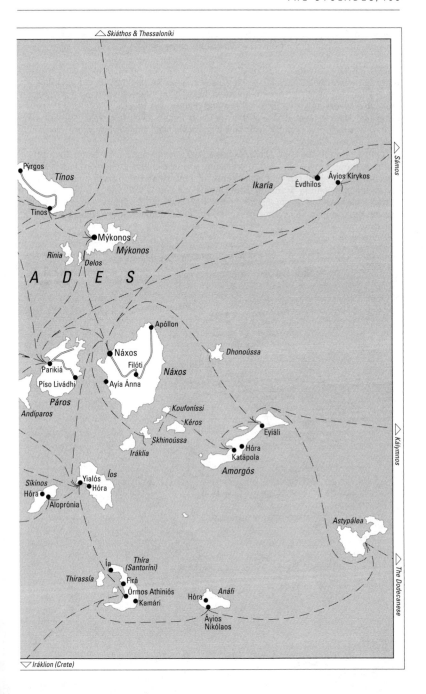

Lagoudera. There's good swimming at **Yialiskári**, a small, eucalyptus-fringed beach between Korissía and Vourkári; the *Yialiskari* rooms (☎0288/21 197; ③) enjoy a good view.

VOURKÁRI, a couple of kilometres to the north, is more compact and arguably more attractive than Korissía, serving as the favourite hangout of the yachting set; there's no real beach or accommodation here. Three fairly expensive and indistinguishable **tavernas** serve up good seafood dishes, and there's a very good ouzerí – *Strofi tou Mimi* – located where the road cuts inland towards Otziás. The few **bars** include *Vourkariani*, popular with an older crowd, and the slightly more happening *Kokko Cafe* and *Emage*.

Another 4km to the east, **OTZIÁS** has a small beach that's a bit better than that at Korissía, though more exposed to prevailing winds; facilities are limited to a couple of tavernas and a fair number of apartments for rent. Kéa's only functioning monastery, the eighteenth-century **Panayía Kastrianí**, is an hour's walk along a dirt road from Otziás. The hostel at the monastery (☎0288/21 348) is the cheapest accommodation deal on the island, albeit rather basic and isolated. Although more remarkable for its

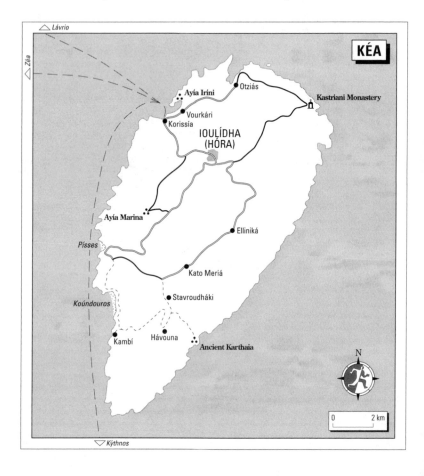

fine setting on a high bluff than for any intrinsic interest, from here you can take the pleasant walk on to the island capital, Ioulídha, in another two hours.

Ioulídha

IOULÍDHA (ancient Ioulis) was the birthplace of the renowned early fifth-century BC poets Simonides and Bacchylides. With its numerous red-tiled roofs, Neoclassical buildings and winding flagstoned paths, it is by no means a typical Cycladic village, but, beautifully situated in an amphitheatric fold in the hills, it is architecturally the most interesting settlement on the island. Accordingly it has "arrived" in recent years, with numerous trendy bars and bistros much patronized on weekends. The **archeological museum** (Tues–Sun 8.30am–3pm; free) displays finds from the four ancient city-states of Kéa, although the best items were long ago spirited away to Athens. The lower reaches of the town stretch across a spur to the **Kástro**, a tumbledown Venetian fortress incorporating stones from an ancient temple of Apollo. Fifteen minutes' walk northeast, on the path toward Panayía Kastrianí, you pass the **Lion of Kea**, a sixth-century BC sculpture carved out of the living rock. Six metres long and two metres high, the imposing beast has crudely powerful haunches and a bizarre facial expression. There are steps right down to the lion, but the effect is most striking from a distance.

Currently there is only one **hotel** in Ioulídha: the somewhat pokey *Filoxenia* (☎0288/22 057; ③), perched above a shoe shop, with no en-suite plumbing and saggy beds; the more comfortable *Ioulis* up in the kástro is due to reopen its doors under new management in the near future.

You're spoiled for choice in the matter of **eating** and **drinking** though, with quality generally higher here than near Korissía. *Iy Piatsa*, just as you enter the lower town from the car park, has a variety of tasty dishes, while *Iy Dafni*, reached by a path from the bus stop, and *To Kalofagadhon*, up on the platía, both enjoy great views, the latter being the best place for a full-blown meat feast. Further up there is good standard fare on the terrace at *To Steki tis Tzias*. The aptly named *Panorama* serves up pastries and coffee and is a good place to watch the sun set, while after-dark action seems to oscillate between such bars as *Kamini*, *Leon* and, best of all, *Mylos*. *Ta Pedhia Pezi* (which means "the guys are playing"), is a lively hangout a few kilometres out off the road towards Písses and is terrific for a full-on *bouzoúki* night. A **post office** and **bank agent** round up the list of amenities.

The south

About 8km southwest of Ioulídha, reached via a mix of tracks and paths, or by mostly paved road, the crumbling Hellenistic watchtower of **Ayía Marína** sprouts dramatically from the grounds of a small nineteenth-century monastery. Beyond, the paved main road twists around the startling scenic head of the lovely agricultural valley at **PÍSSES**, emerging at a large and little-developed beach. There are two tavernas, plus a pleasant **campsite**, *Camping Kea*, which has good turfy ground and also runs the studios (☎0288/31 302; ③) further inland. Of the tavernas, the best is *To Akroyiali*, with a good range of dishes and excellent rosé wine, as well as rooms to rent upstairs (☎0288/ 31 301 or 31 327; ③).

Beyond Písses, the asphalt – and the bus service – peters out along the 5km south to **KOÚNDOUROS**, a sheltered, convoluted bay popular with yachters; there's a taverna behind the largest of several sandy coves, none cleaner or bigger than the beach at Písses. The luxury *Kea Beach* hotel (☎0288/31 230; ⑤) sits out on its own promontory with tennis courts and pool, and there is a hamlet of dummy windmills; built as holiday homes, they are "authentic" right down to their masts, thatching and stone cladding. At the south end of the bay, *St George Bungalows* (☎0288 31 277; ④) has smart rooms at very reasonable prices, as well as its own taverna which is recommended. Admittedly, *Manos* taverna and rooms (☎0288/31 214; ②), a little further south, is cheaper; however the place looks as if it is on its last legs. A further 2km south at **Kambí**, there's a nice little beach and a good taverna, *To Kambi*.

Besides the very scant ruins of ancient Poiessa near Písses, the only remains of any real significance from Kéa's past are fragments of a temple of Apollo at **ancient Karthaia**, tucked away on the southeastern edge of the island above Póles Bay, with an excellent deserted twin beach that's easiest reached by boat. Otherwise, it's a good three-hour round-trip walk from the hamlet of Stavroudháki, some way off the lower road linking Koúndouros, Hávouna and Káto Meriá. Travelling by motorbike, the upper road, which more directly plies between Písses and Káto Meriá, is worth following as an alternative return along the island's summit to Ioulídha; it's paved between Ioulídha and Káto Meriá, and the entire way affords fine views, over the thousands of magnificent oaks which constitute Kéa's most distinctive feature.

Kýthnos (Thermiá)

Though perhaps the dullest and certainly the most barren of the Cyclades, a short stay on **Kýthnos** is a good antidote to the exploitation likely to be encountered elsewhere. Few foreigners bother to visit – the island is much quieter than Kéa. It's a place where Athenians come to buy land for villas, go spear-fishing and sprawl on generally mediocre beaches without having to jostle for space. You could use it as a first or, better, last island stop; in season there are several ferry connections a week with Kéa and Lávrio, a frequent ferry and hydrofoil service to and from Sérifos, Sífnos and Pireás, plus further direct ferry and hydrofoil connections with Mílos and Kímolos.

Mérihas and around

In good weather boats dock on the west coast at **MÉRIHAS**, a rather functional ferry and fishing port with most of the island's facilities. This fact almost obliges you to stay here, and makes Mérihas something of a tourist ghetto, but it's redeemed by proximity to the island's best beaches. The closest beach of any repute is **Episkopí**, a 500m stretch of averagely clean grey sand with a single taverna, thirty minutes' walk north of the town; you can shorten this considerably by sticking to coast-hugging trails and tracks below the road. Far better are the adjacent beaches of **Apókroussi**, which has a canteen, and **Kolóna**, the latter essentially a sandspit joining the islet of Áyios Loukás to Kýthnos. These lie about an hour's walk northwest of Episkopí, and are easiest reached by boat-trip from the harbour. Camping is generally tolerated, even on Martinákia beach, the nearest to Mérihas, which has an eponymous taverna.

Owners of **accommodation** often meet the ferries in high season, and a relative abundance of rooms makes for good bargaining opportunities. Few places have sea views, one exception being the *Kythnos Hotel* (☎0281/32 247; ②), near the ferry dock, which has the added bonus of being open all year round. A little inland, behind the small bridge on the seafront, *Panayiota* (☎0281/32 268; ③) is a decent choice; and there are plenty of other rooms and studios of similar price and quality along the same road. The best **restaurants** are *To Kandouni*, furthest from the ferry, a tasty grill with tables right by the water and specialities like *sfougáto*, and *Kissos*, a little inland, where you are paying for the food rather than the setting. Among purveyors of a modest nightlife, by far the friendliest and liveliest place is *To Vyzantio*, just back from the water, whose animated owner plays varied rock music. *Remezzo* behind the beach has a fine location and plays good music, while eclectic Greek folk can be heard at the mod-

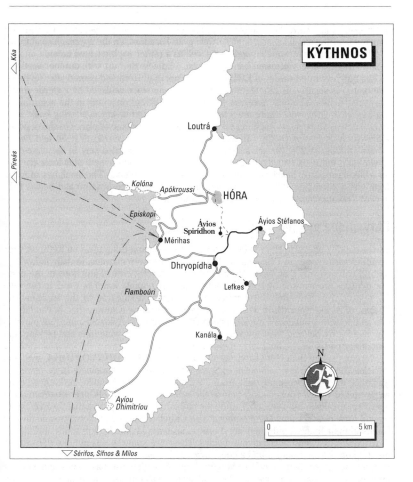

ern *New Corner*, 100m along the road to Dhryopídha. The latest addition of any significance is *Akrotiri Club*, perched up on the headland past *To Kandouni* (see above), playing that popular island blend of summer hits and Greek music.

The **bus service**, principally to Loutrá, Hóra, Dhryopídha and Kanála, is reasonably
reliable, in season at least; the only motorbike rental is through the main Mílos Express
ticket agency and is noticeably more expensive than on many islands. The Cava
Kythnos shop doubles as the official **National Bank** outlet (exchange all day), and is
the agent for hydrofoil tickets and the boat to Kéa.

Hóra and Loutrá

HÓRA lies 6km northeast of Mérihas, set in the middle of the island. Tilting south off
an east–west ridge, and laid out to an approximate grid plan, it's an awkward blend of
Kéa-style gabled roofs, Cycladic churches with dunce-cap cupolas, and concrete mon-
sters. Hóra supports a **post office** (open only until noon); the closest accommodation

at present is at Loutrá (see below). You can **eat** at *To Kentro* taverna run by Maria Tzoyiou near the small square, or at *To Steki* grill; *Paradisos*, on the approach road from Mérihas is another reasonable option. As well as a rather sophisticated kafenío on the square, there is a very pleasant bar, *Apokalypsi*, a little further up, with outdoor seating.

The much-vaunted resort of **LOUTRÁ** (3km north of Hóra and named after its thermal baths) is scruffy, its nineteenth-century spa long since replaced by a sterile modern construction. The best **taverna**, *Katerini*, is a little out on a limb in the neighbouring bay west. Otherwise there are a few seafront bars and tavernas offering basic services, such as showers, to yachting crews. There is no shortage of places to sleep; **pensions** such as *Delfini* (☎0281/31 430; ②), the *Meltemi* (☎0281/31 271; ③) and *Porto Klaras* (☎0281/31 276; ④) are acceptable choices. You can also stay in the state-run *Xenia* baths complex (☎0281/31 217; ③), where a twenty-minute bath plus basic checkup – blood pressure, heart rate and weight – costs about 1000dr. The small bay of Ayía Iríni, just a kilometre east of Loutrá, is a more pleasant place to swim and boasts the decent *Trehandiri* taverna on the hill above the bay.

Dhryopídha and the south

You're handily placed in Hóra to tackle the most interesting thing to do on Kýthnos: the beautiful **walk** south to Dhryopídha. It takes about ninety minutes, initially following the old cobbled way that leaves Hóra heading due south; critical junctions in the first few minutes are marked by red paint dots. The only reliable water is a well in the valley bottom, reached after thirty minutes, just before a side-trail to the triple-naved **chapel of Áyios Spyrídhon** which has recycled Byzantine columns. Just beyond this, you collide with a bulldozed track between Dhryopídha and Áyios Stéfanos, but purists can avoid it by bearing west towards some ruined ridgetop windmills and picking up secondary paths for the final forty minutes of the hike.

More appealing than Hóra by virtue of spanning a ravine, **DHRYOPÍDHA**, with its pleasing tiled roofs, is reminiscent of Spain or Tuscany. A surprisingly large place, it was once the island's capital, built around a famous cave, the Katafíki, at the head of a well-watered valley. Tucked away behind the cathedral is a tiny **folklore museum** that opens erratically in high season. Beside the cathedral is a cheap psistariá, *To Steki*, and a good local ouzerí called *O Apithanos* ("The Unbelievable Guy"). Some people do let rooms in their houses, but the nearest official accommodation is 6km south at Kanála.

KANÁLA is a good alternative to Loutrá. There are some rooms in the older settlement up on the promontory and a good taverna, *Louloudhas*, with a huge terrace overlooking the larger western beach, **Megáli Ámmos**, which also has rooms and a combination snack bar and taverna. Two adjacent pensions on the beach are *Anna* (☎0281/32 035; ②) and the B&B *Margarita* (☎0281/32 265; ② & ④), with the latter warmly recommended.

From Kanála, a succession of small coves extends up the east coast as far as **ÁYIOS STÉFANOS**, a small coastal hamlet with two high-season tavernas opposite a chapel-crowned islet linked by a causeway to the body of the island. Southwest of Dhryopídha, reached by a turning off the road to Kanála, **Flamboúri** is the most presentable beach on the west coast. The recent extension of the asphalted road southwards makes the double bay of **Ayíou Dhimitríou** more accessible than before; although not too exciting, there are however a couple of tavernas and rooms to rent in high season.

Sérifos

Sérifos has long languished outside the mainstream of history and modern tourism. Little has happened here since the legendary Perseus returned with the Gorgon's

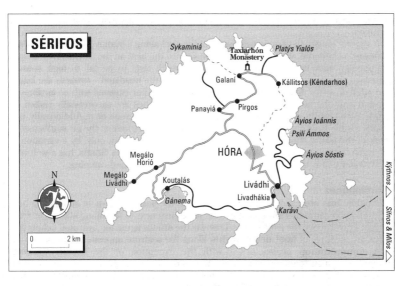

head, in time to save his mother Danaë from being ravished by the local king Polydectes. Many would-be visitors are deterred by the apparently barren, hilly interior which, with the stark, rocky coastline, makes Sérifos appear uninhabited until your ferry turns into Livádhi bay. The island is recommended for serious **walkers**, who can head for several small villages in the little-explored interior, plus some isolated coves. Modern Serifots love seclusion, and here, more than anywhere else in the Cyclades, you will find farmsteads miles from anywhere, with only a donkey path to their door. Everyone here seems to keep livestock, and to produce their own wines, and many also cultivate the wild **narcissus** for the export market.

Few islanders speak much English; even a few select words of amateur Greek will come in handy and will be warmly received. American yachties drop anchor here in some numbers as well, to take on fresh water which, despite appearances, Sérifos has in abundance.

Livádhi and the main beaches

Most visitors stay in the port, **LIVÁDHI**, set in a wide greenery-fringed bay and handy for most of the island's beaches. The usually calm bay here is a magnet for island-hopping yachts, whose crews chug to and fro in dinghies all day and night. It's not the most attractive place on Sérifos – and to stay here exclusively would be to miss some fine walks – but Livádhi and the neighbouring cove of Livadhákia are certainly the easiest places to find rooms and any other amenities you might need, all of which are very scarce elsewhere.

Unfortunately, the long **beach** at Livádhi is nothing to write home about: the sand is hard-packed and muddy, and the water weedy and prone to intermittent jellyfish flotillas – only the far northeastern end is at all usable. Walk uphill along the street from the *Mylos* bakery, or over the southerly headland from the cemetery, to reach the neighbouring, far superior **Livadhákia**. This golden-sand beach, shaded by tamarisk trees, offers snorkelling and other watersports, as well as an acceptable taverna. If you prefer more seclusion, five minutes' stroll across the headland to the south brings you to the smaller **Karávi** beach, which is cleaner and almost totally naturist, but has no shade or facilities.

A slightly longer 45-minute walk north of the port along a bumpy track leads to **Psilí Ámmos**, a sheltered, white-sand beach considered the best on the island. Accordingly, it's popular, with two rival tavernas, both of which tend to be full in high season. Naturists are pointed – via a ten-minute walk across the headland – towards the larger and often deserted **Áyios Ioánnis** beach, but this is rather exposed with no facilities at all, and only the far south end is inviting. Both beaches are theoretically visited by kaïkia from Livádhi, as are two nearby sea caves, but don't count on it. Additionally, and plainly visible from arriving ferries, two more sandy coves hide at the far southeastern flank of the island opposite an islet; they are accessible on foot only, by a variation of the track to Psilí Ámmos. The more northerly of the two, **Áyios Sóstis**, has a well with fresh water and is the most commonly used beach for secluded camping.

Practicalities

The public **bus stop** and posted schedule are at the base of the yacht and fishing-boat jetty, and you can rent a **bike** or **car** from Blue Bird next to the filling station, or from Krinas Travel above the jetty. Krinas Travel is the official agent for hydrofoil tickets and there are a couple of **boat-ticket agents** along the seafront opposite the bus stop.

Accommodation proprietors – with the exception of the *Coralli Camping Bungalows*, which regularly sends a minibus – don't always meet ferries, and in high season you'll have to step lively off the boat to get a decent bed. The most rewarding hunting grounds are on the headland above the ferry dock, or Livadhákia beach (see below); anything without a sea view will be a notch cheaper. Up on the headland, the *Pension Cristi* (☎0281/51 775; ④) has an excellent, quiet position overlooking the bay; the nearby *Areti* (☎0281/51 479; ④) is a little smarter for the same price. Alternatively, down in the flatlands, the inexpensive seafront rooms of *Anna* (☎0281/51 263; ③) and *Fani* (☎0281/51 746; ③) are friendly and spotlessly clean, though the rooms at the front get some traffic noise. The *Hotel Anna* (☎0281/51 666; ③) above the pizzeria by the yacht harbour is another fall-back, while the cheapest rooms in Livádhi are next to each other at the far end of the bay: *Margarita* (☎0281/51 321; ②) and *Adonios Peloponnisos* (☎0281/51 113; ②).

Livadhákia, ten to fifteen minutes' walk south, offers more nocturnal peace, choice and quality, though it has a more touristy feel and the mosquitoes are positively ferocious – bring insecticide coils or make sure your room is furnished with electric vapour pads. One of the oldest and largest complexes of rooms and apartments, close to the beach and with verdant views, is run by Vaso Stamataki (☎0281/51 346; ③). Newer and higher-standard choices include the *Helios Pension* (☎0281/51 066; ③), just above the road as you arrive at Livadhákia, and, further along, the *Medusa* (☎0281/51 127; ③). Cheaper are the rooms in adjacent buildings just after *Helios*, run by two sisters, Yioryia (☎0281/51 336; ②) and Mina (☎0281/51 545; ②–③) – the latter place has sea views. Further along are *Dhorkas* (☎0281/51 422; ④) and, right by the beach above a restaurant, *O Alexandros* (☎0281/51 119; ④). Near the built-up area, beside one of only two public access tracks to the beach and behind the best patch of sand, *Coralli Camping Bungalows* (☎0281/51 500; ④) has a restaurant, bar, shop and landscaped camping area.

A makeshift road runs the length of the Livádhi seafront, crammed with restaurants, shops and all the services you might need. At the strategic southerly crossroads, the *Mylos* bakery has exceptionally good cheese pies and wholegrain bread; a butcher and a handful of fruit shops and **supermarkets** are scattered along the beach, while there's a **pharmacy** at the foot of the quay.

Like most islands, tavernas near the quay tend to be slightly pricier, but *Mokkas* fish taverna is recommended nonetheless. Walk up the beach, and meals get less expensive; the two best traditional tavernas are the busy *Perseus* and the welcoming restaurant under the *Hotel Cyclades*. At the extreme far northeast end of the beach, *Sklavenis* (aka *Margarita's*) has loyal adherents to its down-home feel and courtyard seating, but many find the food overly deep-fried and too pricey. Closer to the yacht harbour, *Meltemi* is a good – if slightly expensive – ouzerí, something out of the ordinary for the island. For crepes and ice cream, try *Meli*, in the commercial centre by the port police.

Nightlife is surprisingly lively, though few establishments stay in business more than two consecutive seasons. The main cluster is about a third of the way along the seafront and includes a mini-mall type affair housing several bars, clubs and eateries. Of the clubs, *Agria Menta* plays a mix of dance music and *bouzoúki*, whereas *Astra Club* upstairs is a conventional disco and *Mythos* has a pool table. *Vitamin C* and *Karnayio* are two popular bars next door, and further along towards the beach is the *Sérifos Yacht Club*, which is actually just a dolled-up kafenío. *Captain Hook* is a new, loud soundproofed club under Krinas Travel.

Buses connect Livádhi with Hóra, 2km away, some ten times daily, but only manage one or two daily trips to Megálo Livádhya, Galaní, and Kállitsos. You may well want to walk, if you're travelling light; it's a pleasant if steep forty minutes up a cobbled way to Hóra, with the *kalderími* leading off from a bend in the road about 300m out of Livádhia. By the beginning of October, you'll have no choice, since the bus – like nearly everything else – ceases operation for the winter.

Hóra

Quiet and atmospheric **HÓRA**, teetering precariously above the harbour, is one of the most spectacular villages of the Cyclades. The best sights are to be found on the town's borders: tiny churches cling to the cliff-edge, and there are breathtaking views across the valleys below. At odd intervals along its alleyways you'll find part of the old castle making up the wall of a house, or a marble statue leaning incongruously in one corner. A pleasant diversion is the hour-long **walk** down to **Psilí Ámmos**: start from beside Hóra's cemetery and aim for the lower of two visible pigeon towers, and then keep close to the phone wires, which will guide you towards the continuation of the double-walled path descending to a bend in the road just above the beach.

Among two or three **tavernas**, the nicest place is *Zorbas*, near the church on the upper square, serving local dishes such as wild fennel fritters; *Stavros*, just east of the bus-stop platía, is consistent and can arrange beds too (☎0281/51 303; ②). The island's **post office** is found in the lowest quarter, and a few more expensive **rooms** for rent lie about 200m north of town, on the street above the track to the cemetery.

The north

North of Hóra, the island's high water-table sometimes breaks the surface to run in delightful rivulets swarming with turtles and frogs, though in recent years many of the open streams seem to have dried up. Reeds, orchards and even the occasional palm tree still take advantage of the unexpected moisture, even if it's no longer visible. This is especially true at **KÁLLITSOS** (Kéndarhos), reached by a ninety-minute path from Hóra, marked by fading red paint splodges along a donkey track above the cemetery. Once at Kállitsos (no facilities), a paved road leads west within 3km to the fifteenth- to seventeenth-century **monastery of Taxiarhón**, designed for sixty monks but presently home only to one of the island's two parish priests, one of a dying breed of farmer-fisherman monks, If he's about, the priest will show you treasures in the monastic church, such as an ivory-inlaid bishop's throne, silver lamps from Egypt (to where many Serifots emigrated) and the finely carved *témblon*.

As you loop back towards Hóra from Kállitsos on the asphalt, the fine villages of Galaní and Panayía (named after its tenth-century church) make convenient stops. In **GALANÍ** you can sometimes get simple **meals** at the central store, which also sells excellent, tawny-pink, sherry-like wine; its small-scale production in the west of the island is highly uneconomic, so you'll find it at few other places on Sérifos. Below the village, trails lead to the remote and often windswept beach of **Sykaminiá**, with no facilities and no camping allowed; a better bet for a local swim is the more sheltered cove of **Platýs Yialós** at the extreme northern tip of the island, reached by a partly paved track (negotiable by moped) that branches off just east of Taxiarhón. The neighbouring beach has a taverna, *Nikoulias*, with a couple of very basic rooms (☎0281/52 174; ②), which nonetheless have great views. The church at **PANAYIÁ** is usually locked, but comes alive on its feast day of Xilopanayía (August 16). Traditionally the first couple to dance around the adjacent olive tree would be the first to marry that year, but this led to unseemly brawls – so the priest always goes first these days.

The southwest

A little way south of Panayía, you reach a junction in the road. Turn left to return to Hóra, or continue straight towards **Megálo Horió** – the site of ancient Sérifos, but with little else to recommend it. **Megálo Livádhi**, further on, is a remote and quiet beach resort 8km west of Hóra, with two lovely tavernas whose tables are practically on the beach. *Iy Mardhitsa* taverna has some simple rooms behind the beach (☎0281/51 003; ②). Iron and copper ore were once exported from here, but cheaper African deposits sent the mines into decline and today most of the idle machinery rusts away, though some gravel-crushing still goes on. There is a monument at the north end of the beach to four workers killed during a protest against unfair conditions in 1916. An alternate turning just below Megálo Horió leads to the small mining and fishing port of **Koutalás**, a pretty sweep of bay with a church-tipped rock, and a long if narrow beach – it has become rather a ghost settlement and the workers' restaurants have all closed down. There is however one snack bar/taverna, catering mainly for yachting crews, which has sprung up recently. The winding track above the village leads to Livádhi, and apart from the pleasant **Gánema** beach, which has a taverna of the same name, there are no places to rest or buy refreshments on the long journey back.

Sífnos

Sífnos is a more immediately appealing island than its northern neighbours: prettier, more cultivated and with some fine architecture. This means that it's also much more popular, and extremely crowded in July or August, when rooms are very difficult to find. Take any offered as you land, come armed with a reservation or, best of all, time your visit for June or early in September, though bear in mind that most of the trendier bars and the souvenir shops will be shut for the winter by the middle of the latter month. In keeping with the island's somewhat upmarket clientele, freelance camping is forbidden (and the two designated sites are substandard), while nudism is tolerated only in isolated coves. The locals tend, if anything, to be even more dour and introverted than on Sérifos.

On the other hand, Sífnos's modest size – no bigger than Kýthnos or Sérifos — makes it eminently explorable. The **bus service** is excellent, most of the roads quite decent, and there's a network of paths that are fairly easy to follow. Sífnos has a strong tradition of pottery and was long esteemed for its distinctive cuisine, although most tourist-orientated cooking is average at best. However, the island's shops and greengrocers are well stocked in season.

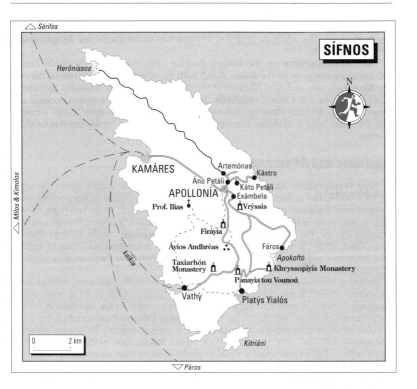

Ferry connections have improved in recent years, keeping pace with the island's increasing popularity. The main lines head south, via Kímolos to Mílos, with occasional extensions to Thíra, Crete and select Dodecanese, or north, via Sérifos and Kýthnos to Pireás. Links with the central Cyclades are provided by the infrequent visits of the Georgios Express to Páros or Sýros and backed up by an almost daily hydrofoil service which also goes to Náxos and Mýkonos several times a week.

Kamáres

KAMÁRES, the island's port, is tucked away at the foot of high, bare cliffs in the west, which enclose a beach. A busy, fairly downmarket resort with concrete blocks of villas edging up to the base of the cliffs, Kamáres' seafront is crammed with bars, travel agencies, ice-cream shops and fast-food places. You can store luggage at the Aegean Thesaurus **travel agency** while hunting for a room (proprietors tend not to meet boats); they also change money and can advise on bed availability throughout the island.

Accommodation is relatively expensive, though bargaining can be productive outside peak season. Try the rooms above the Katzoulakis Tourist Agency near the quay (☎0284/32 362; ③), as well as the reasonable *Hotel Stavros* (☎0284/31 641; ③), a little further along; the good but slightly pricier *Boulis Hotel* (☎0284/32 122; ⑤) is on the beach, across the bay, and has very friendly management. *Ekaterinis* (☎0284/32 392; ④), a short hike up the hill behind the main road leading out of town, consists of rooms in two buildings, one is much newer and more modern than the other; however both are good value and quite adequate. The **campsite** around the bay is rather lacking in shade but has adequate facilities; it is attached to the good-value *Korakis* rooms (☎0284/32 366; ③).

The best **restaurants** are the *Meropi*, ideal for a pre-ferry lunch, the *Boulis* (under the same management as the *Boulis Hotel*) with its collection of huge retsina barrels, the *Kamares* ouzerí and *Kira Mariena* at the far end of the beach. Kamáres also boasts a fair proportion of the island's **nightlife**: try the *Collage Bar* for a sunset cocktail, and move on to the *Mobilize Dancing Club* or the *Cafe Folie*. The best place to hire a moped is at Dionysos, next to Mobilize Dancing Club, the latter is run by the amiable mechanic's son.

Apollonía and Artemónas

A steep twenty-minute bus ride (hourly service until late at night) takes you up to **APOLLONÍA**, the centre of Hóra, an amalgam of three hilltop villages which have merged over the years into one continuous community. With white buildings, flowerdraped balconies, belfries and pretty squares, it is eminently scenic, though not selfconsciously so. On the platía itself, the **folk museum** (daily 9.30am–2pm & 6pm–10pm; 300dr) is well worth a visit. As well as an interesting collection of textiles, lace, costumes and weaponry, there are paintings by Nikolaos Tselemendi, a celebrated teacher of cookery.

Radiating out from the platía is a network of stepped marble footways and the main pedestrian street, flagstoned Odhós Styliánou Prókou, which is lined with shops, churches and restaurants. The garish, cakebox cathedral of **Áyios Spyrídhon** is nearby, while the eighteenth-century church of **Panayía Ouranoforía** stands in the highest quarter of town, incorporating fragments of a seventh-century BC temple of Apollo and a relief of Áyios Yeóryios over the door. **Áyios Athanásios**, next to Platía Kleánthi Triandafýlou, has frescoes and a wooden *témblon*. Some 3km southeast, a short distance from the village of Exámbela, you'll find the active monastery of **Vrýssis** which dates from 1612 and is home to a good collection of religious artefacts and manuscripts.

ARTEMÓNAS, fifteen minutes south of Apollonía on foot, is worth a morning's exploration for its churches and elegant Venetian and Neoclassical houses alone. **Panayía Gourniá** (key next door) has vivid frescoes; the clustered-dome church of **Kohí** was built over an ancient temple of Artemis (also the basis of the village's name); and seventeenth-century **Áyios Yeóryios** contains fine icons. Artemónas is also the point of departure for **Herónissos**, an isolated hamlet with two tavernas and a few potteries behind a deeply indented, rather bleak bay at the northwestern tip of the island. There's a motorable dirt track there – and occasional boat trips from Kamáres, though these are only worth the effort on calm days.

Practicalities

The **post office** and **bus stop** edge onto Apollonía's central platía. The **bank** and **police station** are located on the main road leading north out of town. There are rooms scattered all over the village, making them hard to find; however, there are some obvious choices along the road towards Fáros (thus a bit noisy), the *Margarita* (☎0284/31 032; ②) being fairly representative. If you want quieter premises with a better view, be prepared to pay more: *Margarita Kouki* (☎0284/33 152; ③), above the luxurious *Hotel Petali* (☎0284/33 024; ⑥), is a welcome exception. Probably your best bet is to look on the square for the main branch of the excellent travel agency, Aegean Thesaurus (☎0284/31 151, fax 32 190), which can book you into rooms of all categories. They also sell a worthwhile package consisting of an accurate topographical map, bus/boat schedules and a short text on Sífnos for a few hundred drachmas.

In Hóra there are still a bare handful of quality **tavernas**, the doyen of which is the *Liotrivi* up in Artemónas, which has moved from the old oil-press suggested by its name to extended new premises on the village square. Next to the post office in Apollonía, *Iy Orea Sifnos* has standard fare and a flower-decked garden; there are several tavernas up in the backstreets, of which *To Apostoli to Koutouki* is very reasonable.

Nightlife in Apollonía tends to be dominated by the thirty-something crowd which, having dined early by Greek-island standards, lingers over its oúzo until late. Starting with *Isidora*, a trendy bar at the foot of Odhós Styliánou Prókou, there are several bars further up this street worth visiting. The central *Argo* music bar features the currently fashionable mix of dance music early on and Greek pop later, and *To Doloma* plays an interesting mix of jazz and classic rock; the *Camel Club* on the edge of town has become a new favourite late night hangout.

The east coast

Most of Sífnos's coastal settlements are along the less precipitous eastern shore, within a modest distance of Hóra and its surrounding cultivated plateau. These all have good bus services, and a certain amount of food and accommodation, Kástro being far more appealing than the touristy resorts of Platýs Yialós and Fáros.

Kástro

An alternative east-coast base which seems the last place on Sífnos to fill up in season, **KÁSTRO** can be reached on foot from Apollonía in 35 minutes, all but the last ten on a clear path beginning at the fork in the road to Kástro, threading its way via Káto Petáli hamlet. Built on a rocky outcrop with an almost sheer drop to the sea on three sides, the ancient capital of the island retains much of its medieval character. Parts of its boundary walls survive, along with a full complement of sinuous, narrow streets graced by balconied, two-storey houses and some fine sixteenth- and seventeenth-century churches with ornamental floors. Venetian coats of arms and ancient wall-fragments can still be seen on some of the older dwellings; there are the remains of the ancient acropolis (including a ram's head sarcophagus by one of the medieval gates), as well as a small **archeological museum** (Tues–Sun 8am–2.30pm; free), which does not always stick closely to the official opening hours, installed in a former Catholic church in the higher part of the village.

Among the several **rooms**, the modernized *Aris* apartments (☎0284/31 161; ③–④) have something for most budgets and are open all year. More rooms are available at the lower end of the village, of which the friendly *Marianna* (☎0284/33 681; ③) is a good basic option. The *Star* and *Leonidas* are the obvious tavernas to try out, while the *Cavos Sunrise* café-bar, run by an old hippy, is suitably laid back and has a fantastic view. On the edge of town, the *Castello* disco-bar is a livelier hang-out. There's nothing approximating a beach in Kástro; for a swim you have to walk to the nearby rocky coves of **Serália** (to the southeast, and with more rooms) and **Paláti**. You can also hike – from the windmills on the approach road near Káto Petáli – to either the sixteenth-century monastery of **Khryssostómou**, or along a track opposite to the cliff-face that overlooks the church of the **Eptá Martíres** (Seven Martyrs); nudists sun themselves and snorkel on and around the flat rocks below.

Platýs Yialós

From Apollonía there are almost hourly buses to the resort of **PLATÝS YIALÓS**, some 12km distant, near the southern tip of the island. Despite claims to be the longest beach in the Cyclades, the sand can get very crowded at the end near the watersport facilities rental. Diversions include a pottery workshop, but many are put off by the continuous row of snack bars and rooms to rent, which line the entire stretch of beach, and the strong winds which plague it. **Rooms** are expensive, although the comfortable *Pension Angelaki* (☎0284/71 288; ④), near the bus stop, is more reasonably priced, while the *Hotel Eurosini* (☎0284/71 353; ⑤) next door is comfortable, and breakfast is included in the price. The local **campsite** is rather uninspiring: a stiff hike inland, shadeless and on sloping, stony ground. Among several fairly pricey **tavernas** are the straightforward *To Steki* and *Bus Stop*.

A more rewarding walk uphill from Platýs Yialós brings you to the convent of **Panayía toú Vounoú** (though it's easy to get lost on the way without the locally sold map); the caretaker should let you in, if she's about.

Fáros and around

Less crowded beaches are to be found just to the northeast of Platýs Yialós (though unfortunately not directly accessible along the coast). **FÁROS**, again with regular bus links to Apollonía, makes an excellent fall-back base if you don't strike it lucky elsewhere. A small and friendly resort, it has some of the cheapest **accommodation** on the island, as well as a couple of smarter places, including the recommended *Apéranto* guesthouse (☎0284/71 473; ④) at the far end of the bay. *To Kyma* is a pleasant seafront **taverna**, and the smart *On the Rocks,* perched on the headland at the far end of the beach, serves a tasty selection of snacks as well as full meals. The closest beaches are not up to much: the town strand itself is muddy, shadeless and crowded, and the one to the northeast past the headland not much better. Head off in the opposite direction, however, through the older part of the village, and things improve at **Glyfó**, a longer, wider family beach.

Continuing from Glyfó, a fifteen-minute cliffside path leads to the beach of **Apokoftó**, with a couple of good tavernas, and, up an access road, the *Hotel Flora* (☎0284/71 278; ③), which has superb views. The shore itself tends to collect seaweed, however, and a rock reef must be negotiated to get into the water. Flanking Apokoftó to the south, marooned on a sea-washed spit and featuring on every EOT poster of the island, is the disestablished, seventeenth-century **Khryssopiyís monastery**, where until recently cells were rented out as tourist accommodation. According to legend, the cleft in the rock appeared when two village girls, fleeing to the spit to escape the attentions of menacing pirates, prayed to the Virgin to defend their virtue.

The interior and Vathý

Apollonía is a good base from which to start your explorations of remoter Sífnos. You can rent **bikes** at Moto Apollo, beside the petrol station on the road to Fáros, but the island is best explored on foot.

Taking the path out from Katavatí (the district south of Apollonía) you'll pass, after a few minutes, the beautiful empty **monastery of Firáyia** and – fifteen minutes along the ugly new road – the path climbing up to **Áyios Andhréas**, where you'll be rewarded with tremendous views over the islands of Sýros, Páros, Íos, Folégandhros and Síkinos. Just below the church is an enormous Bronze Age archeological site.

Even better is the all-trail walk to Vathý, around three hours from Katavatí and reached by bearing right at a signed junction in Katavatí. Part way along you can detour on a conspicuous side-trail to the **monastery of Profítis Ilías**, on the very summit of the island, with a vaulted refectory and extensive views.

Vathý

A fishing village on the shore of a stunning funnel-shaped bay, **VATHÝ** is the most attractive and remote base on the island and, remarkably, the 1933-vintage road hasn't promoted much extra development. There are, however, an increasing number of **rooms**, the best deals probably being at *Manolis* taverna (☎0284/71 111; ③), or those attached to the tiny **monastery of the Archangel Gabriel**. Unusually, camping rough meets with little objection from the locals, a reflection of their friendly attitude towards outsiders. For **food**, *Manolis* does excellent grills and has a fascinating gyrating clay oven in the courtyard; *Iy Okeanidha* has good mezédhes such as chickpea balls and cheesy aubergine patties; while *To Tsikali* behind the monastery is cheaper but less varied.

Now that there are regular buses (8 daily in high season, 2 daily at other times) the kaïkia no longer run from Kamáres. It is possible to walk to Platýs Yiálos in ninety minutes, but the path is not marked. At the far end of the bay a traditional pottery still functions.

Mílos

Mílos has always derived prosperity from its strange geology. Minoan settlers were attracted by obsidian, and other products of its volcanic soil made the island – along with Náxos – the most important of the Cyclades in the ancient world. Today the quarrying of barite, perlite and porcelain brings in a steady revenue, but has left deep and unsightly scars on the landscape. The rocks, however, can be beautiful in situ: on the left as your ferry enters Mílos Bay, two outcrops known as the Arkoúdhes (Bears) square off like sumo wrestlers. Off the north coast, accessible only by excursion boat, the Glaroníssia (Seagull Isles) are shaped like massed organ pipes, and there are more weird formations on the southwest coast at Kléftiko. Inland, too, you frequently come across strange, volcanic outcrops, and thermal springs burst forth.

The landscape has been violated, but as with most weathered volcanic terrain, Mílos is incredibly fertile; away from the summits of **Profítis Ilías** in the southwest and lower hills in the east, a gently undulating countryside is intensively cultivated to produce grain, hay and orchard fruits. The island's domestic architecture, with its lava-built, two-up-and-two-down houses, is reminiscent of Níssyros, while parts of the coast, with their sculpted cliffs and inlets, remind some visitors of Cyprus.

Yet the drab whole is less than the sum of the often interesting parts; Mílos is not and never will become another Santoríni, despite a similar geological history, and is probably the better for it. The locals are reconciled to a very short tourist season lasting from late June to early September, and make most of their money during late July and August, when prices are rather high.

Adhámas

The main port of **ADHÁMAS**, known as Adhámandas to locals, was founded by Cretan refugees fleeing a failed rebellion in 1841. Despite sitting on one of the Mediterranean's best natural harbours (created by a volcanic cataclysm similar to, but earlier than, Thíra's), Adhámas is not a spectacularly inviting place, though it's lively enough and has all the requisite facilities.

Most hotel **accommodation** manages to be simultaneously noisy, viewless and relatively expensive. Exceptions are the *Delfíni* (☎0287/22 001; ④), a short way inland from the first beach north of the harbour, the smart, central, double-glazed *Portiani Hotel* (☎0287/22 940; ⑤) and the luxury *Santa Maria Village* (☎0287/21 949; ⑥), 300m behind the beach. Rooms are concentrated on the conical hill above the harbour and on or just off the main road to Pláka, and range from real cheapies with shared facilities, like those of Anna Gozadhinou (☎0287/22 364; ②), to smart rooms with TV and all mod cons, like *Falasistra* (☎0287/23 570; ⑤). During high season the highly organized

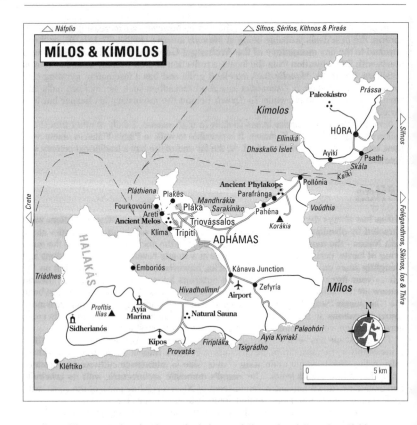

MÍLOS & KÍMOLOS

tourist office opposite the ferry dock has a daily updated list of available rooms around the island, and a handy brochure with all the numbers at any given time. Until recently freelance camping went undisturbed at the small **Frangomnímata** beach, ten minutes' walk northwest by the French war memorial, but with the arrival of the first official campsite at Hivadolímni beach (☎0287/31 410; ①) things seem set to change; as is the case with many campsites in Greece, bungalows are also available (④), which in this case is just as well since the grounds are not well sheltered.

Of the three adjacent **tavernas** along the seafront towards the long tamarisk-lined beach south of town, *Navagio* is the best value, while close to the jetty *Flisvos* is reasonable. Just off the main street inland, *Ta Pitsounakia* is a good cheap psistariá with a pleasant courtyard. Apart from the obvious string of cafés along the main seafront drag, *Akri*, above the jetty is a trendier **bar**, with a pleasant veranda. *Notos Club*, on the way to the first beach north, plays rock music, and *Viagra*, above the far end of the beach, goes on until sunrise playing a mixture of cheesy summer hits and Greek pop.

On the quayside, several travel agencies such as the efficient Vichos Tours have information about coastal boat-trips, sell maps of the island and rent out mopeds. Apricot Tours (☎0287/23 595), up the stairs behind the taxi rank, is particularly friendly and helpful. Otherwise, Adhámas is the hub of the island's **bus services**, which run hourly to Pláka, nine times daily in high season to Pollónia, seven times daily to Paleohóri via Zefíria and to Provatás. Some visitors arrive by plane from Athens: the

airport is 5km southeast of the port, close to Zefíria. There are several banks, a post office and a taxi rank with a posted list of fixed rates. The **Mining Museum of Mílos** (daily 9.30am–1pm & 5pm–8pm; free), housed in a new building towards the south beach, charts the mining history of Mílos. An unmissable day out is the **boat tour** round the island on one of three boats; weather permitting, these normally leave at 9am and make several stops at inaccessible swimming spots like the magnificent Kléftiko, as well as taking in late lunch on Kímolos.

The northwestern villages and ancient Melos

The real appeal of Mílos resides in an area that has been the island's focus of habitation since Classical times, where a cluster of villages huddle in the lee of a crag 4km north-west of the harbour.

PLÁKA (MÍLOS) is the largest of these communities and is the official capital of the island, a status borne out by the presence of the hospital and **post office.** There is also a **motorbike rental** outfit near the archeological museum. **Accommodation** in Pláka is slowly improving, and as well as the three or four modern blocks overlooking the busy approach road, which until recently served as the main accommodation option, there are several room outfits scattered around the village. *Moraitis* (☎0287/41 353; ④) consists of newly refurbished rooms in the house where the Venus de Milo was allegedly hidden following its discovery in 1820 (see archeological museum below). *Vourakis* (☎0287/21 702;④) has rooms with great views, a bit of a trek above the village towards the church, and Maria Kentrota (☎0287/21 572; ③) has a couple of charming, if a little basic, studios close to the archeological museum. A number of ouzeris have opened up in recent years, making it a real **eating** paradise: highly recommended are *Arhondoula*, *Dhiporto* and *To Kastro* up in the centre of the village, as well as *Plakiani Gonia* on the approach road.

The attractive village of **TRYPITÍ** (meaning "perforated" in Greek), which takes its name from the cliffside tombs of the ancient Melian dead nearby, covers a long ridge a kilometre south of Pláka. Despite semi-desolation (many houses are for sale), it probably makes the best base if you're after a village environment, with its three choices of modest **rooms**, two of which are just down the steep street from the tiny platía below the main church. Here also are a couple of café-bars, of which *To Mayeriko* also does simple **meals** and has a fantastic view of the vale of Klíma (see below); more elaborate and expensive fare is available at the *Methismeni Politia* ouzerí, at the top of the road to the catacombs, and at *Ta Glaronisa* fish taverna, along the main village street. From Trypití, it's possible to walk more or less directly down to Adhámas via Skinópi on the old *kalderími*, which begins on the saddle linking Trypití with the hamlet of Klimatovoúni.

TRIOVÁSSALOS and its twin **PÉRAN TRIOVÁSSALOS** are more workaday, less polished than Pláka or Trypití. There are "rooms to rent" signs out here as well, but they'll inevitably be noisier. Péran also offers the idiosyncratic taverna *O Hamos* (which means "a mess") and a naive pebble mosaic in the courtyard of **Áyios Yeóryios church**; created in 1880, the mosaic features assorted animal and plant motifs.

Local sites – and the coast

Pláka boasts **two museums** of moderate interest. Behind the lower car park, at the top of the approach boulevard through the newer district, the **archeological museum** (Tues–Sun 8am–2.30pm; 500dr) contains numerous obsidian implements, plus a whole wing of finds from ancient Phylakopi (see p.503) whose highlights include a votive lamp in the form of a bull and a rather Minoan-looking terracotta goddess. Labelling is scant, but isn't really needed for a plaster cast of the most famous statue in the world, the Venus de Milo, the original of which was found on the island in 1820 and appropriated by the French; her arms were knocked off in the melée surrounding her abduction. Up in a mansion of the old quarter, the **folklore museum** (Tues–Sun 10am–1pm; 500dr, Sun free) offers room re-creations but is otherwise a Greek-labelled jumble of impedimenta pertaining to milling, brewing, cheese-making, baking and weaving, rounded off by old engravings, photos and mineral samples.

A stairway beginning near the police station leads up to the old Venetian **Kástro**, its slopes clad in stone and cement to channel precious rainwater into cisterns. The enormous chapel of **Panayía Thalassítra** looms near the summit, where the ancient Melians made their last stand against the Athenians before being massacred in 416 BC. Today it offers one of the best views in the Aegean, particularly at sunset in clear conditions.

From the archeological museum, signs point you towards the **early Christian catacombs** (Tues–Sun 8am–8pm; free), 1km south of Pláka and just 400m from Trypití village; steps lead down from the road to the inconspicuous entrance. Although some 5000 bodies were buried in tomb-lined corridors which stretch some 200m into the soft volcanic rock, only the first 50m are illuminated and accessible by boardwalk. They're worth a look if you're in the area, but the adjacent ruins of **ancient Melos**, extending down from Pláka almost to the sea, justify the detour. There are huge Dorian walls, the usual column fragments lying around and, best of all, a well-preserved Roman **amphitheatre** (unrestricted access) some 200m west of the catacombs by track, then trail. Only seven rows of seats remain intact, but these evocatively look out over Klíma to the bay. Between the catacombs and the theatre is the signposted spot where the Venus de Milo was found; promptly delivered to the French consul for "safekeeping" from the Turks, this was the last the Greeks saw of the statue until a copy was belatedly forwarded from the Louvre in Paris.

At the very bottom of the vale, **KLÍMA** is the most photogenic of several fishing hamlets on the island, with its picturesque boathouses tucked underneath the principal living areas. There's no beach to speak of, and only one place to stay – the impeccably sited, if a little basic *Panorama* (☎0287/21 623; ④), with an acceptable balcony taverna.

Pláthiena, 45 minutes' walk northwest of Pláka, is the closest proper beach, and thus is vastly popular in summer. There are no facilities, but the beach is fairly well protected and partly shaded by tamarisks. Head initially west from near the police station on the marked footpath towards **ARETÍ** and **FOURKOVOÚNI**, two more cliff-dug, boathouse-hamlets very much in the Klíma mould. Although the direct route to Pláthiena is signposted, it's no longer to go via Fourkovoúni; both hamlets are reached by side-turnings off the main route, which becomes a jeep track as you approach Fourkovoúni. By moped, access to Pláthiena is only from Plakés, the northernmost and smallest of the five northwestern villages.

The south

The main road to the south of the island splits at **Kánava junction**, an unrelievedly dreary place at first glance owing to the large power plant here. But opposite this, indicated by a rusty sign pointing seaward, is the first of Mílos's **hot springs**, which bubble up in the shallows and are much enjoyed by the locals.

Taking the left or easterly fork leads to **ZEFYRÍA**, hidden among olive groves below the bare hills; it was briefly the medieval capital until an eighteenth-century epidemic drove out the population. Much of the old town is still deserted, though some life has returned, and there's a magnificent seventeenth-century church.

South of here it's a further 8km down a winding road to the coarse-sand beach of **Paleohóri**. Actually a triple strand totalling 800m in length, it's indisputably the island's best; clothing's optional at the westerly cove, where steam vents heat both the shallow water and the rock overhangs onshore. There are a number of places to stay, such as the inland *Broutsos* (☎01/34 78 425; ④) and the purpose-built rooms at the *Artemis* restaurant (☎0287/31 221; ④) nearer the beach, but the cheapest are Panayiota Vikelli's rooms (☎0287/31 228; ③). Apart from the *Artemis*, there are a couple of other tavernas including *Pelagos*, which has a large raised patio.

The westerly road from Kánava junction leads past the airport gate to **Hivadholímni**, considered to be the best beach on Mílos bay itself. Not that this is saying much: Hivadholímni is north-facing and thus garbage-prone, with shallow sumpy water offshore, although there is a taverna, a disco-bar and a sizable community of campers during the summer. It's better to veer south to **Provatás**, a short but tidy beach, closed off by colourful cliffs on the east. Being so easy to get at, it hasn't escaped some development: there are two rooms establishments plus, closer to the shore, a newer, luxury complex, *Golden Milos Beach* (☎0287/31 307; ⑥). The best value for food and accommodation is the *Maistrali* (☎0287/31 206; ③).

Some 2km west of Provatás, you'll see a highway sign for **Kípos**. Below and to the left of the road, a small **medieval chapel** dedicated to the Kímisis (Assumption) sits atop foundations far older – as evidenced by the early Christian reliefs stacked along the west wall and a carved, cruciform baptismal font in the *ieron* behind the altar screen. At one time a spring gushed from the low tunnel-cave beside the font – sufficiently miraculous in itself on arid Mílos. Several kilometres before Provatás, a road forks east through a dusty white quarry to the trendy and popular beach of **Firipláka**, beautifully set but sadly dominated in high summer by a noisy canteen pumping out techno. Further east, **Tsigrádho** beach is accessible by boat, or by the novel means of a rope hanging down a crevice in the cliff-face.

For the most part **Hálakas**, the southwestern peninsula centred on the wilderness of 748-metre Profítis Ilías, is uninhabited and little built upon, with the exception of the **monastery of Sidherianós**. The roads are memorable, if a little tiring, and several spots are worth making the effort to see. **Emboriós** on the east side of the peninsula has a fine little beach and a great local taverna with a few cheap rooms (☎0287/21 389; ③). On the mostly rugged west coast, **Triádhes** is one of the finest and least spoilt beaches in the Cyclades, but you'll have to bring your own provisions. **Kléftiko** in the southwest corner is only reachable by boat, but repays the effort to get there with its stunning rock formations, semi-submerged rock tunnels and colourful coral.

The north coast

From either Adhámas or the Pláka area, good roads run roughly parallel to the **north coast** which, despite being windswept and largely uninhabited, is not devoid of interest. **Mandhrákia**, reached from Péran Triovássalos, is another boathouse settlement, and **Sarakíniko**, to the east, is a sculpted inlet with a sandy sea-bed and a summer beach café. About 8km from Adhámas, the little hamlet of **Páhena**, not shown on many maps, has a cluster of rooms and a small beach – the best-value rooms are *Terry's* (☎0287/22 640; ③). About a kilometre beyond this, the remains of three superimposed Neolithic settlements crown a small knoll at **Fylakopí** (ancient Phylakope); the site was important archeologically, but hasn't been maintained and is difficult to interpret. Just before the site is another one of Milos's coastal wonders: the deep-sea inlet of **Papafránga**, set in a ravine and accessible through a gap in the cliffs.

Pollónia

POLLÓNIA, 12km northeast of Adhámas, must be the windiest spot on the island, hence the name of its longest-lived and best **bar**, *Okto Bofor* (meaning "Force 8 gales"), near the church. The second resort on Mílos after Adhámas, it is, not surprisingly, immensely popular with windsurfers, and the new diving centre has further increased its popularity among watersports enthusiasts. Pollónia is essentially a small harbour protected by a storm-lashed spit of land on the northeast, where self-catering units are multiplying rapidly, fringed by a long but narrow, tamarisk-fringed beach to the rear, and closed off on the south by a smaller promontory on which the tiny original settlement huddles. Besides the town beach, the only other convenient, half-decent beach is at **Voúdhia**, 3km east, where you will find more of the island's hot springs, although it is effectively spoiled by its proximity to huge mining works, which lend it the desolate air of a *Mad Max* location.

On the quay are several **tavernas** and a couple of café/snack bars. The best tavernas are *Kapetan Nikolaos* (aka *Koula's*; open year-round) and *Araxovoli*, which has a good selection of seafood. Inland and south of here you'll find a concentration of **accommodation**, more simple rooms and fewer apartments, most with the slight drawback of occasional noise and dust from quarry trucks. Among the highest-quality units here are the *Kapetan Tasos Studios* (☎0287/41 287; ⑤), with good views of the straits between Mílos and Kímolos. *Flora* (☎0287/41 249; ④), on the road towards the spit, is a more reasonable option, as are *Efi* rooms (☎0287/41 396; ④), above the far end of the beach. *Andreas* (☎0287/41 262; ⑤) has triple studios with stunning views and easy access to the quiet neighbouring bay. Pollónia has no bank or post office, but the friendly Axios Rent A Car office (☎0287/41 442) can change money and advise you on accommodation matters. A **motorbike rental** place and a well-stocked **supermarket** complete the list of amenities. There is a huge map fixed on a metal frame near the bus stop, which shows all the facilities and gives telephone numbers.

Getting to Kímolos (see below) may be the main reason you're here. Either the *Tria Adhelfia* or one other kaïki makes the trip daily year-round at 6.45am and 2pm, returning from Kímolos an hour later; during high season, there are five crossings a day.

Kímolos

Of the three islets off the coast of Mílos, Andímilos is home to a rare species of chamois, Políegos has more ordinary goats, but only **Kímolos** has any human habitation. Volcanic like Mílos, with the same little lava-built rural cottages, it profits from its geology and used to export chalk (*kimolía* in Greek) until the supply was exhausted. Fuller's earth is still extracted locally, and the fine dust of this clay is a familiar sight on the island, where mining still outstrips fishing and farming as an occupation. Rugged and barren in the interior, it has some fertile land on the southeast coast where wells provide water, and this is where the population of about eight hundred is concentrated.

Kímolos is sleepy indeed from September to June, and even in August sees hardly any visitors. This is probably just as well, since there are fewer than a hundred beds on the whole island, and little in the way of other amenities.

Psathí and Hóra

Whether you arrive by ferry, or by kaïki from Pollónia, you'll dock at the hamlet of **PSATHÍ**, pretty much a non-event except for the excellent *To Kyma* **taverna** midway along the beach. The laissez-faire attitude towards tourism is demonstrated by the fact that there are no rooms here, but, equally, nobody minds if you sleep on the small beach. **Ferry tickets** are sold only outside the expensive café at the end of the jetty, an hour or so before the anticipated arrival of the boat; the *Tria Adhelfia* kaïki comes and goes unremarked from the base of the jetty five times a day in summer. There is no bus on the island, but a licence has been obtained for a taxi, so now only a driver is required.

Around the bay there are a few old windmills and the dazzlingly white **HÓRA** perched on the ridge above them. Unsung – and neglected, although there are plans to reconstruct it and build government rooms – is the magnificent, two-gated **kástro**, a fortified core of roughly the same design as those at Andíparos and Síkinos; the perimeter houses are intact but its heart is a jumble of ruins. Just outside the kástro on the north stands the conspicuously unwhitewashed, late-sixteenth-century church of **Khryssóstomos**, the oldest and most beautiful on the island. It takes fifteen minutes to walk up to the surprisingly large town, passing the adequate *Villa Maria* (☎0287/51 392; ③), about five minutes along the way and nearer to Psathí. Further accommodation is available in Hóra itself, where Margaro Petraki (☎0287/51 314; ②), has rooms tucked away in the rather unglamorous maze of backstreets, as does Nikos Ventouris (☎0287/51 329; ②) above his kafenío nearby. Sofia Ventouris (☎0287/51 219; ④) has a few new studios with sea views, close to the church. The aptly named *Panorama*, near the east gate of the kástro, is the most elaborate and consistently open **taverna**. *Meltémi* (☎0287/51 360; ③), to the west of the village, is a good, new taverna which also has some rooms. There are a couple of basic psistariés, as well as *1860*, a surprisingly sophisticated **café-bar**. Self-catering is an easy proposition – and may be a necessity before June or after August – with a well-stocked supermarket, produce stalls and a butcher. Finally, there are a couple of boat agencies, and a **post office** in the west of the village. The small **archeological museum** (Tues & Fri 8am–2pm, Wed, Thur, Sat, Sun 8am–1pm), currently on the road into Hóra, is due to move to more spacious premises near the church; its collection comprises pottery from the Geometric to the Roman period.

Around the island

During summer at least, the hamlet of **ALYKÍ** on the south coast is a better bet for staying than Psathí and Hóra; it only takes about thirty minutes to walk there on the paved road that forks left just before the *Villa Maria*. Alykí is named after the salt pan which sprawls between a rather mediocre beach with no shade or shelter, and has a pair of **rooms** – *Sardis* (☎0287/51 458; ④) and *Passamihalis* (☎0287/51 340; ②) – and simple **tavernas**. You can stroll west one cove to **Bonátsa** for better sand and shallow water, though you won't escape the winds. Passing another cove you come to the even more attractive beach of Kalamítsi, with better shade and the good little taverna and rooms of *Ventouris* (③). To the east, between Alykí and Psathí, the smaller, more secluded beach of **Skála** is better for camping.

The 700m coarse-sand beach of **Elliniká** is 45 minutes' walk west of Alykí: starting on the road, bear left – just before two chapels on a slope – onto a narrower track which runs through the fields at the bottom of the valley. Divided by a low bluff, the beach is bracketed by two capes and looks out over Dhaskalió islet; it tends to catch heavy weather in the afternoon, and there are no facilities here.

Another road leads northeast from Hóra to a beach and radioactive springs at **Prássa**, 7km away. The route takes in impressive views across the straits to Políegos, and there are several shady peaceful coves where you could camp out. Innumerable goat tracks invite exploration of the rest of the island; in the far northwest, on Kímolos's summit, are the ruins of an imposing Venetian fortress known as **Paleókastro**. The local community has plans to open an official campsite at Klíma Bay 2km northeast of Hóra, once it has relocated the rubbish dump that currently befouls the place.

Ándhros

Ándhros, the second largest and northernmost of the Cyclades, has a number of fine features to offer the visitor, although you have to search them out. Thinly populated but prosperous, its fertile, well-watered valleys have attracted scores of Athenian holiday villas whose red-tiled roofs and white walls stand out among the greenery. Some of the

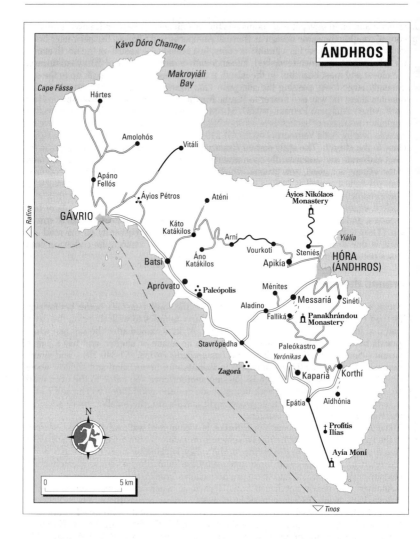

more recent of these have robbed many of the villages of life and atmosphere, turning them into scattered settlements with no nucleus, and have created a weekender mentality manifest in noisy Friday and Sunday evening traffic jams at the ferry dock. The island neither needs nor welcomes independent travellers, and it can be almost impossible to get a bed in between the block-bookings during high season. On the positive side, the permanent population is distinctly hospitable; traditionally working on ships, they are only too happy to practise their English on you. Together with some of the more idiosyncratic reminders of the Venetian period, such as the *peristereónes* (pigeon towers) and the *frákhtes* (dry-stone walls, here raised to the status of an art form), it is this friendliness that lends Ándhros its charm.

Ferries connect the island with Rafína on the mainland, only an hour from Athens on the bus, and you can loop back onto the central Cycladic routes via Mýkonos, Tínos or Sýros. The bus service is poor, and you'd be well advised to consider renting a bike to tour the sights – otherwise you'll face a lot of walking.

Northern and western Ándhros

All ferries and catamarans arrive at the main port, **GÁVRIO**. No longer the nondescript place it once was, Gávrio is moving into the last few stages of its painfully slow transformation from scruffy port to moderately attractive holiday resort. Few venture onto the adjacent windswept beach; however, there are plenty more attractive alternatives just to the south, where you'll find some of the area's better accommodation. A converted dovecote houses a sporadically functioning **tourist office**, and there are half a dozen ferry **ticket agents**. There's also a **bank**, and a **post office** on the waterfront.

The cheapest **accommodation** is in the basic *Galaxy* (☎0282/71 228; ②), which serves as a late-arrival fall-back. There are more room and studio outfits along and above the main coastal road leading out of Gávrio to Batsí: *Aktion* (☎0282/71 607; ④) is fairly representative, and *Andros Holiday Hotel* (☎0282/71 384; ⑥) is a good upmarket choice. **Restaurants** worth trying include the good if basic estiatório, *Tria Asteria*; the *Vengera* taverna 100m inland with its nice leafy courtyard; and the smart *Trehandiri* ouzerí opposite the catamaran dock. **Nightlife** revolves around a string of cafés and bars along the harbourfront, of which *Marlin* is a popular newcomer. Alternatively, there are one or two lively venues on Áyios Pétros beach several kilometres south, including *Marabou* taverna which frequently features live guitar music. Along the same stretch the excellent *Yiannouli* taverna is worth checking out for lunch.

The road north begins behind the *Hotel Gavrion Beach*. Around 3km northwest are two beaches named **Fellós**: one with holiday villas and a taverna, the other hidden beyond the headland and popular with freelance campers. Beyond Ápano Fellós, the countryside is empty except for a few hamlets inhabited by the descendants of medieval Albanians who settled here and in southern Évvia several hundred years ago.

Most traffic heads 8km south down the coast, past the lively Khryssí Ammos beach, and the *Perakkis Hotel* above (☎0282/71 456; ⑥), to **BATSÍ**, the island's main package resort, with large hotels and bars around its fine natural harbour. The beautiful though crowded beach curves round the port, and the sea is cold, calm and clean (except near the taxi park). **Hotels** range from the basic but comfortable *Chryssi Akti* (☎0282/41 236; ④) to the upmarket *Aneroussa Beach Hotel* (☎0282/41 045; ④), south of town past the Stivári area towards Áyia Marína beach (a picturesque cove with *Yiannoulis* fish taverna and studios (☎0282/41 963; ③)). Besides these there are plenty of other rooms, and good food can be had at *Stamatis*, an established taverna with a nice atmosphere, or at *Ta Delfinia,* which has a pleasant, sheltered balcony – both are near the harbour. For something a little different have a shrimp feast at *Restaurant Sirocco*, on the inland path above the village. Further out at **Stivári**, a pleasant café-taverna, *Stivari Gardens*, is run by an Englishwoman, who also has a few rooms (③). As well as several café-bars, of which *Capriccio* and *Select* are the most "in", there are half a dozen or so loud indoor **bars** featuring the standard foreign/Greek musical mix, although *Diva* plays some psychedelic sounds. If a full-blown *bouzoúki* night is what you are after try *Arpa* next door to *Stamatis*. Finally, there are two banks, with cash dispensers, where you can change money.

From Batsí you're within easy walking distance of some beautiful inland villages. At **KÁTO KATÁKILOS**, one hour inland, there are a couple of seasonal **tavernas** including *O Gregos*; a rough track leads to **ATÉNI**, a hamlet in a lush, remote valley, as yet unvisited by the dreaded donkey safaris. **ÁNO KATÁKILOS** has a couple of under-visited tavernas with fine views across the village. A right-hand turning out of Katákilos heads up the mountain to **ARNÍ**, whose lone taverna is often shrouded in mist. Another rewarding trip is to a well-preserved, 20-metre-high **Classical tower** at **Áyios Pétros**, 5km from Gávrio or 9km coming from Batsí.

South of Batsí along the main road are Káto and Áno Apróvato. **Káto** has rooms, including *Galini* (☎0282/41 472; ③), a taverna and a path to a quiet beach, while nearby is the largely unexplored archeological site of **Paleópolis**. Áno has the excellent taverna *To Balkoni tou Egeou*, which can be most easily visited on one of the "Mezédhes Nights" organized from Batsí, though for a more authentic evening you may be better off making your own way there.

Hóra and around

A minimal bus service links the west coast with **HÓRA** or **ÁNDHROS TOWN**, 35km from Gávrio. With its setting on a rocky spur cutting across a huge bay, the capital is the most attractive place on the island. Paved in marble and schist from the still-active local quarries, the buildings around the bus station are grand nineteenth-century affairs, and the squares with their ornate wall fountains and gateways are equally elegant. The hill quarters are modern, while the small port acts as a yacht supply station, and below are the sands of Parapórti – a fine beach, if a little exposed to the *meltémi* winds in summer.

The few **hotels** in town are on the expensive side and tend to be busy with holidaying Greeks: try the *Aigli* (☎0282/22 303; ④), opposite the big church on the main walkway. Most rooms are clustered behind the long **Nimbório** beach north of town, and range from cheap family guesthouses like those of *Firiou* (☎0282/22 921; ②) and good clean rooms like those of *Villa Stella* (☎0282/22 471; ④) to modern apartments such as the *Alkioni Inn* (☎0282/24 522; ⑤). The *Paradise Hotel* (☎0282/22 187, *marlos@mail.otenet.gr*, ⑥), with its swimming pool and tennis court, is the most upmarket choice. For **eating**, most cafés are up in Hóra: *Plátanos* do a generous mezédhes selection which can be enjoyed with an oúzo under the plane trees; the appropriately named *O Stathmos* right by the bus station is good; and there's a decent psistariá on the main drag. The nicest taverna is *O Nonas*, tucked away at the town end of the beach behind the ugly *Xenia* hotel; *Nostos*, a smart new pizzeria nearby on the seafront, is another popular choice. Up in Hóra there's the *Rock Café* for a **drink**, but Nimboúrio beach is the epicentre of nightlife with the two-storey *Veyera*, a thumping disco halfway along, and the huge *Kavo* right at the end, which plays Greek music till after 4am. There's a post office and bank around town, a couple of travel agents and three moped rentals behind the beach.

From the square right at the end of town you pass through an archway and down to windswept **Platía Ríva**, with its statue of the unknown sailor scanning the sea. Beyond lies the thirteenth-century Venetian **kástro**, precariously joined to the mainland by a narrow-arched bridge, which was damaged by German munitions in World War II. The **Modern Art Museum** (Wed–Mon 10am–2pm, also 6–8pm in summer; 1000dr) has a sculpture garden and a permanent collection that includes works by Picasso and Braque, as well as temporary exhibits. Don't be discouraged by the stark modern architecture of the **Archeological Museum** (Tues–Sun 8.30am–2.30pm; 500dr); it proves to be well laid out and labelled, with instructive models. The prize items on view are the fourth-century "Hermes of Ándros", reclaimed from a prominent position in the Athens Archeological Museum, and the "Matron of Herculaneum".

Hiking inland and west from Ándhros, the obvious destination is **MÉNITES**, a hill village just up a green valley choked with trees and straddled by stone walls. The church of the **Panayía** may have been the location of a temple of Dionysos, where water was turned into wine; water still flows continuously from the local rocks. Nearby is the medieval village of **MESSARIÁ**, with the deserted twelfth-century Byzantine church of **Taxiárhis** below and the pleasantly shady *Platanos* taverna. The finest monastery on the island, **Panakhrándou**, is only an hour's (steep) walk away, via the village of Falliká; reputedly tenth-century, it's still defended by massive walls but occupied these days by just three monks. It clings to an iron-stained cliff southwest of Hóra, to which you can return directly with a healthy two- to three-hour walk down the creek valley, guided by red dots.

Hidden by the ridge directly north of Hóra, the prosperous nineteenth-century village of **STENIÉS** was built by the vanguard of today's shipping magnates; just below, at Yiália, there's a small pebble beach with a taverna. Nearby on the road to Strapouriés is a wonderful taverna, *Bozakis*, which boasts a view all the way down to the coast and excellent food. Beyond Steniés is **APIKÍA**, a tidy little village which bottles Sariza-brand mineral water for a living; there are a few **tavernas**, including *O Tassos* which has a lovely garden setting and specialities such as goat and rabbit. There are a very limited number of **rooms** here, as well as the "luxury" hotel *Pigi Sariza* (☎0282/23 799 or 23 899; ⑥), which is getting a bit tatty around the edges. The road is now asphalted up to Vourkotí and even past this point is quite negotiable via Arní to the west coast. There are some stunning views all along this road but bike riders need to take care when the *meltémi* is blowing – it can get dangerously windy.

Southern Ándhros

On your way south, you might stop at **Zagorá**, a fortified Geometric town – unique in having never been built over – that was excavated in the early 1970s. Located on a desolate, flat-topped promontory with cliffs falling away on three sides, it's worth a visit for the view alone. With your own transport, the sheltered cove of Sinéti south of Hóras is also worth a detour.

The village of **KORTHÍ**, the end of the line, is a friendly village which is slowly waking up to its tourist potential. Set on a large sandy bay, cut off from the rest of the island by a high ridge and so relatively unspoiled, it is pleasant enough to merit spending the night at *Villa Aristidou* (☎0282/62 122; ③) or at the austere-looking *Hotel Korthion* (☎0282/61218; ③). There are also several good seafood **restaurants**, and a number of pleasant café-bars including *Erolo Cafe* on the seafront. You could also take in the nearby convent of **Zoödhóhou Piyís** (open to visitors before noon), with illuminated manuscripts and a disused weaving factory.

To the north is **PALEÓKASTRO**, a tumbledown village with a ruined Venetian castle – and a legend about an old woman who betrayed the stronghold to the Turks, then jumped off the walls in remorse, landing on a rock now known as "Old Lady's Leap". In the opposite direction out of Korthí are **AÏDHÓNIA** and **KAPARIÁ**, dotted with pigeon towers (*peristereónes*) left by the Venetians.

Tínos

Tínos still feels one of the most Greek of the larger islands. A few foreigners have discovered its beaches and unspoiled villages, but most visitors are Greek, here to see the church of **Panayía Evangelístria**, a grandiose shrine erected on the spot where a miraculous icon with healing powers was found in 1822. A Tiniote nun, now canonized as Ayía Pelayía, was directed in a vision to unearth the relic just as the War of Independence was getting underway, a timely coincidence which served to underscore the links between the Orthodox Church and Greek nationalism. Today, there are two major annual pilgrimages, on March 25 and August 15, when, at 11am, the icon bearing the Virgin's image is carried in state down to the harbour over the heads of the faithful.

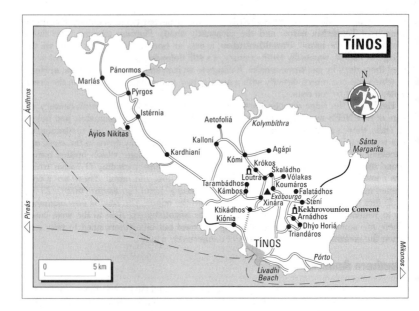

The Ottoman tenure here was the most fleeting in the Aegean. **Exóbourgo**, the crag-gy mount dominating southern Tínos and surrounded by most of the island's sixty-odd villages, is studded with the ruins of a Venetian citadel which defied the Turks until 1715, long after the rest of Greece had fallen. An enduring legacy of the long Venetian rule is a persistent **Catholic minority**, which accounts for almost a half of the population, and a sectarian rivalry said to be responsible for the numerous graceful belfries scattered throughout the island – Orthodox and Catholic parishes vying to build the tallest. The sky is pierced, too, by distinctive and ornate dovecotes, even more in evidence here than on Ándhros. Aside from all this, the inland village architecture is striking and there's a flourishing folk-art tradition which finds expression in the abundant local marble. The islanders have remained open and hospitable to the relatively few foreigners and the steady stream of Greek visitors who touch down here, and any mercenary inclinations seem to be satisfied by booming sales in religious paraphernalia to the faithful.

Tínos Town and the southern beaches

At **TÍNOS Town**, trafficking in devotional articles certainly dominates the streets lead-ing up from the busy waterfront to the Neoclassical **church** (daily 8am–8pm) which towers above. Approached via a massive marble staircase, the famous **icon** inside is all but buried under a dazzling mass of gold and silver *támmata* (votive offerings); below is the crypt (where the icon was discovered) and a mausoleum for the sailors drowned when the Greek warship *Elli*, at anchor off Tínos during a pilgrimage, was torpedoed by an Italian submarine on August 15, 1940. Museums around the courtyard display more objects donated by the faithful (who inundate the island for the two big yearly fes-tivals), as well as icons, paintings and work by local marble sculptors.

The shrine aside – and all the attendant stalls, shops and bustle – the port is none too exciting, with just scattered inland patches of nineteenth-century buildings. You might make time for the **Archeological Museum** (Tues–Sun 8.30am–3pm; 500dr) on the way up to the church, whose collection includes a fascinating sundial from the local Roman sanctuary of Poseidon and Amphitrite (see p.512).

Practicalities

Ferries dock at any of three different **jetties**; which one depends on weather conditions. There are at least two boats a day from Pireás and Sýros, and four from Rafína and Ándhros going on to Mýkonos, as well as a useful hydrofoil, and less frequent ferry connections to Páros, Náxos and Santoríni. When you're leaving, ask your ticket agent which jetty to head for. **Buses** leave from a small parking area in front of a cubbyhole-office on the quay, to Pánormos, Kalloní, Stení, Pórto and Kiónia (timetables available here; no buses after 7.30pm). A **moped** is perhaps a more reliable means of exploring – Vidalis, Zanáki Alavánou 16, is a good rental agency.

Windmills Travel (☎0283/23 398, *tinos@windmills-travel.com*), on the front towards the new jetty, can help with information as well as hotel and **tour bookings**; they even have a book exchange. In season an excursion boat does day-trips taking in Delos (see p.519) and Mýkonos (Tues–Sun; 5000dr round trip); this makes it possible to see Delos without the expense of staying overnight in Mýkonos, but only allows you two and a half hours at the site. The **tourist police** are located on the road to the west of the new jetty.

To have any chance of securing a reasonably priced **room** around the pilgrimage day of March 25 (August 15 is hopeless), you must arrive several days in advance. At other times there's plenty of choice, though you'll still be competing with out-of-season pilgrims, Athenian tourists and the sick and the disabled seeking a miracle cure. Of the hotels, the *Eleana* (☎0283/22 561; ③), east of the quay about 400m inland at the edge of the bazaar, is a good budget option. The conspicuous waterfront *Yannis Rooms* (☎0283/22 515; ③) is just in front of the reasonable *Thalia* (☎0283/22811; ④), all the way around the bay from the old jetty. Slightly pricier options include the *Avra* (☎0283/22 242; ③), a Neoclassical relic on the waterfront, and the *Favie Souzane* just inland (☎0283/22 693 or 22 176; ④). *Hotel Tinion* (☎0283/22 261; ⑤) is a stylish 1920s hotel near the post office. The *Vyzantio*, Zanáki Alavánou 26 (☎0283/22 454; ④), on the road out towards Pórto and the villages, is not especially memorable but it and the *Meltémi* (☎0283/22 881; ④) at Filipóti 7, near Megaloháris, are the only places open out of season. Finally, there is a smart hotel with swimming pool near the beginning of the beach road east of the promontory – *Aeolos Bay Hotel* (☎0283/23 410; ④). Otherwise, beat the crowds by staying at *Tinos Camping*, which also has a few nice rooms to let (☎0283/22 344; ②); follow the signs from the port – it's a ten-minute walk. A farmers' **market** for locally produced fruit and vegetables takes place every morning in the Palládha area (towards the new jetty between the bars and the waterfront).

As usual, most seafront **restaurants** are rather overpriced and indifferent, with the exception of a friendly psitopolió right opposite the bus terminal, and the smarter *Xinari* restaurant and pizzeria on Evangelístrias. A cluster of places around the bazaar just to the left of Megaloháris as you face the church include *Palea Pallada* and *Peristereonas*, both of them reasonable. Tucked away in a small alley near the seafront off Evangelistriás, *Pigada* does a fine clay-pot moussaka, as well as some more unusual dishes, while *1000 + 1 Yevsis*, further inland on Nikoláou Loúvari, is a basic estiatório with reasonable prices. Wash down your meal with the island's very good barrelled retsina, which is available just about everywhere.

There are quite a few **bars**, mostly in a huddle near the new quay. *Fevgatos* has a pleasant atmosphere, *Koutsaros* on the corner plays rock music, and *Kala Kathoumena* is pretty lively with a mixture of international hits and Greek music. At 3am all bars in Tinos Town close, and for those not ready to hit the sack, the *Paradise* and *Vegera* club duplex on the main road out of town to Amphitrite stay open until dawn, the former playing mainly Greek music and the latter favouring trance.

Nearby beaches

Kiónia, 3km northwest (hourly buses), is the site of the **Sanctuary of Poseidon and Amphitrite** which was discovered in 1902; the excavations yielded principally columns (*kiónia* in Greek), but also a temple, baths, a fountain and hostels for the ancient pilgrims. The **beach** is functional enough, lined with rooms to rent and snack bars, but it's better to walk past the large *Tinos Beach Hotel* (☎0283/22 626; ⑤), the last stop for the bus, and follow an unpaved road to a series of sandy coves beyond.

The beach beyond the headland east of town starts off rocky but improves if you walk 500 metres further along. Further east, **Pórto** (six buses daily) boasts two good beaches, with a couple of good tavernas as well as rooms at the reasonably priced restaurant belonging to *Akti Aegeou* (☎0283/24 248; ⑤), on the first beach of Áyios Pandelímon, as well as the smart studios of *Porto Raphael* (☎0283/22 403; ④), above Áyios Ioánnis. *Porto Tango* (☎0283/24 410; ⑥) is an excellent upmarket hotel here, with a lovely pool setting.

Northern Tínos

A good beginning to a foray into the interior is to take the stone stairway – the continuation of Odhós Ayíou Nikoláou – that passes behind and to the left of the Evangelístria. This climbs for ninety minutes through appealing countryside to **KTIKÁDHOS**, a fine village with a good sea-view taverna, *Iy Dhrosia*. You can either flag down a bus on the main road or stay with the trail until Xinára (see "Around Exóbourgo" below).

Heading northwest from the junction flanked by Ktikádhos, Tripótamos and Xinára, there's little to stop for – except the fine dovecotes around Tarambádhos – until you reach **KARDHIANÍ**, one of the most strikingly set and beautiful villages on the island, with its views across to Sýros from amid a dense oasis. Nestled in the small sandy bay below is a fine little restaurant by the name of *Anemos*, which serves octopus stew and other dishes at good prices. Kardhianí has been discovered by wealthy Athenians and expatriates, and now offers the exotic *To Perivoli* taverna. **ISTÉRNIA**, just a little beyond, is not nearly so appealing but there is some accommodation on offer, including the *Lameras Hotel* (☎0283/31215; ③). The *Tavsternia* taverna commands stunning panoramic views and there are a few cafés, perched above the turning for **Órmos Isterníon,** a comparatively small but overdeveloped beach.

Five daily buses along this route finish up at **PÝRGOS**, a few kilometres further north and smack in the middle of the island's marble-quarrying district. A beautiful village, its local artisans are renowned throughout Greece for their skill in producing marble ornamentation; ornate fanlights and bas-relief plaques crafted here adorn houses throughout Tínos. Pýrgos is also home to the School of Arts, and **the Museum of Tinian Artists** (daily 11am–2pm & 5.30–6.30pm; 300dr) contains numerous representative works from some of the island's finest artists. There are two **kafenía** and a **snack bar** on the attractive shady platía, and one acceptable **taverna** opposite the bus station. Pýrgos is popular in summer, and if you want to stay there are some new **studios** for rent on the main road coming into the village; alternatively ask the locals on the platía.

The marble products were once exported from **PÁNORMOS** (Órmos) harbour, 4km northeast, with its tiny but commercialized beach; there's little reason to linger, but if you get stuck there are rooms and some tavernas.

Around Exóbourgo

The ring of villages around **Exóbourgo** mountain is the other focus of interest on Tínos. The fortified pinnacle itself (570m), with ancient foundations as well as the ruins of three Venetian churches and a fountain, is reached by steep steps from **XINÁRA** (near the island's major road junction), the seat of the island's Roman Catholic bishop. Most villages in north central Tínos have mixed populations, but Xinára and its immediate neighbours are purely Catholic; the inland villages also tend to have a more sheltered position, with better farmland nearby – the Venetians' way of rewarding converts and their descendants. Yet **TRIPÓTAMOS**, just south of Xinára, is a completely Orthodox village with possibly the finest architecture in this region – and has accordingly been pounced on by foreigners keen to restore its historic properties.

At **LOUTRÁ**, the next community north of Xinára, there's an Ursuline convent and a good **folk art museum** (summer only 10.30am–3.30pm; free) in the old Jesuit monastery here; to visit, leave the bus at the turning for Skaládho. From Krókos, which has a scenically situated restaurant *O Krokos*, it's a forty-minute walk to **VÓLAKAS** (Vólax), one of the most remote villages on the island, a windswept oasis surrounded by bony rocks. Here, half a dozen elderly Catholic basketweavers fashion some of the best examples of that craft in Greece. There is a small **folklore museum** (free) which you have to ask the lady living in the house opposite the entrance to open, and the charming outdoor **Fontaine Theatre** which in August hosts visiting theatre groups from all over Greece. Accommodation is hard to come by; however there are a couple of places to eat, including the recommended *O Rokos* taverna.

At Kómi, 5km beyond Krókos, you can take a detour for **KOLYMBÍTHRA**, a magnificent double beach: one part wild, huge and windswept (temporary residence to pink flamingos migrating to Africa during May), the other sheltered and with a couple of tavernas including *Kolibithra Beach* (☎0283/51213; ⑤), which also has rooms. The bus to Kallóni goes on to Kolymbíthra twice a day in season; out of season you'll have to get off at Kómi and walk 4km.

From either Skaládho or Vólakas you go on to Koúmaros, where another long stairway leads up to Exóbourgo, or skirt the pinnacle towards Stení and Falatádhos which appear as white speckles against the fertile Livádha valley. From Stení you can catch the bus back to the harbour (seven daily). On the way down, try and stop off at one of the beautiful settlements just below the important twelfth-century **convent of Kekhrovouníou**, where Ayía Pelayía had her vision. Particularly worth visiting are **DHÝO HORIÁ**, which has a fine main square where cave-fountains burble, and **TRIANDÁROS**, which has two reasonable **eating** places: *Iy Lefka* and *Eleni's* (a tiny place at the back of the village). If you have your own transport, there are quite wide and fairly negotiable tracks down to some lovely secluded bays on the east of the island from the area of Stení. One such is **Sánta Margaríta**; given the lack of tourist development here, it's a good idea to take something to drink.

This is hardly an exhaustive list of Tiniot villages; armed with a map and good walking shoes for tackling the many old trails that still exist, you could spend days within sight of Exóbourgo and never pass through the same hamlets twice. Take warm clothing out of season, especially if you're on a moped, since the forbidding mountains behind Vólakas and the Livadhéri plain keep things noticeably cool.

Mýkonos

Originally visited only as a stop on the way to ancient Delos, **Mýkonos** has become easily the most popular (and the most expensive) of the Cyclades. Boosted by direct air links with Britain and domestic flights from Athens, it sees an incredible 800,000 tourists pass through in a good year, producing some spectacular overcrowding in high summer on Mýkonos's 75 square kilometres. But if you don't mind the crowds, or – and this is a much more attractive proposition – you come out of season, the prosperous capital is still one of the most beautiful of all island towns, its immaculately whitewashed houses concealing hundreds of little churches, shrines and chapels.

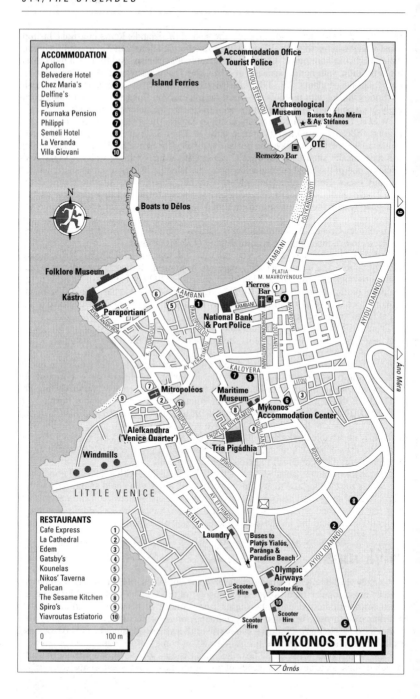

ACCOMMODATION
Apollon	❶
Belvedere Hotel	❷
Chez Maria's	❸
Delfine's	❹
Elysium	❺
Fournaka Pension	❻
Philippi	❼
Semeli Hotel	❽
La Veranda	❾
Villa Giovani	❿

Accommodation Office
Tourist Police
Island Ferries
Archaeological Museum
Buses to Áno Méra & Ay. Stéfanos
OTE
Remezzo Bar
Boats to Délos
Folklore Museum
Kástro
Paraportianí
PLATIA M. MAVROYENOUS
Pierros Bar
KAMBANI
National Bank & Port Police
KALOYERA
Maritime Museum
Mýkonos Accommodation Center
Mitropoléos
Alefkandhra ('Venice Quarter')
Tría Pigádhia
Windmills
LITTLE VENICE
Laundry
Buses to Platýs Yialós, Paránga & Paradise Beach
Olympic Airways
Scooter Hire
Scooter Hire
Scooter Hire

N

RESTAURANTS
Cafe Express	①
La Cathedral	②
Edem	③
Gatsby's	④
Kounelas	⑤
Nikos' Taverna	⑥
Pelican	⑦
The Sesame Kitchen	⑧
Spiro's	⑨
Yiavroutas Estiatorio	⑩

0   100 m

MÝKONOS TOWN

Áno Méra

Órnós

The sophisticated nightlife is pretty hectic, amply stimulated by Mýkonos's former reputation as *the* gay resort of the Mediterranean – a title shared in recent years with places like Ibiza and Sitges in Spain; whatever, the locals take this comparatively exotic clientele in their stride. Unspoiled it isn't, but the island does offer excellent (if crowded) beaches, picturesque windmills and a rolling arid interior. An unheralded Mýkonian quirk is the widespread legality of scuba diving, a rarity in Greece, and dive centres have sprung up on virtually every beach.

Mýkonos Town

Don't let the crowds put you off exploring **MÝKONOS TOWN**, the archetypal postcard image of the Cyclades. Its sugar-cube buildings are stacked around a cluster of seafront fishermen's dwellings, with every nook and cranny scrubbed and shown off. Most people head out to the beaches during the day, so early morning or late afternoon are the best times to wander the maze of narrow streets. The labyrinthine design was intended to confuse the pirates who plagued Mýkonos in the eighteenth and early nineteenth centuries, and it still has the desired effect.

You don't need any maps or hints to explore the convoluted streets and alleys of town; getting lost is half the fun. There are, however, a few places worth seeking out. Coming from the ferry quay you'll pass the **Archeological Museum** (Tues–Sat 9am–3.30pm, Sun 10am–3pm; 500dr) on your way into town, which displays some good Delos pottery; the town also boasts a **marine museum** displaying various nautical artefacts, including a lighthouse re-erected in the back garden (Tues–Sun 8.30am–3pm; 350dr). Alternatively, behind the two banks there's the **library**, with Hellenistic coins and late medieval seals, or, at the base of the Delos jetty, the **Folklore Museum** (Mon–Sat 4–8pm, Sun 5–8pm; free), housed in an eighteenth-century mansion and cramming in a larger-than-usual collection of bric-a-brac, including a vast four-poster bed. The museum shares the same promontory as the old Venetian kástro, the entrance to which is marked by Mýkonos's oldest and best-known church, **Paraportianí**, which is a fascinating asymmetrical hodge-podge of four chapels amalgamated into one.

The shore leads to the area known as "Little Venice" because of its high, arcaded Venetian houses built right up to the water's edge. Its real name is **Alefkándhra**, a trendy district packed with art galleries, chic bars and discos. Away from the seafront, behind Platía Alefkándhra, are Mýkonos's two **cathedrals**: Roman Catholic and Greek Orthodox. Beyond, the famous **windmills** look over the area, a little shabby but ripe for photo opportunities. Instead of retracing your steps along the water's edge, follow Énoplon Dhinaméon (left off Mitropóleos) to **Tría Pigádhia** fountain. The name means "Three Wells", and legend has it that should a maiden drink from all three she is bound to find a husband.

Arrival and information

There is some accommodation information at the **airport**, but unless you know where you're going it's easier to take a taxi for the 3km into town, and sort things out there. The vast majority of visitors arrive by boat at the new northern **jetty**, where a veritable horde of room-owners pounces on the newly arrived. The scene is actually quite intimidating, and so, if you can avoid the grasping talons, it is far better to go a hundred metres further where a row of offices deal with official hotels, rented rooms and camping information, or into town to the extremely helpful Mykonos Accommodation Centre on the corner of Énoplon Dhinaméon and Malamatenías (☎0289/23 160, *mac@mac.myk.forthnet.gr*).

The harbour curves around past the dull, central Polikandhrióti beach, south of which is the **bus station** for Toúrlos, Áyios Stéfanos, Elía and Áno Méra. The **tourist**

police are located at the harbour. A second **bus terminus**, for beaches to the south, is right at the other end of the town, in the Lákka area where the **post office and** Olympic Airways office are. Buses to all the most popular beaches and resorts run frequently, until the early hours. **Taxis** go from Platía Mavroyénous on the seafront, and their rates are fixed and quite reasonable; try Mykonos Radio Taxi (☎0289/22 400). It is also here that the largest cluster of **motorbike rental** agencies is to be found; prices vary little.

Accommodation

Accommodation **prices** in Mýkonos rocket in the high season to a greater degree than almost anywhere else in Greece. One **hotel** that comes recommended despite its unattractive location is *Villa Giovani* (☎0289/22 485; ⑤), on Ayíou Ioánnou, the busy main road above the bus station. **In town**, try *Delfines* on Mavroyénous (☎0289/22 292; ⑤), *Apollon* on Kambáni (☎0289/22 223; ⑤), *Chez Marias* at Kaloyéra 27 (☎0289/22 480; ⑥) or the *Philippi* at Kaloyéra 25 (☎0289/22 294, *chrico@otenet.gr,* ④). There are plenty of very expensive splurge hotels like *Semeli Hotel* (☎0289/27 466; ⑥) on Ayíou Ioánnou, which has a pool, whirlpool and very tastefully decorated rooms, or the *Belvedere Hotel* (☎0289/25 122, *belvedere@myk.forthnet.gr,* ⑥) next door. *La Veranda* (☎0289/23 670; ⑥) is a hidden gem, located on the hillside above town, with rooms set around a small pool. Unsurprisingly, most accommodation is extremely gay-friendly; *Elysium* (☎0289/23 952; ⑥) is almost exclusively gay, and *Fournakia Pension* (☎0289/23 160; ⑤) has clean, modern rooms close to *Pierro's Bar*. There are two **campsites**: *Mykonos Camping* (☎0289/24 578) above Paránga Beach is smaller and has a more pleasant setting than nearby *Paradise Camping* on Paradise Beach (☎0289/22 852, *PARADISE@paradise.myk.forthnet.gr*); however, the latter also has bungalows (③). Both are packed in season, and dance music from the 24-hour bars on Paradise Beach makes sleep difficult. The campsite restaurants are best avoided. Hourly bus services to Paránga and Paradise Beach continue into the early hours but can get very overcrowded.

Eating and nightlife

Even **light meals** and **snacks** are expensive in Mýkonos, but there are several bakeries – the best is *Andhrea's*, just off Platía Mavroyénous – and plenty of supermarkets and takeaways in the backstreets, including *Three Wells* on Énoplon Dhinaméon.

The area around Alefkándhra is a promising place to head for a full **meal**: *La Cathedral*, by the two cathedrals on the platía, has standard fare; *Pelican*, behind the cathedrals, is pricey but well sited; and *Kostas*, also nearby, has competitive prices, a good wine list including barrelled wine (not easily found on Mýkonos) and friendly service. Less than fifty metres further along Mitropóleos, the small *Yiavroutas Estiatorio* is probably the least expensive and most authentically Greek place on the island, again with good barrelled wine. *Kounelas* is a good fish taverna with more reasonable prices than *Spiro's* on the seafront. *Edem*, close to Panakhrándou, offers poolside dining. *El Greco* at Tría Pigádhia is expensive but romantic, and *Gatsby's* on Tourlianís is a popular gay restaurant with an adventurous menu. *The Sesame Kitchen* on Énoplon Dhinaméon is an acceptable vegetarian restaurant; however, most of the smarter restaurants in Mýkonos do cater well for vegetarians anyway. Just behind the town hall is *Nikos' Taverna* – crowded, reasonable and recommended. For **late-night** snacks, most of the cafés on Kambani stay open until the small hours, and *Cafe Express* is open all night.

Nightlife in town is every bit as good as it's cracked up to be – and every bit as pricey. *Remezzo* (near the OTE) is one of the oldest bars, now a bit over the hill but a lively spot nonetheless, and a good place to have a drink before moving onto *Mercedes Club* next door; both are popular with young Athenians. *Skandinavian Bar-Disco* is a cheap-and-cheerful party spot, as is the nearby *Irish Bar*, and there are more sophisti-cated bars on Andhroníkou Matoyiánni and Énoplon Dhinaméon. *Caprice* and *Kastro's*, both around Little Venice, are ideal for sunset cocktails; the latter plays classical music and is popular with an older gay crowd. *La Mer* is a popular disco-bar playing a lively mix of Greek and dance music, while *Porta* is a popular gay haunt. *Pierro's* and *Icarus* (upstairs), just off Platía Mavroyénous, become the focal point of gay activity later on, the latter having great drag shows and welcoming proprietors. *Cavo Paradiso*, near *Paradise Camping*, is the after-hours club where die-hard party animals of all persua-sions come together.

The beaches

The closest beaches to town are those to the north, at **Toúrlos** (only 2km away but horrid) and **Áyios Stéfanos** (4km, much better), both developed resorts and connect-ed by a very regular bus service to Mýkonos Town. There are tavernas and rooms to let (as well as package hotels) at Áyios Stéfanos, away from the beach; *Mocambo Lido* taverna at the far end of the bay has a pleasant setting and good food.

Other nearby destinations include southwest peninsula resorts, with undistin-guished beaches tucked into pretty bays. The nearest to town, 1km away, is **Megáli Ammos**, a good beach backed by flat rocks and pricey rooms, but nearby Kórfos Bay is disgusting, thanks to the town dump and machine noise. Buses serve **Ornós**, an average beach, and **Áyios Ioánnis**, a dramatic bay with a tiny, stony beach, which achieved its moment of fame as a location for the film *Shirley Valentine*. The taverna *To Iliovasilema* has an excellent selection of fish and is highly recommended, if a little pricey.

The south coast is the busiest part of the island. Kaïkia ply from town to all of its beaches, which are among the straightest on the island, and still regarded to some extent as family strands by the Greeks. You might begin with **Platýs Yialós**, 4km south of town, though you won't be alone: one of the longest-established resorts on the island, it's not remotely Greek any more, the sand is monopolized by hotels, and you won't get a room to save your life between June and September. **Psaroú**, next door to the west, is very pretty – 150m of white sand backed by foliage and calamus reeds, crowded with sunbathers. Facilities here include a diving club (☎0289/23 579), waterskiing and wind-surfer rental, but again you'll need to reserve well in advance to secure a room between mid-June and mid-September.

Just over the headland to the east of Platýs Yialós is **Paránga Beach**, which is actu-ally two beaches separated by a smaller headland. The highly recommended *Nicolas* taverna and rooms (☎0289/23 566; ④) on the first beach is worlds apart from its noisy neighbour which is home to a loud beach bar and *Mykonos Camping*. A dusty footpath beyond Platýs Yialós crosses the fields and caves of the headland across the clifftops past Paranga, and drops down to **Paradise Beach**, a crescent of golden sand that is packed in season. Behind are the shops, self-service restaurants and noisy 24-hour beach bars of *Paradise Camping*. The next bay east contains **Super Paradise** (official-ly "Plindhrí") beach, accessible by footpath or by kaïki. One of the most fun beaches on the island, it has a decent taverna and two bars at opposite ends of the beach pumping out cheesy summer hits. One half of the beach is very mixed, getting progressively more gay as you walk away from where the kaïkia dock towards the beach bar perched in the hills, below which the beach is almost exclusively gay and nudist.

Probably the **best beach** on Mýkonos, though, is **Eliá**, the last port of call for the kaïkia. A broad, sandy stretch with a verdant backdrop, it's the longest beach on the island, though split in two by a rocky area. Almost exclusively nudist, it boasts a couple of restaurants, including the excellent *Matheos*. If the crowds have followed you this far, one last escape route is to follow the bare rock footpath over the spur (look for the white house) at the end of Eliá Beach. This cuts upwards for grand views east and west and then winds down to **Kaló Livádhi** (seasonal bus service), a stunning beach adjoining an agricultural valley scattered with little farmhouses; even here there's a restaurant (a good one at that) at the far end of the beach. **Lía**, further on, is smaller but delightful, with bamboo windbreaks and clear water, plus another taverna.

The rest of the island

If time is limited, any of the beaches above will be just fine. There are others, though, away from Mýkonos Town, as well as a few other destinations worth making the effort for.

East of Eliá, roughly 12km by road from the town, **Ayía Ánna** boasts a shingle beach and taverna, with the cliffs above granting some fine vistas. **Tarsaná**, on the other side of the isthmus, has a long, coarse sand beach, with watersports, a taverna and smart bungalows on offer. **Kalafáti**, almost adjacent, is more of a tourist community, its white-sand beach supporting a few hotels, restaurants and a disco. There's a local bus service from here to Áno Méra (see below), or you can jump on an excursion boat to **Tragoníssi**, the islet just offshore, for spectacular coastal scenery, seals and wild birds. The rest of the east coast is difficult – often impossible – to reach: there are some small beaches, really only worth the effort if you crave solitude, and the region is dominated by the peak of Profítis Ilías, sadly spoiled by a huge radar dome and military establish-

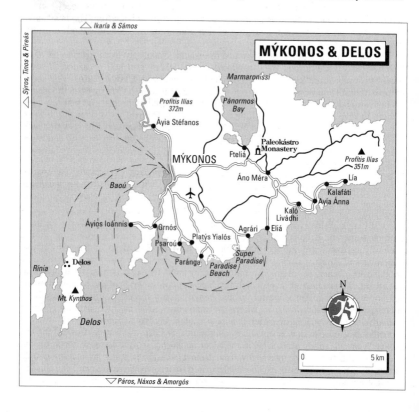

ment. The **north coast** suffers persistent battering from the *meltémi*, plus tar and litter pollution, and for the most part is bare, brown and exposed. **Pánormos Bay** is the
exception to this – a lovely, relatively sheltered beach. Despite a good restaurant, a
relaxed beach bar and the rather conspicuous *Albatros Club Hotel* (☎0289/25 130; ⑥),
Pánormos remains one of the least crowded beaches on the island.

From Pánormos, it's an easy walk to the only other settlement of any size on the
island, **ÁNO MÉRA**, where you should be able to find a **room**. The village prides itself
on striving to maintain a traditional way of life, the result however being rather pseudo
and wishy-washy; the so-called traditional kafenío has long since ditched Greek coffee
for cappuccino and traditional sweets for "ice-cream special". There are, however, several acceptable **tavernas** on the platía, of which *Tou Apostoli to Koutouki* is most popular with locals, and a large **hotel** – *Hotel Ano Mera* (☎0289/71 276; ⑥). The red-roofed
church near the square is the sixteenth-century **monastery of Panayía Tourlianí**,
where a collection of Cretan icons and the unusual eighteenth-century marble baptismal font are worth seeing. It's not far, either, to the late twelfth-century **Paleokástro
monastery** (also known as Dárga), just north of the village, in a magnificent green setting on an otherwise barren slope. To the northwest are more of the same dry and
wind-buffeted landscapes, though they do provide some enjoyable, rocky walking with
expansive views across to neighbouring islands – head to Áyios Stéfanos for buses back
to the harbour.

Delos (Dhílos)

The remains of **ancient Delos**, Pindar's "unmoved marvel of the wide world",
though skeletal and swarming now with lizards and tourists, give some idea of the
past grandeur of this sacred isle a few sea-miles west of Mýkonos. The ancient town
lies on the west coast on flat, sometimes marshy ground which rises in the south to
Mount Kýnthos. From the summit – an easy walk – there's a magnificent view
across the Cyclades: the name of the archipelago means "those [islands] around
[Delos]".

The first excursion boats to Delos leave Mýkonos daily at 8.30am (1900dr round
trip), except Mondays when the site is closed. You have to return on the same boat but
in season each does the trip several times and you can choose what time you leave. The
last return is usually about 3pm, and you'll need to arrive early if you want to make a
thorough tour of the site. In season a daily kaïki makes return trips from the beaches
(3000dr) with pick-up points at Platýs Yialós and Órnos, but only allows you three hours
on the island. It's a good idea to bring your own food and drink as the tourist pavilion's
snack bar is a rip-off.

Some history

Delos's ancient fame was due to the fact that Leto gave birth to the divine twins
Artemis and Apollo on the island, although its fine harbour and central position did
nothing to hamper development. When the Ionians colonized the island around 1000
BC it was already a cult centre, and by the seventh century BC it had become the
commercial and religious centre of the **Amphictionic League**. Unfortunately Delos
also attracted the attention of Athens, which sought dominion over this prestigious
island; the wealth of the Delian Confederacy, founded after the Persian Wars to protect the Aegean cities, was harnessed to Athenian ends, and for a while Athens controlled the Sanctuary of Apollo. Athenian attempts to "purify" the island began with a
decree that no one could die or give birth on Delos – the sick and the pregnant were
taken to the islet of Rheneia – and culminated in the simple expedient of banishing
the native population.

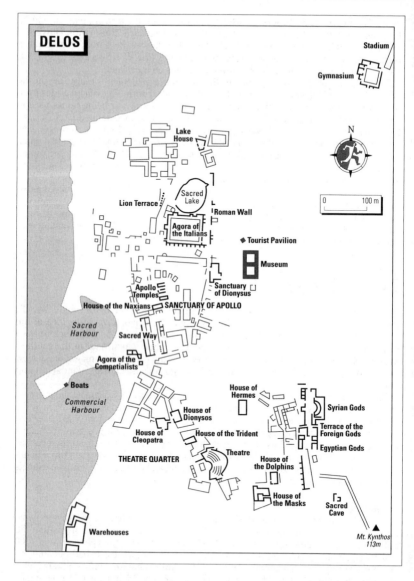

DELOS

Stadium

Gymnasium

Lake House

Sacred Lake

Lion Terrace

Roman Wall

Agora of the Italians

N

0   100 m

Tourist Pavilion

Museum

Apollo Temples

Sanctuary of Dionysus

House of the Naxians   SANCTUARY OF APOLLO

Sacred Harbour

Sacred Way

Agora of the Competialists

Boats

Commercial Harbour

House of Hermes

House of Dionysos

House of the Trident

House of Cleopatra

THEATRE QUARTER   Theatre

House of the Dolphins

House of the Masks

Syrian Gods

Terrace of the Foreign Gods

Egyptian Gods

Sacred Cave

Warehouses

Mt. Kynthos 113m

Delos reached its peak in the third and second centuries BC, after being declared a free port by its Roman overlords. In the end, though, its undefended wealth brought ruin: first Mithridates (88 BC), then Athenodorus (69 BC) plundered the treasures and the island never recovered. By the third century AD, Athens could not even sell it, and for centuries, every passing seafarer stopped to collect a few prizes.

The site

Tues–Sun 8.30am–3pm; 1500dr.

As you land, the Sacred Harbour is on your left, the Commercial Harbour on your right; and straight ahead is the **Agora of the Competialists**. Competialists were Roman merchants or freed slaves who worshipped the Lares Competales, the guardian spirits of crossroads; offerings to Hermes would once have been placed in the middle of the *agora*, their position now marked by a round and a square base. The **Sacred Way** leads north from the far left corner; it used to be lined with statues and the grandiose monuments of rival kings. Along it you reach three marble steps which lead into the **Sanctuary of Apollo**; much was lavished on the god, but the forest of offerings has been plundered over the years. On your left is the Stoa of the Naxians, while against the north wall of the House of the Naxians, to the right, a huge statue of Apollo stood in ancient times. In 417 BC the Athenian general Nikias led a procession of priests across a bridge of boats from Rheneia to dedicate a bronze palm tree; when it was later blown over in a gale it took the statue with it. Three **Temples of Apollo** stand in a row to the right along the Sacred Way: the Delian Temple, that of the Athenians and the Porinos Naos, the earliest of them, dating from the sixth century BC. To the east towards the museum you pass the **Sanctuary of Dionysos**, with its marble phalluses on tall pillars.

The best finds from the site are in Athens, but the **museum** still justifies a visit. To the north stands a wall that marks the site of the **Sacred Lake** where Leto gave birth, clinging to a palm tree. Guarding it are the superb **lions**, their lean bodies masterfully executed by Naxians in the seventh century BC; of the original nine, three have disappeared and one adorns the Arsenale at Venice. On the other side of the lake is the City Wall, built in 69 BC – too late to protect the treasures.

Set out in the other direction from the Agora of the Competialists and you enter the residential area, known as the **Theatre Quarter**. Many of the walls and roads remain, but there is none of the domestic detail that brings such sites to life. Some colour is added by the mosaics: one in the **House of the Trident**, and better ones in the **House of the Masks**, most notably a vigorous portrayal of Dionysos riding on a panther's back. The **theatre** itself seated 5500 spectators, and, though much ravaged, offers some fine views. Behind the theatre, a path leads past the **Sanctuaries of the Foreign Gods** and up **Mount Kýnthos** for more panoramic sightseeing.

Sýros

Don't be put off by first impressions of **Sýros**. From the ferry it looks grimly industrial, but away from the Neórion shipyard things improve quickly. Very much a working island with only a very recent history of tourism, it is probably the most Greek of the Cyclades; there are few holiday trappings and what there is exists for the benefit of the locals. You probably won't find, as Herman Melville did when he visited in 1856, shops full of ". . . fez-caps, swords, tobacco, shawls, pistols, and orient finery . . .", but you're still likely to appreciate Sýros as a refreshing change from the beautiful people. Of course, outsiders do come to the island; in fact there's a thriving permanent foreign community, and the beaches are hardly undeveloped, but everywhere there's the underlying assumption that you're a guest of an inherently private people.

Ermoúpoli

The main town and port of **ERMOÚPOLI** was founded during the War of Independence by refugees from Psará and Híos, becoming Greece's chief port in the

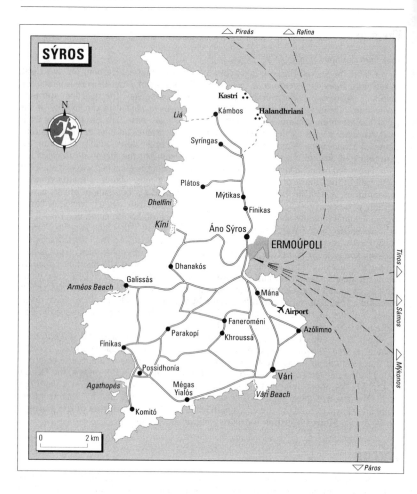

nineteenth century. Although Pireás outstripped it long ago, Ermoúpoli is still the largest town in the Cyclades, and the archipelago's capital. Medieval Sýros was largely a Catholic island, but an influx of Orthodox refugees during the War of Independence created two distinct communities; now almost equal in numbers, the two groups today still live in their respective quarters, occupying two hills that rise up from the sea.

Ermoúpoli itself, the **lower town**, is worth at least a night's stay, with grandiose buildings a relic of its days as a major port. Between the harbour and **Áyios Nikólaos**, the fine Orthodox church to the north, you can stroll through its faded splendour. The **Apollon Theatre** is a copy of La Scala in Milan and once presented a regular Italian opera season; today local theatre and music groups put it to good use. The long, central **Platía Miaoúli** is named after an admiral of the revolution whose statue stands there, and in the evenings the population parades in front of its arcaded kafenía, while the children ride the mechanical animals. Up the stairs to the left of the town hall is the small **Archeological Museum** (Tues–Sun 8.30am–3pm; free), with three rooms of finds from Sýros, Páros and Amorgós. To the left of the clocktower more stairs climb up to **Vrondádho**, the hill that hosts the Orthodox quarter. The wonderful church of the **Anástassi** stands atop the hill, with its domed roof and great views over Tínos and Mýkonos – if it's locked, ask for the key at the priest's house.

On the taller hill to the left is the intricate medieval quarter of **Áno Sýros**, with a clutch of Catholic churches below the cathedral of St George. There are fine views of the town below, and, close by, the **Cappuchin monastery of St Jean**, founded in 1535 to do duty as a poorhouse. It takes about 45 minutes of tough walking up Omírou to reach this quarter, passing the Orthodox and Catholic cemeteries on the way – the former full of grand shipowners' mausoleums, the latter with more modest monuments and French and Italian inscriptions (you can halve the walking time by taking a short cut on to the stair-street named Andhréa Kárga, part of the way along). Once up here it's worth visiting the local art and church exhibitions at the Vamvákeris **museum** (daily 10.30am–1pm & 7–10pm; 500dr), and the Byzantine museum attached to the monastery.

Arrival, facilities and accommodation

The **quayside** is still busy, though nowadays it deals with more tourist than industrial shipping; Sýros is a major crossover point on the ferry-boat routes. Also down here is the **bus station**, along with the **tourist police** and several **bike rental** places, of which Apollon on Andíparou, one block behind the seafront, is recommended. Between them shops sell the *loukoúmia* (Turkish delight) and *halvadhópita* (sweetmeat pie) for which the island is famed. **Odhós Híou**, the market street, is especially lively on Saturday when people come in from the surrounding countryside to sell fresh produce.

Keeping step with a growing level of tourism, **rooms** have improved in quality and number in recent years; many are in garishly decorated, if crumbling, Neoclassical mansions. Good choices include *Kastro* rooms, Kalomenopóulou 12 (☎0281/88 064; ③), *Dream*, on the seafront near the bus station (☎0281/84 356; ④), and *Paradise*, Omírou 3 (☎0281/83 204; ④). Particularly recommended are the traditionally decorated rooms of *Villa Nefeli*, Parou 21 (☎0281/87 076; ③), and *Sea Colours Apartments* (☎0281/88 716; ④), located at Áyios Nikólaos beach, a quieter corner of town. A notch up in price and quality is the well-sited *Hotel Hermes* (☎0281/83 011; ⑥) on Platía Kanári, overlooking the port or, for a slice of good-value opulence, try the *Xenon Ipatias* (☎0281/83 575; ④), beyond Áyios Nikólaos and above *Sea Colours Apartments*. Team Work agency (☎0281/83 400, *teamwork@otenet.gr*), on the waterfront, is a useful source of information and able to help with your accommodation needs. Alternatively, you can try the kiosk belonging to the Rooms and Apartments Association of Sýros (☎0281/87 360) along the waterfront – turn right after disembarking.

Eating, drinking and nightlife

The most authentic and reasonably priced of the harbour **eateries** are the *Yiannena Estiatorio* on Platía Kanári and the popular *Psaropoula Ouzeri*. On or near Platía Miaoúli, the *Manousos* taverna is a good traditional place, as is *Archontariki*. *Ambix*, near where the ferries dock, is a good Italian restaurant; for snacks resist the neon glare of the popular *Goody's* hamburger-joint and have a *yíros* at the more authentic *Fresh Corner* nearby. In Áno Sýros, the *Thea* taverna, signposted in Greek from the car park, is fine and affords the views its name would suggest; *Iy Piatsa* ouzerí is also worth a try.

Incidentally, Sýros still honours its contribution to the development of **rembétika**; *bouzoúki*-great Markos Vamvakaris hailed from here, and a platía in Áno Sýros has been named after him. **Taverna-clubs** such as *Xanthomalis* (up in Áno Sýros) with music on weekends, now take their place beside a batch of more conventional disco-clubs down near the Apollon Theatre. There are several other (often expensive) *bouzoúki* bars scattered around the island, mostly strung along routes to beach resorts. The seafront has a rash of lively **bars**: the *Cotton Club* café seems to be the focal point of activity in this area. There's a more interesting cluster around the Platía Miaoúli: *Clearchos* piano bar is rather smooth, *Agora* has imaginative decor, good DJs and a lovely garden, and *Piramatiko* is heaving, playing a loud and varied mix from indie to house. The big

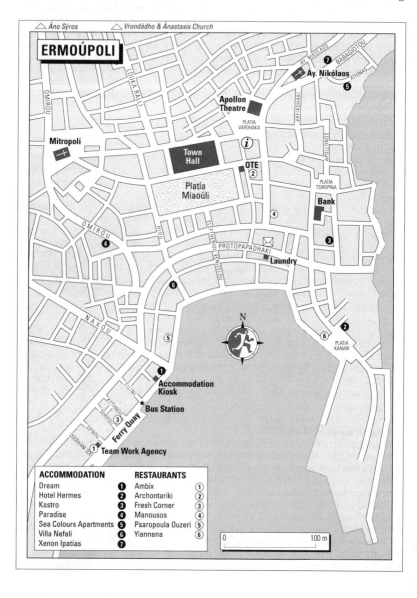

ERMOÚPOLI

△ Áno Sýros   △ Vrondádho & Ánastasis Church

Áy. Nikólaos

Apollon
Theatre

PLATIA
VARDHAKA

Mitropolí

i

Town
Hall

OTE

PLATIA
TSIROPINA

Platía
Miaoúli

Bank

PROTOPAPADHAKI

Laundry

N

PLATIA
KANARI

Accommodation
Kiosk

Bus Station

Ferry Quay

Team Work Agency

ACCOMMODATION		RESTAURANTS	
Dream	❶	Ambix	①
Hotel Hermes	❷	Archontariki	②
Kastro	❸	Fresh Corner	③
Paradise	❹	Manousos	④
Sea Colours Apartments	❺	Psaropoula Ouzeri	⑤
Villa Nefeli	❻	Yiannena	⑥
Xenon Ipatias	❼		

0   100 m

venue for night-owls is *Rodo*, a huge club in a converted warehouse out past the Neórión shipyard opposite the turning to Vári. Finally, the A*egean Casino* on the seafront features live music at the restaurant, and is open till 6am for those who have money to burn (and are sufficiently well-dressed).

Around the island

The main loop road (to Gallissás, Fínikas, Mégas Yialós, Vári and back), and the road west to Kíni, are good: **buses** ply the routes hourly in season, and run until late. Elsewhere, expect potholes – especially to the **north** where the land is barren and high, with few villages. The main route north from Áno Sýros has improved and is quite easily negotiable by bike; en route, the village of **Mýtikas** has a decent taverna just off the road. A few kilometres further on the road forks, with the left turn leading, after another left, to the small settlement of **Syríngas**, where there's an interesting cave to explore. Straight on leads to **Kámbos**, from where a path leads down to Liá Beach; the right fork eventually descends to the northeast coast after passing an excellent kafenío, *Sgouros*, with views across to Tínos.

The well-trodden route **south** offers more tangible and accessible rewards. Closest to the capital, fifteen minutes away by bus, is the twin-beach coastal settlement of **KÍNI**. Good accommodation includes the *Sunset Hotel* (☎0281/71 211; ④–⑤), with the excellent *Zalounis* taverna just below and, just away from the seafront, the *Hotel Elpida* (☎0281/71 224; ③). **GALISSÁS**, a few kilometres south, but reached by different buses, has developed along different lines. Fundamentally an agricultural village, it's been taken over since the mid-1980s by backpackers attracted by the island's only **campsites** (both have good facilities and send minibuses to all boats, but *Camping Yianna* (☎0281/42 418) has the advantage over the newer *Two Hearts* (☎0281/42 052) of being closer to the sea) and a very pretty beach, more protected than Kíni's. This new-found popularity has created a surplus of unaesthetic **rooms**, which at least makes bargaining possible, and six bona fide hotels, of which the cheapest are *Petros* and *Semiramis* (☎0281/42 067; both ③), though the *Benois* (☎0281/42 833; ⑤) is decent value, with buffet breakfast included. Amongst the many **eating** choices, *To Iliovasilema*, next to *Benois*, is an acceptable fish taverna, and *Cavos*, part of a luxury complex, the *Dolphin Bay Hotel* (☎0281/42 924, *dolphinbay@syr.forthnet.gr*, ⑥), has great views overlooking the bay. Galissás's identity crisis is exemplified by the proximity of bemused, grazing dairy cattle, a heavy-metal music pub and upmarket handicrafts shops. Still, the people are welcoming, and if you feel the urge to escape, you can rent a moped, or walk ten minutes past the headland to the nudist beach of **Arméos**, where there's fresh spring water. Note that buses out are erratically routed; to be sure of making your connection you must wait at the high-road stop, not down by the beach. **Dhelfíni** just to the north is also a fine beach, though it's slowly falling prey to the developers under the translated name of Dolphin Bay (not to be confused with aforementioned hotel).

A pleasant forty-minute walk or a ten-minute bus ride south from Galissás brings you to the more mainstream resort of **FÍNIKAS**, purported to have been settled originally by the Phoenicians (although an alternative derivation could be from *fínikas*, meaning "palm tree" in Greek). The beach is narrow and gritty, right next to the road but protected to some extent by a row of tamarisk trees; the pick of the hotels is the *Cyclades* (☎0281/42 255; ④), and there is an acceptable restaurant just in front, while the *Amaryllis* rooms (☎0281/42 894; ④) are slightly cheaper. The fish taverna *O Barpalias* on the seafront is recommended.

Fínikas is separated by a tiny headland from its neighbour **POSSIDHONÍA** (or Delagrazzia), a nicer spot with some idiosyncratically ornate mansions and a bright blue church right on the edge of the village. It's worth walking ten minutes further south, past the naval yacht club and its patrol boat to **Agathopés**, with a sandy beach and a little islet just offshore. Komitó, at the end of the unpaved track leading south from Agathopés, is nothing more than a stony beach fronting an olive grove. **Accommodation** around Possidhonía ranges from the smart *Possidonion* hotel (☎0281/42 100; ④) on the seafront to basic rooms inland, while *Meltémi* is a good seafood taverna.

The road swings east to **MÉGAS YIALÓS**, a small resort below a hillside festooned with brightly painted houses. The long, narrow beach is lined with shady trees and there are pedal boats for hire. Of the **room** set-ups, *Mike and Bill's* (☎0281/43 531; ③) is a reasonable deal, and the pricier *Alexandra Hotel* (☎0281/42 540; ⑥), on the bay, enjoys lovely views. **VÁRI** is more – though not much more – of a town, with its own small fishing fleet. Beach-goers are in a goldfish bowl, as it were, with tavernas and **rooms** looming right overhead, but it is the most sheltered of the island's bays, something to remember when the *meltémi* is up. The *Kamelo* hotel (☎0281/61 217; ⑤) provides the best value and has TV in all the rooms. The adjacent cove of **AKHLÁDHI** is far more pleasant and boasts two small good-value hotels, including the *Emily* (☎0281/61400; ④), on the seafront, and has one taverna.

Páros and Andíparos

Gently and undramatically furled around the single peak of Profítis Ilías, **Páros** has a little of everything one expects from a Greek island – old villages, monasteries, fishing harbours, a labyrinthine capital – and some of the best nightlife and beaches in the Aegean. Parikía, the hóra, is the major hub of inter-island ferry services, so that if you wait long enough you can get to just about any island in the Aegean. However, the island is almost as touristy and expensive as Mýkonos: in peak season, it's touch-and-go when it comes to finding rooms and beach space. At such times, the attractive inland settlements or the satellite island of **Andíparos** handle the overflow. Incidentally, the August 15 festival here is one of the best such observances in Greece, with a parade of flare-lit fishing boats and fireworks delighting as many Greeks as foreigners, but it's a real feat to secure accommodation around this time.

Parikía and around

PARIKÍA sets the tone architecturally for the rest of Páros, with its ranks of typically Cycladic white houses punctuated by the occasional Venetian-style building and church domes. But all is awash in a constant stream of ferry passengers, and the town is relentlessly commercial. The busy waterfront is jam-packed with bars, restaurants, hotels and ticket agencies, while the maze of houses in the older quarter behind, designed to baffle both wind and pirates, has surrendered to an onslaught of chi-chi boutiques.

Just beyond the central clutter, though, the town has one of the most architecturally interesting churches in the Aegean – the **Ekatondapilianí**, or "The One-Hundred-Gated". What's visible today was designed and supervised by Isidore of Miletus in the sixth century, but construction was actually carried out by his pupil Ignatius. It was so beautiful on completion that the master, consumed with jealousy, is said to have grappled with his apprentice on the rooftop, flinging them both to their deaths. They are portrayed kneeling at the column bases across the courtyard, the old master tugging at his beard in repentance and his rueful pupil clutching a broken head. The church was substantially altered after a severe earthquake in the eighth century, but its essentially Byzantine aspect remains, its shape an imperfect Greek cross. Enclosed by a great wall to protect its icons from pirates, it is in fact three interlocking churches; the oldest, the chapel of Áyios Nikólaos to the left of the apse, is an adaptation of a pagan

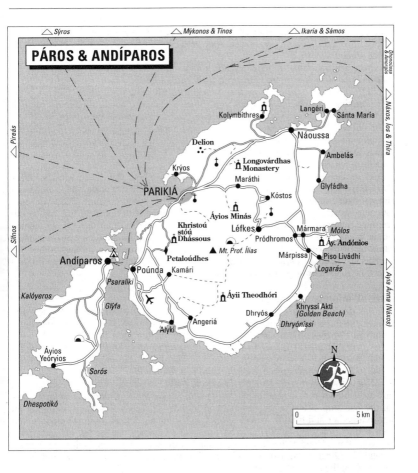

building dating from the early fourth century BC. To the right of the courtyard, the **Byzantine Museum** (daily 9am–1pm & 5.30–9.30pm; 500dr, free on Tues) displays a collection of icons. Behind Ekatondapilianí, the **Archeological Museum** (Tues–Sun 8am–2.30pm; 500dr) has a fair collection of antique bits and pieces, its prize exhibits being a fifth-century winged Nike and a piece of the *Parian Chronicle*, a social and cultural history of Greece up to 264 BC engraved in marble.

These two sights apart, the real attraction of Parikía is simply to wander the town itself. Arcaded lanes lead past Venetian-influenced villas, traditional island dwellings and the three ornate wall-fountains donated by the Mavroyénnis family in the eighteenth century. The town culminates in a seaward Venetian **kástro**, whose surviving east wall incorporates a fifth-century BC round tower and is constructed using masonry pillaged from a temple of Athena. Part of the base of the temple is still visible next to the beautiful, arcaded church of Áyios Konstandínos and Áyia Eléni which crowns the highest point, from where the fortified hill drops sharply to the quay in a series of hanging gardens.

If you're staying in town, you'll want to get out into the surroundings at some stage, if only to the beach. The most rewarding **excursion** is the hour's walk along the road starting just past the museum up to **Áyii Anáryiri** monastery. Perched on the bluff above town, this makes a great picnic spot, with cypress groves, a gushing fountain and some splendid views.

There are **beaches** immediately north and south of the harbour, though none are particularly attractive when compared with Páros's best. In fact, you might prefer to avoid the northern stretch altogether; heading **south** along the asphalt road is a better bet. The first unsurfaced side-track you come to leads to a small, sheltered beach; fifteen minutes further on is **PARASPÓROS**, with a reasonable **campsite** (☎0284/21 100) and beach near the remains of an ancient temple to Asklepios (see p.670), the god of medicine and son of Apollo. Continuing for 45 minutes (or a short hop by bus) brings you to arguably the best of the bunch, **AYÍA IRÍNI**, with good sand and a taverna next to a farm and shady olive grove.

Off in the same direction, but a much longer two-hour haul each way, is **PETA-LOÚDHES**, the so-called "Valley of the Butterflies", a walled-in oasis where millions of Jersey tiger moths perch on the foliage during early summer (June–Sept 9am–8pm; 400dr). The trip pays more dividends when combined with a visit to the eighteenth-century nunnery of **Khristoú stoú Dhássous**, at the crest of a ridge twenty minutes to the north. Only women are allowed in the sanctuary, although men can get as far as the courtyard. The succession of narrow drives and donkey paths linking both places begins just south of Parikía. Petaloúdhes can be reached from Parikía by bus (in summer), by moped or on an overpriced excursion by mule.

Arrival, information and accommodation

Ferries **dock** in Parikía by the windmill; the **bus stop** is 100m or so to the left. Bus routes extend to Náoussa in the north, Poúnda (for Andíparos) in the west, Alikí in the south and Dhrýos on the island's east coast (with another very useful service between Dhrýos and Náoussa). Buses to Náoussa carry on running hourly through the night, while other services stop around midnight. The **airport** is around 12km from town, close to Alykí – from where ten daily buses run to Parikía.

Most of the island is flat enough for bicycle rides, but mopeds are more common and are available for rent at several places in town; Forget-Me-Not, along the seafront west of the bus stop, offers a professional and friendly service. Polos Tours is one of the more together and friendly **travel agencies**, issuing air tickets when Olympic is shut, and acting as agents for virtually all the boats. Luggage can be left at Santorineos Travel, 50m beyond Polos Tours (heading south along the front). Olympic Airways itself is at the far end of Odhós Probóna, while the **tourist police** occupy a building at the back of the seafront square.

As for **accommodation**, Parikía is a pleasant and central base, but absolutely mobbed in summer. You'll be met off the ferry by locals offering rooms, even at the most unlikely hours; avoid persistent offers of rooms or hotels to the north as they'll invariably be a long walk away from town. One of the best deals to be had is at the *Pension Festos* on the back streets inland, managed by young Brits (☎0284/21 635; ① per person); it has beds in shared rooms, making it a good choice for single travellers. Another budget option includes *Kouala Camping* (☎0284/22081), along the seafront west of the bus stop, with good facilities, if a little noisy. Popular **hotels** include *Dina*, (☎0284/21 325; ④), near Platía Veléntza, and *Hotel Oasis* (☎0284/21 227; ④), on Prombóna, very close to the harbour. *Hotel Kypreou* (☎0284/21 383; ⑤) is a small family-run hotel on Prombóna, which, like *Oasis*, stays open through the winter. The smart, family-run *Hotel Argonauta* (☎0284/21440; ④), close to the National Bank, is highly recommended, and also has a pleasant restaurant. Irini Triandafilou (☎0284/23 022; ③) has a few basic rooms within the kástro, some with good sea views, and *Argonauta Appartments* (☎0284/23888; ④) have some smart accommodation in the Livádhia area in the north of town.

Eating, drinking and nightlife

Many Parikía **tavernas** are run by outsiders operating under municipal concession, so year-to-year variation in proprietors and quality is marked. However, the following seem to be long-established and/or good-value outfits. Rock-bottom is the *Koutouki Thanasis*, which serves oven food for locals and bold tourists and lurks in a back street to the left of the town hall. Also in the picturesque backstreets are *Kyriakos Place* on Lohágou Grivári, which has seats out under a fine tree, and the *Garden of Dionysos*. In the exotic department, *May Tey* serves average Chinese food at moderate markup, while Italian dishes can be found at *La Barca Rossa* on the seafront or *Cavo D'Oro* in the Livádhia area. *Trata* behind the post office is recommended for fish, and *Le Coq Fou*, on the same road as *Dionysos*, is a good breakfasting spot, serving excellent crepes. There are a couple of specialist eating places: *The Happy Green Cow*, a friendly café with vegetarian and vegan food behind the National Bank, and *Wired Café* (*stnicolas@bigfoot.com*), an Internet café, on the market street running behind the kástro (2400dr per hour).

Parikía has a wealth of **pubs**, **bars** and low-key **discos**, not as pretentious as those on Mýkonos or as raucous as the scene on Íos, but certainly everything in between. The most popular cocktail bars extend along the seafront, all tucked into a series of open squares and offering competing but staggered (no pun intended) "Happy Hours", so that you can drink cheaply for much of the evening. A rowdy crowd favours the conspicuous *Saloon D'Or*, while the *Pirate Bar* features jazz and blues, and *Havanna* nearby plays a lively Latin mix. *Evinos* and *Pebbles* are more genteel, the latter pricey but with good sunset views and the occasional live gig. The "theme" pubs are a bit rough and ready for some: most outrageous is the *Dubliner Complex*, comprising four bars, a snack section, disco and seating area.

Finally, a thriving cultural centre, *Arhilohos* (near Ekatondapilianí) caters mostly to locals, with occasional **film** screenings – there are also two open-air cinemas, *Neo Rex* and *Paros*, where foreign films are shown in season.

Náoussa and around

The second port of Páros, **NÁOUSSA** was once an unspoiled, sparkling labyrinth of winding, narrow alleys and simple Cycladic houses. Alas, a rash of modern concrete hotels and attendant trappings have all but swamped its character, though down at the small harbour, fishermen still tenderize octopuses by thrashing them against the walls. The local festivals – an annual Fish and Wine Festival on July 2, and an August 23 shindig celebrating an old naval victory over the Turks – are also still celebrated with enthusiasm; the latter tends to be brought forward to coincide with the August 15 festival of the Panayía. Most people are here for the local beaches (see p.530) and the relaxed nightlife; there's really only one sight, a **museum** (daily 9am–1.30pm & 7–9pm; free) in the monastery of Áyios Athanásios, with an interesting collection of Byzantine and post-Byzantine icons from the churches and monasteries around Náoussa.

Despite encroaching development, the town is noted for its nearby beaches and is a good place to head for as soon as you reach Páros. **Rooms** are marginally cheaper here than in Parikía; track them down with the help of the **tourist office** which is just over the bridge, west from the harbour. The *Sea House* (☎0284/52 198; ④) on the rocks above Pipéri beach was the first place in Náoussa to let rooms and has one of the best locations, and the *Manis Inn* (☎0284/51 744, *manisinn@otenet.gr*, ⑥) is an upmarket hotel with pool behind Pipéri Beach; out of season you should haggle for reduced prices at the *Madaki* (☎0284/51 475; ④), just over the bridge west of the harbour, and at the basic, but well-located *Stella* (☎0284/52 198; ④), inland, behind the old harbour. There are two **campsites** in the vicinity: the relaxed and friendly *Naoussa* (☎0284/51 565), out of town towards Kolymbíthres (see p.530), and the newer *Surfing Beach*

(☎0284/51 013) at Sánta Mariá, northeast of Náoussa; both run courtesy minibuses to and from Parikía.

Most of the harbour **tavernas** are surprisingly good, specializing in fresh fish and seafood; *O Barbarossas* ouzerí is the best of these. There are more places to eat along the main road leading inland from just beside the little bridge over the canal. *Glaros*, with good barrelled unresinated wine, and the *Vengera* opposite stay open until the early morning hours. **Bars** cluster around the old harbour: *Linardo* and *Agosta* play dance music, *Camaron* plays mainly Greek music, and *Café Sante*, inland, off the main drag, is a cool spot playing easy-listening, and mellower dance grooves. There are several big clubs around the bus station, including *Slalom* and *Nostos,* popular with a younger late-night crowd.

Local beaches

Pipéri Beach is couple of minutes' walk west of Náoussa's harbour; there are other good-to-excellent beaches within walking distance, and a summer kaïki service to connect them. To the west, an hour's tramp brings you to **Kolymbíthres** (Basins), where there are three tavernas and the wind- and sea-sculpted rock formations from which the place draws its name. A few minutes beyond, **Monastíri** Beach, below the abandoned Pródhromos monastery, is similarly attractive, and partly nudist. If you go up the hill after Monastíri onto the rocky promontory, the island gradually shelves into the sea via a series of flattish rock ledges, making a fine secluded spot for diving and snorkelling, as long as the sea is calm. Go northeast and the sands are better still, the barren headland spangled with good surfing beaches. **Langéri** is backed by dunes; the best surfing is at **Sánta María**, a trendy beach connected with Náoussa by road, which also has a couple of tavernas, including the pleasant *Aristofanes*; and **Platiá Ámmos** perches on the northeastern tip of the island.

The northeast coast and inland

AMBELÁS hamlet marks the start of a longer trek down the **east coast**. Ambelás itself has a good beach, a small taverna and some rooms and hotels, of which the *Hotel Christiana* (☎0284/51 573; ⑤) is good value, with great fresh fish, local wine in the restaurant and extremely friendly proprietors. From here a rough track leads south, passing several undeveloped stretches on the way: after about an hour you reach **Mólos Beach**, impressive and not particularly crowded. **MÁRMARA**, twenty minutes further on, has rooms to let and makes an attractive place to stay, though the marble that the village is built from and named after has largely been whitewashed over.

If Mármara doesn't appeal, then serene **MÁRPISSA**, just to the south, might – a maze of winding alleys and ageing archways overhung by floral balconies, all clinging precariously to the hillside. There are rooms here too: *Hotel Afendakis* (☎0284/41141; ④) is clean and modern, and you can while away a spare hour climbing up the conical Kéfalos hill, on whose fortified summit the last Venetian lords of Páros were overpowered by the Ottomans in 1537. Today the monastery of **Áyios Andónios** occupies the site, but the grounds are locked; to enjoy the views over eastern Páros and the straits of Náxos fully, pick up the key from the priest in Máripissa before setting out (ask in the mini-market of his whereabouts). On the shore nearby, **PÍSO LIVÁDHI** was once a quiet fishing village, but has been ruined by rampant construction in the name of package tourism. The main reason to visit is to catch a (seasonal) kaïki to Ayía Ánna on Náxos; if you need to **stay** overnight here, *Hotel Andromache* (☎0284/41 387 or 42 565; ⑥) is a good place behind the beach, as is the more reasonably priced *Akteon Hotel* (☎0284/ 41873; ④) at **Logarás Beach** next door. The *Captain Kafkis Camping* (☎0284/41 479) – a small quiet site – is out of town on the road up to Márpissa.

Inland

The road runs west from Píso Livádhi back to the capital. A medieval flagstoned path once linked both sides of the island, and parts of it survive in the east between Mármara and the villages around Léfkes. **PRÓDHROMOS**, encountered first, is an old fortified farming settlement with defensive walls girding its nearby monastery, while **LÉFKES** itself, an hour up the track, is perhaps the most beautiful and unspoiled settlement on Páros. The town flourished from the seventeenth century on, its population swollen by refugees fleeing from coastal piracy; indeed it was the island's hóra during most of the Ottoman period. Léfkes' marbled alleyways and amphitheatrical setting are unparalleled and, despite the few rooms, a disco (*Akrovatis*), a taverna on the outskirts and the presence of two oversized hotels – the *Hotel Pantheon* (☎0284/41 646; ④), a large 1970s hotel at the top of the village, and *Lefkes Village* (☎0284/41 827 or 42 398; ⑥), a beautiful hotel on the outskirts, with stunning views – the area around the main square has steadfastly resisted change; the central kafenío and bakery observe their siestas religiously.

Thirty minutes further on, through olive groves, is **KÓSTOS**, a simple village and a good place for lunch in a taverna. Any traces of path disappear at **MARÁTHI**, on the site of the ancient marble quarries which once supplied much of Europe. Considered second only to Carrara marble, the last slabs were mined here by the French in the nineteenth century for Napoleon's tomb. From Maráthi, it's easy enough to pick up the bus on to Parikía, but if you want to continue hiking, strike south for the monastery of **Áyios Minás**, twenty minutes away. Various Classical and Byzantine masonry fragments are worked into the walls of this sixteenth-century foundation, and the friendly custodians can put you on the right path up to the convent of **Thapsaná**. From here, other paths lead either back to Parikía (two hours altogether from Áyios Minás), or on up to the island's summit for the last word in views over the Cyclades.

The south of the island

There's little to stop for south of Parikía until **POÚNDA**, 6km away, and then only to catch the ferry to Andíparos (see below). What used to be a sleepy hamlet is now a concrete jungle, and neighbouring **ALYKÍ** appears to be permanently under construction. The **airport** is close by, making for lots of unwelcome noise; the sole redeeming feature is an excellent beachside restaurant, by the large tamarisk tree. The end of the southern bus route is at Angeriá, about 3km inland of which is the **convent of Áyii Theodhóri**. Its nuns specialize in weaving locally commissioned articles and are further distinguished as *paleomeroloyítes*, or old-calendarites, meaning that they follow the medieval Orthodox (Julian) calendar, rather than the Gregorian one.

Working your way around the **south coast**, there are two routes east to Dhryós. Either retrace your steps to Angeriá and follow the (slightly inland) coastal road, which skirts a succession of isolated coves and small beaches; or keep on across the foothills from Áyii Theodhóri – a shorter walk. Aside from an abundant water supply (including a duck pond) and surrounding orchards, **DHRYÓS** village is mostly modern and characterless, lacking even a well-defined platía. Follow the lane signed "Dhryós Beach", however, and things improve a bit.

Between here and Píso Livádhi to the north are several sandy coves – Khryssí Aktí (Golden Beach), Tzirdhákia, Mezádha, Poúnda and Logarás – prone to pummelling by the *meltémi*, yet all favoured to varying degrees by campers and by windsurfers making a virtue out of necessity. **KHRYSSÍ AKTÍ** is now thoroughly overrun with tavernas, room complexes and the whole range of watersports; there are also tavernas at Logarás, but other facilities are concentrated in Dhryós, which is still the focal point of this part of the island.

Andíparos

Andíparos was once quiet and unspoiled, but now the secret is definitely out. The waterfront is lined with new hotels and apartments, and in high season it can be full of the same young, international crowd you were hoping to leave behind on Páros. It has, however, kept its friendly small island atmosphere and still has a lot going for it, including good sandy beaches and an impressive cave, and the rooms and hotels are less expensive than on Páros.

Most of the population of eight hundred live in the large low-lying northern **village**, across the narrow straits from Páros, the new development on the outskirts concealing an attractive traditional settlement around the kástro. A long, flagstoned pedestrian street forms its backbone, leading from the jetty to the Cycladic houses around the outer wall of the kástro, which was built by Leonardo Loredano in the 1440s as a fortified settlement safe from pirate raids: the Loredano coat of arms can still be seen on a house in the courtyard. The only way into the courtyard is through a pointed archway from the platía, where several cafés are shaded by a giant eucalyptus. Inside, more whitewashed houses surround two churches and a cistern built into the surviving base of the central tower.

Andíparos's **beaches** begin right outside town: **Psaralíki** just to the south with golden sand and tamarisks for shade is much better than Sifnéïko (aka "Sunset") on the opposite side of the island. Villa development is starting to follow the newly paved road down the east coast, but has yet to get out of hand. **Glýfa**, 4km down, is another good beach and, further south, **Sorós** has rooms and tavernas. On the west coast there are some fine small sandy coves at Áyios Yeóryios, the end of the road, and a long stretch of sand at Kalóyeros. Kaïki make daily trips round the island and, less frequently, to the uninhabited islet of Dhespotikó, opposite Áyios Yeóryios.

The great **cave** (summer daily 10.45am–3.45pm; 600dr) in the south of the island is the chief attraction for day-trippers. In these eerie chambers the Marquis de Nointel, Louis XIV's ambassador to Constantinople, celebrated Christmas Mass in 1673 while a retinue of five hundred, including painters, pirates, Jesuits and Turks, looked on; at the exact moment of midnight explosives were detonated to emphasize the enormity of the event. Although electric light and cement steps have diminished its mystery and grandeur, the cave remains impressive. Tour buses (700dr return) and public buses (220dr one-way) run from the port every hour in season; out of season, bus services and opening hours are reduced and in winter you'll have to fetch the key for the cave from the mayor or village council (☎0284 61 218).

Practicalities

To get here, you have a choice of **boats** from Parikía (hourly; 40min), arriving at the jetty opposite the main street, or the car ferry from Poúnda (half-hourly; 10min), arriving 150m to the south. In season there's no need to use the car ferry unless you take a moped over or miss the last boat back to Parikía; the car ferry keeps running until midnight. The service to Parikía is reduced out of season and runs only once a day in winter.

There are plenty of **hotels** along the waterfront, including *Anargyros* (☎0284/61 204; ③), which has good, basic rooms. More upmarket places to the north of the jetty include *Mantalena* (☎0284/61 206; ④) and *Artemis* (☎0284/61 460; ④), while inland there are some cheaper rooms as well as the *Hotel Galini* (☎0284/61 420; ④) to the left of the main street. The popular **campsite** (☎0284/61 221) is a ten-minute walk northeast along a track, next to its own nudist beach; the water here is shallow enough for campers to wade across to the neighbouring islet of Dhipló. For peace and quiet with a degree of comfort try *Studios Delfini* (☎093/275 911; ④) at Áyios Yeóryios, a long stretch of beach with several tavernas, of which *Captain Pipinos* is recommended.

The best of the waterfront **tavernas** is *Anargyros*, below the hotel of the same name. *Klimataria*, 100m inland to the left off the main street, has tables in a pleasant, shady garden, and *To Kastro* is one of the better restaurants outside the kástro. There are plenty of **bars** in the same area but the locals usually stick to the excellent *To Kendro* sweetshop in the eucalyptus-filled platía; *Café Margarita* is a pleasant street-side hang-out on the way up to this platía. For quiet music and views of the mountains try *Café Yam*, an outdoor café-bar near the *Klimataria*. A short-schedule **bank**, a **post office**, a cinema and several **travel agents** round up the list of amenities.

Náxos

Náxos is the largest and most fertile of the Cyclades, and with its green and mountainous highland scenery seems immediately distinct from many of its neighbours. The difference is accentuated by the **unique architecture** of many of the interior villages: the

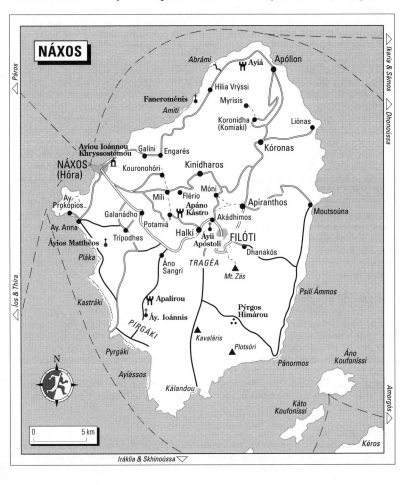

Venetian Duchy of the Aegean, which ruled from the thirteenth to the sixteenth century, left towers and fortified mansions scattered throughout the island, while medieval Cretan refugees bestowed a singular character upon Náxos's eastern settlements.

Today Náxos could easily support itself without tourists by relying on its production of potatoes, olives, grapes and lemons, but it has thrown in its lot with mass tourism, so that parts of the island are now almost as busy and commercialized as Páros in season. But the island certainly has plenty to see if you know where to look: the highest mountains in the Cyclades, intriguing central valleys, a spectacular north coast and marvellously sandy beaches in the southwest.

Náxos Town

A long causeway, built to protect the harbour to the north, connects **NÁXOS TOWN** (or Hóra) with the islet of Palátia – the place where, according to legend, Theseus abandoned Ariadne on his way home from Crete. The huge stone portal of a **temple of Apollo** still stands there, built on the orders of the tyrant Lygdamis in the sixth century BC, but never completed. Most of the town's life goes on down by the crowded port esplanade or just behind it; back streets and alleys behind the harbour lead up through low arches to the fortified **kástro**, from where Marco Sanudo and his successors ruled over the Cyclades. Only two of the kástro's original seven towers – those of the Sanudo and Glezos families – remain, although the north gate (approached from Apóllonos) survives as a splendid example of a medieval fort entrance. The Venetians' Catholic descendants, now much declined in numbers, still live in the old mansions which encircle the site, many with ancient coats of arms above crumbling doorways. Other brooding relics survive in the same area: a seventeenth-century Ursuline convent and the Roman Catholic cathedral, restored in questionable taste in the 1950s, though still displaying a thirteenth-century crest inside. Nearby was one of Ottoman Greece's first schools, the French School; opened in 1627 for Catholic and Orthodox students alike, its pupils included, briefly, Nikos Kazantzakis. The school building now houses an excellent **archeological museum** (Tues–Sun 8.30am–2.30pm; 500dr), with finds from Náxos, Koufoníssi, Keros and Dhonoússa, including an important collection of Early Cycladic figurines. Archaic and Classical sculpture and pottery dating from Neolithic through to Roman times are also on display. On the roof terrace a Hellenistic mosaic floor shows a nereid surrounded by deer and peacocks.

As well as archeological treasures, Náxos has some very good sandal-makers: try the Markos store on Papavassilíou. The island is also renowned for its wines and liqueurs; a shop on the quay sells the Prombonas white and vintage red, plus *kítron*, a lemon firewater in three strengths (there's also a banana-flavoured variant).

Arrival and transport

Large **ferries** dock along the northerly harbour causeway; all small boats and the very useful *Skopelitis* ferry use the jetty in the fishing harbour, not the main car-ferry dock. The **bus station** is at its landward end: buses run five times a day to Apóllon (1100dr), and one of the morning services to Apóllon takes the newly paved coastal road via Engarés and Abrámi, and is much quicker though not any cheaper. There are six buses a day to Apíranthos via Filóti, two of these going on to Moutsoúna on the east coast. Buses run (every 30min; 8am–midnight) to Áyios Prokópios, Ayía Ánna and as far as the Maragás campsite on Pláka beach, and four times a day to Pirgáki. Printed timetables are available from the bus station.

Accommodation

Rooms can be hard to come by and somewhat overpriced in the old quarter of Hóra, and single rooms are non-existent. Naxos Tourist Information (☎0285/25 201), on the seafront near the jetty, is a wealth of information. If you come up with nothing after an hour of hunting, the southern extension of town offers better value, although there's significant night-time noise from the clubs and discos. *Bourgos Rooms* (☎0285/25 979; ④) comprise good new rooms near the kástro, behind *Panorama* (see below); or try *Iliada Studios* (☎0285/23 303 or 24 277, *ILIADA@naxos-island.com*; ⑤) on the cliffs beyond Grotta Beach, with good views over the town and out to sea. *Studios Irene* (☎0285/23 169; ③) consists of good-value, comfortable rooms in the Kristós area, a slightly calmer part of town.

Hotel choices include the *Panorama* on Amfitrítis (☎0285/24 404; ⑤), the nearby *Anixis* (☎0285/22 112; ④), *Hotel Pantheon* (☎0285/24 335; ④), with a few rooms in a traditionally furnished house on Apóllonos, or, as a last resort, the bargain *Dionyssos* (☎0285/22 331; ①) near the kástro, which also has dorm beds (①). Upmarket choices include the traditional *Chateau Zevgoli* (☎0285/22 993; ⑤), with tastefully decorated, air-conditioned rooms near the kástro, and *Hotel Galaxy* (☎0285/22 422; ⑥), an upmarket beach hotel with a pool, behind Áyios Yeóryios beach. *Hotel Anna* (☎0285/22 475; ③), towards the Grótta area, is not particularly remarkable; however it stays open through the winter.

Eating, drinking and nightlife

One of the best quayside breakfast bars is the *Bikini* creperie. Further along to the south are a string of relatively expensive but simple oven-food **tavernas** – *Iy Kali Kardhia* is typical, serving acceptable casserole dishes washed down with barrelled wine. *Iy Platia* on the main square, towards the new south district, serves traditional fare and is popular with Greeks, while the nearby *Cafe Picasso* serves up Mexican food (supper only) for a mixed crowd. On the front *Karnayio* is a good, if a little pricey, fish taverna; *Cafe En Plo* and *Musique Café* are two reasonable places in the middle of the quay, both popular with locals. A hidden gem is *To Roupel*, a good old kafenío in the backstreets between the front and the kástro, with the *Manolis Garden Taverna* nearby one of the most pleasant of the kástro tourist eateries. *Elli Cafe Bar Restaurant* behind Grótta beach is a little more expensive but serves imaginative food, and *Portokali Club* on the headland to the south of town is a club, café and restaurant with good views over Áyios Yeóryios bay.

Much of the evening action goes on at the south end of the waterfront, and slightly inland in the new quarter. **Nightlife** tends more towards drinking places, though there is the lively *Ocean Club*, subsisting on pop-chart fodder, *Ole Club* towards the middle of the quay for dance music and *Vegerra*, a lively cocktail bar behind *Karnayio*. *Lakrindi Jazz Bar*, a tiny place on Apóllonos between the front and the kástro, is recommended. There's also an open-air cinema, the Ciné Astra, on the road to the airport at the southern end of town. It's a fair walk out but the Ayía Ánna bus stops here.

The southwestern beaches

The **beaches** around Náxos Town are worth sampling. For some unusual swimming just to the **north** of the port, beyond the causeway, **Grótta** is easiest to reach. Besides the caves for which the place is named, the remains of submerged Cycladic buildings are visible, including some stones said to be the entrance to a tunnel leading to the unfinished temple of Apollo. The finest spots, though, are all **south** of town, the entire southwestern coastline boasting a series of excellent **beaches** accessible by regular bus. **ÁYIOS YEÓRYIOS**, a long sandy bay fringed by the southern extension of the hotel "colony", is within walking distance. There's a line of cafés and tavernas at the northern end of the beach, and a windsurfing school, plus the first of four **campsites**, whose touts you will no doubt have become acquainted with at the ferry jetty. This first campsite, *Camping Naxos* (☎0285/23 500), isn't recommended; *Maragas* and *Plaka* have far more attractive locations on Pláka beach (see below). A word of warning for campers: although this entire coast is relatively sheltered from the *meltémi*, the plains behind are boggy and you should bring along mosquito repellent.

Buses take you to **ÁYIOS PROKÓPIOS** beach, with plenty of reasonably priced hotels, rooms and basic tavernas, plus the relaxed *Apollon* campsite (☎0285/24 117) nearby. *Hotel Lianos Village* (☎0285/23 366, *lianos-village@nax.forthnet.gr*, ⑥) is an upmarket choice with a pleasant pool setting; of the restaurants *Pizzeria Promponas* has a varied menu and nice setting. Rapid development along this stretch means that this resort has blended into the next resort of **AYÍA ÁNNA** (habitually referred to as "Ayi'Ánna"), further along the busy road; here you will find accommodation of similar price and quality. The seaview *Hotel Ayia Anna* (☎0285/42 576; ③) and adjacent *Gorgona* taverna are recommended, as is *Bar Bagianni* on the road from Áyia Ánna to Áyios Prokópios, a colourful and popular bar which serves vegetarian food. Moving along the coast, away from the built-up area, the beach here is nudist.

Beyond the headland stretch the five kilometres of **PLÁKA** beach, a vegetation-fringed expanse of white sand. Things are not so built up here, and parts of the beach are nudist (past Pláka campsite). There are two suitably laid-back and friendly **campsites** here: *Maragas* campsite (☎0285/24 552) which also has double rooms (②), and the newer *Pláka* campsite (☎0285/42 700), a little further along, which is small and quiet with a few cheap bungalows (①). The *Hotel Orkos Village* (☎0285/75 321, *orkos@nax.forthnet.gr*, ⑥) comprises apartments in an attractive location, on a hillside above the coast between Pláka beach and Mikrí Vígla.

For real isolation, go to the other side of Mikrí Vígla headland, along a narrow footpath across the cliff-edge, to **KASTRÁKI** beach; towards the middle of the beach *Areti* (☎0285/75 292; ⑤) has apartments and a restaurant. A few people camp around the taverna on the small headland a little further down. In summer this stretch, all the way from Mikrí Vígla down to Pyrgáki, attracts camper vans and windsurfers from all over Europe. On the Alíko promontory to the south of Kastráki there is a small nudist beach.

From Kastráki, it's a couple of hours' walk up to the Byzantine castle of **Apalírou** which held out for two months against the besieging Marco Sanudo. The fortifications are relatively intact and the views magnificent. **Pyrgáki** beach has a couple of tavernas and a few rooms; four kilometres further on is **Ayiássos** beach.

The rest of the **southern coast** – indeed, virtually the whole of the southeast of the island – is remote and mountain-studded; you'd have to be a dedicated and well-equipped camper/hiker to get much out of the region.

Central Náxos and the Tragéa

Although buses bound for Apóllon (in the north) link up the central Naxian villages, the core of the island – between Náxos Town and Apíranthos – is best explored by moped or on foot. Much of the region is well off the beaten track, and can be a rewarding excursion if you've had your fill of beaches; Christian Ucke's *Walking Tours on Naxos*, available from bookshops in Náxos Town, is a useful guide for hikers.

Once out of Hóra, you quickly arrive at the neighbouring villages of **GLINÁDHO** and **GALANÁDHO**, forking respectively right and left. Both are scruffy market centres: Glinádho is built on a rocky outcrop above the Livádhi plain, while Galánadho displays the first of Náxos's fortified mansions and an unusual "double church". A combined Orthodox chapel and Catholic sanctuary separated by a double arch, the church reflects the tolerance both by the Venetians during their rule and by the locals to established Catholics afterwards. Continue beyond Glinádho to **TRÍPODHES** (ancient Biblos), 9km from Náxos Town. Noted by Homer for its wines, this old-fashioned agricultural village has nothing much to do except enjoy a coffee at the shaded kafenío. The start of a long but rewarding walk is a rough road (past the parish church) which leads down the colourful Pláka valley, past an old watchtower and the Byzantine church of **Áyios Matthéos** (mosaic pavement), and ends at the glorious Pláka beach (see above).

To the east, the twin villages of **SANGRÍ**, on a vast plateau at the head of a long valley, can be reached by continuing to follow the left-hand fork past Galanádho, a route which allows a look at the domed eighth-century church of **Áyios Mámas** (on the left), once the Byzantine cathedral of the island but neglected during the Venetian period and now a sorry sight. Either way, **Káto Sangrí** boasts the remains of a Venetian castle, while **Áno Sangrí** is a comely little place, all cobbled streets and fragrant courtyards. Thirty minutes' stroll away, on a path leading south out of the village, are the partially reconstructed remains of a Classical temple of Demeter.

The Tragéa

From Sangrí the road twists northeast into the **Tragéa** region, scattered with olive trees and occupying a vast highland valley. It's a good jumping-off point for all sorts of exploratory rambling, and **HALKÍ** is a fine introduction to what is to come. Set high up, 16km from the port, it's a noble and silent town with some lovely churches. The **Panayía Protóthronis** church, with its eleventh- to thirteenth-century frescoes, and the romantic **Grazia (Frangopoulos) Pýrgos**, are open to visitors, but only in the morning. Tourists wanting to stay here are still something of a rarity, although you can usually get a room in someone's house by asking at the store. *Yiannis* taverna is the focal point of village activity and has a good selection of fresh mezédhes to enjoy with a glass of oúzo. Nearby is the distillery and shop of *Vallindras Naxos Citron*, whose charming proprietors explain the proccess of producing this speciality citrus liqueur (*kítron*), followed by a little tasting session. The olive and citrus plantations surrounding Halkí are criss-crossed by paths and tracks, the groves dotted with numerous Byzantine chapels and the ruins of fortified *pyrgi* or Venetian mansions. Between Halkí and Akadhimí, but closer to the latter, sits the peculiar twelfth-century "piggyback" church of **Áyii Apóstoli**, with a tiny chapel (where the ennobled donors worshipped in private) perched above the narthex; there are brilliant thirteenth-century frescoes as well.

The road from Halkí heads north to **MONÍ**. Just before the village, you pass the sixth-century monastery of **Panayía Dhrossianí**, a group of stark grey stone buildings with some excellent frescoes; the monks allow visits at any time, though you may have to contend with coach tours from Náxos Town. Moní itself enjoys an outstanding view of the Tragéa and surrounding mountains, and has four tavernas, plus some rooms. The main road leads on to Kinídharos, with an old marble quarry above the village; a few kilometres beyond, a signpost points you down a rough track to the left, to **FLÉRIO** (commonly called Melanés). The most interesting of the ancient marble quarries on Náxos, this is home to two famous **koúri**, dating from the sixth century BC, that were left recumbent and unfinished because of flaws in the material. Even so, they're finely detailed figures, over five metres in length. One of the statues lies in a private, irrigated orchard; the other is up a hillside some distance above, and you will need to seek local guidance to find it.

From Flério you could retrace your steps to the road and head back to Hóra via Mýli and the ruined Venetian castle at Kouronohóri, both pretty hamlets connected by footpaths. If you're feeling more adventurous, ask to be directed south to the footpath which leads over the hill to the Potamiá villages. The first of these, **ÁNO POTAMIÁ**, has a fine taverna and a rocky track back towards the Tragéa. Once past the valley the landscape becomes craggy and barren, the forbidding Venetian fortress of **Apáno Kástro** perched on a peak just south of the path. This is believed to have been Sanudo's summer home, but the fortified site goes back further, if the Mycenaean tombs found nearby are any indication. From the fort, paths lead back to Halkí in around an hour.

Alternatively, you can continue further southwest down the Potamiá valley towards Hóra, passing first the ruined **Cocco Pýrgos** – said to be haunted by one Constantine Cocco, the victim of a seventeenth-century clan feud – on the way to **MÉSO POTA-MIÁ**, joined by some isolated dwellings with its twin village **KÁTO POTAMIÁ**, nestling almost invisibly among the greenery flanking the creek.

At the far end of the gorgeous Tragéa valley, **FILÓTI**, the largest village in the region, lies on the slopes of Mount Zás (or Zeus) which, at 1000m, is the highest point in the Cyclades. Under the shade of the plane trees on the main platía are several pleasant kafenía, as well as *Babulas Grill-Restaurant* (☎0285/31 426; ②) which has the best rooms in the village. To get an idea of the old village, climb the steps up the hill starting at the platía. A turning at the southern end of the village is signposted to the **Pýrgos Himárou**, a remote 20-metre Hellenistic watchtower, and **Kalándou** beach on the south coast; beyond the turning the road is unpaved. There are no villages in this part of the island, so bring supplies if you're planning to camp. From the village, it's a round-trip walk of two to three hours to the summit of Zás, a climb which rewards you with an astounding panorama of virtually the whole of Náxos and its Cycladic neighbours. From the main Filóti–Apóllon road, take the side-road towards Dhánakos until you reach a small chapel on the right, just beside the start of the waymarked final approach trail.

APÍRANTHOS, a hilly, winding 10km beyond, shows the most Cretan influence of all the interior villages. There are four small **museums** and two Venetian fortified mansions, while the square contains a miniature church with a three-tiered belltower. Ask to be pointed to the start of the spectacular path up over the ridge behind; this ends either in Moní or Kalóxilos, depending on whether you fork right or left respectively at the top. Cafés and tavernas on the main street look out over a terraced valley below. Rooms are available but are not advertised – ask in the cafés or in the embroidery shop. Apíranthos is a good quiet place to stay for a few days, and being high in the mountains is noticeably cooler and greener than the coast.

Apíranthos has a beach annexe of sorts at **Moutsoúna**, 12km east. Emery mined near Apíranthos used to be transported here by means of an aerial funicular and then shipped out of the port. The industry collapsed in the 1980s, and the sandy cove beyond the dock now features a growing colony of holiday villas. An unpaved road heads south along the coast to a remote sandy beach at **Psilí Ámmos** – ideal for self-sufficient campers, but you must take enough water. From here a track carries on to **Pánormos** beach in the southeastern corner of the island.

Northern Náxos

The route through the mountains from Apíranthos to Apóllon is very scenic, and the road surface is in good condition all the way. Jagged ranges and hairpin bends confront you before reaching Kóronos, the halfway point, where a road off to the right threads through a wooded valley to **Liónas**, a tiny and very Greek port with a pebble beach. You'd do better to continue, though, past Skadhó to the remote, emery-miners' village of **KOMIAKÍ** which is a pleasing, vine-covered settlement – the highest village in the island and the original home of *kítron* liqueur.

Back on the main road, a series of slightly less hairy bends leads down a long valley to **APÓLLON** (Apóllonas), a small resort with two beaches: a tiny and crowded stretch of sand backed by cafés and restaurants, and a longer and quieter stretch of shingle, popular mainly with Greek families. If you are staying, try the friendly rooms of *Maria* (☎0285/67 106; ②) behind the harbour. The only major attraction is a **koúros**, approached by a path from the main road just above the village. Lying in situ at a former marble quarry, this largest of Náxos's abandoned stone figures is just over ten metres long, but, compared with those at Flério, disappointingly lacking in detail. Here since 600 BC, it serves as a singular reminder of the Naxians' traditional skill; the famous Delian lions (see p.521) are also made of Apollonian marble. Not surprisingly, bus tours descend upon the village during the day, and Apóllon is now quite a popular little place. The local festival, celebrated on August 28–29, is one of Náxos's best.

From Náxos Town there is now a daily bus service direct to Apóllon (taking about an hour). It's easy to make a round trip by bus of the north coast and inland villages in either direction. The coastal road is spectacularly beautiful, going high above the sea for most of the way – it's more like parts of Crete or the mainland than other islands. Ten kilometres past the northern cape sprouts the beautiful **Ayiá** *pýrgos*, or tower, another foundation (in 1717) of the Cocco family. There's a tiny hamlet nearby, and, 7km further along, a track leads off to **Abrámi** beach, an idyllic spot with a highly recommended family-run taverna and **rooms** to let, *Pension and Restaurant Efthimios* (☎0285/63 244; ③). Just beyond the hamlet of Hília Vrýssi is the abandoned **monastery of Faneroménis**, built in 1606. Carrying on along the coastal road you will reach Engarés valley, at the foot of which is another quiet beach, **Amití**, which can be reached via one of two dirt tracks, the most obvious being the one leading down from Galíni, only 6km from Hóra. On the final stretch back to the port you pass a unique eighteenth-century Turkish fountain-house and the fortified monastery of **Ayíou Ioánnou Khryssostómou**, where a couple of aged nuns are still in residence. A footpath from the monastery and the road below lead straight back to town.

Koufoníssi, Skhinoússa, Iráklia and Dhonoússa

In the patch of the Aegean between Náxos and Amorgós there is a chain of six small islands neglected by tourists and by the majority of Greeks, few of whom have heard of them. **Kéros** – ancient Karos – is an important archeological site but has no permanent population, and **Káto Koufoníssi** is inhabited only by goatherds. However, the other four islands – **Áno Koufoníssi**, **Skhinoússa**, **Iráklia** and **Dhonoússa** – are all inhabited, served by ferry and can be visited. Now increasingly discovered by Greeks and foreigners alike, the islets' popularity has hastened the development of better facilities, but they're still a welcome break from the mass tourism of the rest of the Cyclades, especially during high season. If you want real peace and quiet – what the Greeks call *isyhiá* – get there soon.

A few times weekly in summer a Pireás-based **ferry** – usually the *Olympia Express* or the *Naias Express* – calls at each of the islands, linking them with Náxos and Amorgós and (usually) Páros, and Sýros. A kaḯki, the *Express Skopelitis*, is a reliable daily fixture, leaving Náxos in mid-afternoon for relatively civilized arrival times at all the islets.

Koufoníssi and Kéros

Ano Koufoníssi is the most populous island of the group; there is a reasonable living to be made from fishing and, with some of the best beaches in the Cyclades, it is attracting increasing numbers of Greek and foreign holidaymakers. Small enough to walk round in a morning, the island can actually feel overcrowded in July and August.

The old single-street village of **HÓRA**, on a low hill behind the harbour, is being engulfed by new room and hotel development, but still has a friendly, small-island atmosphere. A map by the jetty shows where to find all the island's **rooms**: *To Limani* (☎0285/71 851 or 71 450; ③) is a café with rooms near the harbour; the popular restaurant and pension *Iy Melissa* (☎0285/71 454; ③) is another good choice. The most upmarket options include *Hotel Aigaion* (☎0285/74 050 or 74 051; ⑥), by the village beach, or *Villa Ostria* (☎0285/71 671; ⑤), on the hillside to the east of the village. *To*

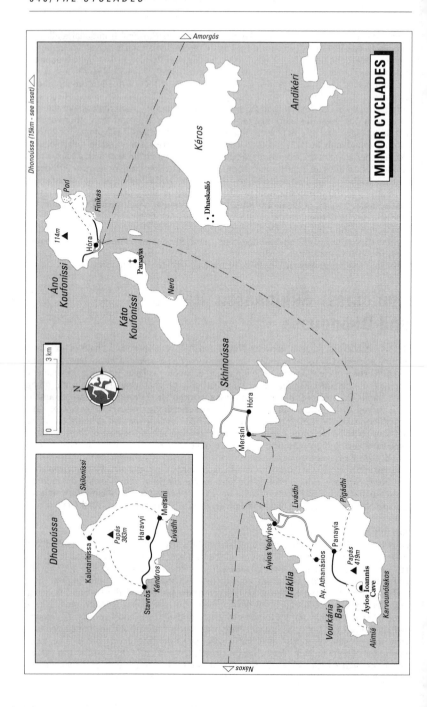

MINOR CYCLADES

Akroyiali (☎0285/71 685; ④) is on the front just beyond the beach; Yeofyia Kouveou has beautifully situated rooms at *Hondros Kavos* (☎0285/71 707; ③), outside the village to the east; and the *Petros Club* (☎0285/71 728; ⑤) is in a quiet position inland, with excellent views.

Koufoníssi is noted for its fish **tavernas**; *To Nikitouri*, up in Hóra, has very personable Greek-American management, and the *Karnayio* ouzerí on the bay to the west of the harbour is cheaper than most and has a fine array of seafood. The nearby *To Steki Tis Marias* is a good breakfast place with a few rooms; ③, and has views over the narrow channel to Káto Koufoníssi. The most popular nightspot is *Soroccos*, a lively café-bar on the front, while good alternatives include *Ta Kalamia*, with a quieter choice of music; *Nikitas*; and *Skholeio*, a creperie and bar. *To Palio Fanari*, to the west of the village, is the club favoured by locals, playing a mix of dance and Greek music. The OTE office and ticket agency are on the main street, and money, unusually, of late, can be changed at the somewhat improvised "post office" (limited hours).

All the good beaches are in the southeast of the island, starting at **Fínikas**, a ten-minute walk from the village, where there are rooms, an acceptable taverna and a **campsite** (☎0285/71 683) with rather poor facilities. Fínikas is the first of a series of small bays and coves of gently shelving golden sand, some with low cliffs hollowed out into sea-caves. Further east, a path round a rocky headland leads to **Porí**, a much longer and wilder beach, backed by dunes and set in a deep bay. It can be reached more easily from the village by following a track heading inland through the low scrub-covered hills.

KÁTO KOUFONÍSSI, the uninhabited island to the southwest, has a seasonal taverna and some more secluded beaches; a kaïki shuttles people across until late in the evening. A festival is held here on August 15, at the church of the Panayía. The island of **Kéros** is harder to reach, but if there is a willing group of people keen to visit the ancient site, a boat and boatmen can be hired at around 15,000dr for the day.

Skhinoússa

A little to the southwest, the island of **Skhinoússa** is just beginning to awaken to its tourist potential. Boats dock at the small port of Mersíni, which has one pension (☎0285/71 157; ④) and a couple of cafés; a road leads up to **HÓRA**, the walk taking just over ten minutes. As you enter the village, the well-stocked shop of the Grispos family is one of the first buildings. Yiorgos Grispos is a mine of information and is personally responsible for the island's map and postcards, as well as being the boat/hydrofoil agent, having a metred phone and selling the Greek and foreign press.

Accommodation is mostly in fairly simple rooms, such as *Pension Meltemi* (☎0285/71 195; ⑤), *Anesis* (☎0285/71180; ③) and the pleasant *Provaloma* (☎0285/71 936; ③), which also has a taverna. The rooms belonging to Anna (☎0285/71 161; ③) are particularly recommended, as is the modern *Hotel Sunset* (☎0285/71 948; ③) which enjoys stunning views of the harbour. The main concentration of **restaurants**, cafés and bars is along the main thoroughfare, including the popular *Bar Ostria* and a lively ouzerí.

There are no fewer than sixteen beaches dotted around the island, accessible by a lacework of trails. **Tsigoúri Beach** is a ten-minute walk from Hóra; largely undeveloped except for the new *Tsigouri Beach Villas* (☎0285/71 175; ③), this was traditonally the beach where freelance campers congregated. The arrival of this new hotel, complete with taverna (great views) may, however, put a damper on things; the only other beach with any refreshments is **Almyrós**, which has a simple canteen.

Iráklia

In an attempt to accommodate increasing visitor numbers, **Iráklia** (pronounced Irakliá by locals), the westernmost of the minor Cyclades, is losing its charm as the number of purpose-built rooms increases.

Ferries and hydrofoils call at **ÁYIOS YEÓRYIOS**, a small but sprawling settlement behind a sandy tamarisk-backed beach. Irini Koveou (☎0285/71 488; ③) has a café-restaurant and rooms opposite the harbour, and more rooms and places to eat can be found along the old road to Livádhi beach. *Anna's Place* (☎0285/71 145; ③) consists of rooms with shared cooking facilities, and *Mestrali* (☎0285/71 807; ③) has newer rooms as well as its own café-cum-taverna. Theofanis Gavalas (☎0285/71 565; ②), Dhimítrios Stefanídhis (☎0285/71 484; ③), Alexandra Tournaki (☎0285/71 482; ②) and Angelos Koveos (☎0285/71 486; ②) all have rooms nearby. *O Pefkos* is a pleasant **taverna**, with tables shaded by a large pine tree, while the café/shop *Melissa* acts as the main ticket agency for ferries. The recommended *Perigiali* taverna also has a small shop selling maps showing the route to a fine **cave** on the far side of the island.

Livádhi, the best beach on the island, is a fifteen-minute walk past a taverna, whose friendly and animated proprietor usually meets ferries at the dock. There is shade, but bring refreshments, since locals seem unsure whether or not the lone taverna on the far side of the beach will reopen. The village of Livádhi, deserted since 1940, stands on the hillside above, its houses ruined and overgrown; among the remains are Hellenistic walls incorporated into a later building, and fortifications from the time of Marco Sanudo. Marietta Markoyianni (☎0285/71 252; ②) has the only rooms on the beach; *Zografos Rooms* (☎0285/71 946; ④), above the road to Panayía, has fine views but is rather remote.

PANAYÍA or **HÓRA**, an unspoiled one-street village at the foot of Mount Papás, is another hour's walk inland along the newly paved road. It has a bakery/mini-market, two café/shops and the excellent and cheap *O Kritikos* ouzerí, but no rooms. A track to the east heads down to Pigádhi, a rocky beach with sea urchins, at the head of a narrow inlet. To the west a track from the near-deserted hamlet of **Áyios Athanásios** leads back to the port.

The **cave of Áyios Ioánnis** lies behind the mountain, at the head of a valley leading to Vourkária bay. From Panayía, follow a signposted track west before zigzagging up to a saddle well to the north of the summit, with views over Skhinoússa, Koufoníssi, Kéros, Náxos and Amorgós; the path drops down to the south around the back of the mountain. A painted red arrow on the left indicates the turning to the cave, just over an hour from Panayía. A church bell hangs from a cypress tree above the whitewashed entrance; inside there's a shrine, and the cave opens up into a large chamber with stalactites and stalagmites. It can be explored to a depth of 120m and is thought to be part of a much larger cave system, yet to be opened up; a festival is held here every year on August 18.

The main trail continues beyond the cave to a small sandy beach at **Alimiá** but this can be reached more easily with the beach boat from Áyios Yeóryios. In season the boat sails daily to either Skhinoússa, Alimiá or the nearby pebble beach of Karvounólakos.

Dhonoússa

Dhonoússa is a little out on a limb compared with the others, and ferries and hydrofoils call less frequently. Island life centres on the pleasant port settlement of **STAVRÓS**, spread out behind the harbour and the village beach.

Rooms, most without signs, tend to be booked up by Greek holidaymakers in August; try Mihalis Prasinos (☎0285/51 578; ④ – based on four people sharing), with rooms along a lane behind the church; Dhimitris Prasinos (☎0285/51 579; ③), with rooms open year-round near the *Iliovasilema* restaurant; or Nikos Prasinos (☎0285/51 551; ④), who has good new studios above the rocks west of the harbour. *Ta Kymata* is the most popular of the four tavernas but *Meltemi* is also good, as is the friendly *Aposperitis*, right on the village beach. Nikitas Roussos (☎0285/51 648) has a **ticket agency** above the harbour and can change money and book rooms.

The hills around Stavrós are low and barren and scarred by bulldozed tracks, but a little walking is repaid with dramatic scenery and a couple of fine beaches. Campers and nudists head for **Kéndros**, a long and attractive stretch of sand fifteen minutes to the east, although shade is limited and there are no facilities. A road has been built on the hillside above, replacing the donkey track to the farming hamlets of Haravyí and Mersíni; these have more hens and goats in the streets than people, and there are no cafés, shops or rooms. **Mersíni** is an hour's walk from Stavrós and has a welcome spring beneath a plane tree, the island's only running water. A nearby path leads down to Livádhi, an idyllic white sand beach with tamarisks for shade. In July and August there's a daily beach boat from the port.

KALOTARÍTISSA in the north can still only be reached on foot or by boat – a track heading inland from Stavrós climbs a valley west of Papás, the island's highest point, before dropping down rapidly to the tiny village with a simple **taverna** and one room to rent (☎0285/51 562; ②). There are two small pebble beaches and a path that continues above the coast to Mersíni. It takes four to five hours to walk round the island.

Amorgós

Amorgós, with its dramatic mountain scenery and laid-back atmosphere, is attracting visitors in increasing numbers; most ferries and hydrofoils call at both Katápola in the southwest and Eyiáli in the northeast. The island can get extremely crowded in mid-summer, the numbers swollen by French paying their respects to the film location of Luc Besson's *The Big Blue*, although few actually venture out to the wreck of the *Olympia*, at the island's west end, which figured so prominently in the movie. In general it's a low-key, escapist clientele, happy to have found a relatively large, interesting and uncommercialized island with excellent walking.

The southwest

KATÁPOLA, set at the head of a deep bay, is actually three separate hamlets: **Katápola** proper on the south flank, **Rahídhi** on the ridge at the head of the gulf and

Xilokeratídhi along the north shore. There is a beach in front of Rahídhi, but the beach to the west of Katápola is better, though not up to the standards of Eyiáli. In season there is also a regular kaḯki to nearby beaches at **Maltézi** and **Plákes** (400dr return) and a daily kaḯki to the islet of **Gramvoússa** off the western end of Amorgós (2000dr return).

There are plenty of small **hotels** and **pensions** and, except in high summer when rooms are almost impossible to find, proprietors tend to meet those boats arriving around sunset – though not necessarily those that show up in the small hours. A good clean place next to the beach at the western end of Katápola is *Eleni Rooms* (☎0285/71 543 or 71 628; ④). *Dhimitri's Place* in Rahídhi (☎0285/71 309; ②) is a compound of interconnecting buildings in an orchard, where shared cooking facilities add to the laid-back atmosphere. On the same road, *Angeliki Rooms* (☎0285/71 280; ③) is well run, friendly and good value, as Angeliki doesn't put up her prices for August; the smart *Hotel Minoa* (☎0285/71 480; ⑤) on the waterfront is noisier than its sister hotel will be when it opens up, round the corner, in the near future. *Panayiotis Rooms* (☎0285/71 890; ③) in Xilokeratídhi is also good value. There is another cluster of hotels behind the port, past *Hotel Anna* (☎0285/71 218; ③), of similar price and quality (③–④), including *Pension Big Blue*. *Hotel Anna* itself is a little old-fashioned; however, it has a lovely setting and basic cooking facilities, and you can enjoy breakfast in the beautiful garden.

In Katápola proper, *Mourayio* is the most popular **taverna** in town; alternatively try the *Akrogiali* taverna. What **nightlife** there is focuses on a handful of cafés and pubs. A bar called *Le Grand Bleu* in Xilokeratídhi regularly shows *The Big Blue* on video but there are other less obvious and less expensive places to drink, such as *The Moon Bar* next door, or *Ippokampos*, a café and bar on the front at Rahídhi.

Prekas is the one-stop **boat ticket agency**, and there are several **moped rental** outlets including the friendly Corner Rentabike, though the local bus service is more than adequate and walking trails delightful. The **campsite** (☎0285/71 802;) is well signed between Rahídhi and Xilokeratídhi; in the latter district are four **tavernas**, of which the first is a friendly fish taverna, and of the others around the corner *Vitzentzos* is by far the best.

Steps, and then a jeep track, lead out of Katápola to the remains of **ancient Minoa**, which are apt to disappoint up close: some Cyclopean wall four or five courses high, the foundations of an Apollo temple, a crumbled Roman structure and bushels of unsorted pottery shards. It's only the setting, with views encompassing Hóra and ancient Arkessíni, that's the least bit memorable. Beyond Minoa the track soon dwindles to a trail, continuing within a few hours to Arkessíni (see below) via several hamlets – a wonderful **excursion** with the possibility of catching the bus back.

The **bus** shuttles almost hourly until 11pm between Katápola and Hóra, the island capital; several times daily the service continues to Ayía Ánna via Hozoviotíssas monastery, and once a day (9.45am) there's a run out to the "Káto Meriá", made up of the hamlets of Kamári, Arkessíni and Kolofána. **HÓRA**, also accessible by an hour-long path beginning from behind the Rahídhi campsite, is one of the best-preserved settlements in the Cyclades, with a scattering of tourist shops, cafés, tavernas and rooms. Dominated by a rock plug wrapped with a chapel or two, the thirteenth-century Venetian fortifications look down on countless other bulbous churches – including Greece's smallest, **Áyios Fanoúrios**, which holds just three worshippers – and a line of decapitated windmills beyond. Of the half-dozen or so **places to stay**, *Pension O Ilias* (☎0285/71 277; ③) is recommended. *Liotrivi* restaurant, down the steps from the bus stop, is probably the best place to **eat** in town. In addition to the pair of traditional tavernas, *Kastanis* and *Klimataria*, there are several noisy bistro-café-pubs, with *To Plateaki* in the upper plaza perennially popular in the late afternoon, and *Giulia Kafeneon*, near the bus stop, livelier later on. Also in the upper square is the island's main **post office**.

From the top of Hóra, next to the helipad, a wide cobbled *kalderími* drops down to two major attractions, effectively short-cutting the road and taking little longer than the bus to reach them. Bearing left at an inconspicuous fork after fifteen minutes, you'll come to the spectacular **monastery of Hozoviotíssas** (daily 8am–1pm & 5–7pm; donation), which appears suddenly as you round a bend, its vast wall gleaming white at the base of a towering orange cliff. Only four monks occupy the fifty rooms now, but they are quite welcoming, considering the number of visitors who file through; you can see the eleventh-century icon around which the monastery was founded, along with a stack of other treasures. The foundation legend is typical for such institutions in outlandish places: during the Iconoclastic period a precious icon of the Virgin was committed to the sea by beleaguered monks at Hózova, somewhere in the Middle East, and it washed up safely at the base of the palisade here. The view from the *katholikón's* terrace, though, overshadows all for most visitors, and to round off the experience, visitors are ushered into a comfy reception room and treated to a sugary lump of *loukoúmi*, a fiery shot of *kítron* and a cool glass of water.

The right-hand trail leads down, within forty minutes, to the pebble **beaches** at **Ayía Ánna**. Skip the first batch of tiny coves in favour of the path to the westernmost bay, where naturists cavort, almost in scandalous sight of the monastery far above. As yet there are no tavernas here, nor a spring, so bring food and water for the day.

For alternatives to Ayía Ánna, take the morning bus out toward modern Arkessíni, alighting at **Kamári** hamlet (where there's a single taverna) for the twenty-minute path down to the adjacent beaches of **Notiná**, **Moúros** and **Poulopódhi**. Like most of Amorgós's south-facing beaches, they're clean, with calm water, and here, too, a freshwater spring dribbles most of the year. The road is paved as far as **Kolofána**, where there is one place with rooms. From here unpaved roads lead to the western tip of the island, and remote beaches at Káto Kámbos and at Paradhísa, facing the islet of Gramvoússa.

Archeology buffs will want to head north from Kamári to Vroútsi, start of the overgrown hour-long route to **ancient Arkessini**, a collection of tombs, six-metre-high walls and houses out on the cape of Kastrí. The main path from Minoa also passes through Vroútsi, ending next to the well-preserved Hellenistic fort known locally as the "Pýrgos", just outside modern **ARKESSÍNI**. The village has a single taverna with rooms, and, more importantly, an afternoon bus back to Hóra and Katápola.

The northeast

The energetically inclined can walk the four to five hours from Hóra to Eyiáli. On the Hóra side you can start by continuing on the faint trail just beyond Hozoviótissas, but the islanders themselves, in the days before the road existed, preferred the more scenic and sheltered valley route through Terláki and Rikhtí. The two alternatives, and the modern jeep road, more or less meet an hour out of Hóra. Along most of the way, you're treated to amazing views of **Nikouriá islet**, nearly joined to the main island, and in former times a leper colony. The only habitations en route are the summer hamlet of **Asfodhilítis**, with well water but little else for the traveller, and **Potamós**, a double village you encounter on the stroll down towards Eyiáli bay.

EYIÁLI (Órmos), smaller than Katápola, is a laid-back beachside place in a 1970s time-warp. The road inland, behind the harbour, leads to a group of **hotels** of similar price and quality. *Nikitas* (☎0285/73 237; ③) is the most pleasant, in that it stands on its own in a field, commanding unobstructed sea views. Above is a row of hotels including *Pension Christine* (☎0285/73 236; ③), *Akrogiali* (☎0285/73 249; ④) and *Hotel Pelagos* (☎0285/73 206; ③). Along the beach is the *Lakki* (☎0285/73 244; ④) and behind this the pleasant *Pension Askas* (☎0285/73 333; ④) – both of which have their own shaded tavernas. Next to *Pension Askas* there is a very friendly official **campsite**, *Amorgos*

Camping (☎0285/ 73 500). Overlooking the bay on the road up to Tholária is a luxury hotel with a swimming pool, the *Aegialis* (☎0285/73 393; ⑥). For **eating out**, try *To Limani* (aka *Katerina's*) on the single inland lane, packed until midnight by virtue of its excellent food and barrel wine. Other good options are the *Amorgialos* kafenío, right by the harbour which serves up octopus, and *Delear*, a smart beach bar with live music some evenings and rather pricey drinks. A few seasonal music **bars**, such as *Blé Café*, attempt to compete with *Katerina's*. The *Corte Club* at the *Aegialis* hotel is a typical holiday resort disco playing the usual mix of northern European dance music and Greek pop. For a more active adventure you can take advantage of the new **diving** centre, Dive Ventures (☎0285/73 611), which organizes daily boat and shore dives.

The main Eyiáli **beach** is more than serviceable, getting less weedy and reefy as you stroll further north, the sand interrupted by the remains of a Roman building jutting into the sea. A trail here leads over various headlands to an array of clothing-optional bays: the first sandy, the second mixed sand and gravel, the last shingle. There are no facilities anywhere so bring along what you need.

Eyiáli has its own **bus service** up to each of the two villages visible above and east, with eight departures daily up and down (a timetable is posted by the harbour bus stop in town), but it would be a shame to miss out on the beautiful **loop walk** linking them with the port. A path starting at the far end of the beach heads inland and crosses the road before climbing steeply to **THOLÁRIA**, named after vaulted Roman tombs found around Vígla, the site of ancient Eyiáli. Vígla is on a hill opposite the village but there is little to see beyond the bases of statues and traces of city walls incorporated into later terracing. Another path winds down behind the hill to a tiny pebble beach at Mikrí Vlihádha far below. There are a few **taverna-cafés**, including a handsome wooden-floored establishment near the church, and there are now several places to stay, including some comfortable **rooms** (reserve through *Pension Lakki* in Eyiáli), the large and upmarket *Vigla* (☎0285/73 288; ⑤) and the *Thalassino Oneiro* (☎0285/73 345; ③), which has a fine restaurant and an extremely friendly owner. **LANGÁDHA** is another hour's walk along a path starting below Tholária; to the left of the trail is the chapel of Astrátios with an altar supported by the capital of a Corinthian column. Past here there are views down to the inlet of Megáli Vlihádha and, on a clear day, across to Ikaría in the north. The path descends through the village of Stroúmbos, abandoned apart from three or four houses restored as holiday homes, and into a small gorge before climbing the steps up to Langádha. The place is home to a sizable colony of expatriates – something reflected in the German-Greek cooking at the beautifully located *Nikos'* **taverna** at the lower end of the village, which also runs the attached *Pagali* hotel (☎0285/73 310; ④). The *Loza* taverna, at the top of the village also runs a more straightforward pension with rooms (☎0285/73 315; ③).

Beyond Langádha, another rocky path leads around the base of the island's highest peak, the 821-metre-high **Kríkellos**, passing on the way the fascinating church of **Theológos**, with lower walls and ground plan dating to the fifth century. Somewhat easier to reach, by a slight detour off the main Tholária–Langádha trail, are the church and festival grounds of **Panayía Panohorianí** – not so architecturally distinguished but a fine spot nonetheless.

Íos

No other island is quite like **Íos**, nor attracts the same vast crowds of young people, although attempts are being made to move the island's tourism upmarket; the island now enforces Greece's early closing laws (3am except Fri & Sat), and bars no longer stay open all night. The only real villages – **Yialós, Hóra** and **Mylopótamos** – are in one small corner of the island, and until recently development elsewhere was restrict-

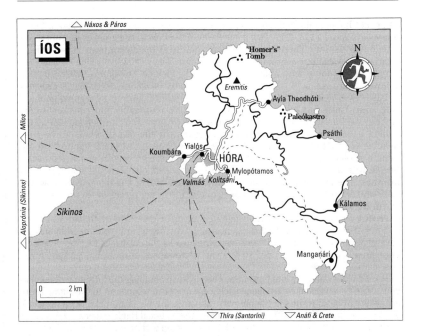

ed by poor roads. As a result there are still some very quiet beaches with just a few rooms to rent. Yialós has one of the best and safest natural harbours in the Cyclades and there is talk of building a new yacht marina.

Most visitors stay along the arc delineated by the port – at Yialós, where you'll arrive (there's no airport), in Hóra above it or at the beach at Mylopótamos; it's a small area, and you soon get to know your way around. **Buses** constantly shuttle between Koumbára, Yialós, Hóra and Mylopótamos, with a daily service running roughly from 8am to midnight; you should never have to wait more than fifteen minutes during high season, but at least once try the short walk up (or down) the stepped path between Yialós and Hóra. Various travel offices run their own buses to the beaches at Manganári and Ayía Theodhóti; they sell return tickets only, and are a bit expensive. To rent your own transport, try Jacob's Car and Bike Rental (☎0286/91 047) in Yialós and Vangelis Bike Rental (☎0286/91 919) in Hóra.

Despite its past popularity, **sleeping on the beach** on Íos is really worth avoiding these days. Crime and police raids are becoming more frequent as the island strains under the sheer impact of increasing youth tourism, and the police have been known to turn very nasty. They prefer you to sleep in the official campsites and, given the problem of theft, you should probably take their advice.

Yialós and Hóra

From **YIALÓS** quayside, **buses** turn around just to the left, while Yialós **beach** – surprisingly peaceful and uncrowded – is another five minutes' walk in the same direction. You might be tempted to grab a room in Yiálos as you arrive: owners meet the ferries, hustling the town's **accommodation**, and there are also a couple of kiosks by the jetty that will book rooms for you. *Hotel Mare Monte* (☎0286/91 585;

④), about half-way down the beach has clean modern rooms and a small pool; *Galini Rooms* (☎0286/91 115; ⑤), down a lane behind the beach, is a good quiet choice, if a little out of the way. There are more rooms on the stepped path from Yialós to Hóra although they can be noisy at night: the *Hotel-Bar Helios* (☎0286/91 500; ④) has a few simple, older rooms, and smarter options nearby include *Armadoras* (☎0286/91 201; ⑤), with a pleasant pool and bar, and *Hotel Poseidon* (☎0286/91 091; ⑤). *Ios Camping* (☎0286/91 329) is friendly and clean and has a rather luxurious swimming pool and café area. Yialós has other essentials, including a reasonable supermarket (to the right of the bus stop), and a few **tavernas**. The *Octopus Tree*, a small kafenío by the fishing boats, serves cheap fresh seafood caught by the owner, while on the front heading towards the beach the *Waves Restaurant* does good Indian food. A twenty-minute stroll over the headland at **KOUMBÁRA**, there's a smaller and less crowded beach, with a rocky islet to explore. *Philippos* taverna on the headland on the way over has excellent squid and romantic views across Yialós, and the *Polydoros* taverna in Koumbára with its homemade food is one of the better places to eat on Iós, and is worth the bus ride.

HÓRA (aka Íos Town) is a twenty-minute walk up behind the port, though you've got a better chance of getting something reasonable by haggling if you intend to stay for several days. The old white village is overwhelmed by the crowds of tourists in season, but with any number of arcaded streets and whitewashed chapels, it does have a certain charm.

Hóra divides naturally into two parts. The old town climbing the hillside to the left as you arrive is separated by an open space from newer development to the right. There are plenty of basic **rooms** in the old part (although the bars can make sleep difficult): *The Hotel Filippou* (☎0286/91 290; ③) is above the National Bank and next to the cathedral; Yannis Stratis (☎0286/91 494; ②) has a few very simple rooms next door; and *Markos Pension* (☎0286/91 059; ④; ask for the ten percent discount for *Rough Guide* readers), with a poolside bar, is one of the best choices in the new part. *Katerina Rooms* (☎0286/91 997; ④), just out of town down a path past the *Iós Club*, is quiet and has fine views over the port, and the friendly *Four Seasons Pension* (☎0286/91 308; winter 0286/92 081; ④), up a turning by Vangelis Bike Rental, is also well away from the noise of the bars and clubs.

What Hóra is still really about, though, is **nightlife**. Every evening the streets throb to music from ranks of competing discos and clubs – mostly free, or with a nominal entrance charge, though drinks tend to be expensive. Most of the smaller **bars** and pubs are tucked into the thronging narrow streets of the old village on the hill, offering something for everyone – unless you just want a quiet drink. A welcome exception to the techno-pop dancing fodder can be found at the *Ios Club*, perched right up on the hill, which plays quieter music, has reasonable food and is a good place to watch the sunset; *Pegasus* and *Super Fly* are also recommended. The larger **dancing clubs**, including the *Mojo*, which plays techno and trance music, and *Disco Scorpion* are to be found on the main road to Mylopótamos.

Eating is a secondary consideration but there are plenty of cheap and cheerful psistariés and takeaway joints: sound choices include the Italian restaurant *Pinocchio*, and the *Lord Byron* mezedhopolí in an alley near the cathedral – it's open year round and tries hard to recreate a traditional atmosphere, with old rembétika music and some good, unusual Greek food.

Culturally things are improving with the recent opening of the **Archeological Museum of Ios** (Tues–Sun 8am–2pm; 500dr), which is hoped will attract a more diverse range of visitors to the island. The outdoor theatre of Odysseus Elytis, behind the windmills, provides a beautiful setting in which to enjoy concerts and plays, details of which can be found from the travel agent/information booth next to the archeological museum.

Around the island

The most popular stop on the island's bus routes is **MYLOPÓTAMOS** (universally abbreviated to Mylópotas), the site of a magnificent beach and a mini-resort. Due to the large number of young travellers in Íos, camping is a popular option. *Far Out* (☎0286/91 468), towards the far end of the beach, consists of a camping ground (2000dr) and bungalows; it has an attractive setting and is very popular but can get very noisy and crowded. *The Purple Pig* (☎0286/91 302, *purplpig@otenet.gr*), a friendly Australian-run **backpackers' complex**, by the road up to Hóra, has clean bungalows, good camping facilities (2000dr) and plenty of other pleasurable distractions, including its own club and a poolside bar. Up the road at the far end of the beach, *Gorgona* (☎0286/91 307; ④) and *Dracos* (☎0286/91 281 or 91 010; ④) have reasonable rooms, but *Dracos* also has a good taverna on its own little quay, serving freshly caught fish. The *Far Out Village* (☎0286/92 305; *farout@otenet.gr*; ⑤), next to the camping site of the same name, the *Far Out Hotel* (☎0286/91 446 or 91 702; ⑤), on the road down from Hóra, and the luxurious *Ios Palace Hotel* (☎0286/91 269; ⑥), above the near end of the beach, are the most upmarket choices. The *Harmony Restaurant* on the rocks beyond the *Ios Palace* is one of the better places to eat, serving pizzas and Mexican food. The restaurants and self-service cafés behind the beach are uninspiring, and only the *Faros Café* rates a mention for staying open through the night to cater for the crowds returning from Hóra in the early hours. Mylopótamos itself has surprisingly little in the way of nightlife.

From Yialós, daily boats depart at around 10am (returning in the late afternoon) to **Manganári** on the south coast, where there's a beach and a swanky hotel; you can also get there by moped. There's an expensive speedboat (4000dr return) from Yialós to Manganári, but most people go by bus (1500dr return). These are private buses run by travel agencies, leaving Yialós about 11am, calling at Hóra and Mylopótamos and returning later in the afternoon. Predominantly nudist, Manganári is the beach to come to for serious tans, although there's more to see, and a better atmosphere at **Ayía Theodhóti** up on the east coast. There's a paved road across the island to Ayía Theodhóti – the daily excursion bus costs 1000dr return. A couple of kilometres south of Ayía Theodhóti is a ruined Venetian castle which encompasses the ruins of a marble-finished town and a Byzantine church. In the unlikely event that the beach – a good one and mainly nudist – is too crowded, try the one at **Psáthi**, 14km to the southeast. Frequented by wealthy Athenians, this small resort has a couple of pricey tavernas, making it better for a day-trip than an extended stay. The road is very poor and not really safe for mopeds, although there are plans to improve it. Another island beach is at **Kálamos**; get off the Manganári bus at the turning for Kálamos, which leaves you with a 4km walk.

"**Homer's**" **tomb** is the only cultural diversion on the island. The story goes that, while on a voyage from Sámos to Athens, Homer's ship was forced to put in at Íos, where the poet subsequently died. The tomb can be reached by moped along a safe new unpaved road (turning left from the paved road to Ayía Theódhoti 4.5km from Hóra). The town itself has long since slipped down the side of the cliff, but the rocky ruins of the entrance to a tomb remain, as well as some graves – one of which is claimed to be Homer's, but which in reality probably dates only to the Byzantine era.

Síkinos

Síkinos has so small a population that the mule ride or walk up from the port to the village was only replaced by a bus late in the 1980s and, until the new jetty was completed at roughly the same time, it was the last major Greek island where ferry passengers were still taken ashore in launches. With no dramatic characteristics, nor any nightlife

SÍKINOS & FOLÉGANDHROS

Paleokástro

KÁSTRO-HÓRA

Áyios Yeóryios

Síkinos

Áyios Nikólaos

Aloprónia

Episkopí

Áyios Pandelímonas

Áyios Yeóryios

Ambéli

Áno Meriá

Livadháki

Khryssospiliá

Angáli

Áyios Nikólaos HÓRA

Vardhiá

Karávostássi

Folégandhros

Loustriá

Katergó

N

0   5 km

▽ *Thíra, Crete & Dodecanese*

to speak of, few foreigners make the short trip over here from neighbouring Íos and Folégandhros or from sporadically connected Páros, Náxos, or Thíra. There is no bank on the island, but there is a **post office** up in Kástro-Hóra, and you can sometimes change cash at the store in Aloprónia.

Aloprónia and Kástro-Hóra

Such tourist facilities as exist are concentrated in the little harbour of **ALOPRÓNIA**, with its long sandy beach and the recent additions of an extended breakwater and jetty. More and more formal **accommodation** is being built here, but it's still possible to camp or just sleep out under the tamarisks behind the beach. For rooms, try *Flora* (☎0286/51 214; ②), near the main road leading to Hóra, *Loukas* (☎0286/51 076; ①–④), who has rooms and studios around town to suit most budgets, or the recommended *The Rock* (☎0286/51 135; ③), above the *Vrachos Rock Cafe*; alternatively, the comfortable and traditional *Hotel Kamares* (☎0286/51 234; ③) has a nicer setting than the conspicuous *Porto Sikinos* luxury complex (☎0286/51 247; ⑥). *To Meltemi* **taverna** on the quay is the locals' hangout, while the fancier *Ostria* is affiliated with the *Hotel Kamares* and the *Loukas* provides standard fare. The *Vrachos Rock Cafe* above the quay plays a more varied music selection than its name would suggest and attracts a good mix of people, while *Vengera* music bar on the opposite side of the bay is a smoother joint.

The double village of **KÁSTRO-HÓRA** is served by the single island bus, which shuttles regularly from early morning till quite late in the evening between the harbour and here, though the route should soon be extended to Episkopí with the completion of the new road. On the ride up, the scenery turns out to be less desolate than initial impressions suggest. Draped across a ridge overlooking the sea, Kástro-Hóra makes for a charming day-trip, and the lovely oil-press **museum** (July to mid-Sept 6.30–8.30pm; free), run privately by a Greek-American is definitely not to be missed. A partly ruined monastery, **Zoödhóhou Piyís** ("Spring of Life", a frequent name in the

Cyclades), crowns the rock above; the architectural highlight of the place, though, is the central quadrangle of **Kástro**, a series of ornate eighteenth-century houses arrayed defensively around a chapel square, their backs to the exterior of the village. The quality of rooms has improved, and both Markos Zagoreos (☎0286/51 263; ②) and Haroula (☎0286/51 212; ②) have competitive prices – the former has great views. A good selection of food is available, along with fine local wine, at both *Klimataria* and *To Steki tou Garbi* next door. The kafenía up here are very traditional affairs and you might feel more welcome at *Kastro* or *Platía*, two newly opened cafe-bars.

Around the island

West of Kástro-Hóra, an hour-plus walk (or mule ride) takes you through a landscape lush with olive trees to **Episkopí**, where elements of an ancient temple-tomb have been ingeniously incorporated into a seventh-century church – the structure is known formally as the Iróön. Ninety minutes from Kástro-Hóra, in the opposite direction, lies **Paleokástro**, the patchy remains of an ancient fortress. The beaches of **Áyios Yeóryios** and **Áyios Nikólaos** are reachable by a regular kaïki from Aloprónia; the former is a better option because it has the daytime *Almira* restaurant. It is possible to walk to them, but there is no real path at the later stages. A more feasible journey by foot is the pebble beach at **Áyios Pandelímonas**: just under an hour's trail walk southwest of Aloprónia, it is the most scenic and sheltered on the island, and is also served by a kaïki in season.

Folégandhros

The cliffs of **Folégandhros** rise sheer in places over 300m from the sea – until the early 1980s as effective a deterrent to tourists as they always were to pirates. It was used as an island of political exile right up until 1974, but life in the high, barren interior has been eased since the junta years by the arrival of electricity and the construction of a lengthwise road from the harbour to Hóra and beyond. Development has been given further impetus by the recent exponential increase in tourism and the mild commercialization this has brought.

A veritable explosion in accommodation for most budgets, and slight improvement in ferry arrival times, means there is no longer much need for – or local tolerance of – sleeping rough on the beaches. The increased wealth and trendiness of the heterogeneous clientele is reflected in fancy jewellery shops, an arty postcard gallery and a helipad. Yet away from the showcase Hóra and the beaches, the countryside remains mostly pristine, and is largely devoted to the spring and summer cultivation of barley, the mainstay of many of the Cyclades before the advent of tourism. Donkeys and donkey paths are also still very much in evidence, since the terrain on much of the island is too steep for vehicle roads.

Karavostássi and around

KARAVOSTÁSSI, the rather unprepossessing port whose name simply means "ferry stop", serves as a last-resort base; it has several **hotels** but little atmosphere. Best value if you do decide to stay is *Hotel Aeolos* (☎0286/41 205; ④), while the *Poseidon* (☎0286/41 272; ⑤) throws in breakfast at its decent restaurant *To Kati Allo*, which means "Something Else". The new *Vrahos Hotel* (☎0286/41 304; ④) has some nice rooms on the far side of the bay. *Iy Kali Kardhia* **taverna** above the harbour is recommended, and there are a couple of pleasant beach bars including the *Smyrna Ouzeri*, housed in a converted boathouse. There are many buses a day in summer to Hóra, and three of those go on to Áno Meriá; if you're feeling adventurous try Jimmy's motorbike rental (☎0286/41 448), which is cheaper than its counterparts in Hóra.

The closest **beach** is the smallish, but attractive enough, sand and pebble **Vardhiá**, signposted just north over the headland. Some twenty minutes' walk south lies **Loustriá**, a rather average beach with tamarisk trees and the island's official **campsite**, *Livadi Camping* (☎0286 41 304), which is good and friendly, although the hot water supply can be erratic.

Easily the most scenic beach on Folégandhros, a 300m stretch of pea-gravel with an offshore islet, is at **Katergó**, on the southeastern tip of the island. Most people visit on a boat excursion from Karavostássi or Angáli, but you can also get there on foot from the hamlet of Livádhi, a short walk inland from Loustriá. Be warned, though, that it's a rather arduous trek, with some nasty trail-less slithering in the final moments.

Hóra

The island's real character and appeal are to be found in the spectacular **HÓRA**, perched on a clifftop plateau some 45 minutes' walk from the dock; an hourly high-season **bus** service (6 daily spring/autumn) runs from morning until late at night. Locals and foreigners – hundreds of them in high season – mingle at the cafés and tavernas under the almond, flowering judas and pepper trees of the two main platías, passing the time unmolested by traffic, which is banned from the village centre. Toward the cliff-edge, and entered through two arcades, the defensive core of the medieval **kástro** is marked by ranks of two-storey houses, whose repetitive, almost identical stairways and slightly recessed doors are very appealing.

From the square where the bus stops, a zigzag path with views down to both coastlines climbs to the crag-top, wedding-cake church of **Kímisis Theotókou**, nocturnally illuminated to grand effect. Beyond and below it hides the **Khryssospiliá**, a large cave with stalactites, accessible only to proficient climbers; the necessary steps and railings have crumbled away into the sea, although a minor, lower grotto can still be visited.

Practicalities

Hóra's **accommodation** seems slightly weighted to favour hotels over rooms, with concentrations around the bus plaza at the eastern entrance to the village and at the western edge. Many of the tavernas and shops advertise rooms in their windows; otherwise try the purpose-built complex run by Irini Dekavalla (☎0286/41 235; ④), east of the bus stop. The nearby *Hotel Polikandia* (☎0286/41 322; ⑤) has an engaging proprietress and lower rates off season. The most luxurious facilities are at the cliff-edge *Anemomilos Apartments* (☎0286/41 309; ⑥), immaculately appointed and with stunning views; the new *Meltemi* (☎0286/41 328; ④), just opposite, has clean, comfortable rooms. The only hotel within Hóra is the *Castro* (☎0286/41 230; ⑤), with three rather dramatic rooms looking directly out on an alarming drop to the sea. At the western edge of Hóra near the police station, a dense cluster of rooms tend to block each other's views; the least claustrophobic is the recently rennovated *Odysseas* (☎0286/41 276; ⑤), which also manages some attractive apartments near the *Anemomilos*, the *Folgeandros Apartments* (☎0286/41 239; ⑤). By the roadside on the way to Áno Meriá, the *Fani-Vevis* (☎0286/41 237; ④), in a Neoclassical mansion overlooking the sea, seems to function only in high season; one hundred metres beyond are some smart new studios managed by *Iy Kali Kardhia* (see p.551) (☎0286/41 274; ⑥).

Hóra's dozen or so **restaurants** are surprisingly varied. The *Folegandhros* ouzerí in water-cistern plaza, is fun, if a bit eccentrically run. Breakfast can be enjoyed on the adjacent Platía Kondaríni at *Iy Melissa*, which does good fruit and yoghurt, omelettes and juices. *Iy Piatsa* has a nightly changing menu of well-executed Greek dishes, while their neighbour and local hangout *O Kritikos* is notable only for its grills. *Iy Pounda* near the bus stop is the most traditional place and has a small garden, while *Apanemo* at the far end of town has good food and a quieter setting, despite its proximity to the main bar area. Self-catering is an attractive option, with two well-stocked fruit shops and two supermarkets. Hóra is inevitably beginning to sprawl unattractively at the edges, but this at least means that the burgeoning **nightlife** – two dancing bars and a quantity of musical pubs and ouzeris – can be exiled to the north, away from most accommodation. *Avli* and *Greco* are two lively bars and both play up-to-date sounds, while *Kellari* is a rustic and charming wine bar where the atmosphere is more relaxed. A **post office** (no bank or OTE) completes the list of amenities, though the single **ferry agent** also does money exchange, as does the friendly and competent Italian-run Sottavento agency, which offers a wide range of services.

The rest of the island

Northwest of Hóra a narrow, paved road threads its way towards **ÁNO MERIÁ**, the other village of the island; after 4km you pass its first houses, clustered around the three churches of Áyios Pandelímonas, Áyios Yeóryios and Áyios Andhréas. Four tavernas operate in high season only: *Barba Kostas* is at the beginning of the village, *O Mimis* is about halfway along, *Iy Sinandisi* is at the turning for Áyios Yeóryios beach, while *Iliovasilema*, at the far end of the sprawling village, completes the list. Several rooms are also available; including *Stella's* (☎0286/41 329; ②) and *Irini's* (☎0286/41 344; ②).

Up to six times a day in high season a **bus** trundles out here to drop people off at the footpaths down to the various sheltered beaches on the southwest shore of the island. Busiest of these is **Angáli** (aka Vathý), with four rather basic room outfits including *Vangelis* (0286/41 105; ②) and *Panagiotis* (☎0286/41 116; ③) and two equally simple summer-only tavernas, reached by a fifteen-minute walk along a dirt road from the bus stop.

Nudists are urged to take the paths which lead twenty minutes east or west to **Firá** or **Áyios Nikólaos** beaches respectively; the latter in particular, with its many tamarisks, coarse sand and view back over the island, is Katergó's only serious rival in the best-beach sweepstakes. At Áyios Nikólaos, a lone taverna operates up by the namesake chapel; Firá has no facilities at all. From the *Iliovasilema* taverna, a motorable track continues north to a point from where a 500-metre path takes you down to the pleasant little bay of **Ambéli**.

Thíra (Santoríni)

As the ferry manoeuvres into the great caldera of **Thíra**, the land seems to rise up and clamp around it. Gaunt, sheer cliffs loom hundreds of feet above, nothing grows or grazes to soften the view, and the only colours are the reddish-brown, black and grey pumice striations layering the cliff-face. The landscape tells of a history so dramatic and turbulent that legend hangs as fact upon it.

From as early as 3000 BC the island developed as a sophisticated outpost of Minoan civilization, until around 1550 BC when catastrophe struck: the volcano-island erupted, its heart sank below the sea, and earthquakes reverberated across the Aegean. Thíra was destroyed and the great Minoan civilizations on Crete were dealt a severe blow. At this point the island's history became linked with legends of Atlantis, the "Happy Isles Submerged by Sea". Plato insisted that the legend was true, and Solon dated the cataclysm to 9000 years before his time – if you're willing to accept a mistake and knock off the final zero, a highly plausible date.

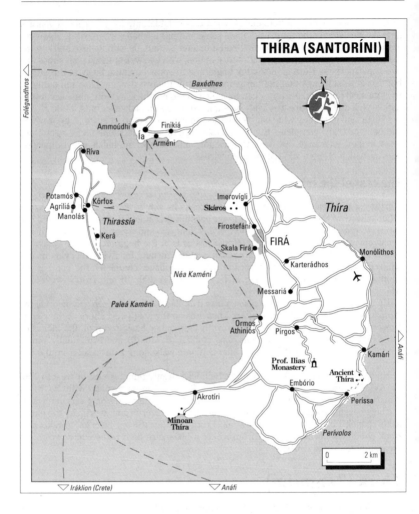

THÍRA (SANTORÍNI)

Folégandhros

Baxédhes

N

Ammoúdhi • Finikiá
Ía • Arméni

Ríva

Potamós •
Agriliá • Kórfos
Manolás

Thirassía

Kerá

Imerovígli
Skáros · ·

Thíra

Firostefáni

FIRÁ

Skala Firá •

Monólithos

Néa Kaméni

Karterádhos •

Paleá Kaméni

Messariá •

Ormos
Athiniós

Pírgos

Kamári

Anáfi

Prof. Ilias
Monastery

Ancient
Thíra · ·

Embório

Akrotíri

Períssa

Minoan
Thíra

Perívolos

0   2 km

▽ Iráklion (Crete)   ▽ Anáfi

These apocalyptic events, though, scarcely concern modern tourists, who are here mostly to stretch out on the island's dark-sand beaches and absorb the peculiar, infernal atmosphere; as recently as a century ago, Thíra was still reckoned to be infested with vampires. Though not nearly so predatory as the undead, current visitors have in fact succeeded in pretty much killing off any genuine island life, creating in its place a rather expensive and stagey playground.

Arrival and departure

Ferries dock at the somewhat grim port of **Órmos Athiniós**; **Skála Firás** and **Ía** in the north are reserved for local ferries, excursion kaïkia and cruise ships. **Buses**, astonishingly crammed, connect Athiniós with the island capital Firá, and, less frequently, with the main beaches at Kamári and Périssa; disembark quickly and take whatever's going, if you want to avoid a long walk. You're also likely to be accosted at Athiniós by people offering rooms all over the island; it may be a good idea to pay attention to them, given the scramble for beds in Firá especially. If you alight at Skála Firás, you have the traditional route above you – 580 mule-shit-splattered steps to Firá itself. It's not that difficult to walk, but the intrepid can also go up by mule or by cable car (summer only 6.40am–10pm, every 20min; 800dr). The **airport** is located towards the other side of the island, near Monólithos; there is a regular shuttle-bus service to the Firá bus station, which runs until 10pm.

When it comes to **leaving** – especially for summer/evening ferry departures – it's best to buy your ticket in advance. Note, too, that although the bus service stops around midnight, a shared taxi isn't outrageously expensive. Incidentally, **ferry information** from any source is notoriously unreliable on Thíra, so departure details should be quadruple-checked. If you do get stranded in Athiniós waiting for a ferry connection, there's no place to stay, and the tavernas are pretty awful. With time on your hands, it's well worth zigzagging the 3500m up to the closest village, **MEGALOHÓRI**. Between Megalohóri and Pýrgos village, near the junction of the main and Athiniós road, is *Hotel Zorbas* (☎0286/31 433; ④), and at the centre of Megalohóri, the *Yeromanolis* is a surprisingly reasonable and tasty grill which offers the increasingly rare homemade Santoríni wine.

Firá

Half-rebuilt after a devastating earthquake in 1956, **FIRÁ** (also known as Thíra or Hóra) still lurches dementedly at the cliff's edge. With a stunningly attractive setting, it appears on postcards and tourist brochures and, naturally, you pay the price for its position. Busy with day-trippers in summer at least, initial impressions of Firá are of gross commercialism, and it is perhaps best avoided in season.

However, Firá's clifftop position does justify a visit, and you should also make time for the **Archeological Museum** (Tues–Sun 8am–2.30pm; 800dr), near the cable car to the north of town, whose collection includes a curious set of erotic Dionysiac figures. The interesting **Museum Megaro Ghyzi** (Mon–Sat 10.30am–1.30pm & 5–8pm, Sun 10.30am–4.30pm; 500dr) is in an old mansion owned by the Catholic diocese of Santoríni and restored as a cultural centre. It has a good collection of old prints and maps as well as photographs of the town before and after the 1956 earthquake.

Practicalities

Caldera-side hotels and studios in **Firá** itself are expensive but there are plenty of rooms without caldera views at the back of town. *Villa Haroula* (☎0286/24 226; ⑤) is a good smart hotel on the road down to *Santorini Camping* (☎0286/22 944), at the back of town, which stays open with heating through the winter. Along the same road *Pension Petros* (☎0286/22 573; ④) and *Pension Soula* (☎0286/ 23 473; ⑤) are two reasonable, if not very exciting alternatives. Otherwise there is the *International Youth Hostel* (☎0286/22 387), in the northern part of town, between Erythroú Stavroú and 25-Martiou, with dorm beds and double rooms; it's a good budget option although it can be a bit noisy at night. Camping Caldera View (☎0286/82 010) is probably the most pleasant **campsite** in Thíra, in between Firá, the port and the nearest beach.

FIROSTEFÁNI, between Firá and Imerovígli, is the best bet for reasonably priced rooms with views over the caldera. Rooms in Firostefáni of varying prices and standards include *Apartments Gaby* (☎0286/22 057; ④), *Hotel Mylos* (☎0286/23 884; ④), *Kafieris Hotel* (☎0286/22 189; ④) and the rooms of Ioannis Roussos (☎0286/22 611 or 22 862; ④). For something smarter, *Manos Apartments* (☎0286/23 202; ⑥) is highly recommended. You might try **KARTERÁDHOS**, a small village about twenty minutes' walk south of Firá, where there are rooms and the pleasant *Hotel Albatross* (☎0286/23 435, fax 23 431; ⑥), or Messariá, another 2km further, with some more expensive hotels.

Firá's **restaurants** are primarily aimed at the tourist market, but there are a few worth trying: the *Flame of the Volcano* is the last of the caldera-side restaurants heading north past the cable-car station (towards Firostefáni) and is better and more reasonably priced than most, although you are still paying extra for the view. *Nikolas* on Erythroú Stavroú is an old-established and defiantly traditional taverna but it can be hard to get a table. Otherwise try *Koutouki* on 25-Martíou, *Mama's Cyclades*, a little further up on the same road, or *Aktaion* in Firostefáni. As for **nightlife**, *Enigma*, a soul disco, occupying a converted house and garden, and *Kyra Thira*, a good jazz bar, are both on Erythroú Stavroú (walking south from the *International Youth Hostel*), along with various other clubs. The best bars from which to admire the caldera are *Franco's*, a rather exclusive and pricey cocktail bar, and the more laid-back *Tropical*, just above, for easy listening which gets funkier as the night progresses.

Nomikos Travel (☎0286/23 660) on 25-Martíou, opposite the OTE, is friendly and organizes excursions and trips to ancient Thira and Thirassía in conjunction with Kamari Tours (☎0286/31 390). **Buses** leave Firá from just south of Platía Theotokopoúlou to Périssa, Perívolos, Kamári, Monólithos, Akrotíri, Athiniós and the airport. **Taxis** (☎0286/22 555) go from near the bus station. If you want to see the whole island in a couple of days a rented **moped** is useful; Moto Chris at the top of the road that leads down to *Santorini Camping* is recommended.

The north

Once outside Firá, the rest of Santoríni comes as a nice surprise, although development is beginning to encroach. The volcanic soil is highly fertile, with every available space terraced and cultivated: wheat, tomatoes (most made into paste), pistachios and grapes are the main crops, all still harvested and planted by hand. The island's *vysándo* and *nikhtéri* wines are a little sweet for many tastes but are among the finest produced in the Cyclades.

A satisfying – if demanding – approach to Ía, 12km from Firá in the northwest of the island, is to walk the stretch from **IMEROVÍGLI**, 3km out of Firá, using a spectacular footpath along the lip of the caldera; the walk takes around two hours. Imerovígli is crowded with luxury, caldera-side **apartments** such as *Chromata* (☎0286/24 850; ⑥) and *Astra* (☎0286/23 641; ⑥), requiring reservations well in advance; *Katerina* (☎0286/22 708; ⑤) is a more moderately priced hotel, with caldera views from the large balcony/bar area only. *Altana* between *Katerina* and *Chromata* is a small caldera-side **café** whose position and relaxed atmosphere make for a pleasing breakfast spot. Continuing to Ía, you'll pass Toúrlos, an old Venetian citadel on Cape Skáros, on the way.

ÍA was once a major fishing port of the Aegean, but it has declined in the wake of economic depression, wars, earthquakes and depleted fish stocks. Partly destroyed in the 1956 earthquake, the town has been sympathetically reconstructed, its pristine white houses clinging to the cliff-face. Apart from the caldera and the village itself there are a couple of things to see, including the **Naval Museum** (daily except Tues 9am–1pm & 5–8pm) and the very modest remains of a Venetian castle. With a **post office**, a couple of travel agencies and several **bike-rental** offices (of which Motor Fun is particularly good), Ía is a fine, and quieter, alternative to Firá. Much of the town's **accommodation** is in its restored old houses, including the troglodytic *Hotel Lauda* (☎0286/71 204; ④), the *Hotel Anemones* (☎0286/71 342; ④) and the *Hotel Fregata* (☎0286/71 221; ④). The highly recommended *Chelidonia Villas* (☎286/71 287; ⑥) are attractive restored cliff-side houses.

Quite near the bus terminal, also reachable by the main road that continues round to the back end of the village, is an excellent new hostel – the *Oia Youth Hostel* (☎0286/71 465), with a terrace and shady courtyard, a good bar, clean dormitories and breakfast included. Generally, the further you go along the central ridge towards the new end of Ía, the better value the **restaurants**; the *Anemomilos* and *Laokastri* are two such examples. The more centrally located *Skala* has standard fare, but you pay that little bit extra for the caldera-side location. **Nightlife** revolves around sunset-gazing, for which people are coached in from all over the island, creating traffic chaos; when this pales, there's *Petra* and *Alitana*, two bars located on the road leading down to the youth hostel, both playing easy listening in pleasant garden surroundings.

Below the town, 200-odd steps switchback hundreds of metres down to two small harbours: **Ammoúdhi**, for the fishermen, and **Arméni**, where the excursion boats dock. Both have excellent fish tavernas. *Sunset* taverna at Ammoúdhi is recommended, and at Arméni there is a taverna which specializes in grilled octopus lunches.

FINIKIÁ, 1km east of Ía, is a very quiet and traditional little village. The reopening of the village taverna looks dubious, and accommodation is not in abundance. *Lotza Rooms* (☎0286/ 71 051; ③) are located in an old house in the middle of the village, while *Hotel Finakia* (☎0286/71 373; ⑤), above the village near the main road, is a smarter option. Just north of Ía is **Baxédhes** beach, a quiet alternative to Kamári and Périssa (see below), with a few tavernas including the *Paradhisos*, which has good food and reasonable prices.

The east and south

Beaches on Santoríni, to the east and south, are bizarre – long black stretches of volcanic sand which get blisteringly hot in the afternoon sun. They're no secret, and in the summer the crowds can be a bit overpowering. Closest to Firá, **MONÓLITHOS** has a couple of tavernas but is nothing special. Further south, **KAMÁRI** has surrendered lock, stock and barrel to the package-tour operators and there's not a piece of sand that isn't fronted by concrete villas.

Nonetheless it's quieter and cleaner than most, with some beachfront **accommodation**, including *Hotel Nikolina* (☎0286/31 702; ③), with basic but cheap rooms towards the southern end of the beach, as well as the *White House* (☎0286/31 441; ④) and the friendly *Sea Side Rooms* (☎0286/33 403; ③) further along the beach. *Rose Bay Hotel* (☎0286/33 650; ⑥) is a far pricier option, with a pleasant pool setting, set back away from the noisy beach thoroughfare. *Kamari Camping* (☎0286/31 453), a fifteen-minute walk on the road out of Kamári, is a small municipal-run site with limited facilities and no points for a warm welcome.

Psistaria O Kritikos, a taverna-grill frequented by locals rather than tourists, is one of the best places to **eat** on the island. It's a long way out of Kamári on the road up to Messariá, and too far to walk, but the bus stops outside. There are plenty of cafés and restaurants behind the beach, though many are expensive or uninspired. *Saliveros*, in front of the *Hotel Nikolina*, has taverna food at reasonable prices, and *Almira*, next to *Sea Side Rooms*, is a smarter restaurant and only a little more expensive. Kamári is a family resort with little in the way of clubs and nightlife, but there is a good open-air **cinema** near the campsite, and in summer buses run until 1am, so there's no problem getting back to Firá after seeing a film.

Things are scruffier at **PÉRISSA**, around the cape. Despite (or perhaps because of) its attractive situation and abundance of cheap rooms, it's noisy and crowded with backpackers. *Camping Perissa Beach* (☎0286/81 343) is right behind the beach and has plenty of shade but is also next to a couple of noisy late-night bars. There is also a youth hostel on the road into Périssa: *Anna* (☎0286/82 182) has dorm beds as well as a few simple studios closer to the beach. There are plenty of cheap rooms in the same area and some upmarket hotels behind the beach, including the smart and expensive *Hotel Veggara* (☎0286/82 060; ⑥). The beach itself extends almost 7km to the west, sheltered by the occasional tamarisk tree, with beach bars dotted along at intervals; *Wet Stories*, about ten minutes' walk from Périssa village, has a fun atmosphere and a varied snack selection.

Kamári and Périssa are separated by the Mésa Vounó headland, on which stood **ancient Thíra** (Tues–Sun 9am–3pm), the post-eruption settlement dating from the ninth century BC. Excursion buses go up from Kamári (5000dr), staying two hours at the site (ask at Kamári Tours behind the beach) but you can walk the **cobbled path** starting from the square in Kamári by the Argo General Store. The path zigzags up to a whitewashed church by a **cave**, containing one of Thira's few freshwater springs, before crossing over to meet the road and ending at a saddle between Mésa Vounó and Profítis Ilías, where a refreshments van sells expensive drinks. From here, the path to the site passes a chapel dating back to the fourth century AD before skirting round to the Temenos of Artemidoros with bas-relief carvings of a dolphin, eagle and lion representing Poseidon, Zeus and Apollo. Next, the trail follows the sacred way of the ancient city through the remains of the agora and past the theatre. Most of the ruins (dating mainly from Hellenistic and Roman times) are difficult to place, but the site is impressively large and the views are awesome. The site can also be reached by a path from Périssa, and either way it's less than an hour's walk.

Inland along the same mountain spine is the monastery of **Profítis Ilías**, now sharing its refuge with Greek radio and TV pylons and the antennae of a NATO station. With just one monk remaining to look after the church, the place only really comes to life for the annual Profítis Ilías festival, when the whole island troops up here to celebrate. The views are still rewarding, though, and from near the entrance to the monastery an old footpath heads across the ridge in about an hour to ancient Thíra. The easiest ascent is the thirty-minute walk from the village of Pýrgos.

PÝRGOS itself is one of the oldest settlements on the island, a jumble of old houses and alleys that still bear the scars of the 1956 earthquake. It climbs to another Venetian fortress crowned by several churches and you can clamber around the battlements for sweeping views over the entire island and its Aegean neighbours. By way of contrast **MESSARIÁ**, a thirty-minute stroll north, has a skyline consisting solely of massive church domes that lord it over the houses huddled in a ravine.

Akrotíri

Evidence of the Minoan colony that once thrived here has been uncovered at the other ancient site of **Akrotíri** (Tues–Sat 8.30am–3pm; 1500dr), at the southwestern tip of the island. Tunnels through the volcanic ash uncovered structures, two and three storeys high, first damaged by earthquake then buried by eruption; Professor Marinatos, the excavator and now an island hero, was killed by a collapsing wall and is also buried on the site. Only a small part of what was the largest Minoan city outside of Crete has been excavated thus far. Lavish frescoes adorned the walls, and Cretan pottery was found stored in a chamber; most of the frescoes are currently exhibited in Athens.

Akrotíri itself can be reached by bus from Firá or Périssa; the excellent *Glaros* taverna, on the way to Kókkini Ámmos beach, has excellent food and barrelled wine. Kókkini Ámmos is about 500m from the site and is quite spectacular with high reddish-brown cliffs above sand the same colour (the name means "red sand"). There's a drinks stall in a cave hollowed into the base of the cliff. It's a better beach than the one below the site, but gets crowded in season.

The Kaméni islets and Thirassía

From either Firá or Ía, boat excursions and local ferries run to the charred volcanic islets of **Paleá Kaméni** and **Néa Kaméni**, and on to the relatively unspoiled islet of

Thirassía, which was once part of Santoríni until shorn off by an eruption in the third century BC. At Paleá Kaméni you can swim from the boat to hot springs with sulphurous mud, and Néa Kaméni, with its own mud-clouded hot springs, features a demanding hike to a volcanically active crater.

The real attraction though, is **Thirassía**, the quietest island in the Cyclades. The views are as dramatic as any on Santoríni, and tourism has little effect on island life. The downside is that there is no sandy beach, no nightlife and nowhere to change money.

Most tour boats head for **Kórfos**, a stretch of shingle backed by fishermen's houses and high cliffs. It has a few tavernas, including *Tonio* which stays open when the daytrippers have gone, but no rooms. From Kórfos a stepped path climbs up to **MANOLÁS**, nearly 200m above. Donkeys are still used for transport, and stables can be seen in both villages. Manolás straggles along the edge of the caldera, an untidy but attractive small island village that gives an idea of what Santoríni was like before tourism arrived there. It has a bakery, a couple of shops and a few tavernas, including the friendly *Panorama*, that opens only for the midday rush: the **restaurant** at the *Hotel Cavo Mare* (☎0286/29 176; ⑤) wins out by giving diners the use of the swimming pool. Dhimítrios Nomikós has **rooms** (☎0286/29 102; ③) overlooking the village from the south.

The best **excursion** from Manolás is to follow the unmade road heading south; about halfway along you pass the church of Profítis Ilías on a hilltop to the left. From here an old and overgrown trail descends through the deserted caldera-side village of **Kerá**, before running parallel with the road to the **monastery of the Kímisis** above the southern tip of the island. Minoan remains were excavated in a pumice quarry to the west of here in 1867, several years before the first discoveries at Akrotíri, but there is nothing to be seen today.

Ferries run to Thirassía four times a week in season and three times a week through the winter. There is no problem taking a car or rental bike over, but fill up with petrol first. Day-trips take in Néa Kaméni and Paleá Kaméni but are expensive (6000dr) and only stay two or three hours on Thirassía.

Anáfi

A ninety-minute boat ride to the east of Thíra, **Anáfi** is the last stop for ferries and hydrofoils and something of a travellers' dead end, with only the occasional high season ferry on to Astypálea in the Dodecanese. Not that this is likely to bother most of the visitors, who intentionally come here for weeks in mid-summer, and take over the island's beaches with a vengeance.

At most other times the place seems idyllic, and indeed may prove too sleepy for some: there are no bona fide hotels, mopeds, discos or organized excursions, and donkeys are still the main method of transport in the interior. Anáfi, though initially enchanting, is a harsh place, its mixed granite/limestone core overlaid by volcanic rock spewed out by Thíra's eruptions. Apart from the few olive trees and vines grown in the valleys, the only plants that seem to thrive are prickly pears.

The harbour and Hóra

The tiny harbour hamlet of **ÁYIOS NIKÓLAOS** has a single taverna, *To Akroyiali*, with a few rooms (☎0286/61 218; ②), while *Dave's Cafe*, with straw umbrellas above the beach, is a colourful English-run drinking spot. Jeyzed Travel (☎0286/61 253, fax 61 352) can provide information as well as issuing ferry tickets, changing money and booking rooms. In August there are enough Greek visitors to fill all the rooms on the island, so it's a good idea to book ahead. Most places to stay are in Hóra. In season a bus runs from the harbour every two hours or so from 9am to 11pm.

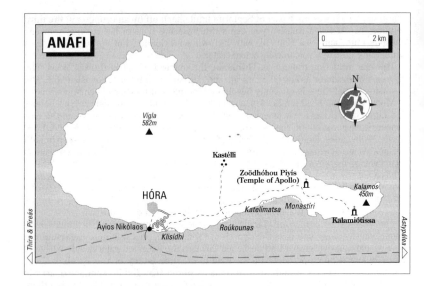

HÓRA itself, adorning a conical hill overhead, is a stiff, 25-minute climb up the obvious old mule path which shortcuts the modern road. Exposed and blustery when the *meltémi* is blowing, Hóra can initially seem a rather forbidding ghost town. This impression is slowly dispelled as you discover the hospitable islanders taking their coffee in sheltered, south-facing terraces, or under the anti-earthquake barrel vaulting that features in domestic architecture here.

The modern, purpose-built **rooms** run by Kalliopi Halari (☎0286/61 271; ②) and Voula Loudharou (☎0286/61 279; ②), and those run by Margarita Kollidha (☎0286/61 292; ③) at the extreme east edge of the village, are about the most comfortable – and boast stunning views south to the islets of Ftená, Pahiá and Makriá, and the distinctive monolith at the southeastern corner of Anáfi. Evening **diners** seem to divide their custom between the simple, welcoming *To Steki*, with reasonable food and barrel wine served on its terrace, and the more upmarket *Alexandhra's* on the central walkway. *Armenaki* is a lively new taverna/ouzerí which hosts regular *bouzoúki* nights. Otherwise nightlife revolves around the two bars: *Mylos Bar*, housed in a converted windmill in the village, and *Mantres* on the main road between the port and Hóra. Several shops, a bakery and a **post office** round up the list of amenities.

East along the coast: beaches and monasteries

The glory of Anáfi is a string of south-facing beaches starting under the cliffs at Áyios Nikólaos. Freelance campers head for **KLISÍDHI**, a short walk to the east of the harbour, where 200m of tan, gently shelving sand is pounded by gentle surf, and splendidly malopropic signs announce that "Nubbism is not allowed". Above the calamus-and-tamarisk oasis backing the beach there are two cafés and a taverna, including the *Kafestiatorion tis Margaritas*, with popular rooms (☎0286/61 237; ③). The *Villa Apollon* on the hillside above has the island's most upmarket accommodation (☎0286/61 348; ③). Klisídhi can be reached by road but it's quicker to take the cliff-top path starting behind the power station at the harbour. East of here the beaches can only be reached by foot or boat.

From a point on the paved road just east of Hóra, the **main path** skirting the south flank of the island is signposted: "Kastélli – Paleá Hóra – Roúkouna – Monastíri". The primary branch of this trail roller-coasters in and out of several agricultural valleys that provide most of Anáfi's produce and fresh water. Just under an hour along, beside a well, you veer down a side trail to **Roúkounas**, easily the island's best beach, with some 500m of broad sand rising to tamarisk-stabilized dunes, which provide welcome shade. A single taverna, *Tou Papa*, operates up by the main trail in season; the suggestively craggy hill of **Kastélli**, an hour's scramble above the taverna, is the site both of ancient Anaphi and a ruined Venetian castle.

Beyond Roúkounas, it's another half hour on foot to the first of the exquisite half-dozen **Katelímatsa** coves, of all shapes and sizes, and 45 minutes to **Monastíri** beach – all without facilities, so come prepared. Nudism is banned on Monastíri, because of its proximity to the monasteries.

The monasteries

Between Katelímatsa and Kálamos, the main route keeps inland, past a rare spring, to arrive at the **monastery of Zoödhóhou Piyís**, some two hours out of Hóra. A ruined temple of Apollo is incorporated into the monastery buildings to the side of the main gate; according to legend, Apollo caused Anáfi to rise from the waves, pulling off a dramatic rescue of the storm-lashed Argonauts. The courtyard, with a welcome cistern, is the venue for the island's major festival, celebrated eleven days after Easter. A family of cheesemakers lives next door and can point you up the start of the spectacular onward path to **Kalamiótissa**, a little monastery perched atop the abrupt pinnacle at the extreme southeast of the island. It takes another hour to reach, but is eminently worthwhile for the stunning scenery and views over the entire south coast. Kalamiótissa comes alive only during its 7–8 September festival; at other times, you could haul a sleeping bag up here to witness the amazing sunsets and sunrises, with your vantage point often floating in a sea of cloud. There is no water up here, so bring enough with you. It's a full day's outing from Hóra to Kalamiótissa and back; you might wish to take advantage, in at least one direction, of the excursion **kaïki** that runs from Áyios Nikólaos to Monastíri (6 times daily in high season). There is also a slightly larger mail and supplies boat (currently Mon & Thurs 11am) which takes passengers to and from Thíra (Athiniós), supplementing the main-line ferries to Pireás.

travel details

Ferries

Most of the Cyclades are served by mainline ferries from **Pireás**, but there are also boats which depart from **Lávrio** (for Kéa) and **Rafína**, which has become increasingly important of late, as work proceeds on the new international airport at nearby Spáta. At the moment there are daily services from Rafína to Ándhros, Tínos and Mýkonos, with less frequent sailings to Sýros, Páros, Náxos and Amorgós, and the North and East Aegean. All three ports are easily reached by bus from Athens. From June to September there are also a few weekly sailings from Thessaloníki to the most popular islands.

The frequency of sailings given below is intended to give an idea of services from April to October, when most visitors tour the islands. During the winter expect departures to be at or below the minimum level listed, with some routes cancelled entirely. Conversely, routes tend to be more comprehensive in spring and autumn, when the government obliges shipping companies to make extra stops to compensate for numbers of boats still in dry dock.

The long-awaited computerized booking system is now in operation, and all agents are required to issue computerized tickets. This move was designed to conform to EU regulations and prevent the overcrowding of ferries so common in the past. It means that in high season, certain popular routes may be booked up days in advance, so if you're visiting a few islands it is important to check availability on arrival in Greece, and book your outward and final pre-flight tickets well ahead. There is not usually so much problem with space between islands as there is to and from Pireás.

Amorgós 6–8 ferries weekly to Náxos and Páros, one of these continuing to Rafína rather than Pireás; 3–4 weekly to Sýros; 2–3 weekly to Tínos and Mýkonos; 2–3 weekly to Ándhros, Koufoníssi, Skhinoússa, Iráklia and Dhonoússa; 2–3 weekly to Astypálea.

Anáfi 6–8 weekly to Pireás (12hr 30min), mostly via Thíra (1hr 30min), Íos, Náxos, Páros; 1 weekly to Astypálea; 1 weekly to Sýros, Síkinos and Folégandhros; 2 weekly mail boats to Thíra (2hr).

Ándhros At least 3 daily to Rafína (2hr), Tínos (2hr) and Mýkonos; 4 weekly to Sýros; 2 weekly to Amorgós and Náxos; 1–4 weekly to Paros.

Dhonoússa 3–4 weekly to Amorgós; 2–3 weekly to Náxos, Koufoníssi, Skhinoússa, Iráklia, and Páros; 1 weekly to Pireás, Mýkonos, Tínos and Sýros; 2 weekly to Astypálea.

Íos At least 3 daily to Pireás (10hr), Páros (5hr), Náxos (3hr) and Thíra (several of which continue to Anáfi); 4–5 weekly to Síkinos and Folégandhros; 1 weekly to Crete; 1 weekly to Mílos, Kímolos, Sérifos and Sífnos; 2–3 weekly to Sýros and Kássos; daily to Mýkonos.

Kéa 1–3 daily to Lávrio (1hr 30min); 4 weekly to Kýthnos; 2 weekly to Sýros.

Kímolos 2 daily kaïkia to Mílos (Pollónia) year-round, 5 in summer; 2–5 weekly to Mílos (Adhámas), Sífnos, Sérifos, Kýthnos and Pireás (7hr); 2 weekly to Folégandhros, Síkinos and Thíra.

Koufoníssi, Skhinoússa, Iráklia 2–3 weekly Náxos; 1–2 weekly to Páros, Sýros and Tínos and Mýkonos; 1 weekly to Dhonoússa, Amorgós and Pireás.

Kýthnos 4–12 weekly to Pireás (3hr 15min); 4–10 weekly to Sérifos, Sífnos, Kímolos and Mílos; 3–4 weekly to Thíra and Folégandhros; 1–2 weekly to Síkinos, Sýros, Íos and Kéa.

Mílos At least daily to Pireás (8hr); Sat–Thurs to Sífnos (2hr), Sérifos and Kýthnos; 2–5 daily kaïkia or 4–6 weekly ferries to Kímolos; 2–3 weekly to Folégandhros, Síkinos, Íos and Thíra; 2 weekly to

Sýros; 2 weekly to Crete (Iráklion or Sitía); 2 weekly to Kássos and Kárpathos; 1 weekly to Hálki and Rhodes.

Mýkonos At least 2 daily to Pireás (5hr), Rafína (3hr 30min), Tínos (1hr), Ándhros (2hr 30min) and Sýros (2hr); 2–3 weekly to Amorgós; 2 weekly to Crete (Iráklion), Skiáthos and Thessaloníki; 1–2 weekly to Dhonoússa, Koufoníssi, Skhinoússa and Iráklia; 1 weekly to Pátmos and Foúrni; 3–4 weekly to Ikaría and Sámos; daily to Íos, Náxos and Páros; daily (except Monday) excursion boats to Delos.

Náxos At least 3 daily to Pireás (8hr), Páros (1hr), Íos and Thíra; 6–8 weekly to Sýros; 5–7 to Amorgós; 3 weekly to Crete (Iráklion); 5–6 weekly to Amorgós; 4–5 weekly to Tínos; 5 weekly to Síkinos and Folégandhros; 2 weekly to Ándhros and Rafína; 3 weekly to Anáfi; 3–4 weekly to Rhodes; 2–6 weekly to Ikaría and Sámos; 4 weekly to Astypálea; 1–2 weekly to Kássos and Kárpathos; 1 weekly to Kós and Foúrni; 2–3 weekly to Skiáthos and Thessaloníki; 3–4 weekly to Iráklia, Skhinoússa, Koufoníssi and Dhonoússa.

Páros At least 3 daily to Pireás (7hr), Andíparos, Náxos, Íos, Thíra; 6–8 weekly to Sýros and Tínos; 4 weekly to Iráklion (Crete); 3–6 weekly to Ikaría and Sámos; 4–6 weekly to Síkinos, Folégandhros and Amorgós; 4 weekly to Rafína and Ándhros; 2–3 weekly to Skiáthos and Thessaloníki; daily to Rhodes; 4–6 weekly to Anáfi; 1–2 weekly to Foúrni, Kós, Kássos and Kárpathos; 4 weekly to Astypálea; 2–4 weekly to Koufoníssi, Skhinoússa, Iráklia and Dhonoússa; 1 weekly to Vólos; 1 weekly to Pátmos and Kálymnos; 3–6 weekly to Ikaría and Sámos; at least 1 daily to Mýkonos; at least hourly (from Parikía) to Andíparos in summer, dropping to 3 weekly in winter. There is also a car ferry from Poúnda to Andíparos at least hourly throughout the year.

Sérifos and Sífnos 5–12 weekly to Pireás (4hr 30min), Kýthnos and each other; 5–10 weekly to Mílos; 2–5 weekly to Kímolos; 2–3 weekly to Folégandhros, Síkinos, and Thíra; once weekly to Íos; 2 weekly to Sýros; 1–2 weekly to Crete from Sífnos only; twice weekly from Sífnos to Páros.

Síkinos and Folégandhros 6 weekly between each other, and to Pireás (10hr); 2 weekly to Sýros, Kýthnos, Sérifos, Sífnos, Mílos and Kímolos; 3–6 weekly to Íos, Thíra, Páros and Náxos.

Sýros At least 2 daily to Pireás (4hr), Tínos (1hr), Mýkonos (2hr), Náxos, and Páros; at least 2 weekly to Rafína (3hr 30min) and Ándhros; 3 weekly to Amorgós and the islets behind Náxos; 2–4 weekly to Íos and Thíra; 1 weekly to Síkinos and Folégandhros; 2 weekly to Ikaría, Sámos and Astypálea; 2 weekly to Kéa, Kýthnos, Sérifos, Sífnos, Mílos and Kímolos; 1 weekly to Pátmos, Léros and Lipsí; 2–4 weekly to Skiáthos and Thessaloníki.

Thíra At least 3 daily to Pireás (10–12hr), Páros, Íos and Náxos; 5–6 weekly to Iráklion, Crete (5hr) and Thessaloníki; 6–8 weekly to Síkinos and Folégandhros; 4–6 weekly to Anáfi and Sífnos; daily to Mýkonos; 6–8 weekly to Sýros; 3–5 weekly to Tínos and Skiáthos; 2–4 weekly to Mílos and Kímolos; 1–2 weekly to Kárpathos, Kássos and Sérifos; 2 weekly to Rhodes; 1 weekly to Vólos; 4–6 weekly to Thirassía (plus lots of expensive daily excursion boats in season); 2 weekly mail boats to Anáfi.

Tínos At least 2 daily to Pireás (5hr), Rafína (4hr), Ándhros, Sýros and Mýkonos; 3–4 weekly to Páros and Náxos; 3 weekly to Thíra and Iráklion (Crete); 2–4 weekly Skiáthos and Thessaloníki; 3 weekly to Amorgós; 1 weekly to Íos, Koufoníssi, Skhinoússa, Iráklia and Dhonoússa; also excursion boats calling at Delos and Mýkonos, 1 daily except Monday.

Other services

To simplify the lists above, certain strategic **hydrofoil** and **small-boat services** have been omitted. Of these, the *Express Skopelitis* plies daily in season between Mýkonos and Amorgós, spending each night at the latter and threading through all of the minor isles between it and Náxos, as well as Náxos and Páros (Píso Livádhi), in the course of a week. For anyone familiar with the old *Skopelitis*, the *Express* is a slight improvement in that refreshments are available on board; however this "newer" boat is as overcrowded and unreliable as her long-lost sister. The Seajet catamaran – a small-capacity (and expensive) jet-boat (☎01 414 12 50 for details) – operates daily during summer out of Rafína and connects Sýros, Ándhros, Tínos, Mýkonos, Páros, Náxos and Thíra. Cycladic routes are pretty well mapped out

by the three hydrofoil companies – Minoan Flying Dolphins, Speed Lines and Cruises (Santorini Dolphin) and Dolphin Sea Line, with regular services from Zéa (Pireás), Thíra and Rafína respectively. Hydrofoil travel is expensive; however when time is an issue, or for more regular connections to some of the less commonly serviced routes such as the minor islets around Náxos, these handy flying machines are a welcome addition to the conventional fleet.

Flights

There are **airports** on **Páros, Mýkonos, Thíra, Sýros, Mílos** and **Náxos**. In season, or during storms when ferries are idle, you have little chance of getting a seat with Olympic Airways at less than three days' notice. Olympic's Athens–Mílos route is probably the best value for money; the other destinations seem deliberately overpriced, in a usually unsuccessful attempt to keep passenger volume manageable. Air Manos has recently introduced June–Sept flights to Thíra, Sýros and Mýkonos. Expect off-season (Oct–April) frequencies to drop by at least eighty percent.

Flights are on Olympic unless otherwise stated.

Athens–Mílos (1–2 daily; 45min)

Athens–Mýkonos (5–6 daily on Olympic; 5 weekly on Air Manos; 45min)

Athens–Náxos (1–2 daily; 45min)

Athens–Páros (3–4 daily; 45min)

Athens–Sýros (1–2 daily on Olympic; 3–4 weekly on Air Manos; 35min)

Athens–Thíra (5–6 daily on Olympic; 6 weekly on Air Manos; 50min)

Mýkonos–Rhodes (2 weekly; 1hr)

Mýkonos–Sámos (2 weekly on Air Manos; 45min)

Mýkonos–Thessaloníki (3 weekly; 1hr 15min)

Mýkonos–Thíra (3–5 weekly; 30min)

Thíra–Iráklion (Crete) (2 weekly; 40min)

Thíra–Rhodes (5 weekly; 1hr)

Thíra–Sámos (2 weekly on Air Manos; 1hr 20min)

Thíra–Thessaloníki (3weekly; 1hr 30min)

CHAPTER EIGHT

CRETE

Crete (Kríti) is a great deal more than just another Greek island. In many places, especially in the cities or along the developed north coast, it doesn't feel like an island at all, but rather a substantial land in its own right – a mountainous, wealthy and surprisingly cosmopolitan one. But when you lose yourself among the mountains, or on the lesser-known coastal reaches of the south, it has everything you could want of a Greek island and more: great beaches, remote hinterlands and hospitable people.

In **history**, Crete is distinguished above all as the home of Europe's earliest civilization. It was only at the beginning of this century that the legends of King Minos and of a Cretan society that ruled the Greek world in prehistory were confirmed by excavations at **Knossós** and **Festós**. Yet the **Minoans** had a remarkably advanced society, the centre of a maritime trading empire as early as 2000 BC. The artworks produced on Crete at this time are unsurpassed anywhere in the ancient world, and it seems clear that life on Crete in those days was good. This apparently peaceful culture survived at least three major natural disasters. Each time the palaces were destroyed, and each time they

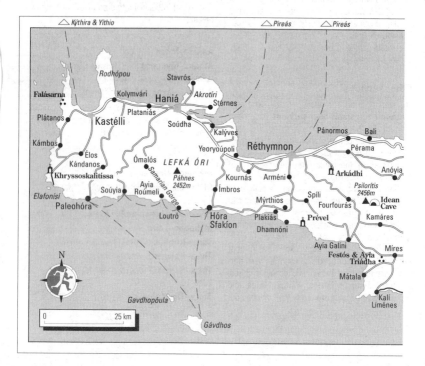

were rebuilt on a grander scale. Only after the last destruction, probably the result of an eruption of Thíra (Santoríni) and subsequent tidal waves and earthquakes, do significant numbers of weapons begin to appear in the ruins. This, together with the appearance of the Greek language, has been interpreted to mean that Mycenaean Greeks had taken control of the island. Nevertheless, for nearly 500 years, by far the longest period of peace the island has seen, Crete was home to a culture well ahead of its time.

The Minoans of Crete probably came originally from Anatolia; at their height they maintained strong links with Egypt and with the people of Asia Minor, and this position as meeting point and strategic fulcrum between east and west has played a major role in Crete's subsequent history. Control of the island passed from Greeks to Romans to Saracens, through the Byzantine empire to Venice, and finally to Turkey for more than two centuries. During World War II, the island was **occupied** by the Germans and attained the dubious distinction of being the first place to be successfully invaded by paratroops.

Today, with a flourishing **agricultural economy**, Crete is one of the few islands which could probably support itself without tourists. Nevertheless, **tourism** is heavily promoted. The northeast coast in particular is overdeveloped, and though there are parts of the south and west coasts that have not been spoiled, they are getting harder to find. By contrast, the high mountains of the interior are still barely touched, and one of the best things to do on Crete is to **rent a vehicle** and explore the remoter villages.

Where to go

Every part of Crete has its loyal devotees and it's hard to pick out highlights, but generally if you want to get away from it all you should head west, towards **Haniá** and the

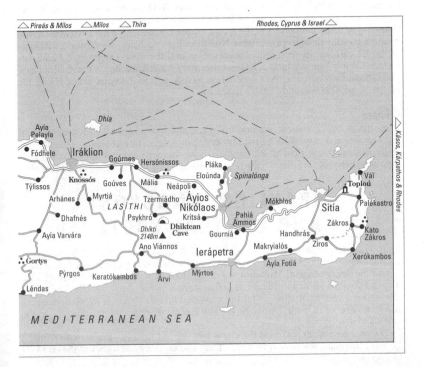

smaller, less well-connected places along the south and west coasts. It is in this part of the island that the White Mountains rise, while below them yawns the famous **Samarian Gorge**. The far east, around **Sitía**, is also relatively unscathed.

Whatever you do, your first main priority will probably be to leave **Iráklion** (Heraklion) as quickly as possible, having paid the obligatory, and rewarding, visit to the **Archeological Museum** and nearby **Knossós**. The other great Minoan sites cluster around the middle of the island: **Festós** and **Ayía Triádha** in the south (with Roman **Górtys** to provide contrast), and **Mália** on the north coast. Almost wherever you go, though, you'll find a reminder of the island's history, whether it's the town of **Gourniá** near the cosmopolitan resort of **Áyios Nikólaos**, the exquisitely sited palace of **Zákros** in the far east, or the lesser sites scattered around the west. Unexpected highlights include Crete's Venetian forts at **Réthymnon** and **Frangokástello**; its hundreds of frescoed Byzantine churches, most famously at **Kritsá**; and, at Réthymnon and Haniá, the cluttered old Venetian and Turkish quarters.

Climate

Crete has by far the longest summers in Greece, and you can get a decent tan here right into October and swim at least from May until November. The one seasonal blight is the *meltémi*, a northerly wind which regularly blows harder here and more continuously than anywhere else in Greece – the best of several reasons for avoiding an **August** visit.

IRÁKLION, KNOSSÓS AND CENTRAL CRETE

Many visitors to Crete arrive in the island's capital, **Iráklion** (Heraklion), but it's not an outstandingly beautiful city, nor one where you'll want to stay much longer than it takes to visit the **Archeological Museum** and nearby **Knossós**. Iráklion itself, though it has its good points – superb fortifications, a fine market, atmospheric old alleys and some interesting lesser museums – is for the most part an experience in survival: despite a recent makeover of central areas by the city hall it remains modern, raucous, traffic-laden and overcrowded.

The area immediately around the city is less touristy than you might expect, mainly because there are few decent beaches of any size on this central part of the coast. To the west, mountains drop straight into the sea virtually all the way to Réthymnon, with just two significant coastal settlements – **Ayía Pelayía**, a sizable resort, and **Balí**, which is gradually becoming one. Eastwards, the main resorts are at least 30km away, at **Hersónissos** and beyond, although there is a string of rather unattractive developments all the way there. Inland, there's agricultural country, some of the richest on the island, Crete's best vineyards, and a series of wealthy but rather dull villages. Directly behind the capital rises **Mount Ioúktas** with its characteristic profile of Zeus; to the west the Psilorítis massif spreads around the peak of **Mount Ídha** (Psilorítis), the island's highest mountain. On the south coast there are few roads and little development of any kind, except at **Ayía Galíni** in the southwest, a nominal fishing village long since swamped with tourists, and **Mátala**, which has thrown out the hippies that made it famous and is now crowded with package-trippers. **Léndas** has to some extent occupied Mátala's old niche.

Despite the lack of resorts, there seem constantly to be thousands of people trekking back and forth across the centre of the island. This is largely because of the superb archeological sites in the south: **Festós**, second of the Minoan palaces, with its attendant villa at **Ayía Triádha**, and **Górtys**, capital of Roman Crete.

Iráklion

The best way to approach **IRÁKLION** is by sea: that way you see the city as it should be seen, with Mount Ioúktas rising behind and the Psilorítis range to the west. As you get closer, it's the city walls that first stand out, still dominating and fully encircling the oldest part of town; finally you sail in past the great **fort** defending the harbour entrance. Unfortunately, big ships no longer dock in the old port but at great modern concrete wharves alongside, which neatly sums up Iráklion itself. Many of the old parts have been restored from the bottom up, but they're of no relevance to the dust and noise that characterizes much of the city today. In recent times, however, Iráklion's administrators have been giving belated attention to dealing with some of the image problems, and large tracts of the centre – particularly the focal Platía Eleftherías – have been landscaped and refurbished with the aim of presenting a less daunting prospect to the visitor.

Orientation, arrival and information

Virtually everything you're likely to want to see in Iráklion lies within the walled city, and even here the majority of the interest falls into a relatively small sector, the northeastern corner. The most vital thoroughfare, **25-Avgoústou**, links the harbour with the commercial city centre. At the bottom it is lined with shipping and travel agencies and rental outlets, but as you climb these give way to banks, restaurants and stores. **Platía Venizélou** (or Fountain Square), off to the right, is crowded with cafés and restaurants; behind Venizélou lies **El Greco Park** (actually a rather cramped garden), with more bars, while on the opposite side of 25-Avgoústou are some of the more interesting of Iráklion's older buildings. Further up 25-Avgoústou, **Kalokerinoú** leads down to Haniá Gate and westwards out of the city; straight ahead, **Odhós 1821** is a major shopping street, and adjacent 1866 is given over to the animated **market**. To the left, Dhikeosínis heads for the city's main square, **Platía Eleftherías**, paralleled by the touristy pedestrian alley, Dhedhálou, the direct link between the two squares. The newly revamped Eleftherías is very much the traditional centre of the city, both for

The telephone code for Iráklion is ☎081

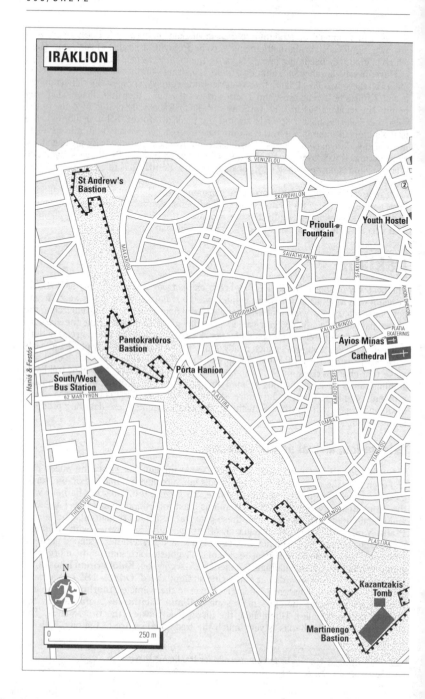

IRÁKLION

St Andrew's Bastion

S. VENIZELOU

SKORDHILÓN

Priouli Fountain

Youth Hostel

MAKARIOU

SAVATHIANON

SFAKION

AYION DHEKA

②

DEDHIDHAKI

KALOKERINOU

PLATIA EKATERINIS

Pantokratóros Bastion

Áyios Minas

Cathedral

Pórta Hanion

KARDIOTISSIS

◁ Haniá & Festós

South/West Bus Station

62 MARTYRON

PLASTIRA

TOMBAZ

YANIKOU

THERISSOU

ROMANOU

THENON

PLASTIRA

N

KONDILAKI

Kazantzakis' Tomb

0   250 m

Martinengo Bastion

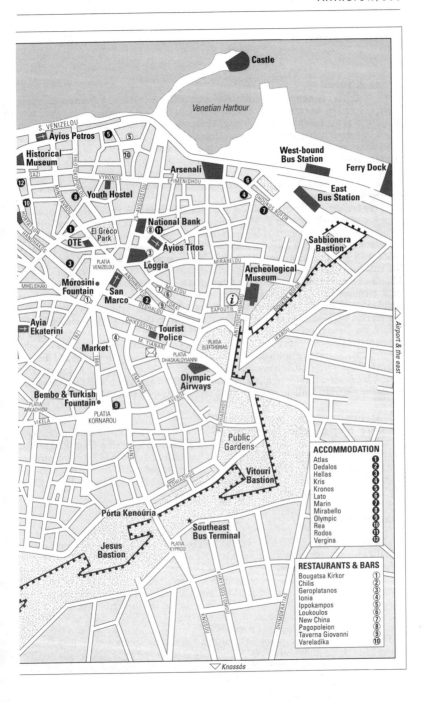

Castle

Venetian Harbour

S. VENIZELOU

Áyios Petros ⑤ ⑤

Historical Museum

GAZI

THEOTOKOPOULOU

VYRONOS

Arsenali

EPIMENIDHOU

West-bound Bus Station

Ferry Dock

⑫

MINOTAVROU

⑧ Youth Hostel

25 AVGOUSTOU

⑥

East Bus Station

DIKNOUKOS BOFOR

⑩

⑩

HORTATSON

HANDHAKOS

① OTE

El Gréco Park

National Bank
⑧ ⑪

Áyios Títos

④

⑦

Sabbionera Bastion

BOFOR

③

PLATIA VENIZELOU

Loggia

ANDHROYEO

MILATOU

MIRABELOU

Archeological Museum

DOUKOS BOFOR

MIHELIDHAKI

Môrosini Fountain ①

San Marco

② DEDHALOU

① ⑤ KORAI

⑨

SAPOUTIE

ⅈ

IKAROU

ANTHOUDHINOU

Ayia Ekaterini

DHIKEOSYNIS

Tourist Police

1821

M. YIANARI

PLATIA ELEFTHERIAS

Market

SFAKNIS

1866

PLATIA DHASKALOYIANNI

Olympic Airways

Bembo & Turkish Fountain

VIKELA

PLATIA ARKADHIOU

⑨

PLATIA KORNAROU

AVEROF

PEDHIADHOS

Public Gardens

▷ Airport & the east

ACCOMMODATION

Atlas ①
Dedalos ②
Hellas ③
Kris ④
Kronos ⑤
Lato ⑥
Marin ⑦
Mirabello ⑧
Olympic ⑨
Rea ⑩
Rodos ⑪
Vergina ⑫

EVANS

PEDHIADHOS

Vitouri Bastion

Pórta Kenoúria

★ Southeast Bus Terminal

PLATIA KYPROU

Jesus Bastion

HRYSSOSTOMOU

KNOSOU

DHIMOKRATIAS

RESTAURANTS & BARS

Bougatsa Kirkor ①
Chilis ②
Geroplatanos ③
Ionia ④
Ippokampos ⑤
Loukoulos ⑥
New China ⑦
Pagopoleion ⑧
Taverna Giovanni ⑨
Vareladika ⑩

▽ *Knossós*

traffic – which swirls around it constantly – and for life in general; it is ringed by more expensive tourist cafés and restaurants and comes alive in the evening with crowds of strolling locals.

Points of arrival

Iráklion **airport** is right on the coast, 4km east of the city. The #1 bus leaves for Platía Eleftherías every few minutes from the car park in front of the terminal; buy your ticket (170dr) at the booth before boarding. There are also plenty of taxis outside (which you'll be forced to use when the buses stop at 10.30pm), and prices to major destinations are posted – it's about 1200–1500dr to the centre of town. Get an agreement on the fare before taking a cab and beware if the driver extols the virtues of a particular place to stay – he'll usually be getting a kick-back from the proprietors. To avoid such hassles ask to be dropped at the central Platía Eleftherías, from where everything is in easy walking distance.

There are three main **bus stations** and a small terminus. Services along the coastal highway to or from the **east** (Mália, Áyios Nikólaos, Ierápetra, Sitía and so on) use the terminal just off the main road between the ferry dock and the Venetian harbour; the #2 local bus to Knossós runs from the city bus stop, adjacent to the east bus station. Main road services **west** (Réthymnon and Haniá) leave from a terminal right next to the east bus station on the other side of the road. Buses for the **southwest** (Festós, Mátala or Ayía Galíni) and along the inland roads west (Týlissos, Anóyia) operate out of a terminal just outside Haniá Gate, a very long walk from the centre along Kalokerinoú (or jump on any bus heading down this street). From the wharves where the **ferries** dock, the city rises directly ahead in steep tiers. If you're heading for the centre, for the archeological museum or the tourist office, cut straight up the stepped alleys behind the bus station onto Dhoúkos Bofór and to Platía Eleftherías; this will take about fifteen minutes. For accommodation though, and to get a better idea of the layout of Iráklion's main attractions, it's simplest to follow the main roads by a rather more roundabout route. Head west along the coast, past the major east-bound bus station and on by the Venetian harbour before cutting up towards the centre on 25-Avgoústou.

Information

Iráklion's **tourist office** (April–Oct Mon–Fri 8am–9pm, Sat & Sun 9am–3pm; Nov–March Mon–Fri 8am–3pm; ☎228 225, fax 226 020) is just below Platía Eleftherías, opposite the Archeological Museum at Zanthoudhídhou 1. A sub-office at the **airport** has the same hours and is good for basic information and maps. The **tourist police** – more helpful than most – are at Dhikeosýnis 10 (☎283 190), halfway between Platía Eleftherías and the market.

Accommodation

Finding a **room** can be difficult in season. The best place to look for inexpensive rooms is in the area around Platía Venizélou, along Hándhakos and towards the harbour to the west of 25-Avgoústou. Other concentrations of affordable places are around El Greco park and in the streets above the Venetian harbour. Better hotels mostly lie closer to Platía Eleftherías, to the south of Platía Venizélou and near the east- and west-bound bus stations. The dusty park between the main bus station and the harbour is often crowded with the sleeping bags of those who failed to find, or couldn't afford, a room; if you're really hard up, crashing here is a possibility, but a pleasant environment it is not.

The **youth hostel** at Výronos 5 (☎286 281), which has operated since 1963, is family run and very friendly and helpful, with plenty of space and up to fifty beds (albeit illegal) on the roof if you fancy sleeping out under the stars. In addition to dormitories, family and double rooms are also available; there are hot showers, breakfast and TV. There are no **campsites** near Iráklion. The nearest sites are both found to the east of the city – *Creta Camping* at Goúves (16km) and *Caravan Camping* at Hersónissos (28km).

Atlas, Kandanoléon 11 (☎288 989). A rather run-down old pension in a convenient but noisy alley between Platía Venizélou and El Greco Park. There's a pleasant roof garden, and freshly squeezed orange juice for breakfast. ①.

Dedalos, Dhedhálou 15 (☎244 812, fax 224 391). Very centrally placed on the pedestrianized alley between Venizélou and Eleftherías. Decent balcony rooms with private bath. ③.

Kris, Dhoúkos Bofór 2, near the Venetian harbour (☎223 221). Apartment-style rooms with kitchenette, fridge, great balcony views and friendly female proprietor. ③.

Kronos, Agaráthou 2, west of 25-Avgoústou (☎282 240, fax 285 853). Pleasant, friendly and modern hotel with seaview and baths in all rooms. ③.

Lato, Epomenídhou 15 (☎228 103, fax 240 350). Stylish and luxurious hotel where the air-con rooms have mini-bar, TV and seaview balcony with breakfast included. ⑥.

Marin, Dhoúkos Bofór 10, (☎224 736, fax 224 730). Comfortable and good-value rooms with bath, overlooking the Venetian harbour; get a balcony room at the front for a great view. Very convenient for the bus stations and the Archeological Museum. ②.

Mirabello, Theotokopoúlou 20 (☎285 052, fax 225 852). Good-value, family-run place with some rooms en-suite in a quiet street close to El Greco Park. ③.

Olympic, Platía Kornárou (☎288 861, fax 222 512). Overlooking the busy platía and the famous Bembo and Turkish fountains. One of the many hotels built in the 1960s, but one of the few that has been refurbished. ④.

Rea, Kalimeráki 1 (☎223 638, fax 242 189). A friendly, comfortable and clean pension in a quiet street. Some rooms with washbasin, others with own shower. ②.

Hellas, Hándhakos 24 (☎280 858, fax 284 442). Hostel-type place with simple doubles, and dormitory rooms favoured by younger travellers. Also has a roof garden and snack bar. ①.

Vergina, Hortátson 32 (☎242 739). Basic but pleasant rooms (with washbasins) in quiet street around a courtyard with a giant banana tree. ①.

Pension Rodos, Platía Áyios Títos (☎228 519). Homely no-frills double and triple rooms place, on a picturesque square with a great breakfast bar next door. ①.

The Town

From the port, the town rises overhead, and you can cut up the stepped alleys for a direct approach to Platía Eleftherías (Liberty Square) and the Archeological Museum. The easiest way to the middle of things, though, is to head west along the coast road, past the main bus stations and the *arsenáli*, and then up 25-Avgoústou, which leads into Platía Venizélou. This is crowded with Iraklian youth, patronizing outdoor cafés (marginally cheaper than those on Eleftherías), and with travellers who've arranged to meet in "Fountain Square". The recently restored Morosini fountain itself is not particularly spectacular at first glance, but on closer inspection is really a very beautiful work; it was built by Venetian governor Francesco Morosini in the seventeenth century, incorporating four lions which were some three hundred years old even then. From the platía you can strike up Dhedhálou, a pedestrianized street full of tourist shops and restaurants, or continue on 25-Avgoústou to a major traffic junction. To the right, Kalokerinoú leads west out of the city, the market lies straight ahead, and Platía Eleftherías is a short walk to the left up Dhikeosínis.

Platía Eleftherías and the Archeological Museum

The recently revamped **Platía Eleftherías**, with seats shaded by palms and eucalyptuses is very much the traditional heart of the city: traffic swirls around it constantly, and on summer evenings strolling hordes jam its expensive cafés and restaurants. Most of Iráklion's more expensive shops are in the streets leading off the platía.

The **Archeological Museum** (Mon 12.30–7pm, Tues–Sun 8am–7pm; 1500dr) is nearby, directly opposite the EOT office. Almost every important prehistoric and Minoan find on Crete is included in this fabulous, if bewilderingly large, collection. The museum tends to be crowded, especially when a guided tour stampedes through, but it's worth taking time over. You can't hope to see everything, nor can we attempt to describe it all (several good museum guides are sold here; the best probably being the glossy one by J.A. Sakellarakis), but highlights include the **mosaics** in Room 2 (galleries are arranged basically in chronological order), the famous **inscribed disc** from Festós in Room 3 (itself the subject of several books), most of Room 4, especially the magnificent bull's head **rhyton** (drinking vessel), the **jewellery** in Room 6 (and everywhere) and the engraved **black vases** in Room 7. Save some of your time and energy for upstairs, where the **Hall of the Frescoes**, with intricately reconstructed fragments of the wall paintings from Knossós and other sites, is especially wonderful.

Walls and fortifications

The massive **Venetian walls**, in places up to fifteen metres thick, are the most obvious evidence of Iráklion's later history. Though their fabric is incredibly well preserved, access is virtually nonexistent. It is possible, just, to walk along them from St Anthony's bastion over the sea in the west, as far as the tomb of Nikos Kazantzakis, Cretan author of *Zorba the Greek*, whose epitaph reads: "I believe in nothing, I hope for nothing, I am free." At weekends, Iraklians gather here to pay their respects and enjoy a free view of the soccer matches played by the island's first-division team, OFI Crete, in the stadium below. If the walls seem altogether too much effort, the **port fortifications** are very much easier to see. Stroll out along the jetty (crowded with courting couples after dark) and you can get inside the sixteenth-century **castle** (Mon–Sat 8am–6pm, Sun 10am–3pm; 500dr) at the harbour entrance, emblazoned with the Venetian Lion of St Mark. Standing atop this, you can begin to understand how Iráklion (or Candia as it was known until the seventeenth century) withstood a 22-year siege before finally falling to the Ottomans. On the landward side of the port, the Venetian **arsenáli** (arsenals) can also be seen, their arches rather lost amid the concrete road system all around.

Churches, icons and the historical museum

From the harbour, 25-Avgoústou will take you up past most of the rest of what's interesting. The **church of Áyios Títos**, on the left as you approach Platía Venizélou, borders a pleasant little platía. It looks magnificent principally because, like most of the churches here, it was adapted by the Turks as a mosque and only reconsecrated in 1925; consequently it has been renovated on numerous occasions. On the top side of this platía, abutting 25-Avgoústou, is the Venetian **city hall** with its famous loggia, again almost entirely rebuilt. Just above this, facing Platía Venizélou, is the **church of San Marco**, its steps usually crowded with the overflow of people milling around in the platía. Neither of these last two buildings has found a permanent role in its refurbished state, but both are generally open to house some kind of exhibition or craft show.

Slightly away from the obvious city-centre circuit, but still within the bounds of the walls, there are a couple of lesser museums worth seeing if you have the time. First of these is the excellent collection of **icons** in the **church of Ayía Ekateríni** (Mon–Sat 9am–1.30pm, Tues, Thurs & Fri also 5–7pm; 500dr), an ancient building just below the undistinguished cathedral, off Kalokerinoú. The finest here are six large scenes by Mihaïl Damaskinos (a near-contemporary of El Greco) who fused Byzantine and Renaissance influences. Supposedly both Damaskinos and El Greco studied at Ayía Ekateríni in the sixteenth century, when it functioned as a sort of monastic art school.

The **historical museum** (Mon–Fri 9am–1pm; 500dr) is some way from here, down near the waterfront opposite the stark *Xenia* hotel. Its display of folk costumes and jumble of local memorabilia includes the reconstructed studies of both Nikos Kazantzakis and Emanuel Tsouderos (Cretan statesman and Greek prime minister). There's enough variety to satisfy just about anyone, including the only El Greco painting on Crete, *View of Mount Sinai and the Monastery of St Catherine*.

The beaches

Iráklion's **beaches** are some way out, whether east or west of town. In either direction they're easily accessible by bus: #6 west from the stop outside the *Astoria* hotel in Platía Eleftherías; #7 east from the stop opposite this, under the trees in the centre of the platía.

Almyrós (or Ammoudhári) to the west has been subjected to a degree of development, comprising a campsite, several medium-size hotels and one giant one (the *Zeus Beach*, in the shadow of the power station at the far end), which makes the beach hard to get to without walking through or past something built up.

Amnissós, to the east, is the better choice, with several tavernas and the added amusement of planes swooping in immediately overhead to land. This is where most locals go on their afternoons off; the furthest of the beaches is the best, although new hotels are encroaching here, too. Little remains here to indicate the once-flourishing port of Knossós aside from a rather dull, fenced-in dig. If you're seriously into antiquities, however, you'll find a more rewarding site in the small villa, known as **Nírou Háni** (Tues–Sun 8.30am–3pm; free) at **Háni Kokkíni**, the first of the full-blown resort developments east of Iráklion.

Eating

Big city as it is, Iráklion disappoints when it comes to eating. The cafés and tavernas of platías **Venizélou** and **Eleftherías** are essential places to sit and watch the world pass, but their food is expensive and mediocre. One striking exception is *Bougatsa Kirkor*, by the Morosini fountain in Venizélou, where you can sample authentic *bougátsa*; alternatively, try a plate of *loukoumádhes*, available from a number of cafés at the top of Dhikeosínis. The cafés and tavernas on **Dhedhálou**, the pedestrian alley linking the two main platías, are very run of the mill, persistent waiters enticing you in with faded photographs of what appears to be food.

A more atmospheric option is to head for the little alley, **Fotíou Theodhosáki**, which runs through from the market to Odhós Evans. It is entirely lined with the tables of rival taverna owners, certainly authentic and catering for market traders and their customers as well as tourists. Compared with some, they often look a little grimy, but they are by no means cheap, which can come as a surprise. Nearby, at the corner of Evans and Yiánari, is the long-established *Ionia* taverna, which is the sort of place to come to if you are in need of a substantial, no-nonsense feed, with a good range of Greek dishes.

A relaxed lunchtime venue in the **centre** of town is *Geroplatanos* with tables on the leafy Platía Ayíou Títou beside the church of the same name. Across from here is a stylish new bar *Pagopoleion* (Ice Factory), good for breakfast, snacks and meals. It's the creation of photographic artist Chrissy Karelli, who has preserved a strident inscription on one wall, left by the Nazi occupiers who used local labour to run what was then Iráklion's only ice factory. Still near the centre, just off Eleftherías at **Platía Dhaskaloyiánni** (where the post office is), are some inexpensive and unexceptional tavernas; by day the platía is however a pleasant and relaxing venue, if not for a meal then to sit at one of its cafés, which transform themselves into more raucous and crowded music bars after dark. Nearer Venizélou, try exploring some of the backstreets to the east, off Dhedhálou and behind the loggia. The *Taverna Giovanni*, on the alley Koraï parallel to Dhedhálou, is one of the better tavernas in Iráklion, although the pricey food and an expensive wine list seem aimed more at Iráklion's smart set than the casual visitor. Should you have a craving for non-Greek food, there is Italian at the equally expensive *Loukoulos* and Chinese at the *New China Restaurant*, both with leafy courtyards and in the same street as the *Taverna Giovanni*. More reasonable prices are on offer at the excellent new taverna *Vareladika*, Monís Agaráthou 13, close to the Venetian harbour which offers a wide range of Cretan specialities in a stylish setting. Mexican tacos and beers are on offer at *Chilis*, Hándhakos 71 on the west side of the central zone – an area with many lively bars and cafés.

The **waterfront** is dotted with fish tavernas with little to recommend them. Instead, turn left at the bottom of 25-Avgoústou and cross the road to *Ippokampos*, which specializes in excellent-value fish dishes and mezédhes at moderate prices. It is deservedly popular with locals and is often crowded late into the evening: you may have to wait in line or turn up earlier than the Greeks eat. Even if you see no space it is worth asking as the owner may suddenly disappear inside the taverna and emerge with yet another table to carry further down the pavement.

For **snacks** and **takeaways**, there's a whole group of *souvláki* stalls clustering around the top of 25-Avgoústou at the entrance to El Greco Park, which is handy if you need somewhere to sit and eat. For *tyrópita* and *spanakópita* (cheese or spinach pies) and other pastries, sweet or savoury, there are no shortage of zaharoplastía and places such as *Everest* – just north of the Morosini fountain – which does takeaways of these as well as a whole bunch of other savouries. If you want to buy your own food, the **market** on Odhós 1866 is the place to go; it's an attraction in itself, and does a great line in modestly priced Cretan herbs (including saffron) to take home.

Drinking, nightlife and entertainment

Iráklion is a bit of a damp squib as far as **nightlife** goes, certainly when compared with many other towns on the island. If you're determined, however, there are a few city-centre possibilities, and plenty of options if all you want to do is sit and **drink**. In addition, there are a number of **cinemas** scattered about: check the posters on the boards by the tourist police office.

Bars

Bars tend to fan out into the streets around Hándhakos; among a number of new-style places, *Jasmin*, Ayiostefanitón 6, is tucked in an alley on the left mid-way down Hándhakos, and serves a variety of teas (including the Cretan *dhíktamo* – a panacea used by the ancients) with easy jazz and rock as background music. At the beginning of Hándhakos is *Tasso's*, a popular hangout for young hostellers, lively at night and with good breakfasts to help you recover in the morning. *Utopia*, also on Hándhakos and the nearby *Bonsai* and *Kallioton* are more places to try in an area that is fast becoming Iráklion's major focus for younger revellers.

Another animated place nearer the centre is Platía Koraï behind Dhedhálou (up from the *Giovanni* restaurant listed above), where there are several pricey bars (including the trendy *Flash* and *Notos*) with outdoor tables, which are popular with students in term time. Enjoy a game of backgammon here during the day or early evening; later it can get extremely lively with many more distractions. In and around **Platía Venizélou** (Fountain Square), there are many bars, again some are very fashionable, with *De Facto* being one of the most popular. This is one of the new breed of kafenío emerging in Iráklion, attracting younger people: the drinks are **cocktails** rather than *rakí*, the music is Western or modern Greek, and there are prices to match. Another is *Rebels*, Perdhikári 3 at the junction with Koraï, which has a good atmosphere with a cluster of similar places nearby; there are similar bars along Kandanoléon, off El Greco Park.

Clubs and discos

For **discos** proper, there is a large selection, even if they are all playing techno at the moment, interspersed with Greek music (not the Greek music you get for tourists). *Genesis* is the most popular, down towards the harbour at the bottom of Dhoúkos Bofór, below the Archeological Museum. The nearby *Kastro* has nightly *lýra* and *bouzoúki* entertainment which you can take in for the price of a drink, although many locals take advantage of their restaurant to have a meal as well. Another cluster of nightclubs can be found on Ikárou, about a twenty-minute walk or easy taxi ride away. Retrace your steps towards the Archeological Museum, but before emerging onto Platía Eleftherías turn left downhill and follow the main road, Ikárou. Here you'll find the *Minoica*, the *Korus Club* and the *Athina*, all playing similar music and popular with young Iraklians.

Listings

Airlines Air Greece, Dhedhálou 36 (☎330 074); Cronus Air, at the airport (☎222 217); Olympic, Platía Eleftherías (☎229 191). Charter airlines flying in to Iráklion mostly use local travel agents as their representatives.

Airport For airport information call ☎245 644. Bus #1 runs from Platía Eleftherías to the airport every few minutes; buy a ticket (170dr) from the booth outside the *Astoria Hotel* first.

Banks There are now 24hr cash dispensers all over town, but the main bank branches are on 25-Avgoústou.

Car and bike rental 25-Avgoústou is lined with rental companies, but you'll often find cheaper rates on the backstreets; it's always worth asking for discounts. Good places to start include: Blue Sea, Kosmá Zótou 7, near the bottom of 25-Avgoústou (☎241 097) for bikes; Motor Club, Platía Ánglon 1 at the bottom of 25-Avgoústou facing the port (☎222 408), Eurocreta, Sapotié 2 (☎226 700) near the Archeological Museum, and Ritz in the *Hotel Rea*, Kalimeráki 1 (☎223 638), are worth trying for cars; Sun Rise, 25-Avgoústou 46 (☎221 609), does both cars and bikes.

Ferry tickets Available from Minoan Lines, 25-Avgoústou 78 (☎229 646; handles the islands and Athens), ANEK Lines, 25-Avgoústou 33 (☎222 481; Athens only), or any of the travel agents listed on p.576.

Hospital Most central is the hospital on Apollónion, southwest of Platía Kornárou, between Albér and Moussoúrou.

Laundry Washsalon, Hándhakos 18 (Mon–Sat 8am–8pm) is reliable and also does service washes (2000dr for 6kg). The new Laundry Perfect at Malikoúti 32, north of the Archeological Museum, will do the same for 1800dr.

Left luggage Offices in the east-bound and southwest bus stations (daily 6am–8pm; 300dr per bag per day), as well as a commercial agency at Hándhakos 18 (open 24hrs; large locker 450dr per day). You can also leave bags at the youth hostel (even if you don't stay there) for 500dr per bag per day. If you want to leave your bag while you go off on a bike for a day or two, the rental company should be prepared to store it.

Newspapers and books For English-language newspapers and novels, as well as local guides and maps, Dhedhálou is the best bet, where Bibliopoleio (no. 6) stocks a wide selection of books in English. Planet International Bookstore, behind Platía Venizélou at the corner of Hándhakos and Kydhonías, has the island's biggest stock of English-language titles.

Pharmacies Plentiful on the main shopping streets – at least one is open 24hr on a rota basis: the others will have a sign on the door indicating which it is. There are traditional herbalists in the market.

Post office Main office in Platía Dhaskaloyiánnis, off Eleftherías (Mon–Fri 7.30am–8pm). There's also a temporary office (a van) at the entrance to El Greco Park (daily 7.30am–2pm).

Taxis Major taxi ranks in Platía Eleftherías and by the Morosini Fountain (Platía Kalergón), or call ☎210 102 or 210 168. Prices displayed on boards at ranks.

Telephones The OTE head office is on the west side of El Greco Park; it's open 8am–11pm, but most overseas destinations can now be phoned from street booths using a phone card (*telekárta*) obtainable from a *períptero* (kiosk).

Toilets In El Greco Park and the public gardens near the cathedral, or at the bus stations and the Archeological Museum (no need to pay entrance charge to use them).

Travel agencies Budget operators and student specialists include the extremely helpful Blavakis Travel, Platía Kallergón 8, just off 25-Avgoústou by the entrance to El Greco Park (☎282 541), and Prince Travel, 25-Avgoústou 30 (☎282 706). For excursions around the island, villa rentals and so on, the bigger operators are probably easier: Irman Travel, Dhedhálou 26 (☎242 527), or Creta Travel Bureau, Epimenídhou 20–22 (☎227 002). The latter is also the local American Express agent.

Knossós

KNOSSÓS, the largest of the **Minoan palaces**, reached its cultural peak more than three thousand years ago, though a town of some importance persisted here well into the Roman era. It lies on a low, largely man-made hill some 5km southeast of Iráklion; the surrounding hillsides are rich in lesser remains spanning 25 centuries, starting at the beginning of the second millennium BC.

Barely a hundred years ago the palace existed only in mythology. Knossós was the court of the legendary King Minos, whose wife Pasiphae bore the Minotaur, half-bull, half-man. Here the labyrinth was constructed by Daedalus to contain the monster, and youths were brought from Athens as human sacrifice until Theseus arrived to slay the beast, and with Ariadne's help, escape its lair. The discovery of the palace, and the interplay of these legends with fact, is among the most amazing tales of modern archeology. Heinrich Schliemann, the German excavator of Troy, suspected that a major Minoan palace lay under the various tumuli here, but was denied the necessary permission to dig by the local Ottoman authorities at the end of the last century. It was left for Sir Arthur Evans, whose name is indelibly associated with Knossós, to excavate the site, from 1900 onwards.

The #2 local **bus** sets off every ten minutes from the Iráklion's city bus stands (adjacent to the east-bound bus station), runs up 25-Avgoústou (with a stop by Platía Venizélou) and out of town on Odhós 1821 and Evans. At Knossós, outside the fenced site, stands the *caravanserai* where ancient wayfarers would rest and water their animals. Head out onto the road and you'll find no lack of watering holes for modern travellers either – a string of rather pricey tavernas and tacky souvenir stands. There are several **rooms** for rent here, and if you're really into Minoan culture, there's a lot to be said for staying out this way to get an early start. Be warned, though, that it's expensive and unashamedly commercial.

The site

Daily: April–Sept 8am–7pm; Oct–March 8.30am–3pm; 1500dr.

As soon as you enter the **Palace of Knossós** through the West Court, the ancient ceremonial entrance, it is clear how the legends of the labyrinth grew up around it. Even with a detailed plan, it's almost impossible to find your way around the site with any success. The best advice is not to try; wander around for long enough and you'll eventually stumble upon everything. If you're worried about missing the highlights, you can always tag along with one of the constant guided tours for a while, catching the patter and then backtracking to absorb the detail when the crowd has moved on. Outside the period December to February you won't get the place to yourself, whenever you come, but exploring on your own does give you the opportunity to appreciate individual parts of the palace in the brief lulls between groups.

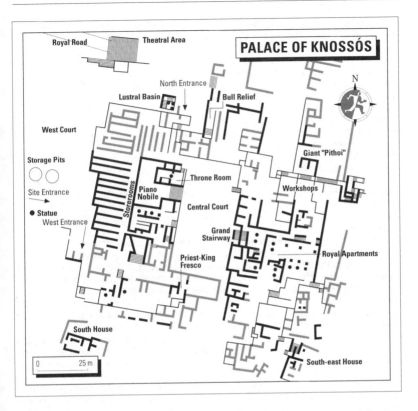

Knossós was liberally "restored" by Evans, and these restorations have been the source of furious controversy among archeologists ever since. It has become clear that much of Evans's upper level – the so-called *piano nobile* – is pure conjecture. Even so, his guess as to what the palace might have looked like is certainly as good as anyone else's, and it makes the other sites infinitely more meaningful if you have seen Knossós first. Without the restorations, it would be almost impossible to imagine the grandeur of the multistorey palace or to see the ceremonial stairways, strange, top-heavy pillars and gaily painted walls that distinguish the site. For some idea of the size and complexity of the palace in its original state, take a look at the cutaway drawings (wholly imaginary but probably not too far off) on sale outside.

Royal Apartments

The superb **Royal Apartments** around the central staircase are not guesswork, and they are plainly the finest of the rooms at Knossós. The **Grand Stairway** itself is a masterpiece of design: not only a fitting approach to these sumptuously appointed chambers, but also an integral part of the whole plan, its large well bringing light into the lower storeys. Light wells such as these, usually with a courtyard at the bottom, are a constant feature of Knossós and a reminder of just how important creature comforts were to the Minoans, and of how skilled they were at providing them.

For evidence of this luxurious lifestyle you need look no further than the **Queen's Suite**, off the grand **Hall of the Colonnades** at the bottom of the staircase. Here, the main living room is decorated with the celebrated **dolphin fresco** (a reproduction; the original is now in the Iráklion archeological museum) and with running friezes of flowers and abstract spirals. On two sides, it opens out onto courtyards that let in light and air; the smaller one would probably have been planted with flowers. The room would have been scattered with cushions and hung with plush drapes, while doors and further curtains between the pillars would have allowed for privacy, and for cool shade in the heat of the day. This, at least, is what they'd have you believe, and it's a very plausible scenario. Remember, though, that all this is speculation and some of it is pure hype; the dolphin fresco, for example, was found on the courtyard floor, not in the room itself, and would have been viewed from an upper balcony as a sort of *trompe l'oeil*, like looking through a glass-bottomed boat. Whatever the truth, this is an impressive example of Minoan architecture, the more so when you follow the dark passage around to the queen's **bathroom**. Here is a clay tub, protected behind a low wall (and again probably screened by curtains when in use), and the famous "flushing" toilet (a hole in the ground with drains to take the waste away – one flushed it by throwing a bucket of water down).

The much perused **drainage system** was a series of interconnecting terracotta pipes running underneath most of the palace. Guides to the site never fail to point these out as evidence of the advanced state of Minoan civilization, and they are indeed quite an achievement, in particular the system of baffles and overflows to slow down the runoff and avoid any danger of flooding. Just how much running water there would have been, however, is another matter; the water supply was, and is, at the bottom of the hill, and even the combined efforts of rainwater catchment and hauling water up to the palace can hardly have been sufficient to supply the needs of more than a small elite.

Going up the Grand Stairway to the floor above the queen's domain, you come to a set of rooms generally regarded as the **King's Quarters**. These are chambers in a considerably sterner vein; the staircase opens into a grandiose reception chamber known as the **Hall of the Royal Guard**, its walls decorated in repeated shield patterns. Immediately off here is the **Hall of the Double Axes**, believed to be have been the ruler's personal chamber, a double room that would allow for privacy in one portion while audiences were held in the more public section. Its name comes from the double-axe symbol carved into every block of masonry.

The Throne Room and the rest of the palace

Continuing to the top of the Grand Stairway, you emerge onto the broad **Central Court**, a feature of all the Minoan palaces. Open now, this would once have been enclosed by the walls of the buildings all around. On the far side, in the northwestern corner of the courtyard, is the entrance to another of Knossós's most atmospheric survivals, the **Throne Room**. Here, a worn stone throne – with its hollowed shaping for the posterior – sits against the wall of a surprisingly small chamber; along the walls around it are ranged stone benches, suggesting a king ruling in council, and behind there's a reconstructed fresco of two griffins. In all probability in Minoan times this was the seat of a priestess rather than a ruler (there's nothing like it in any other Minoan palace), and its conversion into a throne room seems to have been a late innovation wrought by the invading Mycenaeans, during their short-lived domination prior to the palace's final destruction in the fourteenth century BC. The Throne Room is now closed off with a wooden gate, but you can lean over this for a good view, and in the antechamber there's a wooden copy of the throne on which everyone perches to have their picture taken.

The rest you'll see as you wander, contemplating the legends of the place which blur with reality. Try not to miss the giant *pithoi* in the northeast quadrant of the site, an area known as the palace workshops; the storage chambers which you see from behind the Throne Room, and the reproduction frescoes in the reconstructed room above it; the fresco of the Priest-King looking down on the south side of the central court, and the relief of a charging bull on its north side. This last would have greeted you if you entered the palace through its north door; you can see evidence here of some kind of gatehouse and a lustral bath, a sunken area perhaps used for ceremonial bathing and purification. Just outside this gate is the **theatral area**, an open space a little like a stepped amphitheatre, which may have been used for ritual performances or dances. From here the **Royal Road**, claimed as the oldest road in Europe, sets out. At one time, this probably ran right across the island; nowadays it ends after about a hundred yards in a brick wall beneath the modern road. Circling back around the outside of the palace, you get more idea of its scale by looking up at it; on the south side are a couple of small reconstructed Minoan houses which are worth exploring.

Beyond Knossós

If you have transport, the drive beyond Knossós can be an attractive and enjoyable one, taking minor roads through much greener country, with vineyards draped across low hills and flourishing agricultural communities. If you want specific things to seek out, head first for **MYRTIÁ**, an attractive village with the small **Kazantzakis Museum** (Mon, Wed & Sat 9am–1pm & 4pm–8pm, Tues & Fri 9am–1pm; 500dr) in a house where the writer's parents once lived. **ARHÁNES**, at the foot of Mount Ioúktas, is a much larger place that was also quite heavily populated in Minoan times. None of the three archeological sites here is open to the public, but **Anemospiliá**, 2km northwest of the town (directions from the archeological museum below), can be visited and has caused huge controversy since its excavation in the 1980s: many traditional views of the Minoans, particularly that of Minoan life as peaceful and idyllic, have had to be rethought in the light of the discovery of an apparent human sacrifice. An excellent new **archeological museum** (daily, excluding Tues, 8.30am–2.30pm; free) displays finds from here and other nearby excavations, including the strange ceremonial dagger apparently used for human sacrifice. From Arhánes you can also drive (or walk with a couple of hours to spare) to the top of Mount Ioúktas to see the imposing remains of a Minoan **peak sanctuary** and enjoy spectacular panoramic **views** towards Knossós (with which it was linked) and the northern coast beyond. At **VATHÝPETRO**, south of the mountain, is a **Minoan villa and vineyard** (daily 8.30am–3pm, but often fails to open so enquire at the museum in Arhánes; free), which once controlled the rich farmland south of Arhánes. Inside, a remarkable collection of farming implements was found, as well as a unique **wine press** which remains *in situ*. Substantial amounts of the farm buildings remain, and it's still surrounded by fertile vines (Arhánes is one of Crete's major wine-producing zones) three and a half thousand years later – making it probably the oldest still-functioning vineyard in Europe, if not the world.

Southwest from Iráklion: sites and beaches

If you take a **tour** from Iráklion (or one of the resorts), you'll probably visit the **Górtys**, **Festós** and **Ayía Triádha** sites in a day, with a lunchtime swim at **Mátala** thrown in. Doing it by public transport, you'll be forced into a rather more leisurely pace, but there's still no reason why you shouldn't get to all three and reach Mátala within the day; if necessary, it's easy enough to hitch the final stretch. **Bus services** to the Festós site are excellent, with some nine a day to and from Iráklion (fewer run on Sunday), five of which continue to or come from Mátala; there are also services direct to Ayía Galíni. If you're arriving in the afternoon, plan to visit Ayía Triádha first, as it closes early.

The route to Áyii Dhéka

The road from Iráklion towards Festós is a pretty good one by the standards of Cretan mountain roads, albeit rather dull. The country you're heading towards is the richest agricultural land on the island, and right from the start the villages en route are large and business-like. In the biggest of them, Ayía Varvára, there's a great rock outcrop known as the **Omphalos** (Navel) of Crete, supposedly the very centre of the island.

Past here, you descend rapidly to the fertile fields of the Messará plain, where the road joins the main route across the south near the village of **ÁYII DHÉKA**. For religious Cretans Áyii Dhéka is something of a place of pilgrimage; its name, "The Ten Saints", refers to ten early Christians martyred here under the Romans. In a crypt below the modern church you can see the martyrs' tombs. It's an attractive village to wander around, with several places to eat and even some **rooms** along the main road.

Górtys

Daily 8am–5pm; 800dr.

Within easy walking distance of Áyii Dhéka, either through the fields or along the main road, sprawls the site of **Górtys**, ruined capital of the Roman province that included not only Crete but also much of North Africa. After a look at the plan of the extensive site at the entrance, cutting across the fields will give you some idea of the scale of this city, at its zenith in approximately the third century AD; an enormous variety of other remains, including an impressive **theatre**, are strewn across your route. Even in Áyii Dhéka you'll see Roman pillars and statues lying around in people's yards or propping up their walls.

There had been a settlement here from the earliest times, but the extant ruins date almost entirely from the Roman era. Only now is the site being systematically excavated, by the Italian Archeological School. At the main entrance to the fenced site, alongside the road, are the ruins of the still impressive **basilica of Áyios Títos**; the eponymous saint converted the island to Christianity and was its first bishop. Beyond this is the **odeion** which houses the most important discovery on the site, the **Law Code**. These great inscribed blocks of stone were incorporated by the Romans from a much earlier stage of the city's development; they're written in an obscure early Greek-Cretan dialect, and in a style known as *boustrophedon* (ox-ploughed), with the lines reading alternately in opposite directions like the furrows of a ploughed field. At ten metres by three metres, this is reputedly the largest Greek inscription ever found. The laws set forth reflect a strictly hierarchical society: five witnesses were needed to convict a free man of a crime, only one for a slave; raping a free man or woman carried a fine of a hundred staters, violating a serf only five. A small **museum** in a loggia (also within the fenced area) holds a number of large and finely worked sculptures found at Górtys, more evidence of the city's importance.

Míres

Some 20km west of Górtys, **MÍRES** is an important market and focal point of transport for the fertile Messará plain: if you're switching buses to get from the beaches on the south coast to the archeological sites or the west, this is where you'll do it. There are good facilities including a **bank**, a few **restaurants** and a couple of **rooms**, though there's no particular reason to stay unless you are waiting for a bus or looking for work (it's one of the better places for agricultural jobs). Heading straight for Festós, there's usually no need to stop.

Festós (Phaestos)

Daily 8am–7pm; 1200dr.

The **Palace of Festós** was excavated by the Italian, Federico Halbherr (also responsible for the early work at Górtys), at almost exactly the same time as Evans was working at Knossós. The style of the excavations, however, could hardly have been more different. Here, to the approval of most traditional archeologists, reconstruction was kept to an absolute minimum – it's all bare foundations, and walls which rise at most a metre above ground level. This means that despite a magnificent setting overlooking the plain of Messará, the palace at Festós is not as immediately arresting as those at Knossós or Mália. Much of the site is fenced off and, except in the huge central court, it's almost impossible to get any sense of the place as it was; the plan is almost as complex as at Knossós, with none of the reconstruction to bolster the imagination.

It's interesting to speculate why the palace was built halfway up a hill rather than on the plain below – certainly not for defence, for this is in no way a good defensive position. Psychological superiority over the peasants or reasons of health are both possible, but it seems quite likely that it was simply the magnificent view that finally swayed the decision. The site looks over Psilorítis to the north and the huge plain, with the Lasíthi mountains beyond it, to the east. Towards the top of Psilorítis you should be able to make out a small black smudge: the entrance to the Kamáres cave (see p.590).

On the ground closer at hand, you can hardly fail to notice the strong similarities between Festós and the other palaces: the same huge rows of storage jars, the great

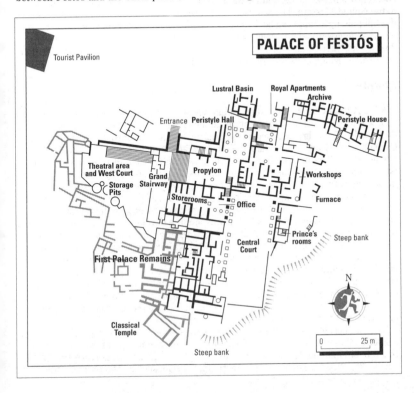

PALACE OF FESTÓS

Tourist Pavilion

Lustral Basin
Royal Apartments
Archive
Entrance Peristyle Hall
Peristyle House
Theatral area and West Court
Grand Stairway
Propylon
Workshops
Storage Pits
Storerooms
Office
Furnace
Prince's rooms Steep bank
Central Court
First Palace Remains
Classical Temple
N
0 25 m
Steep bank

courtyard with its monumental stairway, and the theatral area. Unique to Festós, how-ever, is the third courtyard, in the middle of which are the remains of a **furnace** used for metalworking. Indeed, this eastern corner of the palace seems to have been home to a number of craftsmen, including potters and carpenters. Oddly enough, Festós was much less ornately decorated than Knossós; there is no evidence, for example, of any of the dramatic Minoan wall-paintings.

The **tourist pavilion** at Festós serves drinks and food and also has a few beds, though these are very rarely available (thanks to advance bookings) and expensive when they are. The nearby village of **ÁYIOS IOÁNNIS**, along the road towards Mátala, has a few more **rooms**, including some at *Taverna Ayios Ioannis* (☎0892/42 006; ①), which is also a good place to eat.

Ayía Triádha

Daily 8.30am–3pm; 500dr.

Some of the finest artworks in the museum at Iráklion came from **Ayía Triádha**, about a 45-minute walk (or a short drive) from Festós. No one is quite sure what this site is, but the most common theory has it as some kind of royal summer villa. It's smaller than the palaces, but if anything even more lavishly appointed and beautifully situated. In any event, it's an attractive place to visit, far less crowded than Festós, with a wealth of interesting little details. Look out in particular for the row of **stores** in front of what was apparently a marketplace, and for the remains of the **paved road** that once led down to the Gulf of Messará. The sea itself looks invitingly close, separated from the base of the hill only by Timbáki airfield (mainly used for motor racing these days), but if you try to drive down there, it's almost impossible to find your way around the unmarked dust tracks. There's a fourteenth-century **church** – dedicated to Áyios Yeóryios – at the site, worth visiting in its own right for the remains of ancient frescoes.

Mátala

MÁTALA has by far the best-known **beach** in Iráklion province, widely promoted and included in tours mainly because of the famous **caves** cut into the cliffs above its beau-tiful sands. These are believed to be ancient tombs first used by Romans or early Christians, but more recently inhabited by a sizable hippie community. You'll still meet people who will assure you that this is *the* travellers' beach on Crete. Not any more it isn't. Today, the town is full of package tourists and tries hard to present a respectable image; the cliffs are now cleared and locked up every evening.

A few people still manage to evade the security, or sleep on the beach or in the adja-cent campsite, but on the whole the place has changed entirely. The years since the early 1980s have seen the arrival of crowds and the development of hotels, discos and restaurants to service them; early afternoon, when the tour buses pull in for their swim-ming stop, sees the beach packed to overflowing. If you're prepared to accept Mátala for what it is – a resort of some size – you'll find the place more than bearable. The town beach is beautiful, and if the crowds get excessive, you can climb over the rocks in about twenty minutes (past more caves, many of which are inhabited through the sum-mer) to another excellent stretch of sand, known locally as "Red Beach". In the evening, when the trippers have gone, there are waterside bars and restaurants looking out over invariably spectacular sunsets.

The chief problems concern prices and crowds: rooms are both expensive and over-subscribed, food is good but not cheap. If you want **accommodation**, try looking up the little street to the left as you enter town, just after the *Zafiria* hotel (☎0892/45 112, fax 45 725; ③), where there are several rooms for rent, such as *Matala View* (☎0892/45

114; ①), and *Pension Nikos* (☎0892/42 375, fax 45 120; ②). If these are full, then every-where closer in is likely to be as well, so head back out on the main road, or try the **campsite**, *Camping of Matala* (☎0892/45 720), next to the beach above the car park; *Kommos Camping* (☎0892/45 596) is a nicer site, but a few kilometres out of Mátala and reached by heading back towards Pítsidia and turning left along a signed track. There are places to **eat and drink** all over the main part of town and a solitary summer **disco**, *Neosicos*, competes with a handful of raucous music bars to attract night owls. Also impossible to miss are most other facilities, including stores and a bookshop, currency exchange, car and bike rental, travel agents, post office and a covered market where tourist tat has almost squeezed out the fruit and veg stalls.

Around Mátala: Pitsídhia and Kalamáki

One way to enjoy a bit more peace is to stay at **PITSÍDHIA**, about 5km inland. This has long been a well-used option, so it's not quite as cheap as you might expect, but there are plenty of rooms, lively places to eat and even music bars. If you decide to stay here, the beach at **KALAMÁKI** is an alternative to Mátala. Both beaches are approximately the same distance to walk, though there is a much better chance of a bus or a lift to Mátala. Kalamáki has developed somewhat, with a number of rooms and a couple of tavernas, but it's a messy and unattractive little place. The beach stretches for miles, surprisingly wild and windswept, lashed by sometimes dangerously rough surf. At the southern end (more easily reached by a path off the Pitsídhia–Mátala road) lies **Kómmos**, once a Minoan port serving Festós and now the site of a major archeologi-cal excavation. It's not yet open to the public, but you can peer into the fenced-off area to see what's been revealed so far, which is pretty impressive: dwellings, streets, hefty stonework and even the ship sheds where repairs on the Minoan fleet were carried out.

Iráklion's south coast

South of the Messará plain are two more beach resorts, Kalí Liménes and Léndas, with numerous other little beaches along the coast in between, but nothing spectacular. **Public transport** is very limited indeed; you'll almost always have to travel via Míres (see p.580). If you have your own transport, the roads in these parts are all passable and newly sealed, but most are very slow going; the Kófinas Hills, which divide the plain from the coast, are surprisingly precipitous.

Kalí Liménes

While Mátala itself was an important port under the Romans, the chief harbour for Górtys lay on the other side of Cape Líthinon at **KALÍ LIMÉNES**. Nowadays, this is once again a major port – for oil tankers. This has rather spoiled its chances of becom-ing a major resort, and there are few proper facilities. Some people like Kalí Liménes: it's certainly off the beaten track and the constant procession of tankers gives you something to look at while beach lounging. There are a couple of places offering **rooms** – the best is the *Karavovrousi Beach* (☎0892/42 197; ②), a kilometre or so east of the main village where the main Míres road arrives, which also has a decent **taver-na** attached. The coastline is broken up by spectacular cliffs and, as long as there hasn't been a recent oil spill, the beaches are reasonably clean and totally empty. But (fortunately) not too many share this enthusiasm.

Léndas

LÉNDAS, further east along the coast, is far more popular, with a couple of buses daily from Iráklion and a partly justified reputation for being peaceful (sullied by consider-able summer crowds). Many people who arrive think they've come to the wrong place, as at first sight the village looks shabby, the beach is small, rocky and dirty, and the rooms are frequently all booked. A number of visitors leave without ever correcting that initial impression, but the attraction of Léndas is not the village at all but on the other (west) side of the headland. Here, there's a vast, excellent sandy beach, part of it usually taken over by nudists, and a number of taverna/bars overlooking it from the roadside. The beach is a couple of kilometres from Léndas, along a rough track; if you're walking, you can save time by cutting across the headland. A considerably more attractive prospect than staying in Léndas itself is **camping** on the beach to the west of the village, or with luck getting a **room** at one of the few beach tavernas – try *Tsarakis* (☎0892/95 378, fax 95 377; ②) for seaview rooms. After you've discovered the beach, even Léndas begins to look more welcoming, and at least it has most of the facilities you'll need, including a shop which will change money and numerous places to **eat and drink**.

Once you've come to terms with the place, you can also explore some less good but quite deserted beaches eastwards, and the scrappy remains of **ancient Lebena** on a hilltop overlooking them. There was an important Asclepion (temple of the god Asclepius) here around some now-diverted warm springs, but only the odd broken column and fragments of mosaic survive in a fenced-off area on the village's northern edge.

East of Iráklion: the package-tour coast

East of Iráklion, the startling pace of **tourist development** in Crete is all too plain to see. The merest hint of a beach is an excuse to build at least one hotel, and these are outnumbered by the concrete shells of resorts-to-be. It's hard to find a room in this monument to the package-tour industry, and expensive if you do.

Goúrnes and Goúves

As a general rule, the further you go, the better things get: when the road detours all too briefly inland, the real Crete of olive groves and stark mountains asserts itself. You certainly won't see much of it at **GOÚRNES**, where a former US Air Force base is now occupied by the Greek military, or at nearby Káto Goúves, where there's a **campsite**, *Camping Creta* (☎0897/41 400), which will be quiet unless and until the Greek Air Force moves in next door as planned. From here, however, you can head inland to the old village of **GOÚVES**, a refreshing contrast, and just beyond to the **Skotinó cave**, one of the largest and most spectacular on the island (about an hour's walk from the coast).

Not far beyond Goúrnes is the turning for the direct route up to the Lasíthi plateau, and shortly after that you roll into the first of the big resorts, Hersónissos or, more correctly, Límin Hersoníssou; Hersónissos is the village in the hills just behind, also over-run by tourists.

Hersónissos (Límin Hersoníssou)

HERSÓNISSOS was once just a small fishing village; today it's the most popular of Crete's package resorts. If what you want is plenty of bars, tavernas, restaurants and Eurodisco nightlife, then come here. The resort has numerous small patches of sand beach between rocky outcrops, but a shortage of places to stay in peak season.

Along the modern seafront, a solid line of restaurants and bars is broken only by the occasional souvenir shop; in their midst you'll find a small pyramidal Roman **fountain** with broken mosaics of fishing scenes, the only real relic of the ancient town of Chersonesos. Around the headland above the harbour and in odd places along the seafront, you can see remains of Roman harbour installations, mostly submerged.

Beach and clubs excepted, the distractions of Hersónissos comprise **Lykhnostatis** (Tues–Sun 9.30am–2pm; 1250dr), an open-air "museum" of traditional Crete, on the coast on the eastern edge of the town; a small **aquarium** just off the main road at the west end of town, opposite the *Hard Rock Cafe* (daily 10am–9pm; 800dr); the watersports paradise *Star Water Park* (admission free, charges for individual sports) at the eastern end of the resort; and, a few kilometres inland, the slides, cascades and whirlpools of the newly opened and immense *Aqua Splash Water Park* (daily 10am–7pm; 4000dr per day, discounted rates after 2.30pm).

A short distance inland are the three **hill villages** of Koutoulafári, Piskopianó and "old" Hersónissos, which all have a good selection of tavernas, and are worth searching out for accommodation.

Practicalities

Hersónissos is well provided with all the back-up **services** you need to make a holiday go smoothly. Banks, bike and car rental and post office are all on or just off the main drag, as are the taxi ranks. **Buses** running east and west leave every thirty minutes.

Finding somewhere to stay can be difficult in July and August. Much of the **accommodation** here is allocated to package-tour operators and what remains is not that cheap. To check for availability of accommodation generally, the quickest and best option is to enquire at one of the many travel agencies along the main street, Venizélou, such as Zakros Tours at no. 46. Reasonably priced central options include the *Nancy* on Ayías Paraskevís (☎0897/22 212; ③) and *Virginia* on Máhis Krítis (☎0897/22 466; ②), but be prepared for a fair amount of noise. One place to try on the western edge as you enter the town is *Hotel Ilios* (☎0897/22 500 fax 22 582; ④), just back from the main road, which has a rooftop pool. There are two good **campsites**: one at the eastern end of town, *Caravan Camping* (☎0897/22 025 or 24 718), which also has several reed-roofed bungalows, and *Hersonissos Camping* (☎0897/22 902 or 23 792), just to the west of town. The well-run **youth hostel**, at the east end of Venizélou (☎0897/23 674), is sited opposite *Caravan Camping* (above) and serves meals.

Despite the vast number of **eating places**, there are few in Hersónissos worth recommending, and the tavernas down on the harbourfront should be avoided. One of the few Greek tavernas that stands out is *Kavouri* along Arhéou Theátrou, but it's fairly expensive, so it's better to head out of town on the Piskopianó road where, near the junction to Koutoulafári, the friendly *Fegari* taverna serves good Greek food at reasonable prices. Sitting at your table overlooking the street below you can view the steady trek of clubbers heading down the hill to the bars and nightclubs of Hersónissos. The hill villages have the greatest selection of tavernas, particularly Koutoulafári, where you can have a relaxed evening amongst the narrow streets and small platías. One in-town restaurant definitely worth a try is *Passage to India*, an authentic and extremely good Indian restaurant just off the main street near the church and the war memorial.

Hersónissos is renowned for its **nightlife**, and there's no shortage of it. Most of the better bars and clubs are along the main road. Especially popular are *It*, with up-to-the-minute chart hits, and the *Hard Rock Café*, which often puts on live music. *Aria*, a large glass-fronted disco, is the biggest on Crete and only opens during July and August when it can get the crowds to fill it. Other popular haunts include *Legend* and the beach bar-disco pub *Pirates*, both at the eastern end of town, and, towards the harbour, *Camelot* and *New York*. If you fancy a quiet drink then you have come to the wrong resort, but you could try *Kahluai Beach Cocktail Bar* or *Haris Ouzo* and *Raki Place* (beneath the *Hotel Virginia*). There is an open-air **cinema** showing original version films at the *Creta Maris* hotel at the west end of the town and close to the beach.

Stalídha

STALÍDHA is a Cinderella town, sandwiched in between its two louder, brasher and some would say uglier sisters, Mália and Hersónissos, but it is neither quiet or undeveloped. This rapidly expanding beach resort, with more than sixty tavernas and bars and a few discos, can offer the best of both worlds, with a friendlier and more relaxed setting, a better beach (and usual array of watersports) and very easy access to its two livelier neighbours. The town essentially consists of a single, relatively traffic-free street which rings the seafront for more than two miles, before the apartment blocks briefly become fewer and further, until the mass development of Mália begins.

Finding a place to stay can be difficult, since **accommodation** is almost entirely in studio and apartment blocks which are booked by package companies in high season. Out of season, however, you may well be able to negotiate a very reasonable price for a studio apartment complete with swimming pool; ask in the central travel agencies first, as they will know what is available, and expect to pay at least 8000dr for two. Finding somewhere to **eat** is less difficult as there are plenty of rather ordinary tavernas, the best and most authentic being *Maria's* and the *Hellas Taverna*, both at the western end of the resort.

Stalídha is completely overshadowed by its neighbours when it comes to **nightlife**, though you can dance at *Bells* disco, on the main coast road, or at *Rhythm*, on the beach; the music bars *Sea Wolf Cocktail Bar* and *Akti Bar* are near each other along the beach.

Mália

Much of **MÁLIA** is taken up by the package industry, so in peak season finding a place to stay is not always easy. You're best off, especially if you want any sleep, trying one of the numerous **rooms** and **pensions** signposted in the old town, such as the *Esperia* (☎0897/31 086; ②). Backtracking from here, along the main Iráklion road, there are a number of reasonably priced **pensions** on the left and right including *Hibiscus* (☎0897/31 313, fax 32 042; ③), which has rooms and studios with kitchenette and fridge around a pool in a garden behind. If you really want to be in the centre of things, try *Kostas* (☎0897/31 485; ②), a family-run pension incongruously located behind the mini-golf at the end of the beach road. Otherwise, on arrival visit one of the travel companies along the main road – for example, Stallion Travel, Venizélou 128 (☎0897/33 690) – to enquire about accommodation availability.

Eating in Mália is unlikely to be a problem as **restaurants** jostle for your custom at every step, especially along the beach road. None is particularly good. The best places are around Platía Ayíou Dhimitríou, a pleasant square beside the church in the centre of the old town to the south of the road. Try a meal at *Kalesma*, *Kalimera* or *Petros*, after an aperitif at *Bar Yiannis* just north of the church or *Ouzeri Alisabi* alongside it, where they serve local wine from the wooden barrel. There are a number of other welcoming tavernas and very pleasant bars, including the *Stone House* and *Temple*, lining, or just off, the platía.

The beach road comes into its own at night, when the profusion of **bars**, **discos** and **clubs** erupt into a pulsating cacophony. *Zoo* is a relatively new club, and once past midnight, one of the internal walls parts to reveal an even larger dance area. *Corkers* and *Highway* are the other really popular clubs in Mália. *Desire*, along the beach road, concentrates on rock and has good-quality live music some nights. Unfortunately, a good night's clubbing and dancing is frequently spoiled by groups of drunken youths pouring out of the bars and getting into brawls. The situation got so bad that tour operators threatened to pull out of the resort if action wasn't taken to deal with the hooligans – all rather ironical as it was they who were shipping them in by the plane-load on cut-price packages. Recent years have seen a police clampdown on such activities as drinking on the street, and the situation has considerably improved.

The Palace of Mália

Tues–Sun 8.30am–3pm; 800dr.

Much less imposing than either Knossós or Festós, the **Palace of Mália**, 2km east of Mália town, in some ways surpasses both. For a start, it's a great deal emptier and you can wander among the remains in relative peace. While no reconstruction has been attempted, the palace was never reoccupied after its second destruction, so the ground plan is virtually intact. It's a great deal easier to comprehend than Knossós and, if you've seen the reconstructions there, it's easy to envisage this seaside palace in its days of glory. There's a real feeling of an ancient civilization with a taste for the good life, basking on the rich agricultural plain between the Lasíthi mountains and the sea.

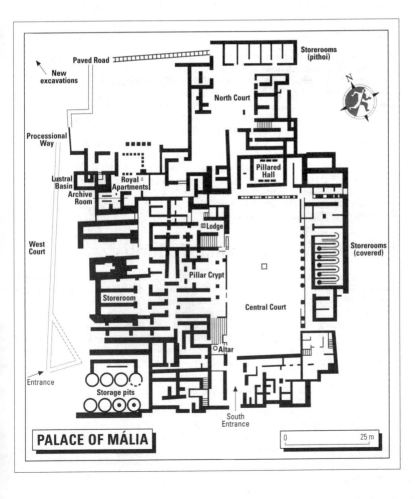

PALACE OF MÁLIA

From this site came the famous **gold pendant** of two bees (which can be seen in the Iráklion museum or on any postcard stand), allegedly part of a horde that was plundered and whose other treasures can now be found in the British Museum in London. The beautiful leopard-head axe, also in the museum at Iráklion, was another of the treasures found here. At the site, look out for the strange indented stone in the central court (which probably held ritual offerings), for the remains of ceremonial stairways and for the giant *pithoi* which stand like sentinels around the palace. To the south and west, digs are still going on as a large town comes slowly to light, and these can now be seen via an overhead walkway.

Any passing **bus** should stop at the site, or you could even rent a **bike** for a couple of hours as it's a pleasant, flat ride from Mália town. Leaving the archeological zone and turning right, you can follow the road down to a lovely stretch of clean and relatively peaceful **beach**, backed by fields, scrubland and a single makeshift taverna, which serves good fresh fish. From here you can walk back along the shore to Mália or take a bus (every thirty minutes in either direction) from the stop on the main road.

Sísi and Mílatos

Head **east** from the Palace of Mália, and it's not long before the road leaves the coast, climbing across the hills towards Áyios Nikólaos. If you want to escape the frenetic pace of all that has gone before, try continuing to **SÍSI** or **MÍLATOS**. These little shore villages are bypassed by the main road as it cuts inland, and are still very much in the early stages of the tourist industry, though both have several tavernas – *Fisherman's Place* in Sísi is worth a try. The more developed of the two, Sísi also has its first disco bar (*Faros*), a large new holiday complex (*Kalimera Krita*) a couple of kilometres to the east, and even a post office – a sure sign of resort status. Accommodation in both is mainly in studios and apartments; it's best to ask in the travel agencies for details of availability. In Sísi there's also a small pension, *Elena* (②) just behind the harbour, and a **campsite** (☎0841/71 247) signposted on the way in, whilst in Mílatos, rooms can be found in the old village, 2km inland. The village beaches aren't great, but the resorts make for a refreshing change of pace, and there are some fine, deep aprons of sand in the rocky coves beyond the resort centres.

West of Iráklion: around Psilorítis

Most people heading west from Iráklion speed straight out on the new **coastal highway**, nonstop to Réthymnon. If you're in a hurry this is not such a bad plan; the road is fast and spectacular, hacked into the sides of mountains which for the most part drop straight to the sea, though there are no more than a couple of places where you might consider stopping. By contrast, the old roads inland are agonizingly slow, but they do pass through a whole string of **attractive villages** beneath the heights of the Psilorítis range. From here you can set out to explore the **mountains** and even walk across them to emerge in villages with views of the south coast.

The coastal route towards Réthymnon

Leaving the city, the **new highway** runs behind a stretch of highly developed coast, where the hotels compete for shore space with a cement works and power station. As soon as you reach the mountains, though, all this is left behind and there's only the clash of rock and sea to contemplate. As you start to climb, look out for **Paleókastro**, beside a bridge which carries the road over a small cove; the castle is so weathered as to be almost invisible against the brownish face of the cliff.

Ayía Pelayía and Fódhele

Some 3km below the highway, as it rounds the first point, lies the resort of **AYÍA PELAYÍA**. It looks extremely attractive from above but, once there, you're likely to find the narrow, taverna-lined beach packed to full capacity; this is not somewhere to roll up without a reserved room, although the Pagasimo travel agency (☎081/811 402, fax 811 424) can usually come up with something, even at the last minute. Out of season you might find a real bargain at an apartment and, despite the high-season crowds, the resort maintains a dignity long since lost in Mália and Hersónissos, and even a certain exclusivity; a couple of Crete's most luxurious hotels, including the enormous *Peninsula* (☎081/811 313, fax 811 219; ⑥), nestle on the headland just beyond the main town beach.

Not far beyond Ayía Pelayía, there's a turning inland to the village of **FÓDHELE**, allegedly El Greco's birthplace. A plaque from the University of Toledo acknowledges the claim and, true or not, the community has built a small tourist industry on that basis. There are a number of craft shops and some pleasant tavernas where you can sit outside along the river. A peaceful 1km walk (or drive) takes you to the spuriously titled "El Greco's house" and the more worthwhile and picturesque fourteenth-century Byzantine **church of the Panayía** (Mon–Fri 9.30am–5pm; free) opposite. None of this amounts to very much but it is a pleasant, relatively unspoiled village if you simply want to sit in peace for a while. A couple of **buses** a day run here from Iráklion, and there's the odd tour; if you arrive on a direct bus, the walk back down to the highway (about 3km), where you can flag down a passing service, is not too strenuous.

Balí and Pánormos

BALÍ, on the coast approximately halfway between Iráklion and Réthymnon, also used to be tranquil and undeveloped, and by the standards of the north coast it still is in many ways. The village is built around a couple of small coves, some 2km from the highway (a hot walk from the bus), and is similar to Ayía Pelayía except that the beaches are not quite as good and there are no big hotels, just an ever-growing proliferation of studios, apartment buildings, rooms for rent and a number of "modest hotels" (brochure-speak). You'll have plenty of company here; the last and best beach, known as "Paradise", no longer really deserves the name; it's a beautiful place to splash about, surrounded by mountains rising straight from the sea, but there's rarely a spare inch on the sand in high season.

Continuing along the coast, the last stop before you emerge on the flat stretch leading to Réthymnon is at **PÁNORMOS**. This makes a good stopover if you're in search of somewhere more peaceful and authentic. The small sandy beach can get crowded when boats bring day-trippers from Réthymnon, but most of the time the attractive village remains relatively unspoiled, and succeeds in clinging to its Cretan identity. There are several decent tavernas and rooms places, one large hotel and the very comfortable *Pension Lucy* (☎0834/51 212, fax 51 434; ②).

Inland towards Mount Psilorítis

Of the **inland routes**, the old main road (via Márathos and Dhamásta) is not the most interesting. This, too, was something of a bypass in its day and there are few places of any size or appeal, though it's a very scenic drive. If you want to dawdle, you're better off on the road which cuts up to **Týlissos** and then goes via **Anóyia**. It's a pleasant ride through fertile valleys filled with olive groves and vineyards, a district (the Malevísi) renowned from Venetian times for the strong, sweet Malmsey wine.

Týlissos and Anóyia

TÝLISSOS has a significant archeological site (daily 8.30am–3pm; 400dr) where three Minoan houses were excavated; unfortunately, its reputation is based more on what was found here (many pieces in the Iráklion museum) and on its significance for archeologists than on anything which remains to be seen. Still, it's worth a look, if you're passing, for a glimpse of Minoan life away from the big palaces, and for the tranquillity of the pine-shaded remains.

ANÓYIA is a much more tempting place to stay, especially if the summer heat is becoming oppressive. Spilling prettily down a hillside close below the highest peaks of the mountains, it looks traditional, but closer inspection shows that most of the buildings are actually concrete; the village was destroyed during World War II and the local men rounded up and shot – one of the German reprisals for the abduction of General Kreipe by the Cretan Resistance. The town has a reputation as a **handicrafts** centre (especially for woven and woollen goods), skills acquired both through bitter necessity after most of the men had been killed and in a conscious attempt to revive the town. At any rate it worked, for the place is thriving today – thanks, it seems, to a buoyant agricultural sector made rich by stockbreeding and the number of elderly widows keen to subject any visitor to their terrifyingly aggressive sales techniques.

Quite a few people pass through Anóyia during the day, but not many of them stay, even though there are some good pensions and rented rooms in the upper half of the town, including the flower-bedecked *Aris* (☎0834/31 460, fax 31 058; ①) and the nearby *Aristea* (☎0834/31 459; ②), which has en-suite rooms. The town has a very different, more traditional ambience at night, and the only problem is likely to be finding a **place to eat**: although there are plenty of snack bars and so-called tavernas, most have extremely basic menus, more or less limited to spit-barbecued lamb, which is the tasty local speciality served up by the grill places on the lower square.

Mount Psilorítis and its caves

Heading for the mountains, a smooth road ascends the 21km from Anóyia to an altitude of 1400m on the **Nídha plateau** at the base of Mount Psilorítis. Here, the *Taverna Nida* (☎0834/31 141; April–Sept daily; Sat & Sun only in winter) serves up hearty taverna standards and has a couple of **rooms** (①), which makes it a good base for hikes in the surrounding mountains. A short path leads from the taverna to the celebrated **Idhéon Ándhron** (Idean cave), a rival of that on Mount Dhíkti (see opposite) for the title of Zeus's birthplace, and certainly associated from the earliest of times with the cult of Zeus. There's a major archeological dig going on inside, which means the whole cave is fenced off, with a miniature railway running into it to carry all the rubble out. In short, there's not a great deal to see.

The taverna also marks the start of the way to the top of **Mount Psilorítis** (2456m), Crete's highest mountain, a climb that for experienced, properly shod hikers is not at all arduous. The route is well marked with the usual red dots, and it should be a six- to seven-hour return journey to the chapel at the summit, although in spring, thick snow may slow you down.

If you're prepared to camp on the plateau (it's very cold, but there's plenty of available water) or find rooms at the taverna, you could continue on foot next day down to the southern slopes of the range. It's a beautiful hike and also relatively easy, four hours or so down a fairly clear path to **VORÍZIA**. If you're still interested in caves, there's a more rewarding one above the nearby village of **KAMÁRES**, a climb of some three hours on a good path. Both Vorízia and Kamáres have a few **rooms** and some tavernas, at least one daily **bus** down to Míres and alternate (more difficult) routes to the peak of Psilorítis if you want to approach from this direction.

EASTERN CRETE

Eastern Crete is dominated by **Áyios Nikólaos**, and while it is a highly developed resort, by no means all of the east is like this. Far fewer people venture beyond the road south to **Ierápetra** and into the eastern isthmus, where only **Sitía** and the famous beach at **Váï** ever see anything approaching a crowd. Inland, too, there's interest, especially on the extraordinary **Lasíthi** plateau, which is worth a night's stay if only to observe its abidingly rural life.

Inland to the Lasíthi plateau

Leaving the palace at Mália, the highway cuts inland towards **NEÁPOLI**, soon beginning a spectacular climb into the mountains. Set in a high valley, Neápoli is a market town little touched by tourism. There is one excellent hotel (*Neapolis* ☎0841/33 966; ③), some rooms, a modern church and a folk museum. Beyond the town, it's about twenty minutes before the bus suddenly emerges high above the Gulf of Mirabéllo and Áyios Nikólaos, the island's biggest resort. If you're stopping, Neápoli also marks the second point of access to the **Lasíthi Plateau**.

Scores of bus tours drive up here daily to view the "thousands of white-cloth-sailed windmills" which irrigate the high plain ringed by mountains, and most groups will be disappointed. There are very few working windmills left, and these operate only for limited periods (mainly in June). This is not to say the trip is not justified, as it would be for the drive alone, and there are many other compensations. The plain is a fine example of rural Crete at work, every inch devoted to the cultivation of potatoes, apples, pears, figs, olives and a host of other crops; stay in one of the villages for a night or two and you'll see real life return as the tourists leave. There are plenty of easy rambles around the villages as well, through orchards and past the rusting remains of derelict windmills. You'll find rooms in the main town of **TZERMIÁDHO**, and at Áyios Konstandínos, Áyios Yeóryios – where you'll find a **folk museum**, and the friendly *Hotel Dias* (☎0844/31 207; ①) – and Psykhró.

Psykhró and the Dhiktean cave

PSYKHRÓ is much the most visited, as it's the base for visiting Lasíthi's other chief attraction, the birthplace of Zeus, the **Dhiktean cave** (daily 8am–6.45pm, reduced hours off-season; 800dr; watch out for slippery stones inside). In legend, Zeus's father, the Titan Kronos, was warned that he would be overthrown by a son and accordingly ate all his offspring; however, when Rhea gave birth to Zeus in the cave, she fed Kronos a stone and left the child concealed, protected by the Kouretes, who beat their shields outside to disguise his cries. The rest, as they say, is history (or at least myth). There's an obvious path running up to the cave from Psykhró and, whatever you're told, you don't have to have a guide if you don't want one, though you will need some form of illumination. On the other hand, it is hard to resist the guides, who do make the visit much more interesting, and they're not expensive if you can get a small group together (around 2000dr for two including lamps or 500–600dr each as part of a larger group). It takes a Cretan imagination to pick out Rhea and the baby Zeus from the lesser stalactites and stalagmites. One of the best guides is Petros Zarvakis, who is also a wildlife expert and leads guided hikes (April–Sept) into the mountains surrounding the plain (☎0844/31 316 for details). **Buses** run around the plateau to Psykhró direct from Iráklion and from Áyios Nikólaos via Neápoli. Both roads offer spectacular views, coiling through a succession of passes guarded by lines of ruined windmills.

Áyios Nikólaos and around

ÁYIOS NIKÓLAOS ("Ag Nik" to the majority of its British visitors) is set around a supposedly bottomless **salt lake**, now connected to the sea to form an inner harbour. It is supremely picturesque and has some style and confidence, which it exploits to the full. There are no sights as such but the excellent **archeological museum** (Tues–Sun 8.30am–3pm; 500dr) and an interesting **folk museum** (daily, excluding Sat, 10am–1.30pm & 7–9.30pm; 300dr) are both worth seeking out. The lake and port are surrounded by restaurants and bars, which charge above the odds, and whilst the

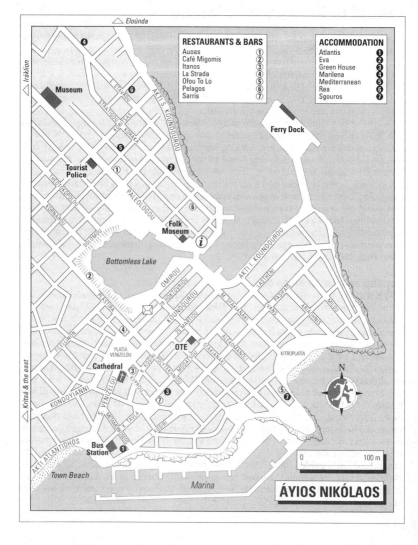

RESTAURANTS & BARS

Auoas ①
Café Migomis ②
Itanos ③
La Strada ④
Ofou To Lo ⑤
Pelagos ⑥
Sarris ⑦

ACCOMMODATION

Atlantis ①
Eva ②
Green House ③
Marilena ④
Mediterranean ⑤
Rea ⑥
Sgouros ⑦

ÁYIOS NIKÓLAOS

resort is still very popular, some tourists are distinctly surprised to find themselves in a place with no decent beach at all.

There are swimming opportunities further north however, where the pleasant low-key resort of **Eloúnda** is the gateway to the mysterious islet of **Spinalónga**, and some great back country to the north – perfect to explore on a scooter. Inland from Áyios Nikólaos, **Kritsá** with its famous church and textile sellers is a tour-bus haven, but just a couple of kilometres away, the imposing ruins of **ancient Lató** are usually deserted.

Áyios Nikólaos practicalities

The greatest concentration of **stores** and **travel agents** are on the hill between the bridge and Platía Venizélou. The main **ferry agent** is LANE (☎0841/26 465 or 23 090) on the corner of 25-Martíou and K. Sfakianáki. The **post office** (Mon–Fri 7.30am–8pm, Sat 7.30am–2pm) is halfway up the newly pedestrianized 28-Oktovríou on the right. The **tourist office** (daily 8.30am–9.30pm; ☎0841/22 357, fax 82 534), situated between the lake and the port, is one of the best on the island for information about accommodation. To **hire a motorbike** or mountain bike try the reliable Mike Manolis (☎0841/24 940), who has a pitch at the junction of 25-Martíou and Sfakianáki. Good **car rental** deals are available at Club Cars, 28-Oktobríou 24 (☎0841/25 868), near the post office. Various **boat trips** to points around the gulf (such as Spinalónga and Eloúnda) leave from the west side of the harbour. **Internet Café** Peripou (daily 9.30am–2am; 1000dr per hour), 28-Oktovríou 25, is Áyios Nikólaos's first of the breed should you want to pick up your emails.

Accommodation

The town is no longer packed solid with tourists, so it is much easier to find a place to stay, though in the peak season you won't have so much choice. One thing in your favour is that there are literally thousands of **rooms**, scattered all around town. The tourist office normally has a couple of boards with cards and brochures about hotels and rooms, including their prices. If the prices seem very reasonable it is because many are for the low season. There is no longer a youth hostel, and the nearest **campsite** is *Gournia Moon*, 17km away (see p.596).

Atlantis, Metamorfoseos, one block east of the bus station (☎0841/28 964). Nothing special but handy for early or late buses; there's a snack bar below for breakfast. ①.

Hotel Eva, Stratigoú Kóraka 20 (☎0841/22587). Decent simple rooms in a misnamed pension close to the centre. ①.

Green House, Modhátsou 15 (☎0841/22 025). Probably the best cheap place to stay in town; clean with shared facilities. ①.

Katerina, Stratigoú Kóraka 30 (☎0841/22 766). A pension close to the *Marilena* and another good choice in the lower price bracket. ②.

Marilena, Érythrou Stavroú 14 (☎0841/22 681, fax 22 681). One of the cheaper pensions for en-suite rooms, this is excellent value. ③.

Mediterranean, S. Dhávaki 27 (☎0841/23 611). Clean, economical rooms without bath close to the lake. ①.

Hotel Rea, Marathónos 1 (☎0841/82 023, fax 28 324). Charming old hotel at top end of this price bracket with stunning views from pleasant balcony rooms overlooking the Mirabéllo Gulf: breakfast included. ③.

Sgouros, Kitroplatía (☎0841/28 931, fax 25 568). Modern hotel overlooking one of the town's beaches, and close to plenty of tavernas. ③.

Eating

At least when it comes to eating there's no chance of missing out, even if the prices are fancier than the restaurants. There are tourist-orientated **tavernas** all around the lake and harbour and little to choose between them, apart from the different perspectives you get on the passing fashion show. Have a drink here perhaps, or a mid-morning coffee, and choose somewhere else to eat. The places around the Kitroplatía are generally fairer value, but again you are paying for the location.

Auoas, Paleológou 44. This taverna serves good, traditional Cretan dishes in and under a plant-covered trellised courtyard, where food and wine prices are among the lowest in town.

Café Migomis, Nikoláou Plastíra 22. Pleasant café high above the bottomless lake with a stunning view. Perfect place for breakfast, afternoon or evening drinks.

Itanos, Kyprou 1, off the east side of Platía Venizélou. Popular with locals, this taverna serves Cretan food and wine and has a terrace across the road opposite.

La Strada, Nikoláou Plastíra 5, just below the west side of Platía Venizélou. Authentic and good-value pizza and pasta, should you fancy a change of cuisine.

Ofou To Lo, Kitroplatía. Best of the moderately priced places on the seafront here: the food is consistently good.

Pelagos, on Stratigoú Kóraka, just back off the lake behind the tourist office. A stylish fish taverna with garden, serving excellent food reflected in the prices.

Sarris, Kýprou 15, off the east side of Platía Venizélou. Great little economical neighbourhood café-diner, especially good for breakfast and *souvláki* served on a leafy terrace.

Drinking and nightlife

After you've eaten you can get into the one thing which Áyios Nikólaos undeniably does well: **bars and nightlife**. Not that you really need a guide to this – the bars are hard to avoid, and you can just follow the crowds to the most popular places centred around the harbour and 25-Martíou. For a quieter drink you could try *Hotel Alexandros* on Paleológou (behind the tourist office), with a rooftop cocktail bar overlooking the lake, or *Zygos* on the north side of the lake which serves low priced cocktails and ices until the small hours. One curiosity worth a look in the harbour itself is *Armida*, a bar inside a beautiful century-old wooden trading vessel, serving cocktails and simple *mezédhes*.

Quiet drinking, however, is not what it's all about in the **disco bars**. *Lipstick*, on the east side of the harbour, as well as *Prince*, *Roxy* and *Santa Maria*, along 25-Martíou ("Soho Street") where it heads up the hill, are very popular and you'll soon be accosted by the greeters on the doors of the nearby *Aquarius*, *Charlie Chan* and *Premiere* as they all try to persuade you to help swell their takings.

The coast north of Áyios Nikólaos

North of Áyios Nikólaos, the swankier hotels are strung out along the coast road, with upmarket restaurants, discos and cocktail bars scattered between them. **ELOÚNDA**, a resort on a more acceptable scale, is about 8km out along this road. Buses run regularly, but if you feel like renting a scooter it's a spectacular ride, with impeccable views over a gulf dotted with islands and moored supertankers. Ask at the bookshop near the post office, on the central square facing the sea, about the attractive seaview *Delfinia Apartments* (☎0841/41 641, fax 41 515; ②). Or you could try the friendly *Pension Oasis* (☎0841/41 076, fax 41 128; ②), which has rooms with kitchenette just off the square, behind the church; there are quite a few similar places along the same road. Alternatively, one of the many travel agents around the main square can help with finding a room or apartment; try the friendly Olous Travel (☎0841/41 324, fax 41 132), which also gives out information and changes money or travellers' cheques. For **eating**, *Britomares*, in a plum spot in the centre of the harbour, is the town's best taverna and although **nightlife** tends to be generally low key, *Aligos* is a lively music bar and *Katafigio* on the Olous road often has *bouzoúki* nights.

Just before the village a track (signposted) leads across a causeway to the "sunken city" of **Oloús**. There are restored windmills, a short length of canal, Venetian salt pans and a well-preserved dolphin mosaic, but of the sunken city itself no trace beyond a couple of walls in about two feet of water. At any rate swimming is good, though there are sea urchins to watch out for.

From Eloúnda, kaïkia run to the fortress-rock of **Spinalónga**. As a bastion of the Venetian defence, this tiny islet withstood the Turkish invaders for 45 years after the mainland had fallen; in more recent decades, it served as a leper colony. As you watch the boat which brought you disappear to pick up another group, an unnervingly real sense of the desolation of those years descends. **PLÁKA**, back on the mainland, and 5km north of Eloúnda, used to be the colony's supply point; now it is a haven from the crowds, with a small pebble beach and a couple of ramshackle fish tavernas which can arrange a boat to take you across to Spinalónga for about 1000dr. There are boat trips daily from Áyios Nikólaos to Oloús, Eloúnda and Spinalónga, usually visiting at least one other island along the way.

Inland to Kritsá and Lató

The other excursion everyone takes from Áyios Nikólaos is to **KRITSÁ**, a "traditional" village about 10km inland. Buses run at least every hour from the bus station, and despite the commercialization it's still a good trip: the local **crafts** (weaving, ceramics and embroidery basically, though they sell almost everything here) are fair value, and it's also a welcome break from living in the fast lane at "Ag Nik". In fact, if you're looking for somewhere to stay around here, Kritsá has a number of advantages: chiefly availability of **rooms**, better prices and something at least approaching a genuinely Greek atmosphere; try *Argyro* (☎0841/51 174; ①) on your way to the village. There are a number of decent places to eat, too – try *Sygonos* near the bus stop for meals – or just to have a coffee and a cake under one of the plane trees.

On the approach road, some 2km before Kritsá, is the lovely Byzantine **church of Panayía Kyrá** (daily 8.30am–2.30pm; 800dr), inside which survives perhaps the most complete set of Byzantine frescoes in Crete. The fourteenth- and fifteenth-century works have been much retouched, but they're still worth the visit. Excellent (and expensive) reproductions are sold from a shop alongside. Just beyond the church, a surfaced road leads off towards the archeological site of **Lató** (Tues–Sun 9am–2.30pm; free), a Doric city with a grand hilltop setting. The city itself is extensive, but neglected, presumably because visitors and archeologists on Crete are more concerned with the Minoan era. Ruins aside, you could come here just for the views: west over Áyios Nikólaos and beyond to the bay and Oloús (which was Lató's port), and inland to the Lasíthi mountains.

The eastern isthmus

The main road south and then east from Áyios Nikólaos is not a wildly exciting one, essentially a drive through barren hills sprinkled with villas and skirting above the occasional sandy cove. Five kilometres beyond a cluster of development at Kaló Hório, a track is indicated on the right for the **Moní Faneroméni**. The track (though partly asphalted) is a rough one and climbs dizzily skywards for 6km, giving spectacular views over the Gulf of Mirabéllo along the way. The **view** from the monastery over the gulf must be among the finest in Crete. To get into the rather bleak-looking monastery buildings, knock loudly. You will be shown up to the chapel, built into a cave sanctuary, and the frescoes are quite brilliant.

Gourniá, Pahiá Ámmos and Mókhlos

Back on the coast road, it's another 2km to the site of **Gourniá** (Tues–Sun 8.30am–3pm; 500dr), slumped in the saddle between two low peaks. The most completely preserved **Minoan town**, its narrow alleys and stairways intersect a throng of one-roomed houses (of which only the ground-floor walls survive – they would have had at least one upper floor) centred on a main square, and the rather grand house of what may have been a local ruler or governor. Although less impressive than the great palaces, the site is strong on revelations about the lives of the ordinary people – many of the dwellings housed craftsmen in wood, metal and clay, who left behind their tools and materials to be found by the excavators. Its desolation today (you are likely to be alone save for a dozing guard) only serves to heighten the contrast with what must have been a cramped and raucous community 3500 years ago.

It is tempting to cross the road here and take one of the paths through the wild thyme to the sea for a swim. Don't bother – the bay and others along this part of the coastline act as a magnet for every piece of floating detritus dumped off Crete's north coast. There is a larger beach (though with similar problems), and rooms to rent, in the next bay along at **PAHIÁ ÁMMOS**, about twenty minutes' walk, where there is also an excellent fish taverna, *Aiolus*; in the other direction, there's the campsite of *Gourniá Moon*, with its own small cove and a swimming pool.

This is the narrowest part of the island, and from here a fast road cuts across the isthmus to Ierápetra (p.600) in the south. In the north though, the route on towards Sitía is one of the most exhilarating in Crete. Carved into cliffs and mountain-sides, the road teeters above the coast before plunging inland at Kavoúsi. Of the beaches you see below, only **MÓKHLOS** is at all accessible, some 5km below the main road. This sleepy village has a few rooms, a hotel or two and a number of tavernas; if you find yourself staying the night, try the rooms at *Limenaria* (☎0843/94 206; ①). Nearer Sitía the familiar olive groves are interspersed with vineyards used for creating wine and sultanas, and in late summer the grapes, spread to dry in the fields and on rooftops, make an extraordinary sight in the varying stages of their slow change from green to gold to brown.

Sitía

SITÍA is the port and main town of the relatively unexploited eastern edge of Crete. It's a pleasantly scenic if unremarkable place, offering a plethora of waterside restaurants, a long sandy beach and a lazy lifestyle little affected even by the thousands of visitors in peak season. There's an almost Latin feel to the town, reflected in (or perhaps caused by) the number of French and Italian tourists, and it's one of those places that tends to grow on you, perhaps inviting a longer stay than intended. For entertainment, there's the **beach**, providing good swimming and windsurfing, and in town a mildly entertaining **folklore museum** (Tues–Sun 9.30am–2.30pm; Wed & Thurs also 6pm–8pm; 500dr), a Venetian fort and Roman fish tanks to explore, plus an excellent **archeological museum** (Tues–Sun 8.30am–3pm; 500dr). Look out, too, for the town's resident and mischievous pelican, Nikos, who has his own living quarters on the harbour quay.

Practicalities

The bus drops you at the new **bus station** (actually an office on the street) on the southwest fringe of the centre and close to the town's main **supermarket**, useful for stocking up on provisions. There are plenty of cheap pensions and **rooms** within easy walking distance, especially in the streets around the folkore museum and beyond here towards the ferry port. A good and friendly **youth hostel** (☎0843/22 693) on the main

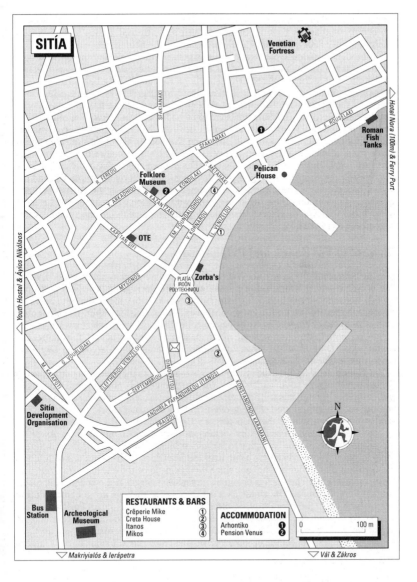

road as it enters town also has a few private rooms and a garden for tents; there's rarely any problem about sleeping on the beach (though it is worth going a little way out of town to avoid any danger of being roused by the police). For rooms, try *Pension Venus*, Kondiláki 60 (☎0843/24 307; ①), *Hotel Arhontiko*, Kondiláki 16 (☎0843/28 172; ①), and *Hotel Nora*, Rouseláki 31 (☎0843/23 017; ②), near the ferry port, for rooms with bath. If you have problems finding somewhere to stay, the **Sitía Development**

Organization (Mon–Fri 8am–3.30pm; ☎0843/23 590) at Anthéon 24, slightly west of the centre, doubles as a tourist office, or there's the **tourist police** at Mysónos 24 (daily 7.30am–2.30pm; ☎0843/24 200), who may also be able to help.

For **food**, the waterside places are rather expensive; the best-value choices near here are the *Itanos Cafe* for mezédhes and *Creta House* serving traditional island dishes, both at the start of the beach road (Konstandínou Karamanlí). Just behind the seafront the popular *Mikos*, Kornárou 117, serves up charcoal-grilled meat and potent local wine, and the waiters run with dishes to a newly aquired terrace fifty metres away on the seafront. Authentic Belgian crepes are to be had at *Creperie Mike*, Venizélou 162, to the east of the focal *Zorbas* restaurant on the seafront. **Nightlife** centres on a few bars and discos near the ferry dock and out along the beach. The town's monster disco, *Planitarion*, attracts crowds from all over the east. It's a kilometre beyond the ferry port (see map), and is best reached by taxi. The in-town alternative is the aptly named *Hot Summer* open-air disco which lies 800m along the beach road towards Váï, and has a pool and gardens. The one major excitement of the year is the August **Sultana Festival** – a celebration of the big local export, with traditional dancing and all the locally produced wine you can consume included in the entrance to the fairground, located beyond the ferry port.

Onward to Váï Beach and Palékastro

Leaving Sitía along the beach, the Váï road climbs above a rocky, unexceptional coastline before reaching a fork to the **monastery of Toploú** (daily 9am–1pm & 2–6pm; 700dr). The monastery's forbidding exterior reflects a history of resistance to invaders, but doesn't prepare you for the gorgeous flower-decked cloister within. The blue-robed monks keep out of the way as far as possible, but their cells and refectory are left discreetly on view. In the church is one of the masterpieces of Cretan art, the eighteenth-century icon *Lord Thou Art Great* by Ioánnis Kornáros. Outside you can buy enormously expensive reproductions.

Váï Beach itself features alongside Knossós or the Lasíthi plateau on almost every Cretan travel agent's list of excursions. Not surprisingly, it is now covered in sunbeds and umbrellas, though it is still a superb beach. Above all, it is famous for its palm trees, and the sudden appearance of the grove is indeed an exotic shock; lying on the fine sand in the early morning, the illusion is of a Caribbean island – a feature seized upon by countless TV-commercial makers seeking an exotic location on the cheap. As everywhere, notices warn that "camping is forbidden by law", and for once the authorities seem to mean it – most campers climb over the headlands to the south or north. If you do sleep out, watch your belongings, since this seems to be the one place on Crete with crime on any scale. There's a café and an expensive taverna at the beach, plus toilets and showers. Because of its status as a nature reserve there is **no accommodation** here whatsoever; the nearest place offering a bed for the night is Palékastro (see below). By day you can find a bit more solitude by climbing the rocks or swimming to one of the smaller beaches which surround Váï. **Ítanos**, twenty minutes' walk north by an obvious trail, has a couple of tiny beaches and some modest ruins of the Classical era.

PALÉKASTRO, some 9km south, is in many ways a better place to stay. Although its beaches can't begin to compare, you'll find several modest places with **rooms** – notably *Hotel Hellas* (☎0843/61 240, fax 61 340; ②), which provides good rooms and food – a number of reasonable restaurants, and plenty of space to camp out without the crowds. The sea is a couple of kilometres down a dirt track, effortlessly reached with a scooter hired from Motor Action (☎0843/61 276) next door to the *Hotel Hellas*. Palékastro is also the crossroads for the road south to Zákros and your own transport presents all kinds of beach and exploration possibilities.

Zákros

ÁNO ZÁKROS is a little under 20km from Palékastro. There are several tavernas and a simple hotel, the *Zakros* (☎0843/43 379, fax 93 379; ④), which has some rooms with bath and great views from its rear rooms; it also offers guests a free minibus service to the Minoan palace and beach. The Minoan palace is actually at Káto (Lower) Zákros, 8km further down towards the sea. Most buses run only to the upper village, but in summer, a couple every day do run all the way to the site. Part way along you can, if on foot, take a short cut through an impressive **gorge** (the "Valley of the Dead", named for ancient tombs in its sides) but it's usually not difficult to hitch if your bus does leave you in the village.

The **Palace of Zákros** (Tues–Sun 8.30am–2.30pm; 500dr) was an important find for archeologists; it had been occupied only once (between 1600 and 1450 BC), and was abandoned hurriedly and completely. Later, it was forgotten almost entirely and as a result was never plundered or even discovered by archeologists until very recently. The first major excavation began only in 1960; all sorts of everyday objects (tools, raw materials, food, pottery) were thus discovered intact among the ruins, and a great deal was learned from being able to apply modern techniques (and knowledge of the Minoans) to a major dig from the very beginning. None of this is especially evident when you're at the palace, except perhaps in a particularly simple ground plan, so it's as well that it is also a rewarding visit in terms of the setting. Although the site is set back from the sea, in places it is often marshy and waterlogged: partly the result of eastern Crete's slow subsidence, partly the fault of a spring which once supplied fresh water to a cistern beside the royal apartments, and whose outflow is now silted up. In wetter periods, among the remains of narrow streets and small houses higher up, you can keep your feet dry and get an excellent view down over the central court and royal apartments. If you want a more detailed overview of the remains, buy the guide to the site on sale at the entrance.

The delightful village of **KÁTO ZÁKROS** is little more than a collection of tavernas, some of which rent out rooms around a peaceful beach and minuscule fishing anchorage. It's a wonderfully restful place, but is often unable to cope with the volume of visitors seeking accommodation in high season, and as rooms are rarely to be had on spec you'd be wise to ring ahead. You should also be aware that villagers are far more hostile these days to wild camping after years of problems, and you should be sensitive to their concerns. Reliable rooms can be found at *Poseidon* (☎0843/93 316; ④), which has fine views, and the friendly *Rooms George* (☎ & fax 0843/93 201; ②), 200m behind the archeological site, is also good.

Ierápetra and the southeast coast

From Sitía, the route south is a cross-country roller-coaster ride until it hits the south coast at **MAKRYIALÓS**. This little fishing village has one of the best beaches at this end of Crete, with fine sand which shelves so gently you feel you could walk the 340km to Africa. Unfortunately, since the early 1990s it has been heavily developed, so while still a very pleasant place to stop for a swim or a bite (the *Porfiria* taverna on the sea is recommended), it's not somewhere you're likely to find a cheap room.

From here to Ierápetra there's little reason to stop; the few beaches are rocky and the coastal plain submerged under ranks of polythene-covered greenhouses. Beside the road leading into Ierápetra, are long but exposed stretches of sand, including the appropriately named "Long Beach", where you'll find a campsite, *Camping Koutsounari* (☎0842/61 213), which has plenty of shade.

Ierápetra

IERÁPETRA itself is a bustling modern supply centre for the region's farmers. It also attracts a fair number of package tourists and not a few backpackers looking for work in the prosperous surrounding agricultural zone, especially out of season. The tavernas along the tree-lined front are scenic enough and the EU blue-flagged beach stretches a couple miles east. But as a town, most people find it pretty uninspiring, despite an ongoing modernization programme which has cleaned up the centre and revamped the seafront. Although there has been a port here since Roman times, only the **Venetian fort** guarding the harbour and a crumbling minaret remain as reminders of better days. What little else has been salvaged is in the one-room **museum** (Tues–Sat 8am–3pm; 500dr) near the post office.

The town hall (*dhimarhío*) on the main square, Platía Kanoupáki, should be able to provide a town map (but not much else) which will help you find your way around. If you want to stay, head up Kazantzákis from the chaotic bus station, and you'll find **rooms** at the *Four Seasons* (✆0842/24 390; ②) or in the nearby *Cretan Villa*, Lakérdha 16 (✆ & fax 0842/28 522; ②), a beautiful 180-year-old house. More central, and also good value, is the *Hotel Ersi*, Platía Eleftherías 20 (✆0842/23 208; ②), which can also rent you a seafront apartment for not much more than the cost of a room. You'll find places to **eat** and **drink** all along the waterfront, the better places such as *Taverna Napoleon* and *Gorgona* being towards the Venetian fort. **Nightlife** centres on a clutch of disco bars and fast-food places along central Kýrba, behind the promenade. Ierapetra's **Internet café**, Orfeas (1400dr per hour), is at Koundouriótou 25, just north of the museum, and serves good breakfasts.

West from Ierápetra

Heading west from Ierápetra, the first stretch of coast is grey and dusty, the road jammed with trucks and lined with drab ribbon development. There are a number of small resorts along the beach, though little in the way of public transport. If travelling under your own steam, there is a scenic detour worth taking at Gría Liyiá: the road, on the right for Anatolí climbs to Máles, a village clinging to the lower slopes of the **Dhíkti range**. Here would be a good starting point if you want to take a walk through some stunning mountain terrain. Otherwise, the dirt road back down towards the coast (signposted Mýthi) has spectacular views over the Libyan Sea, and eventually follows the Mýrtos river valley down to Mýrtos itself.

Mýrtos and Árvi

MÝRTOS is the first resort that might actually tempt you to stop, and it's certainly the most accessible, just off the main road with numerous daily **buses** to Ierápetra and a couple direct to Iráklion. Although developed to a degree, it nonetheless remains tranquil and inexpensive, with lots of young travellers (many of whom sleep on the beach, to the irritation of locals). If you want a **room**, try *Rooms Angelos* (✆0842/51 106; ①), or *Nikos House* (✆0842/51 116; ①), though there are plenty of others. Just off the road from Ierápetra are a couple of excavated **Minoan villas** you might want to explore: Néa Mýrtos and Pýrgos.

After Mýrtos the main road turns inland towards Áno Viánnos, then continues across the island towards Iráklion; several places on the coast are reached by a series of rough sidetracks. That hasn't prevented one of them, **ÁRVI**, from becoming a larger resort than Mýrtos. The beach hardly justifies it, but it's an interesting little excursion (with at least one bus a day) if only to see the bananas and pineapples grown here and to experience the microclimate – noticeably warmer than neighbouring zones, especially in spring or autumn – that encourages them. For rooms you could try the central *Pension Gorgona* (☎0895/71 211; ②).

Beyond Árvi

Two more villages, **KERATÓKAMBOS** and **TSOÚTSOUROS**, look tempting on the map. Keratókambos has a rather stony beach and only basic rooms – the *Morning Star* taverna (☎0895/51 209; ①) is a good bet and the food is tasty too – and although popular with Cretan day-trippers it's a great place to escape the tourist grind for a spell. Tsoútsouros is developed and not really worth the tortuous thirteen-kilometre dirt road in.

If you hope to continue across the **south** of the island, be warned that there are no buses, despite completion of the road towards Mýres after years of work. It's an enjoyable rural drive, but progress can be slow; there's very little traffic if you're trying to hitch.

RÉTHYMNON AND AROUND

The relatively low, narrow section of Crete which separates the Psilorítis range from the White Mountains in the west seems at first a nondescript, even dull part of the island. Certainly in scenic terms it has few of the excitements that the west can offer; there are no major archeological sites and many of the villages seem modern and ugly. On the other hand, **Réthymnon** itself is an attractive and lively city, with some excellent beaches nearby. And on the south coast, in particular around **Plakiás**, there are beaches as fine as any Crete can offer, and as you drive towards them the scenery and villages improve by the minute.

Réthymnon

Since the early 1980s, **RÉTHYMNON** has seen a greater influx of tourists than perhaps anywhere else on Crete, with the development of a whole series of large hotels extending almost 10km along the beach to the east. For once, though, the middle of town has been spared, so that at its heart Réthymnon remains one of the most beautiful of Crete's major cities (only Haniá is a serious rival), with an enduringly provincial air. A wide sandy beach and palm-lined promenade border a labyrinthine tangle of Venetian and Turkish houses lining streets where ancient minarets lend an exotic air to the skyline. Dominating everything from the west is the superbly preserved outline of the **fortress** built by the Venetians after a series of pirate raids had devastated the town.

The town

With a **beach** right in the heart of town, it's tempting not to stir at all from the sands, but Réthymnon repays at least some gentle exploration. For a start, you could try checking out the further reaches of the beach itself. The waters protected by the breakwaters in front of town have their disadvantages – notably crowds and dubious hygiene – but less sheltered sands stretch for miles to the east, crowded at first but progressively less so if you're prepared to walk a bit.

Away from the beach, you don't have far to go for the most atmospheric part of town, immediately behind the **inner harbour**. Almost anywhere here, you'll find unexpected old buildings, wall fountains, overhanging wooden balconies, heavy, carved doors and rickety shops, many still with local craftsmen sitting out front, gossiping as they ply their trades. Look out especially for the **Venetian loggia**, which houses a shop selling

high quality and expensive reproductions of Classical art; the **Rimóndi fountain**, another of the more elegant Venetian survivals; and the **Nerandzés mosque**, the best preserved in Réthymnon but currently serving as a music school and closed to the public. Simply by walking past these three, you'll have seen many of the liveliest parts of Réthymnon. Ethnikís Andistásis, the street leading straight up from the fountain, is also the town's **market** area.

The old city ends at the Porta Guora at the top of Ethnikís Andistásis, the only surviving remnant of the city walls. Almost opposite are the quiet and shady **public gar-**

dens. These are always a soothing place to stroll, and in the latter half of July, the **Réthymnon Wine Festival** is staged here. Though touristy, it's a thoroughly enjoyable event, with spectacular local dancing as the evening progresses and the barrels empty. The entrance fee includes all the wine you can drink, though you'll need to bring your own cup or buy one of the souvenir glasses and carafes on sale outside the gardens.

The museums and fortress

A little further up the street from the Nerandzés mosque at M. Vernárdhou 28, a beautifully restored seventeenth-century Venetian mansion is the home of the small but tremendously enjoyable **Historical and Folk Art Museum** (Mon–Sat 10am–2pm, Mon & Tues also 6–8pm; 500dr). Gathered within four, cool, airy rooms are musical instruments, old photos, basketry, farm implements, an explanation of traditional bread-making techniques, smiths' tools, traditional costumes and jewellery, lace, weaving and embroidery, pottery, knives and old wooden chests. It makes for a fascinating insight into a fast disappearing rural (and urban) lifestyle, which had often survived virtually unchanged from Venetian times to the 1960s, and is well worth a look.

Heading in the other direction from the fountain you'll come to the fortress and **Archeological Museum** (Tues–Sun 8am–2.30pm; 500dr), which occupies a building almost directly opposite the entrance to the fortress. This was built by the Turks as an extra defence, and later served as a prison, but it's now entirely modern inside: cool, spacious and airy. Unfortunately, the collection is not particularly exciting, and really only worth seeing if you're going to miss the bigger museums elsewhere on the island.

The massive **Venetian fortress** (Tues–Sun 8am–8pm; reduced hours out of season; 800dr) is a must, however. Said to be the largest Venetian castle ever built, this was a response, in the last quarter of the sixteenth century, to a series of **pirate raids** (by Barbarossa among others) that had devastated the town. Inside is now a vast open space dotted with the remains of all sorts of barracks, arsenals, officers' houses, earthworks and deep shafts, and at the centre a large domed building that was once a church and later a **mosque** (complete with a surviving but sadly defaced *mihrab*). It was designed to be large enough for the entire population to take shelter within the walls, and you can see that it probably was. Although much is ruined, it remains thoroughly atmospheric, and you can look out from the walls over the town and harbour, or in the other direction along the coast to the west. It's also worth walking around the outside of the fortress, preferably at sunset, to get an impression of its fearsome defences, plus great views along the coast and a pleasant resting point around the far side at the *Sunset* taverna.

Practicalities

The **bus station** in Réthymnon is by the sea to the west of town just off Periferiakós, the road which skirts the waterfront around the fortress. The **tourist office** (Mon–Fri 8am–5.30pm, Sat 9am–2pm; ☎0831/24 143) backs onto the main town beach, close to the mobile post office (summer only). If you arrive by **ferry**, you'll be more conveniently placed, over at the western edge of the harbour. To pick up your emails head for the Galero **Internet café** (1400dr per hr), beside the Rimóndi fountain in the old town.

Accommodation

There's a great number of places to stay in Réthymnon, and only at the height of the season are you likely to have difficulty finding somewhere, though you may get weary looking. The greatest concentration of **rooms** is in the tangled streets west of the inner harbour, between the Rimóndi fountain and the museums; there are also quite a few places on and around Arkadhíou and Platía Frakidháki. The cheapest beds in town are in the **youth hostel**, Tombázi 41 (☎0831/22 848), where you can also sleep (illegally) on the roof. It's large, clean, very friendly and popular, and there's food, showers, clothes-washing facilities and even a library, with books in various languages.

There are a couple of **campsites** 4km east of town; take the bus for the hotels (marked *Scaleta/El Greco*) from the long-distance bus station to get there. *Camping Elizabeth* (☎0831/28 694) is a pleasant, large site on the beach, with all facilities. Only a few hundred metres further east along the beach is *Camping Arkadia* (☎0831/28 825), a bigger and slightly less friendly site.

Anna, Katseháki (☎0831/25 586). Comfortable pension in a quiet position on the street that runs straight down from the entrance to the fortress to Melissínou. ③.

Atelier, Himáras 32 (☎0831/24 440). Pleasant rooms close to *Rooms George*, run by a talented potter, who has her studio in the basement and sells her wares in a shop on the other side of the building. ②.

Barbara Dokimaki, Platía Plastíra 14 (☎0831/22 319). Strange warren of a rooms place, with one entrance at the above address, just off the seafront behind the *Ideon*, and another on Dambérgi; ask for the newly refurbished top-floor rooms, which have balconies. ③.

Byzantine, Vospórou 26 (☎0831/55 609). Excellent-value rooms in a renovated Byzantine palace. The tranquil patio bar is open to all, and breakfast is included in price. ③.

Ideon, Platía Plastíra 10 (☎0831/28 667, fax 28 670). Hotel with a brilliant position just north of the ferry dock; little chance of space in season, though. ⑥.

Leo, Vafé 2 (☎0831/26 197). Good hotel with lots of wood and a traditional feel; the price includes breakfast, and there's a bar. ③.

Olga's Pension, Soulíou 57 (☎0831/53 206, fax 29 851). The star attraction at this very friendly pension on one of Réthymnon's most touristy streets is the resplendent flower-filled roof garden. ②.

Rethymnon House, V. Kornárou 1 (☎0831/23 923). Very pleasant rooms of a high standard in an old building just off Arkadhíou. Bar downstairs. ②.

Rooms George, Makedhonías 32 (☎0831/50 967). Decent rooms (some with fridge), near the Archeological Museum. ②.

Sea-Front Rent Rooms, Arkadhíou 159 (☎0831/51 981, fax 51 062). Rooms with sea views and balconies in an attractively refurbished mansion with ceiling fans and lots of wood. ②.

Zania, Pávlou Vlástou 3 (☎0831/28 169). Pension right on the corner of Arkadhíou; a well-adapted old house, but only a few rooms. ②.

Eating and drinking

Immediately behind the town beach are arrayed the most touristy **restaurants**, the vast majority being overpriced and of dubious quality. One that maintains some integrity (and reasonable prices) is the *Samaria* taverna, almost opposite the tourist office. Around the inner **harbour**, there's a second, rather more expensive group of tavernas, specializing in fish, though as often as not the intimate atmosphere in these places is spoiled by the stench from the harbour itself: *O Zefyros* is one of the less outrageously pricey and maintains reasonable standards. Not far from here and slightly west of Platía Plastíra, *Taverna Fanari* at Makedhonías 5 is a good-value little restaurant serving up tasty lamb and chicken dishes.

The cluster of kafenía and tavernas by the **Rimóndi fountain** and the newer places spreading into the surrounding streets generally offer considerably better value, and a couple of the old-fashioned kafenía serve magnificent yoghurt and honey. Places to try include *Kyria Maria* at Moskhovítou 20, tucked down an alley behind the fountain (after the meal, everyone gets a couple of María's delicious *tyropitákia* with honey on the house); *Agrimia*, a reliable standard on Platía Petiháki, slightly east of the fountain; and the *Zanfoti* kafenío overlooking the fountain which is relatively expensive, but a great place to people-watch over a coffee; and, for a slightly cheaper option *O Psaras* (the Fisherman), a simple, friendly taverna by the church on the corner of Nikifórou

Foká and Koronéou. A good lunchtime stop close to the Archeological Museum is *O Pontios*, Melissinoú 34, a simple place with tables outside and an enthusiastic female proprietor. Healthy, home-baked lunches can also be had at *Stella's Kitchen*, a simple café linked to *Olga's Pension* at Soulíou 55, where meals can be enjoyed up on the leafy roof garden. Tucked behind the church on Platía Martíron, *Mesostrati* is a pleasant little neighbourhood ouzerí/taverna serving well-prepared Cretan country dishes and having a small terrace. A noisier evening alternative is *Taverna O Gounos*, Koronéou 6 in the old town; the family who run it perform live *lyra* every night, and when things get really lively the dancing starts.

If you want takeaway food, there are numerous **souvláki** stalls, including a couple on Arkadhíou and Paleológou and another at Petikháki 52, or you can buy your own ingredients at the **market** stalls set up daily on Ethnikís Andistásis below the Porta Guora. There are small general stores scattered everywhere, particularly on Paleológou and Arkadhíou; east along the beach road you'll even find a couple of mini supermarkets. The **bakery** *I Gaspari* on Mesolongíou, just behind the Rimóndi fountain, sells the usual cheese pies, cakes and the like, and it also bakes excellent brown, black and rye bread. There's a good zaharoplastío, *N.A. Skartsilakos*, at Paleológou 36, just north of the fountain, and several more small cafés which are good for breakfast or a quick coffee.

Nightlife

Nightlife is concentrated in the same general areas as the tavernas. At the west end of Venizélou, in the streets behind the inner harbour, the overflow from a small cluster of noisy music bars – *Templum*, *252*, *Dimmam*, *Karma* and *Venetianikoa* – begins to spill out onto the pavement as party-goers gather for the nightly opening of the *Fortezza Disco* in the inner harbour, which is the glitziest in town, flanked by its competitors *Metropolis*, *NYC* and *Vitro*. Heading up Salamínos, a string of more subdued cocktail bars – *Petaloúda*, *Memphis*, *Santan* and *Pasodia* – cater for those in search of a quieter drink as does *Notas*, Himeras 27 near the *Fortezza* and facing the *Atelier* pension, which puts on live (acoustic) guitar and song every night.

Around Réthymnon

While some of Crete's most drastic resort development spreads ever eastwards out of Réthymnon, to the west a sandy coastline, not yet greatly exploited, runs all the way to the borders of Haniá province. But of all the short trips that can be made out of Réthymnon, the best known and still the most worthwhile is to the **monastery of Arkádhi**.

Southeast to Arkádhi

The **monastery of Arkádhi** (daily 8am–8pm; 300dr), some 25km southeast of the city and immaculately situated in the foothills of the Psilorítis range, is also something of a national Cretan shrine. During the 1866 rebellion against the Turks, the monastery became a rebel strongpoint in which, as the Turks gained the upper hand, hundreds of Cretan guerrillas and their families took refuge. Surrounded and, after two days of fighting, on the point of defeat, the defenders ignited a powder magazine just as the Turks entered. Hundreds (some sources claim thousands) were killed, Cretan and Turk alike, and the tragedy did much to promote international sympathy for the cause of Cretan independence. Nowadays, you can peer into the roofless vault where the explosion occurred and wander about the rest of the well-restored grounds. The sixteenth-century church survived, and is one of the finest Venetian structures left on

Crete; other buildings house a small museum devoted to the exploits of the defenders of the (Orthodox) faith. The monastery is easy to visit by public bus or on a tour.

West to Aryiroúpolis, Yeoryoúpoli and beyond

Leaving Réthymnon to the west, the main road climbs for a while above a rocky coastline before descending (after some 5km) to the sea, where it runs alongside sandy **beaches** for perhaps another 7km. An occasional hotel offers accommodation, but on the whole there's nothing but a line of straggly bushes between the road and the windswept sands. If you have your own vehicle, there are plenty of places you can stop at here for a swim, and rarely anyone else around – but beware of some very strong currents.

One worthwhile detour inland is to **ARYIROÚPOLIS**, a charming village perched above the Mousselás river valley and the seat of ancient Lappa, a Greek and Roman town of some repute. The village is famous for its **springs** which gush dramatically from the hillside and provide most of the city of Réthymnon's water supply. Among the number of **places to stay** try *Rooms Argiroupolis* (0831/81 148; ②), near the springs, while for **places to eat**, you're spoilt for choice, with five tavernas at the springs and a bar in the upper village together with a taverna (*Agnantema*) offering a spectacular terrace view over the valley. A shop under the arch in the main square can provide a village **map** detailing a surprising number of churches, caves and ancient remains to see in and around the village, including an outstanding third-century **Roman mosaic**. An interesting **folklore museum** (daily 9am–9pm; 300dr) – signed from the main square – is worth a look for its collection of tapestries, farm implements, photos and ephemera collected by the Zografakis family who have lived here for countless generations. There are numerous fine **walks** to be had in the surrounding hills, on which the proprietor of the village shop, who speaks English will advise. Although little over 20km from Réthymnon and easy to get to with your own transport, Aryiroúpolis is also served by **buses** from Réthymnon's bus station at 11.30am and 2.30pm, and in the reverse direction at 7.30am, 12.30 and 4pm (all Mon–Fri only).

Back on the coastal route, if you are looking for a place to relax for a while, probably the best base is **YEORYOÚPOLI** just across the provincial border in Haniá, where the beach is cleaner, wider and further from the road. There's been a distinct acceleration in the pace of development at Yeoryoúpoli over the last few years and it's now very much a resort, packed with rooms to rent, small hotels, apartment buildings, tavernas and travel agencies; there's even a small land train to transport visitors along the seafront and on short excursions. But everything remains on a small scale, and the undeniably attractive setting is untarnished, making it a very pleasant place to pass a few days, as long as you don't expect to find many vestiges of traditional Crete. Most of the better rooms, including *Rent Rooms Stelios* (☎0825/61 308; ②), *Irene* (☎0825/61 278; ②) and *Cretan Cactus* (☎0825/61 027; ②), are away from the main platía along the road down towards the beach. More central possibilities include *Rooms Voula* (☎0825/61 359; ①) above a gift shop to the east of the platía and the *Paradise Taverna* (☎0825/61 313; ②) off the southeast corner of the platía, which has rooms and is a good place to eat.

Within walking distance inland – though it can also be visited on the tourist train from Yeoryoúpoli – is **Kournás**, Crete's only lake, set deep in a bowl of hills and almost constantly changing colour. There are a few tavernas with rooms to rent along the shore here (bring mosquito repellent), or you could try for a bed in the nearby village of Moúri. A few kilometres uphill in Kournás village, the *Kali Kardia* taverna is a great place to sample the local lamb and sausages.

Beyond Yeoryoúpoli, the main road heads inland, away from a cluster of coastal villages beyond Vámos. It thus misses the Dhrápano peninsula, with some spectacular views over the sapphire Bay of Soúdha, several quiet beaches and the setting for the film of *Zorba the Greek*. **Kókkino Horió**, the movie location, and nearby **Pláka** are indeed postcard-picturesque (more so from a distance), but **Kefalás**, inland, outdoes both of them. On the exposed north coast there are good beaches at **Almyrídha** and **Kalýves**, and off the road between them. Both are fast developing into resorts in their own right; accommodation is mostly in apartments and rooms are scarce, although there are a few mid-range and more upmarket hotels, and a decent pension, *Katrina* (☎0825/38 775; ②), a short walk uphill from the centre of Almyrídha. With a string of good fish tavernas (try *Dimitri's* or *Manoli's*) along the beach and a pleasantly refreshing sea breeze, Almyrídha makes an enjoyable lunch stop.

South from Réthymnon

There are a couple of alternative routes south from Réthymnon, but the main one heads straight out from the centre of town, an initially featureless road due south across the middle of the island towards **Ayía Galíni**. About 23km out, a turning cuts off to the right for **Plakiás** and **Mýrthios**, following the course of the spectacular Kourtaliótiko ravine.

Plakiás and the south coast

Since the late 1980s, **PLAKIÁS** has undergone a major boom and is no longer the pristine village all too many people arriving here expect. That said, it's still quite low key, and there's a satisfactory beach and a string of good tavernas around the dock. There are hundreds of **rooms**, but at the height of summer you'll need to arrive early if you hope to find one; the last to fill are generally those on the road leading inland, away from the waterside. For rooms try *Christos Taverna* (☎0832/31 472; ③) on the seafront, or the excellent balcony rooms at *Ippokambos* (☎0832/31 525; ④) slightly inland on the road to the relaxed **youth hostel** (☎0832/31 306), which is 500m inland and signed from the seafront.

Once you've found a room there's not a lot else to discover here. You'll find every facility strung out around the waterfront, including a temporary **post office** parked by the harbour, bike rental, money exchange, supermarket and even a laundry. Places to eat are plentiful too. The attractive **tavernas** on the waterfront in the centre are a little expensive; you'll eat cheaper further inland – seek out *Taverna Medusa* at the east end of town – or around the corner from *Christos* at one of the tavernas facing west, where *Sunset* taverna is the first in line.

Mýrthios

For a stay of more than a day or two, **MÝRTHIOS**, in the hills behind Plakiás, also deserves consideration. It's no longer a great deal cheaper, but at least you'll find locals still outnumbering the tourists and something of a travellers' scene based around another popular **youth hostel** (☎0832/31 202), with a friendly taverna and several rooms for rent. The Plakiás bus will usually loop back through Mýrthios, but check; otherwise, it's less than five minutes' walk from the junction. It takes twenty minutes to walk down to the beach at Plakiás, a little longer to Dhamnóni, and if you're prepared to walk for an hour or more, there are some entirely isolated coves to the west – ask for directions at the hostel.

Dhamnóni

Some of the most tempting **beaches** in central Crete hide just to the east of Plakiás, though unfortunately they're now a very poorly kept secret. These three splashes of yellow sand, divided by rocky promontories, are within easy walking distance and together go by the name **Dhamnóni**. At the first, Dhamnóni proper, there's a taverna with showers and a wonderfully long strip of sand, but there's also a lot of new development including a number of nearby rooms for rent and a huge and ugly Swiss-owned holiday village, which has colonized half of the main beach. At the far end, you'll generally find a few people who've dispensed with their clothes, while the little cove which shelters the middle of the three beaches (barely accessible except on foot) is entirely nudist. Beyond this, **Ammoúdhi** beach has another taverna (with good rooms for rent) and a slightly more family atmosphere.

Préveli and "Palm Beach"

Next in line comes **PRÉVELI**, some 6km southeast of Lefkóyia. It takes its name from a **monastery** (daily 8am–7pm; 500dr) high above the sea which, like every other in Crete, has a proud history of resistance, in this case accentuated by its role in the last war as a shelter for marooned Allied soldiers awaiting evacuation off the south coast. There are fine views and a monument commemorating the rescue operations, but little else to see. The evacuations took place from "**Palm Beach**", a sandy cove with a small date-palm grove and a solitary drink stand where a stream feeds a little oasis. The beach usually attracts a summer camping community and is now also the target of day-trip boats from Plakiás. Sadly, these two groups between them have left this lovely place filthy, and despite an ongoing clean-up campaign it seems barely worth the effort. The climb down from the monastery is steep, rocky and surprisingly arduous: it's a great deal easier to come here by boat.

Spíli and Ayía Galíni

Back on the main road south, **SPÍLI** lies about 30km from Réthymnon. A popular coffee break for coach tours passing this way, Spíli warrants time if you can spare it. Sheltered under a cliff are narrow alleys of ancient houses, all leading up from a platía with a famous 24-spouted fountain. If you have your own transport, it's a worthwhile place to stay, peacefully rural at night but with several good **rooms** for rent. Try the *Green Hotel* (☎0832/22 225; ②) or the pleasant *Rooms Herakles* (☎0832/22 411; ②) just behind, the eponymous proprietor of which can advise on some superb **walks** in the surrounding hills.

The ultimate destination of most people on this road is **AYÍA GALÍNI**. If heading here was your plan, maybe you should think again since this picturesque "fishing village" is so busy in high season that you can't see it for the tour buses, hotel billboards and British package tourists. It also has a beach much too small for the crowds that congregate here. Even so, there are a few saving graces – mainly some excellent restaurants and bars, plenty of rooms and a friendly atmosphere that survives and even thrives on all the visitors. Out of season, it can be quite enjoyable, and from November to April the mild climate makes it an ideal spot to spend the winter. A lot of long-term travellers do just that, so it's a good place to find work packing tomatoes or polishing cucumbers. If you want somewhere to stay, start looking at the top end of town, around the main road: the good-value and friendly *Hotel Minos* (☎0832/91 292; ①), with superb views, is a good place to start, with the nearby *Hotel Hariklia* (0832/91 350, fax 91 257; ①) as a backup, but there are dozens of possibilities, and usually something to be found even at the height of summer.

The coastal plain east of Ayía Galíni, hidden under acres of polythene greenhouses and burgeoning concrete sprawl, must be among the ugliest regions in Crete, and **Timbáki** the dreariest town. Since this is the way to Festós and back to Iráklion, however, you may have no choice but to grin and bear it.

The Amári Valley

An alternative route south from Réthymnon, and a far less travelled one, is the road which turns off on the eastern fringe of town to run via the **Amári Valley**. Very few buses go this way, but if you're driving it's well worth the extra time. There's little specifically to see or do (though hidden away are a number of richly frescoed Byzantine churches), but it's an impressive drive under the flanks of the mountains and a reminder of how, in places, rural Crete continues to exist regardless of visitors. The countryside here is delightfully green even in summer, with rich groves of olive and assorted fruit trees, and if you **stay** (there are rooms in Thrónos and Yerákari), you'll find the nights are cool and quiet. It may seem odd that many of the villages along the way are modern; they were systematically destroyed by the Germans in reprisal for the 1944 kidnapping of General Kreipe.

HANIÁ AND THE WEST

The substantial attractions of Crete's westernmost quarter are all the more enhanced by its relative lack of visitors, and despite the now-rapid spread of tourist development, the west is likely to remain one of the emptier parts of the island. This is partly because there are no big sandy beaches to accommodate resort hotels, and partly because it's so far from the great archeological sites. But for mountains and empty (if often pebbly) beaches, it's unrivalled.

Haniá itself is one of the best reasons to come here, perhaps the only Cretan city which could be described as enjoyable in itself. The immediately adjacent coast is relatively developed and not overly exciting; if you want beaches head for the south coast. **Paleohóra** is the only place which could really be described as a resort, and even this is on a thoroughly human scale; others are emptier still. **Ayía Rouméli** and **Loutró** can be reached only on foot or by boat; **Hóra Sfakíon** sees hordes passing through but few who stay; **Frangokástello**, nearby, has a beautiful castle and the first stirrings of development. Behind these lie the **Lefká Óri** (White Mountains) and, above all, the famed walk through the **Gorge of Samariá**.

Haniá

HANIÁ, as any of its residents will tell you, is spiritually the capital of Crete, even if the nominal title was passed back (in 1971) to Iráklion. For many, it is also by far the island's most attractive city, especially if you can catch it in spring, when the Lefká Óri's snow-capped peaks seem to hover above the roofs. Although it is for the most part a modern city, you might never know it as a tourist. Surrounding the small outer harbour is a wonderful jumble of half-derelict **Venetian streets** that survived the wartime bombardments, and it is here that life for the visitor is concentrated. Restoration and gentrification, consequences of the tourist boom, have made inroads of late, but it remains an atmospheric place.

Arrival, information and orientation

Large as it is, Haniá is easy to handle once you've reached the centre; you may get lost wandering among the narrow alleys of the old city but that's a relatively small area, and

---

The phone code for Haniá is ☎0821

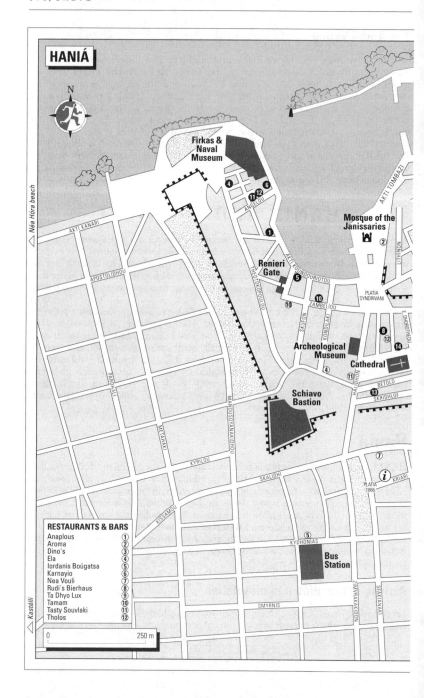

HANIÁ

N

Firkas & Naval Museum

Mosque of the Janissaries

Renieri Gate

Archeological Museum

Cathedral

Schiavo Bastion

Bus Station

Néa Hóra beach

Kastélli

AKTI KANARI

APOSTOLIDHOU

PARHALI

METAHAKI

KYRILOU

KISSAMOU

MANOUSIYANAKIHOU

THEOTOKOPOULOU

ANGELIOU

ALI KOUNDOURIOTOU

ZAMBELIOU

SKUFON

KONDILAKI

HALIDHON

BETOLO

SKRIDHLOF

SKALIDHI

KYDHONIAS

SMYRNIS

ZIMVRAKAKIDON

SFAKIANAKI

AKTI TOMBAZI

LITH...

NIKIFOROU

E. DHORITHEOU

KRIARI

PLATIA SYNDRIVANI

PLATIA 1866

RESTAURANTS & BARS

Anaplous	①
Aroma	②
Dino's	③
Ela	④
Iordanis Boúgatsa	⑤
Karnayio	⑥
Nea Vouli	⑦
Rudí´s Bierhaus	⑧
Ta Dhyo Lux	⑨
Tamam	⑩
Tasty Souvlaki	⑪
Tholos	⑫

0   250 m

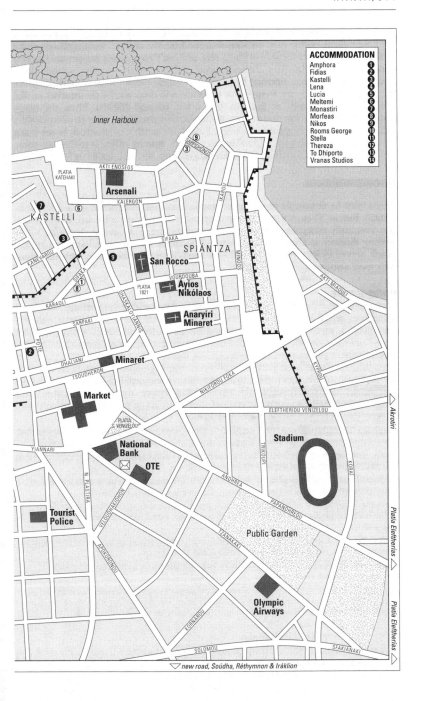

ACCOMMODATION

Amphora	❶
Fidias	❷
Kastelli	❸
Lena	❹
Lucia	❺
Meltemi	❻
Monastiri	❼
Morfeas	❽
Nikos	❾
Rooms George	❿
Stella	⓫
Thereza	⓬
To Dhiporto	⓭
Vranas Studios	⓮

Inner Harbour

PLATIA
KATEHAKI

AKTI ENOSEOS

Arsenali

KALERGÓN

KASTÉLLI

SIFAKA

SPIÁNTZA

San Rocco

VOURDOUBA

PLATIA
1821

Áyios
Nikólaos

KANEVAROU

Anaryíri
Minaret

KARAOLI

SARPAKI

DHASKALOYÁNNIS

POTIE

DHALIANI

Minaret

TSOUDHERON

Market

NIKIFOROU FOKA

ELEFTHERIOU VENIZELOU

PLATIA
S. VENIZELOU

YIANNARI

National
Bank

OTE

Stadium

N. PLASTIRA

VELOUDHAKIDHON

ANDHREA

TRIKOUPI

KYPROU

KORAA

△ Akrotíri

Tourist
Police

Public Garden

APARONDON

TZANAKAKI

PAPANDHREOU

△ Platía Eleftherías

KORNAROU

Olympic
Airways

SOLOMOU

SFAKIANAKI

△ Platía Eleftherías

▽ new road, Soúdha, Réthymnon & Iráklion

SARPIDHONOS

ILAROU

MINOOS

AKTI MIAOULI

you're never far from the sea or from some other obvious landmark. The **bus station** is on Kydhonías, within easy walking distance from the centre – turn right out of the station, then left down the side of Platía 1866 and you'll emerge at a major road junction opposite the top of Halídhon, the main street of the old quarter leading straight down to the Venetian harbour. Arriving by **ferry**, you'll anchor about 10km from Haniá at the port of Soúdha: there are frequent buses which will drop you by the **market** on the fringes of the old town, or you can take a taxi (around 1500dr). From the newly revamped **airport** (15km east of town on the Akrotíri peninsula) taxis (around 2500dr) will almost certainly be your only option, though it's worth a quick check to see if any sort of bus is meeting your flight. The very helpful **tourist office** is in the new town, just off Platía 1866 at Kriári 40 (Mon–Fri 8am–2.30pm ☎92 624, fax 92 943).

Accommodation

There must be thousands of **rooms** to rent in Haniá and, unusually, quite a few comfortable **hotels**. Though you may face a long search for a bed at the height of the season, eventually everyone does seem to find something. The nearest **campsite** within striking distance is *Camping Hania* (☎31 138), some 4km west of Haniá behind the beach, served by local bus (see p.614). The site is lovely, if rather basic, and just a short walk from some of the better beaches.

Harbour area

Perhaps the most desirable rooms of all are those overlooking the **harbour**, which are sometimes available at reasonable rates: be warned that this is often because they're very noisy at night. Most are approached not direct from the harbourside itself but from Zambelíou, the alley behind, or from other streets leading off the harbour further around (where you may get more peace). The nicest of the more expensive places are here, too, equally set back but often with views from the upper storeys. In recent years the popularity of this area has led to anyone with a room near the harbour tarting it up and attempting to rent it out at a ridiculously inflated price. You'll often be touted in the street for these and it's wise not to commit yourself until you've made comparisons with some of the more reasonable places listed below.

Amphora, Theotokopoúlou 20 (☎ & fax 93 224). Large, traditional hotel, and beautifully renovated; worth the expense if you get a view, but probably not for the cheaper rooms with no view. ⑥.

Lucia, Aktí Koundouriótou (☎90 302). Harbourfront hotel with balcony rooms; less expensive than you might expect for one of the best views in town. ②.

Pension Lena, Theotokopoúlou 60 (☎ & fax 72 265). Charming rooms in an old wooden Turkish house restored by friendly German proprietor. Pleasant breakfast café below. ②.

Meltemi, Angélou 2 (☎ 92 802). First of a little row of pensions in a great situation on the far side of the harbour; perhaps noisier than its neighbours, but excellent views and a good café downstairs. ③.

Rooms George, Zambelíou 30 (☎88 715). Old building with steep stairs and eccentric antique furniture; rooms vary in price according to position and size. ①.

Rooms Stella, Angélou 10 (☎73 756). Creaky, eccentric old house above a ceramics shop, close to the *Lucia*, with plain, clean rooms. ②.

Thereza, Angélou 8 (☎ & fax 92 798). Beautiful old house in a great position, with stunning views from roof terrace and some of the rooms; classy decor, too. A more expensive pension than its neighbours but deservedly so; unlikely to have room in season unless you book. ③.

The old town: east of Halídhon

In the eastern half of the old town rooms are far more scattered, usually cheaper, and in the height of the season your chances are much better over here. **Kastélli**, immediately east of the harbour, has some lovely places with views from the heights. Take one of the alleys leading left off Kanevárou if you want to try these, but don't be too hopeful since they are popular and often booked up.

To Dhiporto, Betólo 41, one block north of Skridhlóf (☎53 430). The proprietor of one of Haniá's longest established tavernas with the same name has retired and turned it into a very good-value rooms place with economical doubles and trebles. Recommended. ①.

Fidias, Kalinákou Sarpáki 8 (☎52 494). Signposted from the cathedral, this favourite backpackers' meeting place is rather bizarrely run, but is a friendly pension and has the real advantage of offering single rooms or fixing shares – but watch your baggage with strangers. ①.

Kastelli, Kanevárou 39 (☎57 057, fax 45 314). Not in the prettiest of locations, but a comfortable, modern, reasonably priced pension and very quiet at the back. All rooms come with fans and anti-mosquito machines. The owner is exceptionally helpful and also has a few apartments and a beautiful house (for up to five people) to rent. ②.

Monastiri, Ayíou Márkou 18, off Kanevárou (☎54 776). Pleasant rooms, some with a sea view in the restored ruins of a Venetian monastery. ②.

Morfeas, Isodhíon 15 (☎57 179). Between the cathedral platía and Platía Syndriváni, in the first street parallel to Halídhon. Rather dark, but good value for so central a position. ②.

Nikos, Dhaskaloyiánnis 58 (☎54 783). One of a few down here near the inner harbour; good-value, relatively modern rooms, all with shower. Same owner has economical studios nearby with kitchen and fridge. ①.

Vranas Studios, Ayíon Dhéka & Kalinákou Sarpáki, near the cathedral (☎ & fax 58 618). Pleasant, spacious studio-style rooms with TV, air-con, fridge and kitchenette. ③.

The City

Haniá has been occupied almost continuously since Neolithic times, so it comes as a surprise that a city of such antiquity should offer little specifically to see or do. It is, however, a place which is fascinating simply to wander around, stumbling upon surviving fragments of city wall, the remains of **ancient Kydonia** which are being excavated, and odd segments of Venetian or Turkish masonry.

Kastélli and the harbour

The **port** area is as ever the place to start, the oldest and the most interesting part of town. It's at its busiest and most attractive at night, when the lights from bars and restaurants reflect in the water and crowds of visitors and locals turn out to promenade. By day, things are quieter. Straight ahead from Platía Syndriváni (also known as Harbour Square) lies the curious domed shape of the **Mosque of the Janissaries**, until 1991 the tourist office, but currently without a function.

The little hill that rises behind the mosque is **Kastélli**, site of the earliest habitation and core of the Minoan, Venetian and Turkish towns. There's not a great deal left, but archeologists believe that they may have found the remains of a Minoan palace (logically, there must have been one at this end of the island) in the **excavations** being carried out – and open to view – along Kanevárou. It's also here that you'll find traces of the oldest **walls**; there were two rings, one defending Kastélli alone, a later set encompassing the whole of the medieval city. Beneath the hill, on the inner (eastern) harbour, the arches of sixteenth-century **Venetian arsenals** survive alongside remains of the outer walls; both are currently undergoing restoration.

Following the esplanade around in the other direction leads to a hefty bastion which now houses Crete's **Naval Museum** (daily 10am–4pm; 500dr). The collection is not exactly riveting, although a recently added section on the 1941 **Battle of Crete** with fascinating artefacts, and poignant photos depicting the suffering here under the Nazis, perhaps justifies the entry fee. You might want to wander in anyway for a (free) look at the seaward fortifications and the platform from which the modern Greek flag was first flown on Crete (in 1913). Walk around the back of these restored bulwarks to a street heading inland and you'll find the best-preserved stretch of the outer walls.

The old city

Behind the harbour, lie the less picturesque but more lively sections of the old city. First, a short way up Halídhon on the right, is Haniá's **archeological museum** (Tues–Sun 8am–2.30pm; 500dr) housed in the Venetian-built church of San Francesco. Damaged as it is, especially from the outside, this remains a beautiful building and it contains a fine little display, covering the local area from Minoan through to Roman times. In the garden, a huge fountain and the base of a minaret survive from the period when the Turks converted the church into a mosque; around them are scattered various other sculptures and architectural remnants.

The **cathedral**, ordinary and relatively modern, is just a few steps further up Halídhon on the left. Around it are some of the more animated shopping areas, particularly **Odhós Skrídhlof** ("Leather Street"), with streets leading up to the back of the market beyond. In the direction of the Spiántza quarter are ancient alleys with tumble-down Venetian stonework and overhanging wooden balconies; though gentrification is spreading apace, much of the quarter has yet to feel the effect of the city's modern popularity. There are a couple more **minarets** too, one on Dhaliáni, and the other in Platía 1821, which is a fine traditional platía to stop for a coffee.

The new town

Once out of the narrow confines of the maritime district, the broad, traffic-choked streets of the **modern city** have a great deal less to offer. Up Tzanakáki, not far from the market, you'll find the **public gardens**, a park with strolling couples, a few caged animals (including a few *kri-kri* or Cretan ibex) and a café under the trees; there's also an open-air auditorium which occasionally hosts live music or local festivities. Beyond here, you could continue to the **historical museum** (Mon–Fri 9am–1pm), but the effort would be wasted unless you're a Greek-speaking expert on the subject; the place is essentially a very dusty archive with a few photographs on the wall. Perhaps more interesting is the fact that the museum lies on the fringes of Haniá's desirable residential districts. If you continue to the end of Sfakianáki and then go down Iróön Polytekhníou towards the sea, you'll get an insight into how Crete's other half lives. There are several (expensive) garden restaurants down here and a number of fashionable café-bars where you can sit outside.

The beaches

Haniá's beaches all lie to the west of the city. For the packed **city beach**, this means no more than a ten-minute walk following the shoreline from the naval museum, but for good sand you're better off taking the local bus out along the coast road. This leaves from the east side of Platía 1866 and runs along the coast road as far as **Kalamáki beach**. Kalamáki and the previous stop, **Oásis beach**, are again pretty crowded but they're a considerable improvement over the beach in Haniá itself. In between, you'll find emptier stretches if you're prepared to walk: about an hour in all (on sandy beach virtually all the way) from Haniá to Kalamáki, and then perhaps ten minutes from the road to the beach if you get off the bus at the signs to *Aptera Beach* or *Camping Hania*. Further afield there are even finer beaches at **Ayía Marína** to the west, or **Stavrós** (see p.617) out on the Akrotíri peninsula (reached by KTEL buses from the main station).

Eating

You're never far from something to **eat** in Haniá: in a circle around the harbour is one restaurant, taverna or café after another. All have their own character, but there seems little variation in price or what's on offer. Away from the water, there are plenty of slightly cheaper possibilities on Kondhiláki, Kanevárou and most of the streets off Halídhon. For snacks or lighter meals, the cafés around the harbour on the whole serve cocktails and fresh juices at exorbitant prices, though breakfast (especially "English") can be good value. For more traditional places, try around the market and along Dhaskaloyiánnis (*Synganaki* here is a good traditional bakery serving *tyrópitta* and the like, with a cake shop next door). Fast food is also increasingly widespread, with numerous *souvláki* places on Karaolí; at the end of the outer harbour, near the naval museum; and around the corner of Plastíra and Yiannári, across from the **market** (see "Listings" overleaf, for details of the market and supermarkets).

Anaplous, Sífaka 37. A couple of blocks west of Platía 1821, this is a popular new open-air restaurant inside a stylishly "restored" ruin of a Turkish mansion bombed in the war. Serves both mezédhes and full meals to live guitar music.

Aroma, Aktí Tombázi 4, next to the Mosque of the Janissaries. Pleasant café with great harbour view to savour over lazy breakfasts or late drinks.

Iordanis Bougatsa, Kydhonias 96, opposite the bus station. This place serves little except the traditional creamy *bougátsa*, a sugar-coated cheese pie to eat in or take away.

Ta Dhyo Lux, Sarpidhónos. One of a line of cafés close to the harbour to sit out and be seen in the evening. Try an expensive but sublime lemon *graníta*.

Dino's, inner harbour by bottom of Sarpidhónos. One of the best choices for a pricey seafood meal with a harbour view; *Apostolis*, almost next door, is also good.

Karnayio, Platía Kateháki 8. Set back from the inner harbour near the port police. Not right on the water, but one of the best harbour restaurants nonetheless.

Meltemi, Angélou 2. Slow, relaxed terrace bar beneath the rooms place of the same name; good for breakfast, and where locals (especially expats) sit whiling the day away or playing *tavli*.

Nea Vouli, Yiannári 27, just west of Platía 1866. Excellent and stylish new restaurant serving high-quality standards at modest prices.

Rudi's Bierhaus, Sífaka 24. Austrian Rudi Riegler's bar stocks more than a hundred of Europe's finest beers to accompany mezédhes.

Tamam, Zambelíou just before Renieri Gate. Young, trendy place with adventurous Greek menu including much vegetarian food. Unfortunately only a few cramped tables outside, and inside it's very hot. Slow service.

Tasty Souvlaki, Halídhon 80. Always packed despite being cramped, which is a testimonial to the quality and value of the *souvláki*. Better to take away.

Taverna Ela, top of Kondhiláki. Live Greek music to enliven your meal in yet another roofless taverna townhouse.

Tholos, Ayíon Dhéka 36. Slightly north of the cathedral, *Tholos* is another "restaurant in a ruin", this time Venetian/Turkish, with a wide selection of Cretan specialities.

Bars and nightlife

Haniá's **nightlife** has more than enough venues to satisfy the most insomniac night-owls. Most of the clubs and disco bars are gathered in the area around the inner harbour, whilst there are plenty of terrace bars along both harbourfronts, with more scattered throughout the old quarter.

The smartest and newest places are on and around **Sarpidhónos**, in the far corner of the inner harbour, a good example of which is *Fraise* on Sarpidhónos itself. Heading from here around towards the outer harbour, you'll pass others including the *Four Seasons*, a very popular bar by the port police, and then reach a couple of the older places including *Remember* and *Scorpio* behind the Plaza bar complex on the harbour. Nearby, and running along the **Aktí Miaoúli** seafront just outside the eastern wall are a string of terrace cafés, currently the place to be seen for Haniot late drinkers. At the opposite or **western end of the harbour** *Fagotto*, Angélou 16, is a pleasant, laid-back jazz bar, often with live performers. Other music bars near here are *Mythos* and *Street* on the outer harbour, playing rock and modern Greek sounds until the early hours. **Discos** proper include *Kyvotos* near the mosque, *Ariadni* on the inner harbour (opens 11.30pm, but busy later) and *Millennium*, a big, bright place on Tsoudherón behind the market, which doesn't really get going until 2am. West of here along Skalídhi (no. 39) *Titanic* is another dance place which is a late starter, and, not far away, tucked down a passage near the Schiavo Bastion (Skalídhi and Halídhon), *Game* is a new place that becomes frenetic after midnight.

A couple of venues offering more traditional entertainment are the *Café Kriti*, Kalergón 22, at the corner of Andhroyíou, basically an old-fashioned kafenío where there's **Greek music** and **dancing** virtually every night, and the *Firkas* (the bastion by the naval museum), with Greek dancing at 9pm every Tuesday – pricey but authentic entertainment. It's also worth checking for events at the open-air auditorium in the public gardens, and for performances in restaurants outside the city, which are the ones the locals will go to. Look for posters, especially in front of the market and in the little platía across the road from there.

For **films**, you should also check the hoardings in front of the market. There are open-air screenings at *Attikon*, on Venizélou out towards Akrotíri, about 1km from the centre, and occasionally in the public gardens.

Listings

Airlines Olympic, Tzanakáki 88 (Mon–Fri 9am–4pm; ☎57 701). There's a bus from here connecting with their flights. For airport information call ☎63 264.

Banks and exchange The main branch of the National Bank of Greece is directly opposite the market. Convenient smaller banks for exchange are next to the bus station, at the bottom of Kanevárou just off Platía Syndriváni, or at the top of Halídhon. There are also a couple of exchange places on Halídhon, open long hours.

Bike and car rental Possibilities everywhere, especially on Halídhon, though these are rarely the best value. For bikes, try Kavroulakis, Hálidhon 91 (☎43 342) or Summertime, Daskaloyiánnis 7, slightly northeast of the market (☎98 918); for cars, two reliable local companies are Hermes, Tzanakáki 52 (54 418) or Tellus Rent a Car, Kanevárou 9, east of Platía Syndriváni (☎50 400).

Boat trips Various boat trips are offered by travel agents around town, mostly to Soúdha Bay or out to beaches on the Rodhópou peninsula. Domenico's (☎55 019), on Kanevárou, offers some of the best of these.

Ferry tickets The agent for ANEK is on Venizélou, right opposite the market (☎27 500).

Internet Haniá has two Internet cafés: Sante on the outer harbour at Aktí Koundouriótou 55–56 (2000dr for two hours) and the more tranquil Vranas (30min 500dr), just north of the cathedral and beneath *Vranas Studios* (see p.613).

Laundry There are five laundries, the best of which is Speedy Laundry (☎88 411), junction of Koronéou and Korkidi, just west of Platía 1866; others at Kanevárou 38 (9am–10pm), Episkópou Dhorothéou 7 and Ayíon Dhéka 18; all do service washes. The *Fidias* pension also has its own economical place next door (see p.613).

Left luggage The bus station has a left luggage office open 6am–8.30pm; 300/400dr per item per day depending on size.

Market and supermarkets If you want to buy food or get stuff together for a picnic, the entertaining market is the place to head for. There are vast quantities of fresh fruit and vegetables as well as meat and fish, bakers, dairy stalls and general stores for cooked meats, tins and other standard provisions. There are also several small stores down by the harbour platía which sell cold drinks and a certain amount of food, but these are expensive (though they do open late). A couple of large supermarkets can be found on the edge of the old town, for instance Inka on Platía 1866.

Post office The main post office is on Tzanakáki (Mon–Fri 7am–8pm, Sat 8am–2pm for exchange).

Taxis The main taxi ranks are in Platía 1866. For radio taxis try ☎98 700 or ☎94 300.

Telephones Cardphones (all over town) are the best bet for overseas calls.

Tourist police Inconveniently relocated to Iraklíou 23, in the southern suburb of Koubés (☎53 333 fax 28 708), which means they'll rarely be bothered by visitors – perhaps the thinking behind the move.

Travel agencies For cheap tickets home try Bassias Travel, Halídhon 69 (☎44 295), very helpful for regular tickets too. They also deal in standard excursions. Other travel agents for tours and day trips are everywhere.

Around Haniá: the Akrotíri and Rodhópou peninsulas

Just north of Haniá, the **Akrotíri peninsula** loops around to protect the Bay of Soúdha and a NATO military base and missile-testing area. In an ironic twist, the peninsula's northwestern coastline is fast developing into a luxury suburb; the beach of Kalathás, near Horafákia, long popular with jaded Haniotes, is surrounded by villas and apartments. **STAVRÓS**, further out, has not yet suffered this fate, and its **beach** is absolutely superb if you like the calm, shallow water of an almost completely enclosed lagoon. It's not very large, so it does get crowded, but rarely overpoweringly so. There's a makeshift taverna/*souvláki* stand on the beach, and a couple of tavernas across the road, but for accommodation you need to search slightly south of here, in the area around **Blue Beach**, where there are plenty of apartment buildings.

Inland are the **monasteries** of **Ayía Triádha** (daily 6am–2pm & 5–7pm; 300dr) and **Gouvernétou** (daily 8am–12.30pm & 4.30–7.30pm; free). The former is much more accessible and has a beautiful seventeenth-century church inside its pink-and-ochre cloister, though ongoing renovations have recently caused many of the monks to relocate and on occasions make the normally peaceful enclosure more like a building site. Beyond Gouvernétou, which is in a far better state of preservation and where traditional monastic life can still be observed, you can clamber down a craggy path to the abandoned ruins of the monastery of Katholikó and the remains of its narrow (swimmable) harbour.

West to Rodhópou

The coast to the west of Haniá was the scene of most of the fighting during the German invasion in 1941. As you leave town, an aggressive diving eagle commemorates the German parachutists, and at Máleme there's a big German cemetery; the Allied cemetery is in the other direction, on the coast just outside Soúdha. There are also beaches and considerable tourist development along much of this shore. At **Ayía Marína** there's a fine sandy beach and an island offshore said to be a sea monster petrified by Zeus before it could swallow Crete. Seen from the west, its "mouth" still gapes open.

Between **Plataniás** and **Kolymvári** an almost unbroken strand unfurls, by no means all sandy, but deserted for long stretches between villages. The road here runs through mixed groves of calamus reed (Crete's bamboo) and oranges; the windbreaks fashioned from the reeds protect the ripening oranges from the *meltémi*. At Kolymbári, the road to Kastélli cuts across the base of another mountainous peninsula, **Rodhópou**.

Just off the main road here is a monastery, **Goniá** (daily 8am–12.30pm & 4–8pm; respectable dress), with a view most luxury hotels would envy. Every monk in Crete can tell tales of his proud ancestry of resistance to invaders, but here the Turkish cannon balls are still lodged in the walls to prove it, a relic of which the good fathers are far more proud than of any of the icons.

South to the Samarian Gorge

From Haniá the **Gorge of Samariá** (May–Oct; 1200dr for entry to the national park) can be visited as a day trip or as part of a longer excursion to the south. At 18km, it's Europe's longest gorge and is startlingly beautiful. In the June–Aug period (ring Haniá tourist office for other times) **buses** leave Haniá for the top at 6.15am, 7.30am, 8.30am and 1.30pm (this latter service changes to 4.30pm outside school term time), depositing you at the gorge entrance and then collecting you at the port of Hóra Sfakíon for the return trip to Haniá. Should you take the last bus you will need to spend a night at Ayía Rouméli (the end of the gorge) as you will not get through the gorge in time for the last boat. For the three early buses you'll normally be sold a return ticket (valid from Hóra Sfakíon at any time). It's well worth catching the earliest bus to avoid the full heat of the day while walking through the gorge, though be warned that you will not be alone – there are often as many as five coachloads setting off before dawn for the nail-biting climb into the White Mountains. There are also direct early-morning buses from Iráklion and Réthymnon and bus tours from virtually everywhere on the island, adding up to a couple of thousand plus walkers on most days during high season.

Despite all the crowds, the walk *is* hard work, especially in spring when the stream is a roaring torrent. Early and late in the season, there is a danger of **flash floods**, which are not to be taken lightly: in 1993, a number of walkers perished when they were washed out to sea. For this reason the first and last three weeks of the season are entirely dependent on the weather and you will only be allowed into the gorge if the authorities deem it safe. If in doubt (and to save yourself a wasted journey), phone the Haniá Forest Service (☎0821/67 140) for information. Should you arrive after 4pm you will only be allowed into the first couple of kilometres from each end of the gorge and the wardens ensure that no one remains in the gorge overnight, where camping is strictly forbidden.

Omalós

One way to avoid an early start from the north coast would be to stay at **OMALÓS**, in the middle of the mountain plain from which the gorge descends. There are some ordinary **rooms** for rent and a couple of surprisingly fancy **hotels**; try the *Neos Omalos* (☎0821/67 269 fax 67 190; ①), or *Samaria* (☎0821/67 168; ①), for a cheap and friendly no-frills alternative. But since the village is some way from the start of the path, and the buses arrive as the sun rises, it's almost impossible to get a head start on the crowds. Some people sleep out at the top (where there's a bar-restaurant in the *Tourist Lodge* and kiosks serving drinks and sandwiches), but a night under the stars here can be a bitterly cold experience. The one significant advantage to staying up here would be if you wanted to undertake some other climbs in the White Mountains, in which case there's a **mountain hut** (☎0821/54 560; ①) about ninety minutes' hike (signed) from Omalós or from the top of the gorge.

The gorge

The **gorge** itself begins at the *xylóskala*, or "wooden staircase", a stepped path plunging steeply down from the southern lip of the Omalós plain. Here, at the head of the track, opposite the sheer rock face of Mount Gíngilos, the crowds pouring out of the buses

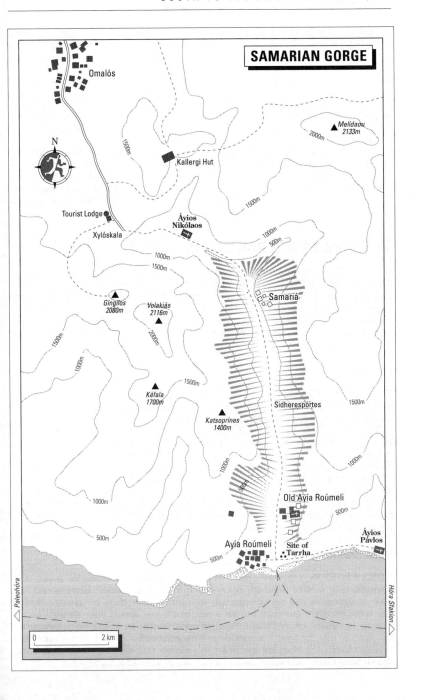

SAMARIAN GORGE

Omalós

Melídaou
2133m

2000m

1500m

Kallergi Hut

1500m

Tourist Lodge

Áyios
Nikólaos

1000m

500m

Xylóskala

1000m

1500m

Gingilos
2080m

Volakiás
2116m

Samariá

2000m

1500m

1000m

1500m

Kéfala
1700m

1500m

Katsoprínes
1400m

Sidherespórtes

1500m

1000m

1000m

1000m

Old Ayía Roúmeli

500m

1500m

Áyios
Pávlos

1000m

500m

Ayía Roúmeli

Site of
Tarrha

500m

N

Paleohóra

Hóra Sfakíon

0   2 km

disperse rapidly as keen walkers march purposefully down while others dally over breakfast, contemplating the sunrise for hours. You descend at first through almost alpine scenery: pine forest, wild flowers and very un-Cretan greenery – a verdant shock in the spring, when the stream is also at its liveliest (and can at times be positively dangerous). Small churches and viewpoints dot the route, and about halfway down you pass the abandoned village of **Samariá**, now home to a wardens' station, with picnic facilities and filthy toilets. Further down, the path levels out and the gorge walls close in until at the narrowest point (the *sidherespórtes* or "iron gates") one can practically touch both tortured rock faces at once, and, looking up, see them rising sheer for almost a thousand feet.

At an average pace, with regular stops, the walk down takes five or six hours, and the upward trek considerably longer. It's strenuous (you'll know all about it next day), the path is rough, and solid shoes are vital. On the way down, there is plenty of water from springs and streams (except some years in September and October), but nothing to eat. The park that surrounds the gorge is a refuge of the Cretan wild ibex, the *kri-kri*, but don't expect to see one; there are usually far too many people around.

Villages of the southwest coast

When you finally emerge from the gorge, it's not long before you reach the village of **AYÍA ROUMÉLI**, which is all but abandoned until you reach the beach, a mirage of iced drinks and a cluster of tavernas with **rooms** for rent. If you want to get back to Haniá, buy your boat tickets now, especially if you want an afternoon on the beach; the last boat (connecting with the final 6.30pm bus from Hóra Sfakíon) tends to sell out first. If you plan to stay on the south coast, you should get going as soon as possible for the best chance of finding a room somewhere nicer than Ayía Rouméli.

Loutró

For tranquillity, it's hard to beat **LOUTRÓ**, two-thirds of the way to Hóra Sfakíon, and accessible only by boat or on foot. The chief disadvantage of Loutró is its lack of a real beach; most people swim from the rocks around its small bay. If you're prepared to walk, however, there are **deserted beaches** along the coast to the east which can also be reached by hired **canoe**. Indeed, if you're really into walking there's a **coastal trail** through Loutró which covers the entire distance between Ayía Rouméli and Hóra Sfakíon, or you could take the daunting zigzag path up the cliff behind to the mountain village of Anópoli. Loutró itself has a number of **tavernas** and **rooms**, though not always enough of the latter. Call the *Blue House* (☎0825/91 127; ①) if you want to book ahead; this is also the best place to eat. There's space to **camp** out on the cape by a ruined fort, but due to a long history of problems, you should be aware that campers are not very popular in the village.

Hóra Sfakíon and beyond

HÓRA SFAKÍON is the more usual terminus for walkers traversing the gorge, with a regular boat service along the coast to and from Ayía Rouméli. Consequently, it's quite an expensive and not an especially welcoming place; there are plenty of rooms and some excellent tavernas, but for a real beach you should jump straight on the evening bus going toward Plakiás. Plenty of opportunities for a dip present themselves en route, one of the most memorable at **Frangokástello**, named after a crumbling Venetian attempt to bring law and order to a district that went on to defy both Turks and Germans. The square, crenellated fort, isolated a few kilometres below a chiselled wall of mountains, looks like it's been spirited out of the High Atlas or Tibet. The place is said to be haunted by ghosts of Greek rebels massacred here in 1829; every May, these *dhrossoulítes* (dewy ones) march at dawn across the coastal plain and disappear into the sea near the fort. The rest of the time Frangokástello is peaceful enough, with a superb beach and a number of tavernas and rooms, but is somewhat stagnant if you're looking for things to do. Slightly further east, and less influenced by tourism or modern life, are the attractive villages of **Skalotí** and **Rodhákino**, each with basic lodging and food.

Soúyia

In quite the other direction from Ayía Rouméli, less regular boats also head to **SOÚYIA** and on to Paleohóra. Soúyia, until World War II merely the anchorage for Koustoyérako inland, is low key, with a long, grey pebble beach and mostly modern buildings (except for a church with a sixth-century Byzantine mosaic as the foundation). Since the 1990 completion of the paved road to Haniá, the village has started to expand; even so, except in the very middle of summer, it continues to make a good fall-back for finding a room or a place to camp, eating cheaply and enjoying the beach when the rest of the island is seething with tourists. Of the **rooms** places try *Hotel Santa Irene* (☎0823/51 342, fax 0821/90 047; ②), where en-suite rooms come with seafront view; for **food**, the nearby *Rembetiko* has a pleasant garden terrace.

Kastélli and the western tip

Apart from being Crete's most westerly town, and the end of the main road, **KASTÉLLI** (Kíssamos, or Kastélli Kissámou as it's variously known) has little obvious attraction. It's a busy town with a rocky beach visited mainly by people using the boat that runs twice weekly to the island of Kýthira and the Peloponnese. The very ordinariness of Kastélli, however, can be attractive: life goes on pretty much regardless of outsiders, but there's every facility you might need. The **ferry agent's office** in Kastélli is one block inland from the main square, Platía Kastellíou (Xirouxákis; ☎0822/22 655). Here there are also good value en-suite rooms at *Koutsanakis* (☎0822/23 416; ③), opposite the *Castelli Hotel*. Heading north from here brings you to the beach promenade where there are a number of **tavernas**. Nothing else is far away from the centre apart from the dock, a two-kilometre walk (or inexpensive taxi ride) from town.

A ROUND TRIP

If you have transport, a circular drive from Kastélli, taking the coast road in one direction and the inland route through Élos and Topólia, makes for a stunningly scenic circuit. Near the sea, villages cling to the high mountainsides, apparently halted by some miracle in the midst of calamitous seaward slides. Around them, olives ripen on the terraced slopes, the sea glittering far below. Inland, especially at **ÉLOS**, the main crop is the chestnut, whose huge old trees shade the village streets.

In **TOPÓLIA**, the chapel of Ayía Sofía is sheltered inside a cave which has been used as a shrine since Neolithic times. Cutting south from Élos, a paved road continues through the high mountains towards Paleohóra. On a motorbike, with a sense of adventure and plenty of fuel, it's great: the bus doesn't come this way, villagers still stare at the sight of a tourist, and a host of small, seasonal streams cascade beside or under the asphalt.

Falásarna to Elafonísi

To the west of Kastélli lies some of Crete's loneliest, and, for many visitors, finest coastline. The first place of note is ancient and modern **Falásarna**, city ruins which mean little to the non-specialist, but they do overlook some of the best beaches on Crete, wide and sandy with clean water. There's a handful of tavernas and an increasing number of rooms for rent; otherwise, you have to sleep out, as many people do. This can mean that the main beaches are dirty (try not to add to the mess), but they remain beautiful, and there are plenty of others within walking distance. The nearest real town is **Plátanos**, 5km up a paved road, along which there are a couple of daily buses.

Further south, the western coastline is still less discovered and there's little in the way of official accommodation. **Sfinári** has several houses which rent rooms, and a quiet pebble beach a little way below the village. **Kámbos** is similar, but even less visited, its beach a considerable walk down a hill. Beyond them both is the **monastery of Khryssoskalítissa**, increasingly visited by tours from Haniá and Paleohóra now the road has been sealed, but well worth the effort for its isolation and nearby beaches; the bus gets as far as Váthy, from where the monastery is another two hours' walk away.

Five kilometres beyond Khryssoskalítissa, a dusty, unpaved road bumps down to the coast opposite the tiny uninhabited islet of **Elafonísi**. You can easily wade out to the islet with its sandy beaches and rock pools, and the shallow lagoon is warm and crystal clear. It looks magnificent, but daily boat trips from Paleohóra and coach tours from elsewhere on the island have attracted a cluster of beach stalls renting loungers and selling tourist tat, which ensures that, in the middle of the day at least, it's far from deserted. To cope with the resulting sanitary problems, a single and totally inadequate Portaloo has been installed by the authorities next to the beach. If you want to stay, and really appreciate the place, there are a couple of seasonal tavernas, but bring some supplies unless you want to be wholly dependent on them.

Kándanos and Paleohóra

Getting down to Paleohóra by the main road, paved the whole way, is a lot easier, and several daily buses from Haniá make the trip. But although this route also has to wind through the western outriders of the White Mountains, it lacks the excitement of the routes to either side. **Kándanos**, at the 58-kilometre mark, has been entirely rebuilt since it was destroyed by the Germans for its fierce resistance to their occupation. The original sign erected when the deed was done is preserved on the war memorial: "Here stood Kándanos, destroyed in retribution for the murder of 25 German soldiers, and never to be rebuilt again." The pleasantly easy-going and once again substantial village had the last laugh.

When the beach at **PALEOHÓRA** finally appears below it is a welcome sight. The little town is built across the base of a peninsula, its harbour and a beach known as Pebble Beach on the eastern side, the wide sands ("Sandy Beach") on the other. Above, on the outcrop, Venetian ramparts stand sentinel. These days Paleohóra has become heavily developed, but it's still thoroughly enjoyable, with a main street filling with tables as diners spill out of the restaurants, and with a pleasantly chaotic social life. A good place to **eat** with some imaginative vegetarian specials is *The Third Eye*, just out of the centre towards Sandy Beach. There are plenty of **places to stay** (though not always many vacancies in high season) – try the basic *Dolphin Rooms* (☎0823/41 703; ①), below the Venetian fort, or *Castello Rooms* (☎0823/41 143; ②), at the south end of Sandy Beach, for a little more en-suite luxury. There's also a fair-sized **campsite** 2km north of Pebble Beach; in extremis, if you are tempted to sleep on the main Sandy Beach – one of the best on the south coast, with showers, trees and acres of sand – be prepared for trouble from police and local residents; your best bet is to get as far away from the town as possible if you want to be left in peace. When you tire of Paleohóra and the excellent **windsurfing** in the bay (boards for hire), there are excursions up the hill to Prodhrómi, for example, or along a five-hour coastal path to Soúyia.

You'll find a helpful **tourist office** (Wed–Mon 10am–1pm & 6–9pm; ☎0823/41 507) in the town hall on Venizélou in the centre of town; they have full accommodation lists and a map (though you'll hardly need this). The **banks** and **travel agents** are all nearby; the **post office** is on the road behind Sandy Beach. **Boats** run from here to Elafonísi, the island of Gávdhos and along the coast to Soúyia and Ayía Rouméli.

Gávdhos

The island of **Gávdhos**, some fifty kilometres of rough sea south of Paleohóra, is the most southerly landmass in Europe. Gávdhos is small (about 10km by 7km) and barren, but it has one major attraction: the enduring **isolation** which its inaccessible position has helped preserve. There are now a few package tours organized by travel agents in Paleohóra such as Interkreta (☎0823/41 393, fax 41 050), who can arrange a room if you want one and also provide current ferry information. There's a semipermanent community of campers through the summer, but if all you want is a beach to yourself and a taverna to grill your fish, this remains the place for you.

travel details

Flights are on Olympic unless otherwise stated

Haniá–Athens (4 daily on Olympic; 2 daily on Cronus; 2 daily on Air Greece)

Haniá–Thessaloníki (1 weekly)

Iráklion–Athens (5–7 daily on Olympic; 4 daily on Cronus; 3–4 daily on Air Greece)

Iráklion–Santorini (2 weekly)

Iráklion–Rhodes (4 weekly, summer only, on Olympic; 3 weekly on Air Greece)

Iráklion–Thessaloníki (3 weekly on Olympic; 3 weekly on Air Greece)

Sitía–Athens (1 weekly, Fri all year)

Ferries

Áyios Nikólaos and Sitía 3–4 sailings a week to Pireás (12hr), 1–3 ferries a week to Kásos, Kárpathos, Hálki and Rhodes; 1–2 weekly to Mílos.

Haniá 1 or 2 ferries daily to Pireás (12hr).

Hóra Sfakíon 5 ferries daily to Loutró/Ayía Rouméli; 3 weekly to Gávdhos in season.

Iráklion 2 ferries daily to Pireás and 3 on Tues & Wed (12hr); 3–5 ferries weekly to Thessaloníki; 1 daily ferry to Thíra (4hr), also fast boats and hydrofoils (2hr 30min); daily ferries to Páros in season; 1–2 weekly to Mýkonos and Íos; weekly to Náxos, Tínos, Skýros, Skíathos.

Kastélli (Kíssamos) 1–2 ferries weekly to Kýthira and Yíthio (8hr).

Paleohóra 3 boats a week in season to Gávdhos. Also daily sailings to Elafonísi and Soúyia.

Réthymnon daily ferries to Pireás (12hr); seasonal day-trips to Thíra.

Buses

Áyios Nikólaos–Sitía (6 daily 6.15am–6pm; 2hr).

Haniá–Hóra Sfakíon (3 daily 8.30am–2pm; 2hr).

Haniá–Paleohóra (3 daily 8.30am–3.30pm; 2hr).

Haniá–Réthymnon–Iráklion (17 daily, two via old road 5.30am–8.30pm; 3hr total).

Iráklion–Ayía Galíni (8 daily 6.30am–6.30pm; 2hr 15min).

Iráklion–Áyios Nikólaos (32 daily 6.30am–9pm; 1hr 30min).

Iráklion–Festós (8 daily 7.30am–4.30pm; 1hr 30min).

Iráklion–Ierápetra (7 daily 7.30am–5.30pm; 2hr 30min).

Kastélli–Haniá (15 daily 6am–7.30pm; 1hr 30min).

Réthymnon–Spíli–Ayía Galíni (4 daily 7am–2.15pm; 45min–1hr 30min).

CHAPTER NINE

THE DODECANESE

T
he furthest Greek island group from the mainland, the **Dodecanese** (Dhodhekánisos) lie close to the Turkish coast – some, like Kós and Kastellórizo, almost within hailing distance of Anatolia. Because of this position, and their remoteness from Athens, the islands have had a turbulent history: they were the scene of ferocious battles between German and British forces in 1943–44, and were only finally included in the modern Greek state in 1948 after centuries of occupation by crusaders, Ottomans and Italians. Even now the threat (real or imagined) of invasion from Turkey is very much in evidence. When you ask about the heavy military presence, some locals answer in terms of *"when* the Turks come", rather than *"if"*.

Whatever the rigours of the various occupations, their legacy includes a wonderful blend of architectural styles and of Eastern and Western cultures. Medieval Rhodes is the most famous, but almost every island has some Classical remains, a crusaders' castle, a clutch of traditional villages and abundant grandiose public buildings. For these last the Italians, who occupied the islands from 1912 to 1943, are mainly responsible. In their determination to beautify the islands and turn them into a showplace for fascism they undertook public works, excavations and reconstruction on a massive scale; if historical accuracy was often sacrificed in the interests of style, only an expert is likely to complain. A more sinister aspect of the Italian administration was the attempted forcible Latinization of the populace: spoken Greek and Orthodox observance were banned in public from 1923 to 1943. The most tangible reminder of this policy is the (rapidly dwindling) number of older people who can still converse – and write – more fluently in Italian than in Greek.

Aside from this bilingualism, the Dodecanese themselves display a marked topographic and economic schizophrenia. The dry limestone outcrops of **Kastellórizo**, **Sými**, **Hálki**, **Kássos** and **Kálymnos** have always been forced to rely on the sea for their livelihoods, and the wealth generated by this maritime culture – especially in the

---

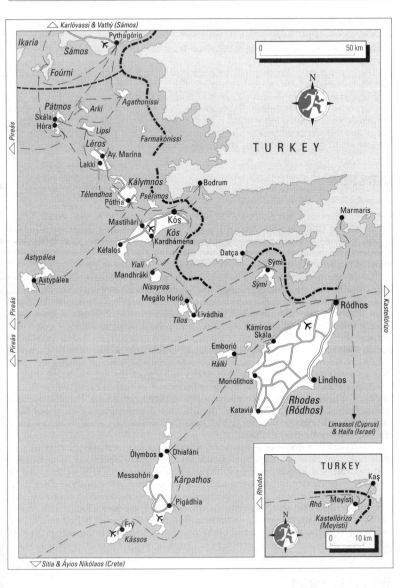

Karlóvassi & Vathý (Sámos)

Ikaría
Samos
Pythágório
Foúrni

Pátmos
Arkí
Agathoníssi
Skála
Hóra
Lipsí
Léros
Farmakónissi
Ay. Marína
Lakkí

Kálymnos
Bodrum
Télendhos
Psérimos
Póthia

TURKEY

Mastihári
Kós
Kós
Kardhámena
Marmaris
Kéfalos
Datça
Astypálea
Yialí
Mandhráki
Sými
Nissyros
Sými
Astypálea
Megálo Horió
Tílos
Livádhia
Ródhos

Kámiros
Skála
Emborió
Hálki
Monólithos
Líndhos
Rhodes
(Ródhos)
Kataviá

Limassol (Cyprus)
& Haifa (Israel)

Ólymbos
Dhiafáni
Messohóri
Kárpathos
Pigádhia

Frý
Kássos

Piréas
Piréas
Piréas
Kastellórizo
Rhodes

TURKEY
Kaş
Rhó
Meyísti
Kastellórizo
(Meyísti)

Sitía & Áyios Nikólaos (Crete)

nineteenth century – fostered the growth of attractive port towns. The sprawling, relatively fertile giants, **Rhodes** (Ródhos) and **Kós**, have recently seen their traditional agricultural economies almost totally displaced by a tourist industry grown up around good beaches and nightlife, as well as the Aegean's most exciting historical monuments. **Kárpathos** lies somewhere in between, with a (formerly) forested north grafted on to a rocky limestone south; **Tílos**, despite its lack of trees, has ample water, though the green volcano-island of **Níssyros** does not. **Léros** shelters softer contours and more amenable terrain than its map outline would suggest, while **Pátmos** and **Astypálea** at the fringes of the archipelago boast architecture and landscapes more appropriate to the Cyclades.

The largest islands in the group are connected by regular ferries, and none (except for Kastellórizo) is hard to reach. Rhodes is the main transport hub, with services to Turkey, Israel and Cyprus, as well as connections with Crete, the northeastern Aegean, the Cyclades and the mainland. Kálymnos and Kós are jointly an important secondary terminus, with a useful ferry based on Kálymnos, hydrofoil services using Kós as a focus and transfer point, and excursion boats based on Kós providing a valuable supplement to larger ferries arriving at uncivil hours.

Kássos

Like Psará islet in the northeast Aegean, **Kássos** contributed its large fleet to the Greek revolutionary war effort, and likewise suffered appalling consequences. In late May 1824, an Ottoman army sent by Ibrahim Pasha, Governor of Egypt, besieged the island; on June 7, aided perhaps by a traitor's tip as to the weak point in Kássos's defences, the invaders descended on the populated north-coastal plain, slaughtered most of the inhabitants and put houses, farms and trees to the torch.

Barren and depopulated since then, Kássos attracts few visitors, despite regular air links with Rhodes and Kárpathos, and being a port of call on ferry lines from those isles to Crete. Numerous sheer gorges slash through lunar terrain, with fenced smallholdings of midget olive trees providing the only permanent relief. Springtime grain crops briefly soften the usually empty terraces, and livestock somehow survives on a thin furze of thornbush. What remains of the population is grouped together in five villages facing Kárpathos, leaving most of the island accessible only on foot or by boat. There's little sign here of the wealth brought into other islands by diaspora Greeks or – since Kássos hasn't much to offer them – tourists; crumbling houses and disused hillside terraces poignantly recall better days. A long pattern of serving as roving pilots, or residence in Egypt (Kassiots were instrumental in digging the Suez Canal), has been eclipsed by subsequent emigration to the US. Thus American logo-T-shirts and baseball caps are de rigueur summer fashion, and the conversation of vacationing expatriates is spiked with Americanisms.

Kássos can be a nuisance to reach; Frý's anchorage just west of Boúka fishing port is so poor that passing ferries won't stop if any appreciable wind is up. In such cases, you disembark at Kárpathos and fly the remaining distance in a light aircraft. The air ticket plus a taxi fare to Kárpathos airport is comparable to the amount charged by Kárpathos-based excursion boats which can manoeuvre into Boúka in most weathers. The airport lies 1km west of Frý (pronounced "free"), an easy enough walk, otherwise a cheap (500dr) ride on one of the island's three taxis. Except in July and August, when a few rental motorbikes and boat excursions are offered, the only method of exploring the island's remoter corners is by hiking along fairly arduous, shadeless tracks.

Frý and Emboriós

Most of the appeal of the capital, **FRÝ**, is confined to the immediate environs of the wedge-shaped fishing port of **Boúka**, protected from the sea by two crab-claws of breakwater and overlooked by the cathedral of Áyios Spyrídhon. Inland, Frý is engagingly unpretentious, even down-at-heel; little attempt has been made to prettify what is essentially a dusty little town poised halfway between demolition and reconstruction.

Accommodation is found at the seafront hotels *Anagenissis* (☎0245/41 323, fax 41 036; ②) and, just behind, the less expensive *Anessis* (☎0245/41 201, fax 41 730; ②). The manager of the *Anagenessis* also has a few pricier apartments, and runs the all-in-one travel agency just below (though Olympic has its own premises). Both hotels tend to be noisy owing to morning bustle on the waterfront – and the phenomenal number of small but lively **bars** in town. During high season a few **rooms** operate; these tend to be more expensive, and also located in the suburb of Emboriós, fifteen minute's walk east.

Perched overlooking the Boúka, *Iy Oraia Bouka* is easily the best of Frý's **tavernas**, and is reasonably priced. *To Meltemi* ouzerí, on the way to Emboriós, is an honourable runner-up. Shops in Frý, including two fruit stalls, are fairly well stocked for self-catering.

Frý's town **beach**, if you can call it that, is at **Ammouá** (Ammoudhiá), a thirty-minute walk beyond the airstrip along the coastal track. This sandy cove, just before the landmark chapel of Áyios Konstandínos, is often caked with seaweed and tar, but persevere five minutes more and you'll find much cleaner pea-gravel coves. Otherwise, it's worth shelling out for high-season boat excursions to far better beaches on a pair of islets visible to the northwest, **Armathiá** and **Makrá**. There are no amenities (or shade) on either islet.

The interior

Kássos's inland villages cluster in the agricultural plain just inland from Frý, and are linked to each other by road; all, except the dull grid of Arvanitohóri, are worth a passing visit, accomplishable by foot in a single day.

Larger in extent and more rural than Frý, **AYÍA MARÍNA**, 1500m inland and uphill, is most attractive seen from the south, arrayed above olive groves; one of its two belfried churches is the focus of the island's liveliest festival, on July 17. Just beyond the hamlet of Kathístres, a further 500m southwest, the cave of **Ellinokamára** is named for the Hellenistic wall partially blocking the entrance; from there a path continues another ninety minutes in the same direction to the larger, more natural cave of **Seláï**, with impressive stalactites in the rear chamber. On the opposite side of the plain, **PANAYÍA** is famous for its now-neglected mansions – many of Kássos's wealthiest ship captains hailed from here – and for the oldest surviving church on the island, the eighteenth-century **Panayía tou Yióryi**. From **PÓLIO**, 2km above Panayía and site of the island's badly deteriorated medieval castle, a track leads southeast within ninety minutes to **Áyios Mámas**, one of two important rural monasteries.

Between Ayía Marína and Arvanitohóri, a dirt track heads southwest from the paved road linking the two villages; having skirted the narrows of a fearsome gorge, you are unlikely to see another living thing aside from goats or an occasional wheeling hawk. After about an hour, the Mediterranean appears to the south, a dull expanse ruffled only by the occasional ship bound for Cyprus and the Middle East. When you finally reach a fork, adopt the upper, right-hand turning, following derelict phone lines and (initially) some cement paving towards the rural monastery of **Áyios Yeóryios Hadhión**, 11km (3hr on foot) from Frý. This is frequented only during its late-April festival time, and during mid-summer by the resident caretaker. There are a few open guest cells and cistern water here if you need to fill up canteens; the only other water en route is a well at the route's high point.

From the monastery it's another 3km – motorbikes can make it most of the way – to **Hélathros**, a lonely cove at the mouth of one of the larger, more forbidding Kassiot canyons. The sand-and-gravel beach itself is small and mediocre, but the water is pristine and – except for the occasional fishing boat – you'll probably be alone. The lower, left-hand option at the fork is the direct track to Hélathros, but this is only 2km shorter, and following severe storm damage, impassable to any vehicle and all but the most energetic hikers.

Kárpathos

A long, narrow island marooned between Rhodes and Crete, wild **Kárpathos** has always been something of an underpopulated backwater, although it is the third largest of the Dodecanese. An habitually cloud-capped mountainous spine rises to over 1200 metres, and divides the more populous, lower-lying south from an exceptionally rugged north. Despite a magnificent windswept coastline of cliffs and promontories interrupted by little beaches, Kárpathos has succumbed surprisingly little to tourism. This has much to do with the appalling road system – rutted where paved, unspeakable otherwise – the paucity of interesting villages and the often high cost of food, which offsets reasonable room prices. Most visitors come here for a glimpse of the traditional village life that prevails in the isolated north of the island, and for the numerous superb, secluded beaches. The airport receives direct international flights – typically several weekly charters from northern Europe – and visitor numbers are on the increase. Since the 1990s, package tourism has more or less dominated several resorts in the southern part of the island, pushing independent travellers up to the remote north.

Kárpathos hasn't the most alluring of interiors: the central and northern uplands were badly scorched by forest fires in the 1980s, and agriculture plays a slighter role than on any other Greek island of comparable size. The Karpathians are too well off to bother much with farming; massive emigration to America and the resulting remittance economy has transformed Kárpathos into one of the wealthiest Greek islands.

Kárpathos's four Mycenaean and Classical cities figure little in ancient chronicles. Alone of the major Dodecanese, the island was held by the Genoese and Venetians after the Byzantine collapse and so has no castle of the crusading Knights of St John, nor any surviving medieval fortresses of consequence. The Ottomans couldn't be bothered to settle or even garrison it; instead they left a single judge or *kadi* at the main town, making the Greek population responsible for his safety during the many pirate attacks.

Pigádhia (Kárpathos Town)

The island capital of **PIGÁDHIA**, often known simply as Kárpathos, nestles at the south end of scenic **Vróndi Bay**, whose sickle of sand extends 3km northwest. The town itself, curling around the jetty and quay where ferries and excursion boats dock, is as drab as its setting is beautiful; an ever-increasing number of concrete blocks contributes to the air of a vast building site, making the Italian-era port police and county governmental buildings seem like heirlooms by comparison. Although there's nothing special to see, Pigádhia does offer just about every facility you might need, albeit with a definite package-tourism slant.

Practicalities

Olympic Airways (book a week minimum in advance) is on Apodhímon Karpathíon, the "Street of the Overseas Karpathians", at the corner of Mitropolítou. The **post office** is a few paces west on Yeoryíou Loízou, while amongst several **banks** there are two cash dispensers.

To explore the island, there are regular **buses** to Pylés, via Apéri, Voládha and Óthos, as well as to Ammopí; the terminal (just a stop with a destination-placard) is at the corner of 28-Oktovriou and Dhimokratías, a couple of blocks back from the front. Set-rate, unmetered **taxis** aren't too expensive to get to these and other points (such as the airport) on the paved road system, but charge a fortune to go anywhere else. Upwards of a dozen outfits **rent cars**, though you may have to try every one to find a free vehicle, rates are vastly over the odds, and the cars themselves often well-worn

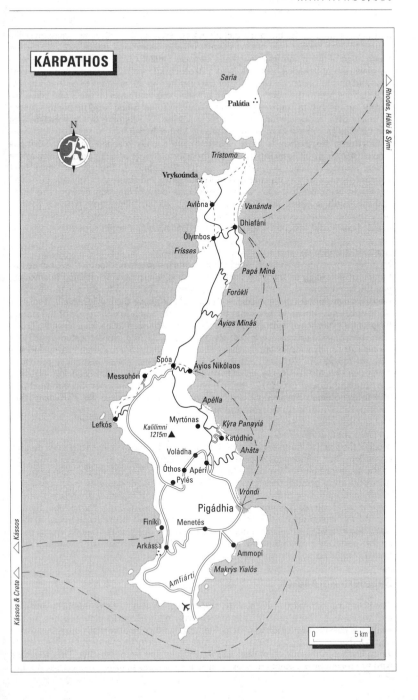

and inferior models. Some to try include Circle (☎0245/22 690), which may give discounts to *Rose Studios* (see below) clients; friendly *Panorama* (☎0245/22 702), at the north edge of town; and less courteous *Gatoulis* (☎0245/22 747), which does, however, have decent vehicles. Hermes Rent a **Motorbike** (☎0245/22 090) has the largest fleet and on-site sevice. Be warned that the only fuel on the island is to be found at several stations just to the north and south of town, and that tanks on the small bikes are barely big enough to complete a circuit of the south, let alone head up north – which is, in any case, expressly forbidden by most outfits. For seagoing jaunts, **windsurfers** and **canoes** are rented from various stalls on Vróndi beach.

Northern Kárpathos is most pleasantly and usually reached **by boat**. Olympos Travel (☎0245/22 993), on the front near the jetty, offers good deals on all-in **day-tours** (from around 5000dr to Ólymbos) on its *Karpathos I*, though the rival boat (*Chrisovalandou III*; pay on board) is more attractive and stable in heavy sea. Less well publicized is the fact that you can use these boats to travel **one-way** between the north and the south in either direction, paying about 2000dr; departures typically 8.30am northbound, 4.30pm southbound. Various agents can also offer trips to Kássos and to isolated east coast beaches without facilities (bring lunch if not included).

ACCOMMODATION

Most ferries are met by people offering **self-catering studios**, though they may be forbidden from touting on the quay itself. Unless you've arranged something in advance, you might consider such offers – the town is so small that no location is too inconvenient, though the best place to stay is on the hillside above the bus terminal. More luxurious places lie north, towards and behind **Vróndi** beach to either side of the ruined fifth-century basilica of **Ayía Fotiní**, but tend to be occupied by package groups. Three of the best hillside premises are *Rose Studios* (☎0245/22 284), well-kept studios (②) and rooms (①) run by a kindly family; the courteous *Amarillis Studios* slightly downhill and east (☎0245/22 375; ②), with enormous units; and *Elias Rooms* just above the *Hotel Karpathos* (☎0245/22 446; ①), en-suite rooms in a converted older house. Lower down, the rambling *Konaki* (☎0245/22 908; ①) on 28-Oktovríou, the upper through-road parallel to Apodhímon Karpathíon, is a backpackers' standby, while the *Karpathos* itself (☎0245/22 347; ②) is serviceable and in a central location.

EATING AND DRINKING

Most of the waterfront **tavernas** are undistinguished and expensive, with a few notable exceptions: fish aficionados should head for *Iy Kali Kardhia*, at the north end of the shore boulevard on the way to the beach, while the *To Perigiali* on the main front is a pricey but fairly genuine ouzerí with good bread, homemade desserts and frozen items clearly indicated. Live **music** can be heard nightly at the *Kafenio Life of Angels*, one of the few surviving old buildings next to the church on Apodhímon Karpathíon, though they're not by any means the best sessions on the island. More trendy bars such as *Rocks* and *Eros* offered taped sounds from perches overlooking the bay. At Vróndi there are two serviceable lunchtime tavernas at the southerly, town end: *To Limanaki* and the *Seaside Snack Bar*.

Southern Kárpathos

The southern extremity of Kárpathos, towards the airport, is extraordinarily desolate and windswept. There are a couple of relatively undeveloped sandy beaches on the southeast coast in the region known as Amfiárti, but they're only really attractive to foreign windsurfers who come to take advantage of the prevailing westerlies. Most people go no further in this direction than **AMMOPÍ**, just 7km from Pigádhia. This, together with the recent development at Vróndi and Arkássa (see opposite), is the closest thing on Kárpathos to a purpose-built beach resort. Two sand-and-gravel, tree-fringed coves fringed by a couple of **tavernas** and numbers of **hotels** and **rooms** are rapidly filling up most of the available space – recommendable among these are the *Votsalakia* (☎0245/22 204; ②) or the *Kastelia Bay* (☎0245/22 678; ②). Heading west from Pigádhia rather than south, the road climbs steeply 9km up to **MENETÉS**, an appealing ridgetop village with handsome old houses, a tiny folklore museum and a spectacularly sited church. There's a single **taverna** here (*Ta Dhyo Adhelfia*) and a World War II memorial with sweeping views north.

Beyond Menetés, you descend to **ARKÁSSA**, on the slopes of a ravine draining to the west coast, with excellent views to Kássos en route. Despite poor, tiny beaches on a mostly rocky shore, Arkássa has been heavily developed, with hotels and restaurants sprouting in clusters. Much of the **accommodation** is aimed squarely at the package market, but independent travellers could try the en-suite *Rooms Irini* (☎0245/61 263 or 61 206; ②) or the more opulent *Hotel Dimitrios* (☎0245/81 256; ③). Most **tavernas** lie north of the ravine in the village centre, for example *Petaloudha* and *Paradhisos* on the dead-end access street.

A few hundred metres south of where the ravine meets the sea, a signposted cement side road leads briefly to the whitewashed chapel of Ayía Sofía, marooned amidst various remains of Classical and Byzantine Arkessia. These consist of several mosaic floors with geometric patterns, including one running diagonally under the floor of a half-buried chapel, emerging from the walls on either side. The Paleókastro headland beyond was the site of Mycenean Arkessia.

The tiny fishing port of **FINÍKI**, just a couple of kilometres north, offers a minuscule beach, occasional excursions to Kássos, half a dozen **tavernas** and several **rooms** establishments lining the road to the jetty; prominent examples include *Taverna Flisvos* and *Giavasis Studios* (☎0245/61 365; ②). The west-coast road is now asphalted all the way to the turning for the attractive resort of **LEFKÓS** (Paraliá Lefkoú). Although this is a delightful place for flopping on the beach, only three weekly buses call, and Lefkós marks the furthest point you can reach from Pighádhia on a small motorbike and return safely without running out of fuel. However, any effort will be rewarded by the striking topography of cliffs, hills, islets and sandspits surrounding a triple bay. There are now nearly two dozen places to stay, and perhaps half as many tavernas, but package companies tend to monopolize the better **accommodation** from June to September. Exceptions include the *Akroyiali Studios* (☎0245/71 178; ②), on stonier fourth bay just south off the access road, or the *Hotel Krinos* (☎0245/71 410; ③), on the final approach just before the fishing port. Overlooking the port itself on the seaward promontory, the *Dhramoundana II* **taverna** has a well-priced menu of Greek and Western specialities, plus drinks, and may be able to help in the search for available rooms.

Back on the main road, you climb northeast through one of the few sections of pine forest not scarred by fire to **MESOHÓRI**. The village tumbles down towards the sea around narrow, stepped alleys, coming to an abrupt halt at the edge of a flat-topped bluff dotted with three tiny, ancient chapels and separated from the village proper by a vast oasis of orchards. These are nurtured by the fountain underneath the church of **Panayía Vryssianí**, wedged against the mountainside just east and invisible from the end of the access road. On the stair-street leading to this church are a taverna and a simple kafenío. The main road, all paved continues on to Spóa, overlooking the east coast.

Central Kárpathos

The **centre** of Kárpathos supports a quartet of villages blessed with superb hillside settings, ample running water – and a cool climate, even in August. Nearly everyone here has "done time" in North America, then returned home with their nest eggs. New Jersey, New York and Canadian car plates tell you exactly where repatriated islanders struck it rich, and it's claimed the area has the highest per capita income in Greece. West-facing **PYLÉS** is the most attractive, set above another oasis, while **ÓTHOS**, noted for its red wine and a private ethnographic museum, is the highest and chilliest, just below 1215-metre Mount Kalilímni. On the east side of the ridge you find **VOLÁDHA** with its tiny Venetian citadel and a pair of nocturnally operating tavernas. From **APÉRI**, the largest, lowest and wealthiest settlement with another pair of night-time eateries, you can drive 6km along a very rough road to the dramatic pebble beach of **Aháta**, with just a drinks-only *kantína*.

Beyond Apéri, the road up the **east coast** is extremely rough in places, passing above beaches most easily accessible by boat trips from Pigádhia. **Kýra Panayiá** is the first encountered, reached via a paved but twisty side road through Katódhio hamlet; there's a surprising number of villas, rooms and tavernas in the ravine behind the 150m of fine gravel and sheltered, turquoise water. **Apélla** is the best of the beaches you can reach by road, though there's a final short path from the single taverna-rooms (the only facility) at the road's end to the scenic 300-metre gravel strand. The end of this route is **SPÓA**, high above the shore just east of the island's spine, with a snack bar (*Fota*) at the edge of the village which might make a better meal stop than the overpriced one down at **Áyios Nikólaos**, 5km below, a small hamlet with an average beach and the overgrown ruins of a Paleo-Christian basilica to explore.

Northern Kárpathos

Although connected by dirt road with Spóa, much the easiest (and usual) way to get to northern Kárpathos is by sea. Inter-island ferries call at Dhiafáni twice a week in season, or there are smaller tour boats from Pigádhia daily. These take a couple of hours, and are met at Dhiafáni by buses for the eight-kilometre transfer up to the traditional village of Ólymbos, the main attraction in this part of the island.

Ólymbos and around

Originally founded as a pirate-safe refuge in Byzantine times, windswept **ÓLYMBOS** straddles a long ridge below slopes studded with mostly ruined windmills. Two restored ones, beyond the main church, grind wheat and barley during late summer only, though one is kept under sail most of the year. Its basement houses a small ethnographic museum (odd hours; free), while a small shop nearby sells locally produced farm products. The village has long attracted foreign and Greek ethnologists, who treat it as a living museum of peasant dress, crafts, dialect and music long since gone elsewhere in Greece. It's still a very picturesque place, yet traditions are vanishing by the year. Nowadays it's only the older women and those working in the several tourist shops who wear the striking and magnificently colourful traditional dress – an instant photo opprtunity in exchange for persistent sales pitches.

After a while you'll notice the prominent role that the women play in daily life: tending gardens, carrying goods on their shoulders or herding goats. Nearly all Ólymbos men emigrate or work outside the village, sending money home and returning only on holidays. The long-isolated villagers also speak a unique dialect, said to maintain traces of its Doric and Phrygian origins – thus "Ólymbos" is pronounced "Élymbos" locally. Live vernacular music is still heard regularly and draws crowds of visitors at festival times, in particular Easter and August 15, when you've little hope of finding a bed.

At other times, the daytime commercialization of Ólymbos makes a good reason to **stay** overnight. The *Rooms Restaurant Olymbos* (☎0245/51 252; ③), near the village entrance, has rooms with baths and traditional furnishings, while *Hotel Aphrodite*

(☎0245/51 307; ②) in the centre offers en-suite facilities and a southerly sea view. There are also several places to **eat**; one of the best and most obvious is *O Mylos*, occupying one of the restored mills and offering locally made wine and home-style specialties. *Parthenonas*, on the square by the church, is also good; try their *makaroúnes*, a local dish of homemade pasta with onions and cheese.

From the village, the west coast and tiny port and beach at **Frísses** are a dizzy, half-hour's drop by path below. Most **local hikes**, however, head north or east, many of them on waymarked paths, though you'll have to stay overnight in the area to enjoy them. The easiest option is the ninety-minute walk back down to Dhiafáni, beginning just below the two working windmills. The way is well marked, with water en route, eventually dropping to a ravine amidst extensive forest – though the last half-hour is mostly over bulldozed riverbed. You could also tackle the trail north to the ruins and beach at **Vrykoúnda** ("Vrougoúnda" in dialect), via sparsely inhabited **Avlóna**, set on a high upland devoted to grain. There's a drinks café at the edge of this hamlet, but best take food and ample water to make a day of it, as it's just under three hours' walk one way to Vrykoúnda, which offers traces of Hellenistic/Roman Brykous, the remote cave-shrine of John the Baptist on the promontory and good swimming. Trístomo, a Byzantine anchorage in the far northeast of Kárpathos, is easiest reached by the recently marked trail from Dhiafáni.

Dhiafáni

Although its popularity is growing – especially since the 1997 completion of a new dock for large ferries – rooms in **DHIAFÁNI** are still inexpensive, and the pace of life slow outside of August. There are plenty of places at which to stay and eat, shops that will change money and even a small travel agency, Orfanos Travel (☎0245/51 410), which has its own en-suite hotel (②). The obvious non-en-suite hotels opposite the quay are noisy; try instead the garrulously friendly *Pansion Delfini* (☎0245/51 391; ①), up on the southern hillside. On the front, the favourite taverna is *Anatoli*, easily recognizable by the folk reliefs that sprout from its roofline.

Boat trips are offered to various nearby **beaches**, as well as to the Byzantine site of Palátia on the uninhabited islet of **Saría** or through the narrow strait to Trístomo anchorage and the ruins of Vrykoúnda. There are several coves within walking distance. Closest is **Vanánda**, a stony beach with an eccentric campsite-snack bar in the oasis behind. To get there, follow the pleasant signposted path north through the pines, but don't believe the signs that say ten minutes – it's over thirty minutes away, short-cutting the more recent road. **Papá Miná**, with a few trees and cliff-shade, lies an hour's walk away via the obvious track starting above the ferry dock.

Rhodes (Ródhos)

It's no accident that **Rhodes** is among the most visited of the Greek islands. Not only is its east coast lined with numerous sandy beaches, but the capital's nucleus is a beautiful and remarkably preserved medieval city, the legacy of the crusading Knights of St John who used the island as their main base from 1309 until 1522. Unfortunately this showpiece is jammed to capacity with over a million tourists in a good year, as against about 100,000 permanent inhabitants (including many foreigners). Of transient visitors, Germans, Brits, Swedes, Italians and Danes predominate in that order; accordingly fish fingers, smörgåsbord and pizza jostle alongside moussaka on tourist menus.

Blessed with an equable climate and strategic position, Rhodes was important from earliest times despite a lack of good harbours. The best natural port spawned the ancient town of Lindos which, together with the other city-states Kameiros and Ialyssos, united in 408 BC to found the new capital of Rhodes at the northern tip of the

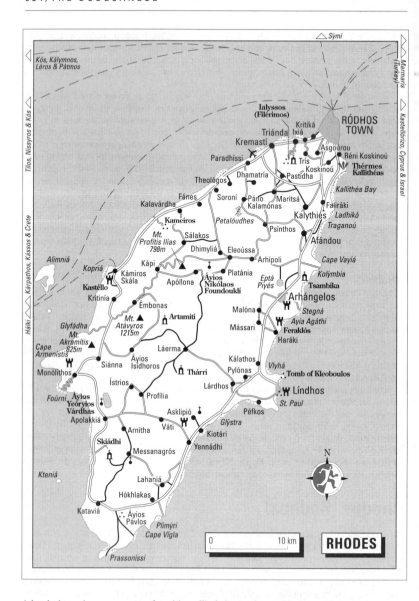

RHODES

0   10 km

island. At various moments the cities allied themselves with Alexander, the Persians, Athenians or Spartans as prevailing conditions suited them, generally escaping retribution for backing the wrong side by a combination of seafaring audacity, sycophancy and burgeoning wealth as a trade centre. Following the failed siege of Demetrios Polyorketes in 305 BC, Rhodes prospered even more, displacing Athens as the major venue for rhetoric and the arts in the east Mediterranean. The town, which lies underneath virtually all of the modern city, was laid out by one Hippodamus in the grid lay-out much in vogue at the time, with planned residential and commercial quarters. Its perimeter walls totalled nearly 15km, enclosing nearly double the area of the present town, and the Hellenistic population was said to exceed 100,000, a staggering figure for late antiquity.

Decline set in when Rhodes became involved in the Roman civil wars, and Cassius sacked the city; by late imperial times, it was a backwater, a status confirmed by numer-ous barbarian raids during the Byzantine period. The Byzantines were compelled to cede the island to the Genoese, who in turn surrendered it to the Knights of St John. The second great siege of Rhodes, during 1522–23, saw Ottoman sultan Süleyman the Magnificent oust the stubborn knights, who retreated to Malta; the town once again lapsed into relative obscurity, though heavily colonized and garrisoned, until its seizure by the Italians in 1912.

Ródhos Town

RÓDHOS TOWN divides into two unequal parts: the compact old walled city, and the new town which sprawls around it in three directions. The latter dates from the Ottoman occupation, when Greek Orthodox natives – forbidden to dwell in the old city – founded several suburb villages or *marásia* in the environs, which have since merged. Commercialization is predictably rampant in the walled town, and in the modern dis-trict of Neohóri west of Mandhráki yacht harbour, the few buildings which aren't hotels are souvenir shops, car rental or travel agencies and bars – easily sixty to seventy in every category. To either side of this stretches the **town beach** (standing room only for latecomers), complete with deckchairs, parasols and showers, particular on the more sheltered east-facing section called **Élli**. At the northernmost point of the island an **Aquarium** (daily April–Sept 9am–9pm, Oct–March 9am–4.30pm; 600dr), officially the "Hydrobiological Institute", offers some diversion with its subterranean maze of seawater tanks. Upstairs is a less enthralling collection of half-rotten stuffed sharks, seals and even a whale. Some 200m southeast stand the **Murad Reis mosque**, an atmospherically neglected Muslim cemetery and the equally dilapidated **Villa Cleobolus**, where Lawrence Durrell lived from 1945 to 1947.

Just a few paces northwest of this, the Italian-built Albergo delle Rose (*Hotel Rodon*) was refurbished and pressed into service in 1999 as the **Playboy Casino Rhodes**, Greece's third largest, complete with "bunnies" serving drinks on the upper floors. Despite parting large sums of money from Rhodians in its first year of operation – uniquely in Greece, locals are allowed to patronize this casino – the outfit has yet to turn a profit.

The old town

Simply to catalogue the principal monuments and attractions cannot do full justice to the infinitely more rewarding **medieval city**. There's ample gratification to be derived from slipping through the eleven surviving gates and strolling the streets, under flying archways built for earthquake resistance, past the warm-toned sandstone and lime-stone walls painted ochre or blue, and over the *hokhláki* (pebble) pavement.

Dominating the northernmost sector of the city's fourteenth-century fortifications is the **Palace of the Grand Masters** (summer Mon noon–7pm, Tues–Fri 8am–7pm; winter Mon 12.30–3pm, Tues–Sun 8.30am–3pm; 1200dr). Largely destroyed by an ammunition depot explosion set off by lightning in 1856, it was reconstructed by the Italians as a summer home for Mussolini and Victor Emmanuel III ("King of Italy and Albania, Emperor of Ethiopia"), neither of whom ever visited Rhodes. The exterior, based on medieval engravings and accounts, is passably authentic, but inside matters are on an altogether grander scale: a marble staircase leads up to rooms paved with

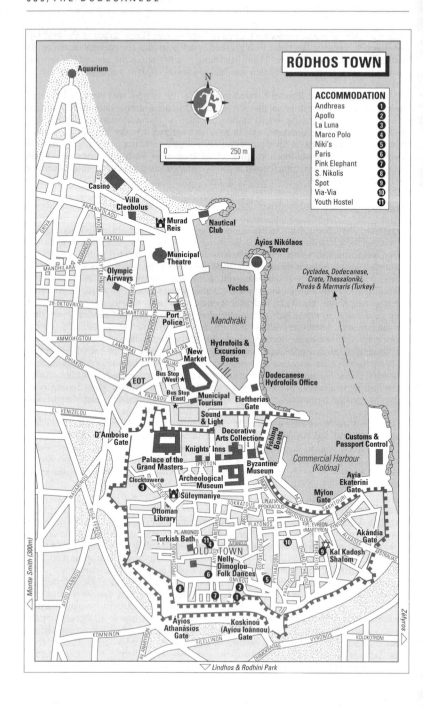

RÓDHOS TOWN

ACCOMMODATION
Andhreas ❶
Apollo ❷
La Luna ❸
Marco Polo ❹
Niki's ❺
Paris ❻
Pink Elephant ❼
S. Nikolis ❽
Spot ❾
Via-Via ❿
Youth Hostel ⓫

Aquarium

Casino

Villa Cleobolus

Murad Reis

Nautical Club

Áyios Nikólaos Tower

Municipal Theatre

Olympic Airways

Yachts

Cyclades, Dodecanese, Crete, Thessaloniki, Pireás & Marmaris (Turkey)

Port Police

Mandhráki

New Market

Hydrofoils & Excursion Boats

Bus Stop (West)

EOT

Bus Stop (East)

Municipal Tourism

Dodecanese Hydrofoils Office

Eleftherias Gate

Sound & Light

Decorative Arts Collection

D'Amboise Gate

Knights' Inns

Fishing Boats

Customs & Passport Control

Palace of the Grand Masters

Byzantine Museum

Commercial Harbour (Kolóna)

Ayia Ekateríni Gate

Clocktower

Archeological Museum

Mýlon Gate

Süleymaniye

Ottoman Library

Akándia Gate

Turkish Bath

OLD TOWN

Kal Kadosh Shalom

Nelly Dimoglou Folk Dances

Áyios Athanásios Gate

Koskinoú (Ayíou Ioánnou) Gate

Monte Smith (300m)

Zéfyros

▽ *Lindhos & Rodhíni Park*

Hellenistic mosaics from Kós, and the ponderous period furnishings rival many a northern European palace. The ground floor is home to the splendid **Medieval Exhibit** and **Ancient Rhodes, 2400 Years** gallery (same hours and admission ticket), together the best museums in town. The medieval collection highlights the importance of Christian Rhodes as a trade centre, with exotic merchandise placing the island in a trans-Mediterranean context. The Knights are represented with a display on their sugar-refining industry and a gravestone of a Grand Master; precious manuscripts and books precede a wing of post-Byzantine icons, moved here permanently from Panayía Kástrou (see below). Across the courtyard in the north wing, "Ancient Rhodes" overshadows the official archeological museum by explaining the everyday life of the ancients, arranged topically (beauty aids, toys, cookware, worship and so on); highlights include a Hellenistic floor mosaic and a household idol of Hecate, goddess of the occult. On Tuesday and Saturday afternoons, there's a supplementary tour of the **city walls** (one hour starting at 2.45pm; 1200dr), beginning from a gate next to the palace and finishing at the Koskinoú gate.

The heavily restored **Street of the Knights** (Odhós Ippotón) leads due east from the Platía Kleovoúlou in front of the Palace; the "Inns" lining it housed the Knights of St John, according to linguistic and ethnic affiliation, until the Ottoman Turks compelled them to leave for Malta after a six-month siege in which the defenders were outnumbered thirty to one. Today the Inns house various government offices and cultural institutions vaguely appropriate to their past, with occasional exhibitions, but the whole effect of the renovation is predictably sterile and stagy (nearby streets were indeed used in the 1987 filming of *Pascali's Island*).

At the bottom of the hill, the Knights' Hospital has been refurbished as the **Archeological Museum** (Tues–Sun 8am–2.30pm; 800dr), though the arches and echoing halls of the building somewhat overshadow the appallingly labelled and presented contents – largely painted pottery dating from the sixth and seventh centuries BC. Behind the second-storey sculpture garden, the Hellenistic statue gallery is more accessible; in a rear corner stands the so-called "Marine Venus", beloved of Lawrence Durrell, but lent a rather sinister aspect by her sea-dissolved face – in contrast to the friendlier *Aphrodite Bathing*. Virtually next door is the **Decorative Arts Collection** (Tues–Sun 8am–2.30pm; 500dr), gleaned from old houses across the Dodecanese; the most compelling artefacts are carved cupboard doors and chest lids painted in naïve style with mythological or historical episodes.

Across the way stands the **Byzantine Museum** (Tues–Sun 8am–2.30pm; 500dr), housed in the old cathedral of the Knights, who adapted the Byzantine shrine of Panayía Kástrou for their own needs. Medieval icons and frescoes lifted from crumbling chapels on Rhodes and Hálki, as well as photos of art still *in situ*, constitute the exhibits; it's worth a visit since most of the Byzantine churches in the old town and outlying villages are locked. Highlights of the collection are a complete cycle from the domes of Thárri monastery (see p.646) dating from 1624, removed in 1967 to reveal much older work beneath.

If instead you head south from the Palace of the Grand Masters, it's hard to miss the most conspicuous Turkish monument in Rhodes, the rust-coloured **Süleymaniye mosque**. Rebuilt in the nineteenth century on foundations three hundred years older, it's currently closed and under scaffolding like most local Ottoman monuments. The old town is in fact well sown with mosques and *mescids* (the Islamic equivalent of a chapel), many of them converted from Byzantine shrines after the 1522 conquest, when the Christians were expelled from the medieval precinct. A couple of these mosques are still used by the sizable **Turkish-speaking minority** here, some of them descended from Muslims who fled Crete between 1898 and 1913. Their most enduring civic contributions are, opposite the Süleymaniye, the **Ottoman Library** (Mon–Fri 7.30am–2.30pm & 6–9pm, Sat–Sun 8am–noon; tip to custodian), with a rich collection of early medieval manuscripts and Korans, and the imposing, still-functioning **hamam**, or Turkish bath, on Platía Ariónos up in the southwest corner of the medieval city (Tues 1–6pm, Wed–Fri 11am–6pm, Sat 8am–6pm; 500dr, 300dr Weds & Sat).

Heading downhill from the Süleymaniye mosque, **Odhós Sokrátous**, once the heart of the Ottoman bazaar, is now the "Via Turista", packed with fur and jewellery stores pitched at cruise-ship tourists. Beyond the tiled central fountain in Platía Ippokrátous, Odhós Aristotélous leads into the Platía tón Evréon Martýron (Square of the Jewish Martyrs), named in memory of the large local community that was almost totally annihilated in summer 1944. Of the four synagogues which once graced Rhodes, only the ornate, arcaded **Kal Kadosh Shalom** (daily 10am–5pm; donation) on Odhós Simíou just to the south survives. It's maintained essentially as a memorial to the approximately 1800 Jews of Rhodes and Kós sent from here to the concentration camps; plaques in French – the language of educated Ottoman Jews across the east Aegean – commemorate the dead. At the rear of the building, a one-room **museum**, set up by a Los Angeles attorney of Jewish Rhodian descent, features archival photos of the community's life on Rhodes and in its far-flung diaspora in the Americas and Africa.

About 2km southwest of Mandhráki, the sparse, unenclosed remains of **Hellenistic Rhodes** – a restored theatre and stadium, plus a few columns of an Apollo temple – perch atop Monte Smith, the hill of Áyios Stéfanos renamed after a British admiral who used it as a watchpoint during the Napoleonic wars. The wooded site is popular with joggers and strollers, but for summer shade and greenery the best spot is probably **Rodini park**, nearly 2km south of town on the road to Líndhos, and served by city bus route #3. The wooded Zimboúli ravine here, fed by natural springs, is home to ducks, peacocks and (in special pens) the native miniature Rhodian deer. Hellenistic **rock-cut tombs**, signposted via a separate side road at the south end of the park, constitute a final possible diversion.

Practicalities

All international and inter-island **ferries** dock at the middle of Rhodes' three ports, the commercial harbour; the only exceptions are local **boats** to and from Sými, all excursion craft, and the **hydrofoils**, which use the yacht harbour of Mandhráki. Its entrance was supposedly once straddled by the Colossus, an ancient statue of Apollo built to celebrate the end of the 305 BC siege; today two columns surmounted by bronze deer are less overpowering replacements.

The **airport** is 13km southwest of town, near the village of Paradhíssi; public urban buses bound for Paradhíssi, Kalavárdha, Theológos or Sálakos pass the stop on the main road opposite the northerly car-park entrance fairly frequently between 6am and midnight. A taxi into town will cost 3000–3700dr, plus bags, depending on time of day. Orange-and-white KTEL **buses** for both the west and east coasts of Rhodes leave from two almost adjacent terminals on Papágou and Avérof, just outside the Italian-built New Market (a tourist trap). Between the lower eastern station and the **taxi** rank at Platía Rimínis there's a **municipal tourist office** (June–Oct Mon–Sat 9am–9pm, Sun 9am–3pm), while some way up Papágou on the corner of Makaríou stands the **EOT office** (Mon–Fri 7.30am–3pm); both dispense bus and ferry schedules.

ACCOMMODATION

Hotels and pensions at all price levels abound in the old town, mostly in the quad bounded by Omírou to the south, Sokrátous to the north, Perikléous to the east and Ippodhámou to the west. At crowded seasons, or late at night, it's prudent to either ring ahead or be prepared to accept the offers of proprietors meeting the ferries and change base next day if necessary – as it frequently is, since standards amongst quay-touted premises tend to be low.

Andreas, Omírou 28d (☎0241/34 156, fax 74 285). Perennially popular (reservations needed), this pension is one of the more imaginative old-house restorations. Rooms in a variety of formats and plumbing arrangements (many en-suite). Terrace view-bar, email facilities, credit cards accepted. Open Mar–Oct. ③.

Apollo, Omírou 28c (☎0241/35 064). Basic but clean and friendly rooms place; the self-catering kitchen makes it good for longer stays. ①.

La Luna, Ierokléous 21 (☎ & fax 0241/25 856). Clean if plain (no en-suite) pension in a converted old Turkish house, complete with still-functioning *hamam* (Turkish bath). Garden bar for breakfast, by the citrus and banana trees. ③.

Marco Polo Mansion, Ayíou Fanouríou 42 (☎ & fax 0241/25 562, *marcopolomansion@ hotmail.com*). Superb, newish (1999) conversion of an old Turkish mansion, again with a *hamam* on site, but here all rooms are en-suite and exquisitely furnished with antiques from the nearby eponymous gallery. Large buffet breakfasts provided by ebullient manageress Efi, and adjoining café after-hours. Three-day minimum stay, breakfast included. ⑥.

Niki's, Sofokléous 39 (☎0241/25 115). Rooms can be on the small side, but ground-floor units are en-suite, and upper-storey ones have fine views. There's a washing machine and common terrace, too. ②.

Paris, Ayíou Fanouríou 88, corner Omírou (☎0241/26 356). Plain but en-suite rooms with fans, the best facing a large courtyard. ③.

Pink Elephant/Roz Elefandas, officially Irodhótou 42 but actually on Timahídhas (☎ & fax 0241/22 469). Simple but clean rooms occupying several levels of a modernized old building; roof deck and card-phone that receives calls too. ②.

S. Nikolis, Ippodhámou 61 (☎0241/34 561, fax 32 034, *nikoliss@hol.gr*). A variety of premises in the west of the old town. Hotel/honeymoon-suite rates ⑥ include breakfast, TV and air con, or there are self-catering apartments (④) or even a simple house pension (③). Bookings essential for hotel and apartments, accepted only with credit-card number. Open Apr–Nov.

Spot, Perikléous 21 (☎0241/34 737). Rooms are a bit dark, but clean enough, and you won't find en-suite rooms elsewhere for this price, except at *Niki's*. ②.

Via-Via, Lysipoú, alley off Pythagóra 31 (☎ & fax 0241/27 895). Efficiently French-run rooms, either shared bathrooms (②) or en-suite (③). Self-catering, roof terrace, email facility, open all year.

Youth Hostel, Eryíou 12 (☎0241/30 491). Both dorms and doubles in this courtyarded house with kitchen facilities; 2000dr for a bunk, but none-YHA-affiliated.

EATING AND DRINKING

Eating well for a reasonable price in and around Ródhos Town is a challenge, but not an insurmountable one. As a general rule, the remoter and further south you go, the better value you'll find.

Araliki, Aristofánous 45, Old Town. Bohemian expatriates and travellers tired of standard resort grub seek out this old-style kafenío on the ground floor of a medieval house. Small plates of exquisitely original mezédhes are provided by Italian proprietors Miriam, Enio and Valeria; count on 4500dr per person with drinks, which include Nissyrot *soumádha*. Open Mar–Dec daily except Sun for supper (and often lunch); also shut two random weeks July–Aug.

Dhiafani, Platía Ariónos, Old Town. Enormous salads and *mayireftá* plates, the cheapest (3000dr a head for the works) in the old town; outdoor seating opposite the *hamam*.

Khristos Ouzeri Inomayerio (O Vlahos), Klavdhíou Pépper 165, at the big bend, Zéfyros Beach, New Town. As the name implies, both ouzerí fare – marinated fish or peppers, great *tzatzíki* – accompanying a vast oúzo list, plus vegetable-strong *mayireftá* (cuttlefish with spinach) that sell out quickly. Not as cheap or big-portioned as formerly, but still worth the trek out.

Le Bistrot de l'Auberge, Praxitélous 21, Old Town. Genuine, popular, French-run bistro with excellent Frenchified food: allow 5000dr per person for three hefty courses plus wine from a well-selected Greek list; jazz soundtrack included. Summer seating in the courtyard of this restored medieval inn; inside under the arches during cooler months. Open Mar–Dec for lunch and supper daily except Mon.

O Meraklis, Aristotélous 30. A *pátsatzídhiko* (tripe-and-trotter soup kitchen) that's only open 3–7am for a motley clientele of post-club lads, Turkish stallholders, night-club singers and travellers just stumbled off an overnight ferry. Great free entertainment, including famously rude staff, and the soup – the traditional Greek hangover cure – is good too.

Metaxi Mas, Klavdhíou Pépper 116, Zéfyros Beach, New Town. No sign or menu in English – look for the elevated boat – at this somewhat pricey seafood ouzerí with various exotic titbits; count on 12,000dr per couple with booze, slightly less in a group. Daily lunch and supper except Sun lunch only.

Mikes (pronounced "mee-kess"), nameless alley behind Sokrátous 17. Inexpensive (for Rhodes, anyway) hole-in-the-wall, serving only grilled fish, salads and wine.

Palia Istoria, Mitropóleos 108, cnr Dhendhrínou, in Ámmos district of New Town. Reckoned to be the best *kultúra* taverna in town, but predictably expensive for such dishes as celery hearts in egg-lemon sauce and scallops with mushrooms and artichokes, washed down by a hundred-strong wine list. Supper only; reservations essential on ☎0241/32 421.

Sheftalies, Tsaldhári 21, New Town, south of Monte Smith past Marinopoulos Supermarket. Direct antithesis to *Palia Istoria*, since you can fill up for 2500dr. Zero atmosphere, but a genuine charcoal griller featuring the namesake *sheftaliés*, dioxin-free chicken and *kokorétsi*, plus a few daily *mayireftá* plates.

To Steno, Ayíon Anaryíron 29, New Town, 400m southwest of the Ayíou Athanasíou Gate. A genuinely welcoming ouzerí, with outdoor seating during the warmer months and limited but superb menu (chickpea soup, courgette croquettes, sausages) at eminently reasonable prices.

Stou Apostoli, Mitropóleos 49, New Town, 500m south of the stadium, past the big church. Inexpensive ouzerí housed on the ground floor of an Italian mansion; brief but well-executed menu of grilled titbits plus vegetable mezédhes.

Vassilis (Kova), Kolokotroni, 80m east of Kanadhá, south of Akándia commercial port. Another place to go when you're down to your last drachma: a friendly working man's canteen, busiest from noon to 2pm, with several *mayireftá* dishes to choose from and shady outdoor seating between the auto-repair shops.

NIGHTLIFE

The old town formerly had a well-deserved reputation for being tomb-silent at night; this has changed drastically since the late 1990s, with an entire alley (Miltiádhou) off Apéllou given over to five loud music bars and clubs, frequented almost exclusively by Greeks. This is just a mini taster for the estimated two hundred foreigner-patronized bars and clubs in Neohóri, where theme nights and various other gimmicks predominate. They are found mostly along the streets and alleys bounded by Alexándhrou Dhiákou, Orfanídhou (aka "Skandi Street", after the latter-day Vikings), Fanouráki and Nikifórou Mandhilará.

Sedate by comparison, Ministry-of-Culture-approved folk dances (May–Oct Mon, Wed, Fri 9.20pm; 2500dr) are presented with live accompaniment by the Nelly Dimoglou Company, performed in the landscaped "Old Town Theatre" off Andhroníkou, near Platía Ariónos. More of a technological extravaganza is the **Sound and Light** show, spotlighting sections of the city walls, staged in a garden just off Platía Rimínis. There's English-language narration nightly except Sunday, its screening time varying from 8.15pm to 10.15pm (1200dr).

Thanks to a large contingent from the local university, there are several year-round **cinemas** in the new town showing first-run fare indoors or open-air according to season. Choose from among the Rodon Municipal Theatre, next to the town hall in Neohóri; the Metropol, southeast of the old town opposite the stadium; and the nearby Pallas on Dhimokratías, completely refurbished in 1999.

Blue Lagoon Pool Bar, 25-Martíou 2, Neohóri. One of the better theme bars, in this case a "desert island" with palm trees, waterfalls, a shipwrecked galleon – and taped music.

Café Besara (very small sign out), Sofokléous 11-13, Old Town. Congenial breakfast café/low-key boozer run by an Australian lady, with interesting mixed clientele and live music some nights.

Christos' Garden/To Dhiporto, Dhilberáki 59, Neohóri. This combination art-gallery/bar/café occupies a carefully restored old house and courtyard with pebble-mosaic floors throughout. Incongruously classy for the area.

Colorado Entertainment Centre, Orfanídhou 57, cnr Aktí Miaouli, Neohóri. Triple venue: "pub" with live in-house band (rock covers), "club" with taped sounds, and quiet upstairs "bar".

Mango Bar, Platía Dhoriéos 3, Old Town. Piped music and a variety of drinks at this durable bar on an otherwise quiet plaza; also a good source of breakfast after 8am, served under a plane tree.

O'Reilly's, Apolloníou Rodhíou 61, Neohóri. Irish theme pub with claimed live music nightly, and Irish draught.

Resalto, Plátonos 6, opposite the mosque. Live Greek rembétika and laikó sounds, rather cheaper than nearby rival *Café Chantant*.

Rolóï, Orféos 1, Old Town. The baroque clocktower erected by Ahmet Fetih Pasha in 1857 is now the focus of possibly the most exclusive café-bar in the old town. Admission charge to climb the tower, and steeply priced drinks, but you are paying for the terrific view.

Sticky Fingers, Anthoúla Zérvou 6, Neohóri. Long-lived music bar with reasonable drinks; live rock several nights weekly from 10pm onwards.

Listings

Airlines British Airways, Platía Kýprou 1 (☎0241/27 756); Olympic, Iérou Lókhou 9 (☎0241/24 571). Air Greece and Cronus Air have no set office; most bona fide travel agents handle them.

Bookshop Second Storey Books, Amarándou 24, Neohóri, has a large stock of used English paperbacks; open all year, normal shop hours.

Car rental Prices at non-international chains are fairly standard at 13,000–14,000dr per day, but can be bargained down to about 10,000–11,000dr a day, all-inclusive, out of peak season and/or for long periods. More flexible local outfits, all in the new town, include Alexander, Afstralías 58, Akándia port (☎0241/27 547); Alamo, 28-Oktovríou 18 (☎0241/73 570); Just, Orfanídhou 45 (☎0241/31 811); Kosmos, Papaloúka 31 (☎0241/74 374); Orion, Yeoryíou Leóndos 36 (☎0241/22 137); and Payless, Íonos Dhragoúmi 29 (☎0241/26 586).

Exchange Most conventional bank branches are near Platía Kýprou in Neohóri, plus there are numerous exchange bureaux keeping long hours. At other times use the cash dispensers of the Commercial Bank (branch in the old town too), Credit Bank, Ionian Bank or National Bank (old town branch).

Ferries Tourist office handouts list the bewildering array of representatives for the several boat and hydrofoil companies which operate here; authoritative schedule information is available at the *limenarhío*, on Mandhráki esplanade near the post office.

Internet cafés The most central and competitive of several are *Rock Style*, Dhimokratías 7, opposite the stadium, and *Café Besara* (see "Nightlife" opposite).

Laundries House of Laundry, Erythroú Stavroú 2, Neohóri; Star, Kostí Palamá 4–6, behind New Market; Wash & Go, Plátonos 33, Old Town.

Motorbike rental Low-volume scooters will make little impact on Rhodes; sturdier Yamaha 125s, suitable for two people, start at about 6000dr a day. In the old town, Mandar Moto at Dhimosthénous 2, cnr Platía Evréon Martýron, has a large stable of medium-sized scooters suitable for short jaunts. Recommended outlets in Neohóri include Margaritis, Ioánni Kazoúli, with a wide range of late models up to 500cc, plus mountain bikes; or (to roll out in style) Rent a Harley at 28-Oktovríou 80 – classic models for two riders start at a whopping 33,000dr per day.

Post office Main branch with outgoing mail, poste restante and exchange windows on Mandhráki harbour, open Mon–Fri 7.30am–8pm.

Radio stations For foreign sounds, try Rodos International at 102 FM, or UK Radio at 107.5 FM.

Scuba diving Waterhoppers and Dive Med both tout for business daily at Mandhráki quay; however days out are expensive (18,000dr for two dives) and you're restricted to one small site at Thérmes, Kallithéa.

Travel agencies Particularly recommended in the old town is Castellania, Evripídhou 1–3, cnr Platía Ippokrátous, which can arrange all domestic air tickets, both domestic and international ferries, and also discount scheduled and charter flights abroad. In Neohóri, Visa at Grigóri Lambráki 54 (☎0241/33 282) and Contours at Ammohóstou 9 (☎0241/36 001) are also worth contacting, while Plaza Travel at Ieroú Lóhou 7 is the main outlet for hydrofoil tickets to Marmaris in Turkey.

The east coast

Heading down the coast from the capital you have to go some way before you escape the crowds from local beach hotels, their numbers swollen by visitors using the regular buses from town or on boat tours out of Mandhráki. You might look in at the decayed, abandoned spa of **Thérmes Kallithéas**, dating in its present spectacle of enjoyable mock-orientalia from the Italian period. Located 3km south of Kallithéa resort proper, down a dirt track through pines, the buildings are set in a palm grove, though an EU-funded restoration begun in 1999 seems stalled indefinitely. Nearby are several hidden sandy coves framed by rock formations, furnished with sunbeds and (in some cases) snack bars. The former fishing village of **FALIRÁKI**, which primarily draws a youngish package clientele, is all too much in the mould of a Spanish *costa* resort, while the scenery just inland – arid, scrubby sand-hills at the best of times – has been made that much bleaker by fire damage that stretches way beyond Líndhos.

The enormous mass of **Tsambíka**, 26km south of town, is the first place at which most non-package visitors will seriously consider stopping. Actually the very eroded flank of a much larger extinct volcano, the hill has a monastery on top offering unrivalled views along some 50km of coastline. From the main highway, a steep, 1500-metre cement drive leads to a small car park and a snack bar, from which steps lead to the summit. The monastery here is unremarkable except for its September 8 festival: childless women climb up – sometimes on their hands and knees – to be relieved of their barrenness, and any children born afterwards are dedicated to the Virgin with the names Tsambikos or Tsambika, which are particular to the Dodecanese. From the top you can survey **Kolýmbia** just to the north, a small beach to one side of a tiny cove ringed with volcanic rocks, backed by a dozen, low-rise hotels. Shallow **Tsambíka** bay on the south side of the headland warms up early in the spring, and the excellent beach, though protected by the forest service from development other than a permanent taverna and a dozen *kantína* caravans, teems with people all summer.

The next beach south, gravelly **Stegná** with its summer cottages for locals, can only be reached by a steep road east from **ARHÁNGELOS**, a large village just inland overlooked by a crumbling castle. Though you can disappear into the warren of alleys between the main road and the citadel, the place is now firmly caught up in package tourism, with a full complement of banks, tavernas, mini-marts and jewellery stores.

A more peaceful overnight base on this stretch of coast would be **HARÁKI**, a pleasant if undistinguished two-street fishing port with mostly self-catering accommodation (generally ③) overlooked by the stubby ruins of **Feraklós castle**, the last stronghold of the Knights to fall to the Turks. You can swim off the town beach if you don't mind an audience from the handful of waterfront cafés and tavernas, but most people head west out of town, then north 800m to the secluded **Agáthi beach**. The best taverna near Haráki is *Efterpi*, 200m south at so-called Massári beach.

Líndhos

LÍNDHOS, the island's second-ranking tourist attraction, erupts from barren surroundings 12km south of Haráki. Like Ródhos old town, its charm is heavily undermined by commercialism and crowds: up to half a million visitors in a typical year. At midday dozens of coaches park nose-to-tail on the narrow southerly access road, with even more on the drives down to the beaches. Back in the village itself, those few vernacular houses not snapped up by package operators have, since the 1960s, been bought up and refurbished by wealthy British, Germans and Italians. The old *agorá* or serpentine high street presents a mass of fairly indistinguishable bars, creperies, mediocre restaurants and travel agents. Although high-rise hotels and all vehicular traffic have been prohibited inside the municipal boundaries, the result is a relentlessly commercialized theme park – hot and airless in August, but deserted and quite ghostly in winter.

Nonetheless, if you arrive before or after peak season, when the pebble-paved streets between the immaculately whitewashed houses are relatively empty of both people and droppings from the donkeys shuttling up to the acropolis (see below), you can still appreciate the beautiful, atmospheric setting of Líndhos. The most imposing fifteenth- to eighteenth-century **captains' residences** are built around *hokhláki* courtyards, their monumental doorways often fringed by intricate stonework, with the number of braids or cables supposedly corresponding to the number of ships owned. A few are open to the public, most notably the **Papakonstandis Mansion**, the most elaborate and now home to an unofficial museum; entrance to the "open" mansions is free but some pressure will probably be exerted on you to buy something, especially lace and embroidery.

On the bluff looming above the town, the ancient acropolis with its 1990s-restored Doric **Temple of Athena** and imposing **Hellenistic stoa** is found inside the Knights' **castle** (summer Tues–Sun 8am–6.40pm, Mon 12.30am–6.40pm; rest of year Tues–Sun 8.30am–3pm; 1200dr) – a surprisingly felicitous blend of ancient and medieval culture. Though the ancient city of Lindos and its original temple date from at least 1100 BC, the present structure was begun by local ruler Kleoboulos in the sixth century BC and replaced by the present structure after a fourth-century fire.

Líndhos's north beach, once the main ancient harbour, is overcrowded and occasionally polluted; if you do base yourself here, cleaner, quieter **beaches** are to be found one cove beyond at Pállas beach (with a nudist annexe around the headland), or 5km north at **Vlyhá** bay. South of the acropolis huddles the small, perfectly sheltered **St Paul's harbour**, where the apostle is said to have landed in 58 AD on a mission to evangelize the island.

PRACTICALITIES

It used to be tempting fate to just turn up and hope for accommodation vacancies on spec, but since certain British tour companies pulled out of Líndhos in the late 1990s, it's something of a buyers' market. If you're not met at the bus stop under the giant fig tree by proprietors touting rooms, *Pallas Travel* (☎0244/31 494, fax 31 595) can arrange a room or even a whole villa for a small fee. The oft-cited backpackers' standbys, 1970s-vintage *Pension Electra* (☎0244/31 226; ②) and *Pension Katholiki* (☎0244/31 445; ②), next door to each other on the way to the north beaches, are both low standard (shared baths) and overpriced.

Local **restaurants** tend to be bland and exploitative, although *Agostino's* by the southerly car park possesses the important virtues of bulk Émbonas wine and real country sausages (not imported hot dogs). You may as well push the boat out at *Mavrikos* on the fig-tree square, founded in 1933 and in the same family ever since. Mezédhes are good, as are quasi-French main courses like cuttlefish in wine; dipping into the excellent (and expensive) Greek wine list as well will land you a bill of 5000–6000dr per person. If your wallet won't stretch that far, the *Panorama* up on the main road, 2km towards Vlyhá, does good fish. For snacks and desserts, try respectively *Il Forno*, an Italian-run bakery, and *Gelo Blu*, still the best of several gelaterie here despite the departure of its Italian founders. There's a unique combination laundry/second-hand bookshop up beyond Pallas Travel, open during normal shop hours, while there are currently three Internet cafés operating in Líndhos. Local **car rental** rates tend to be cheaper than in Ródhos Town, though you've less choice in models and vehicles may be less roadworthy. There are two proper **banks**, working normal hours, each with cash dispensers. And finally, Lindos Suntours (☎0244/31 333) has metred phones (call boxes tend to have huge queues) and a nice line in unclaimed one-way charter seats back to Britain.

The west coast

Rhodes' west coast is the windward flank of the island, so it's damper, more fertile and more forested; most beaches, however, are exposed and decidedly rocky. None of this has deterred development, and as in the east the first few kilometres of the busy shore road down from the capital have been surrendered entirely to tourism. From Neohóri's aquarium down to the airport, the shore is fringed by an almost uninterrupted line of Miami-Beach-style hotels, though such places as Triánda, Kremastí and Paradhíssi are still nominally villages, with real centres. This was the first part of the island to be favoured by the package operators, and tends to be frequented by a decidedly middle-aged, sedate clientele that doesn't stir much from the poolside.

There's not much inducement to stop until you reach the important archeological site of **KAMEIROS**, which together with Líndhos and Ialyssos was one of the three Dorian powers that united during the fifth century BC to found the powerful city-state of Rhodes. Soon eclipsed by the new capital, Kameiros was abandoned and only redis-covered in 1859. As a result it is a particularly well-preserved Doric townscape, doubly worth visiting for its beautiful hillside site (summer Tues–Sun 8am–6.40pm, winter 8.30am–3pm; 800dr). While none of the individual remains are spectacular, you can make out the foundations of two small temples, the re-erected pillars of a Hellenistic house, a Classical fountain, and the stoa of the upper *agora*, complete with a water cis-tern. Because of the gentle slope of the site, there were no fortifications, nor was there an acropolis. On the beach below Kameiros there are several tavernas, highly com-mercialized but acceptable while waiting for one of the two daily buses back to town (if you're willing to walk 4km back to Kalavárdha you'll have a better choice of service).

At the tiny anchorage of **KÁMIROS SKÁLA** (aka Skála Kamírou) 15km south, there are more touristy restaurants which somewht inexplicably have become the target of coach tours. Less heralded is the daily **kaïki** which leaves for the island of **Hálki** at 2.30pm, weather permitting, returning early the next morning; on Wednesdays and Sundays there are day-trips departing at 9am and returning at 4pm. For a decent **meal**, skip the circus here and proceed 400m southwest to off-puttingly named **Paralía Kopriá** (Manure Beach), where *Psarotaverna Johnnys* has superb, non-farmed fish and mezédhes, especially on Sundays when own-made *dolmádhes* and (seasonally) squash blossoms may be on the menu with the usual standards.

A couple of kilometres south of Skála, the "Kastello", signposted as **Kástro Kritinías**, is from afar the most impressive of the Knights' rural strongholds, and the paved access road is too narrow and steep for tour buses. Close up it proves to be no more than a shell, but a glorious shell, with fine views west to assorted islets and Hálki. You make a "donation" to the formidable old harpy at the car park in exchange for fizzy drinks, seasonal fruit or flowers.

Beyond Kritinía itself, a quiet hillside village with a few rooms and tavernas, the main road winds south through the dense forests below mounts Akramítis and Atávyros to **SIÁNNA**, the most attractive mountain settlement on the island, famous for its aro-matic pine-sage honey and *soúma*, a grape-residue distillation similar to Italian *grappa* but far smoother. The rough-and-ready *Elektra*, whose owner spent 27 years in Connecticut, is the place to sample it, with tomato and cheese mezédhes. The tiered, flat-roofed farmhouses of **MONÓLITHOS**, 4km southwest at the end of the public bus line, are scant justification for the long trip out here, and food at the four **tavernas** is indifferent owing to the tour-group trade, but the view over the bay is striking and you could use the village as a base by staying in rooms or at the pricier *Hotel Thomas* (☎0241/22 741 or ☎0246/61 291; ②), self-catering and open most of the year. Diversions in the area include yet another **Knights' castle** 2km west of town, photo-genically perched on its own pinnacle (the "monolith" of the name) but enclosing even less inside than Kastéllo Kritinías, and the sand and gravel beaches (no facilities) at

Foúrni, five paved but curvy kilometres below the castle. In the headland between the first and second beaches are some caves that were hollowed out by early Christians fleeing persecution.

The interior

Inland Rhodes is hilly, and still mostly wooded, despite the recent depredations of arsonists. You'll need a vehicle to see its highlights, especially as enjoyment resides in getting away from it all; no single site justifies the tremendous expense of a taxi or the inconvenience of trying to make the best of sparse bus schedules.

Ialyssos and the Valley of the Butterflies

Starting from the west coast highway, turn inland at the central junction in Tríanda for the five-kilometre uphill ride to the scanty acropolis of ancient **Ialyssos** (Tues–Sun 8am–6.40pm, Mon 8am–2.30pm; 800dr) on flat-topped, strategic Filérimos hill; from its Byzantine castle Süleyman the Magnificent directed the 1522 siege of Rhodes. Filérimos means "lover of solitude", after the tenth-century settlement here by Byzantine hermits. The existing **Filérimos monastery**, restored successively by Italians and British, is the most substantial structure here. As a concession to the Rhodian faithful, the church alone is usually open to pilgrims after the stated hours. Directly in front of the church sprawl the foundations of third-century **temples to Zeus and Athena**, built atop a far older Phoenician shrine. Below this, further towards the car park, lies the partly subterranean church of **Aï-Yeórgis Hostós**, a simple, barrel-vaulted structure with fourteenth- and fifteenth-century frescoes, not as vivid or well preserved as those at Thárri or Asklipió. A bit southeast of the parking area, a hillside **Doric fountain** with a columned facade was only revealed by subsidence in 1926 – and is now off-limits owing to another landslip which has covered it again. Southwest of the monastery and archeological zone, a "Way of the Cross", with the fourteen stations marked out in copper plaques during the Italian era, leads to an enormous concrete crucifix, a recent replacement of an Italian-era one; you're allowed to climb out onto the cross-arms for a supplement to the already amazing view. Illuminated at night, the crucifix is clearly visible from the island of Sými and – perhaps more pertinently – infidel Turkey across the way.

The only highly publicized tourist "attraction" in the island's interior, **Petaloúdhes** or the **"Butterfly Valley"** (May–Sept daily 8.30am–7pm; 300dr–600dr depending on butterfly numbers), reached by a seven-kilometre paved side road bearing inland from the west-coast highway between Paradhíssi and Theológos, is actually a rest stop for Jersey tiger moths (*Panaxia quadripunctaria*). Only in summer do these creatures congregate here, attracted for unknown reasons by the abundant *Liquidambar orientalis* trees. In season, the moths roost in droves on the tree trunks; they cannot eat during this final phase of their life cycle, must rest to conserve energy and die of starvation soon after mating. When sitting in the trees, the moths are a well-camouflaged black and yellow, but flash cherry-red overwings in flight.

Eptá Piyés to Profítis Ilías

Heading inland from Kolýmbia junction on the main east-coast highway, it's a four-kilometre walk or drive to **Eptá Piyés** (Seven Springs), a superb oasis with a tiny dam created by the Italians for irrigation. A shaded streamside **taverna**, immensely popular at weekend with islanders and visitors alike, serves hearty if slightly pricey fare. A trail, or a rather claustrophobic Italian aqueduct-tunnel, both lead from the vicinity of the springs to the reservoir.

Continuing inland, you reach the Italian governor's summer residence at Eleoússa after another 9km, in the shade of the dense forest at the east end of Profítis Ilías ridge.

Two other undisturbed villages, Platánia and Apóllona, nestle on the south slopes of the mountain overlooking the start of the burned area, but most people keep straight on 3km further from Eleoússa to the late Byzantine church of **Áyios Nikólaos Foundoúkli** (St Nicholas of the Hazelnuts). The partly shaded site has a fine view north over cultivated valleys, and locals descend in force for picnics on weekends. The frescoes inside, dating from the thirteenth to the fifteenth centuries, could do with a good cleaning but various scenes from the life of Christ are recognizable.

Heading west from the church along mostly paved roads gets you finally to **Profítis Ilías**, where the Italian-vintage chalet-hotels *Elafos* and *Elafina* (shut down) hide in deep woods just north of the 798-metre peak, Rhodes' third-highest point but out of bounds as a military area. However, there's good, gentle strolling below and around the summit, and a snack bar on the through road is generally open in season.

Atávyros villages

All tracks and roads west across Profítis Ilías converge upon the main road from Kalavárdha bound for **ÉMBONAS**, a large and architecturally nondescript village backed up against the north slope of 1215-metre **Mount Atávyros**. Émbonas, with its two pensions and meat-orientated tavernas, is more geared to handling tourists than you might expect, since it's the venue for summer "folk-dance tours" from Ródhos Town. The village also lies at the heart of the island's most important wine-producing districts, and CAÏR – the Italian-founded vintners' co-operative – produces a choice of acceptable mid-range varieties. However, products of the smaller, family-run Emery winery (☎0246/41 208; Mon–Fri 9am–3pm for tasting tours) at the village outskirts are more esteemed. To see what Émbonas would be like without tourists, carry on clockwise around the peak past the Artamíti monastery, to less celebrated **ÁYIOS ISÍDHOROS**, with as many vines and tavernas, a more open feel, and the **trailhead** for the five-hour return ascent of Atávyros. This path, beginning at the northeast edge of the village, is the safest and easiest way up the mountain, which has extensive foundations of a Zeus temple on top.

Thárri monastery

The road from Áyios Isídhoros to Siána is paved; not so the appalling one that curves for 12km east to Láerma, but it's worth enduring if you've any interest in Byzantine monuments. The **monastery of Thárri**, lost in pine forests five kilometres south, is the oldest religious foundation on the island, re-established as a living community of half a dozen monks in 1990 by the charismatic abbot Amfilohios. The striking *katholikón* (open daily, all day) consists of a long nave and short transept surmounted by barrel vaulting. Various recent cleanings have restored formerly damp-smudged frescoes dating from 1300 to 1450 to their former exquisite glory. The most distinct, in the transept, depict the Evangelists Mark and Matthew, plus the Archangel Gabriel, while the nave boasts various acts of Christ, including such scenes as the *Storm on the Sea of Galilee*, *Meeting the Samaritan Woman at the Well* and *Healing the Cripple*.

The far south

South of a line connecting Monólithos and Lárdhos, you could easily begin to think you had strayed onto another island. Gone are most of the five-star hotels and roads to match, and with them the bulk of the crowds. Gone too are most tourist facilities and public transport. Only one or two daily buses (in season) serve the depopulated villages here, approaching along the east coast; tavernas grace the more popular stretches of sand, but aside from the growing package enclaves of Lárdhos, Péfkos and Kiotári there are few places to stay.

Despite the shelving of plans for a second island airport in the area, new beachfront development mushrooms to either side of **LÁRDHOS**, itself solidly on the tourist circuit despite an inland position between Láerma and the peninsula culminating in Líndhos. The beach 2km away is gravelly and dull, so it's best to continue 3km to Glýstra cove, a small but delightful crescent, with umbrellas and a snack bar, which sets the tone for the coast from here on. Four kilometres east of Lárdhos, **PÉFKOS** (Péfki on some maps) began life as the garden annexe and overflow for Líndhos, but is now a burgeoning package resort in its own right; the sea is clearer than at Lárdhos, with small, well-hidden beaches which are getting harder to find with all the new development on the clifftop.

Asklipió

Nine kilometres beyond Lárdhos, a paved side road heads 3.5km inland to **ASKLIPIÓ**, a sleepy village guarded by a crumbling castle and graced by the Byzantine church of **Kímisis Theotókou** (daily 9am–6pm; free). The building dates from 1060, with a ground plan nearly identical to Thárri's, except that two subsidiary apses were added during the eighteenth century, supposedly to conceal a secret school in a subterranean crypt. The frescoes within are in better condition than those at Thárri owing to the drier local climate; they are also a bit later, though some claim that the final work at Thárri and the earliest here were executed by the same hand, a master from Híos.

The format and subject matter of the frescoes are both rare in Greece: didactic "cartoon strips" which extend completely around the church in some cases, featuring extensive Old Testament stories in addition to the more usual lives of Christ and the Virgin. There's a complete sequence from Genesis, from the Creation to the Expulsion from Eden; note the comically menacing octopus among the fishes in the panel of the Fifth Day, and Eve subsequently being fashioned from Adam's rib. A *Revelation of John the Divine* takes up most of the east transept; pebble-mosaic flooring decorates both the interior and the vast courtyard. Two adjacent buildings house separate museums: an ecclesiastical exhibit (donation requested) and a more interesting folklore gallery full of rural craft tools.

To the southern tip

Back on the coast road, the beachfront hamlet of **KIOTÁRI** has mushroomed as a package venue for Germans and Italians since the mid-1990s, when the Orthodox Church elected to sell up its vast holdings here. There's little local character remaining, so most will choose to continue 4km to **YENNÁDHI**, the only sizable settlement on this coast, with various amenities including **car rental**, a **post office**, some rooms and a few **tavernas** (best of these is *Klimis*) behind the seemingly endless sand and gravel beach. Some 10km south of Yennádhi, and 2km inland, **LAHANIÁ** village with its eponymous **hotel** (☎0244/43 089; ②) and smattering of private rooms makes another possible base. Abandoned after a postwar earthquake, since the 1980s its older houses have been mostly occupied and renovated by Germans on long-term lease agreements. On the main platía at the lower, eastern end of the village, the *Platanos* taverna has decent food and seating between the church and two wonderful fountains, one with an Ottoman inscription.

You can go directly from Lahaniá to **Plimýri**, an attractive sandy bay backed by dunes heaped up by strong afternoon winds; so far the only facility is a good-value rustic **taverna**, next to the church of Zoödhóhou Piyís which has ancient columns upholding its vaulted porch. Beyond Plimýri the road curves inland to **KATAVIÁ**, over 100km from the capital, marooned amidst grain fields; the village, like so many in the south, is three-quarters deserted, the owners of the closed-up houses off working in Australia or North America.

There are a few **rooms** to rent, a vital **filling station** and several **tavernas** at the junction that doubles as the platía – most interesting of these the brightly coloured *Martine's Bakaliko* (shut Thurs), run by folk from Lahanía, which has some vegetarian dishes and attempts to use local organic ingredients when possible.

From Kataviá a paved road leads on to **Prassoníssi**, Rhodes' southernmost extremity and a mecca for European **windsurfers**. The sandspit which tethers Prassoníssi (Leek Island) to Rhodes was partially washed away by storms early in 1998, but enough remains to create flat water on the east side and up to two-metre waves on the west, ideal for different ability levels. Of the two windsurfing centres operating here, Swiss-run Procenter (April–Oct; ☎0244/91 045, *procenter.prasonisi@ EUnet.at*) is the more professional, with hourly rates from 4500dr, and a ten-hour card (valid over several days) from 37,500dr. They're geared for one-week packages, including jeeps and lodged in rooms above the *Lighthouse Restaurant*, one of a half-dozen food and accommodation outfits here; the UK agent is Sportif (☎01273/ 844919, *Sportif@compuserve.com*).

The far southwest

From Lahaniá it's also possible to head 9km northwest along a narrow paved road to the picturesque hilltop village of **MESSANAGRÓS**. This already existed in some form by the fifth century AD, if foundations of a ruined basilica at the village outskirts are anything to go by. A smaller thirteenth-century chapel squats amidst mosaic-floor patches of the larger, earlier church, with a *hokhláki* floor and stone barrel arches (key from the nearby kafenío).

The onward road to Skiádhi monastery, 6km distant, is shown incorrectly on most maps. Take the Kataviá-bound road initially, then bear right onto an unsigned dirt track after about 2km; the last 4km are quite badly surfaced. Known formally as Panayía Skiadhení, **Skiádhi monastery** – despite its undistinguished modern buildings – was founded in the thirteenth century to house a miraculous icon of the Virgin; in the fifteenth century a heretic stabbed the painting, and blood flowed from the wound in the Mother of God's cheek. The offending hand was, needless to say, instantly paralysed; the fissure, and intriguing brown stains around it, are still visible. The immediate surroundings of the monastery are rather dreary since a fire in 1992, but the views west are stunning. Tiny Khténia islet is said to be a petrified pirate ship, rendered into stone by the Virgin in answer to prayers from desperate locals. Except on September 7–8, the festival of the icon, you can stay the night on arrangement with the caretaker.

West of Kataviá, the completely paved island loop road emerges onto the deserted, sandy southwest coast; Skiádhi can more easily be reached from this side as well. If freelance camping and nudism are your thing, this is the place to indulge, though you'll need to be completely self-sufficient, and only strong swimmers should venture far offshore here.

The nearest village is nondescript, agricultural **APOLAKKIÁ**, 7km north of the Skiádhi turning and equipped with a bona fide **hotel**, **tavernas** and shops. Northwest the road leads to Monólithos, while the northeasterly bearing leads quickly and pleasantly back to Yennádhi via Váti. Due north, just below an irrigation reservoir, the tiny frescoed chapel of **Áyios Yeóryios Várdhas** (unlocked) is worth the short detour if you have your own transport.

Hálki

Hálki, a tiny (20 square kilometres), waterless, limestone speck west of Rhodes, is a fully fledged member of the Dodecanese, though all but about three hundred of the former population of three thousand have emigrated (mostly to Rhodes or to Florida) in the wake of a devastating sponge blight during the early 1900s. Despite a renaissance through tourism in recent years, the island is tranquil compared with its big neighbour, with a slightly weird, hushed atmosphere. The big event of the day is the arrival of the regular afternoon kaïki from Kámiros Skála on Rhodes.

Hálki first attracted outside attention in 1983, when UNESCO designated it the "isle of peace and friendship", and the seat of regular international youth conferences. Some 150 crumbling houses were to be restored at UNESCO's expense as accommodation for delegates, but by 1987 just one hotel had been completed, and the only sign of "peace and friendship" was a stream of UNESCO and Athenian bureaucrats staging musical binges under the rubric of "ecological seminars". Confronted with an apparent scam, the islanders sent UNESCO packing and contracted two UK package operators to complete restorations and bring in paying guests.

Emborió

The skyline of **EMBORIÓ**, the port and only habitation, is pierced by the tallest free-standing clocktower in the Dodecanese and the belfry of Áyios Nikólaos church. Emborió's restored houses are pretty much block-booked from April to October by the tour companies mentioned; independent travellers will be lucky to find anything at all on spec, even early or late in the season. Non-package **accommodation**, all requiring advance reservations, includes the delightful, en-suite *Captain's House* (☎0241/45 201; ③), with the feel of a French country hotel, whose English manageress can point you in likely directions if she's full; *Pension Keanthi* (☎0241/45 334; ④) near the school, with high-ceiling rooms and stone walls; or the hillside rooms at *Pension Argyrenia* (☎0241/45 205; ③), below the municipal cistern. Of the half-dozen **tavernas** along the field-stoned, pedestrianized waterfront, *Mavri Thalassa* near the fish depot is one of the best for portion size and freshness, with a stress on seafood, while *Houvardas*, near the opposite end of the quay has proven reliable for *mayireftá* over the years. Amongst several bars and cafés, the standout must be the 1999-opened sweet shop near the base of the jetty, with puddings and own-made ice cream to die for. There's a **post office**, four well-stocked stores, two good bakeries cranking out a range of bread and pies, plus two **travel agencies** which sell boat tickets, change money (there's no bank) and at slow times just might be able to find you a vacancy amongst the studios they manage on behalf of the UK companies.

The rest of the island

Three kilometres west lies the old pirate-safe village of **HORIÓ**, abandoned in the 1950s but still crowned by the Knights' castle. Except during the major August 14–15 festival, the church here is kept securely locked to protect its frescoes. Across the valley, the little monastery of **Stavrós** is the venue for its other big island bash on September 14. There's little else to see or do inland, though you can spend three hours **walking** across the island on the 1998-vintage dirt track, the extension of the cement "Tarpon Springs Boulevard" donated by the expatriate community in Florida. At the end of the road you'll come to the monastery of **Ayíou Ioánnou Prodhrómou**; the caretaking family there can put you up in a cell (except around August 29, the other big festival date), but you'll need to bring supplies. The terrain en route is monotonous, but compensated by views over half the Dodecanese and Turkey.

Longish but narrow **Póndamos**, fifteen minutes' walk west of Emborió, is the only sandy beach on Hálki, and even this has had to be artificially supplemented. The sole facility is the somewhat pricey *Nick's Pondamos Taverna*, serving lunch only. Small and pebbly **Yialí**, west of and considerably below Horió via a jeep track, lies an hour's hike away from Póndamos. A thirty-minute walk north of Emborió lies **Kánia**, with a rocky foreshore and a rather industrial ambience from both power lines and the island's only petrol pump to one side.

Since these three coves are no great shakes, it's worth signing on at Emborió quay for **boat excursions** to more remote beaches. More or less at the centre of Hálki's southern shore, directly below Horió's castle, **Trahiá** consists of two coves to either side of an isthmus. North-coast beaches figuring as excursion-boat destinations include the pretty fjord of **Aréta**, **Áyios Yeóryios** just beyond, and the remote double bay of **Dhýo Yialí**. Of these, Aréta is the most attractive, and the only one accessible overland (in about two hours) by experienced hillwalkers equipped with the *Chalki, Island of Peace and Friendship* map based on the old Italian topographical survey products.

Alimniá (Alimiá) islet

One of the more promoted local boat excursions visits **Alimniá (Alimiá) islet**, roughly halfway between Hálki and Rhodes. Despite more well-water and greenery and a better harbour than Hálki's, the deserted village here, overlooked by a few palm trees and yet another Knights' castle, was completely abandoned by the 1960s. The locals were initially deported during World War II after they admitted to assisting British commandos sent in April 1944 to sabotage the enemy submarines who used the deep harbour here. The seven commandos themselves were captured here by the Nazis, bundled off first to Rhodes, then to Thessaloníki, where six were summarily executed as spies rather than regular prisoners of war; Kurt Waldheim allegedly countersigned their death sentences.

Interesting history acknowledged, Alimniá is probably not a place you'd want to be stuck for an entire day. Excursions on offer are pricey (about 6500dr), beach space very limited, the castle a long, hot walk up and the crumbling village behind its salt marsh unedifying. If you snorkel in the outer bay beyond little Áyios Mínas monastery, you might glimpse outlines of the Italian-built submarine pens to one side of the deep bay. The former inhabitants only show up to graze livestock, or on the date of the annual festival (Áyios Yeóryios).

Kastellórizo (Meyísti)

Kastellórizo's official name, Méyisti (biggest), seems more an act of defiance than a statement of fact. While the largest of a tiny group of islands, it is actually the smallest of the Dodecanese, over seventy nautical miles from its nearest Greek neighbour (Rhodes) but barely more than a nautical mile off the Turkish coast at the narrowest straits. At night its lights are quite outnumbered by those of the Turkish town of Kaş, across the bay, with whom Kastellórizo generally has excellent relations.

Less than a century ago there were almost 14,000 people here, supported by a fleet of schooners that transported goods, mostly timber, from the Greek towns of Kalamaki (now Kalkan) and Andifelos (Kaş) on the Anatolian mainland opposite. But the withdrawal of autonomy after the 1908 "Young Turk" revolution, the Italian seizure of the other Dodecanese in 1912 and an inconclusive 1913–1915 revolt against the Turks sent the island into decline. A French occupation of 1915–21 prompted destructive shelling from the Ottoman-held mainland, a harbinger of worse to come (see below). Shipowners failed to modernize their fleets upon the advent of steam power, preferring to sell ships to the British for the Dardanelles campaign, and the new frontier between the island and republican Turkey, combined with the expulsion of all Anatolian Greeks in 1923, deprived any remaining vessels of their trade. During the 1930s the island enjoyed a brief renaissance when it became a major stopover point for French and Italian seaplanes, but events at the close of World War II put an end to any hopes of the island's continued viability.

When Italy capitulated to the Allies in the autumn of 1943, a few hundred Commonwealth commandos occupied Kastellórizo, departing of their own accord in spring 1944 – leaving the island deserted and vulnerable to the attentions of pirates. In early July, a harbour fuel dump caught (or was set on) fire and an adjacent arsenal exploded, taking with it more than half of the two thousand houses on Kastellórizo. Even before these events most of the population had left for Rhodes, Athens, Australia (especially Perth) and North America. Today there are fewer than two hundred people living permanently on Kastellórizo, largely maintained by remittances from over 30,000 emigrants and by subsidies from the Greek government, which fears that the island will revert to Turkey should their numbers diminish any further.

Yet Kastellórizo may have a future of sorts, thanks to expat "Kassies" who have begun renovating their crumbling ancestral houses as a retirement or holiday home. Each summer, the population is swelled by returnees of Kassie ancestry, some of whom celebrate traditional weddings in the **Áyios Konstandínos** cathedral at Horáfia, which incorporates ancient columns from Patara in Asia Minor. Access has also improved since the 1980s: an airport (domestic flights only) was completed, the harbour dredged to accommodate larger ferries, and the island designated an official port of entry to Greece, which has appealed to both yachties and conventional travellers crossing from Turkey.

Perhaps the biggest recent boost for Kastellórizo was its role as location for the 1990 film *Mediterraneo*, which has resulted in a tidal wave of Italian visitors (though the island in fact gets a broad spectrum of tourists). You will either love it and stay a week, or crave escape after a day; detractors dismiss Kastellórizo as a human zoo maintained by the government for the edification of nationalists, while partisans celebrate an atmospheric, barely commercialized outpost of Hellenism.

Kastellórizo Town

The current population is concentrated in the northern town of **KASTELLÓRIZO** – supposedly the finest natural harbour between Beirut and Fethiye on the Turkish coast – and its little "suburb" of **Mandhráki**, just over the fire-blasted hill with its half-ruined castle of the Knights. Its keep now houses the local **museum** (Tues–Sun 7am–2.30pm; free), with displays including plates from a Byzantine shipwreck, frescoes rescued from decaying churches and a reconstruction of an ancient basilica on the site of today's gaudy Ayíou Yeoryíou Santrapé church at Horáfia. Just below and beyond the museum, in the cliff-face opposite Psorádhia islet, is Greece's only **Lycian house-tomb**; it's sign-posted from the shoreline walkway, up some steps beside the first wooden lamp standard.

Most of the town's surviving mansions are ranged along the waterfront, their tiled roofs, wooden balconies and long, narrow windows having obvious counterparts in the originally Greek-built houses of Kalkan and Kaş just across the water. Just one street back, however, many properties are derelict – abandonment having succeeded where the World War I shelling, a 1926 earthquake and the 1944 explosions failed; sepia-toned posters and postcards on sale of the town in its prime are poignant evidence of its later decline.

Practicalities

Kastellórizo is not really geared up for large numbers of visitors, though **pensions** in the old houses have been upgraded of late to en-suite status. If you're not met off the boat, the best budget en-suite options include the restored mansion-pension of Damian Mavrothalassitis (☎0241/49 208; ②); the nearly adjacent *Kristallo* (☎0241/41 209; ②); and the waterfront *Mediterraneo* (☎0241/49 368; ②), on the northwest quay. Relative luxury is available, for a price, at the *Hotel Meyisti* (☎0241/49 272, fax 49 221; ④; April–Oct), on the opposite side of the bay from the ferry jetty, beyond the *Mediterraneo*.

Apart from fish, goat meat and various fig-based sweets, plus whatever can be smuggled over from Kaş, Kastellórizo has to import foodstuffs and drinking water from Rhodes; prices when eating out can consequently be higher than usual, with the further pretext of the island's celebrity status. The two most prominent waterfront **tavernas** have had a long and pernicious acquaintance with the yacht trade – best to continue to the *Sydney* for reliably fresh and affordable seafood and meat grills. Another good quayside choice is *Kas-Bar*, just left of the Italian market arcade, where a mother and son team serve up fine grills, vegetable dishes and cold mezédhes nightly except perhaps Thursday in off-season. Two to recommend inland are *Iy Orea Meyisti*, run by Savvas Mavrothalassitis and his wife, and *Ta Platania*, opposite Áyios Konstandínos in Horáfia, good for daily-changing *mayireftá* and frequently homemade desserts. **Nightlife** mostly occurs in *barákia* along the quay, though English Kassie Mariana Ftiara's *The Magic Shop*, inland in the ground floor of her restored house, is perhaps the best with its range of drinks and light snacks in an oriental ambience.

The **post office** sits behind *Hotel Meyisti*; there's no bank. Most ferry companies are represented by one of several grocery stores, while the only travel agency, grumpy DiZi Travel, is the Olympic Airways representative; at busy times, you should book return flights immediately on arrival if you've not done so in Ródhos Town. A public transfer van shuttles between town and airstrip at flight times.

It is usually possible to arrange a ride over **to Turkey** on one of five local boats, and possibly one of the three Kaş-based boats which appear regularly. The standard day-return fee is 4000dr, and you may have to leave your passport with the authorities the night before. Since Kastellórizo is a legal port of entry to Greece, they technically cannot prevent EU nationals arriving **from Kaş**, which is also an officially entry–exit point for Turkey.

The rest of the island

Kastellórizo's austere hinterland is predominantly bare rock, flecked with stunted vegetation; incredibly, two generations ago much of the countryside was carefully tended, producing wine of some quality and in quantity. A rudimentary road system links points between Mandhráki and the airport, but there aren't many specific places to go along it and no scooters for rent. Karstic cliffs drop sheer to the sea, offering no anchorage for boats except at the main town, Mandhráki and Návlakas fjord (see below).

Rural monasteries and ruins

Heat permitting, you can hike up the obvious, zigzag stair-path, then south through desolate fire-charred scrub to the rural **monastery of Áyios Yeóryios toú Vounioú**, forty minutes away. The sixteenth to eighteenth-century church boasts fine rib-vaulting and a carved *témblon*, but its highlight is a crypt, with the frescoed, subterranean chapel of **Áyios Harálambos** off to one side; access is via a steep, narrow passage descending from the church floor – bring a flashlight and grubby clothes, and get the key first from the keeper, who lives behind the *Little Paris* taverna. Alternatively, a fifteen-minute track-walk west of the port leads to the peaceful monastery of **Ayías Triádhas**, perched on the saddle marked by the OTE tower, and an army strongpoint (off-limits) – one of many sprung up here since the Ímia crisis (see p.857).

The onward path arrives after 25 minutes at the ancient citadel of **Paleókastro**, where you'll find masonry from Classical to medieval times, a warren of vaulted chambers, tunnels, cisterns plus another, ruined monastery with a *hokhláki* courtyard. From any of the heights above town there are tremendous views north over sixty kilometres of Anatolian coast.

The shoreline and Rhó

Swimming is complicated by a total absence of beaches and an abundance of sea urchins and razor-sharp limestone reefs; the safest entry near town lies beyond the graveyard at Mandhráki, or at the tiny inlet of **Áyios Stéfanos**, a forty-minute walk north of town along the obvious trail beginning behind the post office. Once away from the shore, you're rewarded by clear waters with a rich variety of marine life. From Áyios Yeóryios toú Vounoú, you can continue 45 minutes further on foot, partly on a French-built *kalderími*, to the multi-lobed fjord of **Návlakas**, a favourite mooring spot for yachts and fishing boats. The French built the cobbled way to facilitate offloading supplies here during World War I, safe from Ottoman artillery. Uniquely on Kastellórizo, this bay is sea-urchin-free, with freshwater seeps keeping the temperature brisk; there's superb snorkelling to 25-metre depths off the south wall.

Over on the southeast coast, accessible only by a 45-minute boat ride from town, the grotto of **Perastá** deserves a look for its stalactites and strange blue-light effects; the low entrance, negotiable only by inflatable raft, gives little hint of the enormous chamber within, where seals occasionally are glimpsed. Two-hour raft trips (2000dr minimum per person) visit only the cave, or for 5000dr minimum on a larger kaïki, you can take it in as part of a five-hour tour that includes Rhó islet.

Should you make the trip out to **Rhó**, the tomb of *Iý Kyrá tís Rhó* (**The Lady of Rhó**), aka Dhespina Akhladhiotis (1893–1982) – who resolutely hoisted the Greek flag each day on that islet in defiance of the Turks on the mainland – is the first thing you see when you dock at the sandy, northwestern harbour. From here a path heads southeast for 25 minutes to the islet's southerly port, past the side trail up to the intact Hellenistic fortress on the very summit. The islet has no facilities – just a few soldiers to prevent Turkish military landings or poachings of the hundreds of goats – so bring your own food and water.

Sými

Sými's most pressing problem, lack of water, is in many ways also its saving grace. As with so many dry, rocky Dodecanese, water must be imported at great expense from Rhodes, pending completion of a reservoir in the distant future. As a result the island can't hope to support more than a handful of large hotels; instead, hundreds of people are shipped in daily during the season from Rhodes, relieved of their money and sent back. This arrangement suits both the islanders and those visitors lucky enough to stay longer; many foreigners return regularly, or even own houses here.

Once beyond the inhabited areas, you'll find a surprisingly attractive island that has retained some of its original forest cover of junipers, valonea oaks and even a few pines – ideal walking country in spring or autumn (though not midsummer, when temperatures are among the highest in Greece). Another prominent feature of the landscape are dozens of tiny monasteries, usually locked except on their patron saint's day, though their cisterns with a can on a string to fetch water are usually accessible.

Sými Town

SÝMI, the island's capital and only proper town, consists of **Yialós**, the excellent natural port, and **Horió**, on the hillside above. Incredibly, less than a hundred years ago the place was richer and more populous (25,000) than Rhodes, its wealth generated by shipbuilding and sponge-diving, skills nurtured since pre-Classical times. Under the Ottomans, Sými, like most of the smaller Dodecanese, enjoyed considerable autonomy in exchange for a yearly tribute in sponges to the sultan; but the Italian-imposed frontier, the 1919–22 Greco-Turkish war, the advent of synthetic sponges and the gradual replacement of the

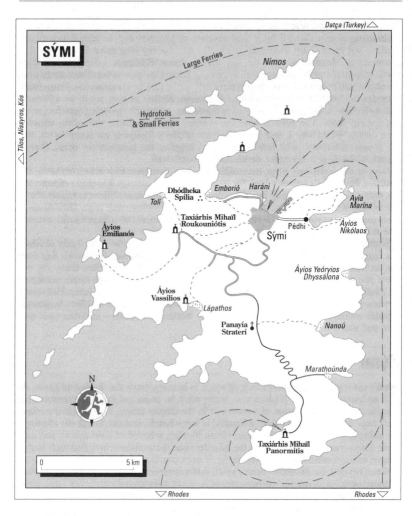

crews by Kalymniots spelt doom for the local economy. Vestiges of past nautical glories remain in still-active boatyards at Pédhi and Haráni, but today the souvenir-shop sponges come entirely from overseas, and the recent boom notwithstanding, a significant fraction of the magnificent nineteenth-century mansions stands roofless and empty.

The approximately three thousand remaining Symiotes are scattered fairly evenly throughout the mixture of Neoclassical and more typical island dwellings; despite the surplus of properties many outsiders have preferred to build anew, rather than restore derelict shells accessible only by donkey or on foot. As on Kastellórizo, a wartime ammunition blast – this time set off by the retreating Germans – levelled hundreds of houses up in Horió. Shortly afterwards, the official surrender of the Dodecanese to the Allies was signed here on May 8, 1945: a plaque marks the spot at the present-day *Restaurant Les Catherinettes*.

At the lively **port**, an architecturally protected area since the early 1970s, spice and sponge stalls plus a few jewellery shops are thronged with Rhodes-based trippers between 11am and 3pm, and exhaust fumes from four or five excursion boats envelop the quay. But one street back from the water the more peaceful pace of village life takes over, with sheep and chickens roaming free-range. Two massive stair-paths, the Kalí Stráta and Katarráktes, effectively deter many of the day-trippers and are most dramatic towards sunset; large ruins along the lower reaches of the Kalí Stráta are lonely and sinister after dark, though these too are now scheduled for restoration.

A series of blue arrows through Horió leads to the excellent local **museum** (Tues–Sun 10am–2pm; 500dr). Housed in a fine old mansion at the back of the village, the collection concentrates on Byzantine and medieval Sými, with exhibits on frescoes in isolated, locked churches and a gallery of medieval icons, as well as antiquarian maps and the inevitable ethnographic wing. The nearby **Hatziagapitos Mansion** has been refurbished as an annexe; there, wonderful carved wooden chests are the main exhibits, along with fragmentary wall-paintings. On the way back to central Horió, the nineteenth-century pharmacy, with its apothecary jars and wooden drawers labelled for exotic herbal remedies, is worth a look.

At the very pinnacle of things, a **castle of the Knights** occupies the site of Sými's ancient acropolis, and you can glimpse a stretch of Cyclopean wall on one side. A dozen churches grace Horió; that of the Ascension, inside the fortifications, is a replacement of the one blown to bits when the Germans detonated the munitions cached there. One of the bells in the new belfry is the nose-cone of a thousand-pound bomb, hung as a memorial.

Practicalities

Excursion boats run daily to Sými from Mandhráki in Ródhos Town, but you'll come under considerable pressure at the quay to buy an expensive (approximately 5000dr) return ticket – not what you want if you're off island-hopping. Instead, take the islanders' own craft – the *Symi I*, the catamaran *Symi II* or the hydrofoil *Aigli* – which between them provide an *epivatikó* (normal passenger) service at 2000–3000dr per person. The *Symi I* or *II* departs Rhodes four days weekly at 6pm, returning the next day at 6–6.30am, while the hydrofoil follows a far more variable service six days weekly, though typically it leaves Mandhráki at 2.30 or 6pm, returning 7am. A few times a week there are mainline ferries as well in either direction. ANES, the outlet for *Symi I/Symi II/Aigli* tickets, maintains a booth on the quay; Sunny Land, in the marketplace lanes, is the agent for most inter-island **ferries** except for DANE Lines.

There's no official tourism bureau but the island's English-language advertiser-newsletter, *The Symi Visitor* (free), is literate and has current island gossip with informative features. The **post office** in the Italian "palace" is open standard hours; of the two **banks**, the Ioniki/Ionian is more efficient and has a cash dispenser. During the season a small green bus shuttles between Yialós and Pédhi via Horió on the hour (returning at the half-hour) until 11pm. There are also four **taxis**, and a few pricey outlets for **motor-scooter hire** (5000dr and up daily), though this is a perfect island for boat and walking excursions. A **laundry** operates in the grid of market lanes, resorted to by those whose hosts forbid clothes-washing in rooms.

ACCOMMODATION

Accommodation for independent travellers is somewhat limited, though the situation isn't nearly so bad as on Hálki; proprietors tend not to meet arriving boats. Studios, rather than simple rooms, predominate, and package operators control most of these. Despite asphyxiating summer heat, air conditioning and ceiling fans are rarely found – go for north-facing and/or balconied units when possible. If you're planning in advance, the BBC-award-winning *www.symi-island.com* site is worth consulting; there's visual information on lodging, and you can make bookings either through the site or by phone (UK: ☎01782/815231, Sými: ☎0241/72 693).

Albatros, marketplace (☎0241/72 784 or 71 829). Partial sea views from this exquisite small hotel; pleasant second-floor breakfast salon, air con. ④. The same family have five apartments at *Villa Thalassa* on the south quay opposite the clock tower, with either air con or balconies, all suitable for families or groups of four. ⑥.

Anastasia, behind the post office (☎0241/71 364). Pleasantly set hotel though with limited views, this has parquet-floored rooms plus a couple of studios, with some package allotment however. ④.

Fiona, at the top of the Kalí Stráta (☎0241/72 088 or 72 755). Mock-traditional hotel building whose large airy rooms have double beds and stunning rooms; breakfast in mid-air on common balcony. ④. Managed by affable returned Greek-Australian Nikos Halkitis and family, who also offer *The Cottages*, four studio units in two adjacent old houses in Horió. ⑤.

Jean Manship, c/o Jean & Tonic Bar (☎0241/71 819 8pm–1am Greek time, fax 72 172). Jean has two traditional houses in Horió, both suitable for couples and with stunning views. ④.

Katerina Tsakiris Rooms (☎0241/71 813). Just a handful of very simple en-suite rooms with common kitchen and grandstand view; reservations essential. ③.

Kokona, at the rear of the marketplace, by the clinic (☎0241/71 451). En-suite if plain hotel, the upstairs rooms with balconies (though no sea views). ③.

Les Catherinettes, above eponymous restaurant, north quay (☎0241/72 698, *marina-epe@rho.forthnet.gr*). Creaky but spotless pension in a historic building with painted ceilings and sea-view balconies for most rooms. ④.

Rooms Egli, base of the Kalí Stráta (☎0241/71 392). Basic (non-en-suite), but clean enough rooms, and usually has vacancies when everyone else is full. ②.

Taxiarhis Apartments, edge of Horió overlooking Pédhi (☎0241/72 012). Secluded, well-designed row of studios with common areas, though some German package groups. ⑤.

EATING

You're best off avoiding most **eateries** on the north and west quays of the port, where menus, prices and attitudes have been terminally warped by the day-trip trade. Away from these areas, you've a fair range of choice among *kultúra* tavernas, old-style *mayireftá* places, a few genuine ouzeris and even a traditional kafenío or two.

To Amoni, far side of main platía, Yialós. An excellent, inexpensive, authentic ouzerí, where big helpings of liver, sausage and seafood titbits accompany the usual fried vegetarian starters and mainland bulk wine. Open most of the year; seating indoors and out.

Dhimitris, south quay, on the way out of town. Excellent, family-run seafood-stressing ouzerí with exotic items such as *hokhlióalo* (sea snails), *foúskes* (mock oysters), *spinóalo* (pinna-shell flesh) and the indigenous miniature shrimps, along with the more usual plates and lots of vegetarian starters. Nov–May this outdoor premises moves inside to *Tasty*, in the bazaar next to *O Meraklis*.

Ellinikon, off main square, Yialós. The more reasonable (6000–7000dr a head) of the *kultúra* tavernas, with own-made pasta and desserts, plus 140 varieties of Greek wine (their main selling point).

Elpidha, north quay. This landmark with wooden chairs, a hundred paces in from the clocktower, is a hallowed snack and drinks café and marvellous people-watching vantage.

O Ilios, west quay. British-run, with "English" or healthy full breakfasts, plus vegetarian meals and own-made cakes all hours. Also does picnic hampers for beach outings – notify them the previous day.

To Klima, near top of Kalí Stráta, Horió. British-run place that's an excellent source of breakfast (after 9.30am); also does Indian food on Saturday nights, and an all-you-can eat buffet on Sundays – Greek food at other times.

O Meraklis, rear of the bazaar. Polite service and fair portions of well-priced *mayireftá* and mezéd-hes make this a reliable bet April–Dec. Sample meal: beans, beets, dips, and roast lamb with potatoes as a tender main course.

Mythos, south quay near taxi rank. Professionally run, Athens-style ouzerí where your host reels off the plates of the day; moderately pricey.

Monastery on Níssyros

Orthodox priest

Venetian houses in the old harbour, Réthymnon

View of Kástro and Hóra, Astypálea

Windmill at sunset, Páros

Tomatoes drying, Híos

Paleohóra, Crete

Ferry at Foúrni

Church in Kástro, Síkinos

Café terrace, Kós

Platía Ippokrátous, Rhodes Town

Shipwreck Bay, Zákynthos

Flagstone colours, Yialós, Sými Island

Kaïki-building, Pátmos, Dodecanese

Pahos, west quay, beside *O Ilios* (no sign). The old-boys' kafenío, in operation since World War II, and a classic spot for a sundown oúzo.

Syllogos, top of Kalí Stráta in Horió. Aspires to be a *kultúra* taverna, and popular with Greeks and Italians in summer; recipes aren't that imaginative, but ingredients are fresh and presentation home-style.

Yiorgos, by Kalí Stráta in Horió. Jolly, supper-only institution since 1977, with seating on a pebble-mosaic courtyard; service is slipshod, but excellent-value food such as feta-stuffed peppers, spinach-rice, chicken in mushroom-wine sauce, and grilled fish when available.

DRINKING

Nightlife is long and occasionally loud, with a number of bars owned by expatriates. Up in Horió, convivial *Jean & Tonic* is the heart and soul of nightlife, catering to a mixed clientele until the small hours most of the year; a short way down the Kalí Stráta, *Kali Strata* is a low-key place with unbeatable views and excellent wide-ranging music. Down at Yialós, *Vapori*, the oldest bar on the island, and former adjacent rival *Mina's* have merged, welcoming customers with desserts and breakfast as well as drinks. However, the local nickname for their noisy alley is still "the Gaza Strip", and some prefer *Katoi* on the south quay, a no-touts, no-hassle, low-key bar.

Around the island

Sými has no big sandy beaches, but there are plenty of pebbly stretches at the heads of the deep, protected bays which indent the coastline. **PÉDHI**, a 45-minute walk from Yialós, retains some of its former identity as a fishing hamlet, with enough water in the plain behind – the island's largest – to support a few vegetable gardens. The beach is poor, though, and patronage from yachts and the giant *Pedhi Beach* hotel (packages only) has considerably bumped up prices at the four local **tavernas**, of which the most reasonably priced and authentic is *Iy Kamares* at the far south end. Many will opt for another twenty minutes of walking via a rough but obvious path along the south shore of the almost landlocked bay to **Áyios Nikólaos**. The only all-sand beach on Sými, this offers sheltered swimming, tamarisks for shade and a mediocre taverna. Alternatively, a paint-splodge-marked path on the north side of the inlet leads in just over half an hour to **Ayía Marína**, where there's a minuscule beach, a shingle and sunbed lido, another snack bar and a monastery-capped islet to which you can easily swim.

Around Yialós, you'll find tiny **NOS (Navtikós Ómilos Sýmis)** "beach" ten minutes past the boatyards at Haráni, but there's sun here only until lunchtime and it's usually packed with day-trippers. You can continue along the cement-paved coast road, or cut inland from the Yialós platía past the abandoned desalination plant, to appealing **Emborió** (Nimborió) bay, with a poor **taverna** (*Metapontis*) and an artificially sand-strewn beach a bit beyond. Inland from this are Byzantine mosaic fragments under a protective shelter, and, nearby, a catacomb complex known locally as **Dhódheka Spília**.

Plenty of other, more secluded coves are accessible by energetic walkers with sturdy footwear, or those prepared to pay a modest sum for the taxi-boats (daily in season 10am–1pm, returning 4–5pm; one-way fares available to the nearer bays cited above). These are the best way to reach the southern bays of **Marathoúnda** and **Nanoú**, and the only method of getting to the spectacular, fjord of **Áyios Yeóryios Dhyssálona**. Dhyssálona lacks a taverna and lies in shade after 1pm, while unalluring Marathoúnda consists of coarse, slimy pebbles, making Nanoú the most popular destination for day-trips. The 200-metre beach there consists of gravel, sand and small pebbles, with a scenic backdrop of pines and a reasonable taverna (squid, chips and salad) behind. It's also possible to reach Nanoú overland, by taking a motor scooter to Panayía Straterí chapel and then descending a scenic gorge for some 45 minutes.

For more hiking adventures, you can cross the island from Horió in ninety minutes to **Áyios Vasílios**, the most scenic of the gulfs with its Lápathos beach; in about the same time to **Tolí**, a deserted, west-facing cove, also accessible from Emborió; or in three hours, partly through forest, to **Áyios Emilianós** at the island's extreme west end, where a little monastery is tethered to the body of Sými by a causeway. On the way to the latter you should look in at the monastery of **Taxiárhis Mihaïl Roukouniótis** (daily 9am–2pm & 4–8pm) Sými's oldest, with naive eighteenth-century frescoes and a peculiar ground plan: the current *katholikón* is actually superimposed on a lower, thirteenth-century structure abandoned after being burnt and pillaged by pirates during the 1400s, though a fine fresco of St Lawrence (Áyios Lavréntios) survives behind the altar screen. Resident, trilingual Father Amfilohios will be able to tell you about anything else you might possibly wish to know about the place.

The Archangel is also honoured at the huge monastery of **Taxiárhis Mihaïl Panormítis** near the southern tip of the island, Sými's biggest rural attraction and generally the first port of call for the excursion boats from Rhodes. These allow only a quick thirty-minute tour; if you want more time, you'll have to come by scooter from Yialós (though the someday-to-be-paved road down from the central escarpment is terrible, with nine hairpin bends), or arrange to stay the night (2000dr minimum donation) in the *xenónas* set aside for pilgrims. There are large numbers of these in summer, as Mihaïl has been adopted as the patron of sailors in the Dodecanese.

Like many of Sými's monasteries, Panormítis is of recent (eighteenth-century) vintage and was thoroughly pillaged during the last war, so don't expect too much of the building or its treasures. An appealing pebble-mosaic court surrounds the central *katholikón*, tended by the monk Gabriel, lit by an improbable number of oil lamps and graced by a fine *témblon*, though the frescoes are recent and mediocre. One of the two small museums (400dr admits to both) contains a strange mix of precious antiques, exotic junk (stuffed crocodiles and koalas, elephant tusks), votive offerings, models of ships and a chair piled with messages-in-bottles brought here by Aegean currents – the idea being that if the bottle or toy boat arrived, the sender got their prayer answered. There's a small beach, a shop/kafenío, a bakery and a **taverna** (*Panormio*) popular with passengers of the many yachts calling in. Near the taverna stands a memorial commemorating three Greeks, including the monastery's abbot, executed in February 1944 by the Germans for aiding British commandos.

Tílos

The small, blissfully quiet island of **Tílos**, with an official population of about three hundred (dwindling to eighty in winter), is one of the least frequented of the Dodecanese, though it can be visited on a day-trip by hydrofoil once or twice a week. Why anyone would want to come for just a few hours is unclear: while it's a great place to rest on the beach or go walking, there is nothing very striking at first glance. After a few days, however, you may have stumbled on several of the seven small castles of the Knights of St John which stud the crags, or found some of the inconspicuous medieval chapels clinging to the hillsides.

Tílos shares the characteristics of its closest neighbours: limestone mountains resembling those of Hálki, plus volcanic lowlands, pumice beds and red-lava sand as on Níssyros. Though rugged and scrubby on its heights, the island has ample water – from springs or pumped up from the agricultural plains – and clusters of oak and terebinth near the cultivated areas. From many points on the island you've startling views across to Kós, Sými, Turkey, Níssyros, Hálki, Rhodes and even (weather permitting) Kárpathos.

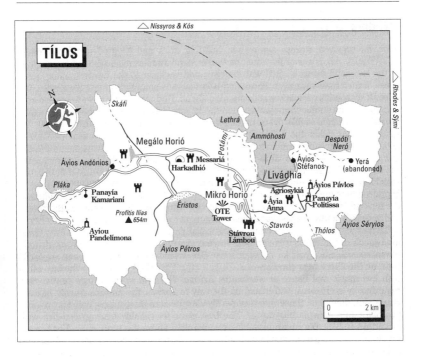

Since the mid-1990s, however, development on Tílos has threatened to reverse the conditions which many visitors have historically come to enjoy; besides the Dodge-City atmosphere of Livádhia (see p.660), a hyperactive bulldozing programme has scarred virtually every mountain in the east of the island. A 1998-vintage road from the telecom-tower hill, heading east along the summit ridge, is intended to facilitate proposed fish farms at Thólos and Áyios Séryios, which will finish those coves as leisure beaches. Other manic schemes proposed for the immediate future include a road down the pristine Potámi ravine to Lethrá beach (to serve a proposed taverna), and around the coast past Áyios Stéfanos towards a planned mega-hotel. The long-running foreigners' interest group, FOTA (Friends of Tílos Association), has effectively decided not to stick its neck out on these issues and to emphasize its role as the expatriates' social-events co-ordinating committee, leaving activist environmental campaigns to new rival organization Tilos 2000 (57 Avenue Jules Malou, Brussels B1040, ☎32/2/646 7098, *nigel.gardner@spp.cec.be*, or c/o Nigel Gardner, Megálo Horió, Tílos).

Tílos's main necessary road, widened in 1999 but awaiting new asphalt, runs 7km from Livádhia, the port village, to Megálo Horió, the capital and only other significant habitation. A public **minibus** links the two, and services are theoretically scheduled to coincide with ferry arrivals; at other times the bus makes up to six runs daily along the Livádhia–Éristos stretch. There are also two **taxis**, or you can rent **scooters** from two outlets in Livádhia. The new filling station lies between Livádhia and Megálo Horió. Non-wheeled transport includes **boat trips** (offered through Blue Sky Restaurant or David's Bikes, summer only) and your own two feet – many visitors come specifically to **walk**, assisted by the extremely accurate map prepared by Baz "Paris" Ward and sold locally.

Livádhia

With its unpaved streets, unfinished building sites and higgledy-piggledy layout, **LIVÁDHIA** makes a poor introduction to the island, but it remains the better equipped of the two settlements to deal with tourists, and is closer to the best remaining path-hikes. If they have vacancies, **room** and **hotel** owners sometimes meet the ferries, but in peak season it's certainly worth phoning ahead. Budget options include several consecutive outfits on the shore just beyond the Italian "palace", for example *Paradise* (aka *Stamatia's*; ☎0241/44 334; ②) or two studios next door at *Paraskevi* (☎0241/44 280; ②). Inland, go for either the 1994-refurbished and good-value *Hotel Livadhia* (☎0241/44 266; ②), with en-suite rooms and two "penthouse" units, or the well-appointed *Studios Irinna* (☎0241/44 305; ②), above the ironmonger's which runs it. More luxury means the friendly *Eleni Beach* on the shore about halfway around the bay (☎0241/44 062; ③), with large airy rooms; the *Faros* at the extreme end of the bay (☎0241/44 068; ②), widely praised for calm and its hospitable managing family; or, 200m inland from mid-beach, the top-end *Irini* (☎0241/44 293, fax 44 238; ③), with a pool, all mod cons in the rooms and generally a few on-spec vacancies in amongst the Laskarina package clients here.

There must be twenty **tavernas** around Livádhia, though some churn out lazy, bland food (such as tinned carrots and peas in your rice) for timid package patrons. Among the more authentic spots for a no-nonsense Greek feed are *Irinna*, doling out *mayireftá* right on the shore near the *Paradise*; *Zorba's* (aka *Vangelis's*), east along the bay, often with live music and dance at weekends; *Kritikos Psistaria* in the village centre, well regarded by carnivores; and inland on the way to *Zorba's*, the *Pantelis Souvla Maria's Pizza* (sic), doing just those things superbly, despite zero atmosphere courtesy of plastic chairs and a purple bug-zapper. The best place for reliably fresh grilled fish with mezédhes is *Blue Sky*, an unmissable eyrie perched above the ferry dock. For **breakfast** (plus evening snacks and homemade desserts), Anglo-Italian *Joanna's Café*, just up from Kritikos, is hard to beat, also with a long list of strong cocktails. *Omonia* – under the trees strung with fairy lights, near the post office – is the enduringly popular "traditional" alternative for a sundowner or breakfast. Livelier organized **nightlife** in or near Livádhia is limited to three bars: *Cafe Ino* on the shore near Irinna for the trendy set, the new *La Luna* at the far east end of bay (nightly in summer, weekends otherwise) and a durable music pub in Mikró Horió (see below).

There's a **post office**, but no bank or cash dispenser, so come with sufficient Greek cash or submit to the mercies of Stefanakis Travel, the sole ferry agency, which also has a metered phone in the unlikely event that both village card-phones are out of order. A **bakery** and several well-stocked **supermarkets** round out the roster of amenities.

Around the island

From Livádhia you can trail-walk an hour north along the obvious path to the pebble bay of **Lethrá**, or in about the same time south on separate itineraries to the secluded coves of **Stavrós** or **Thólos**. The track to the former begins between the *Tilos Mare Hotel* and the *Castellania Apartments*, becoming a trail at the highest new house in the village; once up to the saddle with its new road, there's a sharp drop (some of it cross-country, but cairned) to the beach. The latter route begins by the cemetery and the chapel of **Áyios Pandelímon** with its Byzantine *hokhláki* court, then curls around under the seemingly impregnable castle of **Agriosykiá**; from the saddle overlooking the descent to Thólos, a route marked with cairns leads northwest to the citadel in twenty minutes. It's less than an hour's walk west, with some surviving path sections shortcutting the road curves, up to the ghost village of **Mikró Horió**, whose 1200 inhabitants left for Livádhia during the 1950s. The only intact structures are the church (locked except for the August 15 festival) and an old house which has been restored as a long-hours **music pub**, which operates only during July and August, with a variable formula of Greek/foreign music, and a shuttle van laid on from the port.

Megálo Horió and Éristos

The rest of Tílos's inhabitants live in or near **MEGÁLO HORIÓ**, which has an enviable perspective over the vast agricultural *kámbos* stretching down to Éristos (see below), and is overlooked in turn by the vast castle of the Knights, which encloses a sixteenth-century chapel. The castle was built on the site of ancient Tílos – with recycled masonry evident – and is reached by a stiff, thirty-minute climb that begins on the lane behind the Ikonomou supermarket before threading its way through a vast jumble of cisterns, house foundations and derelict chapels – the remains of the much large medieval Megálo Horió. Two more flanking fortresses stare out across the plain: the easterly one of **Messariá** helpfully marks the location of the **Harkadhió** cave where Pleiocene midget-elephant bones were discovered in 1971. A signposted 500-metre track goes there from the road, ending near a spring and modern amphitheatre (to be used in a new summer festival) just below the cave-mouth, which was hidden for centuries until a World War II artillery barrage exposed it. The bones themselves have been transferred to a tiny, not very compelling **museum** in Megálo Horió, on the ground floor of the town hall (open Mon–Fri 8am–2.30pm on application upstairs to the warden).

Your choices for **accommodation** in the village are the *Pension Sevasti* (☎0241/44 237; ①) at the lower end of town, the central *Miliou Apartments* (☎0241/44 204; ②) or (best) *Studios Ta Elefandakia* (☎0241/44 213; ②), among attractive gardens by the car park. Of the two **tavernas**, the *Kali Kardhia*, next to the *Pension Sevasti*, is more reliably open and has the best view; there's a traditional **kafenío** by the church, and futher up the Athenian-run *Kafenio Ilikati* (May–Sept only), with cakes and drinks.

South of and below Megálo Horió, signs direct you towards the three-kilometre paved side road to the long, pink-to-grey-sand **Éristos** beach, reputedly the island's best, though summer rubbish piles from campers can be disconcerting. Discreet nudism at either end goes unremarked. About halfway down the road on the right amongst the orchards is *Taverna-Rooms Tropikana* (☎0241/44 020; ①), nothing special in either respect, but the most reliable all-season venue for a snack near the beach; its perennial rival on the far side of the access road is the *Navsika*, also with simple rooms (☎0241/44 306; ①). If you ring ahead, one or other may send a van to fetch you from the ferry dock.

The far northwest

The main road beyond Megálo Horió hits the coast again at dreary **Áyios Andónios**, whose single **hotel/taverna**, the *Australia* (☎0241/44 296; ②) sees little trade outside high season. At low tide on the exposed, average beach you can find more lava-trapped skeletons strung out in a row – human this time, presumably tide-washed victims of a Nissyrian eruption in 600 BC, and discovered by the same archeologists who found the miniature pachyderms.

There's better swimming at isolated **Pláka** beach, 2km west of Áyios Andónios, where people camp rough despite a total lack of facilities. The paved road finally ends 8km west of Megálo Hório at the fortified monastery of **Ayíou Pandelímona**, founded in the fifteenth century for the sake of its miraculous spring. Now the place is usually deserted except from July 25 to 27, when it hosts the island's major festival. Its tower-gate and oasis setting more than two hundred forbidding metres above the west coast are the most memorable features, though an eminently photogenic inner courtyard boasts a *hokhláki* surface, and the church a fine marble floor. On the *katholikón* wall, an early eighteenth-century fresco shows the founder-builder holding a model of the monastery, while behind the ornate altar screen hides another fresco of the Holy Trinity.

To guarantee access, you should visit with the regular Sunday-morning minibus tour from Megálo Horió (fare 1000dr; 1hr to look around), or contact Pandelis Yiannourakis, the key-keeper, in Megálo Horió (☎0241/44 213). To vary the return, you can walk back much of the way on a signposted path; it's shown correctly on Baz Ward's map, and ends at the minor monastery of Panayía Kamarianí near Áyios Andónios.

Níssyros

Volcanic **Níssyros** is noticeably greener than its southern neighbours Tílos and Hálki, and unlike them has proven wealthy enough to retain over eight hundred of its population year-round (down, though, from 10,000 in 1900). While remittances from abroad (particularly Astoria, New York) are significant, most of the island's income is derived from the offshore islet of Yialí, where a vast lump of **pumice** is slowly being quarried away by Lava Ltd. The concession fee collected from Lava by the municipality has engendered a huge public payroll and vast per-capita sums available to spend. Under the circumstances, the Nissyrians bother little with agriculture other than keeping cows and pigs; the hillside terraces meticulously carved out for grain and grapes lie fallow, and wine is no longer made locally.

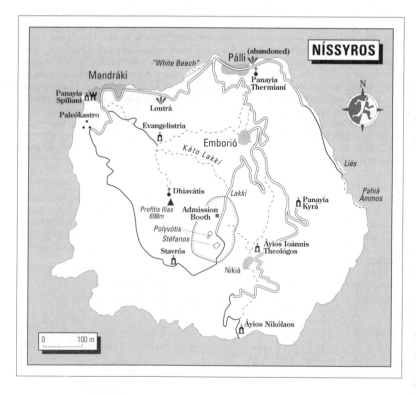

The main island's peculiar geology is potentially a source of other benefits: DEI, the Greek power company, spent the years between 1988 and 1992 sinking exploratory **geothermal** wells and attempting to convince the islanders of the benefits of cheap electricity.

In 1993, a local referendum went massively against the project, and DEI, together with its Italian contractor, took the hint and packed up. The desalination plant, reliant on an expensive fuel-oil generator, scarcely provides enough fresh water to spur a massive growth in package tourism. The relatively few tourists (mostly German) who stay the night, as opposed to the day-trippers from Kós, still find peaceful villages with a minimum of concrete eyesores and a friendly tight-knit population. Níssyros also offers good **walking** opportunities through a countryside planted with oak or terebinth, on a network of trails finally being marked and maintained with EU money; wherever you stroll you'll hear the contented grunting of pigs as they gorge themselves on acorns from the many oak trees. Autumn is a wonderful time, especially when the landscape has perked up after the first rains, and the late-January almond-blossoming is one of the island's glories.

Mandhráki

MANDHRÁKI is the deceptively large port and island capital, with blue patches of sea visible and audible at the end of narrow streets lined with tightly-packed houses whose brightly painted balconies and shutters are mandated by law. Except for the tattier fringes near the ferry dock, where multiple souvenir shops and bad tavernas pitched at day-trippers leave a poor first impression, the bulk of the place is cheerful and villagey, arrayed around the community orchard or *kámbos* and overlooked by two ancient fortresses.

Into a corner of the first of these, the fourteenth-century Knights' castle, is wedged the little monastery of **Panayía Spilianí**, built on this spot in accordance with instructions from the Virgin, who appeared in a vision to one of the first Christian islanders. The monastery's prestige grew after raiding Saracens failed to discover the vast quantities of silver secreted here in the form of a rich collection of Byzantine icons. During 1996–97, the Langadhaki area just below was rocked by a series of earthquakes, damaging a score of venerable houses, and rendering the small **folklore museum** homeless – it's now temporarily on the shore (daily 11am–2pm & 5–8pm; 200dr), but hardly worth the admission fee for a couple of mannequins in traditional dress. A new combination archeological-ethnographical-historical museum is being built on the *kámbos* with money donated by the Nissyrian founder of the Vitex paint company.

As a defensive bastion, the seventh-century BC Doric **Paleókastro** (unrestricted access), twenty minutes' well-signposted walk out of the Langadháki district, is infinitely more impressive than the Knights' castle, and ranks as one of the more underrated ancient sites in Greece. You can clamber up onto the massive, Cyclopean-block walls by means of a broad staircase beside the still-intact gateway.

Practicalities

You'll see a handful of port **hotels** on your left as you disembark; cheapest of these is the waterfront *Three Brothers* (☎0242/31 344; ①) and the *Romantzo* (☎0242/31 340; ①) across the way, which also runs the *Studios Volcano* (②) in town. For more comfort, try the municipally run *Xenon* (☎0242/31 011; ②) just beyond. In the town proper, the main budget option is the small, simple, hillside *Hotel Ypapandi* (☎0242/31 485 or visit *Taverna Panorama*; ①), near Mandhráki's most comfortable accommodation, the *Hotel Porfyris* (☎0242/31 376; ③), also overlooking the sea and *kámbos*, with gardens and a large swimming pool. There's little actually on the shore aside from *Studios Sunset-Iliovasilema* (☎0242/31 159; ③), adequate and quiet, near the converted windmill.

Culinary **specialities** include pickled caper greens, honey, *pittiá* (chickpea croquettes), and *soumádha*, an almond-syrup drink widely sold in recycled wine bottles.
When eating out, it's best to give all of the commercialized, shoddy shoreline **tavernas** a miss – *Manolis* is the honourable exception, often with fresh fish – in favour of
more genuine haunts inland. Top of the heap is evening-only, musical ouzerí *Iy
Fabrika*, with indoor/outdoor tables by season and family recipes from founder Patti
preserved by new owner Manolis, also the miners' chef on Yiali. Runners-up include
Panorama, with bean and mushroom salad and suckling pig on offer, or *Irini* on lively, ficus-shaded Platía Ilikioméni, with more involved *mayireftá* unavailable elsewhere. Two resolutely simple spots are the summer-only *Panayiotis* (no sign) in
Langadháki, with mezédhes served at a half-dozen outside tables, or *Taverna
Nissiros*, the oldest eatery in town, always packed despite predictably average grill
quality. Focuses of **nightlife** are Platía Ilikioméni and a string of *barákia* on the shore
west of *Manolis*.

The most useful of three **travel agencies** is Dhiakomihalis, which acts as a representative for most ferries and hydrofoils, rents cars and exchanges money (albeit for
stiff commissions – there's a post office but no bank). Kentris, near the town hall, does
G&A ferries and Olympic Airways tickets. At the base of the jetty is the **bus stop**, with
(theoretically) up to five daily departures to the hill villages and seven to Pálli; otherwise, there are two set-rate **taxis** and three outlets for **scooter rental**, among which
Alfa provides the best service – rates begin at 3000dr per day.

Beaches and Pálli

Beaches on Níssyros are in even shorter supply than water, so much so that the tour
company here can successfully market excursions to a sandy cove on **Áyios Andónios**
islet, opposite the Yialí mines. Closer at hand, the short, black-rock beach of **Hokhláki**,
behind the Knights' castle, is unusable if the wind is up, and the town beach of
Miramáre at the east edge of the harbour would be a last resort in any weather. It's
best to head east along the main road, passing the refurbished spa of **Loutrá** (hot mineral water only by doctor's prescription) and the smallish **"White Beach"** (properly
Yialiskári), 2km along and dwarfed by an ugly eponymous hotel (☎0242/31 498; ④),
unwelcoming and generally filled by tour groups.

A kilometre or so further, 4km in total from Mandhráki, the fishing village of **PÁLLI**
makes a more attractive base and excellent hangout at lunchtime, when the port fills
with trippers. Tavernas here are multiplying, but stick with the two long-term
favourites: the less expensive *Ellinis*, with spit-roasted meat by night, grilled fish in
season and simple rooms upstairs (☎0242/31 453; ③), or the adjacent *Afroditi* (aka
Nikos & Tsambika), with big portions to match bumped-up prices, Cretan bulk wine
and excellent own-made desserts. They've also a house to rent, all or in part
(☎0242/31 242; ③ for the entire house). A scooter-rental outlet, an excellent bakery
cranking out brown bread and fine pies (branch in Mandhráki), and modest nightlife
make Pálli also worth considering as a base. A tamarisk-shaded, dark-sand beach
extends east of Pálli, improving as it goes, to the abandoned Pantelídhi spa, behind
which the little grotto-chapel of **Panayía Thermianí** is tucked inside the vaulted
remains of a Roman baths complex. To reach Níssyros's best beaches, continue in this
direction for an hour on foot (or twenty minutes by bike along the road), past an initially discouraging seaweed- and cowpat-littered shoreline, to the delightful cove of
Liés (snack bar June 15–Sept 15), where the track ends. Walking a further fifteen minutes along a trail over the headland brings you to the idyllic, 350-metre expanse of
Pahiá Ámmos, with grey-pink sand heaped in dunes, shade at the far end and a large
summer colony of free campers.

The interior

Its central, dormant **volcano** gives Níssyros its special character and fosters the growth of the abundant vegetation – and no stay would be complete without a visit. When excursion boats arrive from Kós, an agency coach and usually one of the public buses are pressed into service to take customers into the interior. Tours tend to monopolize the crater floor between 11am and 2pm, so if you want solitude, use early morning or late afternoon scheduled buses to Nikiá (two daily continue to the crater floor), a scooter or your own two feet to get there.

The road up from Pálli winds first past the virtually abandoned village of **EMBORIÓ**, where pigs and cows far outnumber people, though the place is slowly being bought up and restored by Athenians and foreigners. New owners are often surprised to discover natural saunas, heated by volcano steam, in the basements of the crumbling houses; at the outskirts of the village there's a public **steam bath** in a grotto, its entrance outlined in white paint. If you're descending to Pálli from here, an old cobbled way starting at the sharp bend below the sauna offers an attractive short cut of the four-kilometre road, while another *kalderími* drops from behind *To Balkoni tou Emboriou* **taverna** (Easter–Sept, limited menu) to within a quarter-hour's walk to the craters.

NIKIÁ, the large village on the east side of the volcano's caldera, is with seventy inhabitants more of a going concern, and its spectacular situation 14km from Mandhráki offers views out to Tílos as well as across the volcanic caldera. There are three places to **drink** (and, modestly, **eat**) here: *Porta* and *Platia* on or near the engagingly round *hokhláki* plaza, or *Nikia*, at the entrance to the village. By the bus turn-around area, signs point to the 45-minute **trail** descending to the crater floor; a few minutes downhill, you can detour briefly to the eyrie-like **monastery of Áyios Ioánnis Theológos**, which only comes to life at the September 25 festival. To **drive** directly to the volcanic area you must use the road which veers off just past Emborió.

However you approach the **volcano**, a sulphurous stench drifts out to meet you as fields and scrub gradually give way to lifeless, caked powder. The sunken main crater of **Stéfanos** is extraordinary, a moonscape of grey, brown and sickly yellow; there is another, less-visited double crater (dubbed **Polyvótis**) to the west, equally dramatic, with a clear trail leading up to it from the access road. The perimeters of both are pocked with tiny blowholes from which jets of steam puff constantly and around which form little pincushions of pure sulphur crystals. The whole floor of the larger crater seems to hiss, and standing in the middle you can hear something akin to a huge cauldron bubbling away below you. According to legend this is the groaning of Polyvotis, a Titan crushed here by Poseidon under a huge rock torn from Kós. When there are tour groups around, a small, tree-shaded snack bar operates in the centre of the wasteland, and a booth on the access road sporadically charges admission (500dr) to the volcanic zone.

Since the 1991 destruction of the old direct *kalderími* between the volcano and Mandhráki, finding pleasant options for **walking** back to town requires a bit of imagination and possession of Beate and Jürgen Franke's locally available, GPS-drawn topographical map. First choice involves backtracking along the main crater access road for about 1km from the admission booth to find the start of a clear, crudely marked path which passes the volcanic gulch of **Káto Lákki** and the monastery of **Evangelístria** on its two-hour-plus course back to the port. You can lengthen the trip by detouring from Evangelístria south to **Profítis Ilías**, the island's summit – a two-hour detour round-trip, with the route recently cleaned and well marked with cairns or white paint. An alternative approach to Evangelístria requires returning to Emborió and leaving from the top of the village, near the cemetery and small castle, on a 45-minute course to the monastery – an enjoyable link, despite haphazard 1998 marking and cleaning.

Kós

After Rhodes, **Kós** is the second largest and most popular island in the Dodecanese, and there are superficial similarities between the two. Here also the harbour is guarded by an imposing castle of the Knights of St John; the streets are lined with grandiose Italian public buildings; and minarets and palm trees punctuate extensive Hellenistic and Roman remains. Although its hinterland for the most part lacks the wild beauty of Rhodes' interior, acre for acre Kós is the most fertile of the Dodecanese, blessed with rich soil and abundant ground water.

Mass tourism has largely displaced the old agrarian economy amongst the population of about 27,000, and outside the main town and Kardhámena this is very much a family-holiday isle, where you can turn the kids loose on push-bikes. Except for Kós Town and Mastihári, there aren't many independent travellers, and from early July to early September you'll be lucky to find any sort of room at all without reservations far in advance, or a pre-booked package. The tourist industry is juxtaposed rather bizarrely with cows munching amidst baled hay, and Greek army tanks exercising in the volcanic badlands around the airport. All these peculiarities acknowledged, Kós is still definitely worth a few days' time while island-hopping: its handful of mountain villages are appealing, the tourist infrastructure excellent (including such amenities as regular city buses and cycle paths) and swimming opportunities are limitless – virtually the entire coast is fringed by beaches of various sizes, colours and consistencies.

Kós Town

The town of **KÓS**, home to most of the island's population, spreads in all directions from the harbour, with little charm aside from its scattered ancient and medieval antiquities. Apart from the Knights' castle, the first thing you see on arrival, its attraction lies in the wealth of Hellenistic and Roman remains, many of which were only revealed by an earthquake in 1933, and excavated subsequently by the Italians, who also planned and laid out the "garden suburb" extending east of the central grid. Elsewhere, vast areas of open space alternate with a hotchpotch of Ottoman monuments and later mock-medieval or Art Deco buildings.

The **castle** (Tues–Sun 8.30am–2.30pm; 800dr) is reached via a causeway over its former moat, now filled in and planted with palms (hence the avenue's Greek name, Finíkon). The existing double citadel, which was built in stages between 1450 and 1514, replaced an original fourteenth-century fort deemed not capable of withstanding advances in medieval artillery. A fair proportion of ancient Koan masonry has been recycled into the walls, where the escutcheons of several Grand Masters of the Knights of St John can also be seen.

Immediately opposite the castle entrance stands the riven trunk of Hippocrates' plane tree, its branches now propped up by scaffolding instead of the ancient columns of yore; at seven hundred years of age, it's not really old enough to have seen the great healer, though it has a fair claim to being one of the oldest trees in Europe. Adjacent are two Ottoman fountains (a dry hexagonal one and a working one in an ancient sarcophagus) and the eighteenth-century **mosque of Hassan Pasha**, also known as the Loggia Mosque after the portico on one side; its ground floor – like that of the **Defterdar mosque** on Platía Eleftherías – is taken up by rows of shops.

Opposite the latter stands the Italian-built **Archeological Museum** (Tues–Sun 8.30am–2.30pm; 800dr), with a predictable Latin bias in the choice of exhibits. Four rooms of statuary are arrayed around an atrium with a mosaic of Hippocrates welcoming Asklepios to Kós; the most famous item, purportedly a statue of Hippocrates, is indeed Hellenistic, but most of the other highly regarded works (such as Hermes seated with a lamb) are Roman.

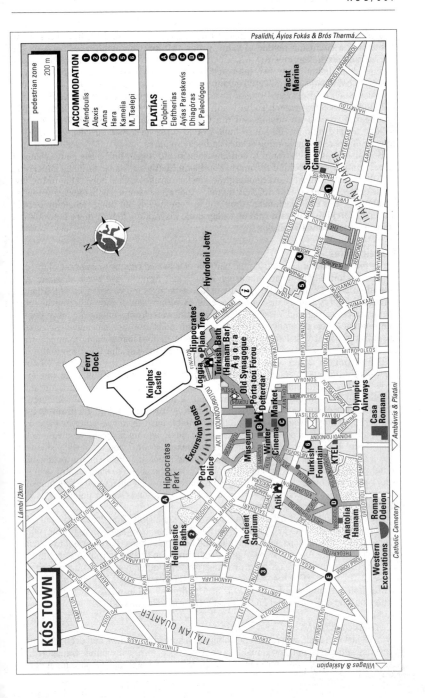

KÓS TOWN

Psalídhi, Áyios Fokás & Brós Thermá △

Yacht Marina

Summer Cinema

ITALIAN QUARTER

Hydrofoil Jetty

Ferry Dock

Knights' Castle

Hippocrates' Plane Tree
Turkish Bath (Hamam Bar)
Loggia
Agora
Old Synagogue
Pórta toú Fórou
Defterdar
Market
Excursion Boats
Port Police
Museum
Winter Cinema
Hippocrates Park
Turkish Fountain
Olympic Airways
Casa Romana
KTEL
Atik
Anatolia Hamam
Roman Odeion
Ancient Stadium
Hellenistic Baths
Western Excavations

Ambávris & Platáni △

Catholic Cemetery △

△ Lámbi (2km)

ITALIAN QUARTER

Villages & Asklepíon △

ACCOMMODATION
1 Afendoulis
2 Alexis
3 Anna
4 Hara
5 Kamelia
6 M. Tselepi

PLATÍAS
A 'Dolphin'
B Eleftherias
C Áyias Paraskevís
D Dhiagóras
E K. Paleológou

pedestrian zone

0   200 m

The largest single section of ancient Kós is the **agora**, a sunken, free-access zone containing a confusing jumble of ruins, owing to repeated earthquakes between the second and sixth centuries AD. More comprehensible are the so-called western excavations, lent definition by two intersecting marble-paved streets and the **Xystos** or restored colonnade of a covered running track. In the same area lie several floor mosaics, such as the famous one of Europa, though these tend to be off-limits or hidden under protective gravel. To the south, across Grigoríou toú Pémptou, are a garishly restored Roman-era odeion and the **Casa Romana** (Tues–Sun 8.30am–2.30pm; 800dr), a third-century AD house built around three atria with suriviving patches of mosaic floors showing hunting scenes and sea creatures.

Kós also boasts a thoroughly commercialized **old town**, lining the pedestrianized street running from behind the market on Platía Eleftherías as far as Platía Dhiagóras and the isolated minaret overlooking the western archeological zone. One of the few areas of town to survive the 1933 earthquake, today it's crammed with expensive tourist boutiques, cafés and snack bars. About the only genuinely old thing remaining here is a capped **Turkish fountain** with an calligraphic inscription, found where the walkway cobbles cross Odhós Venizélou.

Practicalities

Large **ferries** anchor just outside the harbour at a special jetty by one corner of the castle; **excursion boats** to neighbouring islands sail right in and dock all along Aktí Koundouriótou. **Hydrofoils** tie up south of the castle at their own berth, on Aktí Miaoúli. Virtually all ferry and excursion boat agents sit within 50m of each other at the intersection of pedestrianized Vassiléos Pávlou and the waterfront. Among the more helpful and genuinely representative of ferries and hydrofoils, not just expensive excursions, are Adris Nissia at Vassiléos Pávlou 2, and Exas at Andóni Ioannídhi 4. If you just want to clear out, Aeolos Travel at Artemisías 25 often has one-way charters back to the UK.

The **airport** is 26km west of Kós Town in the centre of the island; an Olympic Airways shuttle bus meets Olympic flights for a transfer to the town terminal, but if you arrive on any other flight you'll have to either take a taxi or head towards the giant roundabout outside the airport gate and find a KTEL bus – they run from here to Mastihári, Kardhámena and Kéfalos as well as Kós Town. The **KTEL terminal** in town is a series of stops around a triangular park 400m back from the water, with an info booth adjacent at Kleopátras 7 (tickets on the bus). The municipality also runs a frequent **local bus** service, DEAS, through the beach suburbs and up to the Asklepion, with a ticket and information office at Aktí Koundouriótou 7. Push- or **mountain-bike** rental are popular options for getting around, given the island's relative flatness; if you want a **motor scooter**, try Moto Harley at Kanari, corner Neomartýrou Khrístou, while Autorent/Helen's in Psalídhi suburb, at both the *Ramira* and *Okeanis* hotels (☎0242/28 882), is reputable for good-condition **cars**.

The municipal **tourist office** at Vassiléos Yeoryíou 3 (July–Aug daily 7am–9pm; May & June, Sept & Oct Mon–Fri 7.30am–8pm, Sat 8am–3pm; Nov–April Mon–Fri 8am–3pm) keeps stocks of local maps, bus timetables and ferry schedules (the latter not to be trusted implicitly). The Alpha Pisteos/Alpha Credit **bank** on the waterfront has an automatic note-changer as well as a cash dispenser; several other banks also have cash dispensers. The **post office** is at Vassiléos Pávlou 14; **Internet cafés** include *Café del Mare* at Megálou Alexándhrou 4 and *Taurus* at Mandhilará 9. **Laundries** include Laundry Center on Mandhilará 56 and Laundromat Center at Alikarnassoú 124.

ACCOMMODATION

If you're just in transit, you're virtually obliged to **stay** in Kós Town, and even if you plan a few days on the island, it still makes a sensible base, as it is the public transport hub and has the greatest concentration of transport hire and nightlife. Good budget choices in the centre include the deservedly popular *Pension Alexis* (☎0242/25 594; ②), Irodhótou 9 at the corner of Omírou, across from the Roman *agora*, with wood-floored, non-en-suite rooms and a self-catering kitchen; the same welcoming family has the *Hotel Afendoulis* (☎0242/25 321; April–Nov; ③), about 600m south at Evripýlou 1, with large, balconied en-suite rooms and breakfast included. If they're full, try the nearby *Hotel Kamelia* at Artemisías 3 (☎0242/28 983; ③), claimed open all year, with winter heating; the rear rooms have an orchard view. Other quiet possibilities include the simple but en-suite *Hara* at Hálkonos 6 (☎0242/22 500; ②), the *Pension Anna* at Venizélou 77 (☎024/223 030; ③) or the self-catering rooms let by Moustafa Tselepi (☎0242/28 896; ④) at Venizélou 29, on the corner of Metsóvou. For more comfort and a small private beach, the *Hotel Theodhorou Beach*, 1200m from the centre at the end of town towards Psalídhi (☎0242/22 280; ④) has generous-sized rooms and attractive common areas not completely monopolized by packages. The well-appointed **campsite** lies another 1300m out towards Cape Psalídhi, and can be reached by either the DEAS bus service or its own minibus (which meets ferrries), but is open only during the summer.

EATING, DRINKING AND NIGHTLIFE

Despite an overwhelming first impression of Euro-bland cuisine, it's easy to **eat** well and even reasonably as long as you search inland, away from the harbour. The *Australia-Sydney* on Vassiléos Pávlou opposite the post office is a cheap and cheerful hole-in-the wall with a limited menu of daily dishes where two can eat for about 5000dr; the *Hellas* at Psarón 7, corner of Amerikís, offers more bog-standard *mayireftá*, plus *kléftiko*, in a slightly fancier environment; while *Noufara* at Kanári 45 is carnivore heaven with roast chicken, *kondosoúvli* and the like. Moving up in the world, the nearby *Nikolaos O Psaras*, corner Alikarnassoú and Avérof, is the most genuine fish taverna in town, though expect price hikes since it was refurbished and expanded in 1999. The best one of a number of *kultúra* tavernas is *Petrino* at Theológou 1, open all year with indoor/outdoor seating on Avérof at the corner of Alikarnassoú. Other recommendations are the *Olympiadha* at Kleopátras 2, near Olympic Airways, and *To Kokhili* ouzerí at Alikarnassoú 64, corner of Amerikís. Equal to any of these is *Ambavris* (May–Oct), 800m south out of town by the road from near Casa Romana, in the eponymous village; the "Greek (medley) Plate" in large quantity is a good choice, and again vegetarians will be happy, but expect to wait for a table in summer. For **breakfast** or **dessert**, *Fresko Gelateria-Café*, corner Kleopátras and Ioannídhi, serves crepes and waffles in the morning and sticky cakes or decadent own-made ice cream later on. For a quiet **drink** in atmospheric surroundings, there's the *Anatolia Hamam*, housed partly in a former Ottoman mansion off Platía Dhiagóras (though eating isn't suggested); durable music bars include *Jazz Opera* at Arseníou 5, with varied music for an older crowd, or *Beach Boys* at Kanári 57, with a tiny dance floor and cheapish drinks. If you prefer loud techno and house, look no further than the "Pub Lanes", officially Nafklírou and Dhiákou; every address is a bar, whose identity tends to change each season, so just choose according to the crowd and the noise level. Otherwise there is one active **cinema**, the Orfeas, with summer and winter (Oct–May) premises as shown on the map; the indoor premises also hosts concerts and other special events.

The Asklepion and Platáni

Native son **Hippocrates** is justly celebrated on Kós; not only does he have a tree, a street, a park, a statue and an international medical institute named after him, but the **Asklepion** (Tues–Sun 8.30am–2.30pm; 800dr) 4km south of town, one of just three in Greece, is a major tourist attraction. DEAS buses run to the site via Platáni 8am–2pm and to Platáni only 2–10pm; otherwise it's a 45-minute walk. There is a small snack bar at the Asklepion, or pause for lunch in Platáni (see below) en route.

HIPPOCRATES

Hippocrates (c. 460–370 BC) is generally regarded as the father of scientific medicine, though the Hippocratic oath probably has nothing to with him and is in any case much altered from its original form. Hippocrates was certainly born on Kós, probably at Astypalia near present-day Kéfalos, but otherwise details of his life are few and disputed; what seems beyond doubt is that he was a great physician who travelled throughout the Classical Greek world, but spent at least part of his career teaching and practising at the Asklepion on his native island. A vast number of medical writings have been attributed to Hippocrates, only a few of which he could have actually written; *Airs, Waters and Places*, a treatise on the importance of environment on health, is widely thought to be his, but others were probably a compilation from a medical library kept on Kós. This emphasis on good air and water, and the holistic approach of ancient Greek medicine, now seems positively contemporary.

The Asklepion was actually founded just after the death of Hippocrates, but it's safe to assume that the methods used and taught here were his. Both a temple to Asklepios (god of medicine, son of Apollo) and a renowned curative centre, its magnificent setting on three artificial hillside terraces overlooking Anatolia reflects early recognition of the importance of the therapeutic environment. Until recently, a fountain provided the site with a constant supply of clean, fresh water, and extensive stretches of clay piping are still visible, embedded in the ground.

Today very little remains standing above ground, owing to the chronic earthquakes and the Knights' use of the site as a quarry. The lower terrace in fact never had many structures, being instead the venue for the observance of the *Asklepieia* – quadrennial celebrations and athletic/musical competitions in honour of the healing god. Sacrifices to Asklepios were conducted at an **altar**, the oldest structure on the site, whose foundations can still be seen near the middle of the second terrace. Just to its east, the Corinthian columns of a second-century AD **Roman temple** were partially re-erected by nationalistically minded Italians. A monumental **staircase** leads from the altar to the second-century BC Doric temple of Asklepios on the topmost terrace, the last and grandest of a succession of the deity's shrines at this site.

About halfway to the Asklepion, the village of **PLATÁNI** (also Kermetés, from the Turkish name *Germe*) is, along with the Kós Town, the remaining place of residence for the island's dwindling community of ethnic Turks. Until 1964 there were nearly three thousand of them, but successive Cyprus crises and the worsening of relations between Greece and Turkey prompted mass emigration to Anatolia, and a drop in the Muslim population to currently under a thousand. Near or at the main crossroads junction, with a working Ottoman fountain, are a number of excellent Turkish-run tavernas: *Arap* (summer only), the slightly less touristy *Sherif* (ditto) and *Gin's Palace* (all year), each offering Anatolian-style *mezédhes* (fried vegetables with yoghurt, *bourekákia*, and so on) and kebabs better than most places in Kós Town.

Just outside Platáni on the road back to the port, the island's **Jewish cemetery** lies in a dark conifer grove, 300m beyond the Muslim graveyard. Dates on the Hebrew-Italian-script headstones stop after 1940, after which none of the local Jews were allowed the luxury of a natural death prior to their deportation in summer 1944. Their former synagogue, a wonderfully orientalized Art Deco specimen at Alexándhrou Dhiákou 4, was refurbished in 1991 as a municipal events hall.

Eastern Kós

If you're looking for anything resembling a deserted **beach** near the capital, you'll need to make use of the DEAS bus line connecting the various resorts to either side of town, or else rent a vehicle; pedal-bikes can take advantage of the cycle paths extending as far east as Cape Psalídhi. Closest is **Lámbi**, 3km north towards Cape Skandhári with its military watchpoint, the last vestige of a vast army camp which has deferred to the demands of tourism.

The far end of the city bus line beginning at Lámbi is Áyios Fokás, 8km southeast, with the unusual and remote **Brós Thermá** 5km further on, easiest reached by rented vehicle (though the final kilometre of dirt track was storm-damaged in 1999). Here **hot springs** issue from a grotto and flow through a trench into a shoreline pool protected by boulders, heating the seawater to an enjoyable temperature. Winter storms typically disperse the boulder wall, rebuilt every spring, so that the pool changes from year to year. A taverna above the lower parking area is currently shut but may of course re-open.

Tingáki and Marmári

The two neighbouring beach resorts of Tingáki and Marmári are separated from each other by the salt marsh of **Alykí**, which retains water until June after a wet winter. Between January and April Alykí is host to hundreds of migratory birds, and most of the year you'll find tame terrapins to feed near the outlet to the warm, shallow sea. There's almost always a breeze along this coast, which means plenty of windsurfers for hire at either resort. The profiles of Kálymnos, Psérimos and Turkey's Bodrum peninsula all make for spectacular scenery. If you're aiming for either of these resorts from town, especially on a bike of any sort, it's safest and most pleasant to go by the obvious **minor road** which takes off from the southwest corner of town; the entire way to Tingáki is paved, and involves the same distance as using the main trunk road and marked turnoff. Similarly, a grid of paved rural lanes links the inland portions of Tingáki and Marmári.

TINGÁKI, a busy beachside resort popular with Brits, lies 12km west of the harbour. Oddly, there's very little accommodation near the beach in the dozen or so medium-sized hotels and more numerous studios; most of these are scattered inland through fields and cow pastures. One of the better choices, if heavily subscribed to by packages, is the family-orientated *Hotel Constatinos Ilios* (☎0242/29 411; ③), a well-designed bungalow complex. The best local taverna here is *Ambeli* (supper only), well signposted 2.5km east of the main beachfront crossroads. The beach itself is white sand, long and narrow – it improves, and veers further out of earshot from the frontage road, as you head southwest.

MARMÁRI, 15km from town, has a smaller built-up area than Tingáki, and the beach itself is broader, especially to the west where it forms little dunes. Most hotels here are monopolized by German tour groups, but you might hit on an on-spec vacancy at the 1997-built *Esperia* on the main access road down from the island trunk road (☎0242/42 010; ④), in grassy surroundings. Just inland on the same street stands a pair of adjacent noteworthy **tavernas**: *Apostolis* and the currently superior *Dimitris*, offering *mezedhákia*, seafood and meat grills at reasonable prices and usually open weekends November to April.

The Asfendhioú villages

The main interest of inland Kós resides in the villages on **Mount Dhíkeos**, a handful of settlements collectively referred to as **Asfendhioú**, nestled amidst the island's only natural forest. Together they give a good idea of what Kós looked like before tourism and ready-mix concrete arrived, and all are now severely depopulated by the mad rush to the coast. They are accessible via the curvy side road from Zipári, 8km from Kós Town; a badly marked but paved minor road to Lagoúdhi; or by the shorter access road for Pylí.

The first Asfendhioú village you reach up the Zipári road is Evangelístria, where a major crossroads by the parish church and the recommendable *Asfendhiou* taverna leads to Lagoúdhi and Amanioú (west), Asómati (east) and Ziá (uphill). **ZIÁ**'s spectacular sunsets make it the target of up to six evening tour buses daily, though the village has barely a dozen families still resident, and its daytime tattiness seems to increase by the year. Best of the dozen **tavernas** here is the *Olympiada*, at the start of the pedestrian walkway up to the church, open all year with such dishes as chickpeas, bulgur pilaf, *spédzofai* and good bulk wine; runner up, close to said church and the abandoned school, is *Iliovasilema/Sunset*, with an unbeatable, car-free situation and simple grills. Ziá is also the trailhead for the ascent of 846-metre Dhíkeos peak, a two-and-a-half-hour round-trip, initially on track but mostly by path. The route is fairly obvious, and the views from the pillbox-like summit chapel of Metamórfosis are ample reward for the effort. Up top, you can also ponder the esoteric symbolism of a giant crucifix fashioned of PVC sewer pipe and filled with concrete.

Heading east from Ziá or Evangelístria, roads converge at **ASÓMATI**, home to about thirty villagers and numbers of outsiders restoring abandoned houses; the evening view from the church of Arhángelos with its pebble mosaic rivals that of Ziá, though there are no reliable facilities here. **ÁYIOS DHIMÍTRIOS**, 2km beyond along an exceedingly rough track, is marked by its old name of Haïhoúdhes on some maps, and is today completely abandoned except for a single house next to the attractive church; you can continue from here on 3.5km of more rough road to the junction with the paved road linking Platáni with the municipal rubbish tip.

Pylí

PYLÍ can be reached via the paved road through Lagoúdhi and Amanioú, or from the duck-patrolled Linopótis pond on the main island trunk road. In the upper of its two neighbourhoods, 100m west of the pedestrianized square and church, the simple *Iy Palia Piyi* taverna serves inexpensive but appetizing grills and mezédhes in a superb setting, beside a giant cistern-fountain (*piyí*), decorated with carved lion-head spouts. Pylí's other attraction is the so-called **Harmýlio** (Tomb of Harmylos), signposted near the top of the village as "Heroon of Charmylos". This consists of a subterranean, niched vault (fenced off), probably a Hellenistic family tomb; immediately above, traces of an ancient temple have been incorporated into the medieval chapel of Stavrós.

Paleó (medieval) **Pylí**, roughly 3km southeast of its modern descendant, was the Byzantine capital of Kós. Head there via Amanioú, keeping straight at the junction where signs point left to Ziá and Lagoúdhi. In any case, the castle should be obvious on its rock, straight ahead; the deteriorating road ends next to a spring, opposite which a stair-path leads within fifteen minutes to the roof of the fort. En route you pass the remains of the abandoned town tumbling southward down the slope, as well as three fourteenth-century chapels often locked to protect fresco fragments within.

Western Kós

Near the arid, desolate centre of the island, well sown with military installations, a pair of giant, adjacent roundabouts by the airport funnels traffic northwest towards Mastihári, northeast back towards town, southwest towards Kéfalos, and southeast to Kardhámena.

Mastihári and Andimáhia

The least developed, least "packaged" and least expensive of the northern shore resorts, **MASTIHÁRI** has a shortish, broad beach extending west, and a less attractive one at **Troúllos**, 1.5km east. At the end of the west beach, inside a partly fenced enclosure, lie remains of the fifth-century basilica of **Áyios Ioánnis**, one of several on the island. If you want to **stay**, quieter digs overlooking the west beach include the simple *Hotel Kyma* (☎0242/59 045; ②) or the *Hotel Fenareti* (☎0242/59 024) further up the grade, with rooms (②) and studios (③) in a peaceful garden environement. *O Makis*, one street inland from the quay, and *Kali Kardia*, at the base of the jetty, are the best of a half-dozen tavernas, both well regarded for fresh fish, mezédhes and (at *Kali Kardia*) *mayireftá*. Mastihári is also the port for small ro-ro **ferries** to Kálymnos; there are three well-spaced departures in each direction most of the year, timed more or less to coincide with Olympic Airways' flight schedules – though KTEL buses to or from Kós Town don't (perhaps deliberately) dovetail well.

The workaday village of **ANDIMÁHIA**, 5km southeast of Mastihári, straggles over several ridges; the only concession to tourism is a much-photographed windmill on the main street, operating sporadically as a working museum with its unfurled sails. If open, for a token fee you can climb up to the mast loft and observe its workings. East of Andimáhia, reached via a marked, three-kilometre side road, an enormous, triangular **Knights' castle** overlooks the straits to Níssyros. Once through the imposing north gateway (unrestricted access), you can follow the well-preserved west parapet, and visit two interior chapels: one with a fresco of Áyios Khristóforos (St Christopher) carrying the Christ Child, the other with fine rib-vaulting.

Kardhámena

KARDHÁMENA, on the southeast coast 31km from Kós Town, is the island's largest package resort after the capital itself, with locals outnumbered twenty to one in season by visitors (mostly Brits) intent on getting as drunk as possible as cheaply as possible. Runaway local development has banished whatever redeeming qualities the place may once have had, reducing it to a seething mass of offlicences, bars, trinket shops and excursion agencies. Pubs named the *Black Swan* or *Slug and Lettuce* dispense imported beer, plus you can even find fish and chips. A hefty sand beach stretches to either side of the town, hemmed in to the east with ill-concealed military bunkers and a road as far as Tolári, home to the massive *Norida Beach* all-inclusive complex.

Kardhámena is most worth knowing about as a place to catch a **boat to Níssyros**. There are supposedly two daily sailings in season: the morning tourist excursion kaïki at approximately 9.30am, and another, far less expensive, barely publicized one – the *Chrissula* – at 2.30pm, but in practice the afternoon departure (typically Mon, Wed, Thurs & Fri) can occur any time between 1.30pm and 6.30pm, depending on when the Nissyrians have finished their shopping.

Outside high season, there are generally a few **rooms** not taken by tour companies, and prices are not outrageous. For more comfort, the *Hotel Rio* (☎0242/91 627; ③) gets good reviews, and like most accommodation here is underpriced for its class. **Tavernas** are not very numerous, and predictably poor, though the longest-lived and most reasonable one is *Andreas*.

South-coast beaches

The thinly populated portion of Kós southwest of the airport and Andimáhia boasts the most scenic and secluded beaches on the island, plus a number of minor ancient sites. Though given fanciful names and shown as separate extents on tourist maps, the south-facing **beaches** form essentially one long stretch at the base of a cliff. **Magic**, officially Poléni, is the longest, broadest and wildest. **Sunny**, easily walkable from Magic, has a few sunbeds and a taverna. **Banana** (Langádha) is the cleanest and most picturesque, with junipers tumbling off its dunes. **Paradise**, often dubbed Bubble Beach because of volcanic gas vents in the tidal zone, is small and oversubscribed, with wall-to-wall sunbeds.

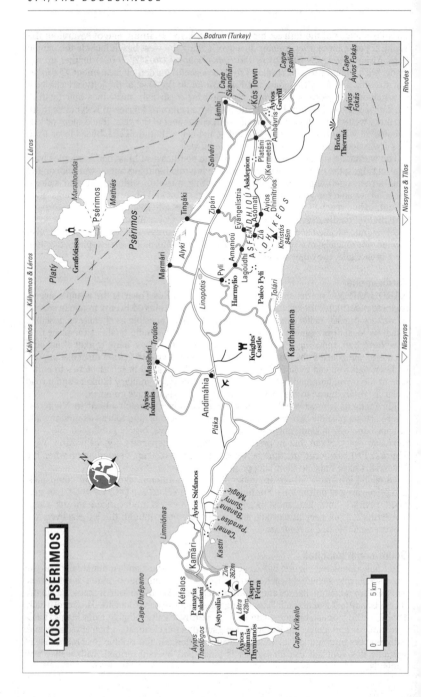

KÓS & PSÉRIMOS

Uninterrupted beach resumes at **Áyios Stéfanos**, overshadowed by a huge Club Med complex, and extends 5km west to Kamári (see below). A marked public access road leads down to the beach just west of a small peninsula, crowned with the exquisite remains of two triple-aisled, sixth-century basilicas. Though the best preserved on the island, several columns have been toppled since the 1980s, and wonderful bird mosaics languish under a permanent layer of "protective" gravel. The basilicas overlook tiny but striking Kastrí islet with its little chapel; in theory it's an easy swim (sometimes wading) across from the westerly beach, with some of the best snorkelling on Kós around the rock formations, but you must run the gauntlet of boats from the local water-ski school.

The far west
Essentially the shore annexe of Kéfalos (see below), **KAMÁRI** is a sprawling package resort of rapidly multiplying breeze-blocks, pitched a few notches above Kardhámena; it's a major watersports centre and an alternative departure point for Níssyros (up to five days weekly in season). One independent hotel that can be recommended is the simple *Maria* (☎0242/71 308; ②), on the seafront west of the main road up to **KÉFALOS**, 43km from Kós Town. Squatting on a bluff looking down the length of the island, this is the end of the line for buses: a dull village but worth knowing about for its post office and as a staging point for expeditions into the rugged peninsula terminating dramatically at Cape Kríkello.

Main highlights of a half-day tour here, beginning along the widened ridge road south, are: a Byzantine church incorporating an ancient temple, 1km beyond the village; the late Classical theatre (unrestricted access), with two rows of seats remaining, of **ancient Astypalia**, 500m further at the side-path signposted "Palatia"; and the cave of **Asprí Pétra** (inhabited during the Neolithic period), marked rather vaguely off the ridge road and requiring a half-hour walk to reach. An improved, soon-to-be-paved road west from just after Astypalia leads to an often windy beach and small chapel at **Áyios Theológos**, 7km from Kéfalos; the *Sunset Wave* taverna is a reliable option for lunch, though quality varies. Keeping to the main paved road until the end of the line brings you to the appealing (but usually locked) monastery of **Áyios Ioánnis Thymianós**, also 7km from the village.

About 1.5km north of Kéfalos on the road tracing the island's summit ridge, a paved side road covers the 2.7 km to **Limniónas**, the only north-facing beach and fishing anchorage on this part of Kós. Of the two fish tavernas here whose signs guide you from the upper road, *Limionas* – the one nearer the jetty – is preferable. Two compact sandy beaches sit either side of the peninsula.

Psérimos

PSÉRIMOS could be an idyllic little island were it not so close to Kós and Kálymnos. Throughout the season, both of these larger neighbours dispatch daily excursion boats, which compete strenuously to dock at the undersized harbour; in mid-summer, day-trippers blanket the main sandy beach stretching around the bay in front of the thirty-odd houses of the single village. Even during May or late September you're guaranteed at least a hundred outsiders daily (nearly double the permanent population), and not surprisingly the islanders are apt to respond in a surly fashion to visitors. There are a couple of other, less attractive beaches to hide away on during the day: **Mathiés** (sand), a thirty-minute walk east, or **Marathoúnda** (pebble), a 45-minute walk north. Nowhere on Psérimos, including the monastery of Grafiótissa, is much more than an hour's walk away.

Even during the season there won't be too many other overnighters, since there's a limited number of **rooms** available. Pick of the several small pensions is *Tripolitis*

(☎0243/23 196; ②) over the *Saroukos* taverna, and rooms managed by Katerina Xyloura (☎0243/23 497; ②) above her taverna on the eastern side of the harbour. There's just one small **store**, and most of the island's supplies are brought in daily from Kálymnos. **Eating out** however, won't break the bank, and there's often fresh fish in the handful of **tavernas**.

Virtually all boats based at Kós harbour operate triangle tours (approximately 6000dr), which involve departure between 9.30am and 10am, followed by a stop for swimming on either Platý islet or adjacent Psérimos, lunch in Póthia, the port of Kálymnos, and another swimming stop at whichever islet wasn't visited in the morning. If you want to spend the entire day on Psérimos, you're much better off departing Póthia at 9.30am daily on the tiny *Pserimos*, returning at 4pm (2000dr round-trip). The islanders themselves use either this boat to haul supplies or their own small craft to visit Kálymnos for shopping on Monday, Wednesday and Friday (returning early afternoon).

Astypálea

Geographically, historically and architecturally, **Astypálea** (alias Astropália) would be more at home among the Cyclades – on a clear day you can see Anáfi or Amorgós in the west far more easily than any of the other Dodecanese (except western Kós), and it looks and feels more like these than its neighbours to the east. Despite an evocative butterfly shape, Astypálea does not immediately impress you as the most beautiful of islands. The heights, which offer modest walking opportunities, are bleak and covered in thornbush. Yet the herb *alisfakiá*, brewed as a tea, flourishes too, and somehow hundreds of sheep survive – as opposed to snakes, which are (uniquely in the Aegean) entirely absent. Lush citrus groves and vegetable patches in the valleys signal a relative abundance of water, hoarded in a reservoir. The various beaches along the generally featureless coastline often have reef underfoot and suffer periodic dumpings of seaweed.

In antiquity the island's most famous citizen was Kleomedes, a boxer disqualified from an early Olympic Games for causing the death of his opponent. He came home so enraged that he demolished the local school, killing all its pupils. Things have calmed down a bit in the intervening 2500 years, and today Astypálea is renowned mainly for its honey and fish; the abundant local catch has only been shipped to Athens since the late 1980s, a reflection of the traditionally poor ferry links in every direction. These have improved recently with the introduction of extra services towards Piréas via select Cyclades, and high-season links with Rhodes via a few intervening islets, but outside July or August you still risk being marooned here for a day or two longer than intended. There is, curiously, no package tourism here since Laskarina Holidays deleted the island from their list in 1995, frustrated by chronically unreliable connections to Kós and its airport.

Despite this relative isolation, plenty of people find their way to Astypálea during the short, intense midsummer season, when the 1100 permanent inhabitants are all but overrun by upwards of 7000 guests a day. Most arrivals are Athenians or Italians, supplemented by large numbers of yachties and foreign owners of holiday homes in the understandably popular Hóra. At such times you won't find a bed without reserving well in advance, and camping rough is expressly frowned upon.

Skála and Hóra

The main harbour of **SKÁLA** or Péra Yialós dates from the Italian era (Astypálea was the first island the Italians occupied in the Dodecanese) and most of the settlement

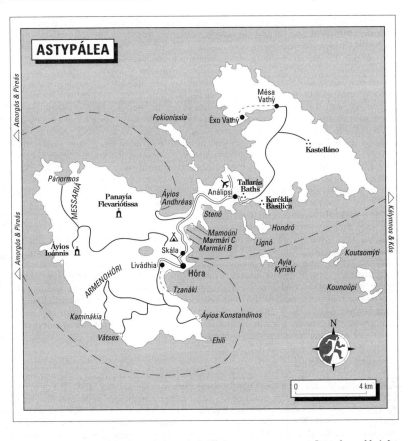

between the quay and the line of nine windmills is even more recent. Its only real bright spot is a 1998-inaugurated **archeological museum** (Tues–Sun 8.30am–2.30pm; free), a single well-lit room crammed with the best local finds spanning all historical periods from the Bronze Age to medieval times.

As you climb up beyond the port towards **HÓRA**, however, the neighbourhoods get progressively older and more attractive, their steep streets enlivened by the *poúndia*, or colourful wooden balconies of the whitewashed houses. The whole culminates in the thirteenth-century **kástro**, one of the finest in the Aegean, erected not by the Knights but by the Venetian Quirini clan and subsequently modified by the Ottomans after 1537. Until well into this century over three hundred people lived inside the *kástro*, but depopulation and World War II damage have combined to leave only a desolate shell today. The fine rib vaulting over the entrance supports the church of Evangelístria Kastrianí, one of two intact here, the other being Áyios Yeóryios (both usually locked).

Skála, and to a lesser extent Hóra, have **accommodation** ranging from spartan, 1970s-vintage rooms to new luxury studios; proprietors meet ferries if they have vacancies. Owing to harbour noise – particularly the sound of ferries dropping anchor at 3am – you might prefer more atmospheric rooms or restored villas (③–④) up in Hóra if uninterrupted sleep is a priority; enquire at the antique shop on the quay or ring ahead on ☎0243/61 430). Otherwise, the obvious port **hotels** are the 1993-refurbished *Astynea* (☎0243/61 040; ②) and the elderly *Paradisos* (☎0243/61 224; ②), both en-suite. A better choice, on the east shore of the bay, are the misnamed *Karlos Studios* (☎0246/61 330; ④, but ② spring and autumn), actually enormous rooms with view balconies, above its own restaurant. A seasonal **campsite** operates amongst calamus reeds and tamarisks behind Dhéftero Marmári bay (see opposite), about 4km along the road to Análipsi, but it's waterlogged in winter and thus mosquito-plagued in summer.

During August, upwards of thirty **tavernas** set up shop across the island, few of them memorable and many concerned primarily with turning a quick profit. Among the more reliable Skála options, *Iy Monaxia* (aka *Viki's*), one block inland from the ferry jetty by the old power plant, has excellent home-style cooking and is open year-round. The *Galini*, up a stairway from the *Hotel Astynea*, is a good grill, though it tends to close by mid-September; *Astropalia*, on the hillside above the one-way street up to Hóra, does fish and stays open longer. At the head of the bay, *Albatros* and *Karavos* are acceptable, but for just a tad more *Etherio* and *Maïstrali*, both near the *Astynea*, are more ambitious and cater to the yacht set.

Most **nightlife** happens up in more atmospheric Hóra, where two traditional kafenía on the main square – *Aigaion* and *Myli* – are joined in season by music bars such as *Kastro* and the newer *Artemis*. The **post office** and most shops are here, though the island's only **bank** (Emboriki/Commercial), complete with cash dispenser, is down at Skála quay.

A single **bus** runs along the paved road between Hóra, Skala, Livádhia and Analípsi, frequently in July and August from 8am until 11pm, less regularly out of season. There are only three official **taxis**, far too few to cope with passenger numbers in season; several places rent out **scooters**, the most reliable being Lakis and Manolis, with branches at Hóra and Skála dock, and also renting out a few jeeps. The island **map** sold locally is grossly inaccurate, even by lenient Greek-island standards, though in compensation rural junctions are adequately signposted.

Around the island

A thirty-minute walk (or a short bus journey) from the capital lies **LIVÁDHIA**, a fertile green valley with a popular, good beach but a rather ramshackle collection of restaurants and cafés immediately behind. You can **rent a room** or studio just inland– for example at *Studios Electra* (☎0243/61 270; ③), near the water, or *Venetos Studios & Bungalows* (☎0243/61 490; ③), on the westerly hillside. Among the half-dozen **tavernas**, *Iy Kalamia* and *To Yerani* are commendable, especially the latter which stays open into October and keeps simple rooms adjacent (☎0243/61 484; ②).

If the busy beach here doesn't suit, continue southwest fifteen minutes on foot to three small single coves at **Tzanáki**, packed out with naturists in mid-summer. The third bay beyond, more easily reached by motorbike, is **Áyios Konstandínos**, a partly shaded, sand and gravel cove with a good seasonal taverna. Around the headland, the lonely beaches of **Vátses** and **Kaminákia** are more usually visited by excursion boat from Skála, subject to weather and captain's whim. By land, Vátses has the easier dirt road in, some twenty minutes by scooter from Livádhia, but it's prone to surf and seaweed; the track to Kaminákia is atrocious but the sheltered, clean scenic cove with a seasonal *kantína* makes the effort worthwhile.

A favourite outing in the west of the island is the two-hour walk or 45-minute motorbike trip from Hóra to the oasis of **Áyios Ioánnis**, 10km distant. Proceed northwest along the initially paved road beginning from the fifth or sixth windmill, then keep left when a side-track goes right to Panayía Flevariotíssas monastery. Beyond this point the main track, briefly dampened by a spring seeping across the road surface, curls north towards farming cottages at Messariá before reaching a junction with gates across each option. Take the left-hand one, and soon the walled orchards of the uninhabited farm-monastery of Áyios Ioánnis come into view. From the balcony of the church, a steep, faint path leads down to the base of a ten-metre waterfall; bathing pools here come and go depending on silt deposit.

Northeast of the harbour, are three coves known as **Próto** (First), **Dhéftero** (Second) and **Tríto** (Third) **Mármari**, and marked as **Marmári A'**, **B'** and **C'** respectively on some maps. The first is home to the power plant and boatyards, the next hosts the campsite (see opposite), while the third, reasonably attractive, also marks the start of the path east to the perfectly decent coves of unfortunately named **Mamoúni** ("Bug" or "Critter" in Greek). Beyond Tríto Marmári, the middle beach at **Stenó** ("narrow", after the isthmus here) with clean sand and a seasonal *kantína*, is the best.

ANÁLIPSI, widely known as Maltezána after medieval Maltese pirates, is a ten-kilometre bus trip or taxi ride from town. Although the second-largest settlement on Astypálea, there's surprisingly little for outsiders save a narrow, sea-urchin-speckled beach (there are better ones east of the main bay) and a nice view south to some islets. Despite this, blocks of **rooms** sprout in ranks well back from the sea, spurred by the proximity of the airport, 700m away. Among a handful of tavernas, the most dependable are *Analipsi*, by the jetty, or the more ambitious-menued *Porto Stampalia*, inland. Behind calamus reeds and eucalyptus near the fishing jetty lie the best-preserved mosaic floors on the island: those of the Byzantine **Tallarás baths**, with somewhat crude figures of zodiacal signs, the seasons personified, and a central androgynous figure (Time or Fortune) holding the cosmic orb.

The motorable road ends at Mésa Vathý, from where an appalling track (or occasional kaïki) continues to **ÉXO VATHÝ**, a sleepy fishing village with a single reasonable taverna and a superb small-craft harbour. Following several accidents, this is no longer the **backup ferry port** in winter, when Skála is buffeted by the prevailing southerlies; foot passengers (but no vehicles) are transferred ashore to the unlit quay at **Áyios Andhréas**, just west of Tríto Marmári.

Kálymnos

Most of the 16,000-strong population of **Kálymnos** lives in or around the large port of Póthia, a wealthy but not conventionally beautiful town famed for its sponge industry. Unfortunately, almost all of the eastern Mediterranean's sponges were devastated by a viral disease in 1986, and only three or four of the fleet of thirty-odd boats are still in use. In response to this catastrophe, the island has recently established a tourist industry – so far confined to one string of beach resorts – and has also retrofitted most of its sponge boats for deep-sea fishing. Warehouses behind the harbour still process and sell sponges all year round, though most of these are imported from Asia and America. There are also still numbers of elderly gentlemen about who rely on two canes, walking frames or even wheelchairs, stark evidence of the havoc wrought in their youth by nitrogen embolism (the "bends"), long before divers understood its crippling effects. The departure of the remaining sponge fleet, usually just after Easter, is preceded by a festive week known as *Yprogrós*, with food, drink and music; the fleet's return, approximately six months later, has historically also been the occasion for more uproarious, male-orientated celebration in the port's bars.

Kálymnos essentially consists of two cultivated and inhabited valleys sandwiched between three limestone ridges, harsh in the full glare of noon but magically tinted towards dusk. The climate, especially in winter, is alleged to be drier and healthier than that of neighbouring Kós or Léros, since the quick-draining limestone strata, riddled with many caves, doesn't retain as much moisture. The rock does, however, admit seawater, which has tainted Póthia's wells; drinking water must be brought in by tanker truck from Vathý, and there are potable springs at Dámos and Hóra.

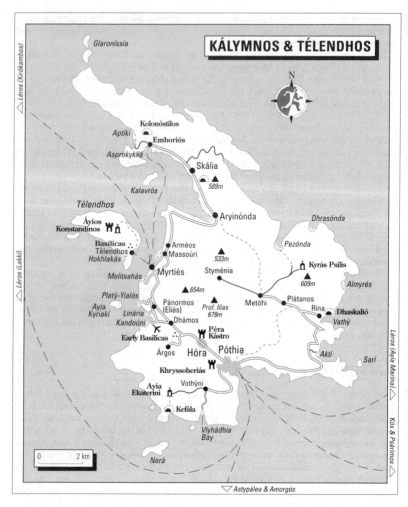

Since Kálymnos is the home port of the very useful local namesake ferry (see p.696), a minor hub for Dodecanese Hydrofoils, and moreover where the long-distance ferry lines from the Cyclades and Astypálea join up with the main Dodecanesian routes, many travellers arrive unintentionally, and are initially most concerned with how to move on quickly. Yet Kálymnos has sufficient attractions to justify a stay of several days while island-hopping – or even longer, as the package industry at the western beaches suggests.

Póthia

PÓTHIA (sometimes pronounced Pothiá), without being obviously picturesque, is colourful and authentically Greek, its houses marching up the valley inland or arrayed in tiers up the sides of the mountains framing it. Your first and overwhelming impression will be of the phenomenal amount of noise engendered by motorbike traffic and the cranked-up sound systems of the dozen waterfront cafés. This is not entirely surprising, since with about 11,000 inhabitants, Póthia ranks as the third largest city in the Dodecanese after the main towns of Rhodes and Kós.

Perhaps the most rewarding way to acquaint yourself with Póthia is by wandering the backstreets, where elegant Neoclassical houses are surrounded by surprisingly large gardens, and craftsmen ply their trade in a genuine workaday bazaar. During the Italian occupation, many local houses were painted blue and white to irritate the colonial overlords, and though the custom has all but died out, the Greek national colours are still evident amongst more traditional pink and ochre buildings.

Of the two local museums, priority should be given to the **Municipal Nautical and Folklore Museum** (Mon–Fri 8am–1.30pm, Sat–Sun 10am–12.30pm; 500dr), on the seaward side of Khristós cathedral. A large photo in the foyer shows Póthia as it was in the 1880s, with no quay, jetty, roads or sumptuous mansions, and with most of the population still up in Hóra, while other photos document sponge-fishing and the Allied liberation of 1945. Three-dimensional exhibits include horribly primitive divers' breathing apparatuses, and "cages" designed to keep propellers from cutting air lines, a constant fear. The local **archeological museum** (Tues–Sun 8.30am–2pm; free guided tours only) is installed in a grand former residence of the Vouvallis family of sponge magnates. A rather eclectic collection, including a kitsch-furnished Second Empire parlour and small troves from the island's several caves, it's not exactly required viewing.

Practicalities

Accommodation is rarely a problem, since pension proprietors usually meet the ferries (though many of the premises touted are substandard, or remote, or both). The town's best, and quietest **hotel**, near the Vouvalis museum, is the *Villa Themelina* (☎0243/22 682; ③), housed in a nineteenth-century mansion plus modern studio annexes, with gardens and a large swimming pool. The high-ceiling, bug-screened, wood-floored rooms in the main house make this Kálymnos's most elegant accommodation. Next niche down, on the west quay but fairly quiet, is occupied by the *Arhondiko* (☎0243/24 061), a refurbished mansion with plain rooms at ② and "luxury" ones (balcony, TV, fridge) at ③; all have heating/air conditioning. Two places in Amoudhára district (west of the harbour) are worth contacting in advance: the en-suite *Pension Greek House* (☎0243/29 559; ②; open most of year) with volubly friendly management and kitsch decor; and considerably above this, the well-signposted *Hotel Panorama* between the *Hotel Porfyris* and Platía Ilikioméni (☎0243/23 138; April–Oct; ③), with balconied view rooms.

When **eating out**, the obvious strategy involves following the waterfront northeast past the Italian-built municipal "palace" to a line of fish **tavernas** and **ouzeris**, where the local speciality is octopus croquettes, more tender than you'd expect. However, recent years have seen touts multiply and prices climb here, so even though the locals still patronize places like *Barba Petros*, you might consider *mayireftá* at *Xefteris*, well signposted inland from Khristós cathedral, with courtyard seating, or *Navtikos Omilos*, at the base of the ferry jetty opposite Áyios Nikólaos church. This has a limited menu of seafood and grills, but portions are large and there's a pleasant terrace. Sticky-cake fans will want to attend the traditional *Zaharoplastiki O Mihalaras* back on restaurant row, while four paces west from here, just before the municipal "palace", *Apothiki* is an old warehouse refurbished as a musical bar for some years now. A summer cinema, Cine Oasis, operates behind the traditional, column-facaded café-tearoom *Ai Musai*, on the front.

All **boat** and **hydrofoil** agents, including the headquarters of the *Nissos Kalymnos*, plus a fairly useless municipal tourist information bureau (sporadic Mon–Fri hours), line the waterfront as you bear right out of the pier-area gate. Olympic Airways has an office at Patriárhou Maxímou 17, 200m inland from the quay, and the new airport near Árgos village may commence operations in 2000. Finally, waterfront branches of the National/Ethniki and Ionian/Ioniki **banks** both have cash dispensers.

Around the island

Buses run as far as Emborió in the northwest and Vathý in the east, from a stop beside the municipal "palace", with schedules helpfully posted and departures in season fairly frequent. Tickets must be bought beforehand from authorized kiosks, and cancelled on board. Otherwise, you can use shared **taxis** from Platía Kýprou (more than KTEL rates, less costly than a normal taxi), or rent a **scooter** from reputable Scootermania, just back from the waterfront, near where it bends south. Avis **car** rental is represented locally (☎0243/28 990), though the island's compact enough that only families would need one.

The castles and basilicas

Heading northwest across the island, the first place you reach after just over a kilometre along is a castle of the Knights of St John, **Kástro Khryssoheriás**, in the suburb of Mýli. From the whitewashed battlements there are wonderful views southeast over town to Kós, and north towards Hóra and Péra Kástro. The former Kalymnian capital of **HÓRA** (aka Horió), 1.5km further along the main road, is still a village of nearly three thousand inhabitants, and guards a critical pass in local geography, focus of settlement in every era. Steep steps lead up from its eastern edge to the Byzantine citadel-town of **Péra Kástro** (daily May–Oct 10am–2pm; tip to guide), appropriated by the Knights of St John and inhabited until late in the eighteenth century. Inside the imposing gate the former heaps of rubble are slowly being re-pieced together; a guided tour by the warden visits five well-maintained, whitewashed chapels, containing late medieval fresco fragments.

Some 200m past the turning for Árgos en route to the northwest coast from Horió, you can detour briefly left to visit two early Byzantine basilicas which are fairly representative, and among the easiest to find, of a vast number on the island. The more impressive of the two, accessed by whitewashed steps on the left just as the highway begins to descend, is that of **Khristós tís Ierousalím**, probably dating from the late fourth century, with its apse fully preserved; the three-aisled **Limniótissa** church in an adjacent field is larger but considerably less intact.

West coast resorts

From the basilicas, the road dips into a tree-shaded valley leading to the consecutive **beach resorts** of Kandoúni, Myrtiés and Massoúri, collectively referred to as "Brostá" by islanders. **KANDOÚNI**, some 200m of brown, hard-packed sand favoured by the locals, is the shore annexe of the rich agricultural valley-village of **Pánormos** (aka Eliés). Accommodation closest to the water here is monopolized by tour companies, and for both bathing and staying you're better off at **Linária**, the north end of the same bay. A smaller cove set apart from Kandoúni proper by a rock outcrop, this has better sand and the possibility of staying at *Skopellos Studios* (☎0243/47 155; ③), on the slope below the church. For eating, there are two worthy options: *Ouzeri Giannis/Ta Linaria* on the shore, with leisurely service but abundant portions of grills and seafood, or *To Steki tis Fanis* in an old mansion up on the hillside, offering local specialities such as *merziméli* (salad with barley rusks) and *mourí* (baked lamb in a clay pot).

The next beach north, **Platý-Yialós**, though again a bit shorter than Kandoúni, is arguably the best on the island: cleaner than its southern neighbours, more secluded, and placed scenically at the base of a cliff, opposite Ayía Kyriakí islet. A lone taverna (*Kyma*), right behind the sand at road's end, will do for lunch. There are two worth-while choices for **staying** on spec: the 1970s-vintage rooms at *Pension Platy-Gialos* (☎0243/47 029; ②), actually overlooking Linária, simple but en-suite, or the mammoth *Mousselis Studios* (☎0243/47 757; ③), with so many units (and on-site snack bar) that they usually have stray vacancies even in summer.

The main road climbs from Pánormos up to a pass, where the *Hotel Kamari* (☎0243/47 278; ③) is another non-packaged possibility, with views from most rooms, before descending in zigzags to meet the sea again 8km from Póthia at **MYRTIÉS**. Together with **MASSOÚRI** (1km north) and **ARMÉOS** (2km north and end of the line for most buses), it sees the lion's share of Kálymnos tourism: all too many neon-lit music bars, "special menus", souvenir shops and the other accoutrements of the pack-age trade. The beach at Myrtiés is narrow, pebbly and cramped by development, though it does improve as you approach Massoúri. The closest all-sand beach to Myrtiés lies 500m south, at **Melitsahás** cove, which also has the only really passable local **taverna** at its fishing anchorage, *Iy Dhrossia*, fish specialists claiming to be open all year. Most local **accommodation** is block-booked by overseas companies; a remote exception enjoying spectacular views is *Studios Nikis* (☎0243/47 201; ②), up on the higher one-way bypass road between Myrtiés and Massoúri. Possibly this coast's most appealing feature is its position opposite the evocatively shaped islet of Télendhos (see below), which frames some of the most dramatic sunsets in Greece. It's also possible to go from Myrtiés directly to Xirókambos on Léros aboard the daily early afternoon **kaïki**.

Some 5km beyond Massoúri, **ARYINÓNDA** has a clean pebble beach backed by a single **rooms** outfit (*Arginonta Beach*, ☎0243/40 000; ②), with a friendly proprietor, and several **tavernas**. It is also the trailhead for the spectacular two-and-a-half-hour walk inland and over two gentle passes to Metóhi in the Vathý valley. From the bus-stop area and small spring, head southwest on a path between rock walls which soon climbs the south flank of the ravine here, sporadically marked by paint dots. Don't believe sources which show the route emerging at Styménia, and be aware that plans are afoot to bull-doze a road from just above the *Arginonta Beach* to Styménia, which may disrupt the first half-hour or so of the trail. You'll need a sunhat, stout shoes and a litre or so of water, as the next source is in Plátanos hamlet, beyond Metóhi.

The end of the bus line, **EMBORIÓ**, 20km from the port, offers a gravel and sand beach, which improves as you head west, **accommodation** (much of it taken up by Laskarina Holidays) and a number of **tavernas**, including the long-running *Harry's Paradise*, with attached garden apartments (☎0243/47061; ④), and *Akti Emborios*, clos-er to the sea. If the twice-daily bus service fails you, there is usually a shuttle boat back to Myrtiés.

Télendhos

The trip across the strait to the striking, volcanic-plug islet of **TÉLENDHOS** is arguably the best reason to come to Myrtiés; little boats shuttle to and fro constantly throughout the day and late into the night. According to local legend, Télendhos is a petrified princess, gazing out to sea after her errant lover; the woman's head profile is most evident at dusk. The hardly less pedestrian geological explanation has the islet sundered from Kálymnos by a cataclysmic earthquake in 554 AD; traces of a sub-merged town are said to lie at the bottom of the straits.

Home to about fifteen families, Télendhos is car-free and blissfully tranquil, though even here package tourism has arrived in a modest way. For cultural edifi-cation you'll find the ruined thirteenth-century **monastery of Áyios Vasílios** and an enormous, 1997-excavated basilica of Ayía Triádha up on the ridge, part way along the ten-minute path to **Hokhlakás** pebble beach, which is small but very scenic, with sunbeds for hire. Accommodation and food can be basic or worse; we've had complaints about *Pension/Restaurant Uncle George*, the obvious place by the jetty. Best perhaps to veer off south to adjacent *Pension Studios Rita* (☎0243/47 914; ②), with rooms and renovated-house studios managed by the namesake dessert café, *Zorba's*, or to *Barba Stathis* tavernas en route to Hokhlakás; or north (beyond Áyios Vasílios) to the Greek-Australian-run *On the Rocks*, which doubles as a decent taverna with homemade desserts, and has a bar that's the heart and soul of local **nightlife**. At one corner of the premises you can visit yet another Byzantine monument, the chapel and sauna of Áyios Harálambos. If you want more (relative) luxury on Télendhos, you'll have to squeeze in between packages at the *Hotel Porto Potha* (☎0243/47 321, fax 48 108; ③), set rather bleakly at the very edge of things but with a large pool.

Vathý

Heading east from Póthia, the first four kilometres (power plant, rubbish tip, multiple gasworks and quarries) seem vastly unpromising, until you round a bend and the ten-kilometre ride ends dramatically at **VATHÝ** a long, fertile valley, carpeted with orange and tangerine groves, whose colour provides a startling contrast to the lifeless greys higher up on Kálymnos. At the simple fjord port of **RÍNA**, more ruined basilicas flank the bay; near the southerly one is the best accommodation option, the helpful *Rooms Manolis* (☎0243/41 300; ②). Some of the five tavernas are pricier than you'd expect, owing to patronage from the numerous yachts which call here; currently the best choice, with shambolic service but good grilled fish, is *The Harbor*, first place on the right at road's end.

The steep-sided inlet has no beach to speak of, so people swim off the artificial lido on the far right; the closest reachable overland are **Aktí**, about 3km back towards Póthia, a functional pebble strand with sunbeds and a single snack bar, and **Pezoúnda**, a little further north, reached by track (and then walking) from Metóhi hamlet. Boat excursions sometimes visit the stalactite cave of **Dhaskalió**, inhabited in Neolithic times, out towards the fjord mouth on its north flank, and the remoter, tiny beaches of **Almyrés** and **Dhrasónda**, accessible only by sea.

It's possible to **walk** back to Póthia along the old direct *kalderími* which existed before the coastal highway – a two-hour jaunt which begins in Plátanos hamlet. The route is tricky to find in this direction, however, so most people start in Póthia, at the church of Ayía Triádha behind the *Villa Themelina* hotel – the way is marked initially by red paint splodges.

The southwest

Some 6km southwest of Póthia, the small bay of **Vlyhádhia** is reached via a narrow ravine draining from the nondescript village of Vothýni. The sand and pebble beach here isn't really worth a special trip, unless you're interested in **scuba**, since the Vlyhádhia area is one of the limited number of legal diving areas in Greece. Stavros Valsamidhes, the local divemaster, has also assembled an impressive **Museum of Submarine Finds** (Mon–Sat 9am–7pm, Sun 10am–2pm; free), which in addition to masses of sponges and shells offers a reconstructed ancient wreck with amphorae and World War II debris. Depending on your ability, dives (arrange in advance on ☎0243/50 662; 10,000dr for one dive, 18,000dr for two) may visit ancient wrecks *in situ*, as well as seal caves.

Póthia-based kaïkia make well-publicized excursions to the cave of **Kefála** just west of Vlyhádhia, the most impressive of half a dozen caverns around the island. You have to walk thirty minutes from where the boats dock, but the vividly coloured formations repay the effort; the cave was inhabited before recorded history, and later served as a sanctuary of Zeus (who is fancifully identified with a particularly imposing stalagmite in the biggest of six chambers).

Léros

Léros is so indented with deep, sheltered anchorages that during World War II it harboured, in turn, the entire Italian, German and British Mediterranean fleets. Unfortunately, many of these magnificent fjords and bays seem to absorb rather than reflect light, and the island's relative fertility can seem scraggly and unkempt when compared with the crisp lines of its more barren neighbours. These characteristics, plus the island's lack of spectacularly good beaches, meant that until the late 1980s just a few thousand foreigners (mostly Italians who grew up on the island), and not many more Greeks, came to visit each August.

Such a pattern is now history, with German, Dutch, Danish and British package operators at the vanguard of those "discovering" Léros and the company of islanders unjaded by mass tourism. Foreign visitor numbers have, however, levelled out of late,

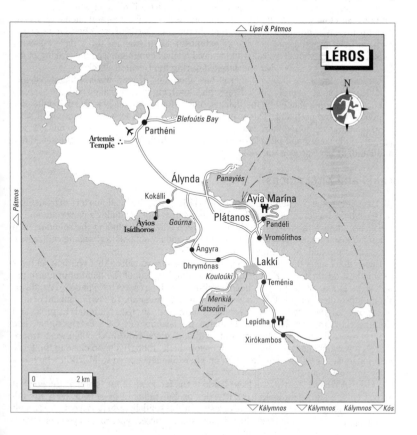

with matters unlikely to change until and unless the tiny airport is expanded to accommodate jets.

Not that Léros needs, or strenuously encourages, mass tourism; various prisons and sanatoriums have dominated the Lerian economy since the 1950s, directly or indirectly employing about a third of the population. During the junta era, the island hosted a notorious detention centre at Parthéni, and today the mental hospital on Léros remains the repository for many of Greece's more intractable psychiatric cases; another asylum is home to hundreds of mentally handicapped children. The island's domestic image problem is compounded by its name, the butt of jokes by mainlanders who pounce on its similarity to the word *lerá*, connoting rascality and unsavouriness.

In 1989, a major scandal emerged concerning the administration of the various asylums, with EU maintenance and development funds found to have been embezzled by administrators and staff, and the inmates kept in degrading and inhumane conditions. Since then, an influx of EU inspectors, foreign psychiatrists and extra funding have resulted in drastic improvements in patient treatment, including the establishment of halfway houses across the island.

More obvious is the legacy of the **Battle of Léros** on November 12–16, 1943, when overwhelming German forces displaced a Commonwealth division which had landed on the island following the Italian capitulation. Bomb nose-cones and shell casings still turn up as gaily painted garden ornaments in the courtyards of churches and tavernas, or have been pressed into service as gateposts. Each year for three days following September 26, memorial services and a naval festival commemorate the sinking of the Greek battleships *Queen Olga* and *Intrepid* during the German attack.

Unusually for a small island, Léros has abundant ground water, channelled into potable cisterns at several points. These, plus low-lying ground staked with the avenues of eucalyptus trees planted by the Italians, makes for an unusually active mosquito contingent, so come prepared. The island is compact enough to walk around, with sufficient hills to give mountain-bikers a good work-out. There is a reasonable bus service, plus several scooter and bicycle rental outfits, of which Motoland (branches at Álinda and Pandéli) have proven the most reliable.

Lakkí and Xirókambos

All large **ferries** arrive at the main port of **LAKKÍ**, once the headquarters of a bustling, purpose-built Italian naval base. Boulevards far too wide for today's paltry amount of traffic are lined with some marvellous Art Deco edifices, including the round-fronted cinema (closed since 1985), the primary and secondary schools, a shopping centre with a round atrium and the defunct *Leros Palace Hotel*.

Buses don't meet the ferries – instead there's a taxi squadron that charges set fares to standard destinations. Few people stay willingly at any of the handful of moribund hotels in Lakkí, preferring to head straight for the resorts of Pandéli, Álynda or Vromólithos (see below). There's just one bona fide **taverna**, *To Petrino*, inland next to the **post office**, two cash dispensers attached to the National/Ethniki and Commercial/Emboriki **banks** and Gribelos, the island's sole G&A Ferries agent. The nearest approximation of a **beach** is at sand and gravel **Kouloúki**, 500m west, where there's a seasonal taverna and some pines for shade, though it's too close to the ferry jetty for most tastes. You can carry on another kilometre or so to **Merikiá** which is a slight improvement and also has a taverna.

XIRÓKAMBOS, nearly 5km from Lakkí in the far south of the island, is the point of arrival for the afternoon kaïki from Myrtiés on Kálymnos (it goes back early the following morning). Though billed as a resort, it's essentially a fishing port where folk also happen to swim – the beach here is poor to mediocre, improving as you head west.

Accommodation is available at *Villa Maria* (✆0247/22 827; ②) on the beach or, for a higher standard, the *Hotel Efstathia* (✆0247/24 099; ③), actually studio apartments with huge, well-furnished doubles as well as family fourplexes, plus a large pool. **Meals** can be had at *Taverna Tzitzifies*, just by the jujube trees at the east end of things, where the road hits the shore. The island's **campsite** is in an olive grove at the village of **LEPÍDHA**, 750m back up the road to Lakkí; just north of the site, an access drive on the far side of the road leads up a tiny acropolis with stretches of ancient masonry and sparse patches of early Christian mosaics.

Pandéli and Vromólithos

Just less than 3km north of Lakkí, Pandéli and Vromólithos together form the fastest-growing resort on the island – and are certainly two of the more attractive and scenic places to stay, if not eat.

   PANDÉLI is still very much a working port, the cement jetty benefiting local fishermen as well as increasing number of yachts which call here. A negligible beach is compensated for by a relative abundance of non-package **accommodation**, such as the *Pension Happiness* (✆0247/23 498; ②) where the road down from Plátanos meets the sea, or, for a higher standard, the *Niki Studios* (✆0247/25 600; ②) at the base of the road to the castle, airy, Aussie-run and with partial sea views. Up on the ridge dividing Pandéli from Vromólithos, the *Pension Fanari* (✆0247/23 152; ②) would seem a good choice for its calm setting below the road and views across to the castle, but hot-water provision was defective at our stay. Further south along the ridge road, the basic *Hotel Rodon* (✆0247/23 524; ②) is another possibility, though a potentially noisy ouzerí operates right next door, as does the musical *Beach Bar*, perched on a rock terrace below, facing Vromólithos. The other long-lived local **bar** is the civilized *Savana*, at the opposite end of Pandéli, beyond the row of waterfront **tavernas** which, alas, have in recent years become tourist traps of the first order. They get less expensive and less pretentious as you head east towards *Maria's*, an unchanging local institution, decked out in coloured lights and whimsically painted gourds; avoid the lousy *mayireftá* here and stick with the generally reliable seafood.

   VROMÓLITHOS boasts the best easily accessible **beach** on the island, car-free and hemmed in by hills studded with massive oaks. The shoreline is gravel and coarse sand, and the sea here is clean, but as so often on Léros you have to cross a nasty, sharp reef at most points before reaching deeper water. Two **tavernas** behind the beach trade more on their location than their cuisine, but the standard of **accommodation** here is higher than at Pandéli, with the result that much of it tends to be monopolized by package companies. One that isn't is the delightful, en-suite *Pension Margarita* (✆0247/22 889; ②), slightly inland but with a fine sea view and kitchen facilities.

Plátanos and Ayía Marína

The Neoclassical and vernacular houses of **PLÁTANOS**, the island capital 1km west of Pandéli, are draped gracefully along a saddle between two hills, one of them crowned by the inevitable Knights' castle. Known locally as the **Kástro**, this is reached either by a paved but potholed road peeling off the Pandéli road, or via a more scenic stair-path from the central square; the battlements, and the views from them, are dramatic, especially near sunrise or sunset. The medieval church of **Panayía tou Kástrou** inside the gate houses a small museum (daily 8.30am–12.30pm, also Wed, Sat & Sun 3.30–7.30pm; token admission), though its carved *témblon* and naive oratory are more remarkable than the sparse exhibits, which incongruously include a certified chunk of the Berlin Wall.

Except for *Hotel Eleftheria* (☎0247/23 550; ②), with a peaceful hillside location, Plátanos is not really a place to stay or eat, although it's well sown with **shops** and **services**. The latter include Olympic Airways, south of the turning for Pandéli, a **post office**, down the road towards Ayía Marína, and two **banks** (one with a cash dispenser). The single **bus** (schedule posted at the stop, opposite the island's main **taxi** rank) plies four to six times daily between Parthéni in the north and Xirókambos in the south.

Plátanos merges seamlessly with **AYÍA MARÍNA**, 1km north on the shore of a fine bay, still graced by a small, Italian-built public market building. If you're travelling to Léros on an excursion boat or hydrofoil, this will be your port of entry. Although there's no accommodation here, it's arguably the best place to **eat** on the island. Just west of the police station, on the water, *Mezedhopolio Kapaniri* is a good, reasonable ouzerí, at its best after dark, featuring plenty of fried vegetable first courses. Just inland opposite the *Agrotiki Trapeza* in a little alley, the *Kapetan Mihalis* ouzerí claims to be open all day and offers a range of inexpensive local specialities, including various fish marinated in salt (*pastós*). Further west, there's the simple but adequate *Lemonis* grill by the water-side and the 1999-opened *Ouzeri Neromylos*, out by the marooned windmill.A semblance of **nightlife** is provided by a half-dozen bars, such as *Remezzo* near the Agricultural Bank, and *Harama* on the quay.

Álynda and the north

ÁLYNDA, 3km northwest of Ayía Marína, ranks as the longest-established resort on Léros, with development just across the road from a long, narrow strip of pea-gravel beach. It's also the first area for accommodation to open in spring, and the last to shut in autumn. Many of the half-dozen **hotels** and **pensions** here are block-booked by tour companies, but you may have better luck at two outfits overlooking the war cemetery: *Hotel Gianna* (☎247/23 153; ③), with fridge-equipped rooms plus a few studios, or the nearby *Studios Diamantis* (☎247/23 213; ③) just inland, with large balconied units but somewhat unpleasant management. At Krithóni, 1.5km south, more comfort is avail-able at the island's top-flight accommodation: the *Crithoni's Paradise* (☎0247/25 120, fax 24 680; ⑥), a mock-traditional low-rise complex with buffet breakfast, a large pool and all mod cons in the rooms. **Restaurant** options aren't brilliant, except for *To Steki* next to the war cemetery, open year round with good grills and rich mezédhes attract-ing a local clientele.

The **Allied War Graves Cemetery**, mostly containing casualties of the November 1943 battle, occupies a walled enclosure at the south end of the beach; immaculately maintained, it serves as a moving counterpoint to the holiday hubbub outside. The other principal sight at Álynda is the privately run **Historical and Ethnographic Museum** (May–Sept only, daily 10am–noon & 6–9pm; 500dr), housed in the unmis-takable castle-like mansion of Paris Bellinis (1871–1957). Most of the top floor is devot-ed to the Battle of Léros: relics from the sunken *Olga*, a wheel from a Junkers bomber, a stove made from a bomb casing. There's also a rather grisly mock-up clinic (mostly gynecological tools) and assorted rural impedimenta, costumes and antiques.

Alternative beaches near Álynda include **Panayiés**, a series of gravel coves (one naturist) at the far northeast of the bay, and **Goúrna**, the turning for which lies 1km or so off the trans-island road. The latter, Léros's longest sandy beach is hard-packed and gently shelving; it's also wind-buffeted, bereft of any nearby facilities, and permanently fringed by an impromptu car park and construction rubble. A separate road beyond the Goúrna turning leads to **Kokálli**, no great improvement beach-wise, but flanked to one side by the scenic islet of **Áyios Isídhoros**, which is tethered to the mainland by a causeway, its eponymous chapel perched on top.

Seven kilometres from Álynda along the main route north, a marked side-track leads left to the purported **Temple of Artemis**, on a slight rise just west of the airport runway. In ancient times, Léros was sacred to the goddess, and the temple here was supposedly inhabited by guinea fowl – the grief-stricken sisters of Meleager, metamorphosed thus by Artemis following their brother's death. All that remains now are some jumbled, knee-high walls, which may in fact have been an ancient fortress, but the view is superb. The onward road skims the shores of sumpy, reed-fringed Parthéni bay, with its dreary army base (formerly the political prison), until the paved road ends 11km along at **Blefoútis**, a rather more inspiring sight with its huge, virtually landlocked bay. The beach (the rough Lerian norm) has tamarisks to shelter under and an adequate taverna, *Iy Thea Artemi*, for *kalamári*-and-chips-type lunch.

Pátmos

Arguably the most beautiful and certainly the best known of the smaller Dodecanese, **Pátmos** has a distinctive, immediately palpable atmosphere. It was in a cave here that St John the Divine (in Greek, *O Theológos* or "The Theologian"), received the New Testament's Book of Revelation and unwittingly shaped the island's destiny. The monastery honouring him, founded here in 1088 by the Blessed Khristodhoulos (1021–93), dominates Pátmos both physically – its fortified bulk towering high above everything else – and, to a considerable extent, politically. While the monks inside no longer run the island as they did for more than six centuries, their influence has nonetheless stopped Pátmos going the way of Rhodes or Kós.

Despite vast numbers of visitors and the island's firm presence on the cruise, hydrofoil and yacht circuits, tourism has not been allowed to take Pátmos over completely. While there are a number of clubs and even one disco around Skála, drunken rowdiness is virtually unknown, and this is one island where you do risk arrest for nudism on all but the most isolated beaches. Package clients have only since the 1990s begun to outnumber independent visitors, and are pretty much confined to Gríkou and a handful of larger hotels at Skála and Kámbos. Day-trippers still exceed overnighters, and Pátmos seems an altogether different place once the last cruise ship has gone at sunset. Away from Skála, development is appealingly subdued if not deliberately retarded, thanks to the absence of an airport.

Skála and around

SKÁLA, with most of the island's population of about three thousand, seems initially to contradict any solemn, otherworldly image of Pátmos. The waterside, with its ritzy cafés and clientele, is a bit too sophisticated for such a small town, and some of the service staff a bit world-weary. During peak season, the quay and commercial district heave by day with hydrofoil and cruise-ship passengers souvenir-hunting or being shepherded onto coaches for the ride up to the monastery; after dark there's still a considerable traffic in well-dressed cliques of visitors on furlough from the cruise ships which weigh anchor after midnight. In winter (which here means October), Skála assumes a ghost-town air as most shops and restaurants close, their owners and staff back in Rhodes or Athens.

Melóï Beach lies 1.5km to the north (see p.691), one of the most convenient and popular coves on the island; Hóra, a bus or taxi ride up the mountain, is a more attractive base but has few rooms. Yet given time – especially in spring or autumn – Skála reveals some more enticing corners in the residential fringes to the east and west, where vernacular mansions hem in pedestrian lanes creeping up the hillsides. The modern town dates only from the 1820s, when the Aegean had largely been cleared of pirates, but at the summit of the westerly rise, **Kastélli**, you can see the extensive foundations of the island's ancient acropolis.

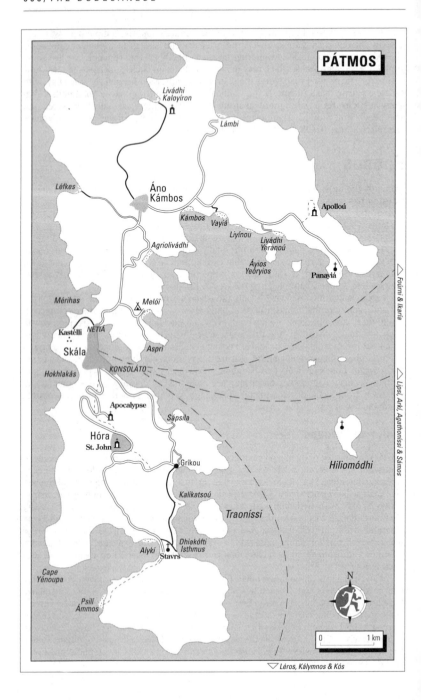

PÁTMOS

Livádhi
Kaloyíron

Lámbi

Léfkes

Áno
Kámbos

Kámbos   Vayiá

Apolloú

Liyínou   Livádhi
Yeranoú

Agriolivádhi

Áyios
Yeóryios

Panayiá

Mérihas

Melóï

Kastélli   NETIÁ

Skála

Aspri

Hokhlakás

KONSOLÁTO

Apocalypse

Sápsila

Hóra
St. John

Hiliomódhi

Gríkou

Kalikatsoú

Traoníssi

Alykí   Dhiakófti
Isthmus
Stavrós

Cape
Yénoupa

Psilí
Ámmos

N

0   1 km

△ Foúrni & Ikaría

△ Lipsí, Arkí, Agathoníssi & Sámos

▽ Léros, Kálymnos & Kós

Practicalities

Almost everything of interest can be found within, or within sight of, the Italian-built municipal "palace": large ferries anchor opposite, the port police occupy the east end, the **post office** one of its corners, while the fairly helpful municipal **tourist information** office (Mon–Sat 9am–1pm) takes up the back. Two banks each have cash dispensers. **Motorbike rental** outfits are common, with lowish rates (3000dr a day) owing to the modest size of the island. **Excursion boats** to Psilí Ámmos, Lipsí and Arkí/Maráthi all leave at about 10am from just in front of Astoria Travel and Apollon Travel, the two most reliable places handling Samos Hydrofoil tickets. G&A Ferries and the *Nissos Kalymnos*/DANE have separate agencies on, or just off, the central square.

ACCOMMODATION

Accommodation touts meet all ferries and hydrofoils, and their offerings tend to be a long walk distant and/or inland – not necessarily a bad thing, as no location is really remote, and anywhere near the waterfront, which doubles as the main road between Gríkou and Kámbos, will be noisy. Pátmos vernacular architecture is quite distinctive, but you wouldn't know it from most lodgings, bland if inoffensive rooms thrown up during the 1980s, with institutional (one might even say monastic) furnishings.

Establishments worth reserving in advance (they'll often then send a van to fetch you) are scattered across several districts. In **central Skála**, good hotel choices include the 1970s-vintage but quiet *Dhiethnes* (☎0247/31 357; ③), back in the fields, or the *Galini*, in a quiet cul-de-sac off the Hóra road (☎0247/31 240; ④).

Konsoláto district, east of the centre near the fishing anchorage, has more high-quality digs, though the worst noise from fishing boats and cruisers coming and going at 4am. Here you'll find the *Captain's House* (☎0247/31 793, fax 32 277; ④), with friendly management, better-than-average furnishings and car rental available, and the **Byzance** a few steps inland (☎0247/31 052; ④), with premises spread over two buildings – go for the larger rooms with balconies looking onto a garden. Some 150m further towards Gríkou, the *Blue Bay* (☎0247/31 165; ④) is not as well appointed but has calm, unbeatable sea views and Skála's only **Internet café** in its favour.

Netiá, the unglamorous area northwest between the power plant and Mérihas cove, is actually a good choice as a base. Various members of a Greek-Australian family run clustered establishments: the *Hotel Australis* (☎0247/31 576; ③), with full breakfast for the price and myriad small kindnesses that guarantee repeat clientele; and the adjacent *Villa Knossos* (☎0247/32 189; ③), whose rooms all have attractive terraces, or the simpler *Pension Sydney* (☎0247/31 139; ③). But the best standard in this area is provided by the *Hotel Asteri* (☎0247/32 465; ④), unimprovably set on a knoll overlooking the bay, in a well-landscaped environment that's also a working farm – guests have own-produced honey, eggs and tomatoes at breakfast.

Pebbly **Hokhlakás** bay, just a ten-minute walk southwest of the central market street, is perhaps the quietest district, with wonderful sunset views. Comfortable options here include the hillside *Summer* (☎0247/31 769; ④); the *Maria* down in the flatlands (☎0247/31 201; ④), where air conditioning and big sea-view balconies make up for tiny bathrooms; the budget en-suite rooms, right on the water, above the *Cactus Restaurant* (☎0247/33 059; ②); or Skála's top accommodation, the *Romeos* (☎0247/31 962; ⑤) on the southerly slope, with a pool, large common areas, and sizable units numerous enough that there's usually a vacancy. Hokhlakás isn't very swimmable; if you're keen to stay nearer a proper beach, there's a well-run, pleasantly set **campsite** (*Stefanos-Flowers*) at **MELÓÏ**, just down the slope from Pátmos's most exclusive digs: the *Porto Scoutari Hotel* (☎0247/33 124, fax 33 175; ⑥), a self-catering bungalow complex open all year, furnished with mock antiques and original art, and arrayed around a pool and sea views. Melóï has an excellent *mayireftá* taverna, *Melloi* (alias *Stefanos*): excellent, reasonably priced and open early or late in the season.

EATING AND DRINKING

Restaurant options are surprisingly limited in Skála; there are altogether too many *souvláki/yíros* joints and not enough good-value sit-down places. Easily the town's best is seafood-only *Ouzeri To Hiliomodhi*, just off the start of the Hóra road, with its vegetarian mezédhes and delicacies such as limpets (served live, be warned), grilled octopus and salted anchovies. Honourable mentions go to *Iy Kalia Kardhia*, well on the way to Hokhlakás, with grilled fish and meat served to a local crowd, and *Cactus* on the beach at Hokhlakás, doing nouvelle-minceur Italian snacks (don't show up too hungry) accompanied by Italian wines and apperitifs. Aside from that, you're best off heading 2km southeast to Sápsila bay, where *Benetos* (June–Sept; reserve on ☎0247/33 089) has since 1998 established a reputation as one of the best spots on the island for seafood and generic Mediterranean dishes. Back in town, the most reliable **breakfast** venue is the second, smaller platía beyond the main one, where *La Frianderie* serves hot drinks and croissants under medieval arches, and the adjacent bakery turns out terrific turnovers. The biggest and most durable **café-bar** is the wood-panelled, barn-like *Café Arion* on the waterside, where local youth play cards; others include open-air *Kafe Aman* in Konsoláto, with music and snacks, or indoor *Pepe Nero*, with a Greek soundtrack.

The monasteries and Hóra

Top of your sightseeing agenda is likely to be the monastery of St John, sheltered behind massive defences in the hilltop capital of Hóra. There is a regular KTEL bus up, or a forty-minute walk by a beautiful old cobbled path. To find its start, proceed through Skála towards Hokhlakás, and once past *Iy Kali Kardhia* bear left onto a lane starting opposite an ironmonger's; follow this uphill to its end on the main road – immediately opposite you'll see the cobbled path. Just over halfway, you might pause at the **monastery of the Apocalypse** (Mon, Wed, Fri & Sat 8am–1.30pm, Tues & Thurs 8am–1.30pm & 4–6pm, Sun 8am–noon & 4–6pm; free) built around the cave where St John heard the voice of God issuing from a cleft in the rock, and where he sat dictating his words to a disciple. In the cave wall, the presumed nightly resting place of the saint's head is fenced off and outlined in beaten silver.

This is merely a foretaste of the **monastery of St John** (Mon, Wed, Fri & Sat 8am–1.30pm, Tues & Thurs 8am–1.30pm & 4–6pm, Sun 8am–noon & 4–6pm; free daily 8am–2pm & Mon, Tues, Thurs & Sun 4–6pm). In 1088, the soldier-cleric Ioannis "The Blessed" Khristodhoulos was granted title to Pátmos by Byzantine Emperor Alexios Komnenos; within three years he and his followers had completed the essentials of the existing monastery, the threats of piracy and the Selçuk Turks dictating a heavily fortified style. A warren of interconnecting courtyards, chapels, stairways, arcades, galleries and roof terraces, it offers a rare glimpse of a Patmian interior; hidden in the walls are fragments of an ancient Artemis temple which stood here before being destroyed by Khristodhoulos. Off to one side, the **treasury** (same hours; 1200dr) justifies its hefty entrance fee for some with its magnificent array of religious treasure, mostly medieval icons of the Cretan school, but pride of place goes to an unusual mosaic icon of Áyios Nikólaos, and the eleventh-century parchment chrysobull (edict) of Emperor Alexios Komnenos, granting the island to Khristodhoulos.

Hóra

The promise of security afforded by St John's stout walls spurred the growth of **HÓRA** immediately outside the fortifications. It remains architecturally homogeneous, with cobbled lanes sheltering dozens of shipowners' mansions from the island's seventeenth- to eighteenth-century heyday. High, windowless walls and imposing wooden doors betray nothing of the opulence within: painted ceilings, pebble-mosaic terraces, flagstoned kitchens, and carved furniture. Inevitably touristic tattiness disfigures the main approaches to the monastery gate, but away from the principal thoroughfares are lanes that rarely see traffic, and by night, when the monastery ramparts are floodlit to startling effect, it's hard to think of a more beautiful Dodecanesian village. Neither should you miss the **view** from Platía Lódza (named after the remnant of an adjacent Venetian *loggia*), particularly at dawn or dusk. Landmasses to the north, going clockwise, include Ikaría, Thýmena, Foúrni, Sámos with the brooding mass of Mount Kérkis, Arkí, and the double-humped Samsun Dağ (ancient Mount Mykale) in Turkey.

Among several tavernas in Hóra, *Vangelis* on the inner square has a wonderful old jukebox, friendly service and view seating on various levels, but alas the cooking has declined of late; you'll probably eat better across the way at *Olympia* (which keeps unpredictable hours), or at *Balkoni* near the monastery. Again on the square, *Kafeteria Stoa* is minimally touristy despite its showcase interior, still functioning as the village kafenío. There are, however, very few places to **stay**; foreigners here are mostly long-term occupants, who have bought up and restored almost a third of the crumbling mansions since the 1960s. Getting a short-term room can be a pretty thankless task, even in spring or autumn; the best strategy is to contact *Vangelis* taverna early in the day, or phone ahead for reservations to Yeoryia Triandafyllou (☎0247/31 963; ③) or Marouso Kouva (☎0247/31 026; ③).

The rest of the island

Pátmos, as a locally published guide once memorably proclaimed, "is immense for those who know how to wander in space and time". Lesser mortals may find it easier to get around on foot, or by bus. There's still scope for **walking** despite a dwindling network of paths; otherwise a single **bus** offers surprisingly reliable service between Skála, Hóra, Kámbos and Gríkou – the main stop, with a posted timetable, is right in front of the main ferry dock.

After its extraordinary atmosphere and magnificent scenery, **beaches** are Patmos's principal attraction. From Hóra, a paved road (partly shortcut by a path) winds east to the sandiest part of rather overdeveloped and cheerless **GRÍKOU**, the main venue for Patmian package tourism – and shut tight as a drum come late September. The beach itself, far from the island's best, forms a narrow strip of hard-packed sand giving way to large pebbles towards the south. En route you pass the hillside *Flisvos* (aka *Floros*) taverna, going since the 1960s with a limited choice of inexpensive *mayireftá*, served on the terrace; they also have simple rooms (②) and fancier apartments (④) – reserve on ☎0247/31 380. Another good **accommodation** option here, open late in the year and not monopolized by packages, is the hillside *Hotel Golden Sun* (☎0247/32 318; ④), with most rooms facing the water.

From Hóra, you can ride a scooter over as far as the Dhiakoftí isthmus, beyond which a thirty-minute walk southwest leads to **Psilí Ámmos** beach. This is the only pure-sand cove on the island, with shade lent by tamarisks, nudism galore at the far south end and a good lunchtime **taverna** that occasionally does roast goat, freshly shot on the surrounding hills. There's also a summer kaïki service here from Skála, departing by 10am and returning at 5pm.

More good beaches are to be found in the north of the island, tucked into the startling eastern shoreline (west-facing bays are uniformly unusable); most are accessible from side roads off the main route north from Skála. **Melóï** is handy and quite appealing, with tamarisks behind the slender belt of sand, and good snorkelling offshore. The first beach beyond Mélóï, **Agriolivádhi (Agriolívadho)**, has mostly sand at its broad centre, kayak rental, and two tavernas: one at mid-beach, the other (*O Glaros*, doing fish) on the south hillside. Hilltop Kámbos is the only other real village on the island, the focus of scattered farms in little oases all around; **Kámbos** beach, 600m downhill, is popular with Greeks, and the most developed remote resort on the island, with seasonal watersports facilities and tavernas (best of these *Ta Kavourakia*), though its appeal is diminished by the road just inland and a rock shelf in the shallows.

East of Kámbos are several less frequented coves, including pebble **Vayiá**, nudist **Liyínou** and sand and gravel **Livádhi Yeranoú**, the latter with more tamarisks, an excellent namesake taverna doing simple but clean grills and salads, and an islet to swim out to. From lower Kámbos you can also journey north to the bay of **Lámbi**, best for swimming when the prevailing wind is from the south, and renowned for an abundance of multicoloured volcanic stones – as well as one of the best beach **tavernas** on the island, *Lambi-Leonidas*, open May to October, with a wide range of fish, mezédhes and grilled meat.

Lipsí

Of the various islets to the north and east of Pátmos, **LIPSÍ** is the largest, most interesting and most populated, and the one that has the most significant summer tourist trade. The presence of a British package company, and the island's appearance on both main-line and off-line ferry routes, mean that it's unwise to show up in peak season without a reservation (though rooms proprietors meet arrivals at other times).

During quieter months, however, Lipsí still makes an idyllic halt, its sleepy pace making plausible a purported link between the island's name and that of Calypso, the nymph who legendarily held Odysseus in thrall. Deep wells provide water for many small farms, but there is only one flowing spring, and pastoral appearances are deceptive – four times the relatively impoverished full-time population of about six hundred live overseas (many in Tasmania, for some reason). Most of those who remain cluster around the fine harbour, as does most of the food and lodging.

A prime **accommodation** choice in all senses is Nikos' and Anna's welcoming *Apartments Galini* (☎0247/41 212, fax 41 012; ②), the first building you see above the ferry jetty; Nikos may take guests for fishing trips on request. Other good options not monopolized by package clients include *Rena's Rooms* (☎0247/41 363 or 41 120; ②), overlooking Liendoú beach, the *Flisvos Pension* at the east end of the port (☎0247/41 261; ②); the *Glaros* (☎0247/41 360; ②) on the hillside behind the *Kalypso Hotel/Restaurant*; and *Studios Paradise* (☎0247/41 125; ③), up on the ridge north of the *Dhelfíni* restaurant which manages it. Top of the heap is the 1997-built *Aphrodite Hotel* (☎0247/41 000 or 41 394; ④), a studio-bungalow complex designed to accommodate package clients, though they're not adverse to walk-ins at slow times.

Among eight or so **tavernas**, mostly on or just behind the quay, *To Dhelfíni* next to the police station and *O Yiannis* next to the eponymous rooms are the best all-rounders, with a good range of grilled items, appetizers and often local bulk wine (white or rosé). *Barbarosa*, on the slope near *Rena's Rooms*, does good vegetable-based *mayireftá*; while *Fish Restaurant* on the quay is reliably fresh. On the waterfront to either side of the *Kalypso*, kafenía and ouzeris with idiosyncratic decor (especially *Asprakis*) offer mezédhes outdoors – an atmospheric and almost obligatory pre-supper ritual. Later on, *The Rock* is the clear winner amongst a handful of **bars** for a congenial crowd and good taped music. Two licensed **travel agents** (Paradhisis and Laid Back) organize excursions and change money, though there's a free-standing Emboriki/Commercial cash dispenser near the former. The **post office** is up a stairway on the attractive cathedral platía, opposite a hilariously indiscriminate **ecclesiastical museum** (theoretically Mon–Fri 9.30am–1.30pm & 4–8pm, Sat/Sun 10am–2pm) featuring such "relics" as oil from the sanctuary on Mount Tabor and water from the Jordan River, as well as archeological finds and two letters from Greek revolutionary hero Admiral Miaoulis.

The island's **beaches** are rather scattered, though none is more than an hour's walk distant. Closest to town, and sandiest, are **Liendoú** and **Kámbos**, but many visitors prefer the attractive duo of **Katsadhiá** and **Papandhriá**, adjacent sand and pebble coves 2km south of the port, with an extremely basic taverna, *Andonis* (May–Sept), just inland from a musical café-bar, *Dilaila* (June–Sept), which dominates the main bay here and runs an informal pine-grove campsite (free but you must buy a snack from them daily).

An hour's walk along the paved road leading west from town brings you to protected **Platýs Yialós**, a small, shallow, sandy bay with a single taverna (June–Sept). During these months a pair of adapted transit vans provides a **minibus** service from the port to all the points cited above; otherwise you can rent a **scooter** from one of two outlets and point them towards isolated east-coast beaches. Of these, **Hokhlakoúra** consists of rather grubby shingle with no facilities, though nearby **Turkómnima** is better. A final ten-minute path scramble gets you from a rough track's end to **Monodhéndhri**, on the northeast coast, notable only for its lone juniper tree and nudist practice – though there's a superior, nameless cove just to the right.

A growing network of roads, paved or otherwise, rather limit opportunities for genuine path-**walks** through the undulating countryside, dotted with blue-domed churches. The most challenging route heads west from the pass between Kámbos and Platýs Yialós to the bay of **Kímisi** (3hr round-trip), where Filippos the octogenarian religious hermit dwells in a tiny monastery above the shore, next to the single island spring. A particularly ugly road has been bulldozed in from the north to disturb his solitude, and partly paved.

Arkí, Maráthi and Agathónissi

About two-thirds the size of Lipsí, **Arkí** is considerably more primitive, lacking drinking water, dynamo electricity (there are solar panels), ferry anchorage or much in the way of a village centre. Just 45 permanent inhabitants eke out a living here, mostly engaged in fishing, though catering for yacht parties attracted here by the superb anchorage is increasingly important. Arkí is an elective, once-weekly stop on the *Nissos Kalymnos* and Miniotis Lines routes: if you want to disembark here, you must warn the captain well in advance, so he can radio for the shuttle service from the island. Most visitors arrive by the more reliable supply boat from Pátmos, which actually docks at the quay. Of the three tavernas around the round harbourside platía, the better two – *Nikolas* (☎0247/32 477) and *O Trypas* ☎0247/32 230) – each control a handful of rooms (②), but avoid August when Italians and Greeks snap up every vacancy in advance. *Nikolas* is more food-orientated, with homemade puddings, while *O Trypas* doubles as the happening music pub, courtesy of the owner's enormous collection of CDs and tapes.

You can swim at the "Blue Lagoon" of **Tiganákia** at the southeast tip of the island – Paradise Travel's excursions stop there – but there are no real beaches to speak of on Arkí. The nearest sandy, tamarisk-shaded one is just offshore on the islet of **Maráthi**, where another pair of **tavernas** cater to day-trippers who come at least several times a week from Pátmos or Lipsí. *Marathi* (☎0247/31 580; ②), run by the engagingly piratical Mihalis Kavouras, is the more traditional, cosy outfit, with waterside seating and simple, adequate rooms; *Pantelis* (☎0247/32 609; ③) is plusher but more commercially minded, and only open June to October.

The small, steep-sided, waterless islet of **Agathoníssi (Gaïdharo)** is too remote – much closer to Turkey than Pátmos, in fact – to be a target of day excursions, though a few are advertised on Sámos. Intrepid German and Italian backpackers (some of whom return annually) form its main clientele, along with a steady trickle of yachts.

Even though hydrofoil connections dovetail well with appearances of the *Nissos Kalymnos*, you should count on staying two to three days, especially if the wind's up. Despite the lack of springs (cisterns are ubiquitous, topped up by tanker shipments from Rhodes), the island is greener and more fertile than apparent from the sea; mastic, carob and scrub oak on the heights overlooks two arable plains in the west. Just 140 people live here, down from several hundred before the last war, but those who've opted to stay seem determined to make a go of raising goats or fishing, and there are virtually no abandoned or neglected dwellings.

Most of the population lives in the hamlet of **MEGÁLO HORIÓ**, just visible on the ridge above the harbour of **Áyios Yeóryios**, and level with tiny **Mikró Horió**. Except for two café-restaurants (*Dhekatria Adherfia* being the more reliable) and the *Katsoulieri Pension* (☎0247/29 035; ②) in Megálo Horió, all amenities are in the port. Here the choice is between *Rooms Theoloyia Yiameou* (☎0247/29 005; ②), the vine-patioed *Hotel Maria Kamitsi* (☎0247/29 003; ②) or *George's Rooms* behind and inland (☎0247/29 064; ②). Worthy **eating/drinking** options in Áyios Yeóryios include *George's* (he of the rooms) near the jetty, local hangout *Limanaki* and the combination breakfast-café and bar, *Yetousa* (incidentally the ancient name for the islet).

With no wheeled transport for hire, exploring involves **walking** along the cement- or dirt-road network, or following a limited number of tracks and paths. If you don't swim at the port, which has the largest beach, you can walk twenty minutes southwest along a track to shingle-gravel **Spiliás**, or continue another quarter-hour along a faint path over the ridge to **Gaïdhourávlakos**, where nudists enjoy a gravel and sand cove. Bays in the east of the island, all served by the paved road system (occasionally shortcut by trails), tend to be dominated by fish farms; **Pálli** is the most pristine of these, though usually visited by boat trip. At **Thóli** in the far southeast, an hour-plus trek away, you can see an arcaded Byzantine structure, probably a combination granary and trading post, and by far the most venerable sight on Agathoníssi.

travel details

To simplify the lists below, several companies/ boats have been left out. DANE or G&A provide a once-weekly link between Rhodes, Kós, Sámos and Thessaloníki, while NEL plies once weekly between Rhodes, Kós, Sámos, Híos, Lésvos, Límnos and Alexandhroúpoli.

The small, slow but reliable **Nissos Kalymnos** (cars carried) is the most regular lifeline of the smaller islands (aside from Kárpathos and Kássos) – it visits them all twice a week between mid-March and mid-January. This ship can be poorly publicized on islands other than its home port; if you encounter difficulties obtaining information, you should phone the central agency on Kálymnos (☎0243/29 612). Specimen schedules, observed for some years now, are as follows:

Mid-March to April, and mid-Sept to mid-Jan: Mon and Fri 7am, leaves Kálymnos for Kós, Níssyros, Tílos, Sými, Rhodes; out to Kastellórizo late afternoon, turns around at midnight. Tues and Sat 9am, departs Rhodes for Sými, Tílos,

Níssyros, Kós, Kálymnos, with a Tues evening return trip to Astypálea. Wed and Sun departs Kálymnos 7am for Léros, Lipsí, Pátmos, Arkí (Wed only), Agathónissi, Pythagório (Sámos), returning from Sámos at 2.30pm bound for Kálymnos via the same islands. Thurs 7am from Kálymnos to Astypálea.

May to mid-June: Mon and Fri 7am, leaves Kálymnos for Kós, Níssyros, Tílos, Sými, Rhodes; out to Kastellórizo late afternoon, turns around at midnight. Tues and Sat 9am, departs Rhodes for Sými, Tílos, Níssyros, Kós, Kálymnos, with an evening return trip both days to Astypálea. Wed and Sun departs Kálymnos 7am for Léros, Lipsí, Pátmos, Arkí (Wed only), Agathónissi, Pythagório (Sámos), returning from Sámos at 2.30pm bound for Kálymnos via the same islands. Thurs, idle.

Mid-June to mid-Sept: Mon and Thurs 7am, leaves Kálymnos for Kós, Níssyros, Tílos, Sými, Rhodes; out to Kastellórizo late afternoon, turns around at midnight. Tues and Fri 9am, departs Rhodes for Sými, Tílos, Níssyros, Kós, Kálymnos, with an evening return trip both days to Astypálea. Wed and Sun departs Kálymnos 7am for Léros, Lipsí, Pátmos, Arkí (Wed only), Agathónissi, Pythagório (Sámos), returning from Sámos at 2.30pm bound for Kálymnos via the same islands. Sat, idle.

Large ferries

Be aware that the following frequencies are only valid for the period mid-June to mid-September; in spring or autumn some of the more esoteric links, such as Astypálea to Tílos/Níssyros, or Lipsí to Sými, will not be operating.

Agathoníssi 1 weekly on Miniotis Lines to Arkí, Lipsí, Pátmos, Sámos (Pythagório).

Astypálea 3–5 weekly to Amorgós, Náxos, Páros & Pireás, 1 to Mýkonos and Sýros, on one of 3 companies; 1–2 weekly to Kós, Kálymnos, Rhodes, Níssyros and Tílos on DANE or G&A.

Hálki 1–2 weekly to Rhodes Town, Kárpathos (both ports), Kássos, Crete and Mílos, all subject to cancellation in bad weather. Once-daily kaïki (6am) to Rhodes (Kámiros Skála).

Kálymnos Similar ferry service to Kós, plus at least 1 weekly to Astypálea, Amorgós (both ports), Náxos, Páros, Sýros; 3 daily ro-ro ferries, well-spaced, to Mastihári; daily morning kaïki to Psérimos; and a daily kaïki (1pm) from Myrtiés to Xirókambos on Léros.

Kárpathos (both ports) and Kássos 2–3 weekly with each other, Crete (Áyios Nikólaos and/or Sitía), Mílos and Rhodes Town, on LANE; 1–2 weekly to Hálki on LANE.

Kastellórizo (Méyisti) 1–2 weekly to Rhodes; 1–2 weekly to Pireás indirectly, via select Dodecanese and Cyclades.

Kós 7–14 weekly to Rhodes and Pireás on G&A or DANE; at least daily to Kálymnos, Léros and Pátmos on G&A or DANE; 1 weekly to Tílos, Níssyros and Sými on DANE or G&A; 1 weekly on G&A or DANE to Astypálea, Sými, Níssyros, Tílos; 3 daily ro-ro ferries year-round from Mastihári to Kálymnos; 1–2 daily from Kós Town to Kálymnos; 4 weekly islanders' kaïkia from Kardhámena to Níssyros.

Léros 7–14 weekly to Pireás, Pátmos, Kálymnos, Kós and Rhodes on G&A or DANE; seasonal daily excursion boats from Ayía Marína to Lipsí and Pátmos (2pm), and from Xirókambos to Myrtiés on Kálymnos (7.30am).

Lipsí 1 weekly to Léros, Kálymnos, Kós, Pátmos, Tílos, Níssyros on DANE or G&A; 1 weekly to Sámos (Vathý) on Nomicos Lines.

Níssyros and Tílos Same as for Sými, plus excursion boats between Níssyros and Kós as follows: to Kardhámena daily at 3.30–4pm; to Kéfalos 4 weekly at 4pm; 4–6 weekly to Kós Town (all of these are seasonal and expensive). The islanders' much cheaper "shopping" kaïki, the *Chrissula*, leaves 4–5 times weekly at 7am.

Pátmos Similar ferry service to Léros, with the addition of 1 weekly to Foúrni, Arkí, Lipsí, Sámos (Pythagório); seasonal tourist boats to Sámos (Pythagório), Lipsí, Arkí and Maráthi on a daily basis; Mon–Thur only to Arkí in low season.

Rhodes 10–12 weekly to Kós and Pireás on G&A or DANE; 7–10 weekly to Kálymnos on G&A or DANE; daily to Léros and Pátmos; 2 weekly to Kárpathos, Kássos, Hálki, Crete (Sitía or Áyios Nikólaos) on LANE; 1–2 weekly to Sými, Lipsí, Tílos, Níssyros, Astypálea on G&A or DANE; 2–3 weekly to Santoríni, Náxos, Páros.

Sými 1–2 weekly to Rhodes, Tílos, Níssyros, Kós, Kálymnos, Léros, Lipsí, Pátmos and Pireás on G&A Ferries or DANE; at least daily catamaran or hydrofoil run by ANES to Rhodes.

Hydrofoils

Two hydrofoil companies, Dodecanese Hydrofoils and Samos Hydrofoils, serve the Dodecanese between mid-May and mid-October, operating out of Rhodes, Kós, Kálymnos and Sámos.

Dodecanese Hydrofoils have three craft, whose schedules are accordingly more complicated; in peak season, there is a daily link Kós–Rhodes and back, usually south in the morning and north in the evening; another craft leaves Kálymnos early in the morning for Kós and a selection of islands north to Pythagório on Sámos; while the third hydrofoil leaves Rhodes at 8am for Kós, returning in the evening; another leaves Kálymnos or Kós at 7 or 8am for Sámos (Pythagório) via select islands, returning at 2.30pm; while the third craft tends to serve a changing cast among the small Dodecanese between Kálymnos and Rhodes, including, once or twice weekly, Hálki, Sými, Tílos, Níssyros and even Astypálea, though some of these runs can get completely booked by transfers of package tour groups. For current routes and schedules, phone ☎0242/25 920.

Samos Hydrofoils, with their GM Caterpillar engines, tend to be more reliable than the Russian-powered Dodecanese Hydrofoils, which did, however, go under new, improved management in 1999. Typically, one craft of Sámos Hydrofoils leaves that island at 7am, reaching Kós along a varying itinerary by 11am or noon, returning via the same islands at 1 or 2pm. Their other craft, based in Kós, departs northward between 7.30am and 8.30am, reaching Pythagório at about 11am and returning via the same ports of call between 1.30pm and 2.30pm. Two to four days weekly, remote or minor ports such as Foúrni, Ikaría, Agathoníssi and Lipsí are served. For precise routes and schedules, ring ☎0273/27 337.

Flights

Note: All are on Olympic Aviation/Olympic Airways unless stated otherwise.

Kárpathos 1–2 daily to Rhodes; 4 weekly to Kássos; 3 weekly to Athens on Olympic, 2 weekly to Athens on Air Manos.

Kássos 1–2 weekly to Kárpathos; 4 weekly to Rhodes.

Kastellórizo (Meyísti) 1 daily to Rhodes June–Sept, 3 weekly otherwise.

Kós 2–3 daily to Athens.

Léros 1 daily to Athens.

Rhodes On Olympic, 5 daily to Athens; 4 weekly to Iráklion; 4–5 weekly to Santoríni; 2 weekly to Thessaloníki; 2 weekly to Mýkonos. On Air Greece, 2 daily to Athens; 3 weekly to Iráklion; 1 daily to Thessaloníki. On Cronus Air, 2 daily to Athens.

International ferries

Kós 2–14 weekly to Bodrum, Turkey (45min), one of the most expensive island–Anatolia services despite the short distance. Greek boat leaves 9am, returns 4pm; 18,000dr return, Greek tax inclusive, 13,000dr one-way; no cheap day-return, no Turkish port tax. Turkish boat, departing 4.30pm, is cheaper at 15,000dr return, 10,000dr one-way, tax inclusive, and provides the only service in winter.

Rhodes Daily in summer to Marmaris, Turkey (1hr) by Greek hydrofoil; 10,000dr one-way, 12,000dr return, plus $10 Turkish port tax. Two to three days weekly a small Turkish ferry (cars carried) puts in appearances. Also 2–3 weekly to Limassol, Cyprus (18hr) and Haifa, Israel (39hr).

CHAPTER TEN

THE EAST AND NORTH AEGEAN

T he seven substantial islands and four minor islets scattered off the north Aegean coast of Asia Minor and northeastern Greece form a rather arbitrary archipelago. Although there are some passing similarities in architecture and landscape, the strong individual character of each island is far more striking. Despite their proximity to modern Turkey, members of the group bear few signs of an Ottoman heritage, especially when compared with Rhodes and Kós. There's the occasional mosque, often shorn of its minaret, but by and large the enduring Greekness of these islands is testimony to the 4000-year Hellenic presence in Asia Minor, which ended only in 1923. This heritage is regularly referred to by the Greek government in an intermittent propaganda war with Turkey over the sovereignty of these far-flung outposts. Tensions here are occasionally worse than in the Dodecanese, aggravated by potential undersea oil deposits in the straits between the islands and the Anatolian mainland. The Turks have also persistently demanded that Límnos, astride the sea lanes to and from the Dardanelles, be demilitarized, but so far Greece has shown no signs of giving in.

The heavy military presence can be disconcerting, and despite the growth of tourism, large tracts of land remain off-limits as military reserves. But as in the Dodecanese, local tour operators do a thriving business shuttling passengers for inflated tariffs between the easternmost islands and the Turkish coast with its amazing archeological sites and busy resorts. Most of these islands' main ports and towns are not quaint, picturesque spots, but urbanized administrative, military and commercial

ACCOMMODATION PRICE CODES

Throughout the book we've used the following **price codes** to denote the cheapest available double room in each establishment in high season. Out of season, rates can drop by more than fifty percent, especially if you are staying for three or more nights. Single rooms, where available, cost around seventy percent of the price of a double.

Rented private rooms on the islands usually fall into the ② or ③ categories, depending on their location and facilities, and the season; a few in the ④ category are more like plush self-catering apartments. They are not generally available from late October through to the beginning of April, when only hotels tend to remain open.

① Up to 6000dr
② 6000–9000dr
③ 9000–12,000dr
④ 12,000–16,000dr
⑤ 16,000–20,000dr
⑥ 20,000dr and upwards

Note: Youth hostels typically charge 2000–2500dr for a dormitory bed.
For more accommodation details, see pp.43–6.

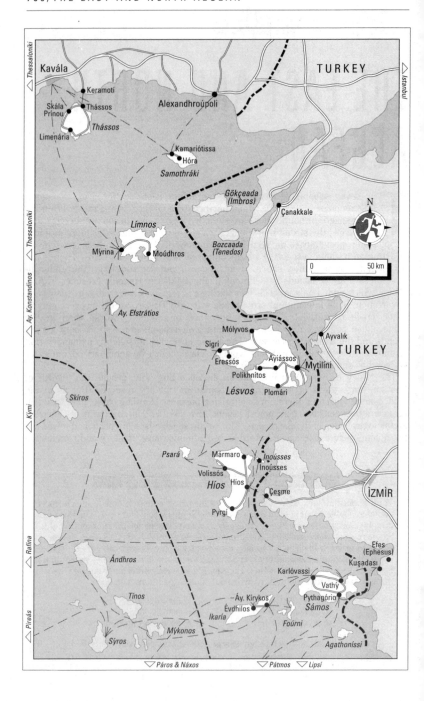

centres. In most cases you should suppress any initial impulse to take the next boat out, and press on into the interiors.

Sámos is the most visited island of the group, but if you can leave the crowds behind, is still arguably the most verdant and beautiful. **Ikaría** to the west remains relatively unspoiled, if a minority taste, and nearby **Foúrni** is a haven for determined solitaries, as are the Híos satellites **Psará** and **Inoússes**, neither of which have any package tourism. **Híos** itself offers far more cultural interest than any of its southern neighbours, but its natural beauty has been ravaged by fires, and the development of tourism was until the late 1980s deliberately retarded. **Lésvos** may not impress initially, though once you get a feel for its old-fashioned, Anatolian ambience, you may find it hard to leave. By contrast virtually no foreigners and few Greeks visit **Áyios Efstrátios**, and with good reason. **Límnos** to the north is a bit livelier, but its appeal is confined mostly to the area around the attractive port town. To the north, Samothráki and Thássos are totally isolated from the others, except via the mainland ports of Kavála or Alexandhroúpoli, and remain easier to visit from northern Greece. **Samothráki** has one of the most dramatic seaward approaches of any Greek island, and one of the more important ancient sites. **Thássos** is more varied, with sandy beaches, mountain villages and minor archeological sites.

Sámos

The lush and seductive island of Sámos was formerly joined to Asia Minor, until sundered from Mount Mykale opposite by Ice Age cataclysms; the resulting 2500-metre strait is now the narrowest distance between Greece and Turkey in the Aegean, except at Kastellórizo. There's little tangible evidence of it today, but Sámos was also once the wealthiest island in the Aegean and, under the patronage of the tyrant Polykrates, home to a thriving intellectual community: Epicurus, Pythagoras, Aristarchus and Aesop were among the residents. Decline set in as the star of Classical Athens was in the ascendant, though Sámos's status was improved somewhat in early Byzantine times when it constituted its own *theme* (imperial administrative district). Towards the end of the fifteenth century, the Genoese abandoned the island to the mercies of pirates; following their attacks, Sámos remained almost uninhabited until 1562, when an Ottoman admiral received permission from the sultan to repopulate it with Greek Orthodox settlers recruited from various corners of the empire.

The heterogeneous descent of today's islanders largely explains an enduring identity crisis and a rather thin topsoil of indigenous culture. Most of the village names are either clan surnames, or adjectives indicating origins elsewhere – constant reminders of refugee descent. Consequently there is no genuine Samiote music, dance or dress, and little that's original in the way of cuisine and architecture. The Samiotes compensated somewhat for their deracination by fighting fiercely for independence during the 1820s, but, despite their accomplishments in sinking a Turkish fleet in the narrow strait and annihilating a landing army, the Great Powers handed the island back to the Ottomans in 1830, with the consoling proviso that it be semi-autonomous, ruled by an appointed Christian prince. This period, referred to as the *Iyimonía* (Hegemony), was marked by a mild renaissance in fortunes, courtesy of the hemp and tobacco trades. However, union with Greece, the ravages of a bitter World War II occupation and mass emigration effectively reversed the recovery until tourism appeared on the horizon during the 1980s.

Today the Samian economy is increasingly dependent on package **tourism**, far too much of it in places; the eastern half of the island, and much of the south coast, has pretty much surrendered to the onslaught of holidaymakers, although the more rugged northwestern part has retained much of its undeveloped grandeur. The rather

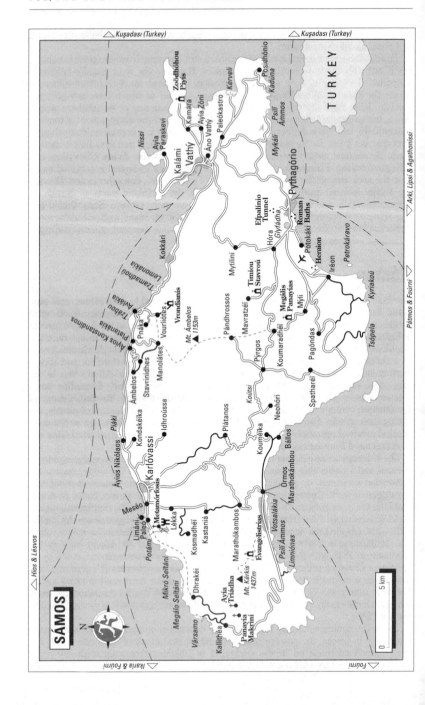

sedate, couples-orientated clientele is overwhelmingly German, Scandinavian, Swiss and Dutch, with a small number of Brits. The absence of an official campsite on such a large island, tame nightlife a world away from that in the Cyclades and phalanxes of self-catering villas hint at the sort of custom expected.

Getting there and getting around

Sámos **airport** lies 14km southwest of Vathý and 3km west of Pythagório. There are no fewer than three **ferry ports**: Karlóvassi in the west, plus Vathý and Pythagório in the east, making it a major hub for travel in every direction. All ferries between Pireás, the Cyclades, Ikaría and Sámos call at both Karlóvassi and Vathý, as do the smaller Miniotis Line ferries linking the island with Híos and, at high season, Foúrni and Ikaría. Vathý also receives the weekly G&A or NEL sailing between northern Greece and the Dodecanese, via most intervening islands, the weekly DANE ferry between Thessaloníki and Rhodes, plus hydrofoils and small ferries from Kuşadası. Pythagório siphons off a bit of the Turkey shipping in high season, and additionally sees two regular weekly ferry connections from as far south as Kós in the Dodecanese, plus a seasonal Miniotis service to Lipsí and Agathonísi. Both ports have hydrofoil services: Vathý is the home base of Samos Hydrofoils, Pythagório the northerly touch-point for Dodecanese Hydrofoils, both lines extending down to Kós.

The **bus terminals** in Pythagório and Vathý lie within walking distance of the ferry dock; at Karlóvassi, you must make your own way the 3km into town from the port. There is no airport bus service; **taxi** fares to various points are stipulated, and in high season taxis to the airport or docks must be booked several hours in advance. The KTEL service itself is excellent along the Pythagório–Vathý and Vathý–Kokkári–Karlóvassi via routes, but poor otherwise; with numerous car and motorbike rental outlets, it's easy to find a good deal outside July or August.

Vathý

Lining the steep northeastern shore of a deep bay, beachless **VATHÝ** is a busy provincial town which grew from a minor anchorage after 1830, when it replaced Hóra as the island's capital. It's an unlikely and somewhat ungraceful resort, which has seen several hotel bankruptcies of late, and minimally interesting for the most part – although the pedestrianized bazaar, tiers of surviving Neoclassical houses and the hill suburb of **ÁNO VATHÝ**, a separate community of tottering, tile-roofed houses have some attraction – and the only real highlight is the excellent **archeological museum** (Tues–Sun 9am–2.30pm; 800dr), set behind the small central park beside the restored Neoclassical town hall. One of the best provincial collections in Greece is housed in both the old Paskhallion building and a modern wing across the way, specially constructed to house the star exhibit: a majestic, five-metre-tall *kouros*, discovered out at the Heraion sanctuary (see p.708). The *kouros*, the largest free-standing effigy to survive from ancient Greece, was dedicated to Apollo, but found together with a devotional mirror to Mut (the Egyptian equivalent of Hera) from a Nile workshop, one of only two discovered in Greece to date.

In the compelling **small-objects collection** of the Paskhallion, more votive offerings of Egyptian design prove trade and pilgrimage links between Sámos and the Nile valley going back to the eighth century BC. The Mesopotamian and Anatolian origins of other artwork confirm the exotic trend, most tellingly in a case full of ivory miniatures: Perseus and Medusa in relief, a kneeling, perfectly formed mini-*kouros*, a pouncing lion and a drinking horn with a bull's head. The most famous local artefacts are the dozen or so bronze griffin-heads, for which Sámos was the major centre of production in the seventh century BC; mounted on the edge of bronze cauldrons, they were believed to ward off evil spirits.

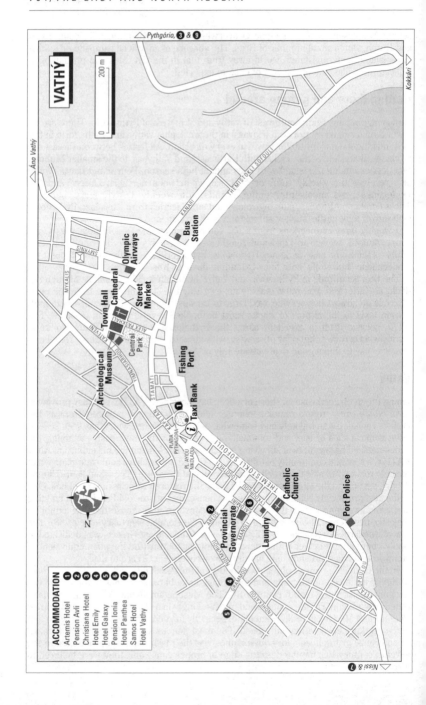

VATHÝ

△ *Áno Vathý*

△ *Pythgório,* ❸ & ❾

▷ *Kokkári*

Bus Station

Olympic Airways

Cathedral

Town Hall

Street Market

Archeological Museum

Central Park

Fishing Port

Taxi Rank

ℹ️

Provincial Governorate

Laundry

Catholic Church

Port Police

N

ACCOMMODATION
- ❶ Artemis Hotel
- ❷ Pension Avli
- ❸ Christiana Hotel
- ❹ Hotel Emily
- ❺ Hotel Galaxy
- ❻ Pension Ionia
- ❼ Hotel Panthea
- ❽ Samos Hotel
- ❾ Hotel Vathy

0   200 m

❼ & *Níssi* ▽

Practicalities

From the **ferry dock** the shore boulevard – Themistoklí Sofoúli – describes a 1300-metre arc around the bay. About 400m along is the traffic circle of Platía Pythagóra, distinguished by its lion statue; some 800m along there's a major turning inland to the **KTEL** terminal, a chaos of buses at a perennially cluttered intersection by the ticket office. The **tourist information** office is at 25-Martíou 4 (May–Oct Mon–Fri 9am–2pm; winter sporadic hours), worth a stop for leaflets, comprehensive bus and ferry schedules and accommodation listings.

The most useful waterfront **ferry/travel agents** for independent travellers are Pythagoras Tours (☎0273/27 337) under the old Catholic church, handling G&A and NEL boats, plus any hydrofoils to Híos; Samos Tours-Horiatopoulos, opposite the jetty, have helpful, native-English-speaking staff and sell most other boat tickets except Agapitos and NEL Lines; By Ship (☎0273/27 337) sells tickets for DANE and Nomikos ferries, as well as being the main agent for Air Manos and Samos Hydrofoils. At present Miniotis Lines representation is in flux; try Nautica or Soutos, both near the *Samos Hotel*. Vathý is chock-a-block with **bike** and **car rental** franchises, which keeps rates reasonable, especially off-season. For motorbikes, try Aramis (☎0273/22 682 at Themistoklí Sofoúli, with a large fleet and recovery service, while for mountain bikes stop at Yiannis at no. 12 (☎0273/23 756). For cars, the preferred outlets are Budget at Themistoklí Sofoúli 31 (☎0273/28 856), Holiday Autos (☎0273/28 833) on Sofoúlis, with branches island wide, or the similarly far-flung Autoplan, a division of Samina Tours (☎0273/23 555). Other amenities include the **post office** on Smýrnis, inland from the Olympic terminal, four waterfront **banks** with cash dispensers and a self-serve **laundry** on pedestrianized Lykoúrgou Logothéti.

ACCOMMODATION

Most **accommodation** available to independent travellers clusters in the hillside district of Katsoúni, more or less directly above the ferry dock; except in August, you'll have little trouble finding affordable vacancies. Budget choices include the rock-bottom, waterfront *Hotel Artemis* (☎0273/27 792; ②) just off "Lion Square"; the *Pension Ionia* (☎0273/28 782; ②), inland at Manoli Kalomíri 5; and the *Pension Avli* (☎0273/22 939; ① non-ensuite, ② en-suite), a wonderful period piece up a nearby stair-street at Aréos 2, the former convent school of the French nuns who ran the Catholic church until 1973.

None of these outfits are palaces by any means; for more luxury start at the surprisingly affordable *Hotel Galaxy* (☎0273/22 665; ③–④), at Angéou 1 near the top of Katsoúni, set in garden surroundings and with a small pool, though you'll have to dodge package allotments. If they're full, try the sympathetic *Emily*, just downhill at the top of Grámmou (☎0273/24 691; ③), a small, personable outfit with a roof garden. The *Samos Hotel* (☎0273/28 377; ③) right by the ferry dock, drops its rates to ② off-season, and is open all year, if a bit noisy. Further afield and a taxi ride uphill, the *Christiana* (☎0273/27 149; ④), the only hotel in Áno Vathý, has a ravine setting, large pool and tie-in (ie discounts) with Budget Car Rental. Some 400m away in Neápoli district near the cemetery, the *Vathy* (☎0273/28 124; ③) is another good choice for its balconied rooms with bay view, small pool and friendly family management. Finally, in Kalámi district 3km north of town, the tiny *Panthea* (☎0273/22 225; ③) enjoys a rural setting, though you'll need transport and advance booking to squeeze in between packages.

Eating and drinking

The only waterfront **tavernas** worth a second glance, at extreme opposite ends of town, are *To Kalami* in the namesake suburb, just before the *Hotel Panthea*, with surprisingly good *mayireftá* and grills, and the pricier *Apanemia Ouzeri*, at the far southwest end of the shore boulevard, with interesting and rather rich recipes – go hungry.

Inland, at the Plátanos junction en route to Áno Vathý, *Ta Kotopoula* is a congenial all-round taverna featuring chicken (as in the name) and mezédhes, open most of the year – most others are shut November to April. Vathý's **nightlife** revolves around its water-front bars, the longest lived of these being *Escape*, on a sea-view terrace at Kefalopoúlou 9 (north of the jetty). The Cine Olympia, inland on Yimnasiarhou Kateveni, is plushly fitted and operates all year with a variable programme of films. There are also two **Internet cafés**: Dhiavlos at Emmanouíl Sofoúli 15, near Olympic Airways, and NetCafe at Themistoklí Sofoúli 175, at the south end of the front.

Around Vathý

The immediate environs of Vathý offer some modest beaches and small hamlets, though you'll usually need your own transport to visit. Two kilometres east and uphill spreads the vast inland plateau of **Vlamarí**, devoted to vineyards and supporting the hamlets of Ayía Zóni and Kamára; from the latter you can climb up a partly cobbled path to the clifftop **monastery of Zoödhóhou Piyís**, for superb views across the end of the island to Turkey.

Heading north out of Vathý, the narrow road ends after 7km at the pebble bay and fishing port of **AYÍA PARASKEVÍ** (or Nissí), with good swimming. Of two tavernas here, *Nissi/O Glaros*, is one of the best this end of the island, with grilled meats and seafoods, well-selected *vegetarian* mezédhes and cheerful terrace service; there's live music at weekends, and it's open weekends in winter.

As you head southeast from Vathý along the main island loop road, the triple chapel at **Trís Ekklisíes** marks an important junction, with another fork 100m along the left-hand turning. Bearing left twice takes you through the hilltop village of Paleókastro, 3km beyond which is another junction. Forking left yet again, after another 3km you reach the quiet, striking bay of **Kérveli**, with a small beach, a pair of tavernas (the friendly *Sea and Dolphins* has good mezédhes and *soúma*, the local spirit) by the water and another characterful favourite with simple grills only, *Iy Kryfi Folia*, about 500m uphill along the access road. Taking the right forks leads to **Possidhónio**, with an even smaller beach and another pair of tavernas (the right-hand one takes its cooking more seriously). Turning right at the junction before Paleókastro leads to the beaches of Mykáli and Psilí Ámmos, the only spots in this section with a bus service. **Mykáli**, a kilometre of windswept sand and gravel, has been encumbered with three package hotels; the best place to try on spec here is *Villa Barbara* (☎0273/25 192; ④), apart-ments behind the *Sirenes Beach* hotel. **Psilí Ámmos**, further east around the headland, is a crowded, sandy cove backed by several commercial tavernas; if you swim to the islet beware of strong currents which sweep through the narrow straits.

Pythagório and around

Most traffic south of Vathý heads for **PYTHAGÓRIO**, the island's premier resort, renamed in 1955 to honour native son Pythagoras, ancient mathematician, philosopher and mystic. Until then it was known as Tigáni (Frying Pan) – in mid-summer you'll learn why. The sixth-century BC tyrant Polykrates had his capital here, now subject to excavations which have forced modern Pythagório to expand northeast and uphill. The village core of cobbled lanes and thick-walled mansions abuts a small **harbour**, fitting almost perfectly into the confines of Polykrates' ancient port, but today devoted almost entirely to pleasure craft and overpriced cocktail bars.

Sámos's most complete **castle**, the nineteenth-century *pýrgos* of local chieftain Lykourgos Logothetis, overlooks both the town and the shoreline. Logothetis, togeth-er with a certain "Kapetan Stamatis" and Admiral Kanaris, chalked up decisive victories over the Turks in the summer of 1824. The final battle was won on Transfiguration Day (6 August), and accordingly the church inside the castle precinct is dedicated to this festival. More antiquities include the fairly dull **Roman baths**, signposted as "Thermai", 400m west of town (Tues–Sun 8.30am–2.45pm; free) and a minuscule **archeological collection** in the town hall on Platía Irínis (Tues–Thur & Sun 9am–2pm, Fri–Sat 10am–2pm; free). Considerably more interesting is the **Efpalínio tunnel** (Tues–Sun 8.45am–2.30pm; 500dr), a 1040-metre aqueduct bored through the mountain just north of Pythagório at the behest of Polykrates. To get there, take the signposted path from the shore boulevard at the west end of town, which meets the vehicle access road towards the end of a twenty-minute walk.

Further subterranean experience can be had at the monastery of **Panayía Spilianí**, high on the hillside over town. Though most of this has been insensitively restored and touristified, behind the courtyard lies a cool, hundred-metre-long grotto, at one end of which is a shrine to the Virgin (open daylight hours; free). This was the presumed residence of the ancient oracular priestess Fyto, and a pirate-safe hideout in medieval times.

Practicalities

If there are any **accommodation** vacancies – and it's best not to assume this in midseason – rooms proprietors meet incoming ferries and hydrofoils. The **tourist information booth** (daily June–Sept 8am–10pm; ☎0273/61 389), on the main thoroughfare Lykoúrgou Logothéti, can help in finding rooms and sells tickets for the *Nissos Kalymnos* ferryboat. Quietly located at the seaward end of Odhós Pythagóra, south of Lykoúrgou Logothéti, the modest *Tsambika* (☎0273/61 642; ②) or the more comfortable *Dora*, a block west (61 456; ③ includes breakfast) are two pensions worth considering. Some 50m inland from the north side of the harbour past the customs house, *Lambis Rooms* on Odhós Íras (☎0273/61 396; ②)is another backpackers' transit stop. Another peaceful area is the hillside north of Platía Irínis, where *Studios Galini* (☎0273/61 167; winter ☎01/98 42 248; ④) has high-quality self-catering units with ceiling fans, balconies and kind English-speaking management.

Eating out can be frustrating in Pythagório, with value for money often a completely alien concept. Away from the water, the *Platania* taverna, under two eucalyptus trees opposite the town hall, is relatively the least touristy option, and okay for a pre-ferry lunch; for waterside dining, you're best off at the far east end of the quay, where the *Remataki* ouzerí features vegetarian dishes such as *angináres ala políta*, and is the only spot the locals themselves will be seen in. Night-owls gather at either *Disco Labito* near the eponymous hotel, or the *Mythos Club* on Platía Irínis. The all-year Cine Rex in Mytilíni village, 7km northwest, is inexpensive with standard first-run fare.

If none of this appeals, the outbound **bus stop** lies just west of the intersection of Lykoúrgou Logothéti and the road to Vathý, with better than average fast food (a creperie, a simple grill) available just adjacent. Two **banks** (both with cash dispensers) and the **post office** are also on Lykoúrgou Logothéti. The flattish country to the west is ideal for cycling, a popular activity, and if you want to rent a **motorbike**, several outfits on Logothéti will oblige you.

Around Pythagório

The main local beach stretches for several kilometres west of the Logothetis "castle", punctuated about halfway along by the end of the airport runway, and the cluster of nondescript hotels known as **POTOKÁKI**. Just before the turnoff to the heart of the beach sprawls the ultra-luxurious *Doryssa Bay* complex, which includes a meticulously concocted fake village, guaranteed to confound archeologists of future eras. No two of the units, joined by named lanes, are alike, and there's even a platía with an expensive café. If you don't mind the hotel crowds and low-flying jets, the sand-and-pebble **beach** here is well groomed and the water clean; you'll have to head out to the end of the road for more seclusion.

The Potokáki access road is a dead end, with the main island loop road pressing on past the turnoff for the airport and Iréon hamlet. Under layers of alluvial mud, plus today's runway, lies the processional Sacred Way joining the ancient city with the **Heraion**, the massive shrine of the Mother Goddess (Tues–Sun 8.30am–2.45pm; 800dr). Much touted in tourist literature, this assumes humbler dimensions – one surviving column and assorted foundations – upon approach. Yet once inside the precinct you sense the former grandeur of the temple, never completed owing to Polykrates' untimely death at the hands of the Persians. The site chosen, near the mouth of the still-active Imvrassós stream, was Hera's legendary birthplace and site of her trysts with Zeus; in the far corner of the fenced-in zone you glimpse a large, exposed patch of the paved Sacred Way.

The modern resort of **IRÉON** nearby is a nondescript grid of dusty streets behind a coarse-shingle beach, attracting a slightly younger and more active clientele than Pythagório. Here you'll find more non-package rooms and two small hotels: *Venetia* (☎0273/61 195; ②) and *Heraion* (☎0273/61 180; ②), both within sight of the water. The oldest and most authentic **taverna** is the *Ireon*, at the far west end by the fishing harbour.

Southern Sámos

Since the circum-island bus only passes through or near the places below once or twice daily, you really need your own vehicle to explore them. Some 5km west of Hóra, a well-marked side road leads up and right to **MAVRATZÉÏ**, one of two Samian "pottery villages"; this one specializes in the *Koúpa tou Pythagóra* or "Pythagorean cup", supposedly designed by the sage to leak over the user's lap if they are over-filled. Slightly more practical wares can be found in **KOUMARADHÉÏ**, back on the main road, another 2km along.

From here you can descend a paved road to the sixteenth-century monastery of **Megális Panayías** (theoretically daily 9am–noon & 5–7pm; ring keeper on ☎61 449 to check), containing the finest frescoes on the island. This route continues to **MÝLI**, submerged in citrus groves and also accessible from Iréon. Four kilometres above Mýli sprawls **PAGÓNDAS**, a large hillside community with a splendid main square and an unusual communal fountain house on the south hillside. From here, a scenic paved road curls 9km around the hill to **SPATHARÉÏ** – its surroundings devastated by fire in 1993 – but set on a natural balcony offering the best sea views this side of the island. From Spatharéï, the road loops back 6km to **PÝRGOS**, lost in pine forests at the head of a ravine and the centre of Samian honey production; the most reliable local **taverna** (June–Oct) lies 3km west, in the plane-shaded Koútsi ravine.

The rugged and beautiful coast south of the Pagóndas–Pýrgos route is largely inaccessible, glimpsed by most visitors for the first and last time from the descending plane bringing them to Sámos. **Tsópela**, a highly scenic sand and gravel cove at a gorge mouth, is the only beach here with marked track access and a good seasonal taverna; you'll need a sturdy motorcycle (not a scooter) or jeep to get down there. The western reaches of this shoreline, which suffered comprehensive fire damage in 1994, are approached via the small village of **KOUMÉÏKA**, with a massive inscribed marble fountain and a pair of kafenía on its square. Below extends the long, pebble bay at **Bállos**, with sand, a cave and naturists at the far east end. Bállos itself is merely a sleepy collection of summer houses, several simple places to **stay** and a few **tavernas**. Returning to Kouméïka, the dubious-looking side road just before the village marked "Velanidhiá" is in fact partly paved and usable by any vehicle – a very useful short cut if you're travelling towards the beaches beyond Órmos Marathokámbou (see p.712).

Kokkári and around

Leaving Vathý on the north coastal section of the island loop road, there's little to stop for until you reach **KOKKÁRI**, the third major Samian tourist centre after Pythagório and the capital. Sadly, while lower Vathý and Pythagório had little beauty to sacrifice, much has been irrevocably lost here. The town's profile, covering two knolls behind twin headlands, remains unaltered, and several families still doggedly untangle their fishnets on the quay, but in general its identity has been altered beyond recognition, with constant inland expansion over vineyards and the abandoned fields of boiling onions that gave the place its name. Since the exposed, rocky beaches here are buffeted by near-constant winds, the promoters have made a virtue of necessity by developing the place as a successful windsurfing resort.

Practicalities

As in Vathý and Pythagório, a fair proportion of Kokkári's **accommodation** is block-booked by tour companies; establishments not completely devoted to such trade include *Lemos* (☎0273/92 250; ④), near the north end of the west beach, and the more modest *Vicky* (☎0273/92 231; ③), facing the same strand. For a guaranteed view of the fishing port, try the *Pension Alkyonis* (☎0273/92 225; ②). Otherwise Yiorgos Mihelios has a wide range of rooms and flats to rent (☎0273/92 456; ②–④), including the *Pension Green Hill*. If you get stuck, seek assistance from the seasonal **EOT post** (☎0273/92 217), housed in a portacabin near the main church.

Most **tavernas** line the north waterfront, and charge above the norm, though they're steadily losing ground to breakfast or cocktail bars. At the far east end of things, *Ta Adhelfia /The Brothers* is a civil, good-value place strong on grilled fish and meat, but with a few oven dishes daily; *Karyatidha*, two doors along, is another good all-rounder, while *Piccolo Porto* still further west does excellent Italian dishes, including wood-fired pizzas. Most (noisy) **bars** ring the little square just west of where the concreted stream (with its family of ducks) meets the sea, but there's also the more elaborate disco the *Cabana Beach Club* on the west beach.

Other amenities include an Emboriki/Commercial Bank **cash dispenser** on the through road, a **post office** in a portacabin on a seaward lane and a long-hours, self-service **laundry** next to that.

West of Kokkári: the coast

The closest sheltered beaches are thirty to forty minutes' walk away to the west, all with sunbeds and permanently anchored umbrellas. The first, **Lemonákia**, is a bit too close to the road, with an obtrusive café; 1km beyond, the graceful crescent of **Tzamadhoú** figures in virtually every EOT poster of the island. With path-only access, it's a bit less spoiled, and each end of the beach (saucer-shaped pebbles) is by tacit consent a nudist zone. There's one more pebble bay, 7km west beyond Avlákia, called **Tzábou**, but it's not worth a special detour when the prevailing northwest wind is up.

The next spot of any interest along the coast road is **Platanákia**, essentially a handful of undistinguished tavernas and rooms for rent at a bridge by the turning for Manolátes (see p.710). Platanákia is actually the eastern suburb of **ÁYIOS KON-STANDÍNOS**, whose surf-pounded esplanade has been prettified. However, there are no usable beaches within walking distance, so the collection of warm-toned stone buildings, with few modern intrusions, constitutes a peaceful alternative to Kokkári. In addition to modest 1970s **hotels**, such as the *Four Seasons* (①) or the *Atlantis* (☎0273/94 329; ①) just above the highway, there's a new generation of more modern rooms below the road, such as *Maria's* (☎0273/94 460; ③). **Eating** out, look no further than the excellent *To Kyma* at the east end of the quay, with good bulk wine and *mayireftá*, or (even better) the *Aeolos* at the far west end of the esplanade (June-Sept), with terrific fish and a few well-chosen baked dishes.

Once past "Áyios", as it's locally abbreviated, the mountains hem the road in against the sea, and the terrain doesn't relent until **Kondakéïka**, whose diminutive shore annexe of **Áyios Nikólaos** has an excellent venue for fish meals in *Iy Psaradhes*, its terrace lapped by the waves. There's also the reasonable beach of **Piáki**, ten minutes' walk east past the last studio units, evidence of a mild explosion in package development here since 1995.

Hill villages

Inland between Kokkári and Kondakéïka, an idyllic landscape of pine, cypress and orchards is overawed by dramatic mountains, so far little burned. Despite destructive nibblings by bulldozers, some of the trail system linking the various **hill villages** is still intact, and walkers can return to the main highway to catch a bus home. Failing that, most of the communities can provide a bed at short notice.

The monastery of **Vrondianís** (Vrónda), directly above Kokkári, is a popular destination, although since the army now uses it as a barracks, the place only really comes alive during its annual festival (7–8 September). **VOURLIÓTES**, 2km west of the monastery, has beaked chimneys and brightly painted shutters sprouting from its typical tile-roofed houses. On the photogenic central square, the oldest and arguably best of several tavernas is *The Blue Chairs*, serving two local specialities: *revithokeftédhes* (chickpea patties) and the homemade *moskháto* dessert wine.

MANOLÁTES, further uphill and an hour-plus walk away via a deep river canyon, also has several simple tavernas (the pick of these being hospitable *Loukas* at the top of the village, with the best views on the island), and is the most popular trailhead for the five-hour round-trip up **Mount Ámbelos** (Karvoúnis), the island's second highest summit. From Manolátes you can no longer easily continue on foot to Stavrinídhes, the next village, but should plunge straight down, partly on a cobbled path, through the shady valley known as **Aïdhónia** (Nightingales), towards Platanákia. Manolátes has accommodation, *Studios Angela* at the edge of town (π0273/94 478; ③), but by far the most characterful base in the area is down in Aïdhónia at the *Hotel Aidonokastro* (π0273/94 404, mobile 093/7069784; ④). Here the kindly, English-speaking Yannis Pamoukis has renovated half the abandoned hamlet of **Valeondátes** as a unique cottage-hotel, each former house comprising a pair of two- or four-person units with traditional touches.

Karlóvassi

KARLÓVASSI, 35km west of Vathý and the second town of Sámos, is decidedly sleepier and more old-fashioned than the capital, despite having roughly the same population. Though lacking in distinction, it's popular as a base for exploring western Sámos's excellent beaches and walking opportunies. The name, despite a vehement denial of Ottoman legacy elsewhere on Sámos, appears to be a corruption of the Turkish for "snowy plain" – the plain in question being the conspicuous saddle of Mount Kérkis overhead. The town divides into four straggly neighbourhoods: Néo, well inland, whose untidy growth was spurred by the influx of post-1923 refugees; Meséo, across the usually dry riverbed, tilting appealingly off a knoll towards the shore; and postcardworthy Paleó (or Áno), above Limáni, the small harbour district.

Most tourists stay at or near **Limáni**, the part of town with most of the tourist facilities. Hotels tend to have road noise and not much view; **rooms**, all in the inland pedestrian lane behind the through road, are quieter – try those of Vangelis Feloukatzis (π0273/33 293; ②). The port itself is an appealing place with a working boatyard at the west end and all the **ferry-ticket agencies** grouped at the middle; often a shuttle-bus service operates from Néo Karlóvassi, timed to boat arrivals and departures. Tavernas and bars are abundant on the quay, though the only remarkable ones are *Rementzo*, tellingly the locals' hangout, and the more touristy *Boussoulas* next door, which does however stay open year-round, with consistent quality. There's also an enjoyable summer cinema on the through road.

Immediately overhead is the partly hidden hamlet of **Paleó**, its hundred or so houses draped on either side of a leafy ravine. The only facilities are the sporadically functioning café *To Mikro Parisi*. **Meséo**, just east, is a conceivable alternative base to Limáni, with the *Hotel Aspasia* (☎0273/32 363; ④), well sited 100m west of the wood-fired bakery, with a pool and air-conditioning. Following the street linking the central square to the waterfront, you pass one of the improbably huge, turn-of-the-century churches, topped with twin belfries and a blue-and-white dome, which dot the coastal plain here. Just at the intersection with the shore road you'll find the friendly, good-value *To Kyma* ouzerí (April–Oct), much improved under new management since 1998, and the best place in town to watch the sunset over a selection of mezédhes.

Néo has little to recommend it besides a wilderness of derelict stone-built warehouses and mansions down near the river mouth, reminders of the long-vanished leather industry which flourished here during the first half of this century. However, if you're staying at Limáni, you'll almost certainly visit one of the three **banks** (cash dispensers), the **post office** or the **bus stop** on the main lower square. There are virtually no **eateries** except the popular, year-round *Dionysos Psistaria*, on the west side of town at the start of the Marathókambos road.

Western Sámos

Visitors tolerate dull Karlóvassi for the sake of western Sámos's excellent **beaches**. Closest of these is **Potámi**, forty minutes' walk away via the coast road from Limáni or an hour by a more scenic, high trail from Paleó. This broad arc of sand and pebbles gets crowded at summer weekends, when virtually the entire population of Karlóvassi descends on the place. Near the end of the trail from Paleó stands *To Iliovasilema*, a friendly fish taverna; there are also a very few **rooms** signposted locally, and many folk camp rough along the lower reaches of the river which gives the beach its name.

A streamside path leads twenty minutes inland, past the eleventh-century church of **Metamórfosis** – the oldest on Sámos – to a point where the river disappears into a small gorge (a new, guard-railed but still perilous stairway takes you up and left here). Otherwise, you must swim and wade 100m in heart-stoppingly cold water through a sequence of fern-tufted rock pools before reaching a low but vigorous waterfall; bring shoes with good tread and perhaps even rope if you want to explore above the first cascade. You probably won't be alone until you dive in, since the canyon is well known to locals and tour agencies. Just above the Metamórfosis church, a clear if precipitous path leads up to a small, contemporaneous **Byzantine fortress**. There's little to see inside other than a subterranean cistern and badly crumbled lower curtain wall, but the views out to sea and up the canyon are terrific, while in October the place is carpeted with pink autumn crocuses.

The coast beyond Potámi ranks among the most beautiful and unspoiled on Sámos; since the early 1980s it has served as a protected refuge for the rare monk seal. The dirt track at the west end of Potámi bay ends after twenty minutes on foot, from which you backtrack 100m or so to find the side trail running parallel to the water. After twenty minutes along this you'll arrive at **Mikró Seïtáni**, a small pebble cove guarded by sculpted rock walls. A full hour's walk from the trailhead, through partly fire-damaged olive terraces, brings you to **Megálo Seïtáni**, the island's finest beach, at the mouth of the intimidating Kakopérato gorge. You'll have to bring food and water, though not necessarily a swimsuit – there's no dress code at either of the Seïtáni bays.

Southwestern beach resorts

Heading south out of Karlóvassi on the island loop road, the first place you reach is **MARATHÓKAMBOS**, a pretty, amphitheatrical village overlooking the eponymous gulf; there's a taverna or two, but no short-term accommodation. Its port, **ÓRMOS MARATHOKÁMBOU**, 18km from Karlóvassi, has recently emerged as a tourist resort, though some character still peeks through in its backstreets. The port has been improved, with kaïkia offering day-trips to Foúrni and the nearby islet of Samiopoúla, while the pedestrianized quay has become the focus of attention, home to several **tavernas** – best of these, by a nod, *Kyra Katina*, with a good range of seafood if somewhat obsequious service. Among the few non-packaged **accommodation** outfits, try *Studios Avra* (☎0273/37 221; ②), unimprovably perched above the jetty.

The beach immediately east from Órmos is hardly the best; for better ones continue 2km west to **VOTSALÁKIA** (officially signposted as "Kámbos"), Sámos' fastest-growing resort, straggling a further 2km behind the island's longest (if not its most beautiful) beach. But for most, Votsalákia is still a vast improvement on the Pythagório area, and the mass of 1437-metre Mount Kérkis overhead rarely fails to impress (see below). As for **accommodation**, Emmanuil Dhespotakis (☎0273/31 258; ③) has numerous premises towards the quieter, more scenic western end of things. Also in this vicinity is *Loukoullos*, an unusual **ouzerí-taverna** overlooking the sea. Other facilities include branches of nearly all the main Vathý travel agencies, offering **vehicle rental** (necessary, as only two daily buses call here) and money exchange.

If Votsalákia doesn't suit, you can continue 3km past to the 600-metre beach of **Psilí Ámmos**, more aesthetic and not to be confused with its namesake beach in the southeast corner of Sámos. The sea shelves very gently here, and cliffs shelter clusters of naturists at the east end. Surprisingly there is still little development: just two small studio complexes in the pines at mid-beach, and two tavernas back up on the road as you approach, either of these fine for a simple lunch. Access to **Limniónas**, a smaller cove 2km further west, passes the *Limnionas Bay Hotel* (☎0273/37 057; ④), much the highest standard accommodation locally with its tiered units arrayed around a garden and pool. Yachts and pleasure kaïkia occasionally call at the protected bay, which offers decent swimming away from a rock shelf at mid-strand, especially at the east end where there's a simple **taverna**.

Mount Kérkis and around

Gazing up from a supine seaside position, you may be inspired to climb **Mount Kérkis**. The classic route begins at the west end of the Votsalákia strip, along the bumpy jeep track leading inland towards Evangelistrías convent. After thirty minutes on the track system, through fire-damaged olive groves and past charcoal pits (a major local industry), the path begins, more or less following power lines up to the convent. A friendly nun may proffer an oúzo in welcome and point you up the paint-marked trail, continuing even more steeply up to the peak. The views are tremendous, though the climb itself is humdrum once you're out of the trees. About an hour before the top there's a chapel with an attached cottage for sheltering in emergencies, and just beyond, a welcome spring. All told, it's a seven-hour outing from Votsalákia and back, not counting rest stops.

Less ambitious walkers might want to circle the flanks of the mountain, first by vehicle and then by foot. The road beyond Limniónas to Kallithéa and Dhrakéï, truly back-of-beyond villages with views across to Ikaría, is paved as far as Kallithéa, making it possible to venture out here on an ordinary motorbike. The bus service is better during the school year, when a vehicle leaves Karlóvassi (1pm, Mon–Fri) bound for these remote spots; during summer it only operates two days a week (currently Mon & Fri).

From **DHRAKÉÏ**, the end of the line with just a pair of very simple kafenía to its credit, a track, then trail, descends ninety minutes through partly burned forest to

Megálo Seïtáni, from where it's easy enough to continue on to Karlóvassi within another two-and-a-half hours. People attempting to reverse this itinerary often discover to their cost that the bus (if any) returns from Dhrakëï early in the day, at about 2.30pm, compelling them to stay at one of two rather expensive **rooms** establishments (summer only) in **KALLITHÉA**, and dine there at either the simple psistariá on the square or a newer, more varied taverna on the western edge of the village. From Kallithéa, a newer track (from beside the cemetery) and an older trail both lead up within 45 minutes to a spring, rural chapel and plane tree on the west flank of Kérkis, with path-only continuation for another thirty minutes to a pair of cave-churches. **Panayía Makriní** stands detached at the mouth of a high, wide but shallow grotto, whose balcony affords terrific views of Sámos's west tip. By contrast, **Ayía Triádha**, a ten-minute scramble overhead, has most of its structure made up of cave wall; just adjacent, another long, narrow, volcanic cavern can be explored with a torch some hundred metres into the mountain.

After these subterranean exertions, the closest spot for a swim is **Vársamo** (Válsamo) cove, 4km below Kallithéa and reached via a well-signposted dirt road. The beach here consists of multicoloured volcanic pebbles, with two caves to shelter in and a single taverna just inland.

Ikaría

Ikaría, a narrow, windswept landmass between Sámos and Mýkonos, is little visited and invariably underestimated by travel journalists who haven't even bothered to show up; the name supposedly derives from the legendary Icarus, who fell into the sea just offshore after the wax bindings on his wings melted. For years the only substantial tourism was generated by a few **hot springs** on the south coast, some reputed to cure rheumatism and arthritis, some to make women fertile, though others are so highly radioactive that they've been closed for some time.

Ikaría, along with Thessaly on the mainland and Lésvos, has traditionally been one of the Greek Left's strongholds. This tendency dates from the long decades of right-wing domination in Greece, when (as in past ages) the island was used as a place of **exile** for political dissidents. Apparently the strategy backfired, with the transportees favourably impressing and proselytizing their hosts; at the same time, many Ikarians emigrated to North America, and ironically their regular capitalist remittances help keep the island going. It can be a bizarre experience to be treated to a monologue on the evils of US imperialism, delivered by a retiree in perfect Alabaman English.

These are not the only Ikarian quirks, and for many the place is an acquired taste, contrasting strongly (for better or worse) with Sámos. Except for forested portions in the west (now being steadily burned off to create land for hotels), it's not a strikingly beautiful island, with most of the terrain consisting of scrub-covered schist put to good use as building material. The mostly desolate south coast is fringed by steep cliffs, while the north face is less sheer but nonetheless furrowed by deep canyons creating hairpin bends extreme even by Greek-island standards. Neither are there many picturesque villages, since the rural schist-roofed houses are generally scattered so as to be next to their famous apricot orchards, vineyards and fields.

Until the mid-1990s, the Ikarians resisted most attempts to develop their island for conventional tourism: charter flights still don't land here, since the northeastern airport can't accommodate jets. Long periods of punitive neglect by Athens (and provincial HQ Sámos) have made the locals profoundly self-sufficient and idiosyncratic, and tolerant of the same in others. Local pride dictates that outside opinion matters not a bit, and locals often seem to have little idea what "modern tourists" expect. This lack of obsequiousness, and a studied eccentricity, are often mistaken for hostility.

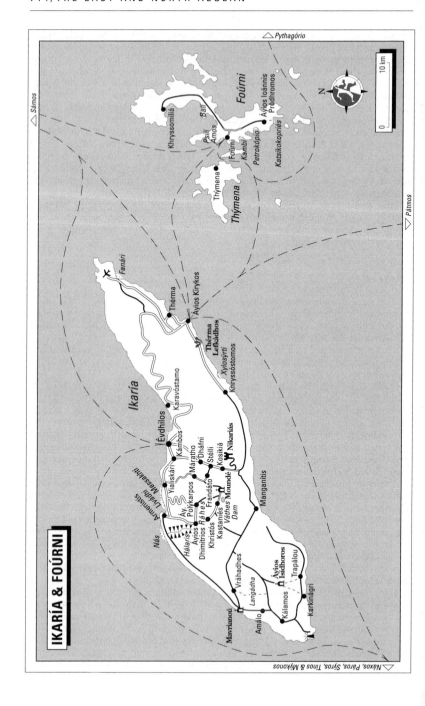

IKARÍA & FOÚRNI

Áyios Kírykos

Roughly half of passing ferries call at the south-coast port and capital of **ÁYIOS KÍRYKOS**, about 1km southeast of the island's main thermal resort. Because of the spa trade, beds are at a premium in town; arriving in the evening from Sámos, accept any reasonable offers of rooms at the jetty, or – if in a group – proposals of a taxi ride to the north coast, which shouldn't cost more than 7500dr per vehicle to Armenistís. A cream and green **bus** sets out across the island from the main square (daily, in theory 10am, & 1.30pm on Mon, Wed & Fri to Armenistís; Mon–Fri noon to Évdhilos only).

The baths (daily 8am–1pm) in **Thérma** are rather old-fashioned stone tubs, with preference given to those under medical care. A better bet for a less formal soak are the more natural, shoreline hot springs at **Thérma Lefkádhos**, 3km southwest of Áyios Kírykos, below a cluster of villas. Here the seaside spa is derelict, leaving the water to boil up right in the shallows, mixing with the sea between giant volcanic boulders to a pleasant temperature.

Practicalities

Hydrofoils, the Miniotis Lines boats and the kaïki for Foúrni use the small east jetty; large ferries dock at the main west pier. There are several **hotels**, such as the *Isabella* (☎0275/22 839; ③), or the friendly, basic but spotless *Akti* (☎0275/22 694; ②), on a knoll east of the hydrofoil and kaïki quay, with views of Foúrni from the garden. Otherwise, **pensions** and **rooms** are not especially cheap: directly behind the base of the ferry jetty and a little to the west there's the well-appointed *Pension Maria-Elena* (☎0275/22 543; ②), with sea views. Both the studios (☎0275/22 276; ③) above the *Snack Bar Dedalos* and the prominently marked, clean *dhomátia* run by Ioannis Proestos (☎0275/23 496; ②), get noise from the several kafenía and snack bars below.

Eating out, you've even less choice than in lodging. Give the obvious quayside eateries a miss in favour of the grilled dishes served up at the *Tzivaeri* ouzerí, just inland from Ioannis Proestos's rooms, or *Iy Klimataria* just around the corner for year-round *mayireftá*. Glitz is all the rage on the front, with *Casino* the last remaining traditional kafenío. There are two **banks** with cash dispensers, a **post office** adjacent on the road out and three ferry/hydrofoil **agents**. You can **rent** motorbikes and cars here, too, but both are cheaper in Armenistís.

Évdhilos and around

The twisting, 41-kilometre road from Áyios Kírykos to Évdhilos is one of the most hairraising on any Greek island, and the long ridge extending the length of Ikaría often wears a streamer of cloud, even when the rest of the Aegean is clear. Karavóstamo, with its tiny, scruffy port, is the first substantial north coast place, beyond which a series of three beaches leads up to **ÉVDHILOS**. Although this is the island's second town and a ferry stop almost every day in summer, it's far less equipped to deal with visitors than Áyios Kírykos. There are two **hotels**, the *Evdoxia* on the slope southwest of the harbour (☎0275/31 502; ④) and the low-lying *Atheras* (☎0275/31 434; ④) with a small pool – plus a few **rooms**, best of these ones run by Apostolos Stenos (☎0275/31 365; ③) just west of town. Among several waterfront **restaurants**, the nameless kafestiatório between *O Flisvos* and the *Blue Nice* travel agency is the most reliable and reasonable option. A **post office** up towards the *Evdoxia*, and a good town **beach** to the east, are also worth knowing about.

KÁMBOS, 2km west, offers a small hilltop museum with finds from nearby **ancient Oinoe**; the twelfth-century church of Ayía Iríni lies just below, with the remains of a fourth-century Byzantine basilica serving as the entry courtyard. Lower down still are the sparse ruins of a Byzantine palace (just above the road) used to house exiled nobles, as well as a large sandy beach. **Rooms** are available from the store run by Vassilis Dhionysos (☎0275/31 300; ③), which also acts as the unofficial and enthusiastic tourist office for this part of Ikaría, keeping the keys for church and museum.

Starting from the large church in Évdhilos, you can also visit the Byzantine **castle of Nikariás** (Koskiná), just over 15km south. The road signposted for Manganítis is paved until Kosikiá, just over 9km away, and for 2km more to the marked side track, along which you can get a bike or jeep to within a short walk of the tenth-century castle, perched on a distinctive conical hill, with an arched gateway and a fine vaulted chapel.

Armenistís and around

Most people carry on to **ARMENISTÍS**, 57km from Áyios Kírykos, and with good reason: this little resort lies below Ikaría's finest (though rapidly dwindling) forest, with two enormous, sandy beaches battered by near-constant surf – **Livádhi** and **Messakhtí** – five and fifteen minutes' walk to the east respectively. Campers in the river-mouth greenery behind each stretch set the tone for the place, though an official campsite functions behind Livádhi in peak season, and the islanders' tolerance doesn't extend to nude bathing, as signs advise you.

A dwindling number of older buildings, plus fishing boats hauled up in a sandy cove, lend Armenistís the air of a Cornish fishing village; it's a tiny place, reminiscent of similar youth-orientated spots in southern Crete, though gentrification has definitely set in. Several "music bars", often with live Greek gigs, operate seasonally behind the nearer beach and at the quay's north end, but for most visitors **nightlife** is mostly about extended sessions in the tavernas and cafés overlooking the anchorage. Along the shore lane, the adjacent *Paskhalia* and *Delfíni* **tavernas** are the best, the former offering full breakfasts as well as good-value, en-suite **rooms** (☎0275/71 302; winter 01/24 71 411; ②). On the hill to the south the *Armena Inn* (☎0275/71 320; ②) is of a similar standard. For more luxury, there are two adjacent hotels about 700m east of the main junction here, both with pools and hosting the local package custom: the *Cavos Bay* (☎0275/71 381; ⑤) and the smaller *Daidalos* (☎0275/71 390; ④). Better than either, just above Messakhtí, is the *Messakhti Village* complex (☎0275/71 331; ④), with a large pool (necessary here, as the deep water off the beach is often unsafe due to undertow) and fine common areas and private terraces making up for the rather plain rooms. Just east of here is the fishing settlement of **YIALISKÁRI**, which has a handful of tavernas and half a dozen rooms looking out to a picturesque church on the jetty.

Among the four travel agencies/car rental/money exchange outfits in Armenistís, Marabou is the most helpful, offering mountain bikes as well as walking tours of western Ikaría; Glaros has reasonably maintained scooters. The sole drawback to staying in Armenistís is getting away, since both taxis and buses are elusive. Theoretically, **buses** head for Áyios Kírykos daily at 2 or 3pm, usually with a change or layover in Évdhilos, and out of school term only at 7am most days, but all these departures are unreliable even by Ikarian standards and should be double-checked. If you've a ferry to catch, it's far easier on the nerves to pre-book a taxi.

Ráhes

Armenistís is actually the shore annexe of four inland hamlets – Áyios Dhimítrios, Áyios Polýkarpos, Kastaniés and Khristós – collectively known as **RÁHES**. Despite the modern, mostly paved access roads through what's left of the pines (trails shortcut them), the settlements retain a certain Shangri-La quality, with the older residents speaking a positively Homeric dialect. On an island not short of foibles, Khristós is particularly strange inasmuch as the locals sleep much of the day, but shop and eat from early afternoon to the small hours; in fact most of the villages west of Évdhilos adhere to this schedule, defy-ing central government efforts to bring them in line with the rest of Greece.

Near the small main square of Khristós, paved in schist and studded with gateways fashioned from the same rock, there's a **post office** and a **hotel/restaurant** (☎0275/71 269; ③), but for lunch you'll have to scrounge something at one of two unmarked tavernas or the more prominent kafenía. The slightly spaced-out demeanour of those serving – plus numbers of old boys shambling around in dirty clothes, with their flies unzipped – may be attributable to over-indulgence in the excellent home-brewed **wine** which everyone west of Évdhilos makes. The local festival is August 6, though better ones take place further southwest in the woods at Langádha valley (August 14–15) or at Áyios Isídhoros monastery (May 14).

Nás

By tacit consent, Greek or foreign hippies and naturists have been allowed to shift 3km west of Armenistís to **Nás**, a tree-clogged river canyon ending in a small but sheltered sand and pebble beach. This little bay is almost completely enclosed by weirdly sculpt-ed rock formations, and as signs warn you, it's unwise to swim outside the cove's nat-ural limits. The crumbling foundations of the fifth-century temple of **Artemis Tavropoleio** (Patroness of Bulls) overlook the permanent deep pool at the mouth of the river. If you continue inland along this past colonies of freelance campers, you'll find secluded rock pools for freshwater dips. Back at the top of the stairs leading down to the beach from the road are several tavernas (best view at *O Nas*, but better food at *Astra*), most offering **rooms**.

Satellite islands: Thýmena and Foúrni

The straits between Sámos and Ikaría are speckled with a mini-archipelago, though the only islets permanently inhabited are Thýmena and Foúrni. More westerly **Thýmena** has one tiny hillside settlement; a regular kaïki calls at the quay below on its way between Ikaría and Foúrni, but there are no tourist facilities, and casual visits are explicitly discouraged. Foúrni is home to a huge fishing fleet and one of the more thriv-ing boatyards in the Aegean; thanks to these, and the improvement of the jetty to receive car ferries, its population is stable, unlike so many small Greek islands. The islets were once the lair of Maltese pirates, and indeed many of the islanders have a dis-tinctly North African appearance.

The above-cited **kaïki** leaves Ikaría at about 1pm several days weekly, stays overnight at Foúrni and returns the next morning. Another twice-weekly kaïki from Karlóvassi, and the larger car ferries which appear every few days, are likewise not tourist excursion boats but exist for the benefit of the islanders. The only practical way to visit Foúrni on a day-trip is by using one of the summer morning hydrofoils out of Sámos (Vathý or Pythagório).

Foúrni

Apart from the remote hamlet of **Khryssomiliá** in the north, where the island's longest (and often roughest) road goes, most of Foúrni's inhabitants are concentrated in the **port** and Kambí hamlet just to the south. The harbour community is larger than it seems from the sea, with a friendly ambience reminiscent of 1970s Greece. Among sev-eral **rooms** establishments, the most popular are the restored mansion-premises run by Manolis and Patra Markakis (☎0275/51 268; ②), immediately to your left as you dis-embark. If they're full you can head inland to the modern blocks of Evtyhia Amoryianou (☎0275/51 364; ②), whose father Nikos Kondylas meets most boats and is a mine of information about the island.

Of four waterfront **tavernas**, the local favourite is *Rementzo*, better known as *Nikos'*; if you're lucky the local *astakós* or Aegean lobster may be on the menu until mid-August. For breakfast and desserts, repair to the tamarisk terrace at the Markakis family's *To Arhondiko tis Kyras Kokonas*, under their inn. The central "high street", field-stoned and mulberry-shaded, ends well inland at a little platía with traditional kafenía under each of two plane trees; between them stands a Hellenistic sarcophagus found in a nearby field, and overhead is a conical hill, site of the ancient acropolis. There's a **post office**, an Ioniki/Ionian Bank **cash dispenser**, plus several surprisingly well-stocked shops.

A fifteen-minute trail-walk south from the school, skirting the cemetery and then slipping over the windmill ridge, brings you to **KAMBÍ**, a scattered community over-looking a pair of sandy, tamarisk-shaded coves which you'll share with chickens and hauled-up fishing boats. There are three cheap and sustaining tavernas, the *Kambi* with tables on the sand and seven **rooms** that are admittedly spartan but have arguably the best views on the island. A path continues to the next bay south, which like Kambí cove, is a preferred anchorage for wandering yachts.

Heading north from the harbour via steps, then a trail, you'll find another **beach: Psilí Ámmos** in front of a derelict fish-processing plant, with shade at one end. At the extreme north of the island, remote **KHRYSSOMILIÁ** is still best approached by the taxi-boat *Evangelistria* rather than the atrocious eighteen-kilometre road. The village, split into a shore district and a hillside settlement, has a decent beach flanked by better but less accessible ones. Simple **rooms** and **meals** can be arranged on the spot, though the locals can be less than welcoming to outsiders. The hamlet and monastery of **Áyios Ioánnis Pródhromos** in the far south of Foúrni is probably a better day-trip target on foot or by motor-scooter (now available for rent), with some good, secluded beaches just below.

Híos

"Craggy Híos", as **Homer** aptly described his putative birthplace, has a turbulent history and a strong identity. It has always been relatively prosperous, in medieval times through the export of mastic **resin** – a trade controlled by Genoese overlords between 1346 and 1566, and later by the **Ottomans**, who dubbed the place Sakız Adası (Resin Island). Since union with Greece in 1912, several shipping dynasties have emerged here, continuing the pattern of wealth. Participation in the maritime way of life is widespread, with someone in almost every family spending time in the merchant navy.

The more powerful ship-owning families and the military authorities did not encourage tourism until the late 1980s, but the worldwide shipping crisis and the saturation of other, more obviously "marketable" islands eroded their resistance. Increasing numbers of foreigners are discovering a Híos beyond its rather daunting port capital: fascinating villages, important Byzantine monuments and a respectable, if remote, complement of beaches. While unlikely ever to be dominated by tourism, the local scene has a distinctly modern flavour – courtesy of numerous returned Greek-Americans and Greek-Canadians – and English is widely spoken.

Unfortunately, the island has suffered more than its fair share of **catastrophes** during the past two centuries. The Turks perpetrated their most infamous, if not their worst, anti-revolutionary atrocity here in March 1822, massacring 30,000 Hiots and enslaving or exiling even more. In 1881, much of Híos was destroyed by a violent **earthquake**, and throughout the 1980s the natural beauty of the island was markedly diminished by devastating forest fires, compounding the effect of generations of tree-

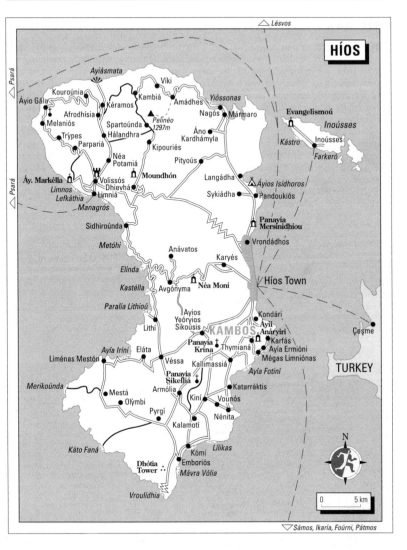

felling by boat-builders. Nearly two-thirds of the majestic pines are now gone, with substantial patches of woods persisting only in the far northeast and the centre of Híos.

In 1988 the first charters from northern Europe were instituted, signalling potentially momentous changes for the island. But there are still only 6000 guest beds on Híos, the vast majority of them in the capital or the nearby beach resort of Karfás. Further expansion, however, is hampered by the lack of direct flights from most countries, and the refusal of property owners to part with land for the extension of the airport runway.

Híos Town

HÍOS, the harbour and main town, will come as a shock after modest island capitals elsewhere; it's a bustling, concrete-laced commercial centre, with little predating the 1881 quake. Yet in many ways it is the most satisfactory of North Aegean ports; time spent exploring is rewarded with a large and fascinating marketplace, several museums and some good, authentic tavernas. Although it's a sprawling town of about 30,000, most things of interest to visitors lie within a hundred or so metres of the water, fringed by Leofóros Egéou.

South and east of the main platía, officially Plastíra but known universally as Vounakíou, extends the marvellously lively tradesmen's **bazaar**, where you can find everything from parrots to cast-iron woodstoves. Opposite the Vounakíou **taxi rank**, the grandiosely titled "Byzantine Museum", occupying the old **Mecidiye Mosque** (Mon–Fri 10am–2pm; 500dr), is little more than an archeological warehouse, with Turkish, Jewish and Armenian marble gravestones testifying to the island's varied population in past centuries.

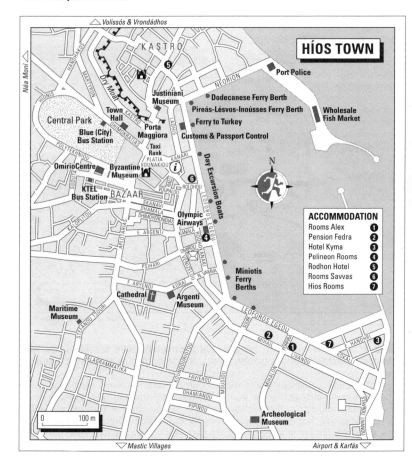

Until the 1881 earthquake, the Genoese **Kástro** was completely intact; thereafter developers razed the seaward walls, filled in much of the moat to the south and made a fortune selling off the real estate thus created around present-day Platía Vounakíou. Today the most satisfying entry to the citadel is via Porta Maggiora behind the town hall. The top floor of a medieval mansion just inside is home to the **Justiniani Museum** (Tues–Sun 9am–3pm; 500dr, 300dr Sun), with a satisfying (and periodically changing) collection of unusual icons and mosaics rescued from local churches. The small dungeon adjacent briefly held 75 Hiot hostages before their execution by the Ottomans in 1822. The old residential quarter inside the surviving castle walls, formerly the Muslim and Jewish neighbourhoods, is well worth a wander; among the wood and plaster houses you'll find assorted Ottoman monuments in various states of decay: a cemetery, a small minaretless mosque, a *hamam* (Turkish bath) and several inscribed fountains.

Further afield, three other museums beckon. The **Maritime Museum** at Stefánou Tsoúri 20 (Mon–Sat 10am–1pm; free) consists principally of model ships and oil paintings of various craft, Greek and foreign, all rather overshadowed by the mansion containing them. In the foyer is enshrined the knife and glass-globe grenade of Admiral Kanaris, who partly avenged the 1822 massacre by ramming and sinking the Ottoman fleet's flagship. In the centre of town, the **Argenti Folklore Museum** (Mon–Fri 8am–2pm, also Fri 5–7.30pm, Sat 8am–12.30pm; 400dr), on the top floor of the Koraï Library at Koraï 2, features ponderous genealogical portraits of the endowing family, an adjoining wing of costumes and rural impedimenta, plus multiple replicas of Delacroix's *Massacre at Hios*, a painting which did much to arouse sympathy for the cause of Greek independence. The **Archeological Museum** on Mihálon (Tues–Sun 8.30am–3pm; 500dr) finally re-opened in late 1999 after an eight-year overhaul – collection unreviewed, but probably worth a look.

Arrival, information and services

Ferries large and small dock at various points as shown on the town map. The **airport** lies 4km south along the coast at Kondári; any blue urban bus labelled "KONDÁRI KARFÁS" departing from the terminal on the north side of the park passes the airport gate. **Ferry** agents cluster to either side of the customs building, towards the north end of the waterfront Egéou and its continuation Neoríon: NEL is a few paces south of customs (☎0271/23 971), while Miniotis Lines, at Neoríon 21–23 (☎0271/24 670) or Egéou 11 (☎0271/21 463), operates small ferries to many neighbouring islands, as well as representing G&A boats. The Turkish evening ferry to Çeşme, as well as the most regular boat to Inoússes (see p.730), are handled by Faros Travel at Egéou 18 (☎0271/27 240). The helpful municipal **tourist office** (May–Sept Mon–Fri 7am–2.30pm & 7–10pm, Sat 10am–1pm, Sun 7–10pm; Oct–April Mon–Fri 7am–2.30pm; ☎0271/44 389) is at Kanári 18, near the Ionian Bank.

The standard green and cream **KTEL buses** leave from a parking area beside their ticket office on the south side of the park, behind the Omírio Cultural Centre. While services to the south of Híos are adequate, those to the centre and northwest of the island are almost non-existent, and to explore you'll need to rent a powerful **motorbike** or a car, or share a **taxi** – they're bright red here, not grey as in most of Greece. Three independent **car rental** agencies sit in a row at Evyenías Handhrí 5–7, behind the *Chandris Hotel*; of these, John Vassilakis Rent a Car (☎0271/29 300), with a branch at Mégas Limniónas, can be particularly recommended. The **post office** is on Omírou, while numerous **banks** all have cash dispensers. A final Hiot idiosyncrasy is afternoon **shopping hours** limited to Monday and Thursday in summer.

Accommodation

Híos Town has a fair bit of affordable accommodation, rarely completely full. Most places line the water or the perpendicular alleys and parallel streets behind, and almost all are plagued by traffic noise to some degree – we've listed the more peaceful establishments.

Fedra, Mihaíl Livanoú 13 (☎0271/41 130). Well-appointed pension in an old mansion, with stone arches in the downstairs winter bar; in summer the bar operates outside, so ask for a rear room to avoid nocturnal noise. ④.

Hios Rooms, Kokáli 1, cnr Egéou (☎0271/27 295). Clean if creaky upper-floor rooms, relatively quiet for a seafront locale; enquire at shop below, or at the Hadzelenis Tourist Information Office on the quay. ①.

Kyma, east end of Evyenías Handhrí (☎0271/44 500). En-suite hotel rooms in a Neoclassical mansion or a modern extension, but splendid service and big breakfasts provided by Theo and Güher really make the place. The old wing saw a critical moment in modern Greek history in September 1922, when Colonel Nikolaos Plastiras commandeered it as his HQ after the Greek defeat in Asia Minor, and announced the deposition of King Constantine I. ④.

Pelineon Rooms, Omírou 9, cnr Egéou (☎0271/28 030). Choose between light, airy and noisy seaview rooms (most en-suite), or quiet, poky ones in back. ②.

Rodhon, Zaharíou 17 (☎0271/24 335). The owners can be crotchety, and the rooms are non-en-suite, but it's just about the only place inside the kástro, and very quiet. ②.

Rooms Alex, Mihaíl Livanoú 29 (☎0271/26 054). The friendly proprietor often meets late-arriving ferries; otherwise ring the bell. There's a roof garden above the well-furnished rooms (TV, fans), some en-suite. ②.

Rooms Savvas, Roïdhou 15 (☎0271/24 892). Modern pension tucked onto a tiny plaza just inland from the water; rear rooms unfortunately overlook the public toilets, but all are en-suite and well equipped. ③.

Eating

Eating out in Híos Town can be more pleasurable than the fast-food joints, touristy tavernas and *barákia* on the waterfront would suggest; it is also usually a lot cheaper than on neighbouring Sámos or Lésvos.

Agrifoglio, Stávrou Livanoú 2 (start of road to Karfás). The place for an Italian blowout; all the pasta standards.

O Hotzas, Yeoryíou Kondhíli 3, corner Stefánou Tsoúri, off map. Oldest taverna in town, much improved recently, with vegetarian dishes (*mavromátika*, cauliflower), sausages, baby fish and *mydhopílafo* (rice and mussels) among the offerings to be washed down by good retsina. Supper only, garden in summer; shut Sun.

Kronos, Filíppou Aryéndi 2, cnr Aplotariás. Own-made ice creams and nothing but, purveyed since 1929; limited seating or take away.

Ta Mylarakia, by three restored windmills in Tambákika district, on the road to Vrondádhos (☎0271/40 412). A large, well-priced seafood selection, every kind of Hiot oúzo and atmospheric waterside seating make reservations advisable in summer. Lunch in summer, supper most of the year.

Ouzeri Theodhosiou, junction Egéou and Neoríon. The genuine article, with a large, reasonable menu, though it's best to wait until the ferries which dock immediately opposite have departed. Supper only; shut Sun.

Drinking, nightlife and entertainment

Cine Kipos, in central park from June to mid-September only. Quality/art-house first-run fare, two screenings nightly; watch for flybills around town or enquire at Pension Fedra.

Iviskos, about halfway along Egéou. This tasteful café is the most popular daylight hangout on the quay, with a range of juices, coffees and alcoholic drinks.

To Loukoumi, alley off Aplotariás 27/c. Old warehouse refitted as a café (8am–2pm), ouzerí (7pm–2am) and occasional events centre. Well executed and worth checking out. Shut Sun and September.

Omirio, south side of the central park. Cultural centre and events hall with frequently changing exhibitions; foreign musicians often come here after Athens concerts to perform in the large auditorium.

Beaches near Híos Town

Híos Town itself has no beaches worth mentioning; the closest decent one is at **KARFÁS**, 7km south beyond the airport and served by frequent blue buses. Once there you can **rent bikes** at Rabbit Motos, or **cars** at MG (☎0271/31 432), both uphill from the bus stop. Most Hiot hotels are planted here, to the considerable detriment of the 500-metre-long beach itself, sandy only at the south end, where all watersports are offered. The main bright spot is a unique **pension**, *Markos' Place* (☎0271/31 990; April–Nov; ②), installed in the disestablished **monastery of Áyios Yeóryios and Áyios Pandelímon**, on the hillside south of the bay. Markos Kostalas, who leases the premises from Thymianá municipality, has created a unique environment much loved by special-activity groups. Guests are lodged in the former pilgrims' cells, with a kitchen available; individuals are more than welcome (there are several single "cells"), though advance reservations are advisable. Two nearby **eating** options are refreshingly at odds with the package ethos here. Amidst it all, on the lane leading to the *Karatzas Hotel*, the *Fakiris Market Taverna* uniquely offers home-marinated aubergine or artichokes and red-pepper dip along with well-executed seafood and pork-based *bekrí mezé* at non-touristy prices; it's open off-season weekends as well. Some 3km back towards town at Kondári, at the end of a side road leading from a right-angle turn to the scrappy beach, *To Tavernaki* has personable service, large portions, magnificent fish and starters, excellent chips or whole-grain bread and decent bulk wine. It's open daily for lunch and supper, though may miss out lunch during slow seasons.

Some 2km further along the coast from Karfás, **AYÍA ERMIÓNI** is not a beach but a fishing anchorage surrounded by a handful of tavernas (*Mayeftiko Akroyiali*, below the church, is adequate, with waterside seating) and apartments to rent. The nearest beach is at **Mégas Limniónas**, a few hundred metres further, smaller than Karfás but more scenic where low cliffs provide a backdrop. *Taverna Angyra* is about the best eating place here, with a good line in mezédhes and a well-chosen wine list. Both Ayía Ermióni and Mégas Limniónas are served by extensions of the blue-bus route to either Karfás or Thymianá, the nearest inland village.

The coast road loops up to Thymianá, from where you can (with your own transport only) continue 3km south towards Kalimassiá to the turning for **Ayía Fotiní**, a 700-metre pebble beach with exceptionally clean water. There's no shade, however, unless you count shadows from the numerous blocks of rooms contracted out to Scandinavian tour operators; a few tavernas cluster around the point where the side road meets the sea.

Southern Híos

Besides olive groves, the gently rolling countryside in the south of the island is also home to the **mastic bush** (*Pistacia lentisca*), found across much of Aegean Greece but only here producing an aromatic resin of any quality or quantity. For centuries it was used as a base for paints, cosmetics and the chewable jelly beans, which became a somewhat addictive staple in the Ottoman harems. Indeed, the interruption of the flow of mastic from Híos to Istanbul by the revolt of spring 1822 was one of the root causes of the brutal Ottoman reaction.

The wealth engendered by the mastic trade supported twenty *mastihohoriá* (mastic villages) from the time the Genoese set up a monopoly in the substance during the fourteenth and fifteenth centuries, but the end of imperial Turkey and the development of petroleum-based products knocked the bottom out of the mastic market. Now it's just a curiosity, to be chewed – try the sweetened *Elma* brand gum – or drunk as a liqueur called *mastíha*, though it has had medicinal applications since ancient times. These days, however, the *mastihohoriá* live mainly off their tangerines, apricots and olives.

The towns themselves, the only settlements on Híos spared by the Ottomans in 1822, are architecturally unique, laid out by the Genoese but retaining a distinct Middle Eastern feel. The basic plan consists of a rectangular warren of tall houses, with the outer row doubling as the town's perimeter fortification, and breached by a limited number of arched gateways.

The mastic villages

ARMÓLIA, 20km from town, is the smallest and least imposing of the mastic villages. Its main virtue is its pottery industry; the best workshop, selling useful kitchen ware as opposed to kitsch souvenirs, is Yeoryios Sfikakis, the third outfit on the right as you head southwest. **PYRGÍ**, 5km further south, is the most colourful of these communities, its houses elaborately embossed with *xystá*, geometric patterns cut into whitewash, revealing a layer of black volcanic sand underneath; strings of sun-drying tomatoes add a further splash of colour in autumn. On the northeast corner of the central square the twelfth-century Byzantine church of **Áyii Apóstoli** (Tues–Thurs & Sat 10am–1pm), embellished with much later frescoes, is tucked under an arcade. Of late, vast numbers of postcard racks and boutiques have sprung up on every main thoroughfare, detracting somewhat from the atmosphere. Pyrgí has a handful of **rooms**, many of them bookable through the Women's Agricultural and Tourist Cooperative (☎0271/72 496; ②). In the medieval core you'll find a bank, a post office and a few *souvláki* grills, but no real tavernas. **OLÝMBI**, 7km further west along the bus route serving Armólia and Pyrgí, is the least visited of the mastic villages, but not devoid of interest. The characteristic tower-keep, which at Pyrgí stands half-inhabited away from the modernized main square, here looms bang in the middle of the platía, its ground floor occupied by two **eateries**: *Kyra Maria's* (no sign), with simple mezédhes, and *Estiatorio Pyrgos*, with more elaborate main dishes.

Sombre, monochrome **MESTÁ**, 4km west of Olýmbi, is considered the finest example of the genre; despite more snack bars and trinket shops than strictly necessary on the outskirts, Mestá remains just the right side of twee as most people here still work the land. From its main square, dominated by the **church of the Taxiárhis** (the largest on the island), a bewildering maze of cool, shady lanes with anti-seismic buttressing and tunnels, leads off in all directions. Most streets end in blind alleys, except those leading to the six gates; the northeast one still has its original iron grate. If you'd like to stay, there are half a dozen **rooms** in restored traditional dwellings managed by Dhimitris Pipidhis (☎0271/76 319; ③); alternatively, three separate premises managed by Anna Floradhi (☎0271/76 455; ②) are somewhat less elaborate. Of the two **tavernas** on the main platía, *O Morias sta Mesta* is renowned for tasty rural specialities like pickled *krítamo* (rock samphire) and locally produced raisin wine: heavy, semi-sweet and sherry-like. However, portions have shrunk of late, and *Mesaionas* – whose tables share the square – is better value and has perhaps the more helpful proprietor.

The south coast

One drawback to staying in Mestá is a lack of nearby beaches; the closest candidate is surf-battered, facility-less **Merikoúnda**, 4km west of Mestá by dirt track. Reached by a seven-kilometre side road starting just west of Pyrgí, the little cove of **Káto Faná** is also bereft of amenities (save for a spring), but more sheltered; by the roadside 400m above the shore, the fragmentary remains of an Apollo temple surround a medieval chapel.

Pyrgí is actually closest to the two major beach resorts in this corner of the island. The nearest, 6km distant, is **EMBORIÓS**, an almost landlocked harbour with four passable **tavernas** (*Porto Emborios* has the edge with homemade desserts and *atherína*-and-onion fry-up); there's· a scanty, British-excavated acropolis on the hill to the northeast, vaguely signposted 1km along the road to Kómi. For swimming, follow the road to its end at an oversubscribed car park and the beach of **Mávra Vólia**, then continue by flagstoned walkway over the headland to two more dramatic pebble (part nudist) strands of red and black volcanic stones, twice as long and backed by impressive cliffs.

If you want sand you'll have to go to **KÓMI**, 3km northeast, also accessible from Armólia via Kalamotí; there are just a few tavernas (most reliable of these being the *Bella Mare*), café-bars and summer apartments behind the pedestrianized beachfront. The bus service is fairly good in season, often following a loop route through Pyrgí and Emboriós.

Central Híos

The portion of Híos extending west and southwest from Híos Town matches the south in terms of interesting monuments, and good roads make touring under your own power an easy matter. There are also several beaches on the far shore of the island which, though not the best on Híos, are fine for a dip at the end of the day.

The Kámbos

The **Kámbos**, a vast fertile plain carpeted with citrus groves, extends southwest from Híos Town almost as far as the village of Halkió. The district was originally settled by the Genoese during the fourteenth century, and remained a preserve of the local aristocracy until 1822. Exploring it by bicycle or motorbike is less frustrating than going by car, since the web of poorly marked lanes sandwiched between high walls guarantee disorientation and frequent backtracking. Behind the walls you catch fleeting glimpses of ornate old mansions built from locally quarried sandstone; courtyards are paved in pebbles or alternating light and dark tiles, and most still contain a pergola-shaded irrigation pond filled by a *mánganos*, or donkey-powered water-wheel, used before the age of electric pumps to draw water up from wells up to 30m deep.

Many of the sumptuous three-storey dwellings, constructed in a hybrid Italo-Turco-Greek style, have languished in ruins since 1881, but a few have been converted for use as unique **accommodation**. The best marked and best publicized are *Mavrokordatiko* (☎0271/32 900; ④), about 1500m south of the airport, with breakfast served by the *mánganos* courtyard, or the *Hotel Perivoli* (☎0271/31 513, fax 32 042; ⑤) slightly inland, with blue urban buses bound for Thymianá passing just 200m to the east. The rooms, no two alike, have fireplaces and (in most cases) en-suite baths and sofas, and it also has a highly regarded garden restaurant with two menus: Italian haute cuisine or postmodern Greek. There's a set price for the multi-plate, vegetarian or carniverous offerings, so best go in a group of four for good value.

Not strictly speaking in Kámbos, but most easily reached from it en route to the *mastihohoriá*, is an outstanding rural Byzantine monument. The thirteenth-century **church of Panayía Krína**, isolated amidst orchards and woods, is well worth the challenge of a maze of dirt tracks beyond Vavýli village, 9km from town. It's currently closed for snail's-pace restoration, but a peek through the apse window will give you a fair idea of the finely frescoed interior, sufficiently lit by a twelve-windowed drum. Some of the late medieval frescoes have been removed, and may be displayed in Híos Town's Justiniani Museum (see p.721). The alternating brick and stonework of the exterior alone justifies the trip here, though architectural harmony is marred by the later addition of a clumsy lantern over the narthex.

Néa Moní

Almost exactly in the middle of the island, the **monastery of Néa Moní** was founded by the Byzantine Emperor Constantine Monomahos ("The Dueller") IX in 1042 on the spot where a wonder-working icon had been discovered. It ranks among the most beautiful and important monuments on any of the Greek islands; the mosaics, together with those of Dháfni and Ósios Loukás on the mainland, are among the finest surviving art of their age in Greece, and the setting – high up in still partly forested mountains 15km west of the port – is no less memorable.

Once a powerful and independent community of six hundred monks, Néa Moní was pillaged in 1822 and most of its residents put to the sword; since then many of its outbuildings have languished in ruins, though a recent EU grant has prompted massive restoration work. The 1881 tremor caused comprehensive damage, while exactly a century later a forest fire threatened to engulf the place until the resident icon was paraded along the perimeter wall, miraculously repelling the flames. Today the monastery, with its giant refectory and vaulted water cisterns, is inhabited by just two elderly, frail nuns and a couple of lay workers.

Bus excursions are provided by the KTEL on Tuesday and Friday mornings, continuing to Anávatos, Lithí and Armólia; otherwise come by motorbike, or walk from Karyés, 7km northeast, to which there is a regular blue-bus service. **Taxis** from town, however, are not prohibitive, at about 5000dr round-trip per carload, including a wait while you look around.

Just inside the main gate (daily 8am–1pm & 4–8pm) stands a **chapel/ossuary** containing some of the bones of those who met their death here in 1822; axe-clefts in children's skulls attest to the savagery of the attackers. The **katholikón**, with the cupola resting on an octagonal drum, is of a design seen elsewhere only in Cyprus; the frescoes in the exonarthex are badly damaged by holes allegedly left by Turkish bullets, but the **mosaics** are another matter. The narthex contains portrayals of the varioussaints of Hios sandwiched between *Christ Washing the Disciples' Feet* and the *Betrayal of Christ*, in which Judas's critical kiss has unfortunately been obliterated, but Peter is clearly visible lopping off the ear of the high priest's servant. In the dome of the sanctuary (currently hidden by scaffolding), which once contained a complete life-cycle of Christ, only the *Baptism*, part of the *Crucifixion*, the *Descent from the Cross*, the *Resurrection* and the Evangelists *Mark* and *John* survived the earthquake.

The west coast

With your own transport, you can proceed 5km west of Néa Moní to **AVGÓNYMA**, a cluster of dwellings on a knoll overlooking the coast; the name means "Clutch of Eggs", an apt description when it's viewed from the ridge above. Since the 1980s, the place has been almost totally restored as a summer haven by descendants of the original villagers, though the permanent population is just seven. A returned Greek-American family runs a reasonable, simple-fare **taverna**, *O Pyrgos*, in an arcaded mansion on the main square; *To Arhondiko*, serving more involved mezédhes on its view terrace at the village entrance, is the alternative. The classiest **accommodation** option here is *Spitakia*, a cluster of small restored houses for up to five people (☎0271/20 513 or 43 051; fax 43 052; ④).

A paved side road continues another 4km north to **ANÁVATOS**, whose empty, dun-coloured dwellings, soaring above pistachio orchards, are almost indistinguishable from the 300-metre-high bluff on which they're built. During the 1822 insurrection, some four hundred inhabitants and refugees threw themselves over this cliff rather than surrender to the besieging Ottomans, and it's still a preferred suicide leap. Anávatos can now only muster five souls, and given a lack of accommodation (there's one small snack bar) plus an eerie, traumatized atmosphere, it's no place to be stranded at dusk.

West of Avgónyma, the main road descends 6km to the coast in well-graded loops. Turning right (north) at the junction leads first to the beach at **Elínda**, alluring from afar but rocky and murky up close; it's better to continue towards more secluded coves to either side of Metóhi, or below **SIDHIROÚNDA**, the only village hereabouts, which enjoys a spectacular hilltop setting overlooking the coast.

All along this coast, as far southwest as Liménas Mestón, are round **watchtowers** erected by the Genoese to look out for pirates – the first swimmable cove you reach by turning left from the junction has the name **Kastélla**, attractive for swimming but with rough track access. A sparse weekday-only bus service resumes 9km south of the junction at **LITHÍ**, a friendly village of whitewashed buildings perched on a wooded ledge overlooking the sea. There are tavernas and kafenía near the bus turnaround area, but must visitors head 2km downhill to **Paralía Lithíou**, a popular weekend target of Hiot townies for the sake of its large but hard-packed, wind-swept beach. You may **stay** and **eat** at *Kyra Despina* (☎0271/73 373; ③), open most of the year, and apparently improved since the demise of the eponymous founder.

Some 5km south of Lithí, the valley-bottom village of **VÉSSA** is an unsung gem, more open and less casbah-like than Mestá or Pyrgí, but still homogeneous. Its honey-coloured buildings are arrayed in a vast grid punctuated by numerous belfries; there's a simple taverna (*Snack Bar Evanemos*) installed in a tower-mansion on the main road, and you can stay at a restored inn, *To Petrino* (☎0271/25 016 or 41 097; ③).

Northern Híos

Northern Híos never really recovered from the 1822 massacre, and the desolation left by fires in 1981 and 1987 will further dampen inquisitive spirits. Since the early 1900s the villages have languished all but deserted much of the year, which means correspondingly sparse bus services. About one-third of the former population now lives in Híos Town, venturing out here only during major festivals or to tend smallholdings; others, based in Athens or the US, visit their ancestral homes for just a few intense weeks in mid-summer, when marriages are arranged between local families.

The road to Kardhámyla

Blue city buses run north from Híos Town up to **VRONDÁDHOS**, an elongated coastal suburb that's a favourite residence of the island's many seafarers. Homer is reputed to have lived and taught here, and in terraced parkland just above the little fishing port and pebble beach you can visit his purported lectern, more probably an ancient altar of Cybele. Accordingly many of the buses out here are labelled "DHASKALÓPETRA", the Teacher's Rock.

Some 15km out of town, just past the tiny bayside hamlet of Pandoukiós, a side road leads to stony **Áyios Isídhoros** cove, home to the rather inconveniently located island **campsite**, *Chios Camping* (☎0271/74 111), though the site itself is shaded and faces Inoússes islet across the water. **LANGÁDHA**, just beyond, is probably the first point on the eastern coast road where you'd be tempted to stop, though there is no proper beach nearby. Set at the mouth of a deep valley, this attractive little harbour settlement looks across its bay to a pine grove, and beyond to Turkey. There are a couple of rooms outfits, but most evening visitors come for the sustaining seafood at two adjacent tavernas on the quay: *Tou Kopelou*, better known as Stelios's, and *Paradhisos*.

Just beyond Langádha an important side road leads 5km up and inland to **Pityoús**, an oasis in a mountain pass presided over by a tower-keep; continuing 4km more brings you to a junction allowing quick access to the west of the island and the Volissós area (see p.728).

Kardhámyla and around

Most traffic proceeds to **ÁNO KARDHÁMYLA** and **KÁTO KARDHÁMYLA**, the latter 37km out of the main town. Positioned at opposite edges of a fertile plain rimmed by mountains, they initially come as welcome relief from Homer's crags. Káto, better known as **MÁRMARO**, is larger, indeed the island's second town, with a bank, post office and filling station. However, there is little to attract a casual visitor other than some Neoclassical architecture: the port, mercilessly exposed to the *meltémi*, is strictly businesslike, and there are few tourist facilities. An exception is *Hotel Kardamyla* (☎0272/23 353; ⑤), co-managed with Híos Town's *Hotel Kyma*. It has the bay's only pebble beach, and its restaurant is a reliable source of lunch if you're touring. *Iy Vlyhadha*, facing the eponymous bay west over the headland, is an excellent independent **taverna** with locally produced suckling pig and squid.

For better swimming head west 5km to **Nagós**, a gravel-shore bay at the foot of an oasis, which is where the summertime bus service terminates. Lush greenery is nourished by active springs up at a bend in the road, enclosed in a sort of grotto overhung by tall cliffs. The place name is a corruption of *naos*, after a large Poseidon temple that once stood near the springs, but centuries of orchard-tending, antiquities-pilfering and organized excavations after 1912 mean that nothing remains visible. Down at the shore the swimming is good, if a bit chilly; there are two mediocre tavernas and a few rooms to rent. Your only chance of relative solitude in July or August lies 1km west at **Yióssonas**; this is a much longer beach, but less sheltered, rockier and with no facilities.

Volissós and around

VOLISSÓS, 42km from Híos Town by the most direct road (45km via the easier Avgónyma route), was once the market town for a dozen remote hill villages beyond, and its old stone houses still curl appealingly beneath the crumbling hilltop Byzantine fort. The towers were improved by the Genoese, from whose era also dates the utterly spuriouus "House of Homer" signposted near the top of town. Volissós can seem depressing at first, with the bulk of its 250 mostly elderly permanent inhabitants living in newer buildings around the main square, but opinions improve with longer acquaintance.

Grouped around the platía you'll find a **post office** (but no bank), two well-stocked shops and three mediocre **tavernas**; far better ones are found up in Pýrgos district, where *Pyrgos* (aka *Vasilis*, disguised by day as a machine shop) and the vegetarian *Kafenio E*, run by Nikos Koungoulios, are your options; reservations (☎0274/21 480) are advised for the latter. A filling station operates 2.5km out of town, the only one hereabouts; you should plan on overnighting since the bus only comes out here on Sundays on a day-trip basis, and on Monday, Wednesday and Friday in the afternoon. This should cause no dismay, since the area has the best beaches, and some of the most interesting **accommodation**, on Híos. Some sixteen old houses, mostly in Pýrgos district, have been meticulously restored by Stella Tsakiri and Argyris Angelou (☎0274/21 421 or 21 413, fax 21 521; ③) and usually accommodate two people – all have terraces, fully equipped kitchens and features such as tree trunks upholding sleeping lofts. Larger families or groups should try for three equally impressive, interlinkable units managed by Elysian Holidays (☎0274/21 128, fax 21 013; ④), very high up near the castle.

LIMNIÁ, (sometimes Limiá), the port of Volissós, lies 2km south, with kaïki skippers coming and going from Psará (mid-June to mid-Sept, Mon, Wed & Fri mid-morning). The best **tavernas** here are the long-established *Ta Limnia* on the jetty, for *mayireftá*, and summer-only *To Limanaki* at the rear of the cove, best for fish. At Limniá you're not far from the fabled beaches either. A 1.5 kilometre walk southeast over the headland brings you to **Managrós**, a seemingly endless sand and pebble beach; nearest **lodgings** are the bungalows of Marvina Alvertou (☎0274/21 335; ③). More intimate, sandy **Lefkáthia** lies just a ten-minute stroll along the cement drive threading over the headland north of the harbour; amenities are limited to a seasonal snack shack on the sand, and Ioannis Zorbas' apartments (☎0274/21 436; ③), beautifully set in a garden where the concrete track joins an asphalt road down from Volissós. This is bound for **Límnos** (not to be confused with Limniá), the next protected cove 400m east of

Lefkáthia, where *Taverna Akroyiali* provides salubrious food and professional service, and the spruce *Latini Apartments* (☎0274/21 461, fax 21 871; ③) are graced with multiple stone terraces.

Ayía Markélla, 5km further northwest of Límnos, stars in many local postcards: a long, stunning beach fronting the monastery of Híos's patron saint, the latter not especially interesting or useful for outsiders, since its cells are reserved for Greek pilgrims. In an interesting variation on the expulsion of the money-changers from the temple, only religious souvenirs are allowed to be sold in the holy precincts, while all manner of plastic junk is on offer just outside. There's the *Taverna Krokos* to hand as well, and around July 22 – the local saint's festival and biggest island bash – the "No Camping" signs are doubtless unenforced.

The dirt road past the monastery grounds is passable to any vehicle, with care, and emerges up on the paved road running high above the northwest coast. Turn left and proceed to the remote village of **ÁYIO GÁLA**, whose claim to fame is a **grotto-church** complex, built into a stream-lapped palisade at the bottom of the village. Signs ("Panayía Ayiogaloúsena") point to a lane crossing the water, but for access, except at the festival on August 23, you'll need to find the key-keeper (ask at the central kafenío), and descend to the complex from a flight of stairs starting beside a eucalypt. Of the two churches inside the cavern, the larger one near the mouth of the complex dates from the fifteenth century but seems newer owing to a 1993 external renovation. Inside, however, a fantastically intricate *témblon* vies for your attention with a tinier, older chapel, built entirely within the rear of the cavern. Its frescoes are badly smudged, except for a wonderfully mysterious and mournful Virgin, surely the saddest in Christendom, holding a knowing Child.

Satellite islands: Psará and Inoússes

There's a single settlement, with beaches and an isolated rural monastery, on both of Híos's satellite isles, but each is surprisingly different from the other, and of course from their large neighbour. Inoússes, the nearer and smaller islet, has a daily kaïki service from Híos Town in season; Psará has less regular services subject to weather conditions (in theory 3 weekly), and is too remote to be done justice on a day-trip.

Psará

The birthplace of revolutionary war hero Admiral Kanaris, **Psará** devoted its merchant fleets – the third largest in 1820s Greece after those of Ídhra and Spétses – to the cause of independence, and paid dearly for it. Vexed beyond endurance, the Turks landed overwhelming forces in 1824 to stamp out this nest of resistance. Perhaps 3000 of the 30,000 inhabitants escaped in small boats which were rescued by a French fleet, but the majority retreated to a hilltop powder magazine and blew it (and themselves) up rather than surrender. The nationalist poet Dhionysios Solomos immortalized the incident in famous stanzas:

> *On the Black Ridge of Psará,*
> *Glory walks alone.*
> *She meditates on her heroes*
> *And wears in her hair a wreath*
> *Made from a few dry weeds*
> *Left on the barren ground.*

Today, it's a sad, stark place fully living up to its name ("the grey things" in Greek), which never really recovered from the holocaust. The Turks burned whatever houses and vegetation the blast had missed, and the permanent population barely exceeds four hundred. The only positive recent development was a 1980s revitalization project insti-gated by a French-Greek descendant of Kanaris and a Greek team. The port was improved, mains electricity and pure water provided, a secondary school opened, and cultural links between France and the island established, though so far this has not been reflected in increased tourist numbers.

Arrival can be something of an ordeal: the regular small ferry from Híos Town can take up to four hours to cover the 57 nautical miles of habitually rough sea. Use the port of Limniá to sail in at least one direction if you can; this crossing takes half the time at just over half the price.

Since few buildings in the east-facing harbour community predate this century, it's a strange hotchpotch of ecclesiastical and secular architecture that greets the eye on dis-embarking. There's a distinctly southern feel, more like the Dodecanese or the Cyclades, and some peculiar churches, no two alike in style.

If you **stay overnight,** there's a choice between a handful of fairly basic rooms and three more professional outfits: *Psara Studios* (☎0274/61 233; ④) and *Apartments Restalia* (☎0274/61 000; ④), both a bit stark but with balconies and kitchens, or the EOT *xenónas* (☎0274/61 293; ③) in a restored prison. For **eating,** the best and cheap-est place is the EOT-run *Spitalia,* housed in a restored medieval hospital at the north edge of the port. A **post office,** bakery and shop complete the list of amenities; there is no full-service bank.

Psará's **beaches** are decent, improving the further northeast you walk from the port. You quickly pass Káto Yialós, Katsoúni and Lazarétta with its off-putting power station, before reaching **Lákka** ("narrow ravine"), fifteen minutes along, apparently named after its grooved rock formations in which you may have to shelter; much of this coast is windswept, with a heavy swell offshore. **Límnos,** 25 minutes from the port along the coastal path, is big and attractive, but there's no reliable taverna here, or indeed at any of the other beaches. The only other thing to do on Psará is to walk north across the island to the **monastery of the Kímisis (Assumption)**; uninhabited since the 1970s, this comes to life only on the first week of August, when its revered icon is carried in ceremonial procession to town and the back on the eve of August 5.

Inoússes

Inoússes has a permanent population of about three hundred – less than half its pre-war figure – and a very different history from Psará. For generations this medium-sized islet has provided the Aegean with many of her wealthiest shipping families: various members of the Livanos, Lemos and Pateras clans (with every street or square named for the last-named family) were born here. This helps explain the large villas and visit-ing summer yachts in an otherwise sleepy Greek backwater – as well as a **maritime museum** (sporadic hours) near the quay, endowed by various shipping magnates. At the west end of the quay, the bigwigs have also funded a large nautical academy, which trains future members of the merchant navy.

Only on Sundays can you make an inexpensive **day-trip** to Inoússes from Híos with the locals' ferry *Inousses*; on other days of the week this arrives at 3pm, returning early the next morning. On weekdays during the tourist season you must participate in the pricey excursions offered from Híos, with return tickets running up to three times the cost of the regular ferry.

Two church-tipped islets, each privately owned, guard the unusually well-protected harbour; the **town** of Inoússes is surprisingly large, draped over hillsides enclosing a ravine. Despite the wealthy reputation, its appearance is unpretentious, the houses dis-playing a mix of vernacular and modest Neoclassical style. There is just one, fairly com-fortable **hotel,** the *Thalassoporos* (☎0272/51 475; ④), on the main easterly hillside lane. **Eating out** is similarly limited to a simple ouzerí just below the nautical academy, or the good-value *Taverna Pateronissia,* conspicuous at the base of the disembarkation jetty. Otherwise, be prepared to patronize one of the three shops (one on the water-front, two up the hill). Beside the museum is a **post office** and a **bank**.

The rest of this tranquil island, at least the southern slope, is surprisingly green and well tended; there are no springs, so water comes from a mix of fresh and brackish wells, as well as a reservoir. The sea is extremely clean and calm on the sheltered southerly shore; among its beaches, choose from **Zepága**, **Biláli** or **Kástro**, respectively five, twenty and thirty minutes' walk west of the port. More secluded **Farkeró** lies 25 minutes east: first along a cement drive ending at a seaside chapel, then by path past pine groves and over a ridge. As on Psará, there are no reliable facilities at any of the beaches.

At the end of the westerly road, beyond Kástro, stands the somewhat macabre convent of **Evangelismoú**, endowed by the Pateras family. Inside reposes the mummified body of the lately canonized daughter, Irini, whose prayers to die of cancer in place of her terminally ill father Panagos were answered early in the 1960s on account of her virtue and piety; he's entombed here also, having outlived Irini by some years. The abbess, presiding over some twenty nuns, is none other than the widowed Mrs Pateras; only women are allowed admission, and even then casual visits are not encouraged.

Lésvos (Mytilíni)

Lésvos, the third largest Greek island after Crete and Évvia, is not only the birthplace of Sappho, but also of Aesop, Arion and – more recently – the Greek primitive artist Theophilos, the Nobel laureate poet Odysseus Elytis and the novelist Stratis Myrivilis. Despite these artistic associations, Lésvos may not at first strike the visitor as particularly beautiful or interesting; much of the landscape is rocky, volcanic terrain, dotted with thermal springs and alternating with vast grain fields, salt pans or even near-desert. But there are also oak and pine forests as well as vast olive groves, some of these over five hundred years old. With its balmy climate and suggestive contours, the island tends to grow on you with prolonged acquaintance.

Lovers of medieval and Ottoman **architecture** certainly won't be disappointed. Castles survive at the main town of Mytilíni, at Mólyvos, Eressós and near Ándissa; most of these date from the late fourteenth century, when Lésvos was given as a dowry to a Genoese prince of the Gateluzzi clan following his marriage to the niece of one of the last Byzantine emperors. Apart from Crete and Évvia, Lésvos was the only Greek island where Turks settled significantly in rural villages (they usually stuck to the safety of towns), which explains the odd Ottoman bridge, shed-like mosque or crumbling minaret often found in the middle of nowhere. Again unusually for the Aegean islands, Ottoman reforms of the eighteenth century encouraged the emergence of a Greek Orthodox land- and industry-owning aristocracy, who built rambling mansions and tower-houses, a few of which survive.

Social and economic idiosyncrasies persist: anyone who has attended one of the extended village *paniyíria*, with hours of music and tables in the streets groaning with food and drink, will not be surprised to learn that Lésvos has the highest alcoholism rate in Greece. Breeding livestock, especially horses, is disproportionately important, and traffic jams caused by mounts instead of parked cars are not unheard of – signs reading "Forbidden to Tether Animals Here" are still common.

Historically, the olive plantations, oúzo distilleries, animal husbandry and fishing industry supported those who chose not to emigrate, but with these enterprises relatively stagnant, mass-market tourism has made visible inroads. However, it still accounts for just five percent of the local economy, there are still few large hotels outside the capital or Mólyvos, villa-type accommodation just barely outstrips rooms, and the first official campsites only opened in 1990. Tourist numbers have in fact levelled

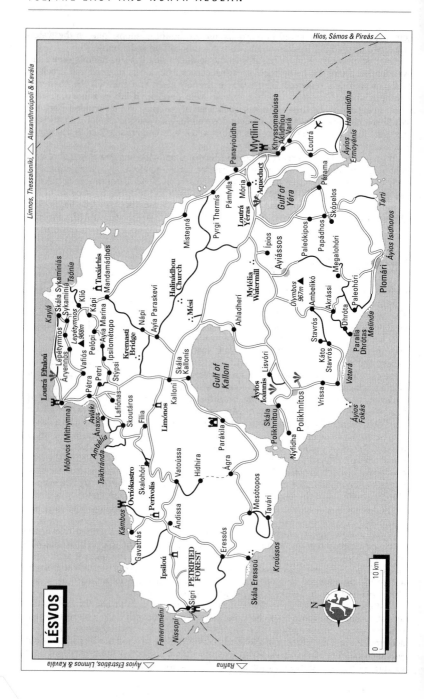

out in recent years, the result of stalled plans to expand the airport, unrealistic hotel pricing and the dropping of the island from several tour operators' programmes.

Public **buses** tends to radiate out from the harbour for the benefit of working locals, not day-tripping tourists. Carrying out such excursions from Mytilíni is next to impossible anyway, owing to the size of the island – about 70km by 45km at its widest points – and a few appalling roads (others have been improved, along with their signposting). Moreover, the topography is complicated by the two deeply indented gulfs of Kallóni and Yéra, with no bridges across their mouths, which means that going from A to B involves an obligatory change of bus at either the port capital, on the east shore, or the town of Kallóni, in the middle of the island. It's best to decide on a base and stay there for a few days, exploring its immediate surroundings on foot or by rented vehicle.

Mytilíni Town

MYTILÍNI, the port and capital, sprawls between and around two bays divided by a fortified promontory, and in Greek fashion often doubles as the name of the island. Most visitors are put off by the combination of urban bustle and slight seediness, and contrive to leave as soon as possible; the town returns the compliment by in fact being a fairly impractical and expensive place to base yourself.

Nonetheless, Mytilíni has enough to justify a layover of a few hours. On the promontory sits the Byzantine-Genoese-Ottoman **fortress** (Tues–Sun 8.30am–2.45pm; 600dr), comprising ruined structures from all these eras and an Ottoman inscription above a Byzantine double-headed eagle at the south gate. Further inland, the town skyline is dominated in turn by the Germanic spire of **Áyios Theodhóros** and the mammary dome of **Áyios Therápon**, the pair of them expressions of the post-Baroque taste of the nineteenth-century Ottoman Greek bourgeoisie. They stand more or less at opposite ends of the bazaar, whose main street, Ermoú, links the town centre with the little-used north harbour of Páno Skála. On its way there Ermoú passes half a dozen expensive but rather picked-over antique shops near the roofless Yeni Tzami, an occasional exhibition venue. Between Ermoú and the castle lies a maze of atmospheric lanes lined with grandiose Belle Epoque mansions and elderly vernacular houses.

The excellent **Archeological Museum** (Tues–Sun 8.30am–3pm; 600dr) is housed partly in the mansion of a large estate just behind the ferry dock. Among the more compelling of the well-labelled exhibits are a complete set of mosaics from a Hellenistic dwelling, rather droll terracotta figurines, votive offerings from a sanctuary of Demeter and Kore excavated in the castle and Neolithic finds from present-day Thermí. A specially built annexe at the rear contains stone-cut inscriptions of various edicts and treaties, and – more interesting than you'd think – *stelae* featuring *nekródhipna*, or portrayals of funerary meals. Yet another annexe for the overflow, 150m up the hill at the base of 8-Noemvríou, is not yet operational.

There's also a worthwhile **Byzantine Art Museum** (summer only Mon–Sat 10am–1pm; 400dr) just behind Áyios Therápon, containing various icons rescued from rural churches, plus a canvas of the *Assumption* by Theophilos (see p.736).

Practicalities

There's no bus link with the **airport**, so a shared taxi for the 7km into Mytilíni is the usual method; Olympic Airways is southwest of the main harbour at Kavétsou 44. As on Híos, there are two bus stations: the *astykó* (blue bus) service departing from the middle of the quay, the *iperastikó* (standard KTEL) buses leaving from a small station near Platía Konstandinopóleos at the southern end of the harbour. If you're intent on getting over to Ayvalık in Turkey, book tickets through either Dimakis Tours at

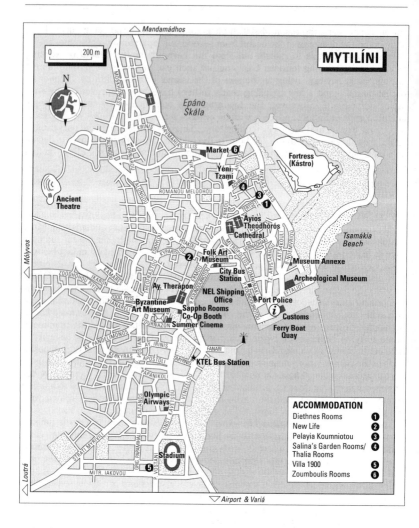

MYTILÍNI

Mandamádhos

0   200 m

N

Epáno
Skála

Market

Yéni
Tzami

Fortress
(Kástro)

Ancient
Theatre

Áyios
Theodhóros
Cathedral

Tsamákia
Beach

Folk Art
Museum

Museum Annexe

City Bus
Station

Archeological Museum

Ay. Therápon

NEL Shipping
Office

Byzantine
Art Museum

Port Police

Sappho Rooms
Co-Op Booth
Summer Cinema

Customs

Ferry Boat
Quay

Olympic
Airways

FANARI

KTEL Bus Station

Stadium

ACCOMMODATION

Diethnes Rooms	❶
New Life	❷
Pelayia Koumniotou	❸
Salina's Garden Rooms/ Thalia Rooms	❹
Villa 1900	❺
Zoumboulis Rooms	❻

Airport & Variá

Mólyvos

Loutrá

Koundouriótou 73 (☎0251/27 865) or Picolo Travel at no. 73a (☎0251/27 000). NEL Ferries has its own agency at no. 47 (☎0251/28 480), while G&A ferries are handled by Picolo Travel.

Car rental is best arranged through reputable chain franchises like Payless at Koundouriótou 49 (☎0251/43 555), Budget, next door (☎0251/25 846), Thrifty at no. 69 (☎0251/41 464) or Just at no. 47 (☎0251/43 080) – though it's generally cheaper to rent at the resort of your choice. Other amenities include the **post office** on Vournázon, behind the central park, and four banks with cash dispensers: the Ethniki/National, Alpha Pisteos/Alpha Credit – both on Koundouriótou – and the Emboriki/Commercial on Ermoú, plus a free-standing booth on the quay. Before leaving town, you might stop at the jointly housed tourist police/EOT office (daily 8.30am–6pm; ☎0251/22 776), behind the customs building, in order to get hold of their excellent town and island maps, plus other brochures. If they're shut, try the EOT regional headquarters 300m away at Aristárhou 6 (Mon–Fri 8am–2.30pm).

ACCOMMODATION

Finding **accommodation** can be difficult: the waterfront hotels are noisy and exorbitantly priced, with few single rooms to speak of. If you need to stay, hunting for better-value rooms has been eased by the formation of the "Sappho's Rented Rooms Association" (☎0251/43 375, booth by the park), with most of the 22 affiliated premises located between the castle and Ermoú. Yeoryíou Tertséti street in particular has two possibilities: the friendly if basic *Pelayia Koumniotou* at no. 6 (☎0251/20 643; ②) or the fancier, en-suite *Vetsikas/Dhiethnes* at no. 1 (☎0251/24 968; ③). Two other quiet establishments sit between the north harbour and fortress: *Salina's Garden Rooms*, behind the Yeni Tzami at Fokéas 7 (☎0251/42 073; ②), co-managed with the *Thalia Rooms* across the street (☎0251/24 640; ②). *Zoumbouli Rooms*, facing the water on Navmahías Ellís (☎0251/29 081; ③), are en-suite, but may get more noise from traffic and the bar below. Moving slightly upmarket, there's *New Life* at the end of Olýmbou, a cul-de-sac off Ermoú (☎0251/46 100), offering antique-furnished rooms in an old mansion, or *Villa 1900*, another restored mansion in the south of town at P. Vostáni 24 (☎0251/43 437; ③), whose en-suite units have fridges, air conditioning and sometimes ceiling murals.

EATING, DRINKING AND NIGHTLIFE

Dining options in Mytilíni are limited, especially since the demise of several more characterful places in the 1990s and the multiplication of fast-food joints in their stead. The obvious, if blatantly touristy, venue for a seafood blowout is the line of three fish tavernas on the southerly quay known as Fanári; *Stratos* at the far end is marginally the best, and the only one that doesn't tout aggressively. Having got this far, you may as well keep going to the end of the jetty and the square lighthouse building which houses a characterful fishermen's kafenío with excellent mezédhes; the only similar establishment left in town is a no-name ouzerí on Thássou, between Ermoú and the front.

If you're stuck here involuntarily, awaiting a dawn-departing ferry, some consolation can be derived from the town's decent **nightlife and entertainment**. *Hott Spott* is a fairly accurate self-description of the durable café-bar at Koundouriótou 63, near the NEL agency; nearby at no. 59, *Papagallino* also does crepes, and has a magnificent interior atrium. Formal live events constitute the Lesviakó Kalokéri, held in the castle from June to August, while the summer cinema Pallas is between the post office and the park on Vournázon.

Around Mytilíni

Beyond the airport and Krátigos village, the paved road becomes dirt up to **Haramídha**, 14km from town and the closest decent beach (the fee-entry town "beach" at Tsamákia is mediocre); the eastern bay has a few tavernas. The double cove at **Áyios Ermoyénis**, 4km west, is more scenic but crowded at weekends, and has no taverna or accommodation. The latter is directly accessible from Mytilíni via Loutrá village. For other pleasant immersions near Mytilíni, make for **Loutrá Yéras**, 8km along the main road to Kalloní. These public baths (daily: June–Aug 8am–7pm; Sept–May 10am–6pm; 500dr) are just the thing if you've spent a sleepless night on a ferry, with ornate spouts that feed 38°C water to marble-lined pools in vaulted chambers; there are separate facilities for each sex.

The Variá museums

The most rewarding single targets near Mytilíni are a pair of museums at **VARIÁ**, 5km south of town (half-hourly buses). The **Theophilos Museum** (Tues–Sun 9am–2pm & 5–8pm; 500dr includes key-catalogue) honours the painter, born here in 1873, with four rooms of wonderful, little-known compositions specifically commissioned by his patron Thériade (see below) during the years leading up to his death in 1934. A wealth of detail is evident in elegiac scenes of fishing, reaping, olive-picking and baking from the pastoral Lésvos which Theophilos obviously knew best; there are droll touches also, such as a cat slinking off with a fish in *The Fishmongers*. In classical scenes – *Sappho and Alkaeos*, a landscape series of Egypt, Asia Minor and the Holy Land, and historical episodes from wars historical and contemporary – Theophilos was clearly on shakier ground. In *Abyssinians Hunting an Italian Horseman*, the subject has been conflated with New World Indians chasing down a conquistador.

The adjacent, imposing **Thériade Museum** (Tues–Sun 9am–2pm & 5–8pm; 500dr) is the brainchild of another native son, Stratis Eleftheriades (1897–1983). Leaving the island at an early age for Paris, he gallicized his name to Thériade and went on to become a renowned avant-garde art publisher, convincing some of the leading artists of the twentieth century to participate in his ventures. The displays consist of lithographs, engravings, wood-block prints and watercolours by the likes of Miró, Chagall, Picasso, Matisse, Le Corbusier, Léger, Rouault and Villon, either annotated by the painters themselves or commissioned as illustrations for the works of prominent poets and authors – an astonishing collection for a relatively remote Aegean island.

Southern Lésvos

The southernmost portion of the island is indented by two great inlets, the gulfs of **Kalloní** and **Yéra**, the first curving in a northeasterly direction, the latter northwesterly, creating a fan-shaped peninsula at the heart of which looms 967-metre Mount Ólymbos. Both shallow gulfs are almost landlocked by virtue of very narrow outlets to the open sea. This is the most verdant and productive olive-producing territory on Lésvos, and the stacks of pressing-mills stab the skyline.

Plomári and around

Due south of Mount Ólymbos, at the edge of the "fan", **PLOMÁRI** is the only sizable coastal settlement in the south, and indeed the second largest town on Lésvos. It presents an unlikely juxtaposition of scenic appeal and its famous oúzo industry, courtesy of several nearby distilleries. Despite a lack of good beaches within walking distance, it's besieged in summer by hordes of Scandinavian tourists, but you can usually find a **room** (they are prominently signposted) at the edge of the old, charmingly dilapidated town, or (better) 1km west in **Ammoudhélli** suburb, which has a small gravel beach. Three specific outfits above Platía Beniamín include *Pension Lida I* and *II* (☎0252/32 620; ③), in adjacent old mansions, and *Pension Kamara* (☎0252/31 901; ③). Rustling up a decent meal may present more difficulties, with the dinner-only *Platanos* taverna at the central plane tree often unbearably busy, and nothing special at that. Ammoudhélli can offer *To Ammoudhelli*, a seafood and grills ouzerí perched over the water, and *Mama Katerina* on the opposite side of the road.

Áyios Isídhoros, 3km east, is where most tourists actually stay; pick of the hotels here, not completely overrun with package tours, is the *Pebble Beach* (☎0252/31 651; ④), with most of the large rooms overlooking a slightly reefy section of beach. Eating out here, try the adjacent *Iy Mouria* or *Mamas Papas* (sic), where the road turns inland to cross the creek draining to the long, popular pebble beach.

Melínda, another 700-metre sand and shingle beach at the mouth of a canyon, lies 6km west of Plomári on a partly paved road (closed to four-wheelers until mid-2000). Here you'll find three inexpensive **taverna-rooms** outfits, of which *Maria's* (☎0252/93 239; ②) is an endearingly ramshackle place with simple but reasonably priced food and lodging; *Melinda* (aka Dhimitris Psaros; ☎0252/93 234; ②) at the west end of the strand has a more elaborate menu and en-suite rooms. Even more unspoiled (thanks partly to a dreadful seven-kilometre side road in, being paved in 1999), *Tárti*, some 22km in total from Plomári, is a 400-metre-wide cove where Lésvos hoteliers and restaurant owners take *their* holidays. Of the three tavernas, the one closest to road's end is the best and cheapest; rooms also line the final stretch of road should you want to stay.

The **bus** into Plomári travels via the attractive villages of Paleókipos and Skópelos (as well as Áyios Isídhoros); the road north from Plomári to Ayiássos has paving and public transport only as far as Megalohóri.

Ayiássos and Mylélia

AYIÁSSOS, nestled in a remote, wooded valley under the crest of Mount Ólymbos, is the most beautiful hill town on Lésvos, its narrow cobbled streets lined by ranks of tiled-roof houses. On the usual, northerly approach, there's no clue of the enormous village until you see huge knots of parked cars at the southern edge of town (where the bus leaves you after the 26-kilometre run from Mytilíni).

Don't be put off by the endless ranks of kitsch wooden and ceramic souvenirs, aimed mostly at Greeks, but continue past the central **church of the Panayía Vrefokratoússa**, originally built in the twelfth century to house an icon supposedly painted by the Evangelist Luke, to the **old bazaar**, with its kafenía, yoghurt shops and butchers' stalls. With such a venerable icon as a focus, the local August 15 *paniyíri* is one of the liveliest in Greece, let alone Lésvos. Ayiássos also takes Carnival very seriously; there's a club dedicated to organizing it, opposite the post office.

The best **restaurants are** *Dhouladhelli*, on your left as you enter the village from the extreme south (bus stop) end, or *Dhayielles*, 70m further along and less subscribed to by Greek coach groups. At either of these spots you can eat for a fraction of the prices asked at the coastal resorts. There are a very few rooms available; ask at the *Anatoli* grill, between the two aforementioned restaurants.

If you're headed for Ayiássos with your own transport, you might visit the **Mylélia water mill**, whose access track takes off 1km west of the turning for Ípios village. The name means "place of the mills", and there were once several hereabouts, powered by a spring up-valley at Karíni. The last survivor (open daily 9am–6pm), restored to working order, has not been twee-ified in the least; the keeper will show you the millrace and paddle-wheel, as well as the flour making its spasmodic exit, after which you're free to buy gourmet pastas at the adjacent shop.

Vaterá, Skála Polikhnítou – and spas en route

A different bus route from Mytilíni leads to Vaterá beach via the inland villages of **Polikhnítos** and **Vríssa**. If you're after a hot bath, the small, vaulted **spa-house** 1.5km east of Polykhnítos has been restored by an EU programme (Mon–Sat 7–11am & 5–7pm, Sun 7–11am; 500dr); there are separate, pink-tinted chambers for each sex. Alternatively there are more **hot springs** at **Áyios Ioánnis** (token admission), fairly well signposted 3km below the village of Lisvóri. Flanking the eponymous chapel are two pools housed in unlocked, whitewashed, vaulted chambers (500dr fee payable when adjacent snack bar attended); the left-hand one's nicer, and there's no gender segregation or dress code.

VATERÁ itself, 9km south of Polikhnítos, is a huge, seven-kilometre-long sand beach, backed by vegetated hills; the sea here is delightfully calm and clean. If you intend to stay here you'll probably want your own transport, as the closest shops are 4km away at Vríssa, and the bus appears only a few times daily. Development straggles for several kilometres to either side of the central T-junction, consisting mostly of seasonal villas and apartments for locals; at the west end of the strip is one of the very few consistently attended and professionally run hotels, the Greek- and American-run *Vatera Beach* (☎0252/61 212, fax 61 164, *hovatera@otenet.gr*, ④). It also has a good attached restaurant with shoreline tables from where you can gaze on the cape of **Áyios Fokás** 3km to the west, where only foundations remain of a temple of Dionysos and a superimposed early Christian basilica. The little tamarisk-shaded anchorage here has an acceptable fish **taverna**, *Akrotiri/Agelerou*; it's better than most eateries east of the T-junction at Vaterá, many of them only operating July and August, but not so good as the half-dozen tavernas at **SKÁLA POLIKHNÍTOU**, 4km northwest of Polikhnítos itself, where *Ta Asteria* and *Exohiko Kendro Tzitzifies* can both be recommended, staying open most of the year. Skála itself is pleasantly workaday, with no beach to speak of but one unusual accommodation option: "Soft Tourism" run by Lefteris and Erika (☎0252/42 678; ②), who also have the concession to run the Polikhnítos spa. They generally have special-interest groups April-to-June and September, but welcome independent travellers during July and August.

East from Vaterá, an intermittently paved road leads via Stavrós, and then either Ambelikó or Akrássi to either Ayiássos or Plomári within ninety minutes. When leaving the area going north towards Kalloní, the short cut via the naval base at Akhladherí is well worth using, and completely paved despite tentative depiction on local maps.

Western Lésvos

The main road west of Loutrá Yéras is surprisingly devoid of settlement, with little to stop for before Kalloní other than the traces of an ancient **Aphrodite temple** at **Mési** (Messon), 1km north of the main road, and signposted just east of the Akhladherí turn-off. At the **site** (Tues–Sun 8.30am–3pm; free) just eleventh-century BC foundations and a few column stumps remain, plus the ruins of a fourteenth-century Genoese-built basilica wedged inside; it was once virtually on the sea but a nearby stream has silted things up in the intervening millennia. All told, it's not worth a special trip, but certainly make the short detour if passing by. With more time and your own transport, you can turn northeast towards **Ayía Paraskeví** village, midway between two more important monuments from diverse eras: the Paleo-Christian **basilica of Halinádhou**, and the **medieval bridge** of Kremastí.

KALLONÍ itself is an unembellished agricultural and market town more or less in the middle of the island, but you may spend some time here since it's the intersection of most bus routes. Some 3km south lies **SKÁLA KALLONÍS**, a somewhat unlikely package resort backing a long but coarse beach on the lake-like gulf. It's mainly distinguished as a bird-watching centre, attracting hundreds of twitchers for the spring nesting season in the adjacent salt marshes. Pick of the handful of hotels is the human-scale bungalow complex *Malemi* (253/22 594; ④), with attractive grounds and a pool. Restaurants are generally unrecommendable except for the *Medusa*, serving succulent seafood (including the gulf's celebrated *sardhélles pastés*, or salt-cured sardines) within sight of the fishing fleet.

Inland monasteries and villages

West of Kalloní, the road winds 4km uphill to the **monastery of Limónos**, founded in 1527 by the monk Ignatios, whose actual cell is maintained in the surviving medieval north wing. It's a huge, rambling complex, with just a handful of monks and lay workers to maintain three storeys of cells around a vast, plant-filled courtyard. The *katho-*

likón, with its carved-wood ceiling and archways, is built in Asia Minor style and is traditionally off-limits to women; a sacred spring flows from below the south foundation wall. A former abbot established a **museum** (daily 9am–3pm, sometimes later as funding permits; 200dr) on two floors of the west wing; the ground-floor ecclesiastical collection is interesting enough, though the upstairs ethnographic gallery (officially shut for "repairs") is better. If denied access, you may have to content yourself with an overflow of farm implements stashed in a corner storeroom below, next to a chamber where giant *pithária* (urns) for grain and olive oil are embedded in the floor.

The main road beyond passes through **VATOÚSSA**, a landlocked and beautiful settlement in the heart of the westerly landmass; besides unspoilt architecture it can offer two sterling examples of the endangered traditional oúzo-mezédhes kafenío in the upper platía: *Tryfon* and *Mihalis*.

Some 8km beyond Vatoússa, a short track leads down to the sixteenth-century **monastery of Perivolís** (daily 8am–one hour before sunset; donation, no photos), built in the midst of a riverside orchard (*perivóli*). Feeble electric light is available to view the narthex's fine if damp-damaged frescoes. In an apocalyptic panel worthy of Bosch (*The Earth and Sea Yield up their Dead*) the Whore of Babylon rides her chimera and assorted sea-monsters disgorge their victims; just to the right, towards the main door, the Three Magi approach the Virgin enthroned with the Christ Child. On the north side you see a highly unusual iconography of *Abraham, the Virgin, and the Penitent Thief of Calvary in Paradise*, with the Four Rivers of Paradise gushing forth under their feet; just right are assembled the Hebrew kings of the Old Testament.

ÁNDISSA, 3km further on, nestles under the west's only pine grove; at the edge of the village a sign implores you to "Come Visit Our Square", not a bad idea for the sake of several kafenía sheltering under three enormous plane trees. For more substantial fare, however, follow the paved road from directly below Ándissa 6km north to **GAVATHÁS**, a fishing hamlet with a narrow, partly protected beach (there's a bigger, surf-buffeted one at Kámbos just to the east) and a few places to eat and stay – the best of these are *Rooms Restaurant Paradise* (☎0253/56 376 or, in winter, call the proprietors in New Jersey ☎302/535-6376; ③); both serve with good fish and locally grown vegetables.

Just west of Ándissa there's an important junction. Keeping straight leads you past the still-functioning **monastery of Ipsiloú**, founded in 1101 atop the extinct volcano of Órdhymnos. The *katholikón*, tucked in one corner of a large, irregular courtyard, has a fine wood-lattice ceiling but had its frescoes repainted to detrimental effect in 1992; more intriguing are portions of Iznik tile stuck in the facade, and the handsome double gateway. Upstairs you can visit a fairly rich **museum** of ecclesiastical treasure (sporadically open; small donation). Ipsiloú's patron saint is John the Theologian, a frequent dedication for monasteries overlooking apocalyptic landscapes like the surrounding parched, boulder-strewn hills.

Signposted just west is the paved, five-kilometre side road to the main concentration of Lésvos's rather overrated **petrified forest** (daily 8am–sunset; 500dr), a fenced-in "reserve" which is toured along 3km of walkways. For once, contemporary Greek arsonists cannot be blamed for the state of the trees, created by the combined action of volcanic ash from Órdhymnos and hot springs some fifteen to twenty million years ago. The mostly horizontal sequoia trunks average a metre or less in length, save for a few poster-worthy exceptions; another more accessible (and free) cluster is found south of Sígri (see below), plus there are a fair number of petrified logs strewn about the courtyard of Ipsiloú.

Sígri

SÍGRI, near the western tip of Lésvos, has an appropriately end-of-the-line feel; the bay here is guarded both by an Ottoman castle, and the long island of Nissopí, which protects the place somewhat from prevailing winds. Accordingly it's an important NATO naval base, with the few weekly NEL **ferries** to Rafína, Áyios Efstrátios and Límnos obliged to dodge numbers of battleships anchored here. The eighteenth-century **castle** sports the sultan's monogram over the entrance, something rarely seen outside Istanbul, and a token of the high regard in which this productive island was held. A vaguely Turkish-looking **church** is in fact a converted mosque, while the town itself presents a drab mix of vernacular and cement dwellings. The town beach, south of the castle headland, is narrow and hemmed in by the road; there are much better beaches at **Faneroméni**, 3.5km north by coastal dirt track from the northern outskirts of town, plus another 2km south, just below the fifteen-kilometre dirt track to Eressós; neither beach has any facilities.

Most **accommodation** is monopolized by British tour companies, but you might try *Nelly's Rooms and Apartments* (☎0253/54 230; ②), overlooking the castle, or the nearby *Rainbow Studios* (☎253/54 310; ②). Among several tavernas, *Galazio Kyma* – the white building with blue trim, opposite the jetty – gets first pick of the fishermen's catch, but is no longer as cheap as it was.

Skála Eressoú

Most visitors to western Lésvos park themselves at the resort of **SKÁLA ERESSOÚ**, accessible via the southerly turning between Ándissa and Ipsiloú. The three-kilometre beach here runs a close second in quality to Vaterá's, and consequently the place is beginning to rival Plomári and Mólyvos for numbers of visitors, who form an odd mix of Brits, Scandinavians, Greek families, neo-hippies and lesbians (of whom, more below). Behind stretches the largest and most attractive agricultural plain on Lésvos, a welcome green contrast to the volcanic ridges above.

There's not much to Skála – just a roughly rectangular grid of perhaps five streets by eight, angling up to the oldest cottages on the slope of **Vígla hill**. The waterfront pedestrian zone (officially Papanikolí) is divided by a café-lined round platía at mid-waterfront dominated by a bust of **Theophrastos**, the renowned botanist who hailed from ancient Eressós. This was not, as you might suppose, on the site of the modern inland village, but atop Vígla hill at the east end of the beach; some of the remaining citadel wall is still visible from a distance. On top, the ruins prove scanty, but it's worth the scramble up for the views – you can discern the ancient jetty submerged beyond the modern fishing anchorage.

Another famous reputed native of ancient Eressós was **Sappho** (c. 615–562 BC), the ancient poetess and reputed lesbian.There are usually appreciable numbers of gay women here paying homage, particularly at the two hotels (see below) devoted to their exclusive use, and in the clothing-optional zone of the beach west of the river mouth. The river itself is home to about a hundred terrapins who have learned to come ashore for bread-feedings and – beware – finger-nippings. Ancient Eressós endured into the Byzantine era, the main legacy of which is the **basilica of Áyios Andhréas** behind the modern church, merely foundations and an unhappily covered floor mosaic; the adjacent museum of local odds and ends is even less compelling.

Skála has countless **rooms and apartments**, but ones near the sea fill early in the day or are block-booked by tour companies; in peak season often the best and quietest you can hope for is something inland overlooking a garden or fields. Late in the day it's wise to entrust the search to an agency, such as Krinellos (☎0253/53 246), just off the round "square"; you pay a small commission but it saves trudging about for vacancies. There are just three bona fide hotels, and two of these – the remote *Antiopi* (☎0253/53 311; ②–③) and the seafront *Sappho the Eressia* (☎0253/53 233; ③) – are run exclusively by and for lesbians. Straights have to make do with the central, inland *Galini* (☎0253/53 138; ②); there is no longer a campsite.

Most **tavernas**, with elevated wooden dining platforms, crowd the beach; none is bad – they wouldn't survive the intense competition – but perhaps the best are two outfits at the far west end of the front. *Adonis* is a good full-on taverna with meat and fish dishes, while adjacent *Blue Sardine* is an excellent seafood ouzerí with good bread, clearly identified frozen items, unusual salads and extra touches to the fish. On the east side of the platía, Canadian-run *Yamas* is the place for pancake breakfasts, veggie burgers, wholemeal bread and decadent chocolate desserts; nearby Austrian-run *Margaratiri* is a Viennese-themed chocolate-coffee-and-Kuchen dessert café, expensive but worth it. The gay women's contingent currently favours *Dhekati Mousa/Tenth Muse*, on the Theophrastos platía; a summer cinema further inland rounds up the nightlife. Skála has a post office and a coin-op laundry near the church, but no bank or cash dispenser; come prepared or pay travel agency commissions.

If you're returning to the main island crossroads at Kalloní, you can complete a loop from Eressós along the western shore of the Gulf of Kalloní via the hill villages of Mesótopos and Ágra; this route is now entirely paved, notwithstanding obsolete maps showing it as a track.

Northern Lésvos

The main road north of Kalloní winds up a piney ridge and then down the other side into increasingly attractive country, stippled with poplars and blanketed by olive groves. Long before you can discern any other architectural detail, the cocks'-comb silhouette of **Mólyvos castle** indicates your approach to the oldest established tourist spot on Lésvos.

Mólyvos (Míthymna)

MÓLYVOS (officially Míthymna), 61km from Mytilíni, is arguably the most beautiful village on Lésvos. Tiers of sturdy, red-tiled houses, some standing defensively with their rear walls to the sea, mount the slopes between the picturesque harbour and the **Genoese castle** (Tues–Sun 8.30am–3pm; 500dr), which provides interesting rambles around its perimeter walls and views of Turkey across the straits. Closer examination reveals a score of weathered Turkish fountains along flower-fragrant, cobbled alleyways, a reflection of the fact that before 1923 Muslims constituted over a third of the local population and owned most of the finest dwellings. You can try to gain admission to the **Krallis and Yiannakos mansions**, or the **municipal art gallery** occupying the former residence of local author Argyris Eftaliotis, which hosts changing exhibits. The small **archeological museum** (Tues–Sun 8.30am–3pm; free), in the basement of the town hall, features finds from the ancient town, including blue Roman beads to ward off the evil eye (belief in this affliction is age-old and pan-Mediterranean). Archival photos depict the Greek conquest of the island in November–December 1912, with Ottoman POWs being dispatched afterwards from Mólyvos port to Anatolia. Barely excavated **ancient Mithymna** to the northwest is of essentially specialist interest, though a necropolis has been unearthed next to the bus stop.

Modern dwellings and hotels have been banned from the municipal core, but this has inevitably sapped all the authentic life from the upper bazaar; just one lonely tailor still plies his trade amongst duplicate souvenir shops, and the last locals' ouzerí shut in 1989 (though the *Salguimi* tries gamely to re-create a traditional kafenío ambience). Cast as an upmarket resort in the early 1980s, Mólyvos is now firmly MOR, with the usual silly T-shirts and other shoddy souvenirs to remind you that you're strolling through a stage-set, however tasteful, for mass tourism.

PRACTICALITIES

The **town beach** is mediocre, improving somewhat as you head towards the southern end and a clothing-optional zone. Advertised **boat excursions** to bays as remote as

Ánaxos and Tsónia (see opposite) seem a frank admission of this failing; there are also six to eight daily minibus shuttles in season, linking all points between Ánaxos and Eftaloú.

The main sea-level thoroughfare, straight past the tourist office, heads towards the harbour; along or just below it stand a number of bona fide **hotels** or **pensions.** These include the *Amfitriti* (☎0253/71 741; ④), with its own pool in a calm garden setting; the *Hermes* very near the beach (253/71 250; ③), with large airy rooms; and the durable *Sea Horse* (☎0253/71 320; ④) down at the fishing harbour, fine if you're not interested in making an early night of it in season. For rooms, seek out the modern studio units of Khryssi Bourdhadonaki (☎0253/72 193; ③), towards Ayía Kyriakí; those of Panayiotis Baxevanellis (☎0253/71 558 or *El Greco* cake-shop; ③), with a preponderance of double beds and a common kitchen; *Studios Voula* below the castle parking lot (☎0253/72 017 or 71 305), studios (③) or a restored four-person house (④), both with knockout views; and the quiet, simple rooms of Varvara Kelesi (☎0253/71 460; ②), way up by the castle. Otherwise, rooms can be reserved through the municipal tourist office by the bus stop (daily: summer theoretically 8am–3pm & 6.30–8.30pm; spring and autumn 8.30am–3pm). The official campsite, *Camping Methymna*, lies 2km northeast of town on the Eftaloú road.

The sea-view tavernas along the lower market lane of 17-Noemvríou are all much of a muchness, where you pay primarily for the view; it's far better to either head for outlying villages (see below) or descend to the fishing port, where *The Captain's Table* (green chairs) combines the virtues of fresh seafood, meat grills and vegetarian mezédhes. On the far side of the Turkish fountain here, 1999-opened *Onar* has some unusual dishes such as stuffed squid, while *To Khtapodhi*, in the old customs house by the port entrance, has fairly consistent quality and treats such as *sardhélles pastés*. Many consider the five-kilometre trip east to Vafiós worth it to patronize either *Taverna Vafios* or *Taverna Ilias*, especially the latter with its wonderful bread and bulk wine – but avoid deep-fried dishes at either place. Also highly recommended, and open most of the year, is *Iy Eftalou*, 4km northeast near the eponymous spa (see below), where the food (mostly grills) and tree-shaded setting are splendid. For dessert, try the pudding and cake shop *El Greco* on the lower market lane, where the proprietor Panayiotis is a wonderful raconteur (in several languages).

Midsummer sees a short **festival of music and theatre** up in the castle, and there's also a well-regarded summer **cinema** next to the taxi rank. Night-owls are well catered for with a selection of music bars: the sedate, retro *Skala* near the harbour; disco-ey young things' hangout *Congas Bar* below the shore road; and the all-season *Gatelousi Piano Bar* near the *Olive Press Hotel*, a more genteel branch of state-of-the-art outdoor disco *Gatelousi*, 3km towards Pétra, the place to be seen on a Saturday night (June–Aug only). Around the tourist office you'll find an automatic money-changing machine and a cash dispenser, plus numerous motorbike and car rental places. The main post office is near the top of the upper commercial street, with a seasonal branch on the shore road Mihaïl Goútou.

Pétra and Ánaxos

Since there are political and practical limits to the expansion of Mólyvos, many package companies have shifted emphasis to **PÉTRA**, 5km due south. The place has sprawled untidily behind its broad sand beach and seafront square, but the core of old stone houses, many with Levantine-style balconies overhanging the street, remains. Pétra takes its name from the giant **rock monolith** located some distance inland and enhanced by the eighteenth-century **church of the Panayía Glykofiloússa**, reached via 103 rock-hewn steps. Other local attractions include the sixteenth-century **church of Áyios Nikólaos**, with three phases of well-preserved frescoes, and the intricately decorated **Vareltzídhena mansion** (closed indefinitely for restoration).

There are a few small **hotels**, the best of these being the *Michaelia* (☎0253/41 573; ④) on the shore road towards Ánaxos – and a Women's Agricultural Tourism Cooperative (☎0253/41 238 or 41 340, fax 41 309), formed by Pétra's women in 1984 to offer something more unusual for visitors. In addition to operating an excellent, inexpensive restaurant on the square, with both grills and *mayireftá* served at rooftop seating, they arrange rooms (②) in a number of scattered premises. Aside from the co-operative's eatery, most tavernas lack distinction, except for the *Pittakos* ouzerí (dinner only) 100m south of the square. You're probably better off out of town – either at the *Taverna Petri* in the *Petrí* village 3km inland, with superb home-recipe *mayireftá* and a view terrace, or at Avláki, 1.5km southwest en route to Ánaxos, where there's an excellent, signposted eponymous taverna (really an ouzerí) behind a tiny beach.

ÁNAXOS, 3km south of Pétra, is a higgledy-piggledy package resort fringing by far the cleanest beach in the area: a kilometre of sand cluttered with sunbeds, pedalos and unmemorable snack bars. From anywhere along here you enjoy beautiful sunsets between and beyond three offshore islets.

Around Mount Lepétymnos

East of Mólyvos, the villages of 968-metre **Mount Lepétymnos**, marked by tufts of poplars, provide a day's rewarding exploration. The first stop, though not exactly up the hill, might be **Loutrá Eftaloú**, some thermal baths 5km along the road passing the campsite. Unfortunately the Ottoman domed structure is kept locked from June to September, when you're obliged to patronize the sterile modern tub-rooms (daily 10am–5pm; 300dr). Nearby, there are a considerable number of fancy hotels and bungalow complexes, friendliest, best value and least packaged of which is the *Eftalou* (☎0253/71 584; ④), with a pool, well-tended garden and loyal repeat clientele.

The main road around the mountain first heads 6km east to **VAFIÓS**, with its two aforementioned tavernas (see opposite), before curling north around the base of the peaks. This route is now entirely paved, but twice-daily bus service back towards Mytilíni does not resume until Áryennos, 6km before the exquisite hill village of **SYKAMINIÁ (Sykamiá)**, birthplace of the novelist Stratis Myrivilis. Below the "Plaza of the Workers' First of May", with its two traditional kafenía and views north to Turkey, one of the imposing basalt-built houses is marked as his childhood home. A marked trail shortcuts the twisting road down to **SKÁLA SYKAMINIÁS**, easily the most picturesque fishing port on Lésvos. Myrivilis used it as the setting for his best-known book, *The Mermaid Madonna*, and the tiny rock-top chapel at the end of the jetty will be instantly recognizable to anyone who has read the novel.

On a practical level, Skála has a few pensions, such as the central *Gorgona* (☎0253/55 301; ③), and four **tavernas**, the best and longest-lived of these being *Iy Skamnia* (aka *Iy Mouria*), with seating under the mulberry tree in which Myrivilis used to sleep on hot summer nights. In addition to good seafood, you can try the late summer island speciality of *kolokytholoúloudha yemistá* (stuffed squash blossoms). The only local beach, however, is the extremely stony one of **Kayiá** 1.5km east, so Skála is perhaps better as a lunch stop rather than a base.

Continuing east from upper Sykaminiá, you soon come to **KLIÓ**, whose single main street (marked "*kentrikí agorá*") leads down to a platía with a plane tree, fountain, kafenía and more views across to Turkey. The village is set attractively on a slope, down which a six-kilometre dirt road, marked in English or Greek and better than maps suggest, descends to **Tsónia beach**, 600m of beautiful pink volcanic sand.

South of Klió, the route forks at Kápi, from where you can complete a loop of the mountain by bearing west along a mostly paved road. **PELÓPI** is the ancestral village of unsuccessful 1988 US presidential candidate Michael Dukakis, and sports a former mosque, now used as a warehouse, on the main square. **IPSILOMÉTOPO,** 5km further along, is punctuated by a minaret (but no mosque) and hosts revels on July 17, the feast of Ayía Marína. By the time you reach sprawling **STÍPSI**, you're just 4km shy of the main Kallloní–Mólyvos road; it's also not a bad start-point for rambles along Lepétymnos's steadily dwindling network of trails. In recent years donkey-trekking has become more popular than walking, and you'll see outfit advertising throughout the north of the island.

Mandamádhos and Taxiárhis monastery

The main highway south from Klió and Kápi leads back to the capital through **MAN-DAMÁDHOS**. This attractive inland village is famous for its pottery, including the Ali Baba style *pithária* (olive oil urns) seen throughout Lésvos, but more so for the "black" icon of the Archangel Michael, whose enormous **monastery of Taxiárhis** (daily: summer 6am–10pm; winter 6.30am–7pm), in a valley just northeast, is the powerful focus of a thriving cult. The image – supposedly made from a mixture of mud and the blood of monks slaughtered in a massacre – is really more idol than icon, both in its lumpy three-dimensionality and in the former rather pagan manner of veneration. First there was the custom of the coin-wish, whereby you pressed a coin to the Archangel's forehead – if it stuck, your wish would be granted. Owing to wear and tear on the image, the practice is now forbidden, with supplicants referred to an alternative icon by the main entrance.

It's further believed that while carrying out his various errands on behalf of the faithful, the Archangel gets through more footwear than Imelda Marcos. Accordingly the icon used to be surrounded not by the usual *támmata* (votive medallions) but by piles of miniature gold and silver shoes. The ecclesiastical authorities, embarrassed by such "primitive" practices, removed all the little shoes in 1986. Since then, a token substitute has reappeared: several pairs of tin slippers which can be filled with money and left in front of the icon. Just why his devotees should want to encourage these perpetual peripatetics is unclear, since in Greek folklore the Archangel Michael is also the one who fetches the souls of the dying, and modern Greek attitudes towards death are as bleak as those of their pagan ancestors.

Límnos

Límnos is a sizable agricultural and garrison island whose remoteness and peculiar ferry schedules have until now protected it from the worst excesses of the holiday trade. Most summer visitors are Greek, and as a foreign traveller, you're still likely to find yourself an object of curiosity and hospitality, though the islanders are becoming increasingly used to numbers of German and British visitors. Accommodation tends to be comfortable if a bit overpriced, with a strong bias towards self-catering units.

Among young Greek males, Límnos has a dire reputation, largely due to its unpopularity as an army posting; there is a conspicuous **military presence**, with the islanders making a reliable living off the soldiers and family members coming to visit them. In recent years, the island has been the focus of disputes between the Greek and Turkish governments; Turkey has a long-standing demand that Límnos should be demilitarized, and Turkish aircraft regularly overfly the island, prompting immediate responses from the Greek Air Force squadron here.

The bays of **Bourniá** and **Moúdhros**, the latter one of the largest natural harbours in the Aegean, almost divide Límnos in two. The west of the island is dramatically bare and hilly, with abundant basalt put to good use as street cobbles and house masonry. Like most volcanic islands, Límnos produces excellent wine from westerly vineyards – good dry whites and rosés, plus excellent retsina – plus oúzo at Kondiás. The east is low-lying and speckled with marshes popular with duck-hunters, where it's not occupied by cattle, combine harvesters and vast corn fields.

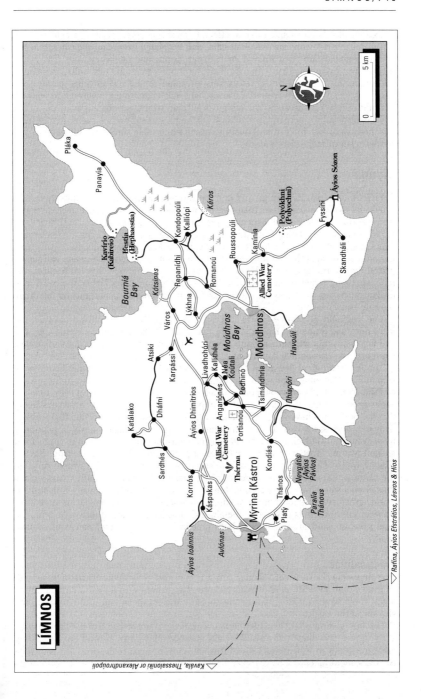

LÍMNOS

Despite off-islander slander to that effect, Límnos is not flat, barren or treeless; much of the countryside consists of rolling hills, well vegetated except on their heights, and with substantial clumps of almond, myrtle, oak, poplar and mulberry trees. The island is, however, extremely dry, with irrigation water pumped from deep wells, and a limited number of potable springs. Yet various terrapin-haunted creeks bring sand to several long, sandy beaches around the coast, where it's easy to find a stretch to yourself – though there's no escaping the stingless jellyfish which periodically pour out of the Dardanelles and die here in the shallows. On the plus side, beaches shelve gently, making them ideal for children and quick to warm up in early summer, with no cool currents except near the river mouths.

Mýrina

MÝRINA (Kástro), the capital and port on the west coast, has the atmosphere of a provincial market town rather than of a resort. With about five thousand inhabitants, it's pleasantly low key, if not especially picturesque, apart from a core neighbourhood of old stone houses dating from the Ottoman occupation, and the ornate Neoclassical mansions at Romeïkos Yialós. Few explicitly Turkish monuments have survived, though a fountain at the harbour end of Kýdha retains its inscription and is still highly prized for its drinking water. Most other things of interest line Kydhá/Karatzá, the main shopping street stretching from the harbour to Romeïkós Yialós, the beach and esplanade to the north of the castle, or Garoufalídhou, its perpendicular offshoot, roughly halfway along.

The originally Byzantine **castle** (access unrestricted), on a headland between the ferry dock and Romeïkós Yialós, is quite ruined despite later additions by the Genoese and Ottomans, but warrants a climb at sunset for views over the town, the entire west coast and – in exceptional conditions – over to Mount Áthos, 35 nautical miles west.

The **Archeological Museum** (Tues–Sun 8.30am–3pm; 600dr) occupies an old mansion behind Romeïkós Yialós, not far from the site of Bronze Age Myrina in the suburb of Rihá Nerá. Finds are assiduously labelled in Greek, Italian and English, and the entire premises are exemplary in terms of presentation – the obvious drawback being that the best items have been spirited away to Athens, leaving a collection that's essentially of specialist interest. The south ground-floor gallery is mainly devoted to pottery from Polyókhni (Polychni); the north wing contains more of the same, plus items from ancient Myrina; upstairs features galleries of post-Bronze Age artefacts from Kavírio (Kabireio) and Ifestía (Hephaestia). The star upper-storey exhibits are votive lamps in the shape of sirens, found in an Archaic sanctuary at Hephaestia. Rather less vicious than Homer's creatures, they are identified more invitingly as the "muses of the underworld, creatures of superhuman wisdom, incarnations of a nostalgia for paradise". Another entire room is devoted to metalwork, of which the most impressive items are gold jewellery and bronze objects, both practical (cheese graters) and whimsical (a snail).

Practicalities

The **airport** is 22km east of Mýrina, almost at the exact geographic centre of the island, sharing a runway with an enormous air-force base; there's no longer a shuttle bus to town, you'll have to take a taxi. Ferries dock at the southern end of the town, in the shadow of the castle.

The **bus station** is on Platía Eleftheríou Venizélou, at the north end of Kydhá. One look at the sparse schedules (only a single daily afternoon departure to most points, slightly more frequently to Kondiás and Moúdhros) will convince you of the need to rent a vehicle. Cars, motorbikes and bicycles can be had from either Myrina Rent a Car (π0254/24

476), Petridou Tours (☎0254/22 039), Holiday (☎0254/24 357 or mobile ☎ 093/2481056) or Auto Europe (☎0254/23 777); rates for bikes are only slightly above the island norm, but cars are expensive. A motorbike is generally enough to explore the coast and the interior, as there are few steep gradients but many perilously narrow village streets.

All three banks have cash dispensers; the post office and Olympic airlines terminal are adjacent to each other on Garoufalídhou, with a laundry across the way by the Hotel Paris.

ACCOMMODATION

Despite Límnos's upmarket reputation, you may still be met off the boat with offers of a **room**. Otherwise, try the *Hotel Lemnos* (☎0254/22 153; ④), by the harbour; the secluded *Studios Despina* (☎0254/23 352; ③) on a cul-de-sac leading north from Garoufalídhou, with spotless, well-furnished apartments in a garden setting; or the quiet *Hotel Ifestos* in Andhróni district (☎0254/24 960, fax 23 623; ④).

Romeïkós Yialós has several **pensions** housed in its restored houses, though all are affected by evening noise from the bars below; best value of the bunch is *Kosmos* at no. 21 (☎0254/22 050; ④). One block inland at Sakhtoúri 7, the *Pension Romeikos Yialos* (☎0254; 23 787; ④) in a stone mansion is quieter. Just north of Romeïkós Yialós, the areas of Rihá Nerá and Áyios Pandelímonas are likely bets for self-catering units; the best positioned are the hilltop *Afroditi Apartments* at Áyios Pandelímonas (☎0254/23 489; ⑤), best bookable through Sunvil Holidays in Britain. Finally, the *Akti Myrina* (☎0254/22 310, fax 22 352; winter ☎01/41 37 907) is a self-contained luxury complex of 110 wood and stone bungalows at the north end of Romeïkós Yialós, with all conceivable diversions and comforts. It's ferociously expensive – £180/$290 double half-board minimum in July – but costs considerably less if booked through one of several British tour operators offering it.

There's no official campsite on Límnos, though Greek caravanners and campers tend to congregate at the north end of Platý beach (see below).

EATING AND DRINKING

About halfway along Kydhá, *O Platanos* serves traditional oven food on an atmospheric little square under two plane trees, while *Avra*, on the quay next to the port police, makes a good choice for a pre-ferry meal or an evening grill. Seafood is excellent on Límnos due to its proximity to the Dardanelles and seasonal fish migrations; accordingly there are no fewer than six tavernas arrayed around the little fishing port. There's little to distinguish their prices or menus, though *O Glaros* at the far end is considered the best – and works out slightly more expensive.

Not too surprisingly given the twee setting, the restaurants and bars along Romeïkós Yialós are pretty poor value, except for a drink in sight of the castle. The tree-shaded tables of *Iy Tzitzifies* on the next bay north are a better option for beachfront dining.

Western Límnos

As town **beaches** go, Romeïkós Yialós is not at all bad, but if you're looking for more pristine conditions, head 3km north past the *Akti Myrina* to Avlónas, unspoiled except for the *Porto Marina Palace* luxury complex flanking it on the south. Some 6km from town you work your way through **KÁSPAKAS**, its north-facing houses in pretty, tiled tiers, before plunging down to **Áyios Ioánnis**. Here, the island's most unusual taverna features seating in the shade of piled-up volcanic boulders, with a sandy beach just north of the fishing anchorage. If it's shut, *Taverna Iliovasilemata* to the south is welcoming, with good (if slightly pricey) fish.

PLATÝ, 2km southeast of Mýrina, is a village of some architectural character, home also to three tavernas. Best of these, 100m south of the pair on the main square, is the

Zimbabwe, where the quality of the food (and the prices) belie its humble appearance. The long sandy beach, 700m below, is popular and usually jellyfish-free; except for the unsightly luxury compound at the south end, the area is still resolutely rural, with sheep parading to and fro at dawn and dusk. The low-rise *Plati Beach Hotel* (☎0254/24 301, fax 23 583; ③) has an enviable position in the middle of the beach, but is often full of package clients; there are basic rooms available at *Tzimis Taverna* (☎0254/24 142; ②), which divides the lunchtime trade with its neighbour *Grigoris* near the south end of the beach. Both lose out in the evenings to the village-centre tavernas, or the nearby poolside bar/restaurant attached to the tastefully landscaped *Villa Afroditi* (☎0254/23 141; winter ☎01/96 41 910; ⑥), co-managed with the *Afroditi Apartments* in town (and also offered advantageously through Sunvil), with one of the best buffet breakfasts in Greece.

THÁNOS, 2km further southeast, seems a bigger version of Platý village, with a few tavernas and "rooms" signs in evidence; **Paralía Thánous**, 1km on a rough track below the village, is perhaps the most scenic of the southwestern beaches, with two tavernas, one (*O Nikos*) renting studio-apartments (☎0254/22 787; ③). Beyond Thános, the road curls over to the enormous beach at **Nevgátis** (Áyios Pávlos), flanked by weird volcanic crags on the west and reckoned to be the island's best. Despite this, there's only a seasonal drinks stall on the sand and a full-service taverna across the road.

Some 3km further along (11km from Mýrina), **KONDIÁS** is the island's third largest settlement, cradled between two hills tufted with Limnos's only pine forest. Stone-built, red-tiled houses combine with the setting to make Kondiás the most attractive inland village, though facilities are limited to a few noisy rooms above one of two kafenía. Eating is better at the two simple tavernas of **Dhiapóri**, 2km east, the shore annexe of Kondiás; the beach is unappealing, with the main interest lent by the narrow isthmus dividing the bays of Kondiás and Moúdhros.

Eastern Límnos

The shores of **Moúdhros bay,** glimpsed south of the trans-island road, are muddy and best avoided. The bay itself enjoyed considerable importance during World War I, culminating in the Ottoman surrender aboard the British warship HMS *Agamemnon* here on October 30, 1918. The port of **MOÚDHROS**, the second largest town on Límnos, is a dreary place, with only a wonderfully kitsch, two-belfried church to recommend it. The closest decent beach is at **Havoúli**, 4km south by dirt track and still far from the open sea. Despite this, there are three hotels here; best of these is *To Kyma* (☎0254/71 333; ⑤), whose moderately priced restaurant is well placed for a lunch break if you're visiting the archeological sites and beaches of eastern Límnos.

About 800m along the Roussopoúli road, you pass an **Allied military cemetery** (unlocked) maintained by the Commonwealth War Graves Commission; its neat lawns and rows of white headstones seem incongruous in such parched surroundings. In 1915, Moúdhros Bay was the principal staging area for the disastrous Gallipoli campaign. Of the roughly 36,000 Allied dead, 887 – mainly battle casualties who died after having been evacuated to the base hospital at Moúdhros – are buried here, with 348 more at another graveyard behind the church in Portianoú.

Indications of the most advanced Neolithic civilization in the Aegean have been unearthed at **Polyókhni (Polyochni)**, 3km from the gully-hidden village of Kamínia (7km east of Moúdhros). Since the 1930s, Italian excavations have uncovered four layers of settlement, the oldest from late in the fourth millennium BC, pre-dating Troy on the Turkish coast opposite; the town met a sudden, violent end from war or earthquake in about 2100 BC. The actual **ruins** (daily 9.30am–5.30pm; free) are of essentially specialist interest, though a *bouleuterion* (assembly hall) with bench seating, a mansion and the landward fortifications are labelled. During August and September the Italian excavators are about, and may be free to show you around the place. The site occupies a bluff overlooking a long, narrow rock and sand beach flanked by stream valleys.

Ifestía and Kavírio, the other significant **ancient** sites on Límnos, are reached via the village of Kondopoúli, 7km northeast of Moúdhros. Both sites are rather remote, and only reachable with your own transport. **Ifestía (Hephaestia)**, 4km from Kondopoúli by rough, signposted track, has little to offer non-specialists. **Kavírio (Kabireio)**, on the opposite shore of Tigáni Bay and accessed by the same road serving a 1996-built luxury complex, is more evocative. The **ruins** (daily 9.30am–3.30pm; free) are those of a sanctuary connected with the cult of the Samothracian Kabiroi (see p.752), though the site here is probably older. Little survives other than the ground plan, but the setting is undeniably impressive. Eleven column stumps stake out a stoa, behind eight spots marked as column bases in the *telestirio* or shrine where the cult mysteries took place. More engaging, perhaps, is a nearby sea grotto identified as the Homeric **Spiliá toú Filoktíti**, where the Trojan war hero Philoctetes was abandoned by his comrades-in-arms until his stinking, gangrenous leg had healed. Landward access to the cave is via steps leading down from the caretaker's shelter.

The beach at **Kéros**, 2.5km by dirt road below **KALLIÓPI** (two snack bar/tavernas), is the best in this part of the island. A 1500-metre stretch of sand with dunes and shallow water, it attracts a number of Greek tourists and Germans with camper vans and windsurfers; a small drinks *kantína* operates near the parking area in season.

On the other side of Kondopoúli, reached via Repanídhi village, the pleasant if somewhat hard-packed beach of **Kótsinas** is set in the protected western limb of Bourniá Bay. The nearby anchorage offers a pair of tavernas and, up on a knoll overlooking the jetty, a corroded, sword-brandishing statue of Maroula, a Genoese-era heroine who delayed the Ottoman conquest by a few years, and a large **church of Zoödhóhou Piyís** (the life-giving spring). This is nothing extraordinary, but beside it 62 steps lead down through an illuminated tunnel in the rock to the brackish spring in question, oozing into a cool, vaulted chamber.

Áyios Efstrátios (Aï Strátis)

Áyios Efstrátios is without doubt one of the quietest and most isolated islands in the Aegean. Historically, the only outsiders to stay here were compelled to do so – it served as a place of exile for political prisoners under both the Metaxas regime of the 1930s and the various right-wing governments that followed the civil war. It's still unusual for travellers to show up on the island, and, if you do, you're sure to be asked why you've come.

You may initially ask yourself the same question, for **ÁYIOS EFSTRÁTIOS** village – the only habitation on the island – must be one of the ugliest in Greece. Devastation caused by an earthquake in early 1968, which killed half the population, was compounded by the reconstruction plan: the contract went to a company with junta connections, who prevented the survivors from returning to their old homes and used army bulldozers to raze even those structures that could have been repaired. From the hillside, some two dozen surviving houses of the old village overlook its replacement, whose grim rows of prefabs constitute a sad monument to the corruption of the junta years. If you're curious, there's a pre-earthquake photograph of the village in the kafenío by the port.

Architecture apart, Áyios Efstrátios still functions as a traditional fishing and farming community, with the prefabs set at the mouth of a wooded stream valley draining to the sandy harbour beach. Tourist amenities consist of just two basic tavernas, plus a growing number of **pensions** where you shouldn't have much trouble finding a bed except in season. Best of these, in one of the surviving old houses, is the *Xenonas Aï-Stratis*

(☎0254/93 329; ③); Popi Panera (☎0254/93 209; ③) has more conventional rooms in one of the prefabs.

As you walk away from the village – there are few cars and no real roads – things improve rapidly. The landscape, dry hills and valleys scattered with a surprising number of oak trees, is deserted apart from wild rabbits, sheep, an occasional shepherd, and some good beaches where you can camp in seclusion. **Alonítsi**, on the north coast – a ninety-minute walk from the village following a track up the north side of the valley – is a two-kilometre stretch of sand with rolling breakers and views across to Límnos.

South of the village, there's a series of greyish sand beaches, most with wells and drinkable water, although with few real paths in this part of the island, getting to them can be something of a scramble. **Lidharío**, at the end of an attractive wooded valley, is the first worthwhile beach, but again it's a ninety-minute walk, unless you can persuade a fisherman to take you by boat. Some of the caves around the coast are home to the rare Mediterranean monk seal, but you're unlikely to see one.

Ferries between Límnos and Kavála to Rafína call at Áyios Efstrátios every two or three days throughout the year; in summer a small Límnos-based ferry, the *Aiolis*, calls twice a week. Despite recent harbour improvements, this is still a very exposed anchorage, and in bad weather you could end up stranded here far longer than you bargained for. If an indefinite stay does not appeal, it's best to visit from Límnos on the day-trip offered by the *Aiolis* (usually on Sunday).

Samothráki (Samothrace)

After Thíra, **Samothráki** has the most dramatic profile of all the Greek islands. Originally colonized by immigrants from Thrace, Anatolia and Lésvos, it rises abruptly from the sea in a dark mass of granite, culminating in 1611-metre Mount Fengári. Seafarers have always been guided by its imposing outline, and in legend its summit provided a vantage point for Poseidon to watch over the siege of Troy. The forbidding coastline provides no natural anchorage, and landing is still very much subject to the vagaries of the notoriously bad local weather. Yet despite these difficulties, for over a millennium pilgrims journeyed to the island to visit the **Sanctuary of the Great Gods** and to be initiated into its mysteries. The Sanctuary remains the outstanding attraction of the island, which, too remote for most tourists (except during July and August), combines earthy simplicity with natural grandeur.

Kamariótissa and Hóra

Ferries and hydrofoils dock at the somewhat shabby and uninteresting port of **KAMARIÓTISSA**, where you're unlikely to want to stay long. There are nonetheless three hotels behind the tree-lined seafront and various rooms for rent in the maze of streets behind. As on most islands with a short season, accommodation is pricey for what you get, and bargaining is usually unproductive, especially in midsummer. Turning left as you step ashore, the first – and cheapest – **hotel** is the spartan *Kyma* (☎0551/41 263; ②, or ③ en-suite); rooms overlooking the water can get noise from the *barákia* which constitute Samothráki's main nightlife. Calmer, but ridiculously pricey, is the *Niki Beach* (☎0551/41 545; ④) at the far north end of the quay. The seafront is also lined with tavernas, but the best one – *Orizontas*, with quick-served *mayireftá* and bulk wine – is slightly inland on the Hóra road.

Motorbikes and **cars** are in short supply, so it's worth grabbing one immediately on disembarkation – or reserving a bike in advance from Hanou Brothers (☎0551/41 511) or a car from Niki Tours (☎0551/41 465). The latter is also the Olympic Airways and main ferry/hydrofoil agent. As with lodging, rented transport is expensive by

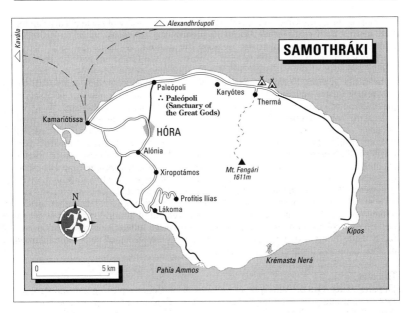

island standards, but if you've the means go for a car, as island roads are dangerously windswept for those on bikes. Note that there is only one fuel pump on the entire island, 1km above the port en route to Hóra. Kamariótissa also has a bank but no post office.

Buses travel eight times daily in season (but only twice weekly in winter) along the north coast to Thermá via Paleópoli (the site of the Sanctuary) or Karyótes, or directly inland seven times daily to **HÓRA**, the largest village and island capital. Far larger than implied by the portion visible from the sea, its attractive, whitewashed Thracian-style houses lie around a hollow in the western flanks of Mount Fengári, dominated by the Genoese Gateluzzi fort, of which little survives other than the gateway. Hóra has no reliable short-term accommodation, though asking for unadvertised rooms in the various kafenía along the winding commercial street can be productive. On the atmospheric, irregularly shaped platía, the *Iy Platia* ouzerí and the more down-to-earth *To Kastro* taverna between them provide the best (and not vastly overpriced) suppers on the island, with such delicacies as stuffed squid and *mýdhia saganáki*. There have been mutterings of moving the administrative capital down to Kamariótissa, but until further notice the island's **post office** is here.

The Sanctuary of the Great Gods

A wide but rough track leads north from Hóra to the hamlet of Paleópoli (see p.753), and, in a stony ravine between it and the plunging northeastern ridge of Mount Fengári, lie the remains of the **Sanctuary of the Great Gods**. From the late Bronze Age until the early Byzantine era, the mysteries and sacrifices of the cult of the Great Gods were performed on Samothráki, indeed in ancient Thracian dialect until the second century BC. The island was the spiritual focus of the northern Aegean, and its importance in the ancient world was comparable (although certainly secondary) to that of the Mysteries of Eleusis.

The religion of the Great Gods revolved around a hierarchy of ancient Thracian fertility figures: the Great Mother Axieros, a subordinate male deity known as Kadmilos, and the potent and ominous twin demons the *Kabiroi*, originally the local heroes Dardanos and Aeton. When the Aeolian colonists arrived (traditionally c. 700 BC) they simply syncretized the resident deities with their own – the Great Mother became Cybele, her consort Hermes and the *Kabiroi* were fused interchangeably with the *Dioskouroi* Castor and Pollux, patrons of seafarers. Around the nucleus of a sacred precinct the newcomers made the beginnings of what is now the Sanctuary.

Despite their long observance, the mysteries of the cult were never explicitly recorded, since ancient writers feared incurring the wrath of the *Kabiroi* (who could brew up sudden, deadly storms), but it has been established that two levels of initiation were involved. Both ceremonies, in direct opposition to the elitism of Eleusis, were open to all, including women and slaves. The lower level of initiation, or *myesis*, may, as is speculated at Eleusis, have involved a ritual simulation of the life, death and rebirth cycle; in any case, it's known that it ended with joyous feasting and it can be conjectured, since so many clay torches have been found, that it took place at night. The higher level of initiation, or *epopteia*, carried the unusual requirement of a moral standard (the connection of theology with morality, so strong in the later Judeo-Christian tradition, was rarely made by the early Greeks). This second level involved a full confession followed by absolution and baptism in bull's blood.

The site

The **site** (Tues–Sun 8.30am–3pm; 600dr) is well labelled, simple to grasp and strongly evokes its proud past. It's a good idea to visit the museum first (open same hours as site; 600dr), with exhibits spanning all eras of habitation, from the Archaic to the Byzantine. Highlights among these include a frieze of dancing girls from the propylon of the temenos, entablatures from different parts of the Sanctuary and Roman votive offerings such as coloured glass vials from the necropolis of the ancient town east of the Sanctuary.

The **Anaktoron**, or hall of initiation for the first level of the mysteries, dates in its present form from Roman times. Its inner sanctum was marked by a warning stele (now in the museum), and at the southeast corner you can make out the **Priestly Quarters**, an antechamber where candidates for initiation donned white gowns. Next to it is the **Arsinoeion**, the largest circular ancient building known in Greece, used for libations and sacrifices. Within its rotunda are the walls of a double precinct (fourth century BC) where a rock altar, the earliest preserved ruin on the site, has been uncovered. A little further south, on the same side of the path, you come to the **Temenos**, a rectangular area open to the sky where the feasting probably took place, and, edging its rear corner, the conspicuous **Hieron**. Five columns and an architrave of the facade of this large Doric edifice (which hosted the higher level of initiation) have been re-erected; dating from the fourth century BC, it was heavily restored in Roman times. The stone steps have been replaced by modern blocks, but Roman benches for spectators remain in situ, along with the sacred stones where confession was heard.

To the west of the path you can just discern the outline of the theatre, while just above it, tucked under the ridge is the **Nymphaeum (Fountain) of Nike**, famous for the exquisitely sculpted marble centrepiece – the *Winged Victory of Samothrace* – which once stood breasting the wind at the prow of a marble ship. It was discovered in 1863 by a French diplomat in the Ottoman empire and carried off to the Louvre, with a copy belatedly forwarded to the local museum. Due west of the theatre, occupying a high terrace, are remains of the main stoa; immediately north of this is an elaborate medieval fortification made entirely of antique material.

The rest of the island

The only accommodation near the site itself is in the tiny hamlet of **PALEÓPOLI,** where the old and basic *Xenia Hotel* (☎0551/41 166 or 41 230; ③) tries hard to compete with the *Kastro Hotel* (☎0551/41 001; ⑤), which comes with pool and restaurant; there are also some basic but en-suite rooms (②) down on the seashore below the *Kastro*. Four kilometres east, near Karyótes, is the much smaller *Elektra* (☎0551/98 242; ④); despite the family management, the lack of a restaurant means you may prefer to be nearer the action – such as it is – in Thermá (Loutrá), a further 2km east.

With its running streams, giant plane trees and namesake hot springs, **THERMÁ** is one of the better places to stay on Samothráki, although it's packed in late July and August, mainly with an odd mixture of foreign hippies and elderly Greeks here to take the waters. These are dispersed in three facilities: the sterile, junta-era main baths (daily 8am–1pm & 5–7pm; 500dr); the *psarováthres* or "fish ponds", a trio of pleasantly rustic open-air pools with a wooden sun-shade; and a small cottage with a very hot pool (keys from the warden of the main baths). The latter two facilities are reached by a dirt road starting above and to the right as you face the "improved" spa. For a cold-water contrast, the low waterfalls and rock pools of **Gría Váthra** are signposted 1.5km up the paved side road leading east from the main Thermá access drive. Thermá is also the base of choice for the tough, six-hour climb up 1611-metre **Fengári**, highest peak in the Aegean islands; the path starts at the top of the village, beside a concrete water tank and huge open-boled plane tree. Tell your accommodation proprietors that you're going, but no one else, as the police may try to stop you – army teams have been summoned on occasion to rescue ill-prepared climbers on what can be an unforgiving mountain.

Thermá is a rather dispersed place, with a small half-built jetty which will probably never receive any hydrofoils. Accommodation includes the *Kaviros Hotel* (☎0551/98 277; ④), just east of the "centre", and – further downhill, 700m from the beach – the *Mariva Bungalows* (☎0551/98 258; ④). None of the four tavernas in "central" Thermá is very inspired, a possible result (or cause) of a predominance in self-catering rooms; *Paradhisos* has the best setting and charges accordingly. At the bus stop, *Kafenio Ta Therma* doubles as the nightspot for Greek and foreign hippies; about halfway along the track to Gría Váthra, *Shelter Pub* occupies the old schoolhouse.

Beyond Thérma, on the wooded coastline, are two municipal campsites: the first, 1.5km from the village, although large, has no facilities except toilets, while the second, 3km from the village, is more expensive but has hot water, electricity, a small shop, restaurant and bar. The bus from Kamariótissa usually passes both sites.

Beaches on Samothráki's north shore are uniformly pebbly and exposed, but it's still worth continuing along the road east from Thermá. At **Cape Foniás** there's a Gateluzzi watchtower, and 45 minutes' walk inland along the stream, there are waterfalls and cold pools much more impressive than those at Gría Váthra. The road surface ends at Foniás, but you can bump along the dirt road beyond to its end, 15km from Thermá at **Kípos beach**, a long strand facing the Turkish-held island of Ímvros. There's a rock overhang for shelter at one end, a spring, shower and seasonal drinks *kantína*, but no food available.

From the warmer south flank of the island, you've fine views out to sea, as well as looming Ímvros, now officially Gökçeada. Up to three daily buses go as far as **PROFÍTIS ILÍAS**, an attractive hill village with good tavernas but no place to stay, via Lákoma. From Lákoma a wide, eight-kilometre dirt track, passable for cars, leads east to **Pahiá Ámmos**, an 800-metre sandy beach with a taverna-rooms place (☎0551/94 235; ③) at the west end. The nearest (meagre) supplies are at Lákoma, but this doesn't deter big summer crowds who also arrive by excursion kaḯkia. These also continue east to **Vátos**, a secluded (nudist) beach also accessible by land, the **Kremastá Nerá** coastal waterfalls and finally Kípos beach (see above).

Thássos

Just 12km from the mainland, **Thássos** has long been a popular resort island for northern Greeks, and since the early 1990s has also attracted a cosmopolitan variety of tourists, in particular Romanians, Serbs, Bulgarians and Hungarians holidaying a tank or so of petrol away from home, plus plenty of Germans and Brits on packages. Accordingly, it's far from unspoiled, with cheerful vulgarity the key-note of vast numbers of rural *bouzoúkia* (music halls) and tavernas which lay on music at weekends, though these haven't completely swamped the ordinary rural industries.

Thássos still makes a substantial living from the pure-white marble which constitutes two-thirds of the landmass, found only here and quarried at forty sites (legal and unlicensed) in the hills between Liménas and Panayía. Olives, honey, fruit and nuts (often

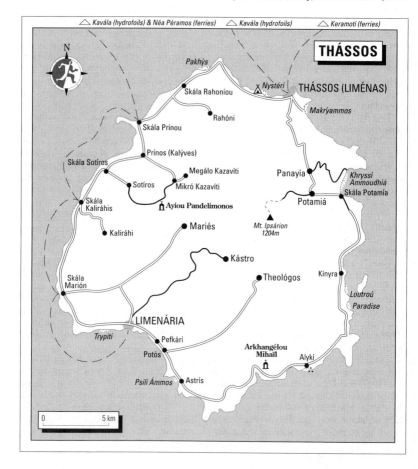

sold candied) are also important products. *Tsípouro* rather than wine is the main local tipple; pear extract, onions or spices like cinnamon or anise are added to homemade batches.

Inhabited since the Stone Age, Thássos was settled by Parians in the seventh century BC, attracted by gold deposits between modern Liménas and Kínyra. Buoyed by revenues from these, and from silver mines under Thassian control on the mainland opposite, the ancient city-state here became the seat of a medium-sized seafaring empire. Commercial acumen did not spell military invincibility however; the Persians under Darius swept the Thassian fleets from the seas in 492 BC, and in 462 Athens permanently deprived Thássos of its autonomy after a three-year siege. The main port continued to thrive into Roman times, but lapsed into Byzantine and medieval obscurity.

The salient fact of the last few decades is a series of devastating, deliberately set **fires** between 1981 and 1993; the worst one, in 1989, began near Rahóni and burnt for three days down to Mariés. Only the northeastern quadrant of the island, plus the area around Astrís and Alykí, escaped, though the surviving forest is still home to numerous pine martens – and well-striped with preventative fire-breaks.

Thássos is just small enough to circumnavigate in one full day on a rented motorbike or car, which would give you an idea where you'd want to base yourself. The KTEL will do the driving for you – albeit with little chance for stopping – some four times daily. **Car rental** is dominated by Potos Care Rental (✆0593/23 969), with branches in all main resorts, or Rent-a-Car Thassos (✆0593/22 535), also widely represented, as are most of the major international chains. Vigorous bargaining with the local one-off outfits is often productive of 35 percent discounts on rack rates – particularly in early June or mid-September. On the other hand, don't bother showing up much before or after these dates, as most facilities will be shut, and the weather dodgy.

Liménas

LIMÉNAS (also known as Limín or Thássos) is the island's capital, though not the only port. Kavála-based ferries stop down the coast at Skála Prínou, with a KTEL bus always on hand to meet arrivals. The town, though largely modern, is partly redeemed by its picturesque fishing harbour and the substantial remains of the ancient city which appear above and below the streets.

With its mineral wealth and safe harbour, **ancient Thassos** prospered from Classical to Roman times. The largest excavated area is the *agora*, a little way back from the fishing harbour. The site (free) is fenced but not always locked, and is most enoyably seen towards dusk. Two Roman stoas are prominent, but you can also make out shops, monuments, passageways and sanctuaries from the remodelled Classical city. At the far end of the site (away from the sea) a fifth-century BC passageway leads through to an elaborate sanctuary of Artemis, a substantial stretch of Roman road and a few seats of the *odeion*. The nearby archeological museum is shut indefinitely for extensive expansion, the new wings designed to accommodate a huge backlog of finds dug up by the French Archeological School.

From a **temple of Dionysos** behind the fishing port, a path curls up to a **Hellenistic theatre**, fabulously positioned above a broad sweep of sea. It's currently open but a chaos of excavation, with summer-festival performances set to resume in the distant future. On the same corner of the headland as the theatre, you can still see the old-fashioned kaïkia being built, and gaze across to the uninhabited islet of Thasopoúla. It's possible to rent boats from the fishing harbour, self-skippered or not, to take you there and elsewhere.

From just before the theatre, the trail winds on to the **acropolis**, where a Venetian-Byzantine-Genoese fort arose between the thirteenth and fifteenth centuries, constructed from recycled masonry of an Apollo temple which stood here. You can con-

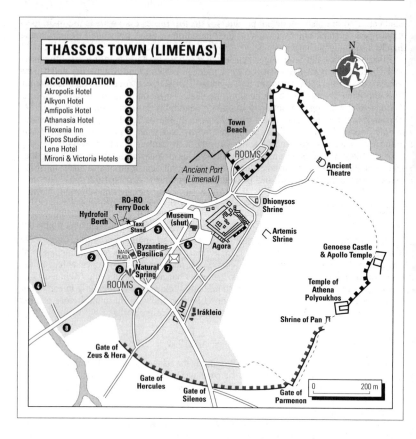

THÁSSOS TOWN (LIMÉNAS)

ACCOMMODATION

Akropolis Hotel	①
Alkyon Hotel	②
Amfipolis Hotel	③
Athanasia Hotel	④
Filoxenia Inn	⑤
Kipos Studios	⑥
Lena Hotel	⑦
Mironi & Victoria Hotels	⑧

Town Beach

ROOMS

Ancient Theatre

Ancient Port (Limenáki)

RO-RO Ferry Dock

Dhionysos Shrine

Hydrofoil Berth

Taxi Stand

Museum (shut)

Artemis Shrine

MAIN PLATIA

Byzantine Basilica

Agora

Genoese Castle & Apollo Temple

Natural Spring

ROOMS

Temple of Athena Polyoukhos

Irákleio

Shrine of Pan

Gate of Zeus & Hera

Gate of Hercules

Gate of Silenos

Gate of Parmenon

0 — 200 m

tinue, following the remains of a massive circuit of fifth-century walls to a high terrace supporting the foundations of the Athena Polyouhos (Athena Patroness of the City) temple, with Cyclopean walls. An artificial cavity in the rock outcrop just beyond was a shrine of Pan, shown in faint relief playing his pipes. From behind the summit, a rock-hewn stairway provided a discreet escape route to the Gate of Parmenon, the only gate to have retained its lintel; it's named from an ancient inscription ("Parmenon Made Me") on a nearby wall slab. From here a track, then a paved lane descend through the southerly neighbourhoods of the modern town, for a satisfying one-hour circuit.

Practicalities

Given the cheap-and-cheerful-package ethos, cuisine is not Liménas's strong point, and eateries are generally overpriced. The picturesque **tavernas** at the old harbour are pre-dictably touristy – *Oraia Simi* is marginally the best of a mediocre bunch there – and it might be better to head for *Syrtaki*, at the far east end of the overly popular town beach. In the town centre, greasy fast food is all too abundant, though a dependable favourite for *mayireftá* is *Iy Piyi*, up at the south corner of the main square, next to the natural sunken spring of the name. Carnivores should head for *Vasilis's Grill/Veryina*, on a pedestrian lane north of the square. Finally, *Orestis*, at the northwest corner of the square near *Iy Piyi*, serves the best ice cream on the island. By contrast, there's plenty of choice in local bars. *Full Moon* and the *Café Anonymous* near the *Hotel Amfípolis* are the Anglophile watering-holes, the former more of a full-on bar and with a paperback swap-library, the latter featuring foreign beers and homemade cakes; *Platia Cafe Bar* on yet another corner of the basilica square, has good music; while *Marina's Bar* near the *Hotel Alkyon* is the best waterfront nightspot, with a mainly Greek clientele.

Mountain and motorbikes can be had from Billy's Bikes (☎0593/22 490), Thomai Tsipou (☎0593/22 815) or *Babis* (☎0593/22 129), in the lane just inland from *Hotel Alkyon*. The KTEL office is on the front, virtually opposite the ferry mooring; the service is good, with regular daily buses to Panayía and Skála Potamiás, Limenária via Potós, Theológos, Kínyra and Alykí. The taxi rank is just in front of the bus stop. Thassos Tours (☎0593/23 250), at the east end of the waterfront, is the agent for Olympic Airways (closest airport is 14km from Keramotí on the mainland). The Ethniki/National and Emboriki/Commercial banks have cash dispensers.

Accommodation

At first glance Liménas – plagued with vehicle traffic and often noisy bars – seems an unlikely resort, with many **hotels** enjoying little in the way of calm or views. Despite this, there are some worthy finds; if none from the list below suits, there are also areas in the southwest of town, plus just behind the town beach, with some relatively quiet rooms (②). The closest campsite to town is the at Nystéri cove, 2.5km west; the beach is okay, its snack bar with tables out on a lawn, but the site is small, basic and on hard ground.

Akropolis (☎0593/22 488, fax 22 441). Occupying a fine traditional house with flagstone floors and a rear garden-bar, though it can get traffic noise; worth a try now that package companies don't use it. ③.

Alkyon (☎0593/22 148, fax 23 662). Certainly the most pleasant of the harbour hotels; English tea and breakfast, plus friendly, voluble management make it a home from home for independent British travellers. Open most of the year; ask also about their cottage in Sotíros and beach villa at Astrís. ③.

Amfípolis (☎0593/23 101, fax 22 110). Housed in a folly, this is the town's most exclusive outfit – and you pay dearly for the privilege; some package commitment. ⑤.

Athanasia (☎0593/23 247). Giant and eccentrically furnished rooms with balconies; take the lane inland from behind the Xenia Hotel to reach it. Run by a friendly fisherman, this place takes the overflow from the Alkyon. ②.

Filoxenia Inn (☎0593/23 331, fax 22 231). Quietly situated behind the archeological museum, this has immaculate new rooms with fridges, dedicated breakfast areas and a garden with a small pool. ④.

Kipos Studios (☎0593/22 469). In a quiet cul-de-sac near *Iy Piyi* taverna, this has cool lower-ground floor doubles (③) and four-person galleried apartments of a fair standard (④); unfortunately, the garden of the name may soon have a pool installed to make premises attractive to package companies.

Lena (☎0593/23 565). Good-value hotel, lightly refurbished in 1998, near the post office, with English-speaking management; no packages. ③.

Myrioni (☎0593/23 256, fax 22 132). Excellent value, well run and allergic to package companies. It's co-managed with the more modest *Victoria* (③) next door, with which it shares a common breakfast room. ④.

Around the coast

Whether you plan to circumnavigate the island clockwise, or in the opposite direction, plan on a lunch stop at **Alykí**, roughly a third of the way along in the sequence described below.

Panayía, Potamiá and Mount Ipsárion

The first beach east of Liménas, Makrýammos, is a purpose-built, controlled-access compound for package tourists, so carry on to **PANAYÍA**, the attractive hillside village overlooking Potamiá Bay. It's a large, thriving place where life revolves around the central square with its large plane trees, multi-spouted fountain and slate-roofed houses. Top **accommodation** choice in all senses is the *Hotel Thassos Inn* (☎0593/61 612, fax 61 027; ④), up in the Trís Piyés district near the Kímisis church, with fine views over the rooftops and the sound of running water to lull you to sleep. Second choice, slightly lower down, is the vine-shrouded *Hotel Theo* (☎0593/61 284; ③), more old-fashioned but with a nice ground-floor bar. Down on the main road, beside the municipal car park, the newish, clean *Pension Stathmos* (☎0593/61 666; ④) is the quietest of several nearby, with stunning views out the back; there are also high-standard rooms (☎0593/61 981; ③) below the school basketball courts. Some readers have complained about high-pressure touting tactics from the hotly competing tavernas on the square; for a low-key approach, try *Iy Thea*, a view-terrace psistariá at the southeast edge of town en route to Potamiá.

POTAMIÁ, much lower down in the river valley, is far less prepossessing and thus little visited, though it has a lively winter carnival. It also offers the **Polygnotos Vayis Museum** (Tues–Sat 9am–1pm, summer also 6–9pm, Sun 10am–2pm; free), devoted to the locally born sculptor; though Vayis emigrated to America when young, he bequeathed most of his works to the Greek state. Potamiá also marks the start of the commonest route up to the 1204-metre summit of **Mount Ipsárion**. Follow the bulldozer track to the big spring near the head of the valley extending west of the village (last water here), where you'll see the first red-painted arrows on trees. Beyond this point, cairns mark the correct turnings in a modern track system; forty minutes above the spring, take an older, wide track, which ends ten minutes later at a gulch and the current trailhead. The path is steep, strenuous and unmaintained, and you'll be dependent on cairns and painted arrows. Go early in the day or season, and allow for three-and-a-half hours up from Potamiá, and nearly as much for the descent.

Skála Potamiás and Khryssí Ammoudhiá

The onward road from Potamiá is lined with *dhomátia*- and apartment-type accommodation which fill in peak season mostly with Germans, judging from the Teutonic establishment names. Just before reaching the coast at **SKÁLA POTAMIÁS** at the southern end of the bay, the road splits – the right fork leads to Skála itself and some fairly uninspired tavernas; the left-hand option brings you to sand dunes extending all the way to the far end. An honourable exception amongst the **tavernas** is *Flor International* (no sign), at the corner where the bus (hourly 7am–8pm to Liménas) turns around; the *Afrodite* next door is also acceptable for *mayireftá*. Worth a mention also is *Eric's Bar* on the approach road, where one Stratos Papafilippou has made a career of his uncanny resemblance to footballer Eric Cantona; full English breakfast (of course) available. The best places to **stay** would be either above the plane-shaded traffic turnaround area by the port – where the *Hera* (☎0593/61 467; ②), just on the left looking inland, or the *Delfini* (☎0593/61 275; ②), 200m straight back, are peaceful – or north along the shore towards the sandy beach, in rooms to either side of the *Arion* (☎0593/61 486; ③) and *Anna* (☎0593/61 070; ②) hotels, which represent the best standard hereabouts. The north end of this beach is called **Khryssí Ammoudhiá**, merely another cluster of tavernas, hotels and a campsite; a separate road (no bus service) descends the 5km from Panayía. Once there, you can choose between the self-catering *Villa Emerald* (☎0593/61 979; ⑤) or the elderly, twin premises of the *Faedra/Golden Sand* (☎0593/61 474; ③). The *Golden Beach* campsite (☎0593/61 472) is the only official one on this side of the island.

Kínyra and Alykí

The tiny hamlet of **KÍNYRA**, some 24km south of Liménas, marks the start of the depressing burnt zone which overlooks it; it's endowed with a poor beach, a couple of grocery stores and several small hotels. Those not block-booked include *Villa Athina* (☎0593/41 214; ②) at the north end of things, whose top-floor rooms see the water over the olive trees, and the welcoming *Pension Marina* (☎0593/31 384; ②). The *Faros* is about the only independent taverna here. Kínyra is convenient for the superior beaches of Loutroú (1km south) and partly nudist Paradise (3km along), officially Makrýammos Kinýron. The latter ranks as most scenic of all Thassian beaches, with still-forested cliffs inland and a namesake islet offshore beyond the extensive shallows, with much cleaner water than at Khryssí Ammoudhiá – but only a single mediocre snack bar which exploits its monopoly.

The south-facing coast of Thássos has the balance of the island's best beaches. **ALYKÍ** hamlet, 35km from Liménas, faces a perfect double bay which almost pinches off a headland. Alone of Thassian seaside settlements, it retains its original architecture as the presence of extensive antiquities here has led to a ban on any modern construction. The ruins include an ancient temple to an unknown deity, and two exquisite early Christian basilicas out on the headland, with a few columns re-erected. The sand and pebble west bay, with its four tavernas, gets oversubscribed in peak season, though you can always stalk off to the less crowded, rocky east cove, or snorkel off the marble formations on the headland's far side. Among the five **tavernas**, *O Glaros* up on the north hillside is the oldest and considered the best for reliably fresh and inexpensive fish by island regulars. The *Koala Café* down on the sand provides desserts, breakfasts and a semblance of nightlife. There are a half-dozen **rooms** establishments, closest to the water being those available through *O Glaros* (☎0593/53 047; ③), four en-suite rooms with a common kitchen, or the rustic, non-en-suite units in the cottage next door to the taverna (☎0593/53 071; ②).

Arhangélou Mihaïl to Potós

Some 5km west of Alykí, the **convent of Arhangélou Mihaïl** (open reasonable daylight hours) clings spectacularly to a cliff on the seaward side of the road. Though founded in the twelfth century above the spot where a spring had gushed forth, it has been hideously renovated by the nuns resident here since 1974. A dependency of Filothéou on Mount Áthos (see p.436), its prize relic is a purported nail from the Crucifixion.

At the extreme south tip of Thássos, 9km further west, **ASTRÍS** (Astrídha) can muster two uninspiring medium-sized hotels, a few rooms and a good beach. Just 1km west is another better but crowded beach, Psilí Ámmos, with watersports on offer. A few kilometres further, **POTÓS** is the island's prime Germanophone package venue, its centre claustrophobically dense, with the few non-block-booked rooms overlooking cramped alleys. However, the kilometre-long beach to the south is still unspoiled, and on the semi-pedestrianized seafront, the original **taverna** *Iy Mouria* remains one of the cheaper and better places; next door, *Michael's Place* has great ice cream and breakfasts. There are plenty of rental outlets for cars, scooters and mountain bikes, including the headquarters of Potos Rent a Car. **Pefkári** with its manicured beach, 1km west, is essentially an annexe of Potós, with a few mid-range **accommodation** options such as *Prasino Veloudho* (☎0593/52 001, fax 51 232; ③).

Limenária and the west coast

LIMENÁRIA, the island's second town, was built to house German mining executives brought in by the Ottomans at the turn of the century. Their remaining mansions, scattered on the slopes above the harbour, lend some character, and the municipality has made a stab at prettifying the waterfront, but it remains one of the least attractive spots on Thássos, handy mainly for its banks (one with cash dispenser), post office and seasonal hydrofoil connections. At the east end of the quay, in some 1960s blocks, are a cluster of very basic hotels such as the *Sgouridis* (☎0593/51 241; ③) and the towering, non-en-suite *Papayioryiou* (☎0593/51 205; ② bathless, ③ en-suite), with mostly Greek clientele. There are also plenty of rooms on offer, and a campsite between Limenária and Pefkári: the *Pefkari* (☎0593/51 190; June–Sept). For eating and drinking, choose from among half-a-dozen each of bars and eateries along the front.

The closest good beach is **Trypití**, a couple of kilometres west – turn left into the pines at the start of a curve right. All development – mostly package villas – is well inland from the broad, 800-metre long strand, though there are umbrellas and chaise longues for rent. The perforation of the name ("pierced" in Greek) is a slender tunnel through the headland at the west end of the beach, leading to a tiny three-boat anchorage.

Continuing clockwise from Limenária to Thássos Town, there's progressively less to stop off for. The various *skáles* such as Skála Kaliráhis and Skála Sotíros are bleak, straggly and windy. **Skála Marión**, 13km from Limenária, is the exception that proves the rule: an attractive little bay, with fishing boats hauled up on the sandy foreshore, and the admittedly modern low-rise village arrayed in a U-shape all around. There are rooms available, a few tavernas, and most importantly two fine beaches to either side. **Skála Prínou** has little to recommend it, other than ferry connections to Kavála. Buses are usually timed to coincide with the ferries, but if you want to stay, there are several hotels, numerous rooms, quayside tavernas and an EOT **campsite** (☎0593/71 171; June–Sept) 1km south of the ferry dock. **Skála Rahoníou**, between here and Liménas, has more accommodation (including the *Perseus* campsite) and fish restaurants, as well as proximity to **Pahýs beach**, 9km short of Liménas, and by far the best strand on the northwest coast. Narrow dirt tracks lead past various tavernas through surviving pines to the sand, partly shaded in the morning.

The interior

Few people get around to exploring inland Thássos – with the post-fire scrub still barely waist-high, it's not always rewarding – but there are several worthwhile excursions to or around the hill villages besides the aforementioned trek up Mount Ipsárion from Potamiá (see p.758).

From Potós you can head 10km up a good road to **THEOLÓGOS**, founded in the sixteenth century by refugees from Constantinople, which was the island's capital under the Ottomans (the last Muslims only departed after 1923). Its houses, most with oversized chimneys and slate roofs, straggle in long tiers to either side of the main street, surrounded by generous kitchen gardens or walled courtyards. A stroll along the single high street, with its two kafenía, soldiers' bar, sandalmaker's and traditional baker, is rewarding and dispels the off-putting effect of vigorous advertising at the outskirts for "Greek Nights" at local tavernas. Two that eschew musical gimmicks and rely on their good fare are the long-running *Psistaria Lambiris*, near the edge of town, and *Kleoniki/Tou Iatrou*, in the very centre past the bus stop and police station. They're at their best in the evening when the *soúvles* loaded with goat and suckling pig start turning.

Despite apparent proximity on the map, there's no straightforward way from Theológos to **KÁSTRO**, the most naturally protected of the anti-pirate redoubts; especially with a car, it's best to descend to Potós and head up a rough, 17-kilometre dirt track from Limenária. Thirty ancient houses and a church surround a rocky pinnacle, fortified by the Byzantines and the Genoese, which has a sheer drop on three sides. Summer occupation by shepherds is becoming the norm after total abandonment in the last century, when mining jobs at Limenária proved irresistible, but there's only one kafenío on the ground floor of the former school, one telephone therein, far more sheep than people and no mains electricity.

From Skála Marión an unmarked but paved road (slipping under the main highway bridge to the north) proceeds 11km inland to attractive **MARIÉS** at the top of a wooded stream valley; of two tavernas here, the well-signed one to the right is more of a going concern. From Skála Sotíros, a steep road heads 3.5km up to **SOTÍROS**, the only interior village with an unobstructed view of sunset over the Aegean and thus popular with foreigners who've bought up about half of the houses for restoration. On the ridge opposite are exploratory shafts left by the miners, whose ruined lodge looms above the church. On the plane-shaded square below the old fountain, *O Platanos* taverna is congenially run by Maria and Manolis, who offer grills plus one *mayireftá* dish-of-the-day, good bulk wine and sometimes their potent, own-made *tsípouro*.

From Prínos (Kalýves) on the coast road, you've a six-kilometre journey inland to the Kazavíti villages, shrouded in greenery that escaped the fires; they're signposted and mapped officially as Megálo and Mikró Prínos but still universally known by their Ottoman name. **MIKRÓ KAZAVÍTI** marks the start of the track south for the convent of Ayíou Pandelímona. **MEGÁLO KAZAVÍTI**, 1km beyond, was once the architectural showcase of the island, a fact apparently lost on the numerous outsiders who bought holiday homes here and proceeded to do appallingly vandalistic renovations. On the magnificent platía are two decent, normal-priced **tavernas**. Some 4km up from its *skála*, **RAHÓNI** is well set at the head of its denuded valley, paired with the small village of Áyios Yeóryios across the way. The road up to the square has plenty of simple tavernas, for example *Iy Dhrosia*.

travel details

To simplify the lists that follow we've excluded three regular sailings in a generally north south direction. These are: the weekly DANE sailing between Rhodes, Kós, Sámos and Thessaloníki (23hr for the full run, usually over the weekend); the G&A sailing between the same points, usually mid-week; the NEL sailing linking Alexandhroúpoli with Límnos, Lésvos, Híos, Sámos, Kós and Rhodes (one-way trip through all ports, total 30hr).

We've also omitted the more convoluted schedules kept by the small ferries of Miniotis Lines, based on Híos. These slow and often tardy craft link Híos with Sámos (both northern ports) twice a week year-round, usually Sun or Mon, & Fri, returning Tues & Fri; from July to mid-Sept there's an extra Tues night/Weds dawn itinerary to Vathý only. Twice weekly (usually Mon/Fri), they venture from Sámos (either port) to Foúrni and Ikaría (Áyios Kírykos) and back, and once weekly (typically Tues) there's an out-and-back run from Pythagório to Agathoníssi, Arkí, Lipsí and Pátmos – these services are reliably available June to mid-Sept.

Áyios Efstrátios 3–4 weekly on NEL Lines to Límnos; 3 weekly to Rafína and Kavála; 1 weekly to Lésvos (Sígri).

Foúrni 3–4 weekly ferries to Sámos (northern ports), Páros and Pireás; morning kaïki to Ikaría on Mon, Wed, Fri; weekends only by demand; twice weekly (usually Mon and Thur) morning kaïki to Karlóvassi (Sámos).

Híos 6–11 weekly on NEL Lines to Pireás (10hr) and Lésvos (3hr 30min); 1–3 weekly to Límnos (10hr); 1 weekly summer only to Sýros or Vólos. Daily afternoon kaïki to Inoússes except Sun morning, and Thurs in off-season; 3 weekly small ferries – usually Tues, Thurs & Sat – from Híos Town to Psará (4hr), 2 weekly kaïkia on different days, mid-June to early September only, from Limniá to Psará (2hr).

Ikaría 1–3 daily from either Áyios Kírykos or Évdhilos to Sámos (both northern ports), and Pireás (at least 3 weekly services year-round); 3–5 weekly to Páros and Náxos; 3–4 weekly full-sized ferries to Foúrni, plus 3 kaïkia weekly from Áyios Kírykos to Foúrni; 1–2 weekly to Mýkonos and Sýros.

Lésvos 6–16 weekly on NEL Lines from Mytilíni to Pireás (11hr direct, 13hr 30min via Híos or Sýros); 6–10 weekly to Híos (3hr 30min); 4–6 weekly to Límnos (6hr from Mytilíni, 5hr from Sígri); 2 weekly to Thessaloníki (14hr); 1 weekly to Áyios Efstrátios (4hr) from Sígri only; 1–2 weekly to Kavála (12hr from Mytilíni, 10hr from Sígri); 1 weekly to Rafína (8hr from Sígri); 1 weekly to Psará (4hr from Sígri); 1 weekly to Vólos or Sýros (early July–early Sept only).

Límnos 4–6 weekly on NEL Lines to Lésvos (Mytilíni or Sígri); 3–4 weekly to Kavála, Áyios Efstrátios and Rafína; 1–3 weekly to Thessaloníki, Pireás, Híos. Also a small local ferry to Áyios Efstrátios 3 times weekly.

Psará 2 weekly on NEL Lines to Lésvos (Mytilíni or Sígri), 1 weekly direct to Pireás (8hr), also Límnos, Samothráki, Kavála, Alexandhroúpoli.

Sámos (Karlóvassi) As for Vathý, plus 2 weekly kaïki departures, usually early Mon and Thurs afternoon, to Foúrni.

Sámos (Pythagório) 1–2 weekly (usually Wed and Sun afternoon) with the *Nissos Kalymnos* to Agathónissi, Lipsí, Pátmos, Léros, Kálymnos, with onward connections to all other Dodecanese (see p.696 for the full schedule).

Sámos (Vathý) 1–3 daily, on G&A, Agapitos or Nomikos Lines, to Ikaría (Áyios Kírykos and/or Évdhilos) and Pireás (14hr); 3–5 weekly to Páros and Náxos; 3-4 weekly to Foúrni; 1–2 weekly to Mýkonos and Sýros; 1 weekly to Pátmos and Lipsí.

Samothráki 2–3 daily ferries to/from Alexandhroúpoli (2hr 30min) in season, dropping to 5–6 weekly out of season. Also 2 weekly late spring and early autumn, up to 4 weekly in peak season, to Kavála (and thence other North Aegean islands). At the time of writing there was weekly summer service on NEL Lines to Lésvos (Sígri) and Psará, though this may not continue in future.

Thássos 8–10 ferries daily, depending on season, between Kavála and Skála Prínou (1hr 15min; 7am–10pm, 6am–9pm to Kavála from the island); 10 daily between Keramotí and Liménas (40min; 7am–10pm, 6am–8.30pm from Thássos).

Hydrofoils

Just one company, Sámos Hydrofoils, operates in the **east Aegean**. Based on Sámos and Kós,

this offers nearly daily early morning service from Vathý and Pythagório to Pátmos, Léros, Kálymnos and Kós (in the Dodecanese), returning from Kós in the late afternoon, and conversely morning service from Kós through the same ports, returning from Pythagório only at mid-afternoon. Lipsí is included 4–7 times weekly; Ikaría and Foúrni are called at 2–4 times weekly, with Agathónissi served once or twice weekly. In 1999 there were also 2 weekly links between Sámos and Híos, but historically these have been unprofitable and cannot be relied on in future. Further, if less reliable, service is provided by Dodecanese Hydrofoils (see p.697), based on Kós and Rhodes, which go northbound in the morning and head south in the afternoon; it's possible in theory to reach Rhodes the same day from Sámos, changing craft at Kós.

Thássos is served by hydrofoils from Kavála, which depart for Liménas 8–15 times daily from 7am–9pm (6am–8pm from Thássos); in summer there are also 2–3 daily departures from Kavála to the west-coast resorts of Skála Kaliráhon, Skála Marión and Limenária.

Samothráki is served by hydrofoil from Alexandhroúpoli from mid-May to mid-June and during late Sept 5-7 times weekly in the morning (1hr 10min); from mid-June through mid-Sept there are 1–2 extra daily departures between 1 and 5pm. Two to four times weekly the morning or early afternoon sailing may continue on to Límnos.

International hydrofoils

Service thrice weekly (in theory), mid-June to mid-Sept, between Vathý (Sámos) and Kuşadası (Turkey). Fares are currently a third more than for a conventional ferry (see section below), though bargains can be had in spring or autumn.

International ferries

Vathý (Sámos)–Kuşadası (Turkey) At least 1 daily, late April to late Oct; otherwise a Turkish boat only by demand in winter, usually Fri or Sat. Morning Greek boat (passengers only), afternoon Turkish boats (usually 2 in season taking 2 cars apiece). Rates are £24/US$39 one way including taxes on both the Greek and Turkish sides, £26/$43 open return; no day-return rate. Small cars £30/$45 one way. Journey time 1hr 30min. Also occasional (2–3 weekly) services in season from Pythagório.

Híos–Çeşme (Turkey) 2–12 boats weekly, depending on season. Thursday night and Saturday morning services tend to run year-round. Passenger rates on the Greek morning boat are £31/$50 one way, £41/$67 open return (no day-return fare), including Greek taxes; no Turkish taxes. Small cars £47/$77 each way, taken on either Greek or Turkish craft. Turkish afternoon boat is usually a bit cheaper. Journey time 45min.

Mytilíni (Lésvos)–Ayvalık (Turkey) 4–8 weekly May–Oct; winter link unreliable, as is the Turkish afternoon boat at any time. Passenger rates on the Greek morning boat are £33/$54 one way, £43/$70 round trip. Small cars £49/$80 each way. Journey time 1hr 30min.

Flights

NB All flights on Olympic Airways/Aviation unless otherwise specified. Frequencies are for the period May–Oct only.

Híos–Athens (4–5 daily on Olympic, 1 daily on Air Manos; 55min)

Lésvos–Athens (4–5 daily; 50min)

Lésvos–Híos (2 weekly; 30 min)

Lésvos–Thessaloníki (6 weekly; 1hr 10min–2hr)

Límnos–Athens (2–3 daily; 1hr)

Límnos–Lésvos (3 weekly; 40min)

Límnos–Thessaloníki (6 weekly; 50min)

Sámos–Athens (3–4 daily on Olympic, 1–2 daily on Air Manos; 1hr)

Sámos–Mýkonos (2 weekly on Air Manos; 40min)

Sámos–Thessaloníki (2 weekly on Olympic, 2 weekly on Air Manos; 1hr 20min)

Sámos–Thíra (2 weekly on Air Manos; 2hr)

CHAPTER ELEVEN

THE SPORADES AND ÉVVIA

The three northern **Sporades**, Skiáthos, Skópelos and Alónissos, are scattered (as their Greek name suggests) just off the mainland, their mountainous terrain betraying their origin as extensions of Mount Pílion in Thessaly. They are archetypal holiday islands, with a wide selection of good beaches, transparent waters and thick pine forests. All are very busy in season, with Skiáthos attracting by far the most package tours.

Skiáthos has the best beaches, and is still the busiest island in the group, though these days **Skópelos** gets very crowded, too. **Alónissos** is the quietest of the three, and has the wildest scenery, so it's really more for nature lovers than night-owls. **Skýros**, further southeast, retains more of its traditional culture than the other three islands, though development is now well under way. The main town doesn't yet feel like a resort, but its main street is not without its fast food and souvenir shops. Unlike the other three islands, the best beaches are those close to the main town. To the south, the huge island of **Évvia** (or Euboea) runs for 150km alongside the mainland. It is one of the most attractive Greek islands, with a forested mountain spine and long stretches of rugged, largely undeveloped coast. Perhaps because it lacks any impressive ruins or real island feel due to its proximity to the mainland, Évvia is explored by few foreign tourists, though Athenians and Thessalians visit the island in force and have erected holiday homes around half a dozen of its major resorts.

The Sporades are well connected by **bus** and **ferry** both with Athens (via Áyios Konstandínos or Kými), Thessaloniki and Vólos, and it's easy to island-hop in the north-

---

ACCOMMODATION PRICE CODES

Throughout the book we've used the following **price codes** to denote the cheapest available double room in each establishment in high season. Out of season, rates can drop by more than fifty percent, especially if you are staying for three or more nights. Single rooms, where available, cost around seventy percent of the price of a double.

Rented private rooms on the islands usually fall into the ② or ③ categories, depending on their location and facilities, and the season; a few in the ④ category are more like plush self-catering apartments. They are not generally available from late October through to the beginning of April, when only hotels tend to remain open.

① Up to 6000dr	④ 12,000–16,000dr
② 6000–9000dr	⑤ 16,000–20,000dr
③ 9000–12,000dr	⑥ 20,000dr and upwards

Note: Youth hostels typically charge 2000–2500dr for a dormitory bed.
For more accommodation details, see pp.43–6.

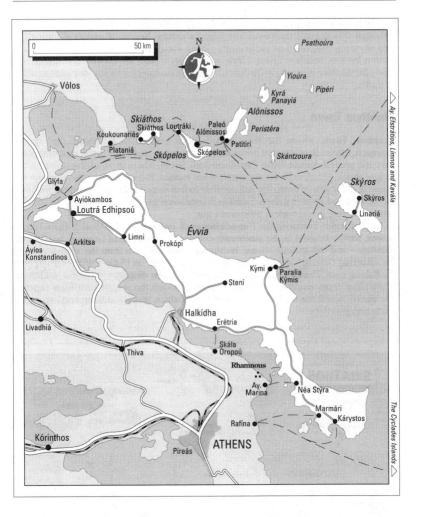

ern group. The only ferry connection to Skýros is from Kými, plus a Flying Dolphin hydrofoil service in summer from Vólos via the other Sporades. Évvia is linked to the mainland by a bridge at its capital Halkídha, and by a series of shuttle ferries. Both Skiáthos and Skýros have airports.

Skiáthos

The commercialization of **Skiáthos** is legendary among foreigners and Greeks: it's a close fourth to that of Corfu, Mýkonos and Rhodes. But if you've some time to spare, or a gregarious nature, you might still break your journey here to sample the best, if most overcrowded, **beaches** in the Sporades. Along the south and southeast coasts, the road serves an almost unbroken line of villas, hotels and restaurants, and although this doesn't take away the island's natural beauty, it makes it difficult to find anything unspoiled or particularly Greek about it all. As almost the entire population lives in Skiáthos Town, a little walking soon pays off. However, camping outside official sites is strongly discouraged, since summer turns the dry pine-needles to tinder.

Skiáthos Town

Skiáthos Town, where the ferries dock, looks great from a distance, but as you approach, tourist development becomes very apparent, especially to the east side of the port and around Alexándhrou Papadhiamándi Street, where most of the services, the tackier shops, "English" pubs and eateries are located. But tucked into the alleys on the western, older side of town, it is still possible to find some pockets of charm: older houses, gardens and flowers galore. Skiáthos boasts some good restaurants and nightclubs, and can be fun, in a crowded, boisterous way.

The few sights comprise the **Papadhiamándi museum** (Tues–Sun 9.30am–1pm & 5–8pm; free) – housed in the nineteenth-century home of one of Greece's best-known novelists – and two antique shops, Archipelago two blocks in from the waterfront, and the enduring Galerie Varsakis (open usual shop hours), on Platía Trión Ierarhón near the fishing port. The latter has one of the best **folklore displays** in Greece, and many of the older items would do the Benaki Museum proud; the proprietor neither expects, nor wants, to sell the more expensive of these, which include antique textiles, handicrafts and jewellery.

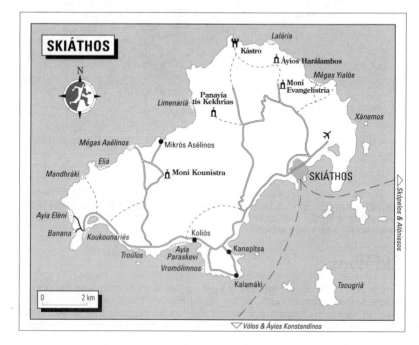

Arrival, transport and other facilities

Buses and **taxis** ply from the area around the **ferry harbour**. To Koukounariés, the bus is the cheapest option (280dr); it runs at least hourly in summer (every fifteen minutes at peak times), the last bus returning at 1am. Sharing a taxi is another option.

A large number of competing **rental outlets** in town, most on the front behind the ferry harbour, offer bicycles, mopeds, motorbikes, cars and motorboats. For bikes, good rates can be had from Makis Dimas, whose workshop is signposted at the far end of Papadhiamándi. The cheapest, small cars go for around 15,000dr a day, as do motorboats; fuel and insurance are extra. Several travel agents organize "round the island" **mule trips** (5900dr a day), and there's **horse-riding** at the Pinewood Riding Club (no phone) at Koukounariés. Most other facilities are on Alexándhrou Papadhiamándi, including the **OTE**, **post office**, **banks** and a branch of American Express.

Accommodation

Much of the island's accommodation is in Skiáthos Town. The few reasonably priced **hotels** or **pensions** are heavily booked in season, though you can usually find a room, albeit slightly more expensively than on most islands. At other times, supply exceeds demand and you can find very cheap **rooms** with a little bargaining. Try for locations in the older quarters to the west; avoid lodgings in the flatlands to the north as they tend to be noisy. There is a room-owners' association kiosk on the quay that opens fitfully in high season but at other times bookings can be made through several tourist agencies. For an honest and helpful approach, try the Mare Nostrum at Papadhiamándi 21 (☎0427/21 463) or the efficient Helotropio (☎0427/22 430, fax 21 952) on the seafront. A more direct option is Adonis Stamelos' rooms just outside town at Megáli Ámmos (☎0427/22 962; ③). Good small hotels include the *Bourtzi* (☎0427/22 694; ⑤) and *Pothos* (☎0427/21 304; ⑤), both immaculate with delightful gardens, and the *Orsa* (☎0427/22 430; ⑥), a remodelled house overlooking the sea on the west side of the port which can be booked through Heliotropio. Other fine options are the *Alkyon Hotel*, on the seafront at the commercial port end (☎0427/22 981; ⑥), or the *Meltemi Hotel*, on the front near the taxi rank (☎0427/22 493; ⑥).

The island has three official **campsites**. Koukounariés and Asélinos are fairly decent with standard facilities. Xanémos beach is 3km northeast of Skiáthos Town, right next to the airport runway, and, apart from being within walking distance of the town, has little to recommend it.

Eating, drinking and nightlife

You're spoiled for choice for **eating places**, but nothing is particularly cheap apart from the few burger/*yíros* joints. One of the best of the cheaper tavernas is *Zorba's*, opposite the taxi rank, while *Mesogeia*, above and to the west of Plátia Trión Ierarkhón, has excellent moussaka and home-cooked dishes. *Ellinikon*, up in the backstreets above the west seafront, also has home-style cooking and good wine in a secluded garden, while *Cuba*, set in a leafy square east of Papadhiamándi, has a huge range of grilled meat, fish and starters. For more elegant dining, head for *Agnantio*, at the start of the road to Evangelístria, for superlative Greek cuisine and views; *The Windmill* at the top of the hill above Áyios Nikólaos, for nouvelle cuisine and views; and *Calypso*, on the east waterfront, for genuine Italian food. Back on the west side, above the flat rocks where people sunbathe, *Tarsanas* is a converted boatbuilders' yard with a picturesque veranda – the best place in town for an evening drink as the harbour lights come on.

Nightlife centres on the clubs on or near Polytekhníou. The best places are *Borzoi*, the oldest club on the island, *Stones* and the *Apothiki Music Hall* for Greek music and a good atmosphere, while on the seafront *BBC* pulses till dawn. In the bars in the back streets around Polytekníou you can hear a wider range of music; places like the *Banana* are pop-orientated and popular among British beer drinkers, the old and much loved *Kentavros* plays jazz and blues, *Adagio* has classical music in the evenings, and *Blue Chips* is a stylish upmarket place. On the east shore, the chic *Remezzo* with its maritime motifs, is a perennial favourite, while *Kavos* and *Kalua* rival it for pumping out the loudest disco sounds.

Skiáthos's outdoor **cinema** *Refresh Paradiso*, on the ring road, shows new releases in their original language. Another source of entertainment is that the little offshore Boúrtzi fortress has been transformed into an outdoor **theatre** and is home to occasional plays and musical performances during the summer.

Around the island

Other than using the buses or the various rental outlets in town (for which see above), you could also get your bearings on a **boat trip** around the island. These cost about 4500dr per person and leave at around 10am. Or try a boat trip to the islet of **Tsougriá** (opposite Skiáthos Town), where there's a good beach and a taverna. Boats leave from the fishing harbour beyond the Boúrtzi, and not the yacht anchorage to the north of the ferry harbour; east-coast boats leave from the quay area in front of the bus station.

If you're interested in seeing more of Skiáthos on foot, the locally produced guide to **walks** (by Rita and Dietrich Harkort; available in larger tourist shops) has detailed instructions and maps for trails all over the island.

Monasteries and Kástro

The **Evangelístria monastery** (daily 8am–noon & 4–8pm) is more than an hour on foot out of Skiáthos Town. Founded in the late eighteenth century, it is exceptionally beautiful, even beyond the grandeur of isolation you find in all Greek monasteries. The Greek flag was raised here in 1807, and heroes of the War of Independence such as Kolokotronis pledged their oaths to fight for freedom here. To reach the monastery, walk 500m out of the centre of town on the road towards the airport until, at the point where the asphalt veers to the right, you take a prominently signposted tarmac track that veers left; be careful to stick to the tarmac and not to wander off onto the dirt roads.

Beyond Evangelístria, a mule track continues to the abandoned **Áyios Harálambos monastery**, from where it's possible to walk across the island to the ruined capital of Kástro (see below) along another dirt road; this takes about two hours. To reach Kástro from Skiáthos Town, it's quicker to take the direct road, though in all it's still a hard five- to six-kilometre uphill slog; the turning is signposted on the road behind town, some distance beyond the turning for Evangelístria. You'll find it much easier if you do the walk in reverse. Just take a round the island kaïki ride and get off at the beach below Kástro. Another option is to ride a motorbike up the hill and then explore on foot.

Just over halfway between Evangelístria and Kástro, a well-used dirt track (signposted) turns left and heads towards the abandoned fifteenth-century monastery of **Panayía tís Kekhriás**, three hours' walk from town. It's said to be the oldest on the island and has a colony of bats inside. It's a beautiful walk (or organized donkey-ride), and there are two pebbly beaches below, one with a welcoming stream that provides a cool shower. Ignoring this excursion, the paved road continues to within a thirty-minute walk of **Kástro** – a spectacular spot, built on a windswept headland. In the past, the entrance was only accessible by a drawbridge, which has been replaced by a flight of steps. The village was built in the sixteenth century, when the people of the island moved here for security from pirate raids. It was abandoned three hundred years later in 1830, following independence from Turkey, when the population moved back to build the modern town on the site of ancient Skiáthos. The ruins are largely overgrown, and only three churches survive intact, the largest still retaining some original frescoes.

From outside the gates, a path leads down the rocks to a good pebble **beach**; with a stream running down from the hills and a daytime café (with slightly overpriced food and drinks), it makes a good place to camp. For an apparently inaccessible spot though, it does attract a surprising number of people. All the island excursion boats call here, and even when they've gone, there's little chance of having the ruins or beach to yourself.

Finally, the seventeenth-century **Kounístra monastery**, can be reached by turning right off the paved road that runs up the island from Tróulos, the last beach before Koukounariés, to the beach at Asélinos. It's a very pretty spot, with a beautiful carved icon screen, splendid icons, a grape arbour and a taverna.

The beaches

The real business of Skiáthos is **beaches**. There are reputed to be more than sixty of them, but that's hardly enough to soak up the numbers of summer visitors: at the height of the season, the local population of five thousand can be swamped by up to fifty thousand visitors. The beaches on the northeast coast aren't easily accessible unless you pay for an excursion kaïki: reaching them on foot requires treks more arduous than those described above. The bus, though, runs along the entire south coast, and from strategic points along the way you can easily reach a good number of beaches. The prevailing summer *meltémi* wind blows from the north, so the beaches on the south coast are usually better protected. Most of the popular beaches have at least a drinks/snacks stall; those at Vromólimnos, Asélinos and Tróulos have proper tavernas.

The beaches before the **Kalamáki peninsula** (where English and rich Greeks have their villas) are unexciting, but on the promontory itself are the highly-rated **Ayía Paraskeví** and **Vromólimnos beaches**, close to Kanapítsa hamlet; Vromólimnos offers windsurfing and waterskiing. For scuba enthusiasts, there is the *Dolphin Diving Centre* (☎0427/22 599) at the *Nostos* hotel, on the eastern side of the Kalamáki peninsula.

Just before Tróulos you can turn right up a paved road, which runs 4km north to **Mégas Asélinos**, a very good beach with a campsite, beach bar and a reasonable taverna. A daily bus and excursion boats stop here, so it's crowded in season. A fork in the paved road leads to Kounístra monastery (see above) and continues to **Mikrós Asélinos**, just east of its larger neighbour and somewhat quieter.

The bus only goes as far as **KOUKOUNARIÉS**, a busy resort with wooden walkways traversing the sand to a series of canteens selling drinks and light snacks, though the three beaches are excellent if you don't mind the crowds. There's a majestic sandy bay of clear, gradually deepening water, backed by acres of pines, which despite its popularity merits at least one visit if only to assess the claim that it's the best beach in Greece. The road runs behind a small lake at the back of the pine trees, and features a string of **hotels**, **rooms** and **restaurants**, as well as a good campsite. Here, the *Strofilia* apartments which sleep four (☎0427/49 251; ⑥) are particularly nicely furnished. The *Lake Hotel*, a smart new place right opposite the lake itself, is also decent value (☎0427/49 362; ⑤). Jet-skis, motorboats, windsurfing and waterskiing are all available off the beach.

"**Banana beach**" (also known as Krassá), the third cove on the far side of Poúnda headland, is one of the trendiest beaches with watersports, a couple of bars and tolerance of nude bathing. For the less adventurous, the turning for **Ayía Eléni**, 1km from the road, leads to a pleasant beach with a drinks kiosk. Further north, **Mandhráki** and **Eliá** beaches have similar facilities, and are accessible by bus.

The famed **Lalária beach**, on the northern stretch of coast, can be reached by taxi-boats from the town. Covered with smooth white stones, it's beautiful, with steep cliffs rising behind it; the swimming is excellent, but beware of the undertow. The island's three natural grottoes – Skotiní, Glazía and Halkiní – are nearby, and are included in many of the "round the island" trips. Southeast of Kástro are the greyish sands of **Mégas Yialós**, one of the less crowded beaches, and **Xánemos**, another nudist beach; both suffer from airport noise.

The only real way to get away from the crowds is to persuade a boat-owner to take you out to one of Skiáthos's **islets. Tsougriá**, in particular, has three beaches, with a taverna on the main one.

Skópelos

Bigger, more rugged and better cultivated than Skiáthos, **Skópelos** is almost as busy, but its concessions to tourism are lower key and in better taste than in Skiáthos. Most of the larger beaches have sunbeds, umbrellas and some watersports, but smaller, secluded coves do exist. Inland, it is a well-watered place, growing olives, plums, pears and almonds. **Glóssa** and **Skópelos**, its two main towns, are also among the prettiest in the Sporades, clambering uphill along paved steps, their houses distinguished by attractive wooden balconies and grey slate roofs. A number of **nationalities** have occupied the island at various stages of its history, among them the Romans, Persians, Venetians, French and, of course, the Turks. The Turkish admiral Barbarossa (Redbeard) had the entire population of the island slaughtered in the sixteenth century.

Loutráki, Glóssa and the west

Most boats call at both ends of Skópelos, stopping first at the small port of **LOUTRÁKI** with its narrow pebble beach, small hotels and rooms for rent. The village has been

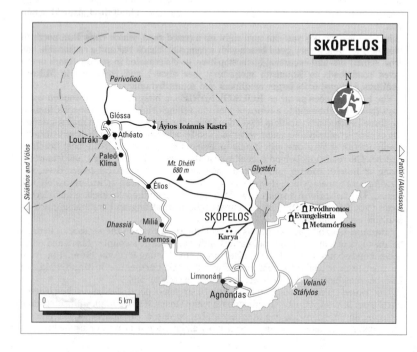

spoiled a little by development at either end, but it's not a bad place to stay if you're after peace and quiet; try *O Stelios* (☎ 0424/33 412; ③), a simple pension above the *Vrahos* taverna, the *Avra* (☎0424/33 550; ④) or any of the rooms advertised just in from the seafront. Though most of the quayside tavernas don't offer value for money, there are exceptions: the *Orea Ellas* taverna by the harbour is shaded by beautiful chestnut trees and sells a highly recommended, homemade retsina; the *Flisvos* is a friendly place with decent pasta dishes, and the small ouzerí *Boukadhoura* is good.

High above Loutráki, **GLÓSSA** would be perhaps a preferable base if it had more places to stay. It is a sizable and quite beautiful, totally Greek town, with several kafenía, a taverna and a few rooms to let, some of which are hot and musty, with erratic water pressure. *Kostas and Nina's* place (☎0424/33 686; ②) has simple, clean rooms, some with a view; they also rent out studios longer term, or you could stay at the *Selinounda Apartments* (☎0424/33 570; ③) on the road between Loutráki and Glóssa. The one central taverna, *To Agnandi*, is a lively and authentic place to eat, and full most evenings, while *Iy Kali Kardhia*, on the road out towards Élios, also serves good food in a pleasant setting. Incidentally, it's a good idea to accept offers of a taxi ride up to Glóssa from Loutráki; it's a stiff walk up even if you know the path shortcuts, and taxi drivers will know if there are any vacancies. If it's really high season, though, and even Glóssa is packed, two nearby villages, **Athéato** and **Paleó Klíma** have rooms, while Élios on the coast below has two big hotels, bungalows and rooms.

Ninety minutes' walk from Glóssa, up to the north coast, will bring you to a **beach** the locals call **Perivolioú**. The walk itself is worthwhile, passing a **monastery** next to a stone cairn containing masses of human bones and skulls. There's also a huge hollow oak tree here, in the heart of which is a small tank of drinking water. The beach, when you get there, is nothing out of the ordinary, but there's spring water for drinking and a cave for shade.

East of Glóssa, a dirt road leads to the splendidly sited church of **Áyios Ioánnis Kastrí**, perched on the top of a rock high above a small sandy cove where you can swim. A new unsightly house nearby has spoiled the isolation somewhat, but the walk from Glóssa (again, about ninety minutes) is beautiful and peaceful, with hawks and nightingales for company.

Skópelos Town

If you stay on the ferry beyond Loutráki – probably the best plan – you reach **SKÓPELOS TOWN**, sloping down one corner of a huge, almost circular bay. The best way to arrive is by sea, with the town revealed slowly as the boat rounds the final headland. Though more and more people seem to have discovered Skópelos Town, the locals are making a tremendous effort to keep it from going the way of Skiáthos. The harbour area is practically wall-to-wall tavernas and cafés, but the shops and eateries in the back alleys tend to be imaginative and tasteful, with wooden, hand-painted name signs; the two real eyesores date from the junta years. Spread below the oddly whitewashed ruins of a Venetian **Kástro**, are an enormous number of churches – 123 reputedly, though some are small enough to be mistaken for houses and most are locked except for their annual festival day. Other sights include a **folklore museum** (Wed–Fri 10am–2pm & 6–8pm, Sat 6–9pm and Sun 11am–1pm & 6–9pm) and photography exhibitions in summer.

Outside town, perched on the slopes opposite the quay, are two convents, worth visiting for their seclusion and views: **Evangelístria** (daily 8am–1pm & 4–7pm), which is within view of the town, and **Pródhromos** (daily 8am–1pm & 5–8pm). The monastery of **Metamórfosis**, also on this promontory, was abandoned in 1980 but is now being restored by the monks and is open to visitors. Access is simplest by following an old road behind the line of hotels along the bay to Evangelístria (an hour's walk). From there it's an extra half-hour's scramble over mule tracks to Pródhromos, the remotest and most beautiful of the three. Ignore the new road that goes part way – it's longer, and misses most of the beauty of the walk.

Practicalities

The **ferry quay** is at the western end of a long promenade, lined with an array of boutiques, bars, stores and restaurants. To get to the **bus station**, turn left where the quay meets the main road, and follow the sea until you pass the children's swings and the second *períptero*; at the point where the road divides around a car park. Opposite the bus station entrance, a short road leads into a maze of lanes and signposts to the **post office**. There are **banks** about 50m from the quay. Among the several **motorbike rental** outlets, friendly service can be had at Panos Bikes (☎0424/23 696), near the start of the road towards Glóssa. For around 5000dr, day-long **boat cruises** offer to take you round the island or on a tour of Alónissos and the marine park.

In the main body of the town there are dozens of **rooms** for rent. These can be arranged through the Association of Room Owners office (☎ & fax 0424/24 567; daily 9am–noon & 6–8pm), on the seafront 100m from the ferry dock. Alternatively, there are a few pleasant small hotels such as *Andromache* (inquire at Madro Travel by the quay ☎0424/22 145; ③), in a quiet old house near the post office, and the relaxed and casual *Kyr Sotos* (☎0424/22 549; ④) nearby. The old style *Georgios* (☎0424/22 308; ④), right by the quay, is a fair standby and the gaily painted *Adonis* (☎0424/22 231; ⑤), just above the mid-seafront is also good though noisy. For larger, more **expensive hotels** higher up from the port, you're unlikely to find a space without having booked through a tour operator, but if you fancy the likes of the cosy *Elli* (☎0424/22 943; ⑥) on the east side of town, the modern *Aperitton* (☎0424/22 256; ⑥) on the ring road above the town, or the neo-rustic *Dionysos* (☎0424/23 210, fax 22 954; ⑥), also on the ring road – each with a pool – ask about vacancies at Madro Travel (see above) on the quay; they're also the local Flying Dolphin agents.

There's a wide variety of **places to eat**, ranging from the acceptable to the truly excellent. Those at the near end of the harbour, like *Angelos-Ta Kymata*, *Molos* and *Klimataria*, all offer decent meals, while *Spyros* in the middle has been a reliable favourite for years. *To Aktaion* is also a good bet, with exceptionally pleasant staff and large, delicious and reasonably priced portions. At the far end of the front *Stergios* also has tasty dishes like chicken in white wine sauce. A little way inland, two *souvláki* places, both named *O Platanos*, compete for the distinction of having the best *yíros*; the one with blue chairs also has a much wider menu. And for a gourmet treat, the *Perivoli* is the place. It is located near the two *Platanos*es – above the waterfront to the east of town.

Nightlife in Skópelos is on the increase, but is more of the late-night bar than the nightclub variety, apart from the *Cocos* disco out of town. That said, *Metro, Ano Kato* and *Panselinos,* which form a cluster on Dhoulídhis street, are pretty jumping on a hot summer evening. Among bars, look out for the classy *Vengera*, in a restored house that compares favourably with the town's folk art museum, and the small, atmospheric *Nemesis*. The *bouzoúki* joint *Meintani* is housed in an old olive press near Souvlaki Square, while the *Skopelitissa* and *Anatoli* on top of the Kástro play Greek music till the early hours.

Around the rest of the island

Buses cover the island's main paved road between Skópelos Town and Loutráki via Glóssa (around 6–8 times daily 7am–10.30pm), stopping at the paths to all the main beaches and villages. **Stáfylos**, 4km south of town, is the closest beach, though rather small and rocky. It's getting increasingly crowded, but the *Terpsis* taverna, which rents

rooms, is a very pleasant spot shaded by a vast pine tree. Among the new room ventures, *Mando* (☎0424/23 917; ⑤) is friendly and quiet.

When Stáfylos gets too busy, it's better to go to **Velanió** beach, a short walk north round the coast, to have a chance of escaping the crowds. Nudity is acceptable and although the official campsite has closed, you shouldn't be hassled if you stay a night or two. There's spring water and a *kantína* too.

Further around the coast to the west, the tiny horseshoe-shaped harbour of **AGNÓNDAS** (with its two fish tavernas and rooms) is the start of a fifteen-minute path (2km by road) or half-hourly kaïki trip to **LIMNONÁRI**, 300m of fine sand set in a closed, rocky bay. The *Limnonari Beach* restaurant serves delicious spiral-shaped local *tyrópittes* and rents rooms (☎0424/23 046; ④).

PÁNORMOS is very much a full-blown, commercial resort, with rooms, tavernas, a campsite, yacht anchorage and watersports. The beach here is gravelly and steeply shelving, but there are small secluded bays close by. The thirty-room *Panormos Beach Hotel* (☎0424/22 711; ⑥) has a beautiful garden and fine views, and is lovingly looked after; beyond it, the *Adrina Beach* (☎0424/23 373; ⑤) is one of the most attractive and most expensive hotels in the Sporades. Slightly further on at **MILIÁ**, there is a tremendous, 1500m sweep of tiny pebbles beneath a bank of pines, facing the islet of Dhassía. There's one taverna and the *Milia Apartments* (☎0424/23 998; ④) in this languid setting; nudist swimming is possible at a lovely five-hundred-metre-long beach a little way north. The shore beyond is indented with many tiny coves, ranging from individual- to family-size.

Further north, **ÉLIOS**, 9km short of Glóssa, is a medium-sized, fairly new resort settled by residents of the earthquake-damaged villages above it, with nothing special to offer besides a pleasant beach. If you want to stay, try the newly done-up *Zanneta* (☎ 0424/33 140, fax 33 717; ⑤). Beyond here, the renovated village of Paleó Klíma marks the start of a beautiful forty-minute **trail** to Glóssa, via the empty hamlet of Áyii Anáryiri and the oldest village on the island, **Athéato**.

West of Skópelos Town, various jeep tracks and old paths wind through olive and plum groves toward **Mount Dhélfi** and the Vathiá forest, or skirt the base of the mountain northeast to Revýthi hill with its fountains and churches, and the site of **Karyá**, with its *sendoúkia*: ancient rock-cut tombs which may be early Christian. To the northwest of Skópelos Town, **Glystéri** is a small pebble beach with no shade, whose taverna is much frequented by locals on Sundays. A fork off the Glystéri and Mount Dhélfi tracks can – in theory – be followed across the island to Pánormos within ninety minutes; it's a pleasant walk though the route isn't always obvious.

Alónissos and some minor islets

The most remote of the Sporades, **Alónissos** is also, at first sight, the least attractive. It has an unfortunate recent history. The vineyards were wiped out by disease in 1950, and the hóra was damaged by an earthquake in 1965. Although its houses were mostly repairable, lack of water, combined with corruption and the social control policies of the new junta, were instrumental in the transfer of virtually the entire population down to the previously unimportant anchorage of Patitíri. The result is a little soulless, but what charm may be lacking in the built environment on the coast is made up for by the hospitality of the islanders.

Patitíri and the old town

PATITÍRI is not a good introduction to the island, but it's trying hard to rectify that. The port, a pretty cove flanked by pine trees, is marred by rows of flat-roofed concrete

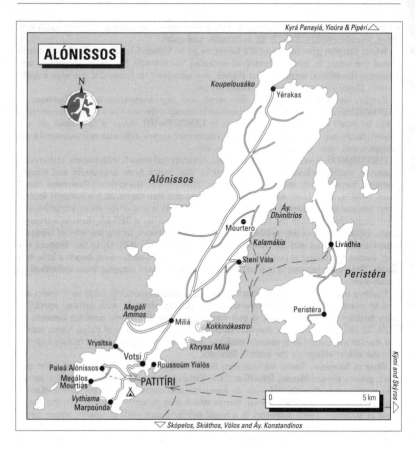

ALÓNISSOS

Kyrá Panayiá, Yioúra & Pipéri

N

Koupelousáko

Yérakas

Alónissos

Áy. Dhimítrios

Mourtero

Kalamákia

Livádhia

Steni Vála

Peristéra

Megáli Ammos

Peristéra

Miliá

Kokkinókastro

Vrysítsa

Khryssí Miliá

Votsi

Paleá Alónissos

Roussoúm Yialós

Megálos Mourtiás

PATITÍRI

Vythisma Marpoúnda

0   5 km

Kými and Skýros

▽ *Skópelos, Skiáthos, Vólos and Áy. Konstandínos*

buildings rising up behind it. Nevertheless, the line of near-identical bars and restaurants that run along the waterfront is not unappealing. Alónissos attracts fewer visitors than Skíathos or Skópelos; most of those who do come stay in Patitíri, and from mid-July to the end of August it can get very crowded. It's easy, though, to pick up connections here for beaches and the old town, and there are several good hotels to choose from. The most interesting place to visit is the **Monk Seal Information Centre** (daily 10am–1pm & 7–10pm) on the first floor of a building halfway along the seafront. The displays include models, photos, video and slide shows; see box on p.776.

PALEÁ ALÓNISSOS is a fine but steep fifty-minute walk via a donkey track – signposted on the left just outside Patitíri. Alternatively, there's a frequent bus service in the mornings and afternoons. Although some houses are still derelict, much of the village has been painstakingly restored, mainly by the English and Germans who bought the properties at knock-down rates. Only a few local families continue to live here, which gives the village a rather odd and un-Greek atmosphere, but it is picturesque, and the views make the trip worthwhile.

Practicalities

All the important facilities are in Patitíri; **buses** and **taxis** congregate next door. The **post office** is on the Hóra road, while kaïkia leave from the quay beside the *Pension Flisvos* (see below). You can rent a moped or motorbike at 2 Trohi or even a car (check with Ikos Travel below) at reasonable prices. The roads between Patitíri, Stení Vála and the northernmost point on the island are paved, and the dirt roads down to the beaches are in good condition: not half as dangerous as the twisting, busy roads on Skiáthos and Skópelos. A couple of the rental places on the waterfront also rent out motorboats and dinghies.

Rooms are easy to find here, as you'll probably be approached with offers as you get off the ferry, sometimes by older women wearing traditional blue and white costumes. The local room-owners' association (☎ & fax 0424/65 577), on the front, can also find you a room (mostly ③) in Patitíri or nearby Vótsi. Other options include the *Ioulieta* pension (☎0424/65 463; ③), *Haravyi* (☎0424/65 090, fax 65 189; ④) and *Pantheon* (☎0424/65 139; ④). *Liadromia* (☎0424/65 521; ⑤) above the port, *Niirides* (☎0424/65 643; ⑤), comprising studio apartments with pool, and *Paradise* (☎0424/65 160; ⑤), on the promontory east of the port with a pool overlooking the sea, are the best in the higher price range. Ikos Travel, the Flying Dolphin agent (☎0424/65 320), can do bookings for a limited number of rooms and apartments in the old town, though accommodation here is in short supply so expect to pay well over the odds, particularly in season. Otherwise, ask around; few people put up "room for rent" signs, but try the simple and clean *Fadasia House* (☎0424/65 186; ③), at the entrance to Hóra.

The **restaurants** along the front of Patitíri are reasonably priced, but the food is nothing special. The best place for breakfast is the *To Korali*; in the evenings, try the friendly *Pension Flisvos*. For the best meal in Patitíri go two blocks up towards the post office from the waterfront to *To Kamaki*, a wonderful ouzerí with a amazing selection of seafood. Two other ouzeris worth a try on the same road are *Kala Krassa* and *Kapetan Spyros*. The *Tzimakis* grill has good food in a splendid setting on the promontary. Up in the old town, *Astrofengia* has the tastiest food, and *Paraport* at the Kástro the most spectacular views.

Nightlife is low-key. The best of the seafront bars is *Pub Dennis*, whose ice-cream concoctions are divine, though both *En Plo* and *La Vie* are popular. Club-wise, *Borio* and *Enigma* are fairly European, while *Rembetika*, on the road to the old town, specializes in Greek music.

The island's beaches

Alónissos has some of the cleanest water in the Aegean, but it's lacking in sand beaches. There's only one really sandy beach on the island (Výthisma), the rest varying from rough to fine pebbles. There's no bus, but kaïkia run half-hourly from Patitíri north to Khrissí Miliá, Kokkinókastro, Stení Vála, Kalamákia and Áyios Dhimítrios, and south around the coast to Marpoúnda, Výthisma and Megálos Mourtiás. Kaïkia also sail occasionally to Livádhia and Peristéra islet.

At Patitíri there's decent swimming from the rocks around the promontory to the north; pick your way along a hewn-out path past the hotels and you're there (ladder provided). To the north, above the headlands, Patitíri merges into two adjoining settlements, **Roussoúm Yialós** and **Vótsi**. For better beaches, you'll have to get in a boat or on a bike.

Khryssí Miliá, the first good beach, has pine trees behind the sand and a taverna; there are a couple of new hotels on the hillside above, such as the posh *Milia Bay* (☎0424/66 035; ⑥), and it can get crowded in summer. At **Kokkinókastro**, over the hill

THE MEDITERRANEAN MONK SEAL

The **Mediterranean monk seal** has the dubious distinction of being the European mammal most in danger of extinction. Fewer than eight hundred survive worldwide, the majority around the Portuguese Atlantic island of Madeira. A large colony off the coast of the West African state of Mauritania was decimated early in 1997: an estimated two hundred seals died, possibly poisoned by algae. Small numbers survive in the Ionian and Aegean seas; the largest population here, of around thirty seals, lives around the deserted islands north of Alónissos.

Monk seals can travel up to 200km a day in search of food, but they usually return to the same places to rear their **pups**. They have one pup every two years, and the small population is very vulnerable to disturbance. Originally, the pups would have been reared on sandy beaches, but with increasing disturbance by man, they have retreated to isolated sea caves, particularly around the coast of the remote islet of Pipéri.

Unfortunately, the seals compete with fishermen for limited stocks of fish, and, in the overfished Aegean, often destroy nets full of fish. Until recently it was common for seals to be killed by fishermen. This occasionally still happens, but in an attempt to protect the seals, the seas around the northern Sporades have been declared a **marine wildlife reserve**: fishing is restricted in the area north of Alónissos and prohibited within 5km of Pipéri. On Alónissos, the conservation effort and reserve have won a great deal of local support, mainly through the efforts of the Hellenic Society for the Protection of the Monk Seal (HSPMS), based at Stení Vála. The measures have been particularly popular with local fishermen, as tighter restrictions on larger, industrial-scale fishing boats from other parts of Greece should help preserve fish stocks, and benefit the fishermen financially.

Despite this, the government has made no serious efforts to enforce the restrictions, and boats from outside the area continue to fish around Pipéri. There are also government plans to reduce the prohibited area around Pipéri to 500m. On a more positive note, the HSPMS, in collaboration with the Pieterburen Seal Creche in Holland, has reared several abandoned seal pups, all of which have been successfully released in the seas north of Alónissos.

For the moment, your chances of actually seeing a seal are remote, unless you plan to spend a few weeks on a boat in the area. It's recommended that you shouldn't visit Pipéri or approach sea caves on other islands which might be used by seals, or try to persuade boat-owners to do so.

to the north, excavations have revealed the site of ancient Ikos and evidence of the oldest known prehistoric habitation in the Aegean. There's nothing much to see, but it's a beautiful spot with a good red pebble beach, and, in July and August, a daytime bar.

STENÍ VÁLA, opposite the island of Peristéra, a haven for the yachts and flotillas that comb the Sporades, has almost become a proper village, with two shops, several houses, a bar, rooms and five tavernas, one of which stays open more or less throughout the year. The Monk Seal Treatment and Rehabilitation Centre, housed in a small hut on the beach, can provide information and insight into the HSPMS's work when manned. There's a campsite (☎0424/65 258) in an olive grove by the harbour, a long pebble beach – Glýfa, where boats are repaired – and some stony beaches within reasonable walking distance in either direction. **KALAMÁKIA**, to the north, also has a couple of tavernas and a few rooms.

If you want real solitude, **Áyios Dhimítrios**, **Megáli Ámmos**, and **Yérakas** (an old shepherds' village at the northernmost point) are possibilities. However, before committing yourself to a Robinson Crusoe existence, check it out by moped or take one of the round the island trips available, and return the next day with enough food for your stay: there are no stores outside the port and Stení Vála. In the opposite direction from Patitíri, **Marpoúnda** features a large hotel and bungalow complex and a rather small beach. It's better to turn left after the campsite towards **Megálos Mourtiás**, a pebble beach with several tavernas linked by dirt track with Paleá Alónissos, 200m above. **Výthisma**, the lovely beach just before Megálos Mourtiás, can only be reached by boat, the path here having been washed out. Further north, visible from Paleá Alónissos, **Vrysítsa** is tucked into its own finger-like inlet. There's sand and a taverna, but little else.

Beyond Alónissos: some minor islets

Northeast of Alónissos, half a dozen tiny **islets** speckle the Aegean. Virtually none of these has any permanent population, or a ferry service, and the only way you can reach them – at least Peristéra, Kyrá Panayía and Yioúra – is by excursion kaḯki (ask at Ikos Travel), weather permitting. No boats are allowed to take you to the other, more remote islets, as they are protected areas within the Sporades National Marine Park. But though it is possible to be left for a night or more on any of the closer islands, when acting out your desert-island fantasies, be sure to bring more supplies than you need: if the weather worsens you'll be marooned until such time as small craft can reach you.

Peristéra is the closest islet to Alónissos, to which it was once actually joined, but subsidence (a common phenomenon in the area) created the narrow straits between the two. It is graced with some sandy beaches and there is rarely anyone around, though some Alónissans do come over for short periods to tend the olive groves, and in season there are regular evening "barbecue boats" from the main island. As on Alónissos, a few unofficial campers are tolerated, but there is only one spot, known locally as "Barbecue Bay", where campfires are allowed.

Kyrá Panayiá (also known as Pelagós) is the next islet out and is equally fertile. It's owned by the Meyístis Lávras monastery of Mount Áthos and there are two monasteries here, one still inhabited. Boats call at a beach on the south shore, one of many such sandy stretches and coves around the island. There's no permanent population other than the wild goats.

Nearby **Yioúra** boasts a stalactite cave reputed to be the previous abode of Polyphemus, the Cyclops who imprisoned Odysseus, but you won't be able to check its credentials. No one is allowed within 500m of the island, since, like Pipéri, it lies inside the restricted zone of the Marine Park.

Pipéri, near Yioúra, is a sea-bird and monk-seal refuge, and permission from a ministry of the environment representative (in Alónissos) is required for visits by specialists; non-scientists are not allowed. Tiny, northernmost **Psathoúra** is dominated by its powerful modern lighthouse, the tallest in the Aegean, although here, as around many of these islands, there's a submerged ancient town, brought low by the endemic subsidence. Roughly halfway between Alónissos and Skýros, green **Skántzoura**, with a single empty monastery and a few seasonal shepherds, is a smaller version of Kyrá Panayiá.

Skýros

Despite its proximity to Athens, **Skýros** remained a very traditional and idiosyncratic island until recently. Any impetus for change had been neutralized by the lack of economic opportunity (and even secondary schooling), forcing the younger Skyrians to live in Athens and leaving behind a conservative gerontocracy. A high school was finally provided in the mid-1980s, and the island has been somewhat "discovered" since that time. It's now the haunt of continental Europeans, chic Athenians and British, many of whom check into the "New Age" Skýros Centre, to "rethink the form and direction of their lives".

Meanwhile, Skýros still ranks as one of the most interesting places in the Aegean. It has a long tradition of painted **pottery** and ornate **woodcarving**, in particular the *salonáki skyrianó* (handmade set of chairs). A very few old men still wear the vaguely Cretan traditional costume of cap, vest, baggy trousers, leggings and *trohádhia* (Skýrian sandals), but this is dying out. Likewise, just a few old women still wear the favoured yellow scarves and long embroidered skirts.

The theory that Skýros was originally two islands seems doubtful, but certainly the character of the two parts of the island is very different. The north has a greener and more gentle landscape, and away from the port and town it retains much of its original pine forest. The sparsely inhabited south is mountainous, rocky and barren; there are few trees and the landscape is more reminiscent of the Cyclades than the Sporades. Compared with Skiáthos, Skópelos and Alónissos, Skýros isn't a great place for beaches. Most **beaches** along the west coast attract a certain amount of sea-borne rubbish, and, although the scenery is sometimes spectacular, the swimming isn't that good. The beaches on the east coast are all close to Skýros Town, and the best option is probably

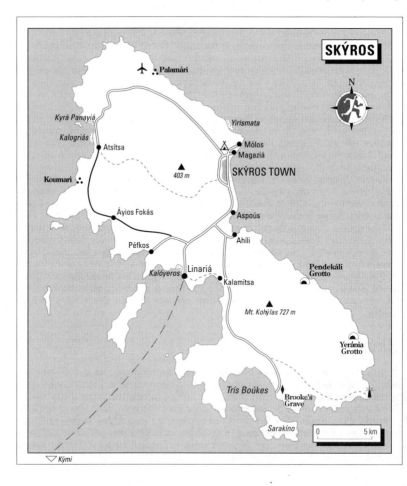

GOAT DANCES AND WILD PONIES

Skýros has some particularly lively, even outrageous, festivals. The *Apokriatiká* (pre-Lenten) Carnival here is structured around the famous **goat dance**, performed by masked revellers in the village streets. The foremost character in this is the Yéros, a menacing figure concealed by a goatskin mask and weighed down by garlands of sheep bells. Accompanying him are Korélles and Kyriés (who are transvestites, as only the men participate) and Frangi (maskers in "Western" garb). For further details, read Joy Koulentianou's *The Goat Dance of Skyros*, available in Athens and occasionally on the island.

The other big annual event takes place near Magaziá beach on August 15, when children race domesticated members of the **wild pony** herd, native to Skýros and said to be related to the Shetland pony (if so, it must be very distantly). They are thought, perhaps, to be the diminutive horses depicted in the Parthenon frieze, and at any time of the year you might find some of the tame individuals tethered and grazing near Skýros Town.

---

to stay here rather than heading for somewhere more isolated. The beaches at the north end have been commandeered by the big air-force base there, which otherwise keeps a low profile.

Linariá

After crossing a seemingly endless expanse of sea, the boat docks at the tiny port of **LINARIÁ**, a functional place on the island's west coast. Although most of the action is around Skýros Town, Linariá does make for a quiet alternative base and is certainly a pleasant spot to while away time waiting for the ferry. If you decide to stay, the smart *King Likomides* hotel on the harbour is very good value (☎0222/93 249, fax 93 412; ③) or cheap rooms in a family atmosphere above the bay can be rented from Khrysoula Strandzi (☎0222/96 378; ②). For eating try out the mezedhopolío next to *Kalí Kardhia* taverna, which has a wide selection of delectable dishes, the *Psariotis* ouzerí or the *Filippos* fish taverna. The splendidly situated *Kavos* bar is open day and night for drinks and snacks, while more raucous nightlife is provided by the *Castro Club* disco. In high season, kaïkia ply from Linariá to the Pentekáli and Yeránia **grottoes**, and to the islet of **Sarakíno**, which has a cave and some of the Skyrian wild ponies. There's a reasonable sandy **beach** called **Kalóyeros** a few minutes' walk along the main road from Linariá, where you can camp.

A tarmac road connects Linariá to Skýros Town, 10km away, and then continues round past the airport to Atsítsa, where the Skyros Centre has a branch; **buses** to Skýros Town and Magaziá, on the coast below, leave from the quay. Midway up the Linariá–Skýros Town route, a side road links Ahíli with Kalamítsa. Most other roads are passable by moped, apart from the direct track between Skýros Town and Atsítsa.

Skýros Town

SKÝROS TOWN (also known as Horió), with its decidedly Cycladic architecture, sits on the landward side of a high rock rising precipitously from the coast. According to legend, King Lycomedes pushed Theseus to his death from its summit. The town has a workaday atmosphere; it doesn't feel like a resort and isn't especially picturesque. The older and more intriguing parts of town are higher up, climbing towards the **Kástro**, a mainly Byzantine building, built on the site of the ancient **acropolis**. There are few traces of the acropolis, although remains of the Classical city walls survive below on the seaward side of the rock. The kástro is open to visitors; to reach its upper parts you pass through a rather private-looking gateway into the monastery, then through an attractive shaded courtyard and up a whitewashed tunnel. There's little to see at the top, apart from a few churches in various states of ruin, but there are great views over the town and the island, and the climb up takes you through the quieter and more picturesque part of town, with glimpses into traditionally decorated houses. With their gleaming copper pots, porcelain plates and antique embroideries decorating the hearth, these dwellings are a matter of intense pride among the islanders, who are often found seated in their doorways on tiny carved chairs.

At the northern end of town is the striking and splendidly incongruous **memorial to Rupert Brooke**. It takes the form of a bronze statue of "Immortal Poetry" and its nakedness caused a scandal among the townspeople when it was first erected. Brooke, who visited the south of the island very briefly in April 1915, died shortly afterwards of blood poisoning on a French hospital ship anchored offshore and was buried in an olive grove above the bay of Trís Boúkes. (The site can be reached on foot from Kalamítsa, by kaïki, or, less romantically, by taxi.) Brooke, who became something of a local hero, despite his limited acquaintance with Skýros, was adopted by Kitchener and later Churchill as the paragon of patriotic youth, in the face of his forthright socialist and internationalist views.

Just below the Brooke statue are two museums. The **Archeological Museum** (Tues–Sun 8am–2pm; 500dr) has a modest collection of pottery and statues from excavations on the island, and a reconstruction of a traditional Skýros house interior. The privately run **Faltaïts Museum** (daily 10am–1pm & 5.30–8pm/6–9pm in summer; free), in a nineteenth-century house built over one of the bastions of the ancient walls, is more interesting, with a collection of domestic items, costumes, embroideries, porcelain and rare books.

Practicalities

The **bus** from Linariá leaves you by the school, 200m below the main platía; the **post office** and **bank** are both nearby. Skýros Travel (☎0222/91 123), on the main street above the platía, can provide **information** or advice, and can find a room or hotel; in high season it's a good idea to telephone them in advance. Of the **motorbike** rental places in the area around the platía, the most prominent and efficient is Trahanas (☎0222/92 032), which also has bicycles for those with strong calf muscles.

You'll probably be met off the bus with offers of **rooms**, which it's as well to accept. If you'd like to stay in a traditional Skyrian house, those of Anna Stergiou (☎0222/91 657; ③) and Maria Mavroyiorgi (☎0222/91 440; ③) are both clean and cosy. Or you could try the pleasant *Nefeli* hotel (☎0222/91 964; ⑤) on the main road before the platía. A more basic option is the *Elena* (☎0222/91 738; ②) next to the post office, which has very cheap singles with shared bath. There's a picturesque **campsite** nearer the beach, at the bottom of the steps below the archeological museum, with basic amenities but a good bar and a friendly management.

The platía and the main street running by it are the centre of village life, with a few noisy pubs and a wide choice of kafenía, tavernas and fast-food places. There are few outstanding **places to eat**; most are overpriced, or serve undistinguished food. *Maryetis* has the best grilled fish and meat, *Sisyphos* has vegetarian specialities, and the *Sweets Workshop* does some wonderful cakes. For a special occasion, try *Kristina's* restaurant below the taxi rank (signposted); its Australian owner has an imaginative menu which has great desserts. The *Panorama*, in the lower town, towards Magaziá, is also good for its home-cooking with a view.

The town's **nightlife** is mostly bar-based until very late, when the few clubs get going. The most popular **bars** are the trendy *Kalypso* which plays jazz and blues, dance-orientated *Kata Lathos* and the rockier *Iroön* and *Rodon*. Later on, *Iy Stasis* is one of the most popular places. The best clubs include the *Skyropoula, Mylos* and the *Stone Club*.

Some bars also serve good breakfasts; here the favourite is *Anemos*, followed by *Kalypso*, which has tasty Danish pastries. Another fine spot for a drink or sweets is *O Anatolikos Anemos*, near the museum, with sweeping views across the bay.

Magaziá and Mólos and nearby beaches

A path leads down past the archeological museum towards the small coastal village of **MAGAZIÁ**, coming out by the official campsite. From Magaziá, an 800-metre-long sandy beach stretches to the adjacent village of **MÓLOS**. In recent years, a sprawl of new development between the road and the beach has more or less joined the two villages together. Despite this, the beach is good, and there are lots of **rooms** down here for the young crowd that uses the beach's watersports and volleyball facilities. *Stamatis Marmaris* (☎0222/91 672; ③) beyond Mólos, and *Manolis Balotis* (☎0222/91 386; ③) near the campsite, are both excellent choices. More upmarket hotels include the *Paliopyrgos* (☎0222/91 014, fax 92 185; ④), halfway between the beach and town with a wonderful view and the *Angela* (☎0222/91 764; ⑤), a new set of bungalows in Mólos. The beachfront **tavernas** compare favourably with those in town: on the Magaziá side *Stefanos* taverna is reliable, while the *Koufari* ouzerí near the *Xenia Hotel* has excellent food for higher prices. At Mólos try *Tou Thoma To Magazi*, the *Maryetis* garden restaurant and the ouzerí at *Balabani's Mill*, all at the end of the beach. It's worth sampling lobster in Skýros: it's a local speciality, often served as a spaghetti dish.

For quieter beaches, take the road past Mólos, or better, try the excellent and undeveloped (unofficial nudist) beach, *Papa tou Houma*, directly below the kástro. The path down to the beach is 150m beyond the *Skyropoula* disco, and isn't obvious from above. However, following the road south of here, the beaches are disappointing until **Aspoús**, which has a couple of tavernas and rooms to rent as well as the smart *Ahillion* hotel (☎0222/93 300, fax 93 303; ⑤). Further south, **Ahíli**, had one of the best beaches on the island until the construction of its new marina. Southeast of Ahíli, the coast is rocky and inaccessible, although you can take a kaïki trip down to the bay of **Trís Boúkes**, passing some picturesque sea caves on the way.

Around the rest of the island

In summer, the whimsical bus service visits the more popular beaches. But if you want to branch out on your own, hire a moped. Roads, tracks and footpaths diverge from the main circle road, leading inward and seaward. Among the most interesting places to head for is **Palamári**, the neglected site of an early Bronze Age settlement and a spectacular beach. Turn right after the road has begun to descend to the airport plain.

For a taste of the wooded interior, a hike on the dirt track from Skýros Town to **ATSÍTSA** is well worth the effort; it takes three to four hours, and is too rough for a moped. Atsítsa is an attractive bay with pine trees down to the sea (tapped by the Skyrian retsina industry), and an increasing number of rooms, in addition to the Skyros Centre buildings. The beach here is rocky and isn't great for swimming, but there are small sandy beaches fifteen and twenty minutes' walk to the north at **Kalogriás** and **Kyrá Panayiá**, with its eponymous taverna, though they are nothing out of the ordinary.

Elsewhere in the coniferous north, **Áyios Fokás** and **Péfkos** bays are easiest reached by a turning from the paved road near Linariá, while access from Atsítsa is via a reasonable dirt road. Both are in the process of being discovered by villa companies, but they have few rooms. Though quite primitive, Áyios Fokás has a very basic, excellent taverna; Péfkos has two, of which *Barba Mitsos* is the more appealing (these are only open in high season, as are all the other tavernas away from Linariá, Skýros Town, Magaziá and Mólos). The bay is beautiful, and the beach reasonable but not that clean – the beaches around Skýros Town are much better for swimming.

As for exploring the great southern mountain of **Kohýlas**, this is best attempted only if you have a four-wheel-drive vehicle, as the tracks are poor away from the main road. A good road runs south of Kalamítsa to the naval base at Trís Boúkes (where Rupert Brooke is buried), which makes getting to the southern beaches easier. Kalamítsa, just east of Linariá, lacks character, but the *Mouries* taverna between it and Linariá is worth a stop, as is the remote beach half way to Trís Boúkes, which has no facilities.

Évvia (Euboea)

Évvia is the second-largest Greek island (after Crete), and seems more like an extension of the mainland to which it was in fact once joined. At **Halkídha**, the gateway to the island, the curious old drawbridge has only a forty-metre channel to span, the island reputedly having been split from Attica and Thessaly by a blow from Poseidon's trident (earthquakes and subsidence being the more pedestrian explanations). Besides the new suspension bridge bypassing Halkídha and linking Évvia to the mainland, there are ferry crossings at no fewer than seven points along its length, and the south of the island is closer to Athens than it is to northern Évvia.

Nevertheless, Évvia *is* an island, in places a very beautiful one. But it has an idiosyncratic history and demography, and an enduringly strange feel that has kept it out of the mainstream of tourism. A marked **Albanian influence** in the south, and scattered Lombard and Venetian watchtowers give it a distinctive flavour. Indeed, the island was the longest-surviving southerly outpost of the Ottoman Turks, who had a keen appreciation of the island's wealth, as did the Venetians and Lombards before them. The last **Ottoman garrison** was not evicted until 1833, hanging on in defiance of the peace settlement that awarded Évvia to the new Greek state. Substantial Turkish communities, renowned for their alleged brutality, remained until 1923.

Economically, Évvia has always been prized. By Greek standards, it's exceptionally **fertile**, producing everything from grain, corn and cotton to kitchen vegetables and livestock. The classical name "Euboea" means "rich in cattle," but nowadays cows are few and far between; its kid and lamb, however, are highly rated, as is the local retsina. Because of the collapse of much of its mining industry, parts of the island are actively seeking foreign tourism. For the moment, however, Greeks predominate, especially in the north around the spa of **Loutrá Edhipsoú**. In July and August, Évvia can seem merely a beach annexe for much of Thessaly and Athens.

In the rolling countryside of the **north**, grain combines whirl on the sloping hay meadows between olive groves and pine forest. This is the most conventionally scenic part of the island, echoing the beauty of the smaller Sporades. The **northeast coast** is rugged and largely inaccessible, its few sandy beaches surf-pounded and often plagued by flotsam and jetsam; the **southwest** is gentler and more sheltered, though much disfigured by industrial operations. The **centre** of the island, between Halkídha and the easterly port of Kými, is mountainous and dramatic, while the far **southeast** is mostly dry and very isolated.

Public **transport** consists of seasonal hydrofoils along the protected southwest coast from Halkídha upwards, and passable bus services along the main roads to Kárystos in the southeast, and Loutrá Edhipsoú in the northwest. Otherwise, explorations are best conducted by rented car; any two-wheeler will make little impact on the enormous distances involved.

Halkídha

The heavily industrialized island-capital of **HALKÍDHA** (the ancient *Chalkis*, an appellation still used) is the largest town on Évvia, with a population of 60,000. A shipyard,

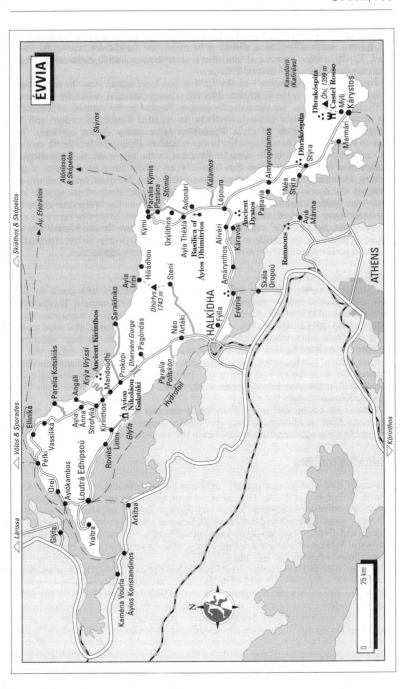

rail sidings and cement works make it a dire place, apart from the old Ottoman quarter, **Kástro**, south of Venizélou, and the area around the Turkish fortress on the mainland. Hardly a trace remains of Halkídha's once-thriving Jewish community, whose presence here dates back around 2500 years.

The entrance to the kástro – on the right as you head inland from the old Euripos bridge – is marked by the handsome fifteenth-century **mosque**, nominally a museum of Byzantine artefacts, but permanently locked. Beyond lie the remains of Karababa, the seventeenth-century Ottoman fortress, an arcaded Turkish aqueduct and the unique basilican **church of Ayía Paraskeví** (shut except during services). The church is an odd structure, converted by the crusaders during the fourteenth century into a Gothic cathedral. In the opposite direction, in the new town, an **archeological museum** at Venizélou 13 (Tues–Sun 8am–2.30pm; 500dr) has a good display of prehistoric, Hellenic and Roman finds from all over the island. The waterside overlooks the **Évripos**, the narrow channel dividing Évvia from the mainland, whose strange currents have baffled scientists for centuries. You can stand on the bridge that spans the narrowest point and watch the water swirling by like a river. Every few hours the current changes and the "tide" reverses. Aristotle is said to have thrown himself into the waters in despair at his inability to understand what was happening, so if you're puzzled you're in good company; there is still no entirely satisfactory explanation.

Practicalities

For most visitors, though, such activities are strictly time-fillers, with much the best view of the place to be had from the bus, train or hydrofoil on the way out. **Trains** arrive on the mainland side of the channel, beneath the old fortress; given numerous, quick rail links with Athens, there's little reason to stay overnight. Should you want to, the basic *Kentrikon* hotel (☎0221/22 375; ②) is a far better deal than the huge waterfront establishments it backs onto. Most other services of interest lie within sight of the old Évripos bridge. The **hydrofoil** terminal sits just northeast, on the mainland side of the channel. The **bus station** is 400m from the bridge along Kótsou, then 50m right; you should get a connection for any corner of the island as long as you show up by 2pm, later for Kými or Límni.

Options for **eating out** range from the restaurants lining the waterfront, where Athenians flock on Sundays to feast on Halkídha's superior seafood, to a handful of acceptable grills serving adequate lunches in the immediate vicinity of the bus station.

Halkídha to Kými

The coast road heading east out of Halkídha is an exceptionally misleading introduction to the interior of Évvia. The industrial zone gives way to nondescript hamlets, which are succeeded between Erétria and Amárynthos by sequestered colonies of Athenian second homes and rather bleak beaches and large hotels frequented by British and German package-tour companies. There are some intriguing **Frankish towers** at **Fýlla**, worth a detour inland from Vasilikó if you have a car, and some easy connections to Athens, but little else.

Modern **ERÉTRIA** is a rather dreary resort laid out on a grid plan; for non-package travellers its main asset is a well-advertised ferry service across to Skála Oropoú in Attica. The site of **ancient Eretria** is more distinguished, though much of it lies under the town. A few scanty remains are dotted around the town centre, most conspicuously an **agora** and a **temple of Apollo**, but more interesting are the excavations in the northwest corner, behind the excellent small museum (Tues–Sun 8am–3pm; 500dr), opened in 1991 in collaboration with the Swiss School of Archeology. Here a **theatre** has been uncovered; steps from the orchestra descend to an underground vault used for sudden entrances and exits. Beyond the theatre are the ruins of a **gymnasium** and a **sanctuary**. The museum guard will be happy to unlock the fourth-century BC **House of Mosaics**, five minutes' walk from the museum. Of the numerous hotels in town the most interesting option is the municipal tourist complex *Dreams Island* (☎0229/61 224, fax 61 268; ⑤), which occupies a tiny offshore island, linked by causeway to the end of the bay.

Nine kilometres further along, **AMÁRYNTHOS** is a smaller and more pleasant resort to stay in. Though the town boasts nothing of particular interest, the seafront square is picturesque enough and there is an ample selection of good eateries, such as *Stefanos* fish taverna right by the square and *To Limenaki* a few minutes west of it. Two good accommodation options are *Iliaktidhes* (☎0229/37 605; ④), just off the main road, and *Stefania* (☎0229/36485, fax 38 384; ⑤), right on the beach.

Just before **Alivéri**, an enormous modern power plant and a virtually intact medieval castle seem incongruously juxtaposed, and more Frankish towers look down from nearby hills. Though Alivéri itself is dreary, the nearby fishing harbour of **Káravos** has several pleasant watering holes, among them the *Vlahos* taverna. Thereafter, the route heads inland. Beyond Lépoura, where the road branches north and south, the scenery improves drastically. Take the north fork towards Kými, and cross some of the most peaceful countryside in Greece. With your own vehicle you can detour east after five kilometres at Neohóri to the excellent beaches at **Kálamos** and **Korasídha**. There is a growing selection of rooms and tavernas at Kálamos.

Twelve kilometres north of Lépoura, at Háni Avlonaríou, stands the Romanesque thirteenth- or fourteenth-century **basilica of Áyios Dhimítrios**, Évvia's largest and finest (ask for the key at the café next door). **AVLONÁRI** proper, 2km east, is dominated by a hill that commands most of the island's centre. At its crown is a huge Lombard or Venetian tower, rearing above the Neoclassical and vernacular houses that tier the lower slopes. There's a single taverna below the platía, though no accommodation.

This part of Évvia is particularly well endowed with Byzantine chapels, since Avlonári was an archiepiscopal see from the sixth century onwards. Back on the road to Kými, a left fork just north of Háni Avlonaríou (the bus goes this way) leads past the hamlet of **Ayía Thékla**, where a small, shed-like **chapel** of that saint, probably slightly later than Áyios Dhimítrios, hides in a lush vale below the modern church. Inside, enough fresco fragments remain with their large-eyed faces to suggest what has been lost over time. The right fork leads towards the coast and takes you past Oxýlithos, with its somewhat more elaborate chapels of **Áyios Nikólaos** and **Ayía Ánna**, both at least a hundred years older than Áyios Dhimítrios.

The road hits the coast at the fine beach of **Stómio** (known also as just Paralía, or "Beach"), some 1500m of sand closing off the mouth of a river, which is deep, swimmable and often cleaner than the sea. To the north and east you glimpse the capes enclosing the broad bay of Kými. Up on the road, there are a couple of cafés and a small pension; most facilities, however, are further round the coast at **PLATÁNA**, where another river is flanked by a line of older houses, many with rooms or flats to rent.

Despite its name, the extremely functional port of **PARALÍA KÝMIS** has no real beach, and is not a particularly congenial place to be stuck overnight waiting for a ferry or hydrofoil to the Sporades. The most substantial and traditional **taverna** is *Spanos/To Egeo*, at the south end of the front, while *To Valanti* is also reasonable and the sweet little *Rock Club* plays eclectic sounds; there are just two **hotels**, *Coralli* (☎0222/22 212, fax 23 353; ④) and *Beis* (☎0222/22 604; ④).

Most travellers get to **KÝMI** (the main ferry port to Skýros) by bus, which takes the inland route via Ayía Thékla. The upper part of town is built on a green ridge overlooking both the sea and Paralía Kými, 4km below. Note that all buses deposit you in the upper town except for the one or two daily that connect with the ferry. At the bottom of the town, on the harbour-bound road, you can visit the **Folklore Museum**, which has an improbably large collection of costumes, household and agricultural implements and old photos recording the doings of Kymians both locally and in the US, where there's a huge community. Among the emigrants was Dr George Papanikolaou, deviser of the "Pap" cervical smear test, and there's a statue honouring him up in the upper-town platía, where you might ask about **rooms**. There are some good **tavernas** like *To Balkoni*, on the main road towards the shore, with its superb view, where you can sample the products of the local vineyards.

To get up into the rugged country west of Kými, you must negotiate jeep tracks through the forest, or return to Halkídha for the bus service up to **STENÍ**, a large and beautiful village at the foot of Mount Dhírfys. The village has a few cheap psistariés and two **hotels**, the *Dirfys* (☎0228/51 217; ③) and the *Steni* (☎0228/51 221; ③). It's a good area for hiking, most notably up the peaks of Dhírfys and Xirovoúni, and beyond to the isolated beach hamlets of Hiliádhou and Ayía Iríni, though you'll need a specialist hiking guide to do this (see "Books", p.910).

Southeast Évvia

The extension of Évvia southeast of Lépoura, so narrow that you can sometimes glimpse the sea on both sides, has a flavour very distinct from the rest of the island. Often bleak and windswept, it forms a geological unit with neighbouring Ándhros, with shared slates and marble. Ethnically, the south also has much in common with that northernmost Cyclade: both were heavily settled by Albanian immigrants from the early fifteenth century onwards, and Arvanítika – a **medieval dialect** of Albanian – was until recently the first language of the remoter villages here. Even non-Arvanítika speakers often betray their ancestry by their startlingly fair colouring and aquiline features. For a place so close to Athens, the south is often surprisingly untouched by modernity; some of the houses have yet to lose their original slate roofs. Others still lack electricity, and the few fields on the steep slopes are far more often worked by donkeys and horses than by farm machinery.

Immediately southeast of Lépoura, most maps persist in showing the lake of Dhýstos in bright blue. In fact, the lake area has been almost totally drained and reclaimed as rich farmland, much to the detriment of the migratory birds who used to stop off here, and to the annoyance of Greek and foreign environmentalists who would prefer that they still did so. Atop the almost perfectly conical hill in the centre of the flat basin are the sparse fifth-century BC ruins of **ancient Dystos** and a subsequent medieval citadel, hard to explore because the surroundings are so swampy.

Beyond the Dhýstos plain, the main road continues along the mountainous spine of the island to Kárystos at the southern end of the paved road system and bus line. If you have your own transport, it's worth stopping off at **STÝRA**, above which are a cluster of **Dhrakóspita** (Dragon Houses), signposted at the north edge of the village and reached by track, then trail. They are so named because only mythological beings were thought capable of shifting into place their enormous masonry blocks. Their origins and uses have yet to be definitively established. The most convincing theory suggests that they are sixth-century BC temples built by immigrants or slaves from Asia Minor working in the nearby marble and slate quarries.

The shore annexe of **NÉA STÝRA**, 5km downhill from the hill village, is a fairly standard package resort, worth knowing about only for its handy ferry connection to Ayía Marína (which gives access to ancient Rhamnous) on the Attic peninsula. Much the same can be said for **MARMÁRI**, 19km south, except in this case the ferry link is with Rafína. Here the smart *Hotel Delfini* (☎0224/31 296, fax 32 300; ③) is surprisingly good value and there are a few decent places to eat; try the *Zygos* mezedhopolío, which serves cheap fish in a nice atmosphere. The road between Marmári and Kárystos is now more or less finished, completing the "superhighway" and allowing you to enjoy the nether reaches of the island as you cruise down to its last major settlement.

Kárystos and around

At first sight **KÁRYSTOS** is a rather boring grid (courtesy of nineteenth-century Bavarian town-planners), which ends abruptly to east and west and is studded with modern buildings. King Otho liked the site so much that he contemplated transferring the Greek capital here, and there are still some graceful Neoclassical buildings dating from that period. Kárystos improves with prolonged acquaintance, though you're unlikely to stay for more than a few days. What it can offer is the superb (if often windy) beach to the west, the smaller, sandier **Psilí Ámmos** ten minutes' walk to the east and a lively, genuine working-port atmosphere. Only one plot of fenced-in foundations, in the central bazaar, bears out the town's ancient provenance, and the oldest obvious structure is the fourteenth-century Venetian **Bourtzi** (locked except for occasional summer evening art exhibitions) on the waterfront. This small tower is all that remains of once-extensive fortifications. Every evening the shore road is blocked with a gate at this point to allow an undisturbed promenade by the locals. There is a small but interesting **archeological museum** (Tues–Sun 8am–3pm; 500dr) inside the Cultural Centre opposite the Bourtzi, displaying finds from the local area – mostly statues and temple carvings plus a few smaller votive objects.

PRACTICALITIES

Rafína-based **ferries** and **hydrofoils** also serve Kárystos; **buses** arrive inland, above the central platía and below the National Bank, near a tiny combination grill/ticket office labelled KTEL. This has information on the extremely infrequent (once daily at best) departures to the remote villages of the Kavodóro (Kafiréas) cape to the east. Information on the August wine festival and sightseeing in the region, including walking routes, is provided by the friendly tourist office in a kiosk near the quay.

Finding affordable **accommodation** is not a big problem. The best value is the *Als* (☎0224/22 202, fax 25 002; ③), right opposite the quay, although it may get noisy in high season. Other options are the big *Galaxy* (☎0224/22 600, fax 22 463; ④) on the west side of the waterfront, the *Karystion* (☎0224/22 391, fax 22 727; ⑤) in the park beyond the Bourtzi on the shore road and the plush new *Apollon Suite* (☎0224/22 045, fax 22 049; ⑥) on Psilí Ámmos beach. Another strategy is to follow up signs in restaurant windows advertising **rooms** inland.

By contrast, you're spoilt for choice when **eating out**, as Kárystos must have more restaurants than the rest of Évvia put together. Among the best choices are the *Kavo Doros*, a friendly and reasonable taverna on Párodos Sakhtoúri one block west of the square, which serves oven food; *Ta Kalamia*, at the west end of the esplanade by the start of the beach is a cheap, filling and popular lunchtime option; while the English-speaking *Ta Ovreika*, in the old Jewish quarter, Sakhtoúri 114, has both Greek and international cuisine and cooked breakfasts. In the road running up from the *Als* there are several fine psistariés, serving the local lamb and goat for which Kárystos is renowned.

AROUND KÁRYSTOS

The obvious excursion from Kárystos is inland towards **Mount Óhi** (1399m) Évvia's highest peak after Dhírfys and Xirovoúni. **MÝLI**, a fair-sized village around a spring-fed oasis, 3km straight inland, makes a good first stop, with its few tavernas. Otherwise, the medieval castle of **Castel Rosso** beckons above, a twenty-minute climb up from the main church (longer in the frequent, howling gales). Inside, the castle is a total ruin, except for an Orthodox **chapel of Profítis Ilías** built over the Venetians' water cistern, but the sweeping views over the sea and the town make the trip worthwhile.

Behind, the ridges of Óhi are as lunar and inhospitable as the broad plain around Kárystos is fertile. From Mýli, it's a three-hour-plus hike up the largely bare slopes, mostly by a path cutting across the new road, strewn with unfinished granite columns, abandoned almost two thousand years ago. The path passes a little-used alpine club shelter (fed by spring water) and yet another *dhrakóspito*, even more impressive than the three smaller ones at Stýra. Built of enormous schist slabs, seemingly sprouting from the mountain, this one is popularly supposed to be haunted.

From Halkídha to Límni

The main road due north from Halkídha crosses a few kilometres of flat farmland and salt marsh on either side of the refugee settlement of Néa Artáki, after which it climbs steeply through forested hills and the **Dhervéni gorge**, gateway to the north of Évvia. With your own transport, a pleasant detour is to take the road left before Psákhna to the long pebbly beach of **Paralía Politikón**, which is dotted with places to stay or eat.

The village of **PROKÓPI** lies beyond the narrows, in a valley defined by the rich and beautiful woods that make it famous. A counterpoint, in the village itself, is the ugly 1960s pilgrimage church of **St John the Russian**, which holds the saint's relics. The "Russian" was actually a Ukrainian soldier, captured by the Turks in the early eighteenth century and taken to Turkey where he died. According to locals, his mummified body began to promote miracles, and the saint's relics were brought here by Orthodox Greeks from Cappadocian Prokópi (today Ürgüp) in the 1923 population exchange – Évvian Prokópi is still referred to by the locals as Akhmétaga, the name of the old Turkish fiefdom here that was bought by an English nobleman, Edward Noel, a cousin of Lord Byron's, right after the War of Independence. His descendants now run summer courses in various crafts, based in the manor house.

Following a shady, stream-fed glen for the 8km north of Prokópi, you suddenly emerge at Mandoúdhi, much the biggest village in the north of the island, though now squarely in the doldrums following the collapse of the local magnesite industry; ignore signs or depictions on certain maps of a beach at Paralía Mandoúdhi, which is nothing more than abandoned quarries and crushing plants. The closest serviceable beach is at **Paralía Kírinthos**, better known as **Krýa Výssi** (take a right-hand turning off the main road, 3km beyond Mandoúdhi). At the coast, a river and an inlet bracket a small beach, with the headland south of the river supporting the extremely sparse remains of **ancient Kírinthos**. The hamlet of Kírinthos, just past Mandoúdhi, has some visitors, owing to the craft school there.

Back on the main road, a fork at Strofiliá, 8km north of Mandoúdhi, offers a choice of routes: continue north to the coastal resorts that curl round the end of the island (see below), east to Pýli and then south to some unspoiled beaches on the way to Cape Sarakíniko, or head west for Límni.

Límni

If you're hunting for a place to stay, **LÍMNI**, on the west coast 19km from Strofiliá, is by far the most practical and attractive base north of Halkídha. The largely Neoclassical, tile-roofed town, built from the wealth engendered by nineteenth-century shipping prowess, is the most appealing on the island, with serviceable beaches and a famous convent nearby. A small **folk art museum** features pottery, coins and sculpture fragments, as well as local costumes, fabrics and furniture.

There is a regular **hydrofoil** service during summer to Halkídha and the Sporades, and buses from Halkídha stop at the north side of the quay. Límni has a **post office** and **two banks**, all inland just off the main through-road into town from Strofiliá.

As yet, Límni gets few package tours, and **accommodation** is usually available in its rooms or hotels, except during August. At the extreme south, quieter, end of the waterfront, the *Límni* (☎0227/31 316; ②) is good value, with singles and doubles; the *Plaza* (☎0227/31 235; ②), beside the bus stop, is very similar, but has no singles and gets some noise from nocturnal revels outside. Smarter rooms with TV can be rented at

Livaditis (☎0227/31 640; ④), above *Pyrofanis*, an ouzerí beyond the *Plaza*. The best **place to eat** in terms of setting, menu and popularity is *O Platanos* (under the enormous quayside plane tree) with the adjacent *Avra* not far behind. Other local favourites are *Kallitsis* inland from the waterfront, and *Lambros* and *O David* on the way to Katoúnia beach to the south of town.

Around Límni

There are no recommendable beaches in Límni itself, though if you continue 2.5km northwest from the town you reach the gravel strand of **Kohýli**, with a basic but leafy **campsite** out on the cape, 500m beyond mid-beach. Here there are some congenial places to stay, most notably *Denis House* (☎0227/31 787; ⑤) and the more luxurious *Ostria* (☎0227/32 247; ⑤), which has a pool and includes breakfast.

ROVIÉS, some 14km west of Límni, doesn't stand out, but with its medieval tower, rooms, hotels, grid of weekenders' apartments and services, it's the last place of any sort along the scenic coast road to Loutrá Edhipsoú.

The outstanding excursion from Límni is 7km south (under your own steam) to the **convent of Ayíou Nikoláou Galatáki**, superbly set on the wooded slopes of Mount Kandhíli, overlooking the north Evvian Gulf. To get there, veer up and left at the unsigned fork off the coast road; there's no formal scheme for visiting, but don't show up in the early afternoon or around sunset as the gates will be shut. Though much rebuilt since its original Byzantine foundation atop a Poseidon temple, the convent retains a thirteenth-century tower built to guard against pirates, and a crypt. One of a dozen or so nuns will show you frescoes in the *katholikón* dating from the principal sixteenth-century renovation. Especially vivid, on the right of the narthex, is the *Entry of the Righteous into Paradise*: the righteous ascend a perilous ladder to be crowned by angels and received by Christ, while the wicked miss the rungs and fall into the maw of Leviathian.

Below Ayíou Nikoláou Galatáki, and easily combined with it to make a full half-day outing, are the pebble and sand beaches of **Glýfa**, arguably the best on Évvia's southwest-facing coast. There are several in succession, leading up to the very base of Mount Kandhíli, some reachable by paths, the last few only by boat. The shore is remarkably clean, considering the number of summer campers who pitch tents here for weeks on end; a single roadside spring, 2km before the coast, is the only facility in the whole zone.

Northern coastal resorts

Returning to the junction at Strofiliá, take the main road north for 8km to **AYÍA ÁNNA** (locally and universally elided to *Ayiánna*), which has long enjoyed the unofficial status of Évvia's most **folkloric village**, by virtue of traditional costumes worn by the older women and an assiduous local ethnographer, Dimitris Settas, who died in 1989. The place itself is nothing extraordinary, and most passers-by are interested in the prominently marked turnoff for **Angáli beach**, 5km east. This is billed as the area's best, and it's sandy enough, the low hills behind lending a little drama but like this entire coast it's exposed and can gather rubbish. A frontage road, set back 200m or so, is lined by a few kilometres of anonymous villas and apartments, with the "village" at the north end. The *Agali Hotel* (☎0227/97 104, fax 97 067; ⑤) is a congenial place to stay, and there is also a campsite. Horse-riding on the beach is a well-advertised and popular diversion.

Ten kilometres north of Ayía Ánna, a side road heads downhill for 6km, past the village of Kotsikiá, to **Paralía Kotsikiás**. The small cove with its taverna and rooms serves primarily as a fishing-boat anchorage, and its tiny, seaweed-strewn beach is of little interest. **Psaropoúli beach**, 2km below Vassiliká village (13km north of the Kotsikiá turnoff), is more usable in its three-kilometre length, but like Ayía Ánna it is scruffy and shadeless, with a smattering of rooms, self-catering units and tavernas not imparting much sense of community. If you choose to stay, you can't do much better than *Motel Canadiana* (☎0226/43 274; ②), where the road down meets the seafront. **Elliniká**, the next signposted beach, lies only 800m below its namesake village inland; it's far smaller than Angáli or Psaropoúli, but cleaner and certainly the most picturesque spot on this coast, with a church-capped islet offshore as a target to swim to. The approach driveway has a very limited number of facilities: a minimarket, one taverna and a few studios. *Motel Aigaio* (☎0226/42 262; ③) is as good as any for a stay.

Beyond Elliniká, the road (and bus line) skirts the northern tip of Évvia to curl southwest towards **PÉFKI**, a seaside resort mobbed with Greeks in summer, which straggles for some two ki lometres along a mediocre beach. The best **restaurants**, near the north end of this strip, include *Ouzeri Ta Thalassina* and *Psitopolio O Thomas*, while *Zaharoplastio O Peristeras* proffers decadent desserts. **Accommodation** is the usual Évvian mix of self-catering units and a few seaside hotels such as *Galini* (☎0226/41 208, fax 41 650; ④) and *Myrtia* (☎0226/41 202; ③), all resolutely pitched at mainlanders; the **campsite**, *Camping Pefki*, is 2km north of town behind the beach, rather pricey and geared to people with caravans. Hydrofoils for the Sporades depart from here regularly in season.

The next resort (14km southwest), **OREÍ**, is a low-key fishing village, whose cafés are favoured by those in the know as the best places to watch the sun set. It has a fine statue of a Hellenistic bull, hauled up from the sea in 1965, and is also the last **hydrofoil stop** en route to Vólos and the Sporades. Nearby Néos Pýrgos beach has a selection of rooms and restaurants. Some 7km further along the coast, **AYIÓKAMBOS** has a frequent ferry connection to Glýfa on the mainland opposite, from where there are buses to Vólos. Ayiókambos is surprisingly pleasant considering its port function, with a patch of beach, two or three tavernas and a few rooms for rent.

The trans-island bus route ends 14km south of Ayiókambos at **LOUTRÁ EDHIPSOÚ**, which attracts older Greeks, who come to bathe at the **spas** renowned since antiquity for curing everything from gallstones to depression. The spas themselves are cheap (300dr for 20min) and quite an experience. The vast number of hotels, some old and creaky, which service the summer influx means good deals can be had off-season. The classy seventy-year-old *Egli* (☎0226/22 215, fax 22 886; ③) on the seafront is a fine choice. Other decent options in the side-streets near the port are *Valar's* (☎0226/22 278, fax 23 419; ④) and the more modern *Lito* (☎0226/22 081; ③). There is an abundance of tavernas strung along the front; try the leafy restaurant of the *Egli* or the traditional *To Fagadhiko tou Barous*, which offers a wide selection of mezédhes.

There are less regimented **hot springs** at **Yiáltra**, 15km west around the head of Edhipsós bay, where the water boils up on the rocky beach, warming the shallows to comfortable bath temperature. From Loutrá Edhipsoú, the coast road heads southeast to Límni.

travel details

Alkyon Tours (in co-operation with Nomicos ferry lines), and the competing Goutos Lines, provide expensive **conventional ferry** services out of Vólos, Áyios Konstandínos and Kými, with fares steeper than those on Cyclades or Dodecanese lines. On the plus side, Alkyon maintain an Athens office (Akadhimías 97; ☎01/38 43 220) for purchase of ferry and combined bus-and-ferry tickets. Between April and October, Flying Dolphin **hydrofoils** operate between various mainland ports and the Sporades. These are pricier than the ferries but cut journey times virtually in half.

SKIÁTHOS, SKÓPELOS AND ALÓNISSOS

Ferries

Áyios Konstandínos to: Skiáthos (14 weekly; 3hr); Skópelos (10 weekly; 5hr, 6 continuing to Alónissos, 6hr).

Vólos to: Skiáthos (3–4 daily; 3hr) and Skópelos (3–4 daily; 4hr); Alónissos (at least one daily; 5hr; this is the most consistent service out of season, and is always the cheapest).

Flying Dolphins (April–Oct only)

Áyios Konstandínos to: Skiáthos, Glóssa, Skópelos and Alónissos (April, May and Oct 1–3 daily; June–Sept 3–5 daily).

Néa Moudhaniá (Halkidhikí) to: Skiáthos, Skópelos, Alónissos (June–Aug 1 daily).

Plataniás (Pílion) to: Skiáthos (June–Aug 4 weekly).

Thessaloníki to: Skiáthos, Glóssa, Skópelos and Alónissos (June–Aug 1–2 daily).

Tríkeri (Pílion) to: Vólos (April–Oct 1–2 daily); Skiáthos, Skópelos and Alónissos (April–Oct 1–2 daily).

Vólos to: Skiáthos, Glóssa and Skópelos (April, May and Oct 2–3 daily; June–Sept 4–6 daily); at least 2 daily (April–Oct) continue from Skópelos to Alónissos.

Flights

Athens to: Skiáthos (mid-June to mid-Sept 1–3 daily, otherwise 6 weekly; 40min).

SKÝROS

Ferries

Skýros is served by conventional ferry, the *Lykomides*, from **Kými** (2hr). Services are at least twice daily mid-June to mid-Sept (usually at around noon and 5pm), once daily (5pm) the rest of the year; ☎0222/96 466 for current information. There is a connecting bus service for the afternoon boat, from the Liossíon 260 terminal in Athens (departs 12.30pm).

Flying Dolphins

A **hydrofoil** (June to mid-Sept; 5 weekly) links Skýros with Skiáthos, Skópelos and Alónissos.

Flights

Athens to: Skýros (mid-June to mid-Sept 3 weekly; 35min).

ÉVVIA

Buses

Athens (Liossíon 260 terminal) to: Halkídha (every 30min 5.30am–9pm; 1hr 15min); Kými (6 daily; 3hr 30min).

Halkídha to: Kárystos (2 daily; 3hr); Límni (5 daily; 1hr 30min); Loutrá Edhipsoú (4 daily; 3hr); Kými (8 daily; 1 hr 45 min).

Trains

Athens (Laríssis station) to: Halkídha (17 daily; 1hr 30min).

Ferries

Arkítsa to: Loutrá Edhipsoú (summer hourly, otherwise 8 daily 6.45am–11pm; 50min).

Ayía Marína to: Néa Stýra (summer 12–14 daily; 50min); Panayía (summer 3–4 daily; 50min).

Glýfa to: Ayiókambos (summer 8 daily, otherwise 4 daily; 30min).

Rafína to: Kárystos (Mon–Thurs 1 daily, Fri, Sat & Sun 2–3 daily; 1hr 30min); Marmári (4–6 daily; 1hr).

Skála Oropoú to: Erétria (summer every 30min 6am–11pm; 25min).

Flying Dolphins

Halkídha to: Límni, Loutrá Edhipsoú, Oreí, Skiáthos and Skópelos (May to mid-Oct 2 weekly; usually late afternoon).

Oreí to: Áyios Konstandinos (July to mid-Sept 2 weekly).

Péfki to: Skiáthos, Glóssa, Skópelos and Alónissos (April, May and Oct 2 weekly; June–Sept 1 daily).

Dolphin Line Hydrofoils

Rafína to: Kárystos (mid-June to late Sept 1 daily).

Tínos/Mýkonos (Cyclades) to: Kárystos (mid-June to late Sept 1 daily).

Connecting buses from Athens run to Rafína (every 30min; 1hr), Ayía Marína (5 daily; 1hr 15min) and Skála Oropoú (hourly; 1hr 30min) all from the Mavromatéon terminal, and to Arkítsa and Glýfa from the Liossíon 260 terminal.

CHAPTER TWELVE

THE IONIAN ISLANDS

T he six **Ionian** islands, shepherding their satellites down the west coast of the
mainland, float on the haze of the Adriatic, their green, even lush, silhouettes
coming as a shock to those more used to the stark outlines of the Aegean. The
fertility is a direct result of the heavy rains that sweep over the archipelago – and
especially Corfu – from October to March, so if you visit in the off-season, come prepared.

The islands were the Homeric realm of Odysseus, centred on Ithaca (modern Itháki)
and here alone of all modern Greek territory (except for Lefkádha) the Ottomans never
held sway. After the fall of Byzantium, possession passed to the **Venetians** and the
islands became a keystone in that city-state's maritime empire from 1386 until its collapse in 1797. Most of the population must have remained immune to the establishment
of Italian as the official language and the arrival of Roman Catholicism, but Venetian
influence remains evident in the architecture of the island capitals, despite damage
from a series of earthquakes.

On Corfu, the Venetian legacy is mixed with that of the **British**, who imposed a military "protectorate" over the Ionian islands at the close of the Napoleonic Wars, before
ceding the archipelago to Greece in 1864. There is, however, no question of the
islanders' essential Greekness: the poet Dhionyssios Solomos, author of the national
anthem, hailed from the Ionians, as did Nikos Mantzelos, who provided the music, and
the first Greek president, Ioannis Kapodistrias.

Today, **tourism** is the dominating influence, especially on **Corfu** (Kérkyra), which
was one of the first Greek islands established on the package-holiday circuit. Its east
coast is one of the few stretches in Greece with development to match the Spanish
costas, and in summer even its distinguished old capital, Kérkyra Town, wilts beneath
the onslaught. However, the island is large enough to retain some of its charms and is
perhaps the most scenically beautiful of the group. Parts of **Zákynthos** (Zante) – which

---

ACCOMMODATION PRICE CODES

Throughout the book we've used the following **price codes** to denote the cheapest
available double room in each establishment in high season. Out of season, rates can
drop by more than fifty percent, especially if you are staying for three or more nights.
Single rooms, where available, cost around seventy percent of the price of a double.

Rented private rooms on the islands usually fall into the ② or ③ categories, depending on their location and facilities, and the season; a few in the ④ category are more
like plush self-catering apartments. They are not generally available from late October
through to the beginning of April, when only hotels tend to remain open.

① Up to 6000dr   ④ 12,000–16,000dr
② 6000–9000dr   ⑤ 16,000–20,000dr
③ 9000–12,000dr   ⑥ 20,000dr and upwards

Note: Youth hostels typically charge 2000–2500dr for a dormitory bed.
For more accommodation details, see pp.43–6.

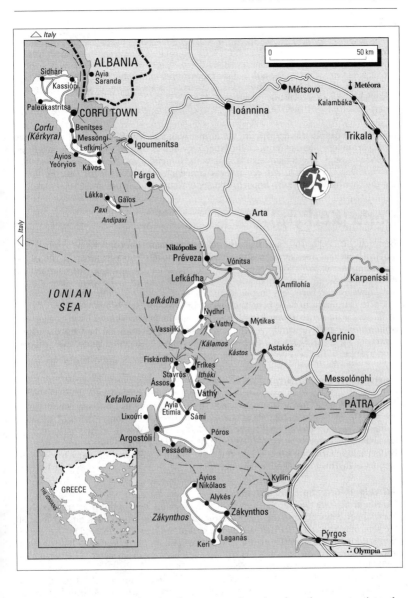

with Corfu has the Ionians' best beaches – seem to be going along the same tourist path, following the introduction of charter flights from northern Europe, but elsewhere the pace and scale of development is a lot less intense. Little **Páxi** is a bit too tricky to reach and lacks the water to support a large-scale hotel, while **Lefkádha** – which is connected to the mainland by a causeway and "boat bridge" – has, so far at least, quite a low-key straggle of ports and only two major resorts. Perhaps the most rewarding duo for island-

> The islands of **Kýthira** and **Andikýthira**, isolated at the foot of the Peloponnese, are historically part of the Ionian islands. However, at some 200km from the nearest other Ionians, and with no ferry connections to the northerly Ionians, they are most easily reached from **Yíthio** or **Neápoli** and are thus covered in Chapter Two.
> Similarly, the island of **Kálamos**, Lefkádha's most distant satellite, is inaccessible from the Ionian group and covered therefore in Chapter Four.

hopping are **Kefalloniá** and **Itháki**, the former with a series of "real towns" and a life in large part independent of tourism, the latter, Odysseus's rugged capital, protected by an absence of sand. The Ionian islands' claims to Homeric significance are manifested in the countless bars, restaurants and streets named after characters in the *Odyssey*, including the "nimble-witted" hero himself, Penelope, Nausicaa, Calypso and Cyclops.

Corfu (Kérkyra)

Between the heel of Italy and the west coast of mainland Greece, green, mountainous **Corfu (Kérkyra)** was one of the first Greek islands to attract mass tourism in the 1960s. Indiscriminate exploitation turned parts into eyesores, but much is still uninhabited olive groves, mountain or woodland. The majority of package holidays are based in the most developed resorts, but unspoiled terrain is often only a few minutes' walk away.

Corfu is thought to have been the model for Prospero and Miranda's place of exile in Shakespeare's *The Tempest*, and was certainly known to writers like Spenser and Milton and – more recently – Lear and Miller, plus Gerald and Lawrence Durrell. Lawrence Durrell's *Prospero's Cell* evokes the island's "delectable landscape", still evident in some of the best beaches of the whole archipelago.

Corfu (Kérkyra) Town

The capital, **Corfu Town**, was renovated for an EU summit in 1994, and is now one of the most elegant island capitals in the whole of Greece. Although many of its finest buildings were destroyed by Nazi bombers in the World War II, its two massive forts, the sixteenth-century church of Áyios Spyrídhon and buildings dating from French and British administrations remain intact. As the island's sole port of entry by ferry or plane, Corfu Town is packed in summer.

Arrivals, information and services

Ferries from Italy dock at the New Port (Néo Limáni) west of the Néo Froúrio (New Fort); those connecting to the mainland (Igoumenítsa and Pátra) dock further west on the seafront. The Old Port (Paleó Limáni), east of the New Port, is used for day excursions and ferries to Paxí. There are ferry offices at both ports; ferries to Italy or south towards Pátra become very busy in summer and booking is advisable. The port police (☎0661/32 655) can advise on services.

The **airport** is 2km south of the city centre. There are no airport buses, although local **blue buses** #5 and #6 can be flagged at the junction where the airport approach meets the main road (500m). It's a forty-minute walk on flat terrain into town (right at the junction then follow the sea road). **Taxis** charge around 2000dr (but agree the fare in advance) or phone (☎0661/33 811) for a radio cab.

The **tourist office** (Mon–Fri 8am–2pm; ☎0661/37 520) on the corner of Vouleftón and Mantzárou has accommodation and transport details. The **post office** is on the corner of Alexándhras and Zafiropoúlou (Mon–Fri 7.30am–8pm).

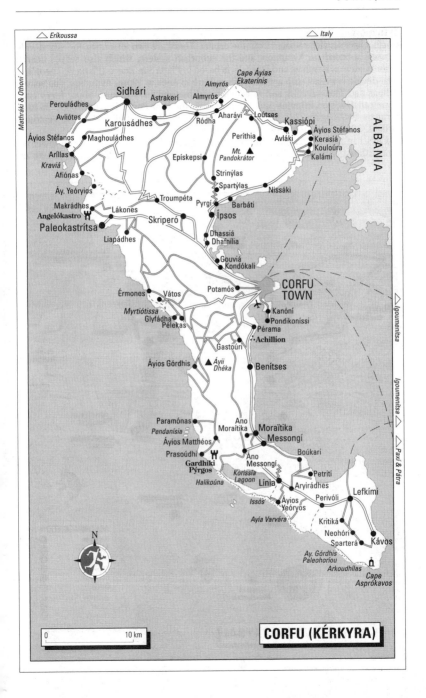

△ Eríkoussa
△ Italy

Mathráki & Othoní △

ALBANIA

Sidhári

Perouládhes
Avliótes
Karousádhes
Áyios Stéfanos
Maghouládhes
Aríllas
Kraviá
Afiónas
Áy. Yeóryios
Makrádhes
Lákones
Angelókastro ※
Paleokastrítsa
Liapádhes
Skriperó

Astrakerí
Almyrós
Almyrós
*Cape Áyias
Ekaterínis*
Aharávi
Ródha
Loútses
Períthia
Kassiópi
Áyios Stéfanos
Kerasiá
Avláki
Kouloúra
Kalámi

Episkepsí
*Mt.
Pandokrátor* ▲

Strinýlas
Spartýlas
Nissáki
Troumpéta
Pyrgí
Barbáti
Ípsos

Dhassiá
Dhafnília

Gouviá
Kondókali

Érmones
Vátos
Potamós

Myrtiótissa
Glyfádha
Pélekas

CORFU
TOWN

Kanóni
Pondikoníssi
Pérama
Achíllion

Gastoúri
Áyios Górdhis
▲ *Áyii
Dhéka*
Benítses

Paramónas
Pendanísia
Áyios Matthéos
Prasoúdhi
**Gardhíki
Pýrgos** ※
Halikoúna

Ano
Moraïtika
Moraïtika
Messongí
Boúkari
Ano
Messongí
Petrití
*Korissía
Lagoon*
Línia
Aryirádhes
Lefkími
PeriVóli
Issós
Áyios
Yeóryos
Kritiká
Ayía Varvára
Neohóri
Spartéra
Kávos
*Ay. Górdhis
Paleohoríou*
Arkoudhílas
*Cape
Asprókavos*

N

0   10 km

CORFU (KÉRKYRA)

Igoumenítsa △

Igoumenítsa △

Paxí & Pétra △

Transport

Corfu's **bus** service radiates from the capital. There are **two** terminals; the island-wide service is based on Avramíou, and the suburban system, which also serves nearby resorts such as Benítses and Dhassiá, is based in Platía San Rocco (Platía G. Theotóki). Island-wide services stop around 6pm, suburban ones at 10pm. Avramíou also serves Athens and Thessaloníki, and sells combined bus-and-ferry tickets. Major **ferry** lines have franchises on Ethnikís Andistásis opposite the New Port: Minoan (☎0661/25 000), Strintzis (☎0661/25 232), ANEK (☎0661/24 504), HML (☎0661/39 747), Ventouris (☎0661/32 664)and Adriatica (☎0661/38 089).

Cars can also be rented from international agencies at the airport or in town; try Avis, Ethnikís Andistásis 42 (☎0661/24 404), Budget, Venízelou 22 (☎0661/49 100; air-

△ *Vidhos*

◁ 3 6 & 8

◁ Paleokastritsa & the north

ARSENIOU
ELEFTHERIOU VENIZELOU
ATHINAGORA
DONZELOT
PIERI
FALIRAKI
CAMPIELLO

Byzantine Museum ❷

Solomos Museum

ZAVITSANOU
AG THEODORA

Palace of Saints Michael & George

Néo Froúrio

PROSALENDIOU
LIPIOU
SOLOMOU
PALEOLOGOU
VELISSARIOU
PALEOKASTRITSA

Orthodox Cathedral ✝

Ayios Spiridhon ✝

KTEL Bus Station

Market

EVANGELISTRIAS
VOLGAREOS
SKARAMAGA
SOTIROS

Liston

Spianádha

LEFTERIOTIS

Paleó Froúrio

I THEOTOKI

WINDMANN

PANDOVA

PADOVA

KAPODHISTRIOU

AG POLITECHNIOU

PLATIA SAN ROCCO
G THEOTOKI
MANFARDOU
DESSYLA
N POLITI
SPIROU
ARSTON

POLYKHRONI KONSTANDA

Blue Bus Station

SAMARA
ZAMBELI

OTE

❹

Maitland Rotunda ●

❺

Kapodhistríou Statue ●

DHIMOULITSA

ℹ️

RIZOSPASTON VOULEFTON
ITALIA
ASPIOTI
AKADHIMIAS

N

◁ Airport, Achillion & the south

LEFKIMIS
KOLOKOTRONI
ALEXANDRAS

Police Station ■

British Cemetery

Archeological Museum ■

Prison

Tomb of Menekrates ■

British Consulate

DHIMOKRATIAS

ACCOMMODATION

Arcadian	❶
Astron	❷
Atlantis	❸
Bella Venezia	❹
Cavalieri	❺
Europa	❻
Hermes	❼
Ionion	❽
Phoenix	❾

CORFU TOWN (KÉRKYRA)

0   200 m

▽ ❾   ▽ *Mon Repos Estate*

port ☎0661/44 017) or Hertz (☎0661/33 547). Among local companies, Sunrise, Ethnikís Andistásis 14, (☎0661/44 325) rents out cars, and **bikes** can be hired from Easy Rider, I. Theotóki 128 (☎0661/43 026), both in the New Port.

Accommodation

Accommodation in Corfu is busy all year round, and expensive. Room owners meet mainland and international ferries, and taxi drivers will often know of decent rooms. Budget travellers might best head straight for the nearest **campsite** at Dhassiá (see p.800).

Arcadian, Kapodhistríou 44 (☎0661/37 670, fax 45 087). Mid-range hotel in a central setting. Street noise can be a problem. ④.

Astron, Dónzelot 15 (☎0661/39 505, fax 33 708). Tastefully renovated and now decidedly upmarket place in the New Port. ⑤.

Atlantis, Xenofóndos Stratigoú 48 (☎0661/35 560, fax 46 480). Large and spacious air-conditioned hotel. ⑥.

Bella Venezia, Zambéli 4 (☎0661/46 500, fax 20 708). Smart and very good-value Neoclassical building just behind the *Cavalieri*, with all the *Cavalieri*'s comforts, but cheaper. ⑤.

Cavalieri, Kapodhistríou 4 (☎0661/39 041 or 39 336, fax 39 283). Smart and friendly, with great views and a roof bar open to the public. ⑥.

Europa, Yitsiáli 10 (☎0661/39 304). Small family hotel one block back from the Igoumenítsa ferry quay. One of the best deals around. ③.

Hermes, Markorá 14 (☎0661/39 268). Another typical lower mid-range hotel in a busy part of town. Overlooks the noisy market. ④.

Ionion, Xenofóndos Stratigoú 46 (☎0661/39 915, fax 44 690). Large, functional, friendly and very reasonably priced. Convenient New Port location. ③.

Phoenix, Khryssostómou Smýrnis 2, Garítsa (☎0661/42 290, fax 42 990). Small, stylish hotel between the airport and the seafront. Good value. ④.

The town

Corfu Town comprises a number of distinct areas. The **Campiello**, the oldest, sits on the hill above the old port, while the streets running between the Campiello and Velisáriou are what remains of the town's **Jewish quarter**. These districts form the core of the old town, and their tall, narrow alleys conceal some of Corfu's most beautiful architecture. **Mandoúki**, beyond the Old Port, is the commercial and dormitory area for the port, and is worth exploring as a living quarter of the city, away from the tourism racket. The town's **commercial area** lies inland from the Spianádha (Esplanade), roughly between Yeoryíou Theotóki, Alexándhras and Kapodhistríou streets, with shops and boutiques around Voulgaréos and Yeoryíou Theotóki and off Platía Theotóki. Tucked behind Platía San Rocco and Odhós Theotóki is the old morning **market** which sells fish and farm produce.

The most obvious sights are the forts, the **Paleó Froúrio** and **Néo Froúrio**, whose designations (*paleó* – "old", *néo* – "new") are a little misleading, since what you see of the older structure was begun by the Byzantines in the mid-twelfth century, just a hundred years before the Venetians began work on the newer citadel. They have both been modified and damaged by various occupiers and besiegers, the last contribution being the Neoclassical shrine of **St George**, built by the British in the middle of Paleó Froúrio during the 1840s. Looming above the old port, the Néo Froúrio (daily 9am–9pm; 500dr), is the more interesting of the two. The entrance, at the back of the fort, gives onto cellars, dungeons and battlements, with excellent views over town and bay; there's a small gallery and café at the summit. The Paleó Froúrio (daily 9am–9pm; 800dr) is rather dull in comparison but hosts daily *son et lumière* shows.

Just west of the Paleó Froúrio, the **Listón**, an arcaded street built during the French occupation by the architect of the Rue de Rivoli in Paris, and the green **Spianádha** (Esplanade) it overlooks, are the focus of town life. At the south end of the Spianádha, the **Maitland Rotunda** was built to honour the first British High Commissioner of Corfu and the Ionian islands. The neighbouring statue of Ioannis Kapodistrias celebrates the local hero and statesman (1776–1831) who led the diplomatic efforts for independence and was made Greece's first president in 1827. At the far northern end of the Listón, the nineteenth-century **Palace of SS Michael and George**, a solidly British edifice built as the residence of their High Commissioner (one of the last of whom was the future British prime minister William Gladstone), and later used as a palace by the Greek monarchy. The former state rooms house the **Asiatic Museum** (Tues–Sun 8am–2.30pm; free) which is a must for aficionados of Oriental culture, although at the time of writing it was being reorganized and only part of the collection was on view. Amassed by Corfiot diplomat Gregorios Manos (1850–1929) and others, it includes Noh theatre masks, woodcuts, wood and brass statuettes, samurai weapons and art works from Thailand, Korea and Tibet. Opened in 1996, the adjoining **Modern Art Museum** (same hours; 500dr) holds a small collection of contemporary Greek art. It's an interesting diversion, as are the gardens and café-bar secreted behind the palace.

In a nearby backstreet off Arseníou, five minutes from the palace, is the **museum** (Mon–Fri 5–8pm; 200dr) dedicated to modern Greece's most famous nineteenth-century poet, **Dhionysios Solomos**. Born on Zákynthos, Solomos was author of the poem *Ímnos stín Eleftheria* (*Hymn to Liberty*), which was to become the Greek national anthem. He studied at Corfu's Ionian Academy, and lived in a house on this site for much of his life.

Up a short flight of steps on Arseníou, the **Byzantine Museum** (Tues–Sun 9am–3pm; 800dr) is housed in the restored church of the Panayía Andivouniótissa. It houses sculptures and sections of mosaic floors from Paleópolis and church frescoes. There are also some pre-Christian artefacts, and a collection of icons dating from the fifteenth to nineteenth centuries. Just to the southwest is Corfu's **cathedral**, packed with icons, including a fine sixteenth-century painting of *St George Slaying the Dragon* by the Cretan artist Mihail Dhamaskinos.

A block behind the Listón, down Odhós Spyrídhonos, is the **church of Áyios Spyrídhon**, whose maroon-domed campanile dominates the town. Here you will find the silver-encrusted coffin of the island's patron saint, **Spyrídhon** – Spyros in the diminutive – after whom about half the male population is named. Four times a year (Palm Sunday and the following Saturday, August 11 and the first Sunday in November), to the accompaniment of much celebration and feasting, the relics are paraded through the streets of Corfu Town. Each of the days commemorates a miraculous deliverance of the island credited to the saint – twice during plague during the seventeenth century, from a famine of the sixteenth century and (a more blessed release than either of those for any Greek) from the Turks in the eighteenth century.

Corfu Town's **Archeological Museum** (Tues–Sun 9am–3pm; 1000dr), just south round the coast, is the best in the archipelago. The most impressive exhibit is a massive (17m) gorgon pediment excavated from the Doric temple of Artemis at Paleópolis; this dominates an entire room, the gorgon flanked by panthers and mythical battle scenes. The museum also has fragments of Neolithic weapons and cookware, and coins and pots from the period when the island was a colony of ancient Corinth.

Just south of Platía San Rocco and signposted on the corner of Methodhíou and Kolokotróni, the **British cemetery** features some elaborate civic and military memorials. It's a quiet green space away from the madness of San Rocco, and in spring and early summer is alive with dozens of species of orchids and other exotic blooms.

The outskirts

Each of the following sights on the outskirts of the city is easily seen in a morning or afternoon, and best visited from the town rather than outlying resorts.

Around the bay from the Rotunda and Archeological Museum, tucked behind Mon Repos beach, the **Mon Repos** estate (8am–8pm; free) contains the most accessible archeological remains on the island. Thick woodland conceals two **Doric temples**, dedicated to Hera and Artemis. The Neoclassical Mon Repos **villa**, built by British High Commissioner Frederic Adam in 1824 and handed over to Greece in 1864, was the birthplace of Britain's Prince Philip and is due to be opened to the public in the near future.

The most famous excursion from Corfu Town is to the islets of **Vlahérna** and **Pondikoníssi**, 2km south of town. A dedicated bus (#2) leaves San Rocco square every half-hour, or it is a pleasant walk of under an hour. Reached by a short causeway, the tiny white convent of Vlahérna is one of the most photographed images on Corfu. Pondikoníssi ("Mouse Island") can be reached by a short boat trip from the dock (500dr). Tufted with greenery and a small chapel, Vlahérna is identified in legend with a ship from Odysseus's fleet, petrified by Poseidon in revenge for the blinding of his son Polyphemus, the Homeric echoes somewhat marred by the thronging masses and low-flying aircraft from the nearby runway. A quieter destination is **Vídhos**, the wooded island visible from the old port, reached from there by a free hourly shuttle kaïki.

Four kilometres further to the south, past the resort sprawl of Pérama, is a rather more bizarre attraction: the **Achillion** (daily 9am–3pm; 800dr), a palace built in a (fortunately) unique blend of Teutonic and Neoclassical styles in 1890 by Elizabeth, Empress of Austria. Henry Miller considered it "the worst piece of gimcrackery" that he'd ever laid eyes on and thought it "would make an excellent museum for surrealistic art". The house is predictably grandiose but the gardens are pleasant to walk around and afford splendid views in all directions.

Eating and drinking

Most **restaurants** are around the old town, with some hard-to-find places favoured by locals concealed in the Campiello. Restaurants on main thoroughfares tend to be indifferent, though the *Averof*, in the old port behind Zavitsiánou, is a Corfu institution, offering above-par taverna cuisine. Nearby and towards the Néo Froúrio the *Tenedos* provides tasteful live music as well as tasty food. Below the Palace of SS Michael and George, the *Faliraki* is reasonably priced for its setting and has an imaginative menu. The *Orestes*, on Xenofóndos Stratigoú in Mandoúki, is probably the best seafood restaurant in town. The *Pizzeria*, on Guildford Street, has a wide range of pizzas with a pleasing choice for vegetarians, as does *Quattro Stagione*, off the north side of N. Theotóki. One of the smartest joints in town is the *Rex*, on Zavitsiánou behind the Listón, and no one staying in Corfu Town should miss the classy *Venetian Well Bistro*, on Platía Kremastí, a tiny square a few alleys to the south of the cathedral. Another excellent choice is the municipally owned *Vidos* restaurant on the island of the same name. It allows you to eat to the gentle accompaniment of a quality duet, whilst surveying the nocturnally lit town; a free kaïki runs until 1.30am.

Nightlife

Corfu Town has plenty to offer in the way of **bars** and nightlife. On the Listón, avoid the mark-ups at the *Magnet* and follow the locals to *Koklia*, *Aegli* or *Olympia*, or drink in one of the hotels; the *Cavalieri* rooftop bar can be heaven at night. For local atmosphere, try *Dirty Dick's*, on the corner of Arseníou and Zavitsiánou, or the expat hangout *Mermaid*, on Ayíon Pantón off the Listón, which will give you a different spin on island culture.

Corfu's self-proclaimed **disco** strip lies a few kilometres north of town, en route to Kondókali. Here, at the (unofficial) *Hard Rock Café*, the *Hippodrome* disco complex (the town's biggest, with its own pool), and the bizarrely decorated *Apokalypsis* and *Coco Flash*, party animals dress up for wild and fairly expensive nights out. In some clubs, women travelling without male partners should beware *kamákia* – slang for Greek males "spearfishing" for foreign women. Corfu Town's two **cinemas** – the Pallas on Yeoryíou Theotóki and the Orfeus on the corner of Akadhimías and Aspióti – both often show English-language films.

The northeast and the north coast

The northeast, at least beyond the immediate suburbs, is the most typically Greek part of Corfu – it's mountainous, with a rocky coastline chopped into pebbly bays and coves, above wonderfully clear seas. Green **buses** between Corfu Town and Kassiópi serve all resorts, along with some blue suburban buses to Dhassiá and Ípsos.

Corfu Town to Ípsos

The landscape between Corfu Town and Kondókali is an industrial wasteland, and things don't improve much at **KONDÓKALI** itself, a small village overrun by holiday developments. The old town consists of a short street with a number of bars and traditional psistariés, the best of which are *Gerekos* and *Takis*, and an international restaurant, *Flags*.

Neighbouring **GOUVIÁ** is also Corfu's largest yachting marina. The village boasts a couple of small **hotels**, notably the *Hotel Aspa* (☎0661/91 165; ④), and some **rooms** – try Maria Lignou (☎0661/91 348; ④) or Yorgos Mavronas (☎0661/91 297 or 90 297; ④). There are a number of decent **restaurants**, including *The Captain's Table* and *Aries Taverna*, and a couple of pizzerias, *Bonito* and *Palladium*. The very narrow shingle **beach**, barely five metres wide in parts, shelves into sand; given the sea traffic the water quality is doubtful.

Two kilometres beyond Goúvia the coastline begins to improve at **DHASSIÁ** and **DHAFNÍLA**, set in two small wooded bays with pebbly beaches. Two large and expensive **hotels**, the *Dassia Chandris* and *Corfu Chandris* both (☎0661/97 100–3, fax 93 458; ⑥), dominate Dhassiá, with extensive grounds, pools and beach facilities. The more reasonable *Hotel Amalia* (☎0661/93 523; ④) has pleasant en-suite rooms and its own pool and garden. **Rooms** are scarce, although Spyros Rengis's minimarket has a few (☎0661/90 282; ③). Dhassiá does, however, have the best **campsite** on the island, *Dionysus Camping Village* (☎0661/91 417, fax 91 760); tents are pitched under terraced olive trees. *Dionysus* also has simple bungalow huts, a pool, shop, bar and restaurant, and the friendly, multilingual owners offer a ten percent discount to Rough Guide readers.

ÍPSOS, 2km north of Dhassiá, can't really be recommended to anyone but hardened bar-hoppers. There isn't room to swing a cat on the thin pebble beach, right beside the busy coast road, and the resort is pretty tacky. Most **accommodation** is pre-booked by package companies, although Ípsos Travel (☎0661/93 661) can offer rooms. *Corfu Camping Ípsos* (☎0661/93 579) has a bar and restaurant, and offers standing tents. Ípsos is also the base for one of the island's major **diving centres**, *Waterhoppers* (☎0661/93 876). **Eating** on the main drag is dominated by fast food, though a more traditional meal and a quieter setting can be found in the *Akrogiali* and *Asteria* tavernas, by the marina to the south of the strip.

North to Áyios Stéfanos

Ípsos has now engulfed the neighbouring hamlet of Pyrgí, which is the main point of access for the villages and routes leading up to **Mount Pandokrátor**; the road, signposted Spartílas, is 200km beyond the junction in Pyrgí. A popular base for walkers is the village of **STRINÝLAS**, 16km from Pyrgí. Accommodation is basic but easy to come by: the *Elm Tree Taverna*, a long-time favourite with walkers, can direct you to rooms. In summer the main routes are busy, but there are quieter walks taking in the handsome Venetian village of Epískepsi, 5km northwest of Strinýlas – anyone interested in walking the Pandokrátor paths is advised to get the **map** of the mountain by island-based cartographer Stephan Jaskulowski or Hilary Whitton-Paipeti's walking book.

The coast road beyond Ípsos mounts the slopes of Pandokrátor towards **BARBÁTI**, 4km further on. Here you'll find the best beach on this coast and ample facilities; it's a favourite with families, and much **accommodation** is pre-booked in advance. However, there are some rooms available on spec – *Paradise* (☎0663/91 320; ③) and *Roula Geranou* (☎0663/92 397; ③).

The mountainside becomes steeper and the road higher beyond Barbáti, and the population thins drastically. **NISSÁKI** is a rather spread-out village with a number of coves, the first and last accessible by road, the rest only by track – one dominated by the gigantic, expensive and rather soulless *Nissaki Beach Hotel* (☎0663/91 232; ⑥). There are a couple of shops and a bakery, and a few travel and **accommodation agencies**. The British-owned *Falcon Travel* (☎0663/91 318, fax 91 070; ⑤) rents out apartments above the first beach, a tiny, white-pebble cove with a trio of fine tavernas. The *Nissaki Holiday Center* (☎0663/91 166, fax 91 206) may have some cheaper rooms.

The two places no one visiting this coast should miss are Kalámi and neighbouring Kouloúra: the first for its Durrell connection, the latter for its exquisite bay (though neither has a beach worth mentioning). **KALÁMI** is on the way to being spoiled, but the village is still small; you can imagine how it would have been in the year Lawrence Durrell spent here on the eve of World War II. The **White House**, where Durrell wrote *Prospero's Cell*, is now split in two: the ground floor is an excellent taverna; the upper floor is let through CV Travel (see p.6). The owner of the *White House*, Tassos Athineos (☎0663/91 251), has rooms, and Yannis Vlahos (☎ and fax 0663/91 077) has rooms, apartments and studios in the bay, as do Sunshine Travel (☎0663/91 170) and Kalami Tourism Services (☎0663/91 062, fax 91 369). The **restaurant** at the White House is recommended, as is *Matella's*, the *Kalami Beach Taverna* and *Pepe's*, which is on the beach.

The tiny harbour of **KOULOÚRA** has managed to keep its charm intact, set at the edge of an unspoiled bay with nothing to distract from the pine trees and kaïkia. The fine **taverna** here has to be the most idyllic setting for a meal in the whole of Corfu.

Around the coast to Aharávi

Two kilometres beyond Kouloúra down a shady lane, the large pebble cove of **Kerasiá** shelters the family-run *Kerasia Beach Taverna*. The most attractive resort on this stretch of coast, 3km down a lane from Agnitsíni on the main road, is **ÁYIOS STÉFANOS**. Most **accommodation** here is upmarket, and the village has yet to succumb to any serious development; so far only the *Kohyli* pizzeria has rooms and apartments (☎0663/81 522; ③). Recommended are the *Garini* and *Kaporelli* **tavernas**, and the *Eucalyptus* over by the village's small beach.

A thirty-minute walk from the coastguard station above Áyios Stéfanos, along a rough track, stretches the beach of **Avláki**, a pebble bay that provides lively conditions for the **windsurfers** who visit the beach's windsurf club. There are two **tavernas**, the *Barbaro* and *Avlaki*, and some **rooms** a few hundred yards back from the beach – *Mortzoukos* (☎0663/81 196; ③), and *Tsirimiagos*, ☎0663/81 522; ④).

Further round the coast is **KASSIÓPI**, a fishing village that's been transformed into a major party resort. The Roman emperor Tiberius had a villa here, and the village's sixteenth-century church is said to stand on the site of a temple of Zeus once visited by

Nero. Little evidence of Kassiópi's past survives, apart from an abandoned Angevin kástro on the headland – most visitors come for the nightlife and the five pebbly beaches. Most **accommodation** in Kassiópi is through village agencies; the largest, Travel Corner (☎0663/81 220, fax 81 108), is a good place to start. An independent alternative, the smart *Kastro* café-pension, overlooks the beach behind the castle (☎0663/81 045; ⑤), and *Theofilos* (☎0663/81 261; ②) offers bargain rooms on Kalamíonas beach. Anglicized cuisine and fast food dominate **eating** in Kassiópi, but for something more traditional, head for the *Three Brothers* taverna on the harbour, or the neighbouring *Porto* fish restaurant. At night, Kassiópi rocks to the cacophony of its music and video bars: the flashiest is the gleaming hi-tech *Eclipse*, closely followed by the *Baron*, *Angelos* and *Jasmine*, all within falling-over distance of the small town square. The *Axis Club* boasts imported British DJs, and frolics sometimes extend onto the beach until dawn. The village is also home to one of the most reliable diving operations, Corfu Divers (☎0663/81 218), which is partly British-run.

The coastline beyond Kassiópi is overgrown and marshy until little-used **Almyrós beach**, one of the longest on the island. It is also the least developed beach, with only a few apartment buildings under construction at the hamlet of **Almyrós**. The Andinióti lagoon, smaller than Korissía (see p.806) but still a haven for birds and twitchers, backs Cape Áyias Ekaterínis to the east. With its wide main road, **AHARÁVI**, the next stop west on the main coast road, resembles an American Midwest truck stop, but the village proper is tucked behind this in a quiet crescent of old tavernas, bars and shops. Aharávi makes a quieter beach alternative to the southerly strands, and should also be considered by those seeking alternative routes up onto **Mount Pandokrátor**. Roads to small hamlets such as Áyios Martínos and Láfki continue onto the mountain, and even a stroll up from the back of Aharávi will find you on the upper slopes in under an hour. **Accommodation** isn't easy to find, but a good place to start is Castaway Travel (☎0663/63 541, fax 63 376) or HN Travel (☎0663/63 458, fax 63 454). There are a number of **restaurants** on Aharávi's main drag; go for the *Pump House* steak and pasta joint, the traditional tavernas *Chris's* and *George's*, or the *Young Tree*, which specializes in Corfiot dishes such as *sofríto* and *pastitsádha*. The bar-restaurants tend to get quite rowdy at night, although the light and airy *Captain's Bar* is a pleasant watering hole. For a quieter drink, head for the leafy awning of the friendly *Vevaiotis* kafenío in the old village.

Ródha, Sidhári and Avliótes

Just to the west, **RÓDHA** has tipped over into overdevelopment, and can't be wholeheartedly recommended for those after a quiet time. Its central crossroads have all the charm of a service station, and the beach is rocky in parts and swampy to the west. "Old Ródha" is a small warren of alleys between the main road and the seafront, where you'll find the best **restaurants** and **bars**: the *Taverna Agra* is the oldest in Ródha and is the best place for fish, and the *Rodha Star Taverna* and *New Harbour* are also good. For bars, try *Nikos* near the *Agra* and the upmarket bar-club *Skouna*. For **accommodation**, the large *Hotel Afroditi* (☎0663/63 147, fax 63 125; ④) has decently priced en-suite rooms with sea views. Both the Anglo-Greek NSK UK Travel (☎0663/63 471, fax 63 274) on the main drag and Nostos Travel on the seafront (☎0663/64 601, fax 64 602) rent rooms and handle car rental. The smart *Roda Beach Camping* (☎0663/93 120) is a little way east of the resort.

The next notable resort, **SIDHÁRI**, is expanding rapidly and is totally dominated by British package tourists; it has a small but pretty town square, with a bandstand set in a small garden, but this is lost in a welter of bars, boutiques and snack joints. The beach is sandy but not terribly clean, and many people tend to head just west to the curious coves, walled by wind-carved sandstone cliffs. However, the main reason to visit Sidhári is to reach the **Dhiapóndia islands**; day-trips to Mathráki, Othoní and Eríkoussa (see p.808) leave weekday mornings around 9am; unless you catch the 5.30am Sidhári bus from Corfu Town, your only option is to stay the night. The boats are run by Nearchos Seacruises (☎0663/95 248) and cost around 5000dr return per person. The best sources of **rooms** are Kostas Fakiolas at the *Scorpion* café-bar at the west of town (☎0663/95 046; ③) and Nikolaos Korakianitis's minimarket on the main road (☎0663/95 058; ③). The biggest accommodation agency is run by young tycoon Philip Vlasseros, whose Vlasseros Travel (☎0663/95 695) also handles car rental, excursions and horse-riding. Sidhári's **campsite**, *Dolphin Camping* (☎0663/31 846), is some way inland from the junction at the western end of town. Most **restaurants** are pitched at those looking for a great night out rather than a quiet meal in a taverna. The *Olympic* is the oldest taverna here; also recommended are the *Diamond* and *Sea Breeze* tavernas. There are no quiet bars in Sidhári, and two **nightclubs** vie for your custom, the *Remezzo* and its younger rival, *Ecstasy*.

The Sidhári bus usually continues to **AVLIÓTES**, a handsome hill town with bars and tavernas but few concessions to tourism. Avliótes is noteworthy for two reasons, however: its accessibility to the quiet beaches below the quiet village of Perouládhes, just over a kilometre away, and the fact that **Áyios Stéfanos** (see p.804) is under thirty minute's walk from here, downhill through lovely olive groves.

Paleokastrítsa and the northwest coast

The northwest conceals some of the island's most dramatic coastal scenery; the interior, violent mountainscapes jutting out of the verdant countryside. The area's honeypot attraction, **Paleokastrítsa**, is the single most picturesque resort on Corfu, but is suffering from its popularity. Further down the west coast, the terrain opens out to reveal long sandy beaches, such as delightful **Myrtiótissa** and the backpackers' haven of **Áyios Górdhis**. Public transport to the west coast is difficult: virtually all buses ply routes from Corfu Town to single destinations, and rarely link resorts.

Paleokastrítsa

PALEOKASTRÍTSA, a small village surrounded by dramatic hills and cliffs, has been identified as the Homeric city of Scheria, where Odysseus was washed ashore and escorted by Nausicaa to the palace of her father Alcinous, king of the Phaeacians. It's a stunning site though, as you would expect, one that's long been engulfed by tourism. The focal point of the village is the car park on the seafront, which backs onto the largest and least attractive of three **beaches**, home to sea taxis and kaïkia. The second beach, to the right and signed by flags for Mike's Ski Club, is stony with clear water, and the best of the three is a small unspoiled strand reached along the path by the *Astakos Taverna*. Protected by cliffs, it's undeveloped apart from the German-run Korfu-Diving Centre (☎0663/41 604) at the end of the cove. From the beach in front of the main car park, **boat trips** (2000dr for a half-hour trip, 3000dr for drop-off and later pick-up) leave for the blue grottoes, a trip worth taking for the spectacular coastal views. Boats also serve as a taxi service to three neighbouring beaches, Áyia Triánda, Platákia and Alípa, which all have snack bars.

On the rocky bluff above the village, the **Theotókou monastery** (7am–1pm & 3–8pm; free, although donations invited) is believed to have been established in the thirteenth century. There's also a museum, resplendent with icons, jewelled Bibles and other impedimenta of Greek Orthodox ritual, though the highlight is the gardens, with spectacular coastal views. Paleokastrítsa's ruined castle, the **Angelókastro**, is around 6km up the coast; only approachable by path from the hamlet of Kríni, it has stunning, almost circular views of the surrounding sea and land.

Unfortunately, perhaps due to the pressure of commerce in such a small space, there's a rather aggressive air about tourism here. **Accommodation** is at a premium, and you may be expected to commit yourself for three to seven days in some places. A good **hotel** is the small, family-run *Odysseus* (☎0663/41 209, fax 41 342; ⑤) on the road into town, and the modern *Akrotiri Beach* (☎0663/41 237, fax 41 277; ⑥) is friendly and unpretentious for such a large and expensive hotel, and accessible on foot. There are good-value **rooms** for rent above Alípa Beach on the road down into Paleokastrítsa: try Andreas Loulis at the *Dolphin Snackbar* (☎0663/41 035; ④), Spiros and Theodora Michalas (☎0663/41 485; ③), or George Bakiras at the *Green House* (☎0663/41 311; ③). Above the village, past Nikos' Bikes, the friendly Korina family also have rooms (☎0663/44 0641; ④). *Paleokastritsa Camping* (☎0663/41 204, fax 41 104), is just off the main road into town, a ten-minute walk from the centre.

There isn't a huge choice of **restaurants** in the centre of Paleokastrítsa. The *Astakos Taverna* and *Corner Grill* are two traditional places, while *Il Pirata* offers a variety of Italian and Greek dishes, including local fish and seafood, and the seafront *Smurfs* has a good seafood menu despite the shocking name. Also recommended are the very smart *St Georges on the Rock*, and the restaurant of the *Odysseus Hotel*. **Nightlife** hangouts include the restaurant-bars in the centre, and those straggling up the hill towards Lákones. By the Lákones turning is Paleokastrítsa's one nightclub, *The Paleo Club*, a small disco-bar with a garden.

Áyios Yeóryios and Áyios Stéfanos

Like many of the west coast resorts, **ÁYIOS YEÓRYIOS**, 6km north of Paleokastrítsa, isn't actually based around a village. The resort has developed in response to the popularity of its large sandy bay, and it's a major **windsurfing** centre, busy even in low season. There are a couple of good **hotels** – the *Alkyon Beach* (0663/96 222; ⑤) and the *Chrisi Akti* (0663/96 207; ⑤) – some rooms such as *Studio Eleana* (☎0663/96 366; ③), and the *San George* campsite (☎0663/51 759) nearly a kilometre back from the beach towards Kavvadhádhes. On the way north towards Áyios Stéfanos, the pleasant sandy beach of **Aríllas** has given rise to gradual development, including several tavernas. Accommodation can be arranged through Arillas Travel (☎0663/51 280, fax 51 381) or there is the smart *Akti Arilla* hotel (☎0663/51 201, fax 51 221; ⑤).

The most northerly of the west coast's resorts, **ÁYIOS STÉFANOS** is a low-key family resort, a quiet base from which to explore the northwest and the Diapóndia islands, visible on the horizon. Day-trips to Mathráki, Othoní and Eríkoussa (see p.808) run every Thursday in season, and cost around 5000dr per person. Áyios Stéfanos's oldest **hotel**, the *Nafsika* (☎0663/51 051, fax 51 112; ③) has a large restaurant, a favourite with villagers, and gardens with a pool and bar. In recent years it has been joined by the upmarket *Thomas Bay* (☎0663/51 767, fax 51 913; ⑤) and *Romanza* hotels (☎0661/22 873, fax 41 878; ⑤). For those on a budget, Peli and Maria's gift shop offers bargain **rooms** (☎0663/51 424; ②), and the *Restaurant Evnios* (☎0663/51 766; ③) and *Hotel Olga* (☎0663/71 252; ③) have apartments above the village. A number of travel agencies handle accommodation, among them San Stefanos (☎0663/51 910, fax 51 771) in the centre. Besides the *Nafsika*, good options for **eating** include the *Golden Beach Taverna*, and the *Waves Taverna*, on the beach, while *O Manthos* taverna serves Corfiot specialities like *sofríto* and *pastitsádha*. For **nightlife**, there's a couple of lively music bars, the *Condor* and the *Athens*, plus the small *Enigma* nightclub.

Central and southern Corfu

Two natural features divide the centre and south of Corfu. The first is the **plain of Rópa**, whose fertile landscape backs on to some of the best beaches on this coast. Settlements and development stop a little to the south of Paleokastrítsa and only resume around **Érmones** and **Pélekas** – a quick bus ride across the island from Corfu Town. Down to the south, a second dividing point is the **Korissía lagoon**, the sandy plains and dunes that skirt this natural feature being great places for botanists and ornithologists. Beyond, a single road trails the interior, with sporadic side roads to resorts on either coast. The landscape here is flat, an undistinguished backdrop for a series of relatively undefiled beaches and, in the far south, **Kávos**, Corfu's big youth resort.

Érmones to the Korissía lagoon: the west coast

ÉRMONES, south of Paleokastrítsa, is one of the busiest resorts on the island, its lush green bay backed by the mountains above the Rópa River. The resort is dominated by the upmarket *Ermones Beach* **hotel** (☎0661/94 241; ⑥), which provides guests with a funicular railway down to the beach. More reasonable accommodation can be found at the *Pension Katerina* (②) and *Georgio's Villas* (③). Head for *George's* **taverna** above the beach for some of the best Greek food here: the mezédhes are often a meal in themselves. Just inland is the Corfu Golf and Country Club (☎0661/94 220), the only golf club in the archipelago, and said to be the finest in the Mediterranean.

The nearby small village of **VÁTOS** has a couple of tavernas, a disco and rooms, and is on the Glyfádha bus route from Corfu Town. Spyros Kousounis, owner of the *Olympic Restaurant and Grill* (☎0661/94 318; ③) has rooms and apartments, as does Prokopios Himarios (☎0661/94 503; ③), next to the Doukakis café-minimarket. The Myrtiótissa **path** is signposted just beyond the extremely handy, if basic, *Vatos Camping* (☎0661/94 393).

Far preferable to the gravelly sand of Érmones are the sandy beaches just south of the resort, at Myrtiótissa and Glyfádha. In *Prospero's Cell*, Lawrence Durrell described **Myrtiótissa** as "perhaps the loveliest beach in the world"; it was until recently a well-guarded secret, and though the place hasn't been entirely swamped, it's best visited at either end of the day or out of high season. Above the beach is the tiny whitewashed **Myrtiótissa monastery**, dedicated to Our Lady of the Myrtles.

The sandy bay of **GLYFÁDHA**, walled in by cliffs, is dominated by the *Louis Grand* (☎0661/94 140, fax 94 146; ⑥), a large and expensive **hotel** in spacious grounds. There's another hotel at the far north end of the beach, the *Glifada Beach* (☎0661/94 258; ④) whose owners, the Megas family, also have a fine taverna. Most of the other accommodation is block-booked – it's a very popular family beach – but the *Gorgona* pool bar and *Restaurant Michaelis* might have rooms. Nightlife centres on two music bars, the *Kikiriko* and *Aloha*.

PÉLEKAS, inland and 2km south of Glyfádha, has long been popular for its views – the **Kaiser's Throne** viewing tower, along the road to Glyfádha, was Wilhelm II's favourite spot on the island. New developments are beginning to swamp the town, but there are still some good **hotels** here, including the elegant, upmarket *Pelekas* (☎0661/94 230; ⑥) and the friendlier *Nicos* (☎0661/94 486; ④), as well as rooms at the *Alexandros* taverna (☎0661/94 215; ③). Among the **tavernas**, the *Alexandros* and *Roula's Grill House* are highly recommended. Pélekas's sandy **beach** is reached down a short path, where *Maria's Place* is an excellent family-run **taverna/rooms** place (☎0661/94 601; ③) with fish caught daily by the owner's husband. Sadly, the beach has been rather spoilt by the monstrous *Pelekas Beach* hotel that now looms over it.

Around 7km south of Pélekas, **ÁYIOS GÓRDHIS** is one of the key play beaches on the island, largely because of the activities organized by the startling **Pink Palace** complex (☎0661/53 101) which dominates the resort. It has pools, games courts, restaurants, a shop and a disco. Backpackers cram into communal rooms for up to ten (smaller rooms and singles are also available) for 6000dr a night, including breakfast and evening meal. Other accommodation is available on the beach, notably at the quieter *Michael's Place* taverna (☎0661/53 041; ③); the neighbouring *Alex-in-the-Garden* **restaurant** is also a favourite.

Inland from the resort is the south's largest prominence, the humpback of **Áyii Dhéka** (576m), reached by path from the hamlet of Áno Garoúna; it is the island's second largest mountain after Pandokrátor. The lower slopes are wooded, and it's possible to glimpse buzzards wheeling on thermals over the higher slopes.

Around 5km south by road from Áyios Górdhis, the fishing hamlet of **PENDÁTI** is still untouched by tourism. There is no accommodation here, but *Angela's* café and minimarket and the *Strofi* grill cater to villagers and the few tourists who wander in. Another 4km on, **PARAMÓNAS** affords excellent views over the coastline, which can be admired from the *Sunset* taverna, and has only a few businesses geared to tourism: the *Paramonas Bridge* restaurant (☎0663/75 761; ③) has **rooms** and **apartments** to rent, as does the *Areti Studios* (☎0661/75 838; ④) on the road in from Pendáti.

The town of **ÁYIOS MATTHÉOS**, 3km inland, is still chiefly an agricultural centre, although a number of kafenía and tavernas offer a warm if bemused welcome to passers-by: head for the *Mouria* snack bar-grill, or the modern *Steki*, which maintains the tradition of spiriting tasty mezédhes onto your table unasked. On the other side of Mount Áyios Matthéos, 2km by road, is the **Gardhíki Pýrgos**, the ruins of a thirteenth-century castle built in this unlikely lowland setting by the despots of Epirus. The road continues on to the northernmost tip of splendid and deserted **Halikoúna** beach on the sea edge of the **Korissía lagoon**, which, if you don't have your own transport, is most easily reached by walking from the village of Línia (on the Kávos bus route) via Íssos Beach; other, longer routes trail around the north end of the lagoon from Áno Messongí and Khlomotianá. Over 5km long and 1km wide at its centre, Korissía is home to turtles, tortoises, lizards, and numerous indigenous and migratory birds. For one of the quietest stays on the island, try *Marin Christel Apartments* (☎0661/75 947; ⑤) just north of Halikoúna beach or *Logara Apartments* (☎0661/76 477; ⑤) 500m inland.

Benítses to Petríti: the east coast

South of Corfu Town, there's nothing to recommend before **BENÍTSES**, a once notorious bonking-and-boozing resort, whose old town at the north end is now reverting to a quiet bougainvillea-splashed Greek village. There's really little to see here, beyond the ruins of a Roman bathhouse at the back of the village, and the tiny **Shell Museum**, part-exhibit, part-shop. **Rooms** are plentiful: try Bargain Travel (☎0661/72 137, fax 72 031; ③) and All Tourist (☎0661/72 223; ③). Visitor numbers are picking up again after a serious decline but some **hotels** can offer good deals. The *Corfu Maris* (☎0661/72 035; ④), on the beach at the southern end of town, has modern en-suite rooms with balconies and views, while the friendly *Hotel Benitsa* and neighbouring *Agis* in the centre (both ☎0661/39 269; ③) offer quiet rooms set back from the main road. Benítses has its fair share of decent if not particularly cheap **tavernas**, notably *La Mer de Corfu* and the Corfiot specialist *Spiros*, as well as the plush *Marabou*. The **bars** at the southern end of town are fairly lively, despite new rules controlling all-night partying, and the *Stadium* **nightclub** still opens occasionally. If you're looking for a quiet drink head for the north end of the village, away from the traffic.

MORAÏTIKA's main street is an ugly strip of bars, restaurants and shops, but its beach is the best between Corfu Town and Kávos. Reasonable beach-side **hotels** include the *Margarita Beach* (☎ & fax 0661/76 267; ⑤) and the *Three Stars* (☎0661/92 457; ④). The *Golden Keys* apartments (☎0661/75 778, fax 75 598; ④) are comfortable and there are **rooms** between the main road and beach, and up above the main road: try Alekos Bostis (☎0661/75 637; ③) or Kostas Vlahos (☎0661/55 350; ②). Much of the main drag is dominated by souvenir shops and minimarkets, as well as a range of **bars**, including the village's oldest, *Charlie's*, which opened in 1939. The *Islands* **restaurant** is recommended for its mix of vegetarian, Greek and international food, as is the unfortunately named beach restaurant *Crabs*, where the seafood and special salads are excellent. The village proper, **ÁNO MORAÏTIKA**, is signposted a few minutes' hike up the steep lanes inland, and is virtually unspoiled. Its tiny houses and alleys are practically drowning in bougainvillea, among which you'll find two **tavernas**: the *Village Taverna* and the *Bella Vista*, which has a basic menu but justifies its name with a lovely garden, sea views and breezes.

Barely a hundred metres on from the Moraïtika seafront, **MESSONGÍ** is disappointing: parts of the resort are sadly moribund. The sandy beach is dominated by the vast *Messonghi Beach* **hotel** complex (☎0661/76 684, fax 75 334; ⑥), one of the plushest on the island. Both the cheaper *Hotel Gemini* (☎0661/75 221, fax 75 213; ⑤) and *Pantheon Hall* (☎0661/75 802, fax 75 801; ③) have pools and gardens, and en-suite rooms with balconies. Despite several closures, Messongí still has a number of good **restaurants**: notably the *Memories* taverna, which specializes in Corfiot dishes and serves its own barrel wine, and the upmarket *Castello*. An alternative is to head for the beach-side *Almond Tree* and *Spanos* tavernas a short walk south on the road to Boúkari.

The quiet road from Messongí to **BOÚKARI** follows the seashore for about 3km, often only a few feet above it. Boukári itself comprises little more than a handful of tavernas, a shop and a few small, family-run hotels; the *Boukari Beach* is the best of the **tavernas**. The very friendly Vlahopoulos family who run the taverna also manage two small hotels nearby, the *Boukari Beach* and *Penelopi* (☎0662/51 269, fax 51 792; ④), as well as good rooms attached to the taverna (③). Boukári is out of the way, but an idyllic little strip of unspoiled coast for anyone fleeing the crowds elsewhere on the island, and inland from here is the unspoiled wooded region around **Aryirádhes**, rarely visited by tourists and a perfect place for quiet walks.

Back on the coastline, the village of **PETRITÍ** fronts onto a small but busy dirt-track harbour, but is mercifully free of noise and commerce; its beach is rock, mud and sand, set among low olive-covered hills. The *Pension Egrypos* (☎0662/51 949; ③) has **rooms** and a **taverna**. At the harbour, three tavernas serve the trickle of sea traffic: the smart *Limnopoula* guarded by caged parrots, and the more basic but friendly *Dimitris* and *Stamatis*. Some way back from the village, near the hamlet of Vassilátika, is the elegant *Regina* **hotel**, with gardens and pool (☎0662/52 132, fax 52 135; ④).

Southern Corfu

Across the island on the west coast, the beach at **ÁYIOS YEÓRYIOS** spreads as far south as Méga Hóro point, and north to encircle the edge of the Korissía lagoon, around 12km of uninterrupted sand. The village itself, however, is an unprepossessing sprawl. British package operators have arrived in force, with bars competing to present bingo, quizzes and video nights. The *Golden Sands* (☎0662/51 225; ⑤) has a pool, open-air restaurant and gardens, but the best **hotel** bargain is the smaller *Blue Sea* (☎0662/51 624, fax 51 172; ③). The most likely place to head for good **rooms** is at the southern end of the strip: the *Barbayiannis* taverna-bar (☎0662/52 110; ③). Besides the Barbayiannis, Áyios Yeóryios has a number of good **restaurants**: *La Perla's* which serves Greek and north European food in a walled garden; the *Napoleon* psistariá; and the *Florida Cove*, with its beachcomber theme. **Nightlife** centres around music and pool bars like the *Gold Hart* and *Traxx*, although the best bar in Áyios Yeóryios is the sea-edge *Panorama*, which has views as far south as Paxí.

A few minutes' walk north of Áyios Yeóryios, **Íssos** is a far better and quieter beach; the dunes north of Íssos are an unofficial nude-bathing area. Facilities around Íssos are sparse: one **taverna**, the *Rousellis Grill* (which sometimes has rooms) a few hundred metres from the beach on the lane leading to Línia on the main road, and the *Friends* snack bar in Línia itself. An English-run **windsurfing school** operates on the beach.

Anyone interested in how a Greek town works away from the bustle of tourism shouldn't miss **LEFKÍMI**, on the island's east coast. The second largest town after Corfu, it's the administrative centre of the south of the island as well as the alternative ferry port to/from Igoumenítsa, and has some fine architecture, including two striking churches: **Áyios Theódoros**, on a mound above a small square, and **Áyios Arsénios**, with a vast orange dome that can be seen for miles. There are some **rooms** at the *Cheeky Face* taverna (☎0661/22 627; ②) and the *Maria Madalena* apartments (☎0661/22 386; ②), both by the bridge over the canal that carries the Himáros River through town. A few **bars** and **restaurants** sit on the edge of the canal – try the *River* psistariá. Away from the centre, the *Hermes* bar has a leafy garden, and there are a number of other good local places where tourists are rare enough to guarantee you a friendly welcome, including the *Mersedes* and *Pacific* bars, and, notably, the *Kavouras* and *Fontana* tavernas.

There are no ambiguities in **KÁVOS**, directly south of Lefkími: either you like 24-hour drinking, clubbing, bungee-jumping, go-karts, video bars named after British sit-coms and chips with almost everything, or you should avoid the resort altogether. Kávos stretches over 2km of decent sandy beach, with watersports galore. This is very much package-tour territory; if you want independent **accommodation**, try Britannia Travel (☎0661/61 400) and Island Holidays (☎0661/23 439), and the nearest to genuine Greek **food** you'll find is at the *Two Brothers* psistariá, at the south end of town. *Future* is still the biggest **club**, with imported north European DJs, followed by *Whispers*. Favourite **bars** include *JCs*, *Jungle*, *The Face* and *Net*, and at night the main drag is one unbroken crowd of young revellers.

Beyond the limits of Kávos, where few visitors stray, a path leaving the road south to the hamlet of Sparterá heads through unspoiled countryside; after around thirty minutes of walking it reaches the cliffs of **Cape Asprókavos** and the crumbling **monastery of Arkoudhílas**. The cape looks out over the straits to Paxí, and down over deserted **Arkoudhílas beach**, which can be reached from Sparterá, 5km by road but only 3km by the signed path from Kávos. Even wilder is **Áyios Górdhis beach**, 3km further on from Sparterá, one of the least visited on the island and not to be confused with the eponymous beach further north.

Corfu's satellite islands

Corfu's three inhabited satellite islands, **Eríkoussa**, **Othoní** and **Mathráki**, in the quintet of **Dhiapóndia islands**, are 20km off the northwest coast. Some travel agencies in the northern resorts offer **day-trips** to Eríkoussa only, often with a barbecue thrown in – fine if you're happy to spend the day on the beach. A trip taking in all three islands from Sidhári or Áyios Stéfanos is excellent value: the islands are between thirty and sixty minutes apart by boat, and most trips allow you an hour on each (longer on sandy Eríkoussa).

Locals use day-trip boats between the islands, so it's possible to pay your way between them. There is also a twice-weekly **ferry** from Corfu Town, the *Alexandros II*, which brings cars and goods to the islands, but given that it has to sail halfway round Corfu first, it's the slowest way to proceed.

Mathráki

Hilly, densely forested and with a long empty beach, beautiful **Mathráki** is the least inhabited of the three islands. The beach begins at the edge of the tiny harbour, and extends south for 3km of fine, dark-red sand, a nesting site for the endangered **loggerhead turtle** (see box on p.834). It's important therefore not to camp anywhere near the beach – and not to make any noise there at night.

A single road rises from the harbour into the interior and the scattered village of **KÁTO MATHRÁKI**, where just one friendly taverna-kafenío-shop overlooks the beach and Corfu. The views are magnificent, as is the sense of isolation. However, construction work above the beach suggests Mathráki is becoming geared towards visitors, and islander Tassos Kassimis (☎0663/71 700; ③) already rents **rooms**. The road continues to the village of **Áno Mathráki**, with its single, old-fashioned kafenío next to the church, but this is beyond walking distance on a day-visit.

Othoní

Six kilometres north, **Othoní** is the largest, and at first sight the least inviting of Corfu's satellite islands. The island has a handful of good tavernas and rooms for rent in its port, **ÁMMOS**, but the reception from islanders who aren't in the tourism trade is rather cool. Ámmos has two beaches, both pebbly, one in its harbour. The village kafenío serves as a very basic shop, and there's one smart **restaurant**, *La Locanda dei Sogni*, which also has **rooms** (☎0663/71 640; ④) – though these tend to be pre-booked by Italian visitors. Three tavernas, *New York*, *Mikros* and tiny *Rainbow*, offer decent but fairly limited menus; the owner of the *New York* also offers rooms for rent (☎0663/71 581; ③). The island's interior is dramatic, and a path up out of the village leads through rocky, tree-covered hills to the central hamlet, **Horió**, after a thirty-minute walk. Horió, like other inland villages, is heavily depopulated – only about sixty people still live on the island through the winter – but it's very attractive, and the architecture is completely traditional.

Eríkoussa

East of Othoní, **Eríkoussa** is the most popular destination for day-trippers. It's invariably hyped as a "desert island" trip, although this is a desert island with a medium-sized hotel, rooms, tavernas and a year-round community. In high season, it gets very busy: Eríkoussa has a large diaspora living in America and elsewhere who return to family homes in their droves in summer, so you may find your *yiá soú* or *kaliméra* returned in a Brooklyn accent.

Eríkoussa has an excellent golden sandy beach right by the harbour, with great swimming, and another, quieter, beach reached by a path across the wooded island interior. The island's cult following keeps its one **hotel**, the *Erikoussa* (☎0663/71 555; ④), busy through the season; rooms are en-suite with balconies and views. Simpler rooms are available from the *Anemomilos* **taverna** (☎0663/71 647; ③). If you're hoping to stay, phoning ahead is essential, as is taking anything you might not be able to buy – the only shop is a snack bar selling basic groceries.

Paxí (Paxos) and Andípaxi

Verdant, hilly and still largely unspoiled, **Paxí (Paxos)** is the smallest of the main Ionian islands. Barely 12km by 4km, it has no sandy beaches, no historical sites, only two hotels and a serious water shortage, yet is so popular it is best avoided in high season. Despite limited ferry connections with Corfu, Igoumenítsa and Párga, it still draws vast crowds, who can make its three harbour villages rather cliquey. It's also popular with yachting flotillas, whose spending habits have brought the island an upmarket reputation, and made it the most expensive place to visit in the Ionian islands (with the possible exception of Fiskárdho on Kefalloniá). There is only one – rather remote – official campsite, due to reopen in 2000 after closure due to infighting, but there are pockets of unauthorized camping. Most accommodation is block-booked by travel companies, though there are local tour operators whose holiday deals are often a fraction of the price. The capital, **Gáïos**, is quite cosmopolitan, with delis and boutiques, but northerly **Lákka** and tiny **Longós** are where hardcore Paxophiles head.

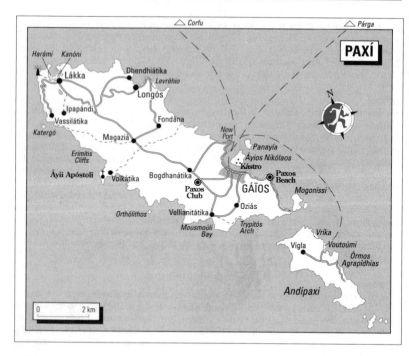

Gáïos

Most visitors arrive at **GÁÏOS**, or at the new port, 1km to the north. Gáïos is a pleasant town built around a small square on the seafront overlooking two islands, Áyios Nikólaos and Panayía. Room owners usually meet ferries, although it's advisable to phone ahead: try Gáïos Travel (☎0661/32 033, fax 32 175), run by the friendly, English-speaking Ioannis Arvanatakis, and Bouas Tours (☎0661/32 401, fax 32 610), both situated on the seafront. Paxí's two seasonal **hotels** are both near Gáïos: the *Paxos Beach Hotel* (☎0661/31 211; ⑨) which has smart en-suite bungalows on a hillside above a pebbly beach 2km south of town, and the fairly luxurious *Paxos Club Hotel* (☎0661/32 450, fax 32 097; ⑥), 2km inland from Gáïos. The island's one (basic) **campsite**, assuming it does reopen, is at Mogoníssi, 45 minutes' walk south (there's no bus), with a taverna above an imported sand beach.

Gáïos boasts a number of decent **tavernas**, the best of them being *Carcoleggio's*, 1.5km out of town towards Bogdhanátika. The menu and wine list are limited, and opening hours unpredictable, but it fills up with islanders who flock for its *souvláki*. Also recommended are the *Blue Grotto*, *Spiro's*, *Dodo's*, inland from the Anemoyiannis statue, and the *Rex* in a side-street off the town square. Of the pricey joints running down one side of the square, the *Volcano* is the best; the kafenía by the ferry ramp and at the bottom of the square are much better bargains. Trendier bars near the square include *Carnayo* and *Red Chairs*. The *Phenix* (sic) disco out by the New Port opens sporadically after midnight and has a terrace for sub-lunar fun, while the inland *Castello* is a more regular disco.

Inland are some of the island's oldest settlements, such as Oziás and Vellianitátika, in prime walking country, but with few if any facilities. Noel Rochford's book,

Landscapes of Paxos (Sunflower), lists dozens of walks, and cartographers Elizabeth and Ian Bleasdale's *Paxos Walking Map* is on sale in most travel agencies.

The rest of the island

Paxí's one main road runs along the spine of the island, with a turning at the former capital Magaziá, leading down to the tiny port of Longós. The main road continues to Lákka, the island's funkiest resort, set in a breathtaking horseshoe bay. Two buses ply the road between Gáïos and Lákka six times a day, most diverting to swing through Longós. The Gáïos–Lákka bus (35min) affords panoramic views, and the route is an excellent walk of under three hours (one way). A taxi between the two costs around 2500dr.

Approached from the south, **LÁKKA** is an unprepossessing jumble of buildings, but once in its maze of alleys and neo-Venetian buildings, or on the quay with views of distant Corfu, you do get a sense of its charm. Lákka's two **beaches**, Harámi and Kanóni, are the best on the island, although there have been complaints in high season of pollution from the yachts that cram the bay. The terraced olive grove behind Kanóni is a favourite with campers but has no facilities. **Accommodation** is plentiful (except in high season) from the island's two biggest agencies: Planos Holidays (☎0661/31 744, fax 31 010) or Routsis (☎0661/31 807, fax 31 161), both on the seafront. The latter runs two bargain rooming houses, *Ilios* and *Lefcothea* (both ②).There's an embarrassment of good tavernas; the friendly *Nionios* and its neighbour *Butterfly*, the *Nautilus*, which has the best view of any Paxiot restaurant, the more upmarket *Pergola* or the exotic *Rosa di Paxos* for a splurge. There's a similar wealth of bars: the lively *Harbour Lights*, the seafront *Romantica* cocktail bar, *Serano's* in the square, or Spyros Petrou's friendly kafenío – the hub of village life. Lákka is also best sited for **walking**: up onto either promontory, to the lighthouse or Vassilátika, or to Longós and beyond. One of the finest walks – if combined with a bus or taxi back – is an early evening visit to the **Erimítis cliffs**, near the hamlet of Voïkátika: on clear afternoons, the cliffs change colour at twilight like a seagoing Ayers Rock.

LONGÓS is the prettiest village on the island, and perfectly sited for morning sun and idyllic alfresco breakfasts. The village is dominated by the upmarket villa crowd, but the Planos office here (☎0661/31 530) is the best place to look for accommodation. It has some of the island's best restaurants: the *Nassos*, with a wide variety of fish and seafood, the seafront *Vassilis*, where you have to squeeze in for the island bus when it rumbles by, and *Kakarantzas*. *To Taxidhi* on the quay is a nice spot for coffee or an early drink, while *Malibu* and *Ores* pander to the night-owls.

Longós has a small, scruffy beach, with sulphur springs favoured by local grannies, but most people swim off Levréhio beach in the next bay south, which gets the occasional camper. (Islanders are touchy about camping for fear of fires; it's politic to ask at the beach taverna if it's acceptable to camp.) Longós is at the bottom of a steep winding hill, making **walking** a chore, but the short circle around neighbouring **Dhendhiátika** provides excellent views, and the walk to **Fondána** and **Magaziá** can be done to coincide with a bus back to Longós.

Andípaxi

A mile south of Paxí, its tiny sibling **Andípaxi** has scarcely any accommodation and no facilities beyond several beach tavernas open during the day in season. The sandy, bluewater coves have been compared with the Caribbean, but you'll have to share them with kaïkia and sea taxis from all three villages, plus larger craft from Corfu (boats from Paxí may also take you to its sea stacks and caves, the most dramatic in the Ionian islands).

Boats basically deposit you either at the sandy **Vríka beach** or the longer pebble beach of **Vatoúmi**. Vríka has a taverna at each end, of which *Spiros* (☎0662/31 172) has good food and can arrange self-catering accommodation up in **Vígla**, the island's hilltop settlement, on a weekly basis. Vatoúmi's only facility is the justifiably named *Bella Vista*, perched on a cliff high above the beach.

For a swim in quieter surroundings the trick is to head south away from the pleasure-craft moorings, although path widening has made even the quieter bays more accessible. Paths also lead inland to connect the handful of homes and the southerly lighthouse, but there are no beaches of any size on Andípaxi's western coastline and thick thorny scrub makes it difficult to approach. In low season, there's also the risk of bad weather keeping pleasure craft in port and stranding you on the island.

Lefkádha (Lefkas)

Lefkádha is an oddity. Connected to the mainland by a long causeway through lagoons, it barely feels like an island, at least on the busier eastern side – and historically in fact it isn't. It is separated from the mainland by a canal cut by Corinthian colonists in the seventh century BC, which has been re-dredged (after silting up) on various occasions since, and today is spanned by a thirty-metre boat-drawbridge built in 1986. Lefkádha was long an important strategic base, and approaching the causeway you pass a series of fortresses, climaxing in the fourteenth-century castle of **Santa Maura** – the Venetian name for the island. These defences were too close to the mainland to avoid an Ottoman tenure, which began in 1479, but the Venetians wrested back control a couple of centuries later. They were in turn overthrown by Napoleon in 1797 and then the British took over as Ionian protectors in 1810. It wasn't until 1864 that Lefkádha, like the rest of the Ionian archipelago, was reunited with Greece.

At first glance Lefkádha is not overwhelmingly attractive, although it is a substantial improvement on the mainland just opposite. The whiteness of its rock strata – *lefkás* has the same root as *lefkós*, "white" – is often brutally exposed by road cuts and quarries, and the highest ridge is bare except for ugly military and telecom installations. With the marshes and sumpy inlets on the east coast, mosquitoes can be a midsummer problem. On the other hand, the island is a fertile place, supporting cypresses, olive groves and vineyards, particularly on the western slopes, and life in the mountain villages remains relatively untouched, with the older women still wearing traditional local dress – two skirts (one forming a bustle), a dark headscarf and a rigid bodice.

Lefkádha has been the home of various literati, including two prominent Greek poets, Angelos Sikelianos and Aristotelis Valaoritis, and the short-story writer Lafcadio Hearn, son of American missionaries. Support for the arts continues in the form of a well-attended international **festival** of theatre and folk-dancing, now extended throughout the summer, with most events staged in the Santa Maura castle. On a smaller scale, frequent village celebrations accompanied by *bouzoúki* and clarinet ensure that the strong local wine flows well into the early hours.

Lefkádha remains relatively undeveloped, with just two major resorts: **Vassilikí**, in its vast bay in the south, claims to be Europe's biggest windsurf centre; **Nydhrí**, on the east coast, overlooks the island's picturesque archipelago, and is the launching point for the barely inhabited island of **Meganíssi**.

Lefkádha Town and around

Lefkádha Town sits at the island's northernmost tip, hard by the causeway. Like other southerly capitals, it was hit by the earthquakes of 1948 and 1953, and the town was devastated, with the exception of a few **Italianate churches**. As a precaution against further quakes, little was rebuilt above two storeys, and most houses acquired second storeys of wood, giving the western dormitory area an unintentionally quaint look. The town is small – you can cross it on foot in little over ten minutes – and despite the

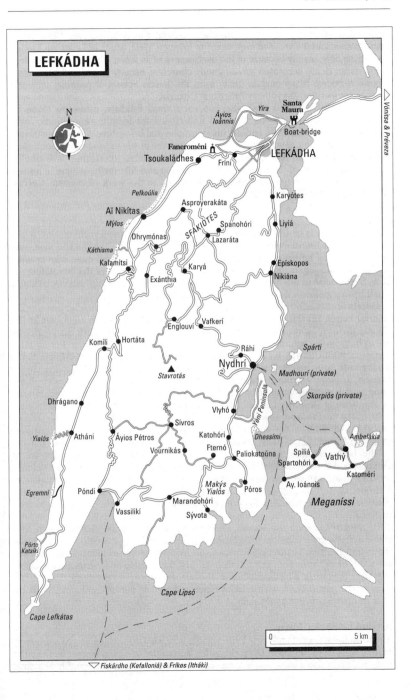

LEFKÁDHA

N

Yíra Santa Maura

Áyios Ioánnis Boat-bridge

Faneroméni LEFKÁDHA
Tsoukaládhes Fríni

Pefkoúlia Karyótes

Asproyerakáta
Aï Nikítas *SFAKIÓTES* Spanohóri Liyiá
Mýlos
Dhrymónas Lazaráta

Káthisma
Kalamítsi Episkopos
Karyá Nikiána
Exánthia

Englouví Vafkerí

Komíli Hortáta Ráhi *Spárti*

▲ Nydhrí
Stavrotás *Madhourí (private)*

Skorpiós (private)

Dhrágano Vlyhó *Ambelákia*

Yialós Athání Sívros Spiliá Vathý
Áyios Pétros Katohóri Spartohóri
Vournikás Fternó Katoméri
Paliokatoúna
Egremní Póndi *Makýs* Póros Ay. Ioánnis
Yialós Marandohóri *Meganíssi*
Vassilikí Sývota

Pórto Katsíki

Cape Lipsó

Cape Lefkátas

Yéni Peninsula
Dhessími

0   5 km

△ *Vónitsa & Préveza*

▽ *Fiskárdho (Kefalloniá) & Fríkes (Itháki)*

destruction still very attractive, especially around the main square, Platía Ayíou Spyridhónos, and the arcaded high street of Ioánnou Méla. Much of Lefkádha Town is pedestrian-only, mainly because of the narrowness of its lanes. The centre boasts over half a dozen richly decorated private family churches, usually locked and best visited around services. Many contain gems from the Ionian School of painting, including work by its founder, Zakynthian Panayiotis Doxaras.

The alleys off Ioánnou Méla also conceal a small **folklore museum** (Mon–Fri 9am–9pm; 200dr), which you may still find closed for lengthy renovations, and a museum/shop dedicated to antique phonographs and bric-a-brac. On the northwestern seafront a brand new Cultural Centre houses the newly expanded **archeological museum** (Tues–Sun 8am–2.30pm; free), which contains interesting, well-labelled displays on aspects of daily life, religious worship and funerary customs in ancient times, as well as a room on prehistory dedicated to the work of eminent German archaeologist Wilhelm Dörpfeld.

Practicalities

The **bus station** is on Odhós Dhimítri Golémi opposite the small yacht marina. It now has services to almost every village on the island, and Nydhrí, Vassilikí and west coast beaches such as Káthisma have extensive daily services. Car and motorbike rental is useful for exploring; try EuroHire, Golémi 5 (☎0645/267 76), near the bus station or I Love Santas next to the *Xenia* hotel. Most resorts have bicycle hire outlets, although you'll need stamina to do any more than local touring.

Hotels are actually dwindling in Lefkádha Town, and currently number just six. The smarter hotels, like the stylish seafront *Nirikos*, Ayías Mávras (☎0645/24 132, fax 23 756; ④) and the cosy *Santa Maura*, Spyridhónos Viánda 2 (☎0645/21 308-9, fax 26 253; ④) are in busy areas, but are glazed against the noise and heat. The *Lefkas*, Pétrou Filípa Panáyou (☎0645/23 916, fax 24 579; ⑥) and *Xenia*, Panágou 2 (☎0645/24 762, fax 25 129; ④) are both large hotels. The *Patras*, Platía Áyiou Spyridhónos (☎0645/22 359; ③) is a bargain, as is the *Byzantio*, Dörpfeld 40 (☎& fax 0645/21 315; ②); both are small and basic, and in very busy and noisy areas of town. There are basic **rooms** in the dormitory area west of Dörpfeld: the Lefkádha Room Owners Association (☎0674/21 266) can help, or try the *Pinelopis Rooms* (☎0645/24 175; ②) in Odhós Pinelópis, off the seafront two short blocks from the pontoon bridge. Lefkádha Town has no campsite, although there are decent sites at Karyótes and Epískopos, a few kilometres to the south.

The best **restaurants** are hidden in the backstreets: the *Reganto* taverna, on Dhimárhou Venióti is the local favourite, but opening hours can be erratic. If it's closed, head for the *Lighthouse*, in its own small garden on Filarmonikís. The *Romantika* on Mitropóleos has nightly performances of Lefkadhan *kantádhes*, while the smartest place in town is the *Adriatica*, Faneroménis and Merarhías, where people tend to dress up to eat.

Of the **bars** in the main square, the *Thalassina* ouzerí is the cheapest, with occasional evening entertainment from buskers, jugglers and even fire-eaters. Further from the action the best is the *Cafe Karfakis*, on Ioánnou Melá, an old-style kafenío with splendid mezédhes. The most stylish bar is the hard-to-find *Vengera*, on Odhós Maxáïra, signposted a block down from the bus station, set in a shady garden and with a hip music policy. The town's outdoor **cinema**, Eleni, on Faneroménis, has two showings and programmes change daily.

Around Lefkádha Town

The town has a decent and fairly large shingle beach across the lagoon at **Yíra**, a forty-minute walk from the top of Dörpfeld, either across the bridge or along Sikelianoú. In season there's also a bus (hourly 10am–2pm) from the bus station. Roughly 4km long, the beach is often virtually deserted even in high season; there's a **taverna** at either end, and at the western end a couple of **bars** in the renovated windmills, as well as the trendy *Club Milos*.

The uninhabited **Faneroméni monastery** (daily 8am–2pm & 4–8pm; free) is reached by any of the west-coast buses, or on foot from town (30min) through the hamlet of Fríni. There's a small museum and chapel, and an ox's yoke and hammer, used when Nazi occupiers forbade the use of bells. There are wonderful views over the town and lagoon from the Fríni road.

The island's **interior**, best reached by bus or car from Lefkádha Town, offers imposing mountainscapes and excellent walking between villages only a few kilometres apart. **KARYÁ** is its centre, with a hotel, the *Karia Village Hotel* (☎0645/41 004; ④), tucked away above the village, and some rooms: try Haritini Vlahou (☎0645/41 634; ②), the Kakiousis family (☎0645/61 136; ②), Olga Lazari (☎0645/61 547; ③) or Michael Halikias (☎0645/61 026; ③). The leafy town square has a popular taverna, *Iy Klimataria*, just off the platía and two psistariés on it, *Ta Platania*, and the smarter *O Rousos*. Karyá is the centre of the island's lace and weaving industry, with a fascinating small **museum** set in a lacemaker's home. The historic villages of **Vafkerí** and **Englouví** are within striking distance, with the west-coast hamlets of **Dhrymónas** and **Exánthia** a hike over the hills.

The east coast to Vassilikí

Lefkádha's east coast is the most accessible and the most developed part of the island. Apart from the campsites at Karyótes (*Kariotes Beach,* ☎0645/71 103) and Epískopos (*Episcopos Beach,* ☎0645/71 388), there's little point stopping before the small fishing ports of **LIYIÁ**, which has some rooms and the hotel *Konaki* (☎& fax 0645 71 127; ⑥), or **NIKIÁNA**, where you'll find the hotel *Pegasus* (☎0645/71 766, fax 25 290; ⑥) and the smarter but considerably cheaper *Ionion* (☎0645/71 721; ⑤), as well as the *Porto Fino* pension (☎ 0645/ 71 389; ③). Nikiána also has a selection of fine tavernas, notably the *Pantazis*, which also has rooms to let and the *Lefko Akroyiali*, a good fish restaurant further south. Beaches here tend to be pebbly and small.

Most package travellers will find themselves in **NYDHRÍ**, the coast's biggest resort with ferry connections to Meganíssi and myriad **boat trips** around the nearby satellite islands. The German archeologist Wilhelm Dörpfeld believed Nydhrí, rather than Itháki, to be the site of Odysseus's capital, and did indeed find Bronze Age tombs on the plain nearby. His theory identifying ancient Ithaca with Lefkádha fell into disfavour after his death in 1940, although his obsessive attempts to give the island some status over its neighbour are honoured by a statue on Nydhrí's quay. Dörpfeld's tomb is tucked away at Ayía Kyriakí on the opposite side of the bay, near the house in which he once lived, visible just above the chapel and lighthouse on the far side of the water.

Nydhrí is an average resort, with some good pebble beaches and a lovely setting, but the centre is an ugly strip with heavy traffic. The best place to stay is the *Hotel Gorgona* (☎0645/92 197, fax 92 268; ④), set in a lush garden away from the traffic a minute along the Ráhi road, which leads to Nydhrí's very own **waterfall**, a forty-five minute walk inland. There are also rooms in the centre – try Emilios Gazis (☎0645/92 703; ③) and Athanasios Konidharis (☎0645/92 749; ④). The town's focus is the Aktí Aristotéli Onássi quay, where most of the rather ritzy **restaurants** and **bars** are found. The *Barrel* and *Il Sappore* restaurants are recommended, as is the *Agra* on the beach. However, eating is better value on the noisy main drag – try *Agrabeli* or *Ta Kalamia*. Nightlife centres around bars like *No Name* and *Byblos*, and the late-night *Status* or *Sail Inn Club*.

Nydhrí sits at the mouth of a deep inlet stretching to the next village, somnolent **VLYHÓ**, with a few good tavernas and mooring for yachts. Over the Yéni peninsula across the inlet is the large **Dhessími Bay**, home to two adjacent campsites: *Santa Maura Camping* (☎0645/95 007, fax 26 087), and *Dessimi Beach Camping* (☎0645/95 374), right on the beach but often packed with outsized mobile homes.

The coast road beyond Vlyhó turns inland and climbs the foothills of Mount Stavrotás, through the hamlets of Katohóri and Paliokatoúna to **Póros**, a quiet village with few facilities. Just south of here is the increasingly busy beach resort of **MAKRÝS YIALÓS**. It boasts a handful of **tavernas**, a few rooms at *Oceanis Studios* (☎and fax 0654/95 095; ③), plus the upmarket *Poros Beach Camping* (☎0654/23 203, fax 95 152), which has bungalows (④), shops and a pool. Try the *Rouda Bay* taverna opposite the beach, which also has rooms (☎ 0645/ 95 634; ⑤).

Along the main road, walkers and drivers are recommended to take the panoramic detour to quiet **Voúrnika** and **Sývros** (the Lefkádha–Vassilíki bus also visits), which both have tavernas and some private rooms. It's around 14km to the next resort, the fjord-like inlet of **SÝVOTA**, 2km down a steep hill (bus twice daily). There's no beach except for a remote cove, but some fine fish tavernas: the *Ionion* is the most popular, but the *Delfinia* and *Kavos* are also good. Thomas Skliros (☎0645/31 151; ③) at the furthest supermarket has a few **rooms**, and there's a basic unofficial campsite by the bus stop at the edge of the village.

Beyond the Sývota turning, the mountain road dips down towards Kondárena, almost a suburb of **VASSILIKÍ**, the island's premiere watersports resort. Winds in the huge bay draw vast numbers of windsurfers, with light morning breezes for learners and tough afternoon blasts for advanced surfers. Booking your **accommodation** ahead is mandatory in high season. The *Paradise* (☎0645/32 156; ③), a basic but friendly hotel overlooking the small rocky beach beyond the ferry dock, is the best bargain. Also good value for its class is the neighbouring upmarket *Hotel Apollo* (☎0645/31 122, fax 31 142; ④). In the centre of town, the two main hotels are the smart and reasonably priced *Vassiliki Bay Hotel* (☎0645/ 31 458, fax 23 567; ⑤) and the *Hotel Lefkatas* (☎0645/31 801, fax 31 804; ⑤), a large, modern building overlooking the busiest road in town. Rooms and apartments are available along the beach road to Póndi: *Billy's House* (☎0645/31 418; ④), *Christina Politi's Rooms* (☎0645/31 440; ④) and the *Samba Pension* (☎0645/31 555; ④) are smart and purpose-built, though not particularly cheap. The largest of the three beach windsurf centres, Club Vassiliki, offers all-in **windsurf tuition** and accommodation deals. Vassilikí's only **campsite**, the large *Camping Vassiliki Beach* (☎0645/31 308, fax 31 458), is about 500m along the beach road; it has its own restaurant, bar and shop.

Vassilikí's pretty quayside is lined with tavernas and bars, notably the *Dolphin Psistaria*, the glitzier *Restaurant Miramare*, the *Penguin* and *Alexander*, which includes a Chinese menu. One of the cheapest places to drink on the entire island is *Livanakis* kafenío next to the bakery. Flyers sometimes advertise **raves** on the beach at Pórto Katsíki.

The beach at Vassilikí is stony and poor, but improves 1km on at tiny **PÓNDI**; most non-windsurfers however, use the daily kaïki trips to nearby Ayiófili or around Cape Lefkátas to the superior beaches at Pórto Katsíki and Egremní on the sandy west coast. There's a gradually increasing amount of accommodation at Póndi, some with great views of the bay and plain behind, particularly from the terrace of the *Ponti Beach Hotel* (☎0645/31 572, fax 31 576; ⑤), which is very popular with holidaying Greeks, and has a restaurant and bar open to non-residents. The *Nefeli* (☎ 0645/ 31 515; ④), right on the beach, is better value though.

The west coast

Tsoukaládhes, just 6km from Lefkádha, is developing a roadside tourism business, but better beaches lie a short distance to the south, so there's very little reason to stay here. Four kilometres on, the road plunges down to the sand-and-pebble **Pefkoúlia beach**, one of the longest on the island, with a taverna at the north end, *Oinilos*, that has rooms, and unofficial camping down at the other end, about 2km away.

Jammed into a gorge between Pefkoúlia and the next beach, Mýlos, is **AÏ NIKÍTAS**, the prettiest resort on Lefkádha, a jumble of lanes and small wooden buildings. The back of the village is a dust-blown car park, which detracts from the appeal of the pleasant, if basic, *O Aï Nikitas* **campsite** (☎0645/97 301, fax 21 173), set in terraced olive groves. The most attractive **accommodation** is in the *Pension Ostria* (☎0645/97 483, fax 97 300; ⑤), a beautiful blue and white building above the village decorated in a mix of beachcomber and ecclesiastical styles. Other options are in the alleys that run off the main drag; the best bets are the *Pansion Aphrodite* (☎0645/97 372; ③), the small *Hotel Selene* (☎0645/97 369; ④) and quieter *Olive Tree* (☎0645/97 453; ④). Best tavernas include the *Sapfo* fish taverna by the sea and the *T'Agnantia*, just above the main street.

Sea taxis (400dr one way) ply between Aï Nikítas and **Mýlos** beach, or it's a 45-minute walk (or bus ride) to the most popular beach on the coast, **Káthisma**, a shadeless kilometre of fine sand. There are two tavernas on the beach: the barn-like *Kathisma Beach* (☎ 0645/ 97 050, fax 97 335; ⑥) with smart apartments, and the *Akroyiali*. Above the beach the *Sunset* has **rooms** (☎0645/97 488; ④). Beyond Káthisma, hairpin bends climb the flank of Mount Méga towards the tiny village of **KALAMÍTSI**, where Spyros Karelis (☎0645/99 214; ②) and Spyros Veryinis (☎0645/99 411; ②) have rooms. *Hermes* (☎0645/99 417; ②), the *Blue and White House* (☎0645/99 413; ②) and *Pansion Nontas* (☎0645/99 451; ③) have larger rooms and apartments. There are also three good tavernas: the *Paradeisos* in its own garden with fountain, the more basic *Ionio* and, just north of the village, the aptly titled *Panorama View*. Three kilometres down a newly paved road is the village's quiet sandy beach, effectively the southern extension of Káthisma.

South of Kalamítsi, past the hamlets of Hortáta, which boasts the excellent *Lygos* taverna with rooms (☎ 0645/33 395; ②), and Komíli, the landscape becomes almost primeval. At 38km from Lefkádha Town, **ATHÁNI** is Lefkádha's most remote spot to stay, with a couple of good tavernas which both have rooms: the *Panorama* (☎0645/33 291; ②) and *O Alekos* (☎0656/33 484; ③).

The road continues 14km to barren **Cape Lefkátas**, which drops abruptly 75 metres into the sea. Byron's Childe Harold sailed past this point, and "saw the evening star above, Leucadia's far projecting rock of woe: And hail'd the last resort of fruitless love". The fruitless love is a reference to Sappho, who in accordance with the ancient legend that you could cure yourself of unrequited love by leaping into these waters, leapt – and died. In her honour the locals termed the place *Kávos tís Kyrás* ("Lady's Cape"), and her act was imitated by the lovelorn youths of Lefkádha for centuries afterwards. And not just by the lovelorn, for the act (known as *katapondismós*) was performed annually by scapegoats – always a criminal or a lunatic – selected by priests from the Apollo temple whose sparse ruins lie close by. Feathers and even live birds were attached to the victims to slow their descent and boats waiting below took the chosen one, dead or alive, away to some place where the evil banished with them could do no further harm. The rite continued into the Roman era, when it degenerated into little more than a fashionable stunt by decadent youth. These days, Greek hang-gliders hold a tournament from the cliffs every July. A turning before the cape leads down an asphalted road to the dramatic twin beach of **Pórto Katsíki**, where there are a couple of large canteens on the cliff above.

Lefkádha's satellites

Lefkádha has four satellite islands clustered off its east coast, although only one, **Meganíssi**, the largest and most interesting, is accessible. **Skorpiós**, owned by the

Onassis family, fields armed guards to deter visitors. **Madhourí**, owned by the family of poet Nanos Valaorítis, is private and similarly off-limits, while tiny **Spárti** is a large scrub-covered rock. Day-trips from Nydhrí skirt all three islands, and some stop to allow swimming in coves.

Meganíssi

MEGANÍSSI, twenty minutes by frequent daily ferries from Nydhrí, is a large island with few facilities but a magical, if bleak landscape, a situation that's made it a favourite with island aficionados. Ferries stop first below **SPARTOHÓRI**, an immaculate village with whitewashed buildings and an abundance of bougainvillea. The locals – many returned émigrés from Australia – live from farming and fishing and are genuinely welcoming. You arrive at a jetty on a pebble beach with a few tavernas and a primitive but free (for a night or two only) campsite behind the *Star Taverna*. The village proper boasts three restaurants: a pizza place called the *Tropicana*, which can direct you to **rooms** (☎0645/51 486; ②–③), the *Gakias* and the traditional taverna *Lakis*. Further west round the coast at Áyios Yiánnis there is a good beach with a taverna and possible future campsite.

The attractive inland village of **KATOMÉRI** is an hour's walk through magnificent country. It has the island's one **hotel**, the *Meganissi*, a comfortable place with a restaurant (☎0645/51 240, fax 51 639; ③), and a few bars. Ten minutes' walk downhill is the main port of **VATHÝ**, with some accommodation (*Different Studios*: ☎0645/22 170; ③) and the island's best restaurants, notably the waterside taverna, *Porto Vathi*, which Lefkádhans flock to on ferries for Sunday lunch. After the high-season madness of Nydhrí, Meganíssi's unspoiled landscape is a tonic, and it's easy to organize a **day-trip** from Nydhrí, getting off at Spartohóri, walking to Katoméri for lunch at the *Meganisi*, and catching a ferry back from Vathý. Paths lead from Katoméri to remote beaches, including popular **Ambelákia**, but these aren't accessible on a day-trip.

Kefalloniá

Kefalloniá is the largest of the Ionian islands – a place that has real towns as well as resorts. Like its neighbours, Kefalloniá was overrun by Italians and Germans in World War II; the "handover" after Italy's capitulation in 1943 led to the massacre of five thousand Italian troops on the island by invading German forces. These events form a key episode in Louis de Bernières' novel, *Captain Corelli's Mandolin*, a tragicomic epic of life on the island from before the war to the present day.

Until the late 1980s, the island paid scant regard to tourism; perhaps this was in part a feeling that Kefalloniá could not easily be marketed. Virtually all of its towns and villages were levelled in the 1953 earthquake, and these masterpieces of Venetian architecture had been the one touch of elegance in a severe, mountainous landscape. A more likely explanation, however, for the island's late emergence on the Greek tourist scene is the Kefallonians' legendary reputation for insular pride and stubbornness.

Having decided on the advantages of an easily exploitable industry, however, Kefalloniá is at present in the midst of a tourism boom. Long favoured by Italians, it has begun attracting British package companies, for whom a new airport terminal has been constructed, while virtually every decent beach has been endowed with restaurants. There are definite attractions here, with some beaches as good as any in the Ionian islands, and a fine (if pricey) local wine, the dry white *Rombola*. Moreover, the island seems able to soak up a lot of people without feeling at all crowded, and the magnificent scenery can speak for itself, the escarpments culminating in the 1632-metre bulk of **Mount Énos**, declared a national park to protect the fir trees (*Abies cephalonica*) named after the island.

Kefalloniá **airport** is 7km south of the capital, Argostóli; there are no airport buses, so you'll have to resort to an overpriced taxi. The **bus** system is basic but expanding, and with a little legwork it can be used to get you almost anywhere on the island. Key routes connect Argostóli with Sámi, Fiskárdho, Skála and Póros. There's a useful connection from Sámi to the tiny resort of **Ayía Evfimía**, which attracts many package travellers. Using a motorbike, take care as the terrain is very rough in places – although an increasing number of roads are being surfaced – and the gradients can sometimes be a bit challenging for underpowered machines. The island has a plethora of **ferry** connections, principally from Fiskárdho to Lefkádha and Itháki, and from Sámi to Lefkádha, Itháki and the mainland, as well as links to Zákynthos, Kyllíni and Pátra.

Sámi and around

Most boats dock at the large and functional port town of **SÁMI**, built and later rebuilt near the south end of the Itháki straits, more or less on the site of ancient Sami. This was the capital of the island in Homeric times, when Kefalloniá was part of Ithaca's maritime kingdom: today the administrative hierarchy is reversed, Itháki being considered the backwater. With ferries to many points of the Ionian islands, and several companies introducing direct links to Italy, the town is clearly preparing itself for a burgeoning future. The long sandy beach that stretches round the bay is quite adequate; 2km beyond ancient Sami, lies a fine pebble beach, **Andísami**.

The town has two smart **hotels**: the *Sami Beach* (☎0674/22 802, fax 22 846; ⑥), actually situated at the far end of the beach in Karavómylos, and the quieter *Pericles* (☎0674/22 780, fax 22 787; ⑤), over a kilometre along the Argostóli road, which has extensive grounds, two pools and sports facilities. The best mid-range bet is the *Ionion* (☎0674/22 035; ③), followed by the *Melissani* (☎0674/22 464; ④), both behind the seafront; on the front itself the *Kastro* (☎ 0674/22 282; ⑤) is very comfortable. The *Kyma* (☎0674/22 064; ③) on Platía Kýprou is a tarted up old-fashioned hotel and rather overpriced. Both *períptera* on the quay offer rooms, as do a variety of private homes a few blocks back from the front. Sámi's **campsite**, *Camping Karavomilos Beach* (☎0674/22 480, fax 22 932), has over 300 well-shaded spaces, a taverna, shop and bar, and opens onto the beach. It is by far the better of the island's two official sites.

Sámi doesn't have a great many **tavernas** beyond those on the seafront; visitors tend to go to the smart *Adonis Restaurant* or the *Delfinia*, but a cheaper and more genuine choice is *O Faros,* which serves a good selection of veg and meat dishes, including the famous local meat pie. Best of all, though, is *To Karnagio,* further towards the beach, where you can sample succulent grilled meat, oven dishes and good local wine. The *Riviera* and *Aqua Marina* are the favourite **bars** in the evenings, while the best place for a snack breakfast or ice cream is *Captain Jimmy's.*

The Dhrogaráti and Melissáni caves

The one good reason to stay in Sámi is its proximity to the Drogharáti and Melissáni caves; the former 5km out of town towards Argostóli, the latter 3km north towards Ayía Efimía. A very impressive stalagmite-bedecked chamber, **Dhrogaráti** (April–Oct daily 8am–9pm; 1000dr) is occasionally used for concerts thanks to its marvellous acoustics – Maria Callas once sang here. **Melissáni** (8am–sunset; 1200dr) is partly submerged in brackish water which, amazingly, emerges from an underground fault which leads the whole way under the island to a point near Argostóli. At that point, known as Katavóthres, the sea gushes endlessly into a subterranean channel – and, until the 1953 earthquake disrupted it – the current was used to drive sea mills. That the water, now as then, still ends up in the cave has been shown with fluorescent tracer dye. The beautiful textures and shades created by the light pouring through the collapsed roof of the cave make it a must.

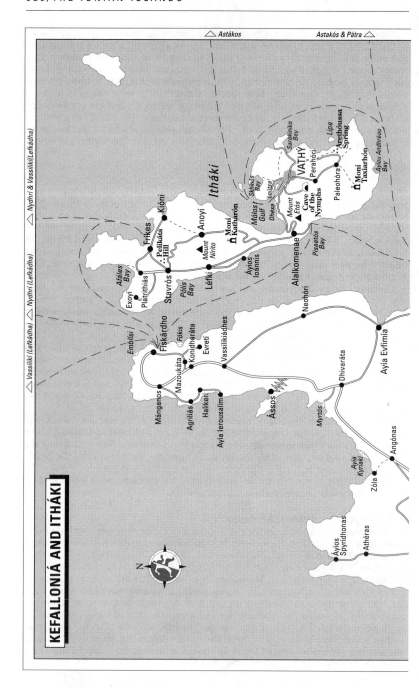

KEFALLONIÁ AND ITHÁKI

△ *Vassilíki (Lefkádha)* △ *Nydhri (Lefkádha)* △ *Nydhri & Vassilíki (Lefkádha)*

Ithaki

Kióni

Anoyí

Frikes

Moní
Katharón

Pelikáta
Hill

Mount
Nirito

Afáles
Bay

Exoyí   Platrithiás

Stavrós

Áyios
Ioánnis

Léfki

Póhis
Bay

Sarakiniko
Bay

Lípa

Arethoússa
Spring

Áyiou Andhréou
Bay

VATHY

Perahóri

Moní
Taxiarhón

Paleohóra

Stylinós
Bay

Mólos
Gulf

Cave
of the
Nymphs

Dhexá
Skhinos

Mount
Étós

Pisaetós
Bay

Alalkomenae

Neohóri

Fiskárdho

Fókis

Emblisi

Konidharáta

Evretí

Vassilikádhes

Dhivaráta

Ayía Evfimía

Mánganos

Mazoukáta

Agriliás

Halkeri

Ayía Ierousalim

Ássos

Myrtós

Angónas

Ayía
Kyriakí

Zóla

Áyios
Spyridhonas

Athéras

N

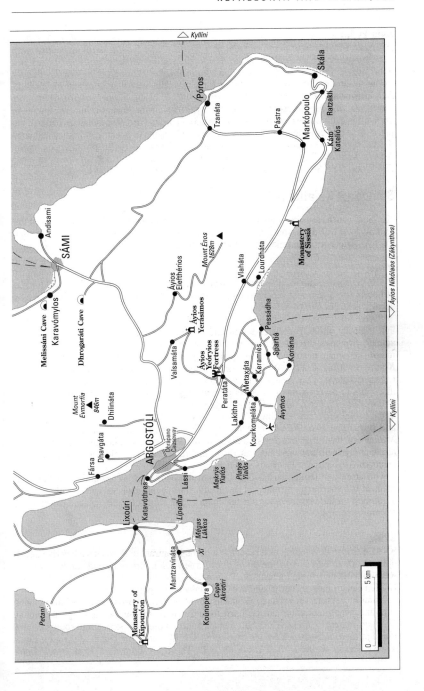

Ayía Evfimía

AYÍA EVFIMÍA, 9km north of Sámi, is a friendly little fishing harbour popular with package operators, yet with no major developments. Its two drawbacks are its beaches – the largest, Paradise Beach, is around 20m of shingle, although there are other coves to the south – and its poor connections (only two daily buses to Sámi and Fiskárdho). **Accommodation** here is good at two small, smart **hotels**: *Pilaros* (☎0674/61 800, fax 61 801; ⑥) and *Moustakis* (☎ & fax 0674/61 030; ④) or the decent-value apartments of Yerasimos Raftopoulos (☎0674/61 233, fax 61 216; ③). The *Dendrinos* **taverna** is the place for island cuisine; the *Pergola* also has a wide range of island specialities and standard Greek dishes. Hipsters head for the *Cafe Triton* at night, philhellenes to the *Asteria* kafenío. The town's night club is *Paranoia*, 700m out of town towards Fiskárdho. The *Strawberry* zaharoplastío is the place for a decadent breakfast.

Southeast Kefalloniá

Heading **southeast from Sámi** has been made a lot easier by the completion of the asphalt road to **Póros** and the consequent addition of a twice-daily bus route between the two. Another route links Póros to **Skála** along the recently paved coastal road.

Póros

PÓROS was one the island's earliest developed resorts, and shows it. Its small huddle of hotels and apartment blocks is almost unique on Kefalloniá, and not enhanced by a scruffy seafront and thin, pebbly beach.

Póros does, however, have a regular ferry link to **Kyllíni** on the mainland, a better link than the one to remote **Astakós** and a viable alternative to Sámi–Pátra. Póros is actually two bays: the first, where most tourists are based, and the actual harbour, a few minutes over the headland. There's plenty of rooms, apartments and a few **hotels**. The *Kefalos* (☎0674/72 139; ④) has en-suite rooms on the seafront, while the elegant *Odysseus Palace* in the centre of town (☎0674/72 036, fax 72 148; ⑥) has offered good discounts in recent summers. Among **travel agents**, Poros Travel by the ferry dock (☎0674/72 476, fax 72 069) offers a range of accommodation, as well as services such as car rental and ferry bookings. The main seafront has the majority of the **restaurants** and **bars**. The *Fotis Family* taverna serves good food in a pleasant setting and the *Mythos* café has Internet access. At night, however, the old port is quieter and has more atmosphere, with tavernas such as *Tzivas* and the *Dionysus*, which are strong on local seafood.

The aforementioned road twists 12km around the rocky coastline from Póros to Skála at the southern extremity of the island. It's a lovely, isolated route, with scarcely a building on the way, save for a small chapel, 3km short of Skála, next to the ruins of a **Roman temple**.

Skála

SKÁLA is also developing as a resort, but in total contrast to Póros it's a low-rise development set among handsome pines above a few kilometres of good sandy beach. A **Roman villa** and some mosaics were excavated here in the 1950s, near the site of the Golden Beach Palace rooms, and are open daily to the public.

Its faithful return crowd keep Skála busy until well after Póros has closed for the season, and accommodation can be hard to find. There are studios and apartments at *Dionysus Rooms* (☎0671/83 283; ③), a block south of the high street, and rooms can be found at the *Golden Beach Palace* (☎0671/83 327; ③) above the beach or through Etam Travel Service (☎0671/83 101, fax 83 142). The more upmarket *Tara Beach Hotel*

(☎0671/83 250, fax 83 344; ⑥) has rooms and individual bungalows in lush gardens on the edge of the beach. Skála boasts a number of good **restaurants**: the *Pines*, the *Flamingo*, and, on the beach, the *Paspalis* and *Sunset*. Drinkers head for *The Loft* cocktail **bar** and the beach-side *Pikiona* pool-bar.

Skála to Lourdháta

Some of the finest sandy beaches on the island are just beyond Skála below the village of Ratzákli, and around the growing micro-resort of **KÁTO KATELIÓS**, which already has couple of hotels: the smart *Odyssia* (☎0671/81 615, fax 81 614; ⑤) and the German-dominated *Galini Resort* (☎0671/81 582; ⑤). There are also some self-contained **apartments** available through the stylish *Arbouro* **taverna** (☎0671/81 192; ③) or the beach-side *Faros* taverna (☎0671/81 355; ③). There is now a row of around half a dozen restaurants and cafés at the seafront. However, the coast around Káto Kateliós is also Kefalloniá's key breeding ground for the **loggerhead turtle** (see box on p.834). Camping is discouraged and would, anyway, strand you miles from any facilities.

At the inland village of **MARKÓPOULO**, claimed by some to be the birthplace of homophonous explorer Marco Polo, the **Assumption of the Virgin festival** (August 15) is celebrated in unique style at the local church with small, harmless snakes with cross-like markings on their heads. Each year, so everyone hopes, they converge on the site to be grasped to the bosoms of the faithful; a few, in fact, are kept by the priests for those years when they don't naturally arrive. The celebrants are an interesting mix of locals and gypsies – some of whom come over from the mainland for the occasion. It's quite a spectacle.

The coastline is largely inaccessible until the village of **VLAHÁTA**, which has some rooms – *Maria Studios* (☎0671/31 055; ③) – and a good taverna, the *Dionysus*, but you're better off continuing to **LOURDHÁTA**, 2km to the south. It has a fine one-kilometre shingle beach and a couple of **tavernas** on a tiny plane-shaded village square – the *New World* and the *Diamond* – as well as the smarter *Spiros* steak and grill house above. *Adonis* (☎0671/31 206; ④) and *Ramona* (☎0671/31 032; ③) have **rooms** just outside the village on the approach road, while the one **hotel**, the *Lara* (☎0671/31 157, fax 31 156; ⑤), towards the beach, has en-suite rooms with sea views and a pool.

Argostóli and around

ARGOSTÓLI, Kefalloniá's capital, is a large and thriving town, virtually a city, with a marvellous site on a bay within a bay. The stone bridge, connecting the two sides of the inner bay, was initially constructed by the British in 1813. A small obelisk remains, but the plaque commemorating "the glory of the British Empire" has disappeared. The town was totally rebuilt after the earthquake but has an enjoyable street life that remains defiantly Greek, especially during the evening vólta around Platía Metaxá – the nerve centre of town.

The **Korgialenio History and Folklore Museum** (Tues–Sun 9am–2pm; 500dr), on Ilía Zervoú behind the Municipal Theatre, has a rich collection of local religious and cultural artefacts, including photographs taken before and after the 1953 quakes. Insight into how the island's nobility used to live can be gained from a visit to the new **Focas-Cosmetatos Foundation**, on Valianoú opposite the provincial government building. It contains elegant furniture and a collection of lithographs and paintings, including works by nineteenth-century British artists Joseph Cartwright and Edward Lear. The **Archeological Museum** (Tues–Sun 8.30am–2pm; 500dr), on nearby R. Vergóti, has a sizable collection of pottery, jewellery, funerary relics and statuary but at the time of writing was closed for a major refurbishment.

Practicalities

Argostóli's shiny new **Kefalloniá airport** lies 7km south of town. There are no airport buses, and suburban bus services are so infrequent or don't go close enough that a taxi (at an inflated flat rate of 3500dr) is the only dependable connection. Those arriving in Argostóli by bus from Sámi or elsewhere will wind up at the KTEL **bus station**, a minute from the Dhrápano causeway and ten minutes' walk south of the main square, **Platía Metaxá**. Argostóli's friendly **tourist office** (Mon–Fri 8am–2pm; open till 10pm in August; ☎0671/22 248 or 24 466) is on Andoníou Trítsi at the north end of the seafront, next to the port authority and has information about rooms, and can advise on transport and other resorts around the island.

Hotels around Platía Metaxá stay open year round, but tend to be pricey: the best bet here is the *Mirabel* (☎0671/25 381, fax 25 384; ⑤). A good mid-range option away from the square is the *Fokas*, Yeroulánou 1–3 (☎0671/22 566, fax 23 109; ④), whereas the *Mouikis*, Výronos 3 (☎0671/23 454; ⑥), has gone decidedly upmarket; the only budget hotel is the friendly *Chara* at the corner of G Vergóti and Dhevossétou near Dhrápano bridge (☎0671/22 427; ①). In a working town with a large permanent population, **private rooms** aren't too plentiful. Some of the best bargains can be found through waterfront tavernas, such as the *Kalafatis* (☎0671/22 627; ②–④), nearest to the Dhrápano bridge on the Metaxá waterfront, the *Tzivras* (☎0671/24 259; ②), on Vandórou, just off the centre of the waterfront, or Spyros Rouhotas' kafenío (☎0671/23 491; ③), opposite the Lixoúri ferry ramp. A number of travel agencies also offer rooms, apartments and villas: try *Filoxenos Travel* (☎0671/23 055) on R. Vergóti or *Myrtos* at A. Trítsi 75 (☎0671/25 895, fax 24 230; ③–⑤). The town's one **campsite**, *Argostoli Camping* (☎0671/23 487), lies 2km north of the centre, just beyond the Katovóthres sea mills; there's only an infrequent bus service in high season, so you'll probably have to walk and it's rather basic and limited in shade.

The *Tzivras Estiatório* (only open until 5pm) just off the seafront or *Kalafatis* **taverna** right on it are the places to try Kefallonian cuisine; the *Captain's Table* just off the platía merits a splurge and to hear Kefalloniá *kantádhes*. The *Demosthenes* opposite the *Mirabel* hotel also features gentle live music in a garden setting. Local posers hang out at the *Da Cappo* café-bar, the *Flonitiko* café and the *Koukos* club-bar, on Vasiléos Yeoryíou off the square; the *Space Girls* bar is rather more esoteric. The quay bars, particularly the kafenío by the Dhrápano bridge, are quiet, cheap and have the best views.

South of Argostóli: beaches and Áyios Yeóryios

Many package travellers will find themselves staying in **LÁSSI**, a short bus ride or twenty-minute walk from town. Lássi sprawls unattractively along a busy four-lane highway, but it does have good sandy beaches, particularly at **Makrýs Yialós** and **Platýs Yialós**, although they're right under the airport flight path. **Beaches** such as **Ávythos** are well worth seeking out, although if you're walking beyond **Kourkomeláta** there is a real if occasional risk of being attacked by farm dogs, particularly during the hunting season (Sept 25–Feb 28). There is very little accommodation in the region, and precious few shops or bars. **Pessádha** has a regular ferry link with Zákynthos in summer, but little else.

With a scooter, the best inland excursion is to **ÁYIOS YEÓRYIOS**, the medieval Venetian capital of the island. The old town here supported a population of 15,000 until its destruction by an earthquake in the seventeenth century: substantial ruins of its **castle** (Tues–Sat 8am–8pm, Sun 8am–2pm; 500dr), churches and houses can be visited on the hill above the modern village of Peratáta. Byron lived for a few months in the nearby village of Metaxáta and was impressed by the view from the summit in 1823; sadly, as at Messolóngi, the house where he stayed no longer exists. Two kilometres south of Áyios Yeóryios is a fine collection of religious icons and frescoes kept in a restored church that was part of the nunnery of Áyios Andhréas.

Mount Énos

At 15km from a point halfway along the Argostóli–Sámi road, **Mount Énos** isn't really a walking option, but roads nearly reach the official 1632-metre summit. The mountain has been declared a national park, to protect the *Abies cephalonica* firs (named after the island) which clothe the slopes. There are absolutely no facilities on or up to the mountain, but the views from the highest point in the Ionian islands out over its neighbours and the mainland are wonderful. In low season, watch the weather, which can deteriorate with terrifying speed.

Lixoúri

Half-hourly ferries (hourly in winter) ply between the capital and **LIXOÚRI** throughout the day. The town was flattened by earthquakes, and hasn't risen much above two storeys since. It's a little drab, but has good restaurants, quiet hotels and is favoured by those who want to explore the eerie quakescapes left in the south and the barren north of the peninsula. The bargain **hotel** is the *Giardino* (☎0671/92 505, fax 92 525; ②), four blocks back from the front. There are also two decent beach hotels just south of town: the *Poseidon* (☎0671/92 518, fax 91 374; ④) and *Summery* (☎0671/91 771, fax 91 062; ⑤). Two agencies offer accommodation in town: A. D. Travel (☎0671/93 142, fax 92 663; from ③) on the main road through town, and Perdikis Travel (☎0671/91 097, fax 92 503; from ③) on the quay. Among the tavernas, *Akrogiali* on the seafront draws admirers from all over the island. Nearby *Antonis* mixes traditional dishes with steaks and European food, while *Maria's* is a good basic family taverna.

Lixoúri's nearest beach is **Lípedha**, a 2km walk south. Like the **Xí** and **Mégas Lákkos** beaches (served by bus from Lixoúri and both with restaurants and accommodation), it has rich red sand and is backed by low cliffs. Those with transport can also strike out for the monastery at **Kipouréon**, and north to the spectacular beach at **Petáni**, where there are two sizable snack bars and signs of future development.

The west coast and the road north

The journey between Argostóli and Fiskárdho, by regular bus or hire vehicle, is the most spectacular ride in the archipelago. Leaving town, the road rises into the Evmorfía foothills and, beyond Agónas, clings to nearly sheer cliffs as it heads for Dhivaráta, the stop for **Mýrtos beach**. It's a four-kilometre hike down on foot (you can also drive down), with just one taverna on the beach, but from above or below, this is the most dramatic beach in the Ionian islands – a splendid strip of pure white sand and pebbles. Sadly, it's shadeless and gets mighty crowded in high season.

Six kilometres on is the turning for the atmospheric village of **ÁSSOS**, clinging to a small isthmus between the island and a huge hill crowned by a ruined fort. Accommodation is scarce – villagers invariably send you to Andhreas Rokos' rooms (☎0674/51 523; ②) on the approach road, which are great value, or you can opt for the posher *Kanakis Apartments* opposite (☎ & fax 0674/51 631; ⑥). Ássos has a small pebble beach, and three tavernas, notably the *Nefeli's Garden* and the *Platanos Grill*, on a plane-shaded village square backed by the shells of mansions ruined in the quake. It can get a little claustrophobic, but there's nowhere else like it in the Ionian islands.

Fiskárdho

FISKÁRDHO, on the northernmost tip of the island, sits on a bed of limestone that buffered it against the worst of the quakes. Two **lighthouses**, Venetian and Victorian, guard the bay, and the ruins on the headland are believed to be from a twelfth-century chapel begun by Norman invader Robert Guiscard, who gave the place his name. The nineteenth-century harbour frontage is intact, nowadays occupied by smart restaurants and chic boutiques.

The island's premier resort, Fiskárdho is very busy through to the end of October, with accommodation at a premium. None of it is cheap even when available but the best deal is at *Regina's* (☎0674/41 125; ③) at the back of the village, next to the car park. *Theodora's Café Bar* has rooms in whitewashed houses along the quay (☎0674/41 297 or 41 310; ④), and the Koria handicraft shop has rooms on the seafront (☎0674/41 270; ④). Another reasonable option is the small *Erissos* pension (☎0674/41 327; ④), just off the seafront. Further up the price range, *Fiskardhona* (☎0674/41 436; ⑤), opposite the post office, and *Philoxenia* (☎ & fax 0674/41 319; ⑤), next to *Erissos*, offer rooms in renovated traditional island homes in the village. There's a wealth of good restaurants: the *Tassia* has a vast range of seafood, and the *Captain's Table* serves succulent Greek and Kefallonian fare, while *Alexis* has a fine selection, including curries, at the most reasonable prices.. *Sirenes* is the favoured bar, although the seafront kafenío's mezédhes are the finest to be had anywhere. The dance spot is *Kastro Club* up at the back of the village. There are two good pebble beaches – **Émblisi** 1km back out of town and **Fókis** just to the south – and a nature trail on the northern headland. Daily **ferries** connect Fiskárdho to Itháki and Lefkádha in season.

Itháki

Rugged **Itháki**, Odysseus' legendary homeland, has had no substantial archeological discoveries but it fits Homer's description to perfection: "There are no tracks, nor grasslands . . . it is a rocky severe island, unsuited for horses, but not so wretched, despite its small size. It is good for goats." In Constantine Cavafy's splendid poem *Ithaca*, the island is symbolized as a journey to life:

When you set out on the voyage to Ithaca
Pray that your journey may be long
Full of adventures, full of knowledge.

Despite the romance of its name, and its proximity to Corfu, very little tourist development has arrived to spoil the place. This is doubtless accounted for in part by a dearth of beaches, though the island is good walking country, with a handful of small fishing villages and various pebbly coves to swim from. In the north, apart from the ubiquitous drone of scooters, the most common sounds are sheep bells jangling and cocks (a symbol of Odysseus) crowing.

Its beaches are minor, mainly pebble with sandy seabeds, but relatively clean and safe; the real attractions are the interior and sites from the **Odyssey**. Some package travellers will find themselves flying into Kefalloniá and being bused to Fiskárdho (sit on the left for the bus ride of your life), for a short ferry crossing to **Fríkes** or the premier resort **Kióni**. Most visitors will arrive at **Vathý**, the capital.

Vathý

Ferries from Pátra, Kefalloniá, Astakós, Corfu and Italy land at the main port and capital of **VATHÝ** (Itháki Town), a bay within a bay so deep that few realize the mountains out "at sea" are actually the north of the island. This snug town is compact, relatively traffic-free and boasts the most idyllic seafront setting of all the Ionian capitals. Like its southerly neighbours, it was damaged by the 1953 earthquake, but some fine examples of pre-quake architecture remain here and in the northern port of **Kióni**. Vathý has a small **archeological museum** on Odhós Kallaníkou (Tues–Sun

8am–2.30pm; 500dr) a short block back from the quay. There are banks, a post office, police and a medical centre in town.

Vathý has two basic but decent **hotels** which bookend the seafront: the *Odysseus* (☎0674/32 381; ④) is to the right of the ferry dock, the *Mentor* (☎0674/32 433, fax 32 293; ⑤) to its left. They have recently been usurped in comfort by the new *Captain Yiannis* (☎0674/33 173, fax 32 849; ⑤), further round the bay from the *Mentor*. Room owners meet ferries until the last knockings of the season, but you can also call ahead to Vassiliki Vlassopoulou (☎0674/32 119; ③), whose rooms are in pleasant gardens by the church above the quay. Also within easy access are those owned by Sotiris Maroulis at Odhós Odysséos 29, near the Perahóri road (☎0674/28 300; ③). Two of the town's travel agents, Polyctor Tours (☎0674/33 120, fax 33 130) and Delas Tours (☎0674/321 104, fax 33 031) on the quay have accommodation throughout the island.

Even though it's tiny, Vathý has a wealth of **tavernas** and **bars**. Many locals head off south around the bay towards *Gregory's*, popular for its lamb and fish, and the more traditional *Tziribis* and *Vlachos*. In town, *O Nikos* is an excellent restaurant in the side-streets that fills early, while *To Kohili* is the best of the half-dozen harbourside tavernas. The *Sirenes Ithaki Yacht Club* is upmarket with a nautical theme; the no-relation *Ithaki Yacht Club* on the front looks private but is actually a bar open to all. Otherwise, head for the town's ancient kafenío one street back from the front.

There are two reasonable pebble **beaches** within fifteen minutes' walk of Vathý: **Dhéxa**, over the hill above the ferry quay, which has a semi-official campsite, and tiny **Loútsa**, opposite it around the bay. Better beaches at **Sarakíniko** and **Skhinós** to the south are an hour's trek by rough track leaving the opposite side of the bay. In season, daily kaïkia ply between the quay and remote coves.

Odysseus sights

Three of the main **Odysseus** sights are just within walking distance of Vathý: the Arethoúsa Spring, the Cave of the Nymphs and ancient Alalkomenae, although the last is best approached by **bus** or **taxi** (no more than 4000dr round-trip).

The Arethóussa Spring

The walk to the **Arethóussa Spring** – allegedly the place where Eumaeus, Odysseus' faithful swineherd, brought his pigs to drink – is a three-hour round trip along a track signposted next to the seafront OTE. The unspoiled landscape and sea views are magnificent, but the walk crosses slippery inclines and might best be avoided if you're nervous of heights. The route is shadeless, so take a hat and plenty of water.

Near the top of the lane leading to the spring path, a signpost points up to what is said to have been the **Cave of Eumaeus**. The route to the spring continues for a few hundred metres, and then branches off onto a narrow footpath through gorse-covered steep cliffs. Parts of the final downhill track involve scrambling across rock fields (follow the splashes of green paint), and care should be taken around the small but vertiginous ravine that houses the **spring**. The spring is sited at the head of a small ravine below a crag known as **Korax** (the raven), which matches Homer's description of the meeting between Odysseus and Eumaeus. In summer it's just a dribble of water.

The spring is a dead end – the only way out is back the way you came. If weather and time allow, there is a small cove for swimming a short scramble down from the spring. If you're uneasy about the gradients involved, it's still worth continuing along the track that runs above it, which loops round and heads back into the village of **Perahóri** above Vathý, which has views as far as Lefkádha to the north. On the way, you'll pass **Paleóhora**, the ruined medieval capital abandoned centuries ago, but with vestiges of houses fortified against pirate attacks and some churches still with Byzantine frescoes.

The Cave of the Nymphs

The **Cave of the Nymphs** (Marmarospíli) is about 2.5km up a rough but navigable road signposted on the brow of the hill above Dhéxa beach. The cave is atmospheric, but it's underwhelming compared to the caverns of neighbouring Kefalloniá and these days is illuminated by coloured lights. The claim that this is the *Odyssey*'s Cave of the Nymphs, where the returning Odysseus concealed the gifts given to him by King Alcinous, is enhanced by the proximity of Dhéxa beach, although there is some evidence that the "true" cave was just above the beach, and was unwittingly demolished during quarrying many years ago.

Alalkomenae and Pisaetós

Alalkomenae, Heinrich Schliemann's much-vaunted "Castle of Odysseus", is signposted on the Vathý–Pisaetós road, on the saddle between Dhéxa and Pisaetós, with views over both sides of the island. The actual site, however, some 300m uphill, is little more than foundations spread about in the gorse. Schliemann's excavations unearthed a Mycenaean burial chamber and domestic items such as vases, figurines and utensils (displayed in the archeological museum), but the ruins actually date from three centuries after Homer. In fact, the most likely contender for the site of Odysseus' castle is above the village of Stavrós (see below).

The road (though not buses) continues to the harbour of **Pisaetós**, about 2km below, with a large pebble beach that's good for swimming and popular with local rod-and-line fishermen. A couple of tavernas here largely serve the regular ferries from Sámi on Kefalloniá.

Northern Itháki

The main road out of Váthy continues across the isthmus and takes a spectacular route to the northern half of Itháki, serving the villages of **Léfki**, **Stavrós**, **Fríkes** and **Kióni**. There are only two daily **buses**, though the north of Itháki is excellent motorscooter country; the close proximity of the settlements, small coves and Homeric interest also make it good rambling country. Once a day a kaïki also visits the last two of those communities – a cheap and scenic ride used by locals and tourists alike to meet the mainline ferries in Vathý. As with the rest of Itháki there is only a limited amount of accommodation.

Stavrós and around

STAVRÓS, the second largest town on the island, discounting Perahóri, is a steep 2km above the nearest beach (Pólis Bay). It's a pleasant enough town nonetheless, with kafenía edging a small square that's dominated by a rather fierce statue of Odysseus. There is even a tiny **museum** (Tues–Sun 9.30am–2.30pm; free) off the road to Platrithiás, displaying local archeological finds. Stavrós's Homeric site is on the side of **Pelikáta Hill**, where remains of roads, walls and other structures have been suggested as the possible site of Odysseus' castle. Stavrós is useful as a base if both Fríkes and Kióni are full up, and is an obvious stopping-off point for exploring the northern hamlets and the road up to the medieval village of Anoyí (see below). Both Polyctor and Delas handle **accommodation** in Stavrós; the traditional *Petra* taverna(☎0674/31 596; ③) offers rooms, or there's the *Porto Thiaki* pension above the pizzeria. The oldest and best taverna is *Fatouros* and the *Margarita* zaharoplastío is a good place for a drink or to sample the local sweet *rovaní*.

A scenic mountain road leads 5km southeast from Stavrós to **ANOYÍ**, whose name translates roughly as "upper ground". Once the second most important settlement on the island, it is almost deserted today. The centre of the village is dominated by a free-standing Venetian campanile, built to serve the (usually locked) church of the **Panayía**, which comes alive for the annual *paniyíri* on August 14, the eve of the Virgin's Assumption; at other times enquire at the kafenío about access to the church, whose Byzantine frescoes have been heavily restored following centuries of earthquake damage. On the outskirts of the village are the foundations of a ruined **medieval prison**, and in the surrounding countryside are some extremely strange rock formations, the biggest being the eight-metre-high Iraklís (Hercules) rock, just east of the village. The **monastery of Katharón**, 3km further south along the road, has stunning views down over Vathý and the south of the island, and houses an icon of the *Panayía* discovered by peasants clearing scrubland in the area. Byron is said to have stayed here in 1823, during his final voyage to Messolóngi. The monastery celebrates its festival on 8 September with services, processions and music.

Two roads leave Stavrós heading north: one, to the right, heads 2km down to Fríkes, while the main road, to the left, loops below the hill village of **Exoyí**, and on to **Platrithiás**. Just off the start of the road up to Exoyí a signpost points about 1km along a rough track to the supposed **School of Homer**, where excavations still in progress have revealed extensive foundations, a well and ancient steps. The site is unfenced and well worth a detour for its views of **Afáles bay** as much as the remains. On the outskirts of Platrithiás a track leads down to Afáles, the largest bay on the entire island, with an unspoiled and little-visited pebble beach. The landscape around here, thickly forested in parts and dotted with vineyards, is excellent walking terrain.

Fríkes

At first sight, tiny **FRÍKES** doesn't appear to have much going for it. Wedged in a valley between two steep hills, it was only settled in the sixteenth century, and emigration in the nineteenth century almost emptied the place – as few as two hundred people live here today – but the protected harbour is a natural year-round port. Consequently, Fríkes stays open for tourism far later in the season than neighbouring Kióni, and has a better range of tavernas. There are no beaches in the village, but plenty of good, if small, pebble strands a short walk away towards Kióni. When the ferries and their cargoes have departed, Fríkes falls quiet and this is its real charm: a downbeat but cool place to lie low.

Fríkes' one **hotel** is the smart but pricey *Nostos* (☎0674/31 644, fax 31 716; ⑤). Kiki Travel (☎ & fax 0674/31 387; ③) has **rooms** and other accommodation, as do the adjacent souvenir shop (☎0674/31 735; ②) and *Ulysses* taverna (☎0674/31733; ④). Phoning ahead is advisable and in peak season chances are slim. Fríkes has a quartet of good seafront **tavernas**, the *Symposium*, the *Rementzo*, the *Penelope* and aforementioned *Ulysses* all being worth a try.

Kióni

KIÓNI sits at a dead end 5km southeast of Fríkes. On the same geological base as the northern tip of Kefalloniá, it avoided the very worst of the 1953 earthquakes, and so retains some fine examples of pre-twentieth-century architecture. It's an extremely pretty village, wrapped around a tiny harbour, and tourism here is dominated by British blue-chip travel companies and visiting yachts.

The bay has a small **beach**, 1km along its south side, a sand and pebble strand below a summer-only snack bar. Better pebble beaches can be found within walking distance towards Fríkes. While the best **accommodation** has been snaffled by the Brits, some local businesses have rooms and apartments to let, among them *Apostolis* (☎0674/31 072; ③), *Dellaportas* (☎0674/31 481, fax 31 090; ④) and *Kioni Vacations* (☎0674/31 668; ③). A quieter option, a short walk uphill on the main road in the hamlet of Ráhi, are the rooms and studios run by Captain Theofilos Karatzis and his family (☎0674/31 679; ③), which have panoramic views. Alternatively, seek out the very helpful Yiorgos Moraitis (☎0674/31 464, fax 31 702), whose boat rental company has access to accommodation in Kióni.

Kióni's **restaurants** are dotted around the picturesque harbour but compare unfavourably with those in Fríkes; the traditional *Avra* and the *Kioni* pizzeria are adequate, while the upmarket *Calypso* taverna has interesting dishes but is overpriced. Village facilities stretch to two well-stocked shops, a post office and a couple of bars and cafes.

Zákynthos (Zante)

Zákynthos, most southerly of the six core Ionian islands, currently teeters between underdevelopment and indiscriminate commercialization. Much of the island is still green and unspoiled, but the sheer intensity of business in some resorts is threatening to spill over into the quieter parts.

The island has three distinct zones: the barren, mountainous northwest; the fertile central plain; and the eastern and southern coasts which house the resorts. The big resort – rivalling the biggest on Corfu – is **Laganás**, on Laganás Bay in the south, a 24-hour party venue that doesn't give up from Easter until the last flight home in October. There are smaller, quieter resorts north and south of the capital, and the southerly Vassilikós peninsula has the best countryside and beaches, including exquisite **Yérakas**.

Although half-built apartment blocks are spreading through the central plain, this is where the quieter island begins: farms and vineyards, ancient villages and the ruins of Venetian buildings levelled in the 1948 and 1953 earthquakes. The island still produces fine wines, such as the white Popolaro, as well as sugar-shock-inducing *mandoláto* nougat, whose honey-sweetened form is best. Zákynthos is also the birthplace of *kantádhes*, the hybrid of Cretan folk song and Italian opera ballad that can be heard in tavernas in Zákynthos Town and elsewhere. It also harbours one of the key breeding sites of the endangered **loggerhead sea turtle** at Laganás Bay. The loggerhead (see box on p.834) is the subject of a continuing dispute between tourism businesses and environmentalists, which has caused an international political scandal and even provoked a bomb attack against the environmentalists.

Zákynthos Town

The town, like the island, is known as both **ZÁKYNTHOS** and Zante. This former "Venice of the East" (*Zante, Fior di Levante*, "Flower of the Levant", in an Italian jingle), rebuilt on the old plan, has bravely tried to recreate some of its style, though reinforced concrete can only do so much.

The town stretches beyond the length of the wide and busy harbour, its main section bookended by the grand **Platía Solomoú** at the north, and the church of **Áyios Dhionýsios**, patron saint of the island, at the south. The square is named after the island's most famous son, the poet Dhionysios Solomos, the father of modernism in Greek literature, who was responsible for establishing demotic Greek (as opposed to the elitist *katharévousa* form) as a literary idiom. He is also the author of the lyrics to the national anthem. There's an impressive **museum** devoted to the life and work of him and other Zakynthian luminaries in nearby Platía Ayíou Márkou (daily 9am–2pm; 800dr) which shares its collection with the museum on Corfu (see p.798), where Solomos spent most of his life. Another local man of letters, who had a museum dedicated to him by the town council in 1998, is novelist and playwright Grigorios Xenopoulos. His eponymous museum (Wed–Sun 9am–1pm; free), to be found in a small house tucked in Gaïta street not far from Áyios Dhionýsios church, displays a modest collection of manuscripts, books and photographs.

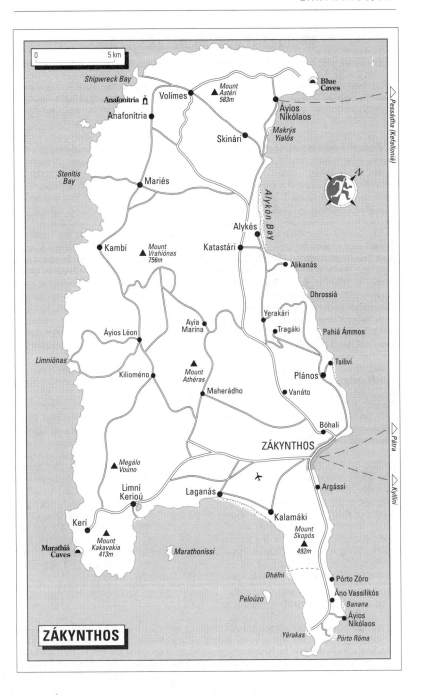

0   5 km

Shipwreck Bay

Anafonítria

Anafonítria

Volímes

Mount
Astéri
583m

Blue
Caves

Áyios
Nikólaos

Skinári

Makrýs
Yialós

Stenítis
Bay

Mariés

Alykón Bay

Alykés

Kambí

Mount
Vrahiónas
756m

Katastári

Alikanás

Dhrossiá

Yerakári

Ayía
Marina

Áyios Léon

Tragáki

Pahiá Ámmos

Limniónas

Kilioméno

Mount
Athéras

Tsiliví

Plános

Maherádho

Vanáto

Bóhali

ZÁKYNTHOS

Megálo
Voúno

Limní
Kerioú

Laganás

Argássi

Kerí

Kalamáki

Mount
Kakavakia
413m

Marathoníssi

Mount
Skopós
492m

**Marathiá
Caves**

Dháfni

Pórto Zóro

Áno Vassilikós

Banana

Peloúzo

Áyios
Nikólaos

Yérakas

Pórto Róma

Pessádha (Kefalloniá)

Pátra

Kyllíni

ZÁKYNTHOS

BOAT TRIPS FROM ZÁKYNTHOS

At least ten pleasure craft offer **day-trips** around the island from the quay in Zákynthos town for 2000–3500dr. All take in sights such as the blue-water grottoes of the **Blue Caves** at Cape Skinári, and moor in **Tó Naváyio (Shipwreck Cove)** and the **Cape Kerí** caves. Shop around for the trip with the most stops, as eight hours bobbing round the coast can become a bore. Check also that the operators actually take you into the caves.

Platía Solomoú is home to the town's **library**, which has a small collection of pre- and post-quake photography, and the massive **Zákynthos Museum** (Tues–Sun 8am–2.30pm; 800dr), sometimes referred to as the Byzantine Museum and notable for its collection of artworks from the Ionian School, the region's post-Renaissance art movement, spearheaded by Zakynthian painter Panayiotis Doxaras. The movement was given impetus by Cretan refugees, unable to practise under Turkish rule. It also houses some secular painting and a fine model of the town before the earthquake.

The town's other main attraction is its massive **kástro**, brooding over the hamlet of Bóhali on its bluff above the town. The ruined Venetian fort (daily 8am–7.30pm in summer, 8am–2pm in winter; 500dr) has vestiges of dungeons, armouries and fortifications, stunning views in all directions and makes a great spot to relax or picnic on its shady carpet of fallen pine needles. Below the kástro walls, **Bóhali** has a couple of good though expensive tavernas, some hosting nightly *kantádhes*, although Zakynthian driving habits make the thirty-minute walk from town a definite no-no after dark. The ugly new **amphitheatre** on the road up from town sometimes hosts concerts. Further towards the kástro the **Maritime Museum** (daily 9am–2pm & 6–9pm; 800dr) contains plenty of naval paraphernalia and is arranged as an interesting chronological history of Hellenic seafaring.

Zákynthos is a working town with few concessions to tourism, although there are hotels and restaurants aplenty, and it's the only place to stay if you want to see the island by public transport. Of the central hotels, the *Egli*, on Loútzi (☎0695/28 317; ③) is the bargain, tucked in beside the gargantuan and more expensive *Strada Marina* (☎0695/42 761, fax 28 733; ⑤). There are quieter hotels in the Répara district beyond Platía Solomoú: try either the *Plaza* (☎0695/48 909, fax 45 733; ④) or the classy *Bitzaro*, Dhionysíou Róma (☎0695/23 644, fax 23 493; ⑥), both near the municipal lido. Cheaper options at the back of town near the airport road include the *Diethnes*, Ayíou Lazárou (☎0695/22 286; ③) and nearby *Haravyi* pension, Xanthopoúlou 4 (☎0695/23 629; ③). The smart **restaurants** and bars of the seafront and Platía Ayíou Márkou are bedevilled by traffic, although the seafront *Village Inn* should be checked out for its bizarre Gothic-Polynesian decor and the miniature jungle at the rear, while the *Psaropoula* does fine meat and fish. First stop though, should be the friendly *Arekia* beyond the lido, which offers succulent taverna staples and nightly *kantádhes*. The neighbouring *Alivizos* also specializes in island cuisine and music. When the bored teens get off their bikes, they go **clubbing**, to bars like *Base* on Ayíou Márkou, which plays anything from Miles Davis to Philip Glass, or the *Jazz Café*, on Tertséti which, despite plundering the London jazz club's logo, is actually a techno bar with DJ and token cover charge.

The south and west

The road heading southeast from Zákynthos passes through **ARGÁSSI**, the busiest resort on this coast, but with a beach barely a few feet wide in parts. Although the independent traveller would be better off basing himself at one of the places further down, it could be used as a jumping-off point for the Vassilikós peninsula; there are rooms at the *Pension Vaso* (☎0695/44 599; ③) and *Andro* (☎0695/22 190; ③) on the main road in the centre of the village, and the seafront boasts some smart hotels, among them the *Locanda* (☎0695/45 386; ⑤) and the *Iliessa Beach* (☎0695/45 345; ⑥). Beyond a few indigenous tavernas – try *Three Brothers* or *The Big Plate* restaurant – culture here is summed up, surreally, by an English caff that advertises a "Greek night" every Saturday. Argási is also home to some of the island's biggest and most popular discos such as *Vivlos* and *Barrage*.

The Vassilikós Peninsula

The peninsula that stretches southeast of Argássi is one of the most attractive parts of the island, with a happy blend of development and natural beauty. Various maps vaguely identify different inland spots as **Vassilikós** villages but the real interest lies in the series of small beach resorts, mainly situated on the east coast. The first two are newly-developed **Kamínia**, with the good-value *Levantino* rooms (☎0695/35 366; ③), and the more established at **Pórto Zóro**, which has a canteen and the eponymous *Porto Zoro* hotel (☎0695/35 304; ④). The only real facilities away from the coast are to be found at the sprawling village of **Áno Vassilikós**, which serves the nearby beaches of **Iónio** and **Banana**. Among accommodation possibilities on the main road are the *Vassilikos Apartments* (☎0695/35 280; ④) and *Villa Maria* (☎0695/35 316; ③). Among the **tavernas**, *O Adherfos tou Kosta* is well worth a try, as is the *Logos Rock Club*. Isolated **Áyios Nikólaos** lures day-trippers from Argási, Kalamáki and Laganás with a **free bus** service in season; its expanding *Vasilikos Beach* (☎0695/24 114; ⑤) complex has a good beach, with a fast-emerging hamlet and some rooms in the moon-like landscape behind it.

The island's star is **Yérakas**, a sublime crescent of golden sand at the very tip of the peninsula, which is also a key loggerhead turtle breeding ground, and which is therefore off-limits between dusk and dawn. There's little here beyond two tavernas back from the beach and some pleasant, if remote, cabin accommodation at *Liuba Apartments* (☎0695/35 372; ④). The beach does draw crowds, but the 6am bus out of Zákynthos Town should secure you a few hours of Yérakas to yourself. Compared with Yérakas, **Pórto Róma**, back on the east coast, is a disappointment, a small sand and pebble bay with a taverna and bar, some rooms on the approach road and occasional hardy campers, although there is a more genuinely Greek flavour to it. Beaches on the west coast, like **Dháfni**, require your own transport and have few facilities, but are worth a visit, especially in the quieter months.

Laganás and Kalamáki

The majority of the 400,000 people or so who visit Zákynthos each year find themselves in **LAGANÁS**. The nine-kilometre beach in the bay is good, if trampled, and there are entertainments from watersports to ballooning, and even an occasional funfair. Beachfront bars and restaurants stretch for over a kilometre; the bars and restaurants on the main drag another kilometre inland. Some stay open around the clock; others just play music at deafening volume until dawn. The competing video and music bars can make Laganás at night resemble the set of *Bladerunner*, but that's how its predominantly English visitors like it. If this is your bag, there's no place better; if it isn't, flee. **Accommodation** is mostly block-booked by package companies. There's a basic campsite on the southern edge of town, where there are also quietish private rooms, or you can contact the Union of Room Owners, who have an office on the main drag (daily 8.30am–2pm & 5–8pm; ☎0695/51 590). As for hotels, try the *Byzantio* (☎0695/51 136; ③), near the crossroads, *Pension Toula* (☎0695/51 560; ④), between the beach and the campsite, or *Ionis* (☎0695/51 141, fax 51 601; ⑤), on the main drag towards the beach. *Nefeli* and *Zougras* are among the more authentic **tavernas**, the former hosting nightly *kantádhes*, and respectable Chinese/Indian food can be had at *Bee Garden* or *Taj Mahal*.

LOGGERHEAD TURTLES

The Ionian islands harbour the Mediterranean's main concentration of **loggerhead sea turtles** (*Caretta caretta*). These creatures, which lay their eggs at night on sandy coves, are under direct threat from the tourist industry in Greece. Each year, many turtles are injured by motorboats, their nests are destroyed by bikes ridden on the beaches, and the newly hatched young die entangled in deckchairs and umbrellas left out at night on the sand. The turtles are easily frightened by noise and lights, too, which makes them uneasy cohabitants with freelance campers and late-night discos.

The Greek government has passed laws designed to protect the loggerheads, including restrictions on camping at some beaches, but local economic interests tend to prefer a beach full of bodies to a sea full of turtles.

On Laganás, nesting grounds are concentrated around the fourteen-kilometre bay, but Greek marine zoologists striving to protect and study the turtles are in angry dispute with locals and the burgeoning tourist industry. Other important locations include the turtles' nesting ground just west of Skála on Kefalloniá, although numbers have dwindled to half their former strength in recent years, and now only about 800 remain. Ultimately, the turtles' main hope of survival may rest in their being appreciated as a unique tourist attraction in their own right.

While capitalists and environmentalists are still at, well, loggerheads, the **World Wildlife Fund** has issued guidelines for visitors:

1. Don't use the beaches of Laganás and Yérakas between sunset and sunrise.

2. Don't stick umbrellas in the sand in the marked nesting zones.

3. Take your rubbish away with you – it can obstruct the turtles.

4. Don't use lights near the beach at night – they can disturb the turtles, sometimes with fatal consequences.

5. Don't take any vehicle onto the protected beaches.

6. Don't dig up turtle nests – it's illegal.

7. Don't pick up the hatchlings or carry them to the water, as it's vital to their development that they reach the sea on their own.

8. Don't use speedboats in Laganás Bay – a 9kph speed limit is in force for vessels in the bay.

Neighbouring **KALAMÁKI** has a better beach than Laganás, and is altogether quieter, although both resorts suffer from airport noise. There are a number of good hotels, notably the *Crystal Beach* (☎0695/42 788, fax 42 917; ⑤), and the friendly Zakyta travel agency (☎0695/27 080) can also arrange accommodation. The two *Stanis* tavernas have extensive menus of Greek and international dishes, although the beachside version is geared more to lunches and its sibling more to evening meals. Alternatives include *Afrodite* and *Merlis*. **Nightlife** centres around bars like *Al'Sandros*, and the *Vios Club* on the hillside above the village, which has a garden with breathtaking views.

Kerí

The village of **KERÍ** is hidden in a fold above the cliffs at the island's southernmost tip. The village retains a number of pre-quake, Venetian buildings, including the church of the **Panayía Keriou**; the Virgin is said to have saved the island from marauding pirates by hiding it in a sea mist. Kerí is also famous for a geological quirk, a series of small tar pools mentioned by both Pliny and Herodotus, but these have mysteriously dried up in recent years. A rough path leaving the southern end of the village leads 1km on to the lighthouse, with spectacular views of the sea, rock arches and stacks. The beach next to **Límni Keriou** at the southern end of Laganás bay is fast growing into a good alternative resort and is home to the *Turtle Beach Diving Centre* (☎0695/48 768).

Maherádho, Kilioméno and Kambí

The bus system does not reach the wild western side of the island, but a hire car or sturdy motorbike will get you there. **MAHERÁDHO** boasts impressive pre-earthquake architecture set in beautiful arable uplands, surrounded by olive and fruit groves. The church of **Ayía Mávra** has an impressive free-standing campanile, and inside a splendid carved iconostasis and icons by Zakynthian painter Nikolaos Latsis. The town's major festival – one of the biggest on the island – is the saint's day, which falls on the first Sunday in June. The other notable church in town, that of the Panayía, commands breathtaking views over the central plain.

KILIOMÉNO is the best place to see surviving pre-earthquake domestic architecture, in the form of the island's traditional two-storey houses. The town was originally named after its church **Áyios Nikólaos**, whose impressive campanile, begun over a hundred years ago, still lacks a capped roof. The road from Kilioméno passes through the nondescript village of Áyios Léon, from where two turnings lead through fertile land and down a newly-paved loop road to the impressive rocky coast at **Limniónas**, where there is a tiny bay and a taverna.

Further along the main road another turning leads to the tiny clifftop hamlet of **KAMBÍ**, destination for numerous coach trips to catch the sunset over the sea.. Its clifftop **tavernas** have extraordinary views over the 300-metre-high cliffs and western horizon. On an incline above the village there's an imposing concrete cross, constructed in memory of islanders killed here during the 1940s, either by nationalist soldiers or Nazis. The tiny village of **Mariés**, 5km to the north and set in a wooded green valley, has the only other coastal access on this side of Zákynthos, a seven-kilometre track leading down to the rocky inlet of **Stenítis Bay,** where there's a taverna and yacht dock, and another road to the uninspiring **Vrómi Bay**, from where speedboats run trips to Shipwreck Beach (see below).

The north

North and west from Zákynthos Town, the roads thread their way through luxuriantly fertile farmland, punctuated with tumulus-like hills. **Tsiliví**, 5km north of the capital, is the first beach resort here, which has now effectively merged with the hamlet of **PLÁNOS**. Unfortunately, this part of the coastline suffers from occasional oil pollution, with nothing but the winter storms to clear it. There's a good, basic **campsite**, *Zante Camping* (☎0695/61 710), beyond Plános, and some rooms – try *Gregory's* (☎0695/61 853; ③), *Dolphin* (☎0695/27 425; ④) or contact *Tsilivi Travel* (☎0695/44 194, fax 22 655)– but most visitors here are on package deals. *The Olive Tree* taverna is the best of a tourist-orientated bunch.

The beaches further along this stretch of coast become progressively quieter and more pleasant and they all have at least a smattering of accommodation and restaurants to choose from. Good choices include **Pahiá Ámmos**, with the *Pension Petra* (☎0695/62 410; ③) and *Porto Roulis* fish taverna, and **Dhrossiá**, where you can find the *Avouris* (☎0695/61 716; ③) and *Drosia* (☎0695/62 256; ④) apartments and eat at another fish taverna, *Andreas*.

Alykés and its bay

Ormós Alykón, 12km north of Tsiliví, is a large sandy bay with lively surf and two of the area's largest resorts. **ALIKANÁS** is a small but expanding village, much of its accommodation being overseas villa rentals and **ALYKÉS**, named after the spooky salt pans behind the village, has the best beach north of the capital. There are **rooms** on the beach (try the *Golden Dolphin* taverna), and a number of **hotels** set back from it, but with sea views – try the *Ionian Star* (☎0695/83 416, fax 83 173; ④) or the

Montreal (☎0695/83 241; ⑤), although the best deal is further back at the *Picadilly* (☎0695/83 606; ②). There are many eating joints, among the best the *Anatolikos* and *Fantasia* tavernas. Alykés is the last true resort on this coast, and the one where the bus service gives out. **Koróni**, 4km north, has sulphur springs flowing into the sea – follow the smell – which provide the odd sensation of swimming in a mix of cool and warm water. The next small beach of **Makrýs Yialós**, which has a good taverna, makeshift campsite and a diving school, makes for an extremely pleasant break on a tour of the north.

Áyios Nikólaos, 6km on, is a small working port serving daily ferries to and from Pessádha on Kefalloniá. From here another good trip is a ride by **kaïki** (1000dr) to the extreme northern tip of the island, where the **Blue Caves** are some of the more realistically named of the many contenders in Greece. They're terrific for snorkelling, and when you go for a dip here your skin will appear bright blue. The road snakes onwards through a landscape of gorse bushes and dry-stone walls until it ends at the lighthouse of **Cape Skinári**. With only a taverna and a cafeteria, and a view of the mountainous expanse of Kefalloniá, it's a good spot for unofficial camping, or you could stay in the unique setting of the converted windmill rented out by *To Faros* taverna (☎0695/31 132; ④).

Volímes, Katastári and Ayía Marína

The northern towns and villages are accessible only to those with cars or sturdy motor-bikes, and although there are guided coach tours from the resorts, none is really geared to tourism. **VOLÍMES** is the centre of the island's embroidery industry – with your own transport, you could make it to the **Anafonítria monastery**, 3km south, thought to have been the cell of the island's patron saint, Dhionysios, whose festivals are celebrated on August 24 and December 17. A newly paved road leads on to the cliffs overlooking **Shipwreck Bay** (Tó Naváyio), with hair-raising views down to the ship-wreck below and a fine taverna to recover your composure in. Two kilometres inland from Alykés, **KATASTÁRI** is the largest settlement after the capital. Although it's unprepared for tourism, it's the place to see Zákynthian life as it's lived away from the tourism racket. Its most impressive edifice is the huge rectangular church of Iperáyia Theotókos, with a twin belfry and small new amphitheatre for festival performances.

AYÍA MARÍNA, a few kilometres south of Katastári, has a church using an impressive Baroque altar screen, and a belfry that's being rebuilt from the remnants left after the 1953 earthquake. As in most Zákynthos churches, the bell-tower is detached, in Venetian fashion. Just above Ayía Marína is the *Parthenonas* taverna, rightly boasting one of the best views on the island. From here you can see the whole of the central plain from beyond Alykés in the north to Laganás Bay in the south.

travel details

Corfu (Kérkyra)

There are three or four daily **flights** between Corfu and Athens (1hr), and one or two daily except Sun to Thessaloníki (1hr). Several **ferries** (Port Authority ☎0661/32 655) per hour (5.15am–10pm) run between Corfu and Igoumenítsa (1hr 15min) in high season. Also 6 daily between Igoumenítsa and Lefkími (40min) Additionally, most ferries between Italy (Brindisi, Bari, Ancona and Venice) and Patra stop at Corfu; stopover is free if specified in advance and there is no problem buying Corfu–Patra tickets. You may also be able to travel between Corfu and Kefalloniá on the few Italy–Corfu–Patra ships that call there. Services to Paxí have improved and there are now two to three daily in season, either direct or via Igoumenítsa. **Buses** to Athens via the Igoumenítsa ferry depart three times daily, once daily to Thessaloníki.

Eríkoussa, Mathráki and Othoní

A **car ferry**, the *Alexandros II*, runs from Corfu Town to all the islands twice weekly (Tues & Sat, 6.30am). The ferry leaves from near the BP station on the seafront, midway between the Old and New Ports, although it involves sailing halfway round the island. Quicker access, favoured by islanders without vehicles, is via daily excursions from **Sidhári** run by Nearchos Seacruises (☎0663/95 248).

Paxí

Ferry connections to Paxí (Port Authority ☎0662/32 259) have stabilized in the last couple of years. To Corfu, there is now one service daily throughout the year, plus one or two extra and a hydrofoil in the summer months. There are unreliable, ferries 2–3 weekly to/from Igoumenítsa. In summer two kaïkia connect daily with Párga.

Lefkádha

5 **buses** daily to and from Athens (7hr), and 5 buses daily to the Áktio ferry (30min) for Préveza, passing Áktio airport (30min). 7 **ferries** daily in season from Nydhrí to Meganíssi; daily connections (several in summer and one all year) from Nydhrí or Vassilikí to Kefaloniá (Fiskárdho and Sámi) and Itháki (Fríkes).

Kefaloniá

1–2 daily **flights** to and from Athens (45min).

Ferries in season from **Sámi** to: Pátra (2 daily; 2hr 30min); Astakós (1 daily; 3hr 30min); Vathý (Itháki; 1–2 daily; 1hr); Pisaetós (Itháki; 5 daily; 30min); Vassilikí (Lefkádha; 1 daily; 3hr). Also ferries from **Póros** to Kyllíni (3 daily; 1hr 15min). **Fiskárdho** to: Fríkes (Itháki; 1 daily; 1hr); Nydhrí (Lefkádha; 2 daily; 2hr); Vassilikí (Lefkádha; 2 daily; 1hr). **Argostóli** to: Kyllíni (2 daily; 1hr 45min); Lixoúri (every 30min; 20min). **Pessádha** to: Áyios Nikólaos (Zákynthos; 2 daily; 1hr 30min). Most routes maintain one daily service in winter – check with Port Authorities (Argostóli ☎0671/22 224; Sámi ☎0674/22 031; Póros ☎0674/72 460).

Buses 3 daily from Argostóli to Athens (6hr). 1 daily from Lixoúri, Póros and Sámi.

Itháki (Ithaca)

Seasonal **ferries** from **Fríkes** to: Fiskárdho (Kefaloniá; 1 daily; 1hr); Nydhrí (Lefkádha; 1 daily; 2hr); Vassilikí (Lefkádha; 1 daily; 1hr). **Pisaetós** to: Sámi (Kefaloniá; 5 daily; 30min). **Váthy** to: Sámi (Kefaloniá; 1–2 daily; 1hr); Astakós (2 daily; 1hr 30min); Pátra (2 daily; 5hr). **Off season**, there is one daily service on each route, weather permitting – check with Port Authority (☎0674 32 909).

Zákynthos

Ferries from: **Zákynthos Town** to: Kyllíni (5 daily all year, up to 10 in season; 1hr 30min). **Áyios Nikólaos** to: Pessádha (Kefaloniá; 2 daily May–Sept; 1hr 30min).

Buses from Zákynthos Town to Athens (3–7 daily, according to season; 6hr).

Flight (on Olympic) from Zákynthos Town to Athens (1 daily; 1hr).

THE HISTORICAL FRAMEWORK

This section is intended just to lend some perspective to travels in Greece, and is heavily weighted towards the era of the modern, post-independence nation – especially the twentieth century. More detailed accounts of particular periods (Mycenae, Minoan Crete, Classical Athens, Byzantine Mystra and so on) are to be found in relevant sections of the guide.

NEOLITHIC, MINOAN AND MYCENAEAN AGES

Other than the solitary discovery of a fossilized Neanderthal skull near Thessaloníki, the earliest **evidence of human settlement** in Greece is to be found at Néa Nikomedhía, near Véria. Here, traces of large, rectangular houses dated to around 6000 BC have been excavated.

It seems that people originally came to this eastern Mediterranean territory in fits and starts, predominantly from Anatolia. These **pre-Hellenes** settled in essentially peaceful farming communities, made pottery and worshipped earth/fertility goddesses – clay statuettes of which are still found on the sites of old settlements. This simple way of life eventually disappeared, as people started to tap the land's resources for profit and to compete and trade.

MINOANS AND MYCENAEANS

The years between around **2000** and **1100 BC** were a period of fluctuating regional dominance, based at first upon sea power, with vast **royal palaces** serving as centres of administration. Particularly important were those at **Knossos** in Crete, and **Mycenae**, **Tiryns** and **Pylos** in the Peloponnese.

Crete monopolized the eastern Mediterranean trade routes during an era subsequently called the **Minoan Age**, with the palace at Knossos surviving two earthquakes and a massive volcanic eruption on the island of Thíra (Santoríni), at some indefinite point between 1500 and 1450 BC. The most obvious examples of Minoan culture can be seen in frescoes, in jewellery and in pottery, the distinctive red-and-white design on a dark background marking the peak period of Minoan achievement. When Knossos finally succumbed to disaster, natural or otherwise, around 1400 BC, it was the flourishing centre of **Mycenae** that assumed the leading role (and gave its name to the civilization of this period), until it in turn collapsed around 1200 BC.

This is a period whose history and remains are bound up with its **legends**, recounted most famously by Homer and his disciples. Knossos was the home of King Minos, while the palaces of Mycenae and Pylos were the respective bases of Agamemnon and Nestor; Menelaos and Odysseus hailed from Sparta and Ithaca. The Homeric and other legends relating to them almost certainly reflect the prevalence of violence, revenge and **war** as increasing facts of life, instigated and aggravated by trade rivalry. The increasing scale of conflict and militarization is exemplified in the massive fortifications – dubbed Cyclopean by later ages, after the only beings thought capable of hefting the huge stones – that were built around many of the palaces.

The Greece of these years was by no means a united nation – as the Homeric legend reflects – and its people were divided into what were in effect a series of splinter groups, defined in large part by sea and mountain barriers and by access to **pasture**. Settlements flourished according to their proximity to and prowess on the sea and the fertility of their land; most were self-sufficient, specializing in the production of particular items for **trade**. Olives, for example, were associated with the region of Attica, and minerals with the island of Mílos.

THE DORIAN AND CLASSICAL ERAS

The Mycenaean-era Greek states had also to cope with and assimilate periodic influxes of new peoples and trade. The traditional view of the collapse of the Mycenaean civilization has it that a northern "barbarian" tribe, the **Dorians**, "invaded" from the north, devastating the existing palace culture and inaugurating a "dark age"; a competing theory has the so-called "Sea Peoples", probably based in southwestern Anatolia, conducting a series of raids over several decades. These days, archeologists see the influx more in terms of shifting trade patterns, though undoubtedly there was major disruption of the palace cultures and their sea power during the eleventh century.

Two other trends are salient to the period: the almost total supplanting of the mother goddesses by **male deities** (a process begun under the Mycenaeans) and the appearance of an **alphabet** still recognizable by modern Greeks, which replaced the so-called "Linear A" and "Linear B" Minoan/Mycenaean scripts.

CITY-STATES: SPARTA AND ATHENS

The ninth century BC ushered in the beginnings of the Greek **city-state** (*polis*). Citizens – rather than just kings or aristocrats – became involved in government and took part in community activities and organized industry and leisure. Colonial ventures increased, as did commercial dealings, and a consequent rise in the import trade was gradually to create a new class of manufacturers.

The city-state was the life of the people who dwelt within it and each state retained both its independence and a distinctive style, with the result that the sporadic attempts to unite in a league against an external enemy were always pragmatic and temporary. The two most powerful states to emerge were Athens and Sparta, who were to exercise rivalry over the next five centuries.

Sparta was associated with the Dorians, who had settled in large numbers on the fertile Eurotas (Évrotas) river plain. The society of Sparta and its environs was based on a highly militaristic, hierarchical ethos, accentuated by the need to defend the exposed and fertile land on which it stood. Rather than build intricate fortifications, the people of Sparta relied upon military prowess and a system of laws decreed by the (semi-legendary) **Lycurgus**. Males were subjected to military instruction between the ages of seven and thirty. Weak babies were known periodically to "disappear"; the majority of the population, the helots, existed in a state of serfdom as they worked to support the elite. Girls too had to perform athletic feats of sprinting and wrestling, and even dwellings were more like barracks than houses.

Athens, the fulcrum of the state of Attica, was dynamic and exciting by contrast, though here too slavery and its variants were vital to the economy. Home to the administrations of **Solon** and **Pericles**, the dramatic talents of Sophocles and Aristophanes, the oratory of the historian Thucydides and Demosthenes, and the philosophical power of Socrates and Plato, it made up in cultural achievement what it lacked in Spartan virtue. Yet Sparta did not deserve all the military glory. The Athens of the sixth and fifth centuries BC, the so-called **Classical period** in Greek history, played the major part in repelling the armies of the Persian king Xerxes at Marathon (490 BC) and Salamis (480 BC), campaigns later described by Aeschylus in *The Persians*.

Athens also gave rise to a tradition of **democracy** (*demokratia*), literally "control by the people" – although at this stage "the people" did not include either women or slaves. In Athens there were three organs of government. The Areopagus, composed of the city elders, had a steadily decreasing authority and ended up dealing solely with murder cases. Then there was the Council of Five Hundred (men), elected annually by ballot to prepare the business of the Assembly and to attend to matters of urgency. The Assembly gave every free man a political voice; it had sole responsibility for law-making and provided an arena for the discussion of important issues. It was a genuinely enfranchised council of citizens.

This was a period of intense creativity, particularly in Athens, whose actions and pretensions were fast becoming imperial in all but name. Each city-state had its **acropolis**, or high town, where religious activity was focused. In Athens, Pericles endowed the acropolis with a complex of buildings, whose climax was the temple of the Parthenon. Meanwhile, the era saw the tragedies of Sophocles performed, and the philosophies of Socrates and Plato expounded.

Religion at this stage was polytheistic, ordering the eleven other main Olympian gods under the aegis of Zeus. Urban temples tended to be dedicated to Zeus, Athena or Poseidon. In the countryside the proliferation of names and of sanctuary finds suggests a preference for Apollo, Hera, Dionysos and Artemis.

THE PELOPONNESIAN WAR

The power struggles between Athens and Sparta, allied with various networks of city-states, eventually culminated in the **Peloponnesian War** of 431–404 BC. After these conflicts, superbly recorded by Thucydides and nominally won by Sparta, the city-state ceased to function so effectively.

This was in part due to drained resources and political apathy, but to a greater degree a consequence of the increasingly commercial and complex pressures on everyday life. Trade, originally spurred by the invention of **coinage** in the sixth century BC, continued to expand; a revitalized Athens, for example, was exporting wine, oil and manufactured goods, getting corn in return from the Black Sea and Egypt.

The amount of time each man had to devote to the affairs of government decreased, and a position in political life became a professional job rather than a natural assumption. Democracy had changed, while in philosophy there was a shift from the idealists and mystics of the sixth and fifth centuries BC to the Cynics, Stoics and Epicureans – followers, respectively, of Diogenes, Zeno and Epicurus.

HELLENISTIC AND ROMAN GREECE

The most important factor in the decline of the city-states was meanwhile developing outside their sphere, in the kingdom of Macedonia.

THE MACEDONIAN EMPIRE

Ruling from the Macedonian capital of Pella, **Philip II** (reigned 359–336 BC) was forging a strong military and unitary force, extending his territories into Thrace and finally establishing control over Athens and southern Greece. His son, **Alexander the Great**, in a brief but glorious thirteen-year reign, extended these gains into Persia and Egypt and parts of modern India and Afghanistan.

This unwieldy empire splintered almost immediately upon Alexander's death in 323 BC, to be divided into the three Macedonian dynasties of **Hellenistic Greece**: the Antigonids in Macedonia, the Seleucids in Syria and Persia and the Ptolemies in Egypt. Each were in turn conquered and absorbed by the new Roman empire, the Ptolemies – under their queen Cleopatra – last of all.

ROMAN GREECE

Mainland Greece was subdued by the Romans over some seventy years of campaigns, from 215 to 146 BC. Once in control, however, **Rome** allowed considerable autonomy to the old territories of the city-states. Greek remained the official language of the eastern Mediterranean, and its traditions and culture coexisted fairly peacefully with that of the overlords during the next three centuries.

In central Greece both **Athens** and **Corinth** remained important cities but the emphasis was shifting north – particularly to towns, such as **Salonica** (Thessaloníki), along the new Via Egnatia, a military and civil road engineered between Rome and Byzantium via the port of Brundisium (modern Brindisi in Italy).

THE BYZANTINE EMPIRE AND MEDIEVAL GREECE

The shift of emphasis to the north was given even greater impetus by the decline of the Roman empire and its apportioning into eastern and western empires. In 330 AD Emperor Constantine moved his capital to the Greek city of Byzantium, and here emerged Constantinople (modern Istanbul), the "new Rome" and spiritual and political capital of the **Byzantine empire**.

While the last western Roman emperor was deposed by barbarian Goths in 476, this eastern portion was to be the dominant Mediterranean power for some seven hundred years; only in 1453 did it collapse completely.

CHRISTIANITY

Christianity had been introduced under Constantine; by the end of the fourth century it was the official state religion, its liturgies (still in use in the Greek Orthodox Church), creed and New Testament all written in Greek. However, a distinction must be drawn between perceptions of Greek as a language and culture and as a concept. The Byzantine empire styled itself Roman, or *Romios*, rather than Hellenic, and moved to eradicate all remaining symbols of pagan Greece. The Delphic Oracle was forcibly closed, and the Olympic Games discontinued, by the emperor Theodosius I in 391–92 AD. Schools of philosophy, especially neo-Platonic ones, did however survive until 529.

The seventh century saw **Constantinople** besieged by Persians, and later Arabs, but the Byzantine empire survived, losing only Egypt, the least "Greek" of its territories. From the ninth to the early eleventh centuries it enjoyed an archetypal "golden age" in culture, confidence and security. Bound up with the Orthodox Byzantine faith was a sense of spiritual superiority, and the emperors saw Constantinople as a "new Jerusalem" for their "chosen people". It was the beginning of a diplomatic and ecclesiastical conflict with the Catholic West that was to have disastrous consequences over the next five centuries. In the meantime the eastern and western patriarchs mutually excommunicated each other.

From the seventh until the eleventh centuries **Byzantine Greece**, certainly in the south and centre, became something of a provincial backwater. Administration was absurdly top-heavy and imperial taxation led to semi-autonomous provinces ruled by military generals, whose lands were usually acquired from bankrupted peasants. This alienation of the poor provided a force for change, with a disaffected populace ready to turn to or co-operate with the empire's enemies if the terms offered were an improvement.

Waves of **Slavic raiders** needed no encouragement to sweep down from the north Balkans throughout this period. At the same time other tribal groups moved down more peaceably from **central Europe** and were absorbed with little difficulty. According to one theory, the nomadic **Vlachs** from Romania eventually settled in the Píndhos Mountains, and later, from the thirteenth century onwards, immigrants from **Albania** repopulated the islands of Spétses, Ídhra, Ándhros and Évvia, as well as parts of Attica and the Peloponnese.

THE CRUSADES: FRANKISH AND VENETIAN RULE

From the early years of the eleventh century, less welcome and less assimilable Western forces began to appear. The **Normans** landed first at Corfu in 1085, and returned again to the mainland with papal sanction a decade later on their way to liberate Jerusalem.

These were only a precursor, though, for the forces that were to descend en route for the **Fourth Crusade** of 1204, when Venetians, Franks and Germans turned their armies directly on Byzantium and sacked and occupied Constantinople. These Latin princes and their followers, intent on new lands and kingdoms, settled in to divide up the best part of the empire. All that remained of Byzantium were four small peripheral kingdoms or **despotates**: the most powerful in Nicaea in Asia Minor, less significant ones at Trebizond on the Black Sea, and (in present-day Greece) in Epirus and around Mystra in the Peloponnese (known in these times as the Morea).

There followed two extraordinarily involved centuries of manipulation and struggle between Franks, Venetians, Genoese, Catalans and Turks. The Paleologos dynasty at Nicaea recovered the city of Constantinople in 1261, but little of its former territory and power. Instead, the focus of Byzantium shifted to the Peloponnese, where the autonomous **Despotate of Mystra**, ruled by members of the imperial family, eventually succeeded in wresting most of the peninsula from Frankish hands. At the same time this despotate underwent an intense cultural renaissance, strongly evoked in the churches and shells of cities still visible at Mystra and Monemvasía.

TURKISH OCCUPATION

Within a generation of driving out the Franks, the Byzantine Greeks faced a much stronger threat in the expanding empire of the **Ottoman Turks**. Torn apart by internal struggles between their own ruling dynasties, the **Palaeologi** and **Cantacuzenes**, and unaided by the Catholic West, they were to prove no match for the Turks. On Tuesday, May 29, 1453, a date still solemnly commemorated by the Orthodox Church, Constantinople fell to besieging Muslim Turks.

Mystra was to follow within seven years, and Trebizond within nine, by which time virtually all of the old Byzantine empire lay under Ottoman domination. Only the **Ionian islands** and the **Cyclades**, which remained Venetian, and a few scattered and remote enclaves – like the Máni in the Peloponnese, Sfákia in Crete and Soúli in Epirus – were able to resist the Turkish advance.

OTTOMAN RULE

Under what Greeks refer to as the "Yurkokratía" or era of **Ottoman rule**, the lands of present-day Greece passed into rural provincialism, taking refuge in a self-protective mode of village life that was only substantially disrupted by World War II. Taxes and discipline, sporadically backed up by the massacre of dissenting communities, were inflicted by the Turkish Porte, but large areas passed into the hands of local chieftains who often had considerable independence.

Greek identity, meanwhile, was preserved through the offices of the **Orthodox Church** which, despite instances of enforced conversion, the sultans allowed to continue. The **monasteries**, sometimes secretly, organized schools and became the trustees of Byzantine culture, though this had gone into stagnation after the fall of Constantinople and Mystra, whose scholars and artists emigrated west, adding impetus to the Renaissance.

As Ottoman administration became more and more decentralized and inefficient, individual Greeks rose to local positions of considerable influence, and a number of communities achieved a degree of autonomy. Ambelákia village in Thessaly, for example, established an industrial co-operative system to export dyed cloth to Europe, paying only direct taxes to the sultan. And on the Albanian-repopulated islands of the Argo-Saronic Gulf, a **Greek merchant fleet** came into being in the eighteenth century, permitted to trade throughout the Mediterranean. Greeks, too, were becoming organized overseas in the sizable expatriate colonies of central Europe, which often had affiliations with the semi-autonomous village clusters of Zagória (in Epirus) and Mount Pílion.

THE STRUGGLE FOR INDEPENDENCE

Despite these privileges, by the eighteenth century opposition to Turkish rule was becoming widespread, exemplified most obviously by the **klephts** (brigands) of the mountains. It was not until the nineteenth century, however, that a resistance movement could muster sufficient support and firepower to prove a real challenge

to the Turks. In 1770 a Russian-backed uprising had been easily and brutally suppressed, but fifty years later the situation was different.

In Epirus the Turks were over-extended in subduing the expansionist campaigns of local ruler **Ali Pasha**. The French Revolution had given impetus to "freedom movements", and the Greek fighters were provided with financial and ideological underpinnings by the Filikí Etería, or "Friendly Society", a secret group recruited among the exiled merchants and intellectuals of central Europe.

This somewhat motley coalition of klephts and theorists launched their insurrection at the monastery of **Ayía Lávra** near Kalávryta in the Peloponnese, where on March 25, 1821, the Greek banner was openly raised by the local bishop, Yermanos.

THE WAR OF INDEPENDENCE

To describe in detail the course of the **War of Independence** is to provoke unnecessary confusion, since much of the rebellion consisted of local and fragmentary guerrilla campaigns. What is important to understand is that Greeks, though fighting for liberation from the Ottomans, were not fighting as and for a nation. Motives differed enormously: landowners assumed their role was to lead and sought to retain and reinforce their traditional privileges, while the peasantry saw the struggle as a means towards land redistribution.

Outside Greece, the prestige of and publicity for the insurrection were promoted by the arrival of a thousand or so European **Philhellenes**, almost half of them German, though the most important was the English poet, **Lord Byron**, who died while training Greek forces at Messolóngi in April 1824.

Though it was the Greek guerrilla leaders, above all **Theodhoros Kolokotronis**, "the old man of the Morea", who brought about the most significant military victories of the war, the death of Byron had an immensely important effect on public opinion in the West. Aid for the Greek struggle had come neither from Orthodox Russia, nor from the Western powers of France and Britain, ravaged by the Napoleonic Wars. But by 1827, when Messolóngi fell again to the Turks, these three "Great Powers" finally agreed to seek autonomy for certain parts of Greece, and they sent a combined fleet to put pressure on the sultan's Egyptian army, then ransacking and massacring in the Peloponnese. Events took over, and an accidental naval battle in **Navarino Bay** resulted in the destruction of almost the entire Turkish-Egyptian fleet. The following spring Russia itself declared war on the Turks and the sultan was forced to accept the existence of an autonomous Greece.

In 1830 Greek independence was confirmed by the Western powers, and **borders** were drawn in 1832. These included just 800,000 of the six million Greeks living within the Ottoman empire, and Greek territories which were for the most part the poorest of the Classical and Byzantine lands, comprising Attica, the Peloponnese and the islands of the Argo-Saronic, Sporades and Cyclades. The rich agricultural belt of Thessaly, Epirus in the west and Macedonia in the north remained in Turkish hands. Meanwhile, the Ionian islands were controlled by a British protectorate and the Dodecanese by the Ottomans (and subsequently by the new Italian nation).

THE EMERGING STATE

Modern Greece began as a republic and **Ioannis Kapodistrias**, its first president, concentrated his efforts on building a viable central authority and government in the face of diverse protagonists from the independence struggle. Almost inevitably he was assassinated – in 1831, by two chieftains from the ever-disruptive Máni – and perhaps equally inevitably the three powers stepped in. They created a monarchy, gave limited aid and set on the throne a Bavarian prince, **Otho (Otto)**.

The new king proved an autocratic and insensitive ruler, bringing in fellow Germans to fill official posts and ignoring all claims by the landless peasantry for redistribution of the old estates. In 1862 he was forced from the country by a popular revolt, and the Europeans produced a new prince, this time from Denmark, who requested that Britain cede the Ionian islands as a condition of accession. **George I**, in fact, proved more capable: he had the first railways and roads built, introduced limited land reforms in the Peloponnese and oversaw the first expansion of the Greek borders.

THE MEGÁLI IDHÉA AND EXPANSIONIST WARS

From the very beginning, the unquestioned motive force of Greek foreign policy was the

Megáli Idhéa (Great Idea) of liberating Greek populations outside the country and incorporating the old territories of Byzantium into the kingdom. In 1878 **Thessaly**, along with southern Epirus, was ceded to Greece by the Turks.

Less illustriously, the Greeks failed in 1897 to achieve *énosis* (union) with **Crete** by attacking Turkish forces on the mainland, and in the process virtually bankrupted the state. The island was, however, placed under a high commissioner, appointed by the Great Powers, and in 1913 became a part of Greece.

It was from Crete, also, that the most distinguished modern Greek statesman emerged. **Eleftherios Venizelos**, having led a civilian campaign for his island's liberation, was elected as Greek prime minister in 1910. Two years later he organized an alliance of Balkan powers to fight the **Balkan Wars** (1912–13), campaigns that saw the Turks virtually driven from Europe. With Greek borders extended to include the northeast Aegean islands, northern Thessaly, central Epirus and parts of Macedonia, the *Megáli Idhéa* was approaching reality. At the same time Venizelos proved himself a shrewd manipulator of domestic public opinion by revising the constitution and introducing a series of liberal social reforms.

Division, however, was to appear with the outbreak of **World War I**. Venizelos urged Greek entry on the British side, seeing in the conflict possibilities for the "liberation" of Greeks in Thrace and Asia Minor, but the new king, Constantine I, who was married to a sister of the German Kaiser, imposed a policy of neutrality. Eventually Venizelos set up a revolutionary government in Thessaloníki, polarizing the country into a state of civil war along Venezelist–Royalist lines, but in 1917 Greek troops entered the war to join the French, British and Serbians in the **Macedonian campaign**. Upon the capitulation of Bulgaria and Ottoman Turkey, the Greeks occupied **Thrace**, and Venizelos presented demands at Versailles for the predominantly Greek region of Smyrna on the Asia Minor coast.

THE KATASTROFI AND ITS AFTERMATH

This was the beginning of one of the most disastrous episodes in modern Greek history, the so-called **Katastrofí** (Catastrophe). Venizelos was authorized to move forces into Smyrna in

1919, but in Turkey itself a new nationalist movement was taking power under Mustafa Kemal, or **Atatürk** as he came to be known. In 1920 Venizelos lost the elections and monarchist factions took over, their aspirations unmitigated by the Cretan's skill in foreign diplomacy. Despite Allied support for such ventures now having completely evaporated, Greek forces were ordered to advance upon Ankara in an attempt to bring Atatürk to terms.

This so-called **Anatolian campaign** ignominiously collapsed in summer 1922 when Turkish troops forced the Greeks back to the coast and a hurried evacuation from **Smyrna**. As they left Smyrna, the Turks moved in and systematically massacred much of the Armenian and Greek population before burning most of the city to the ground.

Although an entire Greek army remained intact in eastern Thrace, Britain, hitherto Greece's only backer, let it be known that Greece would be wisest to accept Atatürk's own terms, formalized by the Treaty of Lausanne in 1923, which ordered the **exchange of religious minorities** in each country – in effect, the first large-scale regulated ethnic cleansing. Turkey was to accept 390,000 Muslims resident on Greek soil. Greece, mobilized almost continuously for the last decade and with a population of under five million, was faced with the resettlement of over 1,300,000 Christian refugees, many of whom had already reached Greece between 1919 and 1922. The *Megáli Idhéa* had ceased to be a viable blueprint.

Changes, inevitably, were intense and far-reaching. The last great agricultural estates of Thessaly were finally redistributed, both to Greek tenants and refugee farmers, and huge shanty towns grew into new quarters around Athens, Pireás and other cities, a spur to the country's then almost nonexistent industry.

Politically, too, reaction was even swifter. By September 1922, a group of Venizelist army officers under **Colonel Nikolaos Plastiras** assembled after the retreat from Smyrna, "invited" King Constantine to abdicate and executed six of his ministers held most responsible for the debacle. Democracy was nominally restored with the proclamation of a republic, but for much of the next decade changes in government were brought about by factions within the armed forces. Meanwhile, among the urban refugee population, unions were being formed

and the Greek Communist Party (KKE) was established.

VENIZELOS'S LAST GASP – AND THE RISE OF METAXAS

Elections in 1928 returned **Venizelos** to power, but a series of economic problems forced him from office in 1932. Venizelos's supporters under Plastiras attempted to reinstate him by means of a putsch in March 1933, but the coup was quashed and Venizelos fled into exile in Paris, where he died three years later.

By 1936 the Communist Party had enough electoral support to hold the balance of power in parliament, and would have done so had not the army and the by-then restored king decided otherwise. **King George (Yeóryios) II** had been returned by a plebiscite held the previous year, and so presided over an increasingly factionalized parliament.

In April 1936 George II appointed **General John Metaxas** as prime minister, despite the latter's being supported by only six elected deputies. Immediately a series of KKE-organized strikes broke out and the king, ignoring attempts to form a broad liberal coalition, dissolved parliament without setting a date for new elections. It was a blatantly unconstitutional move and opened the way for five years of ruthless and at times absurd dictatorship.

Metaxas averted a general strike with military force and proceeded to set up a state based on **fascist** models of the age. Left-wing and trade-union opponents were imprisoned or forced into exile, a state youth movement and secret police set up and rigid censorship, extending even to passages of Thucydides, imposed. But it was at least a Greek dictatorship, and though Metaxas was sympathetic to Nazi organizational methods and economics, he completely opposed German or Italian domination.

WORLD WAR II AND THE GREEK CIVIL WAR

Using a submarine based in the Dodecanese, the Italians tried to provoke the Greeks into prematurely entering **World War II** by surreptitiously torpedoing the Greek cruiser *Elli* in Tínos harbour on August 15, 1940, but they met with no response. However, when Mussolini occupied Albania and sent an ultimatum on October

28, 1940, demanding passage for his troops through Greece, Metaxas responded to the Italian foreign minister with the apocryphal one-word answer **"óhi"** (no). (In fact, his response, in the mutually understood French, was "C'est la guerre.") The date marked the entry of Greece into the war, and the gesture is still celebrated as a national holiday.

Galvanized into brief unity by the crisis, the Greeks drove Italian forces from the country and moreover managed to take control of the long-coveted and predominantly Greek-populated northern Epirus (southern Albania). However, the Greek army subsequently frittered away its strength in the snowy mountains of northern Epirus rather than consolidating its gains or defending the Macedonian frontier, and co-ordination with the British never materialized.

OCCUPATION AND RESISTANCE

In April of the following year Nazi mechanized columns swept through Yugoslavia and across the Greek mainland, effectively reversing the only Axis defeat to date, and by late May 1941, airborne and seaborne **German invasion** forces had completed the occupation of Crete and the other islands. Metaxas had died before their arrival, while King George and his new self-appointed ministers fled into exile in Cairo; few Greeks, of any political persuasion, were sad to see them go.

The joint Italian-German-Bulgarian Axis **occupation** of Greece was among the bitterest experiences of the European war. Nearly half a million Greek civilians starved to death over the winter of 1941–42, as all available food was requisitioned, principally by the Germans, to feed occupying armies. In addition, entire villages throughout the mainland, but especially on Crete, were burned at the least hint of resistance activity and nearly 130,000 civilians slaughtered. In their northern sector, the Bulgarians additionally desecrated ancient sites and churches to support a future bid to annex "Slavic" Macedonia.

Primarily in the north, too, the Nazis supervised during 1944 the deportation to concentration camps of virtually the entire **Greek-Jewish population** of nearly 80,000. Thessaloníki – where the former UN secretary-general and Austrian president Kurt Waldheim worked for Nazi intelligence – contained 57,000, the largest Jewish population of any

Balkan city, and there were significant populations in all the Greek mainland towns and on many of the islands. After the Italians capitulated in September 1943, the Jewish communities in Rhodes, Kós, Crete, Corfu, Vólos, Évvia and Zákynthos in particular were exposed to the full force of **Nazi racial doctrine**, though in the last three places co-operation between courageous church or municipal authorities and the budding Resistance (see below), ensured that most local Jews survived.

With a quisling government in Athens – and an unpopular, discredited royalist government-in-exile in Cairo – the focus of Greek political and military action over the next four years passed largely to the **EAM**, or National Liberation Front. By 1943 it was in virtual control of most areas of the country, working with the British on tactical operations, with its own army (**ELAS**), navy and both civil and secret police forces. Initially it commanded widespread popular support and appeared to offer an obvious framework for the resumption of postwar government.

However, most of its highest-ranking members were communists, and the British prime minister, **Winston Churchill**, was determined to reinstate the monarchy. Even with two years of the war to run, it became obvious that there could be no peaceable post-liberation regime other than a republic. Accordingly, in August 1943, representatives from each of the main resistance movements (including two noncommunist groups) flew clandestinely to Cairo to request that the king not return unless a plebiscite had first voted in his favour. Both the Greek and British authorities refused to consider the proposal, and the best possibility of averting civil war was lost.

The EAM contingent returned divided, as perhaps the British had intended, and a **conflict** broke out between those who favoured taking peaceful control of any government imposed after liberation, and the hard-line Stalinist ideologues, who forbade Popular-Front-type participation in any "bourgeois" regime.

In October 1943, with fears of an imminent British landing force and takeover, ELAS launched a **full-scale attack** upon its Greek rivals; by the following April, they had wiped out all but the EDES, a right-wing grouping suspected of collaboration with the Germans. At the same time other forces were at work, with both the British and Americans infiltrating units into Greece in order to prevent the establishment of a communist government when the Germans began withdrawing their forces.

LIBERATION AND CIVIL WAR

In fact, as the Germans began to leave in October 1944, most of the EAM leadership agreed to join a British-sponsored "official" **interim government**. It quickly proved a tactical error, however. With almost ninety percent of the provinces under their control, the communists were eventually given only one-third representation in Athens, and a new regular army began to formed, based on the extreme-right-wing Mountain Brigade, the Sacred Band and even the fascist Security Battalions, rather than the ELAS officer corps. The king showed no sign of renouncing his claims, and, in November, Allied forces under British general Ronald Scobie ordered ELAS to disarm. On December 3 all pretences of civility or neutrality were dropped; the police fired on an EAM demonstration in Athens, killing at least sixteen, and fighting broke out between ELAS and **British troops**, in the so-called **Dhekemvrianá** battle of Athens.

A truce of sorts was negotiated at Várkiza the following February, but the agreement was never implemented. The army, police and civil service remained in right-wing hands and while collaborationists were often allowed to retain their positions, left-wing sympathizers, many of whom were not communists, were systematically excluded. The elections of March 1946 were won by the right-wing parties (after a left-wing boycott), followed by yet another rigged plebiscite in favour of the king's return. By 1947 guerrilla activity had again reached the scale of a full **civil war**, with ELAS reorganized into the Democratic Army of Greece (**DSE** in Greek).

In the interim, King George had died and been succeeded by his brother Paul (with his consort Frederika), while the **Americans** had taken over the British role, and begun implementing the cold-war **Truman doctrine**. In March 1947 they took virtual control of Greece, their first significant postwar experiment in anti-communist intervention. Massive economic and military aid was given to a client Greek government, with official decrees that had to be countersigned by the American Mission chief in order to become valid.

In the mountains US military advisers trained the initially woeful Nationalist army for **campaigns against the DSE**, and in the cities there were mass arrests, court-martials and imprisonments – a kind of "White Terror" – lasting until 1951. Over three thousand government executions were recorded, including a number of Jehovah's Witnesses, "a sect proved to be under communist domination", according to US Ambassador Grady.

In the autumn of 1949, with the Yugoslav-Greek border closed after Tito's rift with Stalin, the last DSE guerrillas finally admitted defeat, retreating into Albania from their strongholds on Mount Grámmos. Atrocities had been committed on both sides, including, from the Left, rather more than three thousand executions, widescale vandalization of monasteries and the dubious evacuation of children from "combat areas" (as told in Nicholas Gage's virulently anti-communist book *Eleni*). Such errors, as well as the high percentage of openly separatist Slavophones amongst their ranks, and the hopelessness of 30,000 lightly armed guerrillas fighting an American-backed army, undoubtedly doomed the DSE's efforts from the start.

RECONSTRUCTION AMERICAN STYLE 1950–67

It was thus a demoralized, shattered Greece that emerged into the Western political orbit of the 1950s. The country was perforce American-dominated, enlisted into the Korean War in 1950 and NATO the following year. In domestic politics, the US embassy – still giving the orders – foisted upon the Greeks a winner-take-all electoral system, which was to ensure victory for the Right over the next twelve years. All leftist activity was banned; those individuals who were not herded into political "re-education" camps or dispatched by firing squads, legal or vigilante, went into exile throughout Eastern Europe, to return only after 1974.

The American-backed, highly conservative **"Greek Rally"** party, led by General Papagos, won the first decisive post-civil-war elections in 1952. After the general's death, the party's leadership was taken over – and to an extent liberalized – by **Constantine Karamanlis**. Under his rule, stability of a kind was established and some economic advances registered, particularly after the revival of Greece's traditional German markets. However, the 1950s was also a decade that saw wholesale **depopulation** of remote villages as migrants sought work in Australia, America and western Europe, or the larger Greek cities.

The main crisis in foreign policy throughout this period was **Cyprus**, where a long terrorist campaign was waged by Greek-Cypriots opposing British rule, and there were sporadic threats of a new Greco-Turkish war. An ultimately unworkable compromise solution was forced on the island by Britain in 1960, granting independence without the possibility of "self-determination" (union with Greece). Much of the traditional Greek-British goodwill was destroyed by the issue, with Britain seen to be acting with regard primarily for its two military bases (over which, incidentally, it still retains sovereignty).

By 1961, unemployment, the Cyprus issue and the imposition of US nuclear bases on Greek soil were changing the political climate, and when Karamanlis was again elected there was strong suspicion of a fraud arranged by the king and army. Strikes became frequent in industry and even agriculture, and King Paul and autocratic, fascist-inclined Queen Frederika were openly attacked in parliament and at protest demonstrations. The far right grew uneasy about **"communist resurgence"** and, losing confidence in their own electoral influence, arranged the **assassination** of left-wing deputy **Grigoris Lambrakis** in Thessaloníki in May 1963. (The murder, and its subsequent cover-up, is the subject of Vassilis Vassilikos's thriller Z, filmed by Costa-Gavras.) It was against this volatile background that Karamanlis dissolved parliament, lost the subsequent elections and left the country.

The new government – the first controlled from outside the Greek Right since 1935 – was formed by **George Papandreou's Centre Union Party**, and had a decisive majority of nearly fifty seats. It was to last, however, for under two years as conservative forces rallied to thwart its progress. In this the chief protagonists were army officers and their constitutional commander-in-chief, the new king, 23-year-old **Constantine II**.

Since power in Greece depended on a pliant military as well as a network of political appointees, Papandreou's most urgent task in order to govern securely and effectively was to reform the armed forces. His first minister of defence proved incapable of the task and, while

he was investigating the right-wing plot that was thought to have rigged the 1961 election, "evidence" was produced of a leftist conspiracy connected with Papandreou's son Andreas (also a minister in the government). When the allegations grew to a crisis, George Papandreou decided to assume the defence portfolio himself, a move for which the king refused to give the necessary sanction. He then resigned in order to gain approval at the polls but the king would not order fresh elections, instead persuading members of the Centre Union – chief among them **Constantine Mitsotakis** – to defect and organize a coalition government. Punctuated by strikes, resignations and mass demonstrations, this lasted for a year and a half until new elections were eventually set for May 28, 1967. They failed to take place.

THE COLONELS' JUNTA 1967–74

It was a foregone conclusion that Papandreou's party would win popular support in the polls against the discredited coalition partners. And it was equally certain that there would be some sort of anti-democratic action to try and prevent them from reassuming power. Disturbed by the party's leftward shift, King Constantine was said to have briefed senior generals for a coup d'état, to take place ten days before the elections. However, he was caught by surprise, as was nearly everyone else, by the **coup** of April 21, 1967, staged by a group of "unknown" colonels. It was, in the words of Andreas Papandreou, "the first successful CIA military putsch on the European continent".

The **colonels' junta**, having taken control of the means of power, was sworn in by the king and survived the half-hearted counter-coup which he subsequently attempted to organize. It was an ostensibly **fascist regime**, absurdly styling itself as the true "Revival of Greek Orthodoxy" against Western "corrupting influences", though in reality its ideology was nothing more than warmed-up dogma from the Metaxas era mixed with ultra-nationalism.

All **political activity was banned**, independent trade unions were forbidden to recruit or meet, the press was so heavily censored that many papers stopped printing and thousands of "communists" were arrested, imprisoned and often tortured. Among the persecuted were both Papandreous, the composer Mikis Theodorakis (deemed "unfit to stand trial" after three months in custody) and Amalia Fleming (widow of Alexander Fleming). While relatively few people were killed outright, thousands were permanently maimed in the junta's torture chambers. The best-known Greek actress, Melina Mercouri, was stripped of her citizenship in absentia, and thousands of prominent Greeks joined her in exile. Culturally, the colonels put an end to popular music (closing down most of the live rembétika and *néo kýma* clubs) and inflicted ludicrous censorship on literature and the theatre, including (as under Metaxas) a ban on production of the Classical tragedies.

The colonels lasted for seven years, opposed (especially after the first two years) by the majority of the Greek people, officially excluded from the Council of Europe, but propped up and given massive aid by **US presidents Lyndon Johnson** and **Richard Nixon**. To them and the CIA the junta's Greece was an ideal client state: human rights considerations were then considered trivial; orders were placed for sophisticated military technology; and foreign investment on terms highly unfavourable to Greece was made available to multinational corporations. It was a fairly routine scenario for the exploitation of an underdeveloped nation.

Opposition was voiced from the beginning by exiled Greeks in London, the United States and western Europe, but only in 1973 did **demonstrations** break out openly in Greece. On November 17 the students of **Athens Polytechnic** began an occupation of their buildings. The ruling clique lost its nerve; armoured vehicles stormed the Polytechnic gates and a still-undetermined number of students (estimates range from 34 to three hundred) were killed. Martial law was tightened and junta chief **Colonel Papadopoulos** was replaced by the even more noxious and reactionary **General Ioannides**, head of the secret police.

THE RETURN TO CIVILIAN RULE 1975–81

The end of the ordeal, however, came within a year as the dictatorship embarked on a disastrous political adventure in **Cyprus**. By attempting to topple the Makarios government and impose *énosis* (union) on the island, they provoked a Turkish invasion and occupation of forty percent of Cypriot territory. The army finally mutinied and **Constantine Karamanlis** was invited to return from Paris to again take office. He swiftly negotiated a ceasefire (but no solution) in Cyprus, withdrew temporarily from NATO and warned that US bases would have to be removed except where they specifically served Greek interest.

In November 1974 Karamanlis and his **Néa Dhimokratía (New Democracy) party** were rewarded by a sizable majority in elections, with a centrist and socialist opposition. The latter was constituted as the **Panhellenic Socialist Movement (PASOK)**, a new party led by Andreas Papandreou.

The election of Néa Dhimokratía was in every sense a safe conservative option, but to Karamanlis's enduring credit it oversaw an effective and firm return to democratic stability, even legitimizing the KKE (Communist Party) for the first time in its history. Karamanlis also held a **referendum on the monarchy**; 59 percent of Greeks rejected the return of Constantine II, so he instituted in its place a French-style presidency, which he himself occupied from 1980 to 1985 (and again from 1990 to 1995). Economically there were limited advances, although these were more than offset by inflationary defence spending (the result of renewed tension with Turkey), the hastily negotiated entrance into the EC and the decision to let the drachma float after decades of its being artificially fixed at thirty to the US dollar.

Most crucially, Karamanlis failed to deliver vital reforms in bureaucracy, social welfare and education; and while the worst figures of the junta were brought to trial and jailed indefinitely, the face of Greek political life and administration was little changed. By 1981 inflation was hovering around 25 percent, and it was estimated that tax evasion was depriving the state of one-third of its annual budget. In foreign policy the US bases remained and it was felt that Greece, back in NATO, was still acting as little more than an American satellite. The traditional Right was demonstrably inadequate to the task at hand.

PASOK 1981–89

"Change" (*Allayí*) and "Out with the Right" (*Ná Fíyi íy Dhexiá*) were the watchwords of the election campaign that swept **PASOK** and Andreas Papandreou to power on October 18, 1981.

This victory meant a chance for Papandreou to form the first socialist government in Greek history and break a half-century monopoly of authoritarian right-wing rule. With so much at stake, the campaign had been passionate even by Greek standards, and PASOK's victory was greeted with euphoria both by the generation whose political voice had been silenced in the civil war and by a large proportion of the young. Their hopes perhaps ran naively and dangerously high.

The electoral margin, at least, was conclusive. PASOK won 174 of the 300 parliamentary seats and the Communist KKE – though not a part of the new government – returned another thirteen deputies, one of them composer Mikis Theodorakis, while Néa Dhimokratía moved into unaccustomed opposition. There appeared to be no obstacle to the implementation of a **radical socialist programme**: devolution of power to local authorities, the effective nationalization of heavy industry, improvement of the woefully skeletal social services, a purge of bureaucratic inefficiency and malpractice, the end of bribery and corruption as a way of life, an independent and dignified foreign policy following expulsion of US bases and finally withdrawal from NATO and the European Community.

A change of style was promised, too, replacing the country's long traditions of authoritarianism and bureaucracy with openness and dialogue. Even more radically, given that Greek political parties had long been the personal followings of charismatic leaders, PASOK was to be a party of ideology and principle, dependent on no single individual member. Or so, at least, thought some of the youthful PASOK cadres.

The new era started with a bang. The wartime Resistance was officially recognized; hitherto they hadn't been allowed to take part in any celebrations, wreath-layings or other ceremonies. Peasant women were granted pensions for the first time – 3000 drachmas a month ($55 in 1982), the same as their outraged husbands – and wages were indexed to the cost of living. In addition, civil marriage was introduced, family law was reformed in favour of wives and mothers, and equal rights legislation was put on the statute book.

These popular **reformist moves** seemed to mark a break with the past, and the atmosphere had indeed changed. Greeks no longer lowered their voices to discuss politics in public places

or wrapped their opposition newspaper in the respectably conservative *Kathimerini*. At first there were real fears that the climate would be too much for the military who would once again intervene to choke a dangerous experiment in democracy, especially when Andreas Papandreou assumed the defence portfolio himself in a move strongly reminiscent of his father's attempt to remove the king's appointee in 1965. But he went out of his way to soothe military susceptibilities, increasing their salaries, buying new weaponry and being fastidious in his attendance at military functions.

THE END OF THE HONEYMOON

Nothing if not a populist, **Papandreou** promised a bonanza which he must have known, as an academically trained economist, he could not deliver. As a result he pleased nobody on the economic front.

He could not fairly be blamed for the inherited lack of investment, low productivity, deficiency in managerial and labour skills and other chronic problems besetting the **Greek economy**. However, he certainly aggravated the situation in the early days of his first government by allowing his supporters to indulge in violently anti-capitalist rhetoric, which frightened off potential investors, and by the prosecution and humiliation of the Tsatsos family, owners of one of Greece's few competitive businesses (Hercules Cement) for the illegal export of capital, something of which every Greek with any savings was guilty. These were cheap victories, not backed by any rational programme of public investment, and the only nationalizations were of hopelessly lame-duck companies.

Faced with this sluggish economy and burdened with the additional charges of (marginally) improved social benefits and wage indexing, Papandreou's government had also to cope with the effects of **world recession**, which always hits Greece with a delayed effect compared with its more advanced European partners. **Shipping**, the country's main foreign-currency earner, was devastated. Remittances from emigré workers fell off as they joined the lines of the unemployed in their host countries, and tourism diminished under the dual impact of the recession and US President Ronald Reagan's warning to Americans to stay away from allegedly insecure and terrorist-bomb-prone Athens airport.

With huge quantities of imported goods continuing to be sucked into the country in the absence of significant domestic production, the **foreign debt** topped £10 billion in 1986, while inflation remained at 25 percent and the balance of payments deficit approached £1 billion. Greece also began to experience the social strains of unemployment for the first time. Not that it didn't exist before, but it had always been concealed as under-employment by the family and the rural structure of the economy – as well as by the absence of reliable statistics.

THE SECOND TERM

A modest spending spree transparently intended to buy votes, continued satisfaction at the discomfiture of the Right, the popularity of his Greece-for-the-Greeks foreign policy, plus some much-needed reforms, saw **Papandreou** through into a **second term** with an electoral victory in June 1985 scarcely less triumphant than the first. But his complacent and, frankly, dishonest slogan was "Vote PASOK for Even Better Days". By October PASOK had imposed a two-year wage freeze and import restrictions, abolished the wage-indexing scheme and devalued the drachma by fifteen percent.

Papandreou's fat was pulled out of the fire by none other than his former bogeyman, the European Community, which offered a huge two-part loan on condition that an IMF-style **austerity programme** was maintained.

The political fallout from such classic right-wing strategies, accompanied by shameless soliciting for foreign investment, was the alienation of the Communists and most of PASOK's own core constituency. Increasingly autocratic (ironic, given his earlier pledges of openness), Papandreou's response to **dissent** was to fire recalcitrant trade-union leaders and expel some three hundred members of his own party. Assailed by strikes, the government veered off course completely, and in the local elections of October 1986 it lost abundant ground to Néa Dhimokratía, including the mayoralties of the three major cities of Athens, Thessaloníki and Pátra – the first two retained by them ever since.

Papandreou assured the nation that he had taken the message to heart, but all that followed was a minor government reshuffle and a panicky attempt to undo the ill-feeling caused by an incredible freeing of **rent controls** at a time when all wage-earners were badly feeling

---

WOMEN'S RIGHTS IN GREECE

Women's right to vote wasn't universally achieved in Greece until 1956 and, until the mid-1970s, adultery was still a punishable offence, with cases regularly brought to court. The socialist party, PASOK, was elected for terms of government in 1981 and 1985 with a strong theoretical programme for **women's rights**, and their women's council review committees, set up in the early, heady days, effected a landmark reform with the 1983 **Family Law**. This prohibited dowry and stipulated equal legal status and shared property rights between husband and wife.

Subsequently, however, the PASOK governments did little to follow through on **practical issues**, like improved child care, health and family planning. Contraception is not available as part of the skeletal Greek public health service, leaving many women to fall back on abortions – only recently made legal under certain conditions, but running (as for many years past) to an estimated seventy to eighty thousand a year.

By far the largest organization is the **Union of Greek Women**. Founded in 1976, this espouses an independent feminist line and is responsible for numerous consciousness-raising activities across the country, though it remains too closely linked to PASOK for comfort. As a perfect metaphor for this, Margaret Papandreou felt compelled to resign from the Union following her well-publicized divorce from ex-Premier Andreas, leaving it without her effective and vocal leadership. Other, more autonomous groups, have been responsible for setting up advice and support networks, highlighting women's issues within trade unions and campaigning for changes in media representation.

None of this is easy in a country as polarized as Greece. In many rural areas women rely heavily on traditional extended families for security, and are unlikely to be much affected by legislative reforms or city politics. Yet Greek men of all classes and backgrounds are slowly becoming used to the notion of women in positions of power and responsibility, and are taking a substantial share in child-rearing – both utterly unthinkable two decades ago, and arguably one of the few positive legacies with which PASOK can at least in part be credited.

the pinch. Early in 1987 he went further and sacked all the remaining PASOK veterans in his cabinet, including his own son, though this was merely a palliative to public opinion. The new cabinet was so unsocialist that even the right-wing press called it "centrist".

Similar about-faces took place in **foreign policy**. The first-term anti-US, anti-NATO and anti-EC rhetoric had been immensely popular, and understandable for a people shamelessly bullied by bigger powers since 1830. There was some high-profile nose-thumbing, like refusing to join EC partners in condemning Jaruzelski's Polish regime, the Soviet downing of a Korean airliner or Syrian involvement in terrorist bomb-planting.

Much was made of a strategic opening to the Arab world. Yasser Arafat, for example, was the first "head of state" to be received in Athens under the PASOK government. Given Greece's geographical position and historical ties, it was an imaginative and appropriate policy. But if Arab investment was hoped for, it never materialized.

In stark contrast to these early promises and rhetoric, the "realistic" policies that Papandreou increasingly pursued during his second term were far more conciliatory towards his big Western brothers. This was best exemplified by the fact that **US bases** remained in Greece until 1994, largely due to the fear that snubbing NATO would lead to Greece being exposed to Turkish aggression, still the only issue that unites the main parties to any degree. As for the once-reviled **European Community** (soon to be the European Union), Greece had by now become an established beneficiary, and its leader was hardly about to bite the hand that feeds.

SCANDAL

Even as late as mid-1988, despite the many betrayals and failings of Papandreou, it seemed unlikely that PASOK would be toppled in the following year's **elections**. This was due mainly to the lack of a credible alternative. Constantine Mitsotakis, a bitter personal enemy of Papandreou's since 1965, when his defection had brought down his father's government and set in train the events that culminated in the junta, was an unconvincing and antipathetic character at the helm of Néa Dhimokratía. Meanwhile, the liberal centre parties had disappeared, and the main commu-

nist party, the KKE, appeared trapped in a Stalinist timewarp under the leadership of Harilaos Florakis. Only the **Ellenikí Aristerá (Greek Left)**, formerly the European wing of the KKE, seemed to offer any sensible alternative programme, but they had a precariously small following.

However, a combination of spectacular blunders, plus perhaps a general shift to the right, influenced by the cataclysmic events in Eastern Europe, conspired against PASOK. First came the extraordinary **cavortings of the prime minister** himself. Late in 1988, the seventy-year-old Papandreou was flown to Britain for open-heart surgery. He took the occasion, with fear of death presumably rocking his judgement, to make public a year-long liaison with a 34-year-old Olympic Airways hostess, **Dimitra "Mimi" Liani**. Widespread depiction in the media of an old man shuffling about after a young blonde, to the public humiliation of Margaret, his American-born wife, did little to bolster his image (Papandreou subsequently divorced Margaret and married Mimi). His integrity was further questioned when he missed several important public engagements – including a ceremony commemorating the victims of the 1987 Kalamáta earthquake – and was pictured out with Mimi, reliving his youth in flashy nightspots.

The real damage, however, was done by a series of **economic scandals**. The most serious of these involved a self-made, Greek-American con-man, **Yiorgos Koskotas**, director of the Bank of Crete, who managed to embezzle £120 million (US$190 million) in deposits, distribute it lavishly amongst numerous Greek public figures and, worse still, slip though the authorities' fingers on a private jet to the US. Certain PASOK ministers and even Papandreou himself were implicated in the scandal. Further harm was done by allegations of illegal arms dealings and fraudulent farm-produce sales by various government ministers.

United in disgust at this corruption, the other left-wing parties – KKE and Ellinikí Aristerá – formed a coalition, the **Synaspismós**, taking still more support from PASOK.

THREE BITES AT THE CHERRY

In this climate of disaffection, an inconclusive result to the **June 1989 election** was no real surprise. What was less predictable, however, was the formation of a bizarre **"kathársis"** **(purgative) coalition** of conservatives and communists, united in the avowed intent of cleansing PASOK's increasingly Augean stables.

The Synaspismós would have formed a government with PASOK but set one condition for doing so – that Papandreou should step down as prime minister – and the old man would have none of it. In the deal finally cobbled together between the Left and Néa Dhimokratía, Mitsotakis was denied the premiership, too, having to make way for his compromise party colleague, **Ioannis Tzanetakis**.

During the three months that the coalition lasted, the *kathársis* turned out to be largely a matter of burying the knife as deeply as possible into the ailing body of PASOK. Andreas Papandreou and three other ministers were officially accused of involvement in the Koskotas affair – though there was no time to set up their trial before the Greek people returned once again to the polls. In any case, the chief witness and protagonist in the affair, Koskotas himself, was still imprisoned in America, awaiting extradition proceedings.

Contrary to the Right's hope that publicly accusing Papandreou and his cohorts of criminal behaviour would pave the way for a Néa Dhimokratía victory, PASOK actually made a slight recovery in the **November 1989 elections**, though the result was again inconclusive. This time the Left resolutely refused to do deals with anyone, and the result was a consensus caretaker government under the neutral aegis of an academic named Zolotas, who was reluctantly dragged into the prime minister's office from Athens University. His only mandate was to see that the country didn't go off the rails completely while preparations were made for yet another election.

These took place in **April 1990** with the same captains at the command of their ships and with the Synaspismós having completed its about-turn to the extent that in the five single-seat constituencies (the other 295 seats are drawn from multiple-seat constituencies in a complicated system of reinforced proportional representation), they supported independent candidates jointly with PASOK. Greek communists are good at about-turns, though; after all, composer Mikis Theodorakis, musical torchbearer of the Left during the dark years of the junta, and formerly a KKE MP, was by now

standing for Néa Dhimokratía, prior to his resignation from politics altogether.

On the night, Néa Dhimokratía scraped home with a majority of one, later doubled with the defection of a centrist, and Mitsotakis finally got to achieve his dream of becoming prime minister. The only other memorable feature of the election was the first parliamentary representation for a party of the **Turkish minority** in Thrace by activist Ahmet Sadiq, and for the **Greens**, based in Athens – the latter a focus for many disaffected PASOK voters.

A RETURN TO THE RIGHT: MITSOTAKIS

On assuming power, Mitsotakis followed a course of **austerity measures** to try and revive the chronically ill economy. Little headway was made, though; given the world recession, it was hardly surprising. Greek inflation was still approaching twenty percent annually, and at nearly ten percent, unemployment remained chronic. Yet certain menial jobs went begging, taken only (since 1990) by **impoverished Albanians** who have arrived in numbers over half a million strong. They now form something of a permanent underclass, especially those who aren't ethnically Greek, and are blamed for all manner of ills; they have also prompted the first anti-immigration measures with teeth in a country whose population is more used to being on the other side of such laws.

Other conservative measures introduced by Mitsotakis included laws to combat strikes and terrorism. The **terrorist issue** had been a perennial source of worry for Greeks since the appearance in the mid-1970s of a group called **Dhekaeftá Noemvríou** ("November 17", the date of the colonels' attack on the Polytechnic in 1973). Since 1974, they (and more recent, copycat groups) have killed over twenty industrialists, politicians and NATO military personnel and have attacked buildings of foreign corporations in Athens. It hardly seemed likely that Mitsotakis's laws, however, were the solution. They stipulated that statements by the group could no longer be published, which led to one or two newspaper editors being jailed for a few days for defiance – much to everyone's embarrassment. The **anti-strike laws** threatened severe penalties but were equally ineffectual, as prolonged breakdowns in public transport, electricity and rubbish collection all too frequently illustrated.

As for the **Koskotas scandal**, the man himself was eventually extradited and gave evidence for the prosecution against Papandreou and various of his ministers. The trial was televised and proved as popular as any soap opera, as indeed it should have been, given the twists of high drama – which included one of the defendants, Agamemnon "Menios" Koutsoyiorgas, dying in court of a heart attack in front of the cameras. The case against Papandreou gradually lost steam and he was officially acquitted in early 1992. The two other surviving ex-ministers, Tsovolas and Petsos, were convicted, given jail sentences (bought off with a heavy fine) and barred from public life for a time.

The great showcase trial thus went out with a whimper and did nothing to enhance Mitsotakis's position. If anything, it served to increase sympathy for Papandreou, who was felt to have been unfairly victimized. The real villain of the piece, Koskotas, was eventually convicted of major **fraud** and is serving a 25-year sentence at the high-security Korydhallos prison, also home to the ex-junta members.

THE MACEDONIAN QUESTION

Increasingly unpopular due to the desperate austerity measures, and perceived as ineffective on the international scene, the last thing Mitsotakis needed was a major foreign policy headache. That is exactly what he got when, in 1991, one of the breakaway republics of the former Yugoslavia named itself **Macedonia**, thereby injuring Greek national pride and sparking off vehement protests at home and abroad. Diplomatically, the Greeks fought tooth and nail against anyone recognizing the **breakaway state**, let alone using the name "Macedonia", but their position became increasingly isolated, and by 1993 the new country had gained official recognition from both the EU and the UN – albeit under the provisional, convoluted title of the Former Yugoslav Republic of Macedonia (FYROM).

Salt was rubbed into Greek wounds when the FYROM started using the "Star of Vergina" (and of the ancient Macedonian kings) as a national symbol on their new flag, allegedly printed a banknote portraying the White Tower of Thessaloníki (Solun in Macedonian) and

retained passages in its constitution referring to "unredeemed" Aegean territories. Greece still refuses to call its neighbour Macedonia, instead referring to it as Ta Skópia after the capital – and for quite some time you couldn't go anywhere in Greece without coming across officially placed stickers proclaiming that "Macedonia was, is and always will be Greek and only Greek!"

THE PENDULUM SWINGS BACK

In effect, the Macedonian problem more or less directly led to Mitsotakis's **political demise**. In the early summer of 1993 his ambitious foreign minister, **Andonis Samaras**, disaffected with his leader, jumped on the bandwagon of resurgent Greek nationalism to set up his own party, **Politikí Ánixi (Political Spring)**. His platform, still right-wing, was largely based on action over Macedonia, and during the summer of 1993 more **Néa Dhimokratía** (ND) MPs broke ranks, making Politikí Ánixi a force to be reckoned with. When parliament was called upon to approve severe new budget proposals, it became clear that the government lacked sufficient support, and early elections were called for October 1993.

Mitsotakis had also been plagued for nearly a year by accusations of phone-tapping, theft of antiquities to stock his large private collection in Crete and links with a nasty and complicated contracts scandal centred around a national company, AGET.

Many of ND's disillusioned supporters reverted directly to PASOK, and **Papandreou** romped to election victory.

THE MORNING AFTER

And so, a frail-looking Papandreou, now well into his seventies, became prime minister for the third time. He soon realized that the honeymoon was going to be neither as sweet nor as long as it had been in the Eighties.

PASOK immediately fulfilled two of its preelection promises by removing restrictions on the reporting of statements by terrorist groups and de-privatizing the Athens city bus company. The new government also started improving the health system and began to set the wheels in motion for Mitsotakis to be tried for his alleged misdemeanours, although all charges were mysteriously dropped in January 1995, prompting allegations of under-the-table dealings between Papandreou and his old rival.

The root of popular dissatisfaction remained **the economy**, which was still in dire straits. Nor could PASOK claim to have won any diplomatic battles over Macedonia, despite a lot of posturing. The only concrete move was the imposition in October 1993 of a **trade embargo** on the FYROM, which merely landed the Greeks in trouble with the European Court of Justice – and succeeded in virtually shutting down the port of Thessaloníki. By contrast, alone among NATO members, Greece was conspicuous for its open **support of Serbia** in the wars wracking ex-Yugoslavia, breaking that particular embargo with supply trucks to Belgrade via Bulgaria.

In **October 1994**, for the first time ever in a PASOK-sponsored reform, provincial governors were directly elected in regional elections, rather than appointed from Athens. On the municipal level, ND candidate Dhimitris Avramopoulos swept to victory in Athens, ahead of PASOK stalwart Theodhoros Pangalos, and the incumbent ND mayor of Thessaloniki retained office as well, though Pátra reverted to PASOK.

In March 1995, **presidential elections** were held in parliament to designate a successor to the 88-year-old Karamanlis. The winner, supported by Politikí Ánixi and PASOK, was Kostis Stefanopoulos, ex-head of the dissolved party **DIANA** (Democratic Renewal), like Politikí Ánixi a breakaway movement from ND. A former lawyer, untainted by scandal, he had been nominated by Samaras and accepted by Papandreou in a deal that would allow PASOK to see out its four-year term without ructions.

The prime recurring **scandal** for 1995 had to do with the maximum-security prison of Korydhallos, home to Koskotas and the former junta figures. Two mass breakout attempts bracketed the discovery of an extensive drug-dealing ring controlled from inside; a call girl was detected in Koskotas's cell, as were large quantities of guns, ammunition and narcotics in the office of the head warden.

In November 1995, Greece **lifted its embargo** on "Macedonia", opening its mutual borders to tourism and trade in return for the Macedonians suitably editing their constitution and removing the offending emblem from their flag. Relations, in fact, were almost normalized, with only the name still moot; current favourite candidates are

"New Macedonia" or "Upper Macedonia", though as of late 1999 the place was still being referred to as FYROM (the Former Yugoslav Republic of Macedonia) by all outsiders.

THE END OF AN ERA

However, the emerging critical issue was the 76-year-old Papandreou's continued **stewardship of PASOK**, and the country, as he clung obstinately to power despite obvious signs of dotage. Numerous senior members of PASOK became increasingly vocal in their criticism.

By late 1995, Papandreou was desperately ill in intensive care at the Onassis hospital. As there was no constitutional provision for replacing an infirm (but alive) prime minister, the country was essentially rudderless for two months, until the barely conscious old demagogue finally **resigned** as prime minister (though not as party leader) in mid-January 1996. The "palace clique" of Mimi Liani and cohorts was beaten off in the parliamentary replacement vote in favour of the allegedly colourless but widely respected technocrat **Kostas Simitis**.

Upon assuming office, Simitis indicated that he wouldn't necessarily play to the gallery as Papandreou had with a remarkable statement:

> Greece's intransigent nationalism is an expression of the wretchedness that exists in our society. It is the root cause of the problems we have had with our Balkan neighbours and our difficult relations with Europe.

These beliefs were immediately put to the test by a tense armed face-off with Turkey over the uninhabited Dodecanese islet of **Ímia**. Simitis eventually bowed to US and UN pressure, ordering a withdrawal of Greek naval forces.

Andreas finally succumbed to his illness on June 22, 1996, prompting a widespread display of national mourning; it was genuinely the **end of an era**, with only Karamanlis (who died less than two years later) and Papadopoulos (who died, still incarcerated, in June 1999) as the last remaining "dinosaurs" of post-war Greek politics. Already his **canonization** process proceeds apace, with a spate of streets renamed to honour him in provincial towns where he was always revered, but the long-term verdict of history is likely to be harsher.

Papandreou's demise was promptly followed by PASOK's summer conference, where Simitis ensured his survival as party leader by co-opting his main internal foe, Papandreou's former head of staff, Akis Tsohadzopoulos, with a promise of future high office (he is now Minister of Defense). Following the summer congress, Simitis rode the wave of pro-PASOK sympathy caused by Papandreou's death, and called **general elections** a year early in September 1996.

The **results** were as expected: 162 seats for PASOK versus 108 for Néa Dhimokratía. Given that the two main parties' agendas were virtually indistinguishable, it boiled down to which was better poised to deliver results – and whether voters would be swayed by ND chief Miltiades Evert's strident nationalism. The biggest surprise was the collapse of Samaras's Politikí Ánixi, but three leftist splinter parties did well: eleven seats for Aleka Papariga's KKE, ten for the Synaspismós and nine for the Democratic Social Movement (DIKKI). Evert resigned as ND leader, succeeded by Karamanlis's nephew Kostas, who is now attempting to regain the centre ground.

THE CURRENT SITUATION

Néa Dhimokratía is down but by no means out, having actually increased its strength on the mainland in the last parliamentary poll, and done well by its own standards in the closely fought October 1998 provincial/municipal polls. ND repeated its success in the June 1999 **Euroelections**, where it finished first nationwide, and sent forty percent of Greece's Euro MPs to Strasbourg.

Nonetheless, Simitis's position seems secure for the time being, though elections must be called before autumn 2000. First-term problems thus far have arisen from the economic squeeze caused by continuing **austerity measures**. In December 1996, farmers staged dramatic protests, closing off the country's main road and rail arteries for several weeks, before dismantling the blockades in time for people to travel for the Christmas holidays. Much of 1997 saw the teachers or students (or both) on strike over proposed educational reforms. And immediately after the 1998 regional elections, Simitis endorsed a stringent 1999 budget which has seen little support from within his party, let alone outside it.

Simitis, by nature far more pro-European than his maverick predecessor, has devoted himself doggedly to the unenviable task of getting the Greek economy in sufficiently good shape to meet the criteria for **monetary union**. Indeed, the fact that inflation is into single figures for the first time in decades is testament to his ability as an accountant.

Increasingly amicable relations with Greece's Balkan neighbours promise to generate jobs. **Tourism** recovered significantly in the islands during 1999, despite NATO's spring war against Serbia, after having been in the doldrums since 1995. And the *Eforía* or Greek Inland Revenue has made some highly publicized headway in curbing the enormous **black economy**, the largest in the EU, by requiring meticulous documentation of most transactions and by publicly "outing" tax-dodgers.

In September 1997, Greece received a timely boost to national morale and economic prospects with the awarding of the 2004 **Olympic Games** to Athens. One can be fairly confident that both the Athens metro and the new airport at Spáta will be completed on time, even if other infrastructure improvements for the games have yet to materialize.

Carrying these out has been complicated by the aftermath of the **earthquake** which struck northern Athens on September 7, 1999, killing scores, rendering almost 100,000 homeless and immobilizing two of the three national mobile phone networks, whose undamaged base stations couldn't cope with the volume of emergency calls. It came less than a month after the devastating tremor in northwest Turkey, and ironically may prove to be the spur for a **thaw in relations** between the two historical rivals. Greeks donated massive amounts of blood and foodstuffs to the Turkish victims, as well as being the first foreign rescue teams on hand in Turkey, and in turn saw Turkish disaster-relief squads among the first on the scene in Athens. Soon after, Foreign Minister Papandreou announced Greece had dropped its long-time opposition to EU financial aid to Turkey in the absence of a solution to the outstanding Cyprus and Aegean disputes, and further indicated that Greece would not at present oppose Turkish candidacy for accession to the EU.

GREEK SOCIETY TODAY

The foregoing brief summary of recent events doesn't, however, give a full flavour of the massive, ground-level changes which have occurred in Greece since the late 1980s. First and foremost, it is a conspicuously **wealthier society** than before, with vast disparities in income. Athens, Thessaloníki and Pátra have their legions of yuppies, addicted to gourmet wines, designer trinkets, fast cars and travel; even small-town travel agencies successfully promote junkets to Bali and Cuba (the current trendy favourites).

Thanks in part to PASOK's recent policies, the country is now firmly locked into the **global economy**, symbolized by the proliferation of McDonald's, Marks & Spencer and The Body Shop in most larger towns; consumer interest rates, while still high, have plunged, the Athens stock exchange burgeons, and foreign or multinational companies have flocked to invest. It is they who are funding massive **infrastructure improvements** designed to outlast the 2004 Olympics: metros in Athens and Thessaloníki, the Río-Andírio bridge over the Gulf of Corinth and the Via Egnatia expressway across Epirus, Macedonia and Thrace. The imminent end to the ferry practice whereby only Greek companies have been allowed to provide service within Greece should weed out the flakier steamship companies and have the others pulling their socks up.

Domestic companies have engaged in extensive **corporate takeovers**: Alpha Pisteos/ Alpha Credit Bank absorbed troubled Ioniki/Ionian Bank in early 1999 and instantly became the second largest banking group in the country, while Minoan Lines merged with Ceres Hydrofoils to form Minoan Flying Dolphins and acquired majority interest in Air Greece, to become the largest domestic transport company. **Private airlines**, including a number of expensive executive air-taxi outfits, are all the rage, and it seems a new one emerges every few months – and manages to survive.

Greece is infinitely richer than most of its neighbours, and this fact has attracted, besides the aforementioned Albanians, significant **immigrant communities** of Bulgarians, Poles, Arabs, Pakistanis, Africans, Filipinos, Romanians, Ukrainians, Russians and Georgians to what had hitherto been a homogenous, parochial culture. These groups, plus travel, touring bands or dance companies and programmes on the private television channels, have created a taste for **exotic music and foods**. One doesn't always have to wait for the summer festivals to see name jazz, blues or soul acts in Thessaloníki or Athens, and there are decent foreign-cuisine restaurants there as well as in some of the major resorts. All of these factors, however, have had the effect of making Greece less identifiably Greek and of making the Greeks themselves less welcoming than formerly.

THE GREEK MINORITIES

The principal Greek minorities – Vlachs, Sarakatsáni, Turks, Jews, Slavophones, Catholics and Gypsies – are little known, even within Greece. Indeed, to meet Vlachs or Sarakatsáni who remain true to their roots you'll have to get to some fairly remote parts of Epirus. Greco-Turks are another matter, with a sizable (and recently problematic) community living, as they have done for centuries, in Thrace, Rhodes and Kós. The Jews of Greece, as so often, tell the saddest history, having been annihilated by the Nazi occupiers during the latter stages of World War II. Slavophones are officially a taboo subject, and the Catholics largely restricted to the Cyclades, while the Gypsies are admired – from a distance – only for their musicality.

THE VLACHS AND SARAKATSÁNI

The **Vlachs'** homeland is in the remote vastness of the **Píndhos mountains** in northwestern Greece near the Albanian frontier. Traditionally they were transhumant shepherds, although some have long led a more settled existence in Métsovo and a score of villages around. As the town grew in prosperity, the Vlachs traded their sheep products further and further afield. Local merchants established themselves in Constantinople, Vienna, Venice and elsewhere, expanding into other lines of business: Vlachs played a major role in Balkan mule-back haulage and the hotel trade – specifically caravanserais where mule convoys halted.

They are an ancient, close-knit community with a strong sense of identity, like their rival shepherd clan, the Sarakatsáni (see opposite), whom they despise as "tent-dwellers" and who, in turn, just as passionately despise them for living in houses. Unlike the Sarakatsáni, however, their mother tongue is not Greek, but Vlach, a Romance language, which even today is full of words that anyone with a little Latin can easily recognize: *loop* for wolf, *mulier* for women, *pene* for bread. When the Italians invaded Greece in World War II, Vlach soldiers were often used as interpreters, though there were very few instances of collaboration. Incidentally, the Vlachs prefer to call themselves *Roumaní* (Arouman) and their language *Roumaniká*; the word *vláhos* in Greek can mean "yokel" or "bumpkin".

It used to be thought that the Vlachs were descendants of Roman legionaries stationed in the provinces of Illyria and Dacia, who over the centuries had wandered up and down through the Balkans in search of grazing land for their sheep. Those who finally settled in northern Greece were trapped there by the creation of modern frontiers upon the disintegration of the Austro-Hungarian and Ottoman empires. Because of these supposed Romanian connections and enduring official anxieties about the separatist tendencies of northern Greek minorities, the Vlachs have been objects of suspicion to the modern state. To their chagrin many villages with Slavic or Vlach names were officially renamed during the Metaxas dictatorship of the 1930s, and Vlach schoolchildren forbidden to use their mother tongue.

There is, however, a more recent, better supported theory about their origins, which argues that the Greek Vlachs at least are of Greek descent and have always inhabited these same regions of the Píndhos mountains; during Roman times the Romans found it convenient to train local people as highway guards for the high passes on the old Roman road, the Via Egnatia, which connected Constantinople with the Adriatic. Thus the Vlachs learned Latin through their association with the Romans and preserved it in distorted form because of the isolation of their homeland and the exclusive nature of their pastoral way of life.

Sadly, though probably inevitably, the Vlachs' unique traditions are in danger of extinction. Until World War II, a prosperous Vlach family might have 10,000 sheep, and when they set off on the annual migration from their lowland winter pastures to the mountains it was like a small army on the march: two or three complete generations, together with all their animals and belongings. Nowadays few flocks number more than 250 ewes, and the annual migration takes place in lorries – though a few veterans still do it on foot. Hundreds of Vlachs have sold their flocks, and moved to the towns or emigrated. There are depressingly few young men among the remaining shepherds. The hardships of their life are too many and the economic returns too small.

The **Sarakatsáni**, celebrated in Patrick Leigh Fermor's *Roúmeli* (see p.901) and J. K. Campbell's *Honour, Family and Patronage* (see p.907), by contrast appear to be indigenous, and speak an archaic form of Greek. The distinctive costumes and reed tents which Leigh Fermor described are now a thing of the past, to be pulled out only for feast days and ethnographic theme parks, but traces of their former lifestyle persist. Until a few decades ago they were true transhumants, moving between winter quarters well below the snowline and summer pastures in the mountains. After World War II the government required them to establish permanent winter dwellings, but they still return each summer to the heights, where they pasture their sheep on land rented from the village councils – often made up of their hereditary adversaries, the Vlachs.

JEWS AND TURKS

Jews and **Turks** in Greece are, for historical reasons, conveniently considered together. Since the decline of the Ottoman empire, these two minorities have often suffered similar fates as isolated groups in a non-assimilating culture. Yet it seems that enclaves of each will endure for the foreseeable future.

ORIGINS AND SETTLEMENTS

The **Greek Jewish community** is one of the oldest established in Europe, dating back to the early Hellenistic period when Jews were already settled at Rhodes, Corinth, Athens, Thebes, Salonika, Véria, Delos, Crete and Sparta. During the Roman and Byzantine eras, these Jews were termed Romaniot, and urban colonies flourished throughout the Balkans. In Greece these additionally included, by the twelfth to fourteenth centuries, Corfu, Zákynthos, Pátra, Halkídha, Lárissa and, most importantly, Ioánnina.

The most numerically significant Jewish communities in Greece, however, date back to shortly after the taking of Constantinople by the **Ottomans**. In 1493 Sultan Beyazit II invited Spanish and Portuguese Jews expelled from those countries to settle in the Ottoman empire. The great influx of **Sephardim** (Ladino-speaking Jews) soon swamped many of the original

Romaniot centres, particularly at Kós, Rhodes, Véria and Salonika, and within two centuries, Ladino – officially Judeo-Spanish, a mix of medieval Spanish and Portuguese with Turkish, Hebrew and Arabic augments – had largely supplanted Greek as the lingua franca of Balkan Jewry, with Italian and Hungarian refugee Jews nearly as numerous as the Romaniotes. However, *Ladinismo* (the medieval Iberian Jewish culture) never penetrated the Romaniot enclaves of Ioánnina and Halkídha, which remain proudly Greek-speaking to this day. Moreover, the Greek- and non-Greek-speaking Jews differed in religious observance as well as language, resulting in numerous small synagogues being founded in each town for each group – and little intermarriage between the sects.

Ottoman officials and their families fanned out across the Balkans to consolidate imperial administration, thus sowing the seeds of the numerous **Muslim communities** in present-day Bulgaria, Albania, Yugoslavia and Greece. The Ottoman authorities often appointed Jews as civil servants and tax collectors; one, Joseph Nasi, became governor of the Cyclades in 1566, but dared not show his face there, ruling instead through a representative.

As a result of this and other episodes, especially on Crete, Jews became identified with the ruling hierarchy in the eyes of the Orthodox Christian population, and at the outset of the 1821 **War of Independence** inhabitants of the Jewish quarters of Pátra, Trípoli, Athens and virtually all others within the confines of the nascent Greek state, were put to the sword along with the Muslim population. Survivors of the various massacres fled north, to territories that remained under Ottoman control. Within the new Greek kingdom, a small community of Ashkenazi Jews arrived in Athens, along with the Bavarian king Otho, during the 1830s.

UNDER THE GREEK STATE

The **expansion** of the Greek nation thereafter resulted in the decline of both the Greco-Jewish and Greco-Turkish populations. New annexations or conquests (Thessaly in 1878, Epirus, Macedonia, the northeast Aegean and Crete in 1913) provoked a wave of forced or nervous Judeo-Turkish migration to the other side of the receding Ottoman frontier. Although Jews were never forbidden to stay in newly occupied territory, rarely were they explicitly welcome, although the Romaniot communities in Ioánnina and Halkídha were understandably pro-Greek. During the latter half of the nineteenth century – long after such incidents had peaked in Western Europe – there were repeated outbreaks of anti-Semitic riots whenever Jewish communities were falsely accused of murdering Christian children in order to obtain blood thought necessary for ritual use.

The Turks – or more correctly, Muslims, since "Turk" was a generic term for any Muslim, including Albanians, and ethnic Greeks who had converted to Islam for economic advantage – were subject to various expulsion orders. Between 1913 and 1923 the **Muslims of Crete**, mostly converted islanders, were forced to choose between apostasy to Christianity or exile, if they hadn't emigrated voluntarily between 1898 and 1913. (The newly Orthodox can today often be distinguished by their ostentatiously Christian surnames, such as Stavroulakis, Khristakis, and so on.) Those who opted to stand by their faith were summarily deposited in the closest Turkish-Muslim settlements on Greek islands just over the Ottoman border; Kós Town, the nearby village of Plataní, and Rhodes Town were three of the more convenient ones.

When the Italians formally annexed the **Dodecanese** after World War I, the **Muslims** were allowed to remain and were thus rendered exempt from any of the provisions of the 1923 Treaty of Lausanne (stipulating the wholescale exchange of "Turk" and "Greek" populations in the wake of the Asia Minor war). Additionally, the Jewish communities of Kós and Rhodes flourished, as there was little or no anti-Semitism under Italian Fascist rule until the late 1930s. In **Rhodes** there had been a long tradition of co-operation between the Muslim and the Jewish communities. In Ottoman days Jews were the only *millet* (subject ethnic group) allowed out after the city gates were closed at dusk, and since 1948 Muslim and Jewish leaders have consulted on how best to counter government strategies to deprive each of their rights and property. The dilapidated refugee village of Kritiká ("the Cretans") still huddles by the seaside on the way to the airport, and walking through Rhodes' old town it's easy to spot dwindling numbers of Turkish names on the signboards of various jewellers, tinsmiths and

kafenía. Those Turks who live in the old town itself, moreover, have in some cases been there since the sixteenth century and will proudly tell you that they have every right to be considered native Rhodians. This notwithstanding, numbers diminish through emigration to Turkey every year, with (until 1997) those leaving denied any right of return.

In **Kós**, Cretan Muslims settled both in the port town – where they remain active in the antique and shoemaking trades – and at Plataní, which still has a mixed Greek Orthodox and "Turkish" population. However, since the first major Cyprus crisis of 1964, numbers have dropped by two-thirds, and the Turkish-language primary school has been forcibly closed.

During the early 1900s, the same era as the Cretan deportations, the status of mainland Jews and Turks in the path of Greek nationalism was more ambiguous. Even after the respective 1878 and 1913 acquisitions of **Thessaly**, **Epirus** and **Macedonia**, Muslim villages continued to exist in these regions. The Tsamídhes, an Albanian-speaking, nominally Muslim tribe localized in Epirus and Thesprotía, were left alone until World War II, when they made the grievous error of siding with the invading Italian army; after 1944 they were massacred or expelled, first by the National Army and later by guerrilla bands.

Thessaloníki in the late nineteenth and early twentieth century was one of the largest Jewish towns in the world. Jews made up roughly half the population, and dominated the sailing, shipping and chandlery trades, such that the harbour ceased operations on Saturday but functioned on Sunday. In addition there were numerous Dönme, or Ma'min, Jews who had chosen to follow the "false messiah" Sabbatai Zvi into Islam in the 1670s but maintained certain aspects of Jewish worship in secret. As provided for by the Treaty of Lausanne, the authorities insisted on the departure of the Dönme along with other Turkic Muslims. The 20,000 Dönme (Turkish for "renegades", after Zvi's conversion to Islam) insisted that they were "really" Jews, but to no avail. Indeed as early as 1913, with a rapid influx of Greek Orthodox into the conquered city, Thessaloníki had already begun to lose its strong Hebraic character; the fire of 1917, emigration to Palestine, the arrival of Greek Orthodox refugees from Anatolia after 1923 and the tenure of the Nazis effectively brought an era to a close.

The same period, around the time of World War I, also saw the end of Muslim (and minute Jewish) enclaves on the islands of **Thássos**, **Samothráki**, **Límnos**, **Lésvos** and **Híos**, where it is claimed the "Turks" themselves destroyed the fine Turkish bath before departing. On **Sámos** there is a special, tiny Jewish cemetery with the graves of two brothers, who helped start the wine co-op there early in the twentieth century; otherwise there had not been a significant Jewish community here since Byzantine times, and Muslims were uniquely forbidden to settle here after the seventeenth century.

Western Thrace, the area between the Néstos and Évros rivers, was always home to large numbers of Muslims, and it remained their last bastion after the 1919–22 Asia Minor War. The **Treaty of Lausanne** (1923) confirmed the right of this minority to remain in situ, in return for a continued Greek Orthodox presence in Istanbul (still known to Greeks as Konstandinoúpoli), the Princes' Islands and on the islands of Tenedos and Imvros.

Over the years the Turks have repeatedly abrogated the terms of the pact by repressive measures and reduced the Turkish Greek Orthodox population to three percent of pre-1923 levels. The Greeks have acted comparatively leniently, and today Muslims still make up a third of the population of Greek Thrace, being highly visible in the main towns of **Alexandhroúpoli**, **Komotiní** and **Xánthi**. Muslims control much of the tobacco culture hereabouts and the baggy-trousered women can frequently be glimpsed from the trains which pass through their fields.

The loyalty of these Thracian "Turks" to the Greek state was amply demonstrated during **World War II**, when they resisted the invading Bulgarians and Nazis side-by-side with their Christian compatriots. In return the two occupying forces harassed and deported to death camps many local Muslims. During the 1946–49 civil war Thracian Muslims again suffered at the hands of ELAS, who found the deep-seated conservatism of these villagers exasperating and laboured under the misconception that all local Muslims were traitors.

Only the **Pomaks**, a non-Turkic Muslim group of about 40,000 distributed across the Rodhópi ranges north of Xánthi and Komotiní, collaborated to any extent with the Bulgarians, probably on the basis of ethnic affinity. The Pomaks as a group were probably Slavic Bogomil heretics forcibly converted to Islam in the sixteenth century; they speak a degenerate dialect of Bulgarian with generous mixtures of Greek and Turkish. The authorities still keep them on a tight rein; until the early 1990s Pomaks required a travel permit to leave their immediate area of residence, and visitors in turn required a permit to visit certain of their villages near Ehínos. If you do venture up into their Rodhópi homeland, the main reward is some magnificent scenery; there's not much arable land amidst the wild, pine-forested hills, and what there is – down in the river valleys – is devoted entirely to hand-tilled tobacco. Pomaks are occasionally found living outside Thrace, particularly near certain mines in Viotía, the mainland region opposite Évvia, where their skills as sappers and tunnellers are required; apparently they have also prompted the reopening of the mosque in nearby Halkídha for their regular use.

Until recently, the Orthodox and "Turkish" Thracian communities lived in a fairly easy (if distant) relationship with each other, but during the early 1990s a series of ugly intercommunal incidents and official prosecution of Turkish political leaders cast doubt on the carefully cultivated international image of Greece's toleration of its minorities. It has, in fact, always been true that treatment of these Muslims functions as a barometer of relations at a more general level between Greece and Turkey, and as a quid pro quo for perceived maltreatment of the remaining Greek Orthodox in Turkey.

But it is the **Jews** rather than the Muslims who have suffered the greatest catastrophes during and since **World War II**. Jews who chanced to live in the Italian zone of occupation were initially no worse off than their compatriots, but after Italy's capitulation in September 1943 and the German assumption of control, conditions deteriorated drastically. Eighty-five percent of a Jewish population of around 80,000 was rounded up by the Nazis in the spring and summer of 1944, never to return. The Bulgarian occupation forces tended to substitute Greek Jews for Bulgarian ones on the death trains as part of their "Bulgarization" programme, thus earning an unjustified reputation for clemency.

Greek Christians often went to extraordinary lengths to protect their persecuted countrymen, overshadowing the few instances of sordid betrayal; in this respect the Greek record is rather better than many western European countries, France for example. The mayor and bishop of Zákynthos and the bishop of Halkídha put themselves at risk to save the local Jewish communities, virtually ordering their Christian neighbours to hide and feed them; as a result nearly all of them survived. In Athens, the police chief and the archbishop arranged for the issue of false identity cards and baptismal certificates, which again saved huge numbers of Jews. In Athens, Tríkala, Lárissa and Vólos especially, where the rabbi was active in the resistance to occupation, most Jews were warned in good time of what fate the Germans had in store for them, and took to the hills to join the partisans. Romaniot Jews, indistinguishable from their Orthodox neighbours in appearance and tongue, fared best, but the Ladino-speaking Jews of northern Greece, with their distinctive surnames and customs, were easy targets for the Nazis. It must also be said that certain portions of the Greek business community in **Thessaloníki** benefited greatly from the expulsion of the Jews, and needed little encouragement to help themselves to the contents of the abandoned Jewish shops. Jewish sensibilities were further offended in the postwar era when the German desecration of the huge Jewish cemetery was completed by the construction of the University of Thessaloníki and expansion of the fairgrounds.

The paltry number of **survivors** returning from the death camps to Greece was insufficient to form the nucleus of a revival in most provincial towns, and moving to Athens or **emigration** to Israel was often a preferable alternative to living with ghosts. Currently barely six thousand Jews remain in Greece. In Thessaloníki there are around a thousand Sephardim, who generally keep a low profile aside from the Molho family's famous bookstore. Lárissa retains about three hundred Sephardim, who are still disproportionately important in the clothing trade. However, young Jewish women outnumber their male counterparts, so intermarriage with Orthodox men has long been a pattern. Small Romaniot communities of a hundred persons or less continue to exist in Halkídha, Ioánnina, Corfu, Tríkala and Vólos. The Kós, Haniá, and Rhodes congregations were virtually wiped out, and today only about forty Jews – many of these from the mainland – live in Rhodes Town. Here, the Platía ton Evreón Martýron (Square of the Jewish Martyrs), at the edge of the former Jewish quarter, commemorates over 1800 Jews of Kós and Rhodes deported by the Germans. About 3000 of today's Greek Jews live in Athens, which is also home to the **Jewish Museum of Greece**.

SLAVOPHONES

Despite a population exchange between Greece and Bulgaria in 1918, and the flight of many **Slavophones** abroad after 1948, there remain approximately 40,000 individuals in Greece whose at-home language is some approximation of Macedonian. They dwell in a ribbon along the northern frontier, from Préspa to the internal border with Thrace at the Néstos River. If Greeks can seem unreasonable on the question of "Turks", they become positively apoplectic at the mention of any Slavic minority; successive governments of whatever political stripe have indicated that any official recognition of such is out of the question, and counter any activism to the contrary with arrests or unofficial harassment. This position becomes slightly more understandable when such a population is viewed as a potential fifth column for a theoretically expansionist FYROM (Former Yugoslav Republic of Macedonia). Slavophones in Greece did not have their position in Greece made any more tenable during World War II and the civil war, when at various times – until such were suppressed by ELAS as an expression of "bourgeois nationalism" – communist statements contained references to "self-determination for Macedonian peoples", which could be construed to mean dismembering northern Greece and joining parts of it to a hypothetical Macedonian state. In the event, the victorious central government leaned hard on everybody unlucky enough to be dwelling in a northern border zone, regardless of political hue; in some places villages were evacuated, in others Greek-speaking colonists of "healthy national character" were imported to dilute the Slavophone population, along with other discriminatory measures. These had their desired effect, inasmuch as many Slavophones emigrated to Yugoslavia, Canada, America and Australia, where some have become part of the increasingly vocal pro-Macedonian lobby. Since the 1980s there has been some improvement in terms of increased material prosperity, but don't look for Slavic-language schools or public song performances any time soon.

CATHOLICS

The **Catholics** of the Cyclades, numbering no more than 12,000, are a legacy of Venetian settlement in the Aegean following the piratical Fourth Crusade in 1204. Today they live principally on the islands of Sýros and Tínos, with much tinier enclaves on Thíra, Náxos, Sámos, Rhodes and certain provincial towns such as Pátra. Often Italianate last names (Dellaroka) or given names (Leonardhos, Frangiskos) distinguish them from their neighbours. Descended from once-powerful feudal lords, they are today insignificant in civic as well as numerical terms, though they have always attracted suspicion as being less than "one-hundred percent Greek"; in 1994 a civil servant on Náxos was promoted out of harm's way after making an outrageous public pronouncement about "Papist fifthcolumnists in our midst". The Catholic Church hierarchy, for its part, has made periodic complaints about a certain legal disability; like all other non-Orthodox denominations, it is classified as a *xénon dhógma* (foreign creed), and as such its schools (unlike Orthodox academies) are ineligible for state subsidies.

GYPSIES

The **Gypsies** first came to the Balkans in about the eleventh century, probably a low-ranking caste from Rajasthan on the Indian subcontinent, and were soon well enough established to figure in Byzantine chronicles of the 1300s. Nazi policy towards them was even harsher than towards the Jews: they were sent directly to extermination facilities, reckoned not even worth a month of slave labour. Given their elusive, anti-authoritarian nature, no one knows exactly how many Gypsies there are in Greece at present; 150,000, of which ninety percent are nominally Greek Orthodox and the rest Muslim, seems a good guess. They are concentrated on the mainland, especially Thessaly and Étolo-Akarnanía, and in the Athenian neighbourhoods of Kolonós and Ayía Varvára, though they maintain a transient presence on all of the larger islands, and families are a common sight on the ferry-boats. Driving outsized trucks fitted with loud-hailers, Gypsy vendors are a common sight across the country, peddling plastic garden furniture, cheap carpets, house plants, basketry, watermelons and other produce – rather a come-down from their traditional livelihoods of metal-smithing, bear-training, shadow-puppeteering and horse-dealing, which it seems their Rajasthani ancestors also engaged in. Marginalized by centuries of nationalism and industrial advance, they are in Greece – as elsewhere in central Europe – undereducated, increasingly reliant on begging and generally despised by the majority population.

But an echo of the past survives in events such as the **zoöemboropaniyíri** (animal-trading festival), a movable feast which begins at Peloponnesian Stymfalía around September 14 (the Raising of the Cross) and drifts west in stages to meet another party coming from Káto Ahaïa; these then travel jointly to Nafpaktós, where the festival finishes on October 26, the day of Áyios Dhimítrios. Rural tools and spit-roasted meat amongst tatty synthetic goods characterize this as a harvest fair, with Gypsies figuring prominently both as livestock-dealers and evening musicians.

Gypsies are finally (if often grudgingly) being properly credited with disproportionate prominence in the ranks of Greek mainland instrumental **musicians**, among them the *sandoúri* player Aristidhis Moskhos, the late clarinettist Vassilis Soukas, the late crooner Manolis Angelopoulos, the protest guitarist Kostas Hatzis and the *laïkó* star Eleni Vitali. Indeed virtually all of the now-settled clans of mainland clarinettists were originally of Gypsy origin, and for every personality like Vitali who makes no bones about their background, there is another who still feels he or she must conceal it. Incidentally, it is worth emphasizing that Gypsies are not necessarily more talented musically than their host culture; it's just that for many centuries, excluded from bazaar guilds or even fixed residence, they had few other choices of profession. Until recently in many northern towns, there was a designated *kafenío* in the marketplace which acted as an "employment exchange" for Gypsy musicians between engagements. For more on Greek music in general, see p.885.

250 YEARS OF ARCHEOLOGY

Archeology until the second half of the nineteenth century was a very hit-and-miss affair. The early students of antiquity went to Greece to draw and make plaster casts of the great masterpieces of Classical sculpture. Unfortunately, a number soon found it more convenient or more profitable to remove objects wholesale, and might be better described as looters than scholars or archeologists.

EARLY EXCAVATIONS

The British **Society of Dilettanti** was one of the earliest promoters of Greek culture, financing expeditions to draw and publish antiquities. Founded in the 1730s as a club for young aristocrats who had completed the Grand Tour and fancied themselves arbiters of taste, the Society's main qualification for membership (according to most critics) was habitual drunkenness. Its leading spirit was Sir Francis Dashwood, a notorious rake who founded the infamous Hellfire Club. Nevertheless, the society was the first body organized to sponsor systematic research into Greek antiquities, though it was initially most interested in Italy. Greece, then a backwater of the Ottoman empire, was not a regular part of the Grand Tour and only the most intrepid adventurers undertook so hazardous a trip.

In the 1740s, two young artists, **James Stuart** and **Nicholas Revett**, formed a plan to produce a scholarly record of the ancient Greek buildings. With the support of the society they spent three years in Greece, principally around Athens, drawing and measuring the surviving antiquities. The first volume of *The Antiquities of Athens* appeared in 1762, becoming an instant success. The publication of their exquisite illustrations gave an enormous fillip to the study of Greek sculpture and architecture, which became the fashionable craze among the educated classes; many European Neoclassical town and country houses date from this period.

The Dilettanti financed a number of further expeditions to study Greek antiquities, including one to Asia Minor in 1812. The expedition was to be based in Smyrna, but while waiting in Athens for a ship to Turkey, the party employed themselves in excavations at **Eleusis**, where they uncovered the Temple of Demeter. It was the first archeological excavation made on behalf of the society, and one of the first in Greece. After extensive explorations in Asia Minor, the participants returned via Attica, where they excavated the Temple of Nemesis at **Rhamnous** and examined the Temple of Apollo at **Sounion**.

Several other antiquarians of the age were less interested in discoveries for their own sake. A French count, **Choiseul-Gouffier**, removed part of the **Parthenon frieze** in 1787 and his example prompted **Lord Elgin** to detach much of the rest in 1801. These were essentially acts of looting — "Bonaparte has not got such things from all his thefts in Italy", boasted Elgin — and their legality was suspect even at the time.

Other discoveries of the period were more ambiguous. In 1811, a party of English and German travellers, including the architect C.R. Cockerell, uncovered the **Temple of Aphaia** on **Aegina** (Éyina) and shipped away the pediments. They auctioned off the marbles for £6000 to Prince Ludwig of Bavaria and, inspired by this success, returned to Greece for further finds. This time they struck lucky with 23 slabs from the **Temple of Apollo Epikourios** at **Bassae**, for which the British Museum laid out a further £15,000. These were huge sums for the time and highly profitable exercises, but they were also pioneering archeology for the period. Besides, removing the finds was hardly surprising: Greece, after all, was not yet a state and had no public museum; antiquities discovered were sold by their finders — if they recognized their value.

THE NEW NATION

The **Greek War of Independence** (1821–28) and the establishment of a modern Greek nation changed all of this — and provided a major impetus to archeology. Nationhood brought an increased pride in Greece's Classical heritage, nowhere more so than in **Athens**, which succeeded Náfplio as the nation's capital in 1834 largely on the basis of its ancient monuments and past.

As a result of the selection of Prince Otto of Bavaria as the first king of modern Greece in

1832, the **Germans**, whose education system laid great stress on Classical learning, were in the forefront of archeological activity.

One of the dominant Teutonic figures during the early years of the new state was **Ludwig Ross**. Arriving in Greece as a student in 1832, he was on hand to show the new king around the antiquities of Athens when Otto was considering making the town his capital. Ross was appointed deputy keeper of antiquities to the court, and in 1834 began supervising the excavation and restoration of the **Acropolis**. The work of dismantling the accretion of Byzantine, Frankish and Turkish fortifications began the following year. The graceful Temple of Athena Nike, which had furnished many of the blocks for the fortifications, was rebuilt, and Ross's architect, Leo von Klenze, began the reconstruction of the **Parthenon**.

The Greeks themselves had begun to focus on their ancient past when the first stirrings of the independence movement were felt. In 1813 the **Philomuse Society** was formed, which aimed to uncover and collect antiquities, publish books and assist students and foreign philhellenes. In 1829 an orphanage on the island of Éyina, built by Kapodistrias, the first president of Greece, became the first Greek **archeological museum**.

In 1837 the **Greek Archeological Society** was founded "for the discovery, recovery and restoration of antiquities in Greece". Its moving spirit was **Kyriakos Pittakis**, a remarkable figure who during the War of Independence had used his knowledge of ancient literature to discover the Klepsydra spring on the Acropolis – solving the problem of lack of water during the Turkish siege. In the first four years of its existence, the Archeological Society sponsored excavations in Athens at the **Theatre of Dionysos**, the **Tower of the Winds**, the **Propylaia** and the **Erechtheion**. Pittakis also played a major role in the attempt to convince Greeks of the importance of their heritage; antiquities were still being looted or burned for lime.

THE GREAT GERMANS: CURTIUS AND SCHLIEMANN

Although King Otto was deposed in 1862 in favour of a Danish prince, Germans remained in the forefront of Greek archeology in the 1870s. Two men dominated the scene: Heinrich Schliemann and Ernst Curtius.

Ernst Curtius was a traditional Classical scholar. He had come to Athens originally as tutor to King Otto's family and in 1874 returned to Greece to secure permission for conducting the **excavations at Olympia**, one of the richest of Greek sanctuaries and site of the most famous of the ancient panhellenic games. The reigning Kaiser Wilhelm I intended that the excavation would proclaim to the world the cultural and intellectual pre-eminence of his empire. Curtius took steps to set up a **German Archeological Institute** in Athens and negotiated the **Olympia Convention**, under the terms of which the Germans were to pay for and have total control of the dig; all finds were to remain in Greece, though the excavators could make copies and casts; and all finds were to be published simultaneously in Greek and German.

This was an enormously important agreement, which almost certainly prevented the treasure of Olympia and Mycenae following that of Troy to a German museum. But other Europeans were still in very acquisitive mode: French consuls, for example, had been instructed to purchase any "available" local antiquities in Greece and Asia Minor, and had picked up the Louvre's great treasures, the Venus de Milo and Winged Victory of Samothrace, in 1820 and 1863 respectively.

At **Olympia**, digging began in 1875 on a site buried beneath many feet of river mud, silt and sand. Only one corner of the Temple of Zeus was initially visible, but within months the excavators had turned up statues from the east pediment. Over forty magnificent sculptures, as well as terracottas, statue bases and a rich collection of bronzes, were uncovered, together with more than four hundred inscriptions. The laying bare of this huge complex was a triumph for official German archeology.

While Curtius was digging at Olympia, a man who represented everything that was anathema to orthodox Classical scholarship was standing archeology on its head. **Heinrich Schliemann's** beginnings were not auspicious for one who aspired to hunt for ancient cities. The son of a drunken German pastor, he left school at fourteen and spent the next five years as a grocer's assistant. En route to seeking his fortune in Venezuela, he was left for dead on the Dutch coast after a shipwreck; later, working as a book-keeper in Amsterdam, he began to study languages. His phenomenal memory enabled him to master four by the age of 21. Following a six-week study of Russian, Schliemann was sent to St Petersburg as a trading agent and had amassed a fortune by the time he was 30. In 1851 he visited California, opened a bank during the Gold Rush and made another fortune.

His financial position secure for life, Schliemann was almost ready to tackle his life's ambition – the search for **Troy** and the vindication of his lifelong belief in the truth of Homer's tales of prehistoric cities and heroes. By this time he spoke no fewer than seventeen languages, and had excavated on the island of **Ithaca**, writing a book which earned him a doctorate from the University of Rostock.

Although most of the archeological establishment, led by Curtius, was unremittingly hostile to the millionaire amateur, Schliemann sunk his first trench at the hill called Hisarlık, in northwest Turkey, in 1870; excavation proper began in 1871. In his haste to find the city of Priam and Hector and to convince the world of his success, Schliemann dug a huge trench straight through the mound, destroying a mass of important evidence, but he was able nevertheless to identify nine cities, one atop the next. In May of 1873 he discovered the so-called **Treasure of Priam**, a stash of gold and precious jewellery and vessels. It convinced many that the German had indeed found Troy, although others contended that Schliemann, desperate for academic recognition, assembled it from other sources. The finds disappeared from Berlin at the end of World War II, but in 1994 archeologists discovered that artefacts held by some museums in Russia originated in Troy and announced plans to put the Treasure of Priam on display – probably in St Petersburg – in the near future.

Three years later Schliemann turned his attentions to **Mycenae**, again inspired by Homer, again following a hunch. Alone among contemporary scholars, he sought and found the legendary graves of Mycenaean kings inside the existing Cyclopean wall of the citadel rather than outside, unearthing in the process the magnificent treasures that today form the basis of the Bronze Age collection in the National Archeological Museum in Athens.

He dug again at Troy in 1882, assisted by a young architect, Wilhelm Dörpfeld, who was destined to become one of the great archeologists of the next century (though his claim that Lefkádha was ancient Ithaca never found popular acceptance). In 1884 Schliemann returned to Greece to excavate another famous prehistoric citadel, this time at **Tiryns**.

Almost single-handedly, and in the face of continuing academic obstruction, Schliemann had revolutionized archeology and pushed back the knowledge of Greek history and civilization a thousand years. Although some of his results have been shown to have been deliberately falsified in the sacrifice of truth to beauty, his achievement remains enormous.

The last two decades of the nineteenth century saw the discovery of other important Classical sites. Excavation began at **Epidaurus** in 1881 under the Greek archeologist **Panayotis Kavvadias**, who made it his life's work. Meanwhile at **Delphi**, the French, after gaining the permission to transfer the inhabitants of the village to a new site and demolishing the now-vacant village, began digging at the sanctuary of Apollo. Their excavations began in 1892, proved fruitful and continued non-stop for the next eleven years; they have gone on sporadically ever since.

EVANS AND KNOSSOS

The beginning of the twentieth century saw the domination of Greek archeology by an Englishman, **Sir Arthur Evans**. An egotistical maverick like Schliemann, he too was independently wealthy, with a brilliantly successful career behind him when he started his great work and recovered for Greek history another millennium. Evans excavated the **Palace of Minos** at **Knossos** on Crete, discovering one of the oldest and most sophisticated of Mediterranean societies.

The son of a distinguished antiquarian and collector, Evans read history at Oxford, failed to get a fellowship and began to travel. His chief interest was in the Balkans, where he was special correspondent for the *Manchester Guardian* during the 1877 uprising in Bosnia. He took enormous risks in the war-torn country, filing brilliant dispatches and still finding time for exploration and excavation.

In 1884, at the age of 33, Evans was appointed curator of the Ashmolean Museum in Oxford. He travelled whenever he could, and it was in 1893, while in Athens, that his attention was drawn to **Crete**. Evans, though very short-sighted, had almost microscopic close vision. In a vendor's stall he came upon some small drilled stones with tiny engravings in a hitherto unknown language; he was told they came from Crete. He had seen Schliemann's finds from Mycenae and had been fascinated by this prehistoric culture. Crete, the crossroads of the Mediterranean, seemed a good place to look for more.

Evans visited Crete in 1894 and headed for the legendary site of **Knossos**, where a Cretan had already done some impromptu digging, revealing massive walls and a storeroom filled with jars. Evans bought a share of the site and five years later, after the Turks had been forced off the island, returned to purchase the rest of the land. Excavations began in March 1899 and within a few days evidence of a great complex building was revealed, along with artefacts which indicated an astonishing cultural sophistication. The huge team of excavation workers unearthed elegant courtyards and verandas, colourful wall-paintings, pottery, jewellery and sealstones – the wealth of a civilization which dominated the eastern Mediterranean 3500 years ago.

Evans continued to excavate at Knossos for the next thirty years, during which time he established, on the basis of changes in the pottery styles, the system of dating that remains in use today for classifying Greek prehistory: Early, Middle and Late Minoan (Mycenaean on the mainland). He published his account of the excavation in a massive six-volume work, *The Palace of Minos*, which was published between 1921 and 1936. Like Schliemann, Evans attracted criticism and controversy for his methods – most notably his decision to reconstruct parts of the palace – and for many of his interpretations of what he found. Nevertheless, his discoveries and his dedication put him near to the pinnacle of Greek archeology.

INTO THE TWENTIETH CENTURY: THE FOREIGN INSTITUTES

In 1924 Evans gave to the **British School of Archeology** the site of Knossos, along with the Villa Ariadne (his residence there) and all other lands within his possession on Crete. At the time the British School was one of several foreign archeological institutes in Greece; founded in 1886, it had been preceded by the **French School**, the **German Institute** and the **American School**.

Greek archeology owes much to the work and relative wealth of these foreign schools and others that would follow. They have been responsible for the excavation of many of the most famous sites in Greece: the **Heraion on Sámos** (German); the sacred island of **Delos** (French); sites on **Kós** and in **southern Crete** (Italian); **Corinth**, **Samothráki** and the **Athenian Agora** (American), to name but a few. Life as a resident foreigner in Greece at the beginning of the century was not for the weak-spirited (one unfortunate member of the American School was shot and killed by bandits while on a trip to visit sites in the Peloponnese), but there were compensations in unlimited access to antiquities in an unspoiled countryside.

The years between the two world wars saw an expansion of excavation and scholarship, most markedly concerning the **prehistoric civilizations**. Having been shown by Schliemann and Evans what to look for, a new generation of archeologists was uncovering numerous prehistoric sites on the mainland and Crete, and its members were spending proportionately more time studying and interpreting their finds. Digs in the 1920s and 1930s had much smaller labour forces (there were just 55 workmen under Wace at Mycenae, as compared with hundreds in the early days of Schliemann's or Evans's excavations) and they were supervised by higher numbers of trained archeologists. Though perhaps not as spectacular as their predecessors, these scholars would prove just as pioneering as they established the history and clarified the chronology of the newly discovered civilizations.

One of the giants of this generation was **Alan Wace,** who while director of the British School of Archeology from 1913 to 1923 conducted excavations at Mycenae and established a chronological sequence from the nine great **tholos** tombs on the site. This led Wace to propose a new chronology for prehistoric Greece, and put him in direct conflict with Arthur Evans. Evans believed that the mainland citadels had been ruled by Cretan overlords, whereas Wace was convinced of an independent Mycenaean cultural and political development. Evans was by now a powerful member of the British School managing committee, and his published attacks on Wace's claims, combined with the younger archeologist's less than tactful reactions to

Evans's dominating personality, resulted in the abrupt halt of the British excavations at Mycenae in 1923 and the no less sudden termination of Wace's job. Wace was pressured to leave Greece, and it was not until 1939 that he returned. In the interval his theories gained growing support from the archeological community, and are today universally accepted.

Classical archeology was not forgotten in the flush of excitement over the Mycenaeans and Minoans. The period between the wars saw the continuation of excavation at most established sites, and many new discoveries, among them the sanctuary of Asklepios and its elegant Roman buildings on **Kós**, excavated by the Italians from 1935 to 1943, and the Classical Greek city of **Olynthos**, in northern Greece, which was dug by the American School from 1928 to 1934. After the wholesale removal of houses and apartment blocks that had occupied the site, the American School also began excavations in the **Athenian Agora**, the ancient marketplace, in 1931, culminating in the complete restoration of the Stoa of Attalos.

The advent of **World War II** and the invasion of Greece first by the Italians and then the Germans called a halt to most archeological work, although the Germans set to work again at **Olympia**, supposedly due to Hitler's personal interest. A few Allied nation archeologists also remained in Greece, principal among them **Gorham Stevens** and **Eugene Vanderpool**, of the American School, both of whom did charitable work. Back in America and Britain, meanwhile, archeologists were in demand for the intelligence arm of the war effort, both for their intimate knowledge of the Greek terrain and their linguistic abilities, which proved invaluable in decoding enemy messages.

POSTWAR EXCAVATIONS

Archeological work was greatly restricted in the years after World War II, and in the shadow of the Greek civil war. A few monuments and museums were restored and reopened but it was not until 1948 that excavations were resumed with a Greek clearance of the Sanctuary of Artemis at **Brauron** in Attica. In 1952 the American School resumed its activities with a dig at **Lerna** in the Peloponnese. Greek archeologists began work at the Macedonian

site of **Pella**, the **Necromanteion of Ephyra** and, in a joint venture with the French, at the Minoan site of **Káto Zákros** on Crete.

These and many other excavations – including renewed work on the major sites – were relatively minor operations in comparison to earlier digs. This reflected a modified approach to archeology, which laid less stress on discoveries than on documentation. Instead of digging large tracts of a site, archeologists concentrated on small sections, establishing chronologies through meticulous **analysis** of data. Which is not to say that there were no **finds**. At Mycenae, in 1951, a second circle of graves was unearthed; at Pireás (Piraeus), a burst sewer in 1959 revealed four superb Classical bronzes; and a dig at the Kerameikos cemetery site in Athens in 1966 found four thousand potsherds used as ballots for ostracism. Important work has also been undertaken on **restorations** – in particular the **theatres** of the Athens Acropolis, Dodona and Epidaurus, which are used in summer festivals.

The two great postwar excavations, however, have been as exciting as any in the past. At Akrotíri on the island of Thíra (Santoríni), **Spyros Marinatos** revealed, in 1967, a Minoan-era site that had been buried by volcanic explosion around 1550 BC. Its buildings were two or three storeys high, and superbly frescoed. A decade later came an even more dramatic find at **Veryína**, in northern Greece. Here, **Manolis Andronikos** found a series of royal tombs dating from the fourth century BC. Unusually, these had escaped plundering by ancient grave robbers and contained an astonishing hoard of exquisite gold treasures. Piecing together clues – the haste of the tomb's construction, an ivory effigy head, gilded leg armour – Andronikos showed this to have been the tomb of **Philip II of Macedon**, father of **Alexander the Great**. Subsequent forensic examination of the body supported historical accounts of Philip's limp and blindness.

It was an astonishing and highly emotive find, as the artefacts and frescoed walls showed the sophistication and Hellenism of ancient Macedonian culture. With the background of an emerging, self-styled Slavo-Macedonian state on Greece's northern border, archeology had come head-to-head with politics.

MYTHOLOGY, AN A TO Z

While all ancient cultures had their **myths**, it is those from ancient Greece that have had the greatest influence on Western civilization. The Trojan War, the wanderings of Odysseus, the adventures of Heracles – these stories and many more have inspired some of the finest literature, music and art.

Homer and his followers were the first bards to codify some of the stories in around 800 BC, but they had existed in the oral tradition for many years, and it would be another few centuries before Homeric epics would actually be written down, and other legends set forth in **Hesiod's** *Theogeny*. With the enactment of the myths in the rituals of their religious festivals and ceremonies, along with their representation in the designs on their pots and the performances of the stories at the theatre and drama competitions, Greek myth and culture became inextricably blended.

Many versions of the myths exist, some of which are contradictory and confusing. Below is a summary of the principal **gods** and **heroes**. For further reading Robert Graves's *The Greek Myths* is a good source, though perhaps a bit dry and academic; Pierre Grimal's *Dictionary of Classical Mythology* is a better reference, but probably the best starting point and a way into feeling how the myths might have been told is to read Homer's epics *The Iliad* and *The Odyssey*.

Agamemnon, see Atreus, House of; Trojan War

Aphrodite When Kronos castrated Ouranos (see below) and threw his testicles into the sea off Cyprus, the water spumed and foamed and produced Aphrodite, which means "born from sea foam". Aphrodite had a magic girdle which could make the wearer irresistible; she was married to the lame and unprepossessing Hephaistos, but her famed adultery with Ares ended badly when the couple found themselves ensnared in flagrante by the nets that Hephaistos made to expose her infidelity. She later had an affair with Hermes which produced a double-sexed offspring – Hermaphroditos. She particularly favoured the mortal Paris, instigator of the Trojan War. Her most famous ancient shrines were at Paphos (on Cyprus), Knidos (on the Anatolian coast), and on Lésvos.

Apollo was the illegitimate son of Zeus and the nymph Leto, and he was god of the sun, of plagues and, conversely, of healing. His first noteworthy deed was to kill the Python snake that was ravaging the land around Delphi, a location with which he subsequently had a great affinity. His shrine at Delphi was, with Olympia, considered one of the centres of the Hellenic world, and through the priestess of the oracle here, the god gave prophecies to pilgrims. A god of outstanding beauty, he also represented music and poetry, and was usually depicted with either a bow and arrow or a lyre, which was a gift to him from Hermes. He was not unlucky in love, but was famously spurned by Daphne (see p.872).

Ares, the god of war and the only legitimate son of Zeus and Hera, had hardly any temples dedicated to him – not surprisingly in light of Zeus's utterance that of all his offspring, Ares was the most hateful. He was usually attended by his demon henchmen Deimos (Terror) and Phobos (Fear). His violent character, however, did not necessarily render him all-victorious – he was more than once outwitted by Athena in *The Iliad*. The animals associated with Ares – the dog and the vulture – illuminate his character.

Argonauts, see Jason and the Argonauts

Ariadne, see Theseus, Ariadne and the Minotaur

Artemis, Apollo's twin, was the goddess of hunting, the moon, unmarried maidens and indeed all of nature beyond the city; her epithet was "Mistress of the Animals". She was attended by trains of nymphs and lions, frequented wild places, and was always described as a virgin with perpetual youth. She had a dark aspect: human sacrifice was implied or explicitly stated at some of her rites. Moreover, she killed the huntsman Orion who tried to rape her, and instigated the death of Actaeon who had seen her bathe naked by changing him into a stag and setting his own hounds upon him. Of her numerous shrines, the most important were at Brauron in Attica, at Sparta and at Ephesos in Asia Minor.

Athena did not have a conventional birth – she sprang out of the head of Zeus ready for battle, with armour, helmet and spear. She remained a virgin, so her son Ericthonius/Erechtheus was born in an equally unlikely way – he grew from her cast-off garments that had been soaked with Hephaistos' semen. She was the protector of Athens, and was regarded as the goddess of war, reason and wisdom. She discovered olive oil, helped to build the *Argo* and looked after her favourite mortals, particularly Odysseus and Herakles.

Atlas, see Herakles

Atreus, House of A dynasty of revenge, murder, incest and tragedy. Atreus hated his younger brother Thyestes, and when their separate claims for kingship of Mycenae were voiced, the gods favoured Atreus for the task. Atreus banished Thyestes, but when he learned that his wife had had an affair with him, Atreus feigned forgiveness and recalled him from exile. He then had Thyestes' sons murdered, cut up, cooked and fed to Thyestes. When Thyestes had finished eating, Atreus showed him the heads of his children, making it clear to him the true nature of the meal. He again banished Thyestes, who took refuge at Sikyon and, sanctioned by the gods, fathered Aegisthos by his daughter, Pelopia. Pelopia then married Atreus, her uncle, and Aegisthos (who did not know who his real father was) was brought up and cared for by Atreus. When Aegisthos came of age, Atreus instructed him to kill Thyestes, but Aegisthos found out the truth, returned to Mycenae and killed Atreus. Atreus's two sons were Agamemnon and Menelaos. Agamemnon paid for his father's crimes by dying at the hands of his wife Clytemnestra (who had committed adultery with Aegisthos while he Agamemnon was fighting at Troy). She ensnared him in a net while he took a bath and stabbed him to death. She in turn was killed by her son Orestes, who was pursued by the Furies before being absolved of matricide by Athena.

Bacchus, see Dionysos

Centaurs and Lapiths The centaurs were monstrous beings with the heads and torsos of men and the lower bodies of horses. They lived a debauched life, feeding on raw flesh and enjoying the pleasures of wine, but were also considered particularly skilled in the arts of sorcery and herbal healing. There are tales of certain centaurs battling with Herakles on his quest to complete the Twelve Labours, but the most famous story is of the fight that broke out between them and the Lapiths, a race of heroes and warriors who were the descendants of the

river god Pineos (the Piniós flows near Mount Olympus). Pirithous, a Lapith who shared the same father as the centaurs, invited them all to his wedding. At the feast the centaurs tried to abduct all the women, including the bride. A bloody brawl followed, of which the Lapiths were the victors; it is graphically depicted on the pediment reliefs at Olympia, as a metaphor for the triumph of reason over barbarism.

Daphne The nymph Daphne was one of the daughters of the river god Pineos. Apollo took a fancy to her and chased her through the woods, but just as he caught up with her, she prayed to her father to save her. He took pity and turned her into a laurel tree, and she became rooted to the spot. Apollo loved her even as a tree and made the laurel sacred, dedicating wreaths of its leaves as a sign of honour. Her name, to this day, is the Greek word for the laurel tree.

Demeter was the goddess of agriculture, in particular of corn, grain and pigs, as well as of death and regeneration. She exercised her power by making the whole Earth sterile after her daughter Persephone's abduction by Hades. The mother-and-daughter duo were usually revered together, particularly at the major sanctuary at Eleusis; women were her particular devotees, and worship involved the sacrifice of live piglets thrown into deep abysses.

Dionysos, also known as Bacchus, was the god of wine and mystic ecstasy. He was the son of Zeus and because he was ripped from his mother's womb at six months, Zeus sewed him up in his thigh for the remaining three. As a young boy he was disguised as a girl to hide him from Hera, and his feminine demeanour – long hair and dresses – stayed with him. He rode in a chariot drawn by panthers, and followed by a coterie of minor gods and mortal followers brandishing *thyrsoi* (wands topped with pine cones). His semi-mythical women followers, the maenads (see p.875), roamed the countryside in a state of madness; more usually, he was revered in the form of a bearded mask on a column, the antecedent of the comic and tragic masks of theatre. He rescued Ariadne from Náxos following her abandonment there by Theseus.

Eurydice, see Orpheus and Eurydice

Golden Fleece, see Jason and the Argonauts

Hades was the brother of Zeus and Poseidon, and when the cosmos was divided between them he was allotted the underworld. His name means "the invisible", because in the battle with Kronos and the Titans he concealed himself by wearing a magic helmet given to him by the Cyclops. To refer to him as Hades was thought to bring about his awesome anger, so the Greeks called him by his surname Pluto, which means "the rich" and alludes to the wealth that lies hidden underground. His wife was Demeter's daughter, Persephone (see opposite). Rather than temples he had mysterious oracles, most notably at Ephyra in Epirus and that of Trophonios at Livádhia.

Helen was the daughter of Zeus, who appeared in the form of a swan to her mother Leda, and accordingly Helen was hatched from an egg. She was believed to be the most beautiful woman in the world. Her husband Menelaos, king of Sparta, entertained the Trojans Paris and Aeneas and was foolish enough to leave them alone with her; Paris abducted her. Some sources say she went willingly, impressed by his beauty and wealth, others say she was raped. In either event her departure from Sparta was the cause of the Trojan War (see p.877).

Hephaistos was the god of fire, a master craftsman and an important deity for the Bronze Age. In his workshop on volcanic Límnos, where he was especially revered, he made everything from jewellery to armour. He was made lame from injuries sustained when (pick your version) Zeus threw him from Olympus because he had defended Hera in a quarrel, or when Hera, who bore him without a sire, tossed him down to Límnos in disappointment at the unprepossessing result. He was clever but very ugly, yet was married to Aphrodite (see p.871), the most beautiful of the goddesses.

Hera was Zeus's sister and wife and the most powerful of the goddesses – she wreaked jealous vengeance on any whom Zeus seduced, and on the offspring of most of his encounters (see lo). Zeus punished her heavily for her anger against Herakles by suspending her from her wrists from Mount Olympus, weighing her ankles down with anvils and whipping her. Despite her vindictive and irascible Homeric portrayal, she was the protecting deity of wives and the institution of marriage generally. Her totems and sacrificial animals were the cow, the cuckoo and the peacock; her main temples

were the ones on Sámos, near Argos, at Perahóra and at Olympia.

Herakles was the superhero of the ancient world. His father was Zeus and his mother was the mortal Alkmene; as a demigod he had no particular tomb or shrine like other heroes.

Jealous Hera sent two snakes to kill Herakles while he was still in his cradle, which he duly strangled – good preparation for his Twelve Labours. These were commanded by King Eurystheus of the Argolid, who was under the thrall of Hera. The tasks took him to the fringes of the known world, even involving his supporting it on his shoulders while Atlas took a break to lend him a hand in his final task. The labours were: to kill the Nemean lion; to kill the many-headed Hydra monster; to bring back the wild boar Erymanthus alive; to hunt the Keryneian hind that was sacred to Artemis; to kill the man-eating birds at the lake of Stymphaleia; to clean the stables of King Augeas; to bring back the untameable Cretan bull alive; to capture the flesh-eating horses of Diomedes; to fetch the girdle of the Amazon warrior queen; to fetch the herds of Geryon from beyond the edge of the ocean; to fetch Cerberus the guard dog of the underworld gates; and finally to fetch the golden apples from the garden of the Hesperides.

The twelves labours proved that Herakles had the right stuff to be a god, and his death was as dramatic as his life. Deianeira, his second wife, fearing his roving eye, gave him a magic tunic which was supposed to rekindle his affection towards her. When he donned it, it instead clung to his flesh, causing burning agony. She had drenched it in the poisonous blood of the centaur Nessus, whom Herakles had killed when he had tried to carry off Deianeira. Unable to bear the pain, Herakles built a funeral pyre, was conveyed up in the flames to heaven and became fully deified by Zeus – the only mortal or demigod to be so honoured.

Hermes was the son of Zeus and the nymph Maia, and was born in the Kyllene mountains of Arcadia, where his only major temple existed at Pheneos. He is a trickster figure, showing his mettle by inventing the lyre on the day of his birth, then stealing Apollo's sacred cattle, sacrificing two and then returning to his cradle by evening, denying the deed to his disbelieving brother. He was the god of commerce, thievery, herdsmen and travel; rather than shrines he had herms, stone cairns or boundary-markers. In his role as conductor of souls, Hermes crossed the line between the living world and underworld; he's often depicted wearing winged shoes, a wide-brimmed hat and carrying the herald's staff which showed his position as the divine messenger.

Hippolytos and Phaedra Hippolytos, son of the hero Theseus and the Amazon Hippolyta, was an accomplished hunter who revered Artemis and scorned Aphrodite. Aphrodite sought to teach him a lesson and conspired for Phaedra, the new wife of Theseus, to fall in love with the young man. When spurned by Hippolytos she feared he might reveal her advances and so accused him of rape. When Theseus heard this, he called upon Poseidon to kill his son; Hippolytos was then flung from his chariot and torn apart by his horses. Phaedra in shame and remorse hanged herself.

Io was only one of the many mortals Zeus singled out for carnal satisfaction. Having had his way he chose to conceal his misdemeanour by turning her into a cow, denying to Hera (see p.873) that he had ever touched the beast. Hera demanded her as a present, and placed her under the watchful eyes (he had a hundred of them) of Argos the guard. She then proceeded to torment poor Io the cow by sending a stinging gadfly to goad her on her travels. She made for the sea, first to the Ionian Sea, which was named after her, and then crossed the straits into Asia at the Bosporus (literally, the "Cow Ford"). Before settling in Egypt, she wandered all over Asia, even bumping into Prometheus, who was chained for a few centuries to the Caucasus mountain range.

Jason and the Argonauts Jason, a great Greek hero from Iolkos (present-day Vólos), was set an almost impossible task by his step-uncle Pelias to win the power that was his by birthright: to sail to the ends of the earth and bring back the Golden Fleece. He assembled his crew, assorted heroes of the ancient Greek world, and commissioned a ship, called the *Argo* after its maker Argos, which was built with the help of Athena — its prow had the remarkable gift of speech and prophecy. A long journey full of stories and surprises followed. Some of the crew didn't complete the voyage, including Herakles who missed the boat

because he was searching for his favourite, Hylas, a beautiful boy who had been abducted by the nymphs. The seer Phineus gave Jason directions and advice in return for him killing the harpies that were plaguing him; in particular he told Jason how to deal with moving rocks and reefs that might smash his ship. Armed with this knowledge, Jason and the Argonauts reached their destination. On arrival in Colchis, however, the King Aeetes would not hand over the Golden Fleece until Jason had completed various labours. The king's daughter, the sorceress Medea (see opposite), fell in love with Jason and helped him with her magic powers. They stole the fleece and fled, pursued by Aeetes. Medea stalled her father by tearing up her brother Apsyrtus and casting his body parts into the sea; Aeetes had to slow down to collect the pieces. Zeus was greatly angered by this heinous crime and the *Argo* spoke to the crew telling them that they would have to purify themselves at Circe's island. After more adventures and wanderings through treacherous seas, the crew arrived at Corinth where Jason dedicated the Golden Fleece to Poseidon.

Judgement of Paris The goddess Eris (Strife) began a quarrel between Athena, Hera and Aphrodite, by throwing a golden apple between them and saying that it belonged to whichever goddess was the most beautiful. All the gods were too frightened to judge the contest, so Hermes took them to the top of Mount Ida for Paris, the son of Priam of Troy, to decide. Each used bribery to win his favour: Athena offered him wisdom and victory in combat, Hera the kingdom of Asia, but Aphrodite, the winner of the contest, offered him the love of Helen of Sparta.

Kronos The Titan Kronos was the youngest son of the pre-Olympian deities Gaia and Ouranos, who seized power in the heavens by castrating his father. Once on the throne, Kronos lived in perpetual fear of the prediction that one of his offspring would one day overthrow him, and so swallowed all of his children except Zeus (see p.877) — Zeus's mother Rhea had substituted a stone for the bundle that Kronos thought was his baby. Kronos and his Titan brothers were defeated in a cosmic battle by Zeus and his Olympian supporters.

Lapiths, see Centaurs and Lapiths

Maenads The maenads were the possessed or intoxicated female followers of Dionysos (see p.872). They wore scanty clothes, had wreaths of ivy around their heads and played upon tambourines or flutes in their procession. They had power over wild animals, and in their frenzy they believed they drank milk or honey from freshwater springs. In their orgiastic ecstasies they tore limb from limb those who offended them, did not believe or who spied upon their rites – including Orpheus (see below).

Medea exacted gruesome revenge on any who stood against her. She persuaded the daughters of Pelias (see Jason) to cut their father up and put him in a boiling cauldron, having convinced them that if they did so she could rejuvenate him. His body parts, to their extreme disappointment, did not come back together. Akastos, Pelias's son, banished her and Jason as a punishment; they went together to Corinth, where Jason abandoned her to marry Kreusa, the daughter of the local king, Kreon. In revenge, Medea orchestrated a gruesome death for Kreusa, by sending her a tunic which burst into flames upon wearing, and then murdered her own two young sons by Jason.

Minotaur, see Theseus, Ariadne and the Minotaur

Muses The muses were the result of nine nights of lovemaking between Mnemosyne (Memory) and Zeus. They were primarily singers and the inspiration for music (to which they gave their name), but also had power over thought in all its forms: persuasion, eloquence, knowledge, history, mathematics and astronomy. Apollo conducted their singing around the Hippocrene fountain on Mount Helicon, or on Mount Olympus itself.

Nymphs There were various subspecies of nymph: meliads were the nymphs of the ash trees; nereids lived in the springs and streams; naïads in the ocean; dryads were individual tree nymphs; oreads were the mountain nymphs; and the alseids lived in the groves. They were thought to be the daughters of Zeus and attended certain deities, particularly Artemis and Poseidon.

Odysseus Our word "odyssey" derives from Odysseus's ten-year journey home, which was no less fraught with danger, adventure and grief than the ten-year war against the Trojans which preceded it. Shipwrecked, tormented by the gods, held against his will by bewitching women, almost lured to his death by the hypnotic sirens, witnessing his comrades devoured by the giant one-eyed cyclops Polyphemos and all the time missing and desiring his faithful wife Penelope, Odysseus proved himself to be a great and scheming hero. At the end of his arduous journey he arrived in disguise at his palace on Ithaca to find suitors pestering his wife. He contrived a cunning trap and killed them all with the bow which only he could flex.

Oedipus was a man profoundly cursed. The Delphic Oracle said that Laius, king of Thebes, should not father any children, for if he did one would kill him. When Oedipus was born Laius abandoned the baby, piercing his ankles with a nail and tying them together: thus the name, which means "swollen foot". But the baby was discovered and brought up at the court of the neighbouring king, Polybos, at Corinth. The same oracle revealed to the adult Oedipus that he would kill his father and marry his mother. When he heard this news he resolved not to return home to Corinth, but east of Delphi he met with Laius, who was heading west to consult the oracle as to how to rid Thebes of the Sphinx. Because the road was narrow, Laius ordered Oedipus to get out of the way, and when one of the guards pushed him, Oedipus drew his sword in anger and, not knowing that Laius was his father, killed him and his entourage. He then made his way to the Thebes, where Laius had been king, and solved the riddle of the Sphinx. As a reward and in thanks, he was crowned king and offered Laius's widow Iocasta (his mother) in marriage. Plague then fell upon Thebes, because of the crimes of patricide and incest at the heart of the city. The Delphic Oracle instructed Oedipus to expel the murderer of Laius, and in his ignorance he ordered the guilty party cursed and banished. The seer and prophet Teiresias then revealed the full nature of the crime to Iocasta and Oedipus; she hanged herself and he put out his own eyes. He left the city as a vagabond accompanied by his daughter Antigone, and only at his death was granted peace. Attica, the country that received his dead body, became blessed.

Olympus, Mount, see Zeus

Orpheus and Eurydice Orpheus was a great musician who received his lyre from Apollo himself. He played and sang so beautifully that wild beasts were charmed, trees would uproot themselves to come closer, and even the very rocks were moved. He enlisted in the crew of Argonauts and sang for them to row their oars in time. On his return from the *Argo*'s voyage he married the nymph Eurydice. She was bitten by a snake on the banks of the river Pineos and died, and Orpheus was so distraught that he went to the underworld to bring her back to life. His wish was granted by Hades on condition that during the return journey he would not look back at her. As the couple approached daylight, however, his mind became consumed with doubt and, turning around to see if she was behind him, he lost her forever. He preached that Apollo was the greatest god, much to the anger of Dionysos, who set the maenads (see p.875) on him. They tore him apart and cast his head, still singing, into the Thracian river Hebrus; it was finally washed up on the shores of the island of Lésvos, supposedly conferring great musical gifts to the local population.

Ouranos was the personification of the sky and by his union with Gaia (Earth) fathered many children, including Kronos (see p.874) and the Titans (see below). Gaia became so exhausted by her husband's continual advances that she sought protection from her sons. Kronos was the only one to assist; he cut off Ouranos's testicles with a sickle and threw them into the sea, giving rise to Aphrodite (see p.871).

Pan The patron of shepherds and flocks, Pan was the son of Hermes and a nymph and, with his beard, horns, hairy body and cloven hooves, was said to be so ugly that his own mother ran from him in fear. He had an insatiable libido, energetically pursuing both sexes. Apollo learned the art of prophecy from Pan, and hunters looked to him for guidance. He enjoyed the cool woodland shade and streams of Arcadia and relished his afternoon naps so much that he wreaked havoc if he was disturbed.

Pandora, see Prometheus

Pegasus, see Poseidon

Penelope, see Odysseus

Persephone, also known as Kore (the Maiden), was out picking flowers one day when the earth opened up and swallowed her; she had been abducted by Hades in his chariot. Her mother Demeter was distraught and when she found out the truth, she left Olympus in protest and made the earth sterile so that it produced no crops. Zeus ordered Hades to return Persephone, but because she had eaten pomegranate seeds in the underworld she was bound to him. As a compromise, she would be allowed to return to earth for two-thirds of the year but had to reside with Hades for the remaining third. So Demeter divided the year into seasons, so that while Persephone was with Hades the earth would be sterile and suffer winter, but that while Persephone was on earth the ground would be fertile for spring, summer and autumn.

Perseus A son of Zeus, and believed to be a direct ancestor of Herakles, Perseus was cast out to sea in a trunk with his mother Danae, because his grandfather feared a prophecy that Perseus would one day kill him. Danae and Perseus were washed up on Sérifos island, where they were discovered by a fisherman who looked after them. When Perseus came of age, the king of Sérifos demanded that he bring back the head of Medusa the gorgon, whose gaze could turn people to stone. Perseus acquired some special aids to perform the task – Hades' helmet, which made him invisible, and winged sandals to fly through the air – and had the divine assistance of Athena and Hermes. He cut off Medusa's head by looking at her reflection in Athena's polished shield. On his return flight he saw and fell in love with Andromeda, who was being offered as a sacrifice. He rescued her and returned home to find his mother had been raped by the king. He held up the gorgon's head, turned the king to stone and then presented the head as a gift to Athena, who placed it in the middle of her shield. Perseus went on to participate in the king of Lárissa's celebratory games; he competed in the discus-throwing competition but his throw went off course and killed his grandfather, who was a spectator, thus fulfilling the prophecy.

Phaedra, see Hippolytos and Phaedra

Poseidon was the god of the sea, earthquakes and storms, and patron of fishermen. In the battle with Kronos and the Titans, Poseidon, the brother of Zeus, was given the trident by the cyclops which he used to shake both sea and land. After the victory he was awarded, by lot, the realm of the ocean, where he dwelt in the depths. He produced some strange offspring, including the cyclops Polyphemus who had it in for Odysseus (see p.875), and mated with the gorgon Medusa – which resulted in the winged horse Pegasus. He quarrelled frequently with the other gods, competing with them for power over some of the major cities including Athens, Corinth and Argos, but his great hatred was for the Trojans who had double-crossed him by not paying him for helping them to build their city.

Prometheus For someone whose name means "forethought", Prometheus showed a distinct lack of it. In his desire to help mankind, he stole fire from the heavens and was immediately punished by Zeus who bound him in chains, tied him to the Caucasus mountains and then sent an eagle to perpetually peck at his liver. Zeus then dealt with mankind by sending Pandora to Prometheus's brother Epimetheus, whose name means "afterthought". Her curiosity about the contents of his box got the better of her and, peeping inside, she unleashed all the evils and one good (hope) on the world. Prometheus gave some useful advice to Herakles when he passed by on one of his labours and Herakles repaid him by setting him free.

Theseus, Ariadne and the Minotaur Theseus's father, Aegeus of Athens, sent him as a child away from Athens for his own safety. At sixteen the hero returned, in full strength and with the weapons that his father had set aside for him. Theseus was destined for a life of action, and his greatest adventure was to kill the Minotaur on Crete. As tribute from Athens, King Minos was owed six men and six women every nine years for sacrifice to the Minotaur – a gruesome beast, half-man half-bull, born from the bestial copulation of the queen Pasiphae with the huge bull sent by Poseidon. The Minotaur was kept in the labyrinth at Crete. Ariadne, Minos's daughter, contrived to help Theseus kill the Minotaur, having fallen in love with him. She gave him a ball of thread so that he would not lose his way in the labyrinth and then accompanied him in his flight from the island, only to be abandoned later on the island of Náxos. Dionysos saw her there disconsolate on the shore, took pity on her and he married her. Theseus, meanwhile, on his return to Athens forgot to change the black sails to white as a signal to his father that he was alive, and Aegeus – thinking that his son had been killed by the Minotaur – threw himself into the sea which took his name: the Aegean.

Titans The Titans were the six male children of Ouranos and Gaia. Their six sisters, who helped them father numerous gods, were called the Titanides. Kronos was the youngest Titan, and

after he had overthrown his father he helped his brothers to power. The Titans lost their grip when they were toppled by the upstart Olympians, led by Zeus, in the cataclysmic battle called the Titanomachia.

Trojan War When Menelaos of Sparta realized that the Trojan Paris had made off with his wife Helen, he called on his brother Agamemnon of Mycenae. Together they roused the might of Greece to get her back. With just about every hero (Ajax, Achilles, Troilus, Hector, Paris, Odysseus, Priam, Diomedes, Aeneas) making an appearance in this epic, the story of the Trojan War is arguably the greatest tale from the ancient world. Homer's *Iliad* dealt with only one aspect of it, the wrath of Achilles. The ten-year war, fought over a woman and which sent many heroes' souls down to Hades, was finally won by the trickery of the Greeks, who used a huge wooden horse, left ostensibly as a gift to the Trojans, to smuggle an armed platoon inside the city walls. The cunning plan was thought to be the work of Odysseus (see p.875), who, like many of the surviving heroes, had a less than easy journey home.

Zeus was the supreme deity, king of gods and men, but he did not get to this position without a struggle. His father, the Titan Kronos, seized power in the heavens by castrating Ouranos the sky god, and in turn lived in fear that one of his offspring would one day overthrow him. He therefore swallowed all his children except Zeus, whose mother, Rhea, came to the rescue and hid him in a cave on the island of Crete, where the Kouretes warrior, beings, concealed his cries by smashing their swords and shields together. When he came of age, Zeus poisoned Kronos so that he vomited up all Zeus's siblings; with their help, and the assistance of the cyclops, he cast Kronos and the Titans from Mount Olympus, the home of the gods. The cyclops gave Zeus the thunderbolt as a weapon to use in the battle and it became his symbol of power, and emblem of his role as deity of weather and rain. Zeus used his position to maintain cosmic order, control the other gods and men and to get his way with whomever he fancied. Numerous myths tell of his metamorphoses to mate with a variety of mortals out of sight of his jealous wife Hera; all of his liaisons resulted in offspring, which included Herakles (see p.873), Perseus (see opposite) and Helen (see p.873).

WILDLIFE

For anyone who has first seen Greece at the height of summer with its brown parched hillsides and desert-like ambience, the richness of the wildlife – in particular the flora – may come as a surprise. As winter changes to spring, the countryside (and urban waste ground) transforms itself from green to a mosaic of coloured flowers, which attract a plethora of insect life, followed by birds. Isolated areas, whether true islands or remote mountains such as Olympus, have had many thousands of years to develop their own individual species. Overall, Greece has around six thousand species of native flowering plants, nearly four times that of Britain but in the same land area. Many are unique to Greece, and make up about one third of Europe's endemic plants.

SOME BACKGROUND

In early antiquity Greece was thickly forested: Aleppo and Calabrian pines grew in coastal regions, giving way to fir or black pine up in the hills and low mountains. But this **native woodland** contracted rapidly as human activities expanded. By Classical times, a pattern had been set of forest clearance, followed by agriculture, abandonment to scrub and then a resumption of cultivation or grazing. Huge quantities of timber were consumed in the production of charcoal, pottery and smelted metal, and for ships and construction work. Small patches

of virgin woodland have remained, mostly in the north and northeast, but even these are under threat from loggers and arsonists.

Modern Greek **farming** often lacks the rigid efficiency of northern European agriculture. Many peasant farmers still cultivate little patches of land, and even city-dwellers travel at weekends to collect food plants from the countryside. Wild greens under the generic term *hórta* are gathered to be cooked like spinach; grape hyacinth bulbs are boiled as a vegetable. The buds and young shoots of capers, and the fruit of wild figs, carobs, plums, strawberry trees, cherries and sweet chestnuts are harvested. Emergent snails and mushrooms are collected after wet weather. The more resilient forms of wildlife can coexist with these uses, but for many Greeks only those species that have practical uses are regarded as having any value.

Despite an often negative attitude to wildlife, Greece was probably the first place in the world where it was an object of study. Theophrastos (372–287 BC) was the first recorded **botanist** and a systematic collector of general information on plants, while his contemporary, Aristotle, studied the animal world. During the first century AD the distinguished physician Dioscorides compiled a herbal that remained a standard work for over a thousand years.

Since the 1970s, tourist developments have ribboned out along coastlines, sweeping away both agricultural plots and wildlife havens as they do so. These expanding resorts increase local employment, often attracting inland workers to the coast; the generation that would have been shepherds on remote hillsides now works in bars and tavernas for the tourist. Consequently, the pressure of domestic animal grazing, particularly in the larger islands, has been significantly reduced, allowing the regeneration of tree seedlings. Crete, for example, now has more woodland than at any time in the last five centuries.

FLOWERS

Whereas in temperate northern Europe plants flower from spring until autumn, the arid summers of Greece confine the main **flowering period** to the spring, to a climatic window when the days are bright, the temperatures are not too high and the ground water supply still adequate. **Spring** starts in the southeast, in Rhodes in early March, and then travels progressively westwards and northwards. Rhodes, Kárpathos and eastern Crete are at their best in March, western Crete in early April, the Peloponnese and eastern Aegean mid-April to late April, and the Ionian islands in early May, though a cold dry winter can cause several weeks' delay. In the higher mountains the floral spring is held back until the chronological summer, with the alpine zones of central and western Crete in full flower in June, while mainland mountain blooms emerge in July.

The delicate flowers of early spring – orchids, fritillaries, anemones, cyclamen, tulips and small bulbs, are replaced as the season progresses by more robust shrubs, tall perennials and abundant annuals, but many of these close down completely for the fierce **summer**. A few tough plants, like shrubby thyme and savory, continue to flower through the heat and act as magnets for butterflies.

Once the worst heat is over, and the first showers of **autumn** arrive, so does a second "spring", on a much smaller scale but no less welcome after the brown drabness of summer. Squills, autumn cyclamen, crocus in varying shades, pink or lilac colchicum, yellow sternbergia and other small bulbs all come into bloom, while the seeds start to germinate for the following year's crop of annuals. By the new year, early-spring bulbs and orchids are flowering in the south.

SEASHORE

Plants on the **beach** tend to be hardy species growing in a difficult environment where fresh water is scarce. Feathery tamarisk trees are adept at surviving this habitat, and consequently are often planted to provide shade. On hot days or nights you may see or feel them "sweating" away surplus saltwater from their foliage.

Sand dunes in the southern and eastern islands may support the low gnarled trees of the prickly **juniper**. These provide shelter for a variety of colourful small plants like pink campions, yellow restharrow, white stocks, blue alkanet and violet sea-lavender. The flat sandy areas or "slacks" behind the dunes can be home to a variety of plants, where they have not been illegally ploughed for cultivation. Open stretches of beach sand usually have fewer plants, particularly nowadays in resort areas where the bull-dozed "spring cleaning" of the beach removes the local flora along with the winter's rubbish.

WATERCOURSES

Large areas of **freshwater** are scarce, particularly in the warmer south. Many watercourses dry up completely in the hot season, and what seem to be dry river courses are often simply flood-beds, which fill irregularly at times of torrential rain. Consequently, there are few true aquatic plants compared with much of Europe. However, species that survive periodic drying-out can flourish, such as the giant reed or **calamus**, a bamboo-like grass reaching up to 6m in height and often cut for use as canes. It often grows in company with the shrubby, pink- or white-flowered and very poisonous **oleander**.

CULTIVATED LAND

Arable fields can be rich with colourful weeds: scarlet poppies, blue bugloss, yellow or white daisies, wild peas, gladioli, tulips and grape hyacinths. Small **meadows** can be equally colourful, with slower-growing plants such as orchids in extraordinary quantities. The rather dull violet flowers of the mandrake conceal its celebrated history as a narcotic and surgical anaesthetic. In the absence of herbicides, olive groves can have an extensive underflora. In the presence of herbicides there is usually a yellow carpet of the introduced, weedkiller-resistant *Oxalis pescaprae*, which now occurs in sufficient quantity to show up in satellite photographs.

LOWER HILLSIDES

The rocky earth makes cultivation on some hillsides difficult and impractical. Agriculture is often abandoned and areas regenerate to a rich mixture of shrubs and perennials – **garigue** biome. With time, a few good wet winters, and in the absence of grazing, some shrubs develop into small trees, intermixed with tough climbers – the much denser **maquis** vegetation. The colour yellow often predominates in early spring, with brooms, gorse, Jerusalem sage and the three-metre giant fennel followed by the pink and white of large rockroses (*Cistus spp*). An abundance of the latter is often indicative of an earlier fire, since they flourish in the cleared areas. Strawberry trees too are fire-resistant; they flower in winter or early spring, producing an orange-red edible (though disappointingly insipid) fruit in the autumn. The Judas tree flowers on bare wood in spring, making a blaze of pink against the green hillsides.

A third vegetation type is **phrygana** – smaller, frequently aromatic or spiny shrubs, often with a narrow strip of bare ground between each hedgehog-like bush. Many **aromatic herbs** such as lavender, rosemary, savory, sage and thyme are native to these areas, intermixed with other less tasty plants such as the toxic euphorbias and the spiny burnet or wire-netting bush.

Nearly 160 species of **orchid** are believed to occur in Greece; their complexity blurs species' boundaries and keeps botanists in a state of taxonomic flux. In particular, the *Ophrys* bee and spider orchids have adapted themselves, through subtleties of lip colour and false scents, to seduce small male wasps. These insects mistake the flowers for a potential mate, and unintentionally assist the plant's pollination. Other orchids mimic the colours and scents of nectar-producing plants, to lure bees. Though all species are officially protected, many are still picked for decoration – in particular the giant *Barlia* orchid – and fill vases in homes, cafés, tavernas and even on graves.

Irises have a particular elegance and charm. The blue-to-violet winter iris, as its name suggests, is the first to appear, followed by the small blue *Iris gynandriris*. The flowers of the latter open after midday and into the night, to wither by the following morning. The widow iris is sombre-coloured in funereal shades of black and green, while the taller, white *Iris albicans*, the holy flower of Islam, is a relic of Ottoman occupation. On the limestone peaks of Sámos, *Iris suavolens* has short stems, but huge yellow and brown flowers.

MOUNTAINS AND GORGES

The higher **mountains** of Greece have winter snow cover, and cooler weather for much of the year, so flowering is consequently later than at lower altitudes. The **limestone peaks** of the mainland, and of islands such as Corfu, Kefalloniá, Crete, Rhodes, Sámos and Thássos, hold rich collections of attractive rock plants, flowers whose nearest relatives may be from the Balkan Alps or from the Turkish mountains. Gorges are another spectacular habitat, particularly rich in Crete. Their inaccessible cliffs act as refuges for plants that cannot survive the grazing, competition or more extreme climates of open areas. Many of Greece's endemic plants – bellflowers, knapweeds and *Dianthus spp.* in particular – are confined to cliffs, gorges or mountains.

Much of the surviving **original woodland** is in mountain areas. In the south, the woodland includes cypress, Greek fir and several species of pine, with oak and flowering ash. The cypress is native to the south and east Aegean, but in its columnar form it has been planted everywhere with a Mediterranean climate. It is sometimes said that the slim trees are the male and the broader, spreading form is female, but female cones on the thin trees prove this wrong. Further north there are also juniper and yew, with beech, hornbeam, maple, chestnut and poplar. The cooler shade of woodland provides a haven for plants which cannot survive full exposure to the Greek summer. Such species include the wonderful red, pink or white peonies and the scarlet martagon lily, along with helleborine and bird's-nest orchids, and numerous ferns.

With altitude, the forest thins out to scattered individual conifers and kermes oak, before finally reaching a limit at around 1500–2000m on the mainland – much lower on the islands. Above this treeline are summer meadows, and then bare rock. If not severely grazed, these habitats are home to many low-growing, gnarled, but often splendidly floriferous plants, such as aubrieta, alyssum, storksbill, prickly thrift, dwarf rose, saxifrage and viola.

BIRDS

Migratory species which have wintered in East Africa move north in spring through the eastern Mediterranean from mid-March to mid-May, or later, depending on the season and the weather. Some stop to breed in Greece; others move on into the rest of Europe. The southern islands can be the first landfall after a long sea-crossing, and smaller birds recuperate for a few days before moving on north. Larger birds such as storks and ibis often fly very high, and binoculars are needed to spot them as they pass over. In autumn the birds return, but usually in more scattered numbers. Although some species such as quail and turtle dove are shot, there is nothing like the wholesale slaughter that takes place in some other Mediterranean countries.

Swallows, and their relatives the martins, are constantly swooping through the air to catch insects, as are the larger and noisier swifts. Warblers are numerous, with the Sardinian warbler often conspicuous because of its black head, bright red eye and bold habits; the Rüppell's warbler is considerably rarer, and confined to thicker woodland. Other small insect-eaters include stonechats, fly-catchers and woodchat shrikes.

At **night**, the tiny Scops owl has a very distinct, repeated single-note call, very like the sonar beep of a submarine; the equally diminutive little owl is by contrast also visible by **day**, particularly on ruined houses, and has a strange repertoire of cries, chortles and a throaty hiss. Certainly the most evocative nocturnal bird is the nightingale, which requires wooded stream valleys and is most audible around midnight in May, its mating season.

Larger **raptors** occur in remoter areas, particularly around mountain gorges and cliffs. Buzzards are perhaps the most abundant, and mistaken by optimistic birdwatchers for the rarer, shyer eagles. Griffon vultures are unmistakable, soaring on broad, straight-edged wings, whereas the lammergeier is a state-of-the-art flying machine with narrow, swept wings, seen over mountain tops by the lucky few. Lesser kestrels are brighter, noisier versions of the common kestrel, and often appear undisturbed by the presence of humans. Also to be seen in the mountains are ravens, and smaller, colourful birds such as alpine choughs, common choughs, black and white wheatears, wallcreepers and the blue rock thrush.

In lowland areas, hoopoes are a startling combination of pink, black and white, particularly obvious when they fly; they're about the only natural predator of the processionary caterpillar, a major pest in pine forests. The much shyer golden oriole has an attractive song but is rarely seen for more than a few moments before hiding its brilliant colours among the olive trees. Rollers are bright blue and chestnut. Multicoloured flocks of slim and elegant bee-eaters fill the air with their soft calls as they hunt insects. Brightest of all is the kingfisher, more commonly seen sea-fishing than in northern Europe.

In those areas of **wetland** that remain undrained and undisturbed, birds flourish. In saltmarshes, coastal lagoons, estuaries and freshwater ponds, herons and egrets, ducks, osprey, glossy ibis and spoonbills, black storks, white storks, pelicans and many waders can be seen feeding. Cormorants roost on and dive from coastal cliffs from late summer onwards, while greater flamingos sometimes occur, as lone individuals or small flocks, particularly in salt pans in the eastern Aegean.

MAMMALS

Greece's small **mammal** population ranges from small rodents and shrews to hedgehogs, hares and squirrels (a very dark form of the red). Rats are particularly common on Corfu and Sámos. Medium-sized mammals include badgers and foxes, but one of the commonest is the fast-moving, ferret-like, stone (or beech) marten, named for its habit of decorating stones with its droppings to mark territory.

In the mainland mountains, mainly in the north, are found the shy **chamois** and **wild boar**, with even shyer predators like lynx, wolves and brown bear. In the White Mountains of Crete an endemic ibex, known to Cretan hunters as the *agrími* or *krí-krí*, is occasionally seen running wild but more often penned as a zoo attraction. When formerly in danger of extinction, a colony of them was established on offshore islet of Dhía, where they managed in turn to exterminate the rare local flora.

The extremely rare Mediterranean **monk seal** also breeds on some stretches of remote coast in the east Aegean and Sporades; the small world population is now highly endangered since losing many individuals – and most of its main breeding ground – to a toxic algal bloom off Morocco. If spotted, these seals should be treated with deference; they cannot tolerate human disturbance, and on present trends are unlikely to survive much into the new millennium.

REPTILES AND AMPHIBIANS

Reptiles flourish in the hot dry summers of Greece and there are many species, the commonest being **lizards**. Most of these are small, slim, agile and wary, rarely staying around for closer inspection. They're usually brown to grey, with subtle patterns of spots, streaks and stripes, though in adult males the undersides are sometimes brilliant orange, green or blue. The more robust green lizards, with long whip-like tails, can be 50cm or more in length, but equally shy and fast-moving unless distracted by territorial disputes with each other.

On some islands, mainly in the central and eastern Aegean, lives the angular, iguana-like **agama**, sometimes called the Rhodes dragon. Occasionally reaching a robust 30cm in length, their skin is rough and grey to brown with indistinct patterning. Unlike other lizards, they will often stop to study you, before finally disappearing into a wall or under a rock.

Geckos are large-eyed nocturnal lizards, up to 15cm long, with short tails and often rough skins. Their spreading toes have claws and ingenious adhesive pads, allowing them to walk up house walls and onto ceilings in their search for insects. Groups of them lie in wait near bright lights that attract their prey, and small ones living indoors can have very pale, almost transparent skins. Not always popular locally – one Greek name for them, *miaró*, means "defiler" after their outsized faeces – they should be left alone to eat mosquitoes and other bugs. The **chameleon** is a rare, slow-moving and swivel-eyed inhabitant of eastern Crete and some eastern Aegean islands such as Sámos. Although essentially green, it has the ability to adjust its coloration to match the surroundings.

Once collected for the pet trade, **tortoises** can be found on much of the mainland, and some islands, though not on Crete. Usually it is their noisy progress through vegetation on sunny or wooded hills that first signals their presence. They spend their often long lives grazing the vegetation and can reach lengths of 30cm. Closely related **terrapins** are more streamlined, freshwater tortoises which love to bask on waterside mud by streams or ponds, including on many islands. Shy and nervous, they are usually only seen as they disappear under water. They are scavengers and will eat anything, including fingers if handled.

Sea turtles occur mostly in the Ionian Sea, but also in the Aegean. The least rare are the loggerhead turtles (*Caretta caretta*), which nest on Zákynthos and Kefalloniá, and occasionally in Crete. Their nesting grounds are disappearing under tourist resorts, although they are a protected endangered species (see Ionians).

Snakes are abundant in Greece and many islands; most are shy and non-venomous. Several species, including the Ottoman and nose-horned **vipers**, do have a poisonous bite, though they are not usually aggressive. They are adder-like and often have a very distinct, dark zigzag stripe down the back. They are only likely to bite if a hand is put in the crevice of a wall or a rock-face where one of them is resting, or if they are attacked. Unfortunately, the locals in some areas attempt to kill any snake they see, and thus greatly increase the probability of their being bitten. Leave them alone, and they will do the same for you (but if worst comes to worst, see the advice on p.26). Most snakes are not only completely harmless to humans, but beneficial in that they keep down populations of pests such as rats and mice. There are also three species of legless lizards – slow-worm, glass lizard and legless skink – all equally harmless, which suffer because they are mistaken for snakes.

Frogs and **toads** are the commonest and most obvious amphibians in most of Greece, particularly during the spring breeding season. The green toad has green marbling over a pinkish or mud-coloured background, and a cricket-like trill. Frogs prefer the wettest places, and the robust marsh frog particularly revels in artificial water storage ponds, whose concrete sides magnify their croaking impressively. **Tree frogs** are tiny jewels, usually emerald green, with huge and strident voices at night. They rest by day in trees and shrubs, and can sometimes be found in quantity plastered onto the leaves of waterside oleanders.

Newts, complete with lacy external gills, can be seen in a few alpine tarns of the north mainland. Search for **salamanders** in ponds at breeding time, under stones and in moist crevices outside the breeding season. The orange-on-black fire salamander is often found promenading in the mountains after rain.

INSECTS

Greece teems with **insects**. Some pester, like flies and mosquitoes, but most are harmless to humans. The huge, slow-flying, glossy black carpenter bee may cause alarm by its size and noise, but is rarely a problem.

Grasshoppers and **crickets** swarm through open areas of vegetation in summer, with several larger species that are carnivorous on the smaller and can bite strongly if handled. Larger still is the grey-brown locust, which flies noisily before crash-landing into trees and

FLORA AND FAUNA FIELD GUIDES

In case of difficulty obtaining titles listed below from conventional booksellers, there are two reliable mail-order outlets for wildlife field guides within the UK. The **Botanical Society of the British Isles** (BSBI), Green Acre, Wood Lane, Oundle, Peterborough PE8 5TP (☎0132/273388, fax 274 568) specializes in the more popular botanical guides, including many of the nominally out-of-print (o/p) ones, with quite comprehensive listings, and prices including postage within the UK. However, they will cease trading in late 2000. **Summerfield Books**, High Street, Brough, Kirkby Stephen, Cumbria CA17 4BX (☎ & fax 017683/41577, *atkins@summerfield-books.com*) not only has new botanical titles, but also rare or out-of-print natural history books on all topics. Postage is extra, but they often have special offers on select products, and their catalogue descriptions are fuller.

FLOWERS

Hellmut Baumann *Greek Wild Flowers and Plant Lore in Ancient Greece* (Herbert Press, UK). Crammed with fascinating ethnobotany, plus good colour photographs.

Marjorie Blamey and Christopher Grey-Wilson *Mediterranean Wild Flowers* (Harper-Collins, UK). Comprehensive field guide, with coloured drawings; recent and taxonomically up to date.

Lance Chilton *Plant check-lists* (Marengo Publications, UK). Small pamphlets which also include birds, reptiles and butterflies, for a number of Greek islands and resorts. Contact the author directly at ☎01485/532710, *marengo@supanet.com*.

Pierre Delforge *Orchids of Britain and Europe* (HarperCollins, UK). A comprehensive guide, with recent taxonomy, though beware small inaccuracies in the translation.

Anthony Huxley and William Taylor *Flowers of Greece and the Aegean* (Hogarth Press, UK; o/p). The only volume dedicated to the islands and mainland, with colour photos, but now slightly dated for taxonomy.

Oleg Polunin *Flowers of Greece and the Balkans* (Oxford UP, UK). Classic, older field guide (reprinted 1997), also with colour photographs; useful if Huxley and Taylor proves difficult to find.

Oleg Polunin and Anthony Huxley *Flowers of the Mediterranean* (Hogarth Press, UK). The larger scope means that many Greek endemics get missed out, but recent printings have a table of taxonomic changes.

BIRDS

Richard Brooks *Birding in Lesbos* (Brookside Publishing, UK). Superb guide with colour photos which includes a list of birdwatching sites, with detailed maps, plus an annotated species-by-species bird list with much useful information.

George Handrinos and T. Akriotis *Birds of Greece* (A&C Black, UK). A comprehensive guide that includes island birdlife.

Heinzel, Fitter and Parslow *Collins Guide to the Birds of Britain and Europe*; **Petersen, Mountfort and Hollom** *Field Guide to the Birds of Britain and Europe* (Collins, UK; Stephen Green Press, US). Though not specific to Greece, these two field guides have the best coverage of Greek birds outside of Lésvos.

MAMMALS

Corbet and Ovenden *Collins Guide to the Mammals of Europe* (Collins, UK; Stephen Green Press, US). The best field guide on its subject.

REPTILES

Arnold, Burton and Ovenden *Collins Guide to the Reptiles and Amphibians of Britain and Europe* (Collins, UK; Stephen Green Press, US). A useful guide, though it excludes the Dodecanese and east Aegean islands.

Jiri Cihar *Amphibians and Reptiles* (Conran Octopus, UK; o/p). Selective coverage, but includes most endemic species of the Dodecanese and east Aegean isles.

INSECTS

Michael Chinery *Collins Guide to the Insects of Britain and Western Europe* (Collins, UK; Stephen Green Press, US). Although Greece is outside the geographical scope of the guide, it will provide genus identifications for most insects seen.

Lionel Higgins and Norman Riley *A Field Guide to the Butterflies of Britain and Europe* (Collins, UK; Stephen Green Press, US). A thorough and detailed field guide that illustrates nearly all species seen in Greece.

MARINE LIFE

B. Luther and K. Fiedler *A Field Guide to the Mediterranean* (HarperCollins, UK; o/p). Very thorough; includes most Greek shallow-water species.

shrubs. The high-pitched and endlessly repeated chirp of house crickets can drive one to distraction, as can the summer whirring of cicadas on the trunks of trees. The latter insects are giant relatives of the aphids that cluster on roses.

From spring through to autumn Greece is full of **butterflies**, particularly during late spring and early summer. There are three swallowtail species, named for the drawn-out corners of the hind-wings, in shades of cream and yellow, with black and blue markings. Their smaller relatives, the festoons, lack the tails, but add red spots to the palette. The rarer, robust brown and orange pasha is unrelated but is Europe's largest butterfly. In autumn the black and orange plain tiger or African monarch may appear, sometimes in large quantities. In areas of deciduous woodland, look high up and you may see fast-flying large tortoiseshells, while lower down, southern white admirals skim and glide through clearings between the trees. Some of the smallest but most beautiful butterflies are the blues. Their subtle, camouflaging grey and black undersides make them vanish from view when they land and fold their wings.

Some of the Greek **hawkmoths** are equally spectacular, particularly the green and pink oleander hawkmoth. Their large caterpillars can be recognized by their tail horn. The hummingbird hawkmoth, like its namesake, hovers at flowers to feed, supported by a blur of fast-moving wings. Tiger moths, with their black and white forewings and startling bright orange hindwings, are the "butterflies" that occur in huge quantity in sheltered sites of islands such as Rhodes and Páros. The giant peacock moth is Europe's largest, up to 15 cm across. A mixture of grey, black and brown, with big eye-spots, it is usually only seen during the day while resting on tree trunks.

Other insects include the camouflaged praying mantids, holding their powerful forelegs in a position of supplication until another insect comes within reach. The females are voracious, and notorious for eating the males during mating. Ant-lion adults resemble a fluttery dragonfly, but their young are huge-jawed and build pits in the sand to trap ants. Hemispherical carob beetles collect balls of dung and push them around with their back legs, while the huge longhorn beetles of the southern Ionian islands munch their way through tree trunks. Longhorns are named for their absurdly extended, whip-like antennae. Cockroaches of varying species live in buildings, particularly hotels, restaurants and bakeries, attracted by warmth and food scraps.

Corfu is famous for its extraordinary **fireflies**, which flutter in quantities across meadows and marshes on May nights, speckling the darkness with bursts of cold light to attract partners. The Epirot mainland opposite also has its fair share of these creatures; look carefully in nearby hedges, and you may spot the less flashy, more sedentary glow-worm.

Centipedes are not often seen, but the fast-moving 20-centimetre *Scolipendra* should be treated with respect since they can give very painful bites. Other non-vertebrates of interest include the land crabs, which are found in the south and east. They need water to breed, but can cause surprise when found walking on remote hillsides. There are plenty of genuine marine creatures to be seen, particularly in shallow seawater sheltered by rocks – sea cucumbers, sea butterflies, octopus, marine worms, starfish and sea urchins.

Lance Chilton, with Marc Dubin

MUSIC

Music is central to Greek culture; even the most indifferent visitor will be aware of its ubiquitous presence in vehicles, tavernas, ferries and other public spaces. Like most aspects of Greece, it's an amalgamation of native and oriental styles, with occasional contributions from the West. In fact, Western music made little impression until recent decades, when aesthetic disputes arose between adherents of folk- or *laïki*-derived styles and those spurning ethnic roots in favour of jazz/cabaret, symphonic and rock idioms – a reflection of the modernizing-versus-traditionalism debates raging in the nation at large.

Many older songs, invariably in Eastern-flavoured minor scales, have direct antecedents in the forms and styles of both **Byzantine religious chant** and that of the **Ottoman empire**, though the more nationalistically minded musicologists claim their original descent from the now-lost melodies of ancient Greece. Almost all native Greek instruments are near-duplicates of ones used throughout the Islamic world, though it's an open question as to whether the Byzantines, Arabs or Persians first constructed particular instruments. To this broadly Middle Eastern base Slavs, Albanians and Italians have added their share, resulting in an extraordinarily varied repertoire of traditional and modern pieces.

BYZANTINE SACRED MUSIC

Sacred **Byzantine chant** forms the bedrock from which much later Greek secular music sprung. Despite its canonical constancy, and prohibition on instrumentation, it is by no means a museum tradition. Some of the finest liturgical chanting can be heard on Mount Áthos in northern Greece, but only men can visit, by special arrangement (see p.427). More conveniently, tenor **Lycourgos Angelopoulos** and his excellent choir – the best group currently active – used to chant every Sunday at Ayía Iríni church in Athens' flower market, and may once again do so now that its restoration is complete. Greeks get tetchy with foreign critics who fail to give Byzantine music its due, but they are partly to blame themselves; there are a lot of mediocre Greek-originated recordings about – groups headed by Costas Zorbas and Khristodhoulos Halaris being particularly forgettable – while quality musicians go

DISCOGRAPHIES

Each of the following sections is accompanied by a discography. The * symbol denotes a disc **available on CD**. Serial numbers are given for LPs and CDs when known; unless UK or US is stated, all are Greek labels. Cassette pressing has been mostly discontinued in Greece.

For suggestions on **record hunting** in Greece, see the Athens shopping section (p.135). In the UK the best source is Trehantiri, 367 Green Lanes, London N4; (☎020/8802 6530), which also operates a worldwide mail-order service. In North America, try Down Home Music, 10341 San Pablo Ave, El Cerrito, CA (☎510/525-2129). Heritage discs, pressed by Interstate Music in East Sussex,

are uniformly excellent, but can occasionally be difficult to find in shops; if necessary get them mail-order through Swift Record Distributors, 3 Wilton Rd, Bexhill-on-Sea, East Sussex TN40 1HY (☎01424/220028, fax 213440). When in Greece, consider investing in a copy of the monthly music magazine *Dhifono* (1800dr), which includes a CD. It's strictly potluck what you get – it can be lousy new Greek rock or wonderful archival rembétika or folk, but at the price you lose little; instructions in the back (in Greek) tell you where to get back issues – Aristoníkou 1–3, second floor, Mets, Athens; Mon–Fri 9am–3pm (though some of the better ones are sold out).

unrecorded. The great Constantinopolitan *psáltis* (chanter) Thrasyvoulos Stanitsas, who moved to Athens in 1964, has no extant discography, while all of the Angelopoulos recordings in print have been brought out on French labels. Overseas record stores, unsure of whether to stock Byzantine music as "ethnic", "classical" or "sacred", often end up not stocking it at all, or only by special order.

REGIONAL FOLK MUSIC

The most promising times to hear regional folk music live are at the numerous summer *paniyíria* (saints'-day festivals) – or more tourist-orientated cultural programmes – when musicians normally based in Athens or city clubs during winter tour the islands and villages. However, it's as well to know that a marked decline in this type of music began during the 1960s – a trend accelerated by the 1967–74 junta – so that traditional instrumentation is now often replaced by something more appropriate to rock concerts. The musicians themselves, who have been deprived of (or actively scorn) the oral transmission of technique from older master players, are not always what they could be. Furthermore, on the islands at least, most musicians are semi-professionals, required to supplement their income with another trade. All this makes recent re-releases on CD of old archival material more precious, and an increasing number of revival groups (see p.899) are attempting to recapture the musicianship, if not the ethos, of the old-timers.

CRETE, KÁSSOS, HÁLKI AND KÁRPATHOS

This arc of southern islands is one of the most promising areas in Greece for hearing live music

at any season of the year. The dominant instrument here is the **lýra**, a three-stringed fiddle directly related to the Turkish *kemençe*. This is played not on the shoulder but balanced on the thigh, often with tiny bells attached to the bow, which the musician can jiggle for rhythmical accent. The strings are metal, and since the centre string is just a drone, the player improvises only on the outer two. Usually the *lýra* is backed by one or more **laoúta**, similar to the Turkish/Arab *oud* but – especially on Crete where the Venetians ruled for several centuries – more closely resembling a mandolin. These are rarely used to their full potential – a *laoúto* solo is an uncommon treat – but a good player will find the harmonics and overtones of a virtuoso *lýra* piece, at the same time coaxing a pleasing, chime-like tone from his instrument.

In several places in the southern Aegean, notably northern Kárpathos, a primitive bagpipe, the **askómandra** or **tsamboúna**, joins the *lýra* and *laoúto*. During the colonels' dictatorship the playing of the bagpipe in the Cyclades was banned lest tourists think the Greeks "too primitive" – though hopefully all concerned have recovered from any sense of cultural inferiority. If you remember Kazantzakis's classic novel (or the movie), his hero Zorba played a **sandoúri**, or hammer dulcimer, for recreation, but it was actually little known until after 1923 on most islands, being introduced by Asia Minor refugees. Today, accomplished players are few, and in *kritikí* (Cretan music), *nisiótika* (island songs) and rembétika (see p.890), the instrument has been relegated to a supporting role. On older Cretan recordings you may hear solos on the **voúlgari**, a stringed instrument, essentially a small *saz* (Turkish long-necked, fretted lute), which has now all but died out. Modern Cretan artists to look out for on recordings include **Kostas Moundakis**, the late acknowledged *lýra* master, the late **Nikos Xylouris**, justifiably dubbed "the nightingale of Crete" for his soaring voice, and his younger, *lýra*-playing brother Andonis who performs under the name **Psarandonis**.

OTHER AEGEAN ISLANDS

On most of the Aegean islands, and particularly the Cyclades, you'll find the *lýra* replaced by a more familiar-looking **violí**, essentially a Western violin. Accompaniment was provided until recently by *laoúto* or *sandoúri*, though these days you're more likely to be confronted (or affronted) by a bass-guitar and drum rhythm section.

Unlike on Crete, where you can often catch the best music in special clubs or *kéndra*, Aegean island performances tend to be spontaneous and less specialized; festivals and saints' days in village squares offer the most promising opportunities. The melodies, like much folk music the world over, rely heavily on the pentatonic scale. Lyrics, especially on the smaller islands of the central Aegean, touch on the perils of the sea, exile and – in a society where long periods of separation and arranged marriage were the norm – thwarted love. Though since the 1960s the **Konitopoulos clan** from Náxos has become virtually synonymous with *nisiótika*, older stars like **Anna and Emilia Hatzidhaki**, **Effi Sarri** and **Anna Karabesini** – all from the Dodecanese archipelago – offer a warmer, more innocent delivery. Amongst violinists, **Yiorgos Koros**, originally from Évvia, and **Stathis Koukoularis**, born on Náxos, stand out.

Lésvos occupies a special place in terms of island music; before the turbulent decade of 1912–22, its "mainland" was Asia Minor rather than Greece, its urban poles Smyrna and Constantinople rather than Athens. Accordingly its music is far more varied and sophisticated than the Aegean norm, having absorbed melodies and instrumentation from the various groups who lived in neighbouring Anatolia; for example, Lésvos is the only island with a vital tradition of brass bands, and virtually every Greek dance rhythm is represented in local music.

IONIAN ISLANDS

By way of complete contrast, the Ionian islands – except for Lefkádha – alone of all modern Greek territory never saw Turkish occupation and have a predominantly Western musical tradition. The indigenous song-form is Italian both in name (**kantádhes**) and instrumentation (guitar and mandolin); it's most often heard these days on **Lefkádha** and **Zákynthos**.

THE PELOPONNESE, CENTRAL GREECE AND EPIRUS

Many of the folk lyrics of the Peloponnese, central and western Greece hark back to the years of Ottoman occupation and to the War of

Independence; others, in a lighter tone, refer to aspects of pastoral life (sheep, elopements, fetching water from the well and so forth). All these are classified as *dhimotiká tragoúdhia* or folk-songs. The essential instrumentation consists of the *klaríno* (clarinet), which reached Greece during the 1830s, introduced either by Gypsies or by members of King Otto's Bavarian entourage. Backing was traditionally provided by a *koumpanía* consisting of *kithára* (guitar), *laoúto*, *laoutokithára* (a hybrid in stringing and tuning) and *violí*, with *toumberléki* (lap drum) or *défi* (tambourine) for rhythm. Many mainland tunes are danceable, divided by rhythm into such categories as *kalamatianó* (a line dance), *tsámiko*, *hasaposérviko* or *syrtó*, the quintessential circle dance of Greece. Those that are not include the slow, stately *kléftiko*, similar to the *rizítiko* of Crete, both of which relate, baldly or in metaphor, incidents or attitudes from the years of the Ottomans and the rebellions for freedom.

Stalwart vocalists to look for on old recordings include **Yiorgos Papasidheris** and **Yioryia Mittaki**, the latter actually of Arvanitic (Albanian-speaking) origin, as well as **Roza Eskenazi** and **Rita Abatzi** (see under "Rembétika", p.890). Among instrumentalists, the violinist **Yiorgos Koros**, and clarinetists **Yiannis Saleas** and the late **Vassilis Soukas** are especially remarkable, good examples of the Gypsy or Gypsy-descended musicians who virtually dominate instrumental music on mainland Greece (curiously, Gypsies rarely sing *dhimotiká*, preferring *laïkó* – see below).

The music of **Epirus** (Ípiros) still exhibits strong connections with that of northern Epirus (now falling within neighbouring Albania) and the Former Yugoslav Republic of Macedonia, particularly in the polyphonic pieces sung by both men and women. They tend to fall into three basic categories, which are also found further south: **mirolóyia** or laments (the instrumental counterpart is called a *skáros*); drinking songs or **tis távlas**; and various danceable melodies as noted above, common to the entire mainland and many of the islands. Most famous of the Epirot clarinetists are members of the numerous Halkias clan, including the late, great **Tassos Halkias** and the younger, unrelated **Petros Loukas Halkias**.

Since the *paleá dhimotiká* are strongly associated with national identity, it's not surprising

REGIONAL FOLK DISCOGRAPHY

*Songs of... (Society for the Dissemination of National Music, Greece). A thirty-disc-plus series of field recordings from the 1950s through to the 1970s, each covering traditional music of one region or type. All LPs contain lyrics in English and recordings are easily available in Athens in LP, cassette or CD form, especially at the Musicological Museum p.106. Best to date are Thrace 1 (SDNM 106); Epirus 1 (SDNM 111); Peloponnese (SDNM 113); Mytilene and Chios (SDNM 110); Mytilene and Asia Minor (SDNM 125); Rhodes, Chalki and Symi (SDNM 104); and Kassos and Karpathos (SDNM 103).

*Various *Anthology of Greek Folk Songs, vol 4* (CD, FM Records 671). One of the best of a dozen or so discs dedicated to archival *paleá dhimotiká* put out by this company.

*Various *Avthentika Nisiotika tou Peninda* (Lyra CD 0168). Good Cretan and Pontic material from the 1950s, with the Dodecanese also represented, from the collection of the late Ted Petrides, musician and dance master.

*Various *Dhimotiki Paradhosi: Morias* (CD, Minos 7 24383 49042 4). Good, inexpensive anthology of Peloponnesian standards featuring Yiorgos Papasidheris on many tracks.

*Various *Kritiki Mousiki Paradhosi, Iy Protomastores 1920–1953* (Aerakis, 10CD). For many visitors, Cretan music consists of monotonous sawing on the *lýra* and verses in impenetrable dialect; this is the perfect antidote. The whole set's prohibitively pricey, but fortunately discs are available individually; go for no.1 (Baksevanis, *lýra* and small orchestra); no.4 (Stelios Foustalieris, the last master of the tambur-like *voúlgari*, knowledge of which died with him); no.5 (Yiannis Demirtzoyiannis, guitarist and epic singer); and no. 6 (Yiorgis Koutsourelis, on melodic *laoúto*).

*Various *Paniyiria sta Horia mas* (CD, Minos 7 24348 00112 2). Another good general anthology of non-electrified, pre-1960s material.

*Various *Seryiani sta Nisia Mas, vol 1* (CD, MBI 10371). Excellent retrospective of various *nisiótika* hits and artists, mostly from the 1950s; easiest way to hear the vintage stars listed under "Other Aegean Islands".

*Various *Songs and Melodies of Patmos* (CD, Politistikon Idhryma Dhodhekanisou 201). Live 1995 field recordings of pieces as raw but compelling as you'd hear them at an old-time festival.

*Various *Takoutsia, Musiciens de Zagori: Inédit – Grèce – Epiré* (Inédit/Auvidis, France). Drinking songs, dance tunes and dirges performed by one of the last working clans of Epirot Gypsy musicians. Lots of fine fiddle and clarinet, with an all-acoustic *koumpanía* providing support.

*Khronis Aïdhonidhis *T'Aïdhonia tis Anatolis: Songs of Thrace and Asia Minor* (Minos 847/848, Greece). One of the best and most accessible collections available, featuring the top singer of material from Thrace and western Asia Minor, plus an orchestra directed by Ross Daly and solos on four tracks by versatile Yiorgos Dalaras. Aïdhonis sings alone on the equally good *Tragoudhia keh Skopi tis Thrakis/Songs and Tunes of Thrace* (Crete UP 7/8).

*Banda tis Florinas (CD, Ano Kato-Rei 2008, Thessaloníki). Wonderfully twisted brass-band music unique to western Macedonia, verging into ethnic-jazz territory with a nudge from guest saxophonist Floros Floridhis, one of the foremost personalities on Greece's avant-garde/improvisational scene. Recommended for demolishing stereotypes about Greek music. Their more recent

that they were for many years pressed into political service. During election campaigns each party's local store-front headquarters or sound trucks blasted out continuous *paleá dhimotiká* (plus *andártika* – see p.893 – by the Left), interspersed with political harangues. Since 1989, however, this practice has been (officially) banned.

MACEDONIA AND THRACE

Thrace and **Macedonia** remained Ottoman territory until early this century, with a bewilderingly mixed population, so music here can sound more generically Balkan. Meriting a special mention are the brass bands, introduced last century by Ottoman military musicians, peculiar to western Macedonia. Northern Greece has also remained, owing to the huge influx of Anatolian refugees after 1923, a rich treasure-trove for collectors and ethnomusicologists seeking to document the fast-vanishing old music of Asia Minor. *Kálanda* (Christmas carols), carnival dances, wedding processionals and table songs abound. Noteworthy singers –

Banda tis Florinas II on MBI is also of interest, though more explicitly Balkan jazz and less folky.

*Roza Eskenazi and Rita Ambatzi *Se Dhimotika Tragoudhia/In Folk Songs* (CD, Minos 4 802167 29). Mainland standards interpreted with incredible verve, showing the versatility of these two normally associated with rembétika

*Tassos Halkias (CD, EMI 74321 318232). #4 of the long out-of-print "Great Solos" series, this re-release of a 1977 session features the master clarinetist at his most heartfelt.

*Petros Loukas Halkias *Dhromi tis Psykhis* (CD, Papingo/BMG-Ariola 74321 318232) and *Miroloyia ke Yirismata* (LP and CD, Lyra 4717). Technically impeccable updating of the clarinet tradition, but with traditional backing *koumpanía* of *laoúto*, *violí* and percussion; purists prefer *Miroloyia*, but the more orchestrated Papingo disc may be easier to find. However, even better is *Petro-Loukas Chalkias* (sic) *& Kompania* (CD, World Network 46), wonderful improvisations and dialogues in a four-member group.

*Xanthippi Karathanasi *Tragoudhia ke Skopi tis Makedhonias/Songs and Tunes of Macedonia* (CD, UP of Crete). High quality, like all UP Crete releases; the only quibble is that the sidemen are so good that they threaten to overshadow Xanthippi's vocals.

*Irini Konitopoulou-Legaki *Athanata Nisiotika 1* (Tzina-Astir 1020). A 1978 warhorse, beloved of bus drivers across the islands. *Anefala Thalassina* (CD, Lyra 4693) is far less commercial, featuring fellow Naxian lautist Dhimitris Fyroyenis; this is Irini singing her heart out, off the club stage.

*Yiorgos Konitopoulos and Clan *Thalassa ke Paradhosi* (EMI 14C 064 71253). Standard taverna or party fare throughout the islands; slicker than *Athanata Nisiotika* but no worse for it.

*Lesvos Aiolis *Tragoudhia ke Hori tis Lesvou/Songs & Dances of Lesvos* (UP of Crete, double CD 9/10). Two decades' worth (1974–96) of field recordings of the last traditional music extant on the island, a labour of love supervised by musicologist Nikos Dhionysopoulos. Pricey, but the quality and uniqueness of the instrumental pieces especially, and the monstrous illustrated booklet, merit the expense.

*Yiorgos Papasidheris *Tragoudhia Spania Dhimotika Tragoudhia* (FM, CD). An interesting, if rather scratchy, re-release of 1930s sides – some sung in *arvanítika*, a dialect of medieval Albanian, by this native of Salamína.

*Yannis Parios *Ta Nisiotika Vol 1* (CD, Minos 430/431) and *Vol 2* (CD, Minos 1017/1018). Parios sparked a reappraisal of *nisiótika* with the first of these two discs done a decade apart, each accompanied by members of the Konitopoulos clan. Maybe not the most "authentic" versions, but easy on the ear, and both went platinum – vol 1 with sales of nearly a million.

*Tragoudhia tou Pondou *Songs of Pontos* (CD, En Khordais 1910). Songs of the dominant refugee group around Thessaloníki, re-released from the 1960s archives of Macedonian public radio. Pontic music is an acquired taste, but this is the best batch we've sampled.

*Aristeidhis Vasilaris *Floyera* (FM 678). Third issue of FM Records' 12-volume series profiling Greek folk instruments in turn. Excellent documentation, including an interview with Vasilaris.

*Nikos Xylouris *O Arkhangelos tis Kritis*, 1958-1968 (CD, MBI 10376); *Ta Khronia stin Kriti* (2CD, MBI 10677/78). These are the best two retrospectives, with copious notes; the first covers his initial decade of recordings, previously unavailable, with self-accompaniment on the *lýra*.

---

both still alive and active – include **Xanthippi Karathanassi** and **Khronis Aïdhonidhis**. Incidentally, amongst the Pomaks and other local Muslims, the main festival and wedding season in Thrace runs from autumn through spring, the opposite of elsewhere; summer is reserved for tending the precious local tobacco crop.

The Thracian **kaváli**, or end-blown flute, is identical to the Turkish and Bulgarian article (and similar to the disappearing *floyéra* of the south mainland); so too is the northern bagpipe,

or **gáïda**. The **zournás**, a screechy, double-reed oboe similar to the Islamic world's *shenai*, is much in evidence at weddings or festivals, together with the deep-toned **daoúli** drum, as a typically Muslim or Orthodox Gypsy ensemble. Other percussion instruments like the *daïrés* or tambourine and the *darboúka*, the local version of the *toumberléki*, make for some sharply demarcated dance rhythms such as the *zonarádhikos*. The *klaríno* is present here as well, as are two types of *lýres*, but perhaps the most characteristic melodic instrument of

Thrace is the **oúti** or *oud*, whose popularity received a boost after refugee players arrived.

REMBÉTIKA

Rembétika began as the music of the Greek urban dispossessed – criminals, refugees, drug-users, defiers of social norms. It had existed in some form in Greece and Constantinople since at least the turn of the century, perhaps a little before. But it is as difficult to define or get to the origins of as jazz or blues, with which spurious comparisons are often made; although rembétika shares marked similarities in spirit with those American styles, there's none whatsoever in origins or in musical form. The themes of the earlier songs – illicit or frustrated love, drug addiction, police oppression, disease and death – and the tone of the delivery – resignation to the singer's lot, coupled with defiance of authority – will be familiar to Westerners. But even the word "rembétika" is of uncertain derivation, most likely from **harabati**, an old Turkish word meaning, variously, "a shanty town", "a privileged drunkard" and "unconventionally dressed bohemian" – all certainly aspects of rembétika culture. Accordingly, searches for the birth of rembétika must be conducted in the Asia Minor of the last years of the Ottoman empire as well as in Greece proper.

Most outsiders equate Greek music with the **bouzoúki**, a long-necked, fretted, three-stringed lute derived, like the Turkish *saz* and *baglamás*, from the Byzantine *tambourás*. Early in this century, however, only a small proportion of Greek mainland musicians used it. At the same time, across the Aegean in Smyrna and Constantinople, musical cafés, owned and staffed almost entirely by Greeks, Jews, Armenians and even a few Gypsies, had become popular. Groups typically featured a violinist, a *sandoúri* player and a female vocalist, who usually jingled castanets and danced on stage. The metrically free, improvisational singing style was known as *café-aman* or just **amanés** (plural *amanédhes*), after both the setting and the frequent repetition of the exclamation *aman aman* (Turkish for "alas, alas"), used both for its sense and to fill time while the performers searched their imaginations for more explicit lyrics.

Despite the sparse instrumentation, this was an elegant, riveting performance style requiring considerable skill, harking back to similar vocal-

ization in central Asia. Some of its greatest practitioners included **Andonis "Dalgas"** (Wave) **Dhiamandidhis**, so nicknamed for the undulations in his voice; **Roza Eskenazi**, a Greek Jew who grew up in Constantinople; her contemporary **Rita Abatzi**, from Smyrna; **Marika Papagika**, from the island of Kós, who emigrated to America where she made her career; **Agapios Tomboulis**, a *tanbur* and *oud* player of Armenian background; and **Dhimitris "Salonikiyé" Semsis**, a master fiddler from Strumitsa in northern Macedonia. The spectrum of origins for these performers gives a good idea of the range of cosmopolitan influences brought to bear in the years immediately preceding the emergence of "real" rembétika.

The 1919–22 Greco-Turkish war and the resulting 1923 **exchange of populations** were key events in the history of rembétika, resulting in the influx to Greece of over a million Asia Minor Greeks, many of whom settled in shanty towns around Athens, Pireás and Thessaloníki. The *café-aman* musicians, like most of the other refugees, were in comparison to the Greeks of the host country extremely sophisticated; many were highly educated, could read and compose music and had even been unionized in the towns of Asia Minor. Typical of these were **Panayiotis Toundas**, a Smyrniote composer who after arrival in Athens eventually became head of the Greek division of first Odeon and then Columbia Records, succeeding Semsis in that capacity, and **Vangelis Papazoglou**, another composer who failed to survive World War II. It was galling for the less lucky refugees to live initially on the periphery of the new society in poverty and degradation; most had lost all they had in the hasty evacuation, and many, from inland Anatolia, could initially speak only Turkish. In their misery they sought relief in another long-standing Ottoman institution, the *tekés* or hashish den.

In the **tekédhes** of Pireás, Athens and Thessaloníki, a few men would sit around a charcoal brazier, passing around a *nargilés* (hookah) filled with hashish. One of them might improvise a tune on the *baglamás* or the *bouzoúki* and begin to sing. The words, either his own or those of the other *dervíses* ("dervishes" – several rembetic terms were a burlesque of those of mystical Islamic tradition), would be heavily laced with insiders' argot, in the manner of the Harlem jive of the same era. As the *taxími* (long, studied introduction) was completed, one of the smokers might rise and begin to dance a **zeïbékiko**, named after the *zeybeks*, a warrior caste of western Anatolia. It would be a slow, intense, introverted performance following an unusual metre (9/8), not for the benefit of others but for himself.

By the early 1930s, several important male musicians had emerged from the *tekés* culture: the beguiling voiced **Stratos Payioumtzis**, Anestis Delias (aka **Artemis**), who was to die during the World War II occupation, the only *rembétis* to actually succumb to drug addiction; Yiorgos Tsoros, better known as **Batis**, an indifferent musician but generous and engaging; and **Markos Vamvakaris**, the most famous of this quartet, a Catholic from Sýros who had run away to Pireás aged fifteen. Though an indisputable master of the *bouzoúki*, he protested to his friends that his voice, ruined perhaps from too much hash-smoking, was no good for singing. But he soon bowed to their encouragement and his gravelly, unmistakable sound set the standard for male vocals over the next decade. His only close peer as an instrumentalist was **Ioannis Papaïoannou**, with whom he occasionally played; Papaïoannou's some-time vocalist **Rena Dalia** recorded a few famous cuts singing in Turkish – a practice which stopped altogether after the late 1950s, with the dying off of the audience that understood such lyrics, and anti-Turkish sentiment arising from the first Cyprus crises.

Songs about getting stoned, or *mastoúriaka*, were a natural outgrowth of the *tekédhes*. One of the most famous, composed and first recorded in the mid-1930s, included the following lines:

On the sly I went out in a boat
And arrived at the Dhrákou Cave
Where I saw three men stoned on hash
Stretched out on the sand.
It was Batis, and Artemis,
And Stratos the Lazy.
Hey you, Strato! Yeah you, Strato!
Fix us a terrific nargilé,
So old Batis can have a smoke...

It is interesting to observe that the most commonly heard version of this song, from the 1950s, bowdlerizes the lyrics, substituting "Play us a fine bit of *bouzoúki*" for "Fix us a fine *nargilé*", and so forth.

This "Golden Age" of rembétika – as indeed it was, despite the unhappy lives of many performers, and necessarily limited audience – was short lived. The association of the music with a drug-laced underworld would prove its undoing. After the imposition of the Metaxas dictatorship in 1936, harder-core musicians with uncompromising lyrics and lifestyles, were blackballed by the recording industry; anti-hashish laws were systematically enforced, and police harassment of the *tekédhes* was stepped up. Even possession of a *bouzoúki* or *baglamás* became a criminal offence, and several of the big names did time in jail. Others went to Thessaloníki, where the police chief Vassilis Mouskoundis was a big fan of the music and allowed its practitioners to smoke in private.

For a while, such persecution – and the official encouragement of tangos and frothy Italianate love songs, which always had a much wider public – failed to dim the enthusiasm of the **mánges** (roughly translatable as "wide boys" or "hep cats") who frequented the hash dens. Beatings or prison terms were taken in their stride; time behind bars could be used, as it always had been around the Aegean, to make *skaptó* (dug-out) instruments. A *baglamás* could easily be fashioned from a gourd cut in half or even a tortoise shell (the sound box), a piece of wood (the neck), catgut (frets) and wire for strings, and the result would be small enough to hide from the guards. Jail songs were composed and became popular in the underworld. The lyrics below, with some literal translation from the 1930s argot, are from a typical, much-recorded song:

Iy Lahanádhes (The Pickpockets)

Down in Lemonádhika there was a ruckus
They caught two pickpockets who acted innocent
They took 'em to the slammer in handcuffs
They'll get a beating if they don't cough up the loot.
Don't beat us, Mr. Copper, you know very well
This is our job, and don't expect a cut.
We "eat cabbages" and pinch "slippers" so we can
Have a regular rest in jail.
Death don't scare us, it's only hunger we mind,
That's why we nick "cabbage" and get along fine.

Vangelis Papazoglou (1934)

REMBÉTIKA DISCOGRAPHY

EARLY REMBÉTIKA – ANTHOLOGIES

Authentic USA Rembetika, vols 1–4 (CD, Lyra 4644 and 4635-4637). The title is a wild misnomer, unless original 78s were released first in the US, as these feature all the usual suspects, already well established in Greece. Volume 4 is devoted to songs about tuberculosis, the scourge of Greece until the 1950s.

*Amanedhes (LP, Margo 8222/CD, Minos 724383443529). Includes some early cuts made in Istanbul, with Gypsy clarinetists appearing on several tracks.

*The Greek Archives (CD, FM Records, Greece). Luxuriously packaged (though skeletal notes in English), this multi-disc series, uneven but generally worthy, manages usually not to duplicate earlier releases. Discs are arranged in two batches, each title devoted to a theme or particular artist. From the first, twelve-volume series, choose from among no.1 (*Rembetico Song in America 1920–1940*, FM 627); no.6 (*Women of the Rembetico Song*, FM 632); no.7 (*Unknown Smyrna 1922–1940*, FM 633); no.8 (*Armenians, Jews, Turks & Gipsies* [NB, as portrayed, not performing] FM 634) and no.9 (*Constantinople in Old Recordings*, FM 635). From the second, unnumbered batch, *Anthology of Rémbetiko* [sic] *Songs 1933–1940* (FM 654), *Anthology of Smyrnean Songs 1920–1938* (FM 658) and *Songs of the Sea* (FM661) are wonderful.

*Greek Oriental: Smyrneic-Rembetic Songs and Dances (LP/CD, Polylyric 9033, US). Superb collection spanning the 1920s to early 1930s, with Roza, Rita, Marika Papagika and Dhimitris Semsis. Good sleeve notes and lyric translations; the CD version has six extra tracks. *Greek Orientale* (Polylyric, USA, LP/CD).

*Greek Orientale Rembétika 1911–37 (Arhoolie, US). A worthwhile compilation, with Roza Eskenazi, Andonis Dalgas and many more. Includes Roza's "Why I Smoke Cocaine".

*Historic Urban Folk Songs from Greece (Rounder CD 1079, US/Direct Distribution, UK). The above-cited artists, plus many more on terrific selections, mostly from the 1930s; complements *Greek Oriental* well, with no duplications.

*Lost Homelands: The Smyrnaic Song in Greece, 1928–35 (CD, Heritage HT27). Lots of Dalgas, the great rivals Rita Abatzi and Roza Eskenazi, plus instrumental improvisations; as usual for this label, top sound quality and intelligent notes.

*Íy Megali tou Rembetikou (LP, Margo/CD, Minos; Greece). A collection of over twenty albums, but only the first ten are worth it, and available on CD. The best are no.1 (*Early Performers*, CD Minos 4 80193 25), no.3 (Vassilis Tsitsanis, LP/CD Margo 8150), no.4 (Ioannis Papaioannou, LP/CD Margo 8152), no.7 (Stratos Payoumtzis, LP/CD Margo 8217), no.8 (Kostas Roukounas, CD Minos 4 80267 29) and no.9 (Spyros Peristeris composer, mostly Markos Vamvakris playing and singing, LP/CD Margo 8219).

*Mourmourika – Songs of the Greek Underworld, 1930–55 (CD, Round/Direct 1120). Songs of the *mourmourídhes* or street toughs; rare tracks, many censored after 1937, by relatively unknown artists. Decent sound quality, good liner notes.

*Rembétika in Pireaus 1933–37 (Heritage CDs HT 26 and 30). The gang that played – and smoked – together, in top form: Markos, Batis, Stratos and Artemis, plus lesser-known figures.

*Íy Rembetiki Istoria (LP, EMI Regal 14C 034 70364-70380/CD, Minos). Six-volume series which was among the first material reissued after the junta fell, and still a good start to a collection. Nos.1 and 4 are mostly Smyrneic/Asia Minor songs; no.2 is mostly from the 1930s; while nos.3 and 6 are mixed, stressing Tsitsanis and other 1950s material. No.5 is the runt of the litter.

*Smyrneïka 1927–35 (CD, MBI 10557). Duplicates parts of the Polylyric and Rounder discs; worth snagging in Greece only if you can't find the other two.

EARLY REMBÉTIKA – SINGLE ARTISTS

*Rita Abatzi 1933–1938 (CD, Heritage HT 36). With outstanding accompanists, sound quality and notes, this has the edge on *Rita Ambatzi I*

Moreover, the *rembétes* suffered from the disapproval of the puritanical left as well as the puritanical right; the growing Communist Party of the 1930s considered the music and its habitués hopelessly decadent and politically unevolved. When Vamvakaris was about to join the leftist resistance army ELAS in 1943, he was admonished not to sing his own material "lest it corrupt

(Minos 7 24348 040923 3), part of the Arheio series in Greece. The only discs so far devoted exclusively to this refugee Smyrnean, with a huskier, more textured voice than her peer Roza Eskenazi.

*Dalgas *Andonios Dhiamandidhis 1928–33* (Heritage CD HT 34). The best disc devoted entirely to the gifted *amanés* artist; *Periorizmena Antitypa ya Syllektes* (LP, Lyra 4621, Greece) is a second choice. Dalgas also appears on *Great Voices of Constantinople* (Rounder/Direct CD1113), trading tracks with the great Turkish vocalist Hafiz Burhan, though the title is misleading as all the Dalgas cuts were recorded in Athens.

Anestis Dhelias 1912–1944 (Lyra 4642, Greece). Mostly *mastouriaká* (hash songs) by the man known as Artemis, performed by the "Gang of Four"; search bargain bins in Greece.

*Roza Eskenazi 1933–1936 (CD, Heritage HT35). Superb renditions with her usual sidemen Semsis, Tomboulis, plus Lambros on *kanonáki*, extremely varied selection of standards and rare gems make this the best of several collections available.

*Marika Papagika *Greek Popular and Rebetic Music in New York 1918–29* (CD, Alma Criolla, Berkeley California, ACCD802). Her best work, with husband Gus backing on *sandoúri*; includes a superb, rare duet with Marika Kastrouni.

*Vangelis Papazoglou 1897–1943 (CD, Lyra 4713-14). Double album of his compositions from the 1920s and 1930s, sung by most of the top stars of the era, including Stellakis, Roza Eskenazi, Kostas Roukounas and Rita Abatzi. Marred by poor sound quality, but several versions of his classic *Iy Lahanadhes*.

*Markos Vamvakaris *Bouzouki Pioneer 1932–1940* (CD, Rounder, US/Direct, UK 1139). Excellent sound quality, good notes and unusual material – not a trace of his hackneyed and overcovered "Frangosyriani" – make this a top choice. *Afthentika Rembetika tis Amerikis no.2* (CD, Lyra 4635) is mostly Markos, and wonderful; title's a wild misnomer, as Vamvakaris never went to America, though some 78s may have been simultaneously issued there and Greece.

LATER AND CONTEMPORARY REMBÉTIKA

*Elliniki Apolavsis *Apagorevemena Rembetika* (CD, BMG-Falirea 74321/444182). One of the better revival groups from the mid-1980s, with meaty instrumentation (including *cura*, *oud* and *laoúto*) and material from the late 1920s to early 1930s.

*Sotiria Bellou 1946–56 (LP, Margo 8163/CD, Minos 4 80217 24; no.5 in *Iy Megali tou Rembetikou* series). Virtually the only disc under her name without the electric backing of later years; here she performs mostly with Tsitsanis. Includes the original of the classic "Ta Kavourakia".

Marika Ninou *Stou Tzimi tou Hondrou/At Jimmy the Fat's* (LP, Venus-Tzina1053). Poor sound quality since it was a clandestine wire recording, but still a classic. Ninou performs live with Tsitsanis at their habitual club in 1955, Ninou giving it her all; includes two cuts in Turkish. Well worth rooting out.

*Marika Ninou/Vassilis Tsitsanis (LP, Philips 7116 819/CD, Philips 6483004). Not as soulful as the Venus disc, but a far better sound and more than adequate renditions of their favourites, including "Synnefiasmeni Kyriaki" and the gutwrenching "Yennithika".

Vassilis Tsitsanis *Yia Panta 1937–40* vols 1 & 2 (LP, EMI-HMV 401026/401027 Greece); 1938–55 vols 1 & 2 (LP, EMI 70193). First and best vinyl discs of two multivolume series; mostly Stratos on vocals on 1937–40, joined by Ninou and Bellou on 1938–55.

*Vassilis Tsitsanis 1936–1946 (CD 1124, Rounder US/Direct UK). A fine first disc to begin a Tsitsanis collection; again mostly male singers, but includes his reputed first recording, a *mastoúriaka* with Yeoryia Mittaki, and good notes.

*Stavros Xarhakos *Rembetiko* (CD, CBS 70245). Soundtrack to the namesake film, available as a double LP or, in edited form, on one CD. Virtually the only "original" rembétika to be composed in the last forty years, with lyrics by poet Nikos Gatsos.

*Ioanna Yiorgakopoulou *Iy Rembetissa* (CD, EMI 4 80014 29). First and best of four identically titled albums featuring this unjustly neglected singer-composer.

the heroic proletariat". The Left preferred *andártika* (Soviet-style revolutionary anthems), though **Sotiria Bellou**, a *rembétissa* (female rembetic musician) and active communist whose career began late in the 1940s, was a conspicuous exception.

Bellou was one of several important female vocalists to accompany **Vassilis Tsitsanis**, the most significant composer and *bouzoúki* player to emerge after Vamvakaris; the others were **Marika Ninou** and **Ioanna Yiorgakopoulou**, the latter also a composer in her own right. From Tríkala in Thessaly, Tsitsanis abandoned law studies to cut his first record in 1936 for Odeon, directed by rembetic composer **Spyros Peristeris**. The war interrupted his – and everyone else's – recording career from late 1940 until late 1945, a period which Tsitsanis spent running a musical taverna in Thessaloníki; when World War II, and the civil war that followed, ended, a huge backlog of songs composed during the occupation awaited the studios. The traumatic decade between 1939 and 1948 had erased the fashion for *mastoúriaka*; more than ever, audiences instead craved vaguely Neapolitan melodies and words about love. Tsitsanis was happy to oblige, and for the first time rembétika enjoyed something like a mass following, but his love lyrics were anything but insipid, and the demoralization of the war years prompted him to also compose darker works, most famous of these "Synnefiasmeni Kyriaki":

Cloudy Sunday, you seem like my heart
Which is always overcast, Christ and Holy
Virgin!
You're a day like the one I lost my joy.
Cloudy Sunday, you make my heart bleed.
When I see you rainy, I can't rest easy for a
moment;
You blacken my life and I sigh deeply.

(composed 1943, first recorded 1948)

Although Tsitsanis performed almost up to his death in 1984 – his funeral in Athens was attended by nearly a quarter of a million people – 1953 effectively marked the end of the original rembetic style. In that year, Manolis Hiotis added a fourth string to the *bouzoúki*, allowing it to be tuned tonally rather than modally; electrical amplification to reach larger audiences, maudlin lyrics and over-orchestration were not long in following. Performances in huge, barn-like clubs, also called *bouzoúkia*, became debased and vulgarized. Virtuoso *bouzoúki* players, assisted by kewpie-doll-type female vocalists, became immensely rich – the so-called *arhondorembétes* like Hiotis and **Yiorgos Zambetas**. The clubs themselves were clipjoints where Athenians paid large sums to break plates and watch dancing whose flashy

steps and gyrations were a travesty of the simple dignity and precise, synchronized footwork of the old-time *zeïbékiko*.

Ironically, the original rembétika material was rescued from oblivion by the colonels' junta of 1967–74. Along with dozens of other features of Greek culture, rembétika verses were banned. The younger generation coming of age under the dictatorship took a closer look at the forbidden fruit and derived solace, and deeper meanings, from the nominally apolitical lyrics.

When the junta fell in 1974 – and even a little before – there was an outpouring of re-issued recordings of the old masters. Initially these were merely 33rpm pressings of the original 78s, with no re-editing or liner notes, but the industry – prompted in part by growing demand from foreigners – has lately resorted to higher production values, though little in the way of startlingly new finds.

Over the next decade live rembétika also enjoyed a revival, beginning with a clandestine 1979 club near the old Fix brewery in Athens, whose street credentials were validated when it was raided and closed by the police. These smoky attempts to recapture pre-war atmosphere, and eventually larger venues, saw performances by revival groups such as **Ta Pedhia apo tin Patra**, **Rembetiki Kompania** and **Opisthodhromiki Kompania** and (from Thessaloníki) **"Hondronakos"** (Stefanos Kiouproulis), **"Mario"** (Maria Konstandinidhou) and **Agathonas Iakovidhis** with his **Rembetika Synkrotima Thessalonikis**. A feature film by Kostas Ferris, *Rembetiko* (1983), attempted to trace the music from Asia Minor of the 1920s to Greece of the 1950s, and garnered wide acclaim in Greece and abroad. Today, however, the fashion has long since peaked, and only a bare handful of clubs and bands remain from the dozens which made their appearance between 1978 and 1986.

THE ÉNTEKHNO REVOLUTION

The "Westernization" of rembétika that had begun with Tsitsanis and been completed by the *arhondorembétes* paved the way for the *éntekhno* music which emerged during the late 1950s. *Éntekhno*, literally "artistic" or "sophisticated", encompassed an orchestral genre where folk instruments and melodies, where present, would be interwoven into a much larger symphonic fabric.

ÉNTEKHNO DISCOGRAPHY

*Manos Hatzidhakis *Matomenos Gamos; Paramythi horis Onoma* (CD, Columbia GCX107) Nikos Gatsos-translated lyrics, with Lakis Pappas singing.

*Yannis Markopoulos *Thiteia* ((LP/CD, EMI 14C062 70123). With lyrics by Manos Eleftheriou, many consider this – including hits like "Malamatenia Logia" – Markopoulos' best effort, but *Anexartita* (CD, Minos EMI 7243 834897 25) is also a strong contender, with an incredible range of talent and the original live version of the bitter "ly Ellada", recorded just after the junta fell.

*Mikis Theodhorakis *Epitafios* (CD, EMI Columbia) and *To Axion Esti* (CD, EMI Columbia). These are his most influential, reputation-justifying works. The four sessions with the Horodhia Trikalon may still be around on CD (Olympic 1099–1102). If you want to be sure of touching all bases, a recent five-CD set (EMI 14C 045 1702572) includes the best recordings of his best-loved songs, organized roughly chronologically and by type (one disc is entirely soundtracks, another theatre pieces and so forth).

Its first, and most famous, practitioners were exact contemporaries **Manos Hatzidhakis** and **Mikis Theodhorakis**, both classically trained musicians and admirers of rembétika. Already in 1948, Hatzidhakis had defended rembétika in a lecture, suggesting that Greek composers be inspired by it, rather than bow to the prevailing left-wing/middle-class prejudice against it; in a period when most Greek tunes imitated Western light popular music, he had transcribed rembétika for piano and orchestra, keeping only the spirit and nostalgic mood of the original. Theodhorakis, a disciple of Tsitsanis, included *zeïbékiko* and *hasápika* on his earliest albums, with Grigoris Bithikotsis or Stelios Kazantzidhis on vocals and Manolis Hiotis as *bouzoúki* soloist. Other engagingly accessible work was his 1966 sessions with the Horódhia Trikálon (the Trikala Choir). His international reputation became distorted by his overplayed and over-covered 1965 soundtrack for *Zorba the Greek*; indeed soon after this he shunned Byzantine/folk/rembetic influence completely in favour of quasi-classical, overtly political symphonic works and film soundtracks dictated by his communist affiliation.

The *éntekhno* of Theodhorakis and Hatzidhakis combined not only rembetic and Byzantine influences with quasi-classical orchestral arrangements, but also fused Greek music with the country's rich **poetic tradition**. Among Theodhorakis' first albums was his 1963 *Epitafios/Epifaneia*, based on poems by Yiannis Ritsos and George Seferis, and its 1964 successor, *To Axion Esti*, a folk-flavoured oratorio incorporating poetry by Nobel laureate Odysseas Elytis. Hatzidhakis countered in 1965 with *Matomenos Gamos*, a version of Garcia Lorca's *Blood Wedding* translated into Greek by poet-lyricist Nikos Gatsos, and also tried his hand at rendering Elytis in song. Together, these early works changed Greek perceptions of *bouzoúki*-based music, popularized Greek poetry for a mass audience and elevated lyricists such as Gatsos and Manos Eleftheriou to the status of bards.

The down side of this increased sophistication was an inevitable distancing from indigenous roots, in particular the modal scale. The new genre, with its catchy tunes, seemed almost a natural for elevator music and film **soundtracks**. Like Theodhorakis, Hatzidhakis was haunted by soundtracks composed for various movies starring Melina Mercouri, most notably *Never on Sunday* (1960). Hatzidhakis, who died in June 1994, mostly steered clear of political statements; instead he launched, during the 1980s, his own record label Seirios to provide a forum for non-mainstream musicians.

Whatever their shortcomings, Theodhorakis and Hatzidhakis paved the way for successors, less classical and more folk-leaning, such as **Stavros Xarhakos**, most famous abroad for his soundtrack to the film *Rembetiko*. Xarkhakos's exact contemporary, **Yiannis Markopoulos**, also did the all-but-obligatory soundtrack (*Who Pays the Ferryman*, 1978) but otherwise is perhaps the most interesting and consistently Greek-sounding of these four composers to emerge from the 1960s. His best work dates from the early-to-mid-1970s – in retrospect, the Indian summer of *éntekhno*.

LAÏKÓ: SON OF REMBÉTIKA

Diametrically opposed to *éntekhno* was the authentic *laïkó* or "popular" music of the 1950s and 1960s, its gritty, tough style a direct heir to rembétika, undiluted by Western influences. *Laïkó* used not only *zeïmbékiko* and *hasápika* time signatures but also the *tsiftetéli*, another rhythm from Asia Minor mistakenly known as "belly-dance" music overseas. Once again, "debased" oriental influences dominated Greek pop, much to the chagrin of those who objected to the apolitical, decadent, escapist song content. This orientalizing reached its high – or low – point during the brief mid-1960s craze for *indoyíftika*, Indian film music lifted straight from Bollywood and reset to Greek lyrics; chief culprit was the Gypsy singer Manolis Angelopoulos.

The most notable "straight" *laïkó* performer was **Stelios Kazantzidhis**, a man whose volcanic, mournful style was often imitated but never matched. His work, frequently in duets with "Marinella" (Kyriaki Papadhopoulou) and Yiota Lidhia, immortalized the joys and sorrows of the Greek working class which emerged from the 1940s, faced with a choice of life under the restrictive regimes of the time, or emigration. Disgusted with the atmosphere in the *bouzoúkia* clubs, he quit performing live in 1966, but after a brief hiatus returned to the studio under the aegis of Khristos Nikolopoulos and Akis Panou, two of the most influential *laïkó* songwriters.

Any summary of *laïko* singers would be incomplete without **Yiorgos (George) Dalaras**, a musical phenomenon in Greece since he made his 1968 vinyl debut with the composer Manos Loïzos. Born in 1952, the son of a Pireás rembétika player, Dalaras has featured on over eighty records, spanning the range of Greek music from rembétika and *dhimotiká* material, the works of Theodhorakis, Hatzidhakis and Markopoulos, and – more recently – collaborations with the flamenco guitarist Paco de Lucia and American blues star Al Di Meola. Something of a national institution, Dalaras has always – even during the junta years – remained a fierce supporter of popular struggles, with benefit concerts for various worthy causes. In his commitment to quality musicianship he has scrupulously avoided the banalities of the *bouzoúki* scene.

LAÏKÓ DISCOGRAPHY

***Haris Alexiou** From a huge discography, start with *Ta Tragoudhia tis Haroulas* (LP/CD, Minos349) with lyrics by Manolis Rasoulis and Manos Loizos, which secured her position as the queen of *laïkó* for the 1980s, or *Dhodheka Laïka Tragoúdhia* (CD, Minos). Of recent output, go for *Odhos Nefelis* (CD Philips 5426740).

***Yiorgos Dalaras** *Latin* (Minos 671/672). A 1987 team-up with Al Di Meola, Glykeria and others, with Latin rhythms and instrumentalists. Dalaras taught himself enough Spanish to sing passably; nearly half a million copies sold. *A Portrait: George Dalaras* (CD, EMI) is a "best-of" sampler with both live and studio work spanning his entire career, easily found outside Greece.

***The Dance of Heaven's Ghosts** (EMI 7243 8 55644 20, UK). Well-balanced compilation of the most accessible (and slick) *laïko*, with samples of Haris Alexiou, Yiannis Parios, Eleni Vitali and others.

***Glykeria (Kotsoula)** *Me ti Glykeria stin Omorfi Nhykhta* (Lyra, CD). Enduringly popular disc showcases this versatile *laïko* singer and rembétika/ nisiótika revivalist most active in the 1980s.

***Kostas Hatzis and Haris Alexiou** *Iy Alexiou Tragoudhaei Hadzis* (CD, Minos 1002/1003). Hatzis by himself is disappointing; but with Alexiou, singing in Greek or (on two cuts) Romany, it's Greek flamenco.

***Apostolos Kaldharas** *Mikra Asia* (CD, Minos 4800962) marked Haris Alexiou's 1972 debut and helped spark the rembétika revival of the mid-1970s; *Vyzantinos Esperinos* (CD, Minos), with more of Haris and less of Dalaras, is also worth pursuing.

***Stelios Kazantzidhes** *Kazantzidhis 3, 1959-1962* (CD, EMI-Regal). The quintessential early *laïkó* classic that made him a national institution. *Ena Glenda me ton Stelara* (2CD, MBI 10596/7). A recent, intimate acoustic session, essentially Kazantzidhes celebrating his birthday at a taverna.

***Akis Panou** *Ta Megala Tragoudhia* (3LP/2CD, EMI 478938) 1993. Retrospective that's one of the best starts to a *laïkó* collection, and specifically the work of this versatile composer, lyricist and *bouzoúki* virtuoso.

Amongst notable *laïkó* composers and lyricists, **Apostolos Kaldharas** was the most prolific during the 1950s and 1960s; he gave singer **Yiannis Parios**, considered second only to Yiorgos Dalaras, his start, and introduced *laïkó* star **Haris Alexiou** with his landmark 1972 album *Mikra Asia*. **Khristos Nikolopoulos** was a young *bouzoúki* virtuoso who emerged during the 1970s as a composer; his above-noted collaboration with Kazantzidhes peaked in 1975 with the album *Yparho*, and he has since gone on to mega-selling co-efforts with Dalaras and Alexiou – and a spectacular public attack by Kazantzidhis in 1998 over alleged plagiarism. **Akis Panou** has been less prolific and commercially successful, but he too has done noteworthy albums with Dalaras, Bithikotsis and Stratos Dhionysiou as well as Kazantzidhes.

Although *laïkó* and *éntekhno* represented opposite poles, these extremes sometimes met, with *éntekhno* composers – especially Yiannis Markopoulos – often hiring *laïkó* singers for dates, or trying their hand at writing in *laïkó* style.These syntheses became increasingly exceptional (after the success of *Epitafios*/*Epifaneia* and *Axion Esti*) as Greek record labels tried to marginalize *laïkó*; this trend accelerated under the junta, a disaster for many types of music. Not only was the greater portion of *laïkó* banned from the radio as being too "oriental" and "defeatist", but folk music – already disparaged as old-fashioned by a generation coming of age with the Beatles – increasingly fell into disrepute through its use for propaganda purposes. In these conditions, only *elafrolaïkó* (literally "light popular) and *éntekhno*, with its potential for coded messages within oblique lyrics and minority audience, flourished. The dulcet voices of Dalaras and others were soon preferred to the harshness of Kazantzidhes, but the stage was set for the emergence of singer-songwriters – many of them guitarists from Thessaloníki – and groups of folk-rockers, who together wrested back control of Greek music from the purveyors of anodyne pap.

SINGER-SONGWRITERS AND FOLK-ROCK

The first significant musician to break out of the *bouzoúki* mould was Thessalonian **Dhionysis Savvopoulos**, who burst on the scene in 1966 with a maniacal, rasping voice and angst-ridden lyrics, his persona rounded out by shoulder-length hair and outsized glasses. Initially linked with the short-lived *néo kýma* movement – a blend of watered-down *éntekhno* and French *chanson* performed in Athenian *boîtes* soon closed down by the colonels – Savvopoulos's work soon became impossible to piegeonhole: equal parts twisted Macedonian folk, Bob Dylan and Frank Zappa at his jazziest is a useful approximation. Though briefly detained and tortured, he was able to continue performing, and became something of a consolation and password to the generation coming of age under the junta.

Out of Savvopoulos's "Balkan rock" experiments sprung a short-lived movement whose artists alternated electric versions of traditional songs with original material. Few left much trace in discography or longevity of performance except for folk "updater" **Mariza Koch**, the Gypsy protest guitarist-singer **Kostas Hatzis**, and folk/*éntekhno* performer **Arletta**, all still active to various degrees.

Despite a modest discography compared to the *éntekhno* composers, it's difficult to overestimate his effect on subsequent artists. Credit (or blame) for much Greek rock and fusion jazz can be laid at Savvopoulos's door; during his brief tenure as head of Lyra records, and later as an independent producer, Savvopoulos gave breaks to numerous younger artists, many of them also from northern Greece. Among Savvopoulos's protégés and spiritual heirs, the first were **Nikos Xydhakis**, and **Manolis Rasoulis**, whose landmark 1978 pressing, *Iy Ekdhikisi tis Yiftias* (The Revenge of Gypsydom) actually embodied the backlash of *laïkó* culture (*laïkó*, in Greek, means "common" or "low-class" as well as "popular") against the pretentiousness of 1960s and 1970s *éntekhno* and other "politically correct" music. Its spirited, defiant lyrics and *tsiftetéli* rhythms were both homage to and send-up of the music beloved by Greek truck-drivers, Gypsy or otherwise.

As with mainland folk instrumental music, real **Gypsies** have been disproportionately important in *laïkó*, both as performers and composers, though many go to considerably length to conceal the fact; however, for every "assimilated" personality there are others, such as Eleni Vitali, Makis Khristodhoulopoulos and Vassilis Païteris who make no bones about their identity.

SINGER-SONGWRITERS AND CONTEMPORARY MUSIC DISCOGRAPHY

*Eleftheria Arvanitaki *Ta Kormia ke ta Mahairia* (CD, Polydor 527059). Best-selling venture of compositions by Lina Nikolakopoulou and lyrics by Mihala Ganas, that's meatier than her much-publicized work with Ara Dinkjian.

*Eleftheria Arvanitaki *Ektos Programmatos* (CD, Mercury 538659-2). Eleftheria returns to her roots in these rollicking live sessions at Athens and Thessaloníki clubs: a gallop through musical Greece of the last fifty years.

*Himerini Kolymvites (self-produced, 1981). First and arguably best of four discs, with surreal lyrics, *laïko* and *rembétiko* influences and rich, drunken melodies, which has acquired enduring cult status in the years since its 1981 release. *Ohi Lathi Panda Lathi* (CD, Lyra), a live 1997 album shared with Banda tis Florinas, seems a welcome return to form after disappointing efforts in the interim.

*Stamatis Kraounakis and Lina Nikolakopoulou *Kykloforo keh Oploforo* (CD, Polydor 827589). First and most successful of their several collaborations.

*Sokratis Malamas *Kyklos* (LP, Lyra 4744) embodies his latest style; the earlier *Tis Meras ke tis Nykhtas* (LP, Lyra 4654) is more in the mode of Papazoglou.

Notis Mavroudhis and Nikos Houliaras *Ekdhromi* (LP, Zodiac 88002). Rare, guitar–voice duo: one side contains haunting versions of Epirot folk-songs, the other original pieces. Worth scouring the flea market for.

*Thanos Mikroutsikos, Lina Nikolakopoulou, Haris Alexiou *Krataei Khronia Avti iy Kolonia* (Minos 852). Uneven 1990 effort, but Haris is wonderful as ever; the hit single "Mia Pista apo Fosforo" caught on across the Aegean, with a Turkish cover version by Sezen Aksu.

*Nikos Papazoglou *Haratsi* (LP, Lyra 3369) alternates introspective ballads with hard-driving electric rock; the 1990 offering *Synerga* (LP, Lyra 4559, Greece) is gentler, even mystical, more in the mould of later Xydhakis. His more recent *Otan Kindhynevis Paixe tin Pouroudha* (LP, Lyra 4798) is also in a similar vein.

*Dhionysis Savvopoulos Though not his first disc, the radical 1970 *Ballos* (LP, Lyra 3573), a Balkan folk release that set off the brief folk-rock movement, established his position irrevocably; *Dheka Khronia Kommatia* (LP, Lyra 3715/CD, Lyra 0081) is a retrospective anthology of the artist's first (some say best) decade; yet *Trapezakia Exo* (LP, Lyra 3360/CD, Lyra 0041), more digestibly folky, is a personal favourite.

*Nikos Xydhakis and Friends *Konda sti Dhoxa mia Stigmi* (Lyra, Greece/CD Lyra 0039). One of the best Greek discs of the late 1980s, with haunting Xydhakis arrangements and compositions; their 1991 follow-up *Tenedos* (LP, Lyra 4590) was less even but had the wonderful single "Tsigaro Ego sto Stoma mou dhen Evala Oute Ena".

*Nikos Xydhakis, Nikos Papazoglou, Manolis Rasoulis *Iy Ekdhikisi tis Yiftias* (LP, Lyra 3308/CD, Lyra 0019. Ground-breaking recording of the late 1970s, still much loved (and sold) in Greece; its follow-up *Ta Dhithen* (LP, Lyra 3320/CD Lyra 0019) with Manolis Rasoulis is nearly its equal, containing the single "Iy Manges Dhen Yparhoun Pia", covered by Haris Alexiou.

CONTEMPORARY MUSIC: 1980 TO THE PRESENT

After an equally successful 1979 reprise with more or less the same personnel, *Ta Dhithen*, Xydhakis and Papazoglou in particular went on to pursue successful independent careers, Xydhakis in the style that hard-core *laïkó* fans dismiss as *koultouriárika* (high-brow stuff). His most successful venture in this vein was the 1987 *Konda sti Dhoxa mia Stigmi* with **Eleftheria Arvanitaki** guesting on vocals.

Arvanitaki, who began her career on a Savvopoulos album, and next with the rembétika revival group Opisthodhromiki Kompania, went on to participate in a host of *éntekhno* and *laïkó* sessions, and is currently considered Greece's hottest popular vocalist. A Thessalonian like Savvopoulous, **Nikos Papazoglou** is a more varied songwriter than Xydhakis; his material, also based on *laïkó* and folk, often has a harder electric-rock edge, though his 1990 *Synerga* can match Xydhakis for introspection and orientalism. Other performers to emerge from the so-called "Salonica Scene" after 1981 included **Himerini Kolymvites**, a group of architects led by Aryiris Bakirtzis, the *laïkó* composer Yiorgos Zikas and most recently Papazoglou disciple **Sokratis Malamas**.

Back in Athens, *éntekhno* and other Westernizing trends took longer to relax their grip, under the aegis of composers such as classically trained **Thanos Mikroutsikos**, briefly minister of culture after Melina Mercouri's death, who despite his high-brow leanings has worked with Alexiou, Dalaras and top *laïkó éntekhno* vocalist Dhimitra Galani. **Lina Nikolakopoulou** also made a splash with a number of thoughtful, if somewhat slick, albums stretching into the 1990s, exploring the boundaries between rock, jazz-cabaret and *éntekhno*.

BYZANTINE, ANATOLIAN AND FOLK REVIVAL GROUPS

An offshoot of *éntekhno* during the late 1970s and early 1980s involved combining folk and Byzantine traditions. Long before his unfortu-

BYZANTINE, ANATOLIAN AND FOLK REVIVAL GROUPS DISCOGRAPHY

***Manos Achalinotopoulos** *Yakinthos/Hyacinth* (CD, Sony SK60243). Up-and-coming clarinetist joins forces with other young traditional musicians in original compositions encompassing styles from Byzantine chant to Thracian *zournádhes*. Atmospheric and largely a successful experiment.

***Ross Daly** *Selected Works* (CD, BMG Ariola 70205 or Oriente 01, Germany). The best place to start, a compilation from many earlier, out-of-print albums (a chronic problem with Daly's work). Other goodies, still occasionally available, include Ross Daly (LP, RCA-BMG 70184 and *An-Kí* (RCA-BMG 27021), at his most eastern, with Iranian percussionist Jamshid Chemirani.

***Ross Daly and Labryrinth** *Mitos* (CD, World Network 8), 1991 concert recordings with Spyridhoula Toutoudhaki singing; one of the best documents of Daly's musical workshop of the time.

***Haïnidhes** *Haïnidhes* (CD, MBI 10492) and *Kosmos ki Oneiro ine Ena* (CD, MBI 10576) are their first two, and best, albums, with folk-influenced original compositions taking precedence over old standards.

***Khristodhoulos Halaris** *Dhrossoulites* (CD, Minos 7243 480179 25). Still his most riveting and worthy work, with lyrics by Nikos Gatsos and vocals by Khrysanthos and Dhimitra Galani.

***Loudhovikos Ton Anoyion (Yiorgos Dhramoundanis)** *O Erotas stin Kriti ine Melangolikos* (1988, Seirios, CD) His second album, which helped restore the mandolin – downgraded in Crete to the role of rhythm *laoúto* – to its rightful place. *Pyli tis Ammou* (CD, Mylos 009, Thessaloníki) exemplifies his later evolution in a larger group, with guest appearances by Malamas, Papazoglou and Nena Venetsanou.

Prosmoni/Expectation (En Khordais, CD 1901) Original compositions by oudist Kyriakos Kalaitzides, plus music of Lésvos and medieval Constantinople; very spare, late-night sound, hypnotic and tightly executed, originally a theatrical sound track.

***Domna Samiou** *Seryiani me tin Domna Samiou* (LP, Sirios 86003/CD, Minos 7243 4 89781 27). Good 1986 session with the inveterate collector, singer and revivalist – arguably her best work since the 1973 *Ehe Yia Panayia* (LP/CD EMI Columbia 14C 062 70115).

***Vosporos** *Greek Composers of Constantinople* (LP/CD, EMI 064 1701421). First, 1987 exploration of the medieval Constantinopolitan dimension of Greek music; also notable is *Live at the Palas Theatre* (LP, Lyra-Om 51/52). Since 1994, balanced vocals in Greek and Turkish have become pre-eminent, without a loss of instrumental virtuosity and innovation; it's hard to choose between *Ellinika ke Asikika* (CD, MBI 10608-2) and *Valkania Oneira/Balkan Dreams* (CD, MBI 10645).

***Savina Yiannatou** *Anixi sti Saloniki/Spring in Salonika* (LP/CD, Lyra 4765). Recreations of Ladino Sephardic songs, the latest of several such efforts, with Middle Eastern instrumental backing; Savina's voice can take some getting used to, however. The CD has four extra cuts and full notes. Her more recent *Songs of the Mediterranean* (CD, Musurgia 4900) has also been widely acclaimed.

***Ziyia** *Travels with Karagiozis* (CD, Aga Rhythm, USA). Folk and rembetic material by a five-member, bi-coastal American group who are better instrumentalists than many current Greek practitioners – typical of how rembétika has caught on overseas long after the craze for it has subsided in Greece.

nate ventures into speculative Byzantine song, musicologist and arranger **Khristodhoulos Halaris** followed up a version of the Cretan epic *Erotokritos*, showcasing Nikos Xylouris and Tania Tsanaklidou, with the riveting *Dhrossoulites*, which featured Khrysanthos, a high-voiced male singer of Pontic descent, on alternate tracks with Dhimitra Galani.

Ottoman rather than Byzantine Constantinople was the inspiration for **Vosporos**, a group coordinated in Istanbul from 1986 to 1992 by *psáltis* (church chanter) and *kanonáki*-player Nikiforos Metaxas to explore Ottoman classical, devotional and popular music. Since then the group has reformed as Fanari tis Anatolis, with Greek and Turkish singers alternating a variety of Greek folk material with Anatolian songs or mystical Alevi ballads.

Ross Daly, whose interests and style overlap slightly with Vosporos, also merits catching on disc, live in Athens clubs or touring abroad. English-born but Irish by background, Daly plays a dozen traditional instruments and has absorbed influences not only from Crete, where he was long resident, but from throughout the Near East. Alone or with a group, he has recorded strikingly contemporary interpretations of traditional pieces, as well as original compositions.

Occasionally this eclecticism has gone a bit too far, but with lapses of taste reined in, updating of folk material can be manifestly successful, as with two "exports" from Crete: mandolinist **Loudhovikos ton Anoyeion**, originally one of Hatzidhakis's finds at Seirios, and the six-member, all-acoustic group **Haïnidhes**. To foreign ears either sounds more accessible and exciting than more orthodox, scholarly revivalists such as **Domna Samiou**, who has performed both well-known and obscure material from every corner of the Greek world. Newer, crossover performers attempting (again with mixed success) to explore neighbouring influences on Greek music include Notios Ihos, led by Ahilleas Persidhis, and **Night Ark**, featuring Armenian performers Haig Yagdjian and Ara Dinkjian.

Marc Dubin and George Pissalides

BOOKS

Where separate editions exist in the UK and US, publishers are detailed below in the form **UK publisher; US publisher,** unless the publisher is the same in both countries. Where books are published in one country – or Athens – only, this follows the publisher's name.

O/p signifies an out-of-print but still highly recommended book; the recommended Greek-specialist book dealers often have stocks of these. University Press is abbreviated as UP.

Books marked * are part of a highly recommended "Modern Greek Writers" series, currently numbering over thirty titles, issued by the Athenian company Kedros Publishers.

TRAVEL AND GENERAL ACCOUNTS

MODERN ACCOUNTS

Kevin Andrews *The Flight of Ikaros* (Penguin, o/p). Intense and compelling account of an educated, sensitive archeologist loose in the backcountry during the aftermath of the civil war.

Robert Carver *The Accursed Mountains: Journeys in Albania* (Flamingo, UK). It's not usual to include a book on a neighbouring country, but this one's essential to understand why over half a million Albanians have fled the place for Greece. Carver also succinctly captures Greek attitudes towards Albanians (and vice versa), and includes a pithy vignette about the Prespa basin.

Gerald Durrell *My Family and Other Animals* (Penguin, UK). Sparkling, very funny anecdotes of Durrell's childhood on Corfu – and his passion for the island's fauna: toads, tortoises, bats, scorpions, the lot.

Lawrence Durrell *Prospero's Cell* (Faber & Faber; Penguin, o/p); *Reflections on a Marine Venus* (Faber & Faber; Penguin); *The Greek Islands* (Faber & Faber; Penguin, the former o/p). The elder Durrell lived before World War II with Gerald and the family on Corfu, the subject of *Prospero's Cell. Marine Venus* recounts Lawrence's 1945–47 experiences and impressions of Rhodes and other Dodecanese islands. *Greek Islands* is a lyrical but rather dated and occasionally bilious guide to the archipelagos.

John Gill *The Stars over Paxos* (Pavilion, UK). Ex-pat's-eye view of Páxos, with interesting statistics on olives and some acerbic asides on varieties of tourists and (other) ex-pats, amongst long-winded musings on Ionian weather, meteors and yes, stars. Fun for the beach, but lacks depth and marred by some factual clangers.

Yorgos Ioannou *Refugee Capital* (Kedros, Athens*; Central Books, UK). Usually brilliant essays on the city by a native of Thessaloníki; especially good on the reasons for its political powerlessness, the grip of the Orthodox Church and the deportation of the Jews, by way of praise for its flowering shade trees and cruising opportunities at its old cinemas (Ioannou was gay).

Sheelagh Kanneli *Earth and Water: A Marriage in Kalamata* (Efstathiadis, Athens). A classic account of that rare thing – a foreign woman integrating successfully into provincial Greek society. Rich in period detail of pre-tourism and pre-earthquake Kalamáta.

Katherine Kizilos *The Olive Grove: Travels in Greece* (Lonely Planet Journeys, UK). Returned, ambivalent Greek-Australian's musings on the country, and Istanbul, with an excellent final section on how the civil war tore apart her father's natal village in the Peloponnese.

Patrick Leigh Fermor *Roumeli* (Penguin, UK); *Mani* (Penguin; Peter Smith). Leigh Fermor is an aficionado of the vanishing minorities, relict communities and disappearing customs of rural Greece. These two books, written in the late 1950s and early 1960s, are not so much travelogues as scholarship interspersed with strange and hilarious yarns. Though overwritten in parts, they remain among the best books on any aspect of modern Greece.

Peter Levi *The Hill of Kronos* (Harvill, o/p; Dutton, o/p). Beautifully observed landscape, monuments and eventually politics as Levi describes how he is drawn into resistance to the colonels' junta. *A Bottle in the Shade: Journeys in the Peloponnese* (Sinclair Stevenson, UK) describes his return, three decades later, to his old haunts, and proves less engaged and more ruminant.

Willard Manus *This Way to Paradise: Dancing on the Tables* (Lycabettus Press, Athens). American expatriate's memoir of four decades in Líndhos, Rhodes, before its sad descent into mass-tourist tattiness. Wonderful period detail, including hippy excesses and often hilarious cameos by the likes of S. J. Perelman, Germaine Greer and Martha Gellhorn.

Henry Miller *The Colossus of Maroussi* (Minerva, o/p; New Directions). Corfu and the soul of Greece in 1939, with Miller, completely in his element, at his most inspired.

Nikos Pentzikis *Mother Thessaloniki* (Kedros, Athens*; Central Books, UK). About-to-be-issued counterpoint to Ioannou's volume, by another native of the city.

James Pettifer *The Greeks: the Land and People since the War* (Penguin; Viking). A useful, if spottily edited introduction to contemporary Greece – and its recent past. Pettifer charts the state of the nation's politics, food, family life, religion, tourism and other topics.

Tim Salmon *The Unwritten Places* (Lycabettus Press, Athens). Veteran Hellenophile describes his love affair with the Greek mountains, and the Vlach pastoral communities of the Píndhos in particular.

Patricia Storace *Dinner with Persephone* (Granta; Pantheon). A New York poet, resident for a year in Athens (with forays to the provinces) puts the country's psyche on the couch, while avoiding the same position with various predatory males. Storace has a sly sense of humour, and in showing how permeated – and imprisoned – Greece is by its imagined past, gets it right ninety-five percent of the time. Excellent.

Sarah Wheeler *An Island Apart* (Abacus, UK). Entertaining chronicle of a five-month ramble through Évvia, one of the least-visited islands. Wheeler has a sure touch with Greek culture and an open approach to nuns, goatherds or academics; the sole quibble is her success in making Évvia seem more interesting than it really is.

OLDER ACCOUNTS

James Theodore Bent *Aegean Islands: The Cyclades, or Life Among Insular Greeks* (Argonaut, US, o/p). Originally published in 1881, this remains the best account of island customs and folklore; it's also a highly readable, droll account of a year's Aegean travel, including a particularly violent Cycladic winter.

Robert Byron *The Station* (Century, UK, o/p). Travels on Mount Áthos in the 1930s, by one of the pioneering scholars of Byzantine art and architecture.

Nikos Kazantzakis *Travels in Greece: Journey to the Morea* (Bruno Cassirer, UK, o/p). Slightly stilted translation of the Cretan novelist's journey around the Peloponnese, and his increasing alienation from 1930s Greece. Easy to find in specialist shops.

Edward Lear *Journals of a Landscape Painter in Greece and Albania* (Century, UK, o/p). Highly entertaining journals of two journeys through Greece and Albania in autumn 1848 and spring 1849, by the famous landscape painter and author of *The Book of Nonsense*. Further doses of Lear, *The Corfu Years* and *The Cretan Journal*, have been published by Denise Harvey in Athens.

Sidney Loch *Athos, The Holy Mountain* (Molho, Thessaloníki, Greece). A resident of Ouranópoli, on the periphery of Mount Áthos, from 1924 to 1954, Loch recounts the legends surrounding the various monasteries, as gleaned from his years of walking through the monastic republic. Inevitably nostalgic, as the Áthos he knew has been utterly swept away since the 1980s.

Terence Spencer *Fair Greece, Sad Relic: Literary Philhellenism from Shakespeare to Byron* (Denise Harvey, Athens, available in UK; Scholarly Press). Greece – and incipient philhellenism – from the fall of Constantinople to the War of Independence, as conveyed by English poets, essayists and travellers.

Richard Stoneman, ed *A Literary Companion to Travel in Greece* (Getty Centre for the History of Art and the Humanities, US). Ancient and medieval authors, plus Grand Tourists – good for dipping into.

THE CLASSICS

Many of the classics make excellent companion reading for a trip around Greece – especially the historians **Thucydides** and **Herodotus**. Reading **Homer**'s *Odyssey* when you're battling with or resigning yourself to the vagaries of island ferries puts your own plight into perspective. One slightly less well-known source, especially recommended for travels around the Peloponnese, is **Pausanias**'s fourth-century AD *Guide to Greece*, annotated by Peter Levi in its Penguin edition with notes on modern identifications of sites mentioned.

Most of the standard undergraduate staples are part of the **Penguin Classics** paperback series. **Routledge** also has a huge, steadily expanding backlist of Classical Studies, though many titles are expensive and quite specialized; paperback editions are indicated.

Homer *The Iliad; The Odyssey*. The first concerns itself, semi-factually, with the late Bronze Age war of the Achaeans against Troy in Asia Minor; the second recounts the delayed return home, via seemingly every corner of the Mediterranean, of the hero Odysseus. For a verse rendition, Richard Lattimore's translation (University of Chicago, *Iliad*; HarperCollins, *Odyssey*) has yet to be bettered; for prose, the best choices are by the father-and-son team of E.V. Rieu (*Iliad*, Penguin) and D.C.H. Rieu (*Odyssey*, Penguin).

Herodotus *The Histories* (Penguin), or A.D. Godley, tr (Cambridge UP). Revered as the father of systematic history and anthropology, this fifth-century BC Anatolian writer chronicled both the causes and campaigns of the Persian Wars, as well as the contemporary, assorted tribes and nations inhabiting Asia Minor.

Ovid *The Metamorphoses*, A.D. Melville, tr (Oxford UP). Though collected by a first-century AD Roman poet, this remains one of the most accessible renditions of the more piquant Greek myths, involving transformations as divine blessing or curse.

Pausanias *The Guide to Greece* (Penguin, 2 vols). Essentially the first-ever guidebook, intended for Roman pilgrims to the holy sites of the Greek mainland; invaluable for later archeologists in assessing damage or change to temples over the intervening centuries, or (in some cases) locating them at all.

Plutarch *The Age of Alexander; On Sparta; The Rise and Fall of Athens* (Penguin). Another ancient author, writing perhaps with benefit of hindsight – but with the detriment of shaky sources and much conjecture.

Thucydides *History of the Peloponnesian War* (Penguin). Bleak month-by-month account of the conflict, by a cashiered Athenian officer whose affiliation and dim view of human nature usually didn't get in the way of his objectivity; see the review of George Cawkwell's book (below) for a revisionist view.

Xenophon *The History of My Times* (Penguin). Thucydides stopped his coverage of the Peloponnesian War in 411 BC; this work continues events until 362 BC.

ANCIENT HISTORY AND INTERPRETATION OF THE CLASSICS

A.R. Burn *History of Greece* (Penguin). Probably the best general introduction to ancient Greece, though for fuller and more interesting analysis you'll do better with one or other of the following more specialized titles.

George Cawkwell *Thucydides and the Peloponnesian War* (Routledge). Recent, revisionist overview of Thucydides' work and relations with main personalities of the war, challenging previous assumptions of his infallibility.

M.I. Finley *The World of Odysseus* (Penguin). Good on the interrelation of Mycenaean myth and fact.

Simon Hornblower *The Greek World 479–323 BC* (Routledge). An erudite survey of ancient Greece at its zenith, from the end of the Persian Wars to the death of Alexander, which has become a standard university paperback text.

Robin Lane Fox *Alexander the Great* (Penguin). An absorbing study, which mixes historical scholarship with imaginative psychological detail.

Michael Grant and John Hazel *Who's Who in Classical Mythology* (Routledge). Gazetteer of over 1200 mythological personalities, together with historical and geographical background.

Pierre Grimal, ed *Dictionary of Classical Mythology* (Penguin). Though translated from the French, considered to still have the edge on the more recent Grant/Hazel title.

John Kenyon Davies *Democracy and Classical Greece* (Fontana; Harvard UP). Established and accessible account of the Classical period and its political developments.

Oswyn Murray *Early Greece* (Fontana; Harvard UP). The Greek story from the Mycenaeans and

Minoans through to the beginning of the Classical period.

Robin Osborne *Greece in the Making 1200–479 BC* (Routledge). Well-illustrated paperback on the rise of the city-state.

F.W. Walbank *The Hellenistic World* (Fontana; Harvard UP). Greece under the sway of the Macedonian and Roman empires.

ANCIENT RELIGION

Harry Brewster *River Gods of Greece* (I.B. Tauris; St Martin's). Most ancient rivers had a deity associated with them; here are the cults and legends.

Walter Burkert *Greek Religion: Archaic and Classical* (Blackwell). Superb overview of deities and their attributes and antecedents, rites, the protocol of sacrifice and the symbolism of major festivals; especially good on relating Greek worship to its predecessors in the Middle East.

Matthew Dillon *Pilgrims and Pilgrimage in Ancient Greece* (Routledge). Pricey hardback exploring not only the main sanctuaries such as Delphi, but also minor oracles, the role of women and children and the secular festivities attending the rites.

Nano Marinatos and Robin Hagg *Greek Sanctuaries: New Approaches* (Routledge). Form and function of the temples, in the light of recent scholarship.

R. Gordon Wasson, Albert Hoffmann, Carl Ruck *The Road to Eleusis: Unveiling the Secret of the Mysteries* (Harcourt Brace, o/p). Well-argued monograph expounding the theory that the Eleusinian mysteries were at least in part a psychedelic trip, courtesy of grain-ergot fungus. Guaranteed to outrage conventional classicists, though even Burkert (see above) admits they may have a case.

FOOD AND WINE

Andrew Dalby *Siren Feasts* (Routledge). Subtitled "A history of food and gastronomy in Greece", this analysis of Classical and Byzantine texts demonstrates just how little Greek cuisine has changed in three millennia; also excellent on the introduction and etymology of common vegetables and herbs.

Alan Davidson *Mediterranean Seafood* (Penguin, o/p). A 1972 classic, periodically reprinted, this amazingly erudite and witty book catalogues all known edible species, complete with legends, anecdotes, habits, local names and a suggested recipe or two for each; no photos, but useful pen-and-ink sketches.

James Davidson *Courtesans and Fishcakes* (HarperCollins, UK). The politics, class characteristics and etiquette of consumption and consummation – with wine, women, boys and seafood – in ancient Athens, with their bearing on both historical events and modern attitudes. Highly recommended.

Miles Lambert-Gócs *The Wines of Greece* (Faber & Faber). Comprehensive survey of the emerging and improving wines of Greece, with plenty of historical background; unfortunately few of these grace middle-of-the-road taverna tables as yet, and coverage ceases in 1993.

Nikos Stavroulakis *Cookbook of the Jews of Greece* (Lycabettus Press, Athens; Cadmus Press, US). Tasty recipes interspersed with their relation to the Jewish liturgical year, plus potted histories of the communities which produced them.

ARCHEOLOGY AND ART

John Beckwith *Early Christian and Byzantine Art* (Yale UP). Illustrated study placing Byzantine art within a wider context.

William R. Biers *Archeology of Greece: An Introduction* (Cornell UP). A recently revised and excellent standard text.

John Boardman *Greek Art* (Thames & Hudson, UK). A very good concise introduction: part of the "World of Art" series.

Chris Hellier *Monasteries of Greece* (Tauris Parke; St Martin's Press). Magnificently photographed survey of the surviving, active monasteries and their treasures, with insightful accompanying essays.

Reynold Higgins *Minoan and Mycenaean Art* (Thames & Hudson). A clear, well-illustrated round-up.

Sinclair Hood *The Arts in Prehistoric Greece* (Penguin; Yale UP). Sound introduction to the subject.

Roger Ling *Classical Greece* (Phaidon, UK). Another useful illustrated introduction.

Colin Renfrew *The Cycladic Spirit* (Thames & Hudson; Abrams). A fine, illustrated study of the meaning and purpose of Cycladic artefacts.

Gisela Richter *A Handbook of Greek Art* (Phaidon; Da Capo). Exhaustive survey of the visual arts of ancient Greece.

Suzanne Slesin et al *Greek Style* (Thames & Hudson; Crown). Stunning (if sometimes contrived) designer-tweaked interiors from Corfu, Rhodes and Sérifos, among other spots.

R.R.R. Smith *Hellenistic Sculpture* (Thames & Hudson). Modern reappraisal of the art of Greece under Alexander and his successors.

David Talbot Rice *Art of the Byzantine Era* (Thames & Hudson). Talbot Rice was, with Robert Byron, one of the pioneering scholars in the "rediscovery" of Byzantine art; this is an accessible illustrated study.

Peter Warren *The Aegean Civilizations* (Phaidon, o/p; P. Bedrick Books, o/p). Illustrated account of the Minoan and Mycenaean cultures.

BYZANTINE, MEDIEVAL AND OTTOMAN HISTORY

Averil Cameron *The Mediterranean World in Late Antiquity, AD 395–600* (Routledge). Essentially the early Byzantine years.

Nicholas Cheetham *Medieval Greece* (Yale UP, o/p in US). General survey of the period and its infinite convolutions in Greece, with Frankish, Catalan, Venetian, Byzantine and Ottoman struggles for power.

John Julius Norwich *Byzantium: The Early Centuries*; *Byzantium: the Apogee* and *Byzantium: The Decline* (all Penguin; Viking-Knopf). Perhaps the main surprise for first-time travellers to Greece is the fascination of Byzantine monuments, above all at Mystra. This is an astonishingly detailed yet readable trilogy.

Vangelis Pavlidis *Rhodes 1306–1522: A Story* (Rodos Image, Rhodes). Caricature-illustrated history of the Knights of St John's occupation of Rhodes, by one of Greece's leading political cartoonists, but this isn't tourist pap – rigorous research and witty text illuminate a little-known era of the Dodecanese.

Michael Psellus *Fourteen Byzantine Rulers* (Penguin). A fascinating contemporary source, detailing the stormy but brilliant period from 976 to 1078.

Steven Runciman *The Fall of Constantinople, 1453* (Canto-Cambridge UP) is the standard account of the event; *The Great Church in Captivity* (Cambridge UP) follows the vicissitudes of the Orthodox Patriarchate in Constantinople up to the War of Independence. *Byzantine Style and Civilization* (Penguin, o/p in US) and *Mistra* (Thames & Hudson, o/p in US) are more slanted towards art, culture and monuments.

Archbishop Kallistos (Timothy) Ware *The Orthodox Church* (Penguin). Good introduction to what is effectively the established religion of Greece, by the Orthodox archbishop resident in Oxford.

MODERN GREECE

Timothy Boatswain and Colin Nicolson *A Traveller's History of Greece* (Windrush Press; Interlink). Dated (coverage ceases in early 1990s) but well-written overview of the important Greek periods and personalities.

Richard Clogg *A Concise History of Greece* (Cambridge UP). A remarkably clear and well-illustrated account of Greece, from the decline of Byzantium to 1991, with the emphasis on recent decades; there are numerous maps and lengthy feature captions to the artwork.

Douglas Dakin *The Unification of Greece, 1770–1923* (Ernest Benn, o/p; St Martin's, o/p). Benchmark account of the foundation of the Greek state and the struggle to extend its boundaries.

Oriana Falacci *A Man* (Arrow; Pocket Books, o/p). Account of the junta years, relating the author's involvement with Alekos Panagoulis, the anarchist who attempted to assassinate Colonel Papadopoulos in 1968. Issued ostensibly as a "novel" in response to threats by those who were implicated in Panagoulis's own murder in 1975.

H.A. Lidderdale, trs and ed *The Memoirs of General Makriyannis, 1797–1864* (Oxford UP, o/p). The "Peasant General", one of the few honest and self-sacrificing protagonists of the Greek uprising, taught himself to write at age 32 to set down this apologia of his conduct, in vivid demotic Greek. Heartbreaking in its portrayal of the incipient schisms, linguistic and otherwise, that tore the country apart until recently.

Michael Llewellyn Smith *Ionian Vision, Greece in Asia Minor, 1919–22* (C. Hurst; University of Michigan). Standard work, by the recently retired UK ambassador to Greece, on the disastrous Anatolian campaign, which led to the exchange of populations between Greece and Turkey.

Yiannis Roubatis *Tangled Webs: The US in Greece 1947–67* (Pella Publishing, US). Chronicles growing American involvement in Greece during the lead-up to the military coup.

C.M. Woodhouse *Modern Greece, A Short History* (Faber & Faber). Woodhouse was active in the Greek Resistance during World War II. Writing from a more right-wing perspective than Clogg, this history (spanning from the foundation of Constantinople in 324 to the 1980s), is briefer and a bit drier, but scrupulous with facts. *The Rise and Fall of the Greek Colonels* (Granada, o/p; Watts), recounts the (horror) story of the dictatorship.

WORLD WAR II AND ITS AFTERMATH

David H. Close *The Origins of the Greek Civil War* (Longman). Excellent, readable study that focuses on the social conditions in 1920s and 1930s Greece that made the country so ripe for conflict. Draws on primary sources and is relatively objective (though he's no great fan of the Left).

Nicholas Gage *Eleni* (Collins Harvill; Ballantine). Controversial account by a Greek-born *New York Times* correspondent who returns to Epirus to avenge the death of his mother, condemned by an ELAS tribunal in 1948. Superb descriptions of village life, but blinkered political "history" – and the basis of an utterly forgettable 1985 movie. The book inspired a response by a left-wing writer, **Vassilis Kavathas**, whose family had been decimated by the Right, entitled *Iy Alli Eleni* (The Other Eleni), not as yet translated into English.

Iakovos Kambanellis *Mauthausen* (Kedros, Athens*; Central Books, UK). Kambanellis was active in the Resistance, caught by the Germans, and sent to Mauthausen, the concentration camp reserved for those who had opposed the Nazis' rise to power. Harrowing atrocities in flashback there are a-plenty, but the main thrust of the book is post-liberation, describing the author's awkward romance with a Lithuanian Jew, and how the idealist inmates are slowly disillusioned as they see that the "New World Order" will be scarcely different from the old.

Edmund Keeley *The Salonika Bay Murder* (Princeton UP). The assassination in 1948 of a CBS correspondent, apparently by minions of the royalist government, was a major incident. This analysis fingers the colluding Greek and US intelligence services.

Kati Marton *The Polk Conspiracy* (Times Books, US). Another treatment of the Polk case, written as a gripping early Cold War whodunnit, and reaching a similar conclusion.

Mark Mazower *Inside Hitler's Greece: The Experience of Occupation 1941–44* (Yale UP). Somewhat choppily organized, but the standard of scholarship is high and the photos alone justify the price. Demonstrates how the complete demoralization of the country and the incompetence of conventional politicians led to the rise of ELAS and the onset of civil war.

Eddie Myers *Greek Entanglement* (Alan Sutton, UK, o/p). The inside story of the Gorgopotamos viaduct sabotage operation by the British brigadier who led it, and lots else about co-ordinating the Resistance from 1942 to 1944. Myers comes across as under no illusions as to the qualities of the various Greeks he had to deal with. Recommended.

George Psychoundakis *The Cretan Runner* (John Murray, o/p; Transatlantic Arts, o/p; Efstathiadis, Athens). Narrative of the invasion of Crete and subsequent Resistance, by a participant who was a guide and message-runner for all the British protagonists – including Patrick Leigh Fermor, the translator of the book.

Marion Sarafis and Martin Eve *Background to Contemporary Greece, vols 1 & 2* (Merlin, UK). Papers and panel discussion from a late 1980s conference on the civil war, with former belligerents confronting each other across podiums. Left-wing bias, but Sarafis herself – widow of the main DSE commander – is impressive, especially in volume 1.

Adrian Seligman *War in the Islands* (Allan Sutton, UK). Collected oral histories of a little-known Allied unit: a flotilla of kaïkia organized to raid the Axis-held Aegean islands. *Boy's Own* stuff, with service-jargon-laced prose, but lots of fine period photos and detail.

Michael Ward *Greek Assignments: SOE 1943–UNSCOB 1948* (Lycabettus Press, Athens). The author, British consul in Thessaloníki from 1971 to 1983, parachuted into the Píndhos as a guerrilla and walked the width of the country; most amazing is how the Germans controlled only the towns, leaving the countryside to the Resistance. While assigned to discourage other British servicemen from doing so, he married a Greek and later returned to observe the civil war.

C.M. Woodhouse *The Struggle for Greece, 1941–49* (Hart-Davis, o/p; Beekman). A masterly and by no means uncritical account of this crucial decade, explaining how Greece emerged without a communist government.

ETHNOGRAPHY

John K. Campbell *Honour, Family and Patronage* (Oxford UP). Classic study of a Sarakatsáni community in the Píndhos mountains, with much wider applicability to rural Greece.

Costis Copsides *The Jews of Thessaloniki through the Postcards* (sic) *1886–1917* (self-published, Thessaloniki). Jewish personalities, business and monuments, and the pre-fire city in general, as seen by Jewish postcard publishers.

Rae Dalven *The Jews of Ioannina* (Lycabettus Press, Greece, available in the UK/US). History and culture of the thriving pre-Holocaust community, related by a poet and translator of Cavafy (see "Modern Greek Poetry", p.909), herself an Epirot Jew.

Juliet du Boulay *Portrait of a Greek Mountain Village* (Oxford UP, o/p in UK). An account of the village of Ambéli, on Évvia, during the 1960s. The habits and customs of an all-but-vanished way of life are observed and evoked in an absorbing narrative.

Renée Hirschon *Heirs to the Greek Catastrophe: the Social Life of Asia Minor Refugees in Piraeus* (Oxford UP, Clarendon Press UK). Classic 1980s study now reissued in revised edition; shows how this community in Kokkinia has maintained a separate identity three generations after 1923.

Gail Holst-Warhaft *Road to Rembétika: Songs of Love, Sorrow and Hashish* (Denise Harvey, Greece, available in the UK). The most intriguing Greek urban musical style of this century, evocatively traced by a Cornell University musicologist, though the discography has not been updated since the late 1980s.

Anastasia Karakasidou *Fields of Wheat, Hills of Blood* (University of Chicago, US). Excellent but controversial work on the recent formation of Greek national consciousness in Macedonia (see box pp.376–377), declined for publication by Cambridge UP.

John Cuthbert Lawson *Modern Greek Folklore and Ancient Greek Religion: A Study in Survivals* (University Books, New York; o/p). Exactly as the title states, and still highly applicable a century after its writing; well worth scouring libraries and antiquarian dealers for.

Peter Mackridge and Eleni Yannakakis *Ourselves and Others: Development of a Greek Macedonian Identity Since 1912* (Berg, UK). Less provocative than the Karakasidou volume, but covers much the same ground.

Clay Perry *Vanishing Greece* (Conran Octopus; Abbeville Press). Well-captioned photos depict the threatened landscapes and relict ways of life in rural Greece; now in paperback.

Nikos Stavroulakis *Salonika: Jews and Dervishes* (Talos Press, Athens, available in the US). Monograph by the former curator of the Jewish Museum of Greece, lavishly illustrated with old photos, of two of Thessaloníki's most distinctive communities – which have vanished only this century.

T.J. Winnifrith *The Vlachs: The History of a Balkan People* (Duckworth; St Martin's Press). Rather heavy-going hotchpotch on the existing Vlach communities in Greece and the rest of the Balkans, but the only study easily available.

MODERN GREEK LITERATURE

Roderick Beaton *An Introduction to Modern Greek Literature* (Oxford UP). Chronological survey of fiction and poetry from independence to the early 1990s, with a useful discussion on the "Language Question".

FICTION

Maro Douka *Fool's Gold* (Kedros, Athens*; Central Books, UK). Describes an upper-class young woman's involvement, and subsequent disillusionment, with the clandestine resistance to the junta.

Eugenia Fakinou *The Seventh Garment* (Serpent's Tail). Greek history, from the War of Independence to the colonels' junta, told through the life stories (interspersed in counterpoint) of three generations of women; a rather more successful experiment than Fakinou's *Astradeni* (Kedros, Athens; Central Books, UK), in which a young girl – whose slightly irritating narrative voice is adopted throughout – leaves the island of Sými, with all its traditional values, for Athens.

Andreas Franghias *The Courtyard* (Kedros, Athens*; Central Books, UK). Well-observed but relentlessly depressing tale follows the struggling inhabitants of a working-class Athens shanty town during the early 1950s.

Stratis Haviaras *When the Tree Sings* (Picador; Simon & Schuster, both o/p) and *The Heroic Age* (Penguin, o/p). Two-part, faintly disguised autobiography about coming of age in Greece in the 1940s, by the former poetry curator of Harvard University library. Written in English because Haviaris felt his experiences too keenly to set them down in Greek.

Nikos Kazantzakis *Zorba the* Greek; *Christ Recrucified* (published in the US as *The Greek Passion*); *Report to Greco*; *Freedom or Death* (*Captain Mihalis* in the US); *The Fratricides* (all Faber & Faber; Touchstone). The most accessible (and Greece-related) of the numerous novels by the Cretan master. Even with inadequate translation, their strength – especially that of *Report to Greco* – shines through.

Artemis Leontis, ed *Greece: A Traveller's Literary Companion* (Whereabouts Press, San Francisco, US). An overdue idea, brilliantly executed: various regions of the country as portrayed in (very) short fiction or essays by modern Greek writers. A recommended antidote to the often condescending Grand Tourist accounts.

Margarita Liberaki *Three Summers* (Kedros, Athens*; Central Books, UK). Coming-of-age chronicle, mostly from the point of view of the youngest of the adolescent sisters, set in the wealthy estates of Kifissiá during the late 1930s. Slight plot in a rarefied, claustrophobic environment, but it doesn't quite deserve its disparaging dismissal as the Greek *Little Women*.

Kostas Mourselas *Red Dyed Hair* (Kedros, Athens*; Central Books, UK). Politically incorrect picaresque epic, as you'd imagine *Zorba* crossed with *Last Exit to Brooklyn*, of a particularly dysfunctional Pireás *paréa* (the group you hang out

with from youth till middle age). Particularly good translation of an original still selling well, and the basis of a popular TV series.

Stratis Myrivilis *Life in the Tomb* (Quartet; New England UP). A harrowing and unorthodox war memoir, based on the author's experience on the Macedonian front during 1917–18, well translated by Peter Bien. Completing a kind of trilogy are two later novels, set on the north coast of Lésvos, Myrivilis's homeland: *The Mermaid Madonna* and *The Schoolmistress with the Golden Eyes* (Efstathiadis, Athens). Translations of these are not so good, and tend to be heavily abridged.

Alexandhros Papadiamantis *The Murderess* (Writers & Readers). Landmark turn-of-the-century novel set on the island of Skiáthos, in which an old woman, appalled by the fate that awaits them in adulthood, concludes that little girls are better off dead. Also available is a collection of Papadiamantis short stories, *Tales from a Greek Island* (Johns Hopkins UP).

Nick Papandreou *Father Dancing* (Penguin). Thinly veiled *roman à clef* by the late Andreas's younger son. Papandreou Senior, not too surprisingly, comes across as a gasbag and petty domestic tyrant.

Yannis Ritsos *Iconostasis of Anonymous Saints* (Kedros, Athens*). The first three instalments of a projected nine-volume autobiographical novel. The "anonymous saints" are the characters of these vaguely sequentially vignettes.

Dido Sotiriou *Farewell Anatolia* (Kedros, Athens*; Central Books, London). A classic since its initial appearance in 1962 (it has now passed its 56th Greek printing), this epic chronicles the traumatic end of Greek life in Asia Minor, from World War I to the catastrophe of 1922, as narrated by a fictionalized version of the author's father.

Stratis Tsirkas *Drifting Cities* (Kedros, Athens*; Central Books, London). Set by turns in the Jerusalem, Cairo and Alexandria of World War II, this unflinchingly honest and humane epic of a Greek army hero secretly working for the Leftist Resistance got the author denounced by the Communist Party.

Vassilis Vassilikos *Z* (Four Walls Eight Windows). A novel based closely enough on events – the 1963 political assassination of

Gregoris Lambrakis in Thessaloníki – to be banned under the colonels' junta, and brilliantly filmed by Costa-Gavras in 1968.

MODERN GREEK POETRY

With two Nobel laureates in recent years – George Seferis and Odysseus Elytis – modern Greece has an extraordinarily intense and dynamic poetic tradition. Translations of all of the following are excellent.

C.P. Cavafy *Collected Poems* (Chatto & Windus; Princeton UP). The complete works, translated by Edmund Keeley and Philip Sherrard, of perhaps the most accessible modern Greek poet, resident for most of his life in Alexandria. For some, *The Complete Poems of Cavafy* (Harcourt Brace Jovanovich), translated by Rae Dalven, or the volume done by John Mavrokordato (Chatto & Windus, UK) are superior versions.

Odysseus Elytis *The Axion Esti* (Anvil Press; Pittsburgh UP); *Selected Poems* (Anvil Press; Viking Penguin, o/p); *The Sovereign Sun* (Bloodaxe Books; Temple UP, Philadelphia, o/p). The major works in good English versions. Easier to find is *Collected Poems* (Johns Hopkins UP), which includes virtually everything except *The Axion Esti.*

Modern Greek Poetry (Efstathiadis, Athens). Decent anthology of translations, predominantly of Seferis and Elytis.

Yannis Ritsos *Exile and Return, Selected Poems 1967–1974* (Anvil Press; Ecco Press). A fine volume of Greece's foremost leftist poet, from the junta era when he was internally exiled on Sámos.

George Seferis *Collected Poems, 1924–1955* (Anvil Press, o/p; Princeton UP, o/p). Virtually the complete works of the Nobel laureate, with Greek and English verses on facing pages. More recent, but lacking the parallel Greek text, is *Complete Poems* (Anvil Press; Princeton UP).

GREECE IN FOREIGN FICTION

Louis de Bernières *Captain Corelli's Mandolin* (Minerva; Random House). Set on Kefalloniá during the World War II occupation, this is a brilliant tragicomedy by an author best known for his South American extravaganzas. It has won praise from Greek intellectuals despite

its disparagement of ELAS – quite an achievement. Since appearing in 1994 it has acquired seemingly perennial best-seller status, and is soon to be a motion picture.

John Fowles *The Magus* (Vintage; Dell). Fowles's biggest and best novel: a tale of mystery and manipulation – plus Greek island life – inspired by his stay on Spétses as a teacher, in the 1950s.

Olivia Manning *The Balkan Trilogy, vol 3: Friends and Heroes* (Mandarin, UK). In which Guy and Harriet Pringle escape from Bucharest to Athens, in its last months before the invasion of 1941. Wonderfully observed and moving.

Mary Renault *The King Must Die; The Last of the Wine; The Mask of Apollo* (Sceptre; Random House) and others (all Penguin except *Masks*). Mary Renault's imaginative reconstructions are more than the adolescent's reading they're often taken for, with impeccable research and tight writing. The trio above retell, respectively, the myth of Theseus, the life of a pupil of Socrates and that of a fourth-century BC actor. The life of Alexander the Great is told in *Fire from Heaven, The Persian Boy* and *Funeral Games*, available separately or in one economical volume (all Penguin).

Catherine Temma Davidson *The Priest Fainted* (The Women's Press, UK). Autobiographical novel where a Greek-Jewish-American woman tries to find her level in 1980s Athens, and the countryside, and also uncovers what made her mother flee the country three decades before. Lyrical, and not a dissimilar sense of humour to fellow-poet Storace's (see p.902).

Evelyn Waugh *Officers and Gentleman* (Penguin). This volume of the wartime trilogy includes an account of the Battle of Crete and subsequent evacuation.

SPECIFIC GUIDES

ARCHEOLOGY

A.R. and Mary Burn *The Living Past of Greece: A Time Traveller's Tour of Historic and Prehistoric Places* (Herbert Press; Harper-Collins). Unusual in extent, this covers sites from Minoan through to Byzantine and Frankish, with good clear plans and lively text.

Paul Hetherington *Byzantine and Medieval Greece: Churches, Castles and Art* (John Murray). Gazetteer of all major mainland sites, though frustratingly misses the islands. Readable, authoritative and with useful plans.

Evi Melas, ed *Temples and Sanctuaries of Ancient Greece: A Companion Guide* (Thames & Hudson, o/p). Excellent collection of essays on the main sites, written by archeologists who have worked at them.

Alexander Paradissis *Fortresses and Castles of Greece* (Efstathiadis, Athens). Three extremely prolix volumes, widely available in Greek bookshops.

HIKING

Anavasi Mountain Editions New rival to Road Editions (see Basics, p.31,) which in addition to army-map-based cartography offers touring booklets for walks, monuments and ski mountaineering for several mainland alpine regions. To date the expanding series of English-translated titles includes *Mount Parnassós* (the most carefully produced), *Mount Íti*, the Karpenísi area, *Mount Taïyettos* and the *Préspa Basin*. In case of difficulty obtaining them, contact Anavasi at Dhragoúmi 34, 115 28 Athens (☎30/1/72 93 541).

Lance Chilton Various walking pamphlets (Marengo Publications, UK). Small but thorough guides to the best walks at various mainland and island charter resorts, accompanied by three-colour maps. Areas covered to date include: Áyios Yeóryios, Corfu; Yeoryioúpolis and Plakiás, Crete; Stoúpa, Peloponnese; Líndhos, Rhodes; Kokkári, Sámos; and Sými. In specialist UK shops or by mail order; catalogue from 17 Bernard Crescent, Hunstanton PE36 6ER (☎ & fax 01485/532710, *marengo@supanet.com*).

Marc Dubin *Trekking in Greece* (Lonely Planet; o/p). Though some sections are showing their age, still an excellent walkers' guide, expanding on the hikes covered in this book. Includes day-hikes and longer treks, both around the mainland and on the islands, plus extensive preparatory and background information.

Andonis Kaloyirou *Walking Routes on Parnitha* (Road Editions, Athens). Small, pocket-sized booklet, packaged with an encased topo map, enables you to get the best out of the nearest mountain escape from Athens.

Tim Salmon *The Mountains of Greece: A Walker's Guide* (Cicerone Press; Hunter). The emphasis in this practical walkers' handbook updated in 1993, is more specifically on the mainland mountains. Its core is a superb traverse, roughly following the Píndhos crest, from Delphi to Albania.

RAILWAYS

Michael Ward *The Railways of Greece: Their Inception and Development* (self-published, Athens; order on ☎30/1/72 13 894). A history of operations, plus extensive locomotive catalogues and diagrams.

REGIONAL GUIDES

Marc Dubin *The Rough Guide to the Dodecanese and the East Aegean* (Penguin). Exhaustive coverage of the islands described in Chapters Nine and Ten of this book, by a part-time resident of Sámos.

John Fisher and Geoff Garvey *The Rough Guide to Crete* (Penguin). An expanded and practical guide to the island by two Cretophiles, who contributed the Crete chapter to this book.

Peter Greenhalgh and Edward Eliopoulos *Deep Into Mani* (Faber & Faber, o/p). A former member of the wartime Resistance revisits the Máni forty years after first hiding there, and 25 years after Patrick Leigh Fermor's work, in the company of a British scholar. The result is a superb guide to the region and excellent armchair reading.

Lycabettus Press Guides (Athens, Greece). This series takes in many of the more popular islands and certain mainland highlights; most,

---

BOOKSHOPS

Athens has a number of excellent bookshops, at which many of the recommendations above should be available (at fifty per cent mark-up for foreign-published titles): see p.134 for addresses. In **London**, the Hellenic Bookservice, 91 Fortess Rd, Kentish Town, London NW5 1AG (☎020/7267 9499, *www.hellenicbooks.com*), and Zeno's Greek Bookshop, 6 Denmark St, WC2H 8LP (☎020/7836 2522), are knowledgeable and well-stocked specialist dealers in new, secondhand and out-of-print books on all aspects of Greece.

despite decade-long intervals between revisions, pay their way both in interest and usefulness – in particular those on Páros, Kós, Pátmos, Náfplio, Ídhra and the travels of St Paul.

Nikos Stavroulakis *Jewish Sites and Synagogues of Greece* (Talos Press, Athens). Lavishly illustrated alphabetical gazetteer of all Jewish monuments in Greece, with town plans and full histories of the communities that created them. A few have been demolished since publication, however.

YACHTING

H.M. Denham *The Aegean; The Ionian Islands to the Anatolian Coast* (John Murray, UK, o/p). Long the standard references if you were out yachting; still found in secondhand bookshops, but a bit obsolete.

Rod Heikell *Greek Waters Pilot* (Imray, Laurie, Norrie and Wilson, UK). Rather better than the preceding, which it has superseded.

LANGUAGE

So many Greeks have lived or worked abroad in America, Australia and, to a much lesser extent, Britain, that you will find someone who speaks English in the tiniest island village. Add to that the thousands attending language schools or working in the tourist industry – English is the lingua franca of most resorts, with German second – and it is easy to see how so many visitors come back having learned only half a dozen restaurant words between them.

You can certainly get by this way, but it isn't very satisfying, and the willingness and ability to say even a few words will transform your status from that of dumb *tourístas* to the honourable one of *xénos/xéni*, a word which can mean foreigner, traveller and guest all rolled into one.

LEARNING BASIC GREEK

Greek is not an easy language for English speakers but it is a very beautiful one, and even a brief acquaintance will give you some idea of the debt owed to it by Western European languages.

On top of the usual difficulties of learning a new language, Greek presents the additional problem of an entirely separate **alphabet**. Despite initial appearances, this is in practice

LANGUAGE-LEARNING MATERIALS

TEACH-YOURSELF GREEK COURSES

Breakthrough Greece (Pan Macmillan; book and four cassettes). Excellent, basic teach-yourself course; no Greek lettering, but good for classicists who need to unlearn bad habits.

Greek Language and People (BBC Publications, UK; book and two cassettes available). More limited in scope but good for acquiring the essentials, and the confidence to try them.

Anne Farmakides *A Manual of Modern Greek* (Yale UP; McGill UP; 3 vols). If you have the discipline and motivation, this is one of the best for learning proper, grammatical Greek; indeed, mastery of just the first volume will get you a long way.

Hara Garoufalia *Teach Yourself Holiday Greek* (Hodder & Stoughton, UK; book and cassette available). Unlike many quickie courses, this provides a good grammatical foundation, but you'll need a dictionary (see below) to supplement the scanty vocabulary lists.

Niki Watts *Greek in Three Months* (Hugo, Dorling Kindersley; book and four cassettes). Delivers as promised; equals or exceeds *Breakthrough Greek*.

PHRASEBOOKS

Greek, a Rough Guide Phrasebook (Penguin, UK & US). Up-to-date and accurate pocket phrasebook not full of "*plume de ma tante*"-type expressions. The English-to-Greek section is sensibly transliterated, though the Greek-to-English part requires basic mastery of the Greek alphabet. Feature boxes fill you in on dos and don'ts and cultural know-how.

DICTIONARIES

The Oxford Dictionary of Modern Greek (Oxford UP, UK & US). A bit bulky in its wide format, but generally considered the best Greek–English, English–Greek paperback dictionary.

Collins Pocket Greek Dictionary (HarperCollins, UK & US). Very nearly as complete as the Oxford and probably better value for the money. The inexpensive *Collins Gem Greek Dictionary* (UK only) is palm-sized but exactly the same in contents – the best purse or day-pack choice.

Oxford Greek-English, English-Greek Learner's Dictionary (Oxford UP, UK & US). If you're planning a prolonged stay, this pricey, hardbound, two-volume set is unbeatable for usage and vocabulary. There's also a more portable one-volume *Learner's Pocket Dictionary*.

THE GREEK ALPHABET: TRANSLITERATION

Set out below is the Greek alphabet, the system of transliteration used in this book, and a brief aid to pronunciation.

Greek	Transliteration	Pronounced
A, α	a	a as in father
B, β	v	v as in vet
Γ, γ	y/g	y as in yes except before consonants or α, o or oι when its a breathy g as in gap
Δ, δ	dh	th as in then
E, ε	e	e as in get
Z, ζ	z	z sound
H, η	i	i as in ski
Θ, θ	th	th as in theme
I, ι	i	i as in ski
K, κ	k	k sound
Λ, λ	l	l sound
M, μ	m	m sound
N, ν	n	n sound
Ξ, ξ	x	x sound, never z
O, o	o	o as in toad
Π, π	p	p sound
P, ρ	r	r sound
Σ, σ, ς	s	s sound, except z before μ or γ
T, τ	t	t sound
Y, υ	i	i as in ski
Φ, φ	f	f sound
X, χ	h before vowels, kh before consonants	harsh h sound, like ch in loch
Ψ, ψ	ps	ps as in lips
Ω, ω	o	o as in toad, indistinguishable from o

Combinations and diphthongs

AI, αι	e	e as in hey
AY, αυ	av/af	av or af depending on following consonant
EI, ει	i	long i, exactly like ι or η
EY, ευ	ev/ef	ev or ef, depending on following consonant
OI, oι	i	long i, exactly like ι or η
OY, ου	ou	ou as in tourist
ΓΓ, γγ	ng	ng as in angle; always medial
ΓΚ, γκ	g/ng	g as in goat at the beginning of a word, ng in the middle
ΜΠ, μπ	b/mb	b at the beginning of a word, mb in the middle
NT, ντ	d/nd	d at the beginning of a word, nd in the middle
ΤΣ, τσ	ts	ts as in hits
ΤΖ, τζ	tz	j as in jam

Note on diereses

The dieresis is used in Greek over the second of two adjacent vowels to change the pronunciation that you would expect from the preceding table; often in this book it can function as the primary stress. In the word kaïki (caique), the presence of the dieresis changes the pronunciation from "cake-key" to "ki-ee-key" and additionally the middle "i" carries the primary stress. In the word païdhákia (lamb chops), the dieresis again changes the sound of the first syllable from "pay" to "pah-ee", but in this case the primary stress is on the third syllable. It is also, uniquely among Greek accents, used on capital letters in signs and personal-name spellings in Greece, and we have followed this practice.

GREEK WORDS AND PHRASES

Essentials

Yes	*Né*	Yesterday	*Khthés*	Big	*Megálo*
Certainly	*Málista*	Now	*Tóra*	Small	*Mikró*
No	*Óhi*	Later	*Argótera*	More	*Perisótero*
Please	*Parakaló*	Open	*Anikhtó*	Less	*Ligótero*
Okay, agreed	*Endáxi*	Closed	*Klistó*	A little	*Lígo*
Thank you		Day	*Méra*	A lot	*Polý*
(very much)	*Efharistó (polý)*	Night	*Níkhta*	Cheap	*Ftinó*
I (don't)		In the morning	*Tó proï*	Expensive	*Akrivó*
understand	*(Dhén) Katalavéno*	In the afternoon	*Tó apóyevma*	Hot	*Zestó*
Excuse me,	*Parakaló, mípos*	In the evening	*Tó vrádhi*	Cold	*Krýo*
do you speak		Here	*Edhó*	With (together)	*Mazí (mé)*
English?	*miláte angliká?*	There	*Ekí*	Without	*Horís*
Sorry/		This one	*Aftó*	Quickly	*Grígora*
excuse me	*Signómi*	That one	*Ekíno*	Slowly	*Sigá*
Today	*Símera*	Good	*Kaló*	Mr/Mrs	*Kýrios/Kyría*
Tomorrow	*Ávrio*	Bad	*Kakó*	Miss	*Dhespinís*

Other Needs

To eat/drink	*Trógo/píno*	Stamps	*Gramatosímata*	Toilet	*Toualéta*
Bakery	*Foúrnos, psomádhiko*	Petrol station	*Venzinádhiko*	Police	*Astynomía*
Pharmacy	*Farmakío*	Bank	*Trápeza*	Doctor	*Iatrós*
Post office	*Tahydhromío*	Money	*Leftá/Khrímata*	Hospital	*Nosokomío*

Requests and Questions

To ask a question, it's simplest to start with *parakaló*, then name the thing you want in an interrogative tone.

Where is the bakery?	*Parakaló, o foúrnos?*	How many?	*Póssi* or *pósses?*
Can you show me		How much?	*Póso?*
the road to . . . ?	*Parakaló, o dhrómos yiá . . . ?*	When?	*Póte?*
We'd like a room	*Parakaló, éna dhomátio yiá*	Why?	*Yiatí?*
for two	*dhýo átoma*	At what time . . . ?	*Tí óra . . . ?*
May I have a kilo		What is/Which is . . . ?	*Tí íne/pió íne . . . ?*
of oranges?	*Parakaló, éna kiló portokália?*	How much (does it cost)?	*Póso káni?*
Where?	*Poú?*	What time does it open?	*Tí óra aníyi?*
How?	*Pós?*	What time does it close?	*Tí óra klíni?*

Talking to People

Greek makes the distinction between the informal (*esí*) and formal (*esís*) second person, as French does with *tu* and *vous*. Young people, older people and country people nearly always use *esí* even with total strangers. In any event, no one will be too bothered if you get it wrong. By far the most common greeting, on meeting and parting, is *yiá sou/yiá sas* – literally "health to you".

Hello	*Hérite*	My name is . . .	*Me léne . . .*
Good morning	*Kalí méra*	Speak slower, please	*Parakaló, miláte pió sigá*
Good evening	*Kalí spéra*	How do you say it	
Good night	*Kalí níkhta*	in Greek?	*Pos léyete stá Elliniká?*
Goodbye	*Adío*	I don't know	*Dhén xéro*
How are you?	*Ti kánis/Ti kánete?*	See you tomorrow	*Thá sé dhó ávrio*
I'm fine	*Kalá íme*	See you soon	*Kalí andhámosi*
And you?	*Ke esís?*	Let's go	*Páme*
What's your name?	*Pos se léne?*	Please help me	*Parakaló, ná mé voithíste*

Greek's Greek

There are numerous words and phrases which you will hear constantly, even if you rarely have the chance to use them. These are a few of the most common.

Éla!	Come (literally) but also Speak to me! You don't say! etc.	*Ópa!*	Whoops! Watch it!
Oríste!	Literally, "Indicate!"; in effect, "What can I do for you?"	*Po-po-po!*	Expression of dismay or concern, like French "O la la!"
Embrós!		*Pedhí moú*	My boy/girl, sonny, friend, etc.
or *Léyete!*	Standard phone responses	*Maláka(s)*	Literally "wanker", but often used (don't try it!) as an informal term of address.
Ti néa?	What's new?		
Ti yínete?	What's going on (here)?	*Sigá sigá*	Take your time, slow down
Étsi k'étsi	So-so	*Kaló taxídhi*	Bon voyage

Accommodation

Hotel	*Xenodhohío*	Hot water	*zestó neró*
Inn	*Xenónas*	Cold water	*krýo neró*
Youth hostel	*Xenónas neótitos*	Fan	*anamistíra*
A room . . .	*Éna dhomátio . . .*	Can I see it?	*Boró ná tó dhó?*
for one/two/three people	*yiá éna/dhýo/tría átoma*	Can we camp here?	*Boroúme na váloume ti skiní edhó?*
for one/two/three nights	*yiá mía/dhýo /trís vradhiés*	Campsite	*Kamping/Kataskínosi*
with a double bed	*mé megálo kreváti*	Tent	*Skiní*
with a shower	*mé doús*		

On The Move

Aeroplane	*Aeropláno*	Where are you going?	*Poú pás?*
Bus	*Leoforío*	I'm going to . . .	*Páo stó . . .*
Car	*Aftokínito*	I want to get off at . . .	*Thélo ná katévo stó . . .*
Motorbike, scooter	*Mihanáki, papáki*	The road to . . .	*O dhrómos yiá . . .*
Taxi	*Taksí*	Near	*Kondá*
Ship	*Plío/ vapóri/ karávi*	Far	*Makriá*
Bicycle	*Podhílato*	Left	*Aristerá*
Hitching	*Otostóp*	Right	*Dhexiá*
On foot	*Mé tá pódhia*	Straight ahead	*Katefthía*
Trail	*Monopáti*	A ticket to . . .	*Éna isistírio yiá . . .*
Bus station	*Praktorío leoforíon, KTEL*	A return ticket	*Éna isistírio mé epistrofí*
Bus stop	*Stási*	Beach	*Paralía*
Harbour	*Limáni*	Cave	*Spiliá*
What time does it leave?	*Ti óra févyi?*	Centre (of town)	*Kéndro*
What time does it arrive?	*Ti óra ftháni?*	Church	*Ekklisía*
How many kilometres?	*Pósa hiliómetra?*	Sea	*Thálassa*
How many hours?	*Pósses óres?*	Village	*Horió*

Numbers

1	*énas/ éna/ mía*	8	*okhtó*	20	*íkosi*
2	*dhýo*	9	*enyá*	21	*íkosiéna*
3	*trís/ tría*	10	*dhéka*		(all compounds elided thus)
4	*tésseres/ téssera*	11	*éndheka*	30	*triánda*
5	*pénde*	12	*dhódheka*	40	*saránda*
6	*éxi*	13	*dhekatrís*	50	*penínda*
7	*eftá*	14	*dhekatésseres*	60	*exínda*

Numbers (continued)

70	*evdhomínda*	200	*dhiakóssies/ia*	first	*próto*
80	*ogdhónda*	500	*pendakóssies/ia*	second	*dhéftero*
90	*enenínda*	1000	*hílies/hília*	third	*tríto*
100	*ekató*	2000	*dhýo hiliádhes*		
150	*ekatón penínda*	1,000,000	*éna ekatomírio*		

The Time and Days of the Week

Sunday	*Kyriakí*	What time is it?	*Ti óra íne?*
Monday	*Dheftéra*	One/two/three o'clock	*Mía óra, dhýo/trís (óres)*
Tuesday	*Tríti*	Twenty minutes to four	*Tésseres pará íkosi*
Wednesday	*Tetárti*	Five minutes past seven	*Eftá ké pénde*
Thursday	*Pémpti*	Half past eleven	*Éndheka ke misí*
Friday	*Paraskeví*	In half an hour	*Sé misí óra*
Saturday	*Sávato*	In a quarter-hour	*S'éna tétarto*

Months and Seasonal Terms

January	*Yennári*	August	*Ávgoustos*
February	*Fleváris*	September	*Septémvris*
March	*Mártis*	October	*Októvris*
April	*Aprílis*	November	*Noémvris*
May	*Maïos*	December	*Dhekémvris*
June	*Ioúnios*	Summer schedule	*Therinó dhromolóyio*
July	*Ioúlios*	Winter schedule	*Himerinó dhromolóyio*

fairly easily mastered – a skill that will help enormously if you are going to get around independently (see the alphabet box on p.913). In addition, certain combinations of letters have unexpected results. This book's transliteration system should help you make intelligible noises, but you have to remember that the correct **stress** (marked throughout the book with an acute accent or sometimes dieresis) is crucial. With the right sounds but the wrong stress people will either fail to understand you, or else understand something quite different from what you intended.

Greek **grammar** is more complicated still: nouns are divided into three genders, all with different case endings in the singular and in the plural, and all adjectives and articles have to agree with these in gender, number and case. (All adjectives are arbitrarily cited in the neuter form in the boxed lists.) Verbs are even more complex. To begin with at least, the best thing is simply to say what you know the way you know it, and never mind the niceties. "Eat meat hungry" should get a result, however grammatically incorrect. If you worry about your mistakes, you'll never say anything.

KATHARÉVOUSSA, DHIMOTIKÍ AND DIALECTS

Greek may seem complicated enough in itself, but problems are multiplied when you consider that since the early 1800s there has been an ongoing dispute between two versions of the language: **katharévoussa** and **dhimotikí**.

When Greece first achieved independence in the nineteenth century, its people were almost universally illiterate, and the language they spoke – **dhimotikí**, "demotic" or "popular" Greek – had undergone enormous change since the days of the Byzantine empire and Classical times. The vocabulary had assimilated countless borrowings from the languages of the various invaders and conquerors, namely the Turks, Venetians, Albanians and Slavs.

The finance and inspiration for the new Greek state, as well as its early leaders, came largely from the diaspora – Greek families who had been living in the sophisticated cities of central and eastern Europe, in Constantinople or in Russia. With their European notions about the grandeur of Greece's past, and lofty conception of Hellenism, they set about obliterating the memory of subjugation to foreigners in every possible field. And what better way to start than by purging the language of its foreign accretions and reviving its Classical purity?

They accordingly set about creating what was in effect a new form of the language, *katharévoussa* (literally "cleansed" Greek). The complexities of Classical grammar and syntax were reinstated, and Classical words, long out of use, were reintroduced. To the country's great detriment, *katharévoussa* became the language of the schools and the prestigious professions, government, business, the law, newspapers and academia. Everyone aspiring to membership in the elite strove to master it, and to speak it – even though there was no consensus on how many of the words should be pronounced.

The *katharévoussa/dhimotikí* debate remained a highly contentious issue until the early 1980s. Writers – from Solomos and Makriyiannis in the nineteenth century to Seferis, Kazantzakis and Ritsos in the twentieth – have all championed the demotic in their literature. Advocacy of demotic became increasingly linked to left-wing politics, while crackpot right-wing governments forcibly (re)instated *katharévoussa* at every opportunity. Most recently, the **colonels' junta** of 1967–1974 reversed a decision of the previous government to teach using *dhimotikí* in the schools, bringing back *katharévoussa*, even on sweet wrappers, as part of their ragbag of notions about racial purity and heroic ages.

Dhimotikí returned once more after the fall of the colonels and now seems here to stay. It is used in schools, on radio and TV, and after a fashion in newspapers (with the exception of the extreme right-wing *Estia*). The only institutions which refuse to bring themselves up to date are the Church and the legal professions – so beware rental contracts and official documents.

This is not to suggest that there is now any less confusion. The Metaxas dictatorship of the 1930s changed scores of village names from Slavic to Classical forms, and these official **place names** still hold sway on most road signs and maps – even though the local people may use the *dhimotikí* form. Thus you will see "Leonídhio(n)" or "Spétsai" written, while everyone actually says Leonídhi or Spétses.

DIALECTS AND MINORITY LANGUAGES

If the lack of any standard Greek were not enough, Greece still offers a rich field of linguistic diversity, both in its regional dialects and minority languages. Ancient **dialects** are alive and well in many a remote area, and some of them are quite incomprehensible to outsiders. The dialect of Sfákia in Crete is one such. Tsakónika (spoken in the east-central Peloponnese) is another, while the dialect of the Sarakatsáni shepherds is said to be the oldest, a direct descendant of the language of the Dorian settlers.

The language of the Sarakatsáni's traditional rivals, the **Vlachs**, on the other hand, is not Greek at all, but a derivative of early Latin, with strong affinities to Romanian. In the ex-Yugoslav and Bulgarian frontier regions you can still hear Slavic **Macedonian** spoken, while small numbers of Sephardic Jews in the north speak **Ladino**, a medieval form of Spanish. Until a few decades ago **Arvanitika** – a dialect of medieval Albanian – was the first language of many villages of inland Attica, southern Évvia, northern Ándhros, and much of the Argo-Saronic area; it is still widely spoken among the older generation. Lately the clock has been turned back as throngs of Albanian refugees circulate in Athens and other parts of the country. In Thrace there is also a substantial **Turkish**-speaking population, as well as some speakers of **Pomak** (a relative of Bulgarian with a large Greco-Turkish vocabulary).

A GLOSSARY OF WORDS AND TERMS

ACROPOLIS Ancient, fortified hilltop.

AGORA Market and meeting place of an ancient Greek city; also the commercial "high street" of a modern village.

AMPHORA Tall, narrow-necked jar for oil or wine.

ÁNO Upper; common prefix element of village names.

APSE Polygonal or curved recess at the altar end of a church.

ARCHAIC PERIOD Late Iron Age period, from around 750 BC to the start of the Classical period in the fifth century BC.

ARCHITRAVE Horizontal masonry atop temple columns; same as ENTABLATURE.

ARHONDIKÓ A lordly stone mansion, as in Kastoriá, Pílion or Zagóri.

ASTYKÓ (Intra) city, municipal, local; adjective applied to phone calls and bus services.

ATRIUM Open, inner courtyard of an ancient house, usually Roman.

ÁYIOS/AYÍA/ÁYII Saint or holy (m/f/plural). Common place-name prefix (abbreviated Ag or Ay), often spelled AGIOS or AGHIOS.

BASILICA Colonnaded, "hall-" or "barn-" type church adapted from Roman models, most common in northern Greece.

BEMA Rostrum for oratory (and later the chancel) of a church.

BOULEUTERION Auditorium for meetings of an ancient town's deliberative council.

BYZANTINE EMPIRE Created by the division of the Roman empire in 395 AD, this, the eastern half, was ruled from Constantinople (modern Istanbul). In Greece, Byzantine culture peaked twice: in the eleventh century, and again at Mystra in the early fifteenth century.

CAPITAL The flared top, often ornamented, of a column.

CELLA Sacred room of a temple, housing the cult image.

CLASSICAL PERIOD Essentially from the end of the Persian Wars in the fifth century BC until the unification of Greece under Philip II of Macedon (338 BC).

CORINTHIAN Decorative columns, festooned with acanthus florettes; a temple built in this order.

DHIMARHÍO Town hall.

DHOMÁTIA Rooms for rent in purpose-built blocks or private houses.

DORIAN Northern civilization that displaced and succeeded the Mycenaeans and Minoans through most of Greece around 1100 BC.

DORIC Minimalist, unadorned columns, dating from the Dorian period; a temple built in this order.

DRUM Cylindrical or faceted vertical section, usually pierced by an even number of narrow windows, upholding a church cupola.

ENTABLATURE The horizontal linking structure atop the columns of an ancient temple.

EPARHÍA Greek Orthodox diocese, also the smallest subdivision of a modern province, analogous to a county.

EXEDRA Display niche for statuary.

EXONARTHEX The outer vestibule or entrance hall of a church, when a true NARTHEX is present.

FORUM Market and meeting place of a Roman-era city.

FRIEZE Band of sculptures around a temple. Doric friezes consist of various tableaux of figures (METOPES) interspersed with grooved panels (TRIGLYPHS); Ionic ones have continuous bands of figures.

FROÚRIO Medieval castle; also modern military headquarters.

GARSONIÉRA/ES Studio villa/s, self-catering apartment/s.

GEOMETRIC PERIOD Post-Mycenaean Iron Age era named for the style of its pottery; begins in the early eleventh century BC with the arrival of Dorian peoples. By the eighth century BC, with the development of representational styles, it becomes known as the ARCHAIC PERIOD.

HELLENISTIC PERIOD The last and most unified "Greek empire", created in the wake of Alexander the Great's Macedonian empire and finally collapsing with the fall of Corinth to the Romans in 146 BC.

HEROÖN Shrine or sanctuary, usually of a demigod or mortal; war memorials in modern Greece.

HOKHLÁKI Mosaic of coloured pebbles, found in church or house courtyards of the Dodecanese and Spétses.

HÓRA Main town of an island or region; literally it means "the place". An island hóra is often known by the same name as the island.

IERÓN Literally, "sacred" – the space between the altar screen and the apse of a church, reserved for priestly activities.

IKONOSTÁSI Screen between the nave of a church and the altar, supporting at least three icons.

IONIC Elaborate, decorative development of the older DORIC order; Ionic temple columns are slimmer, with deeper "fluted" edges, spiral-shaped capitals and ornamental bases.

IPERASTYKÓ Inter-city, long-distance – as in phone calls and bus services.

JANISSARY Member of the Turkish imperial guard, often forcibly recruited in childhood from the local population.

KAFENÍO Coffee house or café; in a small village the centre of communal life and probably serving as the bus stop, too.

KAΪKI (plural KAΪKIA) Caique, or medium-sized boat, traditionally wooden and used for transporting cargo and passengers; now refers mainly to island excursion boats.

KALDERÍMI A cobbled mule-track or footpath.

KÁMBOS Fertile agricultural plain, usually near a river mouth.

KANTÍNA Shack, caravan or even a disused bus on the beach, serving just drinks and perhaps sandwiches.

KÁSTRO Any fortified hill (or a castle), but most usually the oldest, highest, walled-in part of an island HÓRA.

KATHOLIKÓN Central chapel of a monastery.

KÁTO Lower; common prefix element of village names.

KENDRIKÍ PLATÍA Central square.

KOUROS Nude Archaic or Classical statue of an idealized young man, usually portrayed with one foot slightly forward of the other.

MACEDONIAN EMPIRE Empire created by Philip II in the mid-fourth century BC.

MEGARON Principal hall or throne room of a Mycenaean palace.

MELTÉMI North wind that blows across the Aegean in summer, starting softly from near the mainland and hitting the Cyclades, the Dodecanese and Crete full on.

METOPE see FRIEZE

MINOAN Crete's great Bronze Age civilization, which dominated the Aegean from about 2500 to 1400 BC.

MONÍ Formal term for a monastery or convent.

MOREÁS Medieval term for the Peloponnese; the outline of the peninsula was likened to the leaf of a mulberry tree, *moreá* in Greek.

MYCENAEAN Mainland civilization centred on Mycenae and the Argolid from about 1700 to 1100 BC.

NAOS The inner sanctum of an ancient temple; also, any Orthodox Christian shrine.

NARTHEX Western vestibule of a church, reserved for catechumens and the unbaptized; typically frescoed with scenes of the Last Judgement.

NEOLITHIC Earliest era of settlement in Greece, characterized by the use of stone tools and weapons together with basic agriculture. Divided arbitrarily into Early (*c* 6000 BC), Middle (*c* 5000 BC) and Late (*c* 3000 BC).

NÉOS, NÉA, NÉO "New" – a common prefix to a town or village name.

NOMÓS Modern Greek province – there are more than fifty of them. Village bus services are organized according to their borders.

ODEION Small theatre, used for musical performances, minor dramatic productions or councils.

ORCHESTRA Circular area in a theatre where the chorus would sing and dance.

PALAESTRA Gymnasium for athletics and wrestling practice.

PALEÓS, PALEÁ, PALEÓ "Old" – again a common prefix in town and village names.

PANAYÍA Virgin Mary.

PANIYÍRI Festival or feast – the local celebration of a holy day.

PANDOKRÁTOR Literally "The Almighty"; generally refers to the stern portrayal of Christ in Majesty frescoed or in mosaic in the dome of many Byzantine churches.

PARALÍA Beach or seafront promenade.

PEDIMENT Triangular, sculpted gable below the roof of a temple.

PENDENTIVE Any of four triangular sections of vaulting with concave sides, positioned at a corner of a rectangular space to support a circular or polygonal dome; in churches, often adorned with frescoes of the four Evangelists.

PERÍPTERO Street kiosk.

PERISTEREÓNES Pigeon towers.

PERISTYLE Gallery of columns around a temple or other building.

PINAKOTHÍKI Picture gallery.

PITHOS (plural PITHOI) Large ceramic jar for storing oil, grain etc. Very common in Minoan palaces and used in almost identical form in modern Greek homes.

PLATÍA Square, plaza.

PROPYLAION Monumental columned gateway of an ancient building; often used in the plural, *propylaia*.

PÝRGOS Tower or bastion; also tower-mansions found in the Máni or on Lésvos.

SKÁLA The port of an inland island settlement, nowadays often larger and more important than its namesake, but always younger since built after the disappearance of piracy.

SQUINCH Small concavity across a corner of a columnless interior space, which supports a superstructure such as a dome.

STELE Upright stone slab or column, usually inscribed; an ancient tombstone.

STOA Colonnaded walkway in Classical-era marketplace.

TAVERNA Restaurant; see "Eating and Drinking" in Basics, p.47, for details of the different types of specialist eating places.

TÉMBLON Wooden altar screen of an Orthodox church, usually ornately carved and painted and studded with icons; more or less interchangeable with IKONOSTÁSI.

TEMENOS Sacred precinct, often used to refer to the sanctuary itself.

THEATRAL AREA Open area found in most of the Minoan palaces with seat-like steps around. Probably a type of theatre or ritual area, though this is not conclusively proven.

THOLOS Conical or beehive-shaped building, especially a Mycenaean tomb.

TRIGLYPH see FRIEZE

TYMPANUM The recessed space, flat or carved in relief, inside a pediment.

ACRONYMS

ANEK Anónymi Navtikí Etería Krítis (Shipping Co of Crete, Ltd), which runs most ferries between Pireás and Crete, plus many to Italy.

DANE Dhodhekanisiakí Anónymi Navtikí Etería (Dodecanesian Shipping Company Ltd), which runs many ferries between Rhodes and Pireás via intervening islands.

DIKKI Democrat Social Movement, a party leftward of PASOK.

EAM National Liberation Front, the political force behind ELAS.

ELAS Popular Liberation Army, the main Resistance group during World War II and the basis of the Communist army (DSE) in the civil war.

ELTA Postal service.

EOS Greek Mountaineering Federation, based in Athens.

EOT Ellinikós Organismós Tourismoú, the National Tourist Organization.

FYROM Former Yugoslav Republic of Macedonia.

KKE Communist Party, unreconstructed.

KTEL National syndicate of bus companies. The term is also used to refer to bus stations.

LANE Lasithiakí Anónymi Navtikí Etería (Lasithian Shipping Company Ltd), based in eastern Crete, which runs ferries between Rhodes, Kárpathos, eastern Crete and Pireás.

ND Conservative (Néa Dhimokratía) party.

NEL Navtiliakí Etería Lésvou (Lesvian Shipping Co), which runs most of the northeast Aegean ferries.

OSE Railway corporation.

OTE Telephone company.

PASOK Socialist party (Pan-Hellenic Socialist Movement).

SEO Greek Mountaineering Club, based in Thessaloníki.

INDEX

ROUGH GUIDES: Travel

Amsterdam
Andalucia
Australia

Austria
Bali & Lombok
Barcelona
Belgium &
  Luxembourg
Belize
Berlin
Brazil
Britain
Brittany &
  Normandy
Bulgaria
California
Canada
Central America
Chile
China
Corfu & the
  Ionian Islands
Corsica
Costa Rica
Crete
Cuba
Cyprus
Czech & Slovak
  Republics

Dodecanese
Dominican
  Republic
Egypt
England
Europe
Florida
France
French Hotels &
  Restaurants 1999
Germany
Goa
Greece
Greek Islands
Guatemala
Hawaii
Holland
Hong Kong
  & Macau
Hungary
India
Indonesia
Ireland
Israel & the
  Palestinian
  Territories
Italy
Jamaica
Japan
Jordan

Kenya
Laos
London
London
  Restaurants
Los Angeles
Malaysia,
  Singapore &
  Brunei
Mallorca &
  Menorca
Maya World
Mexico
Morocco
Moscow
Nepal
New England
New York
New Zealand
Norway
Pacific Northwest
Paris
Peru
Poland
Portugal
Prague
Provence & the
  Côte d'Azur
The Pyrenees
Romania

St Petersburg
San Francisco
Sardinia
Scandinavia
Scotland
Scottish Highlands
  & Islands
Sicily
Singapore

South Africa
Southern India
Southwest USA
Spain
Sweden
Syria
Thailand
Trinidad & Tobago
Tunisia
Turkey
Tuscany & Umbria
USA
Venice
Vienna
Vietnam
Wales
Washington DC
West Africa
Zimbabwe &
  Botswana

AVAILABLE AT ALL GOOD BOOKSHOPS

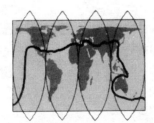